Conversations

CONVERSATIONS
Readings for Writing

Jack Selzer
The Pennsylvania State University

MACMILLAN PUBLISHING COMPANY

NEW YORK

COLLIER MACMILLAN PUBLISHERS

LONDON

Editor: Eben W. Ludlow
Production Supervisor: Betsy Keefer
Production Manager: Aliza Greenblatt
Text Designer: Blake Logan
Cover Designer: Blake Logan

This book was set in 10 pt. Aster by V & M Graphics, printed and bound by Arcata/Fairfield. The cover was printed by Lehigh Press.

Macmillan Publishing Company
866 Third Avenue, New York, New York 10022

Collier Macmillan Canada, Inc.
1200 Eglinton Ave East, Suite 200
Don Mills, Ontario M3C 3N1

Library of Congress Cataloging-in-Publication Data
Conversations: readings for writing/[edited Jack Selzer].
     p.   cm.
   Includes index.
   ISBN 0-02-408975-3
   1. College readers   2. English language—Rhetoric.   I. Selzer, Jack.
PE1417.C6545   1991
808'.0427—dc20   90-42610
                                        CIP

The following have granted permission to reprint material on:
Pages 20–22: From "Education" from *One Man's Meat* by E. B. White. Copyright 1944 by E. B. White. Reprinted by permission of Harper & Row, Publishers, Inc.
Pages 25–38: "What High School Is" from *Horace's Compromise: The Dilemma of the American High School* by Theodore Sizer. Copyright © 1984 by Theodore R. Sizer. Reprinted by permission of Houghton Mifflin Co.
Pages 38–45: Reprinted by permission of *Daedalus*, Journal of the American Academy of Arts and Sciences, "Values, Resources, and Politics in America's Schools," Fall 1984, vol. 113, no. 4, 169–76.
Pages 47–54: Excerpt(s) from *Teaching as a Conserving Activity* by Neil Postman, copyright © 1979 by Neil Postman. Used by permission of Dell Books, a division of Bantam, Doubleday, Dell Publishing Group, Inc.
Pages 54–55: From "What They Learn in School," *All Things Considered*, National Public Radio, March 17, 1989. Copyright © 1989 Jerome Stern. Reprinted by permission of Jerome Stern.
(Continued on page 1025)

Printing: 2 3 4 5 6 7 8   Year: 1 2 3 4 5 6 7 8 9

Main Text: ISBN 0-02-408975-3
Instructor's Edition: ISBN 0-02-439120-4

Preface

Imagine that you enter a parlor. You come late. When you arrive, others have long preceded you, and they are engaged in a heated discussion, a discussion too heated for them to pause and tell you exactly what it is about. In fact, the discussion had already begun long before any of them got there, so that no one present is qualified to retrace for you all the steps that had gone before. You listen for a while, until you decide that you have caught the tenor of the argument; then you put in your oar. Someone answers; you answer him; another comes to your defense; another aligns himself against you, to either the embarrassment or gratification of your opponent, depending upon the quality of your ally's assistance.

This well-known passage from Kenneth Burke's *Philosophy of Literary Form* explains the basic metaphor and the socio-rhetorical orientation of this anthology of readings for freshman composition courses. *Conversations* contains conversations: public discourse on contemporary issues that is calculated to engage students' interests, to encourage and empower their own contributions to contemporary civic discussions, and to represent a broad cross-section of the kinds of conversational styles and genres that are available to writers at the end of the twentieth century.

What's Different About *Conversations*?

Conversations encourages student writing on important current civic issues. The premise of this reader is that writing is less a private act of making personal meaning out of nothing than it is a public and social act of making meaning within a specific rhetorical situation—a specific situation that guides and shapes the meaning-making activity. To put the matter more simply, writing emerges from other writing, other discourse. Though nearly every anthology claims to encourage student responses, those readers just as often actually intimidate students because they present only one or two authoritative voices on a given issue and because those voices are given little context outside the anthology; the student reads an essay by Booth or Didion or Baldwin or Woolf or some other eloquent writer, and says to himself or herself, "Gee, that sure seems right to me. How could I disagree with such an expert?" Therefore, instead of one or two authoritative items on an issue or topic, this reader contains "conversations" on public issues or topics, conversations-with-contexts that will seem less intimidating and therefore invite student responses.

In fact, the book will encourage students to adopt a social and rhetorical model—a "conversation model"—for their own writing: instead of seeing writing merely as private or as debate or point-counterpoint, students should sense that "people are talking about this issue—and I'd like to get in on the talk somewhere." The conversation metaphor does not mean that students should "write like they talk" (since conversational informality is not always appropriate in public discourse); rather, the metaphor simply implies that students should see writing as a response to other writing, a response that they make after considering the implications and importance of what they have read and heard. Students should be encouraged to cooperate as well as compete with other writers, to address sub-issues as well as the main chance, to seek consensus and new syntheses as often as victory.

Thus *Conversations* is organized around focused, topical contemporary public issues (e.g., censorship, what to do about public education, gender at work, affirmative action, legalization of drugs, genetic engineering), each within seven larger thematic groupings (education, language, gender, media, civil liberties and civil rights, crime and punishment, and science and society) that lend additional historical and conceptual perspective to those contemporary issues. "Intertextuality" would be the buzzword from contemporary critical theory: the book includes items which "talk to each other" both directly and indirectly. Some pieces speak directly and explicitly to each other (as in the case of Loren Eiseley's response to C. P. Snow's "two cultures" essay or Milton Friedman's exchange with William Bennett over the legalization of drugs or the exchange among John Wallace, Robert Nadeau, and Nat Hentoff on censoring *Huckleberry Finn*). Some pieces refer only indirectly to others, as in the sections on education and animal rights. And still other items comment on selections in other sections of *Conversations:* e.g., selections on education comment on those on language and race; the section on pornography is informed by the sections on gender and the causes of crime. And so forth. There is certainly no reason why the selections in this anthology cannot be read individually as they are in other books, without reference to other selections, especially since the headnotes orient readers to each item. And there is certainly no reason why the selections could not be read in some other order. Nevertheless, *Conversations* does give students a particular incentive to write because it establishes contexts for writing.

The conversation model should make the book suitable to a range of courses in writing. There is plenty of expository prose here: e.g., comparisons of all kinds; a careful analysis of the justice system by Roger Rosenblatt; Tom Regan's analysis of the religious grounds for animal rights; Mia Klein Anderson's and Mark Gardner's studies of the rhetoric of Martin Luther King, Jr.; cool descriptions of schools, novels, movies, campus politics, television, and a hanging; expositions of the reasons why women are excluded from science and why people commit crimes; and lots of et cetera. The "modes of exposition" are illustrated by numerous selections, as the alternate table of contents makes clear. But *Conversations* will also accommodate courses with an argumentative edge, for this book includes a fair proportion of explicitly or implicitly argumentative writing and tends to encourage a broadly argumentative approach to all discourse. In short, the conversation metaphor implies an inclusive approach to prose, one that subsumes and includes exposition as well as argument, dialogue as well as dialectic. *Conversations* includes not only Neil Postman's prescriptions for the high school classroom, but Theodore Sizer's descriptions as well. It includes not only Trudy J. Sundberg's "Case Against Bilingualism," but the analysis of the issue by Roseann Duenas Gonzalez and her colleagues. It includes not only impassioned pro and con arguments on capital punishment, animal rights, and the "mommy track" for business executives, but also dispassionate analyses of language issues, the appeal of Bruce Springsteen, affirmative action, and more.

Consequently — and this is another notable feature of *Conversations* — this anthology includes a very broad range of genres; the book tries to represent as fully as possible the full spectrum of the "universe of discourse." True, essays are prominent in *Conversations* — familiar and formal essays, academic as well as nonacademic ones — because the essay is a common and important genre and because the form has important correspondences with other genres (e.g., the letter, the sermon, the report, the news story). But essays are not so prominent here as to exclude other genres. Students will find other ways of engaging in public discourse as well: through fiction, poetry, a play, letters of various kinds, public oratory, interviews, congressional hearings and reports, cartoons, advertisements, journals — and more. The occasions for public discourse are many and various. Students and their teachers will find news stories and movie reviews, rhetorical analyses and studies of cultural artifacts, parodies and satires, letters to the editor and counter-responses.

And they will hear a range of voices as well. *Conversations* assumes that students are ready, willing, and able to engage in civic, public discourse, but that does not preclude the possibility for personal inventiveness. Indeed, *Conversations* is committed to the proposition that there are many possible rhetorical stances, that there is no one "correct" way to address a reader. This anthology therefore exposes students to as many rhetorical choices as possible — from the studied erudition of John Simon to the semi-formal, "objective" voice associated with the academy; from the conversational informality of E. B. White, Garrison Keillor, and Woody Allen to satiric invective by Judy Syfers and Douglas R. Hofstadter; from the thrilling oratory of Sojourner Truth to the careful reasoning of Evelyn Fox Keller; from *Rolling Stone, Ms.,* and *The Village Voice* to *Esquire, The New Yorker,* and *The American Scholar;* from Tama Janowitz and James Baldwin to George Orwell, Thomas Jefferson, Richard Rodriguez, and Marcia Ann Gillespie. Students will encounter mainstream texts and dissenting views, conventional rhetorical maneuvers and startlingly inventive ones. They will hear from famous professional writers and anonymous but eloquent fellow citizens; from public figures and fellow students (a half dozen student contributions are included); from women and men; from majority and minority voices. *Conversations* gives students a better chance to find their own voices because they've experienced a full range of possible voices in their reading.

"A rhetorician," says Kenneth Burke in "Rhetoric — Old and New," "is like one voice in a dialogue. Put several such voices together, with each voicing its own special assertion, let them act upon one another in co-operative competition, and you get a dialectic that, properly developed, can lead to views transcending the limitations of each." Fostering that "co-operative competition" is the aim of *Conversations*.

Editorial Apparatus

Substantial editorial assistance has been provided to the users of *Conversations*. The book's Introduction orients students to social motives for writing and domesticates for them the metaphor of conversation. It also introduces students to the notion of critical or rhetorical reading, so that they might have a practical means of approaching every item in *Conversations* — and so that they might understand better how careful reading habits can reinforce effective writing habits. In addition, a headnote is provided for each selection so that students can orient themselves to the rhetoric of each piece. The headnotes provide background on the author (especially when prior knowledge about the author affects one's response to an item), on the topic of the selection (when the matter requires any explanation), and on the specific occasion for the piece (especially on when and where it was originally published). The assumption of most anthologies is that the original context of an essay or story — or whatever — doesn't matter much, or that the anthology itself comprises the context. *Conversations* assumes instead that careful reading must take into account the original circumstances that prompted a given piece of writing. Writing, after all, most often emerges from other writing, so situating each item by means of the headnotes is essential to the concept of *Conversations*. Finally, each part of the book includes an overview of the particular issues under discussion in that part. In sum, the editorial apparatus ensures that the selections in *Conversations* can be used in any order that a teacher or student might wish.

Otherwise, the text of *Conversations* assumes that students are already quite capable readers. On the grounds that students and teachers can handle things on their own and can appropriate readings to their own ends, the book includes no questions at the end of each selection, no suggestions for writing assignments or class discussions, no exercises and few footnotes. Space that might have been devoted to those matters is given over instead to additional selections so that teachers might have as many selections as possible to choose from.

Instructor's Manual

Teacher's who do want additional background on unfamiliar readings or specific suggestions for making the most of *Conversations* will find plenty of help in the detailed Instructor's Manual compiled by Tom Buckley and Linda Ferreira-Buckley. It contains further information on writers, overviews and mini-analyses of each selection, questions for discussion, and ideas for writing assignments. It also offers pointers for how particular selections can be used with other selections. Together, the editorial apparatus and the Instructor's Manual are designed to help *Conversations* engage the intelligence and passions of students and teachers, without getting in the way of either.

Acknowledgments

There may be only one name on the cover of this book, but it too is the product of a conversation — many conversations, in fact — with a number of people who collaborated on its development and production. My greatest debt is to those who assisted me in finding appropriate selections. Dawn Keetley (now of the University of Wisconsin), Tom Buckley (now of the University of Texas) and my Penn State colleague Jay Shuchter deserve special mention; but lots of others affected the outcome: Paul Klemp (University of Wisconsin — Eau Claire); Linda Ferreira-Buckley (University of Texas); Tony O'Keeffe (Bellarmine College); Debra Journet (University of Louisville); and Jim Brasfield, Bob Burkholder, Deb Clarke, Eva Elsmere, Claudia Limbert, Steve Mastrofski, Cynthia Miecznikowski, Jeff Purvis, David Randall, and Linda Selzer (all of Penn State). Several reviewers of the book made excellent suggestions: Stephen

Behrendt, University of Nebraska; John Bodnar, Prince George's Community College; Kitty Dean, Nassau Community College; John Dick, University of Texas at El Paso; Jack Dodds, Harper College; Robert Funk, Eastern Illinois University; Paula Gillespie, Marquette University; Dona Hickey, University of Richmond; Robert Lesman, Northern Virginia Community College; Gerald Levin, University of Akron; George Otte, Baruch College, CUNY; and Richard Zbaracki, Iowa State University. Other colleagues across the country and at Penn State—particularly Davida Charney, Nancy Lowe, Marie Secor, and Jeff Walker—stimulate my thinking on a daily basis. Peggy Keating worked diligently to secure permissions, and Todd Post and Keith Waddle did research for many of the headnotes. And twenty teachers at Penn State tested a prototype of the book in their classes during the fall semester of 1989.

Thanks too to those on the production end of things. Kathy Leitzell and Kim Witherite efficiently and cheerfully typed most of the manuscript; they helped me out of a thousand small scrapes to boot. Another thousand that I don't even know about were taken care of by Nancy Cooperman (at Macmillan) and Betsy Keefer and Durrae Johanek. Eben Ludlow has been an ideal editor: full of excellent suggestions, encouraging without ever being overbearing, supportive at every turn. His confidence in this project brought it into being. I won't forget it.

J. S.

Contents

PREFACE   **v**

Introduction   **1**

I. EDUCATION

Introduction   **18**

What to Do About the Schools?   **20**

E. B. WHITE, Education (essay)   **20**

> Which is better: an intimate, personalized rural school with limited facilities? or a larger urban school with all the modern touches?

CHARLES DICKENS, What Is a Horse? (fiction)   **23**

> A great English novelist describes and satirizes the "progressive" education of his day (and ours?).

THEODORE SIZER, What High School Is (essay)   **25**

> "'Taking subjects' in a systematized, conveyor-belt way is what one does in high school."

NATHAN GLAZER, Some Very Modest Proposals for the Improvement of American Education (essay)   **38**

> A respected educator offers seven suggestions for improving our schools.

MATT GROENING, Life in Hell (cartoon)   **46**

> Who wields power in our schools? Who really asks the questions?

NEIL POSTMAN, Order in the Classroom (essay)   **47**

> "The school is not an extension of the street, the
> movie theatre . . . or a playground. . . . It is a special
> environment that requires the enforcement of certain
> traditional rules."

JEROME STERN, What They Learn in School   **54**
(prose poem)

> "They mainly want to teach them not to question,
> not to challenge, not to imagine, but to be obedient. . . ."

What's College For?   **56**

ALICE WALKER, Everyday Use (fiction)   **56**

> The "child who has made it" confronts her sister who
> "hasn't." What's an education for?

ADRIENNE RICH, Claiming an Education (essay)   **65**

> Especially for women students, does university educa-
> tion mean anything beyond the processing of human
> beings into expected roles, through credit hours and
> tests?

GARRY B. TRUDEAU, Doonesbury (cartoon)   **70**

> Does this cartoon offer a portrait of intellectual life at
> your college or university?

NORMAN COUSINS, How to Make People Smaller   **71**
Than They Are (essay)

> "Nothing is more valuable for anyone who has had
> a professional or vocational education . . . than
> the humanities."

CARRIE TUHY, So Who Needs College? (essay)   **74**

> If a well-paying job is what you seek, college may *not*
> be the best answer.

CAROLINE BIRD, College Is a Waste of Time and   **79**
Money (essay)

> If a little schooling is good for a career, more must be
> better, right? Contrary evidence is beginning to mount up.

Letters to the Editor: Responses to   **90**
    Caroline Bird (letters)

    What is college for? Fourteen people respond — with
    feeling — to Caroline Bird.

CHRISTOPHER JESTER, Not Just a Diploma   **95**
    Factory (student essay)

    A student complains that colleges — and college stu-
    dents — have become too career oriented.

Ads for Hofstra University and Babson College   **99, 100**
    (advertisements)

    What's college for? What's the meaning of success?
    These ads imply an answer.

JAMES THURBER, University Days (essay)   **101**

    An American humorist reminisces about undergraduate
    days at Ohio State.

W. D. SNODGRASS, The Examination (poem)   **107**

    A college education is a sort of surgical procedure,
    isn't it?

II. LANGUAGE

Introduction   **110**

Should There Be — Or Can There Be — A
"Standard" English?   **112**

JAMES BALDWIN, If Black English Isn't   **112**
    a Language, Then Tell Me, What Is? (essay)

    "Language is a political instrument, means and
    proof of power. It is the most vivid and crucial key
    to identity."

RACHEL L. JONES, What's Wrong with Black English   **115**
    (student essay)

    A black student answers Baldwin: "My goal is to see

more black people less dependent on a dialect that
excludes them."

GENEVA SMITHERMAN, White English in   **118**
Blackface, or Who Do I Be? (essay)

"Ain nothin in a long time lit up the English teaching
profession like the current hassle over Black English."

JOHN SIMON, Why Good English Is Good for   **130**
You (essay)

"There is a close connection between the ability to
think and the ability to use English correctly," contends this critic.

GARY LARSON, The Far Side (cartoon)   **142**

A powerful — and funny — dramatization of the relationship between language and power.

Should We Have a National Language?   **143**

RICHARD RODRIGUEZ, Aria: A Memoir of a Bilin-   **143**
gual Childhood (essay)

A writer born into a Spanish-speaking, Mexican-
American family measures the gains and losses that
result when English replaces Spanish.

VICTOR VILLANUEVA, JR., Whose Voice Is It   **155**
Anyway? Rodriguez' Speech in Retrospect (essay)

A professor of English responds to Rodriguez and
defends bilingual education.

WALTER DARLINGTON HUDDLESTON, On   **165**
Behalf of a Constitutional Amendment to Make
English the Official Language of the United States
(speech)

Make English our official language and reduce bilingual education programs, argues a U.S. Senator.

JAMES C. STALKER, Official English or English   **176**
Only? (essay)

Bilingual education is viewed in a historical perspective.

TRUDY J. SUNDBERG, The Case Against 187
Bilingualism (essay)

"The United States is a country of great diversity, and English . . . is the social glue that holds this multicultural country together."

ROSEANN DUENAS GONZALEZ, ALICE A. 189
SCHOTT, AND VICTORIA F. VASQUEZ, The
English Language Amendment: Examining
Myths (essay)

"To equate language diversity with political upheaval is untenable," claim these opponents of the Official Language movement.

THE NATIONAL COUNCIL OF TEACHERS 203
OF ENGLISH, 1986 NCTE Resolution on English
as the "Official Language" (resolution)

An illustration of the rhetoric of official resolutions.

Is English Sexist? 205

CASEY MILLER AND KATE SWIFT, One Small 205
Step for Genkind (essay)

"Our language, like the culture it reflects, is male oriented."

BARBARA LAWRENCE, Four-Letter Words Can 217
Hurt You (essay)

Dirty words are not just innocent expletives. They can express contempt, brutality, and an inhumane attitude toward sex.

DOUGLAS R. HOFSTADTER, A Person Paper on 220
Purity in Language (satire)

"It's high time someone blew the whistle on all the silly prattle about revamping our language to suit certain political fanatics."

III. GENDER

Introduction   **230**

Just How Would You Define Women (and Men)?   **232**

ELIZABETH CADY STANTON, The Seneca Falls   **232**
Declaration (declaration)

> An early advocate of women's rights catalogues the grievances of women against nineteenth-century laws and customs.

SOJOURNER TRUTH, Ain't I a Woman? (speech)   **236**

> "I have plowed and planted, and gathered into barns, and no man could head me. And ain't I a woman?"

SUSAN GLASPELL, *Trifles* (play)   **238**

> A murder in a small community uncovers divisions between the sexes.

SUSAN GLASPELL, A Jury of Her Peers (fiction)   **251**

> A short-story version of *Trifles*: "there was a laugh for the ways of women"—but women get the last laugh.

MARCIA ANN GILLESPIE, A Different Take on   **272**
the Ol' Bump and Grind (essay)

> "In clubs all around this country women are looking, laughing, and carrying on while men come on like Gypsy Rose Lee."

DIANE WAKOSKI, Belly Dancer (poem)   **276**

> A belly dancer watches—and reflects on—those who watch her.

SUSAN BROWNMILLER, Emotion (essay)   **277**

> Do women possess a wider emotional range than men, a greater sensitivity?

CAROL GILLIGAN, Images of Relationships   **289**
(essay)

Contents

Do women and men develop moral sensibilities in different ways?

JUDY SYFERS, Why I Want a Wife (essay) **298**

A satiric account of marriage in twentieth-century America.

KURT FERNSLER, Why I Want a Husband **300**
(student essay)

A response to "Why I Want a Wife": marriage can be a trap for husbands, too.

PAUL THEROUX, Being a Man (essay) **302**

"I have always disliked being a man," confesses this cosmopolitan. "It is normal in America for a man to be apologetic about being a writer."

Do Women and Men Think Differently? **306**

CAMILLA PERSSON BENBOW AND JULIAN C. **306**
STANLEY, Sex Differences in Mathematical Reasoning Ability: More Facts (essay)

Two scientists turn up evidence that "males dominate the highest ranges of mathematical reasoning ability at very young ages."

RUTH BLEIER, Gender and Mathematical **310**
Ability (essay)

A physician and research scientist responds to Benbow and Stanley.

EVELYN FOX KELLER, Women in Science: An **314**
Analysis of a Social Problem (essay)

"Some would argue that the near absence of great women scientists demonstrates that women don't have the minds for true scientific creativity." Not Evelyn Fox Keller.

SAMUEL C. FLORMAN, Engineering and the **325**
Female Mind (essay)

Why don't more young women take up engineering as a profession?

Gender at Work   **335**

VIRGINIA WOOLF, Professions for Women (essay)   **335**

> A distinguished novelist and essayist describes the
> "phantoms and obstacles" that impede professional
> women at work.

JEAN REITH SCHROEDEL, Amy Kelley,   **340**
Machinist (interview)

> The daughter of Japanese immigrants at work in a
> male-dominated profession: Amy Kelley has something
> interesting to say.

LESTER C. THUROW, Why Women Are Paid Less   **350**
Than Men (essay)

> Thurow's answer is both surprising and sensible.

FELICE N. SCHWARTZ, Management Women and   **353**
the New Facts of Life (essay)

> How can companies support the career development of
> talented female managers? A management consultant
> makes some controversial suggestions.

Letters to the Editor of *Harvard Business Review*   **369**
(letters)

> A half-dozen outspoken responses to Felice
> Schwartz's proposals.

SUSAN DUDASH, We've Come a Long Way, But   **376**
Magazines Stayed Behind (student essay)

> Do women's magazines really support women who
> are pursuing careers?

IV.   MEDIA

Introduction   **382**

What Are the Effects of Television?   **384**

EDITH EFRON, The Soaps — Anything But   **384**
99-44/100 Percent Pure (essay)

Soap operas, says a *TV Guide* editor, are built on images of the sickest, most dependent, most immature women in our society.

Television Violence Act of 1989 (law) **391**

The U.S. Congress considers doing something to curb violence on television.

TOM PARADIS, A Child's Other World (student essay) **403**

"Programs aired today are distorting the minds and actions of today's youth."

MARYA MANNES, Television Advertising: The Splitting Image (essay) **407**

Advertising has conditioned Americans to see exaggeration or distortion as normal. And that's only one of the problems.

JULES FEIFFER (cartoon) **415**

Is the problem in your set—or sitting in front of it?

JACK McGARVEY, To Be or Not to Be as Defined by TV (essay) **416**

A teacher learns that TV stations make events, instead of just reporting them.

JOSHUA MEYROWITZ, No Sense of Place (essay) **422**

To a society without roots, maybe television can provide a sense of place—a new sense of place.

Television and the Elections **432**

JOSHUA MEYROWITZ, Whither "1984"? (essay) **432**

Does television really make the electorate susceptible to Big Brother? Or just the opposite?

GARRY WILLS, The Remaking of the Presidents (essay) **437**

What would have happened if television had been here earlier in our history? Could Lincoln have become president in an electronic age?

WILSON CAREY McWILLIAMS, A Republic   **446**
of Couch Potatoes: The Media Shrivel the
Electorate (essay)

> Something is wrong with the way Americans conduct
> election campaigns: something called television.

MORTIMER B. ZUCKERMAN, 1992—A New   **453**
Proposal (essay)

> A simple reform would transform for the better our
> presidential races, says the publisher of *U.S. News &
> World Report.*

Who and What Is Bruce Springsteen?   **456**

MAUREEN ORTH, WITH JANE THUCK AND   **456**
PETER GREENBERG, The Making of a Rock
Star (essay)

> A *Time* magazine cover story that helped launch
> The Boss.

JEFFERSON MORLEY, The Phenomenon (essay)   **466**

> The secret behind the Springsteen "phenomenon"?
> It's a "triumph of the spirit of the Sixties."

GEORGE F. WILL, Bruuuuuce (essay)   **471**

> A conservative explains the appeal of his "friend
> Bruce Springsteen."

MARY ELLEN BANASHEK, Bruce Springsteen: **473**
Why He Makes Us Feel So Good (essay)

> To a middle-ager "Bruce is a real man . . . the sort of
> guy other guys want on their softball team. And he
> has nice buns too."

JOHN LOMBARDI, St. Boss (essay)   **478**

> The sanctification of rock star is traced, from his good works
> to miracles to final apotheosis.

TAMA JANOWITZ, You and The Boss (fiction)   **496**

> Everybody's fantasy is to live with The Boss
> —isn't it?

How Good Is This Film? 502

Three well-known critics size up a major film—but can't agree on its merits.

STUART KLAWANS, On *Born on the Fourth of July*   502

VINCENT CANBY, How an All-American Boy Went to War and Lost His Faith   504

PAULINE KAEL, Potency   507

V. CIVIL LIBERTIES AND CIVIL RIGHTS

Introduction   514

LUIS VALDEZ, *Los Vendidos* (play)   519

The scene of "The Sellouts" is Honest Sancho's Used Mexican Lot, where Mexicans are for sale.

Censorship I: Pornography 531

GLORIA STEINEM, Erotica and Pornography (essay)   531

"Until we untangle the lethal confusion of sex with violence . . . there will be little murders in our beds—and very little love."

President's Commission on Obscenity and Pornography, Majority Report (report)   536

"Exposure to erotic stimuli appears to have little or no effect," according to the majority.

President's Commission on Obscenity and Pornography, Minority Report (report)   541

"Pornography is loveless: it degrades the human being, reduces him to the level of animal."

SUSAN BROWNMILLER, Let's Put Pornography   **544**
Back in the Closet (essay)

"Pornography represents hatred of women," so it
should be eliminated from our society.

SUSAN JACOBY, I Am a First Amendment Junkie   **547**
(essay)

A feminist argues with other feminists over the banning of pornography: "You can't OD on the first
amendment."

ANONYMOUS, Editorial: First Amendment   **551**
Pixillation

An editorial from William F. Buckley's *National Review* contends that pornography is not protected by
the first amendment.

SUSAN BROWNMILLER, Pornography Hurts   **552**
Women (essay)

"Pornography is the undiluted essence of anti-
female propaganda."

ROBERT SHEA, Women at War (essay)   **557**

A *Playboy* magazine analysis of the controversy
among women over restricting pornography.

Censorship II: The Case of
Huckleberry Finn   **571**

MARGOT ALLEN, *Huck Finn:* Two Generations   **571**
of Pain (essay)

A parent describes her son's pain at having to imper-
sonate Twain's Jim.

JOHN H. WALLACE, *Huckleberry Finn* Is   **579**
Offensive (essay)

"Classic or not, *Huck Finn* should not be allowed to
continue to make our children feel bad about themselves."

ROBERT NADEAU, *Huckleberry Finn* Is a Moral   **581**
   Story (essay)

   Twain's novel is "one of the most forceful indictments ever made against the subjugation of any class
   of people."

NAT HENTOFF, Huck Finn Better Get Out of   **584**
   Town by Sundown (essay)

   Is it censorship or sensitivity? A look at both sides of
   the *Huck Finn* question.

Civil Rights, Equal Rights, and the Law   **607**

On Civil Disobedience   **607**

HENRY DAVID THOREAU, Civil Disobedience   **607**
   (essay)

   "Unjust laws exist: shall we be content to
   obey them?"

Public Statement by Eight Alabama Clergymen   **629**
   (essay)

   Convinced that demonstrations in Birmingham are
   "unwise and untimely . . . extreme measures," eight
   clergymen urge an end to those demonstrations.

MARTIN LUTHER KING, JR., Letter from   **631**
   Birmingham Jail (letter/essay)

   The Nobel-Prize-winning civil rights leader defends
   civil disobedience and articulates — from his jail
   cell — the thinking behind civil rights demonstrations.

LEWIS H. VAN DUSEN, JR., Civil Disobedience: **648**
   Destroyer of Democracy (essay)

   Civil disobedience "is an assault on our democratic
   society," argues a successful lawyer.

WOODY ALLEN, A Brief, Yet Helpful, Guide to   **655**
   Civil Disobedience (essay)

   "It is well known that Mahatma Gandhi's insistence
   on eating his salads untossed shamed the British
   government into concessions."

MIA KLEIN ANDERSON, The *Other* Beauty of   **658**
    Martin Luther King, Jr.'s, "Letter from Birming-
    ham Jail" (essay)

    A stylistic analysis of King's letter reveals his rhetori-
    cal artistry.

MARK GARDNER, Appealing to White Moderates   **668**
    (student rhetorical analysis)

    The power of King's argument derives from his per-
    sonal trustworthiness, his careful logic, his appeals to
    powerful emotions.

Affirmative Action   **672**

Affirmative Action: Cure or Contradiction?   **672**
    (discussion)

    A frank, roundtable exchange on the pros and cons of
    affirmative action.

KURT VONNEGUT, JR., Harrison Bergeron   **683**
    (fiction)

    "The year was 2081, and everybody was finally
    equal," thanks to the Handicapper General.

PAUL R. SPICKARD, Why I Believe in   **690**
    Affirmative Action (essay)

    Denied several jobs by affirmative action efforts, a
    white male nevertheless contends that affirmative
    action is good social policy—and a scriptural
    imperative.

ROBERT F. DRINAN, Another Look at   **692**
    Affirmative Action (essay)

    A congressman and Jesuit priest claims that "to get
    beyond racism we must first take account of race."

MIGDIA CHINEA-VARELA, My Life as a "Twofer"   **698**
    (essay)

    To a female Hispanic, there is something insulting
    about affirmative action.

RICHARD RODRIGUEZ, None of This Is   **700**
    Fair (essay)

An eloquent beneficiary of affirmative action explains
what it feels like to be singled out.

Race on Campus   **705**

SHELBY STEELE, The Recoloring of Campus   **705**
Life (essay)

How to explain the presence of racial tension on
campus? A professor proposes a controversial answer,
a controversial solution.

RUTH CONNIFF, Racism 101 (essay)   **719**

"Before they can hope to combat campus racism,
students, professors, and administrators must change
the deeply ingrained attitude that Western culture is
the most important culture."

VICTOR HAO LI, Asian Discrimination: Fact or   **726**
Fiction? (essay)

An analysis of college admissions policies regarding
America's "model minority" generates some hard
questions.

VI.   CRIME AND PUNISHMENT

Introduction   **732**

What Causes Crime?   **734**

CLARENCE DARROW, Address to the Prisoners in   **734**
the Cook County Jail (speech)

People "are in jail because they cannot avoid it on
account of circumstances which are entirely beyond
their control."

RICHARD J. HERRNSTEIN AND JAMES Q.   **745**
WILSON, Are Criminals Made or Born? (essay)

The answer seems to be both, say these
criminologists — but gender and intelligence
are particularly important inherited traits.

STEPHEN JAY GOULD, Of Crime, Cause,   **755**
  and Correlation (essay)

> A noted paleontologist refutes, even ridicules, the
> idea that crime has a biological basis.

GARRISON KEILLOR, The Current Crisis in   **762**
  Remorse (essay)

> "'I'm thinking it was a nutritional thing,' one mass
> murderer remarked . . . 'I'd been doing a lot of deep-
> fried foods.'"

ROGER ROSENBLATT, Why the Justice System   **766**
  Fails (essay)

> Street crime in America can be traced directly to
> inadequacies in the justice system.

What's a Prison For?   772

WARREN BURGER, Prisons Are Designed to   **772**
  Rehabilitate (speech)

> A Supreme Court Chief Justice defends the role of
> prisons as rehabilitative — and suggests some reforms.

J. J. MALONEY, The J. B. Factor (essay)   **779**

> Prisons have become an "acceptable alternative,"
> says a former inmate. "Many prisons offer more com-
> fort than the U.S. Army."

ALLAN C. BROWNFELD, Putting Killers on the   **786**
  Streets (essay)

> The goal of a prison system isn't rehabilitation,
> claims Brownfeld, it's to protect honest citizens from
> criminals.

GEORGE JACKSON, A Letter from Prison (letter) **789**

> Are "criminals" often really "political prisoners"?
> Prisons "have always borne a certain resemblance to
> Dachau," George Jackson claims.

JAMES WRIGHT, American Twilights, 1957   **795**
  (poem)

A Pultizer-Prize-winning poet reflects on our prison system.

Capital Punishment   798

JAMES WRIGHT, At the Executed Murderer's   798
Grave (poem)

"I pity myself, because a man is dead."

GEORGE ORWELL, A Hanging (fiction)   800

"We all had a drink together, quite amicably. The
dead man was a hundred yards away."

H. L. MENCKEN, The Penalty of Death (essay)   805

"The time will come when all people will view with
horror the light way in which society and its courts
now take human life."

EDWARD I. KOCH, Death and Justice (essay)   809

A liberal former mayor of New York defends the
death penalty as an affirmation of life.

HENRY SCHWARZSCHILD, In Opposition to   814
Death Penalty Legislation (speech)

Capital punishment is no deterrent; in fact, it deludes
the public into believing that "something is being
done" about crime.

Should Drugs Be Legalized?   822

KURT SCHMOKE, A War for the Surgeon   822
General, Not the Attorney General (essay)

Our society should fight drugs as a medical problem,
not a legal one, argues the mayor of Baltimore.

MILTON FRIEDMAN, Prohibition and Drugs   829
(essay)

A Nobel Prize winner wonders (in 1972) if we have
the right to prevent an individual from becoming a
drug addict, and if drug laws just make things worse.

MILTON FRIEDMAN, An Open Letter to Bill   **832**
  Bennett (essay/letter)

  Now it's 1989: "The drug war cannot be won without
  undermining the human liberty that we cherish."

WILLIAM BENNETT, A Response to Milton   **834**
  Friedman (letter to the editor)

  President Bush's drug czar answers Milton Friedman:
  legalization would be "irresponsible and reckless
  public policy."

Responses: Letters to the Editor by Milton   **837**
  Friedman and Others (letters)

VII. SCIENCE AND SOCIETY

Introduction   **842**

Nature, Science, and Society: Is Peaceful   **845**
Coexistence Possible?

THOMAS JEFFERSON, Query XIX: Manufactures   **845**
  (from *Notes on the State of Virginia*) (essay)

  "Those who labor in the earth are the chosen people
  of God"; that's the opinion of our third president.

WENDELL BERRY, A Good Scythe (essay)   **847**

  A modern Jeffersonian salutes his "old-fashioned,
  human-powered scythe."

JAMES FENIMORE COOPER, The Slaughter of   **850**
  the Pigeons (fiction)

  In this excerpt from *The Pioneers*, Leather-stocking—
  the ideal western hero—turns away from the slaughter of birds for mere sport.

WILLIAM WORDSWORTH, The Tables Turned   **858**
  (poem)

Contents

"We murder to dissect," but "Sweet is the lore which Nature brings."

C. P. SNOW, The Two Cultures (essay) **859**

A scientist and novelist details the widening separation between the modern arts and sciences.

LOREN EISELEY, The Illusion of the Two Cultures (essay) **865**

The two types of creation—the artistic and the scientific—spring from the same source. That's the opinion of one who has done both.

Genetic Engineering **878**

LEWIS THOMAS, The Hazards of Science (essay) **878**

Are there certain questions scientists should not study? Is it "hubris" to seek a comprehensive understanding of nature?

NATHANIEL HAWTHORNE, The Birth-mark (fiction) **885**

A scientist seeks to perfect nature—but at a terrible cost.

JONATHAN KING, New Genetic Technology: Prospects and Hazards (essay) **901**

Genetic engineering holds great promise and great risks, so scientists must work openly, and closely, with citizens.

To Fight World Hunger (advertisement) **912**

To fight world hunger, ICI is "building" new plants. How could anyone object to that?

SUSAN WRIGHT, Genetic Engineering: The Risks (essay) **914**

Gene splicing offers the potential to redesign life, but the potential problems are very far from being resolved.

Do Animals Have Rights?   **925**

TOM REGAN, Religion and Animal Rights (essay)   **925**

> A careful defense of animal rights on moral,
> philosophical, and especially religious grounds.

TERESA K. RYE, How I Benefited from Animal   **938**
Research (speech)

> The victim of a congenital heart defect credits animal
> research for the surgery that saved her life.

EDWARD C. MELBY, JR., A Statement from the   **942**
Association for Biomedical Research (speech)

> Research on laboratory animals is absolutely essen-
> tial to relieve pain in both animals and people, con-
> tends a dean of veterinary medicine.

NEAL D. BARNARD, Letter from the Physicians   **953**
Committee for Responsible Medicine (letter)

> "Laboratory experiments not only produce inaccurate
> results, they're simply not necessary."

JANE GOODALL, A Plea for the Chimpanzees   **958**
(essay)

> "I shall be haunted forever by the eyes of the chim-
> panzees I saw that day."

GARRY B. TRUDEAU, Doonesbury (cartoons)   **966**

> "Look, I'm against cruelty to animals as much
> as anyone, but these animal rights people are out
> of control!"

What to Do About Acid Rain?   **967**

DIXY LEE RAY, The Great Acid Rain Debate   **967**
(essay)

> "There is no evidence that the problem of acid rain is
> urgent or getting worse."

GEORGE REIGER, What Can Be Done About   **983**
Acid Rain? (essay)

We don't need any more redundant research, says a
respected outdoorsman. We need action. Now.

The Latest Official Report on Acid Rain (report)   **989**

A federal study claims that acid rain has no significant
impact on forests, crops, lakes, or the atmosphere.

JON R. LUOMA, Acid Murder No Longer a   **994**
Mystery (essay)

A Minnesota environmentalist argues that acid rain is
continuing to poison northeastern lakes and forests.

LEO CULLUM, Antacid Rain (cartoon)   **1004**

Is this cartoon purely for laughs?

Euthanasia   **1005**

ANONYMOUS, It's Over, Debbie (essay)   **1005**

"Within seconds her breathing slowed, her eyes
closed and she seemed restful at last."

CHARLES COLSON, It's Not Over, Debbie (essay)   **1006**

"The Debbie story is not over yet, not by a long shot."

JAMES RACHELS, Active and Passive Euthanasia   **1009**
(essay)

The difference between actively ending a life and passively allowing it to end isn't really so clear after all.

SIDNEY HOOK, In Defense of Voluntary   **1016**
Euthanasia (essay)

An octogenarian says that people should have the right
to choose whether to end their lives.

MAY SARTON, From *Recovering: A Journal:*   **1019**
1978–1979 and *At Seventy: A Journal* (journal
entries)

An inside look at growing old — and saying goodbye
to a friend.

Index   **1033**

Contents by Rhetorical Mode

Journal and Personal Report
ELIZABETH CADY STANTON, The Seneca Falls
Declaration of Sentiments and Resolutions: Seneca
Falls Convention, 1848   232
SOJOURNER TRUTH, Ain't I a Woman?   236
MARCIA ANN GILLESPIE, A Different Take on the
Ol' Bump and Grind   272
DIANE WAKOSKI, Belly Dancer   276
JEAN REITH SCHROEDEL, Amy Kelley,
Machinist   340
JACK McGARVEY, To Be or Not to Be as Defined
by TV   416
MARGOT ALLEN, *Huck Finn*: Two Generations
of Pain   571
MIGDIA CHINEA-VARELA, My Life as a
"Twofer"   698
GARRISON KEILLOR, The Current Crisis
in Remorse   762
GEORGE JACKSON, A Letter from Prison   789
JAMES WRIGHT, At the Executed Murderer's
Grave   798
TERESA K. RYE, How I Benefited from
Animal Research   938
JANE GOODALL, A Plea for the Chimpanzees   958
ANONYMOUS, It's Over, Debbie   1005
MAY SARTON, From *Recovering* and
At Seventy   1019, 1022

Description and Narration
CHARLES DICKENS, What Is a Horse?   23
THEODORE SIZER, What High School Is   25
ALICE WALKER, Everyday Use   56
JAMES THURBER, University Days   101
RICHARD RODRIGUEZ, Aria: A Memoir of a
  Bilingual Childhood   143
SUSAN GLASPELL, *Trifles*   238
SUSAN GLASPELL, A Jury of Her Peers   251
JEAN REITH SCHROEDEL, Amy Kelley,
  Machinist   340
TAMA JANOWITZ, You and The Boss   496
MARGOT ALLEN, *Huck Finn:* Two Generations
  of Pain   571
KURT VONNEGUT, JR., Harrison Bergeron   683
RICHARD RODRIGUEZ, None of This Is Fair   700
J. J. MALONEY, The J. B. Factor   779
GEORGE ORWELL, A Hanging   800
WENDELL BERRY, A Good Scythe   847
JAMES FENIMORE COOPER, The Slaughter of
  the Pigeons   850
NATHANIEL HAWTHORNE, The Birth-mark   885

Process
THEODORE SIZER, What High School Is   25
NORMAN COUSINS, How to Make People Smaller
  Than They Are   71
JAMES C. STALKER, Official English or
  English Only?   176
EVELYN FOX KELLER, Women in Science: An Analysis
  of a Social Problem   314
JEAN REITH SCHROEDEL, Amy Kelley,
  Machinist   340
JOHN LOMBARDI, St. Boss   478
JON R. LUOMA, Acid Murder No Longer a
  Mystery   994

Illustration, Example
NATHAN GLAZER, Some Very Modest Proposals for the
  Improvement of American Education   38
JAMES THURBER, University Days   101
GARY LARSON, The Far Side   142
RICHARD RODRIGUEZ, Aria: A Memoir of a
  Bilingual Childhood   143

BARBARA LAWRENCE, Four-Letter Words Can
   Hurt You   217
JEAN REITH SCHROEDEL, Amy Kelley,
   Machinist   340
MARYA MANNES, Television Advertising: The
   Splitting Image   407
JULES FEIFFER cartoon   415
GARRY WILLS, The Remaking of the Presidents   437
JEFFERSON MORLEY, The Phenomenon   466
MARTIN LUTHER KING, JR., Letter from
   Birmingham Jail   631
MIA KLEIN ANDERSON, The *Other* Beauty of
   Martin Luther King Jr., "Letter from
   Birmingham Jail"   658
MARK GARDNER, Appealing to White
   Moderates   668
MIGDIA CHINEA-VARELA, My Life as a
   "Twofer"   698
J. J. MALONEY, The J. B. Factor   779
JAMES WRIGHT, American Twilights, 1957 and At the
   Executed Murderer's Grave   795, 798
EDWARD I. KOCH, Death and Justice   809
To Fight World Hunger   912
ANONYMOUS, It's Over, Debbie   1005
SIDNEY HOOK, In Defense of Voluntary
   Euthanasia   1016

Comparison and Contrast
E. B. WHITE, Education   20
JEROME STERN, What They Learn in School   54
ALICE WALKER, Everyday Use   56
Ads for Hofstra University and Babson
   College   99, 100
W. D. SNODGRASS, The Examination   107
SUSAN GLASPELL, *Trifles* and A Jury of
   Her Peers   238, 251
MARCIA ANN GILLESPIE, A Different Take on the
   Ol' Bump and Grind   272
SUSAN BROWNMILLER, Emotion   277
CAROL GILLIGAN, Images of Relationships   289
THOMAS JEFFERSON, Query XIX:
   Manufactures   845
WENDELL BERRY, A Good Scythe   847
WILLIAM WORDSWORTH, The Tables Turned   858

C. P. SNOW, The Two Cultures   859
LOREN EISELEY, The Illusion of the
    Two Cultures   865
JAMES RACHELS, Active and Passive
    Euthanasia   1009

Analysis
CARRIE TUHY, So Who Needs College?   74
JAMES BALDWIN, If Black English Isn't a Language,
    Then Tell Me, What Is?   112
GENEVA SMITHERMAN, White English in Blackface, or
    Who Do I Be?   118
EVELYN FOX KELLER, Women in Science: An Analysis
    of a Social Problem   314
SUSAN DUDASH, We've Come a Long Way, But
    Magazines Stayed Behind   376
EDITH EFRON, The Soaps—Anything but 99-44/100
    Percent Pure   384
JOSHUA MEYROWITZ, No Sense of Place and Whither
    "1984"?   422, 432
MAUREEN ORTH et al., The Making of a
    Rock Star   456
JEFFERSON MORLEY, The Phenomenon   466
GEORGE F. WILL, Bruuuuuce   471
ROBERT SHEA, Women at War   557
NAT HENTOFF, Huck Finn Better Get Out of Town
    by Sundown   584
MIA KLEIN ANDERSON, The *Other* Beauty of
    Martin Luther King, Jr., "Letter from
    Birmingham Jail"   658
MARK GARDNER, Appealing to White
    Moderates   668
RUTH CONNIFF, Racism 101   719
VICTOR HAO LI, Asian Discrimination: Fact or
    Fiction?   726
H. L. MENCKEN, The Penalty of Death   805
HENRY SCHWARZSCHILD, In Opposition to Death
    Penalty Legislation   814
LEWIS THOMAS, The Hazards of Science   878
JONATHAN KING, New Genetic Technology: Prospects
    and Hazards   901

Cause and Effect
JOHN SIMON, Why Good English Is Good
    for You   130

PAUL THEROUX, Being a Man   302
RUTH BLEIER, Gender and Mathematical
  Ability   310
EVELYN FOX KELLER, Women in Science: An Analysis
  of a Social Problem   314
SAMUEL C. FLORMAN, Engineering and the
  Female Mind   325
VIRGINIA WOOLF, Professions for Women   335
LESTER C. THUROW, Why Women Are Paid Less
  Than Men   350
FELICE N. SCHWARTZ, Management Women and the
  New Facts of Life   353
JEFFERSON MORLEY, The Phenomenon   466
GEORGE F. WILL, Bruuuuuce   471
MARY ELLEN BANASHEK, Bruce Springsteen: Why He
  Makes Us Feel So Good   473
JOHN LOMBARDI, St. Boss   478
Reports of the President's Commission on
  Pornography   536, 541
SHELBY STEELE, The Recoloring of
  Campus Life   705
CLARENCE DARROW, Address to the Prisoners in the
  Cook County Jail   734
RICHARD J. HERRNSTEIN AND JAMES Q. WILSON,
  Are Criminals Made or Born?   745
STEPHEN JAY GOULD, Of Crime, Cause, and
  Correlation   755
ROGER ROSENBLATT, Why the Justice
  System Fails   766

Definition

CHARLES DICKENS, What Is a Horse?   23
W. D. SNODGRASS, The Examination   107
GENEVA SMITHERMAN, White English in Blackface, or
  Who Do I Be?   118
CASEY MILLER AND KATE SWIFT, One Small Step
  for Genkind   205
BARBARA LAWRENCE, Four-Letter Words Can
  Hurt You   217
SOJOURNER TRUTH, Ain't I a Woman?   236
SUSAN BROWNMILLER, Emotion   277
PAUL THEROUX, Being a Man   302
GLORIA STEINEM, Erotica and Pornography   531
SUSAN BROWNMILLER, Pornography Hurts
  Women   552

HENRY DAVID THOREAU, Civil Disobedience   607
LEWIS H. VAN DUSEN, JR., Civil Disobedience:
Destroyer of Democracy   648

Argument: Categorical Proposition ("X is in fact Y")
NEIL POSTMAN, Order in the Classroom   47
CARRIE TUHY, So Who Needs College?   74
CAROLINE BIRD, College Is a Waste of Time
and Money   79
CHRISTOPHER JESTER, Not Just a Diploma
Factory   95
JAMES BALDWIN, If Black English Isn't a Language,
Then Tell Me, What Is?   112
EDITH EFRON, The Soaps—Anything but 99-44/100
Percent Pure   384
SUSAN JACOBY, I Am a First Amendment
Junkie   547
JOHN H. WALLACE, *Huckleberry Finn*
Is Offensive   579
ROBERT NADEAU, *Huckleberry Finn* Is a
Moral Story   581
PAUL R. SPICKARD, Why I Believe in
Affirmative Action   690
HENRY SCHWARZSCHILD, In Opposition to Death
Penalty Legislation   814
LEWIS THOMAS, The Hazards of Science   878
TOM REGAN, Religion and Animal Rights   925
EDWARD C. MELBY, JR., A Statement from the
Association for Biomedical Research   942
DIXY LEE RAY, The Great Acid Rain Debate   967

Argument: Evaluation
NORMAN COUSINS, How to Make People Smaller
Than They Are   71
Ads for Hofstra University and Babson
College   99, 100
RACHEL L. JONES, What's Wrong with
Black English?   115
JOHN SIMON, Why Good English Is Good
for You   130
RUTH BLEIER, Gender and Mathematical
Ability   310
TOM PARADIS, A Child's Other World   403
MARYA MANNES, Television Advertising: The
Splitting Image   407

STUART KLAWANS, VINCENT CANBY, AND
   PAULINE KAEL, On *Born on the Fourth of July*
   502, 504, 507
Reports of the President's Commission on
   Pornography   536, 541
PAUL R. SPICKARD, Why I Believe in Affirmative
   Action   690
ROBERT F. DRINAN, Another Look at Affirmative
   Action   692
RICHARD RODRIGUEZ, None of This Is Fair   700
GEORGE ORWELL, A Hanging   800
EDWARD I. KOCH, Death and Justice   809
WENDELL BERRY, A Good Scythe   847
TOM REGAN, Religion and Animal Rights   925
TERESA K. RYE, How I Benefited from Animal
   Research   938
The Latest Official Report on Acid Rain   989
SIDNEY HOOK, In Defense of Voluntary
   Euthanasia   1016

Argument: Proposal
NATHAN GLAZER, Some Very Modest Proposals for the
   Improvement of American Education   38
ADRIENNE RICH, Claiming an Education   65
WALTER DARLINGTON HUDDLESTON, On Behalf of a
   Constitutional Amendment to Make English the Offi-
   cial Language of the United States   165
EVELYN FOX KELLER, Women in Science: An Analysis
   of a Social Problem   314
Television Violence Act of 1989   391
MARYA MANNES, Television Advertising: The
   Splitting Image   407
MORTIMER B. ZUCKERMAN, 1992 — A New
   Proposal   453
SUSAN BROWNMILLER, Let's Put Pornography Back in
   the Closet   544
MARTIN LUTHER KING, JR., Letter from
   Birmingham Jail   631
WARREN BURGER, Prisons Are Designed to
   Rehabilitate   772
J. J. MALONEY, The J. B. Factor   779
KURT SCHMOKE, A War for the Surgeon General, Not
   the Attorney General   822
MILTON FRIEDMAN, Prohibition and Drugs and An
   Open Letter to Bill Bennett   829, 832

THOMAS JEFFERSON, Query XIX:
  Manufactures   845
SUSAN WRIGHT, Genetic Engineering:
  The Risks   914
JANE GOODALL, A Plea for the Chimpanzees   958
GEORGE REIGER, What Can Be Done About
  Acid Rain?   983

Argument: Refutation
Letters responding to Caroline Bird   90
JOHN SIMON, Why Good English Is Good
  for You   130
VICTOR VILLANUEVA, JR., Whose Voice Is It Anyway?
  Rodriguez' Speech in Retrospect   155
ROSEANN DUENAS GONZALEZ et al., The English
  Language Amendment: Examining Myths   189
KURT FERNSLER, Why I Want a Husband   300
RUTH BLEIER, Gender and Mathematical
  Ability   310
Letters responding to Felice Schwartz   369
Television Violence Act of 1989   391
NAT HENTOFF, Huck Finn Better Get Out of Town
  by Sundown   584
MARTIN LUTHER KING, JR., Letter from
  Birmingham Jail   631
STEPHEN JAY GOULD, Of Crime, Cause, and
  Correlation   755
EDWARD I. KOCH, Death and Justice   809
WILLIAM BENNETT, A Response to Milton
  Friedman   834
Responses to William Bennett   837
LOREN EISELEY, The Illusion of the
  Two Cultures   865
SUSAN WRIGHT, Genetic Engineering:
  The Risks   914
CHARLES COLSON, It's Not Over, Debbie   1006

Irony and Satire
CHARLES DICKENS, What Is a Horse?   23
MATT GROENING, Life in Hell   46
JEROME STERN, What They Learn in School   54
GARRY B. TRUDEAU, Doonesbury   70
W. D. SNODGRASS, The Examination   107

DOUGLAS R. HOFSTADTER, A Person Paper on Purity
   in Language   220
JUDY SYFERS, Why I Want a Wife   298
EVELYN FOX KELLER, Women in Science   314
TAMA JANOWITZ, You and The Boss   496
LUIS VALDEZ, *Los Vendidos*   519
WOODY ALLEN, A Brief, Yet Helpful, Guide to Civil
   Disobedience   655
KURT VONNEGUT, JR., Harrison Bergeron   683
GARRISON KEILLOR, The Current Crisis in
   Remorse   762

Conversations

Introduction

Why Write?

Why do people write?

For lots of reasons, of course. Sometimes the impulse to write derives from a personal need. The motive to write can come from within. Everyone, after all, needs to sort out feelings at one time or another or to make some personal sense of the world and its parts, and a good way to do such sorting is by writing. If you keep a diary or journal, or if you've shared your most intimate feelings through correspondence with a trusted friend, or if you've written essays — or notes toward an essay — in order to explore possible explanations for things, then you know what it means to write for personal reasons. (A root meaning of the word *essay* is "to try out, to experiment.") People do need a means of expressing powerful feelings and personal insights, and writing seems to provide just the tranquility required for a gathering of thoughts.

Other times it is the world itself that motivates a writer. We seem to have a need to note our observations about the world, especially if those observations are noteworthy — if they seem special or unique in some way. Sometimes this process of "taking note" is relatively formalized, as when a scientist records observations in a log of some kind or when the President at the end of a day records significant details for future reference or when you keep score at a baseball game or when a reporter transcribes "just the facts" into a news article. But just as often it is something less formal — when you take notes for a course, for instance, or when I write down something in my journal about the life and times of my two preschoolers. The drive "to hold the mirror up to nature," as Hamlet called it, to record our

1

understanding about the way of the world, accounts for
much of the prose we encounter and produce each day.

The motive to write can also derive from one's vocation.
In other words, some people write because it's their life's
work. They are professional writers — poets, news reporters,
novelists, technical writers, screenwriters. And they are
semiprofessional writers, people who don't think of themselves as writers but who indeed spend a large amount of
their time writing — police officers, engineers, college professors, lawyers, physicians, corporate managers, and so
forth. (You'd be surprised at how much time such people
spend on the writing required by their jobs.) Professional
writers and professionals-who-write sometimes put words
on paper for the reasons that have been named in the previous paragraphs — to express personal feelings or ideas, or
to record their impressions or interpretations of their workaday worlds. But they also often think in terms of a particular kind of writing — a genre — when they compose: newspaper employees think of themselves as writing a news
story or an editorial; poets set out to write a poem; engineers
or police officers think of the report they have to turn in;
lawyers have to produce that legal brief next week. Their
sense of completing a particular genre can sometimes take
precedence over other motives.

Of course all of these motives to write are legitimate, and
seldom do these motives exist in a pure state. It is probably
better to think of motives to write, instead of *a* motive, and
to think of primary and secondary motives, instead of a
single, all-consuming aim. When John Milton wrote
Paradise Lost, for instance, he was certainly out to record
his assessment of the nature of things and to express his
most personal thoughts — and to write an epic. When Henry
David Thoreau wrote *Walden*, he certainly had personal
motives — the book originated in his daily journals — and
he wished "to hold the mirror up to nature" as well (the
very title of *Walden* suggests that Thoreau was attempting
to record his close observations of nature).

But *Walden* and *Paradise Lost* are "public" documents,
too — attempts to sway public opinion and public behavior.
Thoreau advertised *Walden*, after all, as his attempt to "brag
as lustily as Chanticleer [the rooster] in the morning, if
only to wake my neighbor up." He wished to awaken his
fellow citizens to the nature of nature and to persuade them
to renew their own lives after his own example and experi-

ence. Milton's stated purpose—"to justify the ways of God to man"—was just as social. He wished to change how people conceive of their relation to God and to detail his vision of a heroic life to be lived by every wayfaring Christian. Writing to persuade, to have an effect on the thinking of others, does not preclude writing to discover or writing to record or writing in a particular genre. Indeed, writing to persuade nearly always means writing *about something* in a *particular genre* for reasons that are *intensely personal*. But writing to persuade does mean writing something that has designs on the hearts or minds (or both) of particular readers. It is writing that is calculated to have an effect on a real reader. This goes for John Milton and Joan Didion, and it goes for you, too.

For though a writer may work in private, a writer is never really alone. A writer out "to wake people up" or "to justify the ways of God" to men and women is obviously anything but working privately, for the writer out to persuade is inherently social. But every other kind of writing is social as well. The engineer who writes a report on a project is out to influence the project's managers. A physician's report on a patient is used by other caregivers in the short run and long run to direct medical attention in a specific way. The lawyer's brief is meant to sway judges. Even private writing is often quite public in fact. The feelings you pour out in a personal letter get read by sympathetic and responsive friends. The essays you write to discover your version of the truth become written attempts to convert readers to that version. Even journal entries that no one will read but you are shaped to an extent by what society considers to be noteworthy and by what a different "you" will want to read a few years from now; and the very words you choose reflect a vocabulary you share with others and learn from others. Writing is a social act. It is a primary means for touching others, and reading what others have written is a primary way of being touched in turn. The words you read and write are surrounded and shaped by the words and attitudes and beliefs of the many people who share your society, your "social context." People may write to express themselves, or to complete a particular kind of writing, or to say something about their world—or some combination of these—but in some sense they do so in order to have an effect on someone else.

In fact, usually writing emerges quite specifically in response to other writing. When you write, your reasons for writing are nearly always related to the people around you and what they have said or written themselves. A friend expects a letter; a supervisor at work has asked for a report; a professor assigns a paper; a job is advertised that requires a written application; a story or editorial is printed in a local paper or national magazine that arouses your ire; an encouraging teacher or a moving story inspires you to write a journal entry or your own story. That is why this book is titled *Conversations*. It assumes that writing emerges from other writing or from other speech, and that other writing is likely to follow in response to your own. You want to stay in touch, answer a friend's questions, ask your own questions, and maybe gossip or otherwise entertain along the way, so you return a friend's letter; you expect a response in a week or two. You've listened to a controversy or witnessed some expression of confusion in one of your classes, so you write a paper to straighten things out; you anticipate an argument, a counterresponse (or assent and praise) in turn. You want the person who takes your job to have an easier time than you did, so you rewrite the directions on how to do it; you figure the next person will make further revisions next year. Your cousin asks you how you like your school, so you write to encourage her to join you there next year; you end by asking her to let you know if she needs more information. Writing is engaging in conversation. To get in on it, you have to know what others have said about the matter at hand, and you must be able to anticipate possible responses.

This collection of readings is comprised of "public conversations"—conversations on public issues that concern American society (in general and within your local community) in the last decade of the twentieth century. Not every burning issue is represented here, of course; that would be impossible. But this book does include conversations—give-and-take discussions—on many matters that concern you and your community today. What do you want to get out of your years in college? What kind of experience should your college or university be providing? What changes ought to be made to improve American secondary schools? Should English be our official or semiofficial national language? What does it mean (or should it mean) to be a woman or a man these days? Should women be treated differently on the job? Do the news media control elections? Does television promote violence or make people passive? How good is a particular film or recording artist? Should pornography be banned or regulated? Should certain books be kept out of the curriculum? Is affirmative action legitimate? Are college campuses racist—and if so, what should be done about it? What are the causes and cures of crime? Is capital punishment ever justified? Should drugs be legalized? Do animals have rights? Is mercy killing ever legitimate? Should anything be done about acid rain? And so forth. This book assumes that you'll want to get in on some of these conversations, that you'll want to contribute to resolving some of those questions either nationally or within your own community.

For while there is plenty of discussion of these matters in the national media, there is plenty of local discussion as well. What you read here about the reform of secondary education or the control of the curriculum probably frames in many ways discussions of particular school matters in your local community. What you read here about race on campus or animal rights probably is relevant to what is happening someplace on your own campus. What you read here about gender issues will be relevant to your campus (do many women major in science or engineering at your school?), your community (does your town have adequate child-care facilities?), your job (how are women treated where you work?), even your own family (are family chores apportioned in stereotypical ways?). Sometimes you will want to be involved in a debate over The Larger Issue—for instance, should pornography be banned? Other times you'll want to take up more local concerns or subissues: Should x-rated films be shown on your campus? Does pornography demean women—or men? Is a particular item really pornographic? How might pornography be defined? Democracy can be seen as a sometimes messy but always spirited exchange of ideas on how we should conduct ourselves as a society and as individual communities. The readings here are designed to introduce you to the public conversations going on in our democracy, and to encourage you to contribute in some way to those conversations yourself. Even if these particular issues do not always engage you personally, they should provide you with models of how to engage in public discussions when an issue does concern you.

There are plenty of ways to make such contributions. The

contents to follow will introduce you to many different genres, many different kinds of writing. Essays are most prominent because the essay is a common genre and because the essay (or article) has important analogs with other forms, like the letter, the sermon, the report, or the editorial. But you will see other ways of engaging in public discourse as well — through fiction, poetry, speeches, plays, interviews, cartoons, and advertisements, for instance. There are news stories and movie reviews, letters to the editor and counterresponses, parodies and satires, explanations and analyses and outright arguments. As you think about *what* to contribute to discussions going on around you, you'll need to think about *how* to contribute, too — in what form, in what manner.

Indeed there are as many ways of addressing issues as reasons for doing so. Do you want to be formal, less formal, or downright intimate with your reader? Do you want to present yourself as something of an expert on the matter in question, or as someone on the same level as your readers? Do you want to speak dispassionately, or do you want to let your feelings show? Do you want to be explicit in stating your purpose, or less direct? Do you want to compose sentences that are careful and complex and qualified, or ones that are direct and emphatic? You'll see a broad range of tactics illustrated in the following pages, a broad range that will represent the possible ways of engaging in public discourse. You'll encounter mainstream, classic items — and dissenting views. You'll see conventional presentations and startingly inventive ones. You'll see how famous professional writers earned their fame, and you'll hear from anonymous but just-as-eloquent fellow citizens and fellow students. You'll hear from women as well as men, from majority as well as minority voices. The idea is to give you a better chance of finding your own voice in a given circumstance by exposing you to a full range of possible voices in your reading. The idea is to empower you to engage in civic discourse — now, today — on the issues that concern you and your community.

How to Read This Book — And an Example

As the previous section explains, an answer to the question "why write?" ultimately depends on several factors: on the writer's personal needs and motives, on the state of the world or issues within our world, on a genre or form of writing that a writer may be drawn or compelled toward, and on a reader or a community of readers that the writer wishes to influence. Many times all of those factors, in combination, are involved in the decision to write.

All of those factors, in combination, are also involved in decisions on *how* to write. Effective writers consider what they wish to accomplish (aim), on what subject or issue, in what genre, for which particular readers. A writer's decisions on those matters comprise what rhetoricians call a writer's "rhetorical stance"—what *you* decide to say to *someone* on a given *issue* in a particular *genre*. But the matter might be put more simply: your decisions about how to write at a given time are colored by the *occasion* for that writing and your attitude toward that occasion. A football coach will prepare his team for a game by considering the opponent's strengths and weaknesses (audience), by thinking about his own aims (to win, of course, but also perhaps "to establish our running game" or "to get some experience for our younger players"), by assessing his own team's strengths, and so forth. Writers devise their own game plans as well, based on aim, issue, genre, and audience.

Consequently, critical readers committed to understanding prose must attend to those same matters—to how the writer is shaping an idea to an audience in a particular form for a specific purpose. When you read each item in this book, therefore, read with those matters in mind. Consider the issue, of course; consider what the writer has to offer on a given subject. But also consider the writer's purpose, the limitations (or opportunities) that a given genre exerts, and the way the item is adapted by the writer to specific readers' knowledge, attitudes, and needs. Consider how those matters affect *what* is said (what rhetoricians call "invention"—the art of discovering what information and arguments will affect readers), in what *order* it is said (or arrangement), and *how* it is said (style and tone). Reading, like writing, is a social and rhetorical activity. It involves not simply passively decoding a message but actively understanding the designs the message has for the reader and how it is calculated to achieve its effects.

The first item in this book, for example, is E. B. White's essay, "Education." What is its purpose? (If you haven't read "Education" yet, take five minutes to do so now; that way, you can more easily follow the rest of this introduction.) White wrote the essay a half century ago, but you probably find it to be interesting still, in part at least because it concerns a perennial American question: What should our schools be like? Is education better carried out in large, fully equipped, but relatively impersonal settings, or in smaller but intensely personal, teacher-dominated schools? Which should count for more: the efficiencies of an educational system that is "progressive" (the word comes from paragraph two), or the personal traits of the individual classroom teacher? The essay is a personal one, in that it is the education of his son that White is "worried about"; yet it is public matter, too. After all, White published it in the *New Yorker*, a magazine with a readership wide and influential and far more national than its name implies.

What is White's position on the issue? At first it might seem that the author takes no sides, that he simply wishes to describe objectively the two alternatives and to record his son's experiences in each circumstance. He gives equal time to each school, he spends the same amount of space on concrete details about each, and he seems in firm control of his personal biases ("I have always rather favored public schools"). Through his light and comic tone White implies that all will be well for his son — and our children — in either circumstance, that the two schools each are to be neither favored nor feared by us. "All one can say is that the situation is different" (paragraph four), not better, in the two places.

Or is it? Many readers — myself among them — contend that "Education" is less an objective, neutral appraisal than it is a calculated argument that subtly favors the country school. To such readers, White's objective pose is only that — a created pose, an attempt to create a genial, sympathetic, and trustworthy speaker. By caring so obviously for his son (final paragraph), by confessing his biases, and by treating both schools with distance and detachment and reliable detail, White creates what rhetoricians call "ethos" — that quality of a piece of writing that persuades through the character of the speaker or writer. By poking gentle humor at just about everything — his son "the scholar," his wife the prim graduate of Miss Winsor's private schools; himself "the victim of a young ceramist"; and of course both schools — White makes himself seem enormously sympathetic and trustworthy: fair-minded and unflappable, balanced and detached.

But is this reliable speaker arguing or describing? Those who see the essay as an argument for the ways of the country school can point to the emotional aspects of the essay — to its pathos, in other words. The image of the one-room schoolhouse, for instance, is imprinted in positive terms on the American psyche, and White exploits that image for his argumentative purposes. The "scholar" walks miles through the snow to get his education; like the schoolhouse itself, he has the self-reliance and weather-resistance to care for himself and to fit into a class with children both younger and older; and he learns a practical curriculum — there is "no time at all for the esoteric" — "just as fast and as hard as he can." It is all Abraham Lincoln and "The Waltons," isn't it? And the teacher who presides over the country school appeals to the reader's emotions as only The Fairy Tale Mother can. This teacher-mother is not only "a guardian of their health, their clothes, their habits . . . and their snowball engagements," but "she has been doing this sort of Augean task for twenty years, and is both kind and wise. She cooks for the children on the stove that heats the room, and she can cool their passions or warm their soup with equal competence."

No such individual Fairy Tale Mother presides over the city school. Instead, that school is presided over by a staff of Educational Professionals — a busdriver, half a dozen anonymous teachers, a nurse, an athletic instructor, dietitians. The school itself is institutional, regimented, professionalized. There the scholar is "worked on," "supervised," "pulled." Like the one-room schoolhouse, the regimented institution is ingrained in the American psyche. But in this case the emotional appeal is negative, for "The System" is something that Americans instinctively resist. True, the city school is no prison, and true, the scholar in this school learns "to read with a gratifying discernment." But the accomplishments remain rather abstract. Faced with such an education, such a school, no wonder the students literally become ill. At least that is the implication of the end of paragraph three, where the account of the city school is concluded with an account of the networks of professional physicians that discuss diseases that never seem to appear in the country schools.

For these reasons many readers see "Education" as an argument against the city school and an endorsement of the country one. They see the essay as a comparison with an aim like most comparison essays: to show a preference. The evaluative aim is carried out by reference to specific criteria, namely that schools are better if they are less structured and if they make students want to attend (because motivated students learn better); a structured, supervised curriculum and facilities are inferior to a personalized, unstructured environment that makes students love school. Days at the country school pass "just like lightning"; to attend the country school the boy is willing literally to walk through snowdrifts, while to get to the city school he must be escorted to the bus stop — or be "pulled" there. The country school is full of "surprises" and "individual instruction," while the city school is full of supervision; there are no surprises in the "progressive" school. In a real sense, therefore, White persuades not only by the force of his personality or through emotional appeals but also through hard evidence, what rhetoricians call "logos." "Education" amounts to an argument by example wherein the single case — the boy scholar — stands for many such cases. This case study persuades like other case studies: by being presented as representative. White creates through his unnamed son, who is described as typical in every way, a representative example that stands for the education of Everychild. The particular details provided in the essay become not mere "concrete description" but hard evidence, good reasons, summoned to support White's implicit thesis. The logic of the piece seems to go something like this: "Country schools are a bit superior to city ones. They make up for what they lack in facilities with a more personal, less authoritarian atmosphere that children respond to."

E. B. White, then, wins his reader's assent by means of ethos, pathos, and logos. But the country-school approach is also reinforced by the essay's arrangement. Notice, for example, that the essay begins and ends with favorable accounts of the country school. In other words, the emphatic first and final positions of the essay are reserved for the virtues of country schools, while the account of the city school is buried in the unemphatic middle of the essay. The article could easily have begun with the second paragraph (wouldn't sentence two of paragraph two have made a successful opener?), but such a strategy would have promoted the value of the city school. By choosing to add the loving vignette of the Fairy Tale Teacher in his opening paragraph, White disposes his readers to favor country schools from the very start. Notice too that the comparison of the two schools in the body of "Education" proceeds from city to country. Again, it didn't have to be so; White could have discussed the country school first, or he could have gone back and forth from city to country more often (adopting what some handbooks call an "alternating" method of comparison as opposed to the "divided" pattern that White actually did use). By choosing to deal first with the city school, all in one lump, and then to present the country school in another lump, White furthered his persuasive aim. After all, most "preference comparisons" move from the inferior item to the superior one. In other words, writers of comparisons usually move from "this one is good" to "but this other one is even better," rather than vice versa. So when White opts to deal first with the city schools, he subtly reinforces his persuasive end through very indirect means. White's arrangement serves his purpose in two ways, then: it permits him to end with the item he wishes to prefer; and it permits him to add an introductory paragraph that places his country school in that favorable spot as well.

Even the arrangement of details within White's individual paragraphs serves his goals. It appears that the central paragraphs (three, four, and five) are arranged chronologically, that details in those paragraphs are arranged according to the rhythm of the school day. But a closer examination shows that paragraph three closes on a note of sickness. That detail could have come earlier in the paragraph, but White places the negative detail in the emphatic final position. Similarly, the two paragraphs on the country school are manipulated for rhetorical ends. Why does White divide the account of the country school into two paragraphs? (After all, he dealt with the city school in one paragraph.) By doing so he is able to give special emphasis to the first sentence of one of his paragraphs, "There is no supervised play," highlighting thereby a key difference between the two schools.

A critical reading of "Education" must also consider expression, those sentence and word choices that are sometimes equated with the style of a particular essay or author. Like most rhetoricians, I personally resist the idea that "style is the person" — that style is something inherent in a writer, that it amounts to a sort of genetic code or set of fingerprints that are idiosyncratic to each person, that it is possible to speak generically of Didion's style or Martin

Luther King's style or E. B. White's style. It has always seemed to me more appropriate to think of style as characteristic of a particular *occasion* for writing, as something that is as appropriate to reader and subject and genre as it is to a particular author. Words and sentences are chosen in response to rhetorical and social circumstances, and those words and sentences change as the occasion changes. If it is possible to characterize E. B. White's style or Hemingway's style in general (and I'm not sure even of that), then it is so only with respect to certain kinds of writing that they did again and again and again. For when those writers found themselves writing outside the *New Yorker* (in White's case) or outside of fiction (in Hemingway's), they did indeed adopt different stylistic choices. It is probably wiser to focus not on the apparent idiosyncrasies associated with a Didion or a King or a Hemingway or an E. B. White, but on the particular word and sentence choices at work in a particular rhetorical situation.

Take the case at hand. What stylistic choices are worthy of note in "Education"? How has White chosen particular sentence patterns and words in order to further the aims of his essay?

The sentences of White's essay are certainly appropriate for public discourse. There are roughly a thousand words and fifty sentences in "Education," so average sentence length comes to about twenty words. Many are shorter than twenty words though (the shortest is five words), and only one forty-three-word sentence seems particularly long. The result is that this essay can probably be readily comprehended by most adults, without its sentences creating the impression of superficiality or childishness. (The sentences in White's book for children *Charlotte's Web*, by contrast, have an average length of about twelve words.)

Moreover, White's sentences are unpretentious. They move in conventional ways—from subjects and verbs to objects and modifiers. There are no sentence inversions (violations of the normal subject/verb/object order), few distracting interrupters (the parentheses and the "I suspect" in that one long sentence in paragraph two are exceptions), and few lengthy opening sentence modifiers that keep us too long from subjects and verbs. Not only that, the sentences are simple and unpretentious in another sense: White comparatively rarely uses subordinate (or modifying) clauses—clauses containing a subject and verb and beginning with "who" or "although" or "that" or "because" or the like. I count only two such modifying (or dependent) clauses in the first and third paragraphs, for instance, and just five in the second; if you don't think that is a low number, compare it to a six hundred-word sample of your own prose. When White does add length to a sentence, he does it not by adding complex clauses that modify other clauses, but by adding independent clauses (ones that begin with "and" or "but") and by adding phrases and modifiers in parallel series. Some examples? The children's teacher is a guardian "of their health, their clothes, their habits, their mothers, and their snowball engagements"; the boy "learned fast, kept well, and we were satisfied"; the bus "would sweep to a halt, open its mouth, suck the boy in, and spring away." And so forth. The "ands" make White's essay informal and conversational, never remote or scholarly or full of disclaimers and qualifiers.

White uses relatively simple sentence patterns in "Education," then, but his prose is still anything but simple. Some of his sentences are beautifully parallel: "she can cool their passions or warm their soup"; "she conceives their costumes, cleans up their noses, and shares their confidences"; "in a cinder court he played games supervised by an athletic instructor, and in a cafeteria he ate lunch worked out by a dietitian"; "when the snow is deep or the motor is dead"; "rose hips in fall, snowballs in winter." These precise, mirror-image parallel structures are known as isocolons to rhetoricians. White delights in them and in the artful informality they create. He uses parallel structures and relentless coordination — "and" after "and" after "and" — to make his prose accessible to a large audience of appreciative readers. And he uses those lists of specific items in parallel series to give his writing its remarkably concrete, remarkably vivid quality.

That brings us to White's word choices. They too contribute to White's purposes. Remember the sense of detachment and generosity in White's narrative voice, the ethos of involvement and detachment apparent in the speaker? In large measure that is the result of White's word choices. For instance, White has the ability to attach mock-heroic terminology to his descriptions so that he comes across as balanced and wise, as someone who doesn't take himself or his world too seriously. The boy is a "scholar" who "sallied forth" on a "journey" to school or to "make Indian

weapons of a semi-deadly nature." The gentle hyperbole
fits in well with the classical allusion inherent in the word
"Augean" (one of Hercules' labors was to clean the Augean
stables): there is a sophistication and worldly wisdom in
the speaker's voice that qualifies him to speak on this subject. And remember the discussion of whether White's aim
was purely descriptive or more argumentative in character?
White's metaphors underscore his argumentative aim: the
city school bus "was as punctual as death," a sort of macabre
monster that "would sweep to a halt, open its mouth, suck
the boy in, and spring away with an angry growl"; or it is
"like a train picking up a bag of mail." At the country school,
by contrast, the day passes "just like lightning." If the
metaphors do not provide enough evidence of White's persuasive aim, consider the connotations of words—their
emotional charges, that is—that are associated with the
city school: "regimented," "supervised," "worked on," "uniforms," "fevers." And then compare these with the connotation of some words White associates with the country
school: "surprises," a "bungalow," "weather-resistant," "individual instruction," "guardian," and so forth. The diction
and sentence choices made by White indeed do reinforce
his argumentative purpose.

This analysis by no means exhausts the full measure of
rhetorical sophistication that E. B. White brings to the composition of "Education." You may have noticed other tactics
at work, or you might disagree with some of the generalizations presented here. But the purpose of this discussion is
not to detail the rhetoric of White's "Education." It is merely
to illustrate a method of critical reading that you might
employ as you read the selections in this book and the
public rhetoric that you encounter in your life each day.
The point has been to encourage you to read not just for
what is said—though this is crucial—but for *how* it is said
as well. For reading is as "rhetorical" an activity as writing.
It depends on an appreciation of how writer, subject, and
reader are all "negotiated" through a particular document.

If you read for "how" as well as "what," the distinction
between the two may begin to shorten for you. Appreciation
of the rhetoric of public discourse can make you more skeptical of the arguments presented to you and to other citizens.
It can make you a reader less likely to be won over on
slender grounds, more likely to remain the doubter than
the easy victim or trusting soul who accepts all arguments

at face value. Whether you decide to take part in any of the particular "conversations" captured in this book or not, therefore, your thinking can be stimulated by critical reading.

Not only that, you'll find yourself growing as a writer; if you read critically, you'll begin to adopt and adapt for your own purposes the best rhetorical maneuvers on display in this book and elsewhere. What is a particular writer's real aim? What evidence is used to win the assent of readers? How does a particular writer establish credibility? What kind of emotional and logical appeals are at work in a given circumstance? How does the arrangement of a presentation influence its reception? How can sentence style and word choices sustain a writer's aim? By asking and answering questions like these, you can gain confidence as reader and writer. By becoming better able to understand and appreciate the conversations going on around you, you'll learn to make more powerful and sophisticated contributions to the discussions that most engage you personally. Critical reading of the selections in this book can make you a better writer, a better citizen.

I.

EDUCATION

Americans have always been passionate about issues related to education. Why? For one thing, education issues affect every American in a personal way. True, there is an anti-intellectual strain in American life; but it is also true that Americans pursue with passion the ideal of "education for all," both as a means of self-improvement and as the source of the enlightened citizenry required by democratic institutions. For another thing, the decentralized nature of our educational "system" (American education is hardly as monolithic as the term "system" implies) encourages a continuing and sometimes passionate public dialogue among citizens interested in shaping the policies of local schools.

Portions of two current conversations are included in this part. (In addition, education issues emerge later in this book, in the parts on Language, Gender, Media, and Civil Liberties.) The first — "What to Do About the Schools?" — concerns proposals for improving public education, particularly secondary schools. In the past decade, particularly as a response to the economic crises of the early 1980s, a number of committees and commissions launched well-publicized reform efforts aimed at everything from teacher education and school governance to classroom climate and the curriculum — at everything from competency testing and conduct codes to the size of schools, the wisdom of "tracking" students, and the appropriateness of vocational education. The selections here are in one sense more general than those specific issues in that they assume a comprehensive perspective on education. Yet in another sense they dramatize in very specific ways the particular issues that are evident in nearly every discussion of educational policy. Should schools be large, centralized, and comprehensive — have all the advantages of size? Or should they be smaller and more personal — have all the advantages of small size? Is discipline a central problem, and (if so) how can discipline be improved? Or does an overemphasis on discipline make schools confining and constricting — places that value order and conformity over independence and freedom? And what about the curriculum? Should it emphasize mastery of bodies of knowledge, "what every educated person needs to know"? Or should it foster instead learning skills — problem-solving ability, flexibility, independent thinking, and resourcefulness?

The second set of readings in this part addresses the question, "What Is College For?" No doubt on your own campus

you've listened in on discussions of this topic in some form or another, and you've probably pondered the matter yourself. In broad terms, the question can be posed this way: Is college an occasion for personal growth and general intellectual development, or is it the path to social and economic advancement? If college should foster both general education and disciplinary specialization, then in what proportions should it do so? Is college for the intellectual elite who are sophisticated enough to pursue truly advanced learning, or is it something within the reach of most high school graduates? Does college "empower" the democratic citizenry? Does it offer a critical perspective on our institutions and habits? Or is college simply a means of socializing students into willing servants of the modern corporate state?

The perennial nature of debates about education can be frustrating, especially to educational leaders. But the very relentlessness of the debates probably brings out the best feature of a democratic society: the freedom of citizens to shape policy through open and public exchange.

WHAT TO DO ABOUT THE SCHOOLS?

E. B. White
Education

E. B. White (1899–1985), who contributed regularly to the New Yorker *and whose work has been collected into several books, was perhaps America's most popular essayist. You may also know him as the author of the children's classic* Charlotte's Web *(1952). First published in 1939 in* Harper's *and in White's* One Man's Meat, *the following comparison of two educational philosophies remains relevant half a century later.*

1   I have an increasing admiration for the teacher in the country school where we have a third-grade scholar in attendance. She not only undertakes to instruct her charges in all the subjects of the first three grades, but she manages to function quietly and effectively as a guardian of their health, their clothes, their habits, their mothers, and their snowball engagements. She has been doing this sort of Augean task for twenty years, and is both kind and wise. She cooks for the children on the stove that heats the room, and she can cool their passions or warm their soup with equal competence. She conceives their costumes, cleans up their messes, and shares their confidences. My boy already regards his teacher as his great friend, and I think tells her a great deal more than he tells us.

2   The shift from city school to country school was something we worried about quietly all last summer. I have always rather favored public school over private school, if only because in public school you meet a greater variety of children. This bias of mine, I suspect, is partly an attempt to justify my own past (I never knew anything but public schools) and partly an involuntary defense against getting kicked in the shins by a young ceramist on his way to the kiln. My wife was unacquainted with public schools, never having been exposed (in her early life) to anything more

public than the washroom of Miss Winsor's. Regardless of our backgrounds, we both knew that the change in schools was something that concerned not us but the scholar himself. We hoped it would work out all right. In New York our son went to a medium-priced private institution with semi-progressive ideas of education, and modern plumbing. He learned fast, kept well, and we were satisfied. It was an electric, colorful, regimented existence with moments of pleasurable pause and giddy incident. The day the Christmas angel fainted and had to be carried out by one of the Wise Men was educational in the highest sense of the term. Our scholar gave imitations of it around the house for weeks afterward, and I doubt if it ever goes completely out of his mind.

His days were rich in formal experience. Wearing overalls   3 and an old sweater (the accepted uniform of the private seminary), he sallied forth at morn accompanied by a nurse or a parent and walked (or was pulled) two blocks to a corner where the school bus made a flag stop. This flashy vehicle was as punctual as death: seeing us waiting at the cold curb, it would sweep to a halt, open its mouth, suck the boy in, and spring away with an angry growl. It was a good deal like a train picking up a bag of mail. At school the scholar was worked on for six or seven hours by half a dozen teachers and a nurse, and was revived on orange juice in mid-morning. In a cinder court he played games supervised by an athletic instructor, and in a cafeteria he ate lunch worked out by a dietitian. He soon learned to read with gratifying facility and discernment and to make Indian weapons of a semi-deadly nature. Whenever one of his classmates fell low of a fever the news was put on the wires and there were breathless phone calls to physicians, discussing periods of incubation and allied magic.

In the country all one can say is that the situation is   4 different, and somehow more casual. Dressed in corduroys, sweatshirt, and short rubber boots, and carrying a tin dinner-pail pail, our scholar departs at the crack of dawn for the village school, two and a half miles down the road, next to the cemetery. When the road is open and the car will start, he makes the journey by motor, courtesy of his old man. When the snow is deep or the motor is dead or both, he makes it on the hoof. In the afternoons he walks or hitches all or part of the way home in fair weather, gets transported in foul. The schoolhouse is a two-room frame building, bungalow type, shingles stained a burnt brown with weather-resistant stain. It has a chemical toilet in the basement and two teachers above the stairs. One takes the first three grades, the other the fourth, fifth, and sixth. They have little or no time for individual instruction, and no time at all for the esoteric. They teach what they know themselves, just as fast and as hard as they can manage. The pupils sit still at their desks in class, and do their milling around outdoors during recess.

5   There is no supervised play. They play cops and robbers (only they call it "Jail") and throw things at one another — snowballs in winter, rose hips in fall. It seems to satisfy them. They also construct darts, pinwheels, and "pick-up-sticks" (jackstraws), and the school itself does a brisk trade in penny candy, which is for sale right in the classroom and which contains "surprises." The most highly prized surprise is a fake cigarette, made of cardboard, fiendishly lifelike.

6   The memory of how apprehensive we were at the beginning is still strong. The boy was nervous about the change too. The tension, on that first fair morning in September when we drove him to school, almost blew the windows out of the sedan. And when later we picked him up on the road, wandering along with his little blue lunch-pail, and got his laconic report "All right" in answer to our inquiry about how the day had gone, our relief was vast. Now, after almost a year of it, the only difference we can discover in the two school experiences is that in the country he sleeps better at night — and *that* probably is more the air than the education. When grilled on the subject of school-in-country vs. school-in-city, he replied that the chief difference is that the day seems to go so much quicker in the country. "Just like lightning," he reported.

Charles Dickens

What Is a Horse?

Was Charles Dickens (1812–1870) the greatest English novelist? This selection from the opening pages of Hard Times *(1854) illustrates Dickens' satiric edge; designed as a commentary on a "mechanical" system of education devised during the industrial revolution, it may also offer perspective on the schools of today.*

Thomas Gradgrind, sir. A man of realities. A man of fact 1
and calculations. A man who proceeds upon the principle that two and two are four, and nothing over, and who is not to be talked into allowing for anything over. Thomas Gradgrind, sir—peremptorily Thomas—Thomas Gradgrind. With a rule and a pair of scales, and the multiplication table always in his pocket, sir, ready to weigh and measure any parcel of human nature, and tell you exactly what it comes to. It is a mere question of figures, a case of simple arithmetic. You might hope to get some other nonsensical belief into the head of George Gradgrind, or Augustus Gradgrind, or John Gradgrind, or Joseph Gradgrind (all suppositious, nonexistent persons), but into the head of Thomas Gradgrind—no, sir!

In such terms Mr Gradgrind always mentally introduced 2
himself, whether to his private circle of acquaintance, or to the public in general. In such terms, no doubt, substituting the words 'boys and girls', for 'sir', Thomas Gradgrind now presented Thomas Gradgrind to the little pitchers before him, who were to be filled so full of facts.

Indeed, as he eagerly sparkled at them from the cellarage 3
before mentioned, he seemed a kind of cannon loaded to the muzzle with facts, and prepared to blow them clean out of the regions of childhood at one discharge. He seemed a galvanizing apparatus, too, charged with a grim mechanical substitute for the tender young imaginations that were to be stormed away.

'Girl number twenty,' said Mr Gradgrind, squarely point- 4
ing with his square forefinger, 'I don't know that girl. Who is that girl?'

'Sissy Jupe, sir,' explained number twenty, blushing, 5
standing up, and curtseying.

6   'Sissy is not a name,' said Mr Gradgrind. 'Don't call your-
     self Sissy. Call yourself Cecilia.'
7   'It's father as calls me Sissy, sir,' returned the young girl
     in a trembling voice, and with another curtsey.
8   'Then he has no business to do it,' said Mr Gradgrind.
     'Tell him he mustn't. Cecilia Jupe. Let me see. What is your
     father?'
9   'He belongs to the horse-riding, if you please, sir.'
10   Mr Gradgrind frowned, and waved off the objectionable
     calling with his hand.
11   'We don't want to know anything about that, here. You
     mustn't tell us about that, here. Your father breaks horses,
     don't he?'
12   'If you please, sir, when they can get any to break, they
     do break horses in the ring, sir.'
13   'You mustn't tell us about the ring, here. Very well, then.
     Describe your father as a horsebreaker. He doctors sick
     horses, I dare say?'
14   'Oh yes, sir.'
15   'Very well, then. He is a veterinary surgeon, a farrier and
     horsebreaker. Give me your definition of a horse.'
16   (Sissy Jupe thrown into the greatest alarm by this demand.)
17   'Girl number twenty unable to define a horse!' said Mr
     Gradgrind, for the general behoof of all the little pitchers.
     'Girl number twenty possessed of no facts, in reference to
     one of the commonest of animals! Some boy's definition of
     a horse. Bitzer, yours.'
18   The square finger, moving here and there, lighted sud-
     denly on Bitzer, perhaps because he chanced to sit in the
     same ray of sunlight which, darting in at one of the bare
     windows of the intensely whitewashed room, irradiated
     Sissy. For, the boys and girls sat on the face of the inclined
     plane in two compact bodies, divided up the centre by a
     narrow interval; and Sissy, being at the corner of a row on
     the sunny side, came in for the beginning of a sunbeam, of
     which Bitzer, being at the corner of a row on the other side,
     a few rows in advance, caught the end. But, whereas the
     girl was so dark-eyed and dark-haired, that she seemed to
     received a deeper and more lustrous colour from the sun
     when it shone upon her, the boy was so light-eyed and
     light-haired that the self-same rays appeared to draw out
     of him what little colour he ever possessed. His cold eyes
     would hardly have been eyes, but for the short ends of
     lashes which, by bringing them into immediate contrast

with something paler than themselves, expressed their
form. His short-cropped hair might have been a mere continuation of the sandy freckles on his forehead and face.
His skin was so unwholesomely deficient in the natural
tinge, that he looked as though, if he were cut, he would
bleed white.

'Bitzer,' said Thomas Gradgrind. 'Your definition of a 19
horse.'

'Quadruped. Graminivorous. Forty teeth, namely twenty- 20
four grinders, four eye-teeth, and twelve incisive. Sheds
coat in the spring; in marshy countries, sheds hoofs, too.
Hoofs hard, but requiring to be shod with iron. Age known
by marks in mouth.' Thus (and much more) Bitzer.

'Now girl number twenty,' said Mr Gradgrind. 'You know 21
what a horse is.'

Theodore Sizer
What High School Is

*Theodore Sizer (born 1932) chairs the education department
at Brown University. His* Horace's Compromise: The Dilemma of the American High School *(1984) offers a comprehensive analysis of "the American high school"—and a
program for reform. The following passage is excerpted from*
Horace's Compromise.

Mark, sixteen and a genial eleventh-grader, rides a bus 1
to Franklin High School, arriving at 7:25. It is an Assembly
Day, so the schedule is adapted to allow for a meeting of
the entire school. He hangs out with his friends, first outside
school and then inside, by his locker. He carries a pile of
textbooks and notebooks; in all, it weighs eight and a half
pounds.

From 7:30 to 8:19, with nineteen other students, he is in 2
Room 304 for English class. The Shakespeare play being
read this year by the eleventh grade is *Romeo and Juliet*.
The teacher, Ms. Viola, has various students in turn take
parts and read out loud. Periodically, she interrupts the

(usually halting) recitations to ask whether the thread of the conversation in the play is clear. Mark is entertained by the stumbling readings of some of his classmates. He hopes he will not be asked to be Romeo, particularly if his current steady, Sally, is Juliet. There is a good deal of giggling in class, and much attention paid to who may be called on next. Ms. Viola reminds the class of a test on this part of the play to be given next week.

3   The bell rings at 8:19. Mark goes to the boys' room, where he sees a classmate who he thinks is a wimp but who constantly tries to be a buddy. Mark avoids the leech by rushing off. On the way, he notices two boys engaged in some sort of transaction, probably over marijuana. He pays them no attention. 8:24. Typing class. The rows of desks that embrace big office machines are almost filled before the bell. Mark is uncomfortable here. Typing class is girl country. The teacher constantly threatens what to Mark is a humiliatingly female future: "Your employer won't like these erasures." The minutes during the period are spent copying a letter from a handbook onto business stationery. Mark struggles to keep from looking at his work; the teacher wants him to watch only the material from which he is copying. Mark is frustrated, uncomfortable, and scared that he will not complete his letter by the class's end, which would be embarrassing.

4   Nine tenths of the students present at school that day are assembled in the auditorium by the 9:18 bell. The dilatory tenth still stumble in, running down aisles. Annoyed class deans try to get the mob settled. The curtains part; the program is a concert by a student rock group. Their electronic gear flashes under the lights, and the five boys and one girl in the group work hard at being casual. Their movements on stage are studiously at three-quarter time, and they chat with one another as though the tumultuous screaming of their schoolmates were totally inaudible. The girl balances on a stool; the boys crank up the music. It is very soft rock, the sanitized lyrics surely cleared with the assistant principal. The girl sings, holding the mike close to her mouth, but can scarcely be heard. Her light voice is tentative, and the lyrics indecipherable. The guitars, amplified, are tuneful, however, and the drums are played with energy.

5   The students around Mark—all juniors, since they are seated by class—alternately slouch in their upholstered,

hinged seats, talking to one another, or sit forward, leaning on the chair backs in front of them, watching the band. A boy near Mark shouts noisily at the microphone-fondling singer, "Bite it . . . ohhh," and the area around Mark explodes in vulgar male laughter, but quickly subsides. A teacher walks down the aisle. Songs continue, to great applause. Assembly is over at 9:46, two minutes early.

9:53 and biology class. Mark was at a different high school 6 last year and did not take this course there as a tenth-grader. He is in it now, and all but one of his classmates are a year younger than he. He sits on the side, not taking part in the chatter that goes on after the bell. At 9:57, the public address system goes on, with the announcements of the day. After a few words from the principal ("Here's today's cheers and jeers . . ." with a cheer for the winning basketball team and a jeer for the spectators who made a ruckus at the gymnasium), the task is taken over by officers of ASB (Associated Student Bodies). There is an appeal for "bat bunnies." Carnations are for sale by the Girls' League. Miss Indian American is coming. Students are auctioning off their services (background catcalls are heard) to earn money for the prom. Nominees are needed for the ballot for school bachelor and school bachelorette. The announcements end with a "thought for the day. When you throw a little mud, you lose a little ground."

At 10:04 the biology class finally turns to science. The 7 teacher, Mr. Robbins, has placed one of several labeled laboratory specimens — some are pinned in frames, others swim in formaldehyde — on each of the classroom's eight laboratory tables. The three or so students whose chairs circle each of these benches are to study the specimen and make notes about it or drawings of it. After a few minutes each group of three will move to another table. The teacher points out that these specimens are of organisms already studied in previous classes. He says that the period-long test set for the following day will involve observing some of these specimens — then to be without labels — and writing an identifying paragraph on each. Mr. Robbins points out that some of the printed labels ascribe the specimens names different from those given in the textbook. He explains that biologists often give several names to the same organism.

The class now falls to peering , writing, and quiet talking. 8 Mr. Robbins comes over to Mark, and in whispered words asks him to carry a requisition form for science department materials to the business office. Mark, because of his "older" status, is usually chosen by Robbins for this kind of errand. Robbins gives Mark the form and a green hall pass to show to any teacher who might challenge him, on his way to the office, for being out of a classroom. The errand takes Mark four minutes. Meanwhile Mark's group is hard at work but gets to only three of the specimens before the bell rings at 10:42. As the students surge out, Robbins shouts a reminder about a "double" laboratory period on Thursday.

9   Between classes one of the seniors asks Mark whether he plans to be a candidate for schoolwide office next year. Mark says no. He starts to explain. The 10:47 bell rings, meaning that he is late for French class.

10   There are fifteen students in Monsieur Bates's language class. He hands out tests taken the day before: *"C'est bien fait, Etienne . . . c'est mieux, Marie . . . Tch, tch, Robert . . ."* Mark notes his C + and peeks at the A − in front of Susanna, next to him. The class has been assigned seats by M. Bates; Mark resents sitting next to prissy, brainy Susanna. Bates starts by asking a student to read a question and give the correct answer. *"James, question un."* James haltingly reads the question and gives an answer that Bates, now speaking English, says is incomplete. In due course: *"Mark, question cinq."* Mark does his bit, and the sequence goes on, the eight quiz questions and answers filling about twenty minutes of time.

11   "Turn to page forty-nine, *Maintenant, lisez après moi . . ."* and Bates reads a sentence and has the class echo it. Mark is embarrassed by this and mumbles with a barely audible sound. Others, like Susanna, keep the decibel count up, so Mark can hide. This I-say-you-repeat drill is interrupted once by the public address system, with an announcement about a meeting for the cheerleaders. Bates finishes the class, almost precisely at the bell, with a homework assignment. The students are to review these sentences for a brief quiz the following day. Mark takes note of the assignment, because he knows that tomorrow will be a day of busy-work in French class. Much though he dislikes oral drills, they are better than the workbook stuff that Bates hands out. Write, write, write, for Bates to throw away, Mark thinks.

12   11:36. Down to the cafeteria, talking noisily, hanging out, munching. Getting to Room 104 by 12:17: U.S. history. The teacher is sitting cross-legged on his desk when Mark comes

in, heatedly arguing with three students over the fracas that had followed the previous night's basketball game. The teacher, Mr. Suslovic, while agreeing that the spectators from their school certainly were provoked, argues that they should neither have been so obviously obscene in yelling at the opposing cheerleaders nor have allowed Coke cans to be rolled out on the floor. The three students keep saying that "it isn't fair." Apparently they and some others had been assigned "Saturday mornings" (detentions) by the principal for the ruckus.

At 12:34, the argument appears to subside. The uninvolved students, including Mark, are in their seats, chatting amiably. Mr. Suslovic climbs off his desk and starts talking: "We've almost finished this unit, chapters nine and ten . . ." The students stop chattering among themselves and turn toward Suslovic. Several slouch down in their chairs. Some open notebooks. Most have the five-pound textbook on their desks.   13

Suslovic lectures on the cattle drives, from north Texas to railroads west of St. Louis. He breaks up this narrative with questions ("Why were the railroad lines laid largely east to west?"), directed at nobody in particular and eventually answered by Suslovic himself. Some students take notes. Mark doesn't. A student walks in the open door, hands Mr. Suslovic a list, and starts whispering with him. Suslovic turns from the class and hears out this messenger. He then asks, "Does anyone know where Maggie Sharp is?" Someone answers, "Sick at home"; someone else says, "I thought I saw her at lunch." Genial consternation. Finally Suslovic tells the messenger, "Sorry, we can't help you," and returns to the class: "Now, where were we?" He goes on for some minutes. The bell rings. Suslovic forgets to give the homework assignment.   14

1:11 and Algebra II. There is a commotion in the hallway: Someone's locker is rumored to have been opened by the assistant principal and a narcotics agent. In the five-minute passing time, Mark hears the story three times and three ways. A locker had been broken into by another student. It was Mr. Gregory and a narc. It was the cops, and they did it without Gregory's knowing. Mrs. Ames, the mathematics teacher, has not heard anything about it. Several of the nineteen students try to tell her and start arguing among themselves. "O.K., that's enough." She hands out the day's problem, one sheet to each student. Mark sees with dismay   15 that it is a single, complicated "word" problem about some train that, while traveling at 84 mph, due west, passes a car that was going due east at 55 mph. Mark struggles: Is it $d=rt$ or $t=rd$? The class becomes quiet, writing, while Mrs. Ames writes some additional, short problems on the blackboard. "Time's up." A sigh; most students still writing. A muffled "Shit." Mrs. Ames frowns. "Come on, now." She collects papers, but it takes four minutes for her to corral them all.

16   "Copy down the problems from the board." A minute passes. "William, try number one." William suggests an approach. Mrs. Ames corrects and cajoles, and William finally gets it right. Mark watches two kids to his right passing notes; he tries to read them, but the handwriting is illegible from his distance. He hopes he is not called on, and he isn't. Only three students are asked to puzzle out an answer. The bell rings at 2:00. Mrs. Ames shouts a homework assignment over the resulting hubbub.

17   Mark leaves his books in his locker. He remembers that he has homework, but figures that he can do it during English class the next day. He knows that there will be an in-class presentation of one of the *Romeo and Juliet* scenes and that he will not be in it. The teacher will not notice his homework writing, or won't do anything about it if she does.

18   Mark passes various friends heading toward the gym, members of the basketball teams. Like most students, Mark isn't an active school athlete. However, he is associated with the yearbook staff. Although he is not taking "Yearbook" for credit as an English course, he is contributing photographs. Mark takes twenty minutes checking into the yearbook staff's headquarters (the classroom of its faculty advisor) and getting some assignments of pictures from his boss, the senior who is the photography editor. Mark knows that if he pleases his boss and the faculty adviser, he'll take that editor's post for the next year. He'll get English credit for his work then.

19   After gossiping a bit with the yearbook staff, Mark will leave school by 2:35 and go home. His grocery market bagger's job is from 4:45 to 8:00, the rush hour for the store. He'll have a snack at 4:30, and his mother will save him some supper to eat at 8:30. She will ask whether he has any homework, and he'll tell her no. Tomorrow, and virtually every other tomorrow, will be the same for Mark, save

for the lack of the assembly: Each period then will be five
minutes longer.

Most Americans have an uncomplicated vision of what   20
secondary education should be. Their conception of high
school is remarkably uniform across the country, a striking
fact, given the size and diversity of the United States and
the politically decentralized character of the schools. This
uniformity is of several generations' standing. It has, however, two appearances, each quite different from the other,
one of words and the other of practice, a world of political
rhetoric and Mark's world.

A California high school's general goals, set out in 1979,   21
could serve equally well most of America's high schools,
public and private. This school had as its ends:

- Fundamental scholastic achievement ... to acquire
  knowledge and share in the traditionally accepted
  academic fundamentals ... to develop the ability to make
  decisions, to solve problems, to reason independently, and
  to accept responsibility for self-evaluation and continuing
  self-improvement.
- Career and economic competence ...
- Citizenship and civil responsibility ...
- Competence in human and social relations ...
- Moral and ethical values ...
- Self-realization and mental and physical health ...
- Aesthetic awareness ...
- Cultural diversity ...[1]

In addition to its optimistic rhetoric, what distinguishes   22
this list is its comprehensiveness. The high school is to
touch most aspects of an adolescent's existence — mind,
body, morals, values, career. No one of these areas is given

[1]Shasta High School, Redding, California. An eloquent and analogous
statement, "The Essentials of Education," one stressing explicitly the "in-
terdependence of skills and content" that is implicit in the Shasta High
School statement, was issued in 1980 by a coalition of education associations. Organizations for the Essentials of Education (Urbana, Illinois).
[Author's note]

especial prominence. School people arrogate to themselves an obligation to all.

23   An example of the wide acceptability of these goals is found in the courts. Forced to present a detailed definition of "thorough and efficient education," elementary as well as secondary, a West Virginia judge sampled the best of conventional wisdom and concluded that

> there are eight general elements of a thorough and efficient system of education: (a) Literacy, (b) The ability to add, subtract, multiply, and divide numbers, (c) Knowledge of government to the extent the child will be equipped as a citizen to make informed choices among persons and issues that affect his own governance, (d) Self-knowledge and knowledge of his or her total environment to allow the child to intelligently choose life work — to know his or her options, (e) Work-training and advanced academic training as the child may intelligently choose, (f) Recreational pursuits, (g) Interests in all creative arts such as music, theater, literature, and the visual arts, and (h) Social ethics, both behavioral and abstract, to facilitate compatibility with others in this society.[2]

24   That these eight — now powerfully part of the debate over the purpose and practice of education in West Virginia — are reminiscent of the influential list, "The Seven Cardinal Principles of Secondary Education," promulgated in 1918 by the National Education Association, is no surprise.[3] The rhetoric of high school purpose has been uniform and consistent for decades. Americans agree on the goals for their high schools.

25   That agreement is convenient, but it masks the fact that

---

[2]Judge Arthur M. Recht, in his order resulting from *Pauley* v. *Kelly*, 1979, as reprinted in *Education Week*, May 26, 1982, p.10. See also, in *Education Week*, January 16, 1983, pp. 21, 24, Jonathan P. Sher, "The Struggle to Fulfill a Judicial Mandate: How Not to 'Reconstruct' Education in W. Va." [Author's Note]

[3]Bureau of Education, Department of the Interior. "Cardinal Principles of Secondary Education: A Report of the Commission on the Reorganization of Secondary Education, appointed by the National Education Association," *Bulletin*, no. 35 (Washington: U.S. Government Printing Office, 1918). [Author's note]

virtually all the words in these goal statements beg definition. Some schools have labored long to identify specific
criteria beyond them; the result has been lists of daunting
pseudospecificity and numbing earnestness. However, most
leave the words undefined and let the momentum of traditional practice speak for itself. That is why analyzing how
Mark spends his time is important: From watching him
one uncovers the important purposes of education, the ones
that shape practice. Mark's day is similar to that of other
high school students across the country, as similar as the
rhetoric of one goal statement to others. Of course, there
are variations, but the extent of consistency in the shape
of school routine for a large and diverse adolescent population is extraordinary, indicating more graphically than any
rhetoric the measure of agreement in America about what
one does in high school, and, by implication, what it is for.

The basic organizing structures in schools are familiar. 26
Above all, students are grouped by age (that is, freshman,
sophomore, junior, senior), and all are expected to take
precisely the same time — around 720 school days over four
years, to be precise — to meet the requirements for a diploma. When one is out of his grade level, he can feel odd,
as Mark did in his biology class. The goals are the same for
all, and the means to achieve them are also similar.

Young males and females are treated remarkably alike; 27
the schools' goals are the same for each gender. In execution,
there are differences, as those pressing sex discrimination
suits have made educators intensely aware. The students
in metalworking classes are mostly male; those in home
economics, mostly female. But it is revealing how much
less sex discrimination there is in high schools than in other
American institutions. For many young women, the most
liberated hours of their week are in school.

School is to be like a job: You start in the morning and 28
end in the afternoon, five days a week. You don't get much
of a lunch hour, so you go home early, unless you are an
athlete or are involved in some special school or extracurricular activity. School is conceived of as the children's
workplace, and it takes young people off parents' hands
and out of the labor market during prime-time work hours.
Not surprisingly, many students see going to school as little
more than a dogged necessity. They perceive the day-to-day
routine, a Minnesota study reports, as one of "boredom and

lethargy." One of the students summarizes: School is "boring, restless, tiresome, puts ya to sleep, tedious, monotonous, pain in the neck."[4]

29   The school schedule is a series of units of time: The clock is king. The base time block is about fifty minutes in length. Some schools, on what they call modular scheduling, split that fifty-minute block into two or even three pieces. Most schools have double periods for laboratory work, especially in the sciences, or four-hour units for the small numbers of students involved in intensive vocational or other work-study programs. The flow of all school activity arises from or is blocked by these time units. "How much time do I have with my kids" is the teacher's key question.

30   Because there are many claims for those fifty-minute blocks, there is little time set aside for rest between them, usually no more than three to ten minutes, depending on how big the school is and, consequently, how far students and teachers have to walk from class to class. As a result, there is a frenetic quality to the school day, a sense of sustained restlessness. For the adolescents, there are frequent changes of room and fellow students, each change giving tempting opportunities for distraction, which are stoutly resisted by teachers. Some schools play soft music during these "passing times," to quiet the multitude, one principal told me.

31   Many teachers have a chance for a coffee break. Few students do. In some city schools where security is a problem, students must be in class for seven consecutive periods, interrupted by a heavily monitored twenty-minute lunch period for small groups, starting as early as 10:30 A.M. and running to after 1:00 P.M. A high premium is placed on punctuality and on "being where you're supposed to be." Obviously, a low premium is placed on reflection and repose. The student rushes from class to class to collect knowledge. Savoring it, it is implied, is not to be done much in school, nor is such meditation really much admired. The picture that these familiar patterns yield is that of an academic supermarket. The purpose of going to school is

[4]Diane Hedin, Paula Simon, and Michael Robin, *Minnesota Youth Poll: Youth's Views on School and School Discipline*, Minnesota Report 184 (1983), Agricultural Experiment Station, University of Minnesota, p. 13. [Author's note]

to pick things up, in an organized and predictable way, the faster the better.

What is supposed to be picked up is remarkably consis- 32 tent among all sorts of high schools. Most schools specifically mandate three out of every five courses a student selects. Nearly all of these mandates fall into five areas — English, social studies, mathematics, science, and physical education. On the average, English is required to be taken each year, social studies and physical education three out of the four high school years, and mathematics and science one or two years. Trends indicate that in the mid-eighties there is likely to be an increase in the time allocated to these last two subjects. Most students take classes in these four major academic areas beyond the minimum requirements, sometimes in such special areas as journalism and "yearbook," offshoots of English departments.[5]

Press most adults about what high school is for, and you 33 hear these subjects listed. *High school? That's where you learn English and math and that sort of thing.* Ask students, and you get the same answer. High school is to "teach" these "subjects."

What is often absent is any definition of these subjects 34 or any rationale for them. They are just there, labels. Under those labels lie a multitude of things. A great deal of material is supposed to be "covered"; most of these courses are surveys, great sweeps of the stuff of their parent disciplines.

While there is often a sequence *within* subjects — algebra 35 before trigonometry, "first-year" French before "second-year" French — there is rarely a coherent relationship or sequence *across* subjects. Even the most logically related matters — reading ability as a precondition for the reading of history books, and certain mathematical concepts or skills before the study of some of physics — are only loosely coordinated, if at all. There is little demand for a synthesis of it all; English, mathematics, and the rest are discrete items, to be picked up individually. The incentive for picking them up is largely through tests and, with success at these, in credits earned.

Coverage within subjects is the key priority. If some imag- 36

[5]I am indebted to Harold F. Sizer and Lyde F. Sizer for a survey of the diploma requirements of fifty representative secondary schools, completed for A Study of High Schools. [Author's note]

inative teacher makes a proposal to force the marriage of, say, mathematics and physics or to require some culminating challenges to students to use several subjects in the solution of a complex problem, and if this proposal will take "time" away from other things, opposition is usually phrased in terms of what may be thus forgone. If we do that, we'll have to give up colonial history. We won't be able to get to programming. We'll not be able to read *Death of a Salesman.* There isn't time. The protesters usually win out.

37   The subjects come at a student like Mark in random order, a kaleidoscope of worlds: algebraic formulae to poetry to French verbs to Ping-Pong to the War of the Spanish Succession, all before lunch. Pupils are to pick up these things. Tests measure whether the picking up has been successful.

38   The lack of connection between stated goals, such as those of the California high school cited earlier, and the goals inherent in school practice is obvious and, curiously, tolerated. Most striking is the gap between statements about "self-realization and mental and physical growth" or "moral and ethical values"—common rhetoric in school documents—and practice. Most physical education programs have neither the time nor the focus really to ensure fitness. Mental health is rarely defined. Neither are ethical values, save at the negative extremes, such as opposition to assault or dishonesty. Nothing in the regimen of a day like Mark's signals direct or implicit teaching in this area. The "schoolboy code" (not ratting on a fellow student) protects the marijuana pusher, and a leechlike associate is shrugged off without concern. The issue of the locker search was pushed aside, as not appropriate for class time.

39   Most students, like Mark, go to class in groups of twenty to twenty-seven students. The expected attendance in some schools, particularly those in low-income areas, is usually higher, often thirty-five students per class, but high absentee rates push the actual numbers down. About twenty-five per class is an average figure for expected attendance, and the actual numbers are somewhat lower. There are remarkably few students who go to class in groups much larger or smaller than twenty-five.[6]

40   A student such as Mark sees five or six teachers per day;

[6]Education Research Service, Inc. *Class Size: A Summary of Research* (Arlington, Virginia, 1978); and *Class Size Research: A Critique of Recent Meta-Analyses* (Arlington, Virginia, 1980). [Author's note]

their differing styles and expectations are part of his kaleidoscope. High school staffs are highly specialized: Guidance counselors rarely teach mathematics, mathematics teachers rarely teach English, principals rarely do any classroom instruction. Mark, then, is known a little bit by a number of people, each of whom sees him in one specialized situation. No one may know him as a "whole person" — unless he becomes a special problem or has special needs.

Save in extracurricular or coaching situations, such as 41 in athletics, drama, or shop classes, there is little opportunity for sustained conversation between student and teacher. The mode is a one-sentence or two-sentence exchange: *Mark, when was Grover Cleveland president?* Let's see, was 1890 . . . or something . . . wasn't he the one . . . he was elected twice, wasn't he . . . *Yes* . . . *Gloria, can you get the dates right?* Dialogue is strikingly absent, and as a result the opportunity of teachers to challenge students' ideas in a systematic and logical way is limited. Given the rushed, full quality of the school day, it can seldom happen. One must infer that careful probing of students' thinking is not a high priority. How one gains (to quote the California school's statement of goals again) "the ability to make decisions, to solve problems, to reason independently, and to accept responsibility for self-evaluation and continuing self-improvement" without being challenged is difficult to imagine. One certainly doesn't learn these things merely from lectures and textbooks.

Most schools are nice places. Mark and his friends enjoy 42 being in theirs. The adults who work in schools generally like adolescents. The academic pressures are limited, and the accommodations to students are substantial. For example, if many members of an English class have jobs after school, the English teacher's expectations for them are adjusted, downward. In a word, school is sensitively accommodating, as long as students are punctual, where they are supposed to be, and minimally dutiful about picking things up from the clutch of courses in which they enroll.

This characterization is not pretty, but it is accurate, and 43 it serves to describe the vast majority of American secondary schools. "Taking subjects" in a systematized, conveyor-belt way is what one does in high school. That this process is, in substantial respects, not related to the rhetorical purposes of education is tolerated by most people, perhaps because they do not really either believe in those ill-defined goals or, in their heart of hearts, believe that schools can or should even try to achieve them. The students are happy taking subjects. The parents are happy, because that's what they did in high school. The rituals, the most important of which is graduation, remain intact. The adolescents are supervised, safely and constructively most of the time, during the morning and afternoon hours, and they are off the labor market. That is what high school is all about.

Nathan Glazer

Some Very Modest Proposals for the Improvement of American Education

Nathan Glazer (born 1932), professor of education and sociology at Harvard, writes about many public issues, especially as they involve ethnicity: see, for example, his Beyond the Melting Pot *and* Ethnic Dilemmas. *This essay appeared in 1984 in* Daedalus, *the quarterly journal of the American Academy of the Arts and Sciences.*

1   That we can do a great deal for the sorry state of American education with more money is generally accepted. Even apparently modest proposals will, however, cost a great deal of money. Consider something as simple as increasing the average compensation of American teachers — who are generally considered underpaid — by $2,000 a year each. The bill would come to five billion dollars a year. A similar figure is reached by the report of the highly qualified Twentieth Century Fund Task Force on Federal, Elementary, and Secondary Educational Policy, which proposes fellowships and additional compensation for master teachers. Reducing class size 10 percent, or increasing the number of teachers by the same percentage, would cost another five billion dollars: With present-day federal deficits, these look like small sums, but since education is paid for almost entirely by states and local government, these modest proposals

would lead to substantial and painful tax increases. (I leave aside for the moment the views of skeptics who believe that none of these changes would matter.)

But the occasional visitor to American schools will note 2 some changes that would cost much less, nothing at all, or even save money — and yet would improve at least the educational *environment* in American schools (once again, we ignore those skeptics who would insist that even a better educational environment cannot be guaranteed to improve educational achievement). In the spirit of evoking further cheap proposals, here is a small list of suggestions that, to my mind at least — and the mind I believe of any adult who visits American public schools — would mean a clear plus for American education:

1. *Disconnect all loudspeaker systems in American* 3 *schools — or at least reserve them, like the hotline between Moscow and Washington, for only the gravest emergencies.* The American classroom — and the American teacher and his or her charges — is continually interrupted by announcements from central headquarters over the loudspeaker system. These remind teachers to bring in some form or other; or students to bring in some form or other; or students engaged in some activity to remember to come to practice or rehearsal; or they announce a change of time for some activity. There is nothing so unnerving to a teacher engaged in trying to explain something, or a student engaged in trying to understand something, as the crackle of the loudspeaker prepared to issue an announcement, and the harsh and gravelly voice (the systems are not obviously of the highest grade) of the announcement itself.

Aside from questions of personal taste, why would this 4 be a good idea? As I have suggested, one reason is that the loudspeaker interrupts efforts to communicate complicated material that requires undivided attention. Second, it demeans the teacher as professional: every announcement tells her whatever she is doing is not very important and can be interrupted at any time. Third, it accentuates the notion of hierarchy in education — the principal and assistant principal are the important people, and command time and attention even in the midst of instruction. Perhaps I have been softened by too many years as a college teacher, but it would be unimaginable that a loudspeaker, if one existed, would ever interrupt a college class except under conditions of the gravest and most immediate threat to life and limb. One way of showing students that education is important is not to interrupt it for band-rehearsal announcements.

5   2. *Disarm the school.* One of the most depressing aspects of the urban school in the United States is the degree of security manifest within it, and that seems to me quite contradictory to what a school should be. Outer doors are locked. Security guards are present in the corridors. Internal doors are locked. Passes are necessary to enter the school or move within it, for outsiders and for students. Students are marched in groups from classroom to classroom, under the eye of teachers. It is understandable that given the conditions in lower-class areas in our large cities — and not only lower-class areas — some degree of security-mindedness is necessary. There is valuable equipment — typewriters, computers, audio-visual equipment — that can be stolen; vandalism is a serious concern; marauders can enter the school in search for equipment, or teachers' pocketbooks, or to threaten directly personal safety in search of money or sex, and so on. School integration and busing, at least in their initial stages, have contributed to increased interracial tensions in schools and have in part severed the link between community and school. The difference in ethnic and racial composition of faculty, other staff, administrators, and students contributes to the same end.

6   Having acknowledged all this, I still believe the school should feel less like a prison than it does. One should examine to what extent outside doors must be closed; to what extent the security guard cannot be replaced by local parents, volunteer or paid; the degree to which the endless bells indicating "stop" and "go" are really necessary. I suspect that now that the most difficult period of school integration has passed, now that teachers and administrators and staff more closely parallel in race and ethnic background students and community owing to the increase in black and Hispanic teachers and administrators, we may be saddled with more security than we need. Here we come to the sticky problem of *removing* security measures whose need has decreased. What school board will open itself to suit or to public criticism by deliberately providing *less* security? And yet one must consider the atmosphere of the school and a school's primary objective as a teaching agent:

can this be reconciled with a condition of maximum security? Perhaps there are lessons to be learned from colleges and community colleges in older urban areas, which in my experience do seem to manage with less security. One reason is that there are more adults around in such institutions. Is that a hint as to how we could manage better in our public schools?

3. *Enlist the children in keeping the school clean.* Occasionally we see a practice abroad that suggests possible transfer to the American scene. In Japan, the children clean the school. There is a time of day when mops and pails and brooms come out, and the children sweep up and wash up. This does, I am sure, suggest to the children that this is *their* school, that it is not simply a matter of being forced to go to a foreign institution that imposes alien demands upon them. I can imagine some obstacles in the way of instituting regular student clean-up in American schools — custodians' unions, for example, might object. But they can be reassured that children don't do that good a job, and they will still be needed. Once again, as in the case of the security problem, one wants to create in the school, if at all possible, a common enterprise of teachers and students, without the latter being bored and resistant, the former, in response, becoming equally indifferent. The school should be seen as everyone's workplace — and participation in cleaning the school will help.

4. *Save old schools.* Build fewer new ones. It has often surprised me that while in schools such as Eton and Oxford — and indeed well-known private schools and colleges in the United States — old buildings are prized, in so many communities older public schools are torn down when to the naked eye they have many virtues that would warrant their maintenance and use. Only a few blocks from where I live, an excellent example of late nineteenth-century fine brickwork and carved stonework that served as the Cambridge Latin School came down for a remodeling. The carved elements are still displayed about the remodeled school, but why a building of such character should have deserved demolition escaped my understanding, particularly since one can take it almost as a given that a school building put up before the 1940s will be built of heavier and sturdier materials than one constructed today. Even the inconveniences of the old can possess a charm that

makes them worthwhile. And indeed many of the reforms that seemed to require new buildings (for example, class-rooms without walls, concentrated around activities cen-ters in large open rooms) have turned out, on use, to be not so desirable. Our aim should be to give each school a history, a character, something that at least some students respond to. The pressures for new buildings are enormous, and sometimes perfectly legitimate (as when communities ex-pand), but often illegitimate, as when builders and build-ing-trades workers and contract-givers seek an opportunity or when state aid makes it appear as if a new building won't cost anything.

9   5. *Look on new hardware with a skeptical eye.* I think it likely that the passion for the new in the way of teaching-hardware not only does not contribute to higher educa-tional achievement but may well serve as a temporary means to evade the real and hard tasks of teaching — which really require almost no hardware at all, besides textbooks, blackboard, and chalk. Admittedly, when one comes to high-school science, something more is called for. And yet our tendency is to always find cover behind new hardware. It's *fun* to get new audio-visual equipment, new rooms equipped with them in which all kinds of things can be done by flicking a switch or twisting a dial, or, as is now the case, to decide what kind of personal computers and software are necessary for a good educational program. Once again, foreign experience can be enlightening. When Japanese education was already well ahead of American, most Japanese schools were in prewar wooden buildings. (They are now as up-to-date as ours, but neither their age nor up-to-dateness has much to do with their good record of achievement.) Resisting the appeal of new hardware not only saves money, and provides less in the way of saleable goods to burglarize, but it also prevents distraction from the principal tasks of reading, writing, and calculating. When it turns out that computers and new software are shown to do a better job at these key tasks — I am skeptical as to whether this will ever be the case — there will be time enough to splurge on new equipment. The teacher, alone, up front, explaining, encouraging, guiding, is the heart of the matter — the rest is fun, and very helpful to corporate income, and gives an inflated headquarters staff something new to do. But students will have time enough to learn about computers when they get to college, and getting there

will depend almost not at all on what they can do with computers, but how well they understand words and sentences, and how well they do at simple mathematics.

There is nothing wrong with old textbooks, too. Recently, 10 reviewing some recent high-school American history texts, I was astonished to discover they come out in new editions every two years or so, and not because the main body of the text is improved, but because the textbook wants to be able to claim it covers the very last presidential campaign, and the events of the last few years. This is a waste of time and energy and money. There is enough to teach in American history up to 1950 or 1960 not to worry about whether the text includes Reagan's tax cuts. I suspect many new texts in other areas also offer little advantage over the older ones. There is also a virtue in a teacher becoming acquainted with a particular textbook. When I read that a school is disadvantaged because its textbooks are old, I am always mystified. Even the newest advances in physics and biology might well be reserved for college.

6. *Expand the pool from which we draw good teachers.* 11 This general heading covers a number of simple and concrete things, such as: if a teacher is considered qualified to teach at a good private school, that teacher should be considered qualified to teach at a public school. It has always seemed to me ridiculous that teachers accepted at the best private schools in New York City or top preparatory schools in the country would not be allowed to teach in the public school system of New York or Boston. Often, they are willing—after all, the pay is better in public schools and there are greater fringe benefits. They might, it is true, be driven out of those schools by the challenge of lower- and working-class children. But when they are willing, it seems unbelievable that the teacher qualified (or so Brearley thinks) for Brearley will not be allowed to teach at P.S. 122. Greater use of part-time teachers might also be able to draw upon people with qualities that we are told the average teacher unfortunately doesn't possess—such as a higher level of competence in writing and mathematics.

Our recurrent concern with foreign-language teaching 12 should lead us to recruit foreign-born teachers. There are problems in getting teaching jobs today in Germany and France—yet teachers there are typically drawn from pools of students with higher academic skills than is the case in this country. Paradoxically, we make it easy for teachers of Spanish-language background to get jobs owing to the expansion of bilingual programs — but then their teaching is confined to children whose Spanish accent doesn't need improvement. It would make more sense to expose children of foreign-language background more to teachers with native English — and children from English-speaking families to teachers who speak French, German, Spanish, and, why not, Japanese, and Chinese natively. This would mean that rules requiring that a teacher must be a citizen, or must speak English without an accent, should be lifted for special teachers with special tasks. Perhaps we could make the most of the oversupply of teachers in some foreign countries by using them to teach mathematics — a subject where accent doesn't count. The school system in Georgia is already recruiting from Germany. Colleges often use teaching assistants whose English is not native and far from perfect, including Asians from Korea and China, to assist in science and mathematics courses. (There are many state laws which would not permit them to teach in elementary and secondary schools.)

13   All the suggestions above eschew any involvement with some great issues of education — tradition or reform, the teaching of values, the role of religion in the schools — that have in the past dominated arguments over education and still do today. But I add one more proposal that is still, I am afraid, somewhat controversial:

14   7. *Let students, within reason, pick their schools, or let parents choose them for them.* All those informed on school issues will sense the heaving depths of controversy under this apparently modest proposal. Does this mean they might choose parochial schools, without being required to pay tuition out of their own pockets? Or does this mean black children would be allowed to attend schools in black areas, and whites in white areas, or the reverse if each is so inclined? As we all know, the two great issues of religion and race stand in the way of any such simple and common-sensical arrangement. Students are regularly bused from one section of a city to another because of their race, and students cannot without financial penalty attend that substantial sector of schools — 30 percent or so in most Northern and Midwestern cities — that are called "private." I ignore the question of whether, holding all factors constant, students do "better" in private or public schools, in racially well-mixed or hardly mixed schools. The evidence will al-

ways be uncertain. What is perhaps less arguable is that students will do better in a school that forms a community, in which teachers, parents, and students all agree that *that* is the school they want to teach in, to attend, to send their children to. I would guess that this is the kind of school most of the readers of this article have attended; it is the kind of school, alas, that our complex racial and religious history makes it harder and harder for those of minority race or of lower- and working-class status to attend.

I have eschewed the grand proposals — for curriculum 15 change, for improving the quality of entering teachers, for checking on the competence of teachers in service, for establishing national standards for achievement in different levels of education — all of which now form the agenda for many state commissions of educational reform and all of which seem reasonable to me. Rather, I have concentrated on a variety of other things that serve to remove distraction, to open the school to those of quality who would be willing to enter it to improve it, to concentrate on the essentials of teaching and learning as I (and many others) have experienced it. It would be possible to propose larger changes in the same direction: for example, reduce the size of the bureaucracies in urban school systems. Some of my modest proposals are insidiously intended to do this — if there were less effort devoted to building new schools, buying new equipment, evaluating new textbooks, or busing children, there would be no need to maintain quite so many people at headquarters. Or so I would hope.

In the meantime, why not disconnect the loudspeakers? 16

This cartoon by Matt Groening (born 1954), a selection from his popular collection Life in Hell *(1987), captures some of the feelings students associate with high school. Groening cartoons are the basis of the television show* The Simpsons.

From *School is Hell* © 1987 by Matt Groening. All rights reserved. Reprinted by permission of Pantheon Books, a division of Random House, NY.

Neil Postman
Order in the Classroom

An educational reformer, prolific author, and professor of media ecology at New York University, Neil Postman (born 1931) has written many books about language, linguistics, teaching, and education — partly based on his own experiences as a high school and elementary school teacher. The following selection is excerpted from his 1979 book, Teaching As a Conserving Activity.

William O'Connor, who is unknown to me in a personal   1
way, was once a member of the Boston School Committee, in which capacity he made the following remark: "We have no inferior education in our schools. What we have been getting is an inferior type of student."

The remark is easy to ridicule, and I have had some fun   2
with it in the past. But there are a couple of senses in which it is perfectly sound.

In the first place, a classroom is a technique for the   3
achievement of certain kinds of learning. It is a workable technique provided that both the teacher and the student have the skill and, particularly, the attitudes that are fundamental to it. Among these, from the student's point of view, are tolerance for delayed gratification, a certain measure of respect for and fear of authority, and a willingness to accommodate one's individual desires to the interests of group cohesion and purpose. These attitudes cannot be taught easily in school because they are a necessary component of the teaching situation itself. The problem is not unlike trying to find out how to spell a word by looking it up in the dictionary. If you do not know how a word is spelled, it is hard to look it up. In the same way, little can be taught in school unless these attitudes are present. And if they are not, to teach them is difficult.

Obviously, such attitudes must be learned during the   4
years before a child starts school; that is, in the home. This is the real meaning of the phrase "preschool education." If a child is not made ready at home for the classroom experience, he or she usually cannot benefit from any normal school program. Just as important, the school is defenseless against such a child, who, typically, is a source of disorder

in a situation that requires order. I raise this issue because education reform is impossible without order in the classroom. Without the attitudes that lead to order, the classroom is an entirely impotent technique. Therefore, one possible translation of Mr. O'Connor's remark is, "We have a useful technique for educating youth but too many of them have not been provided at home with the attitudes necessary for the technique to work."

5   In still another way Mr. O'Connor's remark makes plain sense. The electronic media, with their emphasis on visual imagery, immediacy, non-linearity, and fragmentation, do not give support to the attitudes that are fundamental to the classroom; that is, Mr. O'Connor's remark can be translated as, "We would not have an inferior education if it were the nineteenth century. Our problem is that we have been getting students who are products of the twentieth century." But there is nothing nonsensical about this, either. The nineteenth century had much to recommend it, and we certainly may be permitted to allow it to exert an influence on the twentieth. The classroom is a nineteenth-century invention, and we ought to prize what it has to offer. It is one of the few social organizations left to us in which sequence, social order, hierarchy, continuity, and deferred pleasure are important.

6   The problem of disorder in the classroom is created largely by two factors: a dissolving family structure, out of which come youngsters who are "unfit" for the presuppositions of a classroom; and a radically altered information environment, which undermines the foundation of school. The question, then, is, What should be done about the increasing tendency toward disorder in the classroom?

7   Liberal reformers, such as Kenneth Keniston, have answers, of a sort. Keniston argues that economic reforms should be made so that the integrity and authority of the family can be restored. He believes that poverty is the main cause of family dissolution, and that by improving the economic situation of families, we may kindle a sense of order and aspiration in the lives of children. Some of the reforms he suggests in his book *All Our Children* seem practical, although they are long-range and offer no immediate response to the problem of present disorder. Some Utopians, such as Ivan Illich, have offered other solutions; for example, dissolving the schools altogether, or so completely

restructuring the school environment that its traditional assumptions are rendered irrelevant. To paraphrase Karl Kraus's epigram about psychoanalysis, these proposals are the Utopian disease of which they consider themselves the cure.

One of the best answers comes from Dr. Howard Hurwitz,   8 who is neither a liberal reformer nor a Utopian. It is a good solution, I believe, because it tries to respond to the needs not only of children who are unprepared for school because of parental failure but of children of all backgrounds who are being made strangers to the assumptions of school by the biases of the electronic media.

During the eleven years Dr. Hurwitz was principal at   9 Long Island City High School, the average number of suspensions each year was three, while in many New York City high schools the average runs close to one hundred. Also, during his tenure, not one instance of an assault on a teacher was reported, and daily student attendance averaged better than 90 percent, which in the context of the New York City school scene represents a riot of devotion.

Although I consider some of Dr. Hurwitz's curriculum   10 ideas uninspired and even wrong-headed, he understands a few things of overriding importance that many educators of more expansive imagination do not. The first is that educators must devote at least as much attention to the immediate consequences of disorder as to its abstract causes. Whatever the causes of disorder and alienation, the consequences are severe and, if not curbed, result in making the school impotent. At the risk of becoming a symbol of reaction, Hurwitz ran "a tight ship." He holds to the belief, for example, that a child's right to an education is terminated at the point where the child interferes with the right of other children to have one.

Dr. Hurwitz also understands that disorder expands pro-   11 portionately to the tolerance for it, and that children of all kinds of home backgrounds can learn, in varying degrees, to function in situations where disorder is not tolerated at all. He does not believe that it is inevitably or only the children of the poor who are disorderly. In spite of what the "revisionist" education historians may say, poor people still regard school as an avenue of social and economic advancement for their children, and do not object in the least to its being an orderly and structured experience.

All this adds up to the commonsense view that the school   12 ought not to accommodate itself to disorder, or to the biases of other communication systems. The children of the poor are likely to continue to be with us. Some parents will fail to assume competent responsibility for the preschool education of their children. The media will increase the intensity of their fragmenting influence. Educators must live with these facts. But Dr. Hurwitz believes that as a technique for learning, the classroom can work if students are oriented toward its assumptions, not the other way around. William O'Connor, wherever he is, would probably agree. And so do I. The school is not an extension of the street, the movie theater, a rock concert, or a playground. And it is certainly not an extension of the psychiatric clinic. It is a special environment that requires the enforcement of certain traditional rules of controlled group interaction. The school may be the only remaining public situation in which such rules have any meaning, and it would be a grave mistake to change those rules because some children find them hard or cannot function within them. Children who cannot ought to be removed from the environment in the interests of those who can.

13   Wholesale suspensions, however, are a symptom of disorder, not a cure for it. And what makes Hurwitz's school noteworthy is the small number of suspensions that have been necessary. This is not the result of his having "good" students or "bad" students. It is the result of his having created an unambiguous, rigorous, and serious attitude — a nineteenth-century attitude, if you will — toward what constitutes acceptable school behavior. In other words, Dr. Hurwitz's school turns out to be a place where children of all backgrounds — fit and unfit — can function, or can learn to function, and where the biases of our information environment are emphatically opposed.

14   At this point I should like to leave the particulars of Dr. Hurwitz's solution and, retaining their spirit, indicate some particulars of my own.

15   Let us start, for instance, with the idea of a dress code. A dress code signifies that school is a special place in which special kinds of behavior are required. The way one dresses is an indication of an attitude toward a situation. And the way one is *expected* to dress indicates what that attitude ought to be. You would not wear dungarees and a T-shirt that says "Feel Me" when attending a church wedding. That would be considered an outrage against the tone and mean-

ing of the situation. The school has every right and reason,
I believe, to expect the same sort of consideration.

Those who are inclined to think this is a superficial point   16
are probably forgetting that symbols not only reflect our
feelings but to some extent create them. One's kneeling in
church, for example, reflects a sense of reverence but also
engenders reverence. If we want school to *feel* like a special
place, we can find no better way to begin than by requiring
students to dress in a manner befitting the seriousness of
the enterprise and the institution. I should include teachers
in this requirement. I know of one high school in which the
principal has put forward a dress code of sorts for teachers.
(He has not, apparently, had the courage to propose one
for the students.) For males the requirement is merely a
jacket and tie. One of his teachers bitterly complained to
me that such a regulation infringed upon his civil rights.
And yet, this teacher will accept without complaint the
same regulation when it is enforced by an elegant restaurant. His complaint and his acquiescence tell a great deal
about how he values schools and how he values restaurants.

I do not have in mind, for students, uniforms of the type   17
sometimes worn in parochial schools. I am referring here
to some reasonable standard of dress which would mark
school as a place of dignity and seriousness. And I might
add that I do not believe for one moment the argument
that poor people would be unable to clothe their children
properly if such a code were in force. Furthermore, I do not
believe that poor people have advanced that argument. It
is an argument that middle-class education critics have
made on behalf of the poor.

Another argument advanced in behalf of the poor and   18
oppressed is the students' right to their own language. I
have never heard this argument come from parents whose
children are not competent to use Standard English. It is
an argument, once again, put forward by "liberal" education critics whose children *are* competent in Standard English but who in some curious way wish to express their
solidarity with and charity for those who are less capable.
It is a case of pure condescension, and I do not think teachers
should be taken in by it. Like the mode of dress, the mode
of language in school ought to be relatively formal and
exemplary, and therefore markedly different from the custom in less rigorous places. It is particularly important that
teachers should avoid trying to win their students' affection

by adopting the language of youth. Such teachers frequently win only the contempt of their students, who sense that the language of teachers and the language of students ought to be different; that is to say, the world of adults is different from the world of children.

19   In this connection, it is worth saying that the modern conception of childhood is a product of the sixteenth century, as Philippe Aries has documented in his *The Centuries of Childhood*. Prior to that century, children as young as six and seven were treated in all important respects as if they were adults. Their language, their dress, their legal status, their responsibilities, their labor, were much the same as those of adults. The concept of childhood as an identifiable stage in human growth began to develop in the sixteenth century and has continued into our own times. However, with the emergence of electronic media of communication, a reversal of this trend seems to be taking place. In a culture in which the distribution of information is almost wholly undifferentiated, age categories begin to disappear. Television, in itself, may bring an end to childhood. In truth, there is no such thing as "children's programming," at least not for children over the age of eight or nine. Everyone sees and hears the same things. We have already reached a point where crimes of youth are indistinguishable from those of adults, and we may soon reach a point where the punishments will be the same.

20   I raise this point because the school is one of our few remaining institutions based on firm distinctions between childhood and adulthood, and on the assumption that adults have something of value to teach the young. That is why teachers must avoid emulating in dress and speech the style of the young. It is also why the school ought to be a place for what we might call "manners education": the adults in school ought to be concerned with teaching youth a standard of civilized interaction.

21   Again those who are inclined to regard this as superficial may be underestimating the power of media such as television and radio to teach how one is to conduct oneself in public. In a general sense, the media "unprepare" the young for behavior in groups. A young man who goes through the day with a radio affixed to his ear is learning to be indifferent to any shared sound. A young woman who can turn off a television program that does not suit her needs at the moment is learning impatience with any stimulus that is not responsive to her interests.

But school is not a radio station or a television program.   22
It is a social situation requiring the subordination of one's
own impulses and interests to those of the group. In a word,
manners. As a rule, elementary school teachers will exert
considerable effort in teaching manners. I believe they refer
to this effort as "socializing the child." But it is astonishing
how precipitously this effort is diminished at higher levels.
It is certainly neglected in the high schools, and where it
is not, there is usually an excessive concern for "bad habits,"
such as smoking, drinking, and in some nineteenth-century
schools, swearing. But, as William James noted, our virtues
are as habitual as our vices. Where is the attention given
to the "Good morning" habit, to the "I beg your pardon"
habit, to the "Please forgive the interruption" habit?

The most civilized high school class I have ever seen was   23
one in which students and teacher said "Good morning" to
each other and in which the students stood up when they
had something to say. The teacher, moreover, thanked each
student for any contribution made to the class, did not sit
with his feet on the desk, and did not interrupt a student
unless he had asked permission to do so. The students, in
turn, did not interrupt each other, or chew gum, or read
comic books when they were bored. To avoid being a burden
to others when one is bored is the essence of civilized behavior.

Of this teacher, I might also say that he made no attempt   24
to entertain his students or model his classroom along the
lines of a TV program. He was concerned not only to teach
his students manners but to teach them how to attend in
a classroom, which is partly a matter of manners but also
necessary to their intellectual development. One of the more
serious difficulties teachers now face in the classroom results
from the fact that their students suffer media-shortened
attention spans and have becomed accustomed, also
through intense media exposure, to novelty, variety, and
entertainment. Some teachers have made desperate attempts to keep their students "tuned in" by fashioning their
classes along the lines of *Sesame Street* or the *Tonight* show.
They tell jokes. They change the pace. They show films,
play records, and avoid *anything* that would take more than
eight minutes. Although their motivation is understandable, this is what their students least need. However difficult it may be, the teacher must try to achieve student
attention and even enthusiasm through the attraction of
ideas, not razzmatazz. Those who think I am speaking here
in favor of "dull" classes may themselves, through media

exposure, have lost an understanding of the potential for excitement contained in an idea. The media (one prays) are not so powerful that they can obliterate in the young, particularly in the adolescent, what William James referred to as a "theoretic instinct," a need to know reasons, causes, abstract conceptions. Such an "instinct" can be seen in its earliest stages in what he calls the "sporadic metaphysical inquiries of children as to who made God, and why they have five fingers. . . ."

25 I trust that the reader is not misled by what I have been saying. As I see it, nothing in any of the above leads to the conclusion that I favor a classsroom that is authoritarian or coldhearted, or dominated by a teacher insensitive to students and how they learn. I merely want to affirm the importance of the classroom as a special place, aloof from the biases of the media; a place in which the uses of the intellect are given prominence in a setting of elevated language, civilized manners, and respect for social symbols.

Jerome Stern

What They Learn in School

Jerome Stern teaches English at Florida State University. This "monologue" aired March 17, 1989 on National Public Radio's "All Things Considered." It was later reprinted in Harper's *magazine.*

1 In the schools now, they want them to know all about marijuana, crack, heroin, and amphetamines,

2 Because then they won't be interested in marijuana, crack, heroin, and amphetamines,

3 But they don't want to tell them anything about sex because if the schools tell them about sex, then they will be interested in sex,

4 But if the schools don't tell them anything about sex,

5 Then they will have high morals, and no one will get pregnant, and everything will be all right,

And they do want them to know a lot about computers so   6
    they will outcompete the Japanese,
But they don't want them to know anything about real   7
    science because then they will lose their faith and become
    secular humanists,
And they do want them to know all about this great land   8
    of ours so they will be patriotic,
But they don't want them to learn about the tragedy and   9
    pain in its real history because then they will be critical
    about this great land of ours and we will be passively
    taken over by a foreign power,
And they want them to learn how to think for themselves   10
    so they can get good jobs and be successful,
But they don't want them to have books that confront them 11
    with real ideas because that will confuse their values,
And they'd like them to be good parents,   12
But they can't teach them about families because that takes 13
    them back to how you get to be a family,
And they want to warn them about how not to get AIDS   14
But that would mean telling them how not to get AIDS,   15
And they'd like them to know the Constitution,   16
But they don't like some of those amendments except when 17
    they are invoked by the people they agree with,
And they'd like them to vote,   18
But they don't want them to discuss current events because 19
    it might be controversial and upset them and make them
    want to take drugs, which they already have told them
    all about,
And they want to teach them the importance of morality,   20
But they also want them to learn that Winning is not every- 21
    thing — it is the Only Thing,
And they want them to be well-read,   22
But they don't want them to read Chaucer or Shakespeare   23
    or Aristophanes or Mark Twain or Ernest Hemingway or
    John Steinbeck, because that will corrupt them,
And they don't want them to know anything about art be-   24
    cause that will make them weird,
But they do want them to know about music so they can   25
    march in the band,
And they mainly want to teach them not to question, not   26
    to challenge, not to imagine, but to be obedient and be-
    have well so that they can hold them forever as children
    to their bosoms as the second millennium lurches toward
    its panicky close.

WHAT'S COLLEGE FOR?

Alice Walker

Everyday Use

for your grandmama

Alice Walker (born 1944) is an essayist, poet, feminist, and activist, but she is best known for her Pulitzer-Prize-winning third novel The Color Purple *(1982). Asked why she writes, she once explained, "I'm really paying homage to people I love, the people who are thought to be dumb and backward but who were the ones who first taught me to see beauty." "Everyday Use" appeared in her acclaimed collection of stories,* In Love and Trouble, *published in 1973.*

1   I will wait for her in the yard that Maggie and I made so clean and wavy yesterday afternoon. A yard like this is more comfortable than most people know. It is not just a yard. It is like an extended living room. When the hard clay is swept clean as a floor and the fine sand around the edges lined with tiny, irregular grooves anyone can come and sit and look up into the elm tree and wait for the breezes that never come inside the house.

2   Maggie will be nervous until after her sister goes: she will stand hopelessly in corners homely and ashamed of the burn scars down her arms and legs, eyeing her sister with a mixture of envy and awe. She thinks her sister has held life always in the palm of one hand, that "no" is a word the world never learned to say to her.

3   You've no doubt seen those TV shows where the child who has "made it" is confronted, as a surprise, by her own mother and father, tottering in weakly from backstage. (A pleasant surprise, of course: What would they do if parent and child came on the show only to curse out and insult each other?) On TV mother and child embrace and smile

into each other's faces. Sometimes the mother and father weep, the child wraps them in her arms and leans across the table to tell how she would not have made it without their help. I have seen these programs.

Sometimes I dream a dream in which Dee and I are sud-   4
denly brought together on a TV program of this sort. Out of a dark and soft-seated limousine I am ushered into a bright room filled with many people. There I meet a smiling, gray, sporty man like Johnny Carson who shakes my hand and tells me what a fine girl I have. Then we are on the stage and Dee is embracing me with tears in her eyes. She pins on my dress a large orchid, even though she has told me once that she thinks orchids are tacky flowers.

In real life I am a large, big-boned woman with rough,   5
man-working hands. In the winter I wear flannel night-gowns to bed and overalls during the day. I can kill and clean a hog as mercilessly as a man. My fat keeps me hot in zero weather. I can work outside all day, breaking ice to get water for washing; I can eat pork liver cooked over the open fire minutes after it comes steaming from the hog. One winter I knocked a bull calf straight in the brain be-tween the eyes with a sledge hammer and had the meat hung up to chill before nightfall. But of course all this does not show on television. I am the way my daughter would want me to be: a hundred pounds lighter, my skin like an uncooked barley pancake. My hair glistens in the hot bright lights. Johnny Carson has much to do to keep up with my quick and witty tongue.

But that is a mistake. I know even before I wake up. Who   6
ever knew a Johnson with a quick tongue? Who can even imagine me looking a strange white man in the eye? It seems to me I have talked to them always with one foot raised in flight, with my head turned in whichever way is farthest from them. Dee, though. She would always look anyone in the eye. Hesitation was no part of her nature.

"How do I look, Mama?" Maggie says, showing just   7
enough of her thin body enveloped in pink skirt and red blouse for me to know she's there, almost hidden by the door.

"Come out into the yard," I say.   8

Have you ever seen a lame animal, perhaps a dog run   9
over by some careless person rich enough to own a car, sidle up to someone who is ignorant enough to be kind to

him? That is the way my Maggie walks. She has been like
this, chin on chest, eyes on ground, feet in shuffle, ever
since the fire that burned the other house to the ground.

10   Dee is lighter than Maggie, with nicer hair and a fuller
figure. She's a woman now, though sometimes I forget.
How long ago was it that the other house burned? Ten,
twelve years? Sometimes I can still hear the flames and
feel Maggie's arms sticking to me, her hair smoking and
her dress falling off her in little black papery flakes. Her
eyes seemed stretched open, blazed open by the flames reflected in them. And Dee. I see her standing off under the
sweet gum tree she used to dig gum out of: a look of concentration on her face as she watched the last dingy gray board
of the house fall in toward the red-hot brick chimney. Why
don't you do a dance around the ashes? I'd wanted to ask
her. She hated the house that much.

11   I used to think she hated Maggie, too. But that was before
we raised the money, the church and me, to send her to
Augusta to school. She used to read to us without pity;
forcing words, lies, other folks' habits, whole lives upon us
two, sitting trapped and ignorant underneath her voice.
She washed us in a river of make-believe, burned us with
a lot of knowledge we didn't necessarily need to know.
Pressed us to her with the serious way she read, to shove
us away at just the moment, like dimwits, we seemed about
to understand.

12   Dee wanted nice things. A yellow organdy dress to wear
to her graduation from high school; black pumps to match
a green suit she'd made from an old suit somebody gave
me. She was determined to stare down any disaster in her
efforts. Her eyelids would not flicker for minutes at a time.
Often I fought off the temptation to shake her. At sixteen
she had a style of her own: and knew what style was.

13   I never had an education myself. After second grade the
school was closed down. Don't ask me why: in 1927 colored
asked fewer questions than they do now. Sometimes Maggie
reads to me. She stumbles along good-naturedly but can't
see well. She knows she is not bright. Like good looks and
money, quickness passed her by. She will marry John
Thomas (who has mossy teeth in an earnest face) and then
I'll be free to sit here and I guess just sing church songs to
myself. Although I never was a good singer. Never could
carry a tune. I was always better at a man's job. I used to

love to milk till I was hooked in the side in '49. Cows are soothing and slow and don't bother you, unless you try to milk them the wrong way.

I have deliberately turned my back on the house. It is   14
three rooms, just like the one that burned, except the roof is tin; they don't make shingle roofs anymore. There are no real windows, just some holes cut in the sides, like the portholes in a ship, but not round and not square, with rawhide holding the shutters up on the outside. This house is in a pasture, too, like the other one. No doubt when Dee sees it she will want to tear it down. She wrote me once that no matter where we "choose" to live, she will manage to come see us. But she will never bring her friends. Maggie and I thought about this and Maggie asked me, "Mama, when did Dee ever *have* any friends?"

She had a few. Furtive boys in pink shirts hanging about   15
on washday after school. Nervous girls who never laughed. Impressed with her they worshiped the well-turned phrase, the cute shape, the scalding humor that erupted like bubbles in lye. She read to them.

When she was courting Jimmy T she didn't have much   16
time to pay to us, but turned all her faultfinding power on him. He *flew* to marry a cheap gal from a family of ignorant flashy people. She hardly had time to recompose herself.

When she comes I will meet — but there they are!   17

Maggie attempts to make a dash for the house, in her   18
shuffling way, but I stay her with my hand. "Come back here," I say. And she stops and tries to dig a well in the sand with her toe.

It is hard to see them clearly through the strong sun. But   19
even the first glimpse of leg out of the car tells me it is Dee. Her feet were always neat-looking, as if God himself had shaped them with a certain style. From the other side of the car comes a short, stocky man. Hair is all over his head a foot long and hanging from his chin like a kinky mule tail. I hear Maggie suck in her breath. "Uhnnnh," is what it sounds like. Like when you see the wriggling end of a snake just in front of your foot on the road. "Uhnnnh."

Dee next. A dress down to the ground, in this hot weather.   20
A dress so loud it hurts my eyes. There are yellows and oranges enough to throw back the light of the sun. I feel my whole face warming from the heat waves it throws out. Earrings gold, too, and hanging down to her shoulders.

Bracelets dangling and making noises when she moves her arm up to shake the folds of the dress out of her armpits. The dress is loose and flows, and as she walks closer, I like it. I hear Maggie go "Uhnnnh" again. It is her sister's hair. It stands straight up like the wool on a sheep. It is black as night and around the edges are two long pigtails that rope about like small lizards disappearing behind her ears.

21   "Wa-su-zo-Tean-o!" she says, coming on in that gliding way the dress makes her move. The short stocky fellow with the hair to his navel is all grinning and he follows up with "Asalamalakim, my mother and sister!" He moves to hug Maggie but she falls back, right up against the back of my chair. I feel her trembling there and when I look up I see the perspiration falling off her chin.

22   "Don't get up," says Dee. Since I am stout it takes something of a push. You can see me trying to move a second or two before I make it. She turns, showing white heels through her sandals, and goes back to the car. Out she peeks next with a Polaroid. She stoops down quickly and lines up picture after picture of me sitting there in front of the house with Maggie cowering behind me. She never takes a shot without making sure the house is included. When a cow comes nibbling around the edge of the yard she snaps it and me and Maggie *and* the house. Then she puts the Polaroid in the back seat of the car, and comes up and kisses me on the forehead.

23   Meanwhile Asalamalakim is going through the motions with Maggie's hand. Maggie's hand is as limp as a fish, and probably as cold, despite the sweat, and she keeps trying to pull it back. It looks like Asalamalakim wants to shake hands but wants to do it fancy. Or maybe he don't know how people shake hands. Anyhow, he soon gives up on Maggie.

24   "Well," I say. "Dee."

25   "No, Mama," she says. "Not 'Dee,' Wangero Leewanika Kemanjo!"

26   "What happened to 'Dee'?" I wanted to know.

27   "She's dead." Wangero said. "I couldn't bear it any longer being named after the people who oppress me."

28   "You know as well as me you was named after your aunt Dicie," I said. Dicie is my sister. She named Dee. We called her "Big Dee" after Dee was born.

29   "But who was *she* named after?" asked Wangero.

30   "I guess after Grandma Dee," I said.

31   "And who was she named after?" asked Wangero.

"Her mother," I said, and saw Wangero was getting tired. 32
"That's about as far back as I can trace it," I said. Though,
in fact, I probably could have carried it back beyond the
Civil War through the branches.

"Well," said Asalamalakim, "there you are." 33

"Uhnnnh," I heard Maggie say. 34

"There I was not," I said, "before 'Dicie' cropped up in 35
our family, so why should I try to trace it that far back?"

He just stood there grinning, looking down on me like 36
somebody inspecting a Model A car. Every once in a while
he and Wangero sent eye signals over my head.

"How do you pronounce this name?" I asked. 37

"You don't have to call me by it if you don't want to," 38
said Wangero.

"Why shouldn't I?" I asked. "If that's what you want us 39
to call you, we'll call you."

"I know it might sound awkward at first," said Wangero. 40

"I'll get used to it," I said. "Ream it out again." 41

Well, soon we got the name out of the way. Asalamalakim 42
had a name twice as long and three times as hard. After I
tripped over it two or three times he told me to just call
him Hakim-a-barber. I wanted to ask him was he a barber,
but I didn't really think he was, so I didn't ask.

"You must belong to those beef-cattle peoples down the 43
road," I said. They said "Asalamalakim" when they met
you, too, but they didn't shake hands. Always too busy:
feeding the cattle, fixing the fences, putting up salt-lick
shelters, throwing down hay. When the white folks poisoned
some of the herd the men stayed up all night with rifles in
their hands. I walked a mile and a half just to see the sight.

Hakim-a-barber said, "I accept some of their doctrines, 44
but farming and raising cattle is not my style." (They didn't
tell me, and I didn't ask, whether Wangero [Dee] had really
gone and married him.)

We sat down to eat and right away he said he didn't eat 45
collards and pork was unclean. Wangero, though, went on
through the chitlins and corn bread, the greens and everything else. She talked a blue streak over the sweet potatoes.
Everything delighted her. Even the fact that we still used
the benches her daddy made for the table when we couldn't
afford to buy chairs.

"Oh, Mama!" she cried. Then turned to Hakim-a-barber. 46
"I never knew how lovely these benches are. You can feel
the rump prints," she said, running her hands underneath

her and along the bench. Then she gave a sigh and her hand closed over Grandma Dee's butter dish. "That's it!" she said. "I knew there was something I wanted to ask you if I could have." She jumped up from the table and went over in the corner where the churn stood, the milk in it clabber by now. She looked at the churn and looked at it.

47   "This churn top is what I need," she said. "Didn't Uncle Buddy whittle it out of a tree you all used to have?"

48   "Yes," I said.

49   "Uh huh," she said happily. "And I want the dasher, too."

50   "Uncle Buddy whittle that, too?" asked the barber.

51   Dee (Wangero) looked up at me.

52   "Aunt Dee's first husband whittled the dash," said Maggie so low you almost couldn't hear her. "His name was Henry, but they called him Stash."

53   "Maggie's brain is like an elephant's," Wangero said, laughing. "I can use the churn top as a centerpiece for the alcove table," she said, sliding a plate over the churn, "and I'll think of something artistic to do with the dasher."

54   When she finished wrapping the dasher the handle stuck out. I took it for a moment in my hands. You didn't even have to look close to see where hands pushing the dasher up and down to make butter had left a kind of sink in the wood. In fact, there were a lot of small sinks; you could see where thumbs and fingers had sunk into the wood. It was beautiful light yellow wood, from a tree that grew in the yard where Big Dee and Stash had lived.

55   After dinner Dee (Wangero) went to the trunk at the foot of my bed and started rifling through it. Maggie hung back in the kitchen over the dishpan. Out came Wangero with two quilts. They had been pieced by Grandma Dee and then Big Dee and me had hung them on the quilt frames on the front porch and quilted them. One was in the Lone Star pattern. The other was Walk Around the Mountain. In both of them were scraps of dresses Grandma Dee had worn fifty and more years ago. Bits and pieces of Grandpa Jarrell's Paisley shirts. And one teeny faded blue piece, about the size of a penny matchbox, that was from Great Grandpa Ezra's uniform that he wore in the Civil War.

56   "Mama," Wangero said sweet as a bird. "Can I have these old quilts?"

57   I heard something fall in the kitchen, and a minute later the kitchen door slammed.

58   "Why don't you take one or two of the others?" I asked.

"These old things was just done by me and Big Dee from some tops your grandma pieced before she died."

"No," said Wangero. "I don't want those. They are stitched 59 around the borders by machine."

"That'll make them last better," I said. 60

"That's not the point," said Wangero. "These are all pieces 61 of dresses Grandma used to wear. She did all this stitching by hand. Imagine!" She held the quilts securely in her arms, stroking them.

"Some of the pieces, like those lavender ones, come from 62 old clothes her mother handed down to her," I said, moving up to touch the quilts. Dee (Wangero) moved back just enough so that I couldn't reach the quilts. They already belonged to her.

"Imagine!" she breathed again, clutching them closely to 63 her bosom.

"The truth is," I said, "I promised to give them quilts to 64 Maggie, for when she marries John Thomas."

She gasped like a bee had stung her. 65

"Maggie can't appreciate these quilts!" she said. "She'd 66 probably be backward enough to put them to everyday use."

"I reckon she would," I said. "'God knows I been saving 67 'em for long enough with nobody using 'em. I hope she will!" I didn't want to bring up how I had offered Dee (Wangero) a quilt when she went away to college. Then she had told me they were old-fashioned, out of style.

"But they're *priceless!*" she was saying now, furiously; for 68 she has a temper. "Maggie would put them on the bed and in five years they'd be in rags. Less than that!"

"She can always make some more," I said. "Maggie knows 69 how to quilt."

Dee (Wangero) looked at me with hatred. "You just will 70 not understand. The point is these quilts, *these* quilts!"

"Well," I said, stumped. "What would *you* do with them?" 71

"Hang them," she said. As if that was the only thing you 72 *could* do with quilts.

Maggie by now was standing in the door. I could almost 73 hear the sound her feet made as they scraped over each other.

"She can have them, Mama," she said, like somebody 74 used to never winning anything, or having anything reserved for her. "I can 'member Grandma Dee without the quilts."

I looked at her hard. She had filled her bottom lip with 75

checkerberry snuff and it gave her face a kind of dopey, hangdog look. It was Grandma Dee and Big Dee who taught her how to quilt herself. She stood there with her scarred hands hidden in the folds of her skirt. She looked at her sister with something like fear but she wasn't mad at her. This was Maggie's portion. This was the way she knew God to work.

76   When I looked at her like that something hit me in the top of my head and ran down to the soles of my feet. Just like when I'm in church and the spirit of God touches me and I get happy and shout. I did something I never had done before: hugged Maggie to me, then dragged her on into the room, snatched the quilts out of Miss Wangero's hands and dumped them into Maggie's lap. Maggie just sat there on my bed with her mouth open.

77   "Take one or two of the others," I said to Dee.

78   But she turned without a word and went out to Hakim-a-barber.

79   "You just don't understand," she said, as Maggie and I came out to the car.

80   "What don't I understand?" I wanted to know.

81   "Your heritage," she said. And then she turned to Maggie, kissed her, and said, "You ought to try to make something of yourself, too, Maggie. It's really a new day for us. But from the way you and Mama still live you'd never know it."

82   She put on some sunglasses that hid everything above the tip of her nose and her chin.

83   Maggie smiled; maybe at the sunglasses. But a real smile, not scared. After we watched the car dust settle I asked Maggie to bring me a dip of snuff. And then the two of us sat there just enjoying, until it was time to go in the house and go to bed.

Adrienne Rich

Claiming an Education

"Claiming an Education" is the transcript of a talk first given to new students at Douglass College, the Women's College of Rutgers University, on September 6, 1977; later it was included in Adrienne Rich's book On Lies, Secrets, and Silence. *Rich (born 1929) is a noted teacher, essayist, and feminist who won the National Book Award for poetry in 1974.*

For this convocation, I planned to separate my remarks 1
into two parts: some thoughts about you, the women students here, and some thoughts about us who teach in a women's college. But ultimately, those two parts are indivisible. If university education means anything beyond the processing of human beings into expected roles, through credit hours, tests, and grades (and I believe that in a women's college especially it *might* mean much more), it implies an ethical and intellectual contract between teacher and student. This contract must remain intuitive, dynamic, unwritten; but we must turn to it again and again if learning is to be reclaimed from the depersonalizing and cheapening pressures of the present-day academic scene.

The first thing I want to say to you who are students, is 2
that you cannot afford to think of being here to *receive* an education; you will do much better to think of yourselves as being here to *claim* one. One of the dictionary definitions of the verb "to claim" is: *to take as the rightful owner; to assert in the face of possible contradiction.* "To receive" is *to come into possession of; to act as receptacle or container for; to accept as authoritative or true.* The difference is that between acting and being acted-upon, and for women it can literally mean the difference between life and death.

One of the devastating weaknesses of university learning, 3
of the store of knowledge and opinion that has been handed down through academic training, has been its almost total erasure of women's experience and thought from the curriculum, and its exclusion of women as members of the academic community. Today, with increasing numbers of women students in nearly every branch of higher learning, we still see very few women in the upper levels of faculty and administration in most institutions. Douglass College

itself is a women's college in a university administered overwhelmingly by men, who in turn are answerable to the state legislature, again composed predominantly of men. But the most significant fact for you is that what you learn here, the very texts you read, the lectures you hear, the way your studies are divided into categories and fragmented one from the other—all this reflects, to a very large degree, neither objective reality, nor an accurate picture of the past, nor a group of rigorously tested observations about human behavior. What you can learn here (and I mean not only at Douglass but any college in any university) is how *men* have perceived and organized their experience, their history, their ideas of social relationships, good and evil, sickness and health, etc. When you read or hear about "great issues," "major texts," "the mainstream of Western thought," you are hearing about what men, above all white men, in their male subjectivity, have decided is important.

4   Black and other minority peoples have for some time recognized that their racial and ethnic experience was not accounted for in the studies broadly labeled human; and that even the sciences can be racist. For many reasons, it has been more difficult for women to comprehend our exclusion, and to realize that even the sciences can be sexist. For one thing, it is only within the last hundred years that higher education has grudgingly been opened up to women at all, even to white, middle-class women. And many of us have found ourselves poring eagerly over books with titles like: *The Descent of Man; Man and His Symbols; Irrational Man; The Phenomenon of Man; The Future of Man; Man and the Machine; From Man to Man; May Man Prevail?; Man, Science and Society;* or *One-Dimensional Man*—books pretending to describe a "human" reality that does not include over one-half the human species.

5   Less than a decade ago, with the rebirth of a feminist movement in this country, women students and teachers in a number of universities began to demand and set up women's studies courses—to *claim* a woman-directed education. And, despite the inevitable accusations of "unscholarly," "group therapy," "faddism," etc., despite backlash and budget cuts, women's studies are still growing, offering to more and more women a new intellectual grasp on their lives, new understanding of our history, a fresh vision of the human experience, and also a critical basis for evaluat-

ing what they hear and read in other courses, and in the society at large.

But my talk is not really about women's studies, much   6
as I believe in their scholarly, scientific, and human necessity. While I think that any Douglass student has everything
to gain by investigating and enrolling in women's studies
courses, I want to suggest that there is a more essential
experience that you owe yourselves, one which courses in
women's studies can greatly enrich, but which finally depends on you, in all your interactions with yourself and
your world. This is the experience of *taking responsibility
toward yourselves*. Our upbringing as women has so often
told us that this should come second to our relationships
and responsibilities to other people. We have been offered
ethical models of the self-denying wife and mother; intellectual models of the brilliant but slapdash dilettante who
never commits herself to anything the whole way, or the
intelligent woman who denies her intelligence in order to
seem more "feminine," or who sits in passive silence even
when she disagrees inwardly with everything that is being
said around her.

Responsibility to yourself means refusing to let others   7
do your thinking, talking, and naming for you; it means
learning to respect and use your own brains and instincts;
hence, grappling with hard work. It means that you do not
treat your body as a commodity with which to purchase
superficial intimacy or economic security; for our bodies
and minds are inseparable in this life, and when we allow
our bodies to be treated as objects, our minds are in mortal
danger. It means insisting that those to whom you give
your friendship and love are able to respect your mind. It
means being able to say, with Charlotte Brontë's *Jane Eyre:*
"I have an inward treasure born with me, which can keep
me alive if all the extraneous delights should be withheld
or offered only at a price I cannot afford to give."

Responsibility to yourself means that you don't fall for   8
shallow and easy solutions — predigested books and ideas,
weekend encounters guaranteed to change your life, taking
"gut" courses instead of ones you know will challenge you,
bluffing at school and life instead of doing solid work, mar-
rying early as an escape from real decisions, getting pregnant as an evasion of already existing problems. It means
that you refuse to sell your talents and aspirations short,

simply to avoid conflict and confrontation. And this, in turn, means resisting the forces in society which say that women should be nice, play safe, have low professional expectations, drown in love and forget about work, live through others, and stay in the places assigned to us. It means that we insist on a life of meaningful work, insist that work be as meaningful as love and friendship in our lives. It means, therefore, the courage to be "different"; not to be continuously available to others when we need time for ourselves and our work; to be able to demand of others — parents, friends, roommates, teachers, lovers, husbands, children — that they respect our sense of purpose and our integrity as persons. Women everywhere are finding the courage to do this, more and more, and we are finding that courage both in our study of women in the past who possessed it, and in each other as we look to other women for comradeship, community, and challenge. The difference between a life lived actively, and a life of passive drifting and dispersal of energies, is an immense difference. Once we begin to feel committed to our lives, responsible to ourselves, we can never again be satisfied with the old, passive way.

9   Now comes the second part of the contract. I believe that in a women's college you have the right to expect your faculty to take you seriously. The education of women has been a matter of debate for centuries, and old, negative attitudes about women's role, women's ability to think and take leadership, are still rife both in and outside the university. Many male professors (and I don't mean only at Douglass) still feel that teaching in a women's college is a second-rate career. Many tend to eroticize their women students — to treat them as sexual objects — instead of demanding the best of their minds. (At Yale a legal suit [*Alexander v. Yale*] has been brought against the university by a group of women students demanding a stated policy against sexual advances toward female students by male professors.) Many teachers, both men and women, trained in the male-centered tradition, are still handing the ideas and texts of that tradition on to students without teaching them to criticize its antiwoman attitudes, its omission of women as part of the species. Too often, all of us fail to teach the most important thing, which is that clear thinking, active discussion, and excellent writing are all necessary for intellectual freedom, and that these require *hard work*. Sometimes, perhaps in discouragement with a culture which is both anti-intellec-

tual and antiwoman, we may resign ourselves to low expectations for our students before we have given them half a chance to become more thoughtful, expressive human beings. We need to take to heart the words of Elizabeth Barrett Browning, a poet, a thinking woman, and a feminist, who wrote in 1845 of her impatience with studies which cultivate a "passive recipiency" in the mind, and asserted that "women want to be made to *think actively:* their apprehension is quicker than that of men, but their defect lies for the most part in the logical faculty and in the higher mental activities." Note that she implies a defect which can be remedied by intellectual training; *not* an inborn lack of ability.

I have said that the contract on the student's part involves that you demand to be taken seriously so that you can also go on taking yourself seriously. This means seeking out criticism, recognizing that the most affirming thing anyone can do for you is demand that you push yourself further, show you the range of what you *can* do. It means rejecting attitudes of "take-it-easy," "why-be-so-serious," "why-worry-you'll-probably-get-married-anyway." It means assuming your share of responsibility for what happens in the classroom, because that affects the quality of your daily life here. It means that the student sees herself engaged *with* her teachers in an active, ongoing struggle for a real education. But for her to do this, her teachers must be committed to the belief that women's minds and experience are intrinsically valuable and indispensable to any civilization worthy the name; that there is no more exhilarating and intellectually fertile place in the academic world today than a women's college — *if* both students and teachers in large enough numbers are trying to fulfill this contract. The contract is really a pledge of mutual seriousness about women, about language, ideas, methods, and values. It is our shared commitment toward a world in which the inborn potentialities of so many women's minds will no longer be wasted, raveled-away, paralyzed, or denied.

Garry B. Trudeau (born 1948) is one of America's most influential (and controversial) political and social commentators. His vehicle is the comic strip "Doonesbury," which appears in over 850 newspapers and whose readership may top 100 million people.

Doonesbury

G. B. TRUDEAU

Norman Cousins

How to Make People Smaller
Than They Are

*Norman Cousins (born 1915) has devoted his life to improving
the fabric of American life. Author of many books and winner
of many awards for public service, and a widely read journalist
with strong feelings on many topics, he is particularly interested
in fostering international cooperation and in improving education for all. The following essay appeared in 1978 as an editorial
in* Saturday Review, *the popular magazine on the arts and
civic affairs that he edited for over thirty years.*

Three months ago in this space we wrote about the costly   1
retreat from the humanities on all the levels of American
education. Since that time, we have had occasion to visit
a number of campuses and have been troubled to find that
the general situation is even more serious than we had
thought. It has become apparent to us that one of the biggest
problems confronting American education today is the increasing vocationalization of our colleges and universities.
Throughout the country, schools are under pressure to become job-training centers and employment agencies.

The pressure comes mainly from two sources. One is the   2
growing determination of many citizens to reduce taxes—
understandable and even commendable in itself, but irrational and irresponsible when connected to the reduction
or dismantling of vital public services. The second source
of pressure comes from parents and students who tend to
scorn courses of study that do not teach people how to
become attractive to employers in a rapidly tightening job
market.

It is absurd to believe that the development of skills does   3
not also require the systematic development of the human
mind. Education is being measured more by the size of the
benefits the individual can extract from society than by the
extent to which the individual can come into possession of
his or her full powers. The result is that the life-giving juices
are in danger of being drained out of education.

Emphasis on "practicalities" is being characterized by   4
the subordination of words to numbers. History is seen not
as essential experience to be transmitted to new generations, but as abstractions that carry dank odors. Art is re-

garded as something that calls for indulgence or patronage and that has no place among the practical realities. Political science is viewed more as a specialized subject for people who want to go into politics than as an opportunity for citizens to develop a knowledgeable relationship with the systems by which human societies are governed. Finally, literature and philosophy are assigned the role of add-ons — intellectual adornments that have nothing to do with "genuine" education.

5   Instead of trying to shrink the liberal arts, the American people ought to be putting pressure on colleges and universities to increase the ratio of the humanities to the sciences. Most serious studies of medical-school curricula in recent years have called attention to the stark gaps in the liberal education of medical students. The experts agree that the schools shouldn't leave it up to students to close those gaps.

6   We must not make it appear, however, that nothing is being done. In the past decade, the National Endowment for the Humanities has been a prime mover in infusing the liberal arts into medical education and other specialized schools. During this past year alone, NEH has given 108 grants to medical schools and research organizations in the areas of ethics and human values. Some medical schools, like the one at Pennsylvania State University, have led the way in both the number and the depth of courses offered in the humanities. Penn State has been especially innovative in weaving literature and philosophy into the full medical course of study. It is ironical that the pressure against the humanities should be manifesting itself at precisely the time when so many medical schools are at long last moving in this direction.

7   The irony of the emphasis being placed on careers is that nothing is more valuable for anyone who has had a professional or vocational education than to be able to deal with abstractions or complexities, or to feel comfortable with subtleties of thought or language, or to think sequentially. The doctor who knows only disease is at a disadvantage alongside the doctor who knows at least as much about people as he does about pathological organisms. The lawyer who argues in court from a narrow legal base is no match for the lawyer who can connect legal precedents to historical experience and who employs wide-ranging intellectual resources. The business executive whose competence in general management is bolstered by an artistic ability to deal with people is of prime value to his company. For the

technologist, the engineering of consent can be just as important as the engineering of moving parts. In all these respects, the liberal arts have much to offer. Just in terms of career preparation, therefore, a student is shortchanging himself by shortcutting the humanities.

But even if it could be demonstrated that the humanities   8
contribute nothing directly to a job, they would still be an essential part of the educational equipment of any person who wants to come to terms with life. The humanities would be expendable only if human beings didn't have to make decisions that affect their lives and the lives of others; if the human past never existed or had nothing to tell us about the present; if thought processes were irrelevant to the achievement of purpose; if creativity was beyond the human mind and had nothing to do with the joy of living; if human relationships were random aspects of life; if human beings never had to cope with panic or pain, or if they never had to anticipate the connection between cause and effect; if all the mysteries of mind and nature were fully plumbed; and if no special demands arose from the accident of being born a human being instead of a hen or a hog.

Finally, there would be good reason to eliminate the   9
humanities if a free society were not absolutely dependent on a functioning citizenry. If the main purpose of a university is job training, then the underlying philosophy of our government has little meaning. The debates that went into the making of American society concerned not just institutions or governing principles but the capacity of humans to sustain those institutions. Whatever the disagreements were over other issues at the American Constitutional Convention, the fundamental question sensed by everyone, a question that lay over the entire assembly, was whether the people themselves would understand what it meant to hold the ultimate power of society, and whether they had enough of a sense of history and destiny to know where they had been and where they ought to be going.

Jefferson was prouder of having been the founder of the   10
University of Virginia than of having been President of the United States. He knew that the educated and developed mind was the best assurance that a political system could be made to work — a system based on the informed consent of the governed. If this idea fails, then all the saved tax dollars in the world will not be enough to prevent the nation from turning on itself.

Carrie Tuhy
So Who Needs College?

Carrie Tuhy composed this article for Money *magazine in 1982.*

1   Career seekers, the want ads are trying to tell you something. Despite the highest unemployment rate since 1941, Sunday papers across America are thick with job postings for specialized skills. Employers seem unable to find enough qualified people for such positions as bank teller, commercial artist, computer programmer, data processor, electronics technician, medical technologist, nurse, office manager, salesperson and secretary. Fewer and fewer classified ads stipulate college as a requirement.

2   The message is clear: even a severe recession hasn't caused a labor surplus in certain occupations. But the message goes deeper. In good times as well as bad, a bachelor's degree is becoming less valuable for some careers. As students head off to college this month, they and their parents may wonder whether the diploma is still worth its price in tuition, room, board and four years of forgone income.

3   The majority of openings, now and for the economic recovery that could be getting under way, require types of skills more likely to be acquired in a technical or trade school or on the job than on an ivied campus. Technical school graduates are routinely landing jobs with higher starting pay than newly minted bachelors of arts can command. A computer programmer fresh from a six-month course can earn up to $14,000 a year while an English major is rewriting his résumé for the umpteenth time. Clearly, the $5,000 certificate of technical competence is gaining on the $50,000 sheepskin.

4   While graduates of four-year colleges still have a small financial edge, that advantage is narrowing. In the 1960s, beginning salaries for college men started an average of 24% higher than for the work force as a whole. That differential is now down to 5%. Projections of the lifetime return on an investment in a college education are still more disillusioning. The foremost specialist in such estimates, Richard Freeman of the National Bureau of Economic Research, predicts that the class of '82 will realize only 6% or 7% a year on its education costs in the form of higher

earnings compared with the 11% return projected for the class of '62. Concludes Finis Welch, an economist at UCLA: "A college degree today is not a ticket to a high-paying job or an insurance policy against unemployment. . . ."

In fact, going to college may even be a hindrance for some   5 people with extraordinary talent or ambition. They often feel that college bottles up their drive. Still, you shouldn't overlook educational values that cannot be measured in dollars. Pursuing a bachelor's degree can stretch the mind, help a young person gain maturity and generally enrich anyone's life. Indisputably too, college remains essential in preparing for the professions and advantageous in getting interviews for some occupations. You may not need a B.A. to do the work of an advertising copywriter, broker or journalist — to cite some conspicuous examples — but a diploma still helps you to get in the door. Degreeless applicants may have to start lower or fight harder to enter such fields, and they may be passed over for promotions, particularly to management levels.

Conversely, doors stand wide open to rewarding careers,   6 especially in technical fields, for those with the right nonacademic training. Trade and technical schools are quickly outgrowing their matchbook-cover image — DRAW THIS DOG AND EARN BIG MONEY! Despite the continuing shabby practices of a few institutions, most of the nation's 7,000 private vocational schools for high school graduates competently provide training for all manner of careers from actor to X-ray technician.

The emphasis in vocational education is switching from   7 training blue-collar factory hands and brown-collar repairmen to preparing gray-collar technicians. Also, high-tech companies with a vested interest in a competent work force have taken it upon themselves to educate people in specialized skills. The list of those companies starts with AT&T, IBM and Xerox but goes on to include such somewhat smaller firms as Bell & Howell, Control Data and Wang. One of several courses sponsored by Bell & Howell's DeVry Institute of Technology in Chicago trains technicians to build product prototypes by following engineering drawings; the course takes 20 months and leads to jobs starting at $18,000 a year.

Profit-making trade schools are flourishing even as uni-   8 versity enrollments dwindle. One of the country's largest commercial schools, National Education Corp. (NEC), based in Newport Beach, Calif., has more than 100,000 students in 70 branches. Graduates repair jets (average starting salary: $15,000), manage radio stations ($30,000), write computer programs and design microprocessor chips (both $12,000).

9   Fees are often substantial at a high-tech school, but because the training is condensed it costs far less than getting a university degree. A six-month course in computers at NEC's National Institute of Technology costs $5,000; a two-year program in electronics engineering is $7,900. Says Wayne Gilpin, president of the institute, with a touch of braggadocio: "Our students may not be able to quote Byron, but they are technically sharp. They can sit alongside four-year graduates from Purdue and MIT."

10   Trade school students should face the fact that they won't sit beside many of those Purdue and MIT graduates. Electrical engineers, for example, can get jobs researching and developing new technology at salaries ranging from $23,000 to $30,000, while technicians are more likely to work at repairing those creations at $18,000 to $22,000.

11   Even so, bright people can advance surprisingly far on trade school training. One example: Ronald Billodeaux, now 29, who completed an electronics course at Little Rock's United Electronics (now called Arkansas College of Technology) and got a job maintaining equipment for Geophysical Services Inc., a Texas Instruments subsidiary that provides exploration data for oil companies. Over the years, Billodeaux helped search for oil in Africa, South America and Australia. Last year the company wanted to move him to London to oversee Middle Eastern and African operations, but he balked at further travel. Almost immediately, Mobil hired him away as a supervisor to scout oil prospects in the Gulf of Mexico.

12   Two-year community colleges and private junior colleges offer vocational training at a considerably lower cost than private technical schools do. Tuition averages $500 a year for such job-oriented studies as auto mechanics, data processing, police science and real estate sales. Says Roger Yarrington, until recently executive director of the American Association of Junior and Community Colleges: "The use of these schools has shifted from university preparation to job preparation." But community colleges, with their multitude of majors, may not have the resources to give as thorough and up-to-date training as you can get at single-

subject technical schools. NEC, for example, is spending more than $1 million this year on new equipment.

What is most valuable in vocational education—whether at a community college or a technical school—is hands-on training. In choosing a program, you should ask about not only the school's resources but also about the time devoted to learning by doing and the companies that hire the most students. Then query those companies' personnel managers on how they rate the school's courses. 13

Employers say the best preparation combines study with work alongside people in the field. At the Fashion Institute of Design and Merchandising, a California junior college with branches in San Francisco and Los Angeles, Constance Bennett, 23, spent her second year working as an intern at Hang Ten, a sportswear manufacturer. The experience serves her well in her present job at Koret of North America, a San Francisco sportswear company. During a 21-month course at the Culinary Institute of America in Hyde Park, N.Y., the Harvard of *haute cuisine*, students get experience in some of the nation's best-known kitchens. John Doherty, 24, spent more than a quarter of his course at the Waldorf Astoria in New York City. After graduation in 1978, he was hired as a cook there; he has since risen to second in command of a kitchen with 170 cooks. 14

The best deal, of course, is getting paid to learn a skill. Competition for apprenticeships is always stiff, and a slack economy has cut the number of openings. But as business revives, so will the need for trainees. Along with the standard apprenticeships for plumbers, pipefitters and carpenters, there are programs in hundreds of occupations including biomedical equipment technician, film and video editor, recording engineer, meteorologist and chef. Frank Ruta, 24, learned to cook and run a kitchen in a three-year apprenticeship arranged by the American Culinary Federation. Instead of forking out more than $13,000 to attend the Culinary Institute of America, he hired on at the Lemon Tree, a restaurant in his home town of McKeesport, Pa., at $3.25 an hour and got a 25¢ raise every six months. Ruta learned to cook well enough to satisfy a range of tastes, in politics as well as palates. As personal chef to the First Family, he has served the Carters and the Reagans. 15

The Labor Department's Bureau of Apprenticeship and Training supervises programs in some 500 trades. Thirty years ago, federal regulation was aimed against racism, 16 favoritism and exploitation in handing out job assignments. Today the bureau mainly monitors wages: apprentices at first average about $6 an hour, 40% to 50% of skilled workers' pay. State agencies with information about apprenticeships are listed in phone directories; look under "state government" for the employment security administration.

17   However, some of the most respected employer-sponsored programs, such as those run by Kodak, General Electric and Westinghouse, are not listed with government offices. You can find them by asking major employers in your chosen field. Apprenticeships are investments of time rather than money; it takes five years to qualify as a journeyman machinist — only a year less than it usually requires to earn a bachelor's degree and an M.B.A. Though apprentices start with no job guarantee, a company that spends up to six years training a person is likely to keep him.

18   Even without training, high school graduates sometimes can land worthwhile jobs in marketing, retailing and a few other fields. Continental Illinois National Bank in Chicago occasionally hires promising teenagers as trainees at $10,000 a year. In five years, they can rise to loan service representative at $27,000 — a position and a salary few people fresh from a liberal arts college would qualify for in less than two or three years.

19   In some government-regulated sales fields — particularly real estate, securities and insurance — a mere office clerk can impress the boss by passing the licensing exam. Judith Briles, 36, started as a secretary in a brokerage house with just a high school diploma and a housewife's experience. She quickly learned the business and got a stockbroker's license. After 10 years in the field, she was earning $150,000 a year in commissions at E.F. Hutton in San Jose.

20   Only after opening her own investment advisory company in 1978 did she go to college — to hone her management skills. At Pepperdine University in Malibu, Calif., she took an entrance exam to determine how much her life's experience should count toward her degree. It counted a lot. In two years of part-time study, she bypassed a bachelor's degree and won an M.B.A.

Caroline Bird

College Is a Waste of Time and Money

Caroline Bird has written a number of books on business and on women in business, but this essay on college may be her best-known piece. It has been frequently reprinted since it appeared in Psychology Today *in 1975 (a much expanded version appeared as* The Case Against College *in the same year). The "Letters to the Editor" responding to Bird appeared in* Psychology Today *in October 1975.*

A great majority of our nine million college students are   1
not in school because they want to be or because they want
to learn. They are there because it has become the thing to
do or because college is a pleasant place to be; because it's
the only way they can get parents or taxpayers to support
them without working at a job they don't like; because
Mother wanted them to go, or some other reason entirely
irrelevant to the course of studies for which college is supposedly organized.

As I crisscross the United States lecturing on college cam-   2
puses, I am dismayed to find that professors and administrators, when pressed for a candid opinion, estimate that
no more than 25 percent of their students are turned on by
classwork. For the rest, college is at best a social center or
aging vat, and at worst a young folks' home or even a prison
that keeps them out of the mainstream of economic life for
a few more years.

The premise — which I no longer accept — that college is   3
the best place for all high-school graduates grew out of a
noble American ideal. Just as the United States was the
first nation to aspire to teach every small child to read and
write, so, during the 1950s, we became the first and only
great nation to aspire to higher education for all. During
the '60s we damned the expense and built great state university systems as fast as we could. And adults — parents,
employers, high-school counselors — began to push, shove
and cajole youngsters to "get an education."

It became a mammoth industry, with taxpayers footing   4
more than half the bill. By 1970, colleges and universities
were spending more than 30 billion dollars annually. But
still only half our high-school graduates were going on.
According to estimates made by the economist Fritz

Machlup, if we had been educating every young person until age 22 in that year of 1970, the bill for higher education would have reached 47.5 billion dollars, 12.5 billion more than the total corporate profits for the year.

The Baby Boom Is Over

5   Figures such as these have begun to make higher education for all look financially prohibitive, particulary now when colleges are squeezed by the pressures of inflation and a drop-off in the growth of their traditional market.

6   Predictable demography has caught up with the university empire builders. Now that the record crop of postwar babies has graduated from college, the rate of growth of the student population has begun to decline. To keep their mammoth plants financially solvent, many institutions have begun to use hard-sell, Madison-Avenue techniques to attract students. They sell college like soap, promoting features they think students want: innovative programs, an environment conducive to meaningful personal relationships, and a curriculum so free that it doesn't sound like college at all.

7   Pleasing the customers is something new for college administrators. Colleges have always known that most students don't like to study, and that at least part of the time they are ambivalent about college, but before the student riots of the 1960s educators never thought it either right or necessary to pay any attention to student feelings. But when students rebelling against the Vietnam war and the draft discovered they could disrupt a campus completely, administrators had to act on some student complaints. Few understood that the protests had tapped the basic discontent with college itself, a discontent that did not go away when the riots subsided.

8   Today students protest individually rather than in concert. They turn inward and withdraw from active participation. They drop out to travel to India or to feed themselves on subsistence farms. Some refuse to go to college at all. Most, of course, have neither the funds nor the self-confidence for constructive articulation of their discontent. They simply hang around college unhappily and reluctantly.

9   All across the country, I have been overwhelmed by the prevailing sadness on American campuses. Too many young people speak little, and then only in drowned voices. Some-

times the mood surfaces as diffidence, wariness, or coolness, but whatever its form, it looks like a defense mechanism, and that rings a bell. This is the way it used to be with women, and just as society had systematically damaged women by insisting that their proper place was in the home, so we may be systematically damaging 18-year-olds by insisting that their proper place is in college.

Sad and Unneeded

Campus watchers everywhere know what I mean when   10
I say students are sad, but they don't agree on the reason for it. During the Vietnam war some ascribed the sadness to the draft; now others blame affluence, or say it has something to do with permissive upbringing.

Not satisfied with any of these explanations, I looked for   11
some answers with the journalistic tools of my trade — scholarly studies, economic analyses, the historical record, the opinions of the especially knowledgeable, conversations with parents, professors, college administrators, and employers, all of whom spoke as alumni too. Mostly I learned from my interviews with hundreds of young people on and off campuses all over the country.

My unnerving conclusion is that students are sad because   12
they are not needed. Somewhere between the nursery and the employment office, they become unwanted adults. No one has anything in particular against them. But no one knows what to do with them either. We already have too many people in the world of the 1970s, and there is no room for so many newly minted 18-year-olds. So we temporarily get them out of the way by sending them to college where in fact only a few belong.

To make it more palatable, we fool ourselves into believ-   13
ing that we are sending them there for their own best interests, and that it's good for them, like spinach. Some, of course, learn to like it, but most wind up preferring green peas.

Educators admit as much. Nevitt Sanford, distinguished   14
student of higher education, says students feel they are "capitulating to a kind of voluntary servitude." Some of them talk about their time in college as if it were a sentence to be served. I listened to a 1970 Mount Holyoke graduate: "For two years I was really interested in science, but in my junior and senior years I just kept saying, 'I've done two

years; I'm going to finish.' When I got out I made up my mind that I wasn't going to school anymore because so many of my courses had been bullshit."

15   But bad as it is, college is often preferable to a far worse fate. It is better than the drudgery of an uninspiring nine-to-five job, and better than doing nothing when no jobs are available. For some young people, it is a graceful way to get away from home and become independent without losing the financial support of their parents. And sometimes it is the only alternative to an intolerable home situation.

16   It is difficult to assess how many students are in college reluctantly. The conservative Carnegie Commission estimates from 5 to 30 percent. Sol Linowitz, who was once chairman of a special committee on campus tension of the American Council on Education, found that "a significant number were not happy with their college experience because they felt they were there only in order to get the 'ticket to the big show' rather than to spend the years as productively as they otherwise could."

17   Older alumni will identify with Richard Baloga, a policeman's son, who stayed in school even though he "hated it" because he thought it would do him some good. But fewer students each year feel this way. Daniel Yankelovich has surveyed undergraduate attitudes for a number of years, and reported in 1971 that 74 percent thought education was "very important." But just two years earlier, 80 percent thought so.

An Inside View of What's Good

18   The doubters don't mind speaking up. Leon Lefkowitz, chairman of the department of social studies at Central High School in Valley Stream, New York, interviewed 300 college students at random, and reports that 200 of them didn't think that the education they were getting was worth the effort. "In two years I'll pick up a diploma," said one student, "and I can honestly say it was a waste of my father's bread."

19   Nowadays, says one sociologist, you don't have to have a reason for going to college; it's an institution. His definition of an institution is an arrangement everyone accepts without question; the burden of proof is not on why you go, but why anyone thinks there might be a reason for not

going. The implication is that an 18-year-old is too young and confused to know what he wants to do, and that he should listen to those who know best and go to college.

I don't agree. I believe that college has to be judged not 20 on what other people think is good for students, but on how good it feels to the students themselves.

I believe that people have an inside view of what's good 21 for them. If a child doesn't want to go to school some morning, better let him stay at home, at least until you find out why. Maybe he knows something you don't. It's the same with college. If high-school graduates don't want to go, or if they don't want to go right away, they may perceive more clearly than their elders that college is not for them. It is no longer obvious that adolescents are best off studying a core curriculum that was constructed when all educated men could agree on what made them educated, or that professors, advisors, or parents can be of any particular help to young people in choosing a major or a career. High-school graduates see college graduates driving cabs, and decide it's not worth going. College students find no intellectual stimulation in their studies and drop out.

If students believe that college isn't necessarily good for 22 them, you can't expect them to stay on for the general good of mankind. They don't go to school to beat the Russians to Jupiter, improve the national defense, increase the GNP, or create a market for the arts — to mention some of the benefits taxpayers are supposed to get for supporting higher education.

Nor should we expect to bring about social equality by 23 putting all young people through four years of academic rigor. At best, it's a roundabout and expensive way to narrow the gap between the highest and lowest in our society anyway. At worst, it is unconsciously elitist. Equalizing opportunity through universal higher education subjects the whole population to the intellectual mode natural only to a few. It violates the fundamental egalitarian principle of respect for the differences between people.

The Dumbest Investment

Of course, most parents aren't thinking of the "higher" 24 good at all. They send their children to college because they are convinced young people benefit financially from those four years of higher education. But if money is the only goal, college is the dumbest investment you can make. I say this because a young banker in Poughkeepsie, New York, Stephen G. Necel, used a computer to compare college as an investment with other investments available in 1974 and college did not come out on top.

25   For the sake of argument, the two of us invented a young man whose rich uncle gave him, in cold cash, the cost of a four-year education at any college he chose, but the young man didn't have to spend the money on college. After bales of computer paper, we had our mythical student write to his uncle: "Since you said I could spend the money foolishly if I wished, I am going to blow it all on Princeton."

26   The much respected financial columnist Sylvia Porter echoed the common assumption when she said last year, "A college education is among the very best investments you can make in your entire life." But the truth is not quite so rosy, even if we assume that the Census Bureau is correct when it says that as of 1972, a man who completed four years of college would expect to earn $199,000 more be-tween the ages of 22 and 64 than a man who had only a high-school diploma.*

27   If a 1972 Princeton-bound high-school graduate had put the $34,181 that his four years of college would have cost him into a savings bank at 7.5 percent interest compounded daily, he would have had at age 64 a total of $1,129,200, or $528,200 more than the earnings of a male college graduate, and more than five times as much as the $199,000 extra the more educated man could expect to earn between 22 and 64.

28   The big advantage of getting your college money in cash now is that you can invest it in something that has a higher return than a diploma. For instance, a Princeton-bound high-school graduate of 1972 who liked fooling around with cars could have banked his $34,181, and gone to work at the local garage at close to $1,000 more per year than the average high-school graduate. Meanwhile, as he was learn-ing to be an expert auto mechanic, his money would be ticking away in the bank. When he became 28, he would have earned $7,199 less on his job from age 22 to 28 than his college-educated friend, but he would have had $73,113

---

*According to the 1984 *Statistical Abstract of the United States*, a person who completed four years of college in 1979 could expect to earn $309,000.

in his passbook—enough to buy out his boss, go into the used-car business, or acquire his own new-car dealership. If successful in business, he could expect to make more than the average college graduate. And if he had the brains to get into Princeton, he would be just as likely to make money without the four years on campus. Unfortunately, few college-bound high-school graduates get the opportunity to bank such a large sum of money, and then wait for it to make them rich. And few parents are sophisticated enough to understand that in financial returns alone, their children would be better off with the money than with the education.

Rates of return and dollar signs on education are fascinating brain teasers, but obviously there is a certain unreality to the game. Quite aside from the noneconomic benefits of college, and these should loom larger once the dollars are cleared away, there are grave difficulties in assigning a dollar value to college at all.   29

Status, Not Money

In fact there is no real evidence that the higher income of college graduates is due to college. College may simply attract people who are slated to earn more money anyway; those with higher IQs, better family backgrounds, a more enterprising temperament. No one who has wrestled with the problem is prepared to attribute all of the higher income to the impact of college itself.   30

Christopher Jencks, author of *Inequality*, a book that assesses the effect of family and schooling in America, believes that education in general accounts for less than half of the difference in income in the American population. "The biggest single source of income differences," writes Jencks, "seems to be the fact that men from high-status families have higher incomes than men from low-status families even when they enter the same occupations, have the same amount of education, and have the same test scores."   31

Jacob Mincer of the National Bureau of Economic Research and Columbia University states flatly that of "20 to 30 percent of students at any level, the additional schooling has been a waste, at least in terms of earnings." College fails to work its income-raising magic for almost a third of those who go. More than half of those people in 1972 who   32 earned $15,000 or more reached that comfortable bracket without the benefit of a college diploma. Jencks says that financial success in the U.S. depends a good deal on luck, and the most sophisticated regression analyses have yet to demonstrate otherwise.

33   But most of today's students don't go to college to earn more money anyway. In 1968, when jobs were easy to get, Daniel Yankelovich made his first nationwide survey of students. Sixty-five percent of them said they "would welcome less emphasis on money." By 1973, when jobs were scarce, that figure jumped to 80 percent.

34   The young are not alone. Americans today are all looking less to the pay of a job than to the work itself. They want "interesting" work that permits them "to make a contribution," "express themselves" and "use their special abilities," and they think college will help them find it.

35   Jerry Darring of Indianapolis knows what it is to make a dollar. He worked with his father in the family plumbing business, on the line at Chevrolet, and in the Chrysler foundry. He quit these jobs to enter Wright State University in Dayton, Ohio, because "in a job like that a person only has time to work, and after that he's so tired that he can't do anything else but come home and go to sleep."

36   Jerry came to college to find work "helping people." And he is perfectly willing to spend the dollars he earns at dull, well-paid work to prepare for lower-paid work that offers the reward of service to others.

Psychic Income

37   Jerry's case is not unusual. No one works for money alone. In order to deal with the nonmonetary rewards of work, economists have coined the concept of "psychic income," which according to one economic dictionary means "income that is reckoned in terms of pleasure, satisfaction, or general feelings of euphoria."

38   Psychic income is primarily what college students mean when they talk about getting a good job. During the most affluent years of the late 1960s and early 1970s college students told their placement officers that they wanted to be researchers, college professors, artists, city planners, social workers, poets, book publishers, archeologists, ballet dancers, or authors.

The psychic income of these and other occupations popu-   39
lar with students is so high that these jobs can be filled
without offering high salaries. According to one study, 93
percent of urban university professors would choose the
same vocation again if they had the chance, compared with
only 16 percent of unskilled auto workers. Even though the
monetary gap between college professor and auto worker
is now surprisingly small, the difference in psychic income
is enormous.

But colleges fail to warn students that jobs of these kinds   40
are hard to come by, even for qualified applicants, and they
rarely accept the responsibility of helping students choose
a career that will lead to a job. When a young person says
he is interested in helping people, his counselor tells him
to become a psychologist. But jobs in psychology are
scarce. The Department of Labor, for instance, estimates
there will be 4,300 new jobs for psychologists in 1975 while
colleges are expected to turn out 58,430 B.A.s in psychology
that year.

Of 30 psych majors who reported back to Vassar what   41
they were doing a year after graduation in 1972, only five
had jobs in which they could possibly use their courses in
psychology, and two of these were working for Vassar.

The outlook isn't much better for students majoring in   42
other psychic-pay disciplines: sociology, English, journalism, anthropology, forestry, education. Whatever college graduates want to do, most of them are going to wind
up doing what there is to do.

John Shingleton, director of placement at Michigan State   43
University, accuses the academic community of outright
hypocrisy. "Educators have never said, 'Go to college and
get a good job,' but this has been implied, and now students
expect it. . . . If we care what happens to students after
college, then let's get involved with what should be one of
the basic purposes of education: career preparation."

In the 1970s, some of the more practical professors began   44
to see that jobs for graduates meant jobs for professors too.
Meanwhile, students themselves reacted to the shrinking
job market, and a "new vocationalism" exploded on campus. The press welcomed the change as a return to the ethic
of achievement and service. Students were still idealistic,
the reporters wrote, but they now saw that they could best
make the world better by healing the sick as physicians or
righting individual wrongs as lawyers.

No Use on the Job

45   But there are no guarantees in these professions either.
If all those who check "doctor" as their career goal succeed
in getting their MDs, we'll immediately have 10 times the
target ratio of doctors for the population of the United
States. Law schools are already graduating twice as many
new lawyers each year as the Department of Labor thinks
we will need, and the oversupply grows annually.

46   And it's not at all apparent that what is actually learned
in a "professional" education is necessary for success.
Teachers, engineers and others I talked to said they find
that on the job they rarely use what they learned in school.
In order to see how well college prepared engineers and
scientists for actual paid work in their fields, The Carnegie
Commission queried all the employees with degrees in these
fields in two large firms. Only one in five said the work
they were doing bore a "very close relationship" to their
college studies, while almost a third saw "very little relationship at all." An overwhelming majority could think
of many people who were doing their same work, but had
majored in different fields.

47   Majors in nontechnical fields report even less relationship
between their studies and their jobs. Charles Lawrence, a
communications major in college and now the producer of
"Kennedy & Co.," the Chicago morning television show,
says, "You have to learn all that stuff and you never use it
again. I learned my job doing it." Others employed as ar-
chitects, nurses, teachers and other members of the so-
called learned professions report the same thing.

48   Most college administrators admit that they don't prepare their graduates for the job market. "I just wish I had
the guts to tell parents that when you get out of this place
you aren't prepared to do anything," the academic head of
a famous liberal-arts college told us. Fortunately, for him,
most people believe that you don't have to defend a liberal-
arts education on those grounds. A liberal-arts education
is supposed to provide you with a value system, a standard,
a set of ideas, not a job. "Like Christianity, the liberal arts
are seldom practiced and would probably be hated by
the majority of the populace if they were," said one defender.

49   The analogy is apt. The fact is, of course, that the liberal
arts are a religion in every sense of that term. When people
talk about them, their language becomes elevated, metaphor-

ical, extravagant, theoretical and reverent. And faith in personal salvation by the liberal arts is professed in a creed intoned on ceremonial occasions such as commencements.

Ticket of Admission

If the liberal arts are a religious faith, the professors are [50] its priests. But disseminating ideas in a four-year college curriculum is slow and most expensive. If you want to learn about Milton, Camus, or even Margaret Mead you can find them in paperback books, the public library, and even on television.

And when most people talk about the value of a college [51] education, they are not talking about great books. When at Harvard commencement, the president welcomes the new graduates into "the fellowship of educated men and women," what he could be saying is, "here is a piece of paper that is a passport to jobs, power and instant prestige." As Glenn Bassett, a personnel specialist at G.E. says, "In some part of G.E., a college degree appears completely irrelevant to selection to, say, a manager's job. In most, however, it is a ticket of admission."

But now that we have doubled the number of young [52] people attending college, a diploma cannot guarantee even that. The most charitable conclusion we can reach is that college probably has very little, if any, effect on people and things at all. Today, the false premises are easy to see:

First, college doesn't make people intelligent, ambitious, [53] happy, or liberal. It's the other way around. Intelligent, ambitious, happy, liberal people are attracted to higher education in the first place.

Second, college can't claim much credit for the learning [54] experiences that really change students while they are there. Jobs, friends, history, and most of all the sheer passage of time, have as big an impact as anything even indirectly related to the campus.

Third, colleges have changed so radically that a freshman [55] entering in the fall of 1974 can't be sure to gain even the limited value research studies assigned to colleges in the '60s. The sheer size of undergraduate campuses of the 1970s makes college even less stimulating now than it was 10 years ago. Today even motivated students are disappointed with their college courses and professors.

Finally, a college diploma no longer opens as many vo- [56]

cational doors. Employers are beginning to realize that when they pay extra for someone with a diploma, they are paying only for an empty credential. The fact is that most of the work for which employers now expect college training is now or has been capably done in the past by people without higher educations.

57   College, then, may be a good place for those few young people who are really drawn to academic work, who would rather read than eat, but it has become too expensive, in money, time, and intellectual effort to serve as a holding pen for large numbers of our young. We ought to make it possible for those reluctant, unhappy students to find alternative ways of growing up, and more realistic preparation for the years ahead.

Letters to the Editor:
Responses to Caroline Bird

1   Some students may be bored with 90 percent of their classes and be "interested" in only the remaining 10 percent. Does that mean that they are wasting their time and money? I don't think so. A valuable learning experience can be wrapped up in that 10 percent.

2   I do agree with Bird that students are unable to recognize the relevance of most of the course work to their jobs. However, I have found that the longer people are out of school, the more they recognize the importance and relevance of many of their college courses.

> Jerry Horgesheimer
> D.B.A.
> Ogden, Utah

3   In some European countries the compulsory attendance age extends to 9th or 10th grade. Much of the emphasis is placed on reading, writing and arithmetic. Many college graduates in the U.S. lack the mastery of these vital skills. The lowering of the compulsory-attendance age in the United States would leave the opportunity of higher educa-

tion only to those students who are attracted to education's liberality.

Sam Maravich Jr.
Steelton, Penn.

High schools should equip students with an awareness   4
of society and the availability of jobs, provide them with
marketable skills, and require courses that will help students examine and develop their own value systems, learn
to make decisions and to achieve "personhood." Giving
high-school students this knowledge would enable them to
make better decisions as to what they chose to do after high
school. Students who opted for work would have difficulty
as the labor market, also, is certainly unprepared to accommodate a good percentage of high-school graduates. So college becomes a good stopgap.

Parents who want their children to have it "as good as   5
they do," if not better, feel that college will guarantee their
children upward mobility (generally equated in dollar
signs). This is unrealistic because of current and predicted
labor demands, as well as the changing role of education
that is becoming a life-long process instead of one ending
at age 23. In addition, jobs will exist that cannot be prepared
for now, as they do not exist. Flexibility is the key word,
as well as societal reappraisal of the value of work and the
prestige of vocational training.

Judith Sacks, Counselor
Baldwin Senior High School
Baldwin, N.Y.

Bird doesn't recognize that a large proportion of the stag-   6
gering sums asked collectively by colleges and universities
are in the forms of loans, scholarships and grants that would
not be available if one chose to invest in the world of business instead.

John Michelsen
Gustavus Adolphus College
Mound, Minn.

I know a number of people with B.A.s who are for all   7
intents and purposes ignorant of 90 percent of what they
supposedly went to college to learn. I attribute this to
immaturity at the time of instruction, poor secondary education, and the lowering of academic standards at many

institutions. I started university study at 28. As an older student, I am self-motivated and have a clear goal I wish to attain. I feel strongly that students not academically inclined (as I was not, at age 18) should not be pushed into or pandered to at a university.

Susan Gilbertsen
Eugene, Ore.

8   We at the Boatshop raise our oar in salute to Caroline Bird.

9   We educators dropped our hammers and saws too soon! Observing that our college-degree success has led to Wall Street failure, we have turned to tools to discover excitement and satisfaction. Using their hands to discipline their minds, our apprentices create marketable products of both.

Stefan P. Galazzi, Director
The Experience on Cape Cod
South Orleans, Mass.

10   College will continue to be a waste of time and money for the taxpayer and the student until colleges start getting what should be their product: trained students that can successfully and skillfully apply what they have learned and do. Of course the first prerequisite to this is that what is taught *can* be used.

Glen J. Doe
Hamilton, Ontario

11   I worked my way through a private college because I wanted to. As one of my professors once said, "The more we know, the more increase of mystery; the more we know, the more unknown we meet." He compared it to a light bulb of 60 watts that illuminates to a certain perimeter of light, and a 100-watt bulb that illuminates only to increase the perimeter of darkness. College, for me, was all this and more.

Christine Masi
Maspeth, N.Y.

12   One overwhelming fact that Bird cannot explain is that once students grow into adulthood, they come back to the university, not for a degree ("that glorious piece of wallpaper," as Mark Twain called it), but to immerse themselves in ideas, literature, and the arts. Although undergraduate programs are finding themselves bankrupt — in

more ways than one — programs for adults, schools of continuing education, are alive and flourishing all over the
country. For the first time in American history, part-time,
adult students outnumber full-time undergraduates. This
does not indicate that our universities are obsolete.

I certainly do not wish to "blame" undergraduates for 13
not living up to our expectations. They, too, are victims of
a society that systematically destroys intellectual curiosity
and interpersonal sensitivity, a society that has replaced
reading and discussion with the TV. But neither must we
blame the universities for the widespread apathy found
among undergraduates. And I suspect Bird knows this very
well.

Victor B. Marrow, Associate Director
Division of Liberal Studies
Assistant Professor of Social Philosophy
School of Continuing Education
New York University

Liberal arts should be taught in high schools, community- 14
based "continuing education" programs, and small colleges.
Vocational curricula should be available, in separate or
coordinated programs, to complement the liberal arts.
Large universities could then stick to academics and research. People could then know what to expect from whatever institution they attend, and clearer purpose would
improve performances by both students and schools.

Eric T. MacKnight
College Dropout
Washington, D.C.

Does Bird make a case against College (*College*, like Plato's 15
Republic) or a case against the American postsecondary-
education system that bores students for four (or more)
years and then has the audacity not to reward those students for their stoical endurance (and dad's dough) with
the lump of sugar, carrot or cigar? Worse, take her use of
the word "good" like a college Freshman would — "I believe
that college has to be judged not on what other people think
is good for students but on how good it feels to students
themselves [outrage mine]." But, Caroline, at least in language one "good" does not another make. What about a
case for wasting more time and money on education?

John M. de Jong
Long Beach, Calif.

16   I lasted one year on a State university campus and three
years later took up in an experimental University Without
Walls program, primarily because I was faced with a salary
cut without a degree. The responsibility of the UWW program was placed squarely upon my shoulders. I learned
not only the necessary academics and some practical skills
that I was able to test out on the job, but I also learned to
direct and take responsibility for my own learning, my own
career, my own life.

17   I think most young people ought to give themselves a few
years between high school and college (if they so desire—
let's not go the other way and say that all 18-year-olds
should delay college). They might see what the world is
really like when one has to support oneself, and they might
get the opportunity to discover what offers "psychic income" to them.

Karen Trisko
Chicago

18   To make higher education more relevant to more people
would certainly make my job (recruiter for Education Opportunity Program applicants) a lot easier and more worthwhile. If the impact of your ideas has this effect, then I
hope more people get wind of your message. If the waste
in higher education is reduced by "better" selection procedures and more effective education methods, then I say
let's push your ideas forward. If, on the other hand, what
occurs is reduced funding that results in less incentives to
create more relevant curricula, or, if "more" selectivity
rather than "better" selectivity results in the continued
"meat-market" tactics of selection based only on GPAS and
test scores (which have proven to discriminate against
minorities and women), then I feel your statements may
amount to a shortcut to the dark ages.

Ramon Cruz, Assistant Director
Educational Opportunity Program
California State University
Long Beach

19   In one sense I can say that college was indeed a waste of
time and money. I am not working in my chosen field of
study and the chances are that I won't be in the future. In
another sense, college was an invaluable experience that I
will never forget. I am not today the person I was when I

entered college. My views on many subjects have made a
180° turnabout. Some of these changes would have occurred anyway as a result of a process of maturing, but
other changes needed the stimulus the university and its
population provided.

Linda Slepicka
Chicago

Christopher Jester

Not Just a Diploma Factory

*Christopher Jester, from Erie, Pennsylvania, graduated in 1989
with a major in international politics and a minor in Russian.
He is now serving in Germany as a second lieutenant in the
Air Force. A version of this essay appeared in* The Daily Collegian, *the student newspaper at Penn State.*

During the 1988 presidential campaign, George Bush   1
acknowledged the current crisis in the American education
system and pledged to be the "education president." So far
Bush has done little to back up that promise, but the situation is beginning to attract more and more attention. Test
scores are dropping and dropout rates in high schools are
on the rise. Illiteracy rates are climbing. Our universities'
graduate programs are becoming increasingly populated
by better-educated foreign students. Each new report
brings more evidence of our educational decline, often with
shocking examples of ignorance.

Americans seem to show no interest in learning anything   2
beyond what they need to know. Few bother to learn
another language, try to understand another nation's culture, or study an opposing point of view. Due to our complacency and ethnocentric isolation we have fallen behind educationally. We prefer the easy entertainment of television
to reading. We have been described as a nation with blinders on—which is as apparent in schools' curricula as in
television. Instant gratification seems to be the requirement
in every aspect of society from music videos to political

campaigns. The majority of Americans lack an understanding of who we are, where we've been, the world around us, or our place in its history.

3   Such deficiencies have been addressed in the recent books *Cultural Literacy* by E. D. Hirsch and *The Closing of the American Mind* by Allan Bloom. Hirsch and Bloom both claim that our schools fail to provide well-prepared students to universities, because the schools fail to teach common, basic knowledge. Hirsch goes into great depth to document modern high school students' lack of intergenerational and "national cultural" information. Bloom also laments the self-centeredness of today's students and associates their inability to think in a broad, contextual way with either an existential nihilism or a sense of detachment and atomization. He sees universities' specialized divisions as "competing and contradictory" and states that students have forgotten that individual areas of study are only parts of a whole.

4   University of Virginia professor Richard Rorty puts forth his own theory of the American education process in the essay "The Opening of American Minds," which appeared in the July 1988 *Harper's*. He describes the current situation as a compromise between liberal and conservative education theories, with the right mainly controlling pre-university education and the left, for the most part, in control at universities.

5   According to Rorty, primary and secondary schools exist to develop the basic concepts, accepted ideas, and commonly believed moral and political assumptions of society — what can be referred to as the socialization process. Post-secondary education, in Rorty's scenario, urges students to question the conventional wisdom, consider opposing ideas, look critically at societal deficiencies, and search for alternative solutions, with the ultimate goal of improving society for the next generation. The problem is that universities are failing both in providing a forum for divergent opinions and in providing students a comparative base of beliefs and knowledge to reshape on their own into an informed opinion and self-image, what Rorty calls "self-individualization."

6   It is hard to determine whether universities or the students themselves are to blame for this problem. Last fall, I had a lower-level political science class with an excellent professor who energetically encouraged his class to look critically at our political system and see how it differs from

standard perceptions. All the students did was whine about how it was too much work to do all of the readings and out-of-class assignments. I heard a few people discuss the idea of dropping the class and taking it when they thought they would have someone easier. Even classmates I've had in 400-level classes seem just as averse to doing any substantive work. In general, today's Reagan-generation college students, weaned on television's fast-moving images and short attention span, can easily be described as pleasure seeking, apolitical, and uninformed.

The typical student apparently thinks mainly of getting   7
a good job that pays well as soon after graduation as possible. The most important aspect of the average senior year involves putting together a slick resume, buying an interview suit, and worrying about on-campus recruiters and rejection letters. The standard measure of success among peers and even parents is the size of the expected starting salary. A desire to learn or quest for knowledge takes second place to a preoccupation with money and career.

The atmosphere on campus and in town can hardly be   8
described as intellectual. A walk down College Avenue reveals an overabundance of trendy clothing stores, gift shops, bars, and other places for spending money. Where there used to be a used-book store, there is now a Subway. More telling is the on-campus bookstore where the majority of available space is devoted to Penn State clothes and memorabilia or leather briefcases and corporate-looking appointment books. Oh, and they sell books, too.

Penn State just doesn't provide an environment very con-   9
ducive to the kinds of discourse Rorty feels a university should provide; instead it merely continues the socialization process, replete with fraternity parties and football games. Students learn what will help them later in life, such as what car to own, how to dress for success, and what music, magazines, and ideas are politically correct. This information on safe displays of status and inoffensive, socially acceptable behavior is provided in college-oriented marketing such as free magazines and bookstore advertising. Much of this socialization process tells us the only way to be happy and successful is to make a lot of money. Penn State mainly serves as a huge vocational school selling very expensive pieces of paper that form the primary ingredient of a resume and serve as tickets to good careers.

Penn State essentially pumps out hordes of careerist, con-   10
sumerist, educated elites—yuppies—instead of enabling

students to think critically, analytically, or independently. The 1988 senior class exemplified this attitude with their class gift — the computerized career placement and interview center. The colleges of Business Administration, Engineering, and Science together dominate the College of Liberal Arts, and the College of Arts and Architecture has a comparatively modest presence on campus.

11   With such emphasis placed on specialization and a career-oriented curriculum, majors in the liberal arts are frowned upon as not "practical" enough — as in "What kind of job can you get with that?" Liberal arts majors, especially philosophy majors, are frequently the object of derision. A question often posed to English or foreign language majors is "What are you going to do, teach?" — with the tone implying the lack of respect (or monetary rewards) associated with teaching. If any given major doesn't appear to lead to a lucrative career, then it is regarded as a waste of time by many Penn Staters.

12   The overemphasis on specialized career training discourages broad conceptual thinking about changing world relationships or social and economic structures; it makes it difficult to develop a philosophy for living. The dominance of business and engineering breeds homogeneity and deprives students of the diversity that serves as an integral part of outside-the-classroom education.

13   Robert Reich points out the fallacy of this career-track thinking with his advice on preparing for future careers. Students' emphasis on "practical" majors is misguided: "The courses to which they now gravitate — finance, law, accounting, management, and other practical arts — may be helpful to understand how a particular job is *now* done (or, more accurately, how your instructors did it years ago when they held such jobs or studied the people who held them), but irrelevant to how such a job *will* be done."

14   Reich stresses the need to learn how to define problems, conceptualize and analyze information, communicate with colleagues to achieve solutions, and convince others. These skills cannot be learned in a strictly career-oriented course. "To the extent to which they can be found in universities at all," Reich writes, "they're more likely to be found in subjects such as history, literature, philosophy, or anthropology — in which students can witness how others have grappled for centuries with the challenge of living good and productive lives."

This ad for Hofstra University appeared in several magazines and newspapers in 1989 and 1990. What does it say about what Hofstra University is for?

What does it take to be the best?

Determination and hard work, at any age, can lead to being the best. Hofstra University, just 50 years old, is already among the top ten percent of American colleges and universities in almost all academic criteria and resources.

Professionally accredited programs in such major areas as business, engineering, law, psychology and education.

A library with over 1.1 million volumes *on campus*—a collection larger than that of 95% of American universities.

Record enrollments with students from 31 states and 59 countries— with a student-faculty ratio of only 17 to 1.

The largest, most sophisticated non-commercial television facility in the East. A high technology undergraduate teaching resource with broadcast-quality production capability.

A ranking in *Barron's Guide to the Most Prestigious Colleges*—one of only 262 colleges and universities chosen from almost 4,000.

At Hofstra, determination, inspiration and hard work are qualities our faculty demands in itself and instills in our students.

These qualities are what it takes to be the best. In anything.

HOFSTRA UNIVERSITY
WE TEACH SUCCESS.

50th Anniversary
Hempstead, L.I., New York 11550

*Babson College placed this ad in several publications in 1990.
What does it imply about the purpose of a college education?*

A BUSINESS MOVE FEW COLLEGES COULD DUPLICATE.

James Thurber
University Days

James Thurber (1894–1961), the great American humorist, wrote essays, plays, stories, and cartoons. His sardonic wit is collected in several books, including My World and Welcome to It *(1942) and* My Life and Hard Times *(1933). This account of his undergraduate education comes from the latter.*

I passed all the other courses that I took at my University, but I could never pass botany. This was because all botany students had to spend several hours a week in a laboratory looking through a microscope at plant cells, and I could never see through a microscope. I never once saw a cell through a microscope. This used to enrage my instructor. He would wander around the laboratory pleased with the progress all the students were making in drawing the involved and, so I am told, interesting structure of flower cells, until he came to me. I would just be standing there. "I can't see anything," I would say. He would begin patiently enough, explaining how anybody can see through a microscope, but he would always end up in a fury, claiming that I could *too* see through a microscope but just pretended that I couldn't. "It takes away from the beauty of flowers anyway," I used to tell him. "We are not concerned with beauty in this course," he would say. "We are concerned solely with what I may call the *mechanics* of flars." "Well," I'd say, "I can't see anything." "Try it just once again," he'd say, and I would put my eye to the microscope and see nothing at all, except now and again a nebulous milky substance — a phenomenon of maladjustment. You were supposed to see a vivid, restless clockwork of sharply defined plant cells. "I see what looks like a lot of milk," I would tell him. This, he claimed, was the result of my not having adjusted the microscope properly, so he would readjust it for me, or rather, for himself. And I would look again and see milk.

I finally took a deferred pass, as they called it, and waited a year and tried again. (You had to pass one of the biological sciences or you couldn't graduate.) The professor had come back from vacation brown as a berry, bright-eyed, and eager to explain cell-structure again to his classes. "Well," he said to me, cheerily, when we met in the first laboratory hour of the semester, "we're going to see cells this time, aren't we?" "Yes, sir," I said. Students to right of me and to left of me and in front of me were seeing cells; what's more, they were quietly drawing pictures of them in their note-books. Of course, I didn't see anything.

3   "We'll try it," the professor said to me, grimly, "with every adjustment of the microscope known to man. As God is my witness, I'll arrange this glass so that you see cells through it or I'll give up teaching. In twenty-two years of botany, I—" He cut off abruptly for he was beginning to quiver all over, like Lionel Barrymore, and he genuinely wished to hold onto his temper; his scenes with me had taken a great deal out of him.

4   So we tried it with every adjustment of the microscope known to man. With only one of them did I see anything but blackness or the familiar lacteal opacity, and that time I saw, to my pleasure and amazement, a variegated constel-lation of flecks, specks, and dots. These I hastily drew. The instructor, noting my activity, came back from an adjoining desk, a smile on his lips and his eyebrows high in hope. He looked at my cell drawing. "What's that?" he demanded, with a hint of a squeal in his voice. "That's what I saw," I said. "You didn't, you didn't, you *did*n't" he screamed, losing control of his temper instantly, and he bent over and squinted into the microscope. His head snapped up. "That's your eye!" he shouted. "You've fixed the lens so that it reflects! You've drawn your eye!"

5   Another course that I didn't like, but somehow managed to pass, was economics. I went to that class straight from the botany class, which didn't help me any in understanding either subject. I used to get them mixed up. But not as mixed up as another student in my economics class who came there direct from a physics laboratory. He was a tackle on the football team, named Bolenciecwcz. At that time Ohio State University had one of the best football teams in the country, and Bolenciecwcz was one of its outstanding stars. In order to be eligible to play it was necessary for him to keep up in his studies, a very difficult matter, for while he was not dumber than an ox he was not any smarter. Most of his professors were lenient and helped him along. None gave him more hints, in answering questions, or asked him simpler ones than the economics professor, a thin, timid man named Bassum. One day when we were on the

subject of transportation and distribution, it came Bolenciecwcz's turn to answer a question. "Name one means of
transportation," the professor said to him. No light came
into the big tackle's eyes. "Just any means of transportation," said the professor. Bolenciecwcz sat staring at him.
"That is," pursued the professor, "any medium, agency, or
method of going from one place to another." Bolenciecwcz
had the look of a man who is being led into a trap. "You
may choose among steam, horse-drawn, or electrically
propelled vehicles," said the instructor. "I might suggest
the one which we commonly take in making long journeys
across land." There was a profound silence in which everybody stirred uneasily, including Bolenciecwcz and Mr. Bassum. Mr. Bassum abruptly broke this silence in an amazing
manner. "Choo-choo-choo," he said, in a low voice, and
turned instantly scarlet. He glanced appealingly around
the room. All of us, of course, shared Mr. Bassum's desire
that Bolenciecwcz should stay abreast of the class in economics, for the Illinois game, one of the hardest and most
important of the season, was only a week off. "Toot, toot,
too-toooooot!" some student with a deep voice moaned,
and we all looked encouragingly at Bolenciecwcz. Somebody else gave a fine imitation of a locomotive letting off
steam. Mr. Bassum himself rounded off the little show.
"Ding, dong, ding, dong," he said, hopefully. Bolenciecwcz
was staring at the floor now, trying to think, his great brow
furrowed, his huge hands rubbing together, his face red.

"How did you come to college this year, Mr. Bolen-   6
ciecwcz?" asked the professor. "*Chuffa* chuffa, *chuffa*
chuffa."

"M'father sent me," said the football player.   7

"What on?" asked Bassum.   8

"I git an 'lowance," said the tackle, in a low, husky voice,   9
obviously embarrassed.

"No, no," said Bassum. "Name a means of transportation. 10
What did you *ride* here on?"

"Train," said Bolenciecwcz.   11

"Quite right," said the professor. "Now, Mr. Nugent, will   12
you tell us—"

If I went through anguish in botany and economics—for   13
different reasons—gymnasium work was even worse. I
don't even like to think about it. They wouldn't let you play
games or join in the exercises with your glasses on and I
couldn't see with mine off. I bumped into professors, hori-

zontal bars, agricultural students, and swinging iron rings.
Not being able to see, I could take it but I couldn't dish it
out. Also, in order to pass gymnasium (and you had to pass
it to graduate) you had to learn to swim if you didn't know
how. I didn't like the swimming pool, I didn't like swimming, and I didn't like the swimming instructor, and after
all these years I still don't. I never swam but I passed my
gym work anyway, by having another student give my gymnasium number (978) and swim across the pool in my place.
He was a quiet, amiable blonde youth, number 473, and
he would have seen through a microscope for me if we
could have got away with it, but we couldn't get away with
it. Another thing I didn't like about gymnasium work was
that they made you strip the day you registered. It is impossible for me to be happy when I am stripped and being
asked a lot of questions. Still, I did better than a lanky
agricultural student who was cross-examined just before I
was. They asked each student what college he was in — that
is, whether Arts, Engineering, Commerce, or Agriculture.
"What college are you in?" the instructor snapped at the
youth in front of me. "Ohio State University," he said
promptly.

14   It wasn't that agricultural student but it was another a
whole lot like him who decided to take up journalism, possibly on the ground that when farming went to hell he could
fall back on newspaper work. He didn't realize, of course,
that that would be very much like falling back full-length
on a kit of carpenter's tools. Haskins didn't seem cut out
for journalism, being too embarrassed to talk to anybody
and unable to use a typewriter, but the editor of the college
paper assigned him to the cow barns, the sheep house, the
horse pavilion, and the animal husbandry department generally. This was a genuinely big "beat," for it took up five
times as much ground and got ten times as great a legislative appropriation as the College of Liberal Arts. The agricultural student knew animals, but nevertheless his
stories were dull and colorlessly written. He took all afternoon on each of them, on account of having to hunt for
each letter on the typewriter. Once in a while he had to ask
somebody to help him hunt. "C" and "L," in particular,
were hard letters for him to find. His editor finally got
pretty much annoyed at the farmer-journalist because his
pieces were so uninteresting. "See here, Haskins," he snapped
at him one day; "Why is it we never have anything hot from

you on the horse pavilion? Here we have two hundred head of horses on this campus—more than any other university in the Western Conference except Purdue—and yet you never get any real lowdown on them. Now shoot over to the horse barns and dig up something lively." Haskins shambled out and came back in about an hour; he said he had something. "Well, start it off snappily," said the editor. "Something people will read." Haskins set to work and in a couple of hours brought a sheet of typewritten paper to the desk; it was a two-hundred-word story about some disease that had broken out among the horses. Its opening sentence was simple but arresting. It read: "Who has noticed the sores on the tops of the horses in the animal husbandry building?"

Ohio State was a land grant university and therefore two   15 years of military drill was compulsory. We drilled with old Springfield rifles and studied the tactics of the Civil War even though the World War was going on at the time. At 11 o'clock each morning thousands of freshmen and sophomores used to deploy over the campus, moodily creeping up on the old chemistry building. It was good training for the kind of warfare that was waged at Shiloh but it had no connection with what was going on in Europe. Some people used to think there was German money behind it, but they didn't dare say so or they would have been thrown in jail as German spies. It was a period of muddy thought and marked, I believe, the decline of higher education in the Middle West.

As a soldier I was never any good at all. Most of the cadets   16 were glumly indifferent soldiers, but I was no good at all. Once General Littlefield, who was commandant of the cadet corps, popped up in front of me during regimental drill and snapped, "You are the main trouble with this university!" I think he meant that my type was the main trouble with the university but he may have meant me individually. I was mediocre at drill, certainly—that is, until my senior year. By that time I had drilled longer than anybody else in the Western Conference, having failed at military at the end of each preceding year so that I had to do it all over again. I was the only senior still in uniform. The uniform which, when new, had made me look like an interurban railway conductor, now that it had become faded and too tight made me look like Bert Williams in his bellboy act. This had a definitely bad effect on my morale. Even so I had become by sheer practise little short of wonderful at squad manoeuvres.

17   One day General Littlefield picked our company out of the whole regiment and tried to get it mixed up by putting it through one movement after another as fast as we could execute them: squads right, squads left, squads on right into line, squads right about, squads left front into line, etc. In about three minutes one hundred and nine men were marching in one direction and I was marching away from them at an angle of forty degrees, all alone. "Company, halt!" shouted General Littlefield. "That man is the only man who has it right!" I was made a corporal for my achievement.

18   The next day General Littlefield summoned me to his office. He was swatting flies when I went in. I was silent and he was silent too, for a long time. I don't think he remembered me or why he had sent for me, but he didn't want to admit it. He swatted some more flies, keeping his eyes on them narrowly before he let go with the swatter. "Button up your coat!" he snapped. Looking back on it now I can see that he meant me although he was looking at a fly, but I just stood there. Another fly came to rest on a paper in front of the general and began rubbing its hind legs together. The general lifted the swatter cautiously. I moved restlessly and the fly flew away. "You startled him!" barked General Littlefield, looking at me severely. I said I was sorry. "That won't help the situation!" snapped the general, with cold military logic. I didn't see what I could do except offer to chase some more flies toward his desk, but I didn't say anything. He stared out the window at the faraway figures of co-eds crossing the campus toward the library. Finally, he told me I could go. So I went. He either didn't know which cadet I was or else he forgot what he wanted to see me about. It may have been that he wished to apologize for having called me the main trouble with the university; or maybe he had decided to compliment me on my brilliant drilling of the day before and then at the last minute decided not to. I don't know. I don't think about it much any more.

W. D. Snodgrass
The Examination

W. D. Snodgrass (born 1926), educated at Geneva College and the University of Iowa, teaches at the University of Delaware. His book of poetry Heart's Needle *won the Pulitzer Prize in 1960.*

Under the thick beams of that swirly smoking light,   1
   The black robes are clustering, huddled in together.
Hunching their shoulders, they spread short, broad
      sleeves like night-
   Black grackles' wings; then they reach bone-yellow
      leather-

y fingers, each to each. And are prepared. Each turns   2
   His single eye—or since one can't discern their eyes,
That reflective, single, moon-pale disc which burns
   Over each brow—to watch this uncouth shape that lies

Strapped to their table. One probes with his ragged nails   3
   The slate-sharp calf, explores the thigh and the lean thews
Of the groin. Others raise, red as piratic sails,
   His wing, stretching, trying the pectoral sinews.

One runs his finger down the whet of that cruel   4
   Golden beak, lifts back the horny lids from the eyes,
Peers down in one bright eye malign as a jewel,
   And steps back suddenly. "He is anaesthetized?"

"He is. He is. Yes. Yes." The tallest of them, bent   5
   Down by the head, rises: "This drug possesses powers
Sufficient to still all gods in this firmament.
   This is Garuda who was fierce. He's yours for hours."

"We shall continue, please." Now, once again, he bends   6
   To the skull, and its clamped tissues. Into the cran-
ial cavity, he plunges both of his hands
   Like obstetric forceps and lifts out the great brain,

Holds it aloft, then gives it to the next who stands   7
   Beside him. Each, in turn, accepts it, although loath,
Turns it this way, that way, feels it between his hands
   Like a wasp's nest or some sickening outsized growth.

8   They must decide what thoughts each part of it must think;
      They tap at, then listen beside, each suspect lobe;
    Next, with a crow's quill dipped into India ink,
      Mark on its surface, as if on a map or globe,

9   Those dangerous areas which need to be excised.
      They rinse it, then apply antiseptics to it;
    Now silver saws appear which, inch by inch, slice
      Through its ancient folds and ridges, like thick suet.

10 It's rinsed, dried, and daubed with thick salves. The smoky
      saws
    Are scrubbed, resterilized, and polished till they gleam.
    The brain is repacked in its case. Pinched in their claws,
      Glimmering needles stitch it up, that leave no seam.

11 Meantime, one of them has set blinders to the eyes,
      Inserting light packing beneath each of the ears
    And calked the nostrils in. One, with thin twine, ties
      The genitals off. With long wood-handled shears,

12 Another chops pinions out of the scarlet wings.
      It's hoped that with disuse he will forget the sky
    Or, at least, in time, learn, among other things,
      To fly no higher than his superiors fly.

13 Well; that's a beginning. The next time, they can split
      His tongue and teach him to talk correctly, can give
    Him opinions on fine books and choose clothing fit
      For the integrated area where he'll live.

14 Their candidate may live to give them thanks one day.
      He will recover and may hope for such success.
    He might return to join their ranks. Bowing away,
      They nod, whispering, "One of ours; one of ours. Yes. Yes."

II.

LANGUAGE

People who use to think of language as neutral — as a transparent window through which ideas are conveyed. Now many people agree that language is not transparent but colored by ideological and social biases. Far from being neutral, language is a product (as well as a producer) of a culture and inevitably reflects (as well as shapes) that particular culture. The three issues included in this part — "Can There Be a 'Standard' English?"; "Should We Have a National Language?"; and "Is English Sexist?" — share the assumption that language is culture-bound, that social issues inevitably mingle with language issues.

The first section includes five items that explore relationships between language and power, particularly questions about the ideology of standard English. Is black English a robust dialect that proceeds according to established conventions of sound and structure, or is it (in its written form) a substandard form of English that impedes communication and clouds opportunities for clear thinking? Do black English and other "nonstandard" dialects empower their users as fully as any other language, or do they undermine literacy, bar people from success in the main streams of American life, and keep their users politically and socially marginalized?

Next come seven items, generally related to those in the previous section, that consider language against the backdrop of America's ethnic diversity. Several of them consider the merits of bilingual education. For many years federal, state, and local governments supported the policy of giving students schoolwork in their native languages and cultures — English for most, but Spanish and Chinese and many other languages, as well — so that students with limited proficiency in English would not fall behind in other subjects while they mastered English "as a second language." In 1974, Congress required schools to promote knowledge of students' native languages and cultures as well as to promote growth in English. During the past decade the policy of bilingual education has come under fire. Some educators have contended that bilingual programs do not work well or that they are too expensive. Other critics, emphasizing the importance of English as a unifying force in American society, contend that bilingual programs — because they interfere with students' mastery of English — prevent non-English-speaking citizens from assuming a central role in American life. A a result, some citizens in over two dozen states have even advocated — and in some cases passed — laws designating English as "the official language" of the United States. They argue partly on the grounds of cost (bilingual education, bilingual ballots, bilingual forms and signs and menus all cost money), partly to enforce a more unified nation, partly to avoid the possibility of states in the Southwest becoming a sort of Spanish-speaking "American Quebecs." Their opponents contend that creating English as an official language would foster intolerance and bigotry, would compromise the civil rights of citizens who have not mastered English, and would compromise our nation's ethnic diversity.

Power is also at the heart of feminist critiques of the English language. As the four selections printed in this part disclose, the English language can favor some groups at the expense of others — particularly men at the expense of women. To what extent does English, as the product of a culture dominated by males, demean and delimit women? To what extent does English perpetuate outworn cultural assumptions about women? In other words, to what extent is English itself sexist? And what can be done about it? Those are the questions addressed here.

Most citizens in this country have been proud of the metaphor of America as melting pot — a place where immigrants are assimilated into the fabric of American life and American language. Recently another metaphor has been proposed: America as salad bowl, as a place where immigrant citizens become American but retain their unique and diverse ethnic culture. Whatever the metaphor, language will continue to be a place where differences between individuals and their society are negotiated, where conflicts between "American society" and diverse individuals are adjudicated. In other words, language itself will remain an issue.

SHOULD THERE BE – OR CAN THERE BE – A "STANDARD" ENGLISH?

James Baldwin
If Black English Isn't a Language, Then Tell Me, What Is?

One of the most powerful American writers of this century, James Baldwin (1924–87) wrote collections of powerful essays, including Notes of a Native Son *(1955) and* The Fire Next Time *(1963). His personal and yet highly analytical accounts illuminate the condition of black and white Americans in the twentieth century. A characteristic theme in his work is the need for identity, a theme inherent in the following analysis of language, published in* The New York Times *in 1979.*

1   The argument concerning the use, or the status, or the reality, of black English is rooted in American history and has absolutely nothing to do with the question the argument supposes itself to be posing. The argument has nothing to do with language itself but with the *role* of language. Language, incontestably, reveals the speaker. Language, also, far more dubiously, is meant to define the other – and, in this case, the other is refusing to be defined by a language that has never been able to recognize him.

2   People evolve a language in order to describe and thus control their circumstances, or in order not to be submerged by a reality that they cannot articulate. (And, if they cannot articulate it, they *are* submerged.) A Frenchman living in Paris speaks a subtly and crucially different language from that of the man living in Marseilles; neither sounds very much like a man living in Quebec; and they would all have great difficulty in apprehending what the man from Guadeloupe, or Martinique, is saying, to say nothing of the man from Senegal – although the "common" language of all these areas is French. But each has paid, and is paying, a different price for this "common" language, in which, as it turns out, they are not saying, and cannot be saying, the

same things: They each have very different realities to articulate or control.

What joins all languages, and all men, is the necessity to 3
confront life, in order, not inconceivably, to outwit death: The price for this is the acceptance, and achievement, of one's temporal identity. So that, for example, though it is not taught in the schools (and this has the potential of becoming a political issue) the south of France still clings to its ancient and musical Provençal, which resists being described as a "dialect." And much of the tension in the Basque countries, and in Wales, is due to the Basque and Welsh determination not to allow their languages to be destroyed. This determination also feeds the flames in Ireland for among the many indignities the Irish have been forced to undergo at English hands is the English contempt for their language.

It goes without saying, then, that language is also a polit- 4
ical instrument, means, and proof of power. It is the most vivid and crucial key to identity: It reveals the private identity, and connects one with, or divorces one from, the larger public, or communal identity. There have been, and are, times, and places, when to speak a certain language could be dangerous, even fatal. Or, one may speak the same language, but in such a way that one's antecedents are revealed, or (one hopes) hidden. This is true in France, and is absolutely true in England: The range (and reign) of accents on that damp little island make England coherent for the English and totally incomprehensible for everyone else. To open your mouth in England is (if I may use black English) to "put your business in the street": You have confessed your parents, your youth, your school, your salary, your self-esteem, and, alas, your future.

Now, I do not know what white Americans would sound 5
like if there had never been any black people in the United States, but they would not sound the way they sound. *Jazz*, for example, is a very specific sexual term, as in *jazz me, baby*, but white people purified it into the Jazz Age. *Sock it to me*, which means, roughly, the same thing, has been adopted by Nathaniel Hawthorne's descendants with no qualms or hesitations at all, along with *let it all hang out* and *right on! Beat to his socks*, which was once the black's most total and despairing image of poverty, was transformed into a thing·called the Beat Generation, which phenomenon was, largely, composed of *uptight*, middle-class white people, imitating poverty, trying to *get down*,

to get *with it*, doing their *thing*, doing their despairing best to be *funky*, which we, the blacks, never dreamed of doing — we *were* funky, baby, like *funk* was going out of style.

6   Now, no one can eat his cake, and have it, too, and it is late in the day to attempt to penalize black people for having created a language that permits the nation its only glimpse of reality, a language without which the nation would be even more *whipped* than it is.

7   I say that this present skirmish is rooted in American history, and it is. Black English is the creation of the black diaspora. Blacks came to the United States chained to each other, but from different tribes: Neither could speak the other's language. If two black people, at that bitter hour of the world's history, had been able to speak to each other, the institution of chattel slavery could never have lasted as long as it did. Subsequently, the slave was given, under the eye, and the gun, of his master, Congo Square, and the Bible — or, in other words, and under these conditions, the slave began the formation of the black church, and it is within this unprecedented tabernacle that black English began to be formed. This was not, merely, as in the European example, the adoption of a foreign tongue, but an alchemy that transformed ancient elements into new language: *A language comes into existence by means of brutal necessity, and the rules of the language are dictated by what the language must convey.*

8   There was a moment, in time, and in this place, when my brother, or my mother, or my father, or my sister, had to convey to me, for example, the danger in which I was standing from the white man standing just behind me, and to convey this with a speed, and in a language, that the white man could not possibly understand, and that, indeed, he cannot understand, until today. He cannot afford to understand it. This understanding would reveal to him too much about himself, and smash that mirror before which he has been frozen for so long.

9   Now, if this passion, this skill, this (to quote Toni Morrison) "sheer intelligence," this incredible music, the mighty achievement of having brought a people utterly unknown to, or despised by "history" — to have brought this people to their present, troubled, troubling, and unassailable and unanswerable place — if this absolutely unprecedented journey does not indicate that black English is a language, I am curious to know what definition of language is to be trusted.

A people at the center of the Western world, and in the 10
midst of so hostile a population, has not endured and transcended by means of what is patronizingly called a "dialect."
We, the blacks, are in trouble, certainly, but we are not
doomed, and we are not inarticulate because we are not
compelled to defend a morality that we know to be a lie.

The brutal truth is that the bulk of the white people in 11
America never had any interest in educating black people,
except as this could serve white purposes. It is not the black
child's language that is in question, it is not his language
that is despised: It is his experience. A child cannot be
taught by anyone who despises him, and a child cannot
afford to be fooled. A child cannot be taught by anyone
whose demand, essentially, is that the child repudiate his
experience, and all that gives him sustenance, and enter a
limbo in which he will no longer be black, and in which
he knows that he can never become white. Black people
have lost too many black children that way.

And, after all, finally, in a country with standards so 12
untrustworthy, a country that makes heroes of so many
criminal mediocrities, a country unable to face why so
many of the nonwhite are in prison, or on the needle, or
standing, futureless, in the streets—it may very well be
that both the child, and his elder, have concluded that they
have nothing whatever to learn from the people of a country
that has managed to learn so little.

Rachel L. Jones

What's Wrong with Black English

*Rachel L. Jones contributed this essay to the "My Turn" column
in* Newsweek *in 1982, while she was a sophomore at Southern
Illinois University. She currently writes for* The River Front
Times, *a weekly newspaper in St. Louis.*

William Labov, a noted linguist, once said about the use 1
of black English, "It is the goal of most black Americans to
acquire full control of the standard language without giving
up their own culture." He also suggested that there are
certain advantages to having two ways to express one's

feelings. I wonder if the good doctor might also consider the goals of those black Americans who have full control of standard English but who are every now and then troubled by that colorful grammar-to-the-winds patois that is black English. Case in point — me.

2   I'm a 21-year-old black born to a family that would probably be considered lower–middle class — which in my mind is a polite way of describing a condition only slightly better than poverty. Let's just say we rarely if ever did the winter-vacation thing in the Caribbean. I've often had to defend my humble beginnings to a most unlikely group of people for an even less likely reason. Because of the way I talk, some of my black peers look at me sideways and ask, "Why do you talk like you're white?"

3   The first time it happened to me I was nine years old. Cornered in the school bathroom by the class bully and her sidekick, I was offered the opportunity to swallow a few of my teeth unless I satisfactorily explained why I always got good grades, why I talked "proper" or "white." I had no ready answer for her, save the fact that my mother had from the time I was old enough to talk stressed the importance of reading and learning, or that L. Frank Baum and Ray Bradbury were my closest companions. I read all my older brothers' and sisters' literature textbooks more faithfully than they did, and even lightweights like the Bobbsey Twins and Trixie Belden were allowed into my bookish inner circle. I don't remember exactly what I told those girls, but I somehow talked my way out of a beating.

4   I was reminded once again of my "white pipes" problem while apartment hunting in Evanston, Illinois, last winter. I doggedly made out lists of available places and called all around. I would immediately be invited over — and immediately turned down. The thinly concealed looks of shock when the front door opened clued me in, along with the flustered instances of "just getting off the phone with the girl who was ahead of you and she wants the rooms." When I finally found a place to live, my roommate stirred up old memories when she remarked a few months later, "You know, I was surprised when I first saw you. You sounded white over the phone." Tell me another one, sister.

5   I should've asked her a question I've wanted an answer to for years: how does one "talk white"? The silly side of me pictures a rabid white foam spewing forth when I speak. I don't use Valley Girl jargon, so that's not what's meant in my case. Actually, I've pretty much deduced what people

mean when they say that to me, and the implications are really frightening.

It means that I'm articulate and well-versed. It means   6
that I can talk as freely about John Steinbeck as I can about Rick James. It means that "ain't" and "he be" are not staples of my vocabulary and are only used around family and friends. (It is almost Jekyll and Hyde-ish the way I can slip out of academic abstractions into a long, lean, double-negative-filled dialogue, but I've come to terms with that aspect of my personality.) As a child, I found it hard to believe that's what people meant by "talking proper"; that would've meant that good grades and standard English were equated with white skin, and that went against everything I'd ever been taught. Running into the same type of mentality as an adult has confirmed the depressing reality that for many blacks, standard English is not only unfamiliar, it is socially unacceptable.

James Baldwin once defended black English by saying   7
it had added "vitality to the language," and even went so far as to label it a language in its own right, saying, "Language [i.e., black English] is a political instrument" and a "vivid and crucial key to identity." But did Malcolm X urge blacks to take power in this country "any way y'all can"? Did Martin Luther King Jr. say to blacks, "I has been to the mountaintop, and I done seed the Promised Land"? Toni Morrison, Alice Walker and James Baldwin did not achieve their eloquence, grace and stature by using only black English in their writing. Andrew Young, Tom Bradley and Barbara Jordan did not acquire political power by saying, "Y'all crazy if you ain't gon vote for me." They all have full command of standard English, and I don't think that knowledge takes away from their blackness or commitment to black people.

I know from experience that it's important for black   8
people, stripped of culture and heritage, to have something they can point to and say, "This is ours, we can comprehend it, we alone can speak it with a soulful flourish." I'd be lying if I said that the rhythms of my people caught up in "some serious rap" don't sound natural and right to me sometimes. But how heartwarming is it for those same brothers when they hit the pavement searching for employment? Studies have proven that the use of ethnic dialects decreases power in the marketplace. "I be" is acceptable on the corner, but not with the boss.

Am I letting capitalistic, European-oriented thinking fog   9 the issue? Am I selling out blacks to an ideal of assimilating, being as much like whites as possible? I have not formed a personal political ideology, but I do know this: it hurts me to hear black children use black English, knowing that they will be at yet another disadvantage in an educational system already full of stumbling blocks. It hurts me to sit in lecture halls and hear fellow black students complain that the professor "be tripping dem out using big words dey can't understand." And what hurts most is to be stripped of my own blackness simply because I know my way around the English language.

10   I would have to disagree with Labov in one respect. My goal is not so much to acquire full control of both standard and black English, but to one day see more black people less dependent on a dialect that excludes them from full participation in the world we live in. I don't think I talk white, I think I talk right.

Geneva Smitherman

White English in Blackface, or Who Do I Be?

Geneva Smitherman is a professor of linguistics at Michigan State University. Her contention printed here, that black English is not slang but a dialect of English that follows careful rules, first appeared in The Black Scholar *in 1973.*

1   Bin nothin in a long time lit up the English teaching profession like the current hassle over Black English. One finds beaucoup sociolinguistic research studies and language projects for the "disadvantaged" on the scene in nearly every sizable black community in the country.[1] And

---

[1]For examples of such programs see *Non-Standard Dialect*, Board of Education of the City of New York (National Council of Teachers of English, 1968); San-Su C. Lin, *Pattern Practices in the Teaching of Standard English to Students with a Non-Standard Dialect* (USOE Project 1339, 1965); Arno Jewett, Joseph Mersand, Doris Gunderson, *Improving English Skills*

educators from K-Grad. School bees debating whether: (1) blacks should learn and use only standard white English (hereafter referred to as WE); (2) blacks should command both dialects, i.e., be bidialectal (hereafter BD); (3) blacks should be allowed (??????) to use standard Black English (hereafter BE or BI). The appropriate choice having everything to do with American political reality, which is usually ignored, and nothing to do with the educational process, which is usually claimed. I say without qualification that we cannot talk about the Black Idiom apart from Black Culture and the Black Experience. Nor can we specify educational goals for blacks apart from considerations about the structure of (white) American society.

And we black folks is not gon take all that weight, for no   2 one has empirically demonstrated that linguistic/stylistic features of BE impede educational progress in communication skills, or any other area of cognitive learning. Take reading. It's don been charged, but not actually verified, that BE interferes with mastery of reading skills.[2] Yet beyond pointing out the gap between the young brother/sistuh's phonological and syntactical patterns and those of the usually-middle-class-WE-speaking-teacher, this claim has not been validated. The distance between the two systems is, after all, short and is illuminated only by the fact that reading is taught *orally*. (Also get to the fact that preceding generations of BE-speaking folks learned to read, despite the many classrooms in which the teacher spoke a dialect different from that of their students.)

For example, a student who reads *den* for *then* probably   3 pronounces initial/th/ as/d/ in most words. Or the one who reads *doing* for *during* probably deletes intervocalic and final/r/ in most words. So it is not that such students can't read, they is simply employing the black phonological system. In the reading classrooms of today, what we bees needin is teachers with the proper attitudinal orientation who thus can distinguish actual reading problems from mere dialect

---

of *Culturally Different Youth in Large Cities* (U.S. Department of Health, Education and Welfare, 1964); *Language Programs for the Disadvantaged* (NCTE, 1965).

    [2]See for example, Joan Baratz and Roger Shuy, ed., *Teaching Black Children to Read* (Center for Applied Linguistics, 1969); A. L. Davis, ed., *On the Dialects of Children* (NCTE, 1968); Eldonna L. Evertts, ed., *Dimensions of Dialect* (NCTE, 1967).

differences. Or take the writing of an essay. The only percentage in writing a paper with WE spelling, punctuation, and usage is in maybe eliciting a positive *attitudinal* response from a prescriptivist middle-class-aspirant-teacher. Dig on the fact that sheer "correctness" does not a good writer make. And is it any point in dealing with the charge of BE speakers being "nonverbal" or "linguistically deficient" in oral communication skills—behind our many Raps who done disproved that in living, vibrant colors?[3]

4   What linguists and educators need to do at this juncture is to take serious cognizance of the Oral Tradition in Black Culture. The uniqueness of this verbal style requires a language competence/performance model to fit the black scheme of things. Clearly BI speakers possess rich communication skills (i.e., are highly *competent* in using language), but as yet there bees no criteria (evaluative, testing, or other instrument of measurement), based on black communication patterns, wherein BI speakers can demonstrate they competence (i.e., *performance*). Hence brothers and sisters fail on language performance tests in English classrooms. Like, to amplify on what Nikki [Giovanni] said, that's why we always lose, not only cause we don't know the rules, but it ain't even our game.

5   We can devise a performance model only after an analysis of the components of BI. Now there do be linguists who supposedly done did this categorization and definition of BE.[4] But the descriptions are generally confining, limited as they are to discrete linguistic units. One finds simply ten to fifteen patterns cited, as for example, the most frequently listed one, the use of *be* as finite verb, contrasting with its deletion: (a) *The coffee be cold* contrasts with (b) *The coffee cold,* the former statement denoting a continuing state of affairs, the latter applying to the present moment only. (Like if you the cook, (a) probably get you fired, and

[3]For the most racist and glaring of these charges, see Fred Hechinger, ed., *Pre-School Education Today* (Doubleday, 1966); for an excellent rebuttal, see William Labov, *Nonstandard English* (NCVE 1970); for a complete overview of the controversy and issues involved as well as historical perspective and rebuttal to the non-verbal claim, see my "Black Idiom and White Institutions," *Negro American Literature Forum,* Fall 1971.

[4]The most thorough and scholarly of these, though a bit overly technical, is Walter Wolfram, *Detroit Negro Speech* (Center for Applied Linguistics, 1969).

(b) only get you talked about.) In WE no comparable grammatical distinction exists and *The coffee is cold* would be used to indicate both meanings. However, rarely does one find an investigation of the total vitality of black expressive style, a style inextricable from the Black Cultural Universe, for after all, BI connects with Black Soul and niggers is more than deleted copulas.[5]

The Black Idiom should be viewed from two important   6 perspectives: linguistic and stylistic. The linguistic dimension is comprised of the so-called nonstandard features of phonology and syntax (patterns like *dis heah* and *The coffee be cold*), and a lexicon generally equated with "slang" or hip talk. The stylistic dimension has to do with *rapping, capping, jiving,* etc., and with features such as cadence, rhythm, resonance, gestures, and all those other elusive, difficult-to-objectify elements that make up what is considered a writer or speaker's "style." While I am separating linguistic and stylistic features, I have done so only for the purpose of simplifying the discussion since the BI speaker runs the full gamut of both dimensions in any given speech event.

I acknowledge from the bell that we's dealing with a   7 dialect structure which is a subsystem of the English language; thus BE and WE may not appear fundamentally different. Yet, though black folks speak English, it do seem to be an entirely different lingo altogether. But wherein lies the uniqueness? Essentially in language, as in other areas of Black Culture, we have the problem of isolating those elements indigenous to black folks from those cultural aspects shared with white folks. Anthropologist Johnnetta Cole suggests that Black Culture has three dimensions: (1) those elements shared with mainstream America; (2) those elements shared with all oppressed peoples; (3) those elements peculiar to the black condition in America.[6] Applying her concepts to language, I propose the accompanying schematic representation.

[5]Kochman is one linguist who done gone this route; see for instance his "Rapping in the Black Ghetto," *Trans-action*, February 1969. However, he makes some black folks mad because of what one of my students called his "superfluity," and others shame cause of his exposure of our "bad" street elements. Kochman's data: jam up with mutafuckas and pussy-copping raps collected from Southside Chicago.

[6]Johnnetta B. Cole, "Culture: Negro, Black and Nigger," *The Black Scholar*, June 1970.

FEATURES SHARED WITH MAINSTREAM AMERICA	FEATURES SHARED WITH ALL OPPRESSED PEOPLES	FEATURES UNIQUE TO BLACK AMERICANS
Linguistic	*Linguistic*	*Linguistic*
1. British/American English lexicon 2. Most aspects of British/American English phonology and syntax	1. Superimpositions of dominant culture's language on native language, yielding 2. Pidginized form of dominant culture's language, subject to becoming extinct, due to 3. Historical evolution, linguistic leveling out in direction of dominant culture's dialect	Unique meanings attributed to certain English lexical items *Stylistic* Unique communication patterns and rhetorical flourishes

8   Referring to the first column, contemporary BE is simply one of the many dialects of contemporary American English, and it is most likely the case that the linguistic patterns of BE differ from those of WE in surface structure only. There's no essential linguistic difference between *dis heah* and *this here,* and from a strictly linguistic point of view, *God don't never change* can be written *God doesn't ever change* (though definitely not from a socio-cultural/political perspective, as Baraka quite rightly notes).[7] Perhaps we could make a case for deep structure difference in the BE use of *be* as finite verb (refer to *The coffee be cold* example above), but we be hard pressed to find any other examples, and even in this case, we could posit that the copula exists in the deep structure, and is simply deleted by some low-level phonological deletion rule, dig: The cof-

[7]Imamu Baraka, "Expressive Language," *Home,* pp. 166–172.

fee is cold . . . The coffee's cold . . . The coffee cold. My conclusion at this point is that despite the claims of some highly respected Creole linguists (with special propers to bad Sistuh Beryl Bailey),[8] the argument for deep structure differences between contemporary BE and WE syntax can not pass the test of rigorous transformational analysis.

Referring to the second column, we note the psychological tendency of oppressed people to adopt the modes of behavior and expression of their oppressors (also, during the African slave trade, the functional necessity of pidginized forms of European language). Not only does the conqueror force his victims into political subjugation, he also coerces them into adopting his language and doles out special rewards to those among the oppressed who best mimic his language and cultural style. In the initial language contact stage, the victims attempt to assemble the new language into their native linguistic mold, producing a linguistic mixture that is termed *pidgin*. In the next stage, the pidgin may develop into a Creole, a highly systematic, widely used mode of communication among the oppressed, characterized by a substratum of patterns from the victim's language with an overlay of forms from the oppressor's language. As the oppressed people's identification with the victor's culture intensifies, the pidgin/Creole begins to lose its linguistic currency and naturally evolves in the direction of the victor's language. Reconstructing the linguistic history of BE, we theorize that it followed a similar pattern, but due to the radically different condition of black oppression in America, the process of *de-creolization* is nearly complete and has been for perhaps over a hundred years. 9

The most important features of BI are, of course, those referred to in column three, for they point us toward the linguistic uniqueness and cultural significance of the Oral Tradition in the Black Experience. It should be clear that all along I been talkin bout that Black Experience associated with the grass-roots folks, the masses, the sho-nuff niggers—in short, all those black folks who do not aspire to white middle-class American standards. 10

Within this tradition, language is used as a teaching/ 11

[8]See her "Toward a New Perspective in Negro English Dialectology," *American Speech* (1965); and "Language and Communicative Styles of Afro-American Children in the United States," *Florida FL Reporter* 7 (Spring/Summer 1969).

socializing force and as a means of establishing one's reputation via his verbal competence. Black talk is never meaningless cocktail chit-chat but a functional dynamic that is
simultaneously a mechanism for acculturation and infor-
mation-passing and a vehicle for achieving group recognition. Black communication is highly verbal and highly
stylized; it is a performance before a black audience who
become both observers and participants in the speech event.
Whether it be through slapping of hands ("giving five" or
"giving skin"), Amen's, or Right on's, the audience influences the direction of a given rap and at the same time
acknowledges or withholds its approval, depending on the
linguistic skill and stylistic ingenuity of the speaker. I mean
like a Brother is only as bad as his rap bees.

I. Toward a Black Language Model: Linguistic

12   While we concede that black people use the vocabulary
of the English language, certain words are always selected
out of that lexicon and given a special black semantic slant.
So though we rappin bout the same language, the reality
referents are different. As one linguist has suggested, the
proper question is not what do words mean but what do
the users of the words mean? These words may be associated with and more frequently used in black street culture but not necessarily. *Muthafucka* has social boundaries,
but not *nigger*.

13   Referring to the lexicon of BI, then, the following general
principles obtain:

14   1. The words given the special black slant exist in a
dynamic state. The terms are discarded when they move
into the white mainstream. (Example: One no longer speaks
of a "hip" brother; now he is a "togetha" brother.) This
was/is necessitated by our need to have a code that was/is
undecipherable by foreigners (i.e., whites).

15   2. In BI, the concept of denotation vs. connotation does
not apply.

16   3. What does apply is shades of meaning along the con-
notative spectrum. For example, depending on contextual
environment, the word *bad* can mean extraordinary; beautiful; good; versatile; or a host of other terms of positive
value. Dig it: after watching a Sammy Davis performance,
a BI speaker testified: "Sammy sho did some *bad* stuff,"

i.e., extraordinary stuff. Or upon observing a beautiful sister: "She sho is *bad*," i.e., beautiful, pretty, or good-looking. Or, noticing how a brother is dressed: "You sho got on some *bad* shit," i.e., *good* shit = attractively dressed.

Note that the above examples are all in the category of *approbation*. It is necessary to rap about *denigration* as well, since certain words in the black lexicon can frequently be used both ways. Consider the word *nigger*, for instance. "He's my main nigger" means my best friend (hence, approbation); "The nigger ain't shit," means he's probably lazy, trifling, scheming, wrong-doing, or a host of other *denigrating* terms, depending on the total context of the utterance.

4. Approbation and denigration relate to the semantic level; we can add two other possible functions of the same word on the grammatical level: *intensification* and *completion*. Slide back to *nigger* for a minute, and dig that often the word is void of real meaning and simply supplies the sentence with a subject. "Niggers was getting out of there left and right, then the niggers was running, and so the niggers said . . ." etc., etc., my point being that a steady stream of overuse means neither denigration nor approbation. Some excellent illustrations of this function of the word are to be found in *Manchild in the Promised Land*, where you can observe the word used in larger contexts.

To give you a most vivid illustration, consider the use of what WE labels "obscenities." From the streets of Detroit: (a) "That's a bad *muthafucka*." Referring to a Cadillac Eldorado, obviously indicating approval. (b) "He's a no-good *muthafucka*." Referring to a person who has just "put some game" on the speaker, obviously indicating disapproval. (c) "You *muthafuckin* right I wasn't gon let him do that." Emphasizing how correct the listener's assessment is, obviously using the term as a grammatical intensifier, modifying "right." (d) "We wasn't doin nothing, just messin round and *shit*." Though a different "obscenity," the point is nonetheless illustrated, "shit" being used neutrally, as an expletive (filler) to complete the sentence pattern; semantically speaking, it is an empty word in this contextual environment.

Where I'm comin from is that the lexicon of BI, consisting of certain specially selected words, requires a unique scheme of analysis to account for the diverse range and multiplicity of meanings attributed to these words. While there do be some dictionaries of Afro-American "slang," they fail to get at the important question: what are the psycho-cultural processes that guide our selection of certain words out of the thousands of possible words in the Anglo-Saxon vocabulary? Like, for instance, Kochman[9] has suggested that we value action in the black community, and so those words that have action implied in them, we take and give positive meanings to, such as *swing, game, hip, hustle,* etc.; whereas words of implied stasis are taken and given negative connotations, such as *lame, square, hung-up, stiffin and jivin,* etc. At any rate, what I've tried to lay here are some suggestions in this particular linguistic dimension; the definitive word on black lexicon is yet to be given.

21   I shall go on to discuss the stylistic dimension of black communication patterns, where I have worked out a more definitive model.

II. Toward a Black Language Model: Stylistic

22   Black verbal style exists on a sacred-secular continuum, as represented by the accompanying scheme. The model allows us to account for the many individual variations in black speech, which can all be located at some point along the continuum.

SACRED	SECULAR
Political Rap Style	*Political Rap Style*
Examples: Jesse Jackson	Examples: Malcolm X
Martin Luther King	Rap Brown
Political Literary Style	*Political Literary Style*
Examples: Barbara Ann Teer's	Examples: Don Lee
National Black Theatre	Last Poets
Nikki Giovanni's	
"Truth Is on Its Way"	

[9]See Thomas Kochman, "The Kinetic Element in Black Idiom," paper read at the American Anthropological Association Convention, Seattle, Washington, 1968; also his *Rappin' and Stylin' Out: Communication in Urban Black America.*

The sacred style is rural and Southern. It is the style of   23
the black preacher and that associated with the black
church tradition. It tends to be more emotive and highly
charged than the secular style. It is also older in time. However, though I've called it "sacred," it abounds in sec-
ularisms. Black church service tends to be highly informal,
and it ain nothin for a preacher to get up in the pulpit and,
say, show off what he's wearing: "Y'all didn't notice the
new suit I got on today, did y'all? Ain the Lord good to
us. . . ."

The secular style is urban and Northern, but since it   24
probably had its beginnings in black folk tales and proverbs,
its *roots* are Southern and rural. This is the street culture;
the style found in barbershops and on street corners in the
black ghettos of American cities. It tends to be more cool,
more emotionally restrained sacred style. It is newer and
younger in time and only fully evolved as a distinct style
with the massive wave of black migration to the citics.

Both sacred and secular styles share the following   25
characteristics:

1. *Call and Response.*   This is basic to black oral tradition.   26
The speaker's solo voice alternates or is intermingled with
the audience's response. In the sacred style, the minister is
urged on by the congregation's Amen's, That's right, Reverend's, or Preach Reverend's. One also hears occasional Take
your time's when the preacher is initiating his sermon, the
congregation desiring to savor every little bit of this good
message they bout to hear. (In both sacred and secular
political rap styles, the "Preach Reverend" is transposed to
"Teach Brother.") In the secular style, the response can take
the form of a back-and-forth banter between the speaker
and various members of the audience. Or the audience
might manifest its response in giving skin (fives) when a
really down verbal point is scored. Other approval responses include laughter and phrases like "Oh, you mean,
nigger," "Get back, nigger," "Git down, baby," etc.

2. *Rhythmic Pattern.*   I refer to cadence, tone, and musi-   27
cal quality. This is a pattern that is lyrical, sonorous, and
generally emphasizing sound apart from sense. It is often
established through repetition, either of certain sounds or
words. The preacher will get a rhythm going, conveying
his message through sound rather than depending on sheer
semantic import. "I-I-I-I-I-Oh-I-I-Oh, yeah, Lord-I-I-heard

the voice of Jesus saying. . . ." Even though the secular style is characterized by rapidity, as in the toasts (narrative tales of bad niggers and they exploits, like Stag-O-Lee, or bad animals and they trickeration, like the Signifying Monkey), the speaker's voice tone still has that rhythmic, musical quality, just with a faster tempo.

28   3. *Spontaneity.* Generally, the speaker's performance is improvisational, with the rich interaction between speaker and audience dictating and/or directing the course and outcome of the speech event. Since the speaker does not prepare a formal document, his delivery is casual, nondeliberate, and uncontrived. He speaks in a lively, conversational tone, and with an ever-present quality of immediacy. All emphasis is on process, movement, and creativity of the moment. The preacher says "Y'all don wont to hear dat, so I'm gon leave it lone," and his audience shouts, "Naw, tell it Reverend, tell it!," and he does. Or, like, once Malcolm [X] mentioned the fact of his being in prison, and sensing the surprise of his audience, he took advantage of the opportunity to note that all black people were in prison: "That's what American means: prison."

29   4. *Concreteness.* The speaker's imagery and ideas center around the empirical world, the world of reality, and the contemporary Here and Now. Rarely does he drift off into esoteric abstractions; his metaphors and illustrations are commonplace and grounded in everyday experience. Perhaps because of his concreteness, there is a sense of identification with the event being described or narrated, as in the secular style where the toast-teller's identity merges with that of the protagonist of his tale, and he becomes Stag-O-Lee or Shine; or when the preacher assumes the voice of God or the personality of a Biblical character. Even the experience of being saved takes on a presentness and rootedness in everyday life: "I first met God in 1925. . . ."

30   5. *Signifying.* This is a technique of talking about the entire audience or some member of the audience either to initiate verbal "war" or to make a point hit home. The interesting thang bout this rhetorical device is that the audience is not offended and realizes—naw, expects—the speaker to launch this offensive to achieve his desired effect. "Pimp, punk, prostitute, Ph.D.—all the P's—you still in slavery!" announces the Reverend Jesse Jackson. Malcolm

puts down the nonviolent movement with: "In a revolution, you swinging, not singing." (Notice the characteristic rhythmic pattern in the above examples — the alliterative poetic effect of Jackson's statement and the rhyming device in Malcolm's.)

An analysis of black expressive style, such as presented [31] here, should facilitate the construction of a performance instrument to measure the degree of command of the style of any given BI speaker. Linguists and educators sincerely interested in black education might be about the difficult, complex business of devising such a "test," rather than establishing linguistic remediation programs to correct a nonexistent remediation. Like in any other area of human activity, some BI rappers are better than others, and today's most effective black preachers, leaders, politicians, writers are those who rap in the black expressive style, appropriating the ritual framework of the Oral Tradition as vehicle for the conveyance of they political ideologies. Which brings me back to what I said from Jump Street. The real heart of this language controversy relates to/is the underlying political nature of the American educational system. Brother Frantz Fanon is highly instructive at this point. From his "Negro and Language," in *Black Skin, White Masks:*

> I ascribe a basic importance to the phenomenon of language. . . . To speak means . . . above all to assume a culture, to support the weight of a civilization. . . . Every dialect is a way of thinking. . . . And the fact that the newly returned [i.e., from white schools] Negro adopts a language different from that of the group into which he was born is evidence of a dislocation, a separation. . . .

In showing why the "Negro adopts such a position . . . with respect to European languages," Fanon continues:

> It is because he wants to emphasize the rupture that has now occurred. He is incarnating a new type of man that he imposes on his associates and his family. And so his old mother can no longer understand him when he talks to her about his *duds*, the family's *crummy joint*, the *dump* . . . all of it, of course, tricked out with the appropriate accent.
>
>   In every country of the world, there are climbers, 'the ones who forget who they are,' and in contrast to them, 'the ones who remember where they came from.' The Antilles Negro

who goes home from France expresses himself in the dialect if he wants to make it plain that nothing has changed.

32   As black people go moving on up toward separation and cultural nationalism, the question of the moment is not which dialect, but which culture, not whose vocabulary but whose values, not *I am* vs. *I be*, but WHO DO I BE?

John Simon
Why Good English Is Good for You

John Simon (born 1925) has reviewed theater and film for several magazines. An eloquent — and sometimes merciless — critic of the misuse of language, for many years he wrote a language column for Esquire. *Several of those columns were collected in* Paradigms Lost, *a book about the "decline of literacy." This essay is from that 1976 collection.*

1   What's good English to you that . . . you should grieve for it? What good is correct speech and writing, you may ask, in an age in which hardly anyone seems to know, and no one seems to care? Why shouldn't you just fling bloopers, bloopers riotously with the throng, and not stick out from the rest like a sore thumb by using the language correctly? Isn't grammar really a thing of the past, and isn't the new idea to communicate in *any* way as long as you can make yourself understood?

2   The usual, basic defense of good English (and here, again, let us not worry about nomenclature — for all I care, you may call it "Standard English," "correct American," or anything else) is that it helps communication, that it is perhaps even a *sine qua non* of mutual understanding. Although this is a crude truth of sorts, it strikes me as, in some ways, both more and less than the truth. Suppose you say, "Everyone in their right mind would cross on the green light" or "Hopefully, it won't rain tomorrow"; chances are very good that the person you say this to will understand you, even though you are committing obvious solecisms or creating needless ambiguities. Similarly, if you write in a letter, "The baby has finally ceased it's howling" (spelling *its* as *it's*), the recipient will be able to figure out what was meant.

But "figuring out" is precisely what a listener or reader should not have to do. There is, of course, the fundamental matter of courtesy to the other person, but it goes beyond that: why waste time on unscrambling simple meaning when there are more complex questions that should receive our undivided attention? If the many cooks had to worry first about which out of a large number of pots had no leak in it, the broth, whether spoiled or not, would take forever to be ready.

It is, I repeat, only initially a matter of clarity. It is also   3
a matter of concision. Space today is as limited as time. If you have only a thousand words in which to convey an important message it helps to know that "overcomplicated" is correct and "overly complicated" is incorrect. Never mind the grammatical explanations; the two extra characters and one space between words are reason enough. But what about the more advanced forms of word-mongering that hold sway nowadays? Take redundancy, like the "hopes and aspirations" of Jimmy Carter, quoted by Edwin Newman as having "a deeply profound religious experience"; or elaborate jargon, as when Charles G. Walcutt, a graduate professor of English at CUNY, writes (again as quoted by Newman): "The colleges, trying to remediate increasing numbers of . . . illiterates up to college levels, are being high-schoolized"; or just obfuscatory verbiage of the pretentious sort, such as this fragment from a letter I received: "It is my impression that effective interpersonal verbal communication depends on prior effective intra-personal verbal communication." What this means is that if you think clearly, you can speak and write clearly — except if you are a "certified speech and language pathologist," like the writer of the letter I quote. (By the way, she adds the letters Ph.D. after her name, though she is not even from Germany, where *Herr* and *Frau Doktor* are in common, not to say vulgar, use.)

But except for her ghastly verbiage, our certified language   4
pathologist (whatever that means) is perfectly right: there is a close connection between the ability to think and the ability to use English correctly. After all, we think in words, we conceptualize in words, we work out our problems inwardly with words, and using them correctly is comparable to a craftsman's treating his tools with care, keeping his materials in good shape. Would you trust a weaver who hangs her wet laundry on her loom, or lets her cats bed down in her yarn? The person who does not respect words and their proper relationships cannot have much respect

for ideas—very possibly cannot have ideas at all. My quarrel is not so much with minor errors that we all fall into from time to time even if we know better as it is with basic sloppiness or ignorance or defiance of good English.

5   Training yourself to speak and write correctly—and I say "training yourself" because nowadays, unfortunately, you cannot depend on other people or on institutions to give you the proper training, for reasons I shall discuss later—training yourself, then, in language, means developing at the very least two extremely useful faculties: your sense of discipline and your memory. Discipline because language is with us always, as nothing else is: it follows us much as, in the old morality play, Good Deeds followed Everyman, all the way to the grave; and, if the language is written, even beyond. Let me explain: if you can keep an orderly apartment, if you can see to it that your correspondence and bill-paying are attended to regularly, if your diet and wardrobe are maintained with the necessary care— good enough; you are a disciplined person.

6   But the preliminary discipline underlying all others is nevertheless your speech: the words that come out of you almost as frequently and—if you are tidy—as regularly as your breath. I would go so far as to say that, immediately after your bodily functions, language is first, unless you happen to be an ascetic, an anchorite, or a stylite; but unless you are a sty*lite*, you had better be a sty*list*.

7   Most of us—almost all—must take in and give out language as we do breath, and we had better consider the seriousness of language pollution as second only to air pollution. For the linguistically disciplined, to misuse or mispronounce a word is an unnecessary and unhealthy contribution to the surrounding smog. To have taught ourselves not to do this, or—being human and thus also imperfect—to do it as little as possible, means deriving from every speaking moment the satisfaction we get from a cap that snaps on to a container perfectly, an elevator that stops flush with the landing, a roulette ball that comes to rest exactly on the number on which we have placed our bet. It gives us the pleasure of hearing or seeing our words—because they are abiding by the rules— snapping, sliding, falling precisely into place, expressing with perfect lucidity and symmetry just what we wanted them to express. This is comparable to the satisfaction of the athlete or ballet dancer or pianist finding his body or legs or fingers doing his bidding with unimpeachable accuracy.

And if someone now says that "in George Eliot's lesser 8
novels, she is not completely in command" is perfectly comprehensible even if it is ungrammatical, the "she" having
no antecedent in the nominative (*Eliot's* is a genitive), I
say, "Comprehensible, perhaps, but lopsided," for the
civilized and orderly mind does not feel comfortable with
that "she" — does not hear that desired and satisfying click
of correctness — unless the sentence is restructured as
"George Eliot, in her lesser novels, is not . . ." or in some
similar way. In fact, the fully literate ear can be thrown by
this error in syntax; it may look for the antecedent of that
"she" elsewhere than in the preceding possessive case. Be
that as it may, playing without rules and winning — in this
instance, managing to communicate without using good
English — is no more satisfactory than winning in a sport
or game by accident or by disregarding the rules: which is
really cheating.

The second faculty good speech develops is, as I have 9
mentioned before, our memory. Grammar and syntax are
partly logical — and to that extent they are also good exer-
cisers and developers of our logical faculty — but they are
also partly arbitrary, conventional, irrational. For example,
the correct "compared to" and "contrasted with" could,
from the logical point of view, just as well be "contrasted
to" and "compared with" ("compared with," of course, is
correct, but in a different sense from the one that concerns
us here, namely, the antithesis of "contrasted with"). And,
apropos *different*, logic would have to strain desperately to
explain the exclusive correctness of "different from," given
the exclusive correctness of "other than," which would seem
to justify "different than," jarring though that is to the cultivated ear.

But there it is: some things are so because tradition, 10
usage, the best speakers and writers, the grammar books
and dictionaries have made them so. There may even exist
some hidden historical explanation: something, perhaps,
in the Sanskrit, Greek, Latin, or other origins of a word or
construction that you and I may very easily never know.
We can, however, memorize; and memorization can be a
wonderfully useful thing — surely the Greeks were right to
consider Mnemosyne (memory) the mother of the Muses,
for without her there would be no art and no science. And
what better place to practice one's mnemonic skills than
in the study of one's language?

There is something particularly useful about speaking 11

correctly and precisely because language is always there
as a foundation—or, if you prefer a more fluid image, an
undercurrent—beneath what is going on. Now, it seems to
me that the great difficulty of life lies in the fact that we
must almost always do two things at a time. If, for example,
we are walking and conversing, we must keep our mouths
as well as feet from stumbling. If we are driving while
listening to music, we must not allow the siren song of the
cassette to prevent us from watching the road and the
speedometer (otherwise the less endearing siren of the
police car or the ambulance will follow apace). Well, it is
just this sort of bifurcation of attention that care for precise,
clear expression fosters in us. By learning early in life to
pay attention both to what we are saying and to how we
are saying it, we develop the much-needed life skill of doing
two things simultaneously.

12   Put another way, we foster our awareness of, and ability
to deal with, form and content. If there is any verity that
modern criticism has fought for, it is the recognition of the
indissolubility of content and form. Criticism won the battle, won it so resoundingly that this oneness has become a
contemporary commonplace. And shall the fact that form
is content be a platitude in all the arts but go unrecognized
in the art of self-expression, whether in conversation or
correspondence, or whatever form of spoken or written utterance a human being resorts to? Accordingly, you are
going to be judged, whether you like it or not, by the correctness of your English as much as by the correctness of your
thinking; there are some people to whose ear bad English
is as offensive as gibberish, or as your picking your nose in
public would be to their eyes and stomachs. The fact that
people of linguistic sensibilities may be a dying breed does
not mean that they are wholly extinct, and it is best not to
take any unnecessary chances.

13   To be sure, if you are a member of a currently favored
minority, many of your linguistic failings may be forgiven
you—whether rightly or wrongly is not my concern here.
But if you cannot change your sex or color to the one that
is getting preferential treatment—Bakke case or no Bakke
case—you might as well learn good English and profit by
it in your career, your social relations, perhaps even in your
basic self-confidence. That, if you will, is the ultimate practical application of good English; but now let me tell you
about the ultimate impractical one, which strikes me as
being possibly even more important.

Somewhere in the prose writings of Charles Péguy, who   14
was a very fine poet and prose writer — and, what is perhaps
even more remarkable, as good a human being as he was
an artist — somewhere in those writings is a passage about
the decline of pride in workmanship among French artisans,
which, as you can deduce, set in even before World War I,
wherein Péguy was killed. In the passage I refer to, Péguy
bemoans the fact that cabinetmakers no longer finish the
backs of furniture — the sides that go against the wall — in
the same way as they do the exposed sides. What is not
seen was just as important to the old artisans as what is
seen — it was a moral issue with them. And so, I think, it
ought to be with language. Even if no one else notices the
niceties, the precision, the impeccable sense of grammar
and syntax you deploy in your utterances, you yourself
should be aware of them and take pride in them as in pieces
of work well done.

Now, I realize that there are two possible reactions among   15
you to what I have said up to this point. Some of you will
say to yourselves: what utter nonsense! Language is a flexible, changing, living organism that belongs to the people
who speak it. It has always been changed according to the
ways in which people chose to speak it, and the dictionaries
and books on grammar had to, and will have to, adjust
themselves to the people and not the other way around.
For isn't it the glory of language that it keeps throwing up
new inventions as surf tosses out differently polished pebbles and bits of bottle glass onto the shore, and that in this
inexhaustible variety, in this refusal to kowtow to dry-as-
dust scholars, lies its vitality, its beauty?

Others among you, perhaps fewer in number, will say to   16
yourselves: quite so, there is such a thing as Standard English, or purity of speech, or correctness of expression —
something worth safeguarding and fostering; but how the
devil is one to accomplish that under the prevailing conditions: in a democratic society full of minorities that have
their own dialects or linguistic preferences, and in a world
in which television, advertising, and other mass media
manage daily to corrupt the language a little further? Let
me try to answer the first group first, and then come back
to the questions of the second.

Of course language is, and must be, a living organism to   17
the extent that new inventions, discoveries, ideas enter the
scene and clamor rightfully for designations. Political, social, and psychological changes may also affect our mode

of expression, and new words or phrases may have to be found to reflect what we might call historical changes. It is also quite natural for slang terms to be invented, become popular, and, in some cases, remain permanently in the language. It is perhaps equally inevitable (though here we are on more speculative ground) for certain words to become obsolescent and obsolete, and drop out of the language. But does that mean that grammar and syntax have to keep changing, that pronunciations and meanings of words must shift, that more complex or elegant forms are obliged to yield to simpler or cruder ones that often are not fully synonymous with them and not capable of expressing certain fine distinctions? Should, for instance, "terrestrial" disappear entirely in favor of "earthly," or are there shades of meaning involved that need to remain available to us? Must we sacrifice "notwithstanding" because we have "in spite of" or "despite"? Need we forfeit "jettison" just because we have "throw overboard"? And what about "disinterested," which is becoming a synonym for "uninterested," even though that means something else, and though we have no other word for "disinterested"?

18   "Language has *always* changed," say these people, and they might with equal justice say that there has always been war or sickness or insanity. But the truth is that some sicknesses that formerly killed millions have been eliminated, that some so-called insanity can today be treated, and that just because there have always been wars does not mean that someday a cure cannot be found even for that scourge. And if it cannot, it is only by striving to put an absolute end to war, by pretending that it can be licked, that we can at least partly control it. Without such assumptions and efforts, the evil would be so widespread that, given our current weaponry, we would no longer be here to worry about the future of language.

19   But we are here, and having evolved linguistically this far, and having the means — books of grammar, dictionaries, education for all — to arrest unnecessary change, why not endeavor with might and mind to arrest it? Certain cataclysms cannot be prevented: earthquakes and droughts, for example, can scarcely, if at all, be controlled; but we can prevent floods, for which purpose we have invented dams. And dams are precisely what we can construct to prevent floods of ignorance from eroding our language, and, beyond that, to provide irrigation for areas that would otherwise remain linguistically arid.

For consider that what some people are pleased to call   20
linguistic evolution was almost always a matter of ignorance prevailing over knowledge. There is no valid reason,
for example, for the word *nice* to have changed its meaning
so many times—except ignorance of its exact definition.
Had the change never occurred, or had it been stopped at
any intermediate stage, we would have had just as good a
word as we have now and saved some people a heap of
confusion along the way. But if *nice* means what it does
today—and it has two principal meanings, one of them, as
in "nice distinction," alas, obsolescent—let us, for heaven's
sake, keep it where it is, now that we have the means with
which to hold it there.

If, for instance, we lose the accusative case *whom*— and   21
we are in great danger of losing it—our language will be
the poorer for it. Obviously, "The man, whom I had never
known, was a thief" means something other than "The man
who I had never known was a thief." Now, you can object
that it would be just as easy in the first instance to use
some other construction; but what happens if *this* one is
used incorrectly? Ambiguity and confusion. And why
should we lose this useful distinction? Just because a million or ten million or a billion people less educated than
we are cannot master the difference? Surely it behooves us
to try to educate the ignorant up to our level rather than
to stultify ourselves down to theirs. Yes, you say, but suppose they refuse to or are unable to learn? In that case, I
say, there is a doubly good reason for not going along with
them. Ah, you reply, but they are the majority, and we must
accept their way or, if the revolution is merely linguistic,
lose our "credibility" (as the current parlance, rather con-
fusingly, has it) or, if the revolution is political, lose our
heads. Well, I consider a sufficient number of people to be
educable enough to be capable of using *who* and *whom*
correctly, and to derive satisfaction from this capability—a
sufficient number, I mean, to enable us to preserve *whom*,
and not to have to ask "for who the bells tolls."

The main problem with education, actually, is not those   22
who need it and cannot get it, but those who should impart
it and, for various reasons, do not. In short, the enemies of
education are the educators themselves: miseducated, underpaid, overburdened, and intimidated teachers (frightened
because, though the pen is supposed to be mightier than
the sword, the switchblade is surely more powerful than
the ferule), and professors who—because they are struc-

tural linguists, democratic respecters of alleged minority rights, or otherwise misguided folk—believe in the sacrosanct privilege of any culturally underprivileged minority or majority to dictate its ignorance to the rest of the world. For, I submit, an English improvised by slaves and other strangers to the culture—to whom my heart goes out in every human way—under dreadfully deprived conditions can nowise equal an English that the best literary and linguistic talents have, over the centuries, perceptively and painstakingly brought to a high level of excellence.

23   So my answer to the scoffers in this or any audience is, in simplest terms, the following: contrary to popular misconception, language does not belong to the people, or at least not in the sense in which *belong* is usually construed. For things can rightfully belong only to those who invent or earn them. But we do not know who invented language: is it the people who first made up the words for *father* and *mother*, for *I* and *thou*, for *hand* and *foot;* or is it the people who evolved the subtler shadings of language, its poetic variety and suggestiveness, but also its unambiguousness, its accurate and telling details? Those are two very different groups of people and two very different languages, and I, as you must have guessed by now, consider the latter group at least as important as the former. As for *earning* language, it has surely been earned by those who have striven to learn it properly, and here even economic and social circumstances are but an imperfect excuse for bad usage; history is full of examples of people rising from humble origins to learn, against all kinds of odds, to speak and write correctly—even brilliantly.

24   *Belong*, then, should be construed in the sense that parks, national forests, monuments, and public utilities are said to belong to the people: available for properly respectful use but not for defacement and destruction. And all that we propose to teach is how to use and enjoy the gardens of language to their utmost aesthetic and salubrious potential. Still, I must now address myself to the group that, while agreeing with my aims, despairs of finding practical methods for their implementation.

25   True enough, after a certain age speakers not aware of Standard English or not exceptionally gifted will find it hard or impossible to change their ways. Nevertheless, if there were available funds for advanced methods in teaching; if teachers themselves were better trained and paid, and had smaller classes and more assistants; if, further-

more, college entrance requirements were heightened and the motivation of students accordingly strengthened; if there were no structural linguists and National Councils of Teachers of English filling instructors' heads with notions about "Students' Rights to Their Own Language" (they have every right to it as a *second* language, but none as a *first*); if teachers in all disciplines, including the sciences and social sciences, graded on English usage as well as on specific proficiencies; if aptitude tests for various jobs stressed good English more than they do; and, above all, if parents were better educated and more aware of the need to set a good example to their children, and to encourage them to learn correct usage, the situation could improve enormously.

Clearly, to expect all this to come to pass is utopian; some 26 of it, however, is well within the realm of possibility. For example, even if parents do not speak very good English, many of them at least can manage an English that is good enough to correct a very young child's mistakes; in other words, most adults can speak a good enough four-year-old's idiom. They would thus start kids out on the right path; the rest could be done by the schools.

But the problem is what to do in the most underprivileged 27 homes: those of blacks, Hispanics, immigrants from various Asian and European countries. This is where day-care centers could come in. If the fathers and mothers could be gainfully employed, their small children would be looked after by day-care centers where — is this asking too much? — good English could be inculcated in them. The difficulty, of course, is what to do about the discrepancy the little ones would note between the speech of the day-care people and that of their parents. Now, it seems to me that small children have a far greater ability to learn things, including languages, than some people give them credit for. Much of it is indeed rote learning, but, where languages are concerned, that is one of the basic learning methods even for adults. There is no reason for not teaching kids another language, to wit, Standard English, and turning this, if desirable, into a game: "At home you speak one way; here we have another language," at which point the instructor can make up names and explanations for Standard English that would appeal to pupils of that particular place, time, and background.

At this stage of the game, as well as later on in school, 28 care should be exercised to avoid insulting the language spoken in the youngsters' homes. There must be ways to convey that both home and school languages have their validity and uses and that knowing both enables one to accomplish more in life. This would be hard to achieve if the children's parents were, say, militant blacks of the Geneva Smitherman sort, who execrate Standard English as a weapon of capitalist oppression against the poor of all races, colors, and religions. But, happily, there is evidence that most black, Hispanic, and other non-Standard English–speaking parents want their children to learn correct English so as to get ahead in the world.

29   Yet how do we defend ourselves against the charge that we are old fogeys who cannot emotionally adjust to the new directions an ever-living and changing language must inevitably take? Here I would want to redefine or, at any rate, clarify, what "living and changing" means, and also explain where we old fogeys stand. Misinformed attacks on Old Fogeydom, I have noticed, invariably represent us as people who shudder at a split infinitive and would sooner kill or be killed than tolerate a sentence that ends with a preposition. Actually, despite all my travels through Old Fogeydom, I have yet to meet one inhabitant who would not stick a preposition onto the tail of a sentence; as for splitting infinitives, most of us O.F.'s are perfectly willing to do that, too, but tactfully and sparingly, where it feels right. There is no earthly reason, for example, for saying "to dangerously live," when "to live dangerously" sounds so much better; but it does seem right to say (and write) "What a delight to sweetly breathe in your sleeping lover's breath"; that sounds smoother, indeed sweeter, than "to breathe in sweetly" or "sweetly to breathe in." But infinitives begging to be split are relatively rare; a sensitive ear, a good eye for shades of meaning will alert you whenever the need to split arises; without that ear and eye, you had better stick to the rules.

30   About the sense in which language is, and must be, alive, let me speak while donning another of my several hats — actually it is not a hat but a cap, for there exists in Greenwich Village an inscription on a factory that reads "CRITIC CAPS." So with my drama critic's cap on, let me present you with an analogy. The world theater today is full of directors who wreak havoc on classic plays to demonstrate their own ingenuity, their superiority, as it were, to the author. These directors — aborted playwrights, for the most part — will stage productions of *Hamlet* in which the prince is a woman, a flaming homosexual, or a one-eyed hunchback.

Well, it seems to me that the same spirit prevails in our   31
approach to linguistics, with every newfangled, ill-in-
formed, know-nothing construction, definition, pronunciation enshrined by the joint efforts of structural linguists,
permissive dictionaries, and allegedly democratic but actually demagogic educators. What really makes a production
of, say, *Hamlet* different, and therefore alive, is that the
director, while trying to get as faithfully as possible at
Shakespeare's meanings, nevertheless ends up stressing
things in the play that strike him most forcefully; and the
same individuality in production design and performances
(the Hamlet of Gielgud versus the Hamlet of Olivier, for
instance — what a world of difference!) further differentiates
one production from another, and bestows on each its particular vitality. So, too, language remains alive because
each speaker (or writer) can and must *within the framework
of accepted grammar, syntax, and pronunciation*, produce a
style that is his very own, that is as personal as his posture,
way of walking, mode of dress, and so on. It is such stylistic
differences that make a person's — or a nation's — language
flavorous, pungent, alive, and all this without having to
play fast and loose with the existing rules.

But to have this, we need, among other things, good   32
teachers and, beyond them, enlightened educators. I shudder when I read in the *Birmingham* (Alabama) *Post-Herald*
of October 6, 1978, an account of a talk given to eight
hundred English teachers by Dr. Alan C. Purves, vice-president of the National Council of Teachers of English. Dr.
Purves is quoted as saying things like "We are in a situation
with respect to reading where . . . ," and culminating in
the following truly horrifying sentence: "I am going to suggest that when we go back to the basics, I think what we
should be dealing with is our charge to help students to be
more proficient in producing meaningful language — language that says what it means." Notice all the deadwood,
the tautology, the anacoluthon in the first part of that sentence; but notice especially the absurdity of the latter part,
in which the dubious word "meaningful" — a poor relation
of "significant" — is thought to require explaining to an audience of English teachers.

Given such leadership from the N.C.T.E., the time must   33
be at hand when we shall hear — not just "Don't ask for who
the bell rings" (*ask not* and *tolls* being, of course, archaic,
elitist language), but also "It rings for you and I."

*Gary Larson grew up in Tacoma, Washington, and graduated
from Washington State University. "The Far Side" is one of
America's most popular (and offbeat) cartoons.*

THE FAR SIDE   By GARY LARSON

"Ha! The idiots spelled 'surrender' with only one 'r'!"

THE FAR SIDE cartoon by Gary Larson is reprinted by permission of
Chronicle Features, San Francisco, CA.

SHOULD WE HAVE A NATIONAL LANGUAGE?

Richard Rodriguez
Aria: A Memoir of a Bilingual Childhood

Richard Rodriguez, born in 1944 into a Spanish-speaking, Mex-ican-American family, was educated at Stanford, Columbia, and Berkeley. Many of his eloquent essays mix memoir and argument, and many measure the gains and losses that result when English replaces Spanish that is spoken at home. This essay, first published in The American Scholar *(1981), was incorporated into his book* Hunger of Memory *(1982). (For another excerpt from* Hunger of Memory, *see page 700.)*

I remember, to start with, that day in Sacramento, in a   1
California now nearly thirty years past, when I first entered
a classroom — able to understand about fifty stray English
words. The third of four children, I had been preceded by
my older brother and sister to a neighborhood Roman Catholic school. But neither of them had revealed very much
about their classroom experiences. They left each morning
and returned each afternoon, always together, speaking
Spanish as they climbed the five steps to the porch. And
their mysterious books, wrapped in brown shopping-bag
paper, remained on the table next to the door, closed firmly
behind them.

An accident of geography sent me to a school where all   2
my classmates were white and many were the children of
doctors and lawyers and business executives. On that first
day of school, my classmates must certainly have been uneasy to find themselves apart from their families, in the
first institution of their lives. But I was astonished. I was
fated to be the "problem student" in class.

The nun said, in a friendly but oddly impersonal voice: 3
"Boys and girls, this is Richard Rodriguez." (I heard her
sound it out: *Rich-heard Road-ree-guess.*) It was the first

time I had heard anyone say my name in English. "Richard," the nun repeated more slowly, writing my name down in her book. Quickly I turned to see my mother's face dissolve in a watery blur behind the pebbled-glass door.

4   Now, many years later, I hear of something called "bilingual education"—a scheme proposed in the late 1960s by Hispanic-American social activists, later endorsed by a congressional vote. It is a program that seeks to permit non-English-speaking children (many from lower class homes) to use their "family language" as the language of school. Such, at least, is the aim its supporters announce. I hear them, and am forced to say no: It is not possible for a child, any child, ever to use his family's language in school. Not to understand this is to misunderstand the public uses of schooling and to trivialize the nature of intimate life.

5   Memory teaches me what I know of these matters. The boy reminds the adult. I was a bilingual child, but of a certain kind: "socially disadvantaged," the son of working-class parents, both Mexican immigrants.

6   In the early years of my boyhood, my parents coped very well in America. My father had steady work. My mother managed at home. They were nobody's victims. When we moved to a house many blocks from the Mexican-American section of town, they were not intimidated by those two or three neighbors who initially tried to make us unwelcome. ("Keep your brats away from my sidewalk!") But despite all they achieved, or perhaps because they had so much to achieve, they lacked any deep feeling of ease, of belonging in public. They regarded the people at work or in crowds as being very distant from us. Those were the others, *los gringos*. That term was interchangeable in their speech with another, even more telling: *los americanos*.

7   I grew up in a house where the only regular guests were my relations. On a certain day, enormous families of relatives would visit us, and there would be so many people that the noise and the bodies would spill out to the backyard and onto the front porch. Then for weeks no one would come. (If the doorbell rang, it was usually a salesman.) Our house stood apart—gaudy yellow in a row of white bungalows. We were the people with the noisy dog, the people who raised chickens. We were the foreigners on the block. A few neighbors would smile and wave at us. We waved back. But until I was seven years old, I did not know the

name of the old couple living next door or the names of the
kids living across the street.

In public, my father and mother spoke a hesitant, ac-   8
cented, and not always grammatical English. And then they
would have to strain, their bodies tense, to catch the sense
of what was rapidly said by *los gringos*. At home, they returned to Spanish. The language of their Mexican past
sounded in counterpoint to the English spoken in public.
The words would come quickly, with ease. Conveyed
through those sounds was the pleasing, soothing, consoling
reminder that one was at home.

During those years when I was first learning to speak,   9
my mother and father addressed me only in Spanish; in
Spanish I learned to reply. By contrast, English (*inglés*) was
the language I came to associate with gringos, rarely heard
in the house. I learned my first words of English overhearing
my parents speaking to strangers. At six years of age, I
knew just enough words for my mother to trust me on
errands to stores one block away—but no more.

I was then a listening child, careful to hear the very dif-   10
ferent sounds of Spanish and English. Wide-eyed with hearing, I'd listen to sounds more than to words. First, there
were English (gringo) sounds. So many words still were
unknown to me that when the butcher or the lady at the
drugstore said something, exotic polysyllabic sounds would
bloom in the midst of their sentences. Often the speech of
people in public seemed to me very loud, booming with
confidence. The man behind the counter would literally
ask, "What can I do for you?" But by being so firm and
clear, the sound of his voice said that he was a gringo; he
belonged in public society. There were also the high, nasal
notes of middle-class American speech—which I rarely am
conscious of hearing today because I hear them so often,
but could not stop hearing when I was a boy. Crowds at
Safeway or at bus stops were noisy with the birdlike sounds
of *los gringos*. I'd move away from them all—all the chirping
chatter above me.

My own sounds I was unable to hear, but I knew that I   11
spoke English poorly. My words could not extend to form
complete thoughts. And the words I did speak I didn't know
well enough to make distinct sounds. (Listeners would usually lower their heads to hear better what I was trying to
say.) But it was one thing for *me* to speak English with
difficulty; it was more troubling to hear my parents speak-

ing in public: their high-whining vowels and guttural consonants; their sentences that got stuck with "eh" and "ah"
sounds; the confused syntax; the hesitant rhythm of sounds
so different from the way gringos spoke. I'd notice, moreover, that my parents' voices were softer than those of gringos we would meet.

12   I am tempted to say now that none of this mattered. (In
adulthood I am embarrassed by childhood fears.) And, in
a way, it didn't matter very much that my parents could
not speak English with ease. Their linguistic difficulties
had no serious consequences. My mother and father made
themselves understood at the county hospital clinic and at
government offices. And yet, in another way, it mattered
very much. It was unsettling to hear my parents struggle
with English. Hearing them, I'd grow nervous, and my
clutching trust in their protection and power would be
weakened.

13   There were many times like the night at a brightly lit
gasoline station (a blaring white memory) when I stood
uneasily hearing my father talk to a teenage attendant. I
do not recall what they were saying, but I cannot forget
the sounds my father made as he spoke. At one point his
words slid together to form one long word — sounds as confused as the threads of blue and green oil in the puddle
next to my shoes. His voice rushed through what he had
left to say. Toward the end, he reached falsetto notes, appealing to his listener's understanding. I looked away at
the lights of passing automobiles. I tried not to hear any
more. But I heard only too well the attendant's reply, his
calm, easy tones. Shortly afterward, headed for home, I
shivered when my father put his hand on my shoulder. The
very first chance that I got, I evaded his grasp and ran on
ahead into the dark, skipping with feigned boyish exuberance.

14   But then there was Spanish: *español*, the language rarely
heard away from the house; *español*, the language which
seemed to me therefore a private language, my family's
language. To hear its sounds was to feel myself specially
recognized as one of the family, apart from *los otros*. A
simple remark, an inconsequential comment could convey
that assurance. My parents would say something to me and
I would feel embraced by the sounds of their words. Those
sounds said: *I am speaking with ease in Spanish. I am addressing you in words I never use with los gringos. I recognize*

you as someone special, close, like no one outside. You belong
with us. In the family. Ricardo.

At the age of six, well past the time when most middle-   15
class children no longer notice the difference between
sounds uttered at home and words spoken in public, I had
a different experience. I lived in a world compounded of
sounds. I was a child longer than most. I lived in a magical
world, surrounded by sounds both pleasing and fearful. I
shared with my family a language enchantingly private—
different from that used in the city around us.

Just opening or closing the screen door behind me was   16
an important experience. I'd rarely leave home all alone or
without feeling reluctance. Walking down the sidewalk,
under the canopy of tall trees, I'd warily notice the (suddenly) silent neighborhood kids who stood warily watching
me. Nervously, I'd arrive at the grocery store to hear there
the sounds of the gringo, reminding me that in this so-big
world I was a foreigner. But if leaving home was never
routine, neither was coming back. Walking toward our
house, climbing the steps from the sidewalk, in summer
when the front door was open, I'd hear voices beyond the
screen door talking in Spanish. For a second or two I'd stay,
linger there listening. Smiling, I'd hear my mother call out,
saying in Spanish, "Is that you, Richard?" Those were her
words, but all the while her sounds would assure me: *You*
are home now. Come closer inside. With us. "Sí," I'd reply.

Once more inside the house, I would resume my place in   17
the family. The sounds would grow harder to hear. Once
more at home, I would grow less conscious of them. It
required, however, no more than the blurt of the doorbell
to alert me all over again to listen to sounds. The house
would turn instantly quiet while my mother went to the
door. I'd hear her hard English sounds. I'd wait to hear her
voice turn to soft-sounding Spanish, which assured me, as
surely as did the clicking tongue of the lock on the door,
that the stranger was gone.

Plainly it is not healthy to hear such sounds so often. It   18
is not healthy to distinguish public from private sounds so
easily. I remained cloistered by sounds, timid and shy in
public, too dependent on the voices at home. And yet I was
a very happy child when I was at home. I remember many
nights when my father would come back from work, and
I'd hear him call out to my mother in Spanish, sounding
relieved. In Spanish, his voice would sound the light and

free notes that he never could manage in English. Some
nights I'd jump up just hearing his voice. My brother and
I would come running into the room where he was with
our mother. Our laughing (so deep was the pleasure!) became screaming. Like others who feel the pain of public
alienation, we transformed the knowledge of our public
separateness into a consoling reminder of our intimacy.
Excited, our voices joined in a celebration of sounds. *We
are speaking now the way we never speak out in public — we
are together,* the sounds told me. Some nights no one seemed
willing to loosen the hold that sounds had on us. At dinner
we invented new words that sounded Spanish, but made
sense only to us. We pieced together new words by taking,
say, an English verb and giving it Spanish endings. My
mother's instructions at bedtime would be lacquered with
mock-urgent tones. Or a word like *sí*, sounded in several
notes, would convey added measures of feeling. Tongues
lingered around the edges of words, especially fat vowels,
and we happily sounded that military drum roll, the twirling roar of the Spanish *r*. Family language, my family's
sounds: the voices of my parents and sisters and brother.
Their voices insisting: *You belong here. We are family members. Related. Special to one another. Listen!* Voices singing
and sighing, rising and straining, then surging, teeming
with pleasure which burst syllables into fragments of laughter. At times it seemed there was steady quiet only when,
from another room, the rustling whispers of my parents
faded and I edged closer to sleep.

19   Supporters of bilingual education imply today that students like me miss a great deal by not being taught in their
family's language. What they seem not to recognize is that,
as a socially disadvantaged child, I regarded Spanish as a
private language. It was a ghetto language that deepened
and strengthened my feeling of public separateness. What
I needed to learn in school was that I had the right, and
the obligation, to speak the public language. The odd truth
is that my first-grade classmates could have become bilingual, in the conventional sense of the word, more easily
than I. Had they been taught early (as upper middle-class
children often are taught) a "second language" like Spanish
or French, they could have regarded it simply as another
public language. In my case, such bilingualism could not
have been so quickly achieved. What I did not believe was
that I could speak a single public language.

Without question, it would have pleased me to have heard   20
my teachers address me in Spanish when I entered the
classroom. I would have felt much less afraid. I would have
imagined that my instructors were somehow "related" to
me; I would indeed have heard their Spanish as my family's
language. I would have trusted them and responded with
ease. But I would have delayed — postponed for how long? —
having to learn the language of public society. I would have
evaded — and for how long? — learning the great lesson of
school: that I had a public identity.

Fortunately, my teachers were unsentimental about their   21
responsibility. What they understood was that I needed to
speak public English. So their voices would search me out,
asking me questions. Each time I heard them I'd look up
in surprise to see a nun's face frowning at me. I'd mumble,
not really meaning to answer. The nun would persist.
"Richard, stand up. Don't look at the floor. Speak up. Speak
to the entire class, not just to me!" But I couldn't believe
English could be my language to use. (In part, I did not
want to believe it.) I continued to mumble. I resisted the
teacher's demands. (Did I somehow suspect that once I
learned this public language my family life would be
changed?) Silent, waiting for the bell to sound, I remained
dazed, diffident, afraid.

Because I wrongly imagined that English was intrinsically   22
a public language and Spanish was intrinsically private, I
easily noted the difference between classroom language and
the language at home. At school, words were directed to a
general audience of listeners. ("Boys and girls . . .") Words
were meaningfully ordered. And the point was not self-expression alone, but to make oneself understood by many
others. The teacher quizzed: "Boys and girls, why do we
use that word in this sentence? Could we think of a better
word to use there? Would the sentence change its meaning
if the words were differently arranged? Isn't there a better
way of saying much the same thing?" (I couldn't say. I
wouldn't try to say.)

Three months passed. Five. A half year. Unsmiling, ever   23
watchful, my teachers noted my silence. They began to
connect my behavior with the slow progress my brother
and sisters were making. Until, one Saturday morning,
three nuns arrived at the house to talk to our parents. Stiffly
they sat on the blue living-room sofa. From the doorway
of another room, spying on the visitors, I noted the incon-

gruity, the clash of two worlds, the faces and voices of school intruding upon the familiar setting of home. I overheard one voice gently wondering, "Do your children speak only Spanish at home, Mrs. Rodriguez?" While another voice added, "That Richard especially seems so timid and shy."

24   *That Rich-heard!*

25   With great tact, the visitors continued, "Is it possible for you and your husband to encourage your children to practice their English when they are home?" Of course my parents complied. What would they not do for their children's well-being? And how could they question the Church's authority which those women represented? In an instant they agreed to give up the language (the sounds) which had revealed and accentuated our family's closeness. The moment after the visitors left, the change was observed."*Ahora*, speak to us only *en inglés*," my father and mother told us.

26   At first, it seemed a kind of game. After dinner each night, the family gathered together to practice "our" English. It was still then *inglés*, a language foreign to us, so we felt drawn to it as strangers. Laughing, we would try to define words we could not pronounce. We played with strange English sounds, often overanglicizing our pronunciations. And we filled the smiling gaps of our sentences with familiar Spanish sounds. But that was cheating, somebody shouted, and everyone laughed.

27   In school, meanwhile, like my brother and sisters, I was required to attend a daily tutoring session. I needed a full year of this special work. I also needed my teachers to keep my attention from straying in class by calling out, *"Richheard"* — their English voices slowly loosening the ties to my other name, with its three notes, *Ri-car-do*. Most of all, I needed to hear my mother and father speak to me in a moment of seriousness in "broken" — suddenly heartbreaking — English. This scene was inevitable. One Saturday morning I entered the kitchen where my parents were talking, but I did not realize that they were talking in Spanish until, the moment they saw me, their voices changed and they began speaking English. The gringo sounds they uttered startled me. Pushed me away. In that moment of trivial misunderstanding and profound insight, I felt my throat twisted by unsounded grief. I simply turned and left the room. But I had no place to escape to where I could grieve in Spanish. My brother and sisters were speaking English in another part of the house.

Again and again in the days following, as I grew increas- 28
ingly angry, I was obliged to hear my mother and father
encouraging me: "Speak to us *en inglés.*" Only then did I
determine to learn classroom English. Thus, sometime afterward it happened: one day in school, I raised my hand
to volunteer an answer to a question. I spoke out in a loud
voice and I did not think it remarkable when the entire
class understood. That day I moved very far from being the
disadvantaged child I had been only days earlier. Taken
hold at last was the belief, the calming assurance, that I
belonged in public.

Shortly after, I stopped hearing the high, troubling 29
sounds of *los gringos.* A more and more confident speaker
of English, I didn't listen to how strangers sounded when
they talked to me. With so many English-speaking people
around me, I no longer heard American accents. Conversations quickened. Listening to persons whose voices sounded
eccentrically pitched, I might note their sounds for a few
seconds, but then I'd concentrate on what they were saying.
Now when I heard someone's tone of voice—angry or questioning or sarcastic or happy or sad—I didn't distinguish
it from the words it expressed. Sound and word were thus
tightly wedded. At the end of each day I was often bemused,
and always relieved, to realize how "soundless," though
crowded with words, my day in public had been. An eight-
year-old boy, I finally came to accept what had been technically true since my birth: I was an American citizen.

But diminished by then was the special feeling of close- 30
ness at home. Gone was the desperate, urgent, intense feeling of being at home among those with whom I felt intimate.
Our family remained a loving family, but one greatly
changed. We were no longer so close, no longer bound
tightly together by the knowledge of our separateness from
los gringos. Neither my older brother nor my sisters rushed
home after school any more. Nor did I. When I arrived
home, often there would be neighborhood kids in the house.
Or the house would be empty of sounds.

Following the dramatic Americanization of their chil- 31
dren, even my parents grew more publicly confident—especially my mother. First she learned the names of all the
people on the block. Then she decided we needed to have
a telephone in our house. My father, for his part, continued
to use the word gringo, but it was no longer charged with
bitterness or distrust. Stripped of any emotional content,
the word simply became a name for those Americans not

of Hispanic descent. Hearing him, sometimes, I wasn't sure if he was pronouncing the Spanish word *gringo*, or saying gringo in English.

32   There was a new silence at home. As we children learned more and more English, we shared fewer and fewer words with our parents. Sentences needed to be spoken slowly when one of us addressed our mother or father. Often the parent wouldn't understand. The child would need to repeat himself. Still the parent misunderstood. The young voice, frustrated, would end up saying, "Never mind" — the subject was closed. Dinners would be noisy with the clinking of knives and forks against dishes. My mother would smile softly between her remarks; my father, at the other end of the table, would chew and chew his food while he stared over the heads of his children.

33   My mother! My father! After English became my primary language, I no longer knew what words to use in addressing my parents. The old Spanish words (those tender accents of sound) I had earlier used — *mamá* and *papá* — I couldn't use any more. They would have been all-too-painful reminders of how much had changed in my life. On the other hand, the words I heard neighborhood kids call their parents seemed equally unsatisfactory. "Mother" and "father," "ma," "papa," "pa," "dad," "pop" (how I hated the all-American sound of that last word) — all these I felt were unsuitable terms of address for *my* parents. As a result, I never used them at home. Whenever I'd speak to my parents, I would try to get their attention by looking at them. In public conversations, I'd refer to them as my "parents" or my "mother" and "father."

34   My mother and father, for their part, responded differently, as their children spoke to them less. My mother grew restless, seemed troubled and anxious at the scarceness of words exchanged in the house. She would question me about my day when I came home from school. She smiled at my small talk. She pried at the edges of my sentences to get me to say something more. ("What . . . ?") She'd join conversations she overheard, but her intrusions often stopped her children's talking. By contrast, my father seemed to grow reconciled to the new quiet. Though his English somewhat improved, he tended more and more to retire into silence. At dinner he spoke very little. One night his children and even his wife helplessly giggled at his garbled English pronunciation of the Catholic "Grace Before

Meals." Thereafter he made his wife recite the prayer at the start of each meal, even on formal occasions when there were guests in the house.

Hers became the public voice of the family. On official   35
business it was she, not my father, who would usually talk to strangers on the phone or in stores. We children grew so accustomed to his silence that years later we would routinely refer to his "shyness." (My mother often tried to explain: both of his parents died when he was eight. He was raised by an uncle who treated him as little more than a menial servant. He was never encouraged to speak. He grew up alone—a man of few words.) But I realized my father was not shy whenever I'd watch him speaking Spanish with relatives. Using Spanish, he was quickly effusive. Especially when talking with other men, his voice would spark, flicker, flare alive with varied sounds. In Spanish he expressed ideas and feelings he rarely revealed when speaking English. With firm Spanish sounds he conveyed a confidence and authority that English would never allow him.

The silence at home, however, was not simply the result   36
of fewer words passing between parents and children. More profound for me was the silence created by my inattention to sounds. At about the time I no longer bothered to listen with care to the sounds of English in public, I grew careless about listening to the sounds made by the family when they spoke. Most of the time I would hear someone speaking at home and didn't distinguish his sounds from the words people uttered in public. I didn't even pay much attention to my parents' accented and ungrammatical speech—at least not at home. Only when I was with them in public would I become alert to their accents. But even then their sounds caused me less and less concern. For I was growing increasingly confident of my own public identity.

I would have been happier about my public success had   37
I not recalled, sometimes, what it had been like earlier, when my family conveyed its intimacy through a set of conveniently private sounds. Sometimes in public, hearing a stranger, I'd hark back to my lost past. A Mexican farm worker approached me one day downtown. He wanted directions to some place. "*Hijito, . . .*" he said. And his voice stirred old longings. Another time I was standing beside my mother in the visiting room of a Carmelite convent, before the dense screen which rendered the nuns shadowy

figures. I heard several of them speaking Spanish in their busy, singsong, overlapping voices, assuring my mother that, yes, yes, we were remembered, all our family was remembered, in their prayers. Those voices echoed faraway family sounds. Another day a dark-faced old woman touched my shoulder lightly to steady herself as she boarded a bus. She murmured something to me I couldn't quite comprehend. Her Spanish voice came near, like the face of a never-before-seen relative in the instant before I was kissed. That voice, like so many of the Spanish voices I'd hear in public, recalled the golden age of my childhood.

38   Bilingual educators say today that children lose a degree of "individuality" by becoming assimilated into public society. (Bilingual schooling is a program popularized in the seventies, that decade when middle-class "ethnics" began to resist the process of assimilation — the "American melting pot.") But the bilingualists oversimplify when they scorn the value and necessity of assimilation. They do not seem to realize that a person is individualized in two ways. So they do not realize that, while one suffers a diminished sense of *private* individuality by being assimilated into public society, such assimilation makes possible the achievement of *public* individuality.

39   Simplistically again, the bilingualists insist that a student should be reminded of his difference from others in mass society, of his "heritage." But they equate mere separateness with individuality. The fact is that only in private — with intimates — is separateness from the crowd a prerequisite for individuality; an intimate "tells" me that I am unique, unlike all others, apart from the crowd. In public, by contrast, full individuality is achieved, paradoxically, by those who are able to consider themselves members of the crowd. Thus it happened for me. Only when I was able to think of myself as an American, no longer an alien in gringo society, could I seek the rights and opportunities necessary for full public individuality. The social and political advantages I enjoy as a man began on the day I came to believe that my name is indeed *Rich-heard Road-ree-guess*. It is true that my public society today is often impersonal; in fact, my public society is usually mass society. But despite the anonymity of the crowd, and despite the fact that the individuality I achieve in public is often tenuous — because it depends on my being one in a crowd — I

celebrate the day I acquired my new name. Those middle-class ethnics who scorn assimilation seem to me filled with decadent self-pity, obsessed by the burden of public life. Dangerously, they romanticize public separateness and trivialize the dilemma of those who are truly socially disadvantaged.

If I rehearse here the changes in my private life after my   40
Americanization, it is finally to emphasize a public gain. The loss implies the gain. The house I returned to each afternoon was quiet. Intimate sounds no longer greeted me at the door. Inside there were other noises. The telephone rang. Neighborhood kids ran past the door of the bedroom where I was reading my schoolbooks — covered with brown shopping-bag paper. Once I learned the public language, it would never again be easy for me to hear intimate family voices. More and more of my day was spent hearing words, not sounds. But that may only be a way of saying that on the day I raised my hand in class and spoke loudly to an entire roomful of faces, my childhood started to end.

Victor Villanueva, Jr.

Whose Voice Is It Anyway?
Rodriguez' Speech in Retrospect

Victor Villanueva, Jr., who teaches at Northern Arizona University, tells a lot about himself in the following essay, which he wrote in 1988 for English Journal, *a magazine for high school and elementary school English teachers. Villanueva's essay appeared in the same issue as the ones by James Stalker (pg. 176), Trudy Sundberg (pg. 187), and Roseann Duenas Gonzalez, Alice A. Schott, and Victoria Vasquez (pg. 189).*

During the 1986 annual conference of the NCTE (National   1
Council of Teachers of English) I attended a luncheon sponsored by the secondary section. Richard Rodriguez, author of *Hunger of Memory*, was the guest speaker. He spoke of how he came to be an articulate speaker of this standard dialect, and he spoke of the conclusions concerning lan-

guage learning that his experiences had brought him to. He was impressive. I was taken by his quiet eloquence. His stage presence recalled Olivier's Hamlet. He spoke well. But for all his eloquence and his studied stage presence, I was nevertheless surprised by the audience's response, an enthusiastic, uncritical acceptance, marked by a long, loud standing ovation. I was surprised because he had blurred distinctions between language and culture, between his experiences and those more typical of the minority in America, between the history of the immigrant and that of the minority, in a way that I had thought would raise more than a few eyebrows. Yet all he raised was the audience to its feet.

2   In retrospect, I think I can understand the rave reception. The message he so softly delivered relieved us all of some anxiety. Classroom teachers' shoulders stoop under the weight of the paper load. They take 150 students through writing and grammar, spelling and punctuation. Within those same forty-five-minute spurts they also work on reading: drama, poetry, literature, the great issues in literature. After that, there's the writers' club or the school paper or the yearbook, coaching volleyball or producing the school play. And throughout it all, they are to remain sensitive to the language of the nonstandard or non-English speaker. They are not really told how—just "be sensitive," while parents, the media, sometimes it seems the whole world, shake their fingers at them for not doing something about America's literacy problems. Richard Rodriguez told the teachers to continue to be sensitive but to forget about doing anything special. The old ways may be painful, but they really are best. There is a kind of violence to the melting pot, he said, but it is necessary. He said that this linguistic assimilation is like alchemy, initially destructive perhaps but magical, creating something new and greater than what was. Do as you have always done. And the teachers sighed.

3   Richard Rodriguez is the authority, after all: a bilingual child of immigrant parents, a graduate of two of the nation's more prestigious schools, Stanford and Berkeley, an English teacher, the well-published author of numerous articles and a well-received, well-anthologized book. He knows. And he says that the teachers who insisted on a particular linguistic form can be credited with his fame. But what is it, really, that has made him famous? He is a fine writer; of that there can be no doubt. But it is his message that has

brought him fame, a message that states that the minority
is no different than any other immigrant who came to this
country not knowing its culture or its language, leaving
much of the old country behind to become part of this new
one, and in becoming part of America subtly changing what
it means to be American. The American who brought his
beef and pudding from England became the American of
the frankfurter, the bologna sandwich, pizza. Typically
American foods—like typical Americans—partake of the
world.

At the luncheon, Richard Rodriguez spoke of a TV ad for   4
Mexican-style Velveeta, "the blandest of American cheeses,"
he called it, now speckled with peppers. This cultural contrast, said Rodriguez, demonstrated how Mexico—no less
than England or Germany—is part of America.

But I think it shows how our times face a different kind   5
of assimilation. Let's put aside for the moment questions
as to why, if Mexicans really are being assimilated, they
have taken so much longer than other groups, especially
since Mexicans were already part of the West and Southwest when the West and Southwest became part of America.
Let's look, rather, at the hyphen in Mexican-Velveeta. Who
speaks of a German-American sausage, for instance? It's a
hot dog. Yet tacos remain ethnic, sold under a mock Spanish
mission bell or a sombrero. You will find refried beans
under "ethnic foods" in the supermarket, not among other
canned beans, though items as foreign-sounding as sauer-
kraut are simply canned vegetables. Mexican foods, even
when as Americanized as the taco salad or Mexican-Velveeta, remain distinctly Mexican.[1]

And like the ethnic food, some ethnic minorities have not   6
been assimilated in the way the Ellis Islanders were. The
fires of the melting pot have cooled. No more soup. America's more a stew today. The difference is the difference
between the immigrant and the minority, a difference having to do with how each, the immigrant and the minority,

---

[1]Mexican food is not the only ethnic food on the market, of course. Asian
and Mediterranean foods share the shelves. But this too is telling, since
Asians alone had had restricted access to the US before the country ended
its Open Door Immigration Policy. When the US closed its doors in 1924,
it was to regulate the flow of less desirable "new immigrants"—the Eastern
and Southern Europeans who remain "ethnic" to this day. See Oscar
Handlin's *Race in American Life*, New York: Anchor, 1957.

came to be Americans, the difference between choice and colonization. Those who emigrated from Europe chose to leave unacceptable conditions in search of better. Choice, I realize, is a tricky word in this context: religious persecution, debtor's prison, potato famine, fascism, foreign takeover, when compared with a chance at prosperity and self-determination doesn't seem to make for much of a choice; yet most people apparently remained in their homelands despite the intolerable, while the immigrants did leave, and in leaving chose to sever ties with friends and families, created a distance between themselves and their histories, cultures, languages, There is something heroic in this. It's a heroism shared by the majority of Americans.

7   But choice hardly entered into most minorities' decisions to become American. Most of us recognize this when it comes to Blacks or American Indians. Slavery, forcible displacement, and genocide are fairly clear-cut. Yet the circumstances by which most minorities became Americans are no less clear-cut. The minority became an American almost by default, as part of the goods in big-time real estate deals or as some of the spoils of war. What is true for the Native American applies to the Alaska Native, the Pacific Islander (including the Asian), Mexican-Americans, Puerto Ricans. Puerto Rico was part of Christopher Columbus' great discovery, Arawaks and Boriquens among his "Indians," a real-estate coup for the Queen of Spain. Then one day in 1898, the Puerto Ricans who had for nearly four hundred years been made proud to be the offspring of Spain, so much so that their native Arawak and Boricua languages and ways were virtually gone, found themselves the property of the United States, property without the rights and privileges of citizenship until — conveniently — World War I. But citizenship notwithstanding, Puerto Rico remains essentially a colony today.[2]

8   One day in 1845 and in 1848 other descendants of Spain who had all but lost their Indian identities found themselves Americans. These were the long-time residents and landowners of the Republic of Texas and the California Republic: the area from Texas to New Mexico, Arizona, Utah, and

---

[2]Nor is it a simple matter of Puerto Rico's deciding whether it wants to remain a commonwealth, gaining statehood, or independence. The interests of US industry, of the US military, and the social and economic ramifications of Puerto Rico's widespread poverty complicate matters.

California. Residents in the newly established US territories were given the option to relocate to Mexico or to remain on their native lands, with the understanding that should they remain they would be guaranteed American Constitutional rights. Those who stayed home saw their rights not very scrupulously guarded, falling victim over time to displacement, dislocation, and forced expatriation. There is something tragic in losing a long-established birthright, tragic but not heroic — especially not heroic to those whose ancestors had fled their homelands rather than acknowledge external rule.

The immigrant gave up much in the name of freedom — and for the sake of dignity. For the Spanish-speaking minority in particular, the freedom to be American without once again relinquishing one's ancestry is also a matter of dignity.   9

This is not to say that Richard Rodriguez forfeited his dignity in choosing not to be Ricardo. The Mexican's status includes not only the descendants of the West and Southwest, Spanish-speaking natives to America, but also immigrants and the descendants of immigrants. Richard Rodriguez is more the immigrant than the minority. His father, he told us, had left his native Mexico for Australia. He fell in love along the way, eventually settling with wife and family in Sacramento. America was not his father's first choice for a new home perhaps, but he did choose to leave his homeland in much the same way European immigrants had. The Rodriguezes no doubt felt the immigrants' hardships, the drive to assimilate, a drive compounded perhaps by the association in their and others' minds between them and the undocumented migrant worker or between them and the minority.   10

And it is this confusion of immigrant and minority in Richard Rodriguez with which we must contend. His message rings true to the immigrant heritage of his audience because it happens to be the immigrant's story. It is received as if it were a new story because it is confused with this story of the minority. The complexities of the minority are rendered simple — not easy — but easily understood.   11

Others tell the story of the minority. I think, for instance, of Piri Thomas and Tato Laviera, since theirs are stories of Puerto Ricans. My own parents had immigrated to New York from Puerto Rico, though not in the way of most. My mother, an American, a US citizen like all Puerto Ricans,   12 fair-skinned, and proud of her European descent, had been sold into servitude to a wealthy Chicago family. My father, recently discharged from the US Army, followed my mother, rescued his sweetheart, and together they fled to New York. I was born a year later, 1948.

13   My mother believed in the traditional idea of assimilation. She and my father would listen to radio shows in English and try to read the American newspapers. They spoke to me in two languages from the start. The local parochial school's tuition was a dollar a month, so I was spared PS 168. Rodriguez tells of nuns coming to his home to suggest that the family speak English at home. For Rodriguez this was something of a turning point in his life; intimacy lost, participation in the public domain gained. A public language would dominate, the painful path to his assimilation, the path to his eventual success. A nun spoke to my parents, too, when I was in kindergarten. I spoke with an accent, they were told. They should speak to me in English. My mother could only laugh: my English was as it was *because* they spoke to me in English. The irony reinforced our intimacy while I continued to learn the "public language."

14   There is more to assimilating than learning the language. I earned my snacks at the Saturday matinee by reading the credits on the screen. I enjoyed parsing sentences, was good at it too. I was a Merriam-Webster spelling bee champ. I was an "A" student who nevertheless took a special Saturday course on how to do well on the standardized test that would gain me entry to the local Catholic high school. I landed in the public vo-tech high school, slotted for a trade. Jarapolk, whose parents had fled the Ukraine, made the good school; so did Marie Engels, the daughter of German immigrants. Lana Walker, a Black girl whose brains I envied, got as far as the alternate list. I don't recall any of the Black or Puerto Rican kids from my class getting in. I never finished high school, despite my being a bright boy who knew the public language intimately.

15   I don't like thinking minorities were intentionally excluded from the better school. I would prefer to think minorities didn't do as well because we were less conscious than the immigrants of the cultural distances we had to travel to be truly Americans. We were Americans, after all, not even seeing ourselves as separated by language by the time most of us got to the eighth grade. I spoke Spanglish

at home, a hybrid English and Spanish common to New York Puerto Ricans; I spoke the Puerto Rican version of Black English in the streets, and as far as I knew, I spoke something close to the standard dialect in the classroom. We thought ourselves Americans, assimilated. We didn't know about cultural bias in standardized tests. I still don't do well on standardized tests.

A more pointed illustration of the difference between the minority and the immigrant comes by way of a lesson from my father. I was around ten. We went uptown one day, apartment hunting. I don't recall how he chose the place. He asked about an apartment in his best English, the sounds of a Spanish speaker attempting his best English. No vacancies. My father thanked the man, then casually slipped into the customary small talk of the courteous exit. During the talk my father mentioned our coming from Spain. By the end of the chat a unit became available. Maybe my father's pleasing personality had gained us entry. More likely, Puerto Rican stereotypes had kept us out. The immigrant could enter where the minority could not. My father's English hadn't improved in the five minutes it had taken for the situation to change. 16

Today I sport a doctorate in English from a major university, study and teach rhetoric at another university, do research in and teach composition, continue to enjoy and teach English literature. I live in an all-American city in the heart of America. And I know I am not quite assimilated. In one weekend I was asked if I was Iranian one day and East Indian the next. "No," I said. "You have an accent," I was told. Yet tape recordings and passing comments throughout the years have told me that though there is a "back East" quality to my voice, there isn't much of New York to it anymore, never mind the Black English of my younger years or the Spanish of my youngest. My "accent" was in my not sounding midwestern, which does have a discernable, though not usually a pronounced, regional quality. And my "accent," I would guess, was in my "foreign" features (which pale alongside the brown skin of Richard Rodriguez). 17

Friends think I make too much of such incidents. Minority hypersensitivity, they say. They desensitize me (and display their liberal attitudes) with playful jabs at Puerto Ricans: greasy hair jokes, knife-in-pocket jokes, spicy food jokes (and Puerto Ricans don't even eat hot foods, unless we're 18 eating Mexican or East Indian foods). If language alone were the secret to assimilation, the rate of Puerto Rican and Mexican success would be greater, I would think. So many Mexican-Americans and Puerto Ricans remain in the barrios — even those who are monolingual, who have never known Spanish. If language alone were the secret, wouldn't the secret have gotten out long before Richard Rodriguez recorded his memoirs? In fact, haven't we always worked with the assumption that language learning — oral and written — is the key to parity, even as parity continues to elude so many?

19   I'm not saying the assumption is wrong. I think teachers are right to believe in the potential power of language. We want our students to be empowered. That's why we read professional journals. That's why we try to accommodate the pronouncements of linguists. That's why we listen to the likes of Richard Rodriguez. But he spoke more of the English teacher's power than the empowerment of the student. "Listen to the sound of my voice," he said. He asked the audience to forget his brown skin and listen to his voice, his "unaccented voice." "This is your voice," he told the teachers. Better that we, teachers at all levels, give students the means to find their own voices, voices that don't have to ask that we ignore what we cannot ignore, voices that speak of their brown or yellow or red or black skin with pride and without need for bravado or hostility, voices that can recognize and exploit the conventions we have agreed to as the standards of written discourse — without necessarily accepting the ideology of those for whom the standard dialect is the language of home as well as commerce, for whom the standard dialect is as private as it is public, to use Rodriguez' terms.

20   Rodriguez said at the luncheon that he was not speaking of pedagogy as much as of ideology. He was. It is an ideology which grew out of the memoirs of an immigrant boy confronting contrasts, a child accommodating his circumstances. He remembers a brown boy in a white middle-class school and is forced to say no to bilingual education. His classmates were the descendants of other immigrants, the products of assimilation, leading him to accept the traditional American ideology of a multiculturalism that manifests as one new culture and language, a culture and language which encompasses and transcends any one culture. I remember a brown boy among other brown boys and

girls, blacks, and olives, and variations on white, and must agree with Richard that bilingualism in the classroom would have been impractical. But my classmates were in the process of assimilation—Polish, German, Ukrainian, and Irish children, the first of their families to enter American schools; my classmates were also Black and Puerto Rican. It seemed to this boy's eyes that the immigrants would move on but the minority would stay, that the colonized do not melt. Today I do not hear of the problems in educating new immigrants, but the problems of Black literacy continue to make the news. And I hear of an eighty per cent dropout rate among Puerto Ricans in Boston, of Mexicans in the Rio Grande Valley, where the dropout rate exceeds seventy per cent, of places where English and the education system do not address the majority—Spanish speakers for whom menial labor has been the tradition and is apparently the future. I must ask how bilingual education in such situations. One person's experiences must remain one person's, applicable to many others, perhaps, but not all others. Simple, monolithic, universal solutions simply can't work in a complex society.

When it comes to the nonstandard speaker, for instance, 21 we are torn between the findings of linguists and the demands of the marketplace. Our attempts at preparing students for the marketplace only succeed in alienating nonstandard speakers, we are told. Our attempts at accommodating their nonstandard dialects, we fear, only succeed in their being barred from the marketplace. So we go back to the basics. Or else we try to change their speech without alienating them, in the process perhaps sensing that our relativism might smack of condescension. Limiting the student's language to the playground and home still speaks of who's right and who's wrong, who holds the power. I would rather we left speaking dialects relatively alone (truly demonstrating a belief in the legitimacy of the nonstandard). The relationship between speaking and writing is complex, as the debate sparked by Thomas Farrell has made clear. My own research and studies, as well as my personal experiences, suggest that exposure to writing and reading affects speaking. My accent changes, it seems, with every book I read. We don't have to give voices to students. If we give them pen and paper and have them read the printed page aloud, no matter what their grade, they'll discover their own voices.

22   And if we let the printed page offer a variety of world
views, of ideologies, those voices should gather the power
we wish them to have. Booker T. Washington, Martin
Luther King, Jr., W. E. B. DuBois all wrote with eloquence.
Each presents a different world view. Maxine Hong Kings-
ton's "voice" resounds differently from Frank Chin's.
Ernesto Galarza saw a different world than Richard
Rodriguez. Rodriguez' is only one view, one voice. Yet it's
his voice which seems to resound the loudest. Rodriguez
himself provided the reason why this is so. He said at the
luncheon that the individual's story, the biography or autobiography, has universal appeal because it strikes at
experiences we have in common. The immigrant's story
has the most in common with the majority.

23   Rodriguez implied that he didn't feel much kinship to
minority writers. He said he felt a special bond with D. H.
Lawrence. It seems appropriate that Rodriguez, who writes
of his alienation from family in becoming part of the
mainstream, would turn to Lawrence. Lawrence, too, was
a teacher turned writer. Lawrence, too, felt alienated from
his working-class background. It was Lawrence who argued, in "Reflections on the Death of the Porcupine," that
equality is not achievable; Lawrence who co-opted, left the
mastered to join the masters. Is this what we want for our
minority students? True, Lawrence's mastery of the English
language cannot be gainsaid. I would be proud to have a
Lawrence credit me with his voice, would appreciate his
acknowledging my efforts as a teacher, and would surely
applaud his accomplishment. But I would rather share
credit in a W. B. Yeats, Anglo and Irish, assimilated but
with a well-fed memory of his ancestry, master of the English language, its beauty, its traditions—and voice of the
colony.

Walter Darlington Huddleston

On Behalf of a Constitutional Amendment to Make English the Official Language of the United States

Walter Darlington Huddleston (born 1926), a Kentuckian, served in the United States Senate from 1973–1985. In 1983 he delivered the following speech to his colleagues; it advocates a constitutional amendment to establish English as the official language of the United States.

Mr. President, the remarks I am about to make will be 1
readily understood by my distinguished colleagues in the Congress. They will be understood by my constituents in Kentucky. They will be understood by the journalists in the press gallery, and by most of their readers across the country.

No simultaneous interpreters will be needed for those in 2
this chamber, and no translators will be needed for most of those who will be reading these words in the *Congressional Record*.

In order to guarantee that this current state of affairs 3
endures, as it has for over two hundred years, I am introducing today a constitutional amendment to make English the official language of the United States.

The amendment addresses something so basic, so very 4
fundamental to our sense of identity as Americans, that some, who are in full agreement with the objectives of this amendment, will nevertheless question the necessity for it. So widely held is the assumption that English already is our national language, that the notion of stating this in our national charter may seem like restating the obvious. However, I can assure my colleagues that this is not the case and that the need for a constitutional amendment grows stronger every day.

Almost alone among the world's very large and populous 5
nations, the United States enjoys the blessings of one primary language, spoken and understood by most of its citizens. The previously unquestioned acceptance of this language by immigrants from every linguistic and cultural background has enabled us to come together as one people.

It has allowed us to discuss our differences, to argue about our problems and to compromise on solutions. It has allowed us to develop a stable and cohesive society that is the envy of many fractured ones, without imposing any strict standards of homogeneity, or even bothering to designate the language, which is ours by custom, as the Nation's official one.

6   As a nation of immigrants, our great strength has been drawn from our ability to assimilate vast numbers of people from many different cultures and ethnic groups into a nation of people that can work together with cooperation and understanding. This process was often referred to as the melting pot and in the past it has been seen as an almost magical concept that helped to make the United States the greatest nation on Earth.

7   But for the last fifteen years, we have experienced a growing resistance to the acceptance of our historic language, an antagonistic questioning of the melting pot philosophy that has traditionally helped speed newcomers into the American mainstream.

8   Initially, the demands to make things easier for the newcomers seemed modest enough; and a generous people, appreciative of cultural diversity, was willing to make some allowances. For example, the English language requirements for naturalization were removed for elderly immigrants living here for twenty years who were still unable to meet them; and the use of a child's home language in the school setting was encouraged, in a well-intentioned attempt to soften the pain of adjustment from the home to the English-speaking society that school represents.

9   However, the demands have sharply escalated, and so has the tone in which they are presented. Bilingual education has gradually lost its role as a transitional way of teaching English, and now mandates a bicultural component. This mandate has been primarily shaped and promoted by the federal government. The unfortunate result is that thousands of immigrant and nonimmigrant children are languishing in near-permanent bilingual/bicultural programs, kept in a state of prolonged confusion suspended between two worlds, and not understanding what is expected of them. They and their parents are given false hopes that their cultural traditions can be fully maintained in this country, and that the mastery of English is not so important, after all.

10   This change in attitude was aptly described by Theodore

H. White in his book *America in Search of Itself* wherein he stated:

> Some Hispanics have, however, made a demand never voiced by immigrants before: that the United States, in effect, officially recognize itself as a bicultural, bilingual nation. . . . [They] demand that the United States become a bilingual country, with all children entitled to be taught in the language of their heritage, at public expense. No better hymn to the American tradition has ever been written than *The Education of Hyman Kaplan*, by Leo Rosten, which describes with tears and laughter the efforts of the earlier immigrants . . . to learn the language of the country in which they wished to live. In New York today, forty years later, Hispanic entitlement has created a college, Hostos Community College — supported by public taxes — which is officially bilingual; half its students receive instruction primarily in Spanish, as they strive to escape from the subculture of the Spanish ghetto. Bilingualism is an awkward word — but it has torn apart communities from Canada to Brittany, from Belgium to India. It expresses not a sense of tolerance but a demand for divisions.

This misdirected public policy of bilingualism has been   11
created primarily by the federal government, at the insistence of special interest groups, and it continues today because elected officials do not want to run the risk of taking a position that could, in some way, offend these groups. An example of how far this special interest influence reaches can be seen by President Reagan's reversal on the issue. At the beginning of his administration he attempted to kill the bilingual program; now he is embracing the concept.

Over the last few years the federal government has spent   12
approximately $1 billion on the bilingual education program and this year alone it cost $139 million. What we have bought with this money is a program that strives to keep separate cultural identities rather than a program that strives to teach English. It is a program which ignores the basic fact that in order to learn another language the student must talk, read and use that language on a regular basis.

The failure of bilingual education programs to teach chil-   13
dren how to speak English in the shortest time has been documented by a study done at the U.S. Department of Education and by the recent report of the Twentieth Cen-

tury Fund Task Force on Federal Elementary and Secondary Education Policy. The latter report stated unequivocally that:

> The Task Force recommends that the federal government clearly state that the most important objective of elementary and secondary education in the United States is the development of literacy in the English language. . . .
> The Task Force recommends that federal funds now going to the bilingual program be used to teach non-English-speaking children how to speak, read, and write English.

14   Even though the bilingual education program has received failing marks by many reputable educators, it still survives because it is a political issue rather than an educational issue. What this means is that we will continue to finance an expensive bilingual program that does more to preserve cultural identities than it does to teach children to speak English.

15   In the area of voting rights we have also formulated a national policy that encourages voting citizens not to learn to speak English. The Voting Rights Act, which was reauthorized in 1982, requires bilingual ballots if more than 5 percent of the citizens of voting age in a jurisdiction are members of specified language minority groups and the illiteracy rate is higher than the national rate. As a result bilingual ballots are required by federal law to be provided in 30 states — even if there is no demand for them.

16   In essence, we have gone far beyond providing a necessary service on a temporary basis; and, we are now engaged in actively encouraging the use of bilingual ballots, even though in many cases they may not be needed. The wisdom of this policy is clearly lacking when you consider that the vast bulk of political debate, whether it is in the printed press or the electronic media, is conducted in English. By failing to provide a positive incentive for voting citizens to learn English, we are actually denying them full participation in the political process. Instead, we are making them dependent upon a few interpreters or go-betweens for information as to how they should vote. Although this process helps to preserve minority voting blocks, it seriously undercuts the democratic concept that every voting individual should be as fully informed as possible about the issues and the candidates.

In many parts of the country foreign language ballots are 17
under attack. In San Francisco, a local initiative petition
has been filed urging that local governments be allowed to
print ballots in English only. In that area ballots are now
printed in English, Spanish, Chinese, and because of the
new census figures, Tagalog ballots will probably be printed
in the future.

There are other less prominent provisions of federal law 18
which now require the use of foreign languages. For example, 28 U.S.C. 1827 requires the Director of the Administrative Office of the U.S. courts to establish a program for the
use of foreign language interpreters in federal civil and
criminal proceedings for parties whose primary language
is other than English; 42 U.S.C. 254 requires the use of
foreign language personnel in connection with federally
funded migrant and community health centers; and 42
U.S.C. 4577 requires the use of foreign language personnel
in the alcohol abuse and treatment programs. Although I
can understand that this kind of assistance is helpful, the
fact that it must be legislated strongly indicates that we
are failing miserably in our efforts to teach immigrants and
many of our native born how to speak, read and write English.

The federal laws requiring the use of interpreters and 19
foreign languages are merely the tip of the iceberg. I recently sent a request to all of the state governors and the
major federal agencies asking for information regarding
non-English forms and publications that their offices produce, which are intended for use in this country. Although
my staff is still in the process of reviewing the data, and I
have not yet received responses to all of my letters, we
know that hundreds of different non-English forms and publications are now being printed and distributed on a wide
scale throughout the United States. These publications
cover a broad spectrum and range from White House press
releases in Spanish to National Labor Relations Board
notices in thirty-two different languages. The non-English
materials which I have received are in a stack that is about
3 feet high, and we are adding to it almost daily. However,
even when all the responses are in we still will not have a
complete picture of the use of official, non-English publications. Many of the states are only sending a few samples of
what they produce, and I am told that if copies of all bilingual educational materials were sent we could fill a large
room. While distribution of these materials may be seen as

providing just another government service, it can also be
seen as reducing the incentive to learn English and demonstrates a growing nationwide problem.

20   At the nongovernment level there is a great deal of emphasis being placed on the use of non-English languages.
In some major metropolitan areas English is the second
language; minorities, who speak only English, are being
told that they must learn a foreign language in order to be
eligible for a job in parts of this country; and, in many
stores non-English languages are the only ones used to conduct business. It is not uncommon to find areas in this
country where an individual can live all of his or her life
having all of his social, commercial, and intellectual needs
met without the use of English.

21   Statistics show a disconcerting trend away from the common use of English. In 1975 the Bureau of the Census reported that about 8 million people in this country used a
language other than English in their households. When the
census was conducted in 1980 the number of people who
spoke a language other than English at home was found to
be over 22 million. Although these numbers are subject to
many interpretations, to me they indicate — very strongly —
that the melting pot is not working as it once did.

22   My assumption is confirmed by a recent population bulletin, "U.S. Hispanics: Changing the Face of America,"
which concluded that because of their common language
and large numbers, Hispanics will take longer than other
immigrant groups to assimilate into the American society.

23   If this situation were static and merely a reflection of the
large scale legal and illegal immigration the United States
has been experiencing over the last few years — in 1980 more
immigrants entered the United States than at any time
other than the peak years at the turn of the century — there
would not be cause for concern. However, what we are
seeing is a decrease in the use of English and a widely
accepted attitude that it is not necessary to learn English.

24   There is a new philosophy taking hold, and it is gaining
more and more acceptance. In the June 13, 1983, *Time* magazine an article stated in regard to this philosophy, that:

> Now, however, a new bilingualism and biculturalism is
> being promulgated that would deliberately fragment the
> Nation into separate, unassimilated groups. . . . The new
> metaphor is not the melting pot but the salad bowl, with

each element distinct. The biculturalists seek to use public services, particularly schools, not to Americanize the young but to heighten their consciousness of belonging to another heritage.

The United States is presently at a crucial juncture. We   25
can either continue down the same path we have walked for the last two hundred years, using the melting pot philosophy to forge a strong and united nation or, we can take the new path that leads in the direction of another Tower of Babel.

There are many nations in the world today that would   26
give a great deal to have the kind of internal social and political stability that a single primary language (English) has afforded us. For us to consciously make the decision to throw away this stabilizing force would be seen as foolish and stupid in countries that have paid a high price for not having a universally accepted language.

We have to look no further than the nation which is closest   27
to us geographically and culturally—Canada. They have had a long-running experience with bilingualism and bicul- turalism, and it is an experience that still generates divisive- ness and still threatens to shatter the nation's unity. The key cause of Canada's internal conflict is language. Accord- ing to the Annual Report, 1981, of the Commissioner of Official Languages, the total cost so far in implementing the Canadian Official Languages Act "is on the order of $4 billion spread over the 12 years. The question of cost-effec- tiveness is more problematical. Measured against the goals of relieving English-French tensions and fostering a com- mon pride in the value of our national languages, the results may be more questionable."

Belgium is another nation that has suffered severe inter-   28
nal dissent, much of which has been caused by language differences. In the last thirty-nine years the political coali- tions that are necessary to govern that country have been broken apart over thirty times by the fights between the French-speaking Walloons and the Dutch-speaking Flemish. This political squabbling has had serious consequences for Belgium, and it is not the kind of situation to which any nation should voluntarily subject itself.

This type of political instability has been repeated   29
throughout history, and is still occurring in many countries today. In countless places, differences in language have

either caused or contributed significantly to political, social, and economic instability. While the absence of language differences does not guarantee that these problems will not occur, I believe that it does significantly reduce the chances that they will occur.

30　　The constitutional amendment which I am proposing is not unusual, and in fact, many nations have one official language. According to the Library of Congress these include, but are not limited to, Austria, Bulgaria, Denmark, France, the German Democratic Republic, the Federal Republic of Germany, Greece, Hungary, Italy, the Netherlands, Norway, Poland, Romania, and Sweden.

31　　Within the United States there is ample tradition and legislation to justify this approach. According to the Library of Congress:

> Several Federal statutes and numerous State laws do require the use of English in a variety of areas.
>
> Thus, the Nationality Act of 1940 (8 U.S.C. 423) requires that—
>
> "No person . . . shall be naturalized as a citizen of the United States upon his own petition who cannot demonstrate—
>
> "1. an understanding of the English language, including an ability to read, write and speak words in ordinary usage in the English language" (with provisos).
>
> Secondly, 28 U.S.C. 865 requires that in determining whether a person is qualified for jury service, the chief judge of a district court "shall deem any person qualified to serve on grand and petit juries in the district court unless he (the prospective juror)—
>
> "2. is unable to read, write, and understand the English language with a degree of proficiency sufficient to fill out satisfactorily the juror qualification form;
>
> "3. is unable to speak the English language. . . ."
>
> At the state level, most states have statutes requiring the use of English as the language of instruction in the public schools. Some states also statutorily require English as the language of legal proceedings and legal notices, of business regulation, etc.

32　　More recently, the U.S Senate has spoken out very strongly in favor of establishing English as the official language. On August 13, 1982, Senator Hayakawa introduced an amendment to the Immigration Reform and Control Act declaring that "the English language is the official language of the United States." On a rollcall vote seventy-eight senators voted for this amendment and it was included in the bill. When this same bill was again reported out of the Judiciary Committee on April 21, 1983 it again contained this language, and the report of the full committee stated:

> If immigration is continued at a high level, yet a substantial portion of these new persons and their descendants do not assimilate into the society, they have the potential to create in America a measure of the same social, political, and economic problems which exist in the countries from which they have chosen to depart. Furthermore, if language and cultural separatism rise above a certain level, the unity and political stability of the nation will — in time — be seriously diminished. Pluralism, within a united American nation, has been the single greatest strength of this country. This unity comes from a common language and a core public culture of certain shared values, beliefs, and customs which make us distinctly "Americans."

The concerns that were expressed by the Senate Judiciary   33
Committee are reflected in the concerns of thousands of citizens throughout this country. In fact, a new national organization has recently been created called U.S. English. The honorary chairman of this organization is former U.S. Senator S. I. Hayakawa, who speaks with a great deal of authority on this issue because he is an immigrant and distinguished scholar of semantics and languages.

U.S. English refers to itself as "a national, non-profit,   34
non-partisan organization . . . founded to defend the public interest in the growing debate on bilingualism and biculturalism."

If we continue along the path we now follow, I believe   35
that we will do irreparable damage to the fragile unity that our common language has helped us preserve for over two hundred years. Cultural pluralism is an established value in our national life, and one which we greatly cherish. Paradoxically, cultural pluralism can only continue if we retain our common meeting ground; namely, the English language. If we allow this bond to erode, we will no longer enjoy the benefits of cultural diversity, but rather, we will suffer the bitterness of ethnic confrontations and cultural separatism.

The constitutional language I am proposing is simple and   36 straightforward: It would serve to establish a principle that would strengthen us as a nation. However, I am aware that adding to the Constitution takes us into uncharted waters, and that there will be many misleading allegations about the extent of the problem and the proposed remedy. This is one of the reasons I have chosen to propose a constitutional amendment in order to address this issue. It will focus national attention on the problem, and subject it to the type of thorough national debate which is necessary.

37   During this constitutional process, all parties, sides, and interests will have the opportunity to present their respective points of view. This will guarantee that the final version submitted to the states for ratification will accomplish only what is needed to be accomplished and that basic individual rights are not interfered with.

38   Even though I believe that the constitutional language I am proposing will work, I am open to all recommendations and I will carefully consider any proposed improvements or modifications. However, regardless of the final language, to a large extent it is the legislative history which determines how the language will be interpreted.

39   Accordingly, it is my intent that the amendment I am proposing would not do a number of things.

40   First. It would not prohibit or discourage the use of foreign languages and cultures in private contexts, such as in homes, churches, communities, private organizations, commerce, and private schools. The United States is rich in ethnic cultures and they would continue to survive as they have in the past.

41   Second. It would not prohibit the teaching of foreign languages in the Nation's public schools or colleges, nor will it prohibit foreign language requirements in academic institutions.

42   Third. It will not prevent the use of second languages for the purpose of public convenience and safety in limited circumstances.

43   On the other hand the amendment would accomplish a number of objectives.

44   First. It would bring national recognition to the proposition that a common language is necessary to preserve the basic internal unity that is required for a stable and growing nation.

45   Second. It would establish English as the official language of federal, state, and local governments throughout the United States.

Third. Since voting by citizens is the method of choosing   46
the representatives of these governments and is the first
step in the official process of governing, it would prevent
the printing of ballots in foreign languages.

Fourth. It would permit bilingual education where it   47
could be clearly demonstrated that the primary objective
and practical result is the teaching of English to students
as rapidly as possible, and not cultural maintenance. It
would not affect the use of total immersion in English,
which is a proven method of teaching English.

Fifth. It would discourage discrimination and exploita-   48
tion by making it clear to immigrant parents and children
that learning English is indispensable for full participation in the American society and economy and by speeding
them into the mainstream of our society and economy as
rapidly as possible.

Sixth. It would reaffirm that we are truly "one Nation   49
. . . indivisible. . . ."

Mr. President, national unity is not a subject to be taken   50
lightly, for without it we would lose much of the strength
which sets us apart as a great nation. I believe that history
has taught us that one of the vital ingredients for obtaining
national unity is a commonly accepted language. This has
been confirmed by our own past experience in this country,
and it has been proven by other countries that have been
divided and weakened by their internal arguments centering around language differences.

National unity does not require that each person think and   51
act like everyone else. However, it does require that there be
some common threads that run throughout our society and
hold us together. One of these threads is our common belief
and support of a democratic form of government, and the
right of every person to fully participate in it. Unfortunately, this right of full participation means very little if
each individual does not possess the means of exercising
it. This participation requires the ability to obtain information and to communicate our beliefs and concerns to others.
Undoubtedly this process is greatly hindered without the
existence of a commonly accepted and used language.

In essence, what a policy of bilingualism/biculturalism   52
does is to segregate minorities from the mainstream of our
politics, economy, and society because we are not making
it possible for them to freely enter into that mainstream.
We are pushing them aside into their own communities,
and denying them the tools with which to break out. I have

always been against segregation of any kind, and by not assuring that every person in this country can speak and understand English we are still practicing segregation. It was wrong when we segregated blacks because of color and it is just as wrong when we create a system which segregates any group of people by language.

53   As Americans we are a unique people and one of the things that makes us uniquely American is our common language — English. My proposed constitutional amendment would assure that anyone in this country can fully take part in the American dream and that future generations also will have this privilege.

54   Mr. President, I ask unanimous consent that the joint resolution be printed in the *Record*.

55   There being no objection, the joint resolution was ordered to be printed in the *Record*, as follows:

S.J. RES. 167

Resolved by the Senate and House of Representatives of the United States of America in Congress assembled (two-thirds of each House concurring therein), That the following article is proposed as an amendment to the Constitution of the United States, which shall be valid to all intents and purposes as part of the Constitution if ratified by the legislatures of three-fourths of the several States within seven years after its submission to the States for ratification:

ARTICLE

"Sec. 1. The English language shall be the official language of the United States.

"Sec. 2. The Congress shall have the power to enforce this article by appropriate legislation."

James C. Stalker

Official English or English Only?

James C. Stalker has been Director of the English Language Center at Michigan State University. Educated at the universities of North Carolina, Louisville, and Wisconsin, he teaches courses in linguistics, the history of English language, and

*rhetoric and composition. This 1988 essay was printed in the
same issue of* English Journal *(a magazine for English and
language arts teachers) as the essay by Victor Villanueva, Jr.,
found on page 155 and the next two essays by Trudy J. Sundberg
and by Roseann Duenas Gonzalez and her colleagues.*

Whether English should be the official language of the   1
United States is a debater's dream — there are no absolutely
right or wrong answers. We can prove pretty conclusively
that a nuclear bomb will kill people; it is somewhat harder
to prove that making English our legally official language
will harm anyone or to prove the opposite, that pursuing
a policy of multilingualism will aid anyone. However, we
can get a clearer view of the topic by avoiding the flaming
rhetoric and the smoke generated from the flames and
exploring the question to see what issues are involved.

"Official English" and "English Only" are apparently   2
synonymous terms. However, the two phrases are not the
same. To call for an "official" English is to call for a law
specifying that English is the language which is to be used
for official government functions, functions which would,
of course, need to be specified in the law. Presumably, if
English were declared the legally official language of the
federal government, it would then be required that all federal documents would be printed in English, that federal
legislative sessions would be conducted in English, perhaps
even that government officials would be required to be
fluent speakers and writers of English. But legislation that
specifies that English be the official language of the United
States need not require that English be the only language
in which the government conducts its business or commu-
nicates with the public it serves. It is quite conceivable that
legislation requiring that English be the official language
should also require that important legislation or legislative
debates be translated into the major languages in use in
the United States.

Legislation requiring that English should be the *only* lan-   3
guage used in the United States is clearly much more restrictive, and although it could have those consequences
touched on in the previous paragraph, other possible consequences might arise as well, consequences not so clearly
obvious. It is possible that English-only legislation could
be used to prohibit children from speaking a language other
than English in public places, such as public school playgrounds. It could mean that languages other than English

could not be spoken in any public places — the street, public offices. It could mean that we must designate certain areas in which languages other than English could be used, much as we now do for cigarette smokers in some states. Such consequences may seem facetious, but they are not. Laws require or prohibit certain specified actions. A law declaring English as the only legal language must inevitably be tested in court to determine the contexts and situations in which the law operates. In California, the recently approved official-English constitutional amendment prohibits printing ballots in any language other than English; that is a specified part of the law as passed. The group that supported the amendment most vigorously, US English, has also sought the prohibition of advertisements in any language other than English, including those in the Yellow Pages (*NY Times*, Trasvina), a quite legal attempt to test how far the law can be extended. In how many and what kinds of situations can the use of a language other than English be prohibited? English as an official language does not necessarily prohibit the use of any other language, although it opens the door for such a prohibition. English as the only legal language opens the prohibitive doors immediately and obviously, and in many cases the call for an official status for English is a thinly disguised call for English as the only legal language.

Clarification of the Issues

4   Before we consider further the practical consequences of our two possibilities — official English and English only, we need to consider the underlying concerns which have brought this question to the level of importance that it now has, and we need to separate the nonlinguistic, political issues from the linguistic ones. One of the primary expressed reasons for the call for an official English centers on bilingual programs and on Hispanic and Asian immigrants. The most common statement is that the Hispanic and Asian populations prefer not to assimilate into mainstream American culture, that they do not want to learn English or adopt traditional, mainstream cultural norms, and that bilingual programs support their desire for separateness by enabling them to maintain their native language under the guise of learning English. The emotional reactions to such a position by many people who regard

themselves as "traditional, mainstream" Americans is all too predictable. Those immigrants who are different and wish to remain different should go back to where they came from, go back to the culture which they hold as more valuable and dear to them than "our" culture. They should go back where they are comfortable and everyone speaks their language.

There are really three issues here: (1) the legitimacy of 5 cultural maintenance, (2) the intention and effectiveness of bilingual programs, and (3) simple communication. For the first of these issues, we can say the obvious; that we are all culturally different in some way or another; that each of us very probably values and wishes to maintain or obtain some part of our native heritage, whatever it is; that we are all immigrants, except for Amerindians; and that we expect others to be tolerant and accepting of our Scots, Polish, Russian, or African heritage. (During periods of high immigration, claims that assimilation is not happening seem to be more prevalent [see e.g., Whitney, *Literary Digest*, Chen and Henderson]). We must also remember that as a nation, we at least give lip service to the notion that our cultural diversity is one of the factors which separates the United States from many other countries in the world, one of the factors that has enabled the US to maintain an open society in the face of political, economic, and social strains which prevent other countries from realizing their full potential. We have been coping with political and cultural diversity since before the Revolution and engaging in cultural maintenance for at least that long.

The second issue, that of the intention and effectiveness 6 of bilingual programs, should be handled as a separate problem. If bilingual programs are ineffective in teaching children English, then something should be done about the programs themselves. Passing a law directed at the official status of English is relatively unlikely to make the bilingual programs better. Outlawing the programs through an English-only law is even less likely to improve the English of the children and adults now in those programs.

The focus on bilingual programs is in part prompted by 7 an often unarticulated fear that we will become a nation which will need interpreters in the legislature. It is a concern over communication, a concern that we might be able to deal with somewhat more objectively than the problem of cultural and political difference.

Historical Background

8   Language diversity was already an issue before the Revolution. As early as 1753, in a letter to a friend, Benjamin
Franklin expressed the fear that German would be so prevalent in Pennsylvania that the legislature would need interpreters. He noted that a good many of the street signs in
Philadelphia were in German, without an English translation (Mencken 140). By 1745 there were approximately
45,000 German speakers in the colonies, and by 1790 there
were some 200,000, nine per cent of the population (Anderson 80). Enough of them settled in Pennsylvania to cause
Franklin to envisage the possibility of that colony's becoming a German-speaking region. In 1795, the Germans of
Virginia (not Pennsylvania) petitioned Congress to print
laws in German for those immigrants in Virginia who had
not yet learned English. The subcommittee turned in a
favorable report on the petition, but it was tabled. A later
request that same year also received a favorable review in
committee but was defeated on the floor of Congress by a
vote of 42 to 41 (Mencken 139).

9   Even with such a rebuff, the German speakers did not go
away or learn English. Rather, their numbers increased:
1.5 million arrived between 1830 and 1860, and another
1.5 million arrived during the decade of the 1880s. In 1900,
the German immigrants and their children numbered approximately 8 million compared to the 2.5 million English
immigrants and their children (Anderson 80). These latter
arrivals were no more eager to abandon their native language than were their cultural ancestors. As a consequence,
there were German bilingual schools in Pennsylvania during the latter half of the nineteenth century; German newspapers were common in New York and Pennsylvania, down
the Ohio River valley, into Missouri and Texas.

10   We can get some retrospective idea of how substantial
the influence of the German immigrants would have been
throughout nineteenth- and early twentieth-century America, linguistically and culturally, by consulting the 1980
census, in which the number of people who reported themselves as being of German heritage was only slightly less
than the number reporting themselves as being of English
heritage — 49.6 million English to 49.2 million German.
Scottish and Irish heritage people add another 50.2 million,
but many of those immigrants did not think of themselves

as English, nor did they speak the same dialect ("The Melting Pot" 30).

Other language groups desired to maintain their native   11
languages when they came to the United States, and a look
into our history turns up some interesting results of that
desire. The Louisiana constitution allowed the publication
of laws in French, and they were so published until about
seventy years ago. California (1849) and Texas allowed the
publication of laws in Spanish, and New Mexico still maintained Spanish and English as official languages of the state
until 1941. In 1842 Texas required the publication of its
laws in German as well as Spanish and English and added
Norwegian in 1858 (Mencken 141). After the Civil War, several states required the use of English as the language of
instruction in the public schools, but several allowed the
use of other languages in one way or another. In Louisiana,
French could be used in those parishes where the French
language was spoken. Hawaii allowed the use of other languages by petition. Minnesota required books in English,
but explanations could be in other languages (Ruppenthal).
What all of this tells us is that we have never been absolutely
certain that we need to or should require that everyone
speak and read and write English. On the other hand, there
has been a rather constant pressure to maintain a common
language, and that language has been English. German had
the strongest chance to displace English; in fact, it had
nearly two hundred years to do so, but it did not succeed.
The conclusion that we can draw is that English is probably not seriously threatened. It has maintained its position as the common language and likely will continue to
do so.

The Status of Spanish: Present and Future

The assumption that Spanish will succeed in displacing   12
English where German did not is probably unfounded, but
we must recognize that the possibility exists. However, certain conditions must prevail for that eventuality to take
place. The Spanish speakers must not only want to maintain
Spanish, but they must also refuse to learn any English at
all. Even in those sections of the country in which there
are large Spanish-speaking populations, it does not seem
to be economically possible for all Spanish immigrants to

remain monolingual. In fact, the evidence points to the opposite conclusion. Results from a 1976 study indicate that of 2.5 million people who spoke Spanish as their native language, 1.6 million adopted English as their principal language (Veltman 14). Fifty per cent of the population switched from Spanish to English as their principal language. In order to offset this large loss of native speakers, Veltman calculates that Spanish-speaking women would need to produce 4.5 children each, but the average Chicano woman has only 2.9 children. A 1985 Rand Corporation study found that "more than 95 percent of first-generation Mexican-Americans born in the United States are proficient in English and that more than half the second generation speaks no Spanish at all" (Nunberg). Another study found that 98 per cent of Hispanic parents in Miami felt it essential that their children read and write English perfectly (Trasvina). In other words, Spanish speakers in the United States show a strong tendency to become English speakers, and as a result we are unlikely to become a Spanish-speaking country.

13   The loss of native speakers might be offset by the immigration of new Spanish speakers, but the evidence is that fifty per cent of Spanish speakers who immigrate to the US already speak some English (Chen and Henderson). They obviously are not Spanish-only speakers and can be reasonably expected to learn more English. It is simply maladaptive and dysfunctional not to do so. If the only way to prevent the maintenance of Spanish among a particular part of the population is to control immigration, then we must take the bull by his horns rather than his tail. We must control immigration through restrictive immigration laws rather than by trying to control immigration through a constitutional amendment mandating English as the official language. Would such an amendment then enable us to control immigration by preventing anyone who does not speak English from migrating to the US? That would be a very interesting law indeed.

14   To be complete, we need to consider the possibility that the statistics I have given are inaccurate—that Spanish speakers are not learning English at any great rate, that Spanish speakers will pour into the country in such large numbers that their number will equal or exceed the number of speakers of English, and that as a consequence, we will become a country with two major languages. If that should

happen, the US could also become a country socially, politically, and linguistically divided, like Canada or Sri Lanka
or any of several African countries. Countries which are
composed of two largely monolingual groups do seem to
have more tensions that tend to pull the nation apart rather
than aid it in retaining unity. It is not generally politically
wise for a nation to possess two major, equally important
languages, especially when each group attaches great emotional value to its own language and culture and becomes
xenophobic about the other language and culture. Will passing a law declaring English as the official language prevent
the rise of a second major language? Only if we also pass
a set of restrictive laws, among them a law which limits
immigration to those people who already speak English,
and a law which prohibits the use of any language other
than English.

Legislation: Effects and Alternatives

We have to question the effectiveness of these two addi-   15
tional laws. Limiting immigration might indeed work, if
we are willing to build an eight-foot concrete wall along
the Mexican-American border and convert a significant portion of our defense budget (or perhaps that portion of our
education budgets now devoted to bilingual education) to
patrolling our Southern borders. We have not been very
effective in enforcing the immigration restrictions that we
already have, and a new, more restrictive law is unlikely
to accomplish any more than the current laws do.

The money for massive enforcement of current or new   16
immigration restrictions is unlikely to materialize, so let's
consider the ramifications of the other major possibility,
prohibition of the use of any language other than English.
If any language group, Spanish or other, chooses to maintain its language, there is precious little that we can do
about it, legally or otherwise, and still maintain that we
are a free country. We cannot legislate the language of the
home, the street, the bar, the club, unless we are willing
to violate the privacy of our people, unless we are willing
to set up a cadre of language police who will ticket and
arrest us if we speak something other than English. What
we can do is disenfranchise all of those who have not yet
learned or cannot learn English. We can exclude them from

the possibility of taking part in our political system and from our schools, and because they will be uneducated, we can prevent them from benefiting from the economic system. We can insure a new oppressed minority. If that minority becomes a majority, through immigration (legal or illegal) and through birth, we will live with the consequences of our actions.

17   I dwelt on the German immigration into our country in the eighteenth and nineteenth centuries because that group very deliberately maintained its language and culture. Thus, those parts of the Spanish and Asian populations which are reluctant to abandon their culture and language because they had to abandon their countries for political and economic reasons are not unique to the United States. This is not a new problem. The Germans, for the most part, have eventually become users of English, not because of repressive linguistic policies or legislation, but for that most effective reason of all—utility. People learn a new language or dialect if they see that that language or dialect has high potential value for them, not because they are legally required to. The very fact that our current evidence says that more Spanish speakers are learning English than are retaining their own language is a pretty good indication that a good many of them believe English to be more useful and therefore more valuable than Spanish. English enables them to gain more than they have, to partake in the political and economic life of the United States more fully than Spanish (or Vietnamese or Chinese) does.

18   Our need is not to insure that everyone in the United States be a monolingual speaker of English but rather to insure that our country continues to hold its own politically and economically in the world at large. To accomplish this task, all Americans must be less provincial and less linguistically ethnocentric. English is now the predominant world language, especially in business, technology, and education, the mainstays of traditional, mainstream American culture. Because of the worldwide importance of English as an international language, it is unlikely that the United States will lose English as its common language at a time when other countries are seeking more speakers of English and teaching their own populations English. However, we will need people who can speak the languages of other countries. For the United States to continue to be an important economic and political power in the world, Americans of whatever variety will need two languages—their first language

and English, or English and a second language. English is indeed a world language, but as every international tourist or business traveler learns, not everyone in the world speaks English. Rather than eliminate the second language of our immigrants, we need to help them learn English and maintain that valuable resource they already have, the use of a second language, and we need to teach our native English speakers a second language.

The United States has always been a polyglot country. 19 It is part of our strength. It is unlikely that nonnative speakers of English, be they immigrants or born here, will remain monolingual, because they need English to talk with other Americans whose native language is not English and with other people in the world who do not speak Vietnamese or Spanish or French or Arabic or whatever. Multilingualism in a country is potentially dangerous only if it becomes the rallying point for cultural divisiveness. Otherwise, it is a benefit of great economic and political value.

Aside from the purely utilitarian economic value of knowing 20 more than one language, there is evidence that knowing a second language increases our abilities to use our first language. People who know two languages generally perform better on tests of verbal ability administered in their native language than do monolingual speakers. That is to say, if your native language is English, and you learn Japanese, you will perform better on tests which measure your knowledge of and abilities in English (Hakuta). Parents who know and accept the research that shows that "bilingual youngsters are more imaginative, better with abstract notions and more flexible in their thinking" are enrolling their children in private language programs to give them the advantage that bilingual programs give other groups of children (Wells).

Conclusion

Neither our Congress nor any other national legislature 21 has ever had much success in legislating morals or beliefs. Making English the official or only language of the United States will not alter my personal beliefs about the value of my language or my beliefs about yours. Rather than taking the path of linguistic legislation, we are much more likely to be successful in maintaining a common language in the United States by pursuing the American tradition of persuasion and demonstration. The very fact that English speakers (whether English is their first or second language) are economically and politically more powerful than non-English speakers is a better argument for learning English than an argument based on the fact that English is the official or only language of the United States. (See Carlin for a similar argument from the viewpoint of politics.)

22   I have tried to point out some distinctions here, perhaps the most important of which is that *official, only* and *common* are not synonymous when coupled with *English*. A great many of us wish to maintain English as the *common* language of the United States, but that goal need not, and probably should not, entail legislating English as the *only* language or the official language. The problems that we have as a multilingual society have been with us since at least 1753 when Benjamin Franklin noted them, and we have managed to overcome them or turn them to our advantage without depriving anyone of the freedom of speech that we value so highly. There are distinct advantages for our culture, for our children, and for each of us individually to be multilingual, especially if we all share a language in common. If we are concerned about the quality and intent of bilingual programs or about the effects of our immigration policies, let's be direct and honest and focus on those and not pretend that legislating language choice will improve or change bilingual programs or slow immigration.

Works Cited

Anderson, Charles. *White Protestant Americans.* Englewood Cliffs, NJ: Prentice, 1970.

Carlin, David R., Jr. "Charm and the English Language Amendment." *The Christian Century* 101.27 (1984): 822–23.

"Charting the Great Melting Pot." *U.S. News & World Report* 7 July 1986: 30.

Chen, Edward M., and Wade Henderson, "New 'English-only' Movement Reflects Old Fear of Immigrants." *Civil Liberties* No. 358 (1986): 8.

Hakuta, Kenji. *The Mirror of Language: The Debate on Bilingualism.* New York: Basic, 1986.

"Immigrants Who Don't." *Literary Digest* 88.11 (1926): 50.

"Is English the Only Language for Government?" *New York Times* 26 Oct. 1986, late ed., sec. 4: 6.

Mencken, H. L. *The American Language: Supplement I.* New York: Knopf, 1945.

Nunberg, Geoffrey. "An 'Official Language' for California?" *New York Times* 2 Oct. 1986, late ed., sec. 3: 23.

Ruppenthal, J. C. "The Legal Status of the English Language in the American School System." *School and Society* 10 (1919): 658–66.

Trasvina, John D. "'Official' English Means Discrimination." *U.S.A. Today* 25 July 1986: 10A.

Veltman, Calvin. *Language Shift in the United States.* The Hague: Mouton, 1983.

Wells, Stacy. "Bilingualism: The Accent Is on Youth." *U.S. News & World Report* 28 July 1986: 60.

Whitney, Parkhurst. "They Want to Know What Their Children Are Saying." *Colliers Magazine* 14 July 1923: 13, 21.

Trudy J. Sundberg

The Case Against Bilingualism

Trudy J. Sundberg teaches at Oak Harbor High School in Washington State. Her 1988 essay appeared in the same issue of English Journal *(a magazine for English and language arts teachers) as the essay by James Stalker (above), the next essay by Roseann Duenas Gonzalez, Alice A. Schott, and Victoria F. Vasquez, and the essay by Victor Villanueva, Jr., found on page 155.*

The case against bilingual education in this country is   1
well made in James Mitchener's novel *Texas* (NY: Random House, 1985) by one of his characters, Professor Roy Aspen, who says,

> For a nation like the United States, which has a workable central tongue used by many countries around the world, consciously to introduce linguistic separatism and to encourage it by the expenditure of public funds is to create and encourage a danger which could in time destroy this nation as other nations with linguistic problems have been destroyed. (1021)

Professor Aspen is referring to India and South Africa.   2
Alan Paton, South African author of *Cry the Beloved Country*, supports Aspen's view of South Africa, which Paton calls "a country of great diversity," and about which he goes on to say,

> But there is no common loyalty that can bind us all together,
> unless it be the physical land itself. We have no Constitution,
> and we have no Bill of Rights. America also has another
> advantage that we do not possess. All Americans speak —
> with different degrees of competency — the same language.
> We have two official languages, English and Afrikaans, but
> we have at least a dozen home languages. ("The Home
> Forum," *The Christian Science Monitor* 26 Feb. 1986: 30)

3   The United States is also a country of great diversity,
and English, our common language, is the social glue that
holds this multicultural country together, making all of us,
regardless of national origin, Americans.

4   For that reason laws proposed in Congress and in some
of the states that would designate English as the official
language of the United States should not be regarded as
xenophobic or anti-immigrant, or even racist as some critics
recklessly contend. Governor Richard Lamm of Colorado
has a good answer to these charges. He says, "We should
be color blind but not linguistically deaf. We should be a
rainbow but not a cacophony. We should welcome different
people but not adopt different languages" (Quoted in "English Spoken Here," *Time* 25 Aug. 1986: 27).

5   John Hughes, Pulitzer Prize-winning journalist, writing
in the *Christian Science Monitor*, makes a related point:

> English is the common tongue of the majority of Americans.
> It might have been Dutch or Italian or some other European
> language. But it is English, and it is important that, what-
> ever other languages they nurture, Americans command the
> primary language that binds them together. ("For US, It's
> English" 28 June 1985: 27)

6   Bilingualism, which became official US policy with the
passage of the Bilingual Education Act in 1968, has made
it harder for immigrants to enter the mainstream of American life by allowing them to avoid learning English, thus
confining many of them to self-perpetuating linguistic ghettos. Since that act was passed, I have seen no statistics that
show that either proficiency in English or the quality of
education in the United States has improved. On the contrary, the National Advisory and Coordinating Council on
Bilingual Education, the body that oversees administration
of this act, wrote in its recent annual report: "There is

simply no evidence that bilingual education should be the preferred approach to instruction in all language-minority students" ("New Directions in Late 80's Pursued," Tenth Annual Report of NACCBE, US Department of Education, March 1986). This attempt to change an educational system which had worked so well to assimilate immigrants into the mainstream of American life for over two hundred years has been a grave error.

There is no reason to fear that repeal of the Bilingual 7 Education Act, or passage of an act declaring English the official language of the United States, would discourage the study of foreign languages. By eliminating bilingual and multilingual courses, the government would have millions of dollars to spend on foreign language courses for all students, as well as on the basic education courses that are suffering severely from lack of funds.

In the Michener novel, Aspen concludes his case against 8 bilingualism by saying,

> India inherited its linguistic jungle; it did not create it willingly. History gave South Africa its divisive bilingualism; it did not seek it. Such nations are stuck with what accident and history gave them, and they cannot justly be accused of having made foolish error, but if the United States consciously invents a linguistic dualism, it deserves the castigation of history. (1021)

Roseann Duenas Gonzalez, *Alice A. Schott, and Victoria F. Vasquez*
The English Language Amendment: Examining Myths

Roseann Duenas Gonzalez, Alice A. Schott, and Victoria F. Vasquez are colleagues at the University of Arizona. You might read their essay in connection with the ones that precede it by Victor Villanueva, Jr., James C. Stalker, and Trudy J. Sundberg because all of them were originally published in the same 1988 issue of English Journal.

1   Current debate on the proposed English Language Amendment (ELA) has created social divisiveness and a political atmosphere described as a veritable "powderkeg" (Marshall 7). A host of nonprofit organizations have sprung up to marshal political and financial support for the ELA, each with its own set of claims, slogans, and titles: English First, the California English Campaign, US English, and other related groups such as the Council on InterAmerican Security and Save our Schools (a group formed to eliminate bilingual education and the threat of bilingualism). These diverse organizations have identified as their common concern the protection of English as the national language. But a number of language scholars and historians view this focus on language and the opposition to bilingualism as nothing less than "veiled hostility" and resentment towards Hispanics and other large minority language groups (Alatis; Heath and Krasner; Judd; Marshall; Reinhold).

2   After careful scrutiny, each of the following language societies passed resolutions opposing the ELA to counteract the letter campaigns used by ELA proponents to enlist the support of their members:

> The NCTE resolution of November 1986 eschewed any movement whose objective it is "to establish English as the official language . . . [and] to render invisible the native languages of any Americans."

> The Linguistic Society of America's resolution of December 1986 focused on the inconsistency of such measures "with basic American ideals of linguistic tolerance."

> The Teachers of English to Speakers of Other Languages (TESOL) sent a letter to its affiliates in March 1987, stating that such a measure would impede rather than facilitate acculturation and national unity.

> The Modern Language Association's resolution of spring 1987 not only strongly opposed ELA measures but encouraged "both foreign language study for native English speakers and programs that enable speakers with other linguistic backgrounds to maintain proficiency in those languages along with English."

3   Because it identifies an enemy and offers easy solutions, the ELA movement is a tempting bandwagon. Unfortunately, the national problems this initiative hopes to rem-

edy are of such scope and complexity as to defy simple solutions. This article explores specific issues raised by Trudy Sundberg in a pro-ELA statement recently submitted to the *English Journal* (pp. 16–17). The statement exemplifies the adoption of a political position by one sincere in intention but for the most part uninformed. In this article we focus on several underlying premises of the ELA movement and refute three of its primary contentions.

Since we believe the group US English best represents the ELA movement overall, we examine this organization and its ideas. US English is the largest, most aggressive, and most successful of the political groups promoting English as the official language in the United States. Its membership has grown rapidly, from 300 in 1983 to 275,000 nationwide as of July 1987 (US English, Personal conversation), with about half of these members in California (Trombley 3). The organization has risen just as quickly in prominence and has availed itself of ample opportunities to both lobby and testify before Congress against bilingual education and bilingual ballots. In a relatively short time, US English has instituted a network of state-level organizations which serve to initiate legislation and muster both political and financial support for its parent organization. As of March 1987, US English has introduced legislation in thirty states — successful in nine (US English, Letter to the authors) — and persists in its efforts to garner national support.

We can best gain insight into the political intentions of ELA proponents by examining the motives of the primary originator of US English, John H. Tanton, a fifty-three-year-old Michigan ophthalmologist. Almost a quarter of a century ago Tanton embarked on his path toward founding US English. Intensely concerned about issues of environmental conservation, he founded US, Inc., an umbrella corporation from which his other organizations stem. Maintaining that the "'population problem . . . is an important barrier to our conservation efforts'" (Trombley 3), Tanton worked for Planned Parenthood and Zero Population Growth. His statement that "excessive immigration, both legal and illegal, was an important reason for the overpopulation problem" (Trombley 3) reveals his insular views.

After failing to convince Zero Population Growth to address the immigration issue, Tanton formed the Federation for American Immigration Reform (FAIR) which lobbied for lower immigration quotas and tougher immigration laws. By 1983, Tanton believed yet another organization was needed to combat, in his words, "'self-serving ethnic politicians' who were promoting bilingual education, bilingual ballots and other multilingual services in order to maintain 'language ghettos' of non-English speakers who would vote as they were told" (Trombley 3). Tanton joined forces with former Senator S. I. Hayakawa of California to promulgate their beliefs nationwide through US English.

7   Fernando Oaxaca, former associate director of the Office of Management and Budget during President Ford's tenure, holds that "'the people behind US English . . . came out of the environmental movement and think the environment is damaged by people, especially people different from themselves. . . . [They are] . . . motivated by xenophobia and probably racism'" (Trombley 20). Jerry Tinker, an aide to Sen. Edward Kennedy, observed that "many of the leaders of US English were also active in FAIR, which has worked hard to restrict immigration" and added, "'Long before they took the garb of US English, this was an anti-immigrant outfit . . . and their newsletters contained barely disguised racism'" (Trombley 20).

8   Thus, US English, the largest and most influential ELA group, derives from an effort to curb population growth and immigration rates, out of a desire to eliminate those linguistic "ghettos," which allegedly were politically planned, and from an effort to curtail any rise in ethnic power which might result from the printing of ballots in languages other than English.

9   It is hardly surprising that the motives of US English — and by association those of ELA — have been called into question. A survey of the literature disseminated to the general public reveals that the arguments fashioned by ELA proponents comprise little more than an "odd mixture of shallow information, misinformation, tangled logic, illogic and xenophobia" (Donohue 100). However, one major strength, and the real danger of US English, is its strategic and unrelenting use of a series of prevalent myths upon which it predicates its ideology.

10   As the Sundberg statement demonstrates, flooding the popular media with these fictions has created the illusion that they are based in fact. And, like Sundberg, the general public, educators, and policymakers can be swayed into believing that these assertions contain some core of truth. The widespread adoption of such views would be disas-

trous. Simply, today's language policies which so many have worked so long and hard to institute in our nation's schools and public institutions would be gone tomorrow. Therefore, in order to clarify the faulty platform of US English, we examine its most commonly advocated myths.

Myth 1: Linguistic Diversity Inevitably Causes Political Conflict

Sundberg cites South Africa as a country whose extreme   11
political tensions result from linguistic pluralism. She then goes on to argue, by analogy, that the United States would share South Africa's fate if we fail to curtail our own linguistic diversity. Both of her beliefs are falsely grounded.

First, only the most superficial analysis would attribute   12
South Africa's racial unrest to linguistic causes alone. To wit, South Africa's current turmoil emanates from the suppression of a black majority's political and economic rights by a white minority who have instituted what are plainly apartheid policies. Although Timothy Reagan, for one, may believe that linguistic and educational policies intermesh closely with political and ideological factors ("Language Policy" 155–64), to conclude that South Africa's political and racial problems stem from its multilingual diversity and language policies distorts reality vastly. For, in spite of its significant political and social shortcomings, South Africa has initiated a language policy that accommodates a multitude of linguistically diversified groups. The dominant linguistic ideology of South Africa is one which "focuses on the right of every child to be educated in his or her mother tongue" (Reagan, "Language Policy" 158) during the child's primary schooling. While critics have assailed this policy as one promoting "ghettoization" and "cultural fragmentation" (qtd. in Kloss, *Problems of Language Policy* 24), the positive intellectual and psychological effects of bilingualism, along with strong support lent by UNESCO, have encouraged the South African government to continue its commitment to a linguistic policy which promotes language addition rather than language shift (Reagan, "Role of Language Policy" 3–5).

Failing to perceive (as many do) that South Africa's lan-   13
guage policies differ radically from its politics, Sundberg and other ELA proponents assume that linguistic diversity

is the cause of political upheaval and strife. Nonetheless, this distinction *is* a valid and significant one. According to Heinz Kloss in *Problems of Language Policy in South Africa*, "Approval or disapproval of a nation's racial, religious, or socioeconomic attitudes and policies, must not, in the minds of sober men, be confounded with its achievement in the realm of language policy" (10).

14   Also, argument by analogy often provides only limited insight: one must question the propriety of transposing the sociopolitical or linguistic difficulties of one nation unto another (Maldoff 105). Each country has its own distinct set of historical, societal, and cultural variables that determines its destiny. To assert that the United States would share South Africa's fate it if did not impede linguistic diversity is a giant and illogical leap.

15   Moreover, proponents of the ELA hardly need look to the events of other nations to determine what circumstances would precipitate political upheaval in our own. The American historical record is clear: to exclude people on the basis of race, religion, *or language* is to engender social and political strife. For example, the struggle for language rights produced intense social conflict when limited- and non-English-speaking persons were denied access to their own legal, political, educational, and social-service systems. It was *not* language diversity which caused this social and political conflict; nor were minority language groups demanding recognition of their native languages — officially or otherwise. The conflict came about because equal opportunity and equal treatment under the law had been withheld from non-English speakers (Gonzalez and others). Once language services and bilingual-education programs were instituted political dissension subsided.

16   Finally, one must question the belief that language diversity would be eliminated by mandating English as the language of government. Even ELA proponents conceded it: the First Amendment guarantees the right of "persons to speak whatever language they want, or to form private associations to foster various languages and cultures" (Bikales 80–81). Exercising their constitutionally protected right to the private use of any language, minority language groups would no doubt continue to maintain their native languages, regardless of any official language enactment. Therefore, to equate language diversity with political upheaval is untenable; despite the official or unofficial status

of any single tongue, language diversity in this nation will continue to exist.

Myth 2: An Official Language Is the Primary Determinant of National Unity

The second myth promoted by ELA supporters is that [17] legislating English as the official language would serve to unify the diverse cultures within our nation. Indeed, this notion that monolingualism is essential for national unity is a propelling force behind the "melting pot" theory. Some ELA advocates have gone so far as to say that language is the pot that all Americans melt in ("Language"). Hayakawa insists that the melting-pot concept is basic to the congruity of our nation and that any other ideological metaphor, such as the "salad bowl," imperils the "future unity of our nation" (Hayakawa 29).

However, this melting-pot theory is illusory at best; it [18] wholly ignores the "social reality of the ethnic, linguistic, and culturally pluralistic society" (Coulmas 106) in which we live; it perpetuates the notion that language homogeneity is synonymous with political, social, and cultural cohesiveness; it implies that political opposition, confrontation, and dissent — all inherent features in the democratic process — can be eradicated through linguistic conformity. Its proponents thereby advocate policies and programs of language shift rather than language maintenance — at the expense of the individual's primary language, ethnic identity, and, ultimately, self-esteem. From a human-rights point of view, the perpetuation and enforcement of the melting-pot theory ignores the rights of differing ethnic, linguistic, and religious groups in all nation-states to maintain their languages — as guaranteed not only constitutionally but internationally by the United Nations on December 16, 1966, in Resolution 2200, Article 27 of the International Covenant on Civil and Political Rights (Djonovich 165–176).

While some countries have found a national language to [19] be an indispensable tool for unification (Kennedy 152), the presently indisputable predominance of English in the United States renders the rallying call for "one nation — one language" irrelevant. Conklin and Lourie have found that specific historical, political, and sociocultural processes in the United States contributed to the dominant status of

English in a manner that "no amount of present or future immigration is likely to challenge" (71). Hayakawa's repeated slogan—"Make English Official: One common language makes our nation work" (36)—is adamantine; national unity is founded on societal support for American political, social, and economic institutions as well as on such common values as freedom of speech. Beardsmore and Willemyns refer to these values, inherent in American culture, as overarching core values, which include not only the right to free speech but equal protection for all people under the law and respect of diverse religious practices (126–127); they conclude that immigrant groups adhere to these overarching values while at the same time maintaining their own core values. Therefore, the belief that an official national language is necessary for immigrants (as well as other groups) to adopt a sense of national unity is a fallacy. America's history and current state of affairs attest to the fact: citizens may be multilingual and yet intensely nationalistic.

Myth 3: Bilingual Education Decelerates the Entrance of Non-English Speakers into the American Mainstream

20   To demonstrate her support for the ELA, Sundberg alludes to yet a third myth—that bilingualism promoted by bilingual education programs deters non-English speakers from entering the American mainstream. She states that immigrants' maintenance of their primary language relegates them to "linguistic ghettos." Three false assumptions underlie this belief. First, there never has been a national language policy promoting bilingualism. The Bilingual Education Act of 1968 served to meet the "special educational needs of children of limited-English-speaking ability in schools having a high concentration of children from families . . . with incomes below $3,000 per year" (Title VII 817). This statute was enacted in response to the outcry of parents whose children "were failing in English-only schools" (qtd. in Hakuta 199). Should we return to mandated English-only instruction, the cycle would repeat itself. Once again we would require a "Bilingual Education Act" to lend children access to an educational system in a

language they can understand until they become proficient in English. This was a hard-learned lesson; as educators and policymakers, we should remember it.

Second, bilingual education programs do *not* promote 21 maintenance of a primary language. The reality is that bilingual education programs have never fully operationalized the maintenance model to produce truly "balanced bilinguals." In spite of the claim that the majority of all bilingual education programs in the United States are maintenance-oriented (Danoff and others), in actuality ninety-nine per cent of all bilingual education programs in the United States are transitional. After two to four years of bilingual instruction, most children exit from bilingual education programs to English-dominant classrooms (National Clearinghouse for Bilingual Education 3).

Transitional bilingual education means that the child's 22 primary language serves to instruct in those content areas appropriate to grade and cognitive level at the same time the child receives instruction in English as a Second Language. The aim is quickly to mainstream the child into an English-dominant classroom. Here the pedagogical and psychological realities have become clear: native-language instruction promotes cognitive growth and increased self-esteem, which in turn produce a healthy attitude towards learning and higher academic achievement (Hakuta 14–44). Thus, bilingual education is a necessity, if only because a limited- or non-English-speaking child (in an English-only classroom) cannot immediately assimilate information presented.

Moreover, advocates of the ELA too often seem to ignore 23 that language acquisition is an arduous, complex process for the non-native speaker and depends on an array of variables, such as age, time, and attitudes. It takes at least seven years for a child to acquire a second language (Cummins, "Role of Primary Language" 3–49); the time required for immigrant adults is yet unknown.

The third false assumption is that bilingual education 24 retards the learning of English and promotes the formation of "linguistic ghettos." Studies show otherwise: Kloss maintains that the "life expectancy of the language of most immigrant groups in an industrialized society is rather low" ("Language Rights" 258). Veltman also has chronicled the rapid language shift by immigrants following their arrival in the United States and has shown how their children do not maintain the immigrant language (*Language Shift* 91). Hernandez-Chavez reports that Spanish-speaking communities are "shifting dramatically to English" (527). Additional studies suggest that a language shift usually marks the third generation, depending on the language group and particular sociological factors which contribute to that shift, such as majority attitudes toward the minority group and its language, the extent of minority isolation from the majority and other minority groups, governmental and educational policies, and other societal pressures to assimilate (Grosjean 107–12). Furthermore, these factors prompt immigrant groups to adopt a host language, even if they choose to maintain their native language. Gilhotra succinctly summarizes immigrant sentiments as follows:

> Members of the minority communities know full well that they must learn the language of the majority to be able to enjoy equal opportunities in the public domain and develop meaningful societal relations with members of the majority community, but at the same time they would also like to maintain their own languages to preserve their self-esteem. (62–63).

25   Three additional factors also do their part to promote this unrealistic perspective of bilingual education: (1) open support of this fiction at the highest governmental levels, (2) unsubstantiated fears about the dangers of bilingual education, and (3) the social stigma attached to bilingualism. In 1981, President Reagan declared that bilingual education prevented non-English speakers from learning English and that it was wrong to maintain native languages. His views were clearly expressed in this statement:

> It is absolutely wrong and against the American concept to have a bilingual program that is now openly, admittedly dedicated to preserving their native language and never getting them adequate in English so they can go out into the job market and participate. (*Public Papers* 181).

26   Unfortunately, the President's own promulgation of this myth has lent it greater legitimacy. The positive effects of this carefully constructed pedagogical approach — called bilingual education — have been interred under a rhetoric of fault and blame. The perpetual goal of bilingual educa-

tion has been to show the child that his or her native language and heritage are indeed of value, so that the child might feel confident and worthy enough to seek academic success while on the road to English proficiency. There are other dividends as well: studies indicate that bilingual instruction correlates significantly with intellectual prowess in reading and nonverbal logic (Hakuta 14–44). In spite of its many positive features, the Reagan administration persists in its negative stance toward bilingualism and bilingual education, a posture leaning toward "effectively deemphasizing the value of bilingualism in the United States" (Levy 125).

Another factor intensifying opposition toward bilingualism and bilingual programs is fear. Cummins defines this fear in sociopolitical and psychoeducational terms ("Construct of Language" 80): sociopolitically, many fear that bilingualism and its educational policies will eventually fragment the social order; there is also a fear of jeopardizing national unity (Kennedy 10), as well as the more universal anti-immigrant fears and xenophobia (Reinhold E6). The general conception of bilingual programs is that the less proficient a child is in English the more instruction he or she should receive in English (Cummins, "Construct of Language" 82); as the general public sees it, too much instructional time is spent in the child's native language. 27

Yet another reason that bilingual education has suffered a backlash is that many look upon bilingualism as an "undesirable social disease" (Troike 9), as a "stigma and a liability" (Grosjean 66), as a societal "deficit" rather than "asset" (Heath 277). The fact that many bilingual education programs receive the label of "compensatory" rather than "academic" encourages such attitudes (Grosjean 79–80; Troike 5). These sentiments are also linked to a perceived language status. Those in need of bilingual education generally speak languages regarded as less prestigious by the linguistically dominant group. 28

Conclusions

Numerous scholars as well as statesmen have pointed out that the current language dispute represents but a surface symptom and functions as a scapegoat mechanism which effectively camouflages deeper, more complex prob- 29 lems rooted in the political, social, and economic structures of our nation. We are in full agreement with this perception. The widespread fear of extensive, uncontrollable immigration, especially of Hispanic and Asian populations; the animosity toward ethnic groups that have become an influential political force; and the apprehension of massive unemployment — all these are indeed symptoms of these deeper problems (Beardsmore and Willemyns; Judd; McArthur; Nelde; Veltman, "Comment"). In this context, language becomes a symbol or a signal that can define particular minority groups and legitimize coercive and discriminative measures against them. The ELA, defining as it does the only "legitimate" language for America, would do much for proponents of such views.

30   Accordingly, we call on American educators to oppose the ELA, to be keenly aware of its destructive potential, to seek alternatives to this amendment that do not threaten the constitutional rights of citizens. Passage of the ELA would set back language rights by at least six decades, render all statutory provisions for serving the needs of non-English speakers unconstitutional — and inevitably precipitate political and social unrest.

31   Passage of the ELA would force our society to address the following practical questions: How would the millions of limited- and non-English speakers learning English at the same time be afforded all the duties, rights, and privileges of American citizenship? How would they vote intelligently? facilitate their children's education if they themselves cannot communicate with teachers? How would they communicate with police? fire departments? emergency medical personnel?

32   Most unfortunate of all is that advocates of the ELA send a plain message to minority-language groups: return to that age of less dignified status — to that time when your children were linguistically excluded from the classroom, to a time when language barred you from voting, to a time when you were unable to understand court proceedings because you could not speak English. To minority-language group members, the picture is clear. The ELA has little to do with language; it has everything to do with oppression.

33   The choice is clear: to adopt an exclusionary language policy or to maintain the status quo. Choosing the former course would no doubt push our nation into a second era of civil-rights turmoil. Should we decide on the latter — ex-

tant language rights — many long and expensive court battles and countless hours of congressional debate that have been spent for their enactment would not have been in vain. Most importantly, limited- and non-English-speaking Americans will continue to enjoy the rights of full participation in our society.

Works Cited

Alatis, James E. "Comment: The Question of Language Policy." *International Journal of the Sociology of Language* 60 (1986): 197–200.

Beardsmore, Hugo Baetens, and Roland Willemyns. "Comment." *International Journal of the Sociology of Language* 60 (1986): 117–28.

Bikales, Gerda. "Comment: The Other Side." *International Journal of the Sociology of Language* 60 (1986): 77–85.

Conklin, Nancy Faires, and Margaret A. Lourie. *A Host of Tongues: Language Communities in the United States*. New York: Free, 1983.

Coulmas, Florian. *Sprache und Staat: Studien zur Sprachplanung und Sprachpolitik*. Berlin: de Gruyter, 1985.

Cummins, James. "The Construct of Language Proficiency in Bilingual Education." *Georgetown University Round Table on Languages and Linguistics 1980*. Ed. James E. Alatis. Washington: GPO, 1980. 81–103.

———. "The Role of Primary Language Development in Promoting Educational Success for Language Minority Students." *Schooling and Language Minority Students: A Theoretical Framework*. Ed. Office of Bilingual Bicultural Education. Los Angeles: Evaluation, Dissemination, and Assessment Center, California State U, 1981. 3–49.

Danoff, Malcolm N., and others. *Evaluation of the Impact of ESEA Title VII Spanish/English Bilingual Education Program*. 3 vols. Palo Alto, CA: American Institutes for Research in the Behavioral Sciences, 1978.

Djonovich, Dusan J., ed. *United Nations Resolution: Resolutions Adopted by the General Assembly*. 22 vols. Dobbs Ferry, NY: Oceana, 1975. Vol. XI.

Donohue, Thomas S. "U.S. English: Its Life and Work." *International Journal of the Sociology of Language* 56 (1985): 99–112.

Gilhotra, Manjit S. "Maintenance of Community Languages in Multicultural Australia." *Journal of Multilingual and Multicultural Development* 6.1 (1985): 59–66.

Gonzalez, Roseann D., and others. *Fundamentals of Court Interpretation: A Handbook for Interpreters, Court Personnel, and Other Users*. Forthcoming.

Grosjean, Francois. *Life with Two Languages: An Introduction to Bilingualism*. Cambridge: Harvard UP, 1982.

202 GONZALEZ, SCHOTT, AND VASQUEZ

Hakuta, Kenji. *Mirror of Language: The Debate on Bilingualism.* New York: Basic, 1986.

Hayakawa, S. I. "Make English Official: One Common Language Makes Our Nation Work." *The Executive Educator* 9.1 (1987): 36+.

Heath, Shirley Brice. "Language and Politics in the United States." *Georgetown University Round Table on Languages and Linguistics 1977.* Ed. Muriel Saville-Troike. Washington: Georgetown UP, 1977. 267–96.

Heath, Shirley Brice, and Lawrence Krasner. "Comment."*International Journal of the Sociology of Language* 60 (1986): 157–62.

Hernandez-Chavez, Eduardo. "Language Maintenance, Bilingual Education, and Philosophies of Bilingualism in the United States." *Georgetown University Round Table on Languages and Linguistics 1978.* Ed. James E. Alatis. Washington: Georgetown UP, 1978. 527–50.

Judd, Elliot L. "The English Language Amendment: A Case Study on Language and Politics." *TESOL Quarterly* 21.1 (1987): 113–33.

Kennedy, Chris, ed. *Language Planning and Language Education.* London: Allen, 1983.

Kloss, Heinz. "Language Rights of Immigrant Groups." *International Migration Review* 5 (1971): 250–68.

———. *Problems of Language Policy in South Africa.* Vienna: Wilhelm Braumüller, 1978.

"The Language Is the Melting Pot." *New York Times* 27 Sept. 1985, natl. ed.: Y28.

Levy, Jack. "Bilingualism, Federal Policy on Bilingual Education and Intercultural Relations." *International Journal of Intercultural Relations* 9 (1985): 113–30.

Maldoff, Eric. "Comment: A Canadian Perspective." *International Journal of the Sociology of Language* 60 (1986): 105–14.

McArthur, Tom. "Comment: Worried About Something Else." *International Journal of the Sociology of Language* 60 (1986): 87–91.

Marshall, David F. "The Question of an Official Language: Language Rights and the English Language Amendment." *International Journal of the Sociology of Language* 60 (1986): 7–75.

National Clearinghouse for Bilingual Education. "Descriptive Phase of National Longitudinal Study Released." *Forum* 8.3 (1985): 1–3.

Nelde, Peter H. "Language Contact Means Language Conflict." *Journal of Multilingual and Multicultural Development* 8.1–2 (1987): 33–42.

The Public Papers of the Presidents of the United States: Ronald Reagan. Washington: GPO, 1981.

Reagan, Timothy. "Language Policy, Politics, and Ideology: The Case of South Africa." *Issues in Education* 2.2 (1984): 155–64.

———. "The Role of Language Policy in South African Education." *Language Problems and Language Planning* 10.1 (1986): 1–13.

Reinhold, Robert. "Resentment Against New Immigrants." *New York Times* 26 Oct. 1986, late ed.: E6.

Title VII-Bilingual Education Programs. Public Law 90–247, 2 Jan. 1968. *U.S. Statutes at Large*. 98 vols. Washington: GPO, 1968. Vol. 81.

Troike, Rudolph. "Developing America's Language Resources for the 21st Century." Unpublished manuscript, U of Illinois, Champaign-Urbana, 1983.

Trombley, William. "Prop. 63 Roots Traced to Small Michigan City." *Los Angeles Times* 20 Oct. 1986: 3 + .

US English. Letter to the authors. 9 March 1987.

——. Personal conversation with the authors. 7 July 1987.

Veltman, Calvin. "Comment." *International Journal of the Sociology of Language* 60 (1986): 177–81.

——. *Language Shifts in the United States*. Berlin: Mouton, 1983.

National Council of Teachers of English

1986 NCTE Resolution on English as the "Official Language"

The National Council of Teachers of English (NCTE), a professional organization that represents thousands of elementary school, high school, and college teachers, passed the following statement on the official language question in 1986.

Background: The proposers of this resolution voiced concern about the current movement in some states to establish English as the official language. Such efforts, successful in one instance so far, can include removal of the native languages of many Americans from official documents, they noted, and called such actions potentially discriminatory.   1

The proposers commended the recent Public Broadcasting System television series *The Story of English* for illustrating the capacity of English to accommodate and incorporate the linguistic characteristics of many peoples and cultures.   2

Resolved, that the National Council of Teachers of English condemn any attempts to render invisible the native lan-   3 guages of any Americans or to deprive English of the rich influences of the languages and cultures of any of the peoples of America;

4   that NCTE urge legislators, other public officials, and citizens to oppose actively action intended to mandate or declare English as an official language or to "preserve," "purify," or "enhance" the language. Any such action will not only stunt the vitality of the language but also ensure its erosion and in effect create hostility toward English, making it more difficult to teach and learn; and

5   that NCTE widely publish this resolution to its affiliates and other professional organizations through news releases, letters to legislators, boards of education and other state officials, especially in those states attempting to legislate English as an official language.

IS ENGLISH SEXIST?

Casey Miller and Kate Swift
One Small Step for Genkind

Casey Miller and Kate Swift, co-authors of Words and Women
(1977) and The Handbook of Nonsexist Writing *(1980), are*
freelance writers and editors. Their interest in language grew
out of editorial work in a range of fields, including science,
religion, history, and the arts. Their articles have appeared in
many prestigious publications; this essay appeared in 1972 in
The New York Times Magazine.

A riddle is making the rounds that goes like this: A man 1
and his young son were in an automobile accident. The
father was killed and the son, who was critically injured,
was rushed to a hospital. As attendants wheeled the unconscious boy into the emergency room, the doctor on duty
looked down at him and said, "My God, it's my son!" What
was the relationship of the doctor to the injured boy?

If the answer doesn't jump to your mind, another riddle 2
that has been around a lot longer might help: The blind
beggar had a brother. The blind beggar's brother died. The
brother who died had no brother. What relation was the
blind beggar to the blind beggar's brother?

As with all riddles, the answers are obvious once you see 3
them: The doctor was the boy's mother and the beggar was
her brother's sister. Then why doesn't everyone solve them
immediately? Mainly because our language, like the culture
it reflects, is male oriented. To say that a woman in
medicine is an exception is simply to confirm that statement. Thousands of doctors are women, but in order to be
seen in the mind's eye, they must be called women doctors.

Except for words that refer to females by definition 4
(mother, actress, Congresswoman), and words for occupations traditionally held by females (nurse, secretary, prostitute), the English language defines everyone as male. The

hypothetical person ("If a man can walk 10 miles in two hours . . . "), the average person ("the man in the street") and the active person ("the man on the move") are male. The assumption is that unless otherwise identified, people in general — including doctors and beggars — are men. It is a semantic mechanism that operates to keep women invisible: *man* and *mankind* represent everyone; *he* in generalized use refers to either sex; the "land where our fathers died" is also the land of our mothers — although they go unsung. As the beetle-browed and mustachioed man in a Steig cartoon says to his two male drinking companions, "When I speak of mankind, one thing I *don't* mean is womankind."

5   Semantically speaking, woman is not one with the species of man, but a distinct subspecies. "Man," says the 1971 edition of the Britannica Junior Encyclopedia, "is the highest form of life on earth. His superior intelligence, combined with certain physical characteristics, have enabled man to achieve things that are impossible for other animals." (The prose style has something in common with the report of a research team describing its studies on "the development of the uterus in rats, guinea pigs and men.") As though quoting the Steig character, still speaking to his friends in McSorley's, the Junior Encyclopedia continues: "Man must invent most of his behavior, because he lacks the instincts of lower animals. . . . Most of the things he learns have been handed down from his ancestors by language and symbols rather than by biological inheritance."

6   Considering that for the last 5,000 years society has been patriarchal, that statement explains a lot. It explains why Eve was made from Adam's rib instead of the other way around, and who invented all those Adam-rib words like *fe*male and *wo*man in the first place. It also explains why, when it is necessary to mention woman, the language makes her a lower caste, a class separate from the rest of man; why it works to "keep her in her place."

7   This inheritance through language and other symbols begins in the home (also called a man's castle) where man and wife (not husband and wife, or man and woman) live for a while with their children. It is reinforced by religious training, the educational system, the press, government, commerce and the law. As Andrew Greeley wrote not long ago in his magazine, "man is a symbol-creating animal. He

orders and interprets his reality by his symbols, and he uses the symbols to reconstruct that reality."

Consider some of the reconstructed realities of American 8 history. When school children learn from their textbooks that the early colonists gained valuable experience in governing themselves, they are not told that the early colonists who were women were denied the privilege of self-government; when they learn that in the 18th century the average man had to manufacture many of the things he and his family needed, they are not told that this "average man" was often a woman who manufactured much of what she and her family needed. Young people learn that intrepid pioneers crossed the country in covered wagons with their wives, children and cattle; they do not learn that women themselves were intrepid pioneers rather than part of the baggage.

In a paper published this year in Los Angeles as a guide 9 for authors and editors of social-studies textbooks, Elizabeth Burr, Susan Dunn and Norma Farquhar document unintentional skewings of this kind that occur either because women are not specifically mentioned as affecting or being affected by historical events, or because they are discussed in terms of outdated assumptions. "One never sees a picture of women captioned simply 'farmers' or 'pioneers,'" they point out. The subspecies nomenclature that requires a caption to read "women farmers" or "women pioneers" is extended to impose certain jobs on women by definition. The textbook guide gives as an example the word *housewife*, which it says not only "suggests that domestic chores are the exclusive burden of females," but gives "female students the idea that they were born to keep house and teaches male students that they are automatically entitled to laundry, cooking and housecleaning services from the women in their families."

Sexist language is any language that expresses such 10 stereotyped attitudes and expectations, or that assumes the inherent superiority of one sex over the other. When a woman says of her husband, who has drawn up plans for a new bedroom wing and left out closets, "Just like a man," her language is as sexist as the man's who says, after his wife has changed her mind about needing the new wing after all, "Just like a woman."

Male and female are not sexist words, but masculine and 11

feminine almost always are. Male and female can be applied
objectively to individual people and animals and, by extension, to things. When electricians and plumbers talk about
male and female couplings, everyone knows or can figure
out what they mean. The terms are graphic and culture free.

12   Masculine and feminine, however, are as sexist as any
words can be, since it is almost impossible to use them
without invoking cultural stereotypes. When people construct lists of "masculine" and "feminine" traits they almost
always end up making assumptions that have nothing to
do with innate differences between the sexes. We have a
friend who happens to be going through the process of pin-
ning down this very phenomenon. He is 7 years old and his
question concerns why his coats and shirts button left over
right while his sister's button the other way. He assumes
it must have something to do with the differences between
boys and girls, but he can't see how.

13   What our friend has yet to grasp is that the way you
button your coat, like most sex-differentiated customs, has
nothing to do with real differences but much to do with
what society wants you to feel about yourself as a male or
female person. Society decrees that it is appropriate for
girls to dress differently from boys, to act differently, and
to think differently. Boys must be masculine, whatever that
means, and girls must be feminine.

14   Unabridged dictionaries are a good source for finding out
what society decrees to be appropriate, though less by definition than by their choice of associations and illustrations.
Words associated with males — *manly, virile* and *masculine*,
for example — are defined through a broad range of positive
attributes like strength, courage, directness and independence, and they are illustrated through such examples of
contemporary usage as "a manly determination to face
what comes," "a virile literary style," "a masculine love of
sports." Corresponding words associated with females are
defined with fewer attributes (though weakness is often one
of them) and the examples given are generally negative if
not clearly pejorative: "feminine wiles," "womanish tears,"
"a womanlike lack of promptness," "convinced that drawing
was a waste of time, if not downright womanly."

15   Male-associated words are frequently applied to females
to describe something that is either incongruous ("a man-
nish voice") or presumably commendable ("a masculine

mind," "she took it like a man"), but female-associated words are unreservedly derogatory when applied to males, and are sometimes abusive to females as well. The opposite of "masculine" is "effeminate," although the opposite of "feminine" is simply "unfeminine."

One dictionary, after defining the word *womanish* as 16 "suitable to or resembling a woman," further defines it as "unsuitable to a man or to a strong character of either sex." Words derived from "sister" and "brother" provide another apt example, for whereas "sissy," applied either to a male or female, conveys the message that sisters are expected to be timid and cowardly, "buddy" makes clear that brothers are friends.

The subtle disparagement of females and corresponding 17 approbation of males wrapped up in many English words is painfully illustrated by "tomboy." Here is an instance where a girl who likes sports and the out-of-doors, who is curious about how things work, who is adventurous and bold instead of passive, is defined in terms of something she is not—a boy. By denying that she can be the person she is and still be a girl, the word surreptitiously undermines her sense of identity: it says she is unnatural. A "tomboy," as defined by one dictionary, is a "girl, especially a young girl, who behaves like a spirited boy." But who makes the judgment that she is acting like a spirited boy, not a spirited girl? Can it be a coincidence that in the case of the dictionary just quoted the editor, executive editor, managing editor, general manager, all six members of the Board of Linguists, the usage editor, science editor, all six general editors of definitions, and 94 out of the 104 distinguished experts consulted on usage—are men?

It isn't enough to say that any invidious comparisons and 18 stereotypes lexicographers perpetuate are already present in the culture. There are ways to define words like womanly and tomboy that don't put women down, though the tradition has been otherwise. Samuel Johnson, the lexicographer, was the same Dr. Johnson who said, "A woman preaching is like a dog's walking on his hind legs. It is not done well; but you are surprised to find it done at all."

Possibly because of the negative images associated with 19 womanish and womanlike, and with expressions like "woman driver" and "woman of the street," the word woman dropped out of fashion for a time. The women at the office and the women on the assembly line and the women one first knew in school all became ladies or girls or gals. Now a countermovement, supported by the very term women's liberation, is putting back into words like woman and sister and sisterhood the meaning they were losing by default. It is as though, in the nick of time, women had seen that the language itself could destroy them.

20   Some long-standing conventions of the news media add insult to injury. When a woman or girl makes news, her sex is identified at the beginning of a story, if possible in the headline or its equivalent. The assumption, apparently, is that whatever event or action is being reported, a woman's involvement is less common and therefore more newsworthy than a man's. If the story is about achievement, the implication is: "pretty good for a woman." And because people are assumed to be male unless otherwise identified, the media have developed a special and extensive vocabulary to avoid the constant repetition of "woman." The results, "Grandmother Wins Nobel Prize," "Blonde Hijacks Airliner," "Housewife to Run for Congress," convey the kind of information that would be ludicrous in comparable headlines if the subjects were men. Why, if "Unsalaried Husband to Run for Congress" is unacceptable to editors, do women have to keep explaining that to describe them through external or superficial concerns reflects a sexist view of women as decorative objects, breeding machines and extensions of men, not real people?

21   Members of the Chicago chapter of the National Organization for Women recently studied the newspapers in their area and drew up a set of guidelines for the press. These include cutting out descriptions of the "clothes, physical features, dating life and marital status of women where such references would be considered inappropriate if about men"; using language in such a way as to include women in copy that refers to homeowners, scientists and business people where "newspaper descriptions often convey the idea that all such persons are male"; and displaying the same discretion in printing generalizations about women as would be shown toward racial, religious and ethnic groups. "Our concern with what we are called may seem trivial to some people," the women said, "but we regard the old usages as symbolic of women's position within this society."

22   The assumption that an adult woman is flattered by being

called a girl is matched by the notion that a woman in a menial or poorly paid job finds compensation in being called a lady. Ethel Strainchamps has pointed out that since lady is used as an adjective with nouns designating both high and low occupations (lady wrestler, lady barber, lady doctor, lady judge), some writers assume they can use the noun form without betraying value judgments. Not so, Strainchamps says, rolling the issue into a spitball: "You may write, 'He addressed the Republican ladies,' or 'The Democratic ladies convened' . . . but I have never seen 'the Communist ladies' or 'the Black Panther ladies' in print."

Thoughtful writers and editors have begun to repudiate   23
some of the old usages. "Divorcée," "grandmother" and "blonde," along with "vivacious," "pert," "dimpled" and "cute," were dumped by the Washington Post in the spring of 1970 by the executive editor, Benjamin Bradlee. In a memo to his staff, Bradlee wrote, "The meaningful equality and dignity of women is properly under scrutiny today. . . because this equality has been less than meaningful and the dignity not always free of stereotype and condescension."

What women have been called in the press — or at least   24
the part that operates above ground — is only a fraction of the infinite variety of alternatives to "women" used in the subcultures of the English-speaking world. Beyond "chicks," "dolls," "dames," "babes," "skirts" and "broads" are the words and phrases in which women are reduced to their sexuality and nothing more. It would be hard to think of another area of language in which the human mind has been so fertile in devising and borrowing abusive terms. In "The Female Eunuch," Germaine Greer devotes four pages to anatomical terms and words for animals, vegetables, fruits, baked goods, implements and receptacles, all of which are used to dehumanize the female person. Jean Faust, in an article aptly called "Words That Oppress," suggests that the effort to diminish women through language is rooted in a male fear of sexual inadequacy. "Woman is made to feel guilty for and akin to natural disasters," she writes; "hurricanes and typhoons are named after her. Any negative or threatening force is given a feminine name. If a man runs into bad luck climbing up the ladder of success (a male-invented game), he refers to the 'bitch goddess' success."

The sexual overtones in the ancient and no doubt honor-   25

able custom of calling ships "she" have become more
explicit and less honorable in an age of air travel: "I'm
Karen. Fly me." Attitudes of ridicule, contempt and disgust
toward female sexuality have spawned a rich glossary of
insults and epithets not found in dictionaries. And the usage
in which four-letter words meaning copulate are interchangeable with cheat, attack and destroy can scarcely be
unrelated to the savagery of rape.

26   In her updating of Ibsen's "A Doll's House," Clare Booth
Luce has Nora tell her husband she is pregnant—"In the
way only men are supposed to get pregnant." "Men, pregnant?" he says, and she nods; "With ideas. Pregnancies there
[*she taps his head*] are masculine. And a very superior form
of labor. Pregnancies here [*taps her tummy*] are feminine—a
very inferior form of labor."

27   Public outcry followed a revised translation of the New
Testament describing Mary as "pregnant" instead of "great
with child." The objections were made in part on esthetic
grounds: there is no attractive adjective in modern English
for a woman who is about to give birth. A less obvious
reason was that replacing the euphemism with a biological
term undermined religious teaching. The initiative and
generative power in the conception of Jesus are understood
to be God's; Mary, the mother, was a vessel only.

28   Whether influenced by this teaching or not, the language
of human reproduction lags several centuries behind scientific understanding. The male's contribution to procreation
is still described as though it were the entire seed from
which a new life grows: the initiative and generative power
involved in the process are thought of as masculine, receptivity and nurturance as feminine. "Seminal" remains a
synonym for "highly original," and there is no comparable
word to describe the female's equivalent contribution.

29   An entire mythology has grown from this biological misunderstanding and its semantic legacy; its embodiment in
laws that for centuries made women nonpersons was a key
target of the 19th-century feminist movement. Today, more
than 50 years after women finally won the basic democratic
right to vote, the word "liberation" itself, when applied to
women, means something less than when used of other
groups of people. An advertisement for the N.B.C. news
department listed Women's Liberation along with crime
in the streets and the Vietnam war as "bad news." Asked
for his views on Women's Liberation, a highly placed politi-

cian was quoted as saying, "Let me make one thing perfectly clear. I wouldn't want to wake up next to a lady pipe-fitter."

One of the most surprising challenges to our male-domi-   30
nated culture is coming from within organized religion, where the issues are being stated, in part, by confronting the implications of traditional language. What a growing number of theologians and scholars are saying is that the myths of the Judeo-Christian tradition, being the products of patriarchy, must be reexamined, and that the concept of an exclusively male ministry and the image of a male god have become idolatrous.

Women are naturally in the forefront of this movement,   31
both in their efforts to gain ordination and full equality and through their contributions to theological reform, although both these efforts are often subtly diminished. When the Rev. Barbara Anderson was ordained by the American Lutheran Church, one newspaper printed her picture over a caption headed "Happy Girl." Newsweek's report of a protest staged last December by women divinity students at Harvard was jocular ("another tilt at the windmill") and sarcastic: "Every time anyone in the room lapsed into what [the students] regarded as male chauvinism — such as using the word 'mankind' to describe the human race in general — the outraged women . . . drowned out the offender with earpiercing blasts from party-favor kazoos. . . . What annoyed the women most was the universal custom of referring to God as 'He.'"

The tone of the report was not merely unfunny; it missed   32
the connection between increasingly outmoded theological language and the accelerating number of women (and men) who are dropping out of organized religion, both Jewish and Christian. For language, including pronouns, can be used to construct a reality that simply mirrors society's assumptions. To women who are committed to the reality of religious faith, the effect is doubly painful. Professor Harvey Cox, in whose classroom the protest took place, stated the issue directly: The women, he said, were raising the "basic theological question of whether God is more adequately thought of in personal or suprapersonal terms."

Toward the end of Don McLean's remarkable ballad   33
"American Pie," a song filled with the imagery of abandonment and disillusion, there is a stanza that must strike

many women to the quick. The church bells are broken, the music has died; then:

> And the three men I admire most,
> The Father, Son and the Holy Ghost,
> They caught the last train for the Coast —
> The day the music died.

34   Three men I admired most. There they go, briefcases in hand and topcoats buttoned left over right, walking down the long cold platform under the city, past the baggage wagons and the hissing steam onto the Pullman. Bye, bye God — all three of you — made in the image of male supremacy. Maybe out there in L.A. where the weather is warmer, someone can believe in you again.

35   The Roman Catholic theologian Elizabeth Farians says "the bad theology of an overmasculinized church continues to be one of the root causes of women's oppression." The definition of oppression is "to crush or burden by abuse of power or authority; burden spiritually or mentally as if by pressure."

36   When language oppresses, it does so by any means that disparage and belittle. Until well into the 20th century, one of the ways English was manipulated to disparage women was through the addition of feminine endings to nonsexual words. Thus a woman who aspired to be a poet was excluded from the company of real poets by the label poetess, and a woman who piloted an airplane was denied full status as an aviator by being called an aviatrix. At about the time poetess, aviatrix, and similar Adam-ribbisms were dropping out of use, H. W. Fowler was urging that they be revived. "With the coming expansion of women's vocations," he wrote in the first edition (1926) of "Modern English Usage," "feminines for vocation-words are a special need of the future." There can be no doubt he subconsciously recognized the relative status implied in the -*ess* designations. His criticism of a woman who wished to be known as an author rather than an authoress was that she had no need "to raise herself to the level of the male author by asserting her right to his name."

37   Who has the prior right to a name? The question has an interesting bearing on words that were once applied to men alone, or to both men and women, but now, having acquired

abusive associations, are assigned to women exclusively.
Spinster is a gentle case in point. Prostitute and many of
its synonyms illustrate the phenomenon better. If Fowler
had chosen to record the changing usage of harlot from
hired man (in Chaucer's time) through rascal and entertainer to its present definition, would he have maintained
that the female harlot is trying to raise herself to the level
of the male harlot by asserting her right to his name? Or
would he have plugged for harlotress?

The demise of most -ess endings came about before the   38
start of the new feminist movement. In the second edition
of "Modern English Usage," published in 1965, Sir Ernest
Gowers frankly admitted what his predecessors had been
up to. "Feminine designations," he wrote, "seem now to be
falling into disuse. Perhaps the explanation of this paradox
is that it symbolizes the victory of women in their struggle
for equal rights; it reflects the abandonment by men of
those ideas about women in the professions that moved Dr.
Johnson to his rude remark about women preachers."

If Sir Ernest's optimism can be justified, why is there a   39
movement back to feminine endings in such words as chair-
woman, councilwoman and congresswoman? Betty Hudson, of Madison, Conn., is campaigning for the adoption of
"selectwoman" as the legal title for a female member of
that town's executive body. To have to address a woman
as "Selectman," she maintains, "is not only bad grammar
and bad biology, but it implies that politics is still, or should
be, a man's business." A valid argument, and one that was,
predictably, countered by ridicule, the surefire weapon for
undercutting achievement. When the head of the Federal
Maritime Commission, Helen D. Bentley, was named "Man
of the Year" by an association of shipping interests, she
wisely refused to be drawn into light-hearted debate with
interviewers who wanted to make the award's name a
humorous issue. Some women, of course, have yet to learn
they are invisible. An 8-year-old who visited the American
Museum of Natural History with her Brownie scout troop
went through the impressive exhibit on pollution and over-
population called "Can Man Survive?" Asked afterward,
"Well, can he?" she answered, "I don't know about him,
but we're working on it in Brownies."

Nowhere are women rendered more invisible by language   40
than in politics. The United States Constitution, in describing the qualifications for Representative, Senator and Pres-

ident, refers to each as *he*. No wonder Shirley Chisholm, the first woman since 1888 to make a try for the Presidential nomination of a major party, has found it difficult to be taken seriously.

41   The observation by Andrew Greeley already quoted— that "man" uses "his symbols" to reconstruct "his reality"— was not made in reference to the symbols of language but to the symbolic impact the "nomination of a black man for the Vice-Presidency" would have on race relations in the United States. Did the author assume the generic term "man" would of course be construed to include "woman"? Or did he deliberately use a semantic device to exclude Shirley Chisholm without having to be explicit?

42   Either way, his words construct a reality in which women are ignored. As much as any other factor in our language, the ambiguous meaning of *man* serves to deny women recognition as people. In a recent magazine article, we discussed the similar effect on women of the generic pronoun *he*, which we proposed to replace by a new common gender pronoun *tey*. We were immediately told, by a number of authorities, that we were dabbling in the serious business of linguistics, and the message that reached us from these scholars was loud and clear: It-is-absolutely-impossible-for-anyone-to-introduce-a-new-word-into-the-language-just-because-there-is-a-need-for-it, so-stop-wasting-your-time.

43   When words are suggested like "herstory" (for history), "sportsoneship" (for sportsmanship) and "mistresspiece" (for the work of a Virginia Woolf) one suspects a not-to-subtle attempt to make the whole language problem look silly. But unless Alexander Pope, when he wrote "The proper study of mankind is man," meant that women should be relegated to the footnotes (or, as George Orwell might have put it, "All men are equal, but men are more equal than women"), viable new words will surely someday supersede the old.

44   Without apologies to Freud, the great majority of women do not wish in their hearts that they were men. If having grown up with a language that tells them they are at the same time men and not men raises psychic doubts for women, the doubts are not of their sexual identity but of their human identity. Perhaps the present unrest surfacing in the Women's Movement is part of an evolutionary change in our particular form of life—the one form of all in the

animal and plant kingdoms that orders and interprets its reality by symbols. The achievements of the species called man have brought us to the brink of self-destruction. If the species survives into the next century with the expectation of going on, it may only be because we have become part of what Harlow Shapley calls the psychozoic kingdom, where brain overshadows brawn and rationality has replaced superstition.

Searching the roots of Western civilization for a word to   45
call this new species of man and woman, someone might come up with *gen*, as in genesis and generic. With such a word, *man* could be used exclusively for males as *woman* is used for females, for gen would include both sexes. Like the words deer and bison, gen would be both plural and singular. Like progenitor, progeny, and generation, it would convey continuity. Gen would express the warmth and generalized sexuality of generous, gentle, and genuine; the specific sexuality of genital and genetic. In the new family of gen, girls and boys would grow to genhood, and to speak of genkind would be to include all the people of the earth.

Barbara Lawrence

Four-Letter Words Can Hurt You

Barbara Lawrence, born in New Hampshire and educated at Connecticut College and New York University, is Professor of Humanities at the State University of New York at Old Westbury. The following essay appeared in The New York Times *in 1973.*

Why should any words be called obscene? Don't they all   1
describe natural human functions? Am I trying to tell them, my students demand, that the "strong, earthy, gut-honest"—or, if they are fans of Norman Mailer, the "rich, liberating, existential"—language they use to describe sexual activity isn't preferable to "phony-sounding, middle-class words like 'intercourse' and 'copulate'"? "Cop You Late!" they say with fancy inflections and gagging grimaces. "Now, what is *that* supposed to mean?"

2   Well, what is it supposed to mean? And why indeed should one group of words describing human functions and human organs be acceptable in ordinary conversation and another, describing presumably the same organs and functions, be tabooed — so much so, in fact, that some of these words still cannot appear in print in many parts of the English-speaking world?

3   The argument that these taboos exist only because of "sexual hangups" (middle-class, middle-age, feminist), or even that they are a result of class oppression (the contempt of the Norman conquerors for the language of their Anglo-Saxon serfs), ignores a much more likely explanation, it seems to me, and that is the sources and functions of the words themselves.

4   The best known of the tabooed sexual verbs, for example, comes from the German *ficken*, meaning "to strike"; combined, according to Partridge's etymological dictionary *Origins*, with the Latin sexual verb *futuere;* associated in turn with the Latin *fustis*, "a staff or cudgel"; the Celtic *buc*, "a point, hence to pierce"; the Irish *bot*, "the male member"; the Latin *battuere*, "to beat"; the Gaelic *batair*, "a cudgeller"; the Early Irish *bualaim*, "I strike"; and so forth. It is one of what etymologists sometimes call "the sadistic group of words for the man's part in copulation."

5   The brutality of this word, then, and its equivalents ("screw," "bang," etc.), is not an illusion of the middle class or a crotchet of Women's Liberation. In their origins and imagery these words carry undeniably painful, if not sadistic, implications, the object of which is almost always female. Consider, for example, what a "screw" actually does to the wood it penetrates; what a painful, even mutilating, activity this kind of analogy suggests. "Screw" is particularly interesting in this context, since the noun, according to Partridge, comes from words meaning "groove," "nut," "ditch," "breeding sow," "scrofula" and "swelling," while the verb, besides its explicit imagery, has antecedent associations to "write on," "scratch," "scarify," and so forth — a revealing fusion of a mechanical or painful action with an obviously denigrated object.

6   Not all obscene words, of course, are as implicitly sadistic or denigrating to women as these, but all that I know seem to serve a similar purpose: to reduce the human organism (especially the female organism) and human functions (especially sexual and procreative) to their least organic,

most mechanical dimension; to substitute a trivializing or deforming resemblance for the complex human reality of what is being described.

Tabooed male descriptives, when they are not openly denigrating to women, often serve to divorce a male organ or function from any significant interaction with the female. Take the word "testes," for example, suggesting "witnesses" (from the Latin *testis*) to the sexual and procreative strengths of the male organ; and the obscene counterpart of this word, which suggests little more than a mechanical shape. Or compare almost any of the "rich," "liberating" sexual verbs, so fashionable today among male writers, with that much-derided Latin word "copulate" ("to bind or join together") or even that Anglo-Saxon phrase (which seems to have had no trouble surviving the Norman Conquest) "make love." 7

How arrogantly self-involved the tabooed words seem in comparison to either of the other terms, and how contemptuous of the female partner. Understandably so, of course, if she is only a "skirt," a "broad," a "chick," a "pussycat" or a "piece." If she is, in other words, no more than her skirt, or what her skirt conceals; no more than a breeder, or the broadest part of her; no more than a piece of a human being or a "piece of tail." 8

The most severely tabooed of all the female descriptives, incidentally, are those like a "piece of tail," which suggest (either explicitly or through antecedents) that there is no significant difference between the female channel through which we are all conceived and born and the anal outlet common to both sexes—a distinction that pornographers have always enjoyed obscuring. 9

This effort to deny women their biological identity, their individuality, their humanness, is such an important aspect of obscene language that one can only marvel at how seldom, in an era preoccupied with definitions of obscenity, this fact is brought to our attention. One problem, of course, is that many of the people in the best position to do this (critics, teachers, writers) are so reluctant today to admit that they are angered or shocked by obscenity. Bored, maybe, unimpressed, aesthetically displeased, but—no matter how brutal or denigrating the material—never angered, never shocked. 10

And yet how eloquently angered, how piously shocked many of these same people become if denigrating language 11 is used about any minority group other than women; if the obscenities are racial or ethnic, that is, rather than sexual. Words like "coon," "kike," "spic," "wop," after all, deform identity, deny individuality and humanness in almost exactly the same way that sexual vulgarisms and obscenities do.

12   No one that I know, least of all my students, would fail to question the values of a society whose literature and entertainment rested heavily on racial or ethnic pejoratives. Are the values of a society whose literature and entertainment rest as heavily as ours on sexual pejoratives any less questionable?

Douglas R. Hofstadter

A Person Paper on Purity in Language

Douglas R. Hofstadter (born 1945) is hard to describe. His enigmatic, difficult, and fascinating bestseller, Godel, Escher, Bach, *which won the 1980 Pulitzer Prize for nonfiction, illustrates the breadth of his knowledge and interests. He works at the edges of computer science, artificial intelligence, neuroscience, and philosophy, and seems to love math and physics and music and language and puns. For two years he wrote a column for* Scientific American; *many of those essays found their way into his 1985 book* Metamagical Themas. *The following essay, though not written for* Scientific American, *also appeared in* Metamagical Themas.

1   It's high time someone blew the whistle on all the silly prattle about revamping our language to suit the purposes of certain political fanatics. You know what I'm talking about — those who accuse speakers of English of what they call "racism." This awkward neologism, constructed by analogy with the well-established term "sexism," does not sit well in the ears, if I may mix my metaphors. But let us grant that in our society there may be injustices here and there in the treatment of either race from time to time, and let us even grant these people their terms "racism" and "racist." How valid, however, are the claims of the self-pro-

claimed "black libbers," or "negrists" — those who would radically change our language in order to "liberate" us poor dupes from its supposed racist bias?

Most of the clamor, as you certainly know by now, re-   2
volves around the age-old usage of the noun "white" and words built from it, such as *chairwhite, mailwhite, repairwhite, clergywhite, middlewhite, Frenchwhite, forewhite, whitepower, whiteslaughter, oneupswhiteship, straw white, whitehandle,* and so on. The negrists claim that using the word "white," either on its own or as a component, to talk about *all* the members of the human species is somehow degrading to blacks and reinforces racism. Therefore the libbers propose that we substitute "person" everywhere where "white" now occurs. Sensitive speakers of our secretary tongue of course find this preposterous. There is great beauty to a phrase such as "All whites are created equal." Our forebosses who framed the Declaration of Independence well understood the poetry of our language. Think how ugly it would be to say "All persons are created equal," or "All whites and blacks are created equal." Besides, as any schoolwhitey can tell you, such phrases are redundant. In most contexts, it is self-evident when "white" is being used in an inclusive sense, in which case it subsumes members of the darker race just as much as fairskins.

There is nothing denigrating to black people in being   3
subsumed under the rubric "white" — no more than under the rubric "person." After all, white is a mixture of all the colors of the rainbow, including black. Used inclusively, the word "white" has no connotations whatsoever of race. Yet many people are hung up on this point. A prime example is Abraham Moses, one of the more vocal spokeswhites for making such a shift. For years, Niss Moses, authoroon of the well-known negrist tracts *A Handbook of Nonracist Writing* and *Words and Blacks*, has had nothing better to do than go around the country making speeches advocating the downfall of "racist language" that ble objects to. But when you analyze bler objections, you find they all fall apart at the seams. Niss Moses says that words like "chairwhite" suggest to people — most especially impressionable young whiteys and blackeys — that all chairwhites belong to the white race. How absurd! It is quite obvious, for instance, that the chairwhite of the League of Black Voters is going to be a black, not a white. Nobody need think twice about it. As a matter of fact, the suffix "white" is usually not

pronounced with a long 'i' as in the noun "white," but like "wit," as in the terms *saleswhite, freshwhite, penwhiteship, first basewhite,* and so on. It's just a simple and useful component in building race-neutral words.

4   But Niss Moses would have you sit up and start hollering "Racism!" In fact, Niss Moses sees evidence of racism under every stone. Ble has written a famous article, in which ble vehemently objects to the immortal and poetic words of the first white on the moon, Captain Nellie Strongarm. If you will recall, whis words were: "One small step for a white, a giant step for whitekind." This noble sentiment is anything but racist; it is simply a celebration of a glorious moment in the history of White.

5   Another of Niss Moses' shrill objections is to the age-old differentiation of whites from blacks by the third-person pronouns "whe" and "ble." Ble promotes an absurd notion: that what we really need in English is a single pronoun covering *both* races. Numerous suggestions have been made, such as "pe," "tey," and others. These are all repugnant to the nature of the English language, as the average white in the street will testify, even if whe has no linguistic training whatsoever. Then there are advocates of usages such as "whe or ble," "whis or bler," and so forth. This makes for monstrosities such as the sentence "When the next President takes office, whe or ble will have to choose whis or bler cabinet with great care, for whe or ble would not want to offend any minorities." Contrast this with the spare elegance of the normal way of putting it, and there is no question which way we ought to speak. There are, of course, some yapping black libbers who advocate writing "bl/whe" everywhere, which, aside from looking terrible, has no reasonable pronunciation. Shall we say "blooey" all the time when we simply mean "whe?" Who wants to sound like a white with as chronic sneeze?

· · ·

6   One of the more hilarious suggestions made by the squawkers for this point of view is to abandon the natural distinction along racial lines, and to replace it with a highly unnatural one along sexual lines. One such suggestion—emanating, no doubt, from the mind of a madwhite—would have us say "he" for male whites (and blacks) and "she" for female whites (and blacks). Can you imagine the outrage with which sensible folk of either sex would greet this "modest proposal"?

Another suggestion is that the plural pronoun "they" be 7
used in place of the inclusive "whe." This would turn the
charming proverb "Whe who laughs last, laughs best" into
the bizarre concoction "They who laughs last, laughs best."
As if anyone in whis right mind could have thought that
the original proverb applied only to the white race! No, we
don't need a new pronoun to "liberate" our minds. That's
the lazy white's way of solving the pseudo-problem of racism. In any case, it's ungrammatical. The pronoun "they"
is a plural pronoun, and it grates on the civilized ear to
hear it used to denote only one person. Such a usage, if
adopted, would merely promote illiteracy and accelerate
the already scandalously rapid nosedive of the average intelligence level in our society.

Niss Moses would have us totally revamp the English 8
language to suit bler purposes. If, for instance, we are to
substitute "person" for "white," where are we to stop? If
we were to follow Niss Moses' ideas to their logical conclusion, we would have to conclude that ble would like to see
small blackeys and whiteys playing the game of "Hangper-
son" and reading the story of "Snow Person and the Seven
Dwarfs." And would ble have us rewrite history to say,
"Don't shoot until you see the *persons* of their eyes!"? Will
pundits and politicians henceforth issue *person* papers? Will
we now have egg yolks and egg *persons*? And pledge allegiance to the good old Red, *Person*, and Blue? Will we
sing, "I'm dreaming of a *person* Christmas?" Say of a
frightened white, "Whe's *person* as a sheet!"? Lament the
increase of *person*-collar crime? Thrill to the chirping of
bob*persons* in our garden? Ask a friend to *person* the table
while we go visit the *persons'* room? Come off it, Niss
Moses—don't personwash our language!

What conceivable harm is there in such beloved phrases 9
as "No white is an island," "Dog is white's best friend," or
"White's inhumanity to white?" Who would revise such
classic book titles as Bronob Jacowski's *The Ascent of White*
or Eric Steeple Bell's *Whites of Mathematics*? Did the poet
who wrote "The best-laid plans of mice and whites gang
aft agley" believe that blacks' plans gang *ne'er* agley? Surely
not! Such phrases are simply metaphors; everyone can see
beyond that. Whe who interprets them as reinforcing racism must have a perverse desire to feel oppressed.

"Personhandling" the language is a habit that not only 10
Niss Moses but quite a few others have taken up recently.
For instance, Nrs. Delilah Buford has urged that we drop

the useful distinction between "Niss" and "Nrs." (which, as everybody knows, is pronounced "Nissiz," the reason for which nobody knows!). Bler argument is that there is no need for the public to know whether a black is employed or not. *Need* is, of course, not the point. Ble conveniently sidesteps the fact that there is a *tradition* in our society of calling unemployed blacks "Niss" and employed blacks "Nrs." Most blacks—in fact, the vast majority—prefer it that way. They *want* the world to know what their employment status is, and for good reason. Unemployed blacks want prospective employers to know they are available, without having to ask embarrassing questions. Likewise, employed blacks are proud of having found a job, and wish to let the world know they are employed. This distinction provides a sense of security to all involved, in that everyone knows where ble fits into the scheme of things.

11   But Nrs. Buford refuses to recognize this simple truth. Instead, ble shiftily turns the argument into one about whites, asking why it is that whites are universally addressed as "Master," without any differentiation between employed and unemployed ones. The answer, of course, is that in America and other Northern societies, we set little store by the employment status of whites. Nrs. Buford can do little to change that reality, for it seems to be tied to innate biological differences between whites and blacks. Many white-years of research, in fact, have gone into trying to understand why it is that employment status matters so much to blacks, yet relatively little to whites. It is true that both races have a longer life expectancy if employed, but of course people often do not act so as to maximize their life expectancy. So far, it remains a mystery. In any case, whites and blacks clearly have different constitutional inclinations, and different goals in life. And so I say, *Vive na différence!*

·   ·   ·

12   As for Nrs. Buford's suggestion that both "Niss" and "Nrs." be unified into the single form of address "Ns." (supposed to rhyme with "fizz"), all I have to say is, it is arbitrary and clearly a thousand years ahead of its time. Mind you, this "Ns." is an abbreviation concocted out of thin air: it stands for absolutely nothing. Who ever heard of such toying with language? And while we're on this subject, have you yet run across the recently founded *Ns.* magazine, ded-

icated to the concerns of the "liberated black"? It's sure to attract the attention of a trendy band of black airheads for a little while, but serious blacks surely will see through its thin veneer of slick, glossy Madison Avenue approaches to life.

Nrs. Buford also finds it insultingly asymmetric that 13 when a black is employed by a white, ble changes bler firmly name to whis firmly name. But what's so bad about that? Every firm's core consists of a boss (whis job is to make sure long-term policies are well charted out) and a secretary (bler job is to keep corporate affairs running smoothly on a day-to-day basis). They are both equally important and vital to the firm's success. No one disputes this. Beyond them there may of course be other firmly members. Now it's quite obvious that all members of a given firm should bear the same firmly name — otherwise, what are you going to call the firm's products? And since it would be nonsense for the boss to change whis name, it falls to the secretary to change bler name. Logic, not racism, dictates this simple convention.

What puzzles me the most is when people cut off their 14 noses to spite their faces. Such is the case with the time-honored colored suffixes "oon" and "roon," found in familar words such as *ambassadroon, stewardoon*, and *sculptroon*. Most blacks find it natural and sensible to add those suffixes onto nouns such as "aviator" or "waiter." A black who flies an airplane may proudly proclaim, "I'm an aviatroon!" But it would sound silly, if not ridiculous, for a black to say of blerself, "I work as a waiter." On the other hand, who could object to my saying that the lively Ticely Cyson is a great actroon, or that the hilarious Quill Bosby is a great comedioon? You guessed it — authoroons such as Niss Mildred Hempsley and Nrs. Charles White, both of whom angrily reject the appellation "authoroon," deep though its roots are in our language. Nrs. White, perhaps one of the finest poetoons of our day, for some reason insists on being known as a "poet." It leads one to wonder, is Nrs. White *ashamed* of being black, perhaps? I should hope not. White needs Black, and Black needs White, and neither race should feel ashamed.

Some extreme negrists object to being treated with polite- 15 ness and courtesy by whites. For example, they reject the traditional notion of "Negroes first," preferring to open doors for themselves, claiming that having doors opened for them suggests implicitly that society considers them inferior. Well, would they have it the other way? Would these incorrigible grousers prefer to open doors for whites? What do blacks want?

·   ·   ·

16   Another unlikely word has recently become a subject of controversy: "blackey." This is, of course, the ordinary term for black children (including teen-agers), and by affectionate extension it is often applied to older blacks. Yet, incredible though it seems, many blacks—even teen-age blackeys—now claim to have had their "consciousness raised," and are voguishly skittish about being called "blackeys." Yet it's as old as the hills for blacks employed in the same office to refer to themselves as "the office blackeys." And for their superior to call them "my blackeys" helps make the ambiance more relaxed and comfy for all. It's hardly the mortal insult that libbers claim it to be. Fortunately, most blacks are sensible people and realize that mere words do not demean; they know it's how they are *used* that counts. Most of the time, calling a black—especially an older black—a "blackey" is a thoughtful way of complimenting bler, making bler feel young, fresh, and hirable again. Lord knows, I certainly wouldn't object if someone told me that I looked whiteyish these days!

17   Many young blackeys go through a stage of wishing they had been born white. Perhaps this is due to popular television shows like *Superwhite* and *Batwhite*, but it doesn't really matter. It is perfectly normal and healthy. Many of our most successful blacks were once tomwhiteys and feel no shame about it. Why should they? Frankly, I think tomwhiteys are often the cutest little blackeys—but that's just my opinion. In any case, Niss Moses (once again) raises a ruckus on this score, asking why we don't have a corresponding word for young whiteys who play blackeys' games and generally manifest a desire to be black. Well, Niss Moses, if this were a common phenomenon, we most assuredly *would* have such a word, but it just happens not to be. Who can say why? But given that tomwhiteys are a dime a dozen, it's nice to have a word for them. The lesson is that White must learn to fit language to reality; White cannot manipulate the world by manipulating mere words. An elementary lesson, to be sure, but for some reason Niss Moses and others of bler ilk resist learning it.

Shifting from the ridiculous to the sublime, let us con- 18
sider the Holy Bible. The Good Book is of course the source
of some of the most beautiful language and profound imagery to be found anywhere. And who is the central character
of the Bible? I am sure I need hardly remind you; it is God.
As everyone knows, Whe is male and white, and that is an
indisputable fact. But have you heard the latest joke promulgated by tasteless negrists? It is said that one of them
died and went to Heaven and then returned. What did ble
report? "I have seen God, and guess what? Ble's female!"
Can anyone say that this is not blasphemy of the highest
order? It just goes to show that some people will stoop to
any depths in order to shock. I have shared this "joke" with
a number of friends of mine (including several blacks, by
the way), and, to a white, they have agreed that it sickens
them to the core to see Our Lord so shabbily mocked. Some
things are just in bad taste, and there are no two ways
about it. It is scum like this who are responsible for some
of the great problems in our society today, I am sorry to
say.

·   ·   ·

Well, all of this is just another skirmish in the age-old 19
Battle of the Races, I guess, and we shouldn't take it too
seriously. I am reminded of words spoken by the great
British philosopher Alfred West Malehead in whis commencement address to my *alma secretaria*, the University
of North Virginia: "To enrich the language of whites is,
certainly, to enlarge the range of their ideas." I agree with
this admirable sentiment wholeheartedly. I would merely
point out to the overzealous that there are some extravagant
notions about language that should be recognized for what
they are: cheap attempts to let dogmatic, narrow minds
enforce their views on the speakers lucky enough to have
inherited the richest, most beautiful and flexible language
on earth, a language whose traditions run back through
the centuries to such deathless poets as Milton, Shakespeare, Wordsworth, Keats, Walt Whitwhite, and so many
others . . . Our language owes an incalculable debt to these
whites for their clarity of vision and expression, and if the
shallow minds of bandwagon-jumping negrists succeed in
destroying this precious heritage for all whites of good will,
that will be, without any doubt, a truly female day in the
history of Northern White.

III.

GENDER

One of the stunning social developments of the twentieth century has been the emergence of women. Beginning with the success of the women's suffrage movement early in the century and continuing with a series of legal and legislative victories in the past quarter of a century, the women's movement has largely achieved the goal of political equality in the United States — at least on paper. But that has not closed discussion on women's concerns, of course, because social, political, and economic parity between women and men remains to be achieved and because the specific terms of social and economic liberation have not yet been agreed upon. In fact, discussion of gender issues has intensified in the past decade as gender roles and their implications — for both men and women — continue to be negotiated through public discourse. This part barely begins to capture the range of issues currently under debate, but it does present discussions of three general matters: How should women (and men) be defined? Are women's brains, are the ways women reason, different somehow from men's? And how do gender issues affect work and careers? (In addition, gender issues are discussed elsewhere in this book, most notably in part two, Language, and in the sections of part five on pornography and affirmative action.)

Until very recently it was men who defined women, mostly in a woman-hating (misogynist) tradition deeply seated in Western culture. But the fact that women are now involved in defining gender roles has not effaced that tradition of misogyny, nor has it ended discussion of the nature of those roles. Just what form will the feminist revolution take? Just what is it that defines the essential natures of women and men? Beyond reproductive differences, are there inevitable distinctions among the sexes in terms of emotions, sexuality, physiology, morals, values, and so forth; or are all distinctions the result of social conditioning — social conditioning that might be altered? That is the basic issue considered in the first section of this part. Eleven selections of various kinds describe or explain or dramatize or argue for various positions on the question of "the essential natures" of women and men, and the extent to which history and culture and environment determine those natures. Those selections also illustrate the range of voices that can be summoned in support of a discussion of gender roles. While most of the selections address women's concerns most directly, each one has direct and indirect implications for men as well. And in the final decade of this century those implications must be faced each day.

It is not hard to notice that women have distinguished themselves comparatively rarely in scientific or applied scientific fields. But why? That question is the topic of discussion in the next section of four essays. Are there "sex differences in mathematical reasoning ability," as one essay contends? Do women *think* any differently than men do? Are women disadvantaged by their sex from excelling at math and science? Or are any such apparent differences the result of social conditioning? How can more women be encouraged to enter scientific and technical fields? What barriers discourage women from careers in engineering? Perhaps those questions have concrete manifestations on your campus or in your own life.

This part concludes with a set of readings somewhat related to the previous set, but dealing more broadly with the conditions women face on the job. What happens—on the job and in the home—when women enter jobs and institutions traditionally dominated by men? How can women cope with unfriendly circumstances? Are the satisfactions of jobs in male-dominated fields worth the hassles? What can men do to reduce the hassles? Can the demands of job and family be balanced successfully? How? Do images of women in the media support or undermine their chances for economic and vocational success? Why do wages for women persistently lag behind those of men? Should corporations and institutions establish separate career tracks for women who want to combine careers and childrearing? Or is a fundamental change in childrearing conventions—a change requiring greater involvement on the part of men— the only route to economic parity? Do biological differences between women and men make such a change unrealistic or undesirable?

And where do you stand on such questions? The selections in this part are intended to provoke further discussion, not to close it off. In fact, a premise of this part on gender is that by engaging in open, public discourse on these questions, writers can hasten the day when the effects of sexual polarization—perhaps sexual polarization itself—might be minimized and when codes of personal behavior might be more freely chosen, to the benefit of both women and men.

JUST HOW WOULD YOU DEFINE WOMEN (AND MEN)?

Elizabeth Cady Stanton
The Seneca Falls Declaration

In 1848 Elizabeth Cady Stanton (1815–1902) proposed a convention to address the "social, civil, and religious condition of women." Her declaration, inspired by an earlier Declaration and revised in part at the convention (which met in Seneca Falls, New York), became an important platform for the women's rights movement in this country.

1   When, in the course of human events, it becomes necessary for one portion of the family of man to assume among the people of the earth a position different from that which they have hitherto occupied, but one to which the laws of nature and of nature's God entitle them, a decent respect to the opinions of mankind requires that they should declare the causes that impel them to such a course.

2   We hold these truths to be self-evident: that all men and women are created equal; that they are endowed by their Creator with certain inalienable rights; that among these are life, liberty, and the pursuit of happiness; that to secure these rights governments are instituted, deriving their just powers from the consent of the governed. Whenever any form of government becomes destructive of these ends, it is the right of those who suffer from it to refuse allegiance to it, and to insist upon the institution of a new government, laying its foundation on such principles, and organizing its powers in such form, as to them shall seem most likely to effect their safety and happiness. Prudence, indeed, will dictate that governments long established should not be changed for light and transient causes; and accordingly all experience hath shown that mankind are more disposed to suffer, while evils are sufferable, than to right themselves by abolishing the forms to which they were accustomed. But when a long train of abuses and usurpations, pursuing

invariably the same object evinces a design to reduce them under absolute despotism, it is their duty to throw off such government, and to provide new guards for their future security. Such has been the patient sufferance of the women under this government, and such is now the necessity which constrains them to demand the equal station to which they are entitled.

The history of mankind is a history of repeated injuries 3 and usurpations on the part of man toward woman, having in direct object the establishment of an absolute tyranny over her. To prove this, let facts be submitted to a candid world.

He has never permitted her to exercise her inalienable 4 right to the elective franchise.

He has compelled her to submit to laws, in the formation 5 of which she had no voice.

He has withheld from her rights which are given to 6 the most ignorant and degraded men — both natives and foreigners.

Having deprived her of this first right of a citizen, the 7 elective franchise, thereby leaving her without representation in the halls of legislation, he has oppressed her on all sides.

He has made her, if married, in the eye of the law, civilly 8 dead.

He has taken from her all right in property, even to the 9 wages she earns.

He has made her, morally, an irresponsible being, as she 10 can commit many crimes with impunity, provided they be done in the presence of her husband. In the covenant of marriage, she is compelled to promise obedience to her husband, he becoming, to all intents and purposes, her master — the law giving him power to deprive her of her liberty, and to administer chastisement.

He has so framed the laws of divorce, as to what shall 11 be the proper causes, and in case of separation, to whom the guardianship of the children shall be given, as to be wholly regardless of the happiness of women — the law, in all cases, going upon a false supposition of the supremacy of man, and giving all power into his hands.

After depriving her of all rights as a married woman, if 12 single, and the owner of property, he has taxed her to support a government which recognizes her only when her property can be made profitable to it.

He has monopolized nearly all the profitable employ- 13

ments, and from those she is permitted to follow, she receives but a scanty remuneration. He closes against her all the avenues to wealth and distinction which he considers most honorable to himself. As a teacher of theology, medicine, or law, she is not known.

14   He has denied her the facilities for obtaining a thorough education, all colleges being closed against her.

15   He allows her in Church, as well as State, but a subordinate position, claiming Apostolic authority for her exclusion from the ministry, and, with some exceptions, from any public participation in the affairs of the Church.

16   He has created a false public sentiment by giving to the world a different code of morals for men and women, by which moral delinquencies which exclude women from society, are not only tolerated, but deemed of little account in man.

17   He has usurped the prerogative of Jehovah himself, claiming it as his right to assign for her a sphere of action, when that belongs to her conscience and to her God.

18   He has endeavored, in every way that he could, to destroy her confidence in her own powers, to lessen her self-respect, and to make her willing to lead a dependent and abject life.

19   Now, in view of this entire disfranchisement of one-half the people of this country, their social and religious degradation—in view of the unjust laws above mentioned, and because women do feel themselves aggrieved, oppressed, and fraudulently deprived of their most sacred rights, we insist that they have immediate admission to all the rights and privileges which belong to them as citizens of the United States.

20   In entering upon the great work before us, we anticipate no small amount of misconception, misrepresentation, and ridicule; but we shall use every instrumentality within our power to effect our object. We shall employ agents, circulate tracts, petition the State and National legislatures, and endeavor to enlist the pulpit and the press in our behalf. We hope this Convention will be followed by a series of Conventions embracing every part of the country.

·   ·   ·

21   Whereas, The great precept of nature is conceded to be, that "man shall pursue his own true and substantial happiness." Blackstone in his Commentaries remarks, that this law of Nature being coeval with mankind, and dictated by

God himself, is of course superior in obligation to any other. It is binding over all the globe, in all countries and at all times; no human laws are of any validity if contrary to this, and such of them as are valid, derive all their force, and all their vitality, and all their authority, mediately and immediately, from this original; therefore,

Resolved, That such laws as conflict, in any way, with the   22
true and substantial happiness of woman, are contrary to the great precept of nature and of no validity, for this is "superior in obligation to any other."

Resolved, That all laws which prevent woman from oc-   23
cupying such a station in society as her conscience shall dictate, or which place her in a position inferior to that of man, are contrary to the great precept of nature, and therefore of no force or authority.

Resolved, That woman is man's equal — was intended to   24
be so by the Creator, and the highest good of the race demands that she should be recognized as such.

Resolved, That the women of this country ought to be   25
enlightened in regard to the laws under which they live, that they may no longer publish their degradation by declaring themselves satisfied with their present position, nor their ignorance, by asserting that they have all the rights they want.

Resolved, That inasmuch as man, while claiming for him-   26
self intellectual superiority, does accord to woman moral superiority, it is preeminently his duty to encourage her to speak and teach, as she has an opportunity, in all religious assemblies.

Resolved, That the same amount of virtue, delicacy, and   27
refinement of behavior that is required of woman in the social state, should also be required of man, and the same transgressions should be visited with equal severity on both man and woman.

Resolved, That the objection of indelicacy and impropri-   28
ety, which is so often brought against woman when she addresses a public audience, comes with a very ill-grace from those who encourage, by their attendance, her appearance on the stage, in the concert, or in feats of the circus.

Resolved, That woman has too long rested satisfied in the   29
circumscribed limits which corrupt customs and a perverted application of the Scriptures have marked out for her, and that it is time she should move in the enlarged sphere which her great Creator has assigned her.

30   *Resolved,* That it is the duty of the women of this country
to secure to themselves their sacred right to the elective
franchise.
31   *Resolved,* That the equality of human rights results necessarily from the fact of the identity of the race in capabilities
and responsibilities.
32   *Resolved, therefore,* That, being invested by the Creator
with the same capabilities, and the same consciousness of
responsibility for their exercise, it is demonstrably the right
and duty of woman, equally with man, to promote every
righteous cause by every righteous means; and especially
in regard to the great subjects of morals and religion, it is
self-evidently her right to participate with her brother in
teaching them, both in private and in public, by writing
and by speaking, by any instrumentalities proper to be
used, and in any assemblies proper to be held; and this
being a self-evident truth growing out of the divinely im-
planted principles of human nature, any custom or authority adverse to it, whether modern or wearing the hoary
sanction of antiquity, is to be regarded as a self-evident
falsehood, and at war with mankind.

.   .   .

33   *Resolved,* That the speedy success of our cause depends
upon the zealous and untiring efforts of both men and
women, for the overthrow of the monopoly of the pulpit,
and for the securing to woman an equal participation with
men in the various trades, professions, and commerce.

Sojourner Truth

Ain't I a Woman?

*Sojourner Truth's story is fascinating and moving. Born into
slavery around 1797 and into the name Isabella in Ulster
County, New York, sold three times before she was twelve,
raped by one of her masters, she fled to freedom in 1827, a year
before slavery was outlawed in New York. In New York City
she worked as a domestic and fell in with an evangelical*

preacher who encouraged her efforts to convert prostitutes. In 1843, inspired by mystical visions, she took the name Sojourner Truth and set off alone and undeterred by her illiteracy to preach and sing about religion and the abolition of slavery. By 1850 huge crowds were coming to witness the oratory of the ex-slave with the resounding voice and message. During the Civil War she was presented to President Lincoln at the White House. After the war she spoke out for women's suffrage, but she never gave up her spiritual and racial themes — or her humor and exuberance. She continued to lecture until near her death in Battle Creek, Michigan, in 1883.

Sojourner Truth accepted neither the physical inferiority of women nor the idea that they should be placed on pedestals; nor did she subordinate women's rights to the pursuit of racial equality. At a religious meeting in May 1851, Sojourner Truth rose extemporaneously to rebut speakers who had impugned the rights and capabilities of women. According to an eyewitness who recorded the scene in his diary, this is what she said:

Well, children, where there is so much racket there must 1 be something out of kilter. I think that 'twixt the negroes of the South and the women at the North, all talking about rights, the white men will be in a fix pretty soon. But what's all this here talking about?

That man over there says that women need to be helped 2 into carriages, and lifted over ditches, and to have the best place everywhere. Nobody ever helps me into carriages, or over mud-puddles, or gives me any best place! And ain't I a woman? Look at me! Look at my arm! I have ploughed and planted, and gathered into barns, and no man could head me! And ain't I a woman? I could work as much and eat as much as a man — when I could get it — and bear the lash as well! And ain't I a woman? I have borne thirteen children, and seen them most all sold off to slavery, and when I cried out with my mother's grief, none but Jesus heard me! And ain't I a woman?

Then they talk about this thing in the head; what's this 3 they call it? [Intellect, someone whispers.] That's it, honey. What's that got to do with women's rights or negro's rights? If my cup won't hold but a pint, and yours holds a quart, wouldn't you be mean not to let me have my little half-measure full?

4   Then that little man in black there, he says women can't
have as much rights as men, 'cause Christ wasn't a woman!
Where did your Christ come from? Where did your Christ
come from? From God and a woman! Man had nothing to
do with Him.

5   If the first woman God ever made was strong enough to
turn the world upside down all alone, these women together
ought to be able to turn it back, and get it right side up
again! And now they is asking to do it, the men better let
them.

6   Obliged to you for hearing on me, and now old Sojourner
ain't got nothing more to say.

Susan Glaspell
Trifles

*Susan Glaspell (1882–1948), an Iowan by birth and education,
moved east in 1911. A Pulitzer-Prize-winning dramatist and a
prolific fictionwriter, she cofounded in 1915 the Provincetown
Playhouse on Cape Cod, which became a center for experimental and innovative drama. In 1916 she wrote* Trifles, *the one-act
play reprinted here; then she adapted it a few months later into
the story "A Jury of Her Peers," which is reprinted here after*
Trifles.

Characters

GEORGE HENDERSON, *County Attorney*   MRS. PETERS
HENRY PETERS, *Sheriff*   MRS. HALE
LEWIS HALE, *A Neighboring Farmer*

1   SCENE
The kitchen in the now abandoned farmhouse of JOHN
WRIGHT, *a gloomy kitchen, and left without having been put
in order — unwashed pans under the sink, a loaf of bread out-
side the breadbox, a dish towel on the table — other signs of
incompleted work. At the rear the outer door opens and the*
SHERIFF *comes in followed by the* COUNTY ATTORNEY *and*
HALE. *The* SHERIFF *and* HALE *are men in middle life, the*

COUNTY ATTORNEY *is a young man; all are much bundled up and go at once to the stove. They are followed by two women — the* SHERIFF'S *wife first; she is a slight wiry woman, a thin nervous face.* MRS. HALE *is larger and would ordinarily be called more comfortable looking, but she is disturbed now and looks fearfully about as she enters. The women have come in slowly, and stand close together near the door.*

COUNTY ATTORNEY. [*Rubbing his hands.*] This feels good.   2
Come up to the fire, ladies.

MRS. PETERS. [*After taking a step forward.*] I'm not — cold.   3

SHERIFF. [*Unbuttoning his overcoat and stepping away from*   4
the stove as if to mark the beginning of official business.]
Now, Mr. Hale, before we move things about, you explain
to Mr. Henderson just what you saw when you came here
yesterday morning.

COUNTY ATTORNEY. By the way, has anything been moved?   5
Are things just as you left them yesterday?

SHERIFF. [*Looking about.*] It's just the same. When it   6
dropped below zero last night I thought I'd better send
Frank out this morning to make a fire for us — no use
getting pneumonia with a big case on, but I told him not
to touch anything except the stove — and you know Frank.

COUNTY ATTORNEY. Somebody should have been left here   7
yesterday.

SHERIFF. Oh — yesterday. When I had to send Frank to Mor-   8
ris Center for that man who went crazy — I want you to
know I had my hands full yesterday, I knew you could
get back from Omaha by today and as long as I went
over everything here myself —

COUNTY ATTORNEY. Well, Mr. Hale, tell just what happened   9
when you came here yesterday morning.

HALE. Harry and I had started to town with a load of   10
potatoes. We came along the road from my place and as
I got here I said, "I'm going to see if I can't get John
Wright to go in with me on a party telephone." I spoke
to Wright about it once before and he put me off, saying
folks talked too much anyway, and all he asked was peace
and quiet — I guess you know about how much he talked
himself; but I thought maybe if I went to the house and
talked about it before his wife, though I said to Harry
that I didn't know as what his wife wanted made much
difference to John —

11 COUNTY ATTORNEY. Let's talk about that later, Mr. Hale. I
    do want to talk about that, but tell now just what hap-
    pened when you got to the house.

12 HALE. I didn't hear or see anything; I knocked at the door,
    and still it was all quiet inside. I knew they must be up,
    it was past eight o'clock. So I knocked again, and I
    thought I heard somebody say, "Come in." I wasn't sure,
    I'm not sure yet, but I opened the door—this door [*In-
    dicating the door by which the two women are still stand-
    ing*] and there in that rocker—[*Pointing to it.*] sat Mrs.
    Wright. [*They all look at the rocker.*]

13 COUNTY ATTORNEY. What—was she doing?

14 HALE. She was rockin' back and forth. She had her apron
    in her hand and was kind of—pleating it.

15 COUNTY ATTORNEY. And how did she—look?

16 HALE. Well, she looked queer.

17 COUNTY ATTORNEY. How do you mean—queer?

18 HALE. Well, as if she didn't know what she was going to do
    next. And kind of done up.

19 COUNTY ATTORNEY. How did she seem to feel about your
    coming?

20 HALE. Why, I don't think she minded—one way or other.
    She didn't pay much attention. I said, "How do, Mrs.
    Wright, it's cold, ain't it?" And she said, "Is it?"—and
    went on kind of pleating at her apron. Well, I was sur-
    prised; she didn't ask me to come up to the stove, or to
    set down, but just sat there, not even looking at me, so
    I said, "I want to see John." And then she—laughed. I
    guess you would call it a laugh. I thought of Harry and
    the team outside, so I said a little sharp: "Can't I see
    John?" "No," she says, kind o' dull like. "Ain't he home?"
    says I. "Yes," says she, "he's home." "Then why can't I
    see him?" I asked her, out of patience. "'Cause he's dead,"
    says she. "*Dead*?" says I. She just nodded her head, not
    getting a bit excited, but rockin' back and forth. "Why—
    where is he?" says I, not knowing what to say. She just
    pointed upstairs—like that [*Himself pointing to the room
    above*]. I got up, with the idea of going up there. I walked
    from there to here—then I says, "Why, what did he die
    of?" "He died of a rope round his neck," says she, and
    just went on pleatin' at her apron. Well, I went out and
    called Harry. I thought I might—need help. We went
    upstairs and there he was lyin'—

21 COUNTY ATTORNEY. I think I'd rather have you go into that

upstairs, where you can point it all out. Just go on now
with the rest of the story.

HALE. Well, my first thought was to get that rope off. It   22
looked... [*Stops, his face twitches*] ... but Harry, he went
up to him, and he said, "No, he's dead all right, and we'd
better not touch anything." So we went back down stairs.
She was still sitting that same way. "Has anybody been
notified?" I asked. "No," says she, unconcerned. "Who did
this, Mrs. Wright?" said Harry. He said it businesslike —
and she stopped pleatin' of her apron. "I don't know,"
she says. "You don't *know*?" says Harry. "No," says she.
"Weren't you sleepin' in the bed with him?" says Harry.
"Yes," says she, "but I was on the inside." "Somebody
slipped a rope round his neck and strangled him and you
didn't wake up?" says Harry. "I didn't wake up," she said
after him. We must 'a looked as if we didn't see how that
could be, for after a minute she said, "I sleep sound."
Harry was going to ask her more questions but I said
maybe we ought to let her tell her story first to the
coroner, or the sheriff, so Harry went fast as he could to
Rivers' place, where there's a telephone.

COUNTY ATTORNEY. And what did Mrs. Wright do when she   23
knew that you had gone for the coroner?

HALE. She moved from that chair to this one over here   24
[*Pointing to a small chair in the corner.*] and just sat there
with her hands held together and looking down. I got a
feeling that I ought to make some conversation, so I said
I had come in to see if John wanted to put in a telephone,
and at that she started to laugh, and then she stopped
and looked at me — scared. [*The* COUNTY ATTORNEY, *who
has had his notebook out, makes a note.*] I dunno, maybe
it wasn't scared. I wouldn't like to say it was. Soon Harry
got back, and then Dr. Lloyd came, and you, Mr. Peters,
and so I guess that's all I know that you don't.

COUNTY ATTORNEY. [*Looking around.*] I guess we'll go up-   25
stairs first — and then out to the barn and around there.
[*To the* SHERIFF] You're convinced that there was nothing
important here — nothing that would point to any motive.

SHERIFF. Nothing here but kitchen things.   26
[*The* COUNTY ATTORNEY, *after again looking around the
kitchen, opens the door of a cupboard closet. He gets up on
a chair and looks on a shelf. Pulls his hand away, sticky.*]

COUNTY ATTORNEY. Here's a nice mess.   27
[*The women draw nearer.*]

28 MRS. PETERS. [*To the other woman.*] Oh, her fruit; it did
    freeze. [*To the* COUNTY ATTORNEY] She worried about
    that when it turned so cold. She said the fire'd go out
    and her jars would break.
29 SHERIFF. Well, can you beat the women! Held for murder
    and worryin' about her preserves.
30 COUNTY ATTORNEY. I guess before we're through she may
    have something more serious than preserves to worry
    about.
31 HALE. Well, women are used to worrying over trifles.
    [*The two women move a little closer together.*]
32 COUNTY ATTORNEY. [*With the gallantry of a young politi-
    cian.*] And yet, for all their worries, what would we do
    without the ladies? [*The women do not unbend. He goes
    to the sink, takes a dipperful of water from the pail and
    pouring it into a basin, washes his hands. Starts to wipe
    them on the roller towel, turns it for a cleaner place.*] Dirty
    towels! [*Kicks his foot against the pans under the sink.*]
    Not much of a housekeeper, would you say, ladies?
33 MRS. HALE. [*Stiffly.*] There's a great deal of work to be done
    on a farm.
34 COUNTY ATTORNEY. To be sure. And yet [*With a little bow
    to her*] I know there are some Dickson county farmhouses
    which do not have such roller towels.
    [*He gives it a pull to expose its full length again.*]
35 MRS. HALE. Those towels get dirty awful quick. Men's hands
    aren't always as clean as they might be.
36 COUNTY ATTORNEY. Ah, loyal to your sex, I see. But you
    and Mrs. Wright were neighbors. I suppose you were
    friends, too.
37 MRS. HALE. [*Shaking her head.*] I've not seen much of her
    of late years. I've not been in this house—it's more than
    a year.
38 COUNTY ATTORNEY. And why was that? You didn't like her?
39 MRS. HALE. I liked her all well enough. Farmers' wives have
    their hands full, Mr. Henderson. And then—
40 COUNTY ATTORNEY. Yes—?
41 MRS. HALE. [*Looking about.*] It never seemed a very cheerful
    place.
42 COUNTY ATTORNEY. No—it's not cheerful. I shouldn't say
    she had the homemaking instinct.
43 MRS. HALE. Well, I don't know as Wright had, either.
44 COUNTY ATTORNEY. You mean that they didn't get on very
    well?

MRS. HALE. No, I don't mean anything. But I don't think a 45
place'd be any cheerfuller for John Wright's being in it.

COUNTY ATTORNEY. I'd like to talk more of that a little 46
later. I want to get the lay of things upstairs now.
[*He goes to the left, where three steps lead to a stair door.*]

SHERIFF. I suppose anything Mrs. Peters does'll be all right. 47
She was to take in some clothes for her, you know, and
a few little things. We left in such a hurry yesterday.

COUNTY ATTORNEY. Yes, but I would like to see what you 48
take, Mrs. Peters, and keep an eye out for anything that
might be of use to us.

MRS. PETERS. Yes, Mr. Henderson. 49
[*The women listen to the men's steps on the stairs, then
look about the kitchen.*]

MRS. HALE. I'd hate to have men coming into my kitchen, 50
snooping around and criticising.
[*She arranges the pans under sink which the* COUNTY AT-
TORNEY *had shoved out of place.*]

MRS. PETERS. Of course it's no more than their duty. 51

MRS. HALE. Duty's all right, but I guess that deputy sheriff 52
that came out to make the fire might have got a little of
this on. [*Gives the roller towel a pull.*] Wish I'd thought of
that sooner. Seems mean to talk about her for not having
things slicked up when she had to come away in such a
hurry.

MRS. PETERS. [*Who has gone to a small table in the left rear 53
corner of the room, and lifted one end of a towel that covers
a pan.*] She had bread set.
[*Stands still.*]

MRS. HALE. [*Eyes fixed on a loaf of bread beside the breadbox, 54
which is on a low shelf at the other side of the room. Moves
slowly toward it.*] She was going to put this in there. [*Picks
up loaf, then abruptly drops it. In a manner of returning to
familiar things.*] It's a shame about her fruit. I wonder if
it's all gone. [*Gets up on the chair and looks.*] I think
there's some here that's all right, Mrs. Peters. Yes—here;
[*Holding it toward the window.*] this is cherries, too. [*Looking again.*] I declare I believe that's the only one. [*Gets
down, bottle in her hand. Goes to the sink and wipes it off
on the outside.*] She'll feel awful bad after all her hard
work in the hot weather. I remember the afternoon I put
up my cherries last summer.
[*She puts the bottle on the big kitchen table, center of the
room. With a sigh, is about to sit down in the rocking-chair.*

Before she is seated realizes what chair it is; with a slow look at it, steps back. The chair which she has touched rocks back and forth.]

55 MRS. PETERS. Well, I must get those things from the front room closet. [*She goes to the door at the right, but after looking into the other room, steps back.*] You coming with me, Mrs. Hale? You could help me carry them.

[*They go in the other room; reappear,* MRS. PETERS *carrying a dress and skirt,* MRS. HALE *following with a pair of shoes.*]

56 MRS. PETERS. My, it's cold in there.

[*She puts the clothes on the big table, and hurries to the stove.*]

57 MRS. HALE. [*Examining her skirt.*] Wright was close. I think maybe that's why she kept so much to herself. She didn't even belong to the Ladies Aid. I suppose she felt she couldn't do her part, and then you don't enjoy things when you feel shabby. She used to wear pretty clothes and be lively, when she was Minnie Foster, one of the town girls singing in the choir. But that—oh, that was thirty years ago. This all you was to take in?

58 MRS. PETERS. She said she wanted an apron. Funny thing to want, for there isn't much to get you dirty in jail, goodness knows. But I suppose just to make her feel more natural. She said they was in the top drawer in this cupboard. Yes, here. And then her little shawl that always hung behind the door. [*Opens stair door and looks.*] Yes, here it is.

[*Quickly shuts door leading upstairs.*]

59 MRS. HALE. [*Abruptly moving toward her.*] Mrs. Peters?

60 MRS. PETERS. Yes, Mrs. Hale?

61 MRS. HALE. Do you think she did it?

62 MRS. PETERS. [*In a frightened voice.*] Oh, I don't know.

63 MRS. HALE. Well, I don't think she did. Asking for an apron and her little shawl. Worrying about her fruit.

64 MRS. PETERS. [*Starts to speak, glances up, where footsteps are heard in the room above. In a low voice.*] Mr. Peters says it looks bad for her. Mr. Henderson is awful sarcastic in a speech and he'll make fun of her sayin' she didn't wake up.

65 MRS. HALE. Well, I guess John Wright didn't wake when they was slipping that rope under his neck.

66 MRS. PETERS. No, it's strange. It must have been done awful crafty and still. They say it was such a—funny way to kill a man, rigging it all up like that.

MRS. HALE. That's just what Mr. Hale said. There was a   67
gun in the house. He says that's what he can't understand.

MRS. PETERS. Mr. Henderson said coming out that what   68
was needed for the case was a motive; something to show
anger, or—sudden feeling.

MRS. HALE. [*Who is standing by the table.*] Well, I don't see   69
any signs of anger around here. [*She puts her hand on the
dish towel which lies on the table, stands looking down at
table, one half of which is clean, the other half messy.*] It's
wiped to here. [*Makes a move as if to finish work, then
turns and looks at loaf of bread outside the breadbox. Drops
towel. In that voice of coming back to familiar things.*]
Wonder how they are finding things upstairs. I hope she
had it a little more red-up up there. You know, it seems
kind of *sneaking*. Locking her up in town and then coming
out here and trying to get her own house to turn against
her!

MRS. PETERS. But Mrs. Hale, the law is the law.   70

MRS. HALE. I s'pose 'tis. [*Unbuttoning her coat.*] Better   71
loosen up your things, Mrs. Peters. You won't feel them
when you go out.

[MRS. PETERS *takes off her fur tippet, goes to hang it on
hook at back of room, stands looking at the under part of
the small corner table.*]

MRS. PETERS. She was piecing a quilt.   72

[*She brings the large sewing basket and they look at the
bright pieces.*]

MRS. HALE. It's log cabin pattern. Pretty, isn't it? I wonder   73
if she was goin' to quilt it or just knot it?

[*Footsteps have been heard coming down the stairs. The
SHERIFF enters followed by HALE and the COUNTY
ATTORNEY.*]

SHERIFF. They wonder if she was going to quilt it or just   74
knot it!

[*The men laugh; the women look abashed.*]

COUNTY ATTORNEY. [*Rubbing his hands over the stove.*]   75
Frank's fire didn't do much up there, did it? Well, let's
go out to the barn and get that cleared up.

[*The men go outside.*]

MRS. HALE. [*Resentfully.*] I don't know as there's anything   76
so strange, our takin' up our time with little things while
we're waiting for them to get the evidence. [*She sits down
at the big table smoothing out a block with decision.*] I
don't see as it's anything to laugh about.

77   MRS. PETERS. [*Apologetically.*] Of course they've got awful
     important things on their minds.
     [*Pulls up a chair and joins* MRS. HALE *at the table.*]
78   MRS. HALE. [*Examining another block.*] Mrs. Peters, look at
     this one. Here, this is the one she was working on, and
     look at the sewing! All the rest of it has been so nice and
     even. And look at this! It's all over the place! Why, it
     looks as if she didn't know what she was about!
     [*After she has said this they look at each other, then start
     to glance back at the door. After an instant* MRS. HALE *has
     pulled at a knot and ripped the sewing.*]
79   MRS. PETERS. Oh, what are you doing, Mrs. Hale?
80   MRS. HALE. [*Mildly.*] Just pulling out a stitch or two that's
     not sewed very good. [*Threading a needle.*] Bad sewing
     always made me fidgety.
81   MRS. PETERS. [*Nervously.*] I don't think we ought to touch
     things.
82   MRS. HALE. I'll just finish up this end. [*Suddenly stopping
     and leaning forward.*] Mrs. Peters?
83   MRS. PETERS. Yes, Mrs. Hale?
84   MRS. HALE. What do you suppose she was so nervous
     about?
85   MRS. PETERS. Oh—I don't know. I don't know as she was
     nervous. I sometimes sew awful queer when I'm just tired.
     [MRS. HALE *starts to say something, looks at* MRS. PETERS,
     then goes on sewing.] Well, I must get these things
     wrapped up. They may be through sooner than we think.
     [*Putting apron and other things together.*] I wonder where
     I can find a piece of paper, and string.
86   MRS. HALE. In that cupboard, maybe.
87   MRS. PETERS. [*Looking in cupboard.*] Why, here's a birdcage.
     [*Holds it up.*] Did she have a bird, Mrs. Hale?
88   MRS. HALE. Why, I don't know whether she did or not—I've
     not been here for so long. There was a man around last
     year selling canaries cheap, but I don't know as she took
     one; maybe she did. She used to sing real pretty herself.
89   MRS. PETERS. [*Glancing around.*] Seems funny to think of
     a bird here. But she must have had one, or why would
     she have a cage? I wonder what happened to it.
90   MRS. HALE. I s'pose maybe the cat got it.
91   MRS. PETERS. No, she didn't have a cat. She's got that feeling
     some people have about cats—being afraid of them. My
     cat got in her room and she was real upset and asked me
     to take it out.
92   MRS. HALE. My sister Bessie was like that. Queer, ain't it?

MRS. PETERS. [*Examining the cage.*] Why, look at this door. 93
It's broke. One hinge is pulled apart.

MRS. HALE. [*Looking too.*] Looks as if someone must have 94
been rough with it.

MRS. PETERS. Why, yes. 95
[*She brings the cage forward and puts it on the table.*]

MRS. HALE. I wish if they're going to find any evidence 96
they'd be about it. I don't like this place.

MRS. PETERS. But I'm awful glad you came with me, Mrs. 97
Hale. It would be lonesome for me sitting here alone.

MRS. HALE. It would, wouldn't it? [*Dropping her sewing.*] 98
But I tell you what I do wish, Mrs. Peters. I wish I had
come over sometimes when *she* was here. I—[*Looking
around the room.*]—wish I had.

MRS. PETERS. But of course you were awful busy, Mrs. 99
Hale—your house and your children.

MRS. HALE. I could've come. I stayed away because it 100
weren't cheerful—and that's why I ought to have come.
I—I've never liked this place. Maybe because it's down
in a hollow and you don't see the road. I dunno what it
is but it's a lonesome place and always was. I wish I had
come over to see Minnie Foster sometimes. I can see
now—
[*Shakes her head.*]

MRS. PETERS. Well, you mustn't reproach yourself, Mrs. 101
Hale. Somehow we just don't see how it is with other
folks until—something comes up.

MRS. HALE. Not having children makes less work—but it 102
makes a quiet house, and Wright out to work all day, and
no company when he did come in. Did you know John
Wright, Mrs. Peters?

MRS. PETERS. Not to know him; I've seen him in town. They 103
say he was a good man.

MRS. HALE. Yes—good; he didn't drink, and kept his word 104
as well as most, I guess, and paid his debts. But he was
a hard man, Mrs. Peters. Just to pass the time of day with
him—[*Shivers.*] Like a raw wind that gets to the bone.
[*Pauses, her eye falling on the cage.*] I should think she
would'a wanted a bird. But what do you suppose went
with it?

MRS. PETERS. I don't know, unless it got sick and died. 105
[*She reaches over and swings the broken door, swings it
again. Both women watch it.*]

MRS. HALE. You weren't raised round here, were you? [MRS. 106
PETERS *shakes her head.*] You didn't know—her?

107 MRS. PETERS. Not till they brought her yesterday.

108 MRS. HALE. She—come to think of it, she was kind of like
     a bird herself—real sweet and pretty, but kind of timid
     and—fluttery. How—she—did—change. [*Silence; then as
     if struck by a happy thought and relieved to get back to
     every day things.*] Tell you what, Mrs. Peters, why don't
     you take the quilt in with you? It might take up her mind.

109 MRS. PETERS. Why, I think that's a real nice idea, Mrs. Hale.
     There couldn't possibly be any objection to it, could
     there? Now, just what would I take? I wonder if her
     patches are in here—and her things.
     [*They look in the sewing basket.*]

110 MRS. HALE. Here's some red. I expect this has got sewing
     things in it. [*Brings out a fancy box.*] What a pretty box.
     Looks like something somebody would give you. Maybe
     her scissors are in here. [*Opens box. Suddenly puts her
     hand to her nose.*] Why—[MRS. PETERS *bends nearer, then
     turns her face away.*] There's something wrapped up in
     this piece of silk.

111 MRS. PETERS. Why, this isn't her scissors.

112 MRS. HALE. [*Lifting the silk.*] Oh, Mrs. Peters—its—
     [MRS. PETERS *bends closer.*]

113 MRS. PETERS. It's the bird.

114 MRS. HALE. [*Jumping up.*] But, Mrs. Peters—look at it! Its
     neck! Look at its neck! It's all—other side *to.*

115 MRS. PETERS. Somebody—wrung—its—neck.
     [*Their eyes meet. A look of growing comprehension, of hor-
     ror. Steps are heard outside.* MRS. HALE *slips box under
     quilt pieces, and sinks into her chair. Enter* SHERIFF *and*
     COUNTY ATTORNEY. MRS. PETERS *rises.*]

116 COUNTY ATTORNEY. [*As one turning from serious things to
     little pleasantries.*] Well, ladies, have you decided whether
     she was going to quilt it or knot it?

117 MRS. PETERS. We think she was going to—knot it.

118 COUNTY ATTORNEY. Well, that's interesting, I'm sure. [*See-
     ing the birdcage.*] Has the bird flown?

119 MRS. HALE. [*Putting more quilt pieces over the box.*] We think
     the—cat got it.

120 COUNTY ATTORNEY. [*Preoccupied.*] Is there a cat?
     [MRS. HALE *glances in a quick covert way at* MRS. PETERS.]

121 MRS. PETERS. Well, not *now.* They're superstitious, you
     know. They leave.

122 COUNTY ATTORNEY. [*To* SHERIFF PETERS, *continuing an in-
     terrupted conversation.*] No sign at all of anyone having

come from the outside. Their own rope. Now let's go up
again and go over it piece by piece. [*They start upstairs.*]
It would have to have been someone who knew just the —
[MRS. PETERS *sits down. The two women sit there not looking at one another, but as if peering into something and at
the same time holding back. When they talk now it is in the
manner of feeling their way over strange ground, as if afraid
of what they are saying, but as if they can not help saying it.*]

MRS. HALE. She liked the bird. She was going to bury it in   123
that pretty box.

MRS. PETERS. [*In a whisper.*] When I was a girl — my kitten —   124
there was a boy took a hatchet, and before my eyes — and
before I could get there — [*Covers her face an instant.*] If
they hadn't held me back I would have — [*Catches herself,
looks upstairs where steps are heard, falters weakly.*] — hurt
him.

MRS. HALE. [*With a slow look around her.*] I wonder how it   125
would seem never to have had any children around.
[*Pause.*] No, Wright wouldn't like the bird — a thing that
sang. She used to sing. He killed that, too.

MRS. PETERS. [*Moving uneasily.*] We don't know who killed   126
the bird.

MRS. HALE. I knew John Wright.   127

MRS. PETERS. It was an awful thing was done in this house   128
that night, Mrs. Hale. Killing a man while he slept, slipping a rope around his neck that choked the life out of him.

MRS. HALE. His neck. Choked the life out of him.   129
[*Her hand goes out and rests on the birdcage.*]

MRS. PETERS. [*With rising voice.*] We don't know who killed   130
him. We don't *know.*

MRS. HALE. [*Her own feeling not interrupted.*] If there'd been   131
years and years of nothing, then a bird to sing to you, it
would be awful — still, after the bird was still.

MRS. PETERS. [*Something within her speaking.*] I know what   132
stillness is. When we homesteaded in Dakota, and my
first baby died — after he was two years old, and me with
no other then —

MRS. HALE. [*Moving.*] How soon do you suppose they'll be   133
through, looking for the evidence?

MRS. PETERS. I know what stillness is. [*Pulling herself back.*]   134
The law has got to punish crime, Mrs. Hale.

MRS. HALE. [*Not as if answering that.*] I wish you'd seen   135
Minnie Foster when she wore a white dress with blue
ribbons and stood up there in the choir and sang. [*A look*

around the room.] Oh, I *wish* I'd come over here once in a while! That was a crime! That was a crime! Who's going to punish that?

136 MRS. PETERS. [*Looking upstairs.*] We mustn't — take on.

137 MRS. HALE. I might have known she needed help! I know how things can be — for women. I tell you, it's queer, Mrs. Peters. We live close together and we live far apart. We all go through the same things — it's all just a different kind of the same thing. [*Brushes her eyes; noticing the bottle of fruit, reaches out for it.*] If I was you I wouldn't tell her her fruit was gone. Tell her it *ain't*. Tell her it's all right. Take this in to prove it to her. She — she may never know whether it was broke or not.

138 MRS. PETERS. [*Takes the bottle, looks about for something to wrap it in; takes petticoat from the clothes brought from the other room, very nervously begins winding this around the bottle. In a false voice.*] My, it's a good thing the men couldn't hear us. Wouldn't they just laugh! Getting all stirred up over a little thing like a — dead canary. As if that could have anything to do with — with — wouldn't they *laugh*!

[*The men are heard coming down stairs.*]

139 MRS. HALE. [*Under her breath.*] Maybe they would — maybe they wouldn't.

140 COUNTY ATTORNEY. No, Peters, it's all perfectly clear except a reason for doing it. But you know juries when it comes to women. If there was some definite thing. Something to show — something to make a story about — a thing that would connect up with this strange way of doing it —

[*The women's eyes meet for an instant. Enter* HALE *from outer door.*]

141 HALE. Well, I've got the team around. Pretty cold out there.

142 COUNTY ATTORNEY. I'm going to stay here a while by myself. [*To the* SHERIFF.] You can send Frank out for me, can't you? I want to go over everything. I'm not satisfied that we can't do better.

143 SHERIFF. Do you want to see what Mrs. Peters is going to take in?

[*The* COUNTY ATTORNEY *goes to the table, picks up the apron, laughs.*]

144 COUNTY ATTORNEY. Oh, I guess they're not very dangerous things the ladies have picked out. [*Moves a few things about, disturbing the quilt pieces which cover the box. Steps back.*] No, Mrs. Peters doesn't need supervising. For that

matter, a sheriff's wife is married to the law. Ever think of it that way, Mrs. Peters?

MRS. PETERS. Not—just that way.   145

SHERIFF. [*Chuckling.*] Married to the law. [*Moves toward*   146 *the other room.*] I just want you to come in here a minute, George. We ought to take a look at these windows.

COUNTY ATTORNEY. [*Scoffingly.*] Oh, windows!   147

SHERIFF. We'll be right out, Mr. Hale.   148

[HALE *goes outside. The* SHERIFF *follows the* COUNTY AT-TORNEY *into the other room. Then* MRS. HALE *rises, hands tight together, looking intensely at* MRS. PETERS, *whose eyes make a slow turn, finally meeting* MRS. HALE's. *A moment* MRS. HALE *holds her, then her own eyes point the way to where the box is concealed. Suddenly* MRS. PETERS *throws back quilt pieces and tries to put the box in the bag she is wearing. It is too big. She opens box, starts to take bird out, cannot touch it, goes to pieces, stands there helpless. Sound of a knob turning in the other room.* MRS. HALE *snatches the box and puts it in the pocket of her big coat. Enter* COUNTY ATTORNEY *and* SHERIFF.]

COUNTY ATTORNEY. [*Facetiously.*] Well, Henry, at least we   149 found out that she was not going to quilt it. She was going to—what is it you call it, ladies?

MRS. HALE. [*Her hand against her pocket.*] We call it—knot   150 it, Mr. Henderson.

CURTAIN

Susan Glaspell

A Jury of Her Peers

For information on Susan Glaspell and "A Jury of Her Peers," see page 238.

When Martha Hale opened the storm-door and got a cut   1 of the north wind, she ran back for her big woolen scarf. As she hurriedly wound that round her head her eye made a scandalized sweep of her kitchen. It was no ordinary thing that called her away—it was probably farther from ordinary than anything that had ever happened in Dickson County. But what her eye took in was that her kitchen was in no shape for leaving: her bread all ready for mixing, half the flour sifted and half unsifted.

2   She hated to see things half done; but she had been at that when the team from town stopped to get Mr. Hale, and then the sheriff came running in to say his wife wished Mrs. Hale would come too—adding, with a grin, that he guessed she was getting scarey and wanted another woman along. So she had dropped everything right where it was.

3   "Martha!" now came her husband's impatient voice. "Don't keep folks waiting out here in the cold."

4   She again opened the storm-door, and this time joined the three men and the one woman waiting for her in the big two-seated buggy.

5   After she had the robes tucked around her she took another look at the woman who sat beside her on the back seat. She had met Mrs. Peters the year before at the county fair, and the thing she remembered about her was that she didn't seem like a sheriff's wife. She was small and thin and didn't have a strong voice. Mrs. Gorman, sheriff's wife before Gorman went out and Peters came in, had a voice that somehow seemed to be backing up the law with every word. But if Mrs. Peters didn't look like a sheriff's wife, Peters made it up in looking like a sheriff. He was to a dot the kind of man who could get himself elected sheriff—a heavy man with a big voice, who was particularly genial with the law-abiding, as if to make it plain that he knew the difference between criminals and non-criminals. And right there it came into Mrs. Hale's mind, with a stab, that this man who was so pleasant and lively with all of them was going to the Wrights' now as a sheriff.

6   "The country's not very pleasant this time of year," Mrs. Peters at last ventured, as if she felt they ought to be talking as well as the men.

7   Mrs. Hale scarcely finished her reply, for they had gone up a little hill and could see the Wright place now, and seeing it did not make her feel like talking. It looked very lonesome this cold March morning. It had always been a lonesome-looking place. It was down in a hollow, and the poplar trees around it were lonesome-looking trees. The men were looking at it and talking about what had happened. The county attorney was bending to one side of the buggy, and kept looking steadily at the place as they drew up to it.

"I'm glad you came with me," Mrs. Peters said nervously, 8
as the two women were about to follow the men in through
the kitchen door.

Even after she had her foot on the door-step, her hand 9
on the knob, Martha Hale had a moment of feeling she
could not cross that threshold. And the reason it seemed
she couldn't cross it now was simply because she hadn't
crossed it before. Time and time again it had been in her
mind, "I ought to go over and see Minnie Foster"—she still
thought of her as Minnie Foster, though for twenty years
she had been Mrs. Wright. And then there was always something to do and Minnie Foster would go from her mind.
But *now* she could come.

The men went over to the stove. The women stood close 10
together by the door. Young Henderson, the county attorney, turned around and said, "Come up to the fire, ladies."

Mrs. Peters took a step forward, then stopped. "I'm not— 11
cold," she said.

And so the two women stood by the door, at first not 12
even so much as looking around the kitchen.

The men talked for a minute about what a good thing it 13
was the sheriff had sent his deputy out that morning to
make a fire for them, and then Sheriff Peters stepped back
from the stove, unbuttoned his outer coat, and leaned his
hands on the kitchen table in a way that seemed to mark
the beginning of official business. "Now, Mr. Hale," he said
in a sort of semi-official voice, "before we move things
about, you tell Mr. Henderson just what it was you saw
when you came here yesterday morning."

The county attorney was looking around the kitchen. 14

"By the way," he said, "has anything been moved?" He 15
turned to the sheriff. "Are things just as you left them yesterday?"

Peters looked from cupboard to sink; from that to a small 16
worn rocker a little to one side of the kitchen table.

"It's just the same." 17

"Somebody should have been left here yesterday," said 18
the county attorney.

"Oh—yesterday," returned the sheriff, with a little ges- 19
ture as of yesterday having been more than he could bear
to think of. "When I had to send Frank to Morris Center for
that man who went crazy—let me tell you, I had my hands
full *yesterday*. I knew you could get back from Omaha by
to-day, George, and as long as I went over everything here
myself—"

20   "Well, Mr. Hale," said the county attorney, in a way of letting what was past and gone go, "tell just what happened when you came here yesterday morning."

21   Mrs. Hale, still leaning against the door, had that sinking feeling of the mother whose child is about to speak a piece. Lewis often wandered along and got things mixed up in a story. She hoped he would tell this straight and plain, and not say unnecessary things that would just make things harder for Minnie Foster. He didn't begin at once, and she noticed that he looked queer — as if standing in that kitchen and having to tell what he had seen there yesterday morning made him almost sick.

22   "Yes, Mr. Hale?" the county attorney reminded.

23   "Harry and I had started to town with a load of potatoes," Mrs. Hale's husband began.

24   Harry was Mrs. Hale's oldest boy. He wasn't with them now, for the very good reason that those potatoes never got to town yesterday and he was taking them this morning, so he hadn't been home when the sheriff stopped to say he wanted Mr. Hale to come over to the Wright place and tell the county attorney his story there, where he could point it all out. With all Mrs. Hale's other emotions came the fear now that maybe Harry wasn't dressed warm enough — they hadn't any of them realized how that north wind did bite.

25   "We come along this road," Hale was going on, with a motion of his hand to the road over which they had just come, "and as we got in sight of the house I says to Harry, 'I'm goin' to see if I can't get John Wright to take a telephone.' You see," he explained to Henderson, "unless I can get somebody to go in with me they won't come out this branch road except for a price I can't pay. I'd spoke to Wright about it once before; but he put me off, saying folks talked too much anyway, and all he asked was peace and quiet — guess you know about how much he talked himself. But I thought maybe if I went to the house and talked about it before his wife, and said all the women-folks liked the telephones, and that in this lonesome stretch of road it would be a good thing — well, I said to Harry that that was what I was going to say — though I said at the same time that I didn't know as what his wife wanted made much difference to John —"

26   Now, there he was! — saying things he didn't need to say. Mrs. Hale tried to catch her husband's eye, but fortunately the county attorney interrupted with:

"Let's talk about that a little later, Mr. Hale. I do want   27
to talk about that, but I'm anxious now to get along to just
what happened when you got here."

When he began this time, it was very deliberately and   28
carefully:

"I didn't see or hear anything. I knocked at the door. And   29
still it was all quiet inside. I knew they must be up — it was
past eight o'clock. So I knocked again, louder, and I thought
I heard somebody say 'Come in.' I wasn't sure — I'm not
sure yet. But I opened the door — this door," jerking a hand
toward the door by which the two women stood, "and there,
in that rocker" — pointing to it — "sat Mrs. Wright."

Every one in the kitchen looked at the rocker. It came   30
into Mrs. Hale's mind that that rocker didn't look in the
least like Minnie Foster — the Minnie Foster of twenty years
before. It was a dingy red, with wooden rungs up the back,
and the middle rung was gone, and the chair sagged to one
side.

"How did she — look?" the county attorney was inquiring.   31

"Well," said Hale, "she looked — queer."   32

"How do you mean — queer?"   33

As he asked it he took out a note-book and pencil. Mrs.   34
Hale did not like the sight of that pencil. She kept her eye
fixed on her husband, as if to keep him from saying unnecessary things that would go into that note-book and make
trouble.

Hale did speak guardedly, as if the pencil had affected   35
him too.

"Well, as if she didn't know what she was going to do   36
next. And kind of — done up."

"How did she seem to feel about your coming?"   37

"Why, I don't think she minded — one way or other. She   38
didn't pay much attention. I said, 'Ho' do, Mrs. Wright?
It's cold, ain't it?' And she said, 'Is it?' — and went on pleatin'
at her apron.

"Well, I was surprised. She didn't ask me to come up to   39
the stove, or to sit down, but just set there, not even lookin'
at me. And so I said: 'I want to see John.'

"And then she — laughed. I guess you would call it a laugh.   40

"I thought of Harry and the team outside, so I said, a   41
little sharp, 'Can I see John?' 'No,' says she — kind of dull
like. 'Ain't he home?' says I. Then she looked at me. 'Yes,'
says she, 'he's home.' 'Then why can't I see him?' I asked
her, out of patience with her now. 'Cause he's dead,' says
she, just as quiet and dull — and fell to pleatin' her apron.

'Dead?' says I, like you do when you can't take in what you've heard.

42   "She just nodded her head, not getting a bit excited, but rockin' back and forth.

43   "'Why—where is he?' says I, not knowing *what* to say.

44   "She just pointed upstairs—like this"—pointing to the room above.

45   "I got up, with the idea of going up there myself. By this time I—didn't know what to do. I walked from there to here; then I says: 'Why, what did he die of?'

46   "'He died of a rope around his neck,' says she; and just went on pleatin' at her apron."

47   Hale stopped speaking, and stood staring at the rocker, as if he were still seeing the woman who had sat there the morning before. Nobody spoke; it was as if every one were seeing the woman who had sat there the morning before.

48   "And what did you do then?" the county attorney at last broke the silence.

49   "I went out and called Harry. I thought I might—need help. I got Harry in, and we went upstairs." His voice fell almost to a whisper. "There he was—lying over the—"

50   "I think I'd rather have you go into that upstairs," the county attorney interrupted, "where you can point it all out. Just go on now with the rest of the story."

51   "Well, my first thought was to get that rope off. It looked—"

52   He stopped, his face twitching.

53   "But Harry, he went up to him, and he said, 'No, he's dead all right, and we'd better not touch anything.' So we went downstairs.

54   "She was still sitting that same way. 'Has anybody been notified?' I asked. 'No,' says she, unconcerned.

55   "'Who did this, Mrs. Wright?' said Harry. He said it business-like, and she stopped pleatin' at her apron. 'I don't know,' she says. 'You don't *know*?' says Harry. 'Weren't you sleepin' in the bed with him?' 'Yes,' says she, 'but I was on the inside.' 'Somebody slipped a rope round his neck and strangled him, and you didn't wake up?' says Harry. 'I didn't wake up,' she said after him.

56   "We may have looked as if we didn't see how that could be, for after a minute she said, 'I sleep sound.'

57   "Harry was going to ask her more questions, but I said maybe that weren't our business; maybe we ought to let her tell her story first to the coroner or the sheriff. So Harry went fast as he could over to High Road—the Rivers' place, where there's a telephone."

"And what did she do when she knew you had gone for   58
the coroner?" The attorney got his pencil in his hand all
ready for writing.

"She moved from that chair to this one over here"—Hale   59
pointed to a small chair in the corner—"and just sat there
with her hands held together and looking down. I got a
feeling that I ought to make some conversation, so I said I
had come in to see if John wanted to put in a telephone;
and at that she started to laugh, and then she stopped and
looked at me—scared."

At the sound of a moving pencil the man who was telling   60
the story looked up.

"I dunno—maybe it wasn't scared," he hastened; "I   61
wouldn't like to say it was. Soon Harry got back, and then
Dr. Lloyd came, and you, Mr. Peters, and so I guess that's
all I know that you don't."

He said that last with relief, and moved a little, as if   62
relaxing. Every one moved a little. The county attorney
walked toward the stair door.

"I guess we'll go upstairs first—then out to the barn and   63
around there."

He paused and looked around the kitchen.   64

"You're convinced there was nothing important here?"   65
he asked the sheriff. "Nothing that would—point to any
motive?"

The sheriff too looked all around, as if to re-convince   66
himself.

"Nothing here but kitchen things," he said, with a little   67
laugh for the insignificance of kitchen things.

The county attorney was looking at the cupboard—a   68
peculiar, ungainly structure, half closet and half cupboard,
the upper part of it being built in the wall, and the lower
part just the old-fashioned kitchen cupboard. As if its queer-
ness attracted him, he got a chair and opened the upper
part and looked in. After a moment he drew his hand away
sticky.

"Here's a nice mess," he said resentfully.   69

The two women had drawn nearer, and now the sheriff's   70
wife spoke.

"Oh—her fruit," she said, looking to Mrs. Hale for sym-   71
pathetic understanding. She turned back to the county attorney and explained: "She worried about that when it
turned so cold last night. She said the fire would go out
and her jars might burst."

72   Mrs. Peters' husband broke into a laugh.

73   "Well, can you beat the woman! Held for murder, and worrying about her preserves!"

74   The young attorney set his lips.

75   "I guess before we're through with her she may have something more serious than preserves to worry about."

76   "Oh, well," said Mrs. Hale's husband, with good-natured superiority, "women are used to worrying over trifles."

77   The two women moved a little closer together. Neither of them spoke. The county attorney seemed suddenly to remember his manners—and think of his future.

78   "And yet," said he, with the gallantry of a young politician, "for all their worries, what would we do without the ladies?"

79   The women did not speak, did not unbend. He went to the sink and began washing his hands. He turned to wipe them on the roller towel—whirled it for a cleaner place.

80   "Dirty towels! Not much of a housekeeper, would you say, ladies?"

81   He kicked his foot against some dirty pans under the sink.

82   "There's a great deal of work to be done on a farm," said Mrs. Hale stiffly.

83   "To be sure. And yet"—with a little bow to her—"I know there are some Dickson County farm-houses that do not have such roller towels." He gave it a pull to expose its full length again.

84   "Those towels get dirty awful quick. Men's hands aren't always as clean as they might be."

85   "Ah, loyal to your sex, I see," he laughed. He stopped and gave her a keen look. "But you and Mrs. Wright were neighbors. I suppose you were friends, too."

86   Martha Hale shook her head.

87   "I've seen little enough of her of late years. I've not been in this house—it's more than a year."

88   "And why was that? You didn't like her?"

89   "I liked her well enough," she replied with spirit. "Farmers' wives have their hands full, Mr. Henderson. And then"— She looked around the kitchen.

90   "Yes?" he encouraged.

91   "It never seemed a very cheerful place," said she, more to herself than to him.

92   "No," he agreed; "I don't think any one would call it cheerful. I shouldn't say she had the home-making instinct."

93   "Well, I don't know as Wright had, either," she muttered.

"You mean they didn't get on very well?" he was quick   94
to ask.

"No; I don't mean anything," she answered, with decision.   95
As she turned a little away from him, she added: "But I
don't think a place would be any the cheerfuler for John
Wright's bein' in it."

"I'd like to talk to you about that a little later, Mrs. Hale,"   96
he said. "I'm anxious to get the lay of things upstairs now."

He moved toward the stair door, followed by the two men.   97

"I suppose anything Mrs. Peters does'll be all right?" the   98
sheriff inquired. "She was to take in some clothes for her,
you know—and a few little things. We left in such a hurry
yesterday."

The county attorney looked at the two women whom they   99
were leaving alone there among the kitchen things.

"Yes—Mrs. Peters," he said, his glance resting on the   100
woman who was not Mrs. Peters, the big farmer woman
who stood behind the sheriff's wife. "Of course Mrs. Peters
is one of us," he said, in a manner of entrusting responsibility. "And keep your eye out, Mrs. Peters, for anything that
might be of use. No telling; you women might come upon
a clue to the motive—and that's the thing we need."

Mr. Hale rubbed his face after the fashion of a show man   101
getting ready for a pleasantry.

"But would the women know a clue if they did come upon   102
it?" he said; and, having delivered himself of this, he followed the others through the stair door.

The women stood motionless and silent, listening to the   103
footsteps, first upon the stairs, then in the room above them.

Then, as if releasing herself from something strange,   104
Mrs. Hale began to arrange the dirty pans under the sink,
which the county attorney's disdainful push of the foot had
deranged.

"I'd hate to have men comin' into my kitchen," she said   105
testily—"snoopin' round and criticizin'."

"Of course it's no more than their duty," said the sheriff's   106
wife, in her manner of timid acquiescence.

"Duty's all right," replied Mrs. Hale bluffly; "but I guess   107
that deputy sheriff that come out to make the fire might
have got a little of this on." She gave the roller towel a pull.
"Wish I'd thought of that sooner! Seems mean to talk about
her for not having things slicked up, when she had to come
away in such a hurry."

She looked around the kitchen. Certainly it was not   108

"slicked up." Her eye was held by a bucket of sugar on a low shelf. The cover was off the wooden bucket, and beside it was a paper bag—half full.

109   Mrs. Hale moved toward it.

110   "She was putting this in there," she said to herself—slowly.

111   She thought of the flour in her kitchen at home—half sifted, half not sifted. She had been interrupted, and had left things half done. What had interrupted Minnie Foster? Why had that work been left half done? She made a move as if to finish it—unfinished things always bothered her,—and then she glanced around and saw that Mrs. Peters was watching her—and she didn't want Mrs. Peters to get that feeling she had got of work begun and then—for some reason—not finished.

112   "It's a shame about her fruit," she said, and walked toward the cupboard that the county attorney had opened, and got on the chair, murmuring: "I wonder if it's all gone."

113   It was a sorry enough looking sight, but "Here's one that's all right," she said at last. She held it toward the light. "This is cherries, too." She looked again. "I declare I believe that's the only one."

114   With a sigh, she got down from the chair, went to the sink, and wiped off the bottle.

115   "She'll feel awful bad, after all her hard work in the hot weather. I remember the afternoon I put up my cherries last summer."

116   She set the bottle on the table, and, with another sigh, started to sit down in the rocker. But she did not sit down. Something kept her from sitting down in that chair. She straightened—stepped back, and, half turned away, stood looking at it, seeing the woman who had sat there "pleatin' at her apron."

117   The thin voice of the sheriff's wife broke in upon her: "I must be getting those things from the front room closet." She opened the door into the other room, started in, stepped back. "You coming with me, Mrs. Hale?" she asked nervously. "You—you could help me get them."

118   They were soon back—the stark coldness of that shut-up room was not a thing to linger in.

119   "My!" said Mrs. Peters, dropping the things on the table and hurrying to the stove.

120   Mrs. Hale stood examining the clothes the woman who was being detained in town had said she wanted.

"Wright was close!" she exclaimed, holding up a shabby   121
black skirt that bore the marks of much making over. "I
think maybe that's why she kept so much to herself. I s'pose
she felt she couldn't do her part; and then, you don't enjoy
things when you feel shabby. She used to wear pretty
clothes and be lively — when she was Minnie Foster, one of
the town girls, singing in the choir. But that — oh, that was
twenty years ago."

With a carefulness in which there was something tender,   122
she folded the shabby clothes and piled them at one corner
of the table. She looked up at Mrs. Peters, and there was
something in the other woman's look that irritated her.

"She don't care," she said to herself. "Much difference it   123
makes to her whether Minnie Foster had pretty clothes
when she was a girl."

Then she looked again, and she wasn't so sure; in fact,   124
she hadn't at any time been perfectly sure about Mrs. Peters.
She had that shrinking manner, and yet her eyes looked as
if they could see a long way into things.

"This all you was to take in?" asked Mrs. Hale.   125

"No," said the sheriff's wife; "she said she wanted an   126
apron. Funny thing to want," she ventured in her nervous
little way, "for there's not much to get you dirty in jail,
goodness knows. But I suppose just to make her feel more
natural. If you're used to wearing an apron — . She said
they were in the bottom drawer of this cupboard. Yes — here
they are. And then her little shawl that always hung on the
stair door."

She took the small gray shawl from behind the door lead-   127
ing upstairs, and stood a minute looking at it.

Suddenly Mrs. Hale took a quick step toward the other   128
woman.

"Mrs. Peters!"   129

"Yes, Mrs. Hale?"   130

"Do you think she — did it?"   131

A frightened look blurred the other things in Mrs. Peters'   132
eyes.

"Oh, I don't know," she said, in a voice that seemed to   133
shrink away from the subject.

"Well, I don't think she did," affirmed Mrs. Hale stoutly.   134
"Asking for an apron, and her little shawl. Worryin' about
her fruit."

"Mr. Peters says — ." Footsteps were heard in the room   135
above; she stopped, looked up, then went on in a lowered

voice: "Mr. Peters says — it looks bad for her. Mr. Henderson is awful sarcastic in a speech, and he's going to make fun of her saying she didn't — wake up."

136   For a moment Mrs. Hale had no answer. Then, "Well, I guess John Wright didn't wake up — when they was slippin' that rope under his neck," she muttered.

137   "No, it's *strange*," breathed Mrs. Peters. "They think it was such a — funny way to kill a man."

138   She began to laugh; at sound of the laugh, abruptly stopped.

139   "That's just what Mr. Hale said," said Mrs. Hale, in a resolutely natural voice. "There was a gun in the house. He says that's what he can't understand."

140   "Mr. Henderson said, coming out, that what was needed for the case was a motive. Something to show anger — or sudden feeling."

141   "Well, I don't see any signs of anger around here," said Mrs. Hale. "I don't — "

142   She stopped. It was as if her mind tripped on something. Her eye was caught by a dish-towel in the middle of the kitchen table. Slowly she moved toward the table. One half of it was wiped clean, the other half messy. Her eyes made a slow, almost unwilling turn to the bucket of sugar and the half empty bag beside it. Things begun — and not finished.

143   After a moment she stepped back, and said, in that manner of releasing herself:

144   "Wonder how they're finding things upstairs? I hope she had it a little more red up up there. You know," — she paused, and feeling gathered, — "it seems kind of *sneaking*: locking her up in town and coming out here to get her own house to turn against her!"

145   "But, Mrs. Hale," said the sheriff's wife, "the law is the law."

146   "I s'pose 'tis," answered Mrs. Hale shortly.

147   She turned to the stove, saying something about that fire not being much to brag of. She worked with it a minute, and when she straightened up she said aggressively:

148   "The law is the law — and a bad stove is a bad stove. How'd you like to cook on this?" — pointing with the poker to the broken lining. She opened the oven door and started to express her opinion of the oven; but she was swept into her own thoughts, thinking of what it would mean, year after year, to have that stove to wrestle with. The thought

of Minnie Foster trying to bake in that oven—and the thought of her never going over to see Minnie Foster—.

She was startled by hearing Mrs. Peters say: "A person gets discouraged—and loses heart." 149

The sheriff's wife had looked from the stove to the sink— to the pail of water which had been carried in from outside. The two women stood there silent, above them the footsteps of the men who were looking for evidence against the woman who had worked in that kitchen. That look of seeing into things, of seeing through a thing to something else, was in the eyes of the sheriff's wife now. When Mrs. Hale next spoke to her, it was gently: 150

"Better loosen up your things, Mrs. Peters. We'll not feel them when we go out." 151

Mrs. Peters went to the back of the room to hang up the fur tippet she was wearing. A moment later she exclaimed, "Why, she was piecing a quilt," and held up a large sewing basket piled high with quilt pieces. 152

Mrs. Hale spread some of the blocks on the table. 153

"It's log-cabin pattern," she said, putting several of them together. "Pretty, isn't it?" 154

They were so engaged with the quilt that they did not hear the footsteps on the stairs. Just as the stair door opened Mrs. Hale was saying: 155

"Do you suppose she was going to quilt it or just knot it?" 156

The sheriff threw up his hands. 157

"They wonder whether she was going to quilt it or just knot it!" 158

There was a laugh for the ways of women, a warming of hands over the stove, and then the county attorney said briskly: 159

"Well, let's go right out to the barn and get that cleared up." 160

"I don't see as there's anything so strange," Mrs. Hale said resentfully, after the outside door had closed on the three men—"our taking up our time with little things while we're waiting for them to get the evidence. I don't see as it's anything to laugh about." 161

"Of course they've got awful important things on their minds," said the sheriff's wife apologetically. 162

They returned to an inspection of the block for the quilt. Mrs. Hale was looking at the fine, even sewing, and preoccupied with thoughts of the woman who had done that sewing, when she heard the sheriff's wife say, in a queer tone: 163

164   "Why, look at this one."

165   She turned to take the block held out to her.

166   "The sewing," said Mrs. Peters, in a troubled way. "All the rest of them have been so nice and even — but — this one. Why, it looks as if she didn't know what she was about!"

167   Their eyes met — something flashed to life, passed between them; then, as if with an effort, they seemed to pull away from each other. A moment Mrs. Hale sat there, her hands folded over that sewing which was so unlike all the rest of the sewing. Then she had pulled a knot and drawn the threads.

168   "Oh, what are you doing, Mrs. Hale?" asked the sheriff's wife, startled.

169   "Just pulling out a stitch or two that's not sewed very good," said Mrs. Hale mildly.

170   "I don't think we ought to touch things," Mrs. Peters said, a little helplessly.

171   "I'll just finish up this end," answered Mrs. Hale, still in that mild, matter-of-fact fashion.

172   She threaded a needle and started to replace bad sewing with good. For a little while she sewed in silence. Then, in that thin, timid voice, she heard:

173   "Mrs. Hale!"

174   "Yes, Mrs. Peters?"

175   "What do you suppose she was so — nervous about?"

176   "Oh, *I* don't know," said Mrs. Hale, as if dismissing a thing not important enough to spend much time on. "I don't know as she was — nervous. I sew awful queer sometimes when I'm just tired."

177   She cut a thread, and out of the corner of her eye looked up at Mrs. Peters. The small, lean face of the sheriff's wife seemed to have tightened up. Her eyes had that look of peering into something. But the next moment she moved, and said in her thin, indecisive way:

178   "Well, I must get those clothes wrapped. They may be through sooner than we think. I wonder where I could find a piece of paper — and string."

179   "In that cupboard, maybe," suggested Mrs. Hale, after a glance around.

180   One piece of the crazy sewing remained unripped. Mrs. Peters' back turned, Martha Hale now scrutinized that piece, compared it with the dainty, accurate sewing of the other blocks. The difference was startling. Holding this

block made her feel queer, as if the distracted thoughts of the woman who had perhaps turned to it to try and quiet herself were communicating themselves to her.

Mrs. Peters' voice roused her.   181

"Here's a bird-cage," she said. "Did she have a bird, Mrs. 182 Hale?"

"Why, I don't know whether she did or not." She turned 183 to look at the cage Mrs. Peters was holding up. "I've not been here in so long." She sighed. "There was a man round last year selling canaries cheap—but I don't know as she took one. Maybe she did. She used to sing real pretty herself."

Mrs. Peters looked around the kitchen.   184

"Seems kind of funny to think of a bird here." She half 185 laughed—an attempt to put up a barrier. "But she must have had one—or why would she have a cage? I wonder what happened to it."

"I suppose maybe the cat got it," suggested Mrs. Hale, 186 resuming her sewing.

"No; she didn't have a cat. She's got that feeling some 187 people have about cats—being afraid of them. When they brought her to our house yesterday, my cat got in the room, and she was real upset and asked me to take it out."

"My sister Bessie was like that," laughed Mrs. Hale.   188

The sheriff's wife did not reply. The silence made Mrs. 189 Hale turn round. Mrs. Peters was examining the bird-cage.

"Look at this door," she said slowly. "It's broke. One hinge 190 has been pulled apart."

Mrs. Hale came nearer.   191

"Looks as if some one must have been—rough with it."   192

Again their eyes met—startled, questioning, apprehen- 193 sive. For a moment neither spoke nor stirred. Then Mrs. Hale, turning away, said brusquely:

"If they're going to find any evidence, I wish they'd be 194 about it. I don't like this place."

"But I'm awful glad you came with me, Mrs. Hale." Mrs. 195 Peters put the bird-cage on the table and sat down. "It would be lonesome for me—sitting here alone."

"Yes, it would, wouldn't it?" agreed Mrs. Hale, a certain 196 determined naturalness in her voice. She had picked up the sewing, but now it dropped in her lap, and she murmured in a different voice: "But I tell you what I *do* wish, Mrs. Peters. I wish I had come over sometimes when she was here. I wish—I had."

197   "But of course you were awful busy, Mrs. Hale. Your house — and your children."

198   "I could've come," retorted Mrs. Hale shortly. "I stayed away because it weren't cheerful — and that's why I ought to have come. I" — she looked around — "I've never liked this place. Maybe because it's down in a hollow and you don't see the road. I don't know what it is, but it's a lonesome place, and always was. I wish I had come over to see Minnie Foster sometimes. I can see now — " She did not put it into words.

199   "Well, you mustn't reproach yourself," counseled Mrs. Peters. "Somehow, we just don't see how it is with other folks till — something comes up."

200   "Not having children makes less work," mused Mrs. Hale, after a silence, "but it makes a quiet house — and Wright out to work all day — and no company when he did come in. Did you know John Wright, Mrs. Peters?"

201   "Not to know him. I've seen him in town. They said he was a good man."

202   "Yes — good," conceded John Wright's neighbor grimly. "He didn't drink, and kept his word as well as most, I guess, and paid his debts. But he was a hard man, Mrs. Peters. Just to pass the time of day with him — ." She stopped, shivered a little. "Like a raw wind that gets to the bone." Her eye fell upon the cage on the table before her, and she added, almost bitterly: "I should think she would've wanted a bird!"

203   Suddenly she leaned forward, looking intently at the cage. "But what do you s'pose went wrong with it?"

204   "I don't know," returned Mrs. Peters; "unless it got sick and died."

205   But after she said it she reached over and swung the broken door. Both women watched it as if somehow held by it.

206   "You didn't know — her?" Mrs. Hale asked, a gentler note in her voice.

207   "Not till they brought her yesterday," said the sheriff's wife.

208   "She — come to think of it, she was kind of like a bird herself. Real sweet and pretty, but kind of timid and — fluttery. How — she — did — change."

209   That held her for a long time. Finally, as if struck with a happy thought and relieved to get back to everyday things, she exclaimed:

"Tell you what, Mrs. Peters, why don't you take the quilt   210
in with you? It might take up her mind."

"Why, I think that's a real nice idea, Mrs. Hale," agreed   211
the sheriff's wife, as if she too were glad to come into the
atmosphere of a simple kindness. "There couldn't possibly
be any objection to that, could there? Now, just what will
I take? I wonder if her patches are in here — and her things."

They turned to the sewing basket.   212

"Here's some red," said Mrs. Hale, bringing out a roll of   213
cloth. Underneath that was a box. "Here, maybe her scissors
are in here — and her things." She held it up. "What a pretty
box! I'll warrant that was something she had a long time
ago — when she was a girl."

She held it in her hand a moment; then, with a little sigh,   214
opened it.

Instantly her hand went to her nose.   215

"Why—!"   216

Mrs. Peters drew nearer — then turned away.   217

"There's something wrapped up in this piece of silk,"   218
faltered Mrs. Hale.

"This isn't her scissors," said Mrs. Peters, in a shrinking   219
voice.

Her hand not steady, Mrs. Hale raised the piece of silk.   220
"Oh, Mrs. Peters!" she cried, "It's—"

Mrs. Peters bent closer.   221

"It's the bird," she whispered.   222

"But, Mrs. Peters!" cried Mrs. Hale, "*Look* at it! Its neck—   223
look at its neck! Its all — other side *to*."

She held the box away from her.   224

The sheriff's wife again bent closer.   225

"Somebody wrung its neck," said she, in a voice that was   226
slow and deep.

And then again the eyes of the two women met — this   227
time clung together in a look of dawning comprehension,
of growing horror. Mrs. Peters looked from the dead bird
to the broken door of the cage. Again their eyes met. And
just then there was a sound at the outside door.

Mrs. Hale slipped the box under the quilt pieces in the   228
basket, and sank into the chair before it. Mrs. Peters stood
holding to the table. The county attorney and the sheriff
came in from outside.

"Well, ladies," said the county attorney, as one turning   229
from serious things to little pleasantries, "have you decided
whether she was going to quilt it or knot it?"

230   "We think," began the sheriff's wife in a flurried voice, "that she was going to—knot it."

231   He was too preoccupied to notice the change that came in her voice on that last.

232   "Well, that's very interesting, I'm sure," he said tolerantly. He caught sight of the bird-cage. "Has the bird flown?"

233   "We think the cat got it," said Mrs. Hale in a voice curiously even.

234   He was walking up and down, as if thinking something out.

235   "Is there a cat?" he asked absently.

236   Mrs. Hale shot a look up at the sheriff's wife.

237   "Well, not *now*," said Mrs. Peters. "They're superstitious, you know; they leave."

238   She sank into her chair.

239   The county attorney did not heed her. "No sign at all of any one having come in from outside," he said to Peters, in the manner of continuing an interrupted conversation. "Their own rope. Now let's go upstairs again and go over it, piece by piece. It would have to have been some one who knew just the—"

240   The stair door closed behind them and their voices were lost.

241   The two women sat motionless, not looking at each other, but as if peering into something and at the same time holding back. When they spoke now it was as if they were afraid of what they were saying, but as if they could not help saying it.

242   "She liked the bird," said Martha Hale, low and slowly. "She was going to bury it in that pretty box."

243   "When I was a girl," said Mrs. Peters, under her breath, "my kitten—there was a boy took a hatchet, and before my eyes—before I could get there—" She covered her face an instant. "If they hadn't held me back I would have"—she caught herself, looked upstairs where footsteps were heard, and finished weakly—"hurt him."

244   Then they sat without speaking or moving.

245   "I wonder how it would seem," Mrs. Hale at last began, as if feeling her way over strange ground—"never to have had any children around?" Her eyes made a slow sweep of the kitchen, as if seeing what that kitchen had meant through all the years. "No, Wright wouldn't like the bird," she said after that—"a thing that sang. She used to sing. He killed that too." Her voice tightened.

Mrs. Peters moved uneasily.   246

"Of course we don't know who killed the bird."   247

"I knew John Wright," was Mrs. Hale's answer.   248

"It was an awful thing was done in this house that night,   249
Mrs. Hale," said the sheriff's wife. "Killing a man while he
slept — slipping a thing round his neck that choked the life
out of him."

Mrs. Hale's hand went out to the bird-cage.   250

"His neck. Choked the life out of him."   251

"We don't *know* who killed him," whispered Mrs. Peters   252
wildly. "We don't *know*."

Mrs. Hale had not moved. "If there had been years and   253
years of — nothing, then a bird to sing to you, it would be
awful — still — after the bird was still."

It was as if something within her not herself had spoken,   254
and it found in Mrs. Peters something she did not know as
herself.

"I know what stillness is," she said, in a queer, monoto-   255
nous voice. "When we homesteaded in Dakota, and my first
baby died — after he was two years old — and me with no
other then — "

Mrs. Hale stirred.   256

"How soon do you suppose they'll be through looking for   257
the evidence?"

"I know what stillness is," repeated Mrs. Peters, in just   258
that same way. Then she too pulled back. "The law has got
to punish crime, Mrs. Hale," she said in her tight little way.

"I wish you'd seen Minnie Foster," was the answer, "when   259
she wore a white dress with blue ribbons, and stood up
there in the choir and sang."

The picture of that girl, the fact that she had lived neigh-   260
bor to that girl for twenty years, and had let her die for
lack of life, was suddenly more than she could bear.

"Oh, I *wish* I'd come over here once in a while!" she cried.   261
"That was a crime! That was a crime! Who's going to punish
that?"

"We mustn't take on," said Mrs. Peters, with a frightened   262
look toward the stairs.

"I might 'a' *known* she needed help! I tell you, it's *queer*,   263
Mrs. Peters. We live close together, and we live far apart.
We all go through the same things — it's all just a different
kind of the same thing! If it weren't — why do you and I
understand? Why do we *know* — what we know this minute?"

She dashed her hand across her eyes. Then, seeing the   264
jar of fruit on the table, she reached for it and choked out:

265   "If I was you I wouldn't *tell* her her fruit was gone! Tell her it *ain't.* Tell her it's all right — all of it. Here — take this in to prove it to her! She — she may never know whether it was broke or not."

266   She turned away.

267   Mrs. Peters reached out for the bottle of fruit as if she were glad to take it — as if touching a familiar thing, having something to do, could keep her from something else. She got up, looked about for something to wrap the fruit in, took a petticoat from the pile of clothes she had brought from the front room, and nervously started winding that round the bottle.

268   "My!" she began, in a high, false voice, "it's a good thing the men couldn't hear us! Getting all stirred up over a little thing like a — dead canary." She hurried over that. "As if that could have anything to do with — with — My, wouldn't they *laugh?*"

269   Footsteps were heard on the stairs.

270   "Maybe they would," muttered Mrs. Hale — "maybe they wouldn't."

271   "No, Peters," said the county attorney incisively; "it's all perfectly clear, except the reason for doing it. But you know juries when it comes to women. If there was some definite thing — something to show. Something to make a story about. A thing that would connect up with this clumsy way of doing it."

272   In a covert way Mrs. Hale looked at Mrs. Peters. Mrs. Peters was looking at her. Quickly they looked away from each other. The outer door opened and Mr. Hale came in.

273   "I've got the team round now," he said. "Pretty cold out there."

274   "I'm going to stay here awhile by myself," the county attorney suddenly announced. "You can send Frank out for me, can't you?" he asked the sheriff. "I want to go over everything. I'm not satisfied we can't do better."

275   Again, for one brief moment, the two women's eyes found one another.

276   The sheriff came up to the table.

277   "Did you want to see what Mrs. Peters was going to take in?"

278   The county attorney picked up the apron. He laughed.

279   "Oh, I guess they're not very dangerous things the ladies have picked out."

280   Mrs. Hale's hand was on the sewing basket in which the box was concealed. She felt that she ought to take her hand

off the basket. She did not seem able to. He picked up one of the quilt blocks which she had piled on to cover the box. Her eyes felt like fire. She had a feeling that if he took up the basket she would snatch it from him.

But he did not take it up. With another little laugh, he   281
turned away, saying:

"No; Mrs. Peters doesn't need supervising. For that mat-   282
ter, a sheriff's wife is married to the law. Ever think of it that way, Mrs. Peters?"

Mrs. Peters was standing beside the table. Mrs. Hale shot   283
a look up at her; but she could not see her face. Mrs. Peters had turned away. When she spoke, her voice was muffled.

"Not — just that way," she said.   284

"Married to the law!" chuckled Mrs. Peters' husband. He   285
moved toward the door into the front room, and said to the county attorney:

"I just want you to come in here a minute, George. We   286
ought to take a look at these windows."

"Oh — windows," said the county attorney scoffingly.   287

"We'll be right out, Mr. Hale," said the sheriff to the   288
farmer, who was still waiting by the door.

Hale went to look after the horses. The sheriff followed   289
the county attorney into the other room. Again — for one final moment — the two women were alone in that kitchen.

Martha Hale sprang up, her hands tight together, looking   290
at that other woman, with whom it rested. At first she could not see her eyes, for the sheriff's wife had not turned back since she turned away at that suggestion of being married to the law. But now Mrs. Hale made her turn back. Her eyes made her turn back. Slowly, unwillingly, Mrs. Peters turned her head until her eyes met the eyes of the other woman. There was a moment when they held each other in a steady, burning look in which there was no evasion nor flinching. Then Martha Hale's eyes pointed the way to the basket in which was hidden the thing that would make certain the conviction of the other woman — that woman who was not there and yet who had been there with them all through that hour.

For a moment Mrs. Peters did not move. And then she   291
did it. With a rush forward, she threw back the quilt pieces, got the box, tried to put it in her handbag. It was too big. Desperately she opened it, started to take the bird out. But there she broke — she could not touch the bird. She stood there helpless, foolish.

There was the sound of a knob turning in the inner door.   292

Martha Hale snatched the box from the sheriff's wife, and got it in the pocket of her big coat just as the sheriff and the county attorney came back into the kitchen.

293   "Well, Henry," said the county attorney facetiously, "at least we found out that she was not going to quilt it. She was going to — what is it you call it, ladies?"

294   Mrs. Hale's hand was against the pocket of her coat.

295   "We call it — knot it, Mr. Henderson."

Marcia Ann Gillespie

A Different Take on the Ol' Bump and Grind

Marcia Ann Gillespie regularly writes for **Ms.** *magazine, where this essay appeared in 1987.*

1   Once upon a time only nasty girls, women my grandmother called floozies, gave men a top-to-bottom once-over checking chests, muscles, behinds, and crotches. Nice girls, ladies, and good women were supposed to keep their eyes, like their skirts, down at all costs. The last thing the ol' patriarchy ever wanted was sexually assertive women knowing, much less talking, about orgasms, discussing our right to sexual pleasure, assessing men's sexual potential or performances, acknowledging that we found men's bodies exciting or simply interesting to look at. But in clubs all around this country women are looking, laughing and carrying on while men come on like Gypsy Rose Lee: who would have thunk it?

2   Recently a friend's mother turned 70 and she knew just where she wanted to celebrate that milestone: Chippendales! Now for those of you who don't know, Chippendales provides a revue where male dancers shake, shimmy, bump, grind, and strip down to their bikini briefs for an almost exclusively female audience who wave dollar bills in the air for their favorites in exchange for slightly sweaty hugs and kisses. In some cities one can even order up a male stripper — who will make house, restaurant, or even office

calls — to shake it down for private parties. All you need do is dial a number and have your credit card handy. Ain't modern life grand!

When asked to join this particular birthday party, in be-   3
tween bursts of laughter, I said yes indeed. My girlfriend was clearly in need of moral support. I think she was a bit shocked that her mother had turned down dinner at The Plaza for Chippendales. (Makes you wonder who the really liberated women are, us or our mothers?) I also will admit to being downright curious about the show. Was it going to be slightly sleazy, or really raunchy? Who went? Who performed? Did the women come on in macha — "hey, baby, shake that thang" — style?

The nightclub scene: dark walls, flashing strobes, speak-   4
ers blasting heavy-bassed hot disco, utilitarian banquettes and benches lining a dance floor. Music videos and pinups of good-looking, well-muscled young men in stock seductive poses, on screens positioned around the room. A bevy of young men moved through the crowd, serving drinks, hug-ging new arrivals, smiling and joking with the customers. Like cocktail waitresses, whose uniforms are designed to expose beaucoup cleavage and much thigh, these waiters are obviously picked for their bodies. Shirtless, wearing tight black pants, collars and bow ties, there's not an inch of excess fat, not an undeveloped pectoral, nary a hairy chest in sight!

The nightclub was filled with women. Women of all ages   5
and sizes, races and ethnicities, married and single, career-ists and workers, students and retirees, suburbanites and city dwellers, they'd come by twos, and in groups large and small. Some appeared to be regulars, who used the club as a girls'-night-out hangout, or came a-cruisin'. And then there were the first-timers: more than a few appeared hesi-tant, with "what in the world am I doing here" looks on their faces; others were obviously revved up and ready to kick it out!

"Ladies, welcome to Chippendales!" The show began with   6
a Las Vegas-style opener, a big dance routine that seemed to include every man in the place. Then the emcee, a Michael J. Fox type, led off with a reverse strip. Starting out in briefs he put it all on, and then proceeded to work the crowd for the rest of the show: a series of vignettes loosely based on a "fantasy weekend." The accommodating Room Service Waiter, the Souvenir Man in a cage, the Macho

Motorcyclist, the James Deanish Rebel who makes a cause
out of oiling his body, and the Friendly Chauffeur—all performed with a fun, shake-it-all-out sense of delivery. The
guys seemed sweet and clearly wished to please their patrons, enjoyed seeing the women have fun, and obviously
loved the attention.

7   The performances are billed as interpretations of
women's fantasies. Very safe middle-of-the-road fantasies
(like those hairless chests), nothing that would shock, rock,
or threaten. (Steve Merritt, the show's choreographer and
director, later told me that he'd discussed the concepts with
women friends and in fact used many of their fantasies in
the show.) Though none of them came close to my Secret
Garden, it's clear that many of the women found them to
be right on the money or maybe they just got a thrill out
of the idea itself. Whatever the reasons, as each guy came
out the women carried on, laughing, acting out a bit, hug-
ging, being hugged and kissed. Kissed with much gusto but
rather chastely (quite sanely given the age), on the cheek.

8   In truth as good-looking and as sexy as the men may
be, I wasn't moved. Some man shaking his family jewels
and flexing his muscles isn't my sexual dish. Besides,
other than Robert DeNiro, white men rarely, as in almost
never, make up the stuff of my erotic dreams. I'm told
that in the Los Angeles and Atlantic City clubs, Chippendales has black performers, providing equal opportunity
erotica. Yet, I hardly think I'd be more turned on if the
stars covered a complete racial spectrum. Fantasies aside,
how many variations of the same old bump and grind
can there be?

9   And yet, though none of it made my toes curl, I clapped
and laughed and had a ball. I knew it was gonna be a good
time from the moment I walked into that room, heard the
music, looked around at the sea of women and felt all their
energy. No matter how good, bad, or simply boring the
show might be, the truly vital dynamic was female.

10   And the women do get down. One woman's enthusiasm
seemed to spur another's, until it was impossible to tell
whether the cheers and clapping and screams were for the
performers, or simply us women saluting ourselves and
each other. As the show progressed, that often repressed,
slightly raunchy girl in even the most sedate of us started
coming out. Across the room in the front row sat an older
black woman, clearly a churchgoing lady, stolid of body,

solemn of mien, who reminded me of my maternal grandmother. From the moment I first spied her, I kept wondering
what in the world she was doing there, and how she was
going to react to the show. Fascinated, I kept my eyes on
her most of the evening. At first she seemed detached from
it all, but then ever so slowly her head began to nod, while
her feet tapped out the beat. And then — with absolutely no
change of expression or position — a dollar bill appeared
like magic in her hand, over the head of one of the younger
women she was with, who, I presumed, was her daughter.
And suddenly to the younger woman's total surprise there
was this very big, very blond, very undressed male dancer
swooping down to give her a hug. Mama cracked up, and
laughed even harder when the same dancer kissed her as
well.

One woman had a lot more contact in mind, which she   11
demonstrated by leaping onto a performer and wrapping
her legs firmly around his waist. She looked like she'd died
and gone to heaven when he danced her around the room.
My friend's mom, head bouncing to the music, got into the
act as well. One minute she was sitting with us, and the
next she was over by the dance floor with her dollar waving
in the air, being swept up in a bare bear hug by another
giant-looking dancer. She returned to the group grinning
from ear to ear.

By the time the show was over everyone seemed to be in   12
a really good, up place. And that's when the real party
began as women singly, and by twos and threes moved out
on the dance floor boogying back. I felt the pull and responded up on my feet out on the floor, dancing with my
friend's mother, energized and feeling a very special high.
High off being with so many other women, and the feeling
of safety and celebration. Where else could women go out
and kick back like that, maybe in a gay women's bar, I
don't know. But here straight women were able to be publicly free in ways we still too rarely are, without a thought
of how we looked or who was looking at us, without giving
a damn about men and about being hit on, when in fact
that was the furthest thing from mind.

I kept contrasting the evening and the place to those   13
clubs where women strip for primarily male audiences. I
recalled a joint I'd been in years before, once again out of
sheer curiosity, with a man friend of mine. The women who
performed seemed deadpan and wary, while the men's eyes

seemed to bore into them, and more than once along with the tucked-in bills came intrusive probing fingers or superior smirks and demeaning remarks. No one seemed to be having a really good time, not the customers, not the dancers, not the waitresses serving the drinks. I could not, cannot imagine those men jumping up as we women did at the end of the show dancing together. Or those women who performed sharing good-time hugs and kisses with the tippers. Too bad, because it will be a better day for all of us when men — as well as women — can raise the roof off of erotic energy.

Diane Wakoski
Belly Dancer

Diane Wakoski (born 1937) has spent much of her life in New York, though she was born in Whittier, California, and educated at Berkeley. She now teaches at Michigan State University. This poem is from Trilogy *(1966), one of several collections of her poetry.*

1   Can these movements which move themselves
    be the substance of my attraction?
    Where does this thin green silk come from that covers
        my body?
    Surely any woman wearing such fabrics
    would move her body just to feel them touching every
        part of her.

2   Yet most of the women frown, or look away, or laugh stiffly.
    They are afraid of these materials and these movements
        in some way.
    The psychologists would say they are afraid of
        themselves, somehow.
    Perhaps awakening too much desire —
    that their men could never satisfy?

3   So they keep themselves laced and buttoned and made up
    in hopes that the framework will keep them stiff enough
        not to feel
    the whole register.

In hopes that they will not have to experience that
  unquenchable desire for rhythm and contact.

If a snake glided across this floor   4
most of them would faint or shrink away.
Yet that movement could be their own.
That smooth movement frightens them —
awakening ancestors and relatives to the tips of the
  arms and toes.

So my bare feet   5
and my thin green silks
my bells and finger cymbals
offend them — frighten their old-young bodies.
While the men simper and leer —
glad for the vicarious experience and exercise.
They do not realize how I scorn them:
or how I dance for their frightened,
unawakened, sweet
women.

Susan Brownmiller

Emotion

*Susan Brownmiller — journalist, novelist, women's rights ac-
tivist — published* Femininity *in 1984; this selection is excerpted from it.* Femininity *attempts to define the term and to
place it in historical perspective. Brownmiller's work also appears elsewhere in this book: see pages 544 and 552.*

A 1970 landmark study, known in the field as *Broverman* 1
and Broverman, reported that "Cries very easily" was rated
by a group of professional psychologists as a highly
feminine trait. "Very emotional," "Very excitable in a minor
crisis" and "Feeling easily hurt" were additional characteristics on the femininity scale. So were "Very easily influenced," "Very subjective," "Unable to separate feelings from
ideas," "Very illogical" and "Very sneaky." As might be ex-

pected, masculinity was defined by opposing, sturdier values: "Very direct," "Very logical," "Can make decisions easily," "Never cries." The importance of *Broverman and Broverman* was not in nailing down a set of popular assumptions and conventional perceptions—masculine-feminine scales were well established in the literature of psychology as a means of ascertaining normality and social adjustment—but in the authors' observation that stereotypic femininity was a grossly negative assessment of the female sex and, furthermore, that many so-called feminine traits ran counter to clinical descriptions of maturity and mental health.

2   Emotional femininity is a tough nut to crack, impossible to quantify yet hard to ignore. As the task of conforming to a specified physical design is a gender mission that few women care to resist, conforming to a prepackaged emotional design is another imperative task of gender. To satisfy a societal need for sexual clarification, and to justify second-class status, an emblematic constellation of inner traits, as well as their outward manifestations, has been put forward historically by some of the world's great thinkers as proof of the "different" feminine nature.

3   "Woman," wrote Aristotle, "is more compassionate than man, more easily moved to tears. At the same time, she is more jealous, more querulous, more apt to scold and to strike. She is, furthermore, more prone to despondency and less hopeful than man, more void of shame or self-respect, more false of speech, more deceptive and of more retentive memory. She is also more wakeful, more shrinking, more difficult to rouse to action, and she requires a smaller amount of nutriment."

4   Addressing a suffrage convention in 1855, Ralph Waldo Emerson had kindlier words on the nature of woman, explicating the nineteenth-century view that her difference was one of superior virtue. "Women," he extolled, "are the civilizers of mankind. What is civilization? I answer, the power of good women. . . . The starry crown of woman is in the power of her affection and sentiment, and the infinite enlargements to which they lead." (In less elevated language, the Emersonian view was perhaps what President Reagan had in mind when he cheerfully stated, "Why, if it wasn't for women, we men would still be walking around in skin suits carrying clubs.")

5   A clarification is in order. Are women believed to possess

a wider or deeper emotional range, a greater sensitivity, say, to the beauties of nature or to the infinite complexities of feeling? Any male poet, artist, actor, marine biologist or backpacker would strenuously object. Rather, it is commonly agreed that women are tossed and buffeted on the high seas of emotion, while men have the tough mental fiber, the intellectual muscle, to stay in control. As for the civilizing influence, surely something more is meant than sophistication, culture and taste, using the correct fork or not belching after dinner. The idealization of emotional femininity, as women prefer to see themselves affirmed, is more exquisitely romantic: a finer temperament in a more fragile vessel, a gentler nature ruled by a twin need to love and to be protected: one who appreciates — without urgency to create — good art, music, literature and other public expressions of the private soul; a flame-bearer of spiritual values by whose shining example the men of the world are inspired to redemption and to accomplish great things.

Two thousand years ago *Dominus flevit*, Jesus wept as he   6
beheld Jerusalem. "Men ceased weeping," proposed Simone de Beauvoir, "when it became unfashionable." Now it is Mary, *Mater Dolorosa*, who weeps with compassion for mankind. In mystical visions, in the reliquaries of obscure churches and miraculous shrines, the figure of the Virgin, the world's most feminine woman, has been seen to shed tears. There are still extant cultures in which men are positively lachrymose (and kissy-kissy) with no seeming detriment to their masculine image, but the Anglo-Saxon tradition, in particular, requires keeping a stiff upper lip. Weeping, keening women shrouded in black are an established fixture in mourning rites in many nations. Inconsolable grief is a feminine role, at least in its unquiet representations. In what has become a stock photograph in the national news magazines, women weep for the multitudes when national tragedy (a terrorist bombing, an air crash, an assassination) strikes.

The catharsis of tears is encouraged in women — "There,   7
there, now, let it all out" — while a man may be told to get a grip on himself, or to gulp down a double Scotch. Having "a good cry" in order to feel better afterward is not usually recommended as a means of raising the spirits of men, for the cathartic relief of succumbing to tears would be tempered by the uncomfortable knowledge that the loss of control was hardly manly. In the 1972 New

Hampshire Presidential primary, Senator Edmund Muskie, then the Democratic front-runner, committed political suicide when he publicly cried during a campaign speech. Muskie had been talking about some harsh press comments directed at his wife when the tears filled his eyes. In retrospect it was his watershed moment: Could a man who became tearful when the going got rough in a political campaign be expected to face the Russians? To a nation that had delighted in the hatless, overcoatless macho posturing of John F. Kennedy, the military successes of General Ike and the irascible outbursts of "Give 'em hell" Harry Truman, the answer was No. Media accounts of Muskie's all-too-human tears were merciless. In the summer of 1983 the obvious and unshakable grief displayed by Israeli prime minister Menachem Begin after the death of his wife was seized upon by the Israeli and American press as evidence that a tough old warrior had lost his grip. Sharing this perception of his own emotional state, perhaps, Begin shortly afterward resigned.

8   Expressions of anger and rage are not a disqualifying factor in the masculine disposition. Anger in men is often understood, or excused, as reasonable or just. Anger in men may even be cast in a heroic mold—a righteous response to an insult against honor that will preclude a manly, aggressive act. Because competitive acts of personal assertion, not to mention acts of outright physical aggression, are known to flow from angry feelings, anger becomes the most unfeminine emotion a woman can show.

9   Anger in a woman isn't "nice." A woman who seethes with anger is "unattractive." An angry woman is hard, mean and nasty; she is unreliably, unprettily out of control. Her face contorts into unpleasant lines: the jaw juts, the eyes are narrowed, the teeth are bared. Anger is a violent snarl and a hostile threat, a declaration of war. The endless forbearance demanded of women, described as the feminine virtue of patience, prohibits an angry response. Picture a charming old-fashioned scene: The mistress of the house bends low over her needlework, cross-stitching her sampler: "Patience is a virtue, possess it if you can/Seldom seen in women, never seen in man." Does the needle jab through the cloth in uncommon fury? Does she prick her thumb in frustration?

10   Festering without a permissible release, women's undissolved anger has been known to seep out in petty, mean-

spirited ways — fits of jealousy, fantasies of retaliation, unholy plots of revenge. Perhaps, after all, it is safer to cry. "Woman's aptitude for facile tears," wrote Beauvoir, "comes largely from the fact that her life is built upon a foundation of impotent revolt."*

Beauvoir hedged her bet, for her next words were these: 11 "It is also doubtless true that physiologically she has less nervous control than a man." Is this "doubtless true," or is it more to the point, as Beauvoir continues, that "her education has taught her to let herself go more readily"?

Infants and children cry out of fear, frustration, discom- 12 fort, hunger, anxiety at separation from a parent, and rage. Surveying all available studies of crying newborns and little children, psychologists Eleanor Maccoby and Carol Jacklin found no appreciable sexual difference. If teenage girls and adult women are known to cry more than men — and there is no reason to question the popular wisdom in this regard — should the endocrine changes of adolescence be held to account? What of those weepy "blue days" of premenstrual tension that genuinely afflict so many women? What about mid-life depression, known in some circles as "the feminine malady"? Are these conditions, as some men propose, a sign of "raging hormonal imbalance" that incapacitates the cool, logical functioning of the human brain? Or does feminine depression result, as psychiatrist Willard Gaylin suggests, when confidence in one's coping mechanism is lost?

Belief in a biological basis for the instability of female 13 emotions has a notorious history in the development of medical science. Hippocrates the physician held that hysteria was caused by a wandering uterus that remained unfulfilled. Discovery in the seventeenth century that the thyroid gland was larger in women inspired that proposition that the thyroid's function was to give added grace to the feminine neck, but other beliefs maintained that the gland served to flush impurities from the blood before it reached the brain. A larger thyroid "was necessary to guard the female system from the influence of the more numerous causes of irritation and vexation" to which the sex was unfortunately disposed. Nineteenth-century doc-

---

*"Facile" is the English translators' match for the French *facile*, more correctly rendered as "easy." Beauvoir did not mean to ascribe a stereotype superficiality to women in her remark.

tors averred that womb-related disorders were the cause of such female complaints as "nervous prostration." For those without money to seek out a physician's care, Lydia E. Pinkham's Vegetable Compound and other patent medicines were available to give relief. In the 1940s and '50s, prefrontal lobotomy was briefly and tragically in vogue for a variety of psychiatric disorders, particularly among women, since the surgical procedure had a flattening effect on raging emotions. Nowadays Valium appears to suffice.

14   Beginning in earnest in the 1960s, one line of research has attempted to isolate premenstrual tension as a contributing cause of accidents, suicide, admittance to mental hospitals and the commission of violent crimes. Mood swings, irritability and minor emotional upsets probably do lead to more "acting out" by females at a cyclical time in the month, but what does this prove beyond the increasingly accepted fact that the endocrine system has a critical influence on the human emotional threshold? Suicide, violent crime and dangerous psychiatric disorders are statistically four to nine times more prevalent in men. Should we theorize, then, that "raging hormonal imbalance" is a chronic, year-round condition in males? A disqualifying factor? By any method of calculation and for whatever reason — hormonal effects, the social inhibitions of femininity, the social pleasure of the masculine role, or all of these — the female gender is indisputably less prone to irrational, antisocial behavior. The price of inhibited anger and a nonviolent temperament may well be a bucketful of tears.

15   Like the emotion of anger, exulting in personal victory is a harshly unfeminine response. Of course, good winners of either sex are supposed to display some degree of sportsmanlike humility, but the merest hint of gloating triumph — "Me, me, me, I did it!" — is completely at odds with the modesty and deference expected of women and girls. Arm raised in a winner's salute, the ritualized climax of a prizefight, wrestling match or tennis championship, is unladylike, to say the least. The powerful feeling that victory engenders, the satisfaction of climbing to the top of the heap or clinching a deal, remains an inappropriate emotion. More appropriate to femininity are the predictable tears of the new Miss America as she accepts her crown and scepter. Trembling lip and brimming eyes suggest a Cinderella who has stumbled upon good fortune through

unbelievable, undeserved luck. At her moment of victory
the winner of America's favorite pageant appears overcome,
rather than superior in any way. A Miss America who raised
her scepter high like a trophy would not be in keeping with
the feminine ideal.

The maidenly blush, that staple of the nineteenth-century   16
lady's novel, was an excellent indicator of innocent virginal
shyness in contrast to the worldliness and sophistication
of men. In an age when a variety of remarks, largely sexual,
were considered uncouth and not for the ears of virtuous
women, the feminine blush was an expected response. On
the other side of the ballroom, men never blushed, at least
not in romantic fiction, since presumably they were knowledgeable and sexually practiced. Lowered eyes, heightened
color, breathlessness and occasional swooning were further
proofs of a fragile and innocent feminine nature that required protection in the rough, indelicate masculine world.
(In the best-selling Harlequin and Silhouette books de-
voured by romance addicts who need the quick fix, the
maidenly blush is alive and well.)

In a new age of relative sexual freedom, or permissive-   17
ness, at any rate, squeals and moans replace the blush and
the downcast eye. Screaming bobbysoxers who fainted in
the aisle at the Paramount Theater when a skinny young
Frank Sinatra crooned his love ballads during the 1940s
(reportedly, the first wave of fainting girls was staged by
promoters) presaged the whimpering orgasmic ecstasy at
rock concerts in huge arenas today. By contrast, young men
in the audience automatically rise to their feet and whistle
and shout when the band starts to play, but they seldom
appear overcome.

Most emphatically, feminine emotion has gotten louder.   18
The ribald squeal of the stereotypic serving wench in
Elizabethan times, a supposed indicator of loose, easy ways,
seems to have lost its lower-class stigma. One byproduct
of our media-obsessed society, in which privacy is considered a quaint and rather old-fashioned human need, has
been the reproduction of the unmistakable sounds of female
orgasm on a record (Donna Summer's "Love to Love You
Baby," among other hits). More than commercialization of
sex is operative here. Would the sounds of male orgasm
suffice for a recording, and would they be unmistakable?
Although I have seen no studies on this interesting sex difference, I believe it can be said that most women do vocalize

more loudly and uncontrollably than men in the throes of sexual passion. Is this response physiological, compensatory or merely symptomatic of the feminine mission to display one's feelings (and the corresponding masculine mission to keep their feelings under control)?

19   Feminine emotion specializes in sentimentality, empathy and admissions of vulnerability — three characteristics that most men try to avoid. Linking these traits to female anatomy became an article of faith in the Freudian school. Erik Erikson, for one, spoke of an "inner space" (he meant the womb) that yearns for fulfillment through maternal love. Helene Deutsch, the grande dame of Freudian feminine psychology, spoke of psychic acceptance of hurt and pain; menstrual cramps, defloration and the agonies of childbirth called for a masochistic nature she believed was innate.

20   Love of babies, any baby and all babies, not only one's own, is a celebrated and anticipated feminine emotion, and a woman who fails to ooh and ahh at the snapshot of a baby or cuddle a proffered infant in her arms is instantly suspect. Evidence of a maternal nature, of a certain innate competence when handling a baby or at least some indication of maternal longing, becomes a requirement of gender. Women with no particular feeling for babies are extremely reluctant to admit their private truth, for the entire weight of woman's place in the biological division of labor, not to mention the glorification of motherhood as woman's greatest and only truly satisfactory role, has kept alive the belief that all women yearn to fulfill their biological destiny out of a deep emotional need. That a sizable number of mothers have no genuine aptitude for the job is verified by the records of hospitals, family courts and social agencies where cases of battery and neglect are duly entered — and perhaps also by the characteristic upper-class custom of leaving the little ones to the care of the nanny. But despite this evidence that day-to-day motherhood is not a suitable or a stimulating occupation for all, the myth persists that a woman who prefers to remain childless must be heartless or selfish or less than complete.

21   Books have been written on maternal guilt and its exploitation, on the endemic feeling that whatever a mother does, her loving care may be inadequate or wrong, with consequences that can damage a child for life. Trends in child care (bottle feeding, demand feeding, not picking up the crying baby, delaying the toilet training or giving up an

outside job to devote one's entire time to the family) illuminate the fear of maternal inadequacy as well as the variability or "expert" opinion in each generation. Advertising copywriters successfully manipulate this feminine fear when they pitch their clients' products. A certain cereal, one particular brand of packaged white bread, must be bought for the breakfast table or else you have failed to love your child sufficiently and denied him the chance to "build a strong body twelve ways." Until the gay liberation movement began to speak for itself, it was a commonplace of psychiatric wisdom that a mother had it within her power to destroy her son's heterosexual adjustment by failing to cut his baby curls, keep him away from dance class or encourage his interest in sports.

A requirement of femininity is that a woman devote her 22 life to love — to mother love, to romantic love, to religious love, to amorphous, undifferentiated caring. The territory of the heart is admittedly a province that is open to all, but women alone are expected to make an obsessional career of its exploration, to find whatever adventure, power, fulfillment or tragedy that life has to offer within its bounds. There is no question that a woman is apt to feel most feminine, most confident of her interior gender makeup, when she is reliably within some stage of love — even the girlish crush or the stage of unrequited love or a broken heart. Men have suffered for love, and men have accomplished great feats in the name of love, but what man has ever felt at the top of his masculine form when he is lovesick or suffering from heartache?

Gloria Steinem once observed that the heart is a sex-dis- 23 tinctive symbol of feminine vulnerability in the marketing of fashion. Heart-shaped rings and heart-shaped gold pendants and heart-shaped frames on red plastic sunglasses announce an addiction to love that is beyond the pale of appropriate design for masculine ornamentation. (A man does not wear his heart on his sleeve.) The same observation applies a little less stringently to flowers.

Rare is the famous girl singer, whatever her age, of popu- 24 lar music (blues, country, Top Forty, disco or rock) who is not chiefly identified with some expression of love, usually its downside. Torchy bittersweet ballads and sad, suffering laments mixed with vows of eternal fidelity to the rotten bastard who done her wrong communicate the feminine message of love at any cost. Almost unique to the female singer, I think, is the poignant anthem of battered survival,

from Fanny Brice's "My Man" to Gloria Gaynor's "I Will
Survive," that does not quite shut the door on further emotional abuse if her man should return.

25   But the point is not emotional abuse (except in extreme,
aberrant cases); the point is feeling. Women are instructed
from childhood to be keepers of the heart, keepers of the
sentimental memory. In diaries, packets of old love letters
and family albums, in slender books of poetry in which a
flower is pressed, a woman's emotional history is preserved.
Remembrance of things past — the birthday, the anniversary, the death — is a feminine province. In the social division of labor, the wife is charged with maintaining the
emotional connection, even with the husband's side of the
family. Her thoughtful task is to make the long-distance
call, select the present and write the thank-you note (chores
that secretaries are asked to do by their bosses). Men are
busy; they move forward. A woman looks back. It is significant that in the Biblical parable it was Lot's wife who
looked back for one last precious glimpse of their city, their
home, their past (and was turned into a pillar of salt).

26   Love confirms the feminine psyche. A celebrated difference between men and women (either women's weakness
or women's strength, depending on one's values) is the ob-
stinate reluctance, the emotional inability of women to
separate sex from love. Understandably. Love makes the
world go round, and women are supposed to get dizzy — to
rise, to fall, to feel alive in every pore, to be undone. In
place of a suitable attachment, an unlikely or inaccessible
one may have to do. But more important, sex for a woman,
even in an age of accessible contraception, has reproductive
consequences that render the act a serious affair. Casual
sex can have a most uncasual resolution. If a young girl
thinks of love and marriage while a boy thinks of getting
laid, her emotional commitment is rooted not only in her
different upbringing but in her reproductive biology as well.
Love, then, can become an alibi for thoughtless behavior,
as it may also become an identity, or a distraction, à la
Emma Bovary or Anna Karenina, from the frustrations of
a limited life.*

---

*The overwhelming influence of feminine love is frequently offered as
a mitigating explanation by women who do unfeminine things. Elizabeth
Bentley, the "Red Spy Queen" of the cold war Fifties, attributed her illegal
activities to her passion for the Russian master spy Jacob Golos. Judith

Christian houses of worship, especially in poor neighbor- 27
hoods, are filled disproportionately by women. This phenomenon may not be entirely attributable to the historic
role of the Catholic and Protestant religions in encouraging
the public devotions of women (which Judaism and Islam
did not), or because women have more time for prayer, or
because in the Western world they are believed to be more
religious by nature. Another contributing factor may be
that the central article of Christian faith, "Jesus loves you,"
has particular appeal for the gender that defines itself
through loving emotions.

Women's special interest in the field of compassion is 28
catered to and promoted. Hollywood "weepies," otherwise
known as four-handkerchief movies, were big-studio productions that were tailored to bring in female box-office
receipts. Columns of advice to the lovelorn, such as the
redoubtable "Dear Dorothy Dix" and the current "Dear
Abby," were by tradition a woman's slot on daily newspapers, along with the coverage of society births and wed-
dings, in the days when females were as rare in a newsroom
as they were in a coal mine. In the heyday of the competitive
tabloids, sob-sister journalism, that newsroom term for a
human-interest story told with heart-wrenching pathos
(usually by a tough male reporter who had the formula
down pat), was held in contempt by those on the paper
who covered the "hard stuff" of politics, crime and war.
(Nathanael West's famous antihero labored under the
byline of Miss Lonelyhearts.) Despite its obvious audience
appeal, "soft stuff" was, and is, on the lower rungs of journalism — trivial, weak and unmanly.

In Government circles during the Vietnam war, it was 29
considered a sign of emotional softness, of lily-livered liberals and nervous nellies, to suggest that Napalmed babies,
fire-bombed villages and defoliated crops were reason
enough to pull out American forces. The peace movement,
went the charge, was composed of cowards and fuzzy thinkers. Suspicion of an unmanly lack of hard practical logic
always haunts those men who espouse peace and nonviolence, but women, the weaker sex, are permitted a certain

---

Coplon's defense for stealing Government documents was love for another
Russian, Valentin Gubichev. More recently, Jean Harris haplessly failed
to convince a jury that her love for "Scarsdale diet" Doctor Herman Tar-
nower was so great that she could not possibly have intended to kill him.

amount of emotional leeway. Feminine logic, after all, is reputedly governed by the heartstrings. Compassion and sentiment are the basis for its notorious "subjectivity" compared to the "objectivity" of men who use themselves as the objective standard.

30   As long as the social division of labor ordains that women should bear the chief emotional burden of caring for human life from the cradle to the grave while men may demonstrate their dimorphic difference through competitive acts of physical aggression, emblematic compassion and fear of violence are compelling reasons for an aversion to war and other environmental hazards. When law and custom deny the full range of public expression and economic opportunity that men claim for themselves, a woman must place much of her hopes, her dreams, her feminine identity and her social importance in the private sphere of personal relations, in the connective tissue of marriage, family, friendship and love. In a world out of balance, where men are taught to value toughness and linear vision as masculine traits that enable them to think strategically from conquest to conquest, from campaign to campaign without looking back, without getting sidetracked by vulnerable feelings, there is, and will be, an emotional difference between the sexes, a gender gap that may even appear on a Gallup poll.

31   If a true shape could emerge from the shadows of historic oppression, would the gender-specific experience of being female still suggest a range of perceptions and values that differ appreciably from those of men? It would be premature to offer an answer. Does a particular emotion ultimately resist separation from its historic deployment in the sexual balance of power? In the way of observation, this much can be said: The entwining of anatomy, history and culture presents such a persuasive emotional argument for a "different nature" that even the best aspects of femininity collaborate in its perpetuation.

Carol Gilligan

Images of Relationships

Carol Gilligan, educator and psychologist, works at Harvard University. In 1984 she was named **Ms.** *magazine's* Woman of the Year, *partly in honor of her 1982 book,* In a Different Voice, *an account of the gender-specific ways that morality is defined and developed. The following is a selection from the book.*

In 1914, with his essay "On Narcissism," Freud swallows   1
his distaste at the thought of "abandoning observation for
barren theoretical controversy" and extends his map of the
psychological domain. Tracing the development of the capacity to love, which he equates with maturity and psychic
health, he locates its origins in the contrast between love
for the mother and love for the self. But in thus dividing
the world of love into narcissism and "object" relationships,
he finds that while men's development becomes clearer,
women's becomes increasingly opaque. The problem arises
because the contrast between mother and self yields two
different images of relationships. Relying on the imagery
of men's lives in charting the course of human growth,
Freud is unable to trace in women the development of relationships, morality, or a clear sense of self. This difficulty
in fitting the logic of his theory to women's experience
leads him in the end to set women apart, marking their
relationships, like their sexual life, as "a 'dark continent'
for psychology."

Thus the problem of interpretation that shadows the   2
understanding of women's development arises from the
differences observed in their experience of relationships.
To Freud, though living surrounded by women and otherwise seeing so much and so well, women's relationships
seemed increasingly mysterious, difficult to discern, and
hard to describe. While this mystery indicates how theory
can blind observation, it also suggests that development
in women is masked by a particular conception of human
relationships. Since the imagery of relationships shapes
the narrative of human development, the inclusion of
women, by changing that imagery, implies a change in
the entire account.

3   The shift in imagery that creates the problem in interpret-
ing women's development is elucidated by the moral judgments of two eleven-year-old children, a boy and a girl,
who see, in the same dilemma, two very different moral
problems. While current theory brightly illuminates the
line and the logic of the boy's thought, it casts scant light
on that of the girl. The choice of a girl whose moral judgments elude existing categories of developmental assessment is meant to highlight the issue of interpretation rather
than to exemplify sex differences per se. Adding a new line
of interpretation, based on the imagery of the girl's thought,
makes it possible not only to see development where previously development was not discerned but also to consider
differences in the understanding of relationships without
scaling these differences from better to worse.

4   The two children were in the same sixth-grade class at
school and were participants in the rights and responsibilities study, designed to explore different conceptions of
morality and self. The sample selected for this study was
chosen to focus the variables of gender and age while maxi-
mizing developmental potential by holding constant, at a
high level, the factors of intelligence, education, and social
class that have been associated with moral development,
at least as measured by existing scales. The two children
in question, Amy and Jake, were both bright and articulate
and, at least in their eleven-year-old aspirations, resisted
easy categories of sex-role stereotyping, since Amy aspired
to become a scientist while Jake preferred English to math.
Yet their moral judgments seem initially to confirm familiar notions about differences between the sexes, suggesting
that the edge girls have on moral development during the
early school years gives way at puberty with the ascendance
of formal logical thought in boys.

5   The dilemma that these eleven-year-olds were asked to
resolve was one in the series devised by Kohlberg to measure moral development in adolescence by presenting a conflict between moral norms and exploring the logic of its
resolution. In this particular dilemma, a man named Heinz
considers whether or not to steal a drug which he cannot
afford to buy in order to save the life of his wife. In the
standard format of Kohlberg's interviewing procedure, the
description of the dilemma itself—Heinz's predicament,
the wife's disease, the druggist's refusal to lower his price—
is followed by the question, "Should Heinz steal the drug?"

The reasons for and against stealing are then explored through a series of questions that vary and extend the parameters of the dilemma in a way designed to reveal the underlying structure of moral thought.

Jake, at eleven, is clear from the outset that Heinz should   6
steal the drug. Constructing the dilemma, as Kohlberg did, as a conflict between the values of property and life, he discerns the logical priority of life and uses that logic to justify his choice:

> For one thing, a human life is worth more than money, and if the druggist only makes $1,000, he is still going to live, but if Heinz doesn't steal the drug, his wife is going to die. *(Why is life worth more than money?)* Because the druggist can get a thousand dollars later from rich people with cancer, but Heinz can't get his wife again. *(Why not?)* Because people are all different and so you couldn't get Heinz's wife again.

Asked whether Heinz should steal the drug if he does not love his wife, Jake replies that he should, saying that not only is there "a difference between hating and killing," but also, if Heinz were caught, "the judge would probably think it was the right thing to do." Asked about the fact that, in stealing, Heinz would be breaking the law, he says that "the laws have mistakes, and you can't go writing up a law for everything that you can imagine."

Thus, while taking the law into account and recognizing   7
its function in maintaining social order (the judge, Jake says, "should give Heinz the lightest possible sentence"), he also sees the law as man-made and therefore subject to error and change. Yet his judgment that Heinz should steal the drug, like his view of the law as having mistakes, rests on the assumption of agreement, a societal consensus around moral values that allows one to know and expect others to recognize what is "the right thing to do."

Fascinated by the power of logic, this eleven-year-old boy   8
locates truth in math, which, he says, is "the only thing that is totally logical." Considering the moral dilemma to be "sort of like a math problem with humans," he sets it up as an equation and proceeds to work out the solution. Since his solution is rationally derived, he assumes that anyone following reason would arrive at the same conclusion and thus that a judge would also consider stealing to

be the right thing for Heinz to do. Yet he is also aware of the limits of logic. Asked whether there is a right answer to moral problems, Jake replies that "there can only be right and wrong in judgment," since the parameters of action are variable and complex. Illustrating how actions undertaken with the best of intentions can eventuate in the most disastrous of consequences, he says, "like if you give an old lady your seat on the trolley, if you are in a trolley crash and that seat goes through the window, it might be that reason that the old lady dies."

9   Theories of developmental psychology illuminate well the position of this child, standing at the juncture of childhood and adolescence, at what Piaget describes as the pinnacle of childhood intelligence, and beginning through thought to discover a wider universe of possibility. The moment of preadolescence is caught by the conjunction of formal operational thought with a description of self still anchored in the factual parameters of his childhood world — his age, his town, his father's occupation, the substance of his likes, dislikes, and beliefs. Yet as his self-description radiates the self-confidence of a child who has arrived, in Erikson's terms, at a favorable balance of industry over inferiority — competent, sure of himself, and knowing well the rules of the game — so his emergent capacity for formal thought, his ability to think about thinking and to reason things out in a logical way, frees him from dependence on authority and allows him to find solutions to problems by himself.

10   This emergent autonomy follows the trajectory that Kohlberg's six stages of moral development trace, a three-level progression from an egocentric understanding of fairness based on individual need (stages one and two), to a conception of fairness anchored in the shared conventions of societal agreement (stages three and four), and finally to a principled understanding of fairness that rests on the free-standing logic of equality and reciprocity (stages five and six). While this boy's judgments at eleven are scored as conventional on Kohlberg's scale, a mixture of stages three and four, his ability to bring deductive logic to bear on the solution of moral dilemmas, to differentiate morality from law, and to see how laws can be considered to have mistakes points toward the principled conception of justice that Kohlberg equates with moral maturity.

11   In contrast, Amy's response to the dilemma conveys a

very different impression, an image of development stunted
by a failure of logic, an inability to think for herself. Asked
if Heinz should steal the drug, she replies in a way that
seems evasive and unsure:

> Well, I don't think so. I think there might be other ways
> besides stealing it, like if he could borrow the money or
> make a loan or something, but he really shouldn't steal the
> drug — but his wife shouldn't die either.

Asked why he should not steal the drug, she considers
neither property nor law but rather the effect that theft
could have on the relationship between Heinz and his wife:

> If he stole the drug, he might save his wife then, but if he
> did, he might have to go to jail, and then his wife might get
> sicker again, and he couldn't get more of the drug, and it
> might not be good. So, they should really just talk it out
> and find some other way to make the money.

Seeing in the dilemma not a math problem with humans   12
but a narrative of relationships that extends over time, Amy
envisions the wife's continuing need for her husband and
the husband's continuing concern for his wife and seeks to
respond to the druggist's need in a way that would sustain
rather than sever connection. Just as she ties the wife's
survival to the preservation of relationships, so she considers the value of the wife's life in a context of relationships,
saying that it would be wrong to let her die because, "if
she died, it hurts a lot of people and it hurts her." Since
Amy's moral judgment is grounded in the belief that, "if
somebody has something that would keep somebody alive,
then it's not right not to give it to them," she considers the
problem in the dilemma to arise not from the druggist's
assertion of rights but from his failure of response.

As the interviewer proceeds with the series of questions   13
that follow from Kohlberg's construction of the dilemma,
Amy's answers remain essentially unchanged, the various
probes serving neither to elucidate nor to modify her initial
response. Whether or not Heinz loves his wife, he still
shouldn't steal or let her die; if it were a stranger dying
instead, Amy says that "if the stranger didn't have anybody
near or anyone she knew," then Heinz should try to save
her life, but he should not steal the drug. But as the inter-

viewer conveys through the repetition of questions that the answers she gave were not heard or not right, Amy's confidence begins to diminish, and her replies become more constrained and unsure. Asked again why Heinz should not steal the drug, she simply repeats, "Because it's not right." Asked again to explain why, she states again that theft would not be a good solution, adding lamely, "if he took it, he might not know how to give it to his wife, and so his wife might still die." Failing to see the dilemma as a self-contained problem in moral logic, she does not discern the internal structure of its resolution; as she constructs the problem differently herself, Kohlberg's conception completely evades her.

14   Instead, seeing a world comprised of relationships rather than of people standing alone, a world that coheres through human connection rather than through systems of rules, she finds the puzzle in the dilemma to lie in the failure of the druggist to respond to the wife. Saying that "it is not right for someone to die when their life could be saved," she assumes that if the druggist were to see the consequences of his refusal to lower his price, he would realize that "he should just give it to the wife and then have the husband pay back the money later." Thus she considers the solution to the dilemma to lie in making the wife's condition more salient to the druggist or, that failing, in appealing to others who are in a position to help.

15   Just as Jake is confident the judge would agree that stealing is the right thing for Heinz to do, so Amy is confident that, "if Heinz and the druggist had talked it out long enough, they could reach something besides stealing." As he considers the law to "have mistakes," so she sees this drama as a mistake, believing that "the world should just share things more and then people wouldn't have to steal." Both children thus recognize the need for agreement but see it as mediated in different ways—he impersonally through systems of logic and law, she personally through communication in relationship. Just as he relies on the conventions of logic to deduce the solution to this dilemma, assuming these conventions to be shared, so she relies on a process of communication, assuming connection and believing that her voice will be heard. Yet while his assumptions about agreement are confirmed by the convergence in logic between his answers and the questions posed, her assumptions are belied by the failure of communication, the interviewer's inability to understand her response.

Although the frustration of the interview with Amy is   16
apparent in the repetition of questions and its ultimate
circularity, the problem of interpretation is focused by the
assessment of her response. When considered in the light
of Kohlberg's definition of the stages and sequence of moral
development, her moral judgments appear to be a full stage
lower in maturity than those of the boy. Scored as a mixture
of stages two and three, her responses seem to reveal a
feeling of powerlessness in the world, an inability to think
systematically about the concepts of morality or law, a
reluctance to challenge authority or to examine the logic
of received moral truths, a failure even to conceive of acting
directly to save a life or to consider that such action, if
taken, could possibly have an effect. As her reliance on
relationships seems to reveal a continuing dependence and
vulnerability, so her belief in communication as the mode
through which to resolve moral dilemmas appears naive
and cognitively immature.

Yet Amy's description of herself conveys a markedly dif-   17
ferent impression. Once again, the hallmarks of the preadolescent child depict a child secure in her sense of herself,
confident in the substance of her beliefs, and sure of her
ability to do something of value in the world. Describing
herself at eleven as "growing and changing," she says that
she "sees some things differently now, just because I know
myself really well now, and I know a lot more about the
world." Yet the world she knows is a different world from
that refracted by Kohlberg's construction of Heinz's dilemma. Her world is a world of relationships and psychological truths where an awareness of the connection between people gives rise to a recognition of responsibility
for one another, a perception of the need for response. Seen
in this light, her understanding of morality as arising from
the recognition of relationship, her belief in communication
as the mode of conflict resolution, and her conviction that
the solution to the dilemma will follow from its compelling
representation seem far from naive or cognitively immature. Instead, Amy's judgments contain the insights central
to an ethic of care, just as Jake's judgments reflect the logic
of the justice approach. Her incipient awareness of the
"method of truth," the central tenet of nonviolent conflict
resolution, and her belief in the restorative activity of care,
lead her to see the actors in the dilemma arrayed not as
opponents in a contest of rights but as members of a network
of relationships on whose continuation they all depend.

Consequently her solution to the dilemma lies in activating the network by communication, securing the inclusion of the wife by strengthening rather than severing connections.

18   But the different logic of Amy's response calls attention to the interpretation of the interview itself. Conceived as an interrogation, it appears instead as a dialogue, which takes on moral dimensions of its own, pertaining to the interviewer's uses of power and to the manifestations of respect. With this shift in the conception of the interview, it immediately becomes clear that the interviewer's problem in understanding Amy's response stems from the fact that Amy is answering a different question from the one the interviewer thought had been posed. Amy is considering not *whether* Heinz should act in this situation (*"should* Heinz steal the drug?") but rather *how* Heinz should act in response to his awareness of his wife's need ("Should Heinz *steal* the drug?"). The interviewer takes the mode of action for granted, presuming it to be a matter of fact; Amy assumes the necessity for action and considers what form it should take. In the interviewer's failure to imagine a response not dreamt of in Kohlberg's moral philosophy lies the failure to hear Amy's question and to see the logic in her response, to discern that what appears, from one perspective, to be an evasion of the dilemma signifies in other terms a recognition of the problem and a search for a more adequate solution.

19   Thus in Heinz's dilemma these two children see two very different moral problems — Jake a conflict between life and property that can be resolved by logical deduction, Amy a fracture of human relationship that must be mended with its own thread. Asking different questions that arise from different conceptions of the moral domain, the children arrive at answers that fundamentally diverge, and the arrangement of these answers as successive stages on a scale of increasing moral maturity calibrated by the logic of the boy's response misses the different truth revealed in the judgment of the girl. To the question, "What does he see that she does not?" Kohlberg's theory provides a ready response, manifest in the scoring of Jake's judgments a full stage higher than Amy's in moral maturity; to the question, "What does she see that he does not?" Kohlberg's theory has nothing to say. Since most of her responses fall through the sieve of Kohlberg's scoring system, her responses appear from his perspective to lie outside the moral domain.

Yet just as Jake reveals a sophisticated understanding of   20
the logic of justification, so Amy is equally sophisticated
in her understanding of the nature of choice. Recognizing
that "if both the roads went in totally separate ways, if you
pick one, you'll never know what would happen if you went
the other way," she explains that "that's the chance you
have to take, and like I said, it's just really a guess." To
illustrate her point "in a simple way," she describes her
choice to spend the summer at camp:

> I will never know what would have happened if I had stayed
> here, and if something goes wrong at camp, I'll never know
> if I stayed here if it would have been better. There's really
> no way around it because there's no way you can do both
> at once, so you've got to decide, but you'll never know.

In this way, these two eleven-year-old children, both   21
highly intelligent and perceptive about life, though in different ways, display different modes of moral understanding, different ways of thinking about conflict and choice.
In resolving Heinz's dilemma, Jake relies on theft to avoid
confrontation and turns to the law to mediate the dispute.
Transposing a hierarchy of power into a hierarchy of values,
he defuses a potentially explosive conflict between people
by casting it as an impersonal conflict of claims. In this
way, he abstracts the moral problem from the interpersonal
situation, finding in the logic of fairness an objective way
to decide who will win the dispute. But this hierarchical
ordering, with its imagery of winning and losing and the
potential for violence which it contains, gives way in Amy's
construction of the dilemma to a network of connection, a
web of relationships that is sustained by a process of communication. With this shift, the moral problem changes
from one of unfair domination, the imposition of property
over life, to one of unnecessary exclusion, the failure of the
druggist to respond to the wife.

Judy Syfers
Why I Want a Wife

Judy Syfers (born 1937), active in support of women's causes, was educated at the University of Iowa. She now lives in San Francisco. This well-known essay appeared in the very first issue of Ms. *in 1972.*

1   I belong to that classification of people known as wives. I am A Wife. And, not altogether incidentally, I am a mother.

2   Not too long ago a male friend of mine appeared on the scene fresh from a recent divorce. He had one child, who is, of course, with his ex-wife. He is looking for another wife. As I thought about him while I was ironing one evening, it suddenly occurred to me that I, too, would like to have a wife. Why do I want a wife?

3   I would like to go back to school so that I can become economically independent, support myself, and, if need be, support those dependent upon me. I want a wife who will work and send me to school. And while I am going to school I want a wife to take care of my children. I want a wife to keep track of the children's doctor and dentist appointments. And to keep track of mine, too. I want a wife to make sure my children eat properly and are kept clean. I want a wife who will wash the children's clothes and keep them mended. I want a wife who is a good nurturant attendant to my children, who arranges for their schooling, makes sure that they have an adequate social life with their peers, takes them to the park, the zoo, etc. I want a wife who takes care of the children when they are sick, a wife who arranges to be around when the children need special care, because, of course I cannot miss classes at school. My wife must arrange to lose time at work and not lose the job. It may mean a small cut in my wife's income from time to time, but I guess I can tolerate that. Needless to say, my wife will arrange and pay for the care of the children while my wife is working.

4   I want a wife who will take care of *my* physical needs. I want a wife who will keep my house clean. A wife who will pick up after my children, a wife who will pick up after me. I want a wife who will keep my clothes clean, ironed, mended, replaced when need be, and who will see to it that

my personal things are kept in their proper place so that I can find what I need the minute I need it. I want a wife who cooks the meals, a wife who is a *good* cook. I want a wife who will plan the menus, do the necessary grocery shopping, prepare the meals, serve them pleasantly, and then do the cleaning up while I do my studying. I want a wife who will care for me when I am sick and sympathize with my pain and loss of time from school. I want a wife to go along when our family takes a vacation so that some-one can continue to care for me and my children when I need a rest and a change of scene.

I want a wife who will not bother me with rambling 5 complaints about a wife's duties. But I want a wife who will listen to me when I feel the need to explain a rather difficult point I have come across in my course of studies. And I want a wife who will type my papers for me when I have written them.

I want a wife who will take care of the details of my 6 social life. When my wife and I are invited out by my friends, I want a wife who will take care of the babysitting arrange-ments. When I meet people at school that I like and want to entertain, I want a wife who will have the house clean, will prepare a special meal, serve it to me and my friends, and not interrupt when I talk about things that interest me and my friends. I want a wife who will have arranged that the children are fed and ready for bed before my guests arrive so that the children do not bother us. I want a wife who takes care of the needs of my guests so that they feel comfortable, who makes sure that they have an ashtray, that they are passed the hors d'oeuvres, that they are offered a second helping of the food, that their wine glasses are replenished when necessary, that their coffee is served to them as they like it. And I want a wife who knows that sometimes I need a night out by myself.

I want a wife who is sensitive to my sexual needs, a wife 7 who makes love passionately and eagerly when I feel like it, a wife who makes sure that I am satisfied. And, of course, I want a wife who will not demand sexual attention when I am not in the mood for it. I want a wife who assumes the complete responsibility for birth control, because I do not want more children. I want a wife who will remain sexually faithful to me so that I do not have to clutter up my intel-lectual life with jealousies. And I want a wife who under-stands that *my* sexual needs may entail more than strict adherence to monogamy. I must, after all, be able to relate to people as fully as possible.

8   If, by chance, I find another person more suitable as a wife than the wife I already have, I want the liberty to replace my present wife with another one. Naturally, I will expect a fresh, new life; my wife will take the children and be solely responsible for them so that I am left free.

9   When I am through with school and have a job, I want my wife to quit working and remain at home so that my wife can more fully and completely take care of a wife's duties.

10   My God, who *wouldn't* want a wife?

Kurt Fernsler

Why I Want a Husband

Kurt Fernsler (born 1969) grew up in State College, Pennsylvania. He is studying business at Penn State in preparation for a career in business or writing. This essay was written for a class of fellow student writers, all of whom had read Judy Syfers' essay (above) "Why I Want a Wife."

1   I am not a husband. I am, however, a male, and have a father who is a husband. I am also fortunate enough to know a great many men who are husbands and will probably become a husband myself someday.

2   I recently read Judy Syfers' essay "Why I Want a Wife" and decided a reply was in order. Though not the most qualified author for such an undertaking, I felt it my duty to make an effort. For I now realize that just as Judy Syfers wants a wife, I want a husband.

3   I want a husband who brings home the bacon. I mean really rakes in the bucks. After all, I certainly can't have anything less than the best. My husband must be driven to succeed; he must climb the corporate ladder quickly and efficiently. He must make every payroll and meet every deadline. Anything less would be completely unacceptable.

4   And I want a husband who bears the burden of being the wage earner without complaint. He must deal with the

stresses of his job without bringing his problems home from the office so as not to upset me. I want a husband who deals patiently and lovingly with screaming, fighting kids even after a tough day. I want a husband who, for fairness sake, does the dishes (even sometimes the wash) for me so that I can put my feet up after dinner. And, I want a husband who will leave the office during a busy day of work to check on a sick child while I'm out on the town shopping.

I want a husband who will gladly eat cold leftovers for 5 a week while I am relaxing with a friend in sunny California. My husband will have to sit through boring PTA meetings and ice-cream socials after a rough day at work. My husband must, of course, be courteous and kind to meddling, gossiping friends. (After all, I am entitled to my friends, too.) I want a husband who listens patiently to my panic about the oversudsing washing machine while he silently sweats about the thousands of dollars he just borrowed from the bank.

I want a husband who keeps the house and lawn looking 6 beautiful in his spare time. He must be willing to spend his Saturday afternoons weeding my garden, and he must give up that tee time with the guys when I decide the grass is a little too long. I want one who makes sure the car is fixed (engines are so complicated and dirty!), and takes care of all the "little" chores around the house — raking leaves in the fall, shoveling snow in the winter, painting the house in spring. And I want one who will take out the garbage. When he's done with these chores, he can take the kids to the zoo or the park or the ballgame because these are things a father should share with his children.

I want a husband who gladly pays for his wife's shopping 7 sprees without ever asking her where all the money goes. He will understand that women need to spend time with their friends. I want a husband who will watch the kids on vacation so my wife can shop and work on her tan. (He must accept the fact that after traveling so many miles, a shopping trip is the only way to wind down.)

And I want my husband to be completely receptive to 8 my sexual needs. He must completely understand when I have a "headache." He will be sensitive to my problems and respect my private life. I want a husband who understands that I must have my freedom. He will be ready to accept the possibility that I may need to "find myself" and may walk out at any time. He will understand, of course, that I will take half of everything we own. He would keep

the kids, however, because I would need to start a brand
new life for myself.

9   I want a husband who will do all these things for me
forever or until I decide we have enough money to retire,
or until he has a heart attack and collapses in a heap. Yes,
I want a husband.

10   How could anyone live without one?

Paul Theroux
Being a Man

*Paul Theroux (born 1941) has spent most of his adult life out-
side the United States — as a Peace Corps volunteer, as a teacher
in East Africa, as a journalist in Singapore, as a novelist and
highly original travel writer. His* The Great Railroad Bazaar:
By Train Through Asia *appeared in 1975, and in 1985 came*
Sunrise with Seamonsters: Travels and Discoveries, *from
which the following essay was taken.*

1   There is a pathetic sentence in the chapter "Fetishism"
in Dr. Norman Cameron's book *Personality Development and
Psychopathology.* It goes, "Fetishists are nearly always men;
and their commonest fetish is a woman's shoe." I cannot
read that sentence without thinking that it is just one more
awful thing about being a man — and perhaps it is an important thing to know about us.

2   I have always disliked being a man. The whole idea of
manhood in America is pitiful, in my opinion. This version
of masculinity is a little like having to wear an ill-fitting
coat for one's entire life (by contrast, I image femininity to
be an oppressive sense of nakedness). Even the expression
"Be a man!" strikes me as insulting and abusive. It means:
Be stupid, be unfeeling, obedient, soldierly and stop thinking. Man means "manly" — how can one think about men
without considering the terrible ambition of manliness?
And yet it is part of every man's life. It is a hideous and
crippling lie; it not only insists on difference and connives
at superiority, it is also by its very nature destructive — emotionally damaging and socially harmful.

The youth who is subverted, as most are, into believing 3
in the masculine ideal is effectively separated from women
and he spends the rest of his life finding women a riddle
and a nuisance. Of course, there is a female version of this
male affliction. It begins with mothers encouraging little
girls to say (to other adults) "Do you like my new dress?"
In a sense, little girls are traditionally urged to please adults
with a kind of coquettishness, while boys are enjoined to
behave like monkeys towards each other. The nine-year-
old coquette proceeds to become womanish in a subtle
power game in which she learns to be sexually indispensable, socially decorative and always alert to a man's sense
of inadequacy.

Femininity — being lady-like — implies needing a man as 4
witness and seducer; but masculinity celebrates the exclusive company of men. That is why it is so grotesque; and
that is also why there is no manliness without inadequacy —
because it denies men the natural friendship of women.

It is very hard to imagine any concept of manliness that 5
does not belittle women, and it begins very early. At an age
when I wanted to meet girls — let's say the treacherous years
of thirteen to sixteen — I was told to take up a sport, get
more fresh air, join the Boy Scouts, and I was urged not to
read so much. It was the 1950s and if you asked too many
questions about sex you were sent to camp — boy's camp,
of course: the nightmare. Nothing is more unnatural or
prison-like than a boy's camp, but if it were not for them
we would have no Elks' Lodges, no pool rooms, no boxing
matches, no Marines.

And perhaps no sports as we know them. Everyone is 6
aware of how few in number are the athletes who behave
like gentlemen. Just as high school basketball teaches you
how to be a poor loser, the manly attitude towards sports
seems to be little more than a recipe for creating bad marriages, social misfits, moral degenerates, sadists, latent
rapists and just plain louts. I regard high school sports as
a drug far worse than marijuana, and it is the reason that
the average tennis champion, say, is a pathetic oaf.

Any objective study would find the quest for manliness 7
essentially right-wing, puritanical, cowardly, neurotic and
fueled largely by a fear of women. It is also certainly philis-
tine. There is no book-hater like a Little League coach. But
indeed all the creative arts are obnoxious to the manly
ideal, because at their best the arts are pursued by uncompetitive and essentially solitary people. It makes it very

hard for a creative youngster, for any boy who expresses the desire to be alone seems to be saying that there is something wrong with him.

8   It ought to be clear by now that I have something of an objection to the way we turn boys into men. It does not surprise me that when the President of the United States has his customary weekend off he dresses like a cowboy — it is both a measure of his insecurity and his willingness to please. In many ways, American culture does little more for a man than prepare him for modeling clothes in the L. L. Bean catalogue. I take this as a personal insult because for many years I found it impossible to admit to myself that I wanted to be a writer. It was my guilty secret, because being a writer was incompatible with being a man.

9   There are people who might deny this, but that is because the American writer, typically, has been so at pains to prove his manliness that we have come to see literariness and manliness as mingled qualities. But first there was a fear that writing was not a manly profession — indeed, not a profession at all. (The paradox in American letters is that it has always been easier for a woman to write and for a man to be published.) Growing up, I had thought of sports as wasteful and humiliating, and the idea of manliness was a bore. My wanting to become a writer was not a flight from that oppressive role-playing, but I quickly saw that it was at odds with it. Everything in stereotyped manliness goes against the life of the mind. The Hemingway personality is too tedious to go into here, and in any case his exertions are well-known, but certainly it was not until this aberrant behavior was examined by feminists in the 1960s that any male writer dared question the pugnacity in Hemingway's fiction. All the bullfighting and arm wrestling and elephant shooting diminished Hemingway as a writer, but it is consistent with a prevailing attitude in American writing: one cannot be a male writer without first proving that one is a man.

10   It is normal in America for a man to be dismissive or even somewhat apologetic about being a writer. Various factors make it easier. There is a heartiness about journalism that makes it acceptable — journalism is the manliest form of American writing and, therefore, the profession the most independent-minded women seek (yes, it is an illusion, but that is my point). Fiction-writing is equated with a kind of dispirited failure and is only manly when it

produces wealth—money is masculinity. So is drinking. Being a drunkard is another assertion, if misplaced, of manliness. The American male writer is traditionally proud of his heavy drinking. But we are also a very literal-minded people. A man proves his manhood in America in old-fashioned ways. He kills lions, like Hemingway; or he hunts ducks, like Nathanael West; or he makes pronouncements like, "A man should carry enough knife to defend himself with," as James Jones once said to a *Life* interviewer. Or he says he can drink you under the table. But even tiny drunken William Faulkner loved to mount a horse and go fox hunting, and Jack Kerouac roistered up and down Manhattan in a lumberjack shirt (and spent every night of *The Subterraneans* with his mother in Queens). And we are familiar with the lengths to which Norman Mailer is prepared, in his endearing way, to prove that he is just as much a monster as the next man.

When the novelist John Irving was revealed as a wrestler, 11 people took him to be a very serious writer; and even a bubble reputation like Eric (*Love Story*) Segal's was enhanced by the news that he ran the marathon in a respectable time. How surprised we would be if Joyce Carol Oates were revealed as a sumo wrestler or Joan Didion active in pumping iron. "Lives in New York City with her three children" is the typical woman writer's biographical note, for just as the male writer must prove he has achieved a sort of muscular manhood, the woman writer—or rather her publicists—must prove her motherhood.

There would be no point in saying any of this if it were 12 not generally accepted that to be a man is somehow—even now in feminist-influenced America—a privilege. It is on the contrary an unmerciful and punishing burden. Being a man is bad enough; being manly is appalling (in this sense, women's lib has done much more for men than for women). It is the sinister silliness of men's fashions, and a clubby attitude in the arts. It is the subversion of good students. It is the so-called "Dress Code" of the Ritz-Carlton Hotel in Boston, and it is the institutionalized cheating in college sports. It is the most primitive insecurity.

And this is also why men often object to feminism but 13 are afraid to explain why: of course women have a justified grievance, but most men believe—and with reason—that their lives are just as bad.

DO WOMEN AND MEN THINK DIFFERENTLY?

Camilla Persson Benbow and Julian C. Stanley

Sex Differences in Mathematical Reasoning Ability: More Facts

In 1983 Camilla Persson Benbow and Julian C. Stanley, then members of the psychology department at Johns Hopkins, published the following essay in Science, *a prestigious academic journal that publishes articles from all fields of science. Professor Benbow now teaches at Iowa State University.*

1   In 1980 we reported large sex differences in mean scores on a test of mathematical reasoning ability for 9,927 mathematically talented seventh and eighth graders who entered the Johns Hopkins regional talent search from 1972 through 1979. One prediction from those results was that there would be a preponderance of males at the high end of the distribution of mathematical reasoning ability. In this report we investigate sex differences at the highest levels of that ability. New groups of students under age 13 with exceptional mathematical aptitude were identified by means of two separate procedures. In the first, the Johns Hopkins regional talent searches in 1980, 1981, and 1982, 39,820 seventh graders from the Middle Atlantic region of the United States who were selected for high intellectual ability were given the College Board Scholastic Aptitude Test (SAT). In the second, a nationwide talent search was conducted for which any student under 13 years of age who was willing to take the SAT was eligible. The results of both procedures substantiated our prediction that before age 13 far more males than females would score extremely high on SAT-M, the mathematical part of SAT.

2   The test items of SAT-M require numerical judgment, relational thinking, or insightful and logical reasoning. This test is designed to measure the developed mathematical reasoning ability of 11th and 12th graders. Most students

in our study were in the middle of the seventh grade. Few had had formal opportunities to study algebra and beyond. Our rationale is that most of these students were unfamiliar with mathematics from algebra onward, and that most who scored high did so because of extraordinary reasoning ability.

In 1980, 1981, and 1982, as in the earlier study, partici-   3
pants in the Johns Hopkins talent search were seventh graders, or boys and girls of typical seventh-grade age in a higher grade, in the Middle Atlantic area. Before 1980, applicants had been required to be in the top 3 percent nationally on the mathematics section of any standardized achievement test. Beginning in 1980, students in the top 3 percent in verbal or overall intellectual ability were also eligible. During that and the next 2 years 19,883 boys and 19,937 girls applied and were tested. Even though this sample was more general and had equal representation by sex, the mean sex difference on SAT-M remained constant at 30 points favor males (males' $\overline{X}$ = 416, S.D. = 87; females' $\overline{X}$ = 386, S.D. = 74; t = 37; P < 0.001). No important difference in verbal ability as measured by SAT-V was found (males' $\overline{X}$ = 367, females' $\overline{X}$ = 365).

The major point, however, is not the mean difference in   4
SAT-M scores but the ratios of boys to girls among the high scorers. The ratio of boys to girls scoring above the mean of talent-search males was 1.5:1. The ratio among those who scored ≥500 (493 was the mean of 1981–82 college-bound 12th-grade males) was 2.1:1. Among those who scored ≥ 600 (600 was the 79th percentile of the 12th-grade males) the ratio was 4.1:1. These ratios are similar to those previously reported but are derived from a broader and much larger data base.

Scoring 700 or more on the SAT-M before age 13 is rare.   5
We estimate that students who reach this criterion (the 95th percentile of college-bound 12th-grade males) before their 13th birthday represent the top one in 10,000 of their age group. It was because of their rarity that the nationwide talent search was created in November 1980 in order to locate such students who were born after 1967 and facilitate their education. In that talent search applicants could take the SAT at any time and place at which it was administered by the Educational Testing Service or through one of five regional talent searches that cover the United States. Extensive nationwide efforts were made to inform school person-

nel and parents about our search. The new procedure (unrestricted by geography or previous ability) was successful in obtaining a large national sample of this exceedingly rare population. As of September 1983, the number of such boys identified was 260 and the number of girls 20, a ratio of 13.0:1. This ratio is remarkable in view of the fact that the available evidence suggests there was essentially equal participation of boys and girls in the talent searches.

6   The total number of students tested in the Johns Hopkins regional annual talent searches and reported so far is 49,747 (9,927 in the initial study and 39,820 in the present study). Preliminary reports from the 1983 talent search based on some 15,000 cases yield essentially identical results. In the ten Middle Atlantic regional talent searches from 1972 through 1983 we have therefore tested about 65,000 students. It is abundantly clear that far more boys than girls (chiefly 12-year-olds) scored in the highest ranges on SAT-M, even though girls were matched with boys by intellectual ability, age, grade, and voluntary participation. In the original study students were required to meet a qualifying mathematics criterion. Since we observed the same sex difference then as now, the current results cannot be explained solely on the grounds that the girls may have qualified by the verbal criterion. Moreover, if that were the case, we should expect the girls to have scored higher than the boys on SAT-V. They did not.

7   Several "environmental" hypotheses have been proposed to account for sex differences in mathematical ability. Fox *et al.* and Meece *et al.* have found support for a social-reinforcement hypothesis which, in essence, states that sex-related differences in mathematical achievement are due to differences in social conditioning and expectations for boys and girls. The validity of this hypothesis has been evaluated for the population we studied earlier and for a subsample of the students in this study. Substantial differences between boys' and girls' attitudes or backgrounds were not found. Admittedly, some of the measures used were broadly defined and may not have been able to detect subtle social influences that affect a child from birth. But it is not obvious how social conditioning could affect mathematical reasoning ability so adversely and significantly, yet have little detectable effect on stated interest in mathematics, the taking of mathematics courses during the high school years before the SAT's are normally taken, and mathematics-course grades.

An alternative hypothesis, that sex differences in mathematical reasoning ability arise mainly from differential course-taking, was also not validated, either by the data in our 1980 study or by the data in the present study. In both studies the boys and girls were shown to have had similar formal training in mathematics.

It is also of interest that sex differences in mean SAT-M scores observed in our early talent searches became only slightly larger during high school. In the selected subsample of participants studied, males improved their scores an average of 10 points more than females (the mean difference went from 40 to 50 points). They also increased their scores on the SAT-V by at least 10 points more than females. Previously, other researchers have postulated that profound differences in socialization during adolescence caused the well-documented sex differences in 11th- and 12th-grade SAT-M scores, but that idea is not supported in our data. For socialization to account for our results, it would seem necessary to postulate (ad hoc) that chiefly early socialization pressures significantly influence the sex difference in SAT-M scores — that is, that the intensive social pressures during adolescence have little such effect.

It is important to emphasize that we are dealing with intellectually highly able students and that these findings may not generalize to average students. Moreover, these results are of course not generalizable to particular individuals. Finally, it should be noted that the boys' SAT-M scores had a larger variance than the girls'. This is obviously related to the fact that more mathematically talented boys than girls were found. Nonetheless, the environmental hypotheses outlined above attempted to explain mean differences, not differences in variability. Thus, even if one concludes that our findings result primarily from greater male variability, one must still explain why.

Our principal conclusion is that males dominate the highest ranges of mathematical reasoning ability before they enter adolescence. Reasons for this sex difference are unclear.

Ruth Bleier
Gender and Mathematical Ability

Ruth Bleier, a physician and research scientist, works in the department of neurophysiology (and in the women's studies program) at the University of Wisconsin. The following selection is excerpted from her 1984 book Science and Gender. *In the course of demonstrating how gender makes it impossible to frame scientific questions in a neutral way, the book considers the relationship of gender to a number of scientific issues: evolution, sociobiology, behavior, hormones, and (her special area of expertise) the brain and nervous system.*

1   In the 1980s the controversy about sex-differentiated cognitive differences rose into overnight prominence in the form of a study that suggested to the news media that some truly new and unexpected scientific discovery had been revealed. Days before the report in *Science*, the official journal of the largest professional science organization in the country, the newspapers announced that Johns Hopkins researchers found that boys are "inherently" better than girls in mathematical reasoning (*New York Times*, Dec. 7, 1980). *Time* magazine carried the story the same week the study appeared and quoted one of its authors, Camilla Benbow, as saying that many women "can't bring themselves to accept sexual difference in aptitude. But the difference in math is a fact. The best way to help girls is to accept it and go from there" (Dec. 15, 1980, p. 57). *Newsweek* of the same date asked in its story headline, "Do Males have a Math Gene?"

2   The study of Camilla Benbow and Julian Stanley (1980) tested about 10,000 students, mainly seventh and eighth graders who were in the upper 3 percent of students in math ability as judged by the College Board Scholastic Aptitude Test (SAT). The students are part of a larger project called the Study of Mathematically Precocious Youth. The mean score for boys in the math SAT was higher than for girls tested during the eight years of the study, and the highest score every year was made by a boy. It is significant that in the last two years, 1978 and 1979, however, the highest score by a boy was 790 and by a girl, 760, the smallest and least significant difference since the beginning

of the study in 1972. (It is highly doubtful that this closing math gap reflects a change in the female *gene* pool for math.) The authors' conclusion was: "We favor the hypothesis that sex differences in achievement in and attitude toward mathematics result from superior male mathematical ability, which may in turn be related to greater male ability in spatial tasks" (p. 1264). The context of the article clearly implied a genetic sex difference.

Since up to the time of testing the girls and boys did not 3 differ in the number of math courses taken, the authors did not seriously consider any other possible social or environmental factors, though they did suggest that their "data are consistent with numerous alternative hypotheses," which they did not explore. (It is important to note that no press reports carried that cautionary statement.) Nor did they think it important to take into account that the subjects were volunteers, despite the evidence that gifted boys are more likely to volunteer to take tests than are gifted girls (Jacklin, 1981). But as two professors of mathematics, Alice Schafer and Mary Gray, wrote in the lead editorial in *Science* five weeks after the Benbow and Stanley article appeared, in criticism of the Benbow and Stanley hypothesis, "Anyone who thinks that seventh graders are free from environmental influences can hardly be living in the real world." Who helps with the math homework, the kinds of toys and games girls and boys are given, and the expectations of parents and teachers are of critical importance. Mathematically gifted boys can confidently expect to use and be rewarded for their skills in math, science, and engineering and will thus be highly motivated to excel, but it has been well documented that, by and large, parents, school counselors, and teachers have traditionally discouraged even talented girls from seriously pursuing mathematics and science skills or, equally damagingly, simply ignored them (Beckwith and Durkin, 1980; Brophy and Good, 1970; Delefes and Jackson, 1972; Ernest, 1976; Leinhardt *et al.*, 1979). One study found that "42 percent of girls interested in careers in mathematics or science reported being discouraged by counselors from taking courses in advanced mathematics" (Haven, 1972). In addition, at an age when pressures are high to conform to expected gender roles and behaviors, many girls do not want to be seen as "unfeminine" in a culture that equates math and science skills with "masculinity." The Benbow and Stanley study and its attendant sensationalized publicity will do little to dispel what Dean Jewell Cobb of Douglass College called the "notion that proficiency in mathematics is a sex-linked characteristic which is widespread among elementary school and high school teachers, college students and young mothers" (quoted in *Science News*, Vol. 113, p. 200, 1978).

4   It is only recently that efforts have been launched to educate teachers and counselors away from sex-typing and channeling. In those schools where the environment is equally challenging to both sexes, studies produce quite different results from those of Benbow and Stanley. Patricia Casserly of the Educational Testing Service in Princeton has studied 20 high schools where all the teachers have science, math, or engineering backgrounds, communicate enthusiasm for math, and *expect* women to advance as well as men. In these schools, girls and boys score equally well in Advanced Placement (college level) examinations (Kolata, 1980).

5   It is faintly ironic that not long after the Benbow and Stanley study, living refutations of sex stereotyping and scientific sex delineations appeared within the same year, though they were not heralded, if noticed at all, by the popular press: 11-year-old Ruth Lawrence of England got the highest score in the mathematics entrance examinations at Oxford University's St. Hugh's College, which she was to enter in 1983 (*Ms*, June 1982); 17-year-old Laura Clark of Long Island was the only student out of 154,000 to score a perfect 800 on *both* sections (verbal and mathematical) of the Scholastic Aptitude Test (*Ms*, June 1982); for the third year in a row, a woman high school student (Reena Gordon of Brooklyn in 1982) was the winner of the National Westinghouse Science Talent Search Award (American Women in Science *Newsletter*, Vol. 11, #4, Aug.–Sept. 1982); Nina Morishige, who received her BA and MA in mathematics at 18 years of age after attending Johns Hopkins University for two years, became one of the youngest recipients ever to receive a Rhodes Scholarship to Oxford in the 78-year history of the award (*Johns Hopkins Journal*, Spring, 1982).

6   There are other problems with the Benbow and Stanley study or with the authors' interpretation of the results. In suggesting inherent (they use the term "endogenous") superiority in mathematical reasoning in males, they overlook the substantial overlap in the distribution of scores of

girls and boys; that is, among talented girls and boys, the scores are more alike than different, with a few exceptional cases. If some girls near the top are superior to most of the boys, then what does male "superiority" mean? Next, Benbow and Stanley state their belief that environmental factors affect mathematical *achievement*, whereas the SAT, which they used, measures aptitude, that is, "natural" ability. There is, however, a real question whether it is possible at all to make a distinction between achievement and aptitude; and, second, there is real doubt that the SAT is indeed capable of measuring aptitude, whatever that may be, as contrasted with achievement. A member of the Educational Testing Service of Princeton has written that "the developers of the SAT do not view it as a measure of fixed capacities," but instead, "The test is intended to measure aspects of developed ability" (Schafer and Gray, 1981). Susan Chipman of the National Institute of Education wrote that the math SAT samples "performance in a domain of learned knowledge and skill. . . . In a fundamental sense, we do not yet know what mathematical ability is . . ."(1981; see the same issue of *Science* for a number of excellent critiques of the Benbow and Stanley study in the *Letters* Section; see also Beckwith and Durkin, 1981).

Finally, Benbow and Stanley's study and conclusions 7 stand in contradiction to a number of other studies that fail to confirm the assumption that boys are invariably superior in mathematics achievement before the grade levels when clear socialization factors appear (Fennema and Sherman, 1977, 1978; Sherman, 1980). Following two years of intensive study of students in grades 6 through 12, Fennema and Sherman (1978) found that "when relevant factors are controlled, sex-related differences in favor of males do not appear often, and when they do, they are not large" (p. 201). Furthermore, Fennema and Sherman have not found sex differences in spatial visualization at any age. But as one might anticipate, these negative results and the innumerable other studies that show *no* differences in performance or aptitude between the sexes do not excite attention or merit headlines and national news service coverage, and many are not accepted by journals for publication.

If the Benbow and Stanley study is flawed, why, one 8 might ask, get so excited about it? It is because the message of the authors' conclusions has undoubtedly already had dire effects; it is an example of a self-perpetuating and reinforcing ideology. Teachers, counselors, and parents are told there is no particular point in encouraging seemingly talented girls because they are ultimately limited, and it tells girls directly that they should spare themselves grief and energy, even though they like math and are good at it. The study itself is likely to widen the sex-differential in performance or at least to offset the advances in confidence and achievement that have been hard-wrought by the women's movement and the more open atmosphere it has created. The predictable effects of the study and the unbridled enthusiasm of its media reception will be to confirm the comfortable stereotypes about women and men, and make it easier to keep women out of those fields that increasingly rely on sophisticated mathematical and computer knowledge — science, business, and the social sciences.

Evelyn Fox Keller

Women in Science:
An Analysis of a Social Problem

Evelyn Fox Keller has taught at several eastern universities, including SUNY — Purchase, MIT, Cornell, and Northeastern; now she is affiliated with the rhetoric, history of science, and women's studies programs at the University of California at Berkeley. This essay appeared in 1974 in Harvard Magazine, *an alumni publication.*

1   Are women's minds different from men's minds? In spite of the women's movement, the age-old debate centering around this question continues. We are surrounded by evidence of *de facto* differences between men's and women's intellects — in the problems that interest them, in the ways they try to solve those problems, and in the professions they choose. Even though it has become fashionable to view such differences as environmental in origin, the temptation to seek an explanation in terms of innate differences remains a powerful one.

TABLE I. *Percentage of Ph.D.'s Earned by Women, 1920–1970*

	1920–29	1940–49	1950–59	1960–69
Physics and Astronomy	5.9	4.2	2.0	2.2
Biological Sciences	19.5	15.7	11.8	15.1
Mathematics	14.5	10.7	5.0	5.7
Psychology	29.4	24.1	14.8	20.7

Source: National Research Council

Perhaps the area in which this temptation is strongest is 2
in science. Even those of us who would like to argue for
intellectual equality are hard pressed to explain the extraordinarily meager representation of women in science, particularly in the upper echelons. Some would argue that the
near absence of great women scientists demonstrates that
women don't have the minds for true scientific creativity.
While most of us would recognize the patent fallacies of
this argument, it nevertheless causes us considerable discomfort. After all, the doors of the scientific establishment
appear to have been open to women for some time now —
shouldn't we begin to see more women excelling?

In the last fifty years the institutional barriers against 3
women in science have been falling. During most of that
time, the percentage of women scientists has declined,
although recent years have begun to show an upswing
(table I). Of those women who do become scientists, few
are represented in the higher academic ranks (table II).

TABLE II. *Percentage Representation of Women, by Rank, in 20 Leading Universities (1962)*

	INSTRUCTOR	ASSISTANT PROFESSOR	ASSOCIATE PROFESSOR	PROFESSOR
Physics	5.6	1.2	1.3	0.9
Biological Sciences	16.3	7.1	6.7	1.3
Mathematics	16.7	10.1	7.3	0.4
Psychology	8.3	10.4	11.1	2.7

Source: J. B. Parrish, A. A. U. W. Journal, 55, 99

In order to have a proper understanding of these data, it is necessary to review the many influences that operate. I would like to argue that the convenient explanation that men's minds are intrinsically different from women's is not only unwarranted by the evidence, but in fact reflects a mythology that is in itself a major contribution to the phenomena observed.

4   As a woman scientist, I have often pondered these questions, particularly at those times when my commitment to science seemed most precarious. Noticing that almost every other woman I had known in science had experienced similar crises of commitment, I sought to explain my ambivalence by concluding that science as a profession is not as gratifying for women as it is for men, and that the reasons for this are to be found in the intrinsic nature of women and science. Several years ago, I endeavored to find out how general my own experiences were. In studying the statistics of success and failure for women in the professions, I indeed found that women fared less well in science than in other professions, although the picture that emerged seemed fairly bleak for all of us.

5   I collected these data during a leave of absence I had taken to accompany my husband to California. At the same time, I was also engaged in completing work I had begun the year before with a (male) colleague — work that seemed less and less compelling as the year wore on. Each week I would receive an enthusiastic telephone call from my colleague, reporting new information and responses he had received from workers he had met while delivering invited lectures on this work. At some point it occurred to me that perhaps there was a relation between my declining interest and isolation on the one hand, and his growing enthusiasm and public recognition on the other. Over the course of the year, he had received a score or more invitations to speak about this work, while I had received none. It began to dawn on me that there were far simpler explanations for both the observations I had made privately and the data I was collecting than that of intrinsic differences between the sexes.

6   I began to realize, for example, that had I been less isolated and more rewarded, my enthusiasm would have been correspondingly greater — a recognition that has been amply corroborated by my subsequent experience. Upon further reflection, I became aware of how much my own, and other similar, attitudes are influenced by a complex

interplay of subtle factors affecting us from birth on. The ways in which we rear our children, train our students, and interact with our colleagues are all so deeply imbued with our expectations and beliefs as to virtually guarantee a fulfillment of these beliefs.

How do men and women develop the characteristics we attribute to them? There are clear differences between the sexes at birth, and there is even some evidence that these differences extend to the brain. Primate studies reveal marked differences in behavior between males and females — differences determined by the prenatal hormonal environment. It seems therefore quite possible that there are even intellectual differences determined prior to birth. For those inclined to believe in such predetermination, such a possibility may appear attractive. It is important to say, however, that there is to date no evidence for biologically determined differences in intelligence or cognitive styles, and that this remains true in spite of a rather considerable desire among many people to find such evidence. 7

An example of this interest is provided by the great enthusiasm with which a recent study was met. This study purported to show that prenatal injection of progestin, a synthetic male hormone, leads to higher than average I.Q.'s in adolescent girls. Although this result was refuted by the original authors shortly after its original announcement, it nevertheless found its way into a rash of textbooks, where it remains. Similarly, there has been a great deal of interest in the measurement of differences in perceptual modes between girls and boys. Tests designed to measure the degree to which one's perception of a figure is independent of its background, or field, show that girls, by the time they enter school, are more field-dependent than boys. Field independence is positively correlated with mathematical and analytic abilities. While the results of these tests are remarkably culturally invariant (the Eskimos are a notable exception), it is important to point out both that the disparities observed are extremely small (of the order of 2 percent) and that they cannot be discerned before the age of five. While the possibility that these disparities are the result of innate differences between the sexes cannot be excluded, there is evidence relating performance on such tests to the individual's environment. What are the environmental differences that could account for such results? 8

We treat our sons and daughters differently from birth 9

onward, although the magnitude of our distinction is largely unconscious. A rude awakening to the extent of our differential treatment can come in those rare instances when a fallacious sex assignment is made at birth, usually as a result of ambiguous genitalia, and must be subsequently corrected. The impact of these early cues can be assessed by the fact that such reassignments are considered unduly traumatic to make after the child is eighteen months old, in spite of the fact that failure to do so dooms the child to an apparent sexual identity at odds with his or her genotype. Sex reassignments made before that time result in apparently normal development. From this and related evidence, workers in this area have concluded that gender identity appears to be established, primarily on the basis of parental treatment, by the age of eighteen months.

10   Children acquire the meaning of their sex identity from the models before them. Their concept of female is based largely on the women they see, as their concept of male is based on the men they see. Their immediate perceptions are later expanded by the images they perceive on TV, and in children's literature. It hardly need be pointed out that both of the latter present to our children extraordinarily rigid stereotypes.

11   It is not surprising, then, that children, even before they enter school, have acquired the belief that certain activities are male and others female. Science is a male activity.

12   The tenacity of this early view is such as to resist easy change. When my daughter was in nursery school, her class was asked one day about the occupation of their fathers. I objected to this, and, as a result, the next day the teacher asked, "Sarah, what does your mother do?" She replied, "My mother cooks, she sews, she cleans, and she takes care of us." "But Sarah, isn't your mother a scientist?" "Oh, yes," said Sarah—clearly implying that this was not a very relevant piece of information.

13   The explanation of her response lies not only in her need to define a conventional image of her mother, but also in the reality of her direct perceptions. Indeed it is true that, like many professional women, I do cook, sew, clean, and take care of my children. My professional identity is not brought into my home, although my husband's is. My daughter, therefore, like my son, continues to view mathematics and science as male, in spite of their information to the contrary.

14   While a child may be concerned with assigning sex labels

only to external attributes, such as clothes, mannerisms, and occupations, the adolescent has already begun to designate internal states as male and female. Thus, in particular, clear thinking is characterized as hard thinking (a male image), and fuzzy thinking as soft thinking (a female image). A girl who thinks clearly and well is told she thinks "like a man." What are the implications of such associations for the girl who (for whatever reasons) does transcend social expectation and finds herself interested in science? Confusion in sexual identity is the inevitable concomitant of a self-definition at variance with the surrounding definitions of sexual norm. The girl who can take pride in "thinking like a man" without cost to her integrity as a girl is rare indeed.

Nevertheless, a considerable number of women, for what- 15 ever reasons, experience enough motivation and have demonstrated enough ability to embark on professional training for a scientific career. Graduate school is a time to prove that one is, in spite of one's aspirations, a woman, and — at one and the same time, because of one's aspirations — "more than" a woman. Social acceptability requires the former, and is considerably facilitated by the acquisition of a husband, while professional respectability requires the latter. The more exclusively male the definition of the profession, the more difficult it is to accomplish these conflicting goals.

My own experience as a graduate student of theoretical 16 physics at Harvard was extreme, but possibly illustrative. I was surrounded by incessant prophecies of failure, independent of my performance. I knew of no counter-examples to draw confidence from, and was led to believe that none existed. (Later, however, I learned that some women in theoretical physics have survived, even at Harvard.) Warned that I would ultimately despair as I came to learn how impossible my ambitions were, I did, though not for the reasons that were then implied. Having denied myself rage, depression was in fact one of the few reasonable responses to the isolation, mockery, and suspicion that I experienced, both within and without my department. Ultimately I did earn my Ph.D. from the Harvard physics department, but only after having adapted my interests and thereby removed myself from the most critical pressures — a course many women have taken before and since.

Hostility, however, was not the only response I received, 17 and not necessarily the usual response experienced by professionally ambitious young women. The necessity of proving one's femininity leaves some women particularly susceptible to another danger — that of accepting, and even seeking, sexual approbation for intellectual and academic performance. There are enough men willing, if not eager, to provide such translated affirmation as to make this a serious problem. The relation between sexuality and intellectuality is an enormously complex subject. I raise it only to point out one perhaps obvious consequence of this confusion for women. Because, unlike men, they are often dependent on sexual and intellectual affirmation from one and the same individual or group, they can never be entirely confident of what is being affirmed. Is it an "A for a Lay" or a "Lay for an A"?

18   Finally, the female scientist is launched. What are her prospects? Many women choose this point to withdraw for a time in order to have children. Although there is a logic to this choice, it reflects a lack of awareness of the dynamics of normal professional growth. For the male scientist, the period immediately following acquisition of the Ph.D. is perhaps the most critical in his professional development. It is the time that he has, free of all the responsibilities that will later come to plague him, to accomplish enough work to establish his reputation. Often it is a time to affiliate himself with a school of thought, to prove his own, independent worth. Although this may have been the original function of the graduate training period, it has in recent times been displaced to the postgraduate years. Awareness of this displacement, of the critical importance of these years, has not permeated to the general public, or even, for the most part, to the science student. Many women therefore take this sometimes fatal step in ignorance. After having been out of a field for a few years, they usually find it next to impossible to return to their field except in the lowest-level positions. Only when it is too late do they learn that it would have been better to have their children first, before completing the Ph.D.

19   I need hardly enumerate the additional practical difficulties involved in combining a scientific (or any other) career with the raising of children. While the practical drains on one's time and energy are generally recognized, perhaps it is worth pointing out that the drains on one's intellectual energy are not generally recognized by men. Only those men who have spent full time, for an extended period, caring for their children are aware of the extraordinary amount

of mental space occupied by the thousand and one details and concerns that mothers routinely juggle. Many have come to the conclusion — beginning with Engels, and more recently including the Swedish government — that equality of the sexes in the work and professional force is not a realistic possibility until the sex roles in the family are radically redefined. Equality must begin at home.

Well, one might ask, what about those women in science 20 who have no children, who never marry? Surely they are freed from all of these difficulties. Why don't they perform better?

First of all, to be freed of responsibilities towards others 21 is not equivalent to having your own responsibilities assumed by others. Nowhere among women is to be found the counterpart of the male scientist who has a wife at home to look after his daily needs. The question, however, deserves a more serious answer, although the answer is almost painfully obvious. Our society does not have a place for unmarried women. They are among the most isolated, ostracized groups of our culture. When one thinks about the daily social and psychological pressures on the unmarried professional woman, one can hardly be surprised to discover that the data reveal that indeed, on the average, married women in science — even with children — publish more and perform better than unmarried women.

The enumeration of obstacles or handicaps faced by 22 women in science would hardly be complete without at least a reference to the inequalities of reward and approval awarded to work done by men and women. The personal anecdote I began with is more than an anecdote — it is evidence of a rather ubiquitous tendency, neither malicious nor necessarily even conscious, to give more public recognition to a man's accomplishments than to a woman's accomplishments. There are many different reasons for this — not least of which includes the habitually lesser inclination of many women to put themselves forward. There is also a simple, although documented, difference in evaluation of the actual work done by men and women.

While all of the above difficulties are hardly exclusive 23 problems of women in science, the question of identity in what has been defined as an almost exclusively male profession is more serious for women in science than in other fields. Not only is the field defined as male by virtue of its membership, it is also defined as male in relation to its methodology, style of thought, indeed its goals. To the extent that analytic thought is conceived as male thought, to the extent that we characterize the natural sciences as the "hard" sciences, to the extent that the procedure of science is to "attack" problems, and its goal, since Bacon, has been to "conquer" or "master" nature, a woman in science *must* in some way feel alien.

24   Traditionally, as in other similar situations, women who have succeeded in scientific careers have dealt with this conflict by identifying with the "aggressor" — incorporating its values and ideals, at the cost, inevitably, of separating themselves from their own sex. An alternative resolution, one opted for frequently in other professions, is to attempt to redefine one's subject so as to permit a more comfortable identification with it. It is in this way, and for this reason, that so many professional women root themselves in subjects that are viewed by the profession as peripheral. In science this is not easy to do, but perhaps not impossible. There is another tradition within science that is as replete with female images as the tradition that dominates today is replete with male images. We all know that the most creative science requires, in addition to a hardness of mind, also fertility and receptivity. The best scientists are those who have combined the two sets of images. It may be that a certain degree of intellectual security is necessary in order to permit the expression of both "male" and "female" thought in science. If women have first to prove their "male" qualifications for admission into the profession, they may never achieve the necessary confidence to allow themselves to use their "female" abilities. What is to be done?

25   The central theme of my discussion is that the differential performance of men and women in science, the apparent differences between conceptual styles of men and women everywhere, are the result, not so much of innate differences between the sexes, but rather of the myth that prevails throughout our culture identifying certain kinds of thinking as male and others as female. The consequent compartmentalization of our minds is as effective as if it had been biologically, and not socially, induced.

26   People conform to the expectations imposed upon them in the evolution of their definition of sexual identity, thus confirming the very myth upon which these expectations are based. Such a process is not easy to change. Myths as deeply rooted and as self-affirming as this one can neither

be wished nor willed away. The only hope is to chip away
at it everywhere, to make enough small inroads so that
future generations may ultimately grow up less hampered. Counter-measures can be effected at every stage
of the process. Each may be of only limited effectiveness,
but cumulatively they may permit enough women to
emerge with intact, fully developed mental capacities—
women who can serve as role models for future generations
of students.

Specifically, we can begin by exerting a conscious effort   27
to raise our children to less rigid stereotypes. Although the
full extent to which we differentiate our treatment of our
sons and daughters is hidden from us, being largely unconscious, we can, by attending to what we do, raise our consciousness of our own behavior.

We can specifically encourage and reward interests and   28
abilities that survive social pressures. As teachers, men
can consciously refrain from mixing academic with sexual
approval. More generally, we can inform women students
interested in science about the realities of the external difficulties they will face. It is all too easy for an individual
experiencing such obstacles to internalize the responsibility
for these obstacles. Specific advice can be given—for instance, to avoid interrupting a career immediately after
the Ph.D. High-quality work by professional women can be
sought out for recognition and encouragement in order to
counteract the normal tendency to grant them less recognition. (The physicist Richard Courant, a very wise man, responded to the news that one of his most talented students
was pregnant by giving her a raise—thus enabling her to
hire competent help, and, simultaneously, obligating her
to continue. After four such raises, she indeed did go on to
become one of the country's better mathematicians.)

Extra care can be taken not to exclude women from pro-   29
fessional interaction on any level. Finally, hiring policies
must take into account the human and political realities.
Women students need role models if they are to mature
properly. Providing such a model is an important part of
the function of a faculty member and should be considered
along with scholarly performance in hiring deliberations.
Similarly, marriage is a social reality, and women scientists
who marry male scientists need jobs in the same area. Anti-
nepotism hiring policies discriminate against women scientists, and even a neutral policy effectively does so as well.
Universities might well consider pro-nepotism policies that

would recognize the limitations of humans and geographical reality.

30   Most of the recommendations I have made require the cooperation of the male scientific community to implement. Why should they? Further, one may ask, why should women even be encouraged to become scientists when the list of odds against them is so overwhelming? Is a career in science intrinsically of so much greater value than other options more available to women?

31   I don't believe it is. Nevertheless, our society has become more and more technologically oriented. As we continue to move in this direction, as we come to attach increasing importance to scientific and technological know-how, women are threatened with a disenfranchisement possibly greater than ever before. The traditional role of the woman becomes increasingly eroded with technology and over-population, while the disparity between the more humanly oriented kinds of knowledge thought to be hers and the more technical kinds of knowledge operating in the real world grows larger. This disparity operates not only at the expense of the women who are thus barred from meaningful roles in society, but also at the expense of the society that has been content to relegate to women those more humanistic values we all claim to support.

32   Finally, myths that compartmentalize our minds by defining certain mental attributes as "male" and others as "female" leave us all functioning with only part of our minds. Though there may well be some innate biological differences between the sexes, there is hardly room for doubt that our preconceptions serve to exaggerate and rigidify any distinctions that might exist. These preconceptions operate as strait jackets for men and women alike. I believe that the best, most creative science, like the most creative human efforts of any kind, can only be achieved with a full, unhampered mind — if you like, an androgynous mind. Therefore, the giving up of the central myth that science is a product of male thought may well lead to a more creative, more imaginative, and, who knows, possibly even a more humanistic science.

Samuel C. Florman

Engineering and the Female Mind

Samuel C. Florman (born 1925), a successful civil engineer, is best known for explaining his profession to the general public in magazine articles like the one reprinted here and in books like The Existential Pleasures of Engineering *(1976). "Engineering and the Female Mind" appeared in* Harper's *in 1978.*

The campus of Smith College in Northampton, Massachu- 1
setts, is one of the most pleasant places in the world to be
on a sunny afternoon in spring. The setting is so lovely, the
academic atmosphere so tranquil, that when I arrived there
on such an afternoon last April I was totally captivated.
The spell of the place, however, made me uneasy about my
mission, which was to convince a few of the students at
this premier, all-female liberal arts college that they ought
to become engineers.

The mission, as it turned out, was destined to fail. Most 2
bright young women today do not want to become engineers. At first hearing this might not seem to be a matter
of grave consequence, but since engineering is central to
the functioning of our society, its rejection as a career option
by female students raises the most profound questions
about the objectives of the women's movement.

It is not generally recognized that at the same time when 3
women are making their way into every corner of our work-
world, only 1 percent of the professional engineers in the
nation are female. A generation ago this statistic would
have raised no eyebrows, but today it is hard to believe.
The engineering schools, reacting to social and governmental pressures, have opened wide their gates and are recruiting women with zeal. The major corporations, reacting to
even more intense pressures, are offering attractive employment opportunities to practically all women engineering
graduates. According to the College Placement Council, engineering is the only field in which average starting salaries
for women are higher than those for men. Tokenism is disappearing, according to the testimony of women engineers
themselves. By every reasonable standard one would expect
women to be attracted to the profession in large numbers.
Yet only 5 percent of last year's 58,000 engineering degrees
were awarded to women (compared to 18 percent in

medicine, 22 percent in law, and 34 percent in the biological sciences). By 1980 the total may reach 10 percent, still a dismal figure when one realizes that more women than men are enrolled in American colleges. Unless this situation changes dramatically, and soon, the proportion of women engineers in practice, among more than a million males, will remain insignificant for many decades. While women are moving vigorously—assertively, demandingly—toward significant numerical representation in industry, the arts, and the other professions, they are, for reasons that are not at all clear, shying away from engineering.

4   At Smith I was scheduled to participate in a seminar entitled "The Role of Technology in Modern Society." The program called for a "sherry hour" before dinner, during which the speakers had an opportunity to chat informally with the students. In a stately paneled room the late-afternoon light sparkled on crystal decanters as we sipped our sherry from tiny glasses. The students with whom I conversed were as elegant as the surroundings, so poised, so ladylike; I found myself thinking, "These girls are *not* going to become engineers. It's simply not their style." The young women were not vapid in the way of country gentry. Far from it. They were alert and sensible, well trained in mathematics and the sciences. I could imagine them donning white coats and conducting experiments in quiet laboratories. But I could not see them as engineers. It is a hopeless cause, I thought. They will not become engineers because it is "beneath" them to do so. It is a question of *class*.

5   This was an intuitive feeling of the moment, although the idea, in the abstract, had occurred to me before. It made sociological sense. Traditionally, most American engineers have come from working-class families. In the words of a post-Sputnik National Science Foundation Study, "engineering has a special appeal for bright boys of lower- and lower-middle-class origins." Girls from blue-collar families have been left behind in the women's crusade for equality in education. Therefore, the only young women who have the educational qualifications to become engineers are likely to come from the upper classes. But the upper classes do not esteem a career in engineering: ergo very few women engineers.

6   Much of our class consciousness we have inherited from England, and so it is with our attitude toward engineering, which the English have always considered rather a "navvy" occupation. Since engineering did not change from a craft

to a profession until the mid-nineteenth century, and never shed completely its craftsman's image, it was fair game for the sneers of pretentious social arbiters. Herbert Hoover, a very successful mining engineer before he became President, and something of a scholar who translated Agricola from the Latin, enjoyed telling about an English lady whom he met during the course of an Atlantic crossing. When, near the end of the voyage, Hoover told her that he was an engineer, the lady exclaimed, "Why, I thought you were a gentleman!"

It may not be realistic to expect women to break down   7 class barriers that were created mostly by men. Yet feminists, if they are serious in their avowed purposes, should by now have taken the lead in changing this situation, encouraging the elite among educated young women to reevaluate their social prejudices. For until upper-class aversion to engineering is overcome, or until lower-class women get out of the kitchen and into the university, engineering will remain a male profession. And while this condition prevails, the feminist movement will be stalled, probably without even knowing it. For, in a man-made world, how can women achieve the equality they seek?

My view, needless to say, is not shared by the feminists   8 of America. Judging by their literature, they seem to attach no particular importance to increasing female enrollment in engineering, perhaps because they are more concerned about battering on closed doors than they are about walking through those that are open. When they do get around to considering the problem, it is not to question or criticize choices being made by women, but only to deplore the effect of external forces.

There is an entire literature devoted to explaining how   9 engineering, and to a lesser degree science and mathematics, has developed a "male image." The terminology of this literature has been ringing in our ears for a long time — "sex role socialization," "undoing sex stereotypes," "self-fulfilling prophecy," and so forth. We know the facts by heart: girls learn early that it is not socially acceptable for them to play with trains and trucks. They learn from teachers that boys perform better than girls in math and science. A condition lately called "math anxiety" is attributed to these social pressures. As girls mature they are persuaded by counselors and family that it is not feminine to enter traditionally male professions. They are afraid to compete with men or to let their intelligence show, lest they seem sexually less desirable. Finally, there is a shortage of "role models" with whom a young girl can identify.

10   Yes, yes, yes, of course, but these facts, which seemed so interesting and important a decade ago, have become stale. As the sociologists busy themselves collating their data and getting it published, the times invariably pass them by. After all, it is now fifteen years since the publication of *The Feminine Mystique* and passage of the Equal Pay Act by Congress, fifteen years of turbulence during which a major social revolution has taken place. Educated young women know well enough that they can become engineers, just as they know all about orgasms and property rights. Surely the women who are planning to be biologists and doctors know that they could choose engineering instead, and those who are crowding into the fields of law, business, and journalism know that they could have opted for engineering if they had been willing to take a little calculus and physics. Women's magazines that used to specialize in menus and sewing patterns are now overflowing with advice on how to compete in what used to be a man's world — how to dress, sit, talk, intimidate, and in general "make it." Engineering's purported male image is no longer an adequate explanation for female aversion to the profession.

11   It has been hypothesized that women avoid engineering because it has to do with technology, an aspect of our culture from which they recoil instinctively. Ruth Cowan, a historian at the State University of New York, has done interesting research on the influence of technology on the self-image of the American woman. The development of household appliances, for example, instead of freeing the housewife for a richer life as advertised, has helped to reduce her to the level of a maidservant whose greatest skill is consumerism. Changing factory technologies have attracted women to the workplace in roles that they have come to dislike. Innovations affecting the most intimate aspects of women's lives, such as the baby bottle and birth-control devices, have been developed almost exclusively by men. Dependent upon technology, but removed from its sources and, paradoxically, enslaved by it, women may well have developed deep-seated resentments that persist even in those who consider themselves liberated.

12   If this phenomenon does exist, however, we might expect that the feminists would respond to it as a challenge. The brightest and most ambitious women should be eager to

bend technology, at long last, to their own will. Obviously this is not happening. The feminists seem content to write articles assuring each other that they have the talent to fix leaky faucets.

Another theory—one which arouses such rancor that I 13 hesitate to bring it up—holds that women are not equipped biologically to excel in engineering. The intellectual factor most closely related to attainment in science is spatial ability, the ability to manipulate objects mentally. Experiments have shown that males are, on average, better at this than females, and that this superiority appears to be related to levels of sex chromosomes and testosterone.

It is a mistake, I think, to argue, as some feminists do, 14 that there is no discernible difference between the male and female brain. It would be more sensible to say that because of substantial overlap in test scores, the differences that do exist are not practically significant when one considers a large group of potential engineers of both sexes. It would be better yet to point out that such differences as there are would serve to enrich the profession, since good engineering requires intuition and verbal imagination as well as mathematical adeptness and spatial ability. In their so-called weakness may be women's hidden strength.

This is considered to be a reactionary view, I learned to 15 my sorrow when I proposed it to Zenith Gross, an executive at RCA whose special interest is the careers of professional women. In response to my remark, Ms. Gross said, "I know that you mean well, but to tell a woman engineer that she has female intuition is like telling a black that he has rhythm."

Inevitably it occurred to me that anyone wondering why 16 women do not become engineers would be well advised to learn something about the few women who *do* become engineers. So I took myself one day to the Engineering Societies Building, a large stone-and-glass structure overlooking the East River near the United Nations in New York City. In this stately edifice are housed most of the major professional societies that represent American engineers. On the third floor, past the imposing offices of the Engineering Foundation and the Engineers Joint Council, there is a single room that serves as the home of the Society of Women Engineers.

The day of my visit, the society's executive secretary, Inez 17 Van Vranken, was alone in the office. She moved about the room answering telephones and pulling papers out of files with enormous energy; energy is what Mrs. Van Vranken exudes, growth and vitality are her themes. The society, founded in 1950 by fifty women engineers, has grown in the past five years from just a few hundred to its present membership of 7,000, half of whom are college students. An organization that looks so pathetically small from the outside seems about to explode within the confines of its tiny headquarters.

18   "Look at these inquiries," Mrs. Van Vranken said, pointing to a pile of letters. "The word is getting around. I wish I could answer all of these letters personally, but we're hard pressed to keep up with sending out printed material.

19   "But here's one I do plan to answer personally," she said, showing me a note from a Princeton freshman who objected to the society sending out mail addressed "Miss" instead of "Ms." "I just won't have that sort of nonsense. We're too busy to play games."

20   I browsed through a pile of career-guidance pamphlets, newsletters full of recruiting ads from DuPont, Boeing, Ford, and IBM, and also a booklet telling about the society's Achievement Award, given annually since 1952. The winners of this award are talented women who have made contributions in many fields: solar energy, circuit analysis, metallurgy, missile launchers, rubber reclamation, computers, fluid mechanics, structural design, heat transfer, radio-wave propagation, and so on. Their undeniable ability adds poignancy to the fact that they and their fellow women engineers are so few that their overall contributions to the profession are in essence negligible.

21   In some of the society's literature I came upon a series of group photos taken at various conferences and luncheons. I do not know what I expected women engineers to look like, but these pictures struck me as slightly incongruous. The ladies in their print dresses looked rather like participants at a pie-baking contest in Dubuque, not at all like the elegantly dressed women I am used to seeing in business magazines. As for the student-chapter members, they appeared to be right out of Andy Hardy's high school yearbook, a different species from the girls I had seen at Smith.

22   Of course the girls at Smith do not study engineering. Neither do the girls at Harvard or Yale, which venerable institutions closed their professional schools of engineering years ago (although they still have some courses in engineering science), and neither of which deigned to respond to a

recent statistical questionnaire from the Society of Women Engineers. Such growth as there is in engineering for women is occurring at places like Purdue, Texas A&M, Georgia Tech, and Ohio State. This middle-America predominance, and the photographs, served to reinforce my ideas about the class origins of the problem. It seemed apparent that these women engineers did not come from homes of wealth or high culture.

Wanting more information, I decided, before leaving the 23 building, to pay a visit to Carl Frey, executive director of the Engineers Joint Council, that organization of organizations to which belong most of the major professional engineering societies. In his position at the top of the organizational pyramid, Frey has long lived with the many discontents and disputes endemic to the sprawling, variegated profession: four-year colleges versus five- and six-year programs (what constitutes a professional education?); state licensing (is an engineer a professional without it?); salaries (why do lawyers make so much more than engineers?); prestige (why do scientists get all the credit for engineering achievements?); leadership (why are there so few engineers in elective office?); conservatism of the self-employed versus radicalism of the hired hands; conscience, responsibility, the environmental crisis. Frey could not survive in his position without a genial disposition and a calm sense of history. From his point of view, women in engineering is just one more problem that the profession will cope with in due time.

"I wouldn't get hung up on any fancy theories about 24 class," Frey said. "It's harder and harder to tell who comes from what class, and things are changing so fast that I wouldn't rely on any old statistics you might have seen about the social origins of engineers."

"Well, how do you explain it?" I asked. "Why aren't more 25 bright young women getting into engineering?"

"I think that it has to do with their perception of power. 26 These kids today — the bright girls particularly — they want to be where the action is, where the sources of power are. They don't see engineers as the ones who have the say in our society. And, let's face it, to a great extent they're right. We may have the know-how, but we don't have the power."

Perception of power. The phrase kept going through my 27 mind. It had a nice ring to it, and it had the ring of truth, as well. It did not seem to contradict my ideas about class so much as to encompass them; for what is the origin of class if not the desire to perpetuate power?

28   Every engineer knows that the profession is relatively impotent. Engineers do not make the laws; they do not have the money; they do not set the fashions; they have no voice in the media; they are not even adequately represented in the highest levels of corporate management. It is one of the most irritating ironies of our time that intellectuals, who apparently are too busy pontificating to look around, constantly complain about being in the grip of a technocratic elite that does not exist.

29   To the extent that today's young women are not fooled by such nonsense, they are deserving of credit. But if intelligent, energetic women reject engineering because of an all-consuming desire to sit on the thrones of power, then woe to us all in the age of feminism.

30   When the National Organization for Women was formed in 1966, its Statement of Purpose spoke of bringing women "into full participation in the mainstream of American society *now*, exercising all the privileges and responsibilities thereof in truly equal partnership with men." Yet judging from the way the most advantaged women are selecting their careers, they seem to be a lot more interested in the privileges than in the responsibilities. In this they are following the lead of those males who appear to be in control of our society — the lawyers, writers, politicians, and business managers. This is all very well, but somebody in our society has to design, create, fabricate, build — to *do*. A world full of coordinators, critics, and manipulators would have nothing in it but words. It would be a barren desert, totally devoid of *things*.

31   Feminist ideology, understandably adopting the values of the extant — i.e., male — establishment, is founded on a misapprehension of what constitutes privilege. The feminist leaders have made the deplorable mistake of assuming that those who work hard without public recognition, and for modest rewards, are necessarily being exploited. "Man's happiness lies not in freedom but in his acceptance of a duty," André Gide said. When the duty turns out to be work that is creative and absorbing, as well as essential, then those who had been patronized for being the worker bees are seen to be more fortunate than the queen.

32   Studies have shown that young engineers, women as well

as men, pursue their career because it promises "interesting work." This is more important to them than money, security, prestige, or any of the other trappings of power. They seem to recognize that a fulfilling career does not have to consist of a continuous ego trip.

Although power, in the popular imagination, is identified 33 with wealth and domination, there is another kind of power that lies beneath the surface of our petty ambitions, and that is the engineer's in full measure. It is the force that Henry Adams had in mind when he wrote of the dynamo and the Virgin. The power of the Virgin raised the medieval cathedrals, although, as Adams noted, the Virgin had been dead for a millennium, and held no real power even when she lived. For better or for worse, technology lies at the heart of our contemporary culture, and the technologist is akin to a priest who knows the secrets of the temple. In this sense—and in this sense only—those who speak of a technocratic elite are touching on a profound truth. Until women share in the understanding and creation of our technology—which is to say, until large numbers of women become engineers—they will suffer from a cultural alienation that ordinary power cannot cure.

Judging from all current signs, women will not achieve 34 active partnership in our society's technology for at least another generation. There is one statistic, however, that I find heartening. It seems that more than 40 percent of the women who are now becoming engineers started college with a different career in mind. (The comparable figure for males is less than 20 percent.) This indicates that the ranks of women in engineering may be swelled by a large number of belated conversions. I recently had a chance to talk to two young women who are representative of this potentially significant trend.

Jane Brechlin graduated in 1975 from Mount Holyoke, a 35 women's liberal arts college every bit as pristine and alien to engineering as Smith. Having majored in mathematics, she found employment with the Westinghouse Company, working in probability and statistics. Only then did she discover, looking around, that engineers were engaged in tangible projects beside which her own work seemed "pale and abstract." She gave up her job and enrolled in the Thayer School of Engineering at Dartmouth College, where she is concentrating in the field of solar energy. She has a

part-time job with a company that installs solar collectors, and plans to continue in that field after she receives
her master's degree.

36   Her roommate at Dartmouth, Diane Knappert, graduated
from Allegheny College as a chemist, only to discover that
chemistry was "too theoretical" to satisfy her creative instincts. Embarked now on a career in chemical engineering,
she has a grant from the National Science Foundation to
study the conversion of waste paper pulp and corn stalks
into ethanol fuel.

37   The prospect of these young women working in the van-
guard of the nation's effort to develop new energy sources
is something I find exhilarating. In speaking about their
careers they make no grandiloquent feminist pronouncements. They seem to be much more interested in the details
of their projects than in the cause of women's liberation.
They do more to serve the cause, in my estimation, than a
hundred militants refighting battles that are already won.

38   The women's liberation movement means different
things to different people. Many of its goals—such as
mutual respect and equality before the law—can be
achieved even if there are no women engineers. But the
ultimate feminist dream will never be realized as long as
women would rather supervise the world than help build it.

GENDER AT WORK

Virginia Woolf
Professions for Women

Virginia Woolf (1882–1942) was one of the greatest writers of her time; perhaps you have read Mrs. Dalloway *(1925) or* To the Lighthouse *(1927) or* The Waves *(1931) or some of her essays. Born and raised in London in a circle of culture and learning known as the Bloomsbury Group, she founded with her husband the Hogarth Press in 1912, which was the first publisher (or first English publisher) of many famous writers. This essay, first given in 1931 to the Women's Service League in London, appeared in 1942 as part of her* Death of the Moth and Other Essays.

When your secretary invited me to come here, she told 1
me that your Society is concerned with the employment of women and she suggested that I might tell you something about my own professional experiences. It is true I am a woman; it is true I am employed, but what professional experiences have I had? It is difficult to say. My profession is literature; and in that profession there are fewer experiences for women than in any other, with the exception of the state—fewer, I mean, that are peculiar to women. For the road was cut many years ago—by Fanny Burney, by Aphra Behn, by Harriet Martineau, by Jane Austen, by George Eliot—many famous women, and many more unknown and forgotten, have been before me, making the path smooth, and regulating my steps. Thus, when I came to write, there were very few material obstacles in my way. Writing was a reputable and harmless occupation. The family peace was not broken by the scratching of a pen. No demand was made upon the family purse. For ten and six pence one can buy paper enough to write all the plays of Shakespeare—if one has a mind that way. Pianos and models, Paris, Vienna and Berlin, masters and mistresses, are not needed by a writer. The cheapness of writing paper is,

of course, the reason why women have succeeded as writers before they have succeeded in the other professions.

2   But to tell you my story—it is a simple one. You have only got to figure to yourselves a girl in a bedroom with a pen in her hand. She had only to move that pen from left to right— from ten o'clock to one. Then it occurred to her to do what is simple and cheap enough after all—to slip a few of those pages into an envelope, fix a penny stamp in the corner, and drop the envelope in the red box at the corner. It was thus that I became a journalist; and my effort was rewarded on the first day of the following month—a very glorious day it was for me— by a letter from an editor containing a check for one pound ten shillings and sixpence. But to show you how little I deserve to be called a professional woman, how little I know of the struggles and difficulties of such lives, I have to admit that instead of spending that sum upon bread and butter, rent, shoes and stockings, or butcher's bills, I went out and bought a cat—a beautiful cat, a Persian cat, which very soon involved me in bitter disputes with my neighbors.

3   What could be easier than to write articles and to buy Persian cats with the profits? But wait a moment. Articles have to be about something. Mine, I seem to remember, was about a novel by a famous man. And while I was writing this review, I discovered that if I were going to review books I should need to do battle with a certain phantom. And the phantom was a woman, and when I came to know her better I called her after the heroine of a famous poem, The Angel in the House. It was she who used to come between me and my paper when I was writing reviews. It was she who bothered me and wasted my time and so tormented me that at last I killed her. You who come of a younger and happier generation may not have heard of her—you may not know what I mean by the Angel in the House. I will describe her as shortly as I can. She was intensely sympathetic. She was immensely charming. She was utterly unselfish. She excelled in the difficult arts of family life. She sacrificed herself daily. If there was chicken, she took the leg; if there was a draught she sat in it—in short she was so constituted that she never had a mind or a wish of her own, but preferred to sympathize always with the minds and wishes of others. Above all—I need not say it— she was pure. Her purity was supposed to be her chief beauty—her blushes, her great grace. In those days—the

last of Queen Victoria—every house had its Angel. And when I came to write I encountered her with the very first words. The shadow of her wings fell on my page; I heard the rustling of her skirts in the room. Directly, that is to say, I took my pen in hand to review that novel by a famous man, she slipped behind me and whispered: "My dear, you are a young woman. You are writing about a book that has been written by a man. Be sympathetic; be tender; flatter; deceive; use all the arts and wiles of our sex. Never let anybody guess that you have a mind of your own. Above all, be pure." And she made as if to guide my pen. I now record the one act for which I take some credit to myself, though the credit rightly belongs to some excellent ancestors of mine who left me a certain sum of money—shall we say five hundred pounds a year?—so that it was not necessary for me to depend solely on charm for my living. I turned upon her and caught her by the throat. I did my best to kill her. My excuse, if I were to be had up in a court of law, would be that I acted in self-defense. Had I not killed her she would have killed me. She would have plucked the heart out of my writing. For, as I found, directly I put pen to paper, you cannot review even a novel without having a mind of your own, without expressing what you think to be the truth about human relations, morality, sex. And all these questions, according to the Angel in the House, cannot be dealt with freely and openly by women; they must charm, they must conciliate, they must—to put it bluntly—tell lies if they are to succeed. Thus, whenever I felt the shadow of her wing or the radiance of her halo upon my page, I took up the inkpot and flung it at her. She died hard. Her fictitious nature was of great assistance to her. It is far harder to kill a phantom than a reality. She was always creeping back when I thought I had despatched her. Though I flatter myself that I killed her in the end, the struggle was severe; it took much time that had better have been spent upon learning Greek grammar; or in roaming the world in search of adventures. But it was a real experience; it was an experience that was bound to befall all women writers at that time. Killing the Angel in the House was part of the occupation of a woman writer.

But to continue my story. The Angel was dead; what then 4
remained? You may say that what remained was a simple and common object—a young woman in a bedroom with an inkpot. In other words, now that she had rid herself of

falsehood, that young woman had only to be herself. Ah, but what is "herself"? I mean, what is a woman? I assure you, I do not know. I do not believe that you know. I do not believe that anybody can know until she has expressed herself in all the arts and professions open to human skill. That indeed is one of the reasons why I have come here — out of respect for you, who are in process of showing us by your experiments what a woman is, who are in process of providing us, by your failures and successes, with that extremely important piece of information.

5   But to continue the story of my professional experiences. I made one pound ten and six by my first review; and I bought a Persian cat with the proceeds. Then I grew ambitious. A Persian cat is all very well, I said; but a Persian cat is not enough. I must have a motor car. And it was thus that I became a novelist — for it is a very strange thing that people will give you a motor car if you will tell them a story. It is a still stranger thing that there is nothing so delightful in the world as telling stories. It is far pleasanter than writing reviews of famous novels. And yet, if I am to obey your secretary and tell you my professional experiences as a novelist, I must tell you about a very strange experience that befell me as a novelist. And to understand it you must try first to imagine a novelist's state of mind. I hope I am not giving away professional secrets if I say that a novelist's chief desire is to be as unconscious as possible. He has to induce in himself a state of perpetual lethargy. He wants life to proceed with the utmost quiet and regularity. He wants to see the same faces, to read the same books, to do the same things day after day, month after month, while he is writing, so that nothing may break the illusion in which he is living — so that nothing may disturb or disquiet the mysterious nosings about, feelings round, darts, dashes and sudden discoveries of that very shy and illusive spirit, the imagination. I suspect that this state is the same both for men and women. Be that as it may, I want you to imagine me writing a novel in a state of trance. I want you to figure to yourselves a girl sitting with a pen in her hand, which for minutes, and indeed for hours, she never dips into the inkpot. The image that comes to my mind when I think of this girl is the image of a fisherman lying sunk in dreams on the verge of a deep lake with a rod held out over the water. She was letting her imagination sweep unchecked round every rock and cranny

of the world that lies submerged in the depths of our unconscious being. Now came the experience, the experience that
I believe to be far commoner with women writers than with
men. The line raced through the girl's fingers. Her imagination had rushed away. It had sought the pools, the depths,
the dark places where the largest fish slumber. And then
there was a smash. There was an explosion. There was foam
and confusion. The imagination had dashed itself against
something hard. The girl was roused from her dream. She
was indeed in a state of the most acute and difficult distress.
To speak without figure she had thought of something,
something about the body, about the passions which it was
unfitting for her as a woman to say. Men, her reason told
her, would be shocked. The consciousness of what men will
say of a woman who speaks the truth about her passions
had roused her from her artist's state of unconsciousness.
She could write no more. The trance was over. Her imagination could work no longer. This I believe to be a very
common experience with women writers — they are im-
peded by the extreme conventionality of the other sex. For
though men sensibly allow themselves great freedom in
these respects, I doubt that they realize or can control the
extreme severity with which they condemn such freedom
in women.

These then were two very genuine experiences of my own.   6
These were two of the adventures of my professional life.
The first — killing the Angel in the House — I think I solved.
She died. But the second, telling the truth about my own
experiences as a body, I do not think I solved. I doubt that
any woman has solved it yet. The obstacles against her are
still immensely powerful — and yet they are very difficult
to define. Outwardly, what is simpler than to write books?
Outwardly, what obstacles are there for a woman rather
than for a man? Inwardly, I think, the case is very different;
she has still many ghosts to fight, many prejudices to overcome. Indeed it will be a long time still, I think, before a
woman can sit down to write a book without finding a
phantom to be slain, a rock to be dashed against. And if
this is so in literature, the freest of all professions for
women, how is it in the new professions which you are now
for the first time entering?

Those are the questions that I should like, had I time, to   7
ask you. And indeed, if I have laid stress upon these professional experiences of mine, it is because I believe that they

are, though in different forms, yours also. Even when the path is nominally open—when there is nothing to prevent a woman from being a doctor, a lawyer, a civil servant—there are many phantoms and obstacles, as I believe, looming in her way. To discuss and define them is I think of great value and importance; for thus only can the labor be shared, the difficulties be solved. But besides this, it is necessary also to discuss the ends and the aims for which we are fighting, for which we are doing battle with these formidable obstacles. Those aims cannot be taken for granted; they must be perpetually questioned and examined. The whole position, as I see it—here in this hall surrounded by women practising for the first time in history I know not how many different professions—is one of extraordinary interest and importance. You have won rooms of your own in the house hitherto exclusively owned by men. You are able, though not without great labor and effort, to pay the rent. You are earning your five hundred pounds a year. But this freedom is only a beginning; the room is your own, but it is still bare. It has to be furnished; it has to be decorated; it has to be shared. How are you going to furnish it, how are you going to decorate it? With whom are you going to share it, and upon what terms? These, I think, are questions of the utmost importance and interest. For the first time in history you are able to ask them; for the first time you are able to decide for yourselves what the answers should be. Willingly would I stay and discuss those questions and answers—but not tonight. My time is up; and I must cease.

Jean Reith Schroedel
Amy Kelley, Machinist

Jean Reith Schroedel (born 1951) worked as a machinist before attending the University of Washington, so it probably seemed natural for her to do oral histories of women in blue-collar trades, the histories collected in her 1985 book Alone in a Crowd: Women in the Trades Tell Their Stories. *One of the twenty-five Seattle-area women that Schroedel profiles in her book is Amy Kelley.*

My parents were divorced when I was nine. My father 1
was a cook at a twenty-four-hour cafe. My mother used to
work two jobs — a pressman at a drycleaner's and also as
a janitress. After the divorce, my mother moved in with
my aunt, who is a widow. My aunt was a journeyman
printer — negative stripper — and she was very independent,
so I learned a lot of that from her. She's also one of the
first women in her field, which subconsciously I wonder
if that's what got me into this, but somehow I really don't
think so. My aunt was more influential in my life than
my mom. Although my mom was around, she was always
working.

When we moved to Ballard I was in the fourth grade, 2
and I made some friends out there, but found them to be
more closed-minded than neighborly. I didn't really care
for the types of kids that were out there, which is why I
continued to commute to the Central District to go to school.
I felt more comfortable there than I did out in Ballard.
Being a minority made it kind of awkward. The school I
went to was more or less for low-income students, so we
didn't have a lot of classes, and it wasn't coed, so we didn't
have classes like shop. There was home ec and sewing, basic
women-type classes. From the time I was a freshman in
high school I worked to put myself through. Right after
school I had to go straight to work, so I was never able to
take extracurricular activities like volleyball.

I started out when I was fourteen years old working for 3
a knitting company based in Ballard. They made ski sweaters. I started out as just a packer. I'd pack the sweaters in
plastic bags and get them ready to ship. Then after awhile
I got really interested in learning to run the knitting
machines. There were no women running the knitting
machines. I wasn't supposed to run the knitting machines
because I was under age. Because of the child labor laws I
had to be sixteen. But I would be able to sneak over and
learn when I didn't have much else to do. The boss didn't
care as long as I wasn't actually running them. I was just
learning how. The knitting was minimum wage. I don't
know what minimum wage was in nineteen sixty-nine. It
was like a dollar twenty-five. It got slack and I got laid off,
so I got a job working in a drive-in restaurant. I started
that in nineteen seventy-one — waitress, whatever you want
to call it. When I turned eighteen I was making a dollar
sixty-five an hour. That was minimum wage, so it had to
be a lot less when I was working at the sweater company.

It was not so great, that's for sure. The conditions at the knitting mill were not that great. I didn't like the fact that the people who owned the place took advantage of immigrants. They'd pay them the minimum wage and work them like they had no feelings. Just produce the work and no money. I didn't like that. But the drive-in job, I enjoyed that. I really liked working with the public. It was fun, and I had a neat boss who was an older guy. He was really good; there are not many places like that. But the pay was lousy.

4   I started thinking about non-traditional work seriously when I was a senior in high school, because I realized there'd be something I'd have to do when I got out. I had just met my husband. When he came back from Vietnam he eventually found employment as a machine operator at a big machine shop in Seattle. At first, during all this time I had known him, we discussed what he was doing at work. I found it fascinating. It was not necessarily machine-type work that I was thinking about. It was more like something automotive.

5   When I finally thought about machine shop work, I liked the money, and I always wanted to do something different. And then, of course, I like working with my hands. But I thought that maybe I might not be smart enough — whether my education was enough or did I know enough to do it. . . .

6   My husband (at that time he was my boy friend) suggested I take some training courses, so he looked around. He had been going to a private fellow who had a private course he was giving in his house, teaching people how to read precision instruments and blueprints. Well, I'd only taken the precision part of it, learning how to use the instruments and stuff. My husband was working in the aircraft industry, and by then they were looking for women and minorities with non-traditional skills. The federal contracts wanted to see more minorities and women in the non-traditional jobs, so they were essentially out looking. They were asking people in the shop if they knew women that would qualify for that kind of thing, so I kind of fell right into place. It helps to know somebody on the inside out there.

7   When I was hired, I was hired as a milling-machine trainee, which is a twenty-two-month program. I didn't know what to expect, because I had never set foot in a machine shop before in my entire life. I didn't know what it would be like to work with a bunch of men. I felt like I

was very naive when I went in there. I had just come out of an all-girl high school and I didn't know a four-letter word from a five-letter word.

. . . As it turned out I was probably the youngest person 8 in the whole shop. And *all* these guys that I saw! I thought, "Gee, these guys don't look very friendly at all." And I'm trying to get enough courage to say, "I'll do all right." The first room was awesome. It was closely packed with machines and noisy. It was the largest machine shop in the company—the machine fabrication shop. The head count at that time was over twelve hundred people on all three shifts. It averages three hundred to four hundred people per shift in the entire building and everybody has plenty of space to breathe. They're not real crowded or cramped. They could easily get two or three airplanes in a building that size. It's like a giant warehouse. And the amount of men compared with the amount of women was—really—I didn't think there were so many men in one place. At the time I was the youngest female in there. Now it's changed, but when I walked in there in nineteen seventy-two all the women were either dispatch clerks or tool room clerks, and all in their upper forties and had been there a long time. There wasn't any woman in the non-traditional jobs, so when I went on the machine it was like I was there all by myself.

When I went in I was wondering what it would be like 9 to work with guys. I was wondering whether the guys would like me, whether I could work with them. I knew at least one person there and that was my husband, so I didn't feel like I'd be totally lost, but the others—they were all white, all male, and probably starting at age thirty-five and up.

After the first or second day there was a supervisor that 10 kind of took me under his wing. He was Japanese and he always reminded me of the way I'd like to have my father be. He made me do and think on my own, but it was like he was looking out for me, which I really appreciated.

After eight months of learning the milling machine, I was 11 approached by the apprenticeship supervisor and asked if I'd be interested in the apprenticeship program. It sounded fascinating, because I was getting bored with what I was doing, so I filled in the application and had to go before the review board, which was made up of three representatives of management, generally from upper management, and three members from the union. . . .

12   My entire interview was tape recorded, and I understand I was the only one tape recorded. The main concern was whether I was going to get married and get pregnant, and I got so tired of hearing it. And then also why I really wanted to become an apprentice, did I really feel I was going to stick it out. Was I going to be there the whole four years or was I going to get pregnant? I would have liked to answer it one way, but I just said, no, I wasn't going to, but I wish I'd told them that nobody has to get married to get pregnant any more. I must have been asked that question four times in my interview. I passed—five people voted for me and one person did not.

13   I got spoiled in my apprenticeship. Everybody was so willing to teach me everything. Like I was saying earlier, women at that time were such a novelty all the guys were hands on, they wanted to train a woman. I think it was a macho thing for them—"Hey, we got a woman here." The only thing I found was some areas in which I worked I think they were afraid to let me go on the machine, because they were afraid of the fact that they didn't really know whether I could handle it or not, so I feel like sometimes I suffered in that respect.

                              .   .   .

14   Right now, because of the lathe I'm on, I do only large work. I run all the large jobs on the machine. It's not really hard. It's kind of funny to see a woman on this machine. You think, "Oh, she's gotta work hard." But it's not really that bad. I do work hard just to get it set up so I can actually get the job going. But you have cranes to work with. You do have to use brute strength, and I'm not afraid to ask somebody else for help if there's something I feel is beyond my capability.

15   I'm quite union active. I'm a shop steward now. I was elected two months ago as a shop steward in the machine shop. I am the first and only woman to be a steward in a machine shop, and I had to work hard at getting that. It's been real political, as far as just getting to *have* the election so I could become shop steward. The union's political for two important reasons. One is whether you support the incumbent that's in office right now, and two, the political incentive. Most men just aren't ready to take on a woman on a committee that's going to speak for them all. They feel

uncomfortable with the fact that a woman has any self-confidence at all. They feel like it's a threat. Basically, they start near the bottom and head towards the top—down the road, like a business rep or staff assistant. They've got some really weird jobs in the union. I don't even understand why they even have those positions. I may not agree with what the elected officials are doing, but I believe in the causes and principles of the union. I believe that every person has a right to fair pay and decent working conditions and somebody to represent them in case of problems. I think the approaches of the union have got to change from what they used to be, like way back in the old days, in how you succeed in getting the things you want. But basically the union is only as strong as its membership, and I'm a firm believer that the union should involve its members more, so it can become strong, not alienate themselves from it.

In relationship to women in non-traditional trades, I   16
don't think the union's done all that much. They just look at it as something they don't talk too much about. If you're a woman and you've got any vocal tendencies to speak your mind, you might as well forget anything for yourself, unless you support their ticket. It's not really a fair game at all, so to speak, within the union. The union, as far as representing women or minorities, is just starting to come out and seeing that justice is done. Basically they don't like to work on problems with women or minorities because it upsets the rest of the membership—the white Caucasian males. They [the rank and file] think that women and minorities are getting preferential treatment, so they [the union officials] keep it all low-key and quiet.

I treat people with respect if they give me respect. And   17
I don't appreciate supervisors, just because they have a little badge that says "supervisor," to treat me just like another employee, another number that doesn't have any feelings. I feel like there's no reason why he can't say, "Please," or "Thank you," or "I appreciate your work." I'm not hesitant to say that. I've had supervisors say, "I need this job done," and I'll say, "What about please?" Or some boss will ask me, "Where the hell were ya?" And I'll ask, "Who the hell wants to know?" I've been wanting to advance in the hourly positions, but I can't seem to, mainly because I'm too outspoken. They want people who are gonna say yes, not why or no, or how come. And I think being a woman doesn't help either. Also, Japanese women

are supposed to be diminutive and quiet and do what they're told. I shock a lot of my co-workers.

18   When I first came into the shop I was a naive girl and I was afraid. I went in one day and opened a cabinet door and there was a nude centerfold. It set me back, but then I realized at the same time that women shouldn't expect to change attitudes of the men. I think, with time, we are showing men we know how to do the work. Then they'll change just naturally. They can't help but respect you if they find out that you can do the work. I think it's very important for women to become more involved with their union and use it to make men realize that they have feelings; they have special problems that men don't understand, like sexual harassment, sexual discrimination. And most of these guys, unless they see it happen to their wives, are oblivious to the whole thing, so they have to be educated, and it has to start with the union, because the management's sure not going to do it.

19   I have had cases of sexual harassment. I have complained to the EEO [Equal Employment Opportunity] commission. The company has an EEO office. I had one supervisor that used to come up behind me and pat me on the butt, and I didn't even know he was back there. And I had another supervisor that would come around, when I didn't know it, and snap my bra strap! It was just something that they thought was cute. I told the supervisor who used to come up and pat me, "Hey, maybe you'd better cut that out, because if *your* supervisor saw you do that, you'd be in a heck of a lot of trouble and I'm not real keen on that." Sexual harassment is one touchy subject. This other supervisor — it wouldn't have done any good to talk to him. I filed a report and it hasn't happened since. They had a meeting and told us that they were getting some complaints, not from who, and it's gotten a lot better. I haven't had to worry about it from the fellow employees. It's the managers. I get a lot of teasing, a lot of jokes from the fellow employees; that doesn't bother me, and I think they have a little more respect for you because they're working *with* you. The supervisors, they're so away and detached from you. They feel like, "Gee, I'm a supervisor, so she should be flattered."

20   My husband understands my position. If you say too much then you can end up — you know, as much as they say they're not supposed to retaliate, there's other ways

they can retaliate. They can make your work a little difficult for you, or they can give you jobs that they know you can't handle, or assign you to a different machine that's a little tricky.

I feel like I've been sexually discriminated against. I guess   21 that's all I can say. Nobody's gonna come out and say, "You're being discriminated against because of your sex." I think that there have been jobs in which I have been sexually discriminated against — mainly the jobs that pay in the higher grades. About two years ago I was able to work a lot of the different jobs that pay higher than I get now. No problems. I was always asked to come back. They would always come and get me for a higher-paying job if they needed someone, if someone was sick or absent. And I'd keep going, keep going, keep going in, and the only time there was a permanent opening I didn't get it. There's no selection process. It's a popularity deal. If the boss likes you, he gets you in the job. They'd put guys in the positions that had less time than I did, who had less experience and less qualifications. And if that's not sexual discrimination, I don't know what to call it. Because they've put me in the positions temporarily before, they're telling me that I'm qualified. All of a sudden the jobs open up permanent, and I'm *not* qualified. That doesn't make sense to me.

In the area I'm working in I'm the most senior employee   22 on second shift. I feel I am respected because I do know quite a bit more, as far as the procedures and where everybody in the area works, which jobs should be lathed on what machines. It makes me real mad when the lead man is not there they will not give me the lead position. I think it's because I'm vocal. I'm not a yes person. If you're not a yes person, you don't get the position. Although it doesn't help that I'm a woman, because there isn't a single woman in our shop that makes higher than a grade 8, which is what I am.

I went to the company's EEO office on a sexual discrim-   23 ination claim when I thought I was being discriminated against in not getting the higher-paying jobs. The guy that got the job had less time than I had, and he didn't even have to go through the connecting jobs like me. I was not really satisfied with the results. They told me I didn't have enough running-time experience, which I disagree with, but I felt like there wasn't a whole lot I could do internally and I wasn't quite ready yet to go on the outside. I think I could have been successful going to the outside, but at the same time I didn't want to cut my own throat. If I had gone to the outside and started a sex-discrimination case and won, then the supervisors may retaliate by giving me hard jobs or putting me in an area that was wrong. I'm not the kind of person who likes to make a whole heck of a lot of trouble. These supervisors know that I want to get ahead. I think they also know I could go to the outside if I wanted to. That's why I'm sort of biding my time. They're gonna realize that I'm gonna run out of patience.

24   I filed a sex-discrimination case with the EEO several years ago. I had been trying and trying to get on the apprenticeship board. EEO said there had never been a case like that before. They said there wasn't anything they could do because it wasn't a paying job. So I was up a creek. But I wanted it real bad, and a group of apprentices wrote up a petition. The men sent it down to the union hall and the next thing I became an alternate to the committee. Of course, they say it's not because of the petition, but funny it didn't happen until the petition had been sent in.

25   Race hasn't been too much of a factor. I think most people realize I'm more American than I am Japanese. Race has only been a problem on the men's bathroom walls. There's stuff about me on the bathroom walls, but, you know, it's kind of touching. Somebody will make a comment about me. Amy is a so-and-so, and somebody will put underneath the graffiti, "What difference does it make, she's nice." And it makes you feel good to think that somebody thinks that the clown who put this up there was crazy. But it's no different than blacks or Chicanos or anybody. There's racism in that shop just like everywhere else. I just live with it. When I first heard about it on the bathroom walls, what am I gonna do, tell 'em to erase it? It can still go back up there again, you know. I believe there are ignorant people out there, and I'll just ignore those ignorant people; I can't waste my time with them.

26   I like doing things around the house. I like to build things — small carpentry things. I built a sixteen-foot work bench in the garage. I've put light fixtures in our house. I've found that my job has made it a little easier to understand all these other things I do at home. My husband doesn't like doing things like that at home. So it's kind of like, if I don't do it, it won't get done. Our marriage is very different. My husband has always been in favor of me be-

coming better, becoming more independently capable, taking care of myself.

My family doesn't quite understand what I do. It's just   27
a language barrier. I feel it's almost like they have learned
to respect me making almost thirteen bucks an hour. And
they also realize I'm a lot more American than they probably want. Most of the women in our family have been
taught to be traditional Japanese. They're from Japan,
where the wife obeys the husband. When he says to get
something to eat, you hop to it and do it right away. Where
I'm more likely to tell him, "There's the kitchen; if you
want something to eat, you can get it yourself." I'm more
independent than they'd like to see a Japanese woman be.

But sometime I miss being able to look like a woman.   28
There's a purpose behind the way I dress. I don't dress to
work at a fashion show, but I mean it isn't glamorous and
there are times I'd like to dress up. That would be the one
thing about work that I don't like. It's hard to relate to
other women about what I do. I get tired of getting stared
at in department stores when I go in with my grubby jeans
and my flannel shirt and my steel-toed shoes. They kind of
look at you like, "What in the world?" It's a whole different
attitude.

As soon as I walk in the door at work it's like I'm not any   29
sex at all. It's no sex at all. It doesn't matter if I'm a man
or a woman. I'm a machinist. I can do the work. They guys
look at me, not because I'm a woman, but because I'm a
machinist. And that feels real good.

I think this is a good job for a woman, but only if she's   30
strong, and I don't mean just physically. I mean mentally.
They need to be strong, secure, emotionally stable, and able
to take some stress. There's more pressure than on other
jobs I've done. You have to make a good part. Because if
you don't make a good part, that's gonna make an unsafe
plane. She has to be able to cope with the stress of wanting
to do good. Somebody that's physically capable—who
knows how to compensate for their weakness. The women
I've noticed, and myself too, they find little ways of doing
things a little different, because you can't do it the same
way the guys do. They didn't build a woman's hip the way
they did unless it was on purpose. I use my hip to a lot of
advantage. I don't have the strength all on my own, so I'll
put my weight into it also.

Some women just don't have the brute strength to do it,   31 but I think the biggest *dis*advantage is from the moment they're born. Somebody's gonna raise them to be a "woman"—not to get their hands dirty, not to go out with Daddy and his hammer and nails. She's not gonna develop the mental skill or the agility. I know I have that problem with hand-eye coordination. On my job it hasn't been a problem, but it has been playing baseball. I think if I had been taught when I was a little girl that it was okay for little girls to play baseball, I would have developed that hand-eye coordination. There are other things that men take for granted. Boys, when they're growing up, learn how to fix their cars, learn what a feeler gauge is or how to set spark plugs, how to understand mechanical levers. Women don't have that advantage, no matter how much training they get. They aren't brought up with it, so I think it's important that they realize that and try to compensate. Also I think it's important they realize not to raise their little girl to do the same thing.

Lester C. Thurow
Why Women Are Paid Less Than Men

Lester C. Thurow (born 1938) grew up in Montana, the son of a Methodist minister. Rhodes Scholar and Harvard Ph.D., member of the Johnson administration and adviser to George McGovern, he is currently Dean of the Sloan School of Management at MIT. Among his books are Poverty and Discrimination, Dangerous Currents, *and the best-selling* Zero-Sum Society. *Thurow writes regularly for the* Los Angeles Times, Newsweek, *and other "generalist" publications; the following appeared in* The New York Times *in 1981.*

1   In the 40 years from 1939 to 1979 white women who work full time have with monotonous regularity made slightly less than 60 percent as much as white men. Why?

2   Over the same time period, minorities have made substantial progress in catching up with whites, with minority women making even more progress than minority men. Black men now earn 72 percent as much as white men (up

16 percentage points since the mid-1950's) but black women earn 92 percent as much as white women. Hispanic men make 71 percent of what their white counterparts do, but Hispanic women make 82 percent as much as white women. As a result of their faster progress, fully employed black women make 75 percent as much as fully employed black men while Hispanic women earn 68 percent as much as Hispanic men.

This faster progress may, however, end when minority 3 women finally catch up with white women. In the bible of the New Right, George Gilder's *Wealth and Poverty*, the 60 percent is just one of Mother Nature's constants like the speed of light or the force of gravity. Men are programmed to provide for their families economically while women are programmed to take care of their families emotionally and physically. As a result men put more effort into their jobs than women. The net result is a difference in work intensity that leads to that 40 percent gap in earnings. But there is no discrimination against women—only the biological facts of life.

The problem with this assertion is just that. It is an asser- 4 tion with no evidence for it other than the fact that white women have made 60 percent as much as men for a long period of time.

"Discrimination against women" is an easy answer but 5 it also has its problems as an adequate explanation. Why is discrimination against women not declining under the same social forces that are leading to a lessening of discrimination against minorities? In recent years women have made more use of the enforcement provisions of the Equal Employment Opportunities Commission and the courts than minorities. Why do the laws that prohibit discrimination against women and minorities work for minorities but not for women?

When men discriminate against women, they run into a 6 problem. To discriminate against women is to discriminate against your own wife and to lower your own family income. To prevent women from working is to force men to work more.

When whites discriminate against blacks, they can at 7 least think that they are raising their own incomes. When men discriminate against women they have to know that they are lowering their own family income and increasing their own work effort.

While discrimination undoubtedly explains part of the 8

male-female earnings differential, one has to believe that men are monumentally stupid or irrational to explain all of the earnings gap in terms of discrimination. There must be something else going on.

9   Back in 1939 it was possible to attribute the earnings gap to large differences in educational attainments. But the educational gap between men and women has been eliminated since World War II. It is no longer possible to use education as an explanation for the lower earnings of women. Some observers have argued that women earn less money since they are less reliable workers who are more apt to leave the labor force. But it is difficult to maintain this position since women are less apt to quit one job to take another and as a result they tend to work as long, or longer, for any one employer. From any employer's perspective they are more reliable, not less reliable, than men.

10   Part of the answer is visible if you look at the lifetime earnings profile of men. Suppose that you were asked to predict which men in a group of 25-year-olds would become economically successful. At age 25 it is difficult to tell who will be economically successful and your predictions are apt to be highly inaccurate. But suppose that you were asked to predict which men in a group of 35-year-olds would become economically successful. If you are successful at age 35, you are very likely to remain successful for the rest of your life. If you have not become economically successful by age 35, you are very unlikely to do so later.

11   The decade between 25 and 35 is when men either succeed or fail. It is the decade when lawyers become partners in the good firms, when business managers make it onto the "fast track," when academics get tenure at good universities, and when blue collar workers find the job opportunities that will lead to training opportunities and the skills that will generate high earnings. If there is any one decade when it pays to work hard and to be consistently in the labor force, it is the decade between 25 and 35. For those who succeed, earnings will rise rapidly. For those who fail, earnings will remain flat for the rest of their lives.

12   But the decade between 25 and 35 is precisely the decade when women are most apt to leave the labor force or become part-time workers to have children. When they do, the current system of promotion and skill acquisition will extract an enormous lifetime price.

13   This leaves essentially two avenues for equalizing male and female earnings. Families where women who wish to

have successful careers, compete with men, and achieve the same earnings should alter their family plans and have their children either before 25 or after 35. Or society can attempt to alter the existing promotion and skill acquisition system so that there is a longer time period in which both men and women can attempt to successfully enter the labor force. Without some combination of these two factors, a substantial fraction of the male-female earnings differentials are apt to persist for the next 40 years, even if discrimination against women is eliminated.

Felice N. Schwartz

Management Women and the New Facts of Life

Felice N. Schwartz is president and founder of Catalyst, a not-for-profit research and advising organization that works with corporations to foster the career development of women. When she published her proposals and analyses in the Harvard Business Review *in 1989, the* Review *was deluged with responses, some of which are reprinted here after the article.*

The cost of employing women in management is greater 1 than the cost of employing men. This is a jarring statement, partly because it is true, but mostly because it is something people are reluctant to talk about. A new study by one multinational corporation shows that the rate of turnover in management positions is 2½ times higher among top-performing women than it is among men. A large producer of consumer goods reports that one-half of the women who take maternity leave return to their jobs late or not at all. And we know that women also have a greater tendency to plateau or to interrupt their careers in ways that limit their growth and development. But we have become so sensitive to charges of sexism and so afraid of confrontation, even litigation, that we rarely say what we know to be true. Unfortunately, our bottled-up awareness leaks out in misleading metaphors ("glass ceiling" is one notable example), veiled hostility, lowered expectations, distrust, and reluctant adherence to Equal Employment Opportunity requirements.

2   Career interruptions, plateauing, and turnover are expensive. The money corporations invest in recruitment, training, and development is less likely to produce top executives among women than among men, and the invaluable company experience that developing executives acquire at every level as they move up through management ranks is more often lost.

3   The studies just mentioned are only the first of many, I'm quite sure. Demographic realities are going to force corporations all across the country to analyze the cost of employing women in managerial positions, and what they will discover is that women cost more.

4   But here is another startling truth: The greater cost of employing women is not a function of inescapable gender differences. Women *are* different from men, but what increases their cost to the corporation is principally the clash of their perceptions, attitudes, and behavior with those of men, which is to say, with the policies and practices of male-led corporations.

5   It is terribly important that employers draw the right conclusions from the studies now being done. The studies will be useless—or worse, harmful—if all they teach us is that women are expensive to employ. What we need to learn is how to reduce that expense, how to stop throwing away the investments we make in talented women, how to become more responsive to the needs of the women that corporations *must* employ if they are to have the best and the brightest of all those now entering the work force.

6   The gender differences relevant to business fall into two categories: those related to maternity and those related to the differing traditions and expectations of the sexes. Maternity is biological rather than cultural. We can't alter it, but we can dramatically reduce its impact on the workplace and in many cases eliminate its negative effect on employee development. We can accomplish this by addressing the second set of differences, those between male and female socialization. Today, these differences exaggerate the real costs of maternity and can turn a relatively slight disruption in work schedule into a serious business problem and a career derailment for individual women. If we are to overcome the cost differential between male and female employees, we need to address the issues that arise when female socialization meets the male corporate culture and mas-

culine rules of career development—issues of behavior and style, of expectation, of stereotypes and preconceptions, of sexual tension and harassment, of female mentoring, lateral mobility, relocation, compensation, and early identification of top performers.

The one immutable, enduring difference between men   7
and women is maternity. Maternity is not simply childbirth but a continuum that begins with an awareness of the ticking of the biological clock, proceeds to the anticipation of motherhood, includes pregnancy, childbirth, physical recuperation, psychological adjustment, and continues on to nursing, bonding, and child rearing. Not all women choose to become mothers, of course, and among those who do, the process varies from case to case depending on the health of the mother and baby, the values of the parents, and the availability, cost, and quality of child care.

In past centuries, the biological fact of maternity shaped   8
the traditional roles of the sexes. Women performed the home-centered functions that related to the bearing and nurturing of children. Men did the work that required great physical strength. Over time, however, family size contracted, the community assumed greater responsibility for the care and education of children, packaged foods and household technology reduced the work load in the home, and technology eliminated much of the need for muscle power at the workplace. Today, in the developed world, the only role still uniquely gender related is childbearing. Yet men and women are still socialized to perform their traditional roles.

Men and women may or may not have some innate   9
psychological disposition toward these traditional roles— men to be aggressive, competitive, self-reliant, risk taking; women to be supportive, nurturing, intuitive, sensitive, communicative—but certainly both men and women are capable of the full range of behavior. Indeed, the male and female roles have already begun to expand and merge. In the decades ahead, as the socialization of boys and girls and the experience and expectations of young men and women grow steadily more androgynous, the differences in workplace behavior will continue to fade. At the moment, however, we are still plagued by disparities in perception and behavior that make the integration of men and women in the workplace unnecessarily difficult and expensive.

10   Let me illustrate with a few broadbrush generalizations. Of course, these are only stereotypes, but I think they help to exemplify the kinds of preconceptions that can muddy the corporate waters.

11   Men continue to perceive women as the rearers of their children, so they find it understandable, indeed appropriate, that women should renounce their careers to raise families. Edmund Pratt, CEO of Pfizer, once asked me in all sincerity, "Why would any woman choose to be a chief financial officer rather than a full-time mother?" By condoning and taking pleasure in women's traditional behavior, men reinforce it. Not only do they see parenting as fundamentally female, they see a career as fundamentally male–either an unbroken series of promotions and advancements toward CEOdom or stagnation and disappointment. This attitude serves to legitimize a woman's choice to extend maternity leave and even, for those who can afford it, to leave employment altogether for several years. By the same token, men who might want to take a leave after the birth of a child know that management will see such behavior as a lack of career commitment, even when company policy permits parental leave for men.

12   Women also bring counterproductive expectations and perceptions to the workplace. Ironically, although the feminist movement was an expression of women's quest for freedom from their home-based lives, most women were remarkably free already. They had many responsibilities, but they were autonomous and could be entrepreneurial in how and when they carried them out. And once their children grew up and left home, they were essentially free to do what they wanted with their lives. Women's traditional role also included freedom from responsibility for the financial support of their families. Many of us were socialized from girlhood to expect our husbands to take care of us, while our brothers were socialized from an equally early age to complete their educations, pursue careers, climb the ladder of success, and provide dependable financial support for their families. To the extent that this tradition of freedom lingers subliminally, women tend to bring to their employment a sense that they can choose to change jobs or careers at will, take time off, or reduce their hours.

13   Finally, women's traditional role encouraged particular attention to the quality and substance of what they did,

specifically to the physical, psychological, and intellectual development of their children. This traditional focus may explain women's continuing tendency to search for more than monetary reward—intrinsic significance, social importance, meaning—in what they do. This too makes them more likely than men to leave the corporation in search of other values.

The misleading metaphor of the glass ceiling suggests an 14 invisible barrier constructed by corporate leaders to impede the upward mobility of women beyond the middle levels. A more appropriate metaphor, I believe, is the kind of cross-sectional diagram used in geology. The barriers to women's leadership occur when potentially counterproductive layers of influence on women—maternity, tradition, socialization—meet management strata pervaded by the largely unconscious preconceptions, stereotypes, and expectations of men. Such interfaces do not exist for men and tend to be impermeable for women.

One result of these gender differences has been to con- 15 vince some executives that women are simply not suited to top management. Other executives feel helpless. If they see even a few of their valued female employees fail to return to work from maternity leave on schedule or see one of their most promising women plateau in her career after the birth of a child, they begin to fear there is nothing they can do to infuse women with new energy and enthusiasm and persuade them to stay. At the same time, they know there is nothing they can do to stem the tide of women into management ranks.

Another result is to place every working woman on a 16 continuum that runs from total dedication to career at one end to a balance between career and family at the other. What women discover is that the male corporate culture sees both extremes as unacceptable. Women who want the flexibility to balance their families and their careers are not adequately committed to the organization. Women who perform as aggressively and competitively as men are abrasive and unfeminine. But the fact is, business needs all the talented women it can get. Moreover, as I will explain, the women I call career-primary and those I call career-and-family each have particular value to the corporation.

Women in the corporation are about to move from a buy- 17 er's to a seller's market. The sudden, startling recognition that 80% of new entrants in the work force over the next decade will be women, minorities, and immigrants has stimulated a mushrooming incentive to "value diversity."

18   Women are no longer simply an enticing pool of occasional creative talent, a thorn in the side of the EEO officer, or a source of frustration to corporate leaders truly puzzled by the slowness of their upward trickle into executive positions. A real demographic change is taking place. The era of sudden population growth of the 1950s and 1960s is over. The birth rate has dropped about 40%, from a high of 25.3 live births per 1,000 population in 1957, at the peak of the baby boom, to a stable low of a little more than 15 per 1,000 over the last 16 years, and there is no indication of a return to a higher rate. The tidal wave of baby boomers that swelled the recruitment pool to overflowing seems to have been a one-time phenomenon. For 20 years, employers had the pick of a very large crop and were able to choose males almost exclusively for the executive track. But if future population remains fairly stable while the economy continues to expand, and if the new information society simultaneously creates a greater need for creative, educated managers, then the gap between supply and demand will grow dramatically and, with it, the competition for managerial talent.

19   The decrease in numbers has even greater implications if we look at the traditional source of corporate recruitment for leadership positions—white males from the top 10% of the country's best universities. Over the past decade, the increase in the number of women graduating from leading universities has been much greater than the increase in the total number of graduates, and these women are well represented in the top 10% of their classes.

20   The trend extends into business and professional programs as well. In the old days, virtually all MBAs were male. I remember addressing a meeting at the Harvard Business School as recently as the mid-1970s and looking out at a sea of exclusively male faces. Today, about 25% of that audience would be women. The pool of male MBAs from which corporations have traditionally drawn their leaders has shrunk significantly.

21   Of course, this reduction does not have to mean a shortage of talent. The top 10% is at least as smart as it always was—smarter, probably, since it's now drawn from a broader segment of the population. But it now consists

increasingly of women. Companies that are determined to recruit the same number of men as before will have to dig much deeper into the male pool, while their competitors will have the opportunity to pick the best people from both the male and female graduates.

Under these circumstances, there is no question that the management ranks of business will include increasing numbers of women. There remains, however, the question of how these women will succeed—how long they will stay, how high they will climb, how completely they will fulfill their promise and potential, and what kind of return the corporation will realize on its investment in their training and development.   22

There is ample business reason for finding ways to make sure that as many of these women as possible will succeed. The first step in this process is to recognize that women are not all alike. Like men, they are individuals with differing talents, priorities, and motivations. For the sake of simplicity, let me focus on the two women I referred to earlier, on what I call the career-primary woman and the career-and-family woman.   23

Like many men, some women put their careers first. They are ready to make the same trade-offs traditionally made by the men who seek leadership positions. They make a career decision to put in extra hours, to make sacrifices in their personal lives, to make the most of every opportunity for professional development. For women, of course, this decision also requires that they remain single or at least childless or, if they do have children, that they be satisfied to have others raise them. Some 90% of executive men but only 35% of executive women have children by the age of 40. The *automatic* association of all women with babies is clearly unjustified.   24

The secret to dealing with such women is to recognize them early, accept them, and clear artificial barriers from their path to the top. After all, the best of these women are among the best managerial talent you will ever see. And career-primary women have another important value to the company that men and other women lack. They can act as role models and mentors to younger women who put their careers first. Since upwardly mobile career-primary women still have few role models to motivate and inspire them, a company with women in its top echelon has   25 a significant advantage in the competition for executive talent.

26   Men at the top of the organization—most of them over 55, with wives who tend to be traditional—often find career women "masculine" and difficult to accept as colleagues. Such men miss the point, which is not that these women are just like men but that they are just like the *best* men in the organization. And there is such a shortage of the best people that gender cannot be allowed to matter. It is clearly counterproductive to disparage in a woman with executive talent the very qualities that are most critical to the business and that might carry a man to the CEO's office.

27   Clearing a path to the top for career-primary women has four requirements:

1. Identify them early.
2. Give them the same opportunity you give to talented men to grow and develop and contribute to company profitability. Give them client and customer responsibility. Expect them to travel and relocate, to make the same commitment to the company as men aspiring to leadership positions.
3. Accept them as valued members of your management team. Include them in every kind of communication. Listen to them.
4. Recognize that the business environment is more difficult and stressful for them than for their male peers. They are always a minority, often the only woman. The male perception of talented, ambitious women is at best ambivalent, a mixture of admiration, resentment, confusion, competitiveness, attraction, skepticism, anxiety, pride, and animosity. Women can never feel secure about how they should dress and act, whether they should speak out or grin and bear it when they encounter discrimination, stereotyping, sexual harassment, and paternalism. Social interaction and travel with male colleagues and with male clients can be charged. As they move up, the normal increase in pressure and responsibility is compounded for women because they are women.

28   Stereotypical language and sexist day-to-day behavior do take their toll on women's career development. Few

male executives realize how common it is to call women by their first names while men in the same group are greeted with surnames, how frequently female executives are assumed by men to be secretaries, how often women are excluded from all-male social events where business is being transacted. With notable exceptions, men are still generally more comfortable with other men, and as a result women miss many of the career and business opportunities that arise over lunch, on the golf course, or in the locker room.

The majority of women, however, are what I call career-and-family women, women who want to pursue serious careers while participating actively in the rearing of children. These women are a precious resource that has yet to be mined. Many of them are talented and creative. Most of them are willing to trade some career growth and compensation for freedom from the constant pressure to work long hours and weekends. 29

Most companies today are ambivalent at best about the career-and-family women in their management ranks. They would prefer that all employees were willing to give their all to the company. They believe it is in their best interests for all managers to compete for the top positions so the company will have the largest possible pool from which to draw its leaders. 30

"If you have both talent and motivation," many employers seem to say, "we want to move you up. If you haven't got that motivation, if you want less pressure and greater flexibility, then you can leave and make room for a new generation." These companies lose on two counts. First, they fail to amortize the investment they made in the early training and experience of management women who find themselves committed to family as well as to career. Second, they fail to recognize what these women could do for their middle management. 31

The ranks of middle managers are filled with people on their way up and people who have stalled. Many of them have simply reached their limits, achieved career growth commensurate with or exceeding their capabilities, and they cause problems because their performance is mediocre but they still want to move ahead. The career-and-family woman is willing to trade off the pressures and demands that go with promotion for the freedom to spend more time 32 with her children. She's very smart, she's talented, she's committed to her career, and she's satisfied to stay at the middle level, at least during the early child-rearing years. Compare her with some of the people you have there now.

33   Consider a typical example, a woman who decides in college on a business career and enters management at age 22. For nine years, the company invests in her career as she gains experience and skills and steadily improves her performance. But at 31, just as the investment begins to pay off in earnest, she decides to have a baby. Can the company afford to let her go home, take another job, or go into business for herself? The common perception now is yes, the corporation can afford to lose her unless, after six or eight weeks or even three months of disability and maternity leave, she returns to work on a full-time schedule with the same vigor, commitment, and ambition that she showed before.

34   But what if she doesn't? What if she wants or needs to go on leave for six months or a year or, heaven forbid, five years? In this worst-case scenario, she works full-time from age 22 to 31 and from 36 to 65—a total of 38 years as opposed to the typical male's 43 years. That's not a huge difference. Moreover, my typical example is willing to work part-time while her children are young, if only her employer will give her the opportunity. There are two rewards for companies responsive to this need: higher retention of their best people and greatly improved performance and satisfaction in their middle management.

35   The high-performing career-and-family woman can be a major player in your company. She can give you a significant business advantage as the competition for able people escalates. Sometimes too, if you can hold on to her, she will switch gears in mid-life and reenter the competition for the top. The price you must pay to retain these women is threefold: you must plan for and manage maternity, you must provide the flexibility that will allow them to be maximally productive, and you must take an active role in helping to make family supports and high-quality, affordable child care available to all women.

36   The key to managing maternity is to recognize the value of high-performing women and the urgent need to retain them and keep them productive. The first step must be a genuine partnership between the woman and her boss. I

know this partnership can seem difficult to forge. One of my own senior executives came to me recently to discuss plans for her maternity leave and subsequent return to work. She knew she wanted to come back. I wanted to make certain that she would. Still, we had a somewhat awkward conversation, because I knew that no woman can predict with certainty when she will be able to return to work or under what conditions. Physical problems can lengthen her leave. So can a demanding infant, a difficult family or personal adjustment, or problems with child care.

I still don't know when this valuable executive will be 37 back on the job full-time, and her absence creates some genuine problems for our organization. But I do know that I can't simply replace her years of experience with a new recruit. Since our conversation, I also know that she wants to come back, and that she *will* come back—part-time at first—unless I make it impossible for her by, for example, setting an arbitrary date for her full-time return or resignation. In turn, she knows that the organization wants and needs her and, more to the point, that it will be responsive to her needs in terms of working hours and child-care arrangements.

In having this kind of conversation it's important to ask 38 concrete questions that will help to move the discussion from uncertainty and anxiety to some level of predictability. Questions can touch on everything from family income and energy level to child care arrangements and career commitment. Of course you want your star manager to return to work as soon as possible, but you want her to return permanently and productively. Her downtime on the job is a drain on her energies and a waste of your money.

For all the women who want to combine career and fam- 39 ily—the women who want to participate actively in the rearing of their children and who also want to pursue their careers seriously—the key to retention is to provide the flexibility and family supports they need in order to function effectively.

Time spent in the office increases productivity if it is 40 time well spent, but the fact that most women continue to take the primary responsibility for child care is a cause of distraction, diversion, anxiety, and absenteeism—to say nothing of the persistent guilt experienced by all working mothers. A great many women, perhaps most of all women who have always performed at the highest levels, are also frustrated by a sense that while their children are babies they cannot function at their best either at home or at work.

41   In its simplest form, flexibility is the freedom to take time off—a couple of hours, a day, a week—or to do some work at home and some at the office, an arrangement that communication technology makes increasingly feasible. At the complex end of the spectrum are alternative work schedules that permit the woman to work less than full-time and her employer to reap the benefits of her experience and, with careful planning, the top level of her abilities.

42   Part-time employment is the single greatest inducement to getting women back on the job expeditiously and the provision women themselves most desire. A part-time return to work enables them to maintain responsibility for critical aspects of their jobs, keeps them in touch with the changes constantly occurring at the workplace and in the job itself, reduces stress and fatigue, often eliminates the need for paid maternity leave by permitting a return to the office as soon as disability leave is over, and, not least, can greatly enhance company loyalty. The part-time solution works particularly well when a work load can be reduced for one individual in a department or when a full-time job can be broken down by skill levels and apportioned to two individuals at different levels of skill and pay.

43   I believe, however, that shared employment is the most promising and will be the most widespread form of flexible scheduling in the future. It is feasible at every level of the corporation except at the pinnacle, for both the short and the long term. It involves two people taking responsibility for one job.

44   Two red lights flash on as soon as most executives hear the words "job sharing": continuity and client-customer contact. The answer to the continuity question is to place responsibility entirely on the two individuals sharing the job to discuss everything that transpires—thoroughly, daily, and on their own time. The answer to the problem of client-customer contact is yes, job sharing requires re-education and a period of adjustment. But as both client and supervisor will quickly come to appreciate, two contacts means that the customer has continuous access to the company's representative, without interruptions for vacation, travel, or sick leave. The two people holding the job can simply cover for each other, and the uninterrupted,

full-time coverage they provide together can be a stipulation of their arrangement.

Flexibility is costly in numerous ways. It requires more 45
supervisory time to coordinate and manage, more office
space, and somewhat greater benefits costs (though these
can be contained with flexible benefits plans, prorated
benefits, and, in two-paycheck families, elimination of duplicate benefits). But the advantages of reduced turnover
and the greater productivity that results from higher energy
levels and greater focus can outweigh the costs.

A few hints: 46

- Provide flexibility selectively. I'm not suggesting
  private arrangements subject to the suspicion of
  favoritism but rather a policy that makes flexible
  work schedules available only to high performers.
- Make it clear that in most instances (but not all) the
  rates of advancement and pay will be appropriately
  lower for those who take time off or who work part-
  time than for those who work full-time. Most career-
  and-family women are entirely willing to make that
  trade-off.
- Discuss costs as well as benefits. Be willing to risk
  accusations of bias. Insist, for example, that half
  time is half of whatever time it takes to do the job,
  not merely half of 35 or 40 hours.

The woman who is eager to get home to her child has a 47
powerful incentive to use her time effectively at the office
and to carry with her reading and other work that can be
done at home. The talented professional who wants to have
it all can be a high performer by carefully ordering her
priorities and by focusing on objectives rather than on the
legendary 15-hour day. By the time professional women
have their first babies — at an average age of 31 — they have
already had nine years to work long hours at a desk, to
travel, and to relocate. In the case of high performers, the
need for flexibility coincides with what has gradually become the goal-oriented nature of responsibility.

Family supports — in addition to maternity leave and flex- 48
ibility — include the provision of parental leave for men,
support for two-career and single-parent families during
relocation, and flexible benefits. But the primary ingredient

is child care. The capacity of working mothers to function effectively and without interruption depends on the availability of good, affordable child care. Now that women make up almost half the work force and the growing percentage of managers, the decision to become involved in the personal lives of employees is no longer a philosophical question but a practical one. To make matters worse, the quality of child care has almost no relation to technology, inventiveness, or profitability but is more or less a pure function of the quality of child care personnel and the ratio of adults to children. These costs are irreducible. Only by joining hands with government and the public sector can corporations hope to create the vast quantity and variety of child care that their employees need.

49   Until quite recently, the response of corporations to women has been largely symbolic and cosmetic, motivated in large part by the will to avoid litigation and legal penalties. In some cases, companies were also moved by a genuine sense of fairness and a vague discomfort and frustration at the absence of women above the middle of the corporate pyramid. The actions they took were mostly quick, easy, and highly visible — child care information services, a three-month parental leave available to men as well as women, a woman appointed to the board of directors.

50   When I first began to discuss these issues 26 years ago, I was sometimes able to get an appointment with the assistant to the assistant in personnel, but it was only a courtesy. Over the past decade, I have met with the CEOs of many large corporations, and I've watched them become involved with ideas they had never previously thought much about. Until recently, however, the shelf life of that enhanced awareness was always short. Given pressing, short-term concerns, women were not a front-burner issue. In the past few months, I have seen yet another change. Some CEOs and top management groups now take the initiative. They call and ask us to show them how to shift gears from a responsive to a proactive approach to recruiting, developing, and retaining women.

51   I think this change is more probably a response to business needs — to concern for the quality of future profits and managerial talent — than to uneasiness about legal requirements, sympathy with the demands of women and minorities, or the desire to do what is right and fair. The nature of such business motivation varies. Some companies

want to move women to higher positions as role models for those below them and as beacons for talented young recruits. Some want to achieve a favorable image with employees, customers, clients, and stockholders. These are all legitimate motives. But I think the companies that stand to gain most are motivated as well by a desire to capture competitive advantage in an era when talent and competence will be in increasingly short supply. These companies are now ready to stop being defensive about their experience with women and to ask incisive questions without preconceptions.

Even so, incredibly, I don't know of more than one or two companies that have looked into their own records to study the absolutely critical issue of maternity leave — how many women took it, when and whether they returned, and how this behavior correlated with their rank, tenure, age, and performance. The unique drawback to the employment of women is the physical reality of maternity and the particular socializing influence maternity has had. Yet to make women equal to men in the workplace we have chosen on the whole not to discuss this single most significant difference between them. Unless we do, we cannot evaluate the cost of recruiting, developing, and moving women up.

Now that interest is replacing indifference, there are four steps every company can take to examine its own experience with women:

1. Gather quantitative data on the company's experience with management-level women regarding turnover rates, occurrence of and return from maternity leave, and organizational level attained in relation to tenure and performance.
2. Correlate this data with factors such as age, marital status, and presence and age of children, and attempt to identify and analyze why women respond the way they do.
3. Gather qualitative data on the experience of women in your company and on how women are perceived by both sexes.
4. Conduct a cost-benefit analysis of the return on your investment in high-performing women. Factor in the cost to the company of women's negative reactions to negative experience, as well as the probable cost of corrective measures and policies. If women's

value to your company is greater than the cost to recruit, train, and develop them — and of course I believe it will be — then you will want to do everything you can to retain them.

54   We have come a tremendous distance since the days when the prevailing male wisdom saw women as lacking the kind of intelligence that would allow them to succeed in business. For decades, even women themselves have harbored an unspoken belief that they couldn't make it because they couldn't be just like men, and nothing else would do. But now that women have shown themselves the equal of men in every area of organizational activity, now that they have demonstrated that they can be stars in every field of endeavor, now we can all venture to examine the fact that women and men are different.

55   On balance, employing women is more costly than employing men. Women can acknowledge this fact today because they know that their value to employers exceeds the additional cost and because they know that changing attitudes can reduce the additional cost dramatically. Women in management are no longer an idiosyncrasy of the arts and education. They have always matched men in natural ability. Within a very few years, they will equal men in numbers as well in every area of economic activity.

56   The demographic motivation to recruit and develop women is compelling. But an older question remains: Is society better for the change? Women's exit from the home and entry into the work force has certainly created problems — an urgent need for good, affordable child care; troubling questions about the kind of parenting children need; the costs and difficulties of diversity in the workplace; the stress and fatigue of combining work and family responsibilities. Wouldn't we all be happier if we could turn back the clock to an age when men were in the workplace and women in the home, when male and female roles were clearly differentiated and complementary?

57   Nostalgia, anxiety, and discouragement will urge many to say yes, but my answer is emphatically no. Two fundamental benefits that were unattainable in the past are now within our reach. For the individual, freedom of choice — in this case the freedom to choose career, family, or a combination of the two. For the corporation, access to the most gifted individuals in the country. These benefits are neither self-indulgent nor insubstantial. Freedom of choice and self-

realization are too deeply American to be cast aside for some wistful vision of the past. And access to our most talented human resources is not a luxury in this age of explosive international competition but rather the barest minimum that prudence and national self-preservation require.

Letters to the Editor of Harvard Business Review

1   The scenarios described by Ms. Schwartz indicate that she based her conclusions on traditional companies where lifetime employment and linear career paths are the norm and where value to the company is measured by the management level achieved. But with the information age, a new kind of corporate environment is emerging, replacing the traditional industrial-age organization. These "third wave" companies are based on flexible structures that support a changing work force, market, and economy.

2   My company is an example of this new type of organization. We don't expect a lifetime commitment from our employees, but we have created an exciting, flexible environment that allows us to attract and retain the most talented individuals in the technology industry. We've done this by providing options—from job sharing to day care to sabbaticals. There are no "tracks" at Apple, only individual paths based on the choices our employees make in balancing career and personal needs. Some choose to emphasize their careers first, others, their families. But many choose *both*— and are successful in doing so.

3   Individuals at all levels in today's work force change jobs, and often careers, several times in their working lives. Many leave the work force part time or temporarily to pursue educational and training opportunities, to raise a child, or for any number of reasons. In this environment, Schwartz's recommended early identification of an individual's career path becomes not only impossible but also undesirable. It establishes barriers instead of providing the options people need.

4   The two-track approach does a disservice to all employees and forces both men and women into predefined roles that are inappropriate today. It is time for corporate America to respond to individual issues, not gender issues, and foster

the kind of environment that leads to satisfying careers *and* personal lives.

Deborah Biondolillo
Vice President
Human Resources
Apple Computer, Inc.
Cupertino, California

5   Felice Schwartz has attempted to answer the question CEOs often ask: What is the best way to retain and promote women? In her attempt to be concise, however, she is too simplistic. Men and women do continue to be socialized differently so that when women join a management culture populated predominantly by men, they must adapt in ways that are often alien to them. If women want to be part of the management ranks, and if the management ranks want to admit them, these differences must be identified and discussed openly. The new twist is that just as women are newly accepted into these ranks, they are raising families and asking for flexibility.

6   Well-intentioned work and family policies directed primarily at talented, high-potential women who ask for flexibility and child care assistance will fail unless certain biases are overcome. The most critical of these include:

1. *Women should be children's primary care givers, even if they work.* This assumes, for example, that mothers working a reduced schedule will be overstressed by unpredictable illnesses, home responsibilities, or guilt. Challenges, work responsibilities, or promotions are not offered to them while on this schedule, and so they lose valuable career momentum.
2. *Time spent at work equals dedication to career.* This assumes that a woman choosing to work half of her work week at home would not relocate or want a promotion to another position where this arrangement isn't possible. One problem is that coworkers don't make the effort to call her at home with critical information.
3. *Taking care of children is like a vacation.* You know this attitude has taken hold when a woman choosing to dedicate one-fourth of her workday to caring for her children hears comments like "Thanks for stopping by" or "I wish I could play on such a nice day" as she leaves the office.

4. *Family issues should not be in the workplace.* While work and family policies ostensibly say the opposite, this assumes that taking time to discuss child care center closings or babysitter illness have no place in the office.

5. *Schedule flexibility is only possible in "softer" jobs.* Many managers' first reaction is that schedule flexibility is not possible in *their* areas but only in "less important" positions. This bias could force women who work reduced hours into areas perceived as "soft," thereby creating a career plateau that they did not choose.

Schwartz's thesis is based on some of these biases. Calling 7 the freedom that women seek "counterproductive" promotes the very inflexibility she criticizes. She suggests that the decision to put career first also requires that women remain single, or at least childless; this would force career mothers to make a permanent choice that is illogical and unnecessary. And as much as I don't like the dichotomy she has created between career and family, I would like to meet the person who can accurately identify early in their careers those women who do not alter their priorities later when they have children. Furthermore, depicting career mothers as distracted, diverted, anxious, and absent only perpetuates the myth that they can't be successful at work during this period of their lives.

And finally, penalizing employees who work reduced 8 hours by advancing them more slowly is absolutely counter to anything I would do. While the first solutions are often schedule flexibility and child care assistance, the next solution will be advancement and challenge. Creating a slower track will surely create a new ghetto of female employees and will certainly not motivate them to stay in corporations.

Karen A. Geiger
Vice President and Director of
   Career Development
NCNB Corporation
Charlotte, North Carolina

This debate takes place in the context of two important 9 historical changes that question the assumptions underlying Felice Schwartz's argument. Schwartz assumes that women who sacrifice having children for their careers will make good managers; I question whether this is true of men or women.

10   The first change is in the nature of corporate work. Companies, especially those customizing products and services, seek ways to transform bureaucracy to increase quality, cut away layers of managerial control, and empower the front line of service employees, technicians, and professionals to solve customer problems. This type of "technoservice" requires a new kind of management, one more competent in both entrepreneurial strategy and human relationships. The most effective managers are not single-minded careerists willing to sacrifice family life to climb the corporate ladder. Though tough-minded, they temper their passion to win with an understanding heart. They are supportive and flexible. The driven managers who did so well in the past, be they men or women, are less adapted to the new competitive environment.

11   The second change is in values, in what people want from work. From my research, I have distinguished two types of values in the workplace. "Traditional" attitudes comprise traditional male values, focused on individual achievement and advancement up the hierarchy, and traditional female values, focused on helping others and gaining appreciation. "New generation" values, on the other hand, are shared by men and women and focus on gaining independence and opportunity for self-development. The new generation struggles to create a balanced life, sacrificing neither work nor family. This value shift is caused not by demographic changes like the "baby boom" or the "baby bust" but by changes in family structure and socialization. One-fifth of all managers, but one-third of those under age 30 and 40% of new college graduates, possess new-generation values. Their numbers will continue to increase with the growth of dual-career families.

12   While Schwartz's double track desegregates the values of women, it will not resolve the issues raised by these historic changes. Many traditional managers at the top believe that the new-generation employees are not as loyal or committed as they should be, even though their work results are better than traditional employees'. Some very competent young managers do not aspire to top positions because they do not feel comfortable with their superiors. Instead of promotions, they seek lateral transfers that prepare them to start or join entrepreneurial businesses.

13   In this age of customized products and services, managers

will also have to customize work arrangements with valued employees, providing, for instance, flexible schedules for new-generation team players. Some new-generation mothers will be satisfied to take limited technical, professional, or managerial roles. Some will let their husbands pursue the major career. Others will be the dominant careerists, while their husbands share a large part of the parenting. And still others will return from mothering to reach for the top. Business should not prejudge or categorize a woman by her attitude toward mothering but rather by her ambition, talent, and ability to balance values.

Michael Maccoby
Director
Project on Technology,
   Work and Character
Washington, D.C.

Much of the comment on Felice Schwartz's recent article 14 seems to be written by people who have not read the essay carefully. They seize on the aspects of her argument that can be taken negatively and ignore the importance of her subject.

The negative reaction undoubtedly comes from the blanket statement that women managers cost their employers 15 more than men do. The natural response is, "What men and in what market conditions?" I know that colleges and universities experience a high turnover rate with their talented women faculty because they are at a premium in the employment market, always being bought away by higher bidders competing for a small pool of talent. This turnover is not a function of their femaleness but of their market position. So it is with many talented corporate women. In a hot market for male employees, such turnover would be viewed philosophically, but with women, it's blamed on "lack of commitment."

Moreover, what costs are calculated in the comparative 16 return on investment among male and female managers? How about the higher rates of heart attacks for men? Or the higher incidence of alcoholism for men? Employers see costs associated with maternity negatively; however, they give time to men to perform community service, develop political savvy, or gain exposure to broader social and cultural concerns and see this as an investment.

Schwartz's division of women into career-primary and 17 career-and-family women is resented because it implies that women with children are deficient in work motivation in ways that men are not and never can be. Such a view overlooks the frequency with which personnel committees hear about reduced performance in men because of divorce, critically ill children, spouses' health problems, and other family matters. Schwartz's formulation may need correction, but it at least raises an issue corporate America needs to think about more. At MIT, a faculty-administration committee is studying how all categories of employees might better combine work and family responsibilities.

18   Schwartz is absolutely right that demography compels attention to women's participation in society above all other factors. The loss of life experienced in Western Europe during two world wars means that there are family and maternal support policies in place in European countries that are totally lacking in the United States. Certainly, the author is correct in pointing out that although women have been encouraged to enter the ranks of management and the professions in large numbers since the 1960s, there has been no corresponding tendency for employers to respond to working women's need for quality day care or to recognize maternity leave as a woman's right rather than an ambiguous threat to her future.

19   As for the glass ceiling, which Schwartz mentions as a misleading metaphor, it is real and clearly observable in many otherwise progressive organizations. It exists because few senior managers are willing to see talented women as real colleagues, although concerns for equity make it easy to impose affirmative action at the middle management level. The author is right to assert that demography will likely compel a change in these attitudes in the 1990s and beyond. Such male bastions as Harvard and Yale quickly welcomed women students when demography required them to, though they have been slow in extending a similar welcome to women faculty.

Jill Conway
President Emerita, Smith College
Visiting Scholar and Professor
Massachusetts Institute of Technology
Cambridge, Massachusetts

20   My husband brought home Felice Schwartz's article for me to read, shaking his head and clucking over the "woman problem," which he said was well treated in the piece.

Schwartz says that women managers cost a little more, but they are worth it. Strangely, this sounds very much like a television commercial for a cosmetic product.

As a mother and former manager, I had two thoughts 21 after reading the article. First, because mothering and managing are so different, I wonder how anyone can combine the two; second, I do not think American business is ready for special parenting-emphasis programs.

Managing is rhythm and control, and when it goes well, 22 there is no feeling like it in the world. But parenting is letting go; it feels more like endlessly trying to push marbles uphill with your nose. When it goes well, it too feels like nothing else in the world. But between parenting and managing there is such a chasm that it is no wonder that many women stop trying to do both and either delegate responsibility for the children to someone else or quit management.

They quit work to get down in the trenches, investing 23 time in their children to ensure that they become productive parts of the future. Endless wars on everything an ad executive can think of are fought daily by mothers — full-time, part-time, managerial, clerical, blue-collar, pink-collar — mothers who, Schwartz tells us, cost more than men to employ.

Schwartz buys into the very mentality that makes enjoy- 24 ing both work and family relationships so difficult: thinking about work as zero-sum competition and approaching it with blind, single-purpose dedication. What service does Schwartz do her avowed cause of creating opportunities for women by embracing this paradigm as the one to govern approaches to the "problem" of mother-managers? There are so many other ways of thinking about the situation. For example, we could look at mothers who interrupt their careers as soldiers performing national service, deserving commendation from the federal department of "mothering affairs" when they return from the "front."

Schwartz is writing to an audience who she assumes is 25 ready to value women managers realistically and fearlessly. I am not convinced by her limited support for this premise. Advocating the segmentation of women managers only serves to make women work harder than ever to be allowed a chance at a rewarding job and to drum up business for Schwartz.

Janet L. Lowden
Mama
The Lowden Family
Scottsdale, Arizona

Susan Dudash

We've Come a Long Way, But Magazines Stayed Behind

Susan Dudash (born 1968) grew up in Telford, Pennsylvania, near Philadelphia; a French major at Penn State, she is considering a career in law, teaching, or pharmacy. This essay (in a slightly different form) appeared in 1989 in The Daily Collegian, *the Penn State student newspaper.*

1   When well-known newscaster Christine Craft lost her job several years ago, many people assumed that she simply was not performing her job effectively. Instead, according to my sociology professor, Dr. Mari Molseed, Craft was fired because her employers found her to be "Too old and unattractive. . . . [Also, she] didn't show enough deference towards men." In an age where a woman sits on the Supreme Court and women may vote, this certainly seems ridiculous. However, this example shows the media's important role in maintaining the status quo as well as in informing the public. The information that we recieve from our media can be especially misleading when they purport to be conveying a different image about women.

2   One media form, working women's magazines, generally presents an image of women as incompetent; its traditional view mars the chance for the status quo perceptions of women to change. Magazines such as *Cosmopolitan, Working Woman, Mademoiselle, Glamour* — even *Ms.* — claim to be up to date, yet still portray women as incompetent in regard to appearance, work and knowledge.

3   The magazines portray women as appearance oriented, which isn't in itself a problem, but the extent to which this image is presented may be. Articles and advertisements deal with clothes, hair, make-up — not business success or how to play the stock market. In three consecutive issues of *Glamour* I found a grand total of four articles that dealt specifically with women's occupations. "Should You Quit Your Job If You're Not Getting Respect?" turned out to be a survey, simply stating the dissatisfaction of women with their superiors, though the author *did* demonstrate that women shouldn't have to put up with disrespect or degradation. Another of these, "Is That Just-Right Job Really All

Wrong?" was a disappointing and patronizing list of do's and don'ts. This particular article gives good hints on what to watch out for in choosing a new occupation, but by the same token, these bits of advice should be common sense. The article tells the reader to beware of jobs whose employees say the company is a bad place to work, or to watch out for companies with high turnover, little financial security and 'nonexistent or vague' job descriptions. The third article, "Managing Your Money in the 90's: Which Old Rules Still Apply? Which Don't?", gave some useful information for those not up to date on expectations for the economy in the 1990's. This is to their credit. However, most women in the business field have probably had an elementary economics course, which makes some of the article's suggestions seem obvious. For example, of course it is better to buy a new car on credit when interest rates are lower in lieu of paying cash or even renting. In sum, even though these articles do deal with the job market, their advice tends to be either common sense or persuades the reader to change occupations.

This may be more apparent with our next example. The 4 final article deals with 'computeritis', a disease the article suggests is primarily caused by the repetitive motion of typing on a keyboard without enough little 'breaks'. Here, the article fails to follow up on the second cause of this disease: namely, thoracic outlet syndrome, a *hereditary* and easily treatable disorder. Here, the emphasis is on the work as a main cause of numb or tingly hands, not on the other causes. The article suggests that the 'inflicted' worker take more breaks, hence work less.

In addition to these articles, I've found only one out of 5 approximately fifty articles had anything to say about the woman and her job. In these same three issues, I also noted a total of three articles on the *work wardrobe*. This is not to say that there weren't countless articles on fashion, methods of seduction, and sex-related issues. These articles, along with those concerning make-up, or parties, constitute the remainder of the approximately fifty articles per issue.

The articles and advertisements in magazines for working 6 women show perfect and unattainable images of women. Most of us don't realize the models themselves don't look this good; trick photography, silk screening, and expert make-up application present the image desired by these magazines.

7   These images lead women to believe their success lies not in their knowledge, but in their appearance. For example, a Nivea Skin Cream advertisement proclaims, "Is Your Face Paying the Price of Success?" A Forever Krystle cologne ad states, "CREATE YOUR OWN DYNASTY"; the accompanying photo shows a woman, arms wrapped around her man as he's dressing for work, a hard day at the office. A Pantene shampoo ad tells you to "Risk everything except your hair." Showing the paramount importance of the perfect appearance, a woman's face dominates the ad — a face devoid of any possible fault of complexion or hair. After skillfully applied make-up, and photo retouching, the woman is nearly perfect. Another ad for cologne, this time from Coty, tells us that we can "Make A Statement Without Saying A Word," and the beautiful flawless woman in the ad reinforces the fact; diligence or competence aren't required here.

8   According to these magazines, success depends on women's appearance, and their accomplishments are secondary. Women may work, state these magazines; however, the importance of their occupations is overshadowed by numerous articles dealing with non-occupational topics and ads. Out of about fifty features in a typical issue of *Cosmopolitan*, I found four articles that were occupation-oriented; one of these even dealt with purchasing real estate. *Cosmo* scored better than most magazines of its type in this category. In place of sound advice for the working woman, this issue chose to emphasize such things as "Living with a Difficult Man," "Women Who Attract Men (And Women Who Don't)," "How Much Sex Is *Enough*?" "Beauty Bar: What a Great Smile You've Got!" The list goes on and on, and these are only the articles dealing with men. The food and decorating section boasts a feature on "Bad Girl Beds," while other sections emphasize health, the importance of staying soft, smooth, young and physically fit. The Beauty and Health Report in October's issue of *Glamour* tells its women readers to "Exercise your breasts." In November's issue, *Glamour* urges women to "Stop obsessing about your thighs, hair, breasts." I'm not making this up. These magazines are sending out conflicting signals, in addition to placing their emphasis on image and appearance.

9   You can take the analysis further by looking at the advertisements yourself. In a particular issue of *Cosmopolitan* (November, 1989) at least 45 ads dealt with skincare, hair-

care, and make-up; 35 ads dealt with cologne; and 19 sold clothing. Also prevalent were cigarette and alcohol advertisements. Nothing occupationally oriented whatsoever was to be found. True, in some ads women were wearing work clothes; but it just so happens that none of the ads mention the workplace. The underlying message is the improvement of a woman's appearance—her skin and hair must look young, healthy; her scent must be attractive, if not seductive.

Advertisements abound demonstrating this point—   10
women are imperfect, but need to be perfect to succeed. Advertisements such as for Episage Ultra (THE CELLU-LITE SOLUTION), or Clairol haircolor (Whether you want to be noticed a little or a lot, the Clairol Highlighting Collection is who you really are), are prime examples. Countless ads for make-up—L'Oreal, Clinique, Estee Lauder, CoverGirl, Max Factor, Almay—all show models with flawless skin and hair, telling us that they use a particular brand of make-up and look so refined. Women just aren't good enough as they are.

The magazines imply that working women must accept   11
double duty—as employees in the workplace and in the traditional roles as mother and housewife. Nona Glazer, an authority in the field of women's studies and a writer for *Women's Studies International Quarterly*, put it this way: from "... cooking ahead... supervising children's homework and spending quality time with them ... relaxing with one's husband, studying to improve oneself for the job," women are expected to retain their traditional homemaker roles in addition to their new jobs.

Advice and articles in women's magazines therefore range   12
from advice for quick one-pot meals to the proper dress-for-success attire. After work, women have to deal with decisions about whether 15-second make-up applications are better than the 12-hour process. A Coors ad states, "Our Women's Work Is Never Done." The tone of some magazines suggests that success comes with sexuality.

Even when these magazines deal specifically with the   13
idea that women work a "double" shift, they usually only address the situation and expect the reader to accept it. Not surprisingly, studies conducted within the last decade show that women are becoming more discontented with their situations in general. Women are expected to perform a double-duty job, yet the magazines often consider them so

incompetent. How are they to perform these duties at all? These magazines consistently show an attitude of patronization. Typical articles give advice such as : "How to Enjoy the Superbowl — Whether You Like It or Not" or "Meeting His Mother: A Survival Guide," or "Create a New You — the Plastic Surgery Primer."

14   The available working women's magazines fail to give women enough suggestions for future success, other than that related to a man. The available magazines take the general attitude that women are incompetent in respect to their appearance and work. Looking at women in this way negates their importance in society. And, the effects of the ideals behind these magazines are all the more powerful because of their subtlety.

15   If these modern working women's magazines are sending out conflicting messages, you can only wonder what the rest of the media are doing. Are women's stereotypes really changing? If so, then why are women in occupations traditionally held by men switching out of these jobs only a few years after entrance? Why are women's *firsts* emphasized (first woman to run for vice president, first woman astronaut)? Even in an issue of *Ms*, only 15% of the articles dealt specifically with women and work; about half of these addressed the problems or obstacles that women are facing on the job. Are things really changing?

16   It is not merely enough to be aware of this misleading perception of women held by the magazines; we must demonstrate the need for more concrete changes to give women the place in society that, according to these magazines, is already theirs.

IV.

MEDIA

Among the revolutions of the twentieth century has been a revolution in communications. Print media—books, newspapers, periodicals, even personal correspondence—dominated public consciousness a century ago, but since then telephones, radio, recordings, films, television, and even computer networks have joined the ranks of public media to great effect. Books and newspapers and magazines and letters have not been supplanted; indeed, they are more prevalent now than ever before. But the new media have given Americans broader and faster and sometimes more dramatic access to information than in the past and additional opportunities for enjoyment and artistic expression, as well.

This does not mean that the new media have been accepted uncritically. Ever since television arrived as a form of mass media forty years ago—in 1950 only 9 percent of U.S. households contained a television; by 1955, 50 percent did—people have worried about its effect on the natural psyche. This worry derives in part from a puritanical distrust of things pleasurable and in part from a traditional national distrust of things technological, but it also derives from an honest concern over the seductive power of TV over the popular imagination. Is television programming "a vast wasteland" (to use a popular formulation)? Do soap operas and sitcoms anesthetize people more than entertain them? Does television make viewers passive observers rather than active inquirers? Does it affect our sense of community? Does it make us into a nation of strangers, a nation of couch potatoes nesting in front of televisions and VCRs? Does violence on television affect our children and ultimately beget the violence in our society? Does the advertising on television propagate destructive stereotypes and promulgate a national cynicism about honesty in general and the honesty of American business in particular? Is television news inevitably biased? Does it deliberately seek out the visual and dramatic as opposed to the truly newsworthy? Does it shape events as much as report them? And if television does have any vices, what, in a world with the First Amendment, can be done about it? Those are some of the questions addressed by the first group of eight readings in this part.

The second set of four essays takes up another specific fear about television: its possible effects on democracy. Does television change our national institutions and compromise access to public office? Do the people who control the airwaves control the electorate? If so, what can be done about it? Furthermore, does television change our sense of what it means to govern? Does it change our attitudes towards our leaders? Ever since John Kennedy debated Richard Nixon on television in 1960 people have worried about the effects of television on the electorate, and the perceived success of Ronald Reagan — the former actor who seemed at ease in front of a camera as no place else — has not made that worry diminish. The essays included in the section on Television and the Elections offer historical and critical perspective on these questions; they offer food for your own thoughts — and your own prose — as the next national election campaign heats up.

But "media" means more than television, and does more than create successful politicians. It creates popular heroes and myths as well, especially through the specific medium of pop music. The next section of this part examines one such figure: Bruce Springsteen. By reading five articles and a work of fiction, you will listen in on a fifteen-year-old conversation on Springsteen, an ongoing conversation that has transformed him into a cultural artifact. The analyses together tell us plenty about Springsteen, plenty about contemporary American culture, and, since writers sometimes have a tendency to make over cultural artifacts in their own images, plenty about the authors as well. As you read, consider how the audience for each analysis — readers of *Time* and *Rolling Stone*, *Esquire*, and *McCall's* — colors each analysis itself. Consider the accuracy of each analysis. And consider the articles as prototypes for your own further meditations on Springsteen or for your own analyses of other cultural artifacts.

The part concludes by considering another twentieth-century medium: film. The three short articles focus on the issue of quality, since judgments about the relative merits of various films frequently occupy the time and the passions of average citizens. What makes a movie "good" or not so good? What are the grounds for aesthetic evaluation? Those questions are made concrete in the three movie reviews printed here, of the popular film *Born on the Fourth of July*. The three reviewers differ markedly in their assessment of the film's merits: How do you account for the differences? On what criteria do the reviewers base their judgments? Are certain important criteria ignored? These readings are likely to sharpen your responses to *Born on the Fourth of July* and your own arguments on the merits of other films (and plays and television shows) that engage your imagination.

WHAT ARE THE EFFECTS
OF TELEVISION?

Edith Efron
The Soaps—Anything But 99-44/100
Percent Pure

*Edith Efron has worked as a reporter and editor for many
magazines, including* Time, Look, *and* Life. *The author of
several books, she was serving as a staff writer for* TV Guide
when she wrote the following piece in 1965.

1   Some months ago, the sleepy, Victorian world of daytime
drama made news. The news was that it had ceased to be
sleepy and Victorian. In fact, said the reports, the soap
operas were doing something no one could quite believe:
"peddling sex."

2   Announced one astounded critic: "Folks squawking about
cheap nighttime sex should harken to the sickly sexuality
of daytime soap opera. *Love of Life* details frank affairs
between married women and men; *Search for Tomorrow*
has a single girl in an affair with a married man, result:
pregnancy; *The Secret Storm* has another single girl expecting a married man's child."

3   And, under the headlines "Era of Souped-Up Soapers"
and "Torrid Days on TV Serial Front," *Variety,* the weekly
newspaper of the entertainment industry, reported that
there was a daytime "race to dredge up the most lurid
incidents in sex-based human wretchedness," and cited "a
torrid couch scene involving a housewife with gown cleaved
to the navel who was sloshed to the gills on martinis, working her wiles on a husband (not hers). The fade to detergent
blurb left little doubt as to the ensuing action."

4   Even a superficial investigation of events in the soap-
opera world confirms that these reports are true.

5   To understand this phenomenon, one must enter the total
universe of the soap operas. And if one does, one soon discovers that the central source of drama is not what it used

384

to be in the old days, when the brave housewife, with husband in wheel chair, struggled helplessly against adversity. The soaps have shifted drastically on their axes; the fundamental theme today is, as Roy Winsor, producer of *Secret Storm*, puts it: "the male-female relationship."

More specifically, the theme of nine of the 10 daytime shows on the air when this study was launched is the mating-marital-reproductive cycle set against a domestic background. The outer world is certainly present — one catches glimpses of hospitals, offices, courtrooms, business establishments — but the external events tend to be a foil for the more fundamental drama, which is rooted in the biological life cycle. Almost all dramatic tension and moral conflict emerge from three basic sources: mating, marriage and babies. 6

The mating process is the cornerstone of this trivalue system. The act of searching for a partner goes on constantly in the world of soap opera. Vacuous teen-age girls have no thought whatever in their heads except hunting for a man. Older women wander about, projecting their intense longing to link themselves to unattached males. Heavily made-up villainous "career women" prowl, relentlessly seeking and nabbing their prey: the married man. Sad, lonely divorcées hunt for new mates. 7

This all-consuming, single-minded search for a mate is an absolute good in the soap-opera syndrome. Morality — and dramatic conflict — emerge from how the search is conducted. Accordingly, there is sex as approached by "good" people, and sex as it is approached by villains. 8

"Good" people's sex is a somewhat extraordinary phenomenon, which can best be described as "icky." In *The Doctors*, Dr. Maggie confides, coyly, to her sister: "He kissed me." Her sister asks, even more coyly: "Did you want him to kiss you?" Maggie wriggles and says: "He says I did." Then archly adds: "You know? I did." Maggie has already been married; her sister has had at least one lover. Coyness, not chastity, is the sign of their virtue. 9

"Good" people's sex is also passive, diffident and apologetic. In *The Doctors*, Sam, after an unendurably long build-up, finally takes Dr. Althea, a troubled divorcée, in his arms, and kisses her once, gently, on the lips. He then looks rueful, says, "I'm sorry," and moves to look mournfully out the window. "I'm not," murmurs Althea softly, and floats out of the room. 10

The "good" people act like saddened goldfish; the villains, 11 on the other hand, are merely grotesque. One gets the impression that villains, both male and female, have read a lot of Ian Fleming, through several layers of cheesecloth.

12   To wit: a dinner between villainess Valerie Shaw and Dr. Matt in *The Doctors* in which Valerie leers, ogles and hints ("A smart woman judges a man by his mouth. . . . Yours is strong and sensual. I'm glad I came to dinner"), announces she will be his "playmate" and boasts throatily, "I play hard and seriously—but not necessarily for keeps."

13   And in *Love of Life* a sinister chap named Ace drinks in a bar with a teen-age girl who used to be his mistress. "We used to ignite," he breathes insinuatingly. They exchange a kiss—presumably so inflammable that the camera nervously cuts the picture off beneath their chins. "Not bad, baby," he gasps heavily.

14   This endless mating game, of course, has a purpose: It leads to marriage, the second arch-value in the soap-opera universe. And the dominant view of marriage in the soaps is also worthy of mention. According to the "good" women, it consists of two ingredients: "love" and homemaking.

15   "Love," in the soaps, tends to be a kind of hospitalization insurance, usually provided by females to male emotional cripples. In these plays, a woman rarely pledges herself to "honor and obey" her husband. She pledges to cure him of his alcoholism, to forgive his criminal record, paranoia, pathological lying, premarital affairs—and, generally, to give him a shoulder to cry on.

16   An expression of love, or a marriage proposal, in the daytime shows, often sounds like a sobbing confession to a psychiatrist. In *Search for Tomorrow* Patti's father, a reformed drinker, took time out from brooding over his daughter's illegitimate pregnancy to express his "love" for his wife. It consisted of a thorough—and convincing—rehash of his general worthlessness and former drinking habits, "I need you," he moaned. "That's all I want," she said.

17   In *General Hospital* Connie's neurotic helplessness proved irresistible some weeks ago; Dr. Doug declared his love. They engaged in a weird verbal competition as to who was more helpless than whom, who was more scared than whom, who "needed" whom more than whom. Doug won. Connie would be his pillar of strength.

18   Homemaking, the second ingredient of a "good" woman's marriage, is actually a symbolic expression of "love." There is a fantastic amount of discussion of food on these shows, and it is all strangely full of marital meaning. On *The Guid-*

ing Light the audience sat through a detailed preview of the plans for roasting a turkey (the stuffing has raisins in it), which somehow would help get separated Julie and Michael together again. On *The Doctors* one ham was cooked, eaten and remorselessly discussed for three days; it played a critical role in the romance of Sam and Dr. Althea.

If domesticity is a marital "good," aversion to it is a serious evil. On *Secret Storm* a husband's arrival from work was greeted by a violent outburst by his wife, who handed him a list of jobs he had not done around the house. His neglect of the curtain rod was a sure sign that he was in love with a temptress who works in his office. Conversely, if a wife neglects her house, the marriage is rocky.   19

After mating and marriage, the third crucial value in the soap-opera universe is reproduction. The perpetuation of the species is the ultimate goal toward which almost all "good" people strive. And "The Baby" is the household god.   20

"Good" people discuss pregnancy endlessly. Young wives are either longing to be pregnant, worried because they are not pregnant, getting pregnant or fighting heroically "not to lose the baby." And at whatever stage of this process they happen to be, it justifies their being inept, irritable, hysterical and irrational.   21

"Good" men, needless to say, are unfailingly sympathetic to the reproductive process and are apparently fascinated by every detail of it. In *The Doctors* you knew one chap was a "good" husband because he referred to himself as "an expectant father" and earnestly discussed his wife's "whoopsing" with his friends.   22

The superlative value of "The Baby" is best revealed when he makes his appearance without benefit of a marriage license. He is usually brought into the world by a blank-faced little girl who has been taught to believe that the only valid goal in life is to mate, marry and reproduce, and who has jumped the gun. The social problem caused by this error in timing is solved in different ways. The girl has an abortion (Patricia, *Another World*); she loses the baby in an accident (Patti, *Search for Tomorrow*); she gives the baby up for adoption (Ellen, *As the World Turns*); she has the baby and marries its father (Julie, *Guiding Light*); she has the baby and marries someone else (Amy, *Secret Storm*).   23

The attitude of the baby-worshipping "good" people to this omnipresent social catastrophe is strangely mixed. The girl is viewed as a helpless victim of male villainy: "She   24 loved the fellow too much," said Angie's father sadly in *General Hospital.* Of course, she has acquired the baby "the wrong way" and must — and does — suffer endlessly because of it. Nonetheless, she is having "The Baby." Thus she receives an enormous amount of sympathy, guidance and help from "good" people.

25   It seems almost unnecessary to say that only "bad" people in soap operas are anti-baby. The fastest bit of characterization ever accomplished in the history of drama was achieved on *Secret Storm,* when Kip's father recently arrived on the scene. He said: "I can't stand all this talk about babies." This instantly established him as a black-hearted villain.

26   The worst people of all, in the soaps, however, are the "career women," unnatural creatures who actually enjoy some activity other than reproducing the species. With the single exception of *The Doctors,* which features two "good" career women, Drs. Maggie and Althea, even the feeblest flicker of a desire for a career is a symptom of villainy in a woman who has a man to support her. Some weeks ago, we could predict that Ann Reynolds, in *The Young Marrieds,* was heading for dire trouble. She was miserable over her lost career, she had no babies, and she said those most evil of words: "I want a purpose in life."

27   It is hardly surprising to discover that even when the female characters achieve their stated ideal, they are almost invariably miserable. A man to support them, an empty house to sit in, no mentally demanding work to do and an endless vista of future pregnancies do not seem to satisfy the younger soap-opera ladies. They are chronically bored and hysterical.

28   They also live in dread of the ever-present threat of adultery, because their husbands go outside every day and meet wicked career women. They also agonize frequently over the clash between their "needs as a woman" and their "needs as a mother."

29   The male denizens of this universe are equally miserable for parallel reasons. They suffer quite a bit from unrequited love. They are often sick with jealousy, tortured by their wives' jealousy of their careers and outer-world existence. They, too, have a remarkable amount of trouble reconciling their "needs as men" with their "needs as fathers."

30   So we find, amid all the gloom in Sudsville, a lot of drinking, epidemic infidelity, and countless cases of acute

neurosis, criminality, psychotic breakdowns and post-maternal psychosis.

And this, dear reader, is the "sex" that the soap operas   31
are "peddling" these days. It is a soggy, dreary spectacle of
human misery, and is unworthy of all those "torrid" headlines. In fact, if one wants to be soured forever on the male-female relationship, the fastest way to achieve this state is
to watch daytime drama.

The real question is not "where did all the sex come   32
from?" but where did this depressing view of the male-female relationship come from? Hardened observers of TV's
manners and mores have claimed that sex is being stressed
in the soaps because it "sells." But the producers of soaps
retort hotly that this has nothing to do with it. Their story
lines, they insist, simply reflect social reality.

Says Frank Dodge, producer of *Search for Tomorrow:* "We   33
always try to do shows that are identifiable to the public.
These shows are a recognition of existing emotions and
problems. It's not collusion, but a logical coincidence that
adultery, illegitimate children and abortions are appearing
on many shows. If you read the papers about what's going
on in the suburbs — well, it's more startling than what's
shown on the air."

"The moral fiber has been shattered in this nation, and   34
nothing has replaced it," says Roy Winsor, producer of *Secret Storm.* "There's a clammy cynicism about life in general. It deeply infects the young. It leads to a generation
that sits, passively, and watches the world go by. The major
interest is the male-female relationship. That's the direction
the daytime shows are going in. Some of the contemporary
sickness has rubbed off onto TV."

A consultation with some authorities on feminine and   35
family psychology seems to support these gentlemen's contentions about the soap operas. "They're realistic," says Dr.
Harold Greenwald, training analyst of the National Psychological Association for Psychoanalysis and supervising
psychologist of the Community Guidance Service in New
York. "I think they're more realistic than many of the evening shows. They're reflecting the changes taking place in
our society. There are fewer taboos. The age of sexual activity in the middle classes has dropped and it has increased
in frequency. There is more infidelity. These plays reflect
these problems."

Dr. William Menaker, professor of clinical psychology at   36

New York University, says: "The theater, the novel, and the film have always reflected people's concern with the sexual life; and in this sense, what's on the air reflects these realities of life. Increasing frankness in dealing with these problems isn't a symptom of moral decay but rather reflects the confused values of a transitional period of sociosexual change.

37   "Unfortunately, the vision of sex that seems to emerge on these shows is mechanical and adolescent, immature. The 'love' seems equally childish; it is interacting dependency, rather than a mutual relating between two autonomous adults. As for the anti-intellectualism of these shows, it is actually antifeminine. It shows the resistance of both writers and audience to the development of the total feminine personality. There is no doubt that these shows are a partial reflection of some existing trends in our society; it is not a healthy picture."

38   Finally, Betty Friedan, author of *The Feminine Mystique,* says: "The image of woman that emerges in these soap operas is precisely what I've called 'The Feminine Mystique.' The women are childish and dependent; the men are degraded because they relate to women who are childish and dependent; and the view of sex that emerges is sick. These plays reflect an image built up out of the sickest, most dependent, most immature women in our society. They do not reflect all women. In reality there are many who are independent, mature, and who possess identity. The soaps are reflecting the sickest aspect of women."

39   On the basis of these comments, one can certainly conclude that all this "sex-based human wretchedness" is on the air because it exists in society. And the producers' claims that this is dramatic "realism" appear to have some validity.

40   But does the fact that a phenomenon exists justify its incessant exploration by the daytime dramas? Two of the three experts consulted actively refrain from making moral judgments. Betty Friedan, however, does not hesitate to condemn the soap operas. "The fact that immature, sick, dependent women exist in our society is no justification for these plays," she says. "The soap operas are playing to this sickness. They are feeding it. They are helping to keep women in this helpless, dependent state."

The Committee on the Judiciary, U.S. House of Representatives
Television Violence Act of 1989

A "Television Violence Act" was proposed by Congress in 1989. After hearings, the Judiciary Committee submitted the following report, together with dissenting views. (The report has been edited very slightly for increased readability.)

The Committee on the Judiciary, to whom was referred 1
the bill (H.R. 1391) to exempt from the antitrust laws certain activities relating to alleviating the negative impact of violence in telecast material, having considered the same, report favorably thereon with an amendment and recommend that the bill as amended do pass.

I. Purpose of H.R. 1391

H.R. 1391 is a response to concerns about the negative 2
impact of violence on television. The purpose of H.R. 1391 is to remove a possible impediment — the antitrust laws — for a limited time should persons in the television industry voluntarily wish to meet and adopt voluntary guidelines in this area. The bill is not meant to coerce any conduct or action whatsoever. Whether or not persons wish to meet as permitted by the bill, or whether or not they wish to develop or abide by guidelines, is entirely voluntary.

II. Procedural Background of H.R. 1391

On March 14, 1989, Congressmen Dan Glickman and Ed- 3
ward Feighan introduced H.R. 1391, legislation to grant a 3-year antitrust exemption to permit persons in the television industry to engage in certain joint voluntary action to develop and disseminate voluntary guidelines designed to alleviate the negative impact of violence in telecast material.

On May 10, 1989, the Subcommittee on Economic and 4
Commercial Law held a hearing on H.R. 1391. Witnesses testifying in support of the legislation were: Senator Paul

Simon of Illinois (sponsor of similar legislation in the Senate), Dr. William Dietz on behalf of the American Academy of Pediatrics, Dr. Brian Wilcox on behalf of the American Psychological Association, and Ms. Joan Dykstra on behalf of the National Parent-Teacher Association.

5   Ms. Beth Waxman Bressan of CBS Broadcast Group testified that CBS neither actively supported nor actively opposed the bill and thought it was unnecessary. Mr. Alan Gerson of the National Broadcasting Company testified that NBC did not oppose the bill but thought it was unnecessary as applied to over-the-air television. Mr. Alfred R. Schneider of Capital Cities/ABC, Inc. testified that ABC did not support the bill because "jointly-developed industry-wide standards to replace those which have been independently arrived at would in our judgment be unnecessary, inappropriate, and exceedingly difficult to implement."

6   Professor Cass R. Sunstein of the University of Chicago Law School testified to his belief that H.R. 1391 was constitutional. Mr. Barry W. Lynn testified in opposition to the bill on behalf of the American Civil Liberties Union, presenting the ACLU's view that the antitrust exemption in the bill "is both unwise and unconstitutional."

7   On June 15, 1989, the subcommittee adopted one clarifying amendment to the bill, offered by Mr. Glickman, and favorably reported the bill as an amendment in the nature of a substitute by a 10 to 4 vote. The amendment was intended to clarify the sponsors' intent that all entities that air or produce programming would fall within the ambit of the bill's coverage.

8   On June 20, 1989, the Committee on the Judiciary ordered the amendment in the nature of a substitute to H.R. 1391 favorably reported, by a vote of 26 to 8.

III. Background and Summary of H.R. 1391

A. Effects of TV Violence on Real Life Violence

9   H.R. 1391 is based upon the premise that there is a causal relationship between violence on television and aggressive behavior in real life, particularly with young viewers. The bulk of the scientific research into this area seems to indicate that there is some link between television violence and real life aggression. Though there is not universal acceptance of this conclusion — a minority of studies have reached

the opposite conclusion—the committee, relying upon the greater weight of the research, accepts the premise that there is some causal relationship between violence on television and real life aggression.

A brief summary of some of the research in this area 10 follows:

1. *Surgeon General's Advisory Committee on Television and Behavior.*—Pursuant to a request by Senator John Pastore in 1969, this Advisory Committee was appointed under the auspices of the National Institute of Mental Health to study whether there was a causal connection between television violence and real life violence and anti-social behavior. Numerous research studies were funded and conducted, and in 1972 the Surgeon General's Report, *Television and Growing Up: The Impact of Televised Violence,* was published. The report's major conclusion was as follows:

> [T]here is a convergence of the fairly substantial experimental evidence for a short-run causation of aggression among some children by viewing violence on the screen and much less certain evidence from field studies that extensive violence viewing precedes some long-run manifestations of aggressive behavior. The convergence of the two types of evidence constitute some preliminary indication of a causal relationship, but a good deal of research remains to be done before one can have confidence in these conclusions.

The report acknowledged that these conclusions were tentative and limited, and were therefore not entirely satisfactory.

Ten years later, an update of the Surgeon General's Report was issued by the National Institute of Mental Health 11 (*Television and Behavior: Ten Years of Scientific Progress and Implications for the 80's*). The update considered the research that had been conducted since the original study, and stated that "[r]ecent research confirms the earlier findings of a causal relationship between viewing televised violence and later aggressive behavior."[1] This conclusion applied to groups, rather than specific types of individuals. Importantly, the update also stated (pp. 89–90):

> [N]o single study unequivocally confirms the conclusion that televised violence leads to aggressive behavior. Similar-

---

[1]*Television and Behavior: Ten Years of Scientific Progress and Implications for the 80's,* Volume 1: Summary Report, page 89 (1982).

ly, no single study unequivocally refutes that conclusion. The scientific support for the causal relationship derives from the convergence of findings from many studies, the great majority of which demonstrates a positive relationship between televised violence and later aggressive behavior.

12   2. *Huesman Longitudinal Study.* — Dr. L. Rowell Huesman, a scientist who has spent many years researching the effects of television violence on behavior, wrote an article for the 1982 NIMH update in which he stated that "[a]t this time, it should be difficult to find any researcher who does not believe that a significant positive relationship exists between viewing television violence and subsequent aggressive behavior under most conditions."[2]

13   Dr. Huesman, along with other colleagues, also conducted a longitudinal study in which the same children were studied first in 1960 at age 8, and then later at ages 22 and 30 (632 persons were studied at all three ages). The researchers concluded that, in boys, "a preference for TV violence viewing at age 8 is related to both current aggressive behavior and later aggressive behavior including criminal behavior as an adult," while for girls, there was no relation between a preference for violent shows and aggression at ages 8 or 19, "but a slight relation between violence viewing and aggression at age 30."[3]

14   3. *Gerbner Prevalence of Violence Studies.* — Dr. George Gerbner, Dean of the Annenberg School of Communications at the University of Pennsylvania, has led a team of researchers that has been analyzing the level of violence in television programs for each television season since 1967. One of the measures studied has been the rate of clear-cut and unambiguous episodes of physical violence. For the year 1985, the latest year for which results have been released, Dr. Gerbner's team found the following number of violent acts to have been committed in an hour of television during the specified period:

    a. All programs on all networks: 9.7 violent acts in an average television hour.

---

[2]"Television Violence and Aggressive Behavior," p. 126, included in *Television and Behavior: Ten Years of Scientific Progress and Implications for the 80's*, Volume 2: Technical Reviews (1982).

[3]Huesman, Eron, et al., "Television Viewing Habits in Childhood and Adult Aggression," p. 9.

b. Between 8 and 9 p.m., in what used to be called the family hour: 7.6 violent acts per hour.
c. Between 9 p.m. and 11 p.m.: 6.4 violent acts per hour.
d. Weekend-Daytime TV (children's programming, largely cartoons): 21.3 violent acts per hour.

Dr. Gerbner's team found that, in 1985, 85 percent of all 15 programs on television contained some act of violence.[4]

The 1985 study contended that viewers of violence, espe- 16 cially viewers who belong to the same group as the most prevalent victims of TV violence — women, young children, and the elderly — tend to identify symbolically with the victims of TV violence and translate this into real fear. The study stated (p. 10) that:

> While the convergence of research indicates that exposure to violence does occasionally incite and often desensitize, our findings show that, for most viewers, television's mean and dangerous world tends to cultivate a sense of relative danger, mistrust, dependence, and — despite its supposedly "entertaining nature" — alienation and gloom.

4. *Attorney General's Task Force on Family Violence.* — In 17 a report issued in September 1984, the Attorney General's Task Force on Family Violence stated that "the evidence is becoming overwhelming that just as witnessing violence in the home may contribute to normal adults and children learning and acting out violent behavior, violence on TV and the movies may contribute to the same result."[5]

5. *Conflicting Research on Television Violence.* — As indi- 18 cated, not all of the studies and literature support a finding that there is some relationship between television violence and real life aggression. For example, the National Broadcasting Company sponsored a study of the effect of exposure to violence on television on aggressive behavior. Exposure to television violence and aggressive behavior among elementary school boys and girls, and among teenage boys, was measured in different schools in two cities, on five (for teenage boys) or six (for elementary school boys and girls)

---

[4]Gerbner, Gross, Signorielli and Morgan, "Television's Mean World: Violence Profile No. 14–15" (September, 1986).

[5]Attorney General's Task Force on Family Violence, Final Report, September, 1984, p. 110.

different occasions between 1970 and 1973. Where possible, the same students were tracked over the course of this three-year period. The study "did not find evidence that television violence was causally implicated in the development of aggressive behavior patterns among children and adolescents over the time periods studied."[6]

19   The committee is persuaded by the majority of studies that indicate there is some relationship between television violence and real life behavior. The committee is therefore concerned about violence on television and its effects. H.R. 1391 addresses the problem of the impact on our Nation's children of violence on television; as formulated, the bill is a limited, narrow, non-coercive response. Television programmers who may wish to take steps to unilaterally alleviate the negative impact of television violence but who do not do so for fear of slipping in the ratings will be able to participate in joint discussions about voluntary guidelines.

IV. Constitutional Issues Raised by H.R. 1391

20   The committee believes that H.R. 1391 presents no constitutional problems. It is a bill that mandates nothing and is completely voluntary. It neither contains nor is meant to imply any sanctions for either failure to meet and hold discussions as permitted by the bill or failure to adhere to any voluntary guidelines that may be developed. The antitrust exemption in the bill is not intended to coerce the industry to either meet or adopt television violence guidelines; it is only intended to remove a possible impediment — the antitrust laws — should members of the industry voluntarily wish to meet and adopt guidelines in this area.[7]

21   The committee believes that H.R. 1391 contains no constitutional infirmities. The bill is entirely voluntary and is reasonably designed to protect impressionable viewers from "developmental" harm. As Professor Cass R. Sunstein of the University of Chicago Law School told the Subcommittee on Economic and Commercial Law at its hearing:

[6]Milavsky, Kessler, Stipp, & Rubens, *Television and Aggression: A Panel Study*, 1982, p. 487.

[7]In this regard, H.R. 1391 is entirely different from the situation in *Writers Guild* v. *ABC*, 609 F. 2d 355 (9th Cir. 1979), where the government, through the Federal Communications Commission, was found to have exerted informal, improper pressure on networks to adopt family viewing guidelines.

H.R. 1391 does not regulate speech. Its only effect is to authorize voluntary action by broadcasters. In this respect, it increases rather than decreases their freedom, by reducing the pressures of the marketplace with respect to television violence. The most powerful attack on the bill would be that the selective exemption it creates is based on the content of speech, and that content-based regulation is subject to careful judicial scrutiny. This attack is, however, unpersuasive in light of the fact that H.R. 1391 (a) is limited to the broadcasting area, (b) does not require or prohibit speech at all, and (c) does not discriminate on the basis of point of view, but is instead a legitimate effort to [combat] genuine harms.

H.R. 1391 is not an effort to regulate a point of view but is, rather, an effort to prevent a legitimate harm.

The bill's efforts to reduce the negative impact of violence 22 has some similarities to the factual situation presented in *Ginsberg* v. *New York*, though the speech involved in Ginsberg was pornography, which, unlike violent speech, is not entitled to First Amendment protections. In *Ginsberg*, the Supreme Court upheld a New York statute that prohibited the sale of pictures or magazines depicting nudity harmful to minors to persons under seventeen years of age. At the time the statute was enacted, there existed scientific studies that concluded exposure to obscenity impaired the development of youth, as well as studies that claimed such exposure did not hinder development. Nevertheless, the Court said "we do not demand of legislatures scientifically certain criteria of legislation." It acknowledged the interest of the government in protecting the welfare of children and safeguarding them from abuses that might hinder children's development. Since the action of the legislature had a rational relation to the objective of safeguarding minors from harm, the statute was upheld.

The Supreme Court has upheld some governmental reg- 23 ulation of broadcasting because of the often uncontrolled or involuntary exposure of children to television, and because of the limited number of airwaves that exist. In *Federal Communications Commission* v. *Pacifica Foundation*, for example, the Court recognized that "it is broadcasting that has received the most limited First Amendment protection." The Court also indicated that "[b]ecause the broadcast audience is constantly tuning in and out, prior warnings cannot completely protect the listener or viewer from unexpected program content."

24   Given that there are not enough broadcast frequencies available to accommodate all parties who want to broadcast, the Supreme Court stated in *Red Lion Broadcasting* v. *FCC* in 1969 that "it is idle to posit an unabridgeable First Amendment right to broadcast comparable to the right of every individual to speak, write, or publish." While the weight of this pronouncement may be somewhat less now because of the recent proliferation of cable and satellite television systems the Government's interest in protecting children from abuse is as strong as ever. In enacting H.R. 1391, the committee believes that it is acting in a reasonable, non-intrusive, non-coercive manner to try to prevent developmental harm to impressionable frequent viewers of television.[8]

V. Antitrust Consideration

25   H.R. 1391 would grant only a temporary exemption from the antitrust laws. It removes a possible impediment to persons in the television industry voluntarily getting together to develop voluntary guidelines to alleviate the negative impact of television violence.

26   The committee does not accept the argument that the antitrust laws now prohibit all joint activities contemplated by the legislation. Under existing law, many joint activities among competitors are not viewed as harmful to competition. Thus, trade associations and industry-wide groups have met for years in order to discuss common problems, to develop standards to improve the safety of the products and even to conduct joint research and development. Because such activities are generally not aimed at restricting competition or decreasing output, but instead are directed at improving competitiveness and efficiencies, the antitrust laws are not needed to restore the operation of a free market economy.[9]

27   The committee does not believe that the decision in *U.S.* v. *National Association of Broadcasters* can be read as pro-

---

[8]In no way does the legislation restrict adults to viewing only what is acceptable for children. The legislation contains no restrictions or bans whatsoever.

[9]*See e.g., Broadcast Music Inc.* v. *CBS*, 441 U.S. 1 (1979); *Continental TV* v. *GTE Sylvania Inc.*, 433 U.S. 36 (1977).

hibiting all joint voluntary agreements in the broadcast industry. In *NAB*, the district court struck down participation by broadcasters in a voluntary code in which there was industry-wide adherence to a rule prohibiting multiple products from being advertised during a single commercial. The court found the multiple product standard to be an artificial device aimed at enhancing the demand for commercial time and/or limiting the supply of commercial time available. Finding the effect to be similar to a tying arrangement, the court found the practice to be a *per se* violation of the antitrust laws. This particular rule was anti-competitive. Other parts of the NAB code were not viewed as anti-competitive, however, and were not invalidated. The committee does not believe that joint, voluntary agreements that are not anti-competitive in their effect, and that do not give rise to ancillary restraints, raise antitrust problems.

Having said this, the committee acknowledges that the antitrust laws are still perceived by some as an impediment to persons in the television industry developing joint voluntary guidelines. Because of its interest in protecting impressionable viewers from abuse, the committee is willing to approve the *limited, temporary,* exemption in H.R. 1391 so that if persons in the television industry wish to voluntarily develop guidelines to reduce the negative impact of television violence, they will not be dissuaded from doing so by possible fears about antitrust exposure. [28]

Perhaps most important, the legislation makes it clear that the antitrust exemption does *not* apply to any joint discussion, consideration, review, action, or agreement which results in a boycott of any person. The exemption is meant only to permit development of voluntary guidelines to alleviate the negative impact of violence on television, not to be used as a subterfuge for a boycott of any person because of adherence to the guidelines developed. [29]

Dissenting Views of Hon. Don Edwards, Hon. Robert W. Kastenmeier, Hon. John Conyers, Jr., Hon. Patricia Schroeder, Hon. Geo. W. Crockett, Hon. Mike Synar, Hon. Howard L. Berman, and Hon. Rick Boucher

As Justice Brennan stated so eloquently in *Bantam Books, Inc.* v. *Sullivan:* "It is characteristic of the freedoms of expression in general that they are vulnerable to gravely [30] damaging yet barely visible encroachments." H.R. 1391 is just such an encroachment. Along with the *Bantam Books* Court, we believe freedom of speech is a precarious, fragile freedom which must be guarded jealously and diligently. Thus, we must dissent from the Committee Report on H.R. 1391.

31   Proponents of H.R. 1391 have cited *Red Lion Broadcasting Co.* v. *FCC, Ginsberg* v. *New York,* and *FCC* v. *Pacifica Foundation* as supportive of their position that the bill does not violate the First Amendment. H.R. 1391 is readily distinguishable from narrow regulations previously upheld by the Supreme Court.

32   H.R. 1391 deals with televised violence. The Court has never suggested that depictions of violence lie outside the full protection of the First Amendment. Rather, the cases relied on by the majority deal primarily with the area of obscenity, an area never viewed by the Court as within the concerns of the First Amendment. As the Court stated in *Roth* v. *United States*: "Obscenity is not within the area of constitutionally protected speech or press."

33   Even in the unprotected area of obscenity, the Court has always required the government to regulate in a manner protective of constitutionally protected speech. "Our insistence that regulations of obscenity scrupulously embody the most rigorous procedural safeguards . . . is . . . but a special instance of the larger principle that the freedoms of expression must be ringed about with adequate bulwarks." (*Bantam Books* v. *Sullivan.*)

34   In contrast, H.R. 1391 operates in a protected area of speech and it manipulates the federal antitrust laws to achieve an impermissible result. The bill exempts the TV industry from the antitrust laws for the express purpose not only of having that industry alter the content of its programs, but also to alter it in the direction the government dictates. That is indirect censorship, clear and simple.

35   Further, as the *Bantam Books* Court pointed out, "People do not lightly disregard public officers' thinly veiled threats to institute . . . proceedings against them if they do not come around." The legislative history of H.R. 1391 is replete with thinly veiled threats of further government action.

36   In *Red Lion Broadcasting* v. *F.C.C.,* the Court merely upheld the Federal Communications Commission's "Fairness Doctrine." This doctrine, as the name implies, requires the presentation of differing viewpoints. The Court upheld the

fairness doctrine in this case because it "enhance[d] rather than abridge[d] the freedoms of speech and press protected by the First Amendment."

In contrast, H.R. 1391 seeks to restrict or eliminate particular viewpoints about the appropriate use of violence. Yet, the Court has said: "It is the purpose of the First Amendment to preserve an uninhibited marketplace of ideas in which truth will ultimately prevail, rather than to countenance monopolization of that market, whether it be by the Government itself or a private licensee." 37

The Court in *F.C.C.* v. *Pacifica Foundation* upheld possible administrative sanctions against a radio station for broadcasting "indecent" material in the early afternoon. The Court noted this would "deter only the broadcasting of patently offensive reference to excretory and sexual organs and activities" which "surely lie at the periphery of First Amendment concerns." In this case, the FCC pointed out that it "never intended to place an absolute prohibition on the broadcast of this type of language, but rather sought to channel it to times of day when children most likely would not be exposed to it." As the *Pacifica* Court emphasized. "It is a central tenet of the First Amendment that the government must remain neutral in the marketplace of ideas." In its decision, the Court merely recognized that certain sexually-oriented speech historically has been outside the protection of the First Amendment, particularly if distributed to minors. 38

In *Ginsberg* v. *New York,* the Court upheld a prohibition on sale to minors of material which was "obscene" as to children, even if not legally "obscene" for adults. The Court was careful to point out that the prohibition did not limit the rights of adults to the same material, and that parents desiring to purchase the magazines for themselves or for their children were *not* barred from doing so. 39

Rather than according with previous Supreme Court decisions, the practical effect of H.R. 1391 is to reach the result forbidden by the Supreme Court in *Butler* v. *Michigan,* that of reducing the adult population to seeing only what is fit for children: "We have before us legislation not reasonably restricted to the evil with which it is said to deal. The incidence of this enactment is to reduce the adult population of Michigan to reading only what is fit for children." 40

The sincere motivations of the proponents of H.R. 1391 are not questioned here. All of us support the goal of a more 41 civil society. But casting aside constitutional concerns and giving content-specific antitrust exemptions to the TV industry is a truly dangerous and constitutionally precluded way to achieve that goal.

42   The words of Justice Brennan in *Pacifica* are particularly salient to H.R. 1391: "Most parents will undoubtedly find understandable as well as commendable the Court's sympathy with the FCC's desire to prevent offensive broadcasts from reaching the ears of unsupervised children. Unfortunately, the facial appeal of this justification for radio censorship masks its constitutional insufficiency."

43   The proper place for TV programming content to be decided is in our homes and our communities. As Justice Douglas pointed out in *Ginsberg*, "It is one thing for parents and the religious organizations to be active and involved. It is quite a different matter for the state to become implicated as a censor." When Congress "signals" to the media what material it deems appropriate, that is informal censorship by the government; and, as such, it can have the same constitutionally impermissible effect as direct restraints on inhibiting communication.

44   S. 593, the Senate companion bill, like H.R. 1391 began with an exemption for violence, but passed the Senate with exemptions for violence, illegal drug use, and sexually explicit material. The action of the Senate demonstrates that once this process is engaged in, there is no rational basis for stopping at any particular point.

45   When they are inclined to do so, power regularly is exercised by our citizens to affect television content. The American people can directly control programming without the interference of the government, and that is how it should be.

46   The Court has in the past "look[ed] through forms to the substance and recognize[d] that informal censorship may sufficiently inhibit the circulation of publications to warrant injunctive relief." Should the Congress proceed in its ill-advised path with H.R. 1391, we can only hope that the Court will do so once again, for it is not only a serious mistake — but also constitutional error — to encourage censorship through the manipulation of the federal antitrust laws.

Tom Paradis
A Child's Other World

*Tom Paradis (born 1970), from Stafford Springs, Connecticut,
is a geography major who anticipates a career in cartography.
He wrote the following essay for a writing course at Penn State;
in 1989 it was included in* Penn Statements, *a magazine of
student writing.*

No one can doubt that society is becoming more career-   1
oriented with time, for more adults than ever are now de-
voting their lives to a specific career. Despite their heavy
workloads, however, many of these people are also maintaining a family at home. This accounts for the fact that
more and more students of all ages have become "latch-key"
kids — kids who come home to an empty house and don't
see their parents until late at night. So, what does a kid do
at home while his parents are at work making millions?
Television is usually the answer. Television has definitely
become an integral part of most students' lives, and ours
has become known as the "video" generation. Recent studies
even indicate that typical American students watch an average of 26 hours of television a week. What are the consequences of spending so much time in front of the tube?
Certainly, the programs aired on television today are distorting the minds and actions of today's youth by providing
them with a false sense of reality and by limiting their
imaginations.

To start with, let's look at how today's television prevents   2
young viewers from obtaining a realistic perspective of our
world. Consider the words of Henry David Thoreau concerning the education of students: "They should not 'play' life
or study it merely, but earnestly live it from beginning to
end. How could youths better learn to live than by at once
trying the experiment of living?" Thoreau makes perfect
sense in saying that a person should not only study and
view the world from afar, but also become actively involved
in it. Indeed, today's young people are only "playing and
studying" the world around them by watching hours of
television. The more time Johnny spends indoors watching
his favorite programs, the less time he spends outdoors
actually experiencing the real world around him.

3   Unfortunately, the world on television which Johnny "studies" so diligently differs considerably from the actual world we live in. Take today's family shows, for example "Little House on the Prairie." For sure, the stories told on this program present a view of western farm life which may appear to be quite appealing to any ten-year-old who has no idea what farm life is actually like. The Ingalls family on "Little House" periodically experiences hardships and dangers, but problems are short-lived and will be worked out in the end. Does this represent the true lifestyle of a farm family? Hardly so. If the kid had to move onto an actual farm, he would not live the happy-go-lucky life Laura Ingalls does. Certain aspects of farm life are not presented on the show — the grueling fifteen-hour work days of the farmers, the never-ending chores which all family members must perform, the long-term hardships of drought or economic instability. When considering a similar Disney depiction of farm life in "Pages from the Life of a Georgia Innocent," Harry Crews's narrator comments, "The hunger and hard work seemed to be a hell of a lot of fun."[1] Indeed it does to a youngster who doesn't know any better and whose parents aren't home to instruct him otherwise.

4   Unlike "Little House," which takes place in a nineteenth-century setting, family sitcoms such as the "Bill Cosby Show" present kids with a taste of upper-middle class lifestyles which are easily mistaken for reality. On the show, Mom's a lawyer, and Dad's a doctor — typical jobs of today's urban professionals. However, they seem to spend an incredible amount of time with their family of four charming, intelligent children. Major quarrels rarely occur, but when brother argues with sister, the matter is quickly and cleverly solved by comical Dad. All have what they need, and problems such as drugs and alcohol would never be found within the Cosby household. In a sense, they are perfect. How many families on our planet can succeed in meeting the standards of the Cosby family? Very few, if any. Many kids, however, will view the Cosbys as a rule rather than as an exception. As a result, children, and even teens, may become envious of the Cosby family and think negatively of their own. Such is the case with one young lady from a broken home who was quoted as saying, "Sometimes when

[1]Harry Crews, "Pages from the Life of a Georgia Innocent," *The Dolphin Reader,* ed. Douglas Hunt (Boston: Houghton Mifflin, 1986), 51.

I see how easy it is for Bill Cosby's kids, I get crazy thinking about my own life."[2] Clearly, sitcoms such as the "Cosby Show" are distorting kids' views of today's modern families.

Almost opposite from family sitcoms, programs which   5
demonstrate a continuously violent nature end up confusing children about their own moral values. What is a boy likely to think, for instance, when he watches the "A-Team" become involved in countless fights, gun battles, and thrilling police chases every week? What about "Kung Fu," a show based entirely on the martial arts? Any young viewer who tunes in to such programs will become brainwashed into believing all problems can be solved with brute force. When a classmate disagrees with Johnny at school, Johnny can just "beat him up"—problem solved. The "A-Team" uses their brains to solve conflicts only when they are inventing some mechanical device which will destroy the enemy. The use of intelligent discussion to settle arguments is certainly not promoted. Like the "A-Team," the action-packed thriller, "Airwolf," keeps its audience amused with numerous violent actions: Stringfellow Hawk takes pleasure in blowing planes out of the sky with his sophisticated warship. It doesn't matter how many people are killed in the process. Such actions are not teaching kids the value of human life, especially when the "hero" cheers and celebrates after the massacre. The youth will undoubtedly obtain more realistic opinions about human values by speaking with any Vietnam veteran. The typical veteran of war certainly will not cheer over the deaths he caused. Thus, television has been successful at portraying violence as a normal, respectable attribute of today's society which kids expect to be part of when they grow up.

In addition to causing viewers to lose touch with society,   6
television has had negative effects on viewers' creativity or imagination. Before the days of television, people were entertained by exciting radio shows such as "Superman," "Batman," and "War of the Worlds." Of course, the listener was required to pay careful attention to the story if all details were to be comprehended. Better yet, while listening to the stories, listeners would form their own images of the actions taking place. When the broadcaster would give brief descriptions of the Martian space ships invading earth, for

---

[2]Ben Stein, "This Is Not Your Life: TV As the Third Parent," *Public Opinion*, Nov. 1988, 41.

example, every member of the audience would imagine a different space ship. In contrast, television's version of "War of the Worlds" will not stir the imagination at all, for everyone can clearly see the actions taking place. All viewers see the same space ship with the same features. Each aspect is clearly defined, and therefore, no one will imagine anything different from what is seen. Thus, television cannot be considered an effective tool for stimulating the imagination.

7   The consequences of planting specific images within the viewers' minds are many. One, which became evident to me during my senior year of high school, is television's ability to dominate the thoughts of the students. The first question to be forwarded by anyone during lunch, for instance, would typically be, "Hey—did you see (such and such a show) last night?" Some would reply in the affirmative, and the rest of their lunch-time conversation would be spent paraphrasing the clever script of the show's cast and describing the specific plot of the show. Such was the case when *Spaceballs* was aired on television last year. For nearly three weeks after it was shown, most of our lunch-time conversation was devoted to it. Of course, no one discussed the ethics or quality of the movie. Someone would be proud to be able to recite the movie's funniest lines and actions at will: "How about the part where Lonestar jammed the radar?" Others would reply, "Ya—ha ha—that was funny." By the time *Spaceballs* finally phased out, I was able to recite half of the movie's script even without first seeing it myself! Certainly, such shows do not stimulate the creativity of students.

8   Similarly, actions of students of all ages are affected by viewing certain occurrences on television. I witnessed a fine example of television's control on student actions when the "Smothers Brothers Show" reappeared last year. After a few weeks, the "Yo Yo Man"—a trademark of the show—became quite popular. It may be no surprise, then, that a large number of students—mostly freshmen—began taking yo-yos to school. In each other's company, they would attempt their best efforts at recreating the exact performance of Tom Smothers—the "Yo Yo Man." In a similar fashion, young children are affected in the same manner by seeing every action take place, for whatever they watch they often recreate during their play time. When a certain battle takes place on a cartoon, for instance, it is likely to be re-enacted

by the child, only because he or she has had the entire sequence of events pre-visualized in his or her mind's eye. To compound the problem, companies produce toys such as transformers which represent the exact figures shown on televison shows. Once these toys are obtained, kids can add to the reality of their unimaginative "fantasies" during play time. These examples effectively demonstrate how television is succeeding at controlling the actions and imaginations of today's youth.

In sum, we can conclude that television is not beneficial 9 to a youth's development. Johnny will spend years enjoying television's fabricated world while recreating its adventures and reviewing them with fellow classmates. It will take him some time to learn what's different about the real world, but in the long run, he will fit into society. Of course, life will be full of surprises: families such as the Cosbys just won't exist; no "Yo Yo Man" will bound out onto the street to entertain him; colleagues at work will indeed discuss topics which relate more to the world they live in. Someday, Johnny will become successful, have a family, and spend plenty of time at work — in order to pay for his son who is at home being introduced to the fictitious world of television.

Marya Mannes

Television Advertising:
The Splitting Image

Marya Mannes (born 1904) was an editor for Vogue *and* Mademoiselle *and published essays in* McCall's, The New York Times, *and* Harper's. *Novelist and social critic, playwright and cultural commentator, she wrote the following analysis in 1970 for* Saturday Review, *a magazine examining the arts and social issues.*

A bride who looks scarcely fourteen whispers, "Oh, Mom, 1 I'm so *happy!*" while a doting family adjust her gown and veil and a male voice croons softly, "A woman is a harder thing to be than a man. She has more feelings to feel." The mitigation of these excesses, it appears, is a feminine deodorant called Secret, which allows our bride to approach the altar with security as well as emotion.

2   Eddie Albert, a successful actor turned pitchman, bestows his attention on a lady with two suitcases, which prompt him to ask her whether she has been on a journey. "No," she says, or words to that effect, as she opens the suitcases. "My two boys bring back their soiled clothes every weekend from college for me to wash." And she goes into the familiar litany of grease, chocolate, mud, coffee, and fruitjuice stains, which presumably record the life of the average American male from two to fifty. Mr. Albert compliments her on this happy device to bring her boys home every week and hands her a box of Biz, because "Biz *is* better."

3   Two women with stony faces meet cart to cart in a supermarket as one takes a jar of peanut butter off a shelf. When the other asks her in a voice of nitric acid why she takes that brand, the first snaps, "Because I'm choosy for my family!" The two then break into delighted smiles as Number Two makes Number One taste Jif for "mothers who are choosy."

4   If you have not come across these dramatic interludes, it is because you are not home during the day and do not watch daytime television. It also means that your intestinal tract is spared from severe assaults, your credibility unstrained. Or, for that matter, you may look at commercials like these every day and manage either to ignore them or find nothing — given the fact of advertising — wrong with them. In that case, you are either so brainwashed or so innocent that you remain unaware of what this daily infusion may have done and is doing to an entire people as the long-accepted adjunct of free enterprise and support of "free" television.

5   "Given the fact" and "long-accepted" are the key words here. Only socialists, communists, idealists (or the BBC) fail to realize that a mass television system cannot exist without the support of sponsors, that the massive cost of maintaining it as a free service cannot be met without the massive income from selling products. You have only to read of the unending struggle to provide financial support for public, noncommercial television for further evidence.

6   Besides, aren't commercials in the public interest? Don't they help you choose what to buy? Don't they provide

needed breaks from programming? Aren't many of them brilliantly done, and some of them funny? And now, with the new sexual freedom, all those gorgeous chicks with their shining hair and gleaming smiles? And if you didn't have commercials taking up a good part of each hour, how on earth would you find enough program material to fill the endless space/time void?

Tick off the yesses and what have you left? You have, I venture to submit, these intangible but possibly high costs: the diminution of human worth, the infusion and hardening of social attitudes no longer valid or desirable, pervasive discontent, and psychic fragmentation. 7

Should anyone wonder why deception is not an included detriment, I suggest that our public is so conditioned to promotion as a way of life, whether in art or politics or products, that elements of exaggeration or distortion are taken for granted. Nobody really believes that a certain shampoo will get a certain swain, or that an unclogged sinus can make a man a swinger. People are merely prepared to hope it will. 8

But the diminution of human worth is much more subtle and just as pervasive. In the guise of what they consider comedy, the producers of television commercials have created a loathsome gallery of men and women patterned, presumably, on Mr. and Mrs. America. Women liberationists have a major target in the commercial image of woman flashed hourly and daily to the vast majority. There are, indeed, only four kinds of females in this relentless sales procession: the gorgeous teen-age swinger with bouncing locks; the young mother teaching her baby girl the right soap for skin care; the middle-aged housewife with a voice like a power saw; and the old lady with dentures and irregularity. All these women, to be sure, exist. But between the swinging sex object and the constipated granny there are millions of females never shown in commercials. These are — married or single — intelligent, sensitive women who bring charm to their homes, who work at jobs as well as lend grace to their marriage, who support themselves, who have talents or hobbies or commitments, or who are skilled at their professions. 9

To my knowledge, as a frequent if reluctant observer, I know of only one woman on a commercial who has a job; a comic plumber pushing Comet. Funny, heh? Think of a dame with a plunger. 10

With this one representative of our labor force, which is 11 well over thirty million women, we are left with nothing but the full-time housewife in all her whining glory: obsessed with whiter wash, moister cakes, shinier floors, cleaner children, softer diapers, and greaseless fried chicken. In the rare instances when these ladies are not in the kitchen, at the washing machine, or waiting on hubby, they are buying beauty soaps (fantasy, see?) to take home so that their hair will have more body. Or out at the supermarket being choosy.

12   If they were attractive in their obsessions, they might be bearable. But they are not. They are pushy, loud-mouthed, stupid, and — of all things now — bereft of sexuality. Presumably, the argument in the tenets of advertising is that once a woman marries she changes overnight from plaything to floor-waxer.

13   To be fair, men make an equivalent transition in commercials. The swinging male with the mod hair and the beautiful chick turns inevitably into the paunchy slob who chokes on his wife's cake. You will notice, however, that the voice urging the viewer to buy the product is nearly always male: gentle, wise, helpful, seductive. And the visible presence telling the housewife how to get shinier floors and whiter wash and lovelier hair is almost invariably a man: the Svengali in modern dress, the Trilby (if only she were!), his willing object.[1]

14   Woman, in short, is consumer first and human being fourth. A wife and mother who stays home all day buys a lot more than a woman who lives alone or who — married or single — has a job. The young girl hell-bent on marriage is the next most susceptible consumer. It is entirely understandable, then, that the potential buyers of detergents, foods, polishes, toothpastes, pills, and housewares are the housewives, and that the sex object spends more of *her* money on cosmetics, hair lotions, soaps, mouthwashes, and soft drinks.

15   Here we come, of course, to the youngest class of consumers, the swinging teen-agers so beloved by advertisers keen on telling them (and us) that they've "got a lot to live, and Pepsi's got a lot to give." This affords a chance to show a squirming, leaping, jiggling group of beautiful kids having a very loud high on rock and — of all things — soda pop. One

[1]In George Du Maurier's novel, *Trilby* (1894), Svengali mesmerizes Trilby and causes her to become a famous singer; when Svengali dies, Trilby loses her voice, dwindles, and soon dies. (Editors' note)

of commercial TV's most dubious achievements, in fact, is the reinforcement of the self-adulation characteristic of the young as a group.

As for the aging female citizen, the less shown of her the   16
better. She is useful for ailments, but since she buys very little of anything, not having a husband or any children to feed or house to keep, nor—of course—sex appeal to burnish, society and commercials have little place for her. The same is true, to be sure, of older men, who are handy for Bosses with Bad Breath or Doctors with Remedies. Yet, on the whole, men hold up better than women at any age—in life or on television. Lines on their faces are marks of distinction, while on women they are signatures of decay.

There is no question, in any case, that television commer-   17
cials (and many of the entertainment programs, notably the soap serials that are part of the selling package) reinforce, like an insistent drill, the assumption that a woman's only valid function is that of wife, mother, and servant of men: the inevitable sequel to her earlier function as sex object and swinger.

At a time when more and more women are at long last   18
learning to reject these assumptions as archaic and demeaning, and to grow into individual human beings with a wide option of lives to live, the sellers of the nation are bent upon reinforcing the ancient pattern. They know only too well that by beaming their message to the Consumer Queen they can justify her existence as the housebound Mrs. America; dumber than dumb, whiter than white.

The conditioning starts very early: with the girl child   19
who wants the skin Ivory soap has reputedly given her mother, with the nine-year-old who brings back a cake of Camay instead of the male deodorant her father wanted. (When she confesses that she bought it so she could be "feminine," her father hugs her, and, with the voice of a child-molester, whispers, "My little girl is growing up on me, huh.") And then, before long, comes the teen-aged bride who "has feelings to feel." It is the little boys who dream of wings, in an airplane commercial; who grow up (with fewer cavities) into the doers. Their little sisters turn into *Cosmopolitan* girls, who in turn become housewives furious that their neighbors' wash is cleaner than theirs.

There is good reason to suspect that this manic obsession   20
with cleanliness, fostered, quite naturally, by the giant soap and detergent interests, may bear some responsibility for the cultivated sloppiness of so many of the young in their

clothing as well as in their chosen hideouts. The compulsive housewife who spends more time washing and vacuuming and polishing her possessions than communicating to, or stimulating her children creates a kind of sterility that the young would instinctively reject. The impeccably tidy home, the impeccably tidy lawn are — in a very real sense — unnatural and confining. Yet the commercials confront us with broods of happy children, some of whom — believe it or not — notice the new fresh smell their clean, white sweat-shirts exhale thanks to Mom's new "softener."

21   Some major advertisers, for that matter, can even cast a benign eye on the population explosion. In another Biz commercial, the genial Eddie Albert surveys with surprise a long row of dirty clothes heaped before him by a young matron. She answers his natural query by telling him gaily they are the products of her brood of eleven "with one more to come!" she adds as the twelfth turns up. "That's great!" says Mr. Albert, curdling the soul of Planned Parenthood and the future of this planet.

22   Who are, one cannot help but ask, the writers who manage to combine the sales of products with the selling-out of human dreams and dignity? Who people this cosmos of commercials with dolts and fools and shrews and narcissists? Who know so much about quirks and mannerisms and ailments and so little about life? So much about presumed wants and so little about crying needs?

23   Can women advertisers so demean their own sex? Or are there no women in positions of decision high enough to see that their real selves stand up? Do they not know, these extremely clever creators of commercials, what they could do for their audience even while they exploit and entertain them? How they could raise the levels of manners and attitudes while they sell their wares? Or do they really share the worm's-eye view of mass communication that sees, and addresses, only the lowest common denominator?

24   It can be argued that commercials are taken too seriously, that their function is merely to amuse, engage, and sell, and that they do this brilliantly. If that were all to this wheedling of millions, well and good. But it is not. There are two more fallouts from this chronic sales explosion that cannot be measured but that at least can be expected. One has to do with the continual celebration of youth at the expense of maturity. In commercials only the young have access to beauty, sex, and joy in life. What do older women feel, day after day, when love is the exclusive possession of

a teen-age girl with a bobbing mantle of hair? What older man would not covet her in restless impotence?

The constant reminder of what is inaccessible must inevitably produce a subterranean but real discontent, just as the continual sight of things and places beyond reach has eaten deeply into the ghetto soul. If we are constantly presented with what we are not or cannot have, the dislocation deepens, contentment vanishes, and frustration reigns. Even for the substantially secure, there is always a better thing, a better way, to buy. That none of these things makes a better life may be consciously acknowledged, but still the desire lodges in the spirit, nagging and pulling. [25]

This kind of fragmentation works in potent ways above and beyond the mere fact of program interruption, which is much of the time more of a blessing than a curse, especially in those rare instances when the commercial is deft and funny: the soft and subtle sell. Its overall curse, due to the large number of commercials in each hour, is that it reduces the attention span of a people already so conditioned to constant change and distraction that they cannot tolerate continuity in print or on the air. [26]

Specifically, commercial interruption is most damaging during that 10 per cent of programing (a charitable estimate) most important to the mind and spirit of a people: news and public affairs, and drama. To many (and among these are network news producers), commercials have no place or business during the vital process of informing the public. There is something obscene about a newscaster pausing to introduce a deodorant or shampoo commercial between an airplane crash and a body count. It is more than an interruption; it tends to reduce news to a form of running entertainment, to smudge the edges of reality by treating death or disaster or diplomacy on the same level as household appliances or a new gasoline. [27]

The answer to this would presumably be to lump the commercials before and after the news or public affairs broadcasts — an answer unpalatable, needless to say, to the sponsors who support them. [28]

The same is doubly true of that most unprofitable sector of television, the original play. Essential to any creative composition, whether drama, music or dance, are mood and continuity, both inseparable from form and meaning. They are shattered by the periodic intrusion of commercials, which have become intolerable to the serious artists who have deserted commercial television in droves because [29] the system allows them no real freedom or autonomy. The selling comes first, the creation must accommodate itself. It is the rare and admirable sponsor who restricts or fashions his commercials so as to provide a minimum of intrusion or damaging inappropriateness.

30   If all these assumptions and imponderables are true, as many suspect, what is the answer or alleviation?

31   One is in the course of difficult emergence: the establishment of a public television system sufficiently funded so that it can give a maximum number of people an alternate diet of pleasure, enlightenment, and stimulation free from commercial fragmentation. So far, for lack of funds to buy talent and equipment, this effort has been in terms of public attention a distinctly minor operation. Even if public television should greatly increase its scope and impact, it cannot in the nature of things and through long public conditioning equal the impact and reach the size of audience now tuned to commercial television.

32   Enormous amounts of time, money, and talent go into commercials. Technically they are often brilliant and innovative, the product not only of the new skills and devices but of imaginative minds. A few of them are both funny and endearing. Who, for instance, will forget the miserable young man with the appalling cold, or the kids taught to use — as an initiation into manhood — a fork instead of a spoon with a certain spaghetti? Among the enlightened sponsors, moreover, are some who manage to combine an image of their corporation and their products with accuracy and restraint.

33   What has to happen to mass medium advertisers as a whole, and especially on TV, is a totally new approach to their function not only as sellers but as social influencers. They have the same obligation as the broadcast medium itself: not only to entertain but to reflect, not only to reflect but to enlarge public consciousness and human stature.

34   This may be a tall order, but it is a vital one at a time when Americans have ceased to know who they are and where they are going, and when all the multiple forces acting upon them are daily diminishing their sense of their own value and purpose in life, when social upheaval and social fragmentation have destroyed old patterns, and when survival depends on new ones.

35   If we continue to see ourselves as the advertisers see us, we have no place to go. Nor, I might add, has commercial broadcasting itself.

Jules Feiffer (born 1929) wrote his first comics in 1949; even the one example printed here suggests why he is regarded as a major influence on the current generation of cartoonists. Feiffer has also written a novel, plays, the musical Little Murders, *and at least one screenplay.*

Jack McGarvey
To Be or Not to Be as Defined by TV

Jack McGarvey (born 1937) has been a teacher for over a quarter century; currently he teaches language arts and computer arts at Coleytown Middle School in Westport, Connecticut. Also a freelance writer, he has published his work in McCall's, Parents, *and other national publications. This essay appeared in 1982 in* Today's Education, *a publication for teachers and other educators.*

1   A couple of years ago, a television crew came to film my ninth grade English class at Bedford Junior High School in Westport, Connecticut. I'm still trying to understand what happened.

2   I was doing some work with my students, teaching them to analyze the language used in television commercials. After dissecting the advertising claims, most of the class became upset over what they felt were misleading — and in a few cases, untruthful — uses of language. We decided to write to the companies that presented their products inaccurately or offensively. Most of them responded with chirpy letters and cents-off coupons. Some did not respond at all.

3   I then decided to contact *Buyline*, a consumer advocate program aired on New York City's WNBC-TV at the time. The show and its host, Betty Furness, were well-known for their investigation of consumer complaints. I sent off a packet of the unanswered letters with a brief explanation of the class's work.

4   About a week later, the show's producer telephoned me. She said that she'd seen the letters and was interested in the class's project. Could she and her director come to Westport to have a look?

5   I said sure and told her about a role-playing activity I was planning to do with my students. I said I was going to organize my class of 24 students into four committees — each one consisting of two representatives from the Federal Trade Commission (FTC), the agency that monitors truth in advertising; two advertising executives anxious to have their material used; and two TV executives caught somewhere in the middle — wanting to please the advertisers while not offending the FTC. Then, I would ask each committee to assume that there had been a complaint about

the language used in a TV commercial, and that the committees had to resolve the complaint. "That sounds great! I'll
bring a crew," she said.

I obtained clearance from my school district's office, and   6
the next morning, as I was walking into school, I met one
of my students and casually let out the word: "WNBC's
coming to film our class this afternoon."

I was totally unprepared for what happened. Word spread   7
around school within five minutes. Students who barely
knew me rushed up to squeal, "Is it true? Is it really, really
true? A TV crew is coming to Bedford to film?" A girl who
was not in my class pinned me into a corner near the
magazine rack in the library to ask me whether she could
sit in my class for the day. Another girl went to her counselor
and requested an immediate change in English classes,
claiming a long-standing personality conflict with her current teacher.

Later, things calmed down a bit, but as I took my regular   8
turn as cafeteria supervisor, I saw students staring wide-
eyed at me, then turning to whisper excitedly to their
friends. I'd become a celebrity simply because I was the
one responsible for bringing a TV crew to school.

Right after lunch, the show's producer and director came   9
to my class to look it over and watch the role-playing activity; they planned to tape near the end of the school day.
The two women were gracious and self-effacing, taking
pains not to create any disturbance; but the students, of
course, knew why they were there. There were no vacant
stares, no hair brushes, no gum chewers, and no note
scribblers. It was total concentration, and I enjoyed one of
my best classes in more than 15 years of teaching.

After the class, I met with the producer and director to   10
plan the taping. They talked about some of the students
they'd seen and mentioned Susan. "She's terribly photogenic and very, very good with words." They mentioned
Steve. "He really chaired his committee well. Real leadership there. Handsome boy, too." They mentioned Jim, Pete,
Randy, and Jenny and their insights into advertising
claims. Gradually I became aware that we were engaged
in a talent hunt; we were looking for a strong and attractive
group to be featured in the taping.

We continued the discussion, deciding on the players. We   11
also discussed the sequencing of the taping session. First,
I'd do an introduction, explaining the role-playing activity

as if the class had never heard of it. Then, I'd follow with the conclusion—summarizing remarks ending with a cheery "See you tomorrow!"—and dismiss the class. The bit players would leave the school and go home. We'd then rearrange the set and film the photogenic and perceptive featured players while they discussed advertising claims as a committee. Obviously, this is not the way I'd conduct an actual class, but it made sense. After all, I wanted my students to look good, and I wanted to look good.

12   "It'll be very hard work," the producer cautioned. "I trust your students understand that."

13   "It's already been hard work," I remarked as I thought of possible jealousies and bruised feelings over our choices of featured players.

14   About a half hour before school's end, the crew set up cameras and lights in the hall near the classroom we'd be working in, a room in an isolated part of the building. But as the crew began filming background shots of the normal passing of students through the hall, near chaos broke out.

15   Hordes of students suddenly appeared. A basketball star gangled through the milling mob to do an imitation of Nureyev, topping off a pirouette by feigning a couple of jump shots. A pretty girl walked back and forth in front of the cameras at least a dozen times before she was snared by a home economics teacher. Three boys did a noisy pantomime of opening jammed lockers, none of which were theirs. A faculty member, seen rarely in this part of the building, managed to work his way through the crowd, smiling broadly. And as members of my class struggled through the press of bodies, they were hailed, clutched at, patted on the back, and hugged.

16   "Knock 'em dead!" I heard a student call.

17   It took the vice-principal and five teachers 10 minutes to clear the hall.

18   We assembled the cast, arranged the furniture, erased several mild obscenities from the chalkboard, and pulled down the window shades—disappointing a clutch of spectators outside. The producer then introduced the crew and explained their work.

19   I was wired with a mike and the crew set up a boom microphone, while the girls checked each other's make-up and the boys sat squirming.

20   Finally, the taping began. It was show business, a performance, a total alteration of the reality I know as a teacher.

As soon as I began the introduction, 26 pairs of eyes focused on me as if I were Billy Joel about to sing. I was instantly startled and self-conscious. When I asked a question, some of the usually quieter students leaped to respond. This so unsettled me that I forgot what I was saying and had to begin again.

The novelty of being on camera, however, soon passed. 21 We had to do retakes because the soundman missed student responses from the rear of the room. The director asked me to rephrase a question and asked a student to rephrase a response. There were delays while technicians adjusted equipment.

We all became very much aware of being performers, 22 and some of the students who had been most excited about making their TV debut began to grumble about the hard work. That pleased me, for a new reality began to creep in: Television is not altogether glamorous.

We taped for almost five hours, on more than 3,200 feet 23 of video tape. That is almost an hour-and-a-half's worth, more than double a normal class period. And out of that mass of celluloid the producer said she'd use seven minutes on the program!

Two days later, five students and I went to the NBC 24 studios at Rockefeller Center to do a taping of a final segment. The producer wanted to do a studio recreation of the role-playing game. This time, however, the game would include real executives—one from advertising, one from the NBC network, and one from the FTC. We'd be part of a panel discussion moderated by Betty Furness. My students would challenge the TV and the advertising executives, asking them to justify some of the bothersome language used in current commercials.

This was the most arduous part of the experience. The 25 taping was live, meaning that the cameras would run for no longer than eight minutes. As we ate turkey and ham during a break with Ms. Furness and the guest executives, I realized that we were with people who were totally comfortable with television. I began to worry. How could mere 14-year-olds compete in a debate with those to whom being on television is as ordinary as riding a school bus?

But my concern soon disappeared. As Ms. Furness began 26 reading her TelePrompTer, Susan leaned over and whispered, "This is fun!" And it was Susan who struck first. "'You can see how luxurious my hair feels' is a perfect example of the silly language your ad writers use," she said with all the poise of a Barbara Walters. "It's impossible to *see* how something feels," she went on.

27   That pleased me, for as an English teacher, I've always emphasized the value of striving for precision in the use of language. The work we'd done with TV commercials, where suggestibility is the rule, had taken hold, I thought, as the ad executive fumbled for a response. The tension vanished, and we did well.

28   The show aired two weeks later, and I had it taped so the class could view it together. It was a slick production, complete with music — "Hey, Big Spender" — to develop a theme for Ms. Furness' introduction. "Teens are big business these days," she said. "Does television advertising influence how they spend their money?" Then followed a shot of students in the hall — edited to show none of the wildness that actually occurred. Next, three of my students appeared in brief clips of interviews. They were asked, "Have you ever been disappointed by television advertising?" The responses were, "Yes, of course," and I was pleased with their detailed answers. Finally, the classroom appeared, and there I was, lounging against my desk, smiling calmly. I looked good — a young, unrumpled Orson Bean, with a cool blue-and-brown paisley tie. My voice was mellifluous. Gee, I thought as I saw the tape, I could have been a TV personality.

29   Now, I am probably no more vain than most people. But television does strange things to the ego. I became so absorbed in studying the image of myself that the whole point of the show passed me by. I didn't even notice that I'd made a goof analyzing a commercial until I'd seen the show three times. The students who participated were the same; watching themselves on videotape, they missed what they had said. I had an enormous struggle to get both them and me to recall the hard work and to see the obvious editing. It was as if reality had been reversed: The actual process of putting together the tape was not real, but the product was.

30   I showed the tape again last year to my ninth grade class. I carefully explained to this delightful gang of fault-finders how the taping had been done. I told them about the changed sequence, the selection of the featured players, the takes and retakes. They themselves had just been through the same role-playing activity, and I asked them to listen carefully to what was said. They nodded happily and set their flinty minds to look at things critically. But as the

tape ended, they wanted to tease me about how ugly and wrinkled I looked. They wanted to say, "That's Randy! He goes to Compo Beach all the time." "Jenny's eye shadow — horrible!" "When will you get us on TV?"

The visual image had worked its magic once again: 31 They had missed the point of the show altogether. And, as I dismissed them, I felt something vibrating in their glances and voices — the celebrity image at work again. I was no longer their mundane English teacher: I was a TV personality.

I decided to show the tape again the next day. I reviewed 32 the hard work, the editing, the slick packaging. I passed out questions so we could focus on what had been said on the program. I turned on the recorder and turned off the picture to let them hear only the sound. They protested loudly, of course. But I was determined to force them to respond to how effectively the previous year's class had taken apart the language used in the claims of commercials. This was, after all, the point of the program. And it worked, finally.

As class ended, one of the students drifted up to me. 33 "What are we going to do next?" she asked.

"We're going to make some comparisons between TV 34 news shows and what's written in newspapers," I replied.

"Do they put together news shows the way they filmed 35 your class?"

"It's similar and usually much quicker," I answered. 36

She smiled and shook her head. "It's getting hard to be- 37 lieve anything anymore."

In that comment lies what every TV viewer should have — 38 a healthy measure of beautiful, glorious skepticism. But as I said, I'm still trying to understand that taping session. And I'm aware of how hard it is to practice skepticism. Every time I see the *Buyline* tape, I'm struck by how good a teacher TV made me. Am I really that warm, intelligent, creative, and good looking? Of course not. But TV made me that way. I like it, and sometimes I find myself still hoping that I am what television defined me to be.

I sometimes think children have superior knowledge of 39 TV. They know, from many years of watching it, that the product in all its edited glory is the only reality. Shortly after the program aired on that February Saturday two years ago, our telephone rang. The voice belonged to my daughter's 11-year-old friend. She said, "I just saw you on TV. May I have your autograph?"

40   I was baffled. After all, this was the boisterous girl who played with my daughter just about every day and who mostly regarded me as a piece of furniture that occasionally mumbled something about lowering your voices. "Are you serious?" I croaked.

41   "May I have your autograph?" she repeated, ignoring my question. "I can come over right now." Her voice was without guile.

42   She came. And I signed while she scrutinized my face, her eyes still aglow with Chromacolor.

43   To Stephanie, television had transformed a kindly grump into something real. And there is no doubt in my mind whatsoever that in the deepest part of her soul is the fervent dream that her being, too, will someday be defined and literally affirmed by an appearance on television.

44   Lately, my ninth grade class has been growing restless. Shall I move up the TV unit and bring out the tape again? Shall I remind them what a great teacher they have? Shall I remind myself what a fine teacher I am? Shall I renew their — and my — hope?

45   To be or not to be as defined by TV? Does that question suggest what makes television so totally unlike any other medium?

Joshua Meyrowitz
No Sense of Place

Joshua Meyrowitz is professor of communication at the University of New Hampshire. This selection and the next one were adapted by the author from the conclusion to his book No Sense of Place: The Impact of Electronic Media on Social Behavior *(1985).*

1   For Americans, the second half of the twentieth century has been marked by an unusual amount and type of social

change. The underprivileged have demanded equal rights, a significant portion of the visible political elite has been discredited, and many of those in between have been maneuvering for new social position and identity. In the past few decades, the United States has experienced extraordinarily rapid and significant changes involving age, race, gender, and other roles.

Perhaps even more confusing than the dimensions of the 2 change has been its seeming inconsistency, even randomness. What is the common thread? We have witnessed peaceful civil rights demonstrations juxtaposed with violent looting and rioting. We have seen the persecution of the people by the agencies of government followed by the virtual impeachment of a president by the people and press, which was followed, in turn, by the near-canonization of a president, even though many viewed him as neither particularly attentive nor extraordinarily intelligent. And angry talk of social revolution has been transformed into the cool and determined pursuit of "affirmative action," community control, and "citizen diplomacy."

Some social observers have comforted themselves by 3 viewing the disruptions of the 1960s as a historical aberration and by pointing gleefully at former hippies who have clipped their locks and become materialistic yuppies. Nothing has really changed, they seem to suggest. What they fail to see, however, are the male police and hardhats who now wear their hair long, the "redneck" farmers who let livestock loose in front of the Capitol (echoes of the yippies?), the wheelchair sit-ins of the disabled, the court battles over returning land (and human remains) to the Indians, the dramatic changes in women's and children's rights and behaviors, and hundreds of other small and large shifts in behavior and attitude.

What does it all mean? Are we witnessing constant change 4 and confusion? Or is there a central mechanism that has been swinging the social pendulum to and fro?

Social change is always too complex to attribute to a 5 single cause and too diverse to reduce to a unitary process, but one common theme that connects many recent and seemingly unrelated phenomena is a change in Americans' "sense of place." Electronic media have broken that age-old connection between location and experience, between *where* we are and what we see and hear, between our location and our access and accessibility to other people. As a result, the logic underlying "appropriate behavior" in a print- and place-oriented society has been radically subverted. Many Americans may no longer seem to "know their place" because the traditionally interlocking components of place — physical location and social position — have been split apart by electronic media. Wherever one is now, one may be in touch and tuned in. Our world may suddenly seem senseless to many observers because, for the first time in history, it is relatively placeless.

6   The greatest impact on the sense of place has been on social groups that were once defined in terms of their physical isolation in specific locations — playgrounds, kitchens, prisons, convents, and so forth.

7   Our children, for example, were once isolated from adult life by being physically isolated at home or school. But television now takes children across the globe even before they have permission to cross the street. Child viewers witness war, starvation, and brutality, as well as a broad spectrum of everyday adult problems, anxieties, and fears. This does not suggest that children simply imitate what they see on TV, but rather that their image of adults and adulthood has been radically altered. No wonder children now seem older and have less fear of, and respect for, adults.

8   Similarly, our society was once based on the assumption that there were two separate worlds: the public, male realm of "rational accomplishments" and brutal competition, and the private, female sphere of childrearing, emotion, and intuition. But TV blurs the difference between public and private. Television close-ups reveal the private, emotional side of public figures and events: We see tears well up in the eyes of presidents, and abstractions such as "glorious victories" and "crushing defeats" are now conveyed through images of blood and limp bodies. Conversely, most public events are now dramas that are played out in the privacy of our living rooms and kitchens. Television has exposed even homebound women to many parts of the culture that were once considered exclusively male domains, just as it has made men more aware of the emotional dimensions and consequences of public actions. It is no surprise, then, that women have demanded integration into the male realm or that men have begun grappling in new ways with their emotions and are becoming more involved fathers.

Lifting Veils

For both better and worse, television has lifted many of   9
the old veils of secrecy that used to exist between the worlds
of children and adults, men and women, and people of
different classes, regions, and levels of education. It has
given us a broader but also a shallower sense of identity
and community.

The intensity of social change in the past thirty years, in   10
particular, may be related to the unique power of television
to break down distinctions between here and there, live
and recorded, and personal and public. More than any other
electronic medium, television tends to involve us in issues
we once thought were "not our business," to thrust us within
a few inches of the faces of murderers and presidents, and
to make physical barriers and passageways relatively
meaningless in terms of patterns of access to social experience. Television has also enhanced the effects of earlier
electronic media by providing us with a better image of
the places experienced through radio and reached through
the telephone.

The widespread social movements and disruptions since   11
the late 1950s may be adjustments in behavior, attitudes,
and laws to match new social settings. Many of the traditional distinctions among groups, among people at various
stages of socialization, and among superiors and subordi-
nates were based on the patterns of information flow that
existed in a print society, where people of different groups,
ages, sexes, and educational background tended to experience very different sets of information. The new and
"strange" behavior of many individuals and of classes of
people may be the result of the steady merging of formerly
distinct social environments. Television has changed "who
knows what about whom" and "who knows what compared
to whom," making it more difficult to stay in one's old
place. For there is nothing more frustrating than being exposed constantly to activities and adventures and excite-
ments that you are told are reserved for someone else.

In spite of its often conservative *content*, television, as a   12
new social *environment*, has been a force of liberation. Television has helped change the deferential Negro into the
proud black, has fostered the merging of the Miss and Mrs.

into a Ms., has supported the transformation of the child into a little adult with expanded rights and responsibilities. Television has encouraged the rise of hundreds of "minorities" — people, who in perceiving a wider world, now see themselves as unfairly isolated in some pocket of it. Television has empowered the elderly, disabled, and disenfranchised by giving them access to social information in spite of their physical isolation. Television has given women an outside view from which their traditional homebound roles appear to be a form of imprisonment. Television has weakened visible authorities by destroying the distance and mystery that once enhanced their aura and prestige. And television has been able to do this without requiring the disabled to leave their wheelchairs, without asking the traditional homemaker to stop cooking dinner, and without demanding that the average citizen leave his or her easy chair.

13   This is not to suggest that information integration leads to instant physical integration or to social harmony. Indeed, the initial outcome of information integration is increased social tension. Information access heightens outsiders' awareness of physical, economic, and legal segregation. Even in the long run, electronic media, in themselves, may continue to encourage a desire for physical and ecomonic equality, but without providing any clear social mechanisms for accomplishing it.

14   Nevertheless, by merging discrete communities of discourse, television has made nearly every topic and issue a valid subject of interest and concern for virtually every member of the public. Further, many formerly private and isolated behaviors have been thrust into the large, unitary public arena. As a result, behaviors that were dependent on great distance and isolation have been largely banished from the social repertoire. The widened public sphere gives nearly everyone a new (and relatively shared) perspective from which to view others and to gain a reflected sense of self. We, our doctors, our police officers, our presidents, our secret agents, our parents, our children, and our friends are all performing roles in new theaters that demand new styles of drama.

15   Many formal reciprocal roles rely on lack of intimate knowledge of the "other." If the mystery and mystification disappear, so do the formal behaviors. Stylized courtship behaviors, for example, must quickly fade in the day-to-day

intimacy of marriage. Similarly, the new access we gain to distant events and to the gestures and actions of the other sex, our elders, and authorities does not simply "educate" us; such access changes social reality.

In both fictional and nonfictional television programs, 16 we have all seen how others prepare for and relax from their traditional "onstage" roles—as "parents who know best," as "masculine men" and "feminine women," and "inspiring leaders." By exposing previously "backstage" behaviors, television has served as an instrument of demystification. It has demystified adults for children, has made traditional sex roles seem transparent and phony, and has led to decline in the image and prestige of political and other leaders.

Our most successful recent president was the one most 17 sensitive to the demands of the new dramatic arena. But even President Reagan's credibility suffered from the public's heightened awareness of the "performance" nature of his presidency. Certainly, we prefer a good performance to a poor one. But we are no longer simply a naive political audience that accepts the onstage role as the only reality.

It is not surprising that the widespread rejection of tradi- 18 tional child and adult, male and female, and leader and follower roles should have begun in the late 1960s with the coming of age of the first generation of Americans to have been exposed to television before learning to read. When this generation was born—around 1950—only 9 percent of U.S. households owned TV sets; only five years later, 50 percent did. By 1966, only 6 percent of households did *not* own a television. In the shared environment of television, women and men, children and adults, and followers and leaders know a great deal about each other's behavior and social knowledge—too much, in fact, for them to play the traditional complementary roles of innocence versus omniscience.

As the experience and knowledge of different people in- 19 creasingly overlap, we are witnessing major social transformations. We are seeing more adultlike children and more childlike adults, more career-oriented women and more family-oriented men, and leaders who act more like the person next door, just as our real neighbors demand to have more of a say in local, national, and international affairs.

The Secret-Exposing Machine

20   Nineteenth-century life entailed many isolated situations
and sustained many isolated behaviors and attitudes. The
current merging of situations does not give us a sum of
what we had before, but rather new, synthesized behaviors
that are qualitatively different. If we celebrate our child's
wedding in an isolated situation where it is the sole "experience" of the day, then our joy may be unbounded. But when
on our way to the wedding, we hear over the car radio of
a devastating earthquake, or the death of a popular entertainer, or the assassination of a political figure, we not only
lose our ability to rejoice fully, but also our ability to mourn
deeply. The electronic combination of many different styles
of interaction from distinct behavioral regions leads to new
"middle region" behaviors that, while containing elements
of formerly distinct roles, are themselves new behavior patterns with new expectations and emotions.

21   Gone, therefore, are many people's "special" behaviors,
those that were associated with distinct and isolated interactions. Gone are the great eccentrics, the passionate
overpowering loves, the massive unrelenting hates, the
dramatic curses and flowery praises. Unbounded joy and
unmitigated misery cannot coexist in the same place and
time. As situations merge, the hot flush and the icy stare
blend into a middle region "cool." The difference between
the reality of behaviors in distinct situations versus the
reality of behaviors in merged situations is as great as
the difference between the nineteenth-century conception
that a man might have a virtuous wife and a raunchy
mistress and the twentieth-century notions of open marriages, living together, friendly divorce, and serial monogamy.

22   The height of print culture was a time of "secrets." The
Victorians were fascinated with the multiple layers and
depths of life: secret passageways, skeletons in the closet,
masks upon masks upon masks. But the awareness of these
layers did not push the Victorians to destroy secrecy, but
rather to maintain and enhance it as an enriching aspect
of the social order. For the most part, skeletons were meant
to stay in the closet, sex was to remain behind closed doors
(perhaps to be spied upon through keyholes), and scandal-
ous acts were to be hidden from peering eyes. The rare

exposures and discoveries were titillating, implicit hints of the vastness of undiscovered reality.

Our own age, in contrast, is fascinated by exposure. In- 23 deed, the act of exposure now seems to excite us more than the content of the secrets exposed. The steady stripping away of layers of social behavior has made the "major scandal" and the exposure of the "deep dark secret" everyday affairs. Ironically, what is pulled from the closets that supposedly contain extraordinary secrets is, ultimately, the potential banality of everyone. The unusual becomes commonplace: famous stars who abuse their children; presidents with hemorrhoids or colon cancer; a pope who gets depressed; televangelists who extort and cavort.

Still we hunger for heroes, and perhaps our search beneath 24 social masks is filled with the hope of finding people whose private selves are as admirable as their public ones. But since most of the people who make enduring contributions to our culture remain under our scrutiny too long to remain pure in our eyes, we have also begun to focus on people who make one grand gesture or who complete a single courageous act that cannot be undermined by scrutiny. Our new heroes are men and women like Lenny Skutnik, who dove into the water—before television cameras—to save an airplane crash survivor, or Reginald Andrews, who saved a blind man's life by pulling him from beneath a New York subway car. Both men were saluted as heroes by the president of the United States. We can admire such isolated heroic acts; the pasts and the futures of such heroes remain comfortably irrelevant and invisible.

The Birth of New Situations

Of course behind the many obvious social changes much 25 of our social order remains the same. There continue to be many distinctions in roles of group identity, different stages of socialization, and different ranks of hierarchy in spite of the homogenizing trend. (And after the dust of change from the current merging of roles settles, we are also likely to rediscover some of the many differences among us.) Further, while electronic media have merged many social situations, direct physical presence and mutual monitoring are still primary experiential modes. And regardless of media access, living in a ghetto, a prison cell, and a middle-class suburb are certainly not equivalent social experiences. Nevertheless, roles and places have changed dramatically and an analysis of how and why they have changed helps to explain many social phenomena that are not otherwise easily understood. While the merging of spheres through electronic media has not given everyone the same knowledge and wisdom, much of the old mystification surrounding other people and places has been pierced. Print still exists and holds many mysteries and secrets for those who master it, but many of the "secrets of secrecy" have been exposed.

26   The changing conceptions of secrecy and place, of gender distinctions, of childhood innocence, and of authority can all be seen in a single social event: the birth of a new human being. Not long ago, this scene was marked by highly isolated environments. Pregnant women were to stay out of public view. Husbands were distanced from the pregnancy and sheltered from the birth. During delivery, the father paced nervously in an isolated waiting room; the mother herself was "removed" from the birthing situation through drugs; young children were kept out of the hospital and were often further isolated through ignorance of the processes of pregnancy and birth. In charge of the birth were the all-powerful doctors, whose authority allowed them to defy gravity and nature and curiosity and mother-love as they wrenched the drugged infant from the womb in a cold stainless steel delivery room.

27   Today, the scene is vastly different. Pregnancy and birth are "family-centered"; fathers and children are often fully involved. A new phrase has entered the language: *"we* are pregnant," and it is now common practice for fathers and mothers to attend childbirth classes together and for fathers to be present at, and assist in, the birth. Siblings as young as two may be involved in the process by attending special "prepared sibling" classes, taking tours of the hospital, and, in some cases, being present at the birth itself.

28   Increasingly, many doctors and nurses are defining themselves more as "educators" than as authorities; the family is expected to make the final choices concerning the variables of delivery. In response to those hospitals and medical personnel who are not willing to allow families to choose their own birthing options, some middle-class families are opting for home deliveries with midwives. Others are giving

birth in "alternative birthing centers," which are a cross between hospitals and motels. But the most significant trend is the move in regular hospitals to blur the differences between labor room and home. Many hospitals are building special birthing rooms that are designed to resemble home bedrooms. Some have double beds, flowery wallpaper, carpeting, and soft chairs. Equipment for delivery is present but kept out of sight until needed. A man and a woman may now give birth to their child while looking out a window or watching television. The specialness of the place in which birth now takes place is further diluted by the increasingly popular trend toward photographing, filming, or videotaping the birth—so that the experience is taken out of the hospital and shared with friends, family, and, perhaps later, with the child itself.

Millions of dollars have been spent studying the effects 29 of television and other modern media. But in searching for effects largely in simple imitation and persuasion, we have been missing the broader impact on social boundaries and hence on social behavior. Electronic media affect us not primarily through their content but by changing the situational geography of everyday life.

TELEVISION AND THE ELECTIONS

Joshua Meyrowitz
Whither "1984"?

[*For an introduction to this essay, see the headnote to the previous selection.*]

1   We have now entered the era of George Orwell's gloomy prophecy. And there are many apparent similarities between Orwell's *1984* and our time. Until stymied, at least temporarily, by the recent changes in the Eastern bloc, our government was presenting us with the image of a world divided into two superpowers, Good versus Evil. Our supposedly unavoidable conflict with The Enemy has served as a backdrop and rationale for many of our domestic and foreign policies. Language, too, has fought the battle. Our actions have always been "defensive," theirs always "aggressive." Our interventions have been "rescue missions to preserve freedom"; theirs have been "invasions to crush the will of the people." Our economic assistance to underdeveloped countries has always been "humanitarian"; theirs has been "propagandistic." And even today, mind-boggling weapons of death are benignly labelled "peacekeepers," while many would-be peacekeepers are surrounded by hints of treason.

2   Many people jump from such observations to the assumption that developments in electronic media are hastening the arrival of an Orwellian nightmare. The evolution of sophisticated surveillance devices and the decline in privacy are seen as concrete manifestations of the type of totalitarianism described by Orwell. Yet these technological developments may actually be signs of a trend in the opposite direction.

3   Orwell offered a vision of society where Big Brother watched all, but was himself invisible. Orwell conceived of an "inner party" elite who observed but were unobservable. The Party demanded and received total loyalty and unques-

tioning obedience. Such a system is conceivable in an electronic age, but if the new technologies have any inherent bias, it may be against such a sharply hierarchical system.

"Leadership" and "authority" are unlike mere "power" in   4
that they depend on performance and appeal; one cannot lead or be looked up to if one is not there to be seen. Yet, paradoxically, authority is weakened by excess familiarity. Awe depends on "distant-visibility" and "mystified-presence." One of the peculiar ironies of our age is that most people who step forward into the media limelight and attempt to gain national visibility become too visible, too exposed, and are thereby demystified. Electronic media may be used by officials to spy on private citizens, but when an electronic medium such as television is used by leaders as a means of communicating with the people, the medium's close-up bias also allows citizens to spy on officials.

Further, for a hierarchy to exist, there must be more   5
followers than leaders. In an era of easy and relatively shared access to information about people, one leader may be able to keep a close watch on thousands of followers, but thousands of followers can keep an even closer watch on one leader. Ironically, the simple mathematics of hierarchy suggests the stronger likelihood of an undermining of the pyramid of status in an electronic age.

The speaker's platform once lifted politicians up and   6
away from average citizens, both literally and symbolically. In newspaper quotes and reports, the politician — as a flesh-and-bones person — was completely absent. And on radio, politicians were disembodied voices. But the television camera now lowers politicians to the level of the common citizen and brings them close for our inspection. In recent years, we've seen our presidents sweat, stammer, and stumble — all in living color. In the face of a "crisis," our presidents once had many hours, sometimes even weeks or months, to consult with advisers and to formulate policy statements to be printed in newspapers. But in live, televised appearances today, even a five-second pause for thought can seriously damage a leader's credibility.

Television not only reduces our awe of politicians; it also   7
increases politicians' self-doubt and lowers self-esteem. A speaker's nervousness and mistakes usually are politely ignored by live audiences and therefore soon forgotten by the speaker too. But with videotape, politicians have permanent records of themselves misspeaking or anxiously licking

their lips. Television may be a prime cause of the complaints of indecisive leadership and hesitant "followership" that we have heard since the mid-1960s.

8   Electronic media not only weaken authority by allowing those low on the ladder of hierarchy to gain access to much information about leaders, but also by affording increased opportunities for the sharing of information horizontally. The telephone and computer, for example, allow people to communicate with each other without going "through channels." Such horizontal flow of information through relatively egalitarian networks and matrices is another significant deterrent to totalitarian central leadership.

9   There is no doubt that new technologies — like old technologies — may be used by bad governments to bad ends. And once a totalitarian government exists, it can stop or control the flow of information. But the assumption that the new media or the lack of privacy they foster will, in and of themselves, support authoritarian hierarchies is based on a misunderstanding of the relationship between privacy and hierarchy. For it is privacy and distance that support strong central authorities. Our notions of privacy have a very short history in Western civilization, and as we know from studies of hunting and gathering societies and of pre-print Western Europe, the virtual lack of privacy tends to weaken rather than support great distinctions in status. It is the person who tries to stand apart or above, not the average citizen, who is most damaged by lack of privacy. We may be aesthetically uncomfortable with the thought of fuller and more open access to information, but, all other things being equal, such access tends to level hierarchies rather than erect them. Even the evidence we have been discovering recently about our leaders' abuses of power may, in this sense, testify more to our relatively increased ability to gather information on leaders rather than to an absolute increase in the abuse of power. The thing to fear is not the loss of privacy per se, but the *nonreciprocal* loss of privacy — that is, where we lose the ability to monitor those who monitor us.

10   As of now, electronic media may be encouraging the slow but steady growth of a "hierarchy of the people." For electronic media give a distinct advantage to the average person. Average people now have access to social information that once was not available to them. Further, they have information concerning the performers of high status roles.

As a result, the distance, mystery, and mystification surrounding high status roles are minimized. There are still many "unusual" people with special knowledge and training, but the average person now knows more about what special individuals know and also more about high status people as people. After seeing so much ordinariness in the close-up views of extraordinary people, we may continue to remain more ignorant and less powerful than they, but we are now more aware of the many things they do not know and cannot do. And even though much of this new information access is reciprocal, the common person has relatively less to lose from exposure and visibility. No one expects the common person to be anything but common. If Joe Smith finds out that the president cheats on his income tax, Joe is likely to be outraged—even if he cheats on his own income tax. Great leaders are not supposed to suffer the frailties of greed, lust, or instability.

Whether this demystification of political leaders is ulti- 11
mately good or bad is not yet entirely clear. On the good side, we seem less willing to follow leaders blindly. On the bad side, the void in confidence in leaders has not yet been filled by wide-scale political awareness or involvement. Nevertheless, at this moment in history, we may be witnessing the prelude to a political revolution of enormous proportions, a revolution that is masked by the conventions of our language and by the form of our traditional ideals. We are moving from a representative government of de facto elites to a government of direct participation with elected "administrators." The change is difficult to see, however, because we refer to both of these systems as "democracy" and because the new system involves the manifestation of many once unattainable ideals such as true "public servants" and "government by and for the people." Reality does not stay the same, however, when ideals become reality.

Electronic media offer the potential of government by 12
direct referendum, and the growth of interactive television promises the mixed blessing of a political system modeled after the structure of the "Gong Show"—where performers can be removed from the stage in midperformance. (A more pleasing metaphor for the same system is the Greek forum.) The new technology fosters the potential of the closest thing the earth has ever witnessed to participatory democracy on an enormous scale—with all the resulting problems and possibilities. Even if this comes to pass, however, we will

need some rethinking of our conceptions of authority if we are to see the system for what it is. For whoever steps before us in the role of leader will seem to be a disappointment compared with our hazy, but glowing images of Washingtons, Jeffersons, and Lincolns, and any step taken without our knowledge, any move taken in opposition to a majority "vote" in a national poll, will be seen as the arrogance of power.

13   Although the political problems of our age may not be the obvious ones many people fear, there remain a number of reasons for caution. The decline in trust in authorities is filled with paradox and some danger. The growth in weapons technology and the increase in speed in global communications have led to an enhancement of the raw power of national leaders even as our faith in governments and leaders has declined. Our recent presidents have had the power to destroy the entire world, but they have often lacked the authority to convince the majority of the population that they are doing a competent job. There is always the danger of leaders using their massive war-making powers in attempts to rally the people behind them — or as an excuse for secrecy and information control.

14   Further, television news continues to follow traditional journalistic conventions of relying primarily on "official sources" and of allowing authorities to set the agenda for news coverage, even as television exposure has encouraged us to question the authority of leaders. Similarly, our increasingly complex technological and social world has made us rely more and more heavily on "expert information," but the general exposure of experts as fallible human beings has lessened our faith in them as people. The change in our image of leaders and experts leaves us with a distrust of power, but also with a seemingly powerless dependence on those in whom we have little trust.

15   The vacuum in our visible political realm of authority may be giving undue power to *in*visible men and women who run large national and multinational corporations. Unlike governments, corporations have no code of "openness." Indeed, competitive business is built on a tradition of secrecy. A business leader who refuses an interview is not viewed as suspiciously as a governor or a president who refuses to speak to the press. We do need to be wary, therefore, of the increasingly complex involvement of many corporations in university research, in government, in domestic and foreign

policy, and in all forms of national and international communication technologies themselves — from book publishing to satellites.

There is also one visible class of "authorities" who, 16 through their unique positions in our society, have been able to become exceptions to the decline in visible authority. These people have managed to maintain both controlled access to the people *and* controlled performances. They are the television newscasters whose daily performances are tightly controlled and scripted. In an implicit professional code, television news programs do not generally expose other news programs or news personalities. A few moments of prime time may be used to show a president fall down while skiing, collapse while jogging, or make a serious slip of the tongue, but there are few, if any, intentional television exposures of Peter Jennings, Tom Brokaw, or Dan Rather falling down, cursing, making serious mistakes, or becoming irritable and tense. Such conventions maintain the fiction that the selectively revealed aspects of newscasters' personalities are representative of their whole selves. This situation may explain why, a few years ago, Walter Cronkite was described as "the most trusted man in America" and was considered to be a viable vice-presidential candidate, even though he had not, at that point, ever expressed his personal political views. Although there is not yet evidence that this power is being abused, we need to be more aware of the staging contingencies that may be enhancing our trust in electronic journalists just as they weaken our faith in the political process.

Garry Wills

The Remaking of the Presidents

Garry Wills (born 1934) is an iconoclastic political essayist who lives in Chicago and teaches at Northwestern. Whether his books concern the Kennedys or Richard Nixon, the Catholic Church or political history, they always raise controversy and careful thought; Inventing America *(1978), an original ac-*

*count of the drafting of the Declaration of Independence, won
a National Book Award. The following essay appeared in 1988
in* Omni, *a general-interest science magazine.*

1   The presidential candidate was on fire with his cause:
"We have petitioned, and our petitions have been scorned.
. . . We have begged, and they have mocked when our calam-
ity came. We beg no longer. . . . We petition no more. We
defy them. . . . You come to us and tell us that the great
cities are in favor of the gold standard. We reply, Burn
down your cities and leave our farms, and your cities will
spring up again as if by magic; but destroy our farms, and
grass will grow in the streets of every city in the country."

2   This speech was not televised from either the Republican
convention in New Orleans or the Democratic convention
in Atlanta, though the powerful images and sense of urgency
are reminiscent of Reverend Jesse Jackson's plea in Atlanta
to move to higher ground, common ground. "We find," said
Jackson, "common ground at the farm auction, where a
good farmer loses his or her land to bad loans or diminishing
markets. . . . Farmers, you seek fair prices, and you are right.
But you cannot stand alone; your patch is not big enough."

3   Television was not even a remote possibility in 1896 when
William Jennings Bryan, author of the opening speech, ran
for president against William McKinley. The thirty-six-
year-old orator, all eloquence and moral glow, stampeded
two parties—the Democratic and the Populist—with his
"Cross of Gold" speech. But if the presence of television had
forced an actual debate between the participants, Bryan
would have had an immense edge—all of the gifts John
Kennedy had in 1960, along with a greater sense of crisis
in the nation. Even without the advantage television might
have given to such an electrifying speaker, he won 6.5 million votes to McKinley's 7 million. Television cameras,
tracking this dynamic young challenger in his restless
moral quest, would most likely have forced McKinley to
get out on the stump for at least some of the time.

4   Many people, when they think of television, consider its
cosmetic possibilities rather than its ability to transmit
information that only insiders knew in the past. This election year has given us nominees for the presidency who are
not, either of them, strikingly telegenic in sheer cosmetic
terms. Even Ronald Reagan, the "Great Communicator,"
spent as much of his time avoiding television (in the form

of press conferences, debates, and questioning opportunities) as in adorning it with ceremonial addresses. Wrong information or historical blunders may doom a candidate's chances on Election Day. In the 1976 debate between Gerald Ford and Jimmy Carter, for example, Ford's mishap — "There's no Soviet domination of Eastern Europe" — gave Carter an edge in the polls.

Even so, the cosmetic power is there, as was demonstrated when Senator Kennedy's image proved so much more attractive than Vice President Richard Nixon's in 1960. Before the first televised debates in American history, voters were evenly split between Kennedy and Nixon. In the four debates that followed, the young Kennedy was calm and relaxed; Nixon, the more experienced debater, appeared tense and ill at ease. Kennedy's forceful image probably was a crucial factor in his narrow victory over Nixon. 5

It is fair to say that modern politics occurs primarily before the TV camera. It is there, under the glare of the lights, that the candidate defines himself and discusses his agenda. A critical factor in the marriage between television and modern politics, however, is the use of image blips and visual symbols to influence the voters' perception of the candidate. According to an August 7, 1988, article in *The New York Times*, an art director at an ad agency in New York who helped design the first Republican Party ads for this year's campaign said that the Dukakis–Bush race "will probably be decided by images you see on television." 6

According to today's media consultants, candidates should avoid appearing uncertain, maintain eye contact, smile under pressure, use proper gestures, give brief but direct answers to questions, and learn how to control difficult interviews. The purpose: to win over the undecided voter. 7

Prior to the advent of television, candidates were just as concerned about their image and the message they conveyed, but they utilized the techniques of their day — banners, slogans, songs, newsprint, and the available technology (railroads, telegraphic and stenographic reporting). In the 1858 debates between Abraham Lincoln and Senator Stephen Douglas for the Senate, Douglas had a flatcar behind his private train coach with a 12-pound cannon announcing his arrival at a site. Lincoln specialized in female processions (which he called his "bouquets"); one of them marched 8 to the scene with a banner held by 32 young women, each symbolizing a state in the Union: "Westward the course of empire takes its way."

9   Large crowds, possibly as many as 15,000 people at one time — gathered to hear Lincoln and Douglas debate. Partisans hissed, booed, and interrupted the speakers up close and fought with one another around the edges of the crowd where "painkiller" was being hawked from various booths — the equivalent of modern TV ads.

10   Hypothetical history is never more than a game: more or less sophisticated, never quite legitimate, though entertaining. To change one factor is to imagine changes in all the other factors dependent upon it. For television to be present in earlier campaigns, other kinds of communications also would have to be assumed (jet airplanes rather than the railroads Douglas rode as the modern marvels of his time), and corresponding political displacements — weakened party control over the contenders for nomination. Mass radio and television would supply channels of information for candidates as well as voters.

11   With all of these factors taken into consideration, we can make some reasonable guesses about what would have happened if television had been present during past campaigns.

Stephen Douglas and Abraham Lincoln, Illinois Senatorial Race, 1858

12   The easiest way to belittle modern debates on television is by referring — with a reverence built on ignorance — to the epic 1858 encounters between Abraham Lincoln and Stephen Douglas. The Lincoln–Douglas debates have become our touchstone of reasoned disagreement at election time, and it hardly matters that they were demagogic exercises in mutual entrapment that backfired for both men. Lincoln lost the debates in the sense that he was not elected senator, his immediate objective. Douglas lost in that he was not elected president two years later, his ulterior objective. Both men lost by failing to save the Union, a goal they shared and that they actually made more difficult for each other and for the rest of the country.

13   This is not a "revisionist" view of the debates. Contemporaries were as harsh on them as we are on our televised

question-and-answer sessions today; newspapers of the
nineteenth century yearned for their own "good old days,"
when the founders of the Republic would not have stooped
to the tricks of stump debaters. "Washington was no speech
maker, neither was Jefferson," huffed a Cincinnati paper.
And the *Norfolk Argus* lamented: "In the earlier days of our
republic such a piece of bold effrontery and impudence
would have met with its merited rebuke." Lincoln himself
would call campaign oratory divisive when he refused to
give any speeches, two years later, as a candidate for the
presidency.

Douglas won the Senate race in 1858. Television might 14
have widened his margin a bit. He was an impressive
speaker, full of jaunty energy of the Jimmy Cagney sort, all
strut and humorous pugnacity — something frozen out of
surviving pictures, which could be focused only if one held
a long pose. Yet his voice gave out easily in the three-hour
contests, making him plead with his own supporters not
to drown his words with cheers — a problem TV would have
obviated.

Lincoln, on the other hand, had some very eccentric plat- 15
form manners, especially at the beginning of a speech, when
he was still nervous. Historian Allan Nevins describes the
problem: "His principal movements when talking — clasp-
ing and unclasping his hands, first behind him and then in
front of himself, an uncouth swing of his long arms, or a
sudden dip at the knees followed by a sharp upward jerk
with much gesticulation of the head — were often indescrib-
ably gauche."

Perhaps with proper coaching he might have modified 16
his style for television, where his logic, humor, and beautiful
prose would have made its impact. His sly remarks would
not have needed the folksy emphasis he gave them when
milking gags for a big audience, especially his references
to Douglas's theories as "homeopathic soup" — made by
boiling the shadow of a pigeon that had starved to death.

The Lincoln–Douglas debates are historically important 17
because they prefigured the breakdown of a nation. Both
men were trying to save the Union from different but overlapping geographic bases. Television, had it been available,
would have made the regional appeal less tempting and
would have thrust other issues into the debate. It would
certainly have improved the decorum of the proceedings,
though it is hard to imagine its changing the outcome.

Designated questioners might have led Lincoln to be less vague about how slavery would die out if people just let it alone. He contented himself with the thought that everyone would someday agree that it was wrong, and "then, and not till then, I think, will we in some way come to an end of the slavery agitation." Douglas might have been forced to say what he thought of slavery personally, a matter he artfully evaded in the debates, to the lasting bewilderment of his admirers.

Theodore Roosevelt and Woodrow Wilson, 1912

18   The presence of television would have given Teddy Roosevelt the visibility he needed to heal the Republican spirit. Television would have undercut the power of the party bosses, who — for good or ill — controlled the nomination process. That power was what made Republicans cling to William Taft after Roosevelt led his "Bull Moose" (Progressive Republican) opposition out of the Chicago convention and held a counterconvention, improvised and full of drama, just made for television. Taft, a stranded whale, held out against his former mentor, calling in all party debts: but all the vitality of Progressivism was with Roosevelt.

19   In the closing weeks of the campaign Roosevelt was shot in Milwaukee by a fanatic who opposed any third-term president. Roosevelt, his shirt bloody, the bullet still in his body, went on to give his scheduled speech, saying, "I will give this speech or die." Television would not only have captured that incident with all its theatrical force, it would have replayed the dramatic moment repeatedly after October 14, magnifying Roosevelt's courage and rallying the Progressives who, doubtful that a third party could win, were defecting to the Democrats

20   Woodrow Wilson, whom the Democrats had nominated late and rather reluctantly (on the forty-sixth ballot), was an inspirational orator of the Adlai Stevenson type, but without the visceral appeal of Roosevelt. Not only the more vital of the two, Roosevelt was the more genuinely learned (despite Wilson's doctorate, barely earned, in political science). In a television debate, Roosevelt would have had an enormous edge on his opponent. As it was, Wilson won only by a plurality of the popular votes, Taft drawing off enough

of the Republican majority party's members to defeat Roosevelt. In retrospect, Roosevelt seems to have been born for TV; 1912 could have proved it.

Thomas E. Dewey and Harry Truman, 1948

The modern polling techniques of 1948 lured Thomas E. 21
Dewey into a false sense of security in his bid against Harry Truman. Ignoring the expertise of the day, Truman invented the modern campaign train (now replaced by the campaign plane) and whistle-stopped himself to a great reversal. If we suppose a greater range and variety of technology available to both candidates, it is hard to imagine the surprise upset occurring. Television would have captured the excitement Truman was creating at distant Western stops; better polls and hot-line reports would have traced changes in the public mood.

Dewey would have had to come out of his ivory tower, 22
where he was putting together his new government, and campaign like a candidate instead of making declarations as if he were already President. Perhaps he would not have been able to stop the extraordinary effort of Truman, but Dewey had been impressive in newsreels as a crusading district attorney in New York; he did have the initial lead that fooled everyone; Truman would have lost some of his underdog appeal if the polls were corrected and expectable countermeasures taken by Dewey.

In Dewey's case television would have forced on the can- 23
didate a bit more boldness but not enough to have altered the outcome. The present tendency seems to inculcate more caution. It is painfully clear that a single gaffe captured on television — Edmund Muskie seeming to cry, Senator Joseph Biden lashing out angrily at a question about his law school performance — can damage if not doom a candidacy. Furthermore, television is always watching. C-SPAN, the cable satellite public-affairs network, is present all the time, at the smallest caucus and primary events, even though the network news shows are drawing smaller audiences. The Biden outburst occurred before a C-SPAN camera, but it was instantly transmitted through the networks, adding a final touch to Biden's troubles over a plagiarism charge.

Today television is making candidates play "defense 24

ball": speaking in predetermined sound bites, avoiding the spontaneous, cutting back on question-and-answer sessions, scheduling debates in less conspicuous time slots. Ironically, apprentice politicians must strive to appear on the tube as often as possible in order to get name recognition (which is now face recognition as well). Then—progressively, as they come into positions where their comments matter more—they begin to ration those comments, hedge them, deliver them in muffled or ambiguous ways. So television has contradictory influences working at one and the same time—toward the wider dissemination of information and toward a tighter control and limitation of what we are to know or hear. This cautious tendency, this fear of any misstep, was there before television but in special cases rather than as a broad influence. It was the strategy that made Lincoln refuse to give any campaign speeches during the emotionally divisive time between his nomination and the 1861 inauguration, a time when several states had already seceded. Television would not have let Lincoln remain so aloof today.

Lincoln and William Seward, Republican Convention, Chicago, 1860

25   If television had been around in 1860, it is extremely unlikely that Lincoln would have been the Republican nominee for President. The best way to see the possible effects of television for accidental evil as well as general good is to go back to the Republican convention and look at the struggle to nominate a candidate. The great favorite in what was offering itself as the healing party was William Seward, who entered the convention in Chicago with a majority of delegates.

26   What followed was a series of deals, bribes, and dirty tricks that could not have endured the scrutiny of TV. Lincoln's managers prevented a balloting when Seward still held the lead, by blocking the printing of ballots. Then they jammed the hall with their supporters while Seward's people were out parading for him and offered posts in the Lincoln administration (which Lincoln later honored) to members of key delegations. As Murat Halstead, the best reporter of political conventions, wrote, "The fact of the

Convention was the defeat of Seward rather than the nomination of Lincoln."

In 1980 television doomed the "dream ticket" of Ronald 27
Reagan and Gerald Ford by airing its possibility and eliciting strong criticism of it before Reagan could make up his mind. In New Orleans in 1988 television speculation on vice presidential bids led to the premature announcement of George Bush's choice of Senator Dan Quayle. And then, in his television debut, the telegenic senator from Indiana, a true child of the television age, appeared rattled and uncertain as he defended himself against allegations of past misconduct involving his military service, a golf trip to Florida with a female lobbyist, and whether he had enough experience to be President should Bush not be able to complete his term.

It is hard to imagine television reporters not swarming 28
around the ballot printers in Chicago in 1860, or the walkie-talkie teams of various networks not alerting camera crews out on the street that Lincoln's men were packing the hall with supporters. Given any of these interventions by television, Seward, not Lincoln, would have been nominated.

Seward was a sentimental favorite with Republicans be- 29
cause of his clear-cut opposition to slavery. Lincoln was, by comparison, more equivocal: His supporters argued that he "had made no records to be defended or explained." As we have seen, he made no public statements at all, not even in response to editors' written requests, during the presidential contest. Seward would not have stayed silent had he been the candidate. But Seward, even if he had not been defeated at the convention, would certainly have been defeated by political passions in the general election. In fact, with Lincoln removed from the race, the most obvious winner would have been Stephen Douglas, his old foe of the Illinois debate—the most moderate candidate left in that field. Some champions of Douglas have argued that he might conceivably have held the Union together. But they ignore the disconcerting fact that he died three months after the 1861 inauguration—which would have left the hellish problems of secession to his running mate, Herschel V. Johnson, a former governor of Georgia.

How such a man, a Southerner, would have coped with 30
the unraveling nation, no one can know. But the outcome could hardly have been as favorable as it was under Lincoln's strong, magnanimous guidance. Would we have had

a successful secession, the President of the United States blessing his sister states as they departed? Would a war have been fought, to an ambiguous conclusion? (Lincoln himself was afraid he could not sustain the war in early 1864.) Would we have had a series of civil wars or trial republics that would be made up of splintering groups of states?

31   Television is a mixed blessing, and in dispelling the corruptions of the 1860 convention, it might have brought upon us curses even greater than those of the Civil War as it was fought—curses, moreover, brought vividly home to people who were frightened enough by Mathew Brady's murky photographs. (Between 1861 and 1865 Brady accompanied the Union armies, taking photographs that became the basis for a pictorial history of the Civil War.) Progress exacts its costs. Abraham Lincoln might have been one of the things the nation would have lost to the unquestionable benefit of modern communications technology.

Wilson Carey McWilliams

A Republic of Couch Potatoes: The Media Shrivel the Electorate

Wilson Carey McWilliams, who teaches political science at Rutgers, has written several books on elections. The following article was published in 1989 in Commonweal, *an influential public affairs magazine.*

1   The election of 1988 sent an urgent signal that something is wrong with the political soul of American democracy. The campaign was more than negative. It was a year when civility "took it on the chin," one in which, on talk shows as in politics, nastiness "became a commodity" (Lena Williams, *New York Times*, December 18, 1988). Even so, it had precedents.

2   In 1888, President Grover Cleveland, who had survived considerable tarring four years earlier, faced smears and

distortions at least the equal of 1988. His former opponent, James G. Blaine, charged that Cleveland had appointed to office 137 convicted criminals, including two murderers, seven forgers, and several brothel keepers. Mrs. Cleveland was forced to deny the rumor that the president beat and abused her. It was said that Cleveland was a dogmatic liberal (of the nineteenth-century variety) and the equivalent of a "secular humanist" because he was reported to have said, "I believe in free trade as I believe in the Protestant religion."

Most notoriously, Matt Quay, the Republican boss of 3
Pennsylvania, engineered a scheme by which a Republican supporter, posing as a former British subject, wrote to the British ambassador asking which candidate would best advance Britain's interest. The ambassador, Mr. Sackville-West, injudiciously replied that Cleveland's free trade sympathies made him preferable, and Republicans exultantly portrayed Cleveland as unpatriotic and, especially in Irish wards, as the tool of British imperialism.

Nevertheless, there is something new and alarming about 4
the incivilities of the presidential campaign in 1988. In the first place, the electronic media give greater force and currency to scurrilities, just as television makes innuendo visible: Blaine's attack on Cleveland's appointments had nothing like the impact of a glowering Willie Horton, illustrating Republican claims that Dukakis had been "soft on crime," or of pictures of garbage afloat in Boston harbor. Moreover, contemporary voters are more exposed to and dependent on mass media.

In Cleveland's day, the press could still be described, in 5
the terms Tocqueville used earlier, as a form of political association. There was a mass press, but the great majority of newspapers were local, the voices and guardians of community. Information from national campaigns and leaders reached most voters only through local editors, leaders, and opinion makers who interpreted it and passed on its propriety and authenticity. In 1988, the media spoke to more and more citizens directly, without intermediaries; gatekeepers could not protect us when the fences had been trampled or pulled down.

In 1888, American politics was still dense with associa- 6
tions, and for both parties, the presidential candidate was only the chief figure in a campaign made up of a myriad of local campaigns in states and wards. Cleveland, in fact,

did not campaign at all, considering huckstering beneath the dignity of his office, and Benjamin Harrison's more active office-seeking was very limited by our standards.

7   Law and technology have combined to create a centralized presidential politics dominated by national media and party committees. In campaigns, as in voting, congressional and local elections are sharply distinct from the presidential contest, so much so that it seemed anomalous, on election night, when candidates for governor and U.S. senator in Montana received about the same percentage of the vote as their party's nominee for president.

8   The "nationalization of the electorate" has been a major political theme of the century, the result of an effort to open politics to individual citizens, freeing them from the control of local elites. Progressive reformers, advocates of the primary system, were also inclined to celebrate the mass media, just as their successors urged a more responsible two-party system. In one respect, the breaking down of racial barriers to political participation, the process has been pure gain. It has become increasingly clear, however, that the grand design of the reform tradition has failed.

9   Despite prolonged campaigning, despite vast expenditure of money (in which, in 1988, the two parties were virtually equal), despite the advice of experts and the easing of rules for voter registration, turnout fell — as it has, with the exception of the New Deal years, throughout this century. This "demobilization" of the electorate is too profound and too persistent to be explained by the requirement of registration or other barriers to voting. In 1988, the fraction of adult Americans who went to the polls was almost 20 percent lower than it was in 1960, when racial discrimination still kept masses of black Americans off the electoral rolls. In Todd Gitlin's axiom, "As politics grows more professional, voting declines."

10   The affective distance between citizens and public life is great and growing. When they vote for president, voters must evaluate candidates, whose characters they know only superficially, for an office in which character is crucial. We lack the peer review that, in earlier years, was provided by party leaders and opinion makers who controlled nominations and guided campaigns. In 1884, the discovery that Grover Cleveland apparently had fathered an illegitimate child provoked the response that such private failings, then as now the focus of media attention, are not the most important indices of *political* character, and Cleveland won the

election. In 1988, by contrast, while Gary Hart's derelictions shattered his candidacy, voters did not appear to notice that, after all his years in the Senate, Hart was endorsed by only one incumbent Democratic senator. Judgment by peers is yielding to an audition by the media, and private proprieties may now outweigh public virtues.

Be that as it may, citizens *are* dependent on mass media 11 for news and for the interpretation needed to make sense out of the bewildering ravelments of contemporary life. At the same time, the media are great concentrations of power, remote and distant "private governments" that decide who will speak to us and on what terms. In the media's version of deliberation, citizens have no voices; one cannot "talk back" to a television set, and citizens can assert their dignity only by refusing to listen. Of course, a displeased viewer can also change channels, but this "receiver control" is almost entirely negative, given the media's tendency toward a homogenized message.

Yet media decision makers know that, while the power 12 of the media as a whole is overawing, any *single* medium is vulnerable, its position still more precarious because media domination invites resentment. Changing channels is as easy as it is because national television has no organic relation to our lives; a local newspaper or radio station is part of, and often indispensable to, the day-to-day life of a community, but there is no reason why I should prefer ABC to NBC or CBS. The older media, especially the local press, had a position that permitted them to offer "cue giving" — guidance as well as protection — and evaluation was an integral part of their reporting. The electronic media are more anxious to "resonate"; more fearful of giving offense, they cultivate nonpartisanship and a professional neutrality.

Better than the Democrats, the Republicans have under- 13 stood that this desperate neutrality makes it easy to neutralize the media. Fairly consistently, Republican candidates criticize the media, appealing to the public's fear of hidden persuaders and joining its resentment of media power. George Bush virtually began his campaign with a contrived face-off with Dan Rather, and he continued to fault the media's coverage of the election. This media bashing takes the form of asking for fair play or balanced treatment, but its real aim is to insulate a candidate — or a president — from criticism, Teflon-coating its beneficiaries.

The success of this strategy was evident in the media 14

response to this year's presidential and vice-presidential debates. After the first debate, the media pronounced the exchange a draw, a defensible stance even if a plurality of viewers thought Dukakis had edged Bush. Even John Chancellor's astonishing claim that Dan Quayle had done well, despite Lloyd Bentsen's one-sided victory, might be explained as a too-rigid refusal to take sides. But television newsmen showed no reluctance to declare that Bush had won the second presidential debate. Taken as a whole, these comments suggest that if the media did not approach Republican candidates "on bended knee" — Mark Hertsgaard's description of the Reagan years — they did bend over backward.

15   Even at its best, however, television reporting (and increasingly, all reporting) shies away from evaluating the substance, or even the accuracy, of what is said in campaigns, preferring to discuss the strategy and process of campaigning. Nominally neutral, this emphasis on stratagems effectively tells citizens that the *public* side of politics — and, especially, those questions being argued — is of secondary importance. Even pure quantities, like results of polls and elections, need to be interpreted in the light of momentum and expectations. In this implicit teaching, "real politics" is covert, a business for professionals that can be approached only through inside information supplied by the media.

16   Parties and candidates, of course, struggle to control the process of interpretation, bypassing the press whenever possible and controlling photo opportunities through carefully contrived events. In 1988, for example, the Dukakis campaign, after beginning with relatively frequent press conferences, followed the Republicans' example in shielding the candidate from the press. Similarly, both national conventions were transparently staged to avoid any appearance of conflict and to project optimism, harmony, and concern for "family values." Ironically, the 1988 conference of the Communist party of the Soviet Union featured heated debate, resembling an old-style American party convention as much as the 1988 American conventions called to mind the traditional, totalitarian gatherings of the Communist party.

17   "Packaging," however, only redefines the role of the media; by pushing debate and decision offstage, it makes citizens even more dependent on the media to search what

is said in public for clues to the real deliberations behind the scenes. Public life, increasingly, is mirroring the media's art. Portrayed as trivial or superficial, political events become lifeless and shallow, arguments for cynicism and indifference.

Inherently, the electronic media emphasize the private, 18 self-protective, and individualistic side of American culture at the expense of citizenship and public life. Traditional politics, like older forms of entertainment, drew citizens into public places; the media bring politics to individuals in private retreats. In those settings, private concerns are naturally uppermost, making it harder than usual — and it is always difficult — to appeal to public goods and goals. Politics is dramaturgical: It asks us to step beyond the day-to-day, to see the present in the light of the possible, judging practice by theory. Great politics, like great theater, requires a special space, a precinct for its particular sort of fantasy, from which we reemerge into everyday life. Such distinctions hone and heighten experience; by blurring fantasy and reality so pervasively, television weakens reality's force and fantasy's charm.

Above all else, television is a visual medium, confined to 19 what can be seen and hence to externalities. Sight is our quickest sense, but it is also superficial, and the media's discontinuity of image and affect encourages emotional detachment, adaptation rather than commitment. A politics of the visible comes naturally to, and teaches us to be, a world of strangers.

At the most fundamental level, politics is about invisible 20 things. A political society can be symbolized — for example, by the flag, George Bush's talisman in 1988 — but it cannot be *seen*. Especially in a polity as diverse as the United States, political community is not a matter of outward semblance but of inward likeness, common ideas and ideals. In this sense, television almost necessarily distorts politics, since it is forced to visualize and personalize things that are impalpable or objective. When events suit the medium, as in television's coverage of the southern civil rights movement, it speaks with unique power, but more often it is apt to be misleading, silly (Dukakis's tank ride), or mischievous.

To classical political theory, speech, not sight, is the 21 most political of the faculties because it is in and through speech that we discover the boundaries and terms of political community. But political speech — and, especially, *listening* to political speech — is a skill and pleasure that must be learned. It demands an extended span of attention, the capacity for critical reflection, and that art of hearing that lets us separate meaning from its disguises. Always difficult, that command of rhetoric is harder to cultivate in a society as supersonic as ours, and the electronic media actually undermine the arts of speech and hearing.

22   Preoccupied with holding their audience, television programmers shun anything that might bore us (the Republican argument, this year, against more than two presidential debates), a logic that tends toward the lowest common public denominator. The 1988 debates were question-and-answer sessions in which no comment could run longer than two minutes; in 1960, Kennedy and Nixon began their debates with eight-minute opening statements. In the 1970s, the average "sound bite" allowed a public figure was fifteen to twenty seconds, and the president was given as much as a minute. Pretty thin at best. But in the 1980s, the figure has declined to ten seconds for *all* public figures. It symbolizes the decline of speech that George Bush, admiring the refrain, made "Don't Worry, Be Happy" into a campaign song, either ignoring the words or trusting that American voters would not notice their very contrary lesson.

23   "Almost the only pleasure of which an American has any idea," Alexis de Tocqueville wrote, "is to take part in government and to discuss the part he has taken," and even women "listen to political harangues after their household labors." More recently, Frank Skeffington, Edwin O'Connor's fictional mayor, spoke of politics as America's "greatest spectator sport," in which performers could, at least, rely on a critical mass of knowledgeable fans, but Skeffington was already sounding "the last hurrah." In 1988, public speech seemed to be degenerating into shouted incivility, the tough talk of playground squabbles, at best a preface to politics.

24   America cannot be an ancient Greek *polis* or a homogeneous community; political life must find room for our diversities and our privacies, just as prudence must acknowledge the impact of technology and economic change. American democracy needs, and can stand, only so many stanzas of epic poetry. Contemporary politics calls for the more prosaic effort to protect and rebuild locality, association, and party, the links between private

individuals and public goods. Even such limited goals, however, presume policy guided by a ruling principle, that middle term between repression and relativism whose better name is citizenship. For both Republicans and Democrats, the election of 1988 indicates the need for a new civility, and for the kinds of word and deed necessary to affirm the dignity of self-government.

Mortimer B. Zuckerman
1992 — A New Proposal

Mortimer B. Zuckerman (1937), who was born into a middle-class home in Montreal, came to the United States in 1961, studied business at Penn and law at Harvard — and parlayed real estate dealings into one of the largest fortunes in America. Recently he has included publishing among his interests — he purchased The Atlantic Monthly *and, in 1984,* U.S. News & World Report, *where he published the following editorial just before the 1988 election.*

America should not endure another presidential election 1
as trivial, negative and evasive as this one. Our Constitution may enshrine the world's greatest democracy, but two phenomena now threaten its proper working: The rise to dominance of television and the decline of the political party. These are irreversible, but need not be malign. There is a simple reform that will transform the 1992 presidential race. It builds on the only redeeming feature of this campaign, the three debates.

The debates attracted millions of Americans. Despite all 2
the limits of the format, they added to our appreciation of the character of the candidates and their positions on a number of issues. Of course, the debates were not entirely spontaneous; the candidates rehearsed their positions, but many of their responses were surprisingly revealing: Dan Quayle's irrelevant reiteration of his qualifications, Michael Dukakis's passionless reaction to the hypothesis that his wife had been raped and murdered and Lloyd Bentsen's

rebuke of Quayle for comparing himself to John F. Kennedy. In all, they illuminated the growth of George Bush and the limits of Dukakis, who revealed all the virtues we dislike and none of the vices we admire.

3   With the debates, we have something to judge. With the nightly newscasts (and with the commercials), we are subject to manipulation and a starvation diet of information. What we have on the nightly newscasts is "PTV," political television, cast in the mold of MTV, Music Television. Symbolism is everything: The medium has indeed become the message. PTV's purpose is entertainment, good pictures and controversy, not information, history and education. The more biting and personal the candidates and the more spectacular their visual backdrops, the more likely they are to get free time on network PTV. So the TV specialists have taken over. They work behind the scenes with the handlers, "spin controllers" and advertising specialists to see that the candidate is packaged and not exposed to experiences that might be revealing.

4   The campaign is thus about style, not about substance. In most industrial democracies, politicians rise to the top by a process in which they are judged by their elected peers and parties, as well as by their electorates. Here, the role of political parties has been virtually wiped out by our system of primaries and caucuses. Anyone, qualified or not, can jump into a national campaign. Money and packaging are all that are required.

5   One result is that campaigns have come to focus on character. The public looks for the best man rather than for the best party, or even the best stance on the issues. Given the complexity of today's issues, that is understandable, for we are comfortable with our capacity to make character judgments. Indeed, the importance of a candidate's response to a question may be in the clues his response gives to the way he approaches a problem. After all, many of the tough decisions a President has to make cannot be imagined in advance. With Nixon and with Carter, character was more important in the end than what they said they would do. But, again, PTV is delusory. It is too easy, using electronic symbolism, to create a false impression of character.

6   Here, then, is the supreme value of the debate and the press conference. Future presidential candidates must be forced into public forums where they will have to talk more

seriously about the major issues, where they cannot just project images of character that might prove false. We cannot confine a presidential election to two debates and virtually no national press conferences. The answer is for the Federal Election Commission to use its power of patronage. It will be giving about $50 million of public money to each candidate in the next presidential election. These grants should depend on a candidate's agreement to five 90-minute debates between Labor Day and Election Day, the last to be held in the week before the election. The debates should involve 45 minutes of questioning by the press and 45 minutes of the candidates questioning each other directly. Each candidate should also be required to have one 60-minute press conference every week.

This must be the last election in which a President may enter the White House by manipulating an electronic back door, for such elections do not provide a mandate with which to govern.

WHO AND WHAT IS BRUCE SPRINGSTEEN?

Maureen Orth, with Jane Thuck and Peter Greenberg

The Making of a Rock Star

The following article was the cover story of Newsweek, *October 27, 1975 — the same day* Time *also ran a cover story on Bruce Springsteen.*

1   The movie marquee in Red Bank, N.J., simply said "HOMECOMING," because everyone knew who was home. Out in the audience was Cousin Frankie, who taught him his first guitar chords. So were the guys from Freehold High who played in his early rock 'n' roll bands. They did not have to be hyped on Bruce Springsteen. This was the scruffy kid they had seen for years in the bars and byways of coastal Jersey. But Bruce was suddenly big time. The rock critics, the media, the music-industry heavies all said so. And in Red Bank, Bruce showed them just how far he had come. With Elvis shimmies and Elton leaps, Springsteen re-created his own electric brand of '50s rock 'n' roll magic. He clowned with saxophonist Clarence Clemons, hustled and bumped his way around the stage and gave a high-voltage performance that lasted more than two hours. When he leaned into the microphone, ripped off his black leather jacket and blasted, "Tramps like us, baby, we were born to run," the Jersey teeny-boppers went wild. After four foot-stomping encores they were ready to crown Bruce Springsteen the great white hope of rock 'n' roll.

2   The official investiture took place last week in Los Angeles at Springsteen's carefully staged West Coast debut at the Roxy Night Club on Sunset Strip. At the kind of opening-night event that defines hip status for at least six months, new Hollywood and rock royalty embraced Bruce Springsteen as one of their own. In a rare ovation that lasted a

full four minutes, Jack Nicholson, Ryan and daughter Tatum O'Neal, Wolfman Jack, and Neil Diamond seconded Cousin Frankie and the boys from Freehold High in Red Bank. Bruce Springsteen was a superstar.

Bruce who? He is still not exactly a household name   3 across America. In San Mateo, California, last week, his 13-year-old sister Pam said, "Only one girl at school has his record." The bus driver's son—who bears a striking resemblance to Dylan, sports black leather jackets like Brando in "The Wild One" and wears a gold hoop earring— was known to only a small coterie of East Coast devotees a year ago. But since the release last August of his highly professional third album, "Born to Run," which rocketed to a million-dollar gold album in six weeks, 26-year-old Bruce Springsteen has exploded into a genuine pop-music phenomenon. He has already been compared to all the great performers—Elvis, Dylan and Mick Jagger. And rock critic Robert Hilburn of *The Los Angeles Times* called him "the purest glimpse of the passion and power of rock 'n' roll in nearly a decade." Springsteen's own insistence on performing in small halls and clubs has created a kind of cult hysteria, and his emergence as one of the most exciting live acts in rock today has only added to the mystique. Springsteen buttons, T-shirts, decals, key charms and three different kinds of wall posters are currently the hot rock paraphernalia. In fact, Bruce Springsteen has been so heavily praised in the press and so tirelessly promoted by his record company, Columbia, that the publicity about his publicity is now a dominant issue in his career. And some people are asking whether Bruce Springsteen will be the biggest superstar or the largest hype of the '70s.

In a $2 billion industry that thrives on smash hits, the   4 artist who grabs the public's emotions the way Elvis or the Beatles once did is the fantasy of rock critics and record industry pros alike. Springsteen's punk image, his husky wailing voice, his hard driving blues based music and his passionate, convoluted lyrics of city lowlife, fast cars and greaser rebellion recall the dreams of the great rock 'n' roll rage of the 1950s:

Well now I'm no hero
That's understood
All the redemption I can offer, girl
Is beneath this dirty hood

But he also injects the images with a new sophistication:

The highways jammed with broken heroes
On a last-chance power drive
Everybody's out on a run tonight
But there's no place left to hide

5   Some critics, however, find Springsteen's music one-dimensional, recycled teen dreams. "Springsteen's lyrics are an effusive jumble," music critic Henry Edwards wrote in *The New York Times*, "his melodies either second-hand or undistinguished and his performance tedious. Given such flaws there has to be another important ingredient to the success of Bruce Springsteen: namely, vigorous promotion." Even some of his champions like disk jockey Denny Sanders of WMMS in Cleveland agree on that point. "Columbia is going overboard on Springsteen," he says. "He is the only unique artist to come out of the '70s, but because the rock 'n' roll well is really dry, they are going crazy for Springsteen."

6   As the real world has caught up with the record world, the penny-pinched economy has begun to erode the record industry. Album sales are down (Warner Brothers, for one, is off by nearly 20 percent), the albums going to the top of the charts are getting there on fewer sales while advertising budgets are being drastically slashed. "Unless an act has a great potential for sales," says one record-company executive, "the companies won't spend the big dollars."

7   Too often, the companies have gotten burned when they spent their money on the sizzle and forgot the steak. Bell Records dished out more than $100,000 last year in parties to promote an act nobody ever heard of—Gary Glitter—and people are still asking who he is. Atlantic bankrolled the rock group Barnaby Bye for an estimated $200,000 but failed to turn up any album sales. MGM decided to promote a singer-songwriter named Judi Pulver. They sent her to a Beverly Hills diet doctor, created a Charles Schulz "Peanuts" ad campaign, rented a Boeing 720 to fly journalists to her opening in San Francisco and even got astronaut Edgar Mitchell to go along for the ride. When the evening was over, the inevitable truth set in. Judi Pulver just couldn't carry the hype. MGM's $100,000 experiment bombed.

8   Everyone in the industry is aware of the pitfalls of The Hype, and insiders think that the current Springsteen mania might inflict damage on his career. "All the attention

Bruce is getting now might hurt him later on," says Hilburn. "What I'm afraid of is that while Springsteen has all the potential everyone says he has, it's still chiefly potential. I just hope he's strong enough to stand up under the pressure." Warner Brothers Records president Joe Smith appreciates the "tumult" Bruce is creating for the industry but is dubious about the extent of his ultimate influence on the development of music. "He's a hot new artist now," says Smith, "but he's not the new messiah and I question whether he will establish an international mania. He's got a very long way to go before he does what Elton has done or Rod Stewart or the Rolling Stones or Led Zeppelin."

Bruce himself is concerned about the effect the publicity   9
campaign will have on his creative equilibrium. "What phenomenon? What phenomenon?" Springsteen asked in exasperation last week while driving up from Jersey to New York. "We're driving around, and we ain't no phenomenon. The hype just gets in the way. People have gone nuts. It's weird. All the stuff you dream about is there, but it gets diluted by all the other stuff that jumped on you by surprise."

Springsteen is experiencing superstar culture shock. He   10
has never strayed far from his best friends like Miami Steve Van Zandt and Garry Tallent, who are in his E Street Band. He has spent hours hanging out on the boardwalk at Asbury Park, N.J., and listening to the barkers tell their tales. For gigs, he used to hitchhike to New York to play his guitar in Greenwich Village. In both places, he found the cast of characters who people his lyrics — Spanish Johnny, the Magic Rat, Little Angel, Puerto Rican Jane. They inspired him but they didn't corrupt him. Springsteen rarely drinks, does not smoke, doesn't touch dope and never swears in front of women.

"I'm a person — people tend to forget that kind of thing,"   11
he says. "I got a rock 'n' roll band I think is one of the best ones. I write about things I believe that are still fun for me. I love drivin' around in my car when I'm 26 and I'll still love drivin' around in my car when I'm 36. Those aren't irrelevant feelings for me." The feelings usually find their way to vinyl. "The record is my life," says Springsteen. "The band is my life. Rock 'n' roll has been everything to me. The first day I can remember lookin' in the mirror and standin' what I was seein' was the day I had a guitar in my hand."

Throughout his unconventional career, Springsteen has   12

found people who felt he was born to star. From the moment
he and his abrasive new manager, Mike Appel, walked into
Columbia Records in 1972 to audition for the legendary
John Hammond—discoverer of Billie Holiday, Aretha
Franklin and Bob Dylan—Springsteen was the subject of
high-pressure salesmanship. "I went into a state of shock
as soon as I walked in," says Springsteen. "Before I ever
played a note Mike starts screamin' and yellin' 'bout me.
I'm shrivelin' up and thinkin,' 'please, Mike, give me a
break. Let me play a damn song.' So, dig this, before I ever
played a note the hype began."

13   "The kid absolutely knocked me out," Hammond recalls.
"I only hear somebody really good once every ten years,
and not only was Bruce the best, he was a lot better than
Dylan when I first heard him." Within a week, Springsteen
was signed to Columbia and although he and Appel had
little previous recording experience, they insisted on producing their own album—the uneven "Greetings from Asbury Park, New Jersey," released in January 1973. At the
time Bruce had no band; he sang alone with an acoustic
guitar. And because of the originality of his lyrics and
perhaps the familiarity of their cadence—he was compared
to Dylan.

Oh some hazard from Harvard
Was skunked on beer playin'
Backyard bombadier
Yes and Scotland Yard was trying
Hard they sent some dude with a
Callin' card
He said "Do what you like but don't do it here"

14   The comparison was so tantalizingly close that Columbia
promoted the best album with ads announcing they had
the new Bob Dylan. The cover letter on the records Columbia sent to the DJ's flatly stated the same thing. But the
hard sell backfired. "The Dylan hype from Columbia was
a turmoil," said Dave Herman, the early morning DJ on
WNEW-FM, the trend-setting pop station in New York. "I
didn't even bother to listen to it. I didn't want Columbia
to think they got me."

15   Without radio airplay—the single most important ingredient in any hit—a record dies. Though the Springsteen
campaign was a special project of then Columbia president

Clive Davis, who personally read Springsteen's lyrics on a promotional film, and even though Bruce got good notices from important rock publications like *Crawdaddy*, only a handful of the 100 or so major FM stations across the country played him. The record sold less than 50,000 copies. "He was just another media hype that failed," said Herman. "He was already a dead artist who bombed out on his first album."

Springsteen's personal appearance at the Columbia Records convention in the summer of 1973 was his biggest bomb. "It was during a period when he physically looked like Dylan," says Hammond. "He came on with a chip on his shoulder and played too long. People came to me and said, 'He really can't be that bad, can he, John?'"   16

That fall, Springsteen's second album, "The Wild, the Innocent & the E Street Shuffle," was released. Again it got some terrific reviews—*Rolling Stone* later named it one of the best albums of 1974—but it sold even less than his first LP. This time, accompanying a stack of favorable reviews, the DJ's got a letter from Springsteen's manager Appel saying "What the hell does it take to get airplay?" Meanwhile, Springsteen had a disastrous experience playing as the opening act for the supergroup Chicago on tour, and he refused to do what most new rock acts must do to get exposure—play short 45-minute sets in huge halls before the main act goes on.   17

Columbia began to ignore Springsteen because he couldn't make a best-selling album or hit-single. But Springsteen was getting better in his live performances and was starting to build followings in towns like Austin and Philadelphia, Phoenix and Cleveland. "The key to Bruce's success was to get people to see him," says Ron Oberman, a Columbia staffer who pushed hard for Springsteen's first album within the company. After a concert in Cleveland, says local DJ Sanders, "Springsteen was a smash and requests zoomed up. We had played him before but now the requests stayed on."   18

In April 1974, Jon Landau, the highly respected record editor of *Rolling Stone*, caught Bruce's act in Boston, went home and wrote an emotional piece for the Real Paper stating, "I saw rock and roll future and its name is Bruce Springsteen." Landau's review was the turning point in Springsteen's faltering career—for the artist as well as the company. "At the time," says Springsteen, "Landau's quote   19 helped reaffirm a belief in myself. The band and I were making $50 a week. It helped me go on. I realized I was gettin' through to somebody." Columbia cannily used the blurb in marketing Springsteen's second album and other critics began to take notice. It was the first time a record label used the prestige of a rock critic to push an artist so hard.

20   "His first two albums' not selling was the best possible thing for Bruce," says the 28-year-old Landau. "It gave him time to develop a strong identity — without anyone pushing him prematurely. For twelve years he has had time to learn how to play every kind of rock 'n' roll. He has far more depth than most artists because he really has roots in a place — coastal Jersey, where no record company scouts ever visit."

21   One month after the Landau review, Springsteen, alone with Mike Appel in a sparsely equipped studio in upstate New York, began to record his third album — his last chance to make it. It took three months to record the title song, "Born to Run," and Columbia immediately sent it out to some key people to review for singles potential. The word came back: "It's not Top 40, forget it, it's too long." Then the ever-assertive Appel released a rough mix of the song to a handful of stations that had played Springsteen.

22   The response was overwhelmingly positive. The stations wanted the record. But the potential superstar was in the studio for the next six months unable to finish his masterpiece. "He told me he was having trouble getting the sound he heard in his head on record," says Landau. In April 1975, a year after his review, Landau became an adviser on the album and quit his job at *Rolling Stone* to become co-producer. He moved them into a better studio and helped shape the album into a heavily produced wall of pulsating sound.

23   Last June, a group of Columbia executives heard a rough cut of the album and decided to launch an unprecedented campaign. Building on the Landau quote and $40,000 worth of radio spots on FM stations in twelve major markets, they promoted the first two dud albums, mentioning a third was on the way. It worked. Sales for the first two LP's climbed back on the charts, more than doubling their original sales.

24   Columbia knew it had a winner; the question was how to showcase the act. Appel, without consulting Springsteen, thought big. He asked a booking agent to get 20,000-seat Madison Square Garden for an artist who had never sold

more than 150,000 records. He finally settled on the 400-seat Bottom Line club in Greenwich Village for the week before the release of the third album last August. The tickets sold out in three and half days, with Columbia picking up 980 of the 4,000 tickets for the media "tastemakers." "Columbia put it on the line," said DJ Richard Neer of WNEW-FM. "They said, 'Go see him. If you don't like him, don't play him—don't write about him.' " With the tickets so limited in number, the ensuing hysteria created more press coverage and critical acclaim for Springsteen—who delivered topnotch shows—than any recent event of its kind. "It was a very intelligent use of an event," says Stan Spadowsky, co-owner of the Bottom Line. "Columbia got all the right people down there." DJ Dave Herman, who refused to even play Springsteen's first album because of the hype, was completely won over. The next day, he apologized on the air. "I saw Springsteen for the first time last night," he told his audience. "It's the most exciting rock 'n' roll show I've ever seen."

Orders for the new album, which had been given an initial   25
press ordering of 175,000, came in at 350,000. The LP has sold 600,000 so far, and Columbia has spent $200,000 promoting it. By the end of the year they will spend an additional $50,000 for TV spots on the album. "These are very large expenditures for a record company; we depend on airplay, which cannot be bought," says Bruce Lundvall, Columbia Records' vice president. "What the public does not understand is that when you spend $100,000 on an album for a major artist, your investment is not so much on media as on the number of people you have out there pushing the artist for airplay." Now, for the first time, a Springsteen single, "Born to Run," has broken through many major AM stations, where the mass audience listens.

The stakes are enormous, since a hot album can earn up   26
to several million dollars for the record company in a matter of a few weeks. Today Bruce Springsteen is still a promising rookie. Nobody knows whether he will sell like Elton John or even lesser publicized groups like Earth, Wind & Fire—a group that will ship more than 750,000 initial orders with the release of its new LP. Because of his enormous build-up, Springsteen now has the awesome task of fulfilling everyone's fantasy of what a new rock hero should be. And most of the country—which isn't even aware of Springsteen yet— may or may not agree that he is born to succeed. "Bruce

is undergoing a backlash right now," says Irwin B. Segel-
stein, president of Columbia Records, "but even his critics
are treating him importantly."

27   Springsteen himself has not yet seen any big bucks. He
keeps 22 people on his payroll. He maintains sophisticated
sound and lighting equipment for his shows and has a video
crew following him everywhere. He only plays small halls
where he can barely cover his expenses, but that hasn't put
a crimp in his style. He has just moved into his first home,
a sparsely furnished cottage overlooking the ocean — about
a 10-minute drive from the Asbury Park boardwalk. His
girlfriend, 20-year-old Karen Darbin, a Springsteen fan
from Texas, lives across the Hudson River in Manhattan.
In Bruce's garage stands his prized possession — a '57 yellow
Chevy convertible customized with orange flames, the same
color as his first guitar.

28   On the eve of his West Coast debut last week, Springsteen
seemed to be down. "People keep telling me I ought to be
enjoying all this but it's sort of depressing to me." He riffled
through his beloved '50s records — Elvis and Dion — from
stacks of albums on the floor, which also included Gregorian
chants, David Bowie and Marvin Gaye. "Now this," Bruce
announces in a faintly Jimmy Durante delivery, "is the
sound of universes colliding." The room fills with Phil Spec-
tor's classic production of the Ronettes' "Baby I Love You."
Springsteen swoons. "Come on, do the greaser two-step,"
he says, beginning to dance.

29   Although Springsteen is a German name, Bruce is mostly
Italian, and he inherited his storytelling ability from his
Neapolitan grandfather, Zuili. "In the third grade . . . [a
nun] stuffed me into a garbage can she kept under her desk
because she told me that's where I belonged," he relates.
"I also had the distinction of being the only altar boy
knocked down by a priest on the steps of the altar during
Mass. The old priest got mad. My Mom wanted me to learn
how to serve Mass but I didn't know what I was doin' so I
was tryin' to fake it."

30   He finally saved $18 to buy his first guitar — "one of the
most beautiful sights I have ever seen in my life" — and at
age 14, Springsteen joined his first band. He was originally
a Rolling Stones fanatic but gradually worked back to early
rock. "We used to play the Elks Club, the Rollerdrome and
the local insane asylum," he says. "We were always terrified
at the asylum. One time this guy in a suit got up and intro-

duced us for twenty minutes sayin' we were greater than the Beatles. Then the doctors came up and took him away."

Springsteen's parents moved to California when he was 31 16, but he stayed behind scuffing in local bands. A year later he drove across country—someone else had to shift because Bruce did not know how to drive—to play a New Year's Eve gig at the Esalen Institute. "I've never been outta Jersey in my life and suddenly I get to Esalen and see all these people walkin' around in sheets," he says. "I see someone playing bongos in the woods and it turns out to be this guy who grew up around the corner from me." "Everybody expected Bruce to come back from California a star," says his old friend "Southside Johnny" Lyon who used to play with Bruce at the Stone Pony bar in Asbury Park. But according to Bruce, "nobody wanted to listen to a guy with a guitar."

They do today. Onstage Springsteen projects the same 32 kind of high school macho and innocence that many young male fans, for whom glitter is dull, strongly identify with. Women think he's sexy and it's likely he'll end up with a movie contract. "He's able to say what we can't about growing up," said John Bordonaro, 23, a telephone dispatcher from the Bronx who traveled to Red Bank to see Bruce in concert. "He's talking about hanging around in cars in front of the Exxon sign. He's talking about getting your hands on your very first convertible. He's telling us it's our last chance to pull something off and he's doing it for us." "The peace and love movement is gone," chimed in his friend, Chris Williams. "We have to make a shot now or settle into the masses."

The question is will Bruce Springsteen be able to reach 33 the masses? "Let's face it," says Joe Smith of Warner Brothers Records. "He's a kid with a beard in his 20s from New Jersey, who happens to sing songs. He's not going to jump around any more than Elton. His voice won't be any sweeter than James Taylor's and his lyrics won't be any heavier than Dylan's."

Springsteen's promoters would disagree, but they don't 34 think it matters. "The industry is at the bottom of the barrel," declares Springsteen's manager Mike Appel, 32, as he paces around the Manhattan office once occupied by Dylan's manager, Albert Grossman. "We've got people scratching around looking for new talent. There's an amazing variety of talent because there hasn't been anyone isolated enough to create a distinctive point of view." He whispers dramatically, "What I'm waiting for, what Bruce Springsteen is waiting for, and we're all waiting for is something that makes you want to dance!" He shouts. "Something we haven't had for seven or eight years! Today anything remotely bizarre is gobbled up as the next thing. What you've got to do is get the universal factors, to get people to move in the same three or four chords. It's the real thing! Look up America! Look up America!" Appel sat down.

35   Hypes are as American as Coca-Cola so perhaps — in one way or another — Bruce Springsteen is the Real Thing.

Jefferson Morley
The Phenomenon

Jefferson Morley, who has written and edited for a number of prestigious magazines, currently works for The Nation. *He published this analysis of Bruce Springsteen in* Rolling Stone *in 1985.*

1   A couple of entrepreneurs recently had a bright idea sure to appeal to a newly patriotic America. They would produce T-shirts invoking the two heroes of the summer of 1985, two muscular, working-class white guys with bandannas and lingering memories of Vietnam. "SPRINGSTEEN: THE RAMBO OF ROCK," the T-shirts proclaimed. In a way, you had to sympathize with the T-shirt hawkers, forced and false as their message might be. Plenty of other clever people, including Lee Iacocca, George Will and Walter Mondale, have tried to grab the Springsteen Phenomenon, and almost all of them have come away with less than they'd hoped. That's because the Springsteen Phenomenon and what Springsteen and his music are all about are two very different things.

2   The Phenomenon is the media's explanation of Springsteen's new status as "something more than a rock icon, something more than an entertainer" (*The New York Times*).

It's also the adulation that kind of coverage encourages. In many respects, this Phenomenon is not unlike the Rambo Phenomenon or the Yuppie Phenomenon or the 1984 Olympics/New Patriotism Phenomenon. Springsteen's working-class origins, his sympathy for Vietnam vets and his desire to feel good about America have made media approval tempting, if facile.

But what is *really* going on "out there" is something very 3 humble, no capital letters, nothing phenomenal and maybe even nothing surprising. Springsteen's music is being shared by a large number of people, and it is making a difference in their lives. We love the bittersweet anthem "Born in the U.S.A.," the reminiscing of "No Surrender," the sheer pride of rocking, the high jinks, the highway, the sorrow. The music is something more than a received pleasure. It touches something you didn't know—or forgot— you had in you.

The media and the businessmen and the politicians can- 4 not fathom all this. The Rambo Phenomenon was easy to handle because fantasies of bitterness and revenge, of exclusion and domination, have shaped public life for the last five years. Springsteen's music and his audience are more elusive because they do not fantasize about revenge or money or social position or glamour or mindless escape or patriotism or any of those things that supposedly everyone wants in 1985.

Baffled by the discrepancy between the familiar explana- 5 tion and what is really going on, the Phenomenologists take refuge in adulation. *Newsweek* said Springsteen is "a kind of American archetype. He is rock and roll's Gary Cooper." The supermarket tabloid *Star* announced: "He has achieved the stratospheric status we reserve for only our mightiest pop heroes—he no longer needs to use a last name. Madonna, Mick, Tina, Sting . . . Bruce."

What makes the drum roll of that ellipsis, and the RAMBO 6 OF ROCK T-shirt, so poignantly laughable is *not* the glib reverse snobbery which holds that Rambo, Madonna and company are tinsel and Springsteen authentic. Nor is it the meaningless boast that Springsteen "puts on a better show." Springsteen would probably be the first to deny both suggestions.

What is silly is the way these pronouncements earnestly 7 urge Springsteen fans to practice the most cynical self-deception. Springsteen couldn't possibly be what he says he is — "a real good journeyman." He must be something else, a megasuperstar or, bigger yet, an archetype.

8   The simple truth is, he and his band started out in the bars of the Jersey shore back in the late 1960s and have gotten more popular since. They play rock and roll, not really complicated, in a kind of Sixties style, but they throw in other things, too: some of Springsteen's songs sound alike, but overall they're pretty great. He recently married a pretty girl from the suburbs. And that's it, nothing more. Why does the Springsteen Phenomenon insist we not take Springsteen at his word?

9   Perhaps out of habit — a lot of Phenomenons turn out to be fake. Perhaps out of fatalism. You can't help thinking this is why the *Star* article seemed sadly eager to wheel the Boss into Madame Tussaud's: "Brucemania, like Michael-mania of last year, will no doubt subside and the fanfare will fade, but true fans will always cherish . . ." Springsteen may sing, "I don't want to fade away," but he's sure to fail.

10   Also, just maybe, the Phenomenon is subconsciously hostile to its subject. To make Springsteen something he's not, to make him a liar, is to get rid of him. Springsteen confronted the built-in obsolescence offered by the Phenomenon when Lee Iacocca reportedly offered him $12 million for the right to use "Born in the U.S.A." in a Chrysler commercial. One imagines the offer was appallingly sincere. Iacocca might have really thought that he was just doing his part (he himself a much-admired Phenomenon) for the country and for Bruce. He might have truly believed that those few seconds would help people keep feeling good ("Chrysler's back" and "America's back") and at the same time Do Good by reducing the trade deficit caused by the yellow man.

11   Of course, if you're a twisted and bitter individual, you might think that Iacocca wanted nothing more than to prove who's really the Boss, that he wanted the power to discard Springsteen into the oblivion of old ad slogans. And if you're not that cynical, you might wonder if it makes any difference. In any case, Springsteen answered Iacocca with three words, rock lyrics from before there was rock music: *No thanks, mister.*

12   If some have missed Springsteen's truth by elevating him, others have missed it by trivializing him. Reporter Sara Rimer closed her August 16th article in *The New York Times*

by quoting a fan: "It's rock 'n' roll. It's just rock 'n' roll."
This is closer to the truth in that Rimer understands Springsteen's uniqueness begins in his music. But her insinuation
is as false as the Rambo T-shirt.

We can be fairly sure that the fan Rimer was quoting   13
meant something like, "Don't deny Springsteen's truth by
making him something he isn't." In other words, if you're
not going to shut up, Walter and Ronald, don't bother coming to the party. As for you, Rambo, please check your
grenade launcher at the door. But we can be fairly sure
that our unthinkingly dutiful *New York Times* reporter was
quoting the fan for the purpose of saying, "Everybody knows
rock is basically trivial but, hey, that doesn't mean it can't
be fun for a night." Rimer's implication here is utterly
wrong. And if she doesn't know it, she should just ask Bruce
Springsteen.

"Until I realized that [rock music was my connection   14
to the rest of the human race], I felt like I was dying, for
some reason, and I didn't really know why," Springsteen
told *Rolling Stone*'s Kurt Loder last fall. Some of Springsteen's most touching and thrilling songs are about wryly
("Glory Days") or chillingly ("State Trooper") recognizing
that you are dying. Sure, some of Springsteen's other songs
are "just" rock and roll: fast cars ("Cadillac Ranch") and
girls ("Rosalica"). All of them helped save Bruce's life and
change ours.

What unites these songs is not the genius of some godlike   15
superstar nor some progressive political sensibility, but a
very out-of-fashion, much-derided article of faith from the
Sixties: the promise and power of rock music. Rock and
roll is fun, but it is also something more: a means of holding
on to life, of blasting away self-deception, joining with
others and discovering why one should keep on living. Its
spirit is democratic, its pain redeemable, its joys communal. If it were "merely" rock and roll, then Springsteen's
talk of dying would be phony or foolish. It's a special pleasure to note that George Will and President Reagan have
corroborated for us that Springsteen's music is neither pretentious nor phony.

Plenty of Springsteen's more politically inclined fans   16
(myself included) pouted when Will claimed Springsteen
on behalf of Reaganism last fall. In retrospect, though, I
think we should thank Will. Of course, Americans were
"gettin' manipulated and exploited" (Bruce's words) by the

Reaganites' sudden attention. And Will and the fashionable conservatives did not dare resurrect their 1984 hucksterism in the summer of 1985. But their attempted co-optation and its failure provided inadvertent acknowledgment from an unlikely source of what is "political" — and powerful — about Springsteen's music.

17   Imagine, for a moment, that it is 1965 and you pull aside former actor Ronald Reagan after he has just denounced Martin Luther King. "I have bad news, sir," you tell him. "Twenty years from now there will be a guy who is very popular with people of all ages and who plays one of those electric guitars at deafeningly loud levels. He'll give piles of money to union bosses. He'll have a colored guy in his band. He'll tell everybody in sight that this three-chord racket saved his life. And people will take him seriously!"

18   Reagan asks if the guy will sing any better than that awful guy on the radio, Bob Dillon (*sic*). "Well, a little. But there's more. This guy, call him Bruce — no, he's not a queer, thank God, sir — will be a national hero. He'll be on the cover of magazines, the toast of political columnists. Conservatives will be scared to attack him. Democratic, even Republican presidential candidates, will try to associate themselves with him."

19   "This is exactly what I've said all along," Reagan says with a grim laugh. "America's on a perilous path, and if we are to rescue our country from such a liberal, decadent future, well, like I say: There *are* simple answers. There just aren't easy answers."

20   The conservatives' testimonials to Springsteen are a useful reminder that even the most powerful and fashionable people have to admit that what is absurd, scorned, silly, impractical, can come smashingly true. Even they have to recognize that the outsiders, the people who are scorned by conventional wisdom — losers, sad highway patrolmen, former high-school baseball players, even humiliated criminals — are worthy and can command the attention of people who run the country. It's no accident that the Reaganites tried to snatch Springsteen and haul him into the country club. They may have been ever so slightly worried.

21   That Springsteen's music is a triumph of the spirit of the Sixties is the one thing that the Springsteen Phenomenon could not bear to admit. Not the Sixties spirit as it exists behind glass in the museum — peace, drugs, liberation, love beads, long hair. That's all part of the Sixties Phenomenon

and doesn't mean much to those of us who were in second grade in 1965. Not the Sixties spirit as renovated in the Yuppie Phenomenon. But the Sixties spirit as it arrived belatedly in a small, unpolitical New Jersey town, the same way it arrived belatedly in countless other places. It has something to do with liberation and something to do with self-respect. It is the spirit that says you can't start a fire sitting around crying of a broken heart.

George F. Will
Bruuuuuce

George F. Will's nationally syndicated political column is probably read by more Americans than any other. He also contributes regularly to Newsweek. *Erudite and witty and substantial, conservative yet surprisingly independent, Will (born 1941) won a Pulitzer Prize in 1977 for his commentaries, which have been collected into several books. This essay on Bruce Springsteen appeared in 1984.*

What I did on my summer vacation: 1

My friend Bruce Springsteen . . . 2

Okay, he's only my acquaintance, but my children now 3
think I am a serious person. I met him because his colleague Max Weinberg and Max's wife, Rebecca, invited me to enjoy Max's work, which I did. He plays drums for Springsteen, who plays rock and roll for purists, of whom there are lots. For ten shows in New Jersey, he recently sold 16,000 $16 tickets in the first hour, all 202,000 in a day. His albums can sell one million copies on the first day of release.

There is not a smidgen of androgyny in Springsteen who, 4
rocketing around the stage in a T-shirt and headband, resembles Robert DeNiro in the combat scenes of *The Deerhunter*. This is rock for the United Steelworkers, accompanied by the opening barrage of the battle of the Somme. The saintly Rebecca met me with a small pouch of cotton — for my ears, she explained. She thinks I am a poor specimen, I thought. I made it three beats into the first number before packing my ears.

5   I may be the only 43-year-old American so out of the swim that I do not even know what marijuana smoke smells like. Perhaps at the concert I was surrounded by controlled substances. Certainly I was surrounded by orderly young adults earnestly—and correctly—insisting that Springsteen is a wholesome cultural portent.

6   For the uninitiated, the sensory blitzkrieg of a Springsteen concert is stunning. For the initiated, which included most of the 20,000 the night I experienced him, the lyrics, believe it or not, are most important. Today, "values" are all the rage, with political candidates claiming to have backpacks stuffed full of them. Springsteen's fans say his message affirms the right values. Certainly his manner does.

7   Many of his fans regarded me as exotic fauna at the concert (a bow tie and double-breasted blazer is not the dress code) and undertook to instruct me. A typical tutorial went like this:

8   Me: "What do you like about him?"

9   Male fan: "He sings about faith and traditional values."

10   Male fan's female friend, dryly: "And cars and girls."

11   Male fan: "No, no, it's about community and roots and perseverance and family."

12   She: "And cars and girls."

13   Let's not quibble. Cars and girls are American values, and this lyric surely expresses some elemental American sentiment: "Now mister the day my number comes in/ I ain't never gonna ride/ in no used car again."

14   Springsteen, a product of industrial New Jersey, is called the "blue-collar troubadour." But if this is the class struggle, its anthem—its "Internationale"—is the song that provides the title for his 18-month, worldwide tour: "Born in the U.S.A."

15   I have not got a clue about Springsteen's politics, if any, but flags get waved at his concerts while he sings songs about hard times. He is no whiner, and the recitation of closed factories and other problems always seems punctuated by a grand, cheerful affirmation: "Born in the U.S.A.!"

16   His songs, and the engaging homilies with which he introduces them, tell listeners to "downsize" their expectations—his phrase, borrowed from the auto industry, naturally. It is music for saying good-bye to Peter Pan: Life is real, life is earnest, life is a lot of work, but . . .

17   "Friday night's pay night, guys fresh out of work/ Talking about the weekend, scrubbing off the dirt . . . / In my head

I keep a picture of a pretty little miss/ Someday mister I'm gonna lead a better life than this."

An evening with Springsteen—an evening tends to wash 18 over into the A.M., the concerts lasting four hours—is vivid proof that the work ethic is alive and well. Backstage there hovers the odor of Ben-Gay: Springsteen is an athlete draining himself for every audience.

But, then, consider Max Weinberg's bandaged fingers. 19 The rigors of drumming have led to five tendonitis operations. He soaks his hands in hot water before a concert, in ice afterward, and sleeps with tight gloves on. Yes, of course, the whole E Street Band is making enough money to ease the pain. But they are not charging as much as they could, and the customers are happy. How many American businesses can say that?

If all Americans—in labor and management, who make 20 steel or cars or shoes or textiles—made their products with as much energy and confidence as Springsteen and his merry band make music, there would be no need for Congress to be thinking about protectionism. No "domestic content" legislation is needed in the music industry. The British and other invasions have been met and matched.

In an age of lackadaisical effort and slipshod products, 21 anyone who does anything—anything legal—conspicuously well and with zest is a national asset. Springsteen's tour is hard, honest work and evidence of the astonishing vitality of America's regions and generations. They produce distinctive tones of voice that other regions and generations embrace. There still is nothing quite like being born in the U.S.A.

Mary Ellen Banashek

Bruce Springsteen: Why He Makes Us Feel So Good

Mary Ellen Banashek contributed the following piece to McCall's *in 1985.*

True story: Michele and Alice, friends of a friend, are 1 beside themselves. They've just obtained the impossible—

tickets to see Bruce Springsteen. Now they must decide what to wear to the concert. Several times a day they're on the phone, mentally going through their respective wardrobes in search of appropriate attire. During the course of one conversation, Alice reveals that her family has asked her to cool it already with the Bruce Springsteen tapes. She thinks a Walkman may be the only solution.

2 Michele is an executive vice-president for a major pharmaceutical company, and Alice is a lawyer. Both women are in their early 40s.

3 Bruce Springsteen may be fond of proclaiming "I'm just a prisoner of rock 'n' roll!" but this is not a mere rocker we're dealing with. As he entered the 14th month of worldwide touring last August, he may just have been the single most popular man born in the U.S.A.

4 Consider the following: Some 236,000 tickets for four Springsteen concerts in New Jersey were sold in less than a day, shattering the old sales record (previous title holder: the King Tut exhibit).

5 The announcement of concert dates in Washington, D.C., and Chicago paralyzed phone systems from Virginia to New Jersey and all around the Midwest.

6 Bruce's surprise wedding to model and actress Julianne Phillips last May was front-page news for days.

7 During last year's presidential campaign, both the Republicans and the Democrats tried to associate themselves with Springsteen, who chose to remain politically noncommittal. ("I don't know that much about politics. I guess my politics are in my songs, whatever they may be," he said before the election.) Actually, Springsteen has had more magazine covers and front-page stories lately than many politicians.

8 Last year the Pennsylvania House of Representatives passed a resolution designating Bruce "The Boss of Rock and Roll" (a nickname he reportedly dislikes, by the way).

9 *Born in the U.S.A.*, his most recent album, has sold 7.5 million copies in the United States alone and has remained in the Top 10 for over a year.

10 It is rumored that Lee Iacocca offered $12,000,000 for the use of the song "Born in the U.S.A." and a cameo appearance by Bruce in a Chrysler commercial. Bruce said no thanks.

11 Tickets to the instantly sold-out Springsteen concerts in New Jersey were harder to find last August than pictures of Madonna with all her clothes on. Among those who

begged Governor Tom Kean, Springsteen's manager, and anyone else who would listen were New York Mayor Ed Koch (he got tickets) and the entire Yankee baseball team (they didn't).

Before the summer was over, it was obvious that Bruce Springsteen was America's sweetheart. By the time you read this, it may even be un-American not to like him. All this for a 35-year-old, middle-class, blue-collar rocker from Freehold, New Jersey, whose following defies all notions of what a rock audience should look like.   12

Go to a Springsteen concert, and you see a cross-section of America—pre-teens and teenagers, yuppies and blue-collar workers, parents along with their kids, parents without their kids. "I just had to share this moment with my daughter," one beaming mother gushed as she exited the first Jersey concert.   13

There have been rock stars in the past, but the hysteria known as "Bruce-mania" transcends anything ever witnessed before. What is it about him that sends adults on the far side of 30 scrambling for tickets and causes grown women (like myself) to start feeling giddy? How has he managed to tap into the American imagination?   14

Some say his popularity lies in his own middle-class background. Working-class heroes are hard to come by in rock—now middle America has found one of their own who proudly proclaims where his roots are.   15

His songs, actually more like stories set to music, are peopled by Vietnam vets, the unemployed, factory workers, cops, convicts—each a microcosm of life in these United States. But, while some may be losers, they're all survivors, like the embittered veteran from *Born in the U.S.A.* who can still call himself "a cool rocking Daddy."   16

But humble beginnings and thought-provoking lyrics set to catchy dance tunes do not a living legend make. Scratch Springsteen's surface, and you hit upon more good reasons why he's become Mr. America.   17

Bruce just seems like a real nice guy. It sounds simple, but it's extremely appealing. He may be a millionaire many times over by now, but he acts more like the ordinary Joe from Jersey who can't believe he's being paid to have all this fun—not far from the real Bruce, say those close to him. "Do they really want me?" he reportedly asked when invited to take part in the recording of "We Are the World." He doesn't give many interviews, but he'll stop and talk to   18 fans who recognize him on the street. He still likes to stroll along the boardwalk at Asbury Park sans entourage or fanfare. He even uses Ben-Gay to unkink worn-out muscles after a grueling performance — how plebeian can you get? This is the sort of guy other guys want to get on their softball teams.

19   Springsteen believes in putting his money where his heart is. "I guess my view of America is of a real bighearted country, real compassionate," he's said. "But the difficult thing out there right now is that the social consciousness that was part of the sixties has become, like, old-fashioned or something." To stir up some of those old social feelings during this last — long — tour, he's donated significant amounts along the way to local charities and community groups. He also proselytizes from the stage for food banks and groups that help the homeless. He's helped publicize the plight of Vietnam veterans, small farmers, the unemployed. And all without any chest-thumping, self-aggrandizing histrionics. After all, you can't dance to Rambo.

20   Bruce is a man who loves his work. And it shows. He's been called "the best rock performer ever" and "the hardest working man in show business." He goes out on stage with no light shows, no special effects, no outrageous costumes or custom-built mechanical stage — just a man and his band, kicking bass. He's mastered the art of giving pleasure by experiencing his own pleasure in his work. That in itself is no mean feat, since so few of us enjoy what we do for a living, according to all those psychological studies. For years I've been stymied by that old parlor-game question, "If you could switch places with anyone, who would it be?" Recently I thought of my answer: Bruce Springsteen.

21   Bruce also loves the fans who make it possible for him to work. "When I'm onstage I always feel, What would I want to see if I was the guy in the fifth row?" he's revealed. And the fans, who know all the lyrics to all the songs, love him back. To attend one of his concerts is to understand the meaning of mutual adoration. Bruce can play to an arena packed with more than 50,000 delirious followers and not seem to disappoint a single one. To leave your first Springsteen concert after three and a half hours plus of singing, dancing, story-telling and sweating is a little reminiscent of what being in love for the first time was like — you know you've just experienced something truly wonderful.

Bruce is a real man. Masculine without being obnoxiously   22
macho, capable of gentleness and strength—beloved by
both men and women. For a role model you could do a lot
worse. He doesn't smoke or use drugs. (When his peers were
into experimenting, he explains, he was locked in his room,
practicing the guitar.) He's not a heavy drinker, though he
has been seen in the company of a beer. He's not known
for trashing hotel rooms or encouraging groupies. He's
never bitten the head off a bat, urinated on stage, blown
up his guitar or performed other acts of questionable taste
common to some rock performers. He never looks as if he's
borrowed his wife's clothes, and no kid will ever come home
wearing red lipstick and blue glitter eyeshadow because
he's trying to emulate Bruce Springsteen. Parents notice
these things. And they appreciate them.

Bruce has nice buns. Actually, Bruce has nice everything   23
these days, thanks to a cutback in junk food and a program
of weight training and running undertaken a while back.
(He used to be sort of wimpy and undernourished looking,
thanks to a steady diet of fast food.) Now he's built like a
brick outhouse (or something close to it) and seems to know
it by the way he dresses. This is not a complaint. No way.

Check out the front cover of the *Born in the U.S.A.* album—   24
even the big guys at the record company knew a good thing
when they saw it. As Bruce explained, "We took a lot of
different types of pictures, and in the end the picture of my
ass looked better than the picture of my face. . . ." That's
okay, Bruce—it's hard to beat a perfect ten.

Bruce Springsteen is growing older, like the rest of us.   25
And, if that's what middle age is all about, bring it on! For
those of us brought up on rock 'n' roll who aren't ready to
give it up, it's refreshing to have someone whose records
we can play openly without having to feel sheepish about
the fact that we were in college when he was born.

"I'm getting old, I gotta slow down," Bruce mockingly   26
lamented during his Washington, D.C., show. But he's
proven that maturity is not instant death to rock. At the
same time, he's acquired the trappings of adulthood—a
home (a mansion in Rumson, New Jersey, of course), a wife
(he went from saying, "I'm just not really lookin' to get
married at this point," last December to "I do" in May) and
maybe soon a family (rumors circulated at the end of the
summer that Bruce and Julianne were telling friends they
were anxious to have a baby).

27   And, by golly, you really want him to be happy, with the
house and the beautiful wife and the kids. Because he works
hard for it. And because the longer he's around, happy about
what he's doing, the happier a lot of the rest of us will be, too.

28   "Maybe you can't dream the same dreams when you're
thirty-four that you did when you were twenty-four," he's
said, "but you can still dream something." As I hurl myself
through my 34th year, trailing a new mortgage behind —
symbol of my newfound maturity — I can look back over
the last ten years and see how my own dreams and ambitions have changed.

29   I'm not a teeny-bopper any more, so I've learned to make
concessions — Bruce's poster is hanging in my office, not in
my bedroom. But one dream I'm not about to give up is
the long shot that I'll get to meet Bruce Springsteen someday and ask him to dance (one fast, one slow). And whenever
I hear "Thunder Road" and he gets to the line, "You ain't
a beauty, but hey you're alright/Oh and that's alright with
me," I can still close my eyes and pretend he's singing to
me. Because he sure isn't singing that one to Julianne.

John Lombardi

St. Boss

John Lombardi, a free-lance writer, is a contributing editor at
Esquire, *where the following article appeared in 1988.*

1   True fame is a commodity like fiberboard or soybean
meal in 1988, and suprastar true fame — not the legless stuff
of also-ran politicians or reliable Mookie Wilsons or
number-six-on-the-charts-but-no-higher pop stars — I mean
the ones that last — Cosby, Michael, Reagan, Bruce — suprastar true fame is corporate grace in perpetuity, brand-
name canonization like Carson and Hope have, a nation
fondly recognizing itself as a perfect sales culture, coming
to terms at last with its own bottom line. . . .

2   The man (or woman — Madonna's almost there) who
achieves this degree of fame is no longer measured in con-

ventional terms: "talent," "intelligence," "character," even
"looks" seem fogey calipers, the anemic mutterings of those
consigned to life's cheap seats, outside the power loop and
consequently unable to sense what really counts: so what
if Cosby's jokes and expression suggest a demonic frog—the
man earns $57 million a year and quietly helps Philly's
poor!; sure Reagan's an aging anchorman, capable of rab-
bity surliness, but he rolled America back from the Carter
pieties, didn't he, sat asses down at defense-industry computers the way they used to during Vietnam; and yeah,
Michael's a little bionic now, after all that reconstruction,
but he's *sweet*, you have to admit, a real-life E.T., narcissism
mitigated by ingenuousness and cold cash ($31 million a
year, according to *Forbes*); last, of course, out of Letterman-
land endlessly rocking, the white suburban cradle of the
twenty-first century, incarnating Mass Hip, the Mall as
Church, bumps Bruce.

You have to hear the crowd—*Broooce!*—curling off the   3
aural wave that smashes the stage seconds after the synthe-
sizer's last notes on "Tougher Than the Rest," sounding
eerily like boos and with, perhaps, an eighth note of petu-
lance leavening the adulation, that adolescent mulishness
of total self-regard, years of combing, of sidelong dreams
reflected in car windows, gym mirrors, storefront plate
glass—*Bruce is Us!*—and yet, and yet, he's *not* us, not anymore, he's thirty-nine, he married a model (why do rock
stars always marry models?), made $56 million in eighteen
months (*Forbes* again), is pumped up like Schwarzenegger,
sleeked down like television, as high-concept as Sonny in
Miami Vice . . .

The Bruce Mythos, as Springsteen chronicler Dave Marsh   4
probably put it in one of his unreadable tomes, is rooted
in the early '70s, the tatty end of the '60s; its heart is the
"populist voyager" image, *The Sorrows of Young Werther* in
(until recently) Levis and boots, the Road, the Night, the
Girl. According to legend, Springsteen and his E Street
Band arose from the ashes of Asbury Park on the Jersey
Shore, a garage-group Phoenix come to dribble the basketball of American popular culture after Bob Dylan fouled
out. Back in those days, Mass Hip was busy becoming;
except for the extreme *initiati*—folkies like Dave Van Ronk,
Patrick Sky, Tony "Little Sun" Glover; writers like Charles
Bukowski, Gregory Corso, and Sam Shepard; scenies like
Bobby Neuwirth and the late Lillian Roxon—nobody knew
that hip was dead. They knew that Hendrix was dead, along

with Joplin and Morrison, the Kennedys and King, and that the salutary experience of sweating on buses filled with their music on the way to protest the war or fight for civil rights was no more; they knew that something had happened to Dylan's spirit after his (greatly exaggerated) motorcycle accident, that he'd stopped licking around the edges of conceits so mean that they'd tried to fuse *Billboard* to Rimbaud, limousines to the Apocalypse, Albert Grossman to Diaghilev. Dylan had stretched American hip culture until it broke, and broke him. He was expected to die, but he didn't. Well, America is more of a relay race than a Dantean journey anyway. *Broooce!*

5   In the early photos he's a skinny little guy in a cut-off denim jacket, greaser jeans, rag around his head, needing a shave — a gofer for the Hell's Angels or the Rolling Stones. Except that his dark eyes (Dutch/Irish/Italian, it turns out) are dense with ambition, yearning and burning at the same time, a macho sensitive. What did Bruce want?

6   To be hip and famous like Elvis Presley and Bob Dylan, except that he'd seen Elvis implode, Dylan retract, one from selling out, the other from giving out: "Dylan was a revolutionary. So was Elvis. I always saw myself as a nuts-and-bolts kind of person." Bruce's dad drove buses, guarded prisoners. His mom typed letters. He came from a section of Freehold called "Texas," where a bunch of Appalachian hillbillies had set up in one of the country's less-noted internal migrations. The kid was street smart. It took a while, he knew, for the urban vibe to penetrate the suburban. That's why the bridge-and-tunnel crowd got status-snubbed every weekend, when they ragtagged into Greenwich Village and the Lower East Side, wearing the first of their mall pseudo-French "designer" jeans, their hair too long and fluffy clean, their baby wattles rosy white, eyes grave, then glassy.

7   Bruce was tougher than the rest. He banged on his guitar at the Cafe Wha? and the Gaslight in the Village, then Chevvied on home to Freehold to mythologize the experience for less mobile Jerseyans. He could make a windswept song out of *anything* — a traffic ticket at Exit 8 off the Jersey Turnpike, where he was, in fulsome, suspended disbelief, "thinkin' about makin' a peanut butter and jelly sandwich and seein' my girl" when the trooper struck ("Open All Night"). In his signature songs, "Thunder Road," "Backstreets," "Born to Run," nothing much happened except the rapid evocation of blurry teen angst, rendered in language

as self-consciously prosaic as a pair of stonewashed 501's would be ten years later. Which was the point: Bruce anticipated Mass Hip, the effect of looking stressed out, nicely worn for the right reasons, without the actual experience of being buffeted by circumstances beyond his control: the idea was not to get as beat up as Dylan, or, heaven forfend, as dead as Brian Jones; Springsteen knew his audience couldn't really relate to something as bizarre as *"a motorcycle black madonna/two-wheeled gypsy queen,"* whatever that was (Dylan's "Gates of Eden"), but they'd probably seen a few "Spanish Johnnys" and "Puerto Rican Janes" ("Incident on 57th Street") hanging around on their weekend sorties into the big city and had talked them up all the way home.

By 1973, when he released his first album, *Greetings from* 8 *Asbury Park, New Jersey,* the "truth" of the working-class American life Springsteen allegedly chronicled was profound frustration, the legacy of post-industrial corporatism and unionism, and, in youthful reaction, bursts of ersatz energy as synthetic as the video cracklings after the 3:00 A.M. John Ford movie clicked off in the "shot and beer" bars Bruce so loved to conjure. The actual Jersey Shore, though, had always been a service economy; the "mill" and "factory" closings Bruce plaintively identified as tangible representations of a "runaway American dream" were located up north in Jersey City, Paterson, and the Oranges, or way down south in Camden, where RCA and Campbell Soup were going on the skids. Bruce and his crowd were bored, not desperate. You could *shoop* by quite nicely at the Stone Pony or the Upstage or the Keyport Rollerdome in Asbury Park on $300- to $3,000-a-week gigs—they got you loaded and laid on beer, pizza, subs, the local *nubilia,* and, provided you were in your twenties or under, the sustaining romance of a kind of East Coast, cut-rate surfer narcissism. Asbury Park was Huntington Beach, California, for kids whose families looked something like Archie Bunker's but who tuned in from breezeways; Coney Island without black and Spanish shooters; 116th Street with natural air conditioning.

A "mall" environment, in short. If Clive Davis, the CBS 9 Records Group president responsible for the initial $40,000 hype that tried to establish Springsteen as "the new Bob Dylan," had been as much of a heads-up *mensch* as his eventual successor, Walter Yetnikoff, was, CBS would simply have optioned the boardwalk and presented Bruce and the E Street Band as a daytime soap: *As the Tide Turns,* the rollback of netherworld teen alienation, the Dead End Kids with $5,000 worth of good orthodontics and the occasional B-12 shot. Bruce was famous for being drug-free, alcohol-free, for working hard (three- and four-hour sets where "youthful" energy bursts knocked audiences out as wholesomely as good aerobics classes would) for being on the right side of social issues . . . Before Springsteen, rock had been about rebelling; after him, it was about conforming, and that's what pierced the hearts of a little group of formerly leftish "rock critics" who got CBS re-interested after Springsteen's first two records, *Greetings* and *The Wild, the Innocent & the E Street Shuffle*, flopped.

10   Bruce was a "rock critic's" dream, a means of rationalizing nostalgic feelings of "rebellion" and blue-collar sympathy with comfortable middle-aged incomes and "life-styles." Bruce's explainers—Robert Christgau of Dartmouth and *The Village Voice*; Jon Landau of Brandeis and *Rolling Stone*; John Rockwell of Harvard and *The New York Times*; Greil Marcus of U. Berkeley and *ArtForum*; and Marsh, unlettered but strident and a sometime contributor to most of the above—saw in him a way of focusing their intellectual/artistic/activist inclinations. All were kids in the '60s, energized by the possibilities they thought they saw in rock 'n' roll. Christgau and Marsh actually belonged to the G.I. Antiwar movement and the White Panther party, respectively, while Marcus established written solidarity with "anarchist" stick-up types like George Jackson, and Landau mused at length on culturopolitical overviews and produced the "revolutionary" Detroit band the MC_5 (into the ground, as it turned out).

11   For these fellows, Bruce was the perfect punk, a street guy with boundless energy who wouldn't beat you up. A person who looked like Rockwell—steel-rimmed, turtle-necked, Capote-toned—or Christgau—swaybacked, smirking, in stale promo T-shirts—appreciated a little absence of malice. In the '60s it had been exhilarating to find yourself lip-deep in scurftroll fans, waiting for Joe Cocker to spasm or Van Morrison to levitate in presumed contradiction of the established order, but as Delmore Schwartz had warned, "in dreams begin responsibilities," and by the '70s, all these boys were supporting families and titles like "King of Rock 'n' Roll Writers" (Landau) or "Dean of Rock Critics" (Christgau). Talking to Bruce wasn't like talking to Mick Jagger, whose formidable IQ threatened to peel the paint off your pet theories, or Sly Stone, who before his cocaine collapse

was capable of throwing a washrag in your face as a test of your willingness to rock out. "The Boss," as Springsteen was known for a while, ducked his head, dropped his *g*'s nicely, seemed boyishly earnest when telling his stories about getting asked to leave Ocean County College for dressing like a biker, or being stuffed in a trash bin by a nun in the third grade (for unspecified sins). Christgau, Landau, et cetera, had little direct experience of white prole life, except in its transplanted form in cultural petri dishes like the Lower East Side or Cambridge, or when they listened to it on the radio, then mulled it over in marathon telephone sessions that could have paid for the medical relief of entire villages in Guatemala. Bruce was becoming Mailer's White Negro for rock's gourmet intelligentsia, five middle-class white men sitting around talking.

In 1975–76, this worked out felicitously. Rock 'n' roll had become effete techno-pop. The industry needed something "vital" to counteract the moon-goon mincings of David Bowie and the disco movement, and the country needed to distract itself from the consensus politics of Ford/Carter. *Born to Run*, Bruce's breakout album, was an Alka-Seltzer fizz for the media department of a sales culture with an upset tummy. Its songs, racing up and down the American highway, cruising the romance of boardwalk detritus, necking on the abstract beach of memory, entertained editors, executives, and fans who didn't get around much anymore. In fact, the circumstance that all of Springsteen's images were utterly familiar helped more than hurt, as did his recycled delivery—Dylan as Elvis, Gary "U.S." Bonds as Woody Guthrie, Little Richard as Mitch Ryder as *Broooce!* Hell, the kid wasn't trying to pull anything, he was right up front, and to tell the truth, it was a *relief* not to feel artistically or intellectually or sexually unhip anymore, as one tended to with the originators of the Boss's inspirations. You could relate to Bruce because he lived vicariously, too—for all his driving imagery, he couldn't shift gears! The other crucial factor was that in an emergent VCR moonscape of cable hook-up and instant replay and mass numbers, where consciousness itself tended to get overwhelmed, high recognition factor (HRF) was beginning to seem fundamental: to be "unique" and "original" now just meant to be remembered, and to be remembered, you had to be a cliché.

Three practical things happened to put Bruce over the top:

12

13

- In May 1974, Landau caught him at a Boston club, wrote "I saw rock 'n' roll's future and its name is Bruce Springsteen," then quit fooling around as a critic and did a Carl Icahn move on Mike Appel, Bruce's naive handler; within two years he was Springsteen's manager and main producer.
- The faceless culture editors of *Time* and *Newsweek*, responding to what they perceived as a prescient swell on the part of the five rock-crit experts charged with knowing about popular music, put Springsteen on the covers of their respective magazines on the same day, October 27, 1975, something that only happens to world leaders.
- Noting the above, CBS uncorked $250,000 in publicly earmarked promotion funds to support twenty-three weeks of touring by the Boss and the E Street Band, and an undisclosed amount to shadowy independent promo men to ensure solid "rotation" airplay for selected songs from *Born to Run* in twelve crucial radio markets in the U.S. The album eventually sold five million units, and renews itself whenever Bruce tours. As Al Teller, CBS's smiling former V.P. for domestic sales, has remarked, "With enough rotation, *Aida* could go Top Ten."

Ped-Xing Suburbia

14   The Met Center, just outside Minneapolis, off 35 W, is a big round building in the golden light, a popular culture cake for the Scandinavians poised on the edge of the Great Plains. There is a Lutheran calm in the air, even though the sound check inside is pumping out the E Street Band's version of the great John Lee Hooker's maximum blues, "Boom-Boom." This diffusive quality seems crucial. Springsteen and his audience are perfectly agreed: in 1988, rock 'n' roll's job is to render frenzy sensible.

15   As if to illustrate the point, Marilyn Percansky, who is forty-eight now but still hitting them safely in black tights and cumulus-cloud black hair (the skinnyfat Tama Janowitz look), is talking things over with her kids, Lisa, twenty-five, and Marc, twenty-two. All three had been to The Registry the night before, the hotel where Bruce and the band encamped, clearing out the cocktail lounge, rolling

up the figurative rug to blast out four hours of "Spare Parts"
and "Cover Me" and "Rosalita," the emotional buzz songs
of the live show. "He's so *cute*," Marilyn gushes professionally, tempering the effusions of her children slightly. Marilyn's father-in-law, it develops, ran a funky club in Minneapolis where Dylan himself used to hang out when he
first came down from Hibbing, up on the Iron Range in the
real north country. Did she know him? She flashes a smile
that contains all of Germaine Greer ("Dr. G." in her groupie
days), all of Edie Sedgwick and Patti Smith and the great
long girls with perfect legs who once lubricated rock's erotic
garden, sliding in and out of limos, brushing past the sumo
hunks guarding the fragile male stars: "I'm with the band"
. . . girls who knew rock better than any straight man will
ever understand—they got down on all fours for it, they let
it bleed them, they rolled it over and plugged their fingers
into it, then straightened their skirts and laughed. She knew
him all right, in the cracked-up way that Edie photo-
graphed; rock was masculine energy turning feminine, the
degenderizing force of technology placed at the service of
the marketing department (because sales are ultimately
sexless), Jagger reading Shelley in Hyde Park in arch
memoriam to Brian Jones, wearing a little white dress . . .
"Bruce is cute," Marilyn repeats, like a vet in a well-lit room
remembering a jungle fire fight. "The kids really dig him."

Rick Cheney certainly does. For him, the mysteries of   16
sexual balance of power are not worth pondering. Bruce is
a *dude*, anyone can see that. Where does all this analyzing
get you? In St. Louis, where Cheney edits *The River*, one of
the foremost Springsteen fanzines, Bruce's popularity turns
on his involvement with food banks and unions and veterans' groups. "Did you know that Bruce writes regular
$5,000 checks to Bobby Muller of the Vietnam Veterans of
America? To Becky Aiello of the Berkeley Emergency Food
Project? And George Cole of the Steelworkers Oldtimers'
Foundation?" Well, I'd heard about it, but what about the
PR mileage that accrues to him from such generosity—after
all, at $22.50 a pop for two sold-out dates at the Met Center,
which holds 17,500 believers, Landau Management, commanding a 95–5 percent split with promoters, will gross
more than $1 million! To say nothing of T-shirt revenues!
And the show's been on the road for three months!

"Well, he doesn't *have* to give anything away," Cheney   17
points out coldly. "What other rock stars do as much?

Christ, the media is maddening with its niggling drive to 'expose' everything."

18   His tone has attracted a little crowd: Lori, thirty, who describes herself as "driven" when it comes to Bruce, maybe "a child in some creepy way," but who nevertheless "hates" some of Bruce's more commercial stuff, like "Dancing in the Dark" and "Hungry Heart" (this observation sets off a fit of Cerberean barking from Cheney: "How can you *say* that?"); John Pugh, thirty-two, and Mark Silver, twenty-seven, out of Toronto, who'd come down to Crosby, Minnesota, to buy wet bikes, heard the Springsteen tour was conquering the Midwest, picked it up in Lexington, Kentucky, and stayed with it wherever they could, driving hundreds of miles, red-eyed, popping tops and sucking smoke, letting their photo business in Canada fend for itself, getting happily strung out in an '80s sense — they're both stocky, tanned, grounded in a way that would have been unthinkable in, say, 1973, when young people hitting the rockfest summer route became virtual Tuaregs . . .

19   Now, finally, they're broke, and paying for their variegated road fuel by scalping a little: "See, Bruce has ticket drops at 5:30 and 6:00 for 8:00 shows," Pugh explains, through a cloud of euphoriant. "He'll let forty or fifty garbage seats (rear floor locations) go, and then between 6:00 and 6:30, twenty or thirty blue-line seats (off-the-floor but close). This is for the true fans, those he knows follow him, because his shows always sell out. We go in and buy a few, enough to cover ourselves. What do we get? Anywhere from $50 to $150 apiece. But if we were *really* tryin' to make money, we'd scarf up thirty tickets, right?" (Lori is yelling that anyone who charges more than face value for a Springsteen ticket is going against the Boss's populist spirit and is consequently full of shit.)

20   Silver nods, like a wise rabbi: "You've got pure people [he indicates Lori] and you've got people who are okay but know what life's really like. We think that's what Bruce is. He tells *true* stories . . . That's why we're followin' him around."

21   Not because you're bored with life in Toronto?

22   "*Phew*, man," Pugh protests. "Of course we are — a little bit. But really, that's not it. Bruce is successful; he's clean; he's like a guy you'd watch the ball game with. Toronto's a clean city, we're *proud* of it; so is Minneapolis. People go to *war* for what we've got. Bruce represents all that. He's one

of us who made it. I feel a one-to-one relationship with him. If that's just show biz, he's the best actor in the world . . ."

But why give him credit for ticket policy? Why not man-   23
agement?

"It's Bruce, man," Pugh says.   24

"Bruce, for sure," Silver confirms.   25

The need to apotheosize pop stars is hardly new — Homer   26
and Rodin had a little of Dave Marsh and John Rockwell
in them. But what's curious about the Boss is the vastness
of the live audience's uncritical response. A pound of
Springsteen *kitsch* trades for a ton of *Broooce!*, orange subway earplugs *de rigueur* among the Rambo security guards
sweating in the photographers' pit at the lip of the stage
and high in the "garbage" seats too. No matter how bland
it was, the instant that a song ends the fans triple the decibel
level, freezing the eardrums, ringing in a tinnitus that can
last for hours. The crowd is louder than the band because
it apparently needs to be. Sensing this, Springsteen proceeds to demonstrate a lesson in modern coping: he au-
tohypes himself into an obsessive but contained and so
profoundly safe fury, and the audience, recognizing his effort and knowing its own more puny struggles to hold it
all in in less than wonderful marriages and jobs and schools,
breaks the sound barrier for him. There is an emotional
downward mobility in this, as if for Bruce and his fans,
noise had replaced action in the modern scheme of things

At the Met Center, the "Tunnel of Love" show, named for 27
the current album, starts at climax and keeps trying to top
itself. After a corny "amusement park" entrance where the
E Street Band straggles onstage to "buy tickets," Bruce
enters in a hot pink jacket and a black silk shirt and pants,
high-heeled cowboy boots with silver-tipped toes (he's five
feet nine), carrying a bouquet of roses: "Ready for a ride?"
he yells, and flings his flowers. "Tunnel of Love," the title
track, occurs. It's meant to be a medium-slow "think piece"
about the vicissitudes of marriage (*"You've got to learn to
live with what you/can't rise above"*), but Springsteen is so
charged-up he rushes the lyrics, can't wait to start sweating,
hunching over his guitar as if it were a gun or a tool, his
lower body locked up tight, the torso swiveling on ball
bearings.

He's no longer the waif of *Born to Run*, though he's   28
pumped down some from the body-builder *massif* he'd

achieved during the "Born in the U.S.A." tour of 1984. Springsteen, via Landau/Marsh, his media advisers, possesses one of the keenest senses of what will play in America today, complete with a built-in timer that separates unsalable hip from high-turnover Mass Hip: in 1975 (*Born to Run*), for example, he presented himself as a ragged road hippie to a suburbia just getting comfortable with images abandoned by the urban cool six years before, after *Easy Rider*; in 1978 (*Darkness on the Edge of Town*) and 1980 (*The River*), he did his versions of Dylan's brooding, post-hip, post-accident *John Wesley Harding* album, originally released in 1968; in 1984, ten years after Schwarzenegger, he'd pumped so much iron he practically clanked, and opened "Born in the U.S.A." against a monolithic American flag motif. This was consonant with the peaking of the fitness craze, with Reagan's huge plurality in the presidential election, and with CREEP's Orwellian "Morning in America" media campaign (though the actual words to "Born in the U.S.A." — *"Had a brother at Khe Sahn/Fightin' off the Viet Cong/They're still there/He's all gone"* — were crafted so ambiguously that President Reagan and Walter Mondale, George Will and Democratic senator Bill Bradley could all claim them as "endorsements"). The resulting "flap" over whether "Born in the U.S.A." was really jingo or pinko rock was in fact the second brilliant media coup for Landau/Marsh, eclipsing even the dual *Born to Run Time/Newsweek* covers they'd helped pull off a decade before, because it was fuel for an eighteen-month tour that eventually grossed $100 million in ticket sales, with unit sales of twenty million. "Pop stars at that level are like surfers," confides one insider, who wants to keep his job—let's call him "Deep Squeak." "They pick a wave and try to ride it to the beach. In '84, the wave was Vietnam veterans, unions, and food banks. No other pop star had defined his image in that 'populist' way. But I can tell you it was charity [50 percent deductible], not conviction with Bruce—and with Landau and Barbara [Carr, Landau's assistant and Dave Marsh's wife] too. You'll notice there are no donations this year, none of those wheelchair geeks and sugar-tit suckers hanging around waiting to get their pictures taken with him!"

29   On one level, though, the populism stuck. Seen from below, say in the first row, Springsteen has taken on a chiseled, Rushmore quality, but instead of resembling Lincoln or Jefferson, he suggests Jimmy Caan as "Sonny" in

The Godfather. He's become the image of the prole ideal, while leaving true proledom to scratch its worn behind in a way that Frank Sinatra, with all his ethnic anger, could never have managed. Bruce is as self-conscious as a logo now, and as hard as a penny.

He's doing "Boom-Boom," a number that features Clar-   30
ence "Big Man" Clemons, his tenor-sax player and longtime stage "buddy." There have been a lot of complaints from rock critics and fans about Clarence's reduced role on the tour, and the growing prominence of blond, microskirted backup singer Patti Scialfa, Bruce's new girlfriend. "Boom-Boom" is there to dispel all of this chatter, in the way that TV images of the President chucking Russian babies under the chin are meant to make us feel generally better about him. Clemons grins, struts, and honks on cue, his biceps gleaming, his eyes mirrored by shades. Springsteen plays off him, *to* him in a sense, acknowledging the debt all white pop owes to black funk, while at the same time continuing to exploit it. (In the five shows I saw, Clarence was virtually the only black face in the place.) Clarence and Bruce no longer do their famous "soul kiss," but at one point Clemons literally backs Springsteen up, humping dryly, and Bruce slides sensually down Clarence's brawny chest to his belly, his head finally lolling on the Big Man's crotch. The fans go into paroxysms over this display of racial/sexual "harmony," but before anyone can get any funny ideas, Bruce is over to stage left, being belly-bumped by Patti. Erotically and politically, he works both sides of the street.

Which is not to say that all of the songs lack power. "Two   31
Faces," "Cover Me," and "Brilliant Disguise" have a whirling, guitar/synthesizer melancholy appropriate for a man about to turn forty; "Tougher Than the Rest" evokes the dusty, hokey grandeur of "Streets of Laredo" and "This Land Is Your Land"; "Spare Parts," despite a dumb intro, is graphic and unforgiving: *"Bobby said he'd pull out/Bobby stayed in/Janey had a baby/It wasn't any sin."* And I very much like the adolescent goofiness and hell-bent for Top Forty hooks of "Dancing in the Dark" and "Glory Days," where, for once, Clarence's lame riffing and the E Street Band's charts, which rival the Blues Brothers for authenticity, don't matter. But then there is the Mass Hip patter. Bruce, stark in a blue light:

"There was this girl, an' she was a little older, an' she fell   32
in love with this guy, an' they got a little garage apartment

down by the beach. . . . He was a house painter, kinda wild,
but he was fun. She got pregnant, they were gonna get married
. . . But I dunno what happened, he got scared an' took off
. . . She waited an' waited, and finally went home to her
Mom. . . ." (Dramatic pause).

33   *"There comes a time when you've got to put the past behind*
you . . . This song is about a woman lookin' for her own
individual identity!"

34   Obvious, meretricious little homilies like this happen an
average of four times in the live show, and are as dulling
as anything on prime time. Springsteen has glued together
a badly imagined shantytown of "blue collar" images and
buzz words — "mill," "car," "street," "girl" — meant to touch
a suburban generation that only knows the "working class"
through sitcoms and "nostalgia" films and old black-and-
whites in granddad's wallet. His atomized material, delivered in what quickly becomes a tiring ritual of "energetic"
striding up and down the stage, of cultivated hoarseness,
rolled-up shirt sleeves, spraying sweat — macho for the age
of lib — passes for romance, but exhaustion seems to be the
point. After four and a half hours (the longest show in rock
'n' roll by half), fan and star are wrung out like mops,
though real emotion — the kind you get at great football
games and fights, or old-time rock shows (the Stones were
in and out in ninety minutes) — hasn't happened. And that's
precisely why Bruce is a suprastar. His "TV" audience has
been weaned off depth. It only wants to mime emotion. It's
more interested in avoiding risk than experiencing anything
"real," having a strenuous workout while pressing remote
buttons — as if life were a VCR — that allow a year's worth
of unexpressed feeling to be acted out in some okay format.
How else explain Stallone? Or Spielberg/Lucas? Or MTV?
A veteran sybarite like Marilyn Percansky doesn't get off
on Springsteen as much as her kids do because the closest
he comes to sex is masturbation.

Hip into Mass Hip

35   Can there have been an enzyme change among his fans?
They're such nice people. In the well-mannered nuttiness
of the Met Center, while trying to scribble notes, I felt a
tap on my shoulder. It was Tom Boehland, a vendor of
"institutional juices" to hospitals and nursing homes in

Minneapolis/St. Paul. He was celebrating his twenty-fifth birthday right there with Bruce. He'd seen my triangular "Tunnel of Love" press pass, pasted on my lapel at the insistence of Barbara Carr, the iron-faced number-two man in Landau Management, and guessed I might be Dave Marsh. Evil thought! No, I explained, Barbara Carr was closer to Dave than I was, and the triangular pass was useless, a kind of placebo for rock-crit types. All it could do was get you into the "hospitality area," where they serve up fruit juice and potato chips. To really get backstage you need a big rectangular pass, and that only holds the security guards off for a little while. Eventually they go for your legs, snarling like pit bulls: "Wheresa photo pass? Huh? *You're* not Full Access!"

Boehland thought I was exaggerating, so on the way to   36
the men's room I tried a quick dash past a security guard by way of demonstration. One of the guard's hands flew to his bat; the other groped his Securo-Phone, ready to beep in reinforcements. "Landau Management! Just testing!" I smiled broadly and went to join Boehland on the long line waiting to micturate.

Springsteen was a veritable elder statesman to Tom, like   37
John Lennon. Jagger was too kinky, a sort of degenerate monkey, and Dylan a Salinger hermit. Steve Tyler of Aerosmith and Bono of U2 were all right, but they didn't have any business longevity. What interested Boehland about Bruce was his ability to put rear ends in seats and keep them there, year after year. As entertainers go, the guy was as practical as a can opener. Plus, he was optimistic. Everybody Boehland knew was fed up with irony. Where could it lead? (He liked George Bush too.)

The West sisters, up from Tracy, Minnesota, felt no need   38
to philosophize their presence. They were plucked out of their "garbage" seats by two members of Landau Management and installed in the middle of the first row. "He *always* does that," Jill, sixteen, a high school student, gasps, "but we never thought it'd happen to *us*!" Landau Management, it seems, has a policy of reserving the two best seats in the house and then going into the crowd and selecting the most deserving-looking fans it can find and *moving them up*, no strings, no charge. Obviously, it's of a piece with the Boss's last-minute ticket-drop beneficence, part of Landau's populist humanism, a way of compensating loyalists for the necessary but depersonalizing sales procedures of the last

few years: because of the great demand for them and in
order to avoid "price discrimination," all Springsteen tickets cost the same; when a Bruce concert is announced, you
rush to predetermined outlets and get your hand stamped;
this entitles you to rush to a later line to get a number; *this*
guarantees you a seat, though you have to stand in a third
line to get it, and you never know where the seat will be:
"Ours were *way* in back, up top," Jill says. She's pretty but
flushed and sickly looking, and her eyes are bugging
slightly, as if someone had just hit her in the liver with a
left hook. "You see how great he is? He *knew* we were here!
He wanted us up front!" She twists around, literally unable
to sit still, adrift in the hormonal sea that has helped populate the earth since Circe came on to Ulysses . . . Oddly, her
sister Julie, twenty-six, a graphic artist, is behaving in
exactly the same way.

39   Susan Hamre, thirty-four, a blond Minneapolis book
editor, is far cooler: "Why do I like him? His songs tell
stories; he's not a little kid; he's got *great* buns."

40   Rock music, like hip, from which it drank a long transfu-
sion, lost its cultural teeth years ago, as the '60s were becoming the '70s. You could see it when John Lennon, in thrall
to a woman as ruthlessly unhip as Mike Tyson's is now,
rolled the Beatles up; when Keith Richards, like a rich
dowager, began having his blood changed in Switzerland;
when a California group called the Eagles managed to sell
millions of records by idealizing a life in the fast lane. Suddenly rock was Mass Hip, as shiny as a Porsche, as skinny
and neutral as a line on a mirror. In a sense, it was the
perfect resolution to an American paradox: real hip had
been about rebellion, but rebellion sold so well! Look at
Rolling Stone.

41   Old-fashioned hip, which drew on a strange mélange of
outlaw traditions from Camus and Genet to runaway slaves,
was an attitude not easily translated in economic or
philosophic terms (though great claims were made for its
"existential" potential). Born in an era before the mass
media consolidated public opinion, it produced some fixed
ideas—that moral vision is best arrived at through sin
(Rimbaud); that conformity can give you cancer (Mailer)—
but basically, you either dug hip or you didn't. Mostly it
assumed that man was a drag, and the cultures he invented
were hopeless. In response, it posited a simple code: live

fast, die young, be cool. It was a minimalist view, comfortable with the pessimism of modern art (post-modern art is equally pessimistic but more cynically acquisitive — Mass Hip.) Thus, hip was a cult, 300,000 people in a society of 240 million with a brilliant if melancholy membership: Jackson Pollock, James Dean, Jack Kerouac, Yardbird Parker . . . But America isn't interested in cults.

Enter Springsteen. If the country's first response to its   42
weirdest cultural vectors was to package and sell them, Bruce would find a way. Rock had already institutionalized rebellion. What was truly dangerous among the beatniks — a deep contempt for the profit motive, an amused indifference to status, a commitment to interracial sex and drug experimentation — was reduced in kind and substance. At its height, rock was a fashion revolution of long hair, costume clothes, and lost weight. Remaining young became a revolutionary act — "Don't trust anyone over thirty" — as if part of America's brain had seized in a fourth gear of adolescent attention, where novels sped by as three-minute songs, paintings were blurred album covers, and ideas flashed as epigrams (*"To live outside the law you must be honest"*) . . . Really hip rockers confused speed with youth; that's why they snorted coke.

Still, until Springsteen (and Michael and Prince), rock's   43
middle-class performers and audience were responding to songs based on real emotion — even if the emotion was borrowed. Keith and Mick were genuinely moved by Muddy Waters's "I'm a Man," for example, and updated it with the polymorphous energy of swinging London; Lennon was in flight from the sooty grimness of Liverpool life and cheered himself up with music-hall versions of Fats Domino and Chuck Berry; Jeff Beck split the atom of pop with power-chord variations on 2/4 and 4/4 time, extending the blues scale. Hip may have proved inadequate for dealing with the neuroses and psychoses of the times, but as music it was still dangerous.

Springsteen simplified rock in the way Mao simplified   44
Marx. He eliminated spontaneity. His guitar lines were as elementary as his words. Few of his songs were hummable, and his articulation — through canniness? — was so tortured that you couldn't understand him. Was the chorus of "Blinded by the Light" really *"Wrapped up like a douche/In the rumor of the night"*? (No, of course not!) Thus, he could mean anything you liked — you'd never be wrong!

45   His borrowed emotion, too, was twice removed—he
didn't get it from primary sources but interpreters (Big Boy
Crudup to Elvis to Bruce), and he'd had no interesting experiences of his own to reroute it through. Like most of his
audience, Bruce had grown up in front of twenty-one-inch
screens, wearing headsets, having his consciousness compromised by fifteen-second spots. For him, feeling and
thinking were *a priori* abstract, something you could click
off, or pay for then leave in a theater or on a turntable (it
was a sophisticated moment in Mass Hip when audiences
realized they could buy experiences instead of having
them). In a sense, Bruce was the greatest member of the
audience, a kind of superfan that lesser fans elected to the
stage, not because he had anything new to offer but because
he was one of them, the best recycler of lowered expectations, the greatest retailer of mass taste, the finest smoother
of distinctions (like TV itself), a Xerox facsimile of the Hip
Hetero as Michael and Prince were facsimiles of Hip An-
drogynes and Reagan was a facsimile of the Straight Statesman. In a sales culture like ours, the fans inevitably take
over, preferring copies to originals because they're cheaper
and last longer.

46   Hip itself was fully pacified by now, on sale at any mall;
heroic posters of the Boss and Michael and Prince shone
down from record-shop walls like May Day portraits in the
Soviet Union; hip's sole mission was to move units; it even
laughed at its former self—first on *Saturday Night Live*,
then in silly movies like *The Blues Brothers*, then on the
Letterman show, then in "comedy stores" across the country, and finally in callow, trust-funder magazines like *Spy*.
If hip had once served to remind the culture that it should
feel as well as sell, the joke was on all those dead rockers.

47   Meanwhile, Bruce chugged on like a carburetor—if Mass
Hip hadn't been there to incarnate he might have become
the hottest Toyota dealer in Matawan!—growing wealthier
and moodier. He'd spend months in the studio, only to
come up dry; he'd fine old employees like Obie Dziedzic
for failing to bring him his soup and sandwich on time, or
for buying an insufficiently faded denim jacket to wear
onstage (one hundred bucks to the Vietnam Vets!); Mike
Batlan had to forfeit a week's pay for missing an air-condi-
tioning cue at Three Rivers Stadium in Pittsburgh and
$311.11 when one of the Boss's favorite canoes floated away

in a storm; he married and unmarried model Julianne Phillips (amid rumors of proletarian manhandling); he began a tabloid-reported affair with Patti Scialfa, a liaison virtually mandated by the public, which had never liked the tall, unassuming Julianne, preferring Springsteen single. Personnel left the band: "Miami" Steve Van Zandt, a longtime E Street stalwart, after fights with Landau over money and producing credits; Doug Sutphin, after being docked a week's pay for touching Nils Lofgren's guitar; Marc Brickman, Bruce's veteran lighting man, over personality clashes with Landau and George Travis, Springsteen's authoritarian road manager. As the European leg of the "Tunnel of Love" tour ended last summer, rumors had Bruce breaking up the band because it "was no longer efficient" (Deep Squeak), that, as with any winning enterprise, "fine tuning" was necessary. Look at the 3M Company! Or the Yankees!

At the end of the American tour, in Madison Square Garden, Springsteen committed eleven *faux* finales—multiple climaxes seem to be his way of resolving a show that is *all* climax: "Part Man, Part Monkey" (no acknowledgment to Jagger) smashed into "Dancing in the Dark" which blitzed into "Light of Day" which was cooled down by the new, acoustically revised "Born to Run" (*Brooocers* are now constrained from just digging out in their ol' cars because "*all you're lookin' for is home an' family anyway!*"); he then geared up again with "Hungry Heart," "Glory Days," and "Raise Your Hand." 48

Scialfa and the E Street Band were sagging, but Springsteen wore the crazed look of De-Niro as LaMotta in *Raging Bull*, wringing wet, hair plastered, stomping relentlessly . . . He led the band down a hole in the middle of the stage, punching at the rafters, only to return a moment later with a towel around his neck and his clenched rictus grin: "DO YA LIKE GOOD MUSIC?" he roared, and here came E Street, doggedly blaring, like Our Lady of Perpetual Sorrows Italian-American Brass Band on the Feast of Saint Anthony in South Philly . . . The suburban fans obviously took this soldiering for ecstasy and began to ululate like mandrills: *Broooce! Brooooooce!!* Jon Landau was up there now, playing guitar, fifty pounds heavier than I remembered him from *Rolling Stone*, balding, but with that same "I got the goldfish bowl" smile . . . Barbara Carr was banging a tambourine, too, wearing a tiny microskirt just like 49

Scialfa's, matte black, a sealskin in the sun, and perhaps
fusion-tailored by the scientists at CBS to lie precisely on
the no-man's-land of decency *without riding up* . . .

50   It was ten basketball crowds from ten middling schools,
no drugs, no beer even, Dad waiting on Eighth Avenue in
the Acura for the young ones, so clean and nice and unde-
manding in their canonization. One girl, Stephanie Cata-
lano, twenty-four, of Allenhurst, New Jersey, who sold
jewelry, had taken the train to the city, had stood dripping
in all the ticket lines (it had been raining for three days),
had stood in more lines for hamburgers and Cokes, and
now didn't even mind her terrible seat at the far end of the
hall, halfway up the wall. Did she, you know, want to *meet*
Bruce, or anything? "Oh *no!*" she said quickly. "It's not like
that at all . . ."

51   Dr. Ruth Westheimer, the well-known TV sex-therapist
personality, happened to be sitting nearby, and I asked her
what she thought of Springsteen and hipness and all these
kids' reactions:

52   "Hip, schmip," she beamed. "It just proves what I've been
saying all along. You don't have to act crazy to have fun
and make money! Bruce is a national *monument.* This is
what America's about!"

Tama Janowitz
You and The Boss

*The sardonic, quirky fiction of Tama Janowitz has appeared
in the* New Yorker, Harper's, Spin, *and* The Paris Review,
and in strange novels like American Dad *and* A Cannibal in
Manhattan. *"You and The Boss" is one of the twenty-two
satiric vignettes collected in* Slaves of New York *(1986).*

1   First, you must dispose of his wife. You disguise yourself
as a chambermaid and get a job at a hotel where Bruce is
staying with his wife on the tour. You know you are doing
the right thing. Bruce will be happier with you. Does Bruce

really need a wife with chipmunk cheeks, who probably talks baby talk in bed? You are educated, you have studied anthropology. You can help Bruce with his music, give him ideas about American culture. You are a real woman.

You go into Bruce's room. His wife is lying on the bed, 2 wearing a T-shirt that says "Number 1 Groupie" and staring straight up at the ceiling. You tell Bruce's wife that Bruce has arranged for you to give her a facial and a massage: it's a surprise. "Isn't he sweet?" she says with a giggle.

You whip out an ice pick, hidden under your clothes, and 3 quickly give her a lobotomy: you've watched this technique in the Frances Farmer story on TV. Bruce's wife doesn't even flinch.

After the operation, you present her with a bottle of Val- 4 ium and an airplane ticket to Hollywood; the taxi's waiting outside. To your amazement, she does exactly as you tell her.

You're a bit worried about how Bruce will adjust to her 5 absence, and your presence, but when he returns to the room, at three in the morning, he doesn't even seem to notice the difference. You're dressed in her nightie, lying in bed, looking up at the ceiling. Bruce strips down to his Jockey shorts and gets into bed with you. "Good night, honeybunch," he says.

In the morning he still doesn't seem to realize there's 6 been a change in personnel. In real life, Bruce is larger than life. Though he appears small on television and on record covers, when you stand next to him for the first time you understand that Bruce is the size of a monster. His hands are as large as your head, his body might take up an entire billboard. This is why, you now know, he must have guitars made specially for him.

At breakfast Bruce puts away a dozen eggs, meatballs, 7 spaghetti, and pizza. He sings while he eats, American songs about food. He has plans, projects, he discusses it all with his business manager: the Bruce Springsteen Amusement Park, the Bruce Springsteen Las Vegas Casino, a chain of Bruce Springsteen bowling alleys.

Bruce decides that today you will buy a new home.   8

You are very excited about this prospect: you imagine 9 something along the lines of Graceland, or an elegant Victorian mansion. "I'm surprised at you," Bruce says. "We agreed not to let my success go to your head."

10   He selects a small ranchhouse on a suburban street of an industrial New Jersey town. "You go rehearse, darling," you say. "I'll pick out the furnishings."

11   But Bruce wants to help with the decoration. He insists on ordering everything from Sears: a plaid couch, brown and white, trimmed with wood; a vinyl La-Z-Boy recliner; orange wall-to-wall carpeting. The bedroom, Bruce decides, will have mirrors on the ceiling, a water bed with purple satin sheets, white shag carpeting, and two pinball machines. Everything he has chosen, he tells you, was made in the U.S.A.

12   In the afternoon, Bruce has a barbecue in the backyard. "Everybody's got to have a hobby, babe," he tells you. He wears a chef's hat and has his own special barbecue sauce — bottled Kraft's, which he doctors with ketchup and mustard. Though he only knows how to make one thing — dried-out chicken — everyone tells him it is the best they've ever had. You think it's a little strange that no one seems to notice his wife is gone and you are there instead; but perhaps it's just that everyone is so busy telling Bruce how talented he is that they don't have time.

13   Soon you have made the adjustment to life with Bruce.

14   The only time Bruce ever feels like making love is when the four of you — you, Bruce, and his two bodyguards — are driving in his Mustang. He likes to park at various garbage dump sites outside of Newark and, while the bodyguards wait outside, Bruce insists that you get in the back seat. He finds the atmosphere — rats, broken refrigerators, old mattresses, soup cans — very stimulating. He prefers that you don't remove your clothes; he likes you to pretend to fight him off. The sun, descending through the heavy pollution, sinks slowly, a brilliant red ball changing slowly into violet and then night.

15   When Bruce isn't on tour, rehearsing with his band, recording a record or writing new songs, his favorite pastime is visiting old age homes and hospitals, where he sings to senior citizens until they beg him to stop. His explanation for why he likes this is that he finds it refreshing to be with real Americans, those who do not worship him, those who do not try to touch the edges of his clothing. But even the sick old people discover, after a short time, that when Bruce plays to them they are cured.

16   The terminally ill recover after licking up just one drop

of Bruce's sweat. Soon Bruce is in such demand at the
nursing homes that he is forced to give it up. There is nothing Bruce can do that doesn't turn to gold.

One day Bruce has a surprise for you. "I'm going to take   17
you on a vacation, babe," he says. "You know, we were born
to run." You are thrilled. At last you will get that trip to
Europe; you will be pampered, you will visit the couture
houses and select a fabulous wardrobe, you will go to Bul-
gari and select a handful of jewels, you will go to Fendi
and pick out a sable coat. You will be deferred to, everyone
will want to be your friend in the hope of somehow getting
close to Bruce.

"Oh, Bruce, this is wonderful," you say, "Where will we   18
go?"

"I bought a camper," Bruce says. "I thought we'd drive   19
around, maybe even leave New Jersey."

You have always hated camping, but Bruce has yet   20
another surprise—he's stocked the camper with food. De-
hydrated scrambled eggs, pancake mix, beef jerky. "No
more fast food for us," he says.

You travel all day; Bruce has decided he wants to visit   21
the Baseball Hall of Fame. While Bruce drives he plays
tapes of his music and sings along. You tell him you're
impressed with the fact he's memorized all the words. "So
what do you think?" he says. "You like the music?"

Though your feet hurt—Bruce has bought you a pair of   22
hiking boots, a size too small—you tell him you think the
music is wonderful. Never has a greater genius walked the
face of the earth.

Unfortunately, Bruce is irritated by this. The two of you   23
have your first fight. "You're just saying that," Bruce says.
"You're just the same as all the rest. I thought you were
different, but you're just trying to get on my good side by
telling me I'm brilliant."

"What do you want from me?" you say.   24

Bruce starts to cry. "I'm not really any good," he says.   25

"That's not true, Bruce," you say. "You mustn't feel dis-   26
couraged. Your fans love you. You cured a small boy of
cancer just because he saw you on TV. You're up there with
the greats: the Beatles, Christ, Gandhi, Lee Iacocca. You've
totally restored New Jersey to its former glory: once again
it's a proud state."

"It's not enough," Bruce says. "I was happier in the old   27
days, when I was just Bruce, playing in my garage."

28   You're beginning to find that you're unhappy in your life
with Bruce. Since Bruce spends so much time rehearsing,
there is little for you to do but shop. Armed with credit
cards and six bodyguards (to protect you from Bruce's angry
women fans), you search the stores for some gift for Bruce
that might please him. You buy foam coolers to hold beer,
Smurf dolls, candy-flavored underwear, a television set he
can wear on his wrist, a pure-bred Arabian colt. You hire
three women to wrestle on his bed covered in mud.

29   Bruce thanks you politely but tells you, "There's only one
thing I'm interested in."

30   "Me?" you say.

31   Bruce looks startled. "My music," he says.

32   To your surprise you learn you are pregnant, though you
can't figure out how this could have happened. You think
about what to name the baby. "How about Benjamin
Springsteen?" you say.

33   "Too Jewish immigrant," Bruce says. "This kid is going
to be an American, not some leftist from Paterson."

34   "How about Sunny Von?" you say.

35   "Sunny von Springsteen?" Bruce says. "I don't get it. No,
there's only one name for a kid of mine."

36   "What?" you say, trying to consider the possibilities.
Bruce is sitting on the couch, stroking his guitar. The three
phones are ringing nonstop, the press is banging on the
door. You haven't been out of the house in three days. The
floor is littered with boxes from Roy Rogers, cartons of
White Castle burgers, empty cans of Coke. You wonder how
you're going to fill up the rest of the day; you've already
filed your nails, studied the Sears, Roebuck catalog, made
a long-distance call to your mother.

37   At last Bruce speaks. "I'm going to call the kid Elvis," he
says.

38   "What if it's a girl?" you say.

39   "Elvis," Bruce says. "Elvis, either way."

40   You fly to Hollywood to try to find his real wife. Finally
you track her down. She's working as a tour guide at the
wax museum. "Admission to the museum is five dollars,"
she says at the door. "The museum will be closing in fifteen
minutes."

41   "Don't you remember me?" you say. "I'm the person who
gave you a lobotomy, who shipped you off to Hollywood."

42   "If you say so," Bruce's wife says. "Thank you."

"I made a mistake," you say. "I did wrong. I have your   43
ticket here; you'll go back to Bruce."

His wife is willing, though she claims not to know what   44
you're talking about. "But what about my job here?" she
says. "I can't just leave."

You tell her you'll take over for her. Quickly you rush   45
her to the airport, push her onto the plane. You tell her to
look after Bruce. "He can't live without you, you know,"
you say.

You wait to make sure her plane takes off on time. A   46
sense of relief comes over you. You have nowhere to go,
nothing to do; you decide to return to the wax museum
and make sure it's properly locked up for the night.

You have the keys to the door; the place is empty, the   47
lights are off. Now you wander through the main hall. Here
are Michael Jackson, Jack the Ripper, President Reagan,
Sylvester Stallone, Muhammad Ali, Adolf Hitler. You are
alone with all these men, waxy-faced, unmoving, each one
a superstar.

Something violent starts to kick, then turns, in your   48
stomach.

HOW GOOD IS THIS FILM?

Born on the Fourth of July was released late in 1989; later it was nominated for an Academy Award for Best Picture of the Year.

The three reviews that follow represent the range of opinions recorded on the movie. On January 1, 1990, Stuart Klawans reviewed the film for The Nation *(a magazine on current public affairs, books, and the arts generally considered "liberal" in perspective). On December 20, 1989, Vincent Canby's review appeared in* The New York Times; *Canby (born 1924) is a well known essayist, novelist, and playwright who has reviewed films for over two decades. Pauline Kael, the author of many books on film, published her review in the January 22, 1990, issue of* The New Yorker; *she has been one of America's most influential movie critics for many years.*

Stuart Klawans

On *Born on the Fourth of July*

1   Most movies never reach an emotional simmer; a rare few boil over. And then there's *Born on the Fourth of July,* which shoots off the screen like pressurized steam. Directed with furious, relentless energy by Oliver Stone, the film keeps hitting moments that feel like climaxes and then pushes them further. Stone doesn't seem to think that it's enough to strand a pair of Vietnam veterans in the Mexican desert, as if they were Vladimir and Estragon in fatigues and wheelchairs. Whereas other directors might cut on that image, Stone has to go on, making the vets get into a fight over primacy in being damned. (The prize goes to the one who killed more babies.) And still the scene won't end. In case the audience should be insufficiently appalled, Stone doesn't quit until the vets have knocked each other out of their wheelchairs and lie sprawled in the sand.

2   It's about time, too. *Born on the Fourth of July* has the urgency of a truth told — or screamed — against a deafening

Muzak of lies. Based on the memoir of the same name by
Ron Kovic (who collaborated on the screenplay), the film
wants to shout down the sentimentalization of the Vietnam
War, the sweet-talk about national healing, most of all the
current pieties about the war's veterans. This is perhaps
the first I-was-there picture (including Stone's own *Platoon*)
to vent full-blast the self-doubt and self-pity and justifiable
rage so many veterans have felt.

In outline, its story is simple. Kovic came from a working-   3
class Catholic family on Long Island, enlisted in the Marines
and served two tours in Vietnam. Wounded in battle, he
returned home in a wheelchair, paralyzed from the chest
down but still convinced he had done his duty, still certain
that anybody who opposed the war should move to Russia.
Then he started to think. He despaired; he drank; after a
long, messy period, he turned to literature and activism.
His memoir won him respect as a writer; his work with
Vietnam Veterans Against the War made him a public figure.

But this is like summarizing *Il Trovatore* by calling it a   4
story about mistaken identity. What makes *Born on the
Fourth of July* so remarkable is the way it inflates Kovic's
testimony to epic proportions. For the price of your ticket,
you get a grand-scale re-creation of American life, 1956–76;
a psychohistory of the Vietnam War; a drama about Every-
vet. The action stays tightly focused on Kovic (portrayed
by Tom Cruise with more grit and self-abandon than I'd
thought him capable of). The focus is so tight, in fact, that
some of the close-ups threaten to burst the frame. The camera generally stays right on the surface of Cruise's eyes or
else substitutes for them; with Stone's nonstop dollies and
pans and tilts, you might come out of the theater feeling
as if you had been fighting battles personally, rolling around
drunkenly in a wheelchair and getting hit on the head by
cops. And yet, for all the hyperkinetic, subjective camera
movement, the unrelenting focus on one character, the film
probably tells you more about American society and politics
than all previous Vietnam movies combined, with *Easy
Rider* thrown in for good measure.

In particular, it dramatizes Kovic's notion that he re-   5
ceived a military education just by living in Massapequa.
The first time we see this all-American boy, in a sequence
that looks unnervingly like a conventional war movie, he
is 10 years old and playing soldier with his friends. "We
couldn't wait to be men," Cruise says on the soundtrack.
And then we see what a man's upbringing entailed: admir-

ing the veterans in Independence Day parades, listening raptly to John Kennedy talk of sacrifice, attending to the bloodthirsty rantings of the high-school wrestling coach. It also meant a fear of women. In a remarkable extended sequence, with a 1960s *mise en scène* so thickly layered that the actors almost have to wade through the period detail, we see Kovic fumble his chance for a date, all because he's so caught up in getting out of Long Island and into the Marines. He quakes at asking his sweetheart to the prom, as if she were the very incarnation of those impure thoughts he's been warned against. The best he can do is talk modestly about the job he's got to do in Vietnam, hoping she'll be impressed. Then, in his final moral conflict before leaving for boot camp, he gets down on his knees on prom night and prays to know whether he's done the right thing. Should he dance with a girl or go to Asia and fight Communism?

6   It's possible to see the rest of the film as the story of how Kovic realized he'd made the wrong choice and then learned to live with the consequences. I could go into detail; but rather than regale you with the rest of the eighteen pages of notes I scribbled so frantically in the dark, let me just encourage you to go. The film is long, overbearing, brutal and indispensable. It gives you more of one man's reality than you can easily handle, combined with more political honesty than anyone could expect from Hollywood. Just how far does it go to get things right? Put it this way: In the big campus demonstration scene, the main speaker is Abbie Hoffman. May the dear man rest in peace—he finally made it into that major motion picture.

Vincent Canby

How an All-American Boy Went to War and Lost His Faith

1   As a teen-ager in Massapequa, L.I., in the 1960's, Ron Kovic believed in all of the right things, including God, country and the domino theory. He was Jack Armstrong, the all-American boy, good-looking, shy around girls and

a surreptitious reader of Playboy. He was the archetypal son in a large archetypal lower-middle-class Roman Catholic family.

When he competed as a member of the high school wres- 2 tling team, he wanted to win, and when he lost a match, he wept. Winning was the way he measured his belief in himself. He didn't question the values that shaped his optimism.

On graduating from high school, he enlisted in the Marine 3 Corps to fight in Vietnam. "Communists are moving in everywhere," he told his somewhat more skeptical classmates. Home and hearth were endangered. Ron Kovic, who really was born on the Fourth of July, was ready when his country called.

In 1968, during his second tour of duty in Vietnam, a 4 bullet tore through his spinal column. He returned home a paraplegic, paralyzed from the waist down, emotionally as well as physically shattered. That was the beginning of a long, painful spiritual rehabilitation that coincided with his political radicalization.

By the time the war ended, Ron Kovic had become one 5 of the most restless and implacable spokesmen for Vietnam Veterans Against the War. Childhood was forever gone.

Taking "Born on the Fourth of July," Mr. Kovic's fine 6 spare memoir about this coming of age, published in 1976, Oliver Stone has made what is, in effect, a bitter, seething postscript to his Oscar-winning "Platoon."

It is a film of enormous visceral power with, in the central 7 role, a performance by Tom Cruise that defines everything that is best about the movie. He is both particular and emblematic. He is innocent and clean-cut at the start; at the end, angry and exhausted, sporting a proud mustache and a headband around his forehead and hippie-length hair.

Though ideally handsome, Mr. Cruise looks absolutely 8 right, which is not to underrate the performance itself. The two things cannot be easily separated. Watching the evolution of his Ron Kovic, as he comes to terms with a reality for which he was completely unprepared, is both harrowing and inspiring.

Written by Mr. Stone and Mr. Kovic, the screenplay is 9 panoramic, sometimes too panoramic for its own good. It covers Ron's childhood, his teen-age years, his enlistment, the tour of duty in Vietnam and his long recuperation in a Bronx veterans' hospital, an institution that makes Bedlam look like summer camp.

10   No other Vietnam movie has so mercilessly evoked the casual, careless horrors of the paraplegic's therapy, or what it means to depend on catheters for urination, or the knowledge that sexual identity is henceforth virtually theoretical.

11   One of the film's problems is that it becomes increasingly generalized as it attempts to dramatize Mr. Kovic's transformation from a wide-eyed Yankee Doodle boy to an antiwar activist.

12   The film is stunning when it is most specific. There is the nighttime mission when Ron's outfit slaughters a group of Vietnamese peasants in the belief that a Vietcong patrol has been ambushed.

13   In the confusion of a fire fight, Ron shoots one of his own corporals through the neck. When he tries to confess to murder, he is given absolution by an officer who tells him that he is probably mistaken and that, anyway, these things happen.

14   Equally agonizing are the posthospital sequences when Ron returns to his well-meaning but bewildered family in Massapequa, where he is presented as the grand marshal of the annual Fourth of July parade. People are always trying to help. "I'm O.K.," he says, or "I'm all right" or "O.K. O.K." But there is no understanding.

15   There is a fine old family row when Ron comes home one night from the local bar, drunk as has become his habit. In a fury, he pulls out the catheter. His mother calls him a drunk. His father tries to get him into his room. Ron cries out about his inoperative penis. His mother screams, "I will not have you use the word penis in this house."

16   The film turns less persuasive as Ron acquires his new political consciousness, possibly because, given everything that has gone before, the transformation is so obligatory to the drama. Mr. Stone's penchant for busy, jittery camera movements and cutting also do not help. Though they reflect Ron's earlier state of mind, they start to obscure the character of the man they mean to reveal.

17   Every member of the large cast is exemplary. It includes Raymond J. Barry and Caroline Kava as Ron's parents; Kyra Sedgwick as his high school girlfriend; Frank Whaley, who is especially good as a fellow vet, one of the few people

with whom Ron can communicate when he comes home, and Cordelia Gonzalez as the Mexican whore who tries to persuade Ron that he's still a man.

The two stars of "Platoon" appear in cameo roles: Tom   18
Berenger, as the marine who recruits Ron with his rousing pep talk at Ron's high school, and Willem Dafoe, as a fellow paraplegic vet Ron meets during a brief interlude in Mexico. An aging Abbie Hoffman, an icon of the Vietnam years, makes a sad, curious appearance, more or less playing himself during an antiwar demonstration set in the 1960's. (Hoffman committed suicide in April at the age of 52.)

"Born on the Fourth of July" is a far more complicated   19
movie than "Platoon." It's the most ambitious nondocumentary film yet made about the entire Vietnam experience. More effectively than Hal Ashby's "Coming Home" and even Michael Cimino's "Deer Hunter," it connects the war of arms abroad with the war of conscience at home.

As much as anything else, Ron Kovic's story is about the   20
vanishing of one man's American frontier.

Pauline Kael

Potency

Ron Kovic (Tom Cruise), the hero of "Born on the Fourth   1
of July," believes everything he hears at the Independence Day ceremonies in Massapequa, Long Island. Pure of heart and patriotic, he trusts in Mom, the Catholic Church, and the flag-waving values John Wayne stands for. Ron thinks war is glamorous; it's how he'll prove himself a man. And so he joins the Marine Corps, goes to Vietnam, and is shocked to discover brutality, dirt, and horror.

It's inconceivable that Ron Kovic was as innocent as the   2
movie and the 1976 autobiography on which it's based make him out to be. Was this kid kept in a bubble? At some level, everybody knows about the ugliness of war. Didn't he ever read anything on the Civil War—not even "The Red Badge of Courage"? When he was growing up, kids were into black humor, sarcasm, and put-ons. If he was as vulnerable to

media influences as the movie and the book indicate, wouldn't he have heard of "Catch-22" and "One Flew Over the Cuckoo's Nest"? Wouldn't he have looked at *Mad*? Ron seems to have blotted out everything that didn't conform to his priggish views. When his younger brother is singing "The Times They Are A-Changin'," it doesn't mean anything to him.

3   "Born on the Fourth of July," directed by Oliver Stone, who wrote the script with Kovic, is committed to the idea of Ron's total naïveté. He's presented as a credulous boy whose country lied to him. Wherever you look in this movie, people are representative figures rather than people, and the falseness starts during the opening credits, with the dusty, emotionally charged Fourth of July celebration in 1956 — Ronnie's tenth birthday. Massapequa is less than an hour from New York City on the Long Island Rail Road, but this set (constructed in Texas) looks like Oliver Stone's vision of Midwestern America in the fifties — clapboard picturesque. He uses slow motion to mythologize the drum majorettes. Even the kids' baseball game is a slo-mo elegy. A lyrical glow fuses sports and kids playing soldier and civic boosterism and imperialism. And John Williams' music is like a tidal wave. It comes beating down on you while you're trying to duck Robert Richardson's frenzied camera angles. So much rapture, so soon. I was suffering from pastoral overload before the credits were finished.

4   Of course Ronnie's country lied to him. Part of growing up is developing a bullshit detector, and kids usually do a pretty fair job of wising each other up. Ron Kovic's Candide-like innocence matches that hazy archetypal parade: they're both fantasies. But they make it easier for him (and the movie) to blame everybody for not stopping him when he wanted to be a hero. To Ron, the Marine recruiter (Tom Berenger) who comes to the Massapequa high school is like a god. Ron's virginal high-mindedness makes him the perfect patsy for a before-and-after movie. What's in between is Vietnam and the rise of the antiwar movement.

5   On Ron Kovic's second tour of duty, in 1968, when he was a twenty-one-year-old sergeant, his spine was severed, and he was left paralyzed from the chest down. The movie is a scream of rage at how he was betrayed, mutilated, neglected; it's also an uplifting account of how he boozed, quarrelled with everyone, and despaired until he stopped being contemptuous of the war protesters and became ac-

tive in Vietnam Veterans Against the War. Kovic's book is simple and explicit; he states his case in plain, angry words. Stone's movie yells at you for two hours and twenty-five minutes. Stone tells you and he shows you at the same time; everything is swollen with meaning. The movie is constructed as a series of blackout episodes that suggest the Stations of the Cross; rising strings alert you to the heavy stuff. Then the finale — Resurrection — takes Ron into white light, and John Williams lays on the trumpets.

The central question that's raised is "Why did you tell 6 me lies about what war would be like?" It's not "Why did you tell me lies about what the Vietnam War was about?" — although it shifts into that at times. Stone's most celebrated film, "Platoon," culminated in the young hero's shooting the man who represented evil, but "Born on the Fourth of July" appears to be a pacifist movie, an indictment of all war, along the lines of Dalton Trumbo's 1939 protest novel "Johnny Got His Gun." You can't be sure, because there's never a sequence where Ron figures out the war is wrong; we simply see him go from personal bitterness to a new faith. The morality of taking up arms in Vietnam (or anywhere else) isn't really what the movie is about anyway. The audience is carried along by Tom Cruise's Ronnie yelling that his penis will never be hard again. The core of the movie is Ron's emotional need to make people acknowledge what he has lost. There's a shrill, demanding child inside the activist — a child whose claims we can't deny. And Stone's visual rant slips by because this kid's outrage at losing his potency is more graphic and real to us than anything else. It affects us in a cruder, deeper way than Ron's sloganeering and his political denunciations of the war.

What we hear when Ron causes a commotion at the 1972 7 Republican Convention and shouts at Nixon is a kid who knows he has lost something and who is going to make an unholy fuss about it. He's going to be heard. Yes, he's expressing the rage of other disabled veterans who feel betrayed — wasted in a war we shouldn't have got into. But what really reaches us is that Ron finds his lost potency when the Convention cameras are on him. He finds it in forcing the country to recognize what it did to him and others like him. He's saying, "You owe me this," or, "Activism is all you've left me, and you can't take it away." And he's saying, "I paid for what I did over there, and I go on paying for it. You haven't paid — your shame is greater."

He doesn't really say that, but it's what filmgoers hear and
respond to. The movie, having presented him as the innocent Catholic boy going to war for the glory of God, now
reaps the reward: the audience — some of the audience — experiences a breast-beating catharsis.

8   Almost everything else in this anti-war Fourth of July
parade that spans twenty years is chaotic sensationalism.
When Ron, in an argument with his mother, drunkenly
pulls out his catheter and says, "It's what I've got instead
of a penis," and she shrieks, "Don't say 'penis' in this house!"
she becomes a comic-strip uptight mom. And when he gets
back at her by yelling "Penis! Penis!" at the top of his lungs,
so the whole neighborhood can hear him, it's a phony, easy
scene. We're supposed to see that his mother denies the
realities of war and every other kind of reality — that this
repressive mom who told him the Communists had to be
stopped was part of the system that deluded him. We're
invited to jeer at her villainy.

9   A scraping-bottom scene that takes place on a roadside
in the Mexican desert has a druggy, "El Topo" flavor. The
burned-out, drunken Kovic brawls with another burned-
out, drunken paraplegic (Willem Dafoe), and they spit in
each other's faces, knock each other out of their wheelchairs,
and go on wrestling. The two men, fighting over which one
takes the prize for committing the worst atrocities in Vietnam, are like bugs screaming in the sand; they're right out
of the theatre of the absurd — they've even got dry, rattle-
snake sounds for accompaniment — and you have to laugh.
But it's too showy, too style-conscious; it makes you aware
of how overblown the whole movie is.

10   In Vietnam, Ron's platoon, thinking they're attacking
Vietcong, massacre a group of village women and children.
Then, during the confusion of a skirmish, Ron kills a nine-
teen-year-old soldier from Georgia, but can't fully accept
it — it happened so fast. He tells his major about it, and the
major doesn't want to hear it; he doesn't know how to
handle Ron's confession, so Ron is stuck with the sickening
guilt. After Ron is paralyzed and in a wheelchair, he makes
a trip to Georgia to confess to the soldier's parents and
young widow. That may relieve Ron's pain, but what about
the pain he causes the others? (The father had been proud
of the honor guard that came with the body.) The scene
might be affecting if it were staged to show that Ron's need
is so overpowering he can't consider the family's grief. In-

stead, it suggests that Stone thinks even blind self-expression is good. (In the book, there's no visit to Georgia. Maybe the trip took place, and Kovic left it out. But I remember the scene from an earlier movie, where after the war the protagonist went to the dead soldier's family and asked forgiveness; there, though, the dead soldier was part of the enemy forces, and the protagonist was offering the family solace.)

Oliver Stone has an instinct for the symbolism that stirs 11 the public. He clung to the Ron Kovic story that he first worked on as a screenwriter more than ten years ago. But he must never have been able to think the material through. "Born on the Fourth of July" seems to ride on its own surface, as if moviemaking were a form of surfing. Kovic doesn't turn against the Vietnam War until long after he gets home, expecting to be welcomed as a hero, and is put in the rat-infested Bronx Veterans Hospital. (The exposure of conditions there is the most straightforward, honest part of the movie.) What would have happened if people had been considerate and kind to Ron, and talked up his bravery? Would he have gone on being a warmongering patriot? I didn't expect the movie to answer this kind of question, but I expected it to show enough about Ron's character for us to make some guesses for ourselves. We come out knowing nothing about him except that his self-righteousness — his will to complain and make a ruckus — is rather glorious. I don't think I've ever seen another epic about a bad loser; I wish Stone had recognized what he was on to, and shaped the conception. (In essence, "Born" is satire played straight. The impotent Ron Kovic holds the nation hostage.)

How is Tom Cruise? I forgot he was there. Cruise is on 12 magazine covers. Of course he is — he's a cute kid and his face sells magazines. And magazine editors may justify their cover stories by claiming he's turning into a terrific actor. They may believe it, and moviegoers may assent. Moviegoers like to believe that those they have made stars are great actors. People used to say that Gary Cooper was a fine actor — probably because when they looked in his face they were ready to give him their power of attorney. Cruise has the right All-American-boy look for his role here, but you wait for something to emerge, and realize the look goes all the way through. He has a little-boy voice and no depth of emotion. (In Vietnam, when Ron barks orders to his squad there's no authority in his tone; he still has no authority when he goes in to speak, by invitation, at the Democratic Convention in 1976.) Cruise does have a manic streak, and Stone uses it for hysteria. (He might be a tennis pro falling to his knees and throwing his fists up in the air.) Cruise gets through Stone's noisy Stations of the Cross without disgracing himself, but he's negligible. Nothing he does is unexpected. He's likable in his boyish, quieter moments, but when those are over he disappears inside Ron Kovic's receding hairline, Fu Manchu mustache, and long, matted hair.

13   Oliver Stone has a taste for blood and fire, and for the anguish and disillusionment that follow. Everything is in capital letters. He flatters the audience with the myth that we believed in the war and then we woke up; like Ron Kovic, we're turned into generic Eagle Scouts. The counterculture is presented in a nostalgic, aesthetically reactionary way; it's made part of our certified popular memories. "Born on the Fourth of July" is like one of those commemorative issues of *Life*—this one covers 1956 to 1976. Stone plays bumper cars with the camera and uses cutting to jam you into the action, and you can't even enjoy his uncouthness, because it's put at the service of sanctimony.

V.

CIVIL LIBERTIES
AND
CIVIL RIGHTS

As you know, a basic premise of this book of readings is that writing typically emerges from other writing. As a demonstration of that premise, consider what a very large body of writing has emerged from some very basic texts in our political history. Consider, for instance, these words — the words of the First Amendment to the Constitution:

> Congress shall make no law respecting an establishment of religion, or prohibiting the free exercise thereof; or abridging the freedom of speech, or of the press; or the right of the people peaceably to assemble, and to petition the Government for a redress of grievances.

Or consider section one of the Fourteenth Amendment, ratified in 1868:

> All persons born or naturalized in the United States, and subject to the jurisdiction thereof, are citizens of the United States and of the State wherein they reside. No State shall make or enforce any law which shall abridge the privileges or immunities of citizens of the United States; nor shall any State deprive any person of life, liberty, or property, without due process of law; nor deny to any person within its jurisdiction the equal protection of the laws.

Or this fragment from the Declaration of Independence:

> We hold these Truths to be self-evident, that all Men are created equal, that they are endowed by their Creator with certain unalienable Rights, that among these are Life, Liberty, and the Pursuit of Happiness. That to secure these rights, Governments are instituted among Men. . . .

The readings in this part test out some of the implications of these seminal passages. First you will encounter a sort of prologue in the form of the Luis Valdez play *Los Vendidos*, a work that dramatizes a number of issues relating to race, gender, liberty, equality, economic justice, and civil rights that reverberate through the remainder of this part of the book. Then you will encounter conversations on a number of specific issues related to civil liberties and civil rights, conversations that in a sense began with the documents quoted above that articulate our central political assumptions.

First come two sets of readings on the issue of censorship,

one (on pornography) that picks up gender and language concerns from part two and the other (the case of *Huckleberry Finn*) that picks up racial issues from that same part of this book; the discussion of *Huckleberry Finn* also anticipates further discussions on the topic of race later in this part.

Is pornography harmful? Should it be censored or restricted? Speaking for the affirmative, many women contend that pornography does indeed have harmful effects — that pornography provides the "theory" on how to treat women and rape or other forms of misogyny, the "practice." But other people see pornography as neutral in its effects or contend that the First Amendment protects all varieties of speech and writing from censorship. Did the framers of the Constitution intend to protect free speech and a free press in an absolute sense? Or were they speaking only of political speech and writing? Is it constitutional to restrict pornography? (After all, we do restrict libel and ban cigarette ads on TV, on the grounds of their harmful effects and apolitical content.) And just what is pornography, anyway? Can it be defined in a way that makes restrictions practical, or would such definitions and restrictions undermine artistic and political freedom? The issue of pornography makes for strange bedfellows; it is an issue about which liberals and conservatives disagree among themselves.

Liberals and conservatives also break ranks over *Huckleberry Finn* and its place in the school curriculum. Does reading *Huckleberry Finn* have either harmful or beneficial effects? Is the book a racist one that reflects and perpetuates stereotypes that are offensive to African-Americans? Or does the book reflect those stereotypes only in order to subvert them? If the book does in fact subvert racial stereotypes but only in a very subtle way, does that suggest that the book should be kept for readers who have completed high school? Or do its merits as an American classic or as a central American document outweigh its demerits? If *Huckleberry Finn* is kept out of the curriculum, is that censorship or merely a defensible pedagogical decision? If we keep *Huckleberry Finn* out of the classroom, will we also have to restrict works that reflect and possibly perpetuate stereotypical roles for women and men and native Americans too? Or should all works remain possible for consideration within a curriculum that foregrounds the inevitable social and political content of all art?

In a famous passage in *Huckleberry Finn*, Huck ponders

his legal and moral predicament in harboring the runaway slave Jim rather than turning him in to the authorities. Should Huck accede to the legal system that makes Jim a slave and that requires Huck to turn in the runaway? Or should he listen to the call of his conscience, continue to hide Jim, and in effect put his private morality before the public system of laws? The conflict between the individual and society is central to American culture because we value both the dignity of the private individual and the importance of public institutions sanctioned through the democratic process. Faced with the dilemma of paying taxes to support a popular war, which he disagreed with, Henry David Thoreau proposed civil disobedience—a private act of personal conscience against "the tyranny of the majority." Later Mahatma Gandhi and Martin Luther King, Jr., refined civil disobedience into an effective tactic for achieving public justice and political equality. Were they right to do so? What is civil disobedience anyway? Is it a legitimate political tool or an invitation to anarchy that would destroy the principle of democratic rule? What should people do when "higher laws" put them in conflict with majority rule? What else can a democratic society do except be ruled by a majority? Can such a majority be a "tyranny," or is it the resistance to legitimate, democratic authority that is arrogant and tyrannical? Could civil disobedience even exist in a truly tyrannical society, one without a free press and trial by jury, one in which political minorities disappear in the middle of the night? The selections in this section articulate and debate the question of the legitimacy of civil disobedience and also offer critical analysis of and commentary on a central document of civil disobedience and the American civil rights movement: King's "Letter from Birmingham Jail."

Another central document of the civil rights movement was the Civil Rights Act of 1964, which attempted to eradicate discrimination from a range of public institutions in America. Part of Title VII of that act prohibited discrimination on the job because of race, color, religion, sex, or national origin:

It shall be an unlawful employment practice for an employer . . . to fail or refuse to hire or to discharge any individual, or other wise to discriminate against any individual with respect to his compensation, terms, conditions, or privileges of employment, because of such individual's race, color, religion, sex, or national origin. . . . It shall be an unlawful employment practice for any employer, labor organization, or joint labor-management committee controlling apprenticeship or other training or retraining, including on-the-job training programs, to discriminate against any individual because of his race, color, religion, sex, or national origin in admission to, or employment in, any program established to provide apprenticeship or other training. . . . If the court finds that the respondent has intentionally engaged in an unlawful employment practice . . . the court may enjoin the respondent from engaging in such unlawful employment practice, and order such affirmative action as may be appropriate. . . .

Title VII thus initiated a period of "affirmative action" to redress past injustices and to establish for everyone the possibility of equal opportunity.

But just what should affirmative action mean? Should it be a means of ensuring that everyone has a chance to compete on equal terms for jobs and education? Or should it denote a more active process of ensuring equal results, especially for people who arrive at jobs and schools with disadvantages that arise from past inequality? For some people, affirmative action means the former; in the words of Hubert Humphrey, nothing in Title VII should "give any power to the [Civil Rights] Commission or any court to require hiring, firing, or promotion of employees in order to meet a racial quota." For others, however, affirmative action means action: active measures (at least in the short run) such as goals, timetables, guidelines and quotas designed to promote balanced results.

Are such actions fair? Is affirmative action a legitimate, short-term measure for breaking up a rigid caste system and for ameliorating the long-term effects of Jim Crow laws, sexist traditions, and inequitable education policies? Or is it inherently unfair? Has the "short-term" expired by now? Can we now justify passing over someone or favoring someone else because of the group one is born into? Is the goal of affirmative action the reduction of social injustice or proportional representation of all races and both sexes? Is affirmative action inefficient, in that it favors racial and sexual factors over job performance? Or is it more efficient, in that it speeds the progress of women and minorities and therefore allows those people a chance, at last, to show their right stuff? Does affirmative action damage self-esteem or promote it? These sensitive questions are discussed in the selections reprinted here on affirmative action.

The part concludes with selections about race on campus. In recent years racial issues have troubled many campuses — hardly surprising, considering a larger society in which race presents continuing challenges and opportunities, but troubling nonetheless (especially since colleges consider themselves among the more enlightened sectors of our society). The appearance of racist slogans and graffiti, even cross burnings; insensitive stereotypings; harassment of black students by whites (and vice versa); charges that African-American, Hispanic-American, and Asian-Americans are culturally isolated on many campuses; the decreasing presence of black students on campus and high dropout rates among other minorities; frustrating shortages of minority faculty members: all these factors and others bring racial issues into the spotlight at many campuses. Just what is at the heart of racial tensions on campus? What would ameliorate those tensions? Would curricular reforms reduce cultural isolation and racial and gender insensitivity?

Those are some of the questions discussed in the final section of this central part of this textbook. No doubt questions like them — and like the others posed in the paragraphs above — are being discussed on every American campus this year.

Luis Valdez
Los Vendidos

Luis Valdez (born 1940), a key figure in the Chicano Theatre movement, has shaped drama that speaks to all Americans. The son of migrant farmworkers, Valdez grew up around San Jose, California, and acquired Spanish as a second language. In the mid-1960s he began devising skits that could be given on the back of flatbed trucks in support of Cesar Chavez's union of farm workers; you can see the influence of that circumstance on Los Vendidos *("The Sellouts"), written in 1967. Valdez, who now lives in San Juan Bautista, California, wrote and directed the movie* La Bamba.

Characters

HONEST SANCHO	JOHNNY
SECRETARY	REVOLUCIONARIO
FARM WORKER	MEXICAN-AMERICAN

Scene: Honest Sancho's Used Mexican Lot and Mexican Curio Shop. Three models are on display in Honest Sancho's shop: to the right, there is a Revolucionario, complete with sombrero, carrilleras,[1] and carabina 30-30. At center, on the floor, there is the Farm Worker, under a broad straw sombrero. At stage left is the Pachuco, filero[2] in hand.

(Honest Sancho is moving among his models, dusting them off and preparing for another day of business.)

SANCHO: Bueno, bueno, mis monos, vamos a ver a quien   1
vendemos ahora, ¿no? *(To audience.)* ¡Quihubo![3] I'm Honest Sancho and this is my shop. Antes fui contratista pero ahora logré tener mi negocito.[4] All I need now is a customer. *(A bell rings offstage.)* Ay, a customer!

---

[1]*carrilleras:* literally chin straps, but may refer to cartridge belts.
[2]*Pachuco:* Chicano slang for a 1940s zoot suiter; *filero:* blade.
[3]*Bueno, bueno, . . . Quihubo:* "Good, good, my cute ones, let's see who we can sell now, O.K.?"
[4]*Antes fui . . . negocito:* "I used to be a contractor, but now I've succeeded in having my little business."

2 SECRETARY *(Entering)*: Good morning, I'm Miss Jiménez
    from —
3 SANCHO: ¡Ah, una chicana! Welcome, welcome Señorita
    Jiménez.
4 SECRETARY *(Anglo pronunciation)*: JIM-enez.
5 SANCHO: ¿Qué?
6 SECRETARY: My name is Miss JIM-enez. Don't you speak
    English? What's wrong with you?
7 SANCHO: Oh, nothing, Señorita JIM-enez. I'm here to help
    you.
8 SECRETARY: That's better. As I was starting to say, I'm a
    secretary from Governor Reagan's office, and we're look-
    ing for a Mexican type for the administration.
9 SANCHO: Well, you come to the right place, lady. This is
    Honest Sancho's Used Mexican lot, and we got all types
    here. Any particular type you want?
10 SECRETARY: Yes, we were looking for somebody suave —
11 SANCHO: Suave.
12 SECRETARY: Debonair.
13 SANCHO: De buen aire.
14 SECRETARY: Dark.
15 SANCHO: Prieto.
16 SECRETARY: But of course not too dark.
17 SANCHO: No muy prieto.
18 SECRETARY: Perhaps, beige.
19 SANCHO: Beige, just the tone. Así como cafecito con leche,[5]
    ¿no?
20 SECRETARY: One more thing. He must be hard-working.
21 SANCHO: That could only be one model. Step right over
    here to the center of the shop, lady. *(They cross to the
    Farm Worker.)* This is our standard farm worker model.
    As you can see, in the words of our beloved Senator George
    Murphy, he is "built close to the ground." Also take spe-
    cial notice of his four-ply Goodyear huaraches, made from
    the rain tire. This wide-brimmed sombrero is an extra
    added feature — keeps off the sun, rain, and dust.
22 SECRETARY: Yes, it does look durable.
23 SANCHO: And our farm worker model is friendly. Muy am-
    able.[6] Watch. *(Snaps his fingers.)*

[5]*Así como . . . leche:* like coffee with milk.
[6]*Muy amable:* very friendly.

FARM WORKER *(Lifts up head)*: Buenos días, señorita. *(His* 24
head drops.)*

SECRETARY: My, he's friendly. 25

SANCHO: Didn't I tell you? Loves his patrones! But his most 26
attractive feature is that he's hard-working. Let me show
you. *(Snaps fingers. Farm Worker stands.)*

FARM WORKER: ¡El jale![7] *(He begins to work.)* 27

SANCHO: As you can see, he is cutting grapes. 28

SECRETARY: Oh, I wouldn't know. 29

SANCHO: He also picks cotton. *(Snap. Farm Worker begins* 30
to pick cotton.)*

SECRETARY: Versatile isn't he? 31

SANCHO: He also picks melons. *(Snap. Farm Worker picks* 32
melons.)* That's his slow speed for late in the season. Here's
his fast speed. *(Snap. Farm Worker picks faster.)*

SECRETARY: ¡Chihuahua! . . . I mean, goodness, he sure is 33
a hard worker.

SANCHO *(Pulls the Farm Worker to his feet)*: And that isn't 34
the half of it. Do you see these little holes on his arms
that appear to be pores? During those hot sluggish days
in the field, when the vines or the branches get so entan-
gled, it's almost impossible to move; these holes emit a
certain grease that allow our model to slip and slide right
through the crop with no trouble at all.

SECRETARY: Wonderful. But is he economical? 35

SANCHO: Economical? Señorita, you are looking at the 36
Volkswagen of Mexicans. Pennies a day is all it takes.
One plate of beans and tortillas will keep him going all
day. That, and chile. Plenty of chile. Chile jalapenos, chile
verde, chile colorado. But, of course, if you do give him
chile *(Snap. Farm Worker turns left face. Snap. Farm*
Worker bends over.)* then you have to change his oil filter
once a week.

SECRETARY: What about storage? 37

SANCHO: No problem. You know these new farm labor 38
camps our Honorable Governor Reagan has built out by
Parlier or Raisin City? They were designed with our
model in mind. Five, six, seven, even ten in one of those
shacks will give you no trouble at all. You can also put
him in old barns, old cars, river banks. You can even
leave him out in the field overnight with no worry!

[7]*El jale:* the job.

39   SECRETARY: Remarkable.

40   SANCHO: And here's an added feature: Every year at the
      end of the season, this model goes back to Mexico and
      doesn't return, automatically, until next Spring.

41   SECRETARY: How about that. But tell me: does he speak
      English?

42   SANCHO: Another outstanding feature is that last year this
      model was programmed to go out on STRIKE! *(Snap.)*

43   FARM WORKER: ¡HUELGA! ¡HUELGA! Hermanos, sálganse
      de esos files.[8] *(Snap. He stops.)*

44   SECRETARY: No! Oh no, we can't strike in the State Capitol.

45   SANCHO: Well, he also scabs. *(Snap.)*

46   FARM WORKER: Me vendo barato, ¿y qué?[9] *(Snap.)*

47   SECRETARY: That's much better, but you didn't answer my
      question. Does he speak English?

48   SANCHO: Bueno . . . no pero[10] he has other —

49   SECRETARY: No.

50   SANCHO: Other features.

51   SECRETARY: NO! He just won't do!

52   SANCHO: Okay, okay pues. We have other models.

53   SECRETARY: I hope so. What we need is something a little
      more sophisticated.

54   SANCHO: Sophisti — ¿qué?

55   SECRETARY: An urban model.

56   SANCHO: Ah, from the city! Step right back. Over here in
      this corner of the shop is exactly what you're looking for.
      Introducing our new 1969 JOHNNY PACHUCO model!
      This is our fast-back model. Streamlined. Built for speed,
      low-riding, city life. Take a look at some of these features.
      Mag shoes, dual exhausts, green chartreuse paint-job,
      dark-tint windshield, a little poof on top. Let me just turn
      him on. *(Snap. Johnny walks to stage center with a pachuco
      bounce.)*

57   SECRETARY: What was that?

58   SANCHO: That, señorita, was the Chicano shuffle.

59   SECRETARY: Okay, what does he do?

60   SANCHO: Anything and everything necessary for city life.
      For instance, survival: He knife fights. *(Snap. Johnny pulls
      out switch blade and swings at Secretary.)*

---

[8]*HUELGA! HUELGA! . . . esos files:* "Strike! Strike! Brothers, leave those
rows."

[9]*Me vendo . . . qué:* "I come cheap, so what?"

[10]*Bueno . . . no, pero:* "Well, no, but . . ."

(Secretary screams.)

SANCHO: He dances. *(Snap.)*   61

JOHNNY *(Singing):* "Angel Baby, my Angel Baby . . ." *(Snap.)*   62

SANCHO: And here's a feature no city model can be without.   63
He gets arrested, but not without resisting, of course.
(Snap.)

JOHNNY: ¡En la madre, la placa![11] I didn't do it! I didn't do   64
it! *(Johnny turns and stands up against an imaginary wall,
legs spread out, arms behind his back.)*

SECRETARY: Oh no, we can't have arrests! We must main-   65
tain law and order.

SANCHO: But he's bilingual!   66

SECRETARY: Bilingual?   67

SANCHO: Simón que yes.[12] He speaks English! Johnny, give   68
us some English. *(Snap.)*

JOHNNY *(Comes downstage.):* Fuck-you!   69

SECRETARY *(Gasps.):* Oh! I've never been so insulted in my   70
whole life!

SANCHO: Well, he learned it in your school.   71

SECRETARY: I don't care where he learned it.   72

SANCHO: But he's economical!   73

SECRETARY: Economical?   74

SANCHO: Nickels and dimes. You can keep Johnny running   75
on hamburgers, Taco Bell tacos, Lucky Lager beer, Thun-
derbird wine, yesca—

SECRETARY: Yesca?   76

SANCHO: Mota.   77

SECRETARY: Mota?   78

SANCHO: Leños[13] . . . Marijuana. *(Snap; Johnny inhales on   79
an imaginary joint.)*

SECRETARY: That's against the law!   80

JOHNNY *(Big smile, holding his breath):* Yeah.   81

SANCHO: He also sniffs glue. *(Snap. Johnny inhales glue, big   82
smile.)*

JOHNNY: Tha's too much man, ése.   83

SECRETARY: No, Mr. Sancho, I don't think this—   84

SANCHO: Wait a minute, he has other qualities I know you'll   85
love. For example, an inferiority complex. *(Snap.)*

---

[11]*En la . . . placa:* "Wow, the police!"

[12]*Simón . . . yes:* yeah, sure.

[13]*Leños:* "joints" of marijuana.

86 JOHNNY *(To Sancho)*: You think you're better than me, huh
    ése? *(Swings switch blade.)*
87 SANCHO: He can also be beaten and he bruises, cut him
    and he bleeds; kick him and he — *(He beats, bruises and
    kicks Pachuco.)* would you like to try it?
88 SECRETARY: Oh, I couldn't.
89 SANCHO: Be my guest. He's a great scapegoat.
90 SECRETARY: No, really.
91 SANCHO: Please.
92 SECRETARY: Well, all right. Just once. *(She kicks Pachuco.)*
    Oh, he's so soft.
93 SANCHO: Wasn't that good? Try again.
94 SECRETARY *(Kicks Pachuco)*: Oh, he's so wonderful! *(She
    kicks him again.)*
95 SANCHO: Okay, that's enough, lady. You ruin the merchan-
    dise. Yes, our Johnny Pachuco model can give you many
    hours of pleasure. Why, the L.A.P.D. just bought twenty
    of these to train their rookie cops on. And talk about
    maintenance. Señorita, you are looking at an entirely
    self-supporting machine. You're never going to find our
    Johnny Pachuco model on the relief rolls. No, sir, this
    model knows how to liberate.
96 SECRETARY: Liberate?
97 SANCHO: He steals. *(Snap. Johnny rushes the Secretary and
    steals her purse.)*
98 JOHNNY: ¡Dame esa bolsa, vieja![14] *(He grabs the purse and
    runs. Snap by Sancho. He stops.)*

*(Secretary runs after Johnny and grabs purse away from him,
kicking him as she goes.)*

99 SECRETARY: No, no, no! We can't have any *more* thieves in
    the State Administration. Put him back.
100 SANCHO: Okay, we still got other models. Come on, Johnny,
    we'll sell you to some old lady. *(Sancho takes Johnny back
    to his place.)*
101 SECRETARY: Mr. Sancho, I don't think you quite understand
    what we need. What we need is something that will at-
    tract the women voters. Something more traditional,
    more romantic.
102 SANCHO: Ah, a lover. *(He smiles meaningfully.)* Step right
    over here, señorita. Introducing our standard Revolu-

[14]*Dame esa . . . , vieja:* "Gimme that bag, old lady!"

cionario and/or Early California Bandit type. As you can see he is well-built, sturdy, durable. This is the International Harvester of Mexicans.

SECRETARY: What does he do?   103

SANCHO: You name it, he does it. He rides horses, stays in the mountains, crosses deserts, plains, rivers, leads revolutions, follows revolutions, kills, can be killed, serves as a martyr, hero, movie star — did I say movie star? Did you ever see *Viva Zapata? Viva Villa? Villa Rides? Pancho Villa Returns? Pancho Villa Goes Back? Pancho Villa Meets Abbot and Costello* —   104

SECRETARY: I've never seen any of those.   105

SANCHO: Well, he was in all of them. Listen to this. *(Snap.)*   106

REVOLUCIONARIO *(Scream)*: ¡VIVA VILLAAAAA!   107

SECRETARY: That's awfully loud.   108

SANCHO: He has a volume control. *(He adjusts volume. Snap.)*   109

REVOLUCIONARIO *(Mousey voice)*: ¡Viva Villa!   110

SECRETARY: That's better.   111

SANCHO: And even if you didn't see him in the movies, perhaps you saw him on TV. He makes commercials. *(Snap.)*   112

REVOLUCIONARIO: Is there a Frito Bandito in your house?   113

SECRETARY: Oh yes, I've seen that one!   114

SANCHO: Another feature about this one is that he is economical. He runs on raw horsemeat and tequila!   115

SECRETARY: Isn't that rather savage?   116

SANCHO: Al contrario,[15] it makes him a lover. *(Snap.)*   117

REVOLUCIONARIO *(To Secretary)*: ¡Ay, mamasota, cochota, ven pa'ca! *(He grabs Secretary and folds her back — Latin-lover style.)*   118

SANCHO *(Snap. Revolucionario goes back upright.)*: Now wasn't that nice?   119

SECRETARY: Well, it was rather nice.   120

SANCHO: And finally, there is one outstanding feature about this model I KNOW the ladies are going to love: He's a GENUINE antique! He was made in Mexico in 1910!   121

SECRETARY: Made in Mexico?   122

SANCHO: That's right. Once in Tijuana, twice in Guadalajara, three times in Cuernavaca.   123

SECRETARY: Mr. Sancho, I thought he was an American product.   124

SANCHO: No, but —   125

---

[15]*Al contrario:* on the contrary

126 SECRETARY: No, I'm sorry. We can't buy anything but American-made products. He just won't do.

127 SANCHO: But he's an antique!

128 SECRETARY: I don't care. You still don't understand what we need. It's true we need Mexican models such as these, but it's more important that he be *American*.

129 SANCHO: American?

130 SECRETARY: That's right, and judging from what you've shown me, I don't think you have what we want. Well, my lunch hour's almost over; I better—

131 SANCHO: Wait a minute! Mexican but American?

132 SECRETARY: That's correct.

133 SANCHO: Mexican but ... *(A sudden flash.)* AMERICAN! Yeah, I think we've got exactly what you want. He just came in today! Give me a minute. *(He exits. Talks from backstage.)* Here he is in the shop. Let me just get some papers off. There. Introducing our new 1970 Mexican-American! Ta-ra-ra-ra-ra-ra-RA-RAAA!

(Sancho brings out the Mexican-American model, a clean-shaven middle-class type in business suit, with glasses.)

134 SECRETARY *(Impressed)*: Where have you been hiding this one?

135 SANCHO: He just came in this morning. Ain't he a beauty? Feast your eyes on him! Sturdy US STEEL frame, stream-lined, modern. As a matter of fact, he is built exactly like our Anglo models except that he comes in a variety of darker shades: naugahyde, leather, or leatherette.

136 SECRETARY: Naugahyde.

137 SANCHO: Well, we'll just write that down. Yes, señorita, this model represents the apex of American engineering! He is bilingual, college educated, ambitious! Say the word "acculturate" and he accelerates. He is intelligent, well-mannered, clean—did I say clean? *(Snap. Mexican-American raises his arm.)* Smell.

138 SECRETARY *(Smells)*: Old Sobaco, my favorite.

139 SANCHO *(Snap. Mexican-American turns toward Sancho.)*: Eric! *(To Secretary.)* We call him Eric Garcia. *(To Eric.)* I want you to meet Miss JIM-enez, Eric.

140 MEXICAN-AMERICAN: Miss JIM-enez, I am delighted to make your acquaintance. *(He kisses her hand.)*

141 SECRETARY: Oh, my, how charming!

142 SANCHO: Did you feel the suction? He has seven especially

engineered suction cups right behind his lips. He's a charmer all right!

SECRETARY: How about boards? Does he function on boards? [143]

SANCHO: You name them, he is on them. Parole boards, draft boards, school boards, taco quality control boards, surf boards, two-by-fours. [144]

SECRETARY: Does he function in politics? [145]

SANCHO: Señorita, you are looking at a political MACHINE. Have you ever heard of the OEO, EOC, COD, WAR ON POVERTY? That's our model! Not only that, he makes political speeches. [146]

SECRETARY: May I hear one? [147]

SANCHO: With pleasure. *(Snap.)* Eric, give us a speech. [148]

MEXICAN-AMERICAN: Mr. Congressman, Mr. Chairman, members of the board, honored guests, ladies and gentlemen. *(Sancho and Secretary applaud.)* Please, please, I come before you as a Mexican-American to tell you about the problems of the Mexican. The problems of the Mexican stem from one thing and one thing alone: He's stupid. He's uneducated. He needs to stay in school. He needs to be ambitious, forward-looking, harder-working. He needs to think American, American, American, AMERICAN, AMERICAN, AMERICAN. GOD BLESS AMERICA! GOD BLESS AMERICA! GOD BLESS AMERICA!! *(He goes out of control.)* [149]

(Sancho snaps frantically and the Mexican-American finally slumps forward, bending at the waist.)

SECRETARY: Oh my, he's patriotic too! [150]

SANCHO: Sí, señorita, he loves his country. Let me just make a little adjustment here. *(Stands Mexican-American up.)* [151]

SECRETARY: What about upkeep? Is he economical? [152]

SANCHO: Well, no, I won't lie to you. The Mexican-American costs a little bit more, but you get what you pay for. He's worth every extra cent. You can keep him running on dry martinis, Langendorf bread. [153]

SECRETARY: Apple pie? [154]

SANCHO: Only Mom's. Of course, he's also programmed to eat Mexican food on ceremonial functions, but I must warn you: an overdose of beans will plug up his exhaust. [155]

SECRETARY: Fine! There's just one more question: HOW MUCH DO YOU WANT FOR HIM? [156]

157   SANCHO: Well, I tell you what I'm gonna do. Today and
      today only, because you've been so sweet, I'm gonna let
      you steal this model from me! I'm gonna let you drive
      him off the lot for the simple price of—let's see taxes and
      license included—$15,000.

158   SECRETARY: Fifteen thousand DOLLARS? For a MEXICAN!

159   SANCHO: Mexican? What are you talking, lady? This is a
      Mexican-AMERICAN! We had to melt down two
      pachucos, a farm worker and three gabachos to make
      this model! You want quality, but you gotta pay for it!
      This is no cheap run-about. He's got class!

160   SECRETARY: Okay, I'll take him.

161   SANCHO: You will?

162   SECRETARY: Here's your money.

163   SANCHO: You mind if I count it?

164   SECRETARY: Go right ahead.

165   SANCHO: Well, you'll get your pink slip in the mail. Oh, do
      you want me to wrap him up for you? We have a box in
      the back.

166   SECRETARY: No, thank you. The Governor is having a lun-
      cheon this afternoon, and we need a brown face in the
      crowd. How do I drive him?

167   SANCHO: Just snap your fingers. He'll do anything you want.

(Secretary snaps. Mexican-American steps forward.)

168   MEXICAN-AMERICAN: RAZA QUERIDA, ¡VAMOS LEVAN-
      TANDO ARMAS PARA LIBERARNOS DE ESTOS DES-
      GRACIADOS GABACHOS QUE NOS EXPLOTAN!
      VAMOS.[16]

169   SECRETARY: What did he say?

170   SANCHO: Something about lifting arms, killing white
      people, etc.

171   SECRETARY: But he's not supposed to say that!

172   SANCHO: Look, lady, don't blame me for bugs from the
      factory. He's your Mexican-American; you bought him,
      now drive him off the lot!

173   SECRETARY: But he's broken!

174   SANCHO: Try snapping another finger.

---

[16]*RAZA QUERIDA, . . . VAMOS:* "Beloved Raza, let's pick up arms to
liberate ourselves from those damned whites that exploit us! Let's go."

(Secretary snaps. Mexican-American comes to life again.)

MEXICAN-AMERICAN: ¡ESTA GRAN HUMANIDAD HA 175
DICHO BASTA! Y SE HA PUESTO EN MARCHA!
¡BASTA! ¡BASTA! ¡VIVA LA RAZA! ¡VIVA LA CAUSA!
¡VIVA LA HUELGA! ¡VIVAN LOS BROWN BERETS!
¡VIVAN LOS ESTUDIANTES! ¡CHICANO POWER![17]

(The Mexican-American turns toward the Secretary, who gasps and backs up. He keeps turning toward the Pachuco, Farm Worker, and Revolucionario, snapping his fingers and turning each of them on, one by one.)

PACHUCO *(Snap. To Secretary)*: I'm going to get you, baby! 176
¡Viva La Raza!
FARM WORKER *(Snap. To Secretary)*: ¡Viva la huelga! ¡Viva 177
la Huelga! ¡VIVA LA HUELGA!
REVOLUCIONARIO *(Snap. To Secretary)*: ¡Viva la revolución! 178
¡VIVA LA REVOLUCIÓN!

(The three models join together and advance toward the Secretary who backs up and runs out of the shop screaming. Sancho is at the other end of the shop holding his money in his hand. All freeze. After a few seconds of silence, the Pachuco moves and stretches, shaking his arms and loosening up. The Farm Worker and Revolucionario do the same. Sancho stays where he is, frozen to his spot.)

JOHNNY: Man, that was a long one, ése. *(Others agree with* 179
him.)
FARM WORKER: How did we do? 180
JOHNNY: Perty good, look all that lana, man! *(He goes over* 181
to Sancho and removes the money from his hand. Sancho
stays where he is.)
REVOLUCIONARIO: En la madre, look at all the money. 182
JOHNNY: We keep this up, we're going to be rich. 183
FARM WORKER: They think we're machines. 184
REVOLUCIONARIO: Burros. 185

---

[17]*ESTA GRAN. . . CHICANO POWER:* "This great mass of humanity has said enough! And it begins to march! Enough! Enough! Long live La Raza! Long live the Cause! Long live the strike! Long live the Brown Berets! Long live the students! Chicano Power!"

186   JOHNNY: Puppets.
187   MEXICAN-AMERICAN: The only thing I don't like is—how
       come I always got to play the godamn Mexican-American?
188   JOHNNY: That's what you get for finishing high school.
189   FARM WORKER: How about our wages, ése?
190   JOHNNY: Here it comes right now. $3,000 for you, $3,000
       for you, $3,000 for you, and $3,000 for me. The rest we
       put back into the business.
191   MEXICAN-AMERICAN: Too much, man. Heh, where you vatos
       going tonight?
192   FARM WORKER: I'm going over to Concha's. There's a party.
193   JOHNNY: Wait a minute, vatos. What about our salesman?
       I think he needs an oil job.
194   REVOLUCIONARIO: Leave him to me.

(The Pachuco, Farm Worker, and Mexican-American exit, talking loudly about their plans for the night. The Revolucionario goes over to Sancho, removes his derby hat and cigar, lifts him up and throws him over his shoulder. Sancho hangs loose, lifeless.)

195   REVOLUCIONARIO *(To audience):* He's the best model we
       got! ¡Ajua! *(Exit.)*

CENSORSHIP I: PORNOGRAPHY

Gloria Steinem
Erotica and Pornography

Gloria Steinem, born in 1934 in Toledo, has written for many prestigious magazines and in 1971–72 was a founding editor of Ms. *magazine, a forum for women's issues. She also helped found the National Women's Political Caucus, Women Against Pornography, and other activist groups. The following analysis appeared in* Ms. *in 1978.*

Human beings are the only animals that experience the 1
same sex drive at times when we can—and cannot—conceive.

Just as we developed uniquely human capacities for lan- 2
guage, planning, memory, and invention along our evolutionary path, we also developed sexuality as a form of expression; a way of communicating that is separable from
our need for sex as a way of perpetuating ourselves. For
humans alone, sexuality can be and often is primarily a
way of bonding, of giving and receiving pleasure, bridging
differentness, discovering sameness, and communicating
emotion.

We developed this and other human gifts through our 3
ability to change our environment, adapt physically, and
in the long run, to affect our own evolution. But as an
emotional result of this spiraling path away from other
animals, we seem to alternate between periods of exploring
our unique abilities to change new boundaries, and feelings of loneliness in the unknown that we ourselves have
created; a fear that sometimes sends us back to the comfort of the animal world by encouraging us to exaggerate
our sameness.

The separation of "play" from "work," for instance, is a 4
problem only in the human world. So is the difference between art and nature, or an intellectual accomplishment
and a physical one. As a result, we celebrate play, art, and

invention as leaps into the unknown; but any imbalance can send us back to nostalgia for our primate past and the conviction that the basics of work, nature, and physical labor are somehow more worthwhile or even moral.

5　　In the same way, we have explored our sexuality as separable from conception: a pleasurable, empathetic bridge to strangers of the same species. We have even invented contraception — a skill that has probably existed in some form since our ancestors figured out the process of birth — in order to extend this uniquely human difference. Yet we also have times of atavistic suspicion that sex is not complete — or even legal or intended-by-god — if it cannot end in conception.

6　　No wonder the concepts of "erotica" and "pornography" can be so crucially different, and yet so confused. Both assume that sexuality can be separated from conception, and therefore can be used to carry a personal message. That's a major reason why, even in our current culture, both may be called equally "shocking" or legally "obscene," a word whose Latin derivative means "dirty, containing filth." This gross condemnation of all sexuality that isn't harnessed to childbirth and marriage has been increased by the current backlash against women's progress. Out of fear that the whole patriarchal structure might be upset if women really had the autonomous power to decide our reproductive futures (that is, if we controlled the most basic means of production), right-wing groups are not only denouncing prochoice abortion literature as "pornographic," but are trying to stop the sending of all contraceptive information through the mails by invoking obscenity laws. In fact, Phyllis Schlafly recently denounced the entire Women's Movement as "obscene."

7　　Not surprisingly, this religious, visceral backlash has a secular, intellectual counterpart that relies heavily on applying the "natural" behavior of the animal world to humans. That is questionable in itself, but these Lionel Tigerish studies make their political purpose even more clear in the particular animals they select and the habits they choose to emphasize. The message is that females should accept their "destiny" of being sexually dependent and devote themselves to bearing and rearing their young.

8　　Defending against such reaction in turn leads to another temptation: to merely reverse the terms, and declare that *all* nonprocreative sex is good. In fact, however, this human activity can be as constructive as destructive, moral or immoral, as any other. Sex as communication can send messages as different as life and death; even the origins of "erotica" and "pornography" reflect that fact. After all, "erotica" is rooted in *eros* or passionate love, and thus in the idea of positive choice, free will, the yearning for a particular person. (Interestingly, the definition of erotica leaves open the question of gender.) "Pornography" begins with a root meaning "prostitution" or "female captives," thus letting us know that the subject is not mutual love, or love at all, but domination and violence against women. (Though, of course, homosexual pornography may imitate this violence by putting a man in the "feminine" role of victim.) It ends with a root meaning "writing about" or "description of" which puts still more distance between subject and object, and replaces a spontaneous yearning for closeness with objectification and a voyeur.

The difference is clear in the words. It becomes even more 9
so by example.

Look at any photo or film of people making love; really 10
making love. The images may be diverse, but there is usually a sensuality and touch and warmth, an acceptance of bodies and nerve endings. There is always a spontaneous sense of people who are there because they *want* to be, out of shared pleasure.

Now look at any depiction of sex in which there is clear 11
force, or an unequal power that spells coercion. It may be very blatant, with weapons or torture or bondage, wounds and bruises, some clear humiliation, or an adult's sexual power being used over a child. It may be much more subtle: a physical attitude of conqueror and victim, the use of race or class difference to imply the same thing, perhaps a very unequal nudity, with one person exposed and vulnerable while the other is clothed. In either case, there is no sense of equal choice or equal power.

The first is erotic: a mutually pleasurable, sexual expres- 12
sion between people who have enough power to be there by positive choice. It may or may not strike a sense-memory in the viewer, or be creative enough to make the unknown seem real; but it doesn't require us to identify with a conqueror or a victim. It is truly sensuous, and may give us a contagion of pleasure.

The second is pornographic: its message is violence, 13
dominance, and conquest. It is sex being used to reinforce

some inequality, or to create one, or to tell us the lie that pain and humiliation (ours or someone else's) are really the same as pleasure. If we are to feel anything, we must identify with conqueror or victim. That means we can only experience pleasure through the adoption of some degree of sadism or masochism. It also means that we may feel diminished by the role of conqueror, or enraged, humiliated, and vengeful by sharing identity with the victim.

14   Perhaps one could simply say that erotica is about sexuality, but pornography is about power and sex-as-weapon — in the same way we have come to understand that rape is about violence, and not really about sexuality at all.

15   Yes, it's true that there are women who have been forced by violent families and dominating men to confuse love with pain; so much so that they have become masochists. (A fact that in no way excuses those who administer such pain.) But the truth is that, for most women — and for men with enough humanity to imagine themselves into the predicament of women — true pornography could serve as aversion therapy for sex.

16   Of course, there will always be personal differences about what is and is not erotic, and there may be cultural differences for a long time to come. Many women feel that sex makes them vulnerable and therefore may continue to need more sense of personal connection and safety before allowing any erotic feelings. We now find competence and expertise erotic in men, but that may pass as we develop those qualities in ourselves. Men, on the other hand, may continue to feel less vulnerable, and therefore more open to such potential danger as sex with strangers. As some men replace the need for submission from childlike women with the pleasure of cooperation from equals, they may find a partner's competence to be erotic, too.

17   Such group changes plus individual differences will continue to be reflected in sexual love between people of the same gender, as well as between women and men. The point is not to dictate sameness, but to discover ourselves and each other through sexuality that is an exploring, pleasurable, empathetic part of our lives; a human sexuality that is unchained both from unwanted pregnancies and from violence.

18   But that is a hope, not a reality. At the moment, fear of change is increasing both the indiscriminate repression of all nonprocreative sex in the religious and "conservative"

male world, and the pornographic vengeance against women's sexuality in the secular world of "liberal" and "radical" men. It's almost futuristic to debate what is and is not truly erotic, when many women are again being forced into compulsory motherhood, and the number of pornographic murders, tortures, and woman-hating images are on the increase in both popular culture and real life.

It's a familiar division: wife or whore, "good" woman   19 who is constantly vulnerable to pregnancy or "bad" woman who is unprotected from violence. *Both* roles would be upset if we were to control our own sexuality. And that's exactly what we must do.

In spite of all our atavistic suspicions and training for   20 the "natural" role of motherhood, we took up the complicated battle for reproductive freedom. Our bodies had borne the health burden of endless births and poor abortions, and we had a greater motive for separating sexuality and conception.

Now we have to take up the equally complex burden of   21 explaining that all nonprocreative sex is *not* alike. We have a motive: our right to a uniquely human sexuality, and sometimes even to survival. As it is, our bodies have too rarely been enough our own to develop erotica in our own lives, much less in art and literature. And our bodies have too often been the objects of pornography and the woman-hating, violent practice that it preaches. Consider also our spirits that break a little each time we see ourselves in chains or full labial display for the conquering male viewer, bruised or on our knees, screaming a real or pretended pain to delight the sadist, pretending to enjoy what we don't enjoy, to be blind to the images of our sisters that really haunt us — humiliated often enough ourselves by the truly obscene idea that sex and the domination of women must be combined.

Sexuality *is* human, free, separate — and so are we.   22

But until we untangle the lethal confusion of sex with   23 violence, there will be more pornography and less erotica. There will be little murders in our beds — and very little love.

Report of the President's Commission on Obscenity and Pornography (Majority Report)

In 1967, Congress by law established an eighteen-member special commission (appointed by President Nixon) to study the impact of obscenity and pornography on American life. After gathering testimony, reviewing research, and conferring at length, the commission in 1970 recommended against legislation that would restrain pornography. A minority of the members of the commission, feeling differently, submitted their own dissenting report. Excerpts from both follow.

1   Discussions of obscenity and pornography in the past have often been devoid of fact. Popular rhetoric has often contained a variety of estimates of the size of the "smut" industry and assertions regarding the consequences of the existence of these materials and exposure to them. Many of these statements, however, have had little anchoring in objective evidence. Within the limits of its time and resources, the Commission has sought, through staff and contract research, to broaden the factual basis for future continued discussion. The Commission is aware that not all issues of concern have been completely researched nor all questions answered. It also recognizes that the interpretations of a set of "facts" in arriving at policy implications may differ even among men of good will. Nevertheless, the Commission is convinced that on most issues regarding obscenity and pornography the discussion can be informed by important and often new facts. It presents its Report, hopeful that it will contribute to this discussion at a new level. . . .

2   Exposure to erotic stimuli appears to have little or no effect on already established attitudinal commitments regarding either sexuality or sexual morality. A series of four studies employing a large array of indicators found practically no significant differences in such attitudes before and after single or repeated exposures to erotica. One study did find that after exposure persons became more tolerant in reference to other persons' sexual activities although their own sexual standards did not change. One study reported that some persons' attitudes toward premarital intercourse became more liberal after exposure, while other persons'

attitudes became more conservative, but another study found no changes in this regard. The overall picture is almost completely a tableau of no significant change. . . .

Statistical studies of the relationship between availability of erotic materials and the rates of sex crimes in Denmark indicate that the increased availability of explicit sexual materials has been accompanied by a decrease in the incidence of sexual crime. Analysis of police records of the same types of sex crimes in Copenhagen during the past 12 years revealed that a dramatic decrease in reported sex crimes occurred during this period and that the decrease coincided with changes in Danish law which permitted wider availability of explicit sexual materials. Other research showed that the decrease in reported sexual offenses cannot be attributed to concurrent changes in the social and legal definitions of sex crimes or in public attitudes toward reporting such crimes to the police, or in police reporting procedures.   3

Statistical studies of the relationship between the availability of erotic material and the rates of sex crimes in the United States presents a more complex picture. During the period in which there has been a marked increase in the availability of erotic materials, some specific rates of arrest for sex crimes have increased (*e.g.*, forcible rape) and others have declined (*e.g.*, overall juvenile rates). For juveniles, the overall rate of arrests for sex crimes decreased even though arrests for nonsexual crimes increased by more than 100%. For adults, arrests for sex offenses increased slightly more than did arrests for nonsex offenses. The conclusion is that, for America, the relationship between the availability of erotica and changes in sex crime rates neither proves nor disproves the possibility that availability of erotica leads to crime, but the massive overall increases in sex crimes that have been alleged do not seem to have occurred. . . .   4

I. Non-Legislative Recommendation

The Commission believes that much of the "problem" regarding materials which depict explicit sexual activity stems from the inability or reluctance of people in our society to be open and direct in dealing with sexual matters. . . .   5

The Commission believes that accurate, appropriate sex   6

information provided openly and directly through legitimate channels and from reliable sources in healthy contexts
can compete successfully with potentially distorted,
warped, inaccurate, and unreliable information from clandestine, illegitimate sources; and it believes that the attitudes and orientations toward sex produced by the open
communication of appropriate sex information from reliable sources through legitimate channels will be normal
and healthy, providing a solid foundation for the basic institutions of our society.

7   The Commission, therefore, ... *recommends that a massive sex education effort be launched.* ... The Commission
feels that such a sex education program would provide a
powerful positive approach to the problems of obscenity
and pornography. By providing accurate and reliable sex
information through legitimate sources, it would reduce
interest in and dependence upon clandestine and less legitimate sources. By providing healthy attitudes and orientations toward sexual relationships, it would provide better
protection for the individual against distorted or warped
ideas he may encounter regarding sex. By providing greater
ease in talking about sexual matters in appropriate contexts, the shock and offensiveness of encounters with sex
would be reduced. ...

II. Legislative Recommendation

8   *The Commission recommends that federal, state, and local
legislation prohibiting the sale, exhibition, or distribution of
sexual materials to consenting adults should be repealed.* ...
Our conclusion is based upon the following considerations:
       1. Extensive empirical investigation, both by the Com-
mission and by others, provides no evidence that exposure
to or use of explicit sexual materials plays a significant
role in the causation of social or individual harms such as
crime, delinquency, sexual or nonsexual deviancy or severe
emotional disturbances. ... Empirical investigation thus
supports the opinion of a substantial majority of persons
professionally engaged in the treatment of deviancy, delinquency and antisocial behavior, that exposure to sexually
explicit materials has no harmful causal role in these areas.
Studies show that a number of factors, such as disorganized
family relationships and unfavorable peer influences, are
intimately related to harmful sexual behavior or adverse

character development. Exposure to sexually explicit materials, however, cannot be counted as among these determinative factors.

2. On the positive side, explicit sexual materials are sought as a source of entertainment and information by substantial numbers of American adults. At times, these materials also appear to serve to increase and facilitate constructive communication about sexual matters within marriage. The most frequent purchaser of explicit sexual materials is a college-educated, married male, in his thirties or forties, who is of above average socio-economic status. Even where materials are legally available to them, young adults and older adolescents do not constitute an important portion of the purchasers of such materials.

3. Society's attempts to legislate for adults in the area of obscenity have not been successful. Present laws prohibiting the consensual sale or distribution of explicit sexual materials to adults are extremely unsatisfactory in their practical application. The Constitution permits material to be deemed "obscene" for adults only if, as a whole, it appeals to the "prurient" interest of the average person, is "patently offensive" in light of "community standards," and lacks "redeeming social value." These vague and highly subjective aesthetic, psychological and moral tests do not provide meaningful guidance for law enforcement officials, juries or courts. As a result, law is inconsistently and sometimes erroneously applied and the distinctions made by courts between prohibited and permissible materials often appear indefensible. Errors in the application of the law and uncertainty about its scope also cause interference with the communication of constitutionally protected materials.

4. Public opinion in America does not support the imposition of legal prohibitions upon the right of adults to read or see explicit sexual materials. While a minority of Americans favors such prohibitions, a majority of the American people presently are of the view that adults should be legally able to read or see explicit sexual materials if they wish to do so.

5. The lack of consensus among Americans concerning whether explicit sexual materials should be available to adults in our society, and the significant number of adults who wish to have access to such materials, pose serious problems regarding the enforcement of legal prohibitions upon adults, even aside from the vagueness and subjectivity of present law. Consistent enforcement of even the clearest

prohibitions upon consensual adult exposure to explicit sexual materials would require the expenditure of considerable law enforcement resources. In the absence of a persuasive demonstration of damage flowing from consensual exposure to such materials, there seems no justification for thus adding to the overwhelming tasks already placed upon the law enforcement system. Inconsistent enforcement of prohibitions, on the other hand, invites discriminatory action based upon considerations not directly relevant to the policy of the law. The latter alternative also breeds public disrespect for the legal process.

6. The foregoing considerations take on an added significance because of the fact that adult obscenity laws deal in the realm of speech and communication. Americans deeply value the right of each individual to determine for himself what books he wishes to read and what pictures or films he wishes to see. Our traditions of free speech and press also value and protect the right of writers, publishers, and booksellers to serve the diverse interests of the public. The spirit and letter of our Constitution tell us that government should not seek to interfere with these rights unless a clear threat of harm makes that course imperative. Moreover, the possibility of the misuse of general obscenity statutes prohibiting distributions of books and films to adults constitutes a continuing threat to the free communication of ideas among Americans — one of the most important foundations of our liberties.

7. In reaching its recommendation that government should not seek to prohibit consensual distributions of sexual materials to adults, the Commission discussed several arguments which are often advanced in support of such legislation. The Commission carefully considered the view that adult legislation should be retained in order to aid in the protection of young persons from exposure to explicit sexual materials. We do not believe that the objective of protecting youth may justifiably be achieved at the expense of denying adults materials of their choice. It seems to us wholly inappropriate to adjust the level of adult communication to that considered suitable for children. Indeed, the Supreme Court has unanimously held that adult legislation premised on this basis is a clearly unconstitutional interference with liberty. . . .

8. The Commission has also taken cognizance of the concern of many people that the lawful distribution of explicit

sexual materials to adults may have a deleterious effect upon the individual morality of American citizens and upon the moral climate in America as a whole. This concern appears to flow from a belief that exposure to explicit materials may cause moral confusion which, in turn, may induce antisocial or criminal behavior. As noted above, the Commission has found no evidence to support such a contention. Nor is there evidence that exposure to explicit sexual materials adversely affects character or moral attitudes regarding sex and sexual conduct. . . .

Report of the President's Commission on Obscenity and Pornography (Minority Report)

Overview

The Commission's majority report is a Magna Carta for 1 the pornographer. . . . The fundamental "finding" on which the entire report is based is: that "empirical research" has come up with "no reliable evidence to indicate that exposure to explicit sexual materials plays a significant role in the causation of delinquent or criminal behavior among youth or adults." The inference from this statement, i.e., pornography is harmless, is not only insupportable on the slanted evidence presented; it is preposterous. How isolate one factor and say it causes or does not cause criminal behavior? How determine that one book or one film caused one man to commit rape or murder? A man's entire life goes into one criminal act. No one factor can be said to have caused that act.

The Commission has deliberately and carefully avoided 2 coming to grips with the basic underlying issue. The government interest in regulating pornography has always related primarily to the prevention of moral corruption and *not* to prevention of overt criminal acts and conduct, or the protection of persons from being shocked and/or offended. The basic question is whether and to what extent society may establish and maintain certain moral standards. If it is conceded that society has a legitimate concern in maintaining moral standards, it follows logically that government has a legitimate interest in at least attempting to protect such standards against any source which threatens them. . . .

3   Sex education, recommended so strongly by the majority, is the panacea for those who advocate license in media. The report suggests sex education, with a plaint for the dearth of instructors and materials. it notes that three schools have used "hard-core pornography" in training potential instructors. The report does not answer the question that comes to mind immediately: Will these instructors not bring the hard-core pornography into the grammar schools? Many other questions are left unanswered: How assure that the instructor's moral or ethical code (or lack of same) will not be communicated to children? Shouldn't parents, not children, be the recipients of sex education courses?

4   Children cannot grow in love if they are trained with pornography. Pornography is loveless; it degrades the human being, reduces him to the level of animal. And if this Commission majority's recommendations are heeded, there will be a glut of pornography for teachers and children.

5   In contrast to the Commission report's amazing statement that public opinion in America does not support the imposition of legal prohibitions upon the consensual distribution of pornography to adults, we find, as a result of public hearings conducted by two of the undersigned in eight cities throughout the country, that the majority of the American people favor tighter controls. Twenty-six out of twenty-seven witnesses at the hearing in New York City expressed concern and asked for remedial measures. Witnesses were a cross section of the community, ranging from members of the judiciary to members of women's clubs. This pattern was repeated in the cities of New Orleans, Indianapolis, Chicago, Salt Lake City, San Francisco, Washington, D.C., and Buffalo. . . . Additionally, law enforcement officers testifying at the Hill-Link hearings were unanimous in declaring that the problem of obscenity and pornography is a serious one. . . . We point also to the results of a Gallup poll, published in the summer of 1969. Eighty-five out of every 100 adults interviewed said they favored stricter state

and local laws dealing with pornography sent through the mails, and 76 of every 100 wanted stricter laws on the sort of magazines and newspapers available on newsstands. . . .

Some have argued that because sex crimes have appar- 6 ently declined in Denmark while the volume of pornography has increased, we need not be concerned about the potential effect in our country of this kind of material (because, essentially, of Denmark's benign experience). However two considerations must be noted. First we are a different culture with a greater commitment to the Judeo-Christian tradition; and secondly, we are actually only a year or so behind Denmark in the distribution and sale of pornography. Hardcore written pornography can be purchased anywhere in the U.S. now. Hardcore still pictures and movies can now be purchased over the counter in some cities. Anything can be purchased through the mails. And in a few cities people can attend hardcore pornographic movies. About the only thing we don't have, which Denmark has, are live sex shows. What is most relevant are sex crime statistics in this country, not Denmark . . . :

> *Reported Rapes (verified)*
> Up 116% 1960–69 (absolute increase)
> Up 93% 1960–69 (controlled for Pop. Growth)
>
> *Rape Arrests*
> Up 56.6% all ages 1960–69
> Up 85.9% males under 18 1960–69

However, it should be stated that conclusively proving 7 causal relationships among social science type variables is extremely difficult if not impossible. Among adults whose life histories have included much exposure to pornography it is nearly impossible to disentangle the literally hundreds of causal threads or chains that contributed to their later adjustment or maladjustment. Because of the extreme complexity of the problem and the uniqueness of the human experience it is doubtful that we will ever have absolutely convincing scientific proof that pornography is or isn't harmful. And the issue isn't restricted to, "Does pornography cause or contribute to sex crimes?" The issue has to do with how pornography affects or influences the individual in his total relationship to members of the same as well as opposite sex, children and adults, with all of its ramifications.

Susan Brownmiller

Let's Put Pornography Back in the Closet

Susan Brownmiller, founder of Women Against Pornography, *states her case against pornography in her 1975 book* Against Our Will: Men, Women, and Rape *and in this essay, which appeared in* Newsday *(a Long Island newspaper) in 1979 and a year later in* Take Back the Night, *a collection of essays against pornography. Brownmiller's work also appears elsewhere in this book: see pages 277 and 552.*

1   Free speech is one of the great foundations on which our democracy rests. I am old enough to remember the Hollywood Ten, the screenwriters who went to jail in the late 1940s because they refused to testify before a congressional committee about their political affiliations. They tried to use the First Amendment as a defense, but they went to jail because in those days there were few civil liberties lawyers around who cared to champion the First Amendment right to free speech, when the speech concerned the Communist Party.

2   The Hollywood Ten were correct in claiming the First Amendment. Its high purpose is the protection of unpopular ideas and political dissent. In the dark, cold days of the 1950s, few civil libertarians were willing to declare themselves First Amendment absolutists. But in the brighter, though frantic, days of the 1960s, the principle of protecting unpopular political speech was gradually strengthened.

3   It is fair to say now that the battle has largely been won. Even the American Nazi Party has found itself the beneficiary of the dedicated, tireless work of the American Civil Liberties Union. But—and please notice the quotation marks coming up—"To equate the free and robust exchange of ideas and political debate with commercial exploitation of obscene material demeans the grand conception of the First Amendment and its high purposes in the historic struggle for freedom. It is a misuse of the great guarantees of free speech and free press."

4   I didn't say that, although I wish I had, for I think the words are thrilling. Chief Justice Warren Burger said it in 1973, in the United States Supreme Court's majority opin-

ion in *Miller* v. *California*. During the same decades that the right to political free speech was being strengthened in the courts, the nation's obscenity laws also were undergoing extensive revision.

It's amazing to recall that in 1934 the question of whether   5
James Joyce's *Ulysses* should be banned as pornographic actually went before the Court. The battle to protect *Ulysses* as a work of literature with redeeming social value was won. In later decades, Henry Miller's *Tropic* books, *Lady Chatterley's Lover* and the *Memoirs of Fanny Hill* also were adjudged not obscene. These decisions have been important to me. As the author of *Against Our Will*, a study of the history of rape that does contain explicit sexual material, I shudder to think how my book would have fared if James Joyce, D. H. Lawrence and Henry Miller hadn't gone before me.

I am not a fan of *Chatterley* or the *Tropic* books, I should   6
quickly mention. They are not to my literary taste, nor do I think they represent female sexuality with any degree of accuracy. But I would hardly suggest that we ban them. Such a suggestion wouldn't get very far anyway. The battle to protect these books is ancient history. Time does march on, quite methodically. What, then, is unlawfully obscene, and what does the First Amendment have to do with it?

In the Miller case of 1973 (not Henry Miller, by the   7
way, but a porn distributor who sent unsolicited stuff through the mails), the Court came up with new guidelines that it hoped would strenthen obscenity laws by giving more power to the states. What it did in actuality was throw everything into confusion. It set up a three-part test by which materials can be adjudged obscene. The materials are obscene if they depict patently offensive, hard-core sexual conduct; lack serious scientific, literary, artistic or political value; and appeal to the prurient interest of an average person — as measured by contemporary community standards.

"Patently offensive," "prurient interest" and "hard-core"   8
are indeed words to conjure with. "Contemporary community standards" are what we're trying to redefine. The feminist objection to pornography is not based on prurience, which the dictionary defines as lustful, itching desire. We are not opposed to sex and desire, with or without the itch, and we certainly believe that explicit sexual material has its place in literature, art, science and education. Here we part company rather swiftly with old-line conser-

vatives who don't want sex education in the high schools,
for example.

9   No, the feminist objection to pornography is based on
our belief that pornography represents hatred of women,
that pornography's intent is to humiliate, degrade and dehumanize the female body for the purpose of erotic stimulation and pleasure. We are unalterably opposed to the
presentation of the female body being stripped, bound,
raped, tortured, mutilated and murdered in the name of
commercial entertainment and free speech.

10   These images, which are standard pornographic fare,
have nothing to do with the hallowed right of political
dissent. They have everything to do with the creation of a
cultural climate in which a rapist feels he is merely giving
in to a normal urge and a woman is encouraged to believe
that sexual masochism is healthy, liberated fun. Justice
Potter Stewart once said about hard-core pornography,
"You know it when you see it," and that certainly used to be
true. In the good old days, pornography looked awful. It was
cheap and sleazy, and there was no mistaking it for art.

11   Nowadays, since the porn industry has become a multimillion dollar business, visual technology has been employed in its service. Pornographic movies are skillfully
filmed and edited, pornographic still shots using the newest
tenets of good design artfully grace the covers of *Hustler*,
Penthouse and *Playboy*, and the public — and the courts —
are sadly confused.

12   The Supreme Court neglected to define "hard-core" in
the Miller decision. This was a mistake. If "hard-core" refers
only to explicit sexual intercourse, then that isn't good
enough. When women or children or men — no matter how
artfully — are shown tortured or terrorized in the service of
sex, that's obscene. And "patently offensive," I would hope,
to our "contemporary community standards."

13   Justice William O. Douglas wrote in his dissent to the
Miller case that no one is "compelled to look." This is hardly
true. To buy a paper at the corner newsstand is to subject
oneself to a forcible immersion in pornography, to be demeaned by an array of dehumanized, chopped-up parts of
the female anatomy, packaged like cuts of meat at the supermarket. I happen to like my body and I work hard at the
gym to keep it in good shape, but I am embarrassed for
my body and for the bodies of all women when I see the
fragmented parts of us so frivolously, and so flagrantly,
displayed.

Some constitutional theorists (Justice Douglas was one) 14
have maintained that any obscenity law is a serious
abridgement of free speech. Others (and Justice Earl Warren was one) have maintained that the First Amendment
was never intended to protect obscenity. We live quite com-
patibly with a host of free-speech abridgements. There are
restraints against false and misleading advertising or statements — shouting "fire" without cause in a crowded movie
theater, etc. — that do not threaten, but strengthen, our
societal values. Restrictions on the public display of pornography belong in this category.

The distinction between permission to publish and per- 15
mission to display publicly is an essential one and one
which I think consonant with First Amendment principles.
Justice Burger's words which I quoted above support this
without question. We are not saying "Smash the presses"
or "Ban the bad ones," but simply "Get the stuff out of our
sight." Let the legislatures decide — using realistic and
humane contemporary community standards — what can
be displayed and what cannot. The courts, after all, will be
the final arbiters.

Susan Jacoby

I Am a First Amendment Junkie

*Susan Jacoby, born 1946, has written numerous articles on
women's issues for popular magazines such as* Glamour,
McCall's, *and* The Nation, *as well as several books. She has
also served as a columnist for the* Washington Post *and* The
New York Times; *in fact, the following argument appeared in
her syndicated "Hers" column in 1978.*

It is no news that many women are defecting from the 1
ranks of civil libertarians on the issue of obscenity. The
conviction of Larry Flynt, publisher of *Hustler* magazine —
before his metamorphosis into a born-again Christian —
was greeted with unabashed feminist approval. Harry
Reems, the unknown actor who was convicted by a Memphis jury for conspiring to distribute the movie *Deep Throat,*

has carried on his legal battles with almost no support from women who ordinarily regard themselves as supporters of the First Amendment. Feminist writers and scholars have even discussed the possibility of making common cause against pornography with adversaries of the women's movement — including opponents of the equal rights amendment and "right-to-life" forces.

2   All of this is deeply disturbing to a woman writer who believes, as I always have and still do, in an absolute interpretation of the First Amendment. Nothing in Larry Flynt's garbage convinces me that the late Justice Hugo L. Black was wrong in this opinion that "the Federal Government is without any power whatsoever under the Constitution to put any type of burden on free speech and expression of ideas of any kind (as distinguished from conduct)." Many women I like and respect tell me I am wrong; I cannot remember having become involved in so many heated discussions of a public issue since the end of the Vietnam War. A feminist writer described my views as those of a "First Amendment junkie."

3   Many feminist arguments for controls on pornography carry the implicit conviction that porn books, magazines and movies pose a greater threat to women than similarly repulsive exercises of free speech pose to other offended groups. This conviction has, of course, been shared by everyone — regardless of race, creed or sex — who has ever argued in favor of abridging the First Amendment. It is the argument used by some Jews who have withdrawn their support from the American Civil Liberties Union because it has defended the right of American Nazis to march through a community inhabited by survivors of Hitler's concentration camps.

4   If feminists want to argue that the protection of the Constitution should not be extended to *any* particularly odious or threatening form of speech, they have a reasonable argument (although I don't agree with it). But it is ridiculous to suggest that the porn shops on 42d Street are more disgusting to women than a march of neo-Nazis is to survivors of the extermination camps.

5   The arguments over pornography also blur the vital distinction between expression of ideas and conduct. When I say I believe unreservedly in the First Amendment, someone always comes back at me with the issue of "kiddie porn."

But kiddie porn is not a First Amendment issue. It is an issue of the abuse of power — the power adults have over children — and not of obscenity. Parents and promoters have no more right to use their children to make porn movies than they do to send them to work in coal mines. The responsible adults should be prosecuted, just as adults who use children for back-breaking farm labor should be prosecuted.

Susan Brownmiller, in *Against Our Will: Men, Women and Rape,* has described pornography as "the undiluted essence of anti-female propaganda." I think this is a fair description of some types of pornography, especially of the brutish subspecies that equates sex with death and portrays women primarily as objects of violence.

The equation of sex and violence, personified by some glossy rock record album covers as well as by *Hustler,* has fed the illusion that censorship of pornography can be conducted on a more rational basis than other types of censorship. Are all pictures of naked women obscene? Clearly not, says a friend. A Renoir nude is art, she says, and *Hustler* is trash. "Any reasonable person" knows that.

But what about something between art and trash — something, say, along the lines of *Playboy* or *Penthouse* magazines? I asked five women for their reactions to one picture in *Penthouse* and got responses that ranged from "lovely" and "sensuous" to "revolting" and "demeaning." Feminists, like everyone else, seldom have rational reasons for their preferences in erotica. Like members of juries, they tend to disagree when confronted with something that falls short of 100 percent vulgarity.

In any case, feminists will not be the arbiters of good taste if it becomes easier to harass, prosecute and convict people on obscenity charges. Most of the people who want to censor girlie magazines are equally opposed to open discussion of issues that are of vital concern to women: rape, abortion, menstruation, contraception, lesbianism — in fact, the entire range of sexual experience from a woman's viewpoint.

Feminist writers and editors and film makers have limited financial resources: Confronted by a determined prosecutor, Hugh Hefner will fare better than Susan Brownmiller. Would the Memphis jurors who convicted Harry Reems for his role in *Deep Throat* be inclined to take a more positive view of paintings of the female genitalia done by sensitive

6

7

8

9

10

feminist artists? *Ms.* magazine has printed color reproductions of some of those art works; *Ms.* is already banned from a number of high school libraries because someone considers it threatening and/or obscene.

11   Feminists who want to censor what they regard as harmful pornography have essentially the same motivation as other would-be censors: They want to use the power of the state to accomplish what they have been unable to achieve in the marketplace of ideas and images. The impulse to censor places no faith in the possibilities of democratic persuasion.

12   It isn't easy to persuade certain men that they have better uses for $1.95 each month than to spend it on a copy of *Hustler?* Well, then, give the men no choice in the matter.

13   I believe there is also a connection between the impulse toward censorship on the part of people who used to consider themselves civil libertarians and a more general desire to shift responsibility from individuals to institutions. When I saw the movie *Looking for Mr. Goodbar,* I was stunned by its series of visual images equating sex and violence, coupled with what seems to me the mindless message (a distortion of the fine Judith Rossner novel) that casual sex equals death. When I came out of the movie, I was even more shocked to see parents standing in line with children between the ages of 10 and 14.

14   I simply don't know why a parent would take a child to see such a movie, any more than I understand why people feel they can't turn off a television set their child is watching. Whenever I say that, my friends tell me I don't know how it is because I don't have children. True, but I do have parents. When I was a child, they did turn off the TV. They didn't expect the Federal Communications Commission to do their job for them.

15   I am a First Amendment junkie. You can't OD on the First Amendment, because free speech is its own best antidote.

Editorial: First Amendment Pixillation

The National Review—a forum for conservative thought that was launched by William F. Buckley in 1955—helped fashion the conservative agenda that prevailed during the 1980s. The following unsigned editorial appeared in The National Review *in 1977.*

Freedom of the press is in mortal peril again, this time 1
out in Kansas, where pseudonymous postal officials tricked New York pornographer Al Goldstein into mailing them his brainchildren, *Screw* and *Smut*. Civil libertarians are swarming to the defense of Goldstein and his former partner, one James Buckley (don't even ask), who are now on trial on federal charges of mailing obscene materials. "*Screw* is a despicable publication," says Harvard's Alan Dershowitz, "but that's what the First Amendment was designed to protect." False. That's what the First Amendment is currently *used* to protect, but . . . well, class, let's have a short review.

Until very recently nobody suggested that the First 2
Amendment had been intended to protect obscenity. Or that it should be *stretched* to protect it. As for the first point, the record is clear: obscenity, like incitement to riot, has traditionally been illegal. And the intentions of the Framers are limned with shocking clarity in Leonard Levy's *Legacy of Suppression*. Judge Wolsey's famous ruling in *Ulysses*, let it be recalled, denied that *Ulysses* was obscene simply as a matter of fact (more emetic than aphrodisiac, he sniffed), without faintly suggesting that nothing was obscene, or that the law should not take cognizance of—and punish—obscene publications. As a matter of fact, the U.S. struggled along for almost two centuries uninundated by the likes of *Screw*, and is it suggested that during those years American thought was stultified? As for the contention that the First Amendment should be stretched, well, that is incompatible with the principle of the rule of law. Let those who want it changed get another Amendment. Of course they can't: their whole case depends heavily on forging a phony constitutional pedigree for their libertarianism, and only deludes people because they have succeeded in intimating that the Constitution has already committed us, whether we like it or not, to . . . *Screw*.

3   Yet here is Geoffrey Stone of the University of Chicago:
"If a publisher wants to play it safe, he has to attempt to
figure out what is the most restrictive, conservative notion
of obscenity in the country and not publish anything that
violates that standard. The net effect is that the rights of
citizens in every other location are impaired." And Dershowitz: "Any community can act as the censor of any other
community—that's small-town censorship." If *Screw* is illegal in Paw Paw, Michigan, you see, it will be impossible
or unprofitable to publish it in New York, and the mind of
every American is manacled. One might as well argue that
the remaining dry counties in Kansas inexorably will bring
Prohibition back to New York. Actually it is the "libertarian" forces who are battling to impose a single rule everywhere—and who, in the name of "individual" rights, would
deny citizens the right to act as a community for certain
purposes. As usual, their demand for "freedom" is for a kind
of freedom that in fact must come at the expense of a structural principle of real freedom: the principle of federalism.

4   By all means *do* shed a tear for the First Amendment—not
because it is threatened in Kansas, but because it is ex-
pounded in the nation's top law schools by such minds as
those of Messrs. Stone and Dershowitz.

Susan Brownmiller

Pornography Hurts Women

This essay by Susan Brownmiller appeared in her 1975 book
Against Our Will: Men, Women, and Rape. *For more of Ms.
Brownmiller's work, see pages 277 and 544.*

1   Pornography has been so thickly glossed over with the
patina of chic these days in the name of verbal freedom
and sophistication that important distinctions between
freedom of political expression (a democratic necessity),
honest sex education for children (a societal good) and ugly
smut (the deliberate devaluation of the role of women
through obscene, distorted depictions) have been hopelessly

confused. Part of the problem is that those who traditionally have been the most vigorous opponents of porn are often those same people who shudder at the explicit mention of any sexual subject. Under their watchful, vigilante eyes, frank and free dissemination of educational materials relating to abortion, contraception, the act of birth, and female biology in general is also dangerous, subversive and dirty. (I am not unmindful that a frank and free discussion of rape, "the unspeakable crime," might well give these righteous vigilantes further cause to shudder.) Because the battle lines were falsely drawn a long time ago, before there was a vocal women's movement, the anti-pornography forces appear to be, for the most part, religious, Southern, conservative and right-wing, while the pro-porn forces are identified as Eastern, atheistic and liberal.

But a woman's perspective demands a totally new align-   2
ment, or at least a fresh appraisal. The majority report of the President's Commission on Obscenity and Pornography (1970), a report that argued strongly for the removal of all legal restrictions on pornography, soft and hard, made plain that 90 percent of all pornographic material is geared to the male heterosexual market (the other 10 percent is geared to the male homosexual taste), that buyers of porn are "predominantly white, middle-class, middle-aged married males" and that the graphic depictions, the meat and potatoes of porn, are of the naked female body and of the multiplicity of acts done to that body.

Discussing the content of stag films, "a familiar and   3
firmly established part of the American scene," the commission report dutifully, if foggily, explained, "Because pornography historically has been thought to be primarily a masculine interest, the emphasis in stag films seems to represent the preferences of the middle-class American male. Thus male homosexuality and bestiality are relatively rare, while lesbianism is rather common."

The commissioners in this instance had merely verified   4
what purveyors of porn have always known: hard-core pornography is not a celebration of sexual freedom; it is a cynical exploitation of female sexual activity through the device of making all such activity, and consequently all females, "dirty." Heterosexual male consumers of pornography are frankly turned on by watching lesbians in action (although never in the final scenes, but always as a curtain raiser); they are turned off with the sudden swiftness of a

water faucet by watching naked men act upon each other. One study quoted in the commission report came to the unastounding conclusion that "seeing a stag film in the presence of male peers bolsters masculine esteem." Indeed. The men in groups who watch the films, it is important to note, are *not* naked.

5   When male response to pornography is compared to female response, a pronounced difference in attitude emerges. According to the commission, "Males report being more highly aroused by depictions of nude females, and show more interest in depictions of nude females than [do] females." Quoting the figures of Alfred Kinsey, the commission noted that a majority of males (77 percent) were "aroused" by visual depictions of explicit sex while a majority of females (68 percent) were not aroused. Further, "females more often than males reported 'disgust' and 'offense.' "

6   From whence comes this female disgust and offense? Are females sexually backward or more conservative by nature? The gut distaste that a majority of women feel when we look at pornography, a distaste that, incredibly, it is no longer fashionable to admit, comes, I think, from the gut knowledge that we and our bodies are being stripped, exposed and contorted for the purpose of ridicule to bolster that "masculine esteem" which gets its kick and sense of power from viewing females as anonymous, panting playthings, adult toys, dehumanized objects to be used, abused, broken and discarded.

7   This, of course, is also the philosophy of rape. It is no accident (for what else could be its purpose?) that females in the pornographic genre are depicted in two cleanly dilineated roles: as virgins who are caught and "banged" or as nymphomaniacs who are never sated. The most popular and prevalent pornographic fantasy combines the two: an innocent, untutored female is raped and "subjected to unnatural practices" that turn her into a raving, slobbering nymphomaniac, a dependent sexual slave who can never get enough of the big, male cock.

8   There can be no "equality" in porn, no female equivalent, no turning of the tables in the name of bawdy fun. Pornography, like rape, is a male invention, designed to dehumanize women, to reduce the female to an object of sexual access, not to free sensuality from moralistic or parental inhibition. The staple of porn will always be the naked female body, breasts and genitals exposed, because as man

devised it, her naked body is the female's "shame," her private parts the private property of man, while his are the ancient, holy, universal, patriarchal instrument of his power, his rule by force over *her*.

Pornography is the undiluted essence of anti-female prop- 9 aganda. Yet the very same liberals who were so quick to understand the method and purpose behind the mighty propaganda machine of Hitler's Third Reich, the conscious-ly spewed-out anti-Semitic caricatures and obscenities that gave an ideological base to the Holocaust and the Final Solution, the very same liberals who, enlightened by blacks, searched their own conscience and came to understand that their tolerance of "nigger" jokes and portrayals of shuffling, rolling-eyed servants in movies perpetuated the degrading myths of black inferiority and gave an ideological base to the continuation of black oppression — these very same lib-erals now fervidly maintain that the hatred and contempt for women that find expression in four-letter words used as expletives and in what are quaintly called "adult" or "erotic" books and movies are a valid extension of freedom of speech that must be preserved as a Constitutional right.

To defend the right of a lone, crazed American Nazi to 10 grind out propaganda calling for the extermination of all Jews, as the ACLU has done in the name of free speech, is, after all, a self-righteous and not particularly courageous stand, for American Jewry is not currently threatened by storm troopers, concentration camps and imminent exter-mination, but I wonder if the ACLU's position might change if, come tomorrow morning, the bookstores and movie theaters lining Forty-second Street in New York City were devoted not to the humiliation of women by rape and tor-ture, as they currently are, but to a systematized, commer-cially successful propaganda machine depicting the sadistic pleasures of gassing Jews or lynching blacks?

Is this analogy extreme? Not if you are a woman who is 11 conscious of the ever-present threat of rape and the prolif-eration of a cultural ideology that makes it sound like "lib-erated" fun. The majority report of the President's Commis-sion on Obscenity and Pornography tried to pooh-pooh the opinion of law enforcement agencies around the country that claimed their own concrete experience with offenders who were caught with the stuff led them to conclude that pornographic material is a causative factor in crimes of sexual violence. The commission maintained that it was not possible at this time to scientifically prove or disprove such a connection.

12   But does one need scientific methodology in order to conclude that the anti-female propaganda that permeates our nation's cultural output promotes a climate in which acts of sexual hostility directed against women are not only tolerated but ideologically encouraged? A similar debate has raged for many years over whether or not the extensive glorification of violence (the gangster as hero; the loving treatment accorded bloody shoot-'em-ups in movies, books and on TV) has a causal effect, a direct relationship to the rising rate of crime, particularly among youth. Interestingly enough, in this area — nonsexual and not specifically related to abuses against women — public opinion seems to be swinging to the position that explicit violence in the entertainment media does have a deleterious effect; it makes violence commonplace, numbingly routine and no longer morally shocking.

13   More to the point, those who call for a curtailment of scenes of violence in movies and on television in the name of sensitivity, good taste and what's best for our children are not accused of being pro-censorship or against freedom of speech. Similarly, minority group organizations, black, Hispanic, Japanese, Italian, Jewish, or American Indian, that campaign against ethnic slurs and demeaning portrayals in movies, on television shows and in commercials are perceived as waging a just political fight, for if a minority group claims to be offended by a specific portrayal, be it Little Black Sambo or the Frito Bandido, and relates it to a history of ridicule and oppression, few liberals would dare to trot out a Constitutional argument in theoretical opposition, not if they wish to maintain their liberal credentials. Yet when it comes to the treatment of women, the liberal consciousness remains fiercely obdurate, refusing to be budged, for the sin of appearing square or prissy in the age of the so-called sexual revolution has become the worst offense of all.

Robert Shea
Women at War

Robert Shea, an editor, novelist, and free-lance writer, has written articles for several men's magazines. He wrote "Women at War" for Playboy *in 1980.*

For one wing of the feminist movement, the hot issue   1
these days is not equal pay, job opportunities, day-care
centers, the Equal Rights Amendment or abortion rights
but pornography. Last September, a New York–based organization called Women Against Pornography (WAP) sponsored a two-day conference at which an audience of 700
heard Gloria Steinem, Bella Abzug and other luminaries
inveigh against Demon Porn. Susan Brownmiller, author
of *Against Our Will*, a book on rape, has been leading widely
publicized tours of the Times Square pornography bazaar,
starting from a storefront that WAP opened in the area.
Similar groups have appeared elsewhere around the country. In San Francisco, Women Against Violence in Pornography and Media (WAVPM) held a Take Back the Night
march which climaxed with a demonstration in the com-
mercial-sex district on Broadway Avenue. Similar marches
have been staged in other cities; one in Minneapolis drew
4500 supporters.

Other feminists have been attacking porn in less conven-   2
tional ways. Women's groups have prevented showings of
Story of O in several cities by such tactics as bomb threats
and disturbances in the theaters. In Perth, Australia,
feminists confiscated sex movies outright. In Denver, the
Bluebird Five spray-painted and pasted leaflets on a local
porn theater. In Cologne, West Germany, a feminist stole
$50,000 worth of merchandise from sex shops, leaving a
leaflet signed "Red Zora, Avenger of the Oppressed."

Nor are pornography outlets the only targets for angry   3
feminists. At 3:15 one morning a woman named Marcia
Womongold fired a rifle bullet through the window of Reading International, a respected bookstore in Harvard Square.
The store's offense was selling *Playboy*, *Oui* and *Penthouse*.
Elaine Noble, a member of Boston mayor Kevin White's
staff, quickly spoke up in Womongold's support: "I think
she has guts," she said. "We're going to have to give her a
mayor's citation."

4   As Womongold's exploit shows, this feminist crusade is not aimed at hardcore pornography alone but against any sexy material that arouses its ire, including newspaper ads and men's magazines. Using the term loosely in this way, the women attacking pornography say it is linked with rape and other sex crimes. Some believe it is a direct cause of such crimes. They charge that pornography creates a cultural climate in which men are encouraged to abuse and humiliate women. And they say that porn is an insult to women, just as racist propaganda is offensive to minority groups.

5   What do they want to do about it? The dominant position in this movement at the moment seems to be to avoid an outright call for censorship . . . . About 5000 antipornography protesters, mostly women, marched down Broadway through Times Square to the beat of a big bass drum, with Abzug, Brownmiller and Steinem in the lead, waving hand-lettered placards and chanting slogans like "Two, four, six, eight, pornography is woman hate." Every so often, the marchers broke ranks to slap Day-Glo stickers on advertisements and ticket windows. Rallying in Bryant Park, just behind the New York Public Library, they heard speeches claiming that pornography is filled with murder, rape, mutilation and torture. They also heard Lynn Campbell, a WAP organizer, call for a boycott of stores that sell *Playboy*. The women hope to arouse public indignation through demonstrations and other publicity, thereby making pornography socially unacceptable.

6   Many women in the movement favor outright censorship. Brownmiller applauds what the U.S. Supreme Court has done to uphold the constitutionality of bans on obscenity and argues that it just hasn't gone far enough. WAP's literature calls for a rewriting of the legal definition of obscenity.

7   Still other feminists advocate what they call the direct-action approach — the sabotage of pornography outlets, destruction of material and harassment of customers. The WAP conference devoted one of its workshops to such action.

8   This drive against porn gets its steam from fear of rape and other violent crimes against women and children. While no one knows whether the actual number or rate of sex crimes is going up or down (because historically so few were reported to the police), there is a wide-spread impression that they are on the rise. We do know that the annual rate of reported forcible rapes nearly doubled between 1969 and 1977. At the same time, the sale of sexually explicit

books, magazines and films has been a booming business, and some of this material portrays violence against women and the sexual abuse of children.

Women are alarmed and angered when they are told that   9
there is a subculture out there that pays money to see depictions of women being raped, tortured and killed. When the news page of the morning paper brings stories of sexual atrocities and the amusements page carries ads for movies in which women are brutalized, it is easy to become enraged and to want to strike out against pornography.

Easy, yes. But is it reasonable or useful?   10

A great many feminists do not think so. Commenting on   11
the September WAP conference, *Village Voice* columnist Ellen Willis, a founder of the radical feminist organization Redstockings, points out that an attack on pornography can be an attack on women's sexuality: "Over the years, I've enjoyed various pieces of pornography — some of them of the sleazy 42nd Street paperback sort — and so have most women I know. If feminists define pornography, per se, as the enemy, the result will be to make a lot of women ashamed of their sexual feelings and afraid to be honest about them. And the last thing women need is more sexual shame, guilt and hypocrisy — this time served up as feminism."

Some feminists see a positive value in pornography. Artist   12
Betty Dodson, quoted in *Ms.* magazine, says, "I call myself a pornographer . . . because I think the word ought to be legitimized. I think that anything that has to do with sex should be good. Sex is something people do, and there should be nothing bad about showing it. If women shy away from this kind of art, it's only because of their conditioning."

Like many people who urge the suppression of pornog-   13
raphy, Susan Brownmiller admits that it has not been scientifically proved that sexually explicit material helps cause sex crimes. "But," she writes in *Against Our Will,* "does one need scientific methodology in order to conclude that the antifemale propaganda that permeates our nation's cultural output promotes a climate in which acts of sexual hostility directed against women are not only tolerated but ideologically encouraged?" Another feminist author, Robin Morgan, puts it more succinctly: "Pornography is the theory and rape is the practice."

There is a good deal of ambiguity in such accusations.   14
Foes of pornography tend to use language implying that it

causes sex crimes in intangible ways not amenable to scientific investigation. They have taken this tack ever since the Federally appointed Commission on Obscenity and Pornography spent two years and some $2,000,000 to sponsor and sift through 39 investigations on the subject. In 1970, the commission issued its findings: "Empirical research designed to clarify the question has found no reliable evidence to date that exposure to explicit sexual material plays a significant role in the causation of delinquent or criminal sexual behavior."

15   At the time the commission published its report, material fusing sexual activity with violence was a minor item on the pornography market — therefore, the commission spent little of its resources on investigating the connection between sexuality and aggression. Since then, though, there has been an increase in hard-core pornography that includes violent elements. And researchers are publishing studies that raise such questions as whether or not erotic material can arouse aggression and whether or not violent, aggressive pornography promotes increased aggressiveness toward women.

16   Edward Donnerstein of the University of Wisconsin has carried out a series of experiments measuring the effects of various kinds of erotic material on aggression in male college students. In a recent study, men were made angry by receiving low ratings on essays they had written. To add injury to insult, they were punished for their poor performance with electric shocks. Then they were shown a neutral film or a film of sexual intercourse without violence or one in which a man with a gun rapes a woman. They were then given a chance to give electric shocks to either male or female victims. Donnerstein found that males who had seen the neutral film administered the mildest shocks. Those who had seen the rape film delivered the most severe shocks, and they gave the strongest shocks of all to the women. "Given the increase in sexual and other forms of violence against women that is depicted in the media," Donnerstein concluded, "a concern over such presentations would seem warranted."

17   Measuring people's aggressiveness by having them administer electric shocks to others is quite a popular experimental device these days. It has also been used at UCLA by Seymour Feshbach and Neal Malamuth , who have been trying to learn whether or not reducing sexual inhibition will release people from internal restraints on aggressive

behavior. They found that men and women who had read erotic passages gave more severe shocks to others than did members of a group that had read neutral passages. In another experiment, they gave students two versions of a detailed description of a rape. In one, the victim was in pain throughout the experience; in the other, she gave in and enjoyed it. Women were not aroused by either version, but the men who read about the victim's enjoying the rape were aroused. Feshbach and Malamuth reasoned that erotic material does not turn people on when it violates their ethical standards but that intensified sexual fantasy can overcome this inhibition in men. "We share the belief," they announced, "that the depiction of violence in erotica and pornography could be harmful."

The Report of the Commission on Obscenity and Pornog- 18 *raphy* has been under heavy fire ever since it came out, nine years ago. Critics say the commission was remiss in not paying more attention to the relationship between sex and aggression. Writing in *Psychology Today*, journalist Garry Wills, for instance, weighs in with a comprehensive critique of the commission's report, charging it with "failure to examine in any thorough way the connection between depictions of sex and of violence." A paper published in WAVPM's antipornography newsletter points out that one commission-sponsored study, by Percy H. Tannenbaum, found that exposure to erotic material, and especially erotic-aggressive material, heightens aggressiveness — yet that finding was barely mentioned in the report.

Some attacks have zeroed in on the commission's studies 19 of pornography and sex crime in Denmark. In 1965, erotic material became widely available in Denmark, and by 1967, the Danish parliament took all legal restrictions off the sale of written and pictorial erotica. The commission reported that the annual number of sex crimes, including the combined figure for rape and attempted rape, had decreased between 1965 and 1967. The report's detractors now argue that the drop in Danish sex crime is due to changes in the laws, legalizing such activities as homosexual prostitution. Also, critics say, there was no decline in the number of rapes per year.

Even after allowances are made for changes in the laws, 20 the fact is that Danish sex-crime statistics really did drop. There was a decline in many individual types of sex crime from 1965 on, the most significant being in peeping and the molesting of preadolescent girls. Berl Kutchinsky, one of the Danish researchers for the commission, suggests that in those two areas, but only those two, legalization of pornography may have provided a safety valve for antisocial impulses. Rape, considered by itself, did not decline between 1965 and 1970, but neither did it increase. If pornography did encourage rape, one would expect the incidence of rape to have risen in those five years. Last September, attending a seminar on pornography and sex crime at Simon Fraser University, British Columbia, Kutchinsky stated that rape had neither increased nor decreased in Denmark by 1973 and that the rate of all sex crimes other than rape went down by about 75 percent from 1967, when pornography was legalized, to 1973.

21   Those who want pornography banned hail all the new research and the recent criticisms of the report as evidence that the commission's findings amount to a scientific house of cards. The researchers themselves are careful to point out that their work scarcely adds up to an indictment of pornography; they've even come up with findings that will never be reported in antiporn literature, such as Donnerstein's discovery that when angry men look at nude and seminude pictures from *Playboy* their aggressive feelings fade away. And even when they are considering violent images, which they do think may be connected with actual violence, these researchers stop well short of calling for a ban on such material. "As psychologists," say Feshbach and Malamuth, "we would support community efforts to restrict violence in erotica to adults who are fully cognizant of the nature of the material and who choose knowingly to buy it."

22   Nine years after the commission's report, we still have no proof that pornography, even the violent sort, causes sex crime. We have only studies that show that in a laboratory setting, for a brief period, men who have previously been made angry and who see erotic or erotic-violent films will act more aggressively toward women *when permitted to do so by an authority figure*. It is doubtful that it ever will be possible to prove that exposure to literary or pictorial works can move a person to criminal behavior. . . .

.   .   .

23   Still, the pattern of evidence that emerges supports the commission's conclusions. For example, in the commission-funded study of pornography and sexual deviance by Michael J. Goldstein and colleagues — the study that discovered that such a high percentage of rapists had seen explicit

sexual photos in early childhood — the other findings about rapists point to a sexually inhibited, repressive childhood environment, a lack of experience with sexual material and a generally negative attitude toward it. For example, 18 percent of the rapists as children had been caught with erotic materials, and in all cases, their parents had become angry and punished them. In the control group, 37 percent had read erotic materials with their parents' knowledge; only seven percent had been punished. It was on that overall pattern, rather than on the one anomalous statistic, that the commission based its conclusion that erotic material has little influence on rape.

To examine in detail the efforts of WAP, WAVPM and 24 their supporters to prove that pornography is dangerous is to make the rather disheartening discovery that this supposedly new movement is, for the most part, reiterating the tired and fallacious arguments conservative procensorship outfits such as CDL have been spouting for decades. Brownmiller, Womongold and the rest haven't advanced an inch in their thinking beyond earlier crusading prudes such as Charles H. Keating, Jr., and J. Edgar Hoover, for whom the fact that some sex criminals were found by police to possess porn was proof enough that pornography incites men to sexual violence.

The women's antipornography movement recognizes 25 that many feminists respect the First Amendment and are unwilling to advocate censorship. In an attempt to deal with this issue, WAP has issued a leaflet titled "Where We Stand on the First Amendment" that states:

> We do not advocate censorship. We respect First Amendment strictures against the imposition of prior restraints on any form of speech, and we do not wish to deprive pornographers of their due-process rights. . . . We have not put forth any repressive legislative proposals, and we are not carving out any new exceptions to the First Amendment. . . . We want to change the definition of obscenity so that it focuses on violence, not sex, but we do not propose to alter the basic process by which obscenity laws must be enforced, in accordance with the procedural guarantees of the First Amendment.

In other words, on the First Amendment, WAP stands 26 shoulder to shoulder with the current U.S. Supreme Court. That puts it well to the right of most civil libertarians. It is no concession to say that one is against censorship by prior restraint. The Court has traditionally held that prior restraint — forbidding the publication of disapproved material — is unconstitutional, and even CDL accepts that. The way censorship operates in this country is to prosecute the offender after the book, magazine or movie has been offered to the public. WAP is saying, in short, that it isn't asking for any new laws, because it is satisfied with the laws already on the books. An important exception is its desire "to change the definition of obscenity so that it focuses on violence, not sex."

27   Civil libertarians have long been arguing that such terms as obscenity and pornography express subjective value judgments differing greatly from one person to the next. Obscenity is a legal term; pornography is not. Pornography, however, is the term this feminist movement usually uses to describe what it is against. Pornography, from *pornographos* — writings of, or about, prostitutes — has always had a connotation of sinfulness. The Commission on Obscenity and Pornography avoided using "pornography" in its report: "The term 'pornography' is not used at all in a descriptive context because it appears to have no legal significance and because it most often denotes subjective disapproval of certain materials, rather than their content or effect. The report uses the phrases 'explicit sexual materials,' 'sexually oriented materials,' 'erotica,' or some variant thereof, to refer to the subject matter of the commission's investigations."

28   A classic definition of pornography was offered by Phyllis and Eberhard Kronhausen in *Pornography and the Law*, in which they describe it as the depiction of sexual acts for the sole purpose of arousing the beholder in such a way as to violate all conventional morality, with no emotion displayed other than lust and its satisfaction. The Kronhausens contrast that with erotic realism, which may also depict sexual activity explicitly, but in the context of a full range of human feelings and concerns.

29   How do those on opposite sides of the porn fence define the subject of their disagreement? The various definitions put forward in the WAP literature and its public statements have a clear central theme but tend to be fuzzy around the edges. Most definitions are some variant of Brownmiller's statement in a newspaper essay that "pornography's intent is to degrade and dehumanize the female body for the purpose of erotic stimulation and pleasure. We are unalterably

opposed to the presentation of the female body being stripped, bound, raped, tortured, mutilated and murdered in the name of entertainment and free speech." This definition is usually presented with the qualification Brownmiller offers in her essay, that "we believe that explicit sexual material has its place in literature, art, science and education."

So much for generalities. But once we get into specifics, 30 that old devil subjectivity intrudes. One might suppose that a large portion of the sexy writings and pictures available today would be acceptable to WAP and its sister organizations, but, in fact, they find hatred of women everywhere. Among examples of pornographic materials displayed in the slide show that introduces its tour of the Times Square area, WAP shows the posters for the movies *Dracula* and *The Wanderers*, a department-store ad showing two smiling little girls modeling sweaters and skirts, a record-album cover featuring a nude girl barely into pubescence and an advertisement for Gloria Vanderbilt jeans.

In an antipornography pamphlet, Womongold, the rifle- 31 person of Harvard Square, includes in a list of horrible examples of pornography "a Bloomingdale's full-page ad in *The New York Times* of July 10, 1978, showing a nude woman, flat on her back, face obscured by a sun hat, with her empty swimsuit lying in the foreground." In her newspaper article, Brownmiller describes as pornographic "still shots using the newest tenets of good design" on the covers of *Playboy, Penthouse* and *Hustler*. Brownmiller also finds the daily newspapers full of pornography: "To buy a paper at the newsstand," she says, "is to subject oneself to a forcible immersion in pornography, to be demeaned by an array of dehumanized, chopped-up parts of the female anatomy, packaged like cuts of meat at the supermarket."

Throughout the movement's literature, the ritualistic 32 hostile references to *Playboy* and other magazines crop up frequently. *Playboy*, of course, refuses to be defined by its detractors. "Nobody can agree on what pornography is, though nearly all definitions have a negative connotation," says *Playboy*'s Associate Publisher, Nat Lehrman. "*Playboy*'s popularity is not based on pornography, hard- or soft-core. All the sexual images we originate are positive. They have no implication of aggressiveness, hostility or exploitation. Eros was the god of love. And our erotic images are exactly what that word implies — loving images. Anyone who sees anything else in a *Playboy* picture of a beautiful and unadorned woman should remember the motto '*Honi soit qui mal y pense*' — 'Evil is as evil thinks.' "

33   Clearly, there can be no such thing as a definition of pornography that satisfies everyone. Perhaps Ellen Willis sums it up best: "What turns me on is erotic; what turns you on is pornographic."

·   ·   ·

34   Our courts still have not found a satisfactory way to draw a line between obscenity and legitimate portrayals of sexual activity. Drawing the line is even more impossible when it comes to aggression. Violence has been an essential element in our literature and art from the *Iliad* and the Bible to *The Deer Hunter* and *Apocalypse Now*.

35   WAP cannot accept the notion of obscenity and also say, "We do not advocate censorship." Obscenity is the key concept that makes censorship possible in this country in spite of the First Amendment. In *Roth*, the Supreme Court stated that "implicit in the history of the First Amendment is the rejection of obscenity as utterly without redeeming social importance . . . . We hold that obscenity is not within the area of constitutionally protected speech or press." Unable to find that sexually explicit material is measurably dangerous, but unwilling to declare that it could circulate freely, the Court came up with a new justification for banning it; it lacks "redeeming social importance." The implications of that principle, as it might be applied to almost any kind of speech, from advertising and TV shows to unorthodox religious, political or scientific opinions, could be disastrous for freedom of expression.

36   As if that were not enough, Brownmiller has gone the Supreme Court one better and come up with yet another justification for depriving people of their First Amendment rights. "In San Francisco, a Jewish community went in and tore down a Nazi bookstore," she writes in WAVPM's newsletter. "It was just not allowed to exist because its message was so hateful. Women must do the same for the pornography establishment." We now have a new principle to set up beside Oliver Wendell Holmes's dictum that free speech does not include the right to shout "Fire!" in a crowded theater: "It was just not allowed to exist because its message was so hateful."

37   No doubt, Brownmiller would hasten to explain that the privilege of destroying bookstores extends only to good guys and may be exercised only against bad guys. The trouble

is, all of us are good guys, and all whose views we find
intolerable are bad guys. The Right to Lifers who were
arrested in Chicago for blocking the doors of an abortion
clinic might plead the Brownmiller principle in their defense: The thought of all those babies being murdered in
there was just too hateful.

The comparison between pornography and Nazi pro-   38
paganda is one that springs easily to Brownmiller's pen.
In *Against Our Will*, she writes:

> To defend the right of a lone, crazed American Nazi to grind
> out propaganda calling for the extermination of all Jews, as
> the A.C.L.U. has done in the name of free speech, is, after
> all, a self-righteous and not particularly courageous stand,
> for American Jewry is not currently threatened by storm
> troopers, concentration camps and imminent extermina-
> tion, but I wonder if the A.C.L.U.'s position might change
> if, come tomorrow morning, the bookstores and movie the-
> aters lining 42nd Street in New York City were devoted not
> to the humiliation of women by rape and torture, as they
> currently are, but to a systematized, commercially success-
> ful propaganda machine depicting the sadistic pleasures of
> gassing Jews or lynching blacks?

The statement that the pornography outlets of Times   39
Square and places like it are "devoted . . . to the humiliation
of women by rape and torture" is a gross exaggeration. The
women's antiporn literature would have us believe that in
the past few years, pornography has come to consist almost
entirely of depictions of torture, mutilation and murder,
that garden-variety sex is now quite passé. "Where We
Stand on the First Amendment" claims, "Most hard-core
pornography consists of pictures or graphic descriptions of
women being raped, bound, beaten or mutilated." But, if
WAP's own tour is any indication, what is actually being
purveyed in the bookstores and peep-show parlors of Times
Square is a good deal tamer than that.

For instance, on one such tour, conducted last October   40
for 16 men and women (most WAP tours are for women
only, but one each month admits men as well), the group
was shown little other than pictures of straight sex acts
between men and women, as well as various well-known,
nonviolent deviations. There was one sickening photograph
of a woman being tortured, but that was in WAP's pretour
slide show, not on the street itself. In one bookstore, the

worst that could be seen was a small section devoted to bondage magazines. WAP believes that normal men can be turned on by the pictures in those magazines and develop the desire to tie real women up, but to a man who is not into bondage, those photos of women trussed up like mummies look extremely odd and not at all inviting. The tour visited two peepshow emporiums called Peep Land and Show World, where there were dozens of booths for private viewing of the short, silent pornographic films called loops (because they run continuously as long as you keep feeding quarters), as well as other booths from which patrons could watch live, nude female dancers. For an extra five dollars, Show World customers could see a live sex act being performed.

41   Of the several hundred films offered for viewing in both places, only a dozen, at the most generous estimate, had titles suggesting that they dealt with violent themes. One of those, called *Hang Her High*, showed a woman being tortured with an elaborate arrangement of ropes and a belt buckled around her neck. It was every bit as ugly, frightening and offensive as the antipornography literature describes, but it wasn't at all representative of what was being shown on 42nd Street. The tour leader claimed that films such as *Hang Her High* are increasing in number (and, in fairness, it should be mentioned also that *Snuff* was playing on 42nd Street that night), but such films are still only a tiny minority.They are far outnumbered, for example, by those depicting anal intercourse. Presumably, the WAP tour shows the worst Times Square has to offer. If so, the picture WAP paints of the current pornographic scene as saturated by images of rape, torture and mutilation is, to put it kindly, hyperbole.

42   Those impressions gathered during one night are substantiated by the observations of long-term pornography watchers. Joseph Slade, who monitors the industry's annual output for the Kinsey Institute for Sex Research, estimates that about eight percent of the feature-length films currently being shown are of the aggressive or violent variety. For the short films displayed in peep shows and sold by mail, the figure rises to about 12 percent. That represents an increase since those innocent days when the Commission on Obscenity and Pornography issued its report. But it is nothing like the take-over usually described in feminist antiporn propaganda.

43   Still, the violent stuff does exist, and, more to the point, Brownmiller and some of her sisters find even ordinary

erotica offensive. That is the way they perceive it, and there's really no point in arguing that issue, any more than one would argue over the "real" meaning of a Rorschach ink blot. But if, as they claim, pornography is "fascistic, misogynist propaganda," then, as propaganda—the communication of ideas, good or bad—it is entitled to First Amendment protection. "All ideas having even the slightest redeeming social importance—unorthodox ideas, controversial ideas, even ideas hateful to the prevailing climate of opinion—have the full protection of the guaranties, unless excludable because they encroach upon the limited area of more important interests," declared the Supreme Court in that crucial *Roth* decision. The enemies of pornography cannot have it both ways.

· · ·

Modern woman's struggle for autonomy goes back to the   44
days when Margaret Sanger was going to jail under the Comstock Act for sending birth-control information through the mail—the same Comstock Act that led to the law under which participants in the movie *Deep Throat* were prosecuted in 1976. Over the past 100 years, a steady liberalizing process has rescued more and more kinds of communication from the power of the censor. This gradual elimination of censorship has opened the door to the pornographer. It has *also* made possible the flow of information and public honesty about sex that revolutionized sexual attitudes in this country and was a necessary background for the women's movement.

Pornography and feminism linked? Some feminists would   45
find that suggestion singularly hateful. True, much of our pornography . . . sexually explicit material . . . erotica . . . is tasteless and hostile to women. It reflects the values of a civilization that for thousands of years has treated sexuality as shameful and women as inferior. At one time, pornography was despised by its own makers and consumers, who often despised themselves as well. But the values of our civilization are evolving; just in the past ten years, erotica has undergone the most dramatic change of circumstances since Vesuvius buried the bawdy walls of Pompeii. To an extent unprecedented in history, the organs and acts of sex are being displayed in openly available works of art and entertainment. As a result, the aesthetic quality of our erotica has improved a hundredfold, and, in turn, erotic realism has permeated and enriched all our arts.

46   But are we paying too high a price for this cultural growth? The women fighting pornography say that the cost of freedom of sexual expression is to be reckoned in another kind of growth, that of the annual numbers of women abused, crippled, killed. How can a man's right to see a dirty movie outweigh a woman's right to health, safety and bodily integrity? But that is a false dichotomy. If, tomorrow, we were to shut down all the porno bookstores and peep-show parlors in all the Times Squares across the country, it would have no effect on the rape rate. If, as seems probable, the rapist is the product of a sexually ignorant, repressed environment, a return to severe censorship might actually make matters worse. In the end, what evidence is there that pornography motivates sex crime? The studies of sexual arousal and aggression show only that those two emotional states can be briefly linked in an artificial situation. The incessant pecking of the critics of the Commission on Obscenity and Pornography has left intact a mountain of evidence for the essential harmlessness of pornography that is impossible to ignore. The word from Denmark is still loud and clear: Total legalization of pornography has done some good and no harm whatever. That evidence takes on more significance when we realize that most of today's porn is still of the garden variety, claims of a new violence-oriented pornography that is sweeping the field being alarmist and much exaggerated. The notion that pornography causes sex crime is magical thinking, on a par with the medieval belief that witches caused plagues.

47   Fighting pornography may give people the feeling that they are doing something about the frightful problem of sexual crime, just as reinstating capital punishment gives them the feeling that they are doing something about murder. In both instances, the sense of accomplishment is illusory. Human beings through history have expended incalculable quantities of energy, wealth and blood trying to impose false solutions on real problems. Myths about magical causes of disease long retarded the development of modern medicine, costing many lives. Only when we put superstition behind us is there any hope of doing something constructive about society's woes. It is not pornography that needs eliminating but, rather, that perennial and terrible and human impulse, in time of trouble, to single out and persecute a scapegoat.

CENSORSHIP II: THE CASE OF *HUCKLEBERRY FINN*

Margot Allen

Huck Finn: Two Generations of Pain

Margot Allen lived in State College, Pennsylvania, when the following account of her family's experience with Huckleberry Finn *appeared in the* Interracial Books for Children Bulletin *in 1984. She now resides in Gladstone, Oregon.*

My adventure with *Huckleberry Finn* has been a stinging 1 and bitter one, one which has left a dull pain that spans two generations, mine and my son's.

Today, during the book's centenary, while Mark Twain 2 specialists and scholars laud this book as one of the "most profound, most transcendent literary images the human imagination has ever come up with,"* it is easy for me to recall a time nearly 30 years ago, a time that seemed like an eternity of teeth-clenching and inner contortions that threatened to betray my extreme discomfort when reading this book in the ninth grade. Had I shared my tension and stress with my teacher or classmates, I would have literally frightened them, and my Blackness would have stood out even more than it did as I read the book along with everyone else and kept my feelings in check.

But such negative experiences with *Huck Finn* are not a 3 thing of the past. Just three years ago, when my son was thirteen, he too was victimized by those same negative images. I am sharing our story with you now in the hopes that teachers, school administrators and parents will be more sensitive to the negative racial elements of this book and will begin to question, research and speak out regarding how and when this book can best be taught.

---

*The comment of novelist John Barth at the Conference on American Comedy: A Celebration of 100 Years of *Huckleberry Finn*, held at Pennsylvania State University, April 26–28.

4   My story begins with two different classroom experiences
some 30 years apart. In both accounts I focus on feelings
and reactions because I believe these represent the very
foundation upon which most complaints about the book
rest. They are personal but real, and to ignore these feelings,
to intellectualize them or to misconstrue them as an excuse
to charge censorship, would be to continue with a status
quo that oppresses people of color. We need to come to
grips with *Huck Finn*'s powerful imagery and the *feelings*
evoked by those images.

An Introduction to *Huck*

5   I was first introduced to *Huck Finn* in 1957. I was thirteen
and in the ninth grade of a large middle-class, suburban,
predominantly white high school in Portland, Oregon. I
was the only Black student in the class. When *Huck Finn*
was assigned, there was no advance preparation; we simply
started to read the book, a classic whose name held a familiar—and friendly—ring for most students. As we began to
get into the story, however, the dialect alone made me feel
uneasy. And as we continued, I began to be apprehensive,
to fear being singled out, being put on the spot, being
ridiculed or made fun of because of my color, and only
because of my color! It was the exact same feeling I'd had
as a child when a supposedly "fun game" turned into a
hurting one. The feelings that I had as a ninth grader reading *Huck Finn* very much resembled those that I had as a
child playing "eenie, meenie, minie, moe: catch a ___ by
the toe." While it never occurred to me to refuse to play
such games, I would pray like the dickens that no one
would use that awful word—the very word my parents
had taught me was used only by people who were ignorant
or of low moral character. And there it was, in print, that
word, staring me in the face over and over again throughout the entire book.

6   I need not tell you that I hated the book! Yet, while we
read it, I pretended that it didn't bother me. I hid, from
my teacher and my classmates, the tension, discomfort and
hurt I would feel every time I heard that word or watched
the class laugh at Jim and felt some white youngster's stare
being directed my way, as if to say, "Hey, it's you and your

kind we're talking about in this book." I think the hardest part was keeping my composure while being stared at. Somehow I thought that a blank face would protect me from not only this book's offensiveness and open insults, but the silent indicting, accusing and sometimes apologetic stares of my classmates. After all, the very last thing I wanted anyone to think was that I was ashamed of being Black, even though I could not identify with Jim or other Blacks in the novel.

I suffered silently through the reading of *Huck Finn*; at times, I pretended to fake a certain easiness with the book that I thought my classmates had. I learned very little from this experience about literature, the antebellum South or slavery. I learned precious little, if anything, about the novel as a form and the elements of irony and satire.

7

I was so glad to move on to something else that I completely suppressed the experience (a not uncommon experience for Black people)—until my son ran into *Huck Finn* in his English class three years ago. My son, the only Black youngster in his class, was asked by his teacher to read the part of Jim aloud. When a curious white youngster immediately asked why he was selected, the teacher replied, "He has the perfect voice for it." At that, the class laughed. My son was humiliated, though he, too, tried to hide his feelings, just as I had so many years before. After class a number of his friends came up to him and made comments like, "Gee, I'm sorry, the teacher's a real jerk." Others were not so supportive. One child said, "That must tell you what the teacher thinks of you," and there were those who took the opportunity to snicker "nigger" under their breath to him.

8

Greatly distressed by my son's experience, I called the Vice-Principal who, in turn, had the teacher call me later that same morning. In our discussion, I asked why she chose my son to read Jim's part and told her emphatically that I did not want him to read that part. The teacher reported that in years past, whenever she had Black students in her class, she'd asked them to read Jim's part and without exception, they had been "proud" to do so. (She also said that she felt that since slavery was a part of the Black heritage, my son should be proud to authenticate that history by reading Jim's part aloud . . . and after all, since he is Black, he could read the part better than the white students.)

9

Use of *Huck Finn* Questioned

10   Incensed by this teacher's lack of sensitivity and understanding, I wrote to the [school] asking that *Huck Finn* be
immediately discontinued as required reading. I felt that
any book that leads a teacher to openly discriminate and
to offend a student should be seriously questioned for its
appropriateness as a tool of instruction. I also questioned
the real educational value of *Huck Finn* as it was currently
taught.

11   The Principal responded immediately to my letter by
pulling my son out of English class and sending him to the
library where he was instructed to work on something else.
When the Principal called to tell me of his actions, I did
not immediately object to his taking my son out of class
because I was more concerned as to what the school's response was going to be to my request to have the book
discontinued as required reading. Our phone conversation
was very brief, however, and the Principal said very little
beyond informing me that the forms needed to challenge
class materials were being mailed to me.

12   In retrospect, the school's first action was awkward at
best, perhaps symptomatic of the staff's inexperience in
dealing with matters relating to race. Had officials been
more willing to discuss the "incident," it certainly would
have gone a long way towards reducing the racial tension
and suspicion on both sides which, in turn, may have had
an ameliorative effect on the final resolution of this matter.
Since this was not the case, I had no alternative but to
proceed to formally challenge the book's use. In effect, the
battlelines were drawn before there was ample opportunity
to discuss the nature of the conflict or even establish a
climate for discussion.

13   Fortunately, Christmas vacation intervened, providing
time to step back from the situation, to reflect and to do
some research in this area. I had, however, no further contact with the Principal, the teacher or any of the school
district officials until March of 1982, when the paperwork
detailing objections to the book was formally submitted to
the district. (The "Citizen's Request for Reconsideration of
a Book" was a one-page questionnaire asking for specific
examples from the book for each stated objection. I gave
seven objections and the completed form was some five

pages long. I am grateful that I had the expert assistance of Dr. Jane Madsen, a professor of education at Penn State, whose specialty is identifying racism and sexism in children's literature.)

In April, my husband and I participated in two rather   14 heated meetings involving the Supervisor of Secondary Education and the District English Coordinator. During these discussions, while apologies were offered for the teacher's blunder (the words "stupidity" and "insensitivity" were used) and for the embarrassment and pain it caused our son, neither the Supervisor nor the English Coordinator could understand that the teacher's remarks were, in and of themselves, racist and discriminatory in nature.

In fact, the English Coordinator, who spent a good deal   15 of time explaining the desired educational objectives involved in teaching the book, preferred that we avoid any discussion regarding the teacher's competence. We were asked to focus our concerns *solely* on the book. That focus led to an agreement between the School District and ourselves to put our "Request for Reconsideration" on hold while a Study Group was formed to identify the positive and negative effects of reading *Huck Finn* at the ninth-grade level. I consented to be part of the Study Group because the Supervisor of Secondary Education seemed to be very empathetic about our concerns, and both my husband and I had every hope that the issue would be resolved to our satisfaction. (The English Coordinator, however, continued to defend the book's literary and educational value.)

In the initial meetings of this Study Group, I was adamant   16 in expressing my feeling that any book that permits an otherwise competent teacher to openly discriminate in class should not be required reading. My inclination was still to find fault with the book rather than the teacher; this may have been a strategic and critical error on my part.

During the next 18 months, the Study Group met some 16   17 times. Eventually — after much struggle — two recommendations were made. They were, very briefly:

1. To use a book other than *Huck Finn* as required reading for ninth-grade classes but make it available for use in courses for grades eleven and twelve; and

2. To undertake a comprehensive study of the schools' sensitivity to and treatment of minority groups in the cur-

ricula for grades K–12. (A Task Force on Understanding Others was set up to meet this recommendation.)

Racism Not Addressed

18   Reasonable as these recommendations sound, they unfortunately failed to address the real underlying issue of institutional racism. This often happens when educators over-intellectualize problems rooted in racial prejudice. Whites, in particular, find it very hard to identify, accept and understand their own racism and the way in which institutions, including the educational system, contribute to and perpetuate this racism.

19   At any rate, pressure from the School District to bring closure to this whole matter resulted in conclusions being drawn from the study that were not totally sound and which warranted further statistical analysis. Even worse, the study seemed to suggest (in the face of evidence to the contrary) that reading *Huck Finn* did not encourage stereotypic thinking in ninth graders. This study, which, to my dismay, bears my name as a group member, has been distributed in a number of arenas, the most significant being the 1983 National Council of Teachers of English Convention.

20   Significantly, the printed study's recommendation that the book be held for the last two grades of high school was ignored. The School Board stated that it was not the Board's prerogative to decide the grade placement of the book, and that decision was referred to an English Advisory Committee made up of the English Coordinator and classroom teachers. At a School Board meeting in October, 1983, the final decision was to retain *Huck Finn* in the ninth grade.

21   The District did give the assurance that, prior to teaching the novel this year, in order to allow parents and youngsters to decide whether they wanted to read the book or not, letters would be sent to all parents informing them that the book had recently come under scrutiny because of the controversy surrounding its negative racial stereotyping of Blacks and its abundant use of racial slurs. The School District never sent such a letter; it later decided to offer *Huck Finn* as one of three titles ninth graders could select for English class. (The other two books were also about adolescence: *Great Expectations* and *A Separate Peace*.)

Complaints Filed

After the School Board condoned the continued use of *Huck*   22
Finn, and with the support and urging of Ida Belle Minnie,
Education Chairperson of the State NAACP standing committee, I filed formal complaints with the Pennsylvania
Human Relations Commission and the Pennsylvania NAACP.
It was clear that my original concerns about the impact of
this book on youngsters (both Black and white) had been
lost between the cracks of committee bureaucracy and
School Board politics. I asked that an investigation be held
to ascertain what corrective action had taken place to ensure
the appropriateness of teaching methodologies used with
this book, and the competence and sensitivity of teachers
to carry out those methodologies without racial overtones.

I filed my complaint with both organizations in Novem-   23
ber 1983. Although my son's experience had occurred more
than two years earlier, I felt a compelling need to continue
the challenge. Accordingly, I sent copies of my complaint
to several legislators and state agencies. I got a supportive
response from K. Leroy Irvis, Pennsylvania House Minority
Leader, and from the Office of the Secretary of Education.
In addition, the NAACP delegated Virginius Thornton, a
Black historian, to speak against the continued use of *Huck
Finn* at a School Board meeting, but I heard from no one
locally — not the School Board President, not a single School
Board member, and certainly not the Superintendent of
Schools.

In January 1984, I received a notice from the Pennsyl-   24
vania Human Relations Commission, indicating that my
complaint had been assigned a docket number. This was
encouraging, but everything seemed to be moving at a
snail's pace. I felt very much alone and the occasional support from a parent here and a couple of parents there, an
English professor here and a psychology professor there, were
not enough to brighten what seemed to be a bleak horizon.

Two Supportive Events

Two separate but related events occurred in March of   25
this year to change this entire picture for me. The first of

these was reading the article, "*Huckleberry Finn* and the Traditions of Blackface Minstrelsy" in the CIBC *Bulletin* (Vol.15, Nos.1&2). This comprehensive piece, which brought some new historical and scholarly insights to understanding the negative characterization of Jim, underpinned academically many of the concerns that had been expressed nationwide about the book at a more emotional level.

26   The second thing that happened was that I was asked to participate in a panel on the teaching of *Huck Finn* in the public schools, at the Conference on American Comedy: A Celebration of 100 Years of *Huckleberry Finn*, hosted by Penn State in April (see Vol. 15, No. 4). The panel presentation resulted in a very extensive and positive dialogue. And, while there was by no means a consensus, there was substantive agreement that indeed there are problems in teaching the novel; that it should be held for use in college or, at the earliest, in the upper grades of high school; and that new teaching strategies *must* be developed to properly teach the novel.

27   I came out of this conference buoyed and more committed than ever to the belief that no youngsters should be required to read literature which demeans, dehumanizes and caricatures their racial or ethnic heritage. Several years ago, *The Merchant of Venice* was dropped from a required reading list for this very reason. Why is *Huck Finn* immune from similar scrutiny?

28   Currently, the Pennsylvania NAACP Education Committee is fully supportive of my complaint, but the bureaucratic wheels of the Human Relations Commission are moving at a much slower pace. With or without their support, I intend to continue to fight this issue. The District hired a new superintendent in July, and I have already written him about my concerns. Dr. Fredrick Woodard, co-author of the *Bulletin's* article on *Huck Finn*, is conducting new research on the negative racial elements of the book and I do not see how it can be ignored. In addition, Roy L. Austin, a professor of sociology at Penn State, James Stewart, a professor of economics as well as President of the Penn State Forum on Black Affairs (an organization of Black faculty, staff and graduate students), and the aforementioned Jane Madsen recently reviewed the study on "The Effects of Reading *Huckleberry Finn* on the Racial Attitudes of Ninth Grade Students." Their conclusions were such that the Forum's membership voted to issue a public statement

affirming that the Study's findings had been published prematurely and were misleading and biased. The statement appeared in the local newspapers and has led to some constructive dialogue between the Black community and the School District. In addition, I understand that the School District's Task Force on Understanding Others, which until this summer had been very inactive, is now meeting again.

Bringing new insights, visions and perspectives to the 29 teaching of *Huck Finn* is no easy matter. The book is cherished; its worth is passed down from professor to graduate student, from teacher to teacher, from teacher to student. But whatever the book's merits, there is a cost to pay in reading it, and unfortunately that cost is borne in large part by young Black students who may experience a complex range and mix of feelings from indifference to anger, from insult to humiliation. (There is also a cost to white students, whose out-dated notions of white superiority are reinforced.) No one has yet proven that the price we pay is reflected in positive educational gains for any student.

John H. Wallace
Huckleberry Finn Is Offensive

John H. Wallace had been a high school administrator at the Mark Twain School in northern Virginia for over twenty years when he wrote this guest column for the Washington Post *in 1982.*

Ever since it was written, Mark Twain's "The Adventures 1 of Huckleberry Finn" has provoked great controversy, and it runs on unabated even now in Fairfax County. After reading the book at least six times, I think it's perfectly all right for college class use, especially at the graduate level, where students can gain insight into the use and writing of satire and an uncensored flavor of the times. The caustic and abusive language is less likely to offend students of that age level because they tend to be mature enough to understand the ridicule.

2   "Huckleberry Finn" uses the pejorative term "nigger" pro-
fusely. It speaks of black Americans with implications that
they are not honest, they are not as intelligent as whites
and they are not human. All of this, of course, is meant to
be satirical. It is. But at the same time, it ridicules blacks.
This kind of ridicule is extremely difficult for black youngsters to handle. I maintain that it constitutes mental
cruelty, harassment and outright racial intimidation to
force black students to sit in a classroom to read this kind
of literature about themselves.

3   I read "Huck Finn" when I was in high school and I can
remember feeling betrayed by the teacher. I felt humiliated
and embarrassed. Ten years ago, my oldest son went
through the same experience in high school, until I went
to talk to the teachers about it and he lost all interest in
English classes. Before reading this book, this bright,
energetic youngster was inquisitive and liked school; but
afterward—after he had been asked to participate in the
reading with an all-white class—I could see a definite negative change in his attitude toward teachers and school. (I'm
happy to say he has recovered now.)

4   For years, black families have trekked to schools in just
about every district in America to say that "this book is
bad for our children," only to be turned away by insensitive
and often unwittingly racist teachers and administrators
responding that "this is a classic." Classic or not, it should
not be allowed to continue to make our children feel bad
about themselves.

5   I am convinced that the assignment and reading aloud
of "Huck Finn" in our classrooms causes black children to
have a low esteem of themselves and of their race. It also
causes white students to have little or no respect for blacks.
The resulting attitudes can lead to tension, discontent and
fights. If the book is removed from the curriculums of our
schools, there will be much better student-to-student, stu-
dent-to-teacher and teacher-to-teacher relationships; and
black students will definitely enjoy school a little bit more.

6   Every black child is the victim of the history of his race
in this country. As John Fisher, former president of Columbia Teachers College, has noted, "On the day he enters kindergarten, he carries a burden no white child can ever know,
no matter what handicaps or disabilities he may suffer."
Add to this the reading of a book like "Huckleberry Finn,"
and the experience can be devastatingly traumatic.

Many of my friends have cited First Amendment rights.   7
But I am convinced that the continued use of pejorative
materials about one particular racial group is a violation
of the equal protection clause of the 14th Amendment. It
also may violate the right to liberty as applied to reputation,
in that the book maligns all black people.

I have no problem with "Huckleberry Finn" being on the   8
library shelf, for any youngster or his parents to check out
and read to their hearts' content, in school or at home. But
as a professional educator with 28 years of teaching at all
levels, I cannot see the slightest need to use disparaging
language to identify any racial, ethnic or religious group.
If the lesson cannot be taught in positive terms, maybe it
should not be taught.

We must be sensitive, creative teachers, encouraged to   9
understand the special factors in the backgrounds of all the
children — with curriculums that reflect these varied needs.
And no sensitive, loving teacher would use "Huckleberry
Finn" in class.

Robert Nadeau

Huckleberry Finn Is a Moral Story

Robert Nadeau, professor of English at George Mason University, wrote this essay in 1982. It appeared on the same page of the Washington Post *as the previous essay by John H. Wallace.*

When the principal of Mark Twain Intermediate School   1
in Fairfax County followed the advice of the school's racially
mixed human relations committee and recommended that
"The Adventures of Huckleberry Finn" be removed from
the school's curriculum, he was not acting without prece-
dent. Misguided guardians of the moral integrity of school-
children have often attempted, particularly in Twain's own
lifetime, to prevent young minds from being exposed to the
profoundly moral views of the 13-year-old, pipe-smoking,
marvelously imaginative liar whose love for the runaway
slave, Jim, grows to such proportions that he would risk
eternal damnation to protect him.

2   A letter written by Twain to a Brooklyn librarian who
was seeking to ban both "Tom Sawyer" and "Huckleberry
Finn" from the children's room of the library has not, I
suspect, been read by most faculty members teaching at a
school named in honor of one of our greatest American
artists. Let me share a portion of it with them: "I wrote
'Tom Sawyer' and 'Huck Finn' for adults exclusively, and
it always distresses me when I find that boys and girls have
been allowed access to them. The mind that becomes soiled
in youth can never again be washed clear. I know this by
my own experience, and to this day I cherish an unappeas-
able bitterness against the unfaithful guardians of my
young life, who not only permitted but compelled me to
read an unexpurgated Bible before I was 15 years old. . . .
More honestly do I wish that I could say a softening word
or two in defense of Huck's character since you wish it, but
really, in my opinion, it is no better than those of Solomon,
David, and the rest of the sacred brotherhood."

3   That Twain firmly believed that the behavior and character of his first person narrator was designed to be morally
instructive to young people is obvious. Countless individuals in this culture, including myself, know from the experience of reading the book at an early age that he was absolutely correct.

4   Apparently the faculty members as well as the parents
and the administrators who concurred with the recommendation to bar teachers from assigning the novel—or even
reading it aloud in class—feel otherwise. They object, we
are told, to "the flagrant use of the word 'nigger' and the
demeaning way in which black people are portrayed in the
book." "Nigger" is, of course, a terribly offensive word in
our own time and should definitely not be used by anyone
who respects the rights and integrities of others. But it
might help to explain to those students who might continue
to study the book at the intermediate school that in slave
states the word was merely the ordinary colloquial term
for a slave, and not necessarily abusive.

5   More important, however, as the historical record also
shows, Twain was a violent opponent of the institution of
slavery, and "Huckleberry Finn" can and should be read as
one of the most forceful indictments ever made against the
subjugation of any class of human beings by another.

6   Anyone, including adolescents, who has carefully read
the book should have little difficulty recognizing the many

instances in which this theme is abundantly obvious. Since there is not sufficient space here to detail all of them, I will only touch briefly on that climactic moment when Huck, in defiance of what he has been taught to be the will of God in his own morally bankrupt society, elects to imperil his mortal soul.

Subjected, as many children in this country continue to 7 be, to a religious education in which the interpreters of spiritual verities seek to sanction the view of black people as innately inferior, Huck reflects late in the narrative upon his many efforts to help Jim to escape and concludes: "And at last, when it hit me all of a sudden that here was the plain hand of Providence slapping me in the face and letting me know my wickedness was being watched all the time from up there in Heaven, whilst I was stealing a poor old woman's nigger that hadn't ever done me no harm, and now was showing me there's One that's always on the look-out, and ain't agoing to allow such miserable doing to go only just so fur and no further, I almost dropped in my tracks I was so scared." Feeling oppressed with guilt, realizing that "people that acts as I'd been acting about that nigger goes to everlasting fire," Huck writes a letter to Mrs. Watson indicating where Jim can be found. But then immediately thereafter he recalls — in a passage that is one of the best illustrations in literature of the power of agape love — the many acts of kindness displayed by Jim toward himself, looks once again at the letter, and says to himself, "'All right, then, I'll go to hell' — and tore it up."

The message here, which is pervasive in this marvelous 8 novel, is that truly moral acts are, often enough, undertaken in defiance of a so-called moral majority. And it is that which this particular member of the sacred brotherhood has chosen to do. If studying "Huckleberry Finn" is in any way to hurt students at Mark Twain Intermediate School, it can only be because those who teach the book have failed to understand it.

But there is, of course, a larger issue here. When we pre- 9 vent our children from being exposed in the classroom to the best that has been known and said in our literary tradition, we not only narrow the range of their educational experience, but we also — unintentionally to be sure — help them to grow into individuals, like the members of the Shepherdson and Grangerford families in the novel, who might commit senseless acts of destruction out of a lack of understanding of the complexities of moral life. If "Huckleberry Finn" is, as an administrative aide at the school put it, "poison," then I suspect my own 11-year-old daughter must have a remarkably immune system. She even appears to thrive on it.

Nat Hentoff

Huck Finn Better Get Out of Town by Sundown

As a novelist, Nat Hentoff (born in 1925) has written several books for teenagers, including one— The Day They Came to Arrest the Book *(1982)—that dramatizes a parent's demand that* Huckleberry Finn *be withdrawn from a high school. As a social critic and civil libertarian and defender of the First Amendment, he has written numerous books and articles for prestigious magazines. He is a regular contributor to* The Village Voice, *the influential New York weekly that published his analysis of the controversy over* Huckleberry Finn *in May, 1982.*

> We have not abrogated anybody's First Amendment rights. We've just said we don't want any kid to be forced to read this racist trash. . . . The book is poison. . . . It is anti-American. . . . It works against the idea that all men are created equal. . . . Anybody who teaches this book is racist.
> — *John H. Wallace, administrative aide, Mark Twain Intermediate School, Fairfax County, Virginia*

> The last damn thing blacks should do is get into the vanguard of banning books. The next step is banning blacks.
> —*Dr. Kenneth B. Clark*

> The rush for racism-free literature is not a call for censorship, but rather a push for

responsibility on the part of educators, librarians and authors.
                    — *Dorothy Gilliam, columnist,*
                    Washington Post, *April 12*

The proof that *Huckleberry Finn* has to be
taught in our schools is that some people
can read great books and not know what
the hell they're about.
                    — *Stephen Altman, on the letters page,*
                    Washington Post, *April 12*

I

The recent attempt by black administrator John Wallace   1
to roust the perennially troublesome *Huckleberry Finn* from
his school's curriculum made the network newscasts, wire
services, and most papers around the country. A teacher in
Houston told me that when it came over the radio, she had
to stop her car, she was so agitated. On the other hand, a
group of black parents in Houston who are also trying to
get this white trash out of *their* schools were pleased to
hear they had an ally up there in Fairfax, Virginia.

My guess is that this wouldn't have been such a widely   2
played story if the name of the school where Mr. Wallace
works were not the Mark Twain Intermediate School. Mr.
Clemens would have whooped long and loud over that one.
Maybe even longer and louder over the name of the racially
integrated six-member faculty committee that *unanimously*
voted to protect the kids from his book. It's called the
Human Relations Committee of the Mark Twain Intermediate School.

Dr. Kenneth Clark of *Brown* v. *Board of Education* and   3
Dark Ghetto told me the other day that he first came upon
Huck Finn in the public library at 135th Street and Lenox
Avenue when he was about 12 years old. No one was around
at the time to protect Kenneth from certain books, and he
got all caught up in *Huckleberry Finn.*

"I loved the book," Dr. Clark says. "I just loved it. Espe-   4
cially the relationship between Huck and Jim. It was such
an easy, *understanding* relationship. The kind a boy wishes
he could have."

Then, as now, the book was full of the word "nigger."   5
Why, John Martin, the principal of the Mark Twain Intermediate School in Fairfax County—who agreed with the

Human Relations Committee that *Huckleberry Finn* is racist — told National Public Radio that the word is repeated
some 160 times in the book. How come Kenneth Clark, when
he was just 12 years old, didn't recoil from this "racist" book?

6   Because he read it, he really read it. Without some adult
censoring what he read beforehand to make sure it did him
no harm. Someone like John Wallace, who told me a couple
of weeks ago: "It's books like *Huckleberry Finn* that are
screwing up black children — books that make black children feel bad about themselves. How can a black child,
reading that racist trash, be proud of being black?"

7   Maybe Kenneth Clark didn't get the message. Or maybe
it's John Wallace, who has read *Huckleberry Finn* eight
times in the last five months, as he tells me, who can't see
past that word. Just as the whites in pre-Civil War Missouri
whom Twain was writing about couldn't see past that word.
They had no idea who "Miss Watson's big nigger, named
Jim" was. Though Huck came to know Jim, underneath
that word. And being able to do that changed his whole life.

8   We are about to begin what has become an annual journey
into the minds of those who would censor for the most
fervent of motives — the shielding of young minds from
books that debase them. Although the focus this trip is on
Huckleberry Finn — in Virginia; in the Spring Independent
School District of Houston; in Davenport, Iowa; in Warrington, Pennsylvania — we shall also stop in Midland,
Michigan, to look into a long, bitter conflict over how *The
Merchant of Venice* should be taught in school — if at all.
And farther on down the line, we shall visit a Sunday service
in Baltimore's First Unitarian Church where "sexist" pas-
sages by "patriarchal" theologians (from St. Augustine to
Karl Barth) are burned in front of the altar.

9   And to show that no enclave in our society is immune
from those who would uplift our souls and purge our minds,
we shall hear from the managing editor of a daily newspaper in New Hampshire who has been striving mightily
to cleanse the comic strips of sexism — much to the ungrateful fury of most of his readers, who are clamoring that they
do not wish to be delivered from this sin.

10   To begin with Huck: my interest in the ceaseless assault
on this well-known drifter has to do with my own ceaseless
delight in the book. I keep going back to it, as I do to certain
jazz recordings, when I feel tempted to agree with Mr.
Twain's gloomy assessment, in his last years, of our species'

prospects. "Why *was* the human race created?" he wrote
William Dean Howells in 1900. "Or at least why wasn't
something creditable created in place of it? God had his
opportunity. He could have made a reputation. But no, He
must commit this grotesque folly. . . ."

But then I become a Musteite again, a believer in the   11
perfectibility of us all, when I listen to Ben Webster. Or to
Huck: "It was kind of solemn, drifting down the big still
river, laying on our backs, looking up at the stars, and we
didn't ever feel like talking loud, and it warn't often that
we laughed — only a little kind of low chuckle."

Another reason I have been charting the present perils of   12
Huck Finn — talking both to those chasing the boy and those
offering him succor — concerns a book of my own. It's a Y/A
(young adult) novel that Delacorte Press will publish this
fall, and it's called *The Day They Came To Arrest the Book.*

The story is about the fierce civil war in a high school —   13
and in the town as a whole — when an otherwise unharmoni-
ous alliance of parents and other citizens moves to rid the
school of *Huckleberry Finn.* Among the attackers are black
students and their parents; "progressive" white students;
and white churchgoing folk who consider Huck's stealing,
lying, and irreverence, both general and particular, the very
worst kind of model for youngsters. Also readying the guil-
lotine are some feminists, though not all, who see the
women in the novel as subservient to men, and empty-
headed besides.

It's not a tract. In my novel, the enemies of Huck are as   14
skillfully compelling as you or I, because I want the reader
to make up his or her own mind. I don't think anybody's
going to like the principal, though. Anyway, as I thought
about my book, and researched the embattled odyssey of
Huckleberry Finn, I came to understand more about the
complex, seductive dynamics of censorship than I had
before.

Although *Catcher in the Rye* and the works of Kurt Von-   15
negut and Judy Blume are currently the most frequently
censored books in school libraries, no novel has been on
the firing line so long and so continuously as *Huckleberry
Finn.* What is there about this book that manages to in-
furiate, differently, each generation of Americans? What
does it tell us that we don't want to hear?

As for the history of Huck-the-fugitive, I noticed that none 16
of the New York papers, covering the attempt to get the

book thrown out of the Mark Twain Intermediate School in Virginia, mentioned *this* city's involvement in the censorship of Huck. In September 1957, under pressure from the NAACP and the Urban League — which called the novel "racially offensive" — the New York City Board of Education removed Huck from the approved textbook reading lists in all elementary and junior high schools.

17   So you thought the Big Apple was too hip to banish so free a spirit as Huck because of certain words in his book? Well, as I shall recount later, *The Village Voice* — and who are more hip than we? — had its own civil war in 1979 when Jules Feiffer used "nigger" in a cartoon strip that a less-than-average third-grader would have known was an antiracist gibe. God forbid they should ever be contaminated by such impurity.

18   Herewith a brief chronicle of the ways in which *Huckleberry Finn* has been buked and scorned, and loved. At first, it was not that word but rather the uncivilized, unsocialized nature of the wandering boy himself that kept getting him into trouble with decent citizens.

19   A year after the book was published, *The Boston Transcript* reported on March 17, 1885:

20   "The Concord [Massachusetts] Public Library committee has decided to exclude Mark Twain's latest book from the library. One member of the committee says that, while he does not wish to call it immoral, he thinks it contains but little humor, and that of a very coarse type. He regards it as the veriest trash. The librarian and other members of the committee entertain similar views, characterizing it as rough, coarse, and inelegant, dealing with a series of experiences not elevating, the whole book being more suited to the slums than to intelligent, respectable people."

21   Concord, where Emerson and Thoreau had incandescently lived! Where Louisa May Alcott still lived. And she — as quoted in Michael Patrick Hearn's invaluable *The Annotated Huckleberry Finn*, Clarkson N. Potter, 1981 — said derisively, "If Mr. Clemens cannot think of something better to tell our pure-minded lads and lasses, he had best stop writing for them."

22   Mr. Twain refused to be chastened: "Those idiots in Concord are not a court of last resort, and I am not disturbed by their moral gymnastics. No other book of mine has sold so many copies within 2 months after issue as this one. . . ."

Actually, the idiots in Concord had done him a good turn: "[They] have given us a rattling tip-top puff which will go into every paper in the country.... That will sell 25,000 copies for us sure."

In 1902, Huck was thrown out of the Denver Public Library   23
("immoral and sacrilegious"); and three years later, he was taken by the scruff of his neck and booted out of the children's room of the Brooklyn Public Library as "a bad example for ingenuous youth."

And so it went. By 1907, it was reported at the time, Huck   24
had been "turned out of some library every year." Not only did he lie his way out of danger, and steal — if only to stay alive — but his grammar was terrible. So was everybody else's in the book. Worse yet, said an editorial in the Springfield *Republican*, Mr. Clemens indulges in "a gross trifling with every fine feeling . . . he has no reliable sense of propriety." And his "moral level is low."

Over the decades, however, the direction and nature of   25
the attacks on *Huckleberry Finn* changed. From the 1950s on, groups of black parents — with some white sympathizers among school faculties and administrators — have been concentrating on the 160 appearances of "nigger" in the book. In 1976, at the New Trier High School in Winnetka, Illinois, for instance, after a five-year struggle, black parents succeeded in getting the novel taken off all required-reading lists on the charge that it is "morally insensitive" and "degrading and destructive to black humanity."

Four years earlier, Huck had also been stricken from re-   26
quired reading lists in Indianapolis. Said the curriculum director: "There's simply no reason to use books that offend minorities if other books may be used instead."

Said a protesting letter from a bunch of Indianapolis   27
students — self-described as white, black, Catholics, Jews, and agnostics — "This is a pointless withdrawal from reality."

But black parents I have spoken to in Texas could not be   28
more convinced that Huck Finn is, in reality, a clear and present danger to *their* children.

II

The easy way to think you're dealing effectively with   29
censors is to see them as indistinguishable. On one side of the deep, clear Manichaean line, wearing white hats, are

us — the forces of light, the boon companions of Madison and Jefferson. On the other side, shrouded in ignorance, pinched in spirit, are the dark hordes ready to start the bonfires. And whatever particular book each of these censors wants to toss into the flames, all of the censors are alike. They're all Yahoos. Barely literate.

30   I used to think that way until some of my own books started to get into trouble, and I tried to find out why. For instance, a novel for young readers, *This School Is Driving Me Crazy*, has been tossed out of a school in Maryland and is on permanent probation in Mobile. I couldn't figure it out. There's not even *implicit* sex in the book. It's what might be called a moral adventure story. As for the language, there are a few "damns" and "hells." And that's it. Not one of George Carlin's seven dirty words. Even more puzzling is that a lot of teachers and — more to the point — kids dig the book, without anybody at all getting upset. It only gets busted in a few places, but the parents in those places are very angry indeed at the book and at me.

31   One of those places is a small town in southern Illinois. At a conference in Chicago, I met the librarian from there. She is as stubborn a free speech fighter as any Wobbly before the First World War, but she doesn't think of her opponents as if they were in cartoons.

32   "There are kids in my town," she told me, "who come from very religious families. What they see on television, what movies they go to, are controlled. They are taught at home that certain words, used in certain ways, are blasphemous. Sure, they hear other kids say them, but when they see those words in a *book* — and 'damn' and 'hell' are among them — these children are really stunned. And their parents go up the wall. And so would I. If I were them.

33   "I fight for your book," the librarian went on. "I tell the parents who want it ridden out of town that they cannot decide what *all* the children in my library are going to read. But I do tell these parents that I will give *their* children alternative books to read."

34   That is standard American Library Association policy, with which the American Civil Liberties Union concurs. An individual parent should have some say in what the state does with his or her child's mind. Education up to a certain age is compulsory. But when a parent's values conflict fundamentally with those of a book assigned for school reading — in the matter of blasphemy, let's say — should the par-

ent have no recourse at all? *For his or her own child?* Give
the kid another book.

But what happens when a parent informs the school that   35
his child must not read a certain book, and the kid insists
that he does too want to read that damn book? The child,
it seems to me, must be allowed to prevail. But at what
age? Depends on the child. For example—though this is
not about books—from what I've read of the record in the
Walter Polovchak case, I think he was capable of deciding
at 12 that he did not want to leave the United States and
go back to the Ukraine with his parents. For this, and other
reasons, I also think the Illinois affiliate of the ACLU has
been dead wrong in taking the side of Walter's parents in
this battle.

Anyway, if under ALA and ACLU standards, it's okay for   36
individual parents to censor certain books *for their own children only*, what's the First Amendment answer when *groups*
of parents charge that because a book is debasing to their
own kids, it has to be removed from the curriculum entirely?
Why? Because otherwise, that book will create or intensify
animus *towards their own kids* from the rest of the student
body. In this context, I mean protesting parental groups of
the same race or religion. Blacks, or Jews, for example.

The standard answer—"We'll give *your* kids alternative   37
books"—had been unacceptable to black parents in most
places where *Huckleberry Finn* is under intense attack. It
is not acceptable, the black parents say, because the book—
by its incessant use of the word "nigger," and by the way
it portrays blacks—incites racism. Right now. And some
of these parents point to the black eighth-grader in Warrington, Pennsylvania, who last year, his father says, was
verbally and physically abused by his white classmates
after they had all read *Huckleberry Finn* in class. The novel
was required reading in the eighth grade then. It no longer
is in Warrington. In another column, we shall journey to
this Pennsylvania town and find out about the Huck Finn
"compromise" that school personnel and black parents are
very pleased with. That snorting you hear from way down
below is a dissenting view from Mr. Clemens.

From Texas to Virginia, I've talked to black objectors to   38
Huckleberry Finn, as I've talked to Jewish objectors to the
Merchant of Venice. They're not Yahoos. I think they were
wrong in wanting to throw out or hide these works, but

they do raise questions about how to teach certain books. Questions that go even more deeply into the very nature of teaching itself.

39   But first, it's useful to understand the depth of these protesters' feelings. Consider John Wallace, the black administrator at the Mark Twain Intermediate School in Fairfax County, Virginia, who has led the thus far unsuccessful fight to remove *Huckleberry Finn* from that school's curriculum.

40   "The press has cut me down something terrible," Wallace told me. Yes, it has, if only by quoting him. ("Anybody who teaches this book is racist.") But where's he coming from? There wasn't much in the press about that. "I grew up in Aurora, Illinois," Wallace told me, "and there were very few black kids there. When I was a kid, I had to study *Huckleberry Finn* in that school; and every time the teacher, reading it aloud, mentioned the word 'nigger,' I flinched. There was only one other black kid in the room, and every time he heard the teacher say that word, he put his head down on the desk."

41   Wallace's mother was dead by the time he was 12, but he remembers how an aunt, and the minister of his church, led the battle to kick *Huckleberry Finn* out of that school. They failed. But Wallace, who has worked in schools for 28 years, has never stopped trying to save black kids from this book which, as he sees it, will make them feel unworthy. It's become a family mission, he tells me, as he looks at a photograph of his two heroes, Malcolm X and Martin Luther King, shaking hands. His son in Chicago, Wallace adds, is also involved in the jihad against Huck Finn.

42   "You want to know why it's so important to get rid of this book?" Wallace says. "We are always lamenting that black students don't learn or progress as well as whites. Well, if you give them this kind of crap about themselves, how are they going to feel good about themselves?"

43   I tried to tell Wallace what Twain had done in the book. Russell Baker put it pretty good in the *Times* on April 14 when he wrote about Huck and Jim on the Mississippi:

44   "The people they encounter are drunkards, murderers, bullies, swindlers, lynchers, thieves, liars, frauds, child abusers, numbskulls, hypocrites, windbags and traders in human flesh. All are white. The one man of honor in this phantasmagoria is black Jim, the runaway slave. 'Nigger Jim,' as Twain called him to emphasize the irony of a society in which the only true gentleman was held beneath contempt."

I didn't get anywhere with Mr. Wallace about what the   45
book is saying. I didn't get anywhere with Mrs. Dora Durden, mother of an 11th-grade student at Westfield High
School in the Spring Independent School District of Houston. She is one of the leaders of a black parent "Sensitivity
Committee" which has been trying for months to get
Huckleberry Finn off the required reading list there. The
committee claims that the book is degrading to blacks, that
no book is worth the humiliation of their children, and that
to compound the harm, the book has been taught insensi-
tively. (More about how Mr. Twain's novel has been taught
in that district later. Intriguingly, the perceptions of the
teachers and the black parents could not be more dissimilar.)

Dora Durden is no Yahoo either. Crisply articulate, she   46
points out how difficult it is for black kids in a school district
where they make up only about 4.4 percent of the student
body. "When a child, like my daughter, is the only black
in her class, teachers have to be more sensitive about what
and how they teach. But they're not, and they make some
of our kids feel like dogs."

If *Huckleberry Finn* has to be taught, Mrs. Durden said,   47
"then at least don't mention the word 'nigger.' But actually,
why does it have to be taught? Surely there are other good
American novels without that word in it? I myself would
just as soon have *Huckleberry Finn* removed not only from
the reading list, but taken out of the school entirely. And
that may not be the only book that should go. I have asked
the curriculum director for a list of all the books used in
all the courses so that we can examine them and determine
which are good for our children and which are harmful to
them. And that means any book that degrades *any* race."

So far, Mrs. Durden and her allies have failed to get *Huck*   48
Finn taken off the required reading list. But they're pushing
on to the school board, and then the Texas Education
Agency, and then the state courts. A Westfield High School
review committee (two teachers and a librarian), set up
to deal with the complaint, has reported: " . . . no other
literary selection illustrates the mid-nineteenth century
and its evils of slavery as well as this novel, Mark Twain's
satirical masterpiece."

In Fairfax County, Virginia, John Wallace reacts with   49
derision to the notion that Mark Twain's satire can get
through to kids. "It's asinine to think that," says Wallace.
"How many children understand satire?"

And back in Texas, Mrs. Durden tells me that eight black   50 youngsters at Westfield High School took the option of not reading *Huckleberry Finn*, and instead chose another book. One of those students was her daughter. I asked which book she had chosen.

51   *"Fahrenheit 451,"* Mrs. Durden said.

52   I wonder if her daughter told Mrs. Durden what the book is about. By the way, that Ray Bradbury novel—about official arsonists of the future torching subversive books—was taken off the required reading list at another Texas high school in 1981. The school principal decided it gave students "too negative" an outlook.

53   But the business at hand here is still to persuade you that censors are not indistinguishable, that they are as heterogeneous, and can be as well-read, as you or I.

54   For instance, from the October 5, 1981, issue of the *Baltimore Sun*, a story by religion editor Frank P. L. Somerville:

55   "Baltimore's First Unitarian Church had a symbolic book-burning yesterday—midway through its 11 a.m. service—in which centuries of Jewish, Christian, Islamic and Hindu writings were 'expurgated' because of sections described as 'sexist.'

56   "Touched off by a candle and consumed in a pot on a table in front of the altar were slips of paper containing 'patriarchal' excerpts from Martin Luther King, Thomas Aquinas, the Koran, St. Augustine, St. Ambrose, St. John Chrysostom, the Hindu Code of Manu V, and the Old Testament.

57   "Also included were references from the writings of such relatively recent theologians as Kierkegaard and Karl Barth.

58   "Nine women—some in dressy gowns, others wearing pants—filed to the altar from the congregation and read 11 'sexist' passages aloud in turn, adding their commentary. . . .

59   "Then the group 'shared a fantasy' with the congregation of men and women, burning 'these slanderous statements, aimed at half the human race.' As the last flame died in the pot and the organ pealed, there was applause.

60   "In his remarks from the pulpit, First Unitarian's minister, the Rev. Robert L. Zoerheide, inquired: 'Do you ever have the feeling you are making history in this historic church?' "

61   I don't know about *making* history, Reverend, but you and your congregation have moved us a mite closer to *Fahrenheit 451*.

Mr. Twain once said: "No civilization can be perfect until   62
exact equality between man and woman is included."

But then, you know what Mr. Twain and Huck thought   63
about civilization, both the male and female of it.

III

The way it used to be in Warrington—about 25 miles   64
north of Philadelphia—most junior high school students
had to read *Huckleberry Finn*. That is, the teachers were
required to pick their class reading assignments from a
small list of books, and from only those books. Huck was
on that list, and was often chosen because, as Mr. Hemingway once said, "All modern American literature comes from
one book by Mark Twain called *Huckleberry Finn*."

Then came the complaint. Last year, the parents of a   65
black eighth-grader asked that Mr. Twain's book be removed from junior high school reading lists and from the
school libraries. Their son, they said, had been harassed
verbally and physically by white kids in his class because
of the infectious use of the word "nigger" in the novel.

These parents agreed that Mr. Twain himself was not a   66
racist. Why, *Huckleberry Finn*, they said, is strongly anti-
slavery and anti-racist. But the book is too subtle, too difficult, for eighth-graders to understand in terms of Mr.
Twain's intentions. All that the kids, white and black, see
is: "nigger."

I have been unable to find out the nature and extent of   67
the abuse of the black eighth-grader by his classmates.
School officials told me they just don't know. They had
heard the charges, but they had no specifics, nor had they
gone after any. (Wouldn't you think they'd try?) The black
parents involved do not wish to speak to the press. Since
they are not public officials or public figures, I did not try to
crack their unlisted phone number or work through intermediaries. The right to say "No" to the press is—or should
be—one of the most sacred American liberties.

But, for the sake of argument, let me stipulate that a very   68
bad scene did occur—the actual beating of the black child.
(Though if that had happened, I would think his parents
would have insisted the white hooligans be at least suspended.) And let me stipulate there was constant taunting
of the boy as a "nigger."

69   Do you keep *Huckleberry Finn* on a required reading list when it leads to such baleful results?

70   In recent weeks, I've asked this question of a good many citizens, black and white, including teachers — most recently, teachers and librarians at the International Reading Association convention in Chicago. The overwhelming consensus has been that what happened in that eighth-grade classroom in Warrington is a boon to any reasonably awake teacher. What a way to get Huck and Jim, on the one hand, and all those white racists they meet, on the other hand, off the pages of the book and into that very classroom. Talk about a book coming alive!

71   Look at that Huck Finn. Reared in racism, like all the white kids in his town. And then, on the river, on the raft with Jim, shucking off that blind ignorance because this runaway slave is the most honest, perceptive, fair-minded man this white boy has ever known. What a book for the children, all the children, in Warrington, Pennsylvania, in 1982!

72   "To miss that teaching opportunity, to not confront what happened to that black kid in Warrington head-on by really exploring this book," Dr. Kenneth Clark told me, "is to underestimate every child in that classroom. And by underestimating them — while also 'protecting' the black child from this book — you deprive them all of what they should know. And what they can especially learn from *Huckleberry Finn*."

73   Ah, but the book is too difficult for eighth-grade kids! We'll hear a rebuttal of this rationale for overprotecting black and white children in a conversation with a school official in a town very much like Warrington. But keep this in mind: *Huckleberry Finn* is not *The Magic Mountain* or *The Castle* or *Remembrance of Things Past*. It is a novel by a writer who, as he put it, "never cared what became of the cultured classes; they could go to the theater and the opera, they had no use for me and the melodeon." Instead, Mr. Twain, in his words, "always hunted for the bigger game — the masses."

74   All the more so in 1884, when *Huckleberry Finn* was published, because Twain was in need of money and wanted to attract as many bookbuyers as he could that year. He even went on a three-and-a-half-month reading tour of 70 cities to advertise *Huckleberry Finn*. In every way, this was intended to be a popular novel.

And surely, kids in 1982 — after all the television pro- 75
grams and movies they've seen — are at least as able as
children were in 1884 to fathom what Mr. Twain is saying
in this novel. Kids have not grown dumber. I will grant
you that reading it again last summer, I found more in
Huckleberry Finn than when I first read it the summer I
was 14. Or, as Lionel Trilling wrote:

"One can read it at ten and then annually ever after, and 76
each year find that it is as fresh as the year before, that it
has changed only in becoming somewhat larger. To read
it young is like planting a tree young — each year adds a
new growth ring of meaning, and the book is as little likely
as the tree to become dull. So, we may imagine, an Athenian
boy grew up together with the *Odyssey*. There are few other
books which we can know so young and love so long."

But at 10, or 12, or 14, even with only the beginning ring 77
of meaning, any child who can read will not miss the dol-
tishness and sheer meanness and great foolishness of most
of the whites in the book, particularly in their attitudes
toward blacks. Nor will the child miss the courage and
invincible decency of the white boy and the black man on
the river.

And if any child, black or white, does miss — through 78
being blocked in one way or another — these points as big
as barn doors, then what the hell is the teacher for?

Well, what *did* happen in Warrington after the incident 79
connected with *Huckleberry Finn*? Were the teachers told
that now is the time to really teach that thing? No, they
were not. The novel was removed from the required reading
list at Tamamend Junior High School, where the incident
took place. And starting next September, it will be gone
from the reading lists in all junior high schools in Central
Bucks County School District. But Huck will still have shelf
room in all school libraries, and he'll be taught in high
school. Well, maybe he'll be taught in high school. More of
that later.

Although the black parents had started by urging that 80
Huckleberry Finn be taken off all reading lists, and from all
school libraries, they were pleased by the compromise. So
were the white school officials. They had shown themselves
to be sensitive to the feelings of this very small minority
in the district (about 200 black kids out of 11,000 students).
One of the school officials told me, by the way, that "it's
unfortunate that most of our kids don't have experiences
with people of other races."

81   In years past, many of them did get to know Jim, though, but he's been told to make himself scarce.

82   I don't know how many Jewish kids there are in the Central Bucks County schools; but the educators there are so nice, so eager to insulate youngsters from having to think beyond platitudes, that they've removed *The Merchant of Venice* from all the junior high schools. It'll be optional in high school. No one had even complained about Shylock, but as one administrator told me, "We had become concerned with the way the Jewish people are presented in that play."

83   How *do* the teachers spend their time in those classrooms? Reading *TV Guide*?

84   As for Huck, now that the junior high kids have been protected from him, what will take his place? Well, it looks as if three books will replace Mr. Twain's misguided novel on that small required reading list from which teachers are to choose what the junior high kids can absorb without harm, and without their imaginations being unduly stimulated. The winners are: William H. Armstrong's *Sounder*; Allen Eckert's *Incident at Hawk's Hill*; and Chaim Potok's *The Chosen*.

85   With all respect to fans of any or all of the above, ain't none of them *Huckleberry Finn*. It's like removing Duke Ellington from a music course, and substituting Oscar Peterson, Dave Brubeck, and Chick Corea.

86   But what the hell, the kids will be able to get on that raft with Huck and Jim when they reach the safety zone, the 10th grade. There, *Huckleberry Finn* will be one of eight titles from which teachers must choose. Kind of long odds against Huck, and all the longer when you realize that the book now has a stigma attached to it in Central Bucks County. After all, Huck had to be bodily removed from junior high, so how many 10th-grade teachers are going to take a chance on maybe getting into trouble with this book, even though it's permitted by then? Who needs a grim visit from black parents when you can teach something that minds its manners and never gets anybody into trouble?

87   There's much more to be learned from the Incident in Warrington, and its aftermath. The reason I have done this much inquiring is because this victory for niceness in the Central Bucks County School District is much more insidiously harmful to kids than the Armageddons of censorship

that get widespread press play. In most of the latter battles, the enemy is clear. There are folks out there who want to censor, ban, burn (if they can) certain books.

But in Warrington, and in an increasing number of other 88 places, offending books are *not* banned. They're just put in the back of the bus. They're taken off reading lists, but kept in the library. Often, moreover, they're kept in the library on restricted shelves, or are just plain hidden. Or they're taken out of lower-school curriculums and placed, maybe, on high school lists. Usually optional lists. Whatever the device, the books are made less accessible to kids. And so they're less often read. If they're read at all.

This is not the kind of stuff that makes for pungent news- 89 paper or broadcast coverage. Actually, this sort of "com- promise" is seldom covered at all. I was only the second reporter in two years to talk to school officials about the Incident in Warrington. The principal of Tamamend Junior High School was surprised to hear from me. "We're not having any racial riots, any racial problems here," he told me. "That takes the fun out of your story, I guess. And we're not banning anything either. I don't believe in going into the censorship business. Besides, then the civil liberties groups get after you."

"The only story here," another school official told me, "is 90 that we worked out a compromise by which everybody wins."

Except the kids, black and white, who are being treated 91 with such "sensitivity" and "kindness" — but not with re- spect. Respecting a child means you work with him so that he can keep discovering more and more of his potential. So that he can keep learning what his strengths are. Like the capacity to see past words like "nigger" or "kike" or "wop" into what the writer is actually *saying*. What's going to happen to a kid when he gets into the world if he's going to let a word paralyze him so he can't think?

But the principal of Tamamend Junior High School told 92 me Huck had to be taken out of his school because black kids' feelings were hurt. Again, where the hell were the teachers — to connect those feelings to Huck and Jim?

And the principal of Mark Twain Intermediate School in 93 Fairfax County, Virginia, went along with the banning of *Huckleberry Finn* (before he was overruled) because: "I just felt that a student of any race or nationality shouldn't be made to feel uncomfortable in a classroom."

94   And in school districts around the country, similar nice people have said similar nice things in justifying the removal of *Huckleberry Finn* and other books from required high school as well as junior high school reading lists. Some school folks, however, refuse to yield to this milky niceness. They figure kids aren't that fragile. And they figure that when educators *are* softly obeisant to those who want to shortchange kids, the result is yet another generation of adults who never learned in school how to think for themselves.

95   So it was in Davenport, Iowa, recently when an attack was made on that good old boy, Huck, who is required reading in an American literature high school course called "Great American Authors." A black student and the parent of another black student wanted this "racist" novel taken off all required reading lists.

96   The demand was turned down. The student was told she could read another book if she wanted to, but, said the English faculty, "It's impossible to have a class called 'Great American Authors' without including Mark Twain." And Huck.

97   Back in Warrington, Pennsylvania, a black girl in junior high asked for *Huckleberry Finn* this year. She'd heard somewhere it was a good book. Although still available in *her* lower school (until September), it had not been chosen by her teacher. The black student got *Huckleberry Finn* and thought it was one hell of a book. She liked it a whole lot. Didn't find it racist at all. Quite the opposite.

98   Better keep an eye on that young woman. Another one of those independent thinkers who'll always be getting into trouble. Like that kid on the raft.

IV

99   If I were to name the town, most of you would have to look it up in an atlas. It's not a village — being big enough for a school population of 16,000 — but it's no metropolis. Hardly any news comes out of this town that's of interest to anyone but the folks who live there, and they'd like to keep it that way.

100   Especially, these days, the man in charge of coordinating the English program in the town's classrooms isn't looking to be on the nightly news. A black parent has just complained to him about *Huckleberry Finn*, which is required

reading in the ninth grade. I mean it's really required. No child leaves the ninth grade in this town without getting on the raft with Huck and Jim.

The black parent is disturbed that his child, that any 101 child for that matter—but especially a black child—should have to read a book with the word "nigger" in it. All the way through it. At this point, the black parent is not demanding that *Huckleberry Finn* be removed from the curriculum and the library. He is objecting to the book being *required* reading.

So far, the discussions have been low-key and informal. 102 No newspaper or wire service or broadcast station has any idea that this place may join Fairfax County, Virginia; Davenport, Iowa; Warrington, Pennsylvania; and Houston as yet another battleground over whether Mr. Twain's novel does injury to young readers, particularly young black readers.

The school official in this unnamed town agreed to let 103 me hear him think out what he's going to do—he's not sure yet—provided I didn't name him or the town.

"You see," he said, "I've kept a file on the attacks on 104 *Huckleberry Finn* around the country, and one thing that's clear to me is that as soon as the press gets into this, it gets a lot harder to keep the talks between the school and the parents low-key. Anyway, there is no story here. Yet. We're trying to figure things out. The parent doesn't want to come across as a censor. And I don't want to come across as being callous on this thing."

He paused, and then said slowly, "When a person is of- 105 fended, a person is offended. You can't say to him, 'Well, you shouldn't have been offended, or it's ridiculous to be offended by this book.' But on the other hand, it's difficult for me to agree to allow any child to go through our school system without reading *Huckleberry Finn*. There's no other book I know of that is so important—in so many different ways—for kids to know. Especially ninth-grade kids. It seems to me I'd be falling down on my job if I didn't keep that book on the required list. On the other hand, I've got to be sensitive to other people's sensitivities. So I don't know what I'm going to do."

Before hearing why this schoolman felt so strongly that 106 all kids who don't read *Huckleberry Finn* are culturally deprived, a note about the impact of the press on these matters. On the one hand, as I tell librarians around the country, as soon as the censor draws a battle line, go to the press. Illumination works wonders, even in those areas where most folks attend fundamentalist churches.

107   The majority of citizens, anywhere, do not like appearing, in newspapers or on television, as if they're being manipulated by organized pressure groups deciding for them what they and their children are going to read. Knowing this element of the American grain is how librarian Kathy Russell triumphed over the censors in conservative Washington County in Virginia. Through the newspapers and broadcast stations there, she kept reminding people that the library belonged to *all* of them, not just the Baptist minister and his allies who wanted to purge it. And the people got angry — at the Baptist minister.

108   Press attention, however, does not always have salutary effects. Last week, I wrote about the travails of *Huckleberry Finn* in Warrington, Pennsylvania, and the ultimate grand compromise there which took the book out of the junior high schools and removed it to the high school where it will be only one of eight titles from which teachers can choose.

109   In Warrington, the protest began with one set of black parents. The wire services picked up the story, followed by some of the big papers in the area, notably the *Philadelphia Inquirer*.

110   Thereupon, other black parents came forward. They reported — and this impressed school officials — that their children had not only suffered emotional harm because they'd had to read *Huckleberry Finn*, but their classwork in other subjects as well had been adversely affected. All because of Mr. Twain's creature.

111   I asked the language arts supervisor in the Warrington school system whether there had been any such reports of damage to black children during all the previous years in which *Huckleberry Finn* had been on the required reading list in the junior high schools.

112   No, there had been no such reports.

113   I asked if she and other school officials had investigated this alleged correlation between Huck and those black children's failing grades. A correlation that revealed itself only after the press reports on the single initial complaint against the novel.

114   Well, no, the school officials had not really looked into whether such a connection could actually be demonstrated.

My own theory, which I also can't prove, is that a kind 115
of group loyalty was in operation among the black kids
who claimed to have been injured by the book. The parents
of one of their own had complained about *Huckleberry Finn*,
and in a show of solidarity, other black children began
protesting against the book. And to make their points all
the more vivid, they also began showing symptoms that
the presence of that book was so malign that they couldn't
concentrate on their other studies either.

Every one of those black children may well have 116
thoroughly believed all this to be true. The function of
the school, however, is to try to find out if it is true. And
it didn't even try.

But let us suppose it is true, that Huck had paralyzed 117
those black kids. All the more reason for them to get all
the way into *Huckleberry Finn*. Otherwise, what a terrible
thing for a child to learn! That he is so fragile, so vulnerable,
so without intellectual and emotional resources that a book
can lay him low. And that is what the teachers and supervisors of the junior high schools in Warrington, Pennsylvania, have allowed the black children in their care to
learn.

To return to the conflict still aborning in the small town 118
which I will not name. The coordinator of the English curriculum was saying one recent morning that he is riven
between his desire to avoid a racial conflict in the community and his desire to "keep the best literature we can in
the classroom."

If he wanted a way out, I told him, Russell Baker, among 119
others, had given him one. In the April 14 *New York Times*,
Baker, an admirer of *Huckleberry Finn*, nonetheless
claimed: "It's a dreadful disservice to Mark Twain for
teachers to push *Huckleberry Finn* on seventh-, eighth-, and
ninth-graders. . . . *Huckleberry Finn* can be partly enjoyed
after the age of 25, but for fullest benefit it probably
shouldn't be read before age 35, and even then only if the
reader has had a broad experience of American society."

Dr. Kenneth Clark had snorted when I read him that 120
Russell Baker passage on the phone. So had I when I
saw it.

But how did this schoolman—worrying about a possible 121
racial confrontation over this book—react to what Baker
had said? He *could* tell the black parents that on reflection,

he had decided that this book was not right for any child in the secondary schools. And, for that matter, he could recommend that even on their own time, all teachers under 35 stay away from the novel.

122   "No," the man decided not to take this escape route. "No. Neither Russell Baker nor my concern about other people's concern over the use of the word 'nigger' is going to change my mind about what's right educationally. *Huckleberry Finn* is well placed, very well placed, in the ninth grade. And I'll tell you why.

123   "First, the story is told by an adolescent: and there are very few *quality* novels where a youth is dealing with adults entirely from his perspective, in his language, through his experiences.

124   "Second, in terms of craftsmanship and flow, it's a simple novel. At the ninth grade, students are just learning the structure of the novel. It's really our first opportunity to teach the novel as a form, and there's nothing better to do that with than *Huckleberry Finn*. Especially the way it's tied in so nicely with the river.

125   "Also, it's a chronological novel. Not all novels are. For instance, when you jump into Charles Dickens at grade 10, you've got a different, more complicated structure to the novel than you have with *Huckleberry Finn*. So Twain's book is a great introduction to the form of the novel.

126   "Then," the schoolman continued, "it ties in very well with the pre-Civil War history that this school district, and most others, are studying at this grade. Twain has a lot to say about America during that period. He gives adolescent kids a great deal to learn and think about.

127   "Take the word 'nigger.' It's during the *adolescent* years that kids ought to be dealing with that word, its history, and the kind of people who used it then, and those who still use it. Good Lord, Twain spends three-quarters of his book trying to make clear what a damnable word 'nigger' is, because it shows the whites who used it didn't *see*, didn't begin to understand the people they were talking about."

128   I mentioned a letter I'd received recently from a librarian in Twain's home state, Missouri. She was focusing on books as a vital part of what she calls the initiation rights of children. Books, she insisted, are among the ways teenagers move into adulthood. "And," she continued, "to deny them the books that can most help them make that transition is inhumane."

"Well, sure," said the schoolman. "That's another reason 129
I've insisted on requiring that all kids in this town read
Huckleberry Finn. That book is *about* Huck's rites of passage.
To put it more prosaically, a large part of it has to do
with an adolescent's growth. But that book also has such
a sweeping magnitude to it. It has so many things in it.
It's about adolescence; it's about the race thing; it's about
con men, the Duke and the Dauphin; it's about the murderous foolishness of pride, the Grangerfords. Oh, I could
go on all morning."

The schoolman's voice became low. "It would be such a 130
shame for a kid never to get to read this book."

I asked him how he felt about such "compromises" as the 131
one that had been worked out in Warrington, Pennsylvania,
to spare kids from Huck Finn in junior high and maybe
allow them to read the book in high school. But even then,
in the majority of such "compromises," *Huckleberry Finn*
has carefully been removed from *required* reading lists in
high schools.

"It's insidious," the schoolman in the small town said. "I 132
mean, it's not outright censorship, so nobody has to defend
himself against that charge. But this kind of 'compromise'
does make it harder and harder for the kid and the book
to come together. Oh, some self-starters will seek out
Huckleberry Finn in the library or ask if they can choose it
for independent study; but in those school districts that
have compromised, *most* kids will never get to read the
book.

"And you know what that's an extension of? The way we 133
underestimate kids. This is a classic case of just that. We
underestimate the capacity of black kids to understand why
and how 'nigger' is used in *Huckleberry Finn*. And God
knows we underestimate Mark Twain."

"Yeah, but so much of this book is Twain's satire," I said. 134
"And John Wallace, the black administrator at Mark Twain
Intermediate School in Fairfax County, said that it was
asinine to think that most children understand satire."

The schoolman laughed. "What could be a more perfect 135
underestimation of kids than that? Look at what kids read
on their own. Sometimes I think they live on satire."

"Well, it seems to me you've made up your mind that 136
Huck's going to stay here," I said. "In the ninth grade. And
on the *required* reading list."

137   "I don't know," he sighed. "I know I'm right about the
book, but the key thing is this — you have to be sensitive to
someone else's sensitivities. I can talk about the book to
the black parents, just the way I've been talking to you
about it now. And I can assure them we teach it sensitively,
and they'll say, 'It still hurts my child.' And I'll say the
child can choose another book. But what book can replace
Huckleberry Finn?"

138   The schoolman had another appointment. "I'd say," he
bade me farewell, "that it's a toss-up right now as to what's
going to happen. This is just one of those little battles fought
in remote places. Only we'll know how it turns out."

CIVIL RIGHTS, EQUAL RIGHTS, AND THE LAW

ON CIVIL DISOBEDIENCE

Henry David Thoreau
Civil Disobedience

Henry David Thoreau (1817–1862) is best known for his classic Walden *(1854), an autobiographical, satiric, spiritual, scientific, and naturalistic "self-help book" based on his two years' stay at Walden Pond, near Boston. A friend of Ralph Waldo Emerson and other transcendentalists, Thoreau expressed his idealism in a number of concrete ways, for example in his opposition to slavery and the Mexican War. His refusal to pay taxes to support the Mexican War inspired his essay "Civil Disobedience" (1849). First delivered as a lecture in 1848, "Civil Disobedience" influenced the thinking of Mahatma Gandhi and Martin Luther King, Jr.*

I heartily accept the motto, — "That government is best 1 which governs least"; and I should like to see it acted up to more rapidly and systematically. Carried out, it finally amounts to this, which also I believe, — "That government is best which governs not at all;" and when men are prepared for it, that will be the kind of government which they will have. Government is at best but an expedient; but most governments are usually, and all governments are sometimes, inexpedient. The objections which have been brought against a standing army, and they are many and weighty, and deserve to prevail, may also at last be brought against a standing government. The standing army is only an arm of the standing government. The government itself, which is only the mode which the people have chosen to execute their will, is equally liable to be abused and perverted before the people can act through it. Witness the present Mexican war, the work of comparatively a few individuals using the standing government as their tool; for, in the outset, the people would not have consented to this measure.

2   This American government — what is it but a tradition, though a recent one, endeavoring to transmit itself unimpaired to posterity, but each instant losing some of its integrity? It has not the vitality and force of a single living man; for a single man can bend it to his will. It is a sort of wooden gun to the people themselves. But it is not the less necessary for this; for the people must have some complicated machinery or other, and hear its din, to satisfy that idea of government which they have. Governments show thus how successfully men can be imposed on, even impose on themselves, for their own advantage. It is excellent, we must all allow. Yet this government never of itself furthered any enterprise, but by the alacrity with which it got out of its way. *It* does not keep the country free. *It* does not settle the West. *It* does not educate. The character inherent in the American people has done all that has been accomplished; and it would have done somewhat more, if the government had not sometimes got in its way. For government is an expedient by which men would fain succeed in letting one another alone; and, as has been said, when it is most expedient, the governed are most let alone by it. Trade and commerce, if they were not made of India-rubber, would never manage to bounce over the obstacles which legislators are continually putting in their way; and, if one were to judge these men wholly by the effects of their actions and not partly by their intentions, they would deserve to be classed and punished with those mischievous persons who put obstructions on the railroads.

3   But, to speak practically and as a citizen, unlike those who call themselves no-government men, I ask for, not at once no government, but *at once* a better government. Let every man make known what kind of government would command his respect, and that will be one step toward obtaining it.

4   After all, the practical reason why, when the power is once in the hands of people, a majority are permitted, and for a long period continue, to rule is not because they are most likely to be in the right, nor because this seems fairest to the minority, but because they are physically the strongest. But a government in which the majority rule in all cases cannot be based on justice, even as far as men understand it. Can there not be a government in which majorities do not virtually decide right and wrong, but conscience? — in

which majorities decide only those questions to which the rule of expediency is applicable? Must the citizen ever for a moment, or in the least degree, resign his conscience to the legislator? Why has every man a conscience, then? I think that we should be men first, and subjects afterward. It is not desirable to cultivate a respect for the law, so much as for the right. The only obligation which I have a right to assume is to do at any time what I think right. It is truly enough said, that a corporation has no conscience; but a corporation of conscientious men is a corporation *with* a conscience. Law never made men a whit more just; and, by means of their respect for it, even the well-disposed are daily made the agents of injustice. A common and natural result of an undue respect for law is, that you may see a file of soldiers, colonel, captain, corporal, privates, powder-monkeys, and all, marching in admirable order over hill and dale to the wars, against their will, ay, against their common sense and consciences, which makes it very steep marching indeed, and produces a palpitation of the heart. They have no doubt that it is a damnable business in which they are concerned; they are all peaceably inclined. Now, what are they? Men at all? or small movable forts and magazines, at the service of some unscrupulous man in power? Visit the Navy-Yard, and behold a marine, such a man as an American government can make, or such as it can make a man with its black arts, — a mere shadow and reminiscence of humanity, a man laid out alive and standing, and already, as one may say, buried under arms with funeral accompaniments, though it may be, —

"Not a drum was heard, not a funeral note,
    As his corse to the rampart we hurried;
Not a soldier discharged his farewell shot
    O'er the grave where our hero we buried."[1]

The mass of men serve the state thus, not as men mainly, 5 but as machines, with their bodies. They are the standing army, and the militia, jailers, constables, posse comitatus, etc. In most cases there is no free exercise whatever of the judgment or of the moral sense; but they put themselves on a level with wood and earth and stones; and wooden men can perhaps be manufactured that will serve the pur-

[1]From "Burial of Sir John Moore at Corunna" by Charles Wolfe (1817).

pose as well. Such command no more respect than men of straw or a lump of dirt. They have the same sort of worth only as horses and dogs. Yet such as these even are commonly esteemed good citizens. Others — as most legislators, politicians, lawyers, ministers, and office-holders — serve the state chiefly with their heads; and, as they rarely make any moral distinctions, they are as likely to serve the Devil, without *intending* it, as God. A very few, as heroes, patriots, martyrs, reformers in the great sense, and *men*, serve the state with their consciences also, and so necessarily resist it for the most part; and they are commonly treated as enemies by it. A wise man will only be useful as a man, and will not submit to be "clay," and "stop a hole to keep the wind away," but leave that office to his dust at least: —

"I am too high-born to be propertied,
To be a secondary at control,
Or useful serving-man and instrument
To any sovereign state throughout the world."[2]

6   He who gives himself entirely to his fellow-men appears to them useless and selfish; but he who gives himself partially to them is pronounced a benefactor and philanthropist.

7   How does it become a man to behave toward this American government to-day? I answer, that he cannot without disgrace be associated with it. I cannot for an instant recognize that political organization as *my* government which is the *slave's* government also.

8   All men recognize the right of revolution; that is, the right to refuse allegiance to, and to resist, the government, when its tyranny or its inefficiency are great and unendurable. But almost all say that such is not the case now. But such was the case, they think, in the Revolution of '75. If one were to tell me that this was a bad government because it taxed certain foreign commodities brought to its ports, it is most probable that I should not make an ado about it, for I can do without them. All machines have their friction; and possibly this does enough good to counterbalance the evil. At any rate, it is a great evil to make a stir about it. But when the friction comes to have its machine, and oppression and robbery are organized, I say, let us not have

---

[2]The line before the indented quotation is from *Hamlet* V. i. 236–37; the indented quotation is from Shakespeare's *King John* V. ii. 79–82.

such a machine any longer. In other words, when a sixth of the population of a nation which has undertaken to be the refuge of liberty are slaves, and a whole country is unjustly overrun and conquered by a foreign army, and subjected to military law, I think that it is not too soon for honest men to rebel and revolutionize. What makes this duty the more urgent is the fact that the country so overrun is not our own, but ours is the invading army.

Paley,[3] a common authority with many on moral questions, in his chapter on the "Duty of Submission to Civil Government," resolves all civil obligation into expediency; and he proceeds to say, "that so long as the interest of the whole society requires it, that is, so long as the established government cannot be resisted or changed without public inconveniency, it is the will of God that the established government be obeyed, and no longer .... This principle being admitted, the justice of every particular case of resistance is reduced to a computation of the quantity of the danger and grievance on the one side, and of the probability and expense of redressing it on the other." Of this, he says, every man shall judge for himself. But Paley appears never to have contemplated those cases to which the rule of expediency does not apply, in which a people, as well as an individual, must do justice, cost what it may. If I have unjustly wrested a plank from a drowning man, I must restore it to him though I drown myself. This, according to Paley, would be inconvenient. But he that would save his life, in such a case, shall lose it. This people must cease to hold slaves, and to make war on Mexico, though it cost them their existence as a people. 9

In their practice, nations agree with Paley; but does any one think that Massachusetts does exactly what is right at the present crisis? 10

"A drab of state, a cloth-o'-silver slut,
To have her train borne up, and her soul trail in the dirt."

Practically speaking, the opponents to a reform in Massachusetts are not a hundred thousand politicians at the South, but a hundred thousand merchants and farmers here, who are more interested in commerce and agriculture

[3]William Paley (1743–1805), English theologian.

than they are in humanity, and are not prepared to do justice to the slave and to Mexico, *cost what it may*. I quarrel not with far-off foes, but with those who, near at home, coöperate with, and do the bidding of, those far away, and without whom the latter would be harmless. We are accustomed to say, that the mass of men are unprepared; but improvement is slow, because the few are not materially wiser or better than the many. It is not so important that many should be as good as you, as that there be some absolute goodness somewhere; for that will leaven the whole lump. There are thousands who are *in opinion* opposed to slavery and to the war, who yet in effect do nothing to put an end to them; who, esteeming themselves children of Washington and Franklin, sit down with their hands in their pockets, and say that they know not what to do, and do nothing; who even postpone the question of freedom to the question of free-trade, and quietly read the prices-current along with the latest advices from Mexico, after dinner, and, it may be, fall asleep over them both. What is the price-current of an honest man and patriot to-day? They hesitate, and they regret, and sometimes they petition; but they do nothing in earnest and with effect. They will wait, well disposed, for others to remedy the evil, that they may no longer have it to regret. At most, they give only a cheap vote, and a feeble countenance and Godspeed, to the right, as it goes by them. There are nine hundred and ninety-nine patrons of virtue to one virtuous man. But it is easier to deal with the real possessor of a thing than with the temporary guardian of it.

11   All voting is a sort of gaming, like checkers or backgammon, with a slight moral tinge to it, a playing with right and wrong, with moral questions; and betting naturally accompanies it. The character of the voters is not staked. I cast my vote, perchance, as I think right; but I am not vitally concerned that that right should prevail. I am willing to leave it to the majority. Its obligation, therefore, never exceeds that of expediency. Even voting *for the right* is *doing* nothing for it. It is only expressing to men feebly your desire that it should prevail. A wise man will not leave the right to the mercy of chance, nor wish it to prevail through the power of the majority. There is but little virtue in the action of masses of men. When the majority shall at length vote for the abolition of slavery, it will be because they are indifferent to slavery, or because there is but little slavery left

to be abolished by their vote. *They* will then be the only slaves. Only *his* vote can hasten the abolition of slavery who asserts his own freedom by his vote.

I hear of a convention to be held at Baltimore, or else- 12 where, for the selection of a candidate for the Presidency, made up chiefly of editors, and men who are politicians by profession; but I think, what is it to any independent, intelligent, and respectable man what decision they may come to? Shall we not have the advantage of his wisdom and honesty, nevertheless? Can we not count upon some independent votes? Are there not many individuals in the country who do not attend conventions? But no: I find that the respectable man, so called, has immediately drifted from his position, and despairs of his country, when his country has more reason to despair of him. He forthwith adopts one of the candidates thus selected as the only *available* one, thus proving that he is himself *available* for any purposes of the demagogue. His vote is of no more worth than that of any unprincipled foreigner or hireling native, who may have been bought. O for a man who is a *man*, and, as my neighbor says, has a bone in his back which you cannot pass your hand through! Our statistics are at fault: the population has been returned too large. How many *men* are there to a square thousand miles in this country? Hardly one. Does not America offer any inducement for men to settle here? The American has dwindled into an Odd Fellow, —one who may be known by the development of his organ of gregariousness, and a manifest lack of intellect and cheerful self-reliance; whose first and chief concern, on coming into the world, is to see that the Almshouses are in good repair; and, before yet he has lawfully donned the virile garb, to collect a fund for the support of the widows and orphans that may be; who, in short, ventures to live only by the aid of the Mutual Insurance company, which has promised to bury him decently.

It is not a man's duty, as a matter of course, to devote 13 himself to the eradication of any, even the most enormous wrong; he may still properly have other concerns to engage him; but it is his duty, at least, to wash his hands of it, and, if he gives it no thought longer, not to give it practically his support. If I devote myself to other pursuits and contemplations, I must first see, at least, that I do not pursue them sitting upon another man's shoulders. I must get off him first, that he may pursue his contemplations too. See what gross inconsistency is tolerated. I have heard some of my townsmen say, "I should like to have them order me out to help put down an insurrection of the slaves, or to march to Mexico; — see if I would go"; and yet these very men have each, directly by their allegiance, and so indirectly, at least, by their money, furnished a substitute. The soldier is applauded who refuses to serve in an unjust war by those who do not refuse to sustain the unjust government which makes the war; is applauded by those whose own act and authority he disregards and sets at naught; as if the state were penitent to that degree that it hired one to scourge it while it sinned, but not to that degree that it left off sinning for a moment. Thus, under the name of Order and Civil Government, we are all made at last to pay homage to and support our own meanness. After the first blush of sin comes its indifference; and from immoral it becomes, as it were, *un*moral, and not quite unnecessary to that life which we have made.

14   The broadest and most prevalent error requires the most disinterested virtue to sustain it. The slight reproach to which the virtue of patriotism is commonly liable, the noble are most likely to incur. Those who, while they disapprove of the character and measures of a government, yield to it their allegiance and support are undoubtedly its most conscientious supporters, and so frequently the most serious obstacles to reform. Some are petitioning the state to dissolve the Union, to disregard the requisitions of the President. Why do they not dissolve it themselves, — the union between themselves and the state, — and refuse to pay their quota into its treasury? Do not they stand in the same relation to the state that the state does to the Union? And have not the same reasons prevented the state from resisting the Union which have prevented them from resisting the state?

15   How can a man be satisfied to entertain an opinion merely, and enjoy *it?* Is there any enjoyment in it, if his opinion is that he is aggrieved? If you are cheated out of a single dollar by your neighbor, you do not rest satisfied with knowing that you are cheated, or with saying that you are cheated, or even with petitioning him to pay you your due; but you take effectual steps at once to obtain the full amount, and see that you are never cheated again. Action from principle, the perception and the performance of right, changes things and relations; it is essentially revolutionary,

and does not consist wholly with anything which was. It not only divides states and churches, it divides families; ay, it divides the *individual*, separating the diabolical in him from the divine.

Unjust laws exist: shall we be content to obey them, or 16 shall we endeavor to amend them, and obey them until we have succeeded, or shall we transgress them at once? Men generally, under such a government as this, think that they ought to wait until they have persuaded the majority to alter them. They think that, if they should resist, the remedy would be worse than the evil. But it is the fault of the government itself that the remedy *is* worse than the evil. *It* makes it worse. Why is it not more apt to anticipate and provide for reform? Why does it not cherish its wise minority? Why does it cry and resist before it is hurt? Why does it not encourage its citizens to be on the alert to point out its faults, and *do* better than it would have them? Why does it always crucify Christ, and excommunicate Copernicus and Luther, and pronounce Washington and Franklin rebels?

One would think, that a deliberate and practical denial 17 of its authority was the only offense never contemplated by government; else, why has it not assigned its definite, its suitable and proportionate penalty? If a man who has no property refuses but once to earn nine shillings for the state, he is put in prison for a period unlimited by any law that I know, and determined only by the discretion of those who placed him there; but if he should steal ninety times nine shillings from the state, he is soon permitted to go at large again.

If the injustice is part of the necessary friction of the 18 machine of government, let it go, let it go; perchance it will wear smooth, — certainly the machine will wear out. If the injustice has a spring, or a pulley, or a rope, or a crank, exclusively for itself, then perhaps you may consider whether the remedy will not be worse than the evil; but if it is of such a nature that it requires you to be the agent of injustice to another, then, I say, break the law. Let your life be a counter friction to stop the machine. What I have to do is to see, at any rate, that I do not lend myself to the wrong which I condemn.

As for adopting the ways which the state has provided 19 for remedying the evil, I know not of such ways. They take too much time, and a man's life will be gone. I have other affairs to attend to. I came into this world, not chiefly to make this a good place to live in, but to live in it, be it good or bad. A man has not everything to do, but something; and because he cannot do *everything*, it is not necessary that he should do *something* wrong. It is not my business to be petitioning the Governor or the Legislature any more than it is theirs to petition me; and if they should not hear my petition, what should I do then? But in this case the state has provided no way; its very Constitution is the evil. This may seem to be harsh and stubborn and unconciliatory; but it is to treat with the utmost kindness and consideration the only spirit that can appreciate or deserves it. So is all change for the better, like birth and death, which convulse the body.

20   I do not hesitate to say, that those who call themselves Abolitionists should at once effectually withdraw their support, both in person and property, from the government of Massachusetts, and not wait till they constitute a majority of one, before they suffer the right to prevail through them. I think that it is enough if they have God on their side, without waiting for that other one. Moreover, any man more right than his neighbors constitutes a majority of one already.

21   I meet this American government, or its representative, the state government, directly, and face to face, once a year—no more—in the person of its tax-gatherer; this is the only mode in which a man situated as I am necessarily meets it; and it then says distinctly, Recognize me; and the simplest, the most effectual, and, in the present posture of affairs, the indispensablest mode of treating with it on this head, of expressing your little satisfaction with and love for it, is to deny it then. My civil neighbor, the tax-gatherer, is the very man I have to deal with,—for it is, after all, with men and not with parchment that I quarrel,—and he has voluntarily chosen to be an agent of the government. How shall he ever know well what he is and does as an officer of the government, or as a man, until he is obliged to consider whether he shall treat me, his neighbor, for whom he has respect, as a neighbor and well-disposed man, or as a maniac and disturber of the peace, and see if he can get over this obstruction to his neighborliness without a ruder and more impetuous thought or speech corresponding with his action. I know this well, that if one thousand, if one hundred, if ten men whom I could name,—if ten

honest men only, — ay, if *one* HONEST man, in this State of
Massachusetts, *ceasing to hold slaves*, were actually to withdraw from this copartnership, and be locked up in the
county jail therefor, it would be the abolition of slavery in
America. For it matters not how small the beginning may
seem to be; what is once well done is done forever. But we
love better to talk about it: that we say is our mission.
Reform keeps many scores of newspapers in its service, but
not one man. If my esteemed neighbor, the State's ambassador, who will devote his days to the settlement of the
question of human rights in the Council Chamber, instead
of being threatened with the prisons of Carolina, were to
sit down the prisoner of Massachusetts, that State which
is so anxious to foist the sin of slavery upon her sister, —
though at present she can discover only an act of inhospi-
tality to be the ground of a quarrel with her, — the Legislature would not wholly waive the subject the following
winter.

Under a government which imprisons any unjustly, the   22
true place for a just man is also a prison. The proper place
to-day, the only place which Massachusetts has provided
for her freer and less desponding spirits, is in her prisons,
to be put out and locked out of the State by her own act,
as they have already put themselves out by their principles.
It is there that the fugitive slave, and the Mexican prisoner
on parole, and the Indian come to plead the wrongs of his
race should find them; on that separate, but more free and
honorable ground, where the State places those who are
not *with* her, but *against* her, — the only house in a slave
State in which a free man can abide with honor. If any
think that their influence would be lost there, and their
voices no longer afflict the ear of the State, that they would
not be as an enemy within its walls, they do not know by
how much truth is stronger than error, nor how much more
eloquently and effectively he can combat injustice who has
experienced a little in his own person. Cast your whole
vote, not a strip of paper merely, but your whole influence.
A minority is powerless while it conforms to the majority;
it is not even a minority then; but it is irresistible when it
clogs by its whole weight. If the alternative is to keep all
just men in prison, or give up war and slavery, the State
will not hesitate which to choose. If a thousand men were
not to pay their tax-bills this year, that would not be a
violent and bloody measure, as it would be to pay them,

and enable the State to commit violence and shed innocent blood. This is, in fact, the definition of a peaceable revolution, if any such is possible. If the tax-gatherer, or any other public officer, asks me, as one has done, "But what shall I do?" my answer is, "If you really wish to do anything, resign your office." When the subject has refused allegiance, and the officer has resigned his office, then the revolution is accomplished. But even suppose blood should flow. Is there not a sort of blood shed when the conscience is wounded? Through this wound a man's real manhood and immortality flow out, and he bleeds to an everlasting death. I see this blood flowing now.

23   I have contemplated the imprisonment of the offender, rather than the seizure of his goods, — though both will serve the same purpose, — because they who assert the purest right, and consequently are most dangerous to a corrupt State, commonly have not spent much time in accumulating property. To such the State renders comparatively small service, and a slight tax is wont to appear exorbitant, particularly if they are obliged to earn it by special labor with their hands. If there were one who lived wholly without the use of money, the State itself would hesitate to demand it of him. But the rich man—not to make any invidious comparison—is always sold to the institution which makes him rich. Absolutely speaking, the more money, the less virtue; for money comes between a man and his objects, and obtains them for him; and it was certainly no great virtue to obtain it. It puts to rest many questions which he would otherwise be taxed to answer; while the only new question which it puts is the hard but superfluous one, how to spend it. Thus his moral ground is taken from under his feet. The opportunities of living are diminished in proportion as what are called the "means" are increased. The best thing a man can do for his culture when he is rich is to endeavor to carry out those schemes which he entertained when he was poor. Christ answered the Herodians according to their condition. "Show me the tribute-money," said he; — and one took a penny out of his pocket; — if you use money which has the image of Caesar on it, and which he has made current and valuable, that is, *if you are men of the State*, and gladly enjoy the advantages of Caesar's government, then pay him back some of his own when he demands it. "Render therefore to Caesar that which is Caesar's, and to God those things which are

God's,"—leaving them no wiser than before as to which was which; for they did not wish to know.

When I converse with the freest of my neighbors, I perceive that, whatever they may say about the magnitude and seriousness of the question, and their regard for the public tranquillity, the long and the short of the matter is, that they cannot spare the protection of the existing government, and they dread the consequences to their property and families of disobedience to it. For my own part, I should not like to think that I ever rely on the protection of the State. But, if I deny the authority of the State when it presents its tax-bill, it will soon take and waste all my property, and so harass me and my children without end. This is hard. This makes it impossible for a man to live honestly, and at the same time comfortably, in outward respects. It will not be worth the while to accumulate property; that would be sure to go again. You must hire or squat somewhere, and raise but a small crop, and eat that soon. You must live within yourself, and depend upon yourself always tucked up and ready for a start, and not have many affairs. A man may grow rich in Turkey even, if he will be in all respects a good subject of the Turkish government. Confucius said: "If a state is governed by the principles of reason, poverty and misery are subjects of shame; if a state is not governed by the principles of reason, riches and honors are the subjects of shame." No: until I want the protection of Massachusetts to be extended to me in some distant Southern port, where my liberty is endangered, or until I am bent solely on building up an estate at home by peaceful enterprise, I can afford to refuse allegiance to Massachusetts, and her right to my property and life. It costs me less in every sense to incur the penalty of disobedience to the State than it would to obey. I should feel as if I were worth less in that case.

Some years ago, the State met me in behalf of the Church, and commanded me to pay a certain sum toward the support of a clergyman whose preaching my father attended, but never I myself. "Pay," it said, "or be locked up in the jail." I declined to pay. But, unfortunately, another man saw fit to pay it. I did not see why the schoolmaster should be taxed to support the priest, and not the priest the schoolmaster; for I was not the State's schoolmaster, but I supported myself by voluntary subscription. I did not see why the lyceum should not present its tax-bill, and have the

State to back its demand, as well as the Church. However, at the request of the selectmen, I condescended to make some such statement as this in writing: — "Know all men by these presents, that I, Henry Thoreau, do not wish to be regarded as a member of any incorporated society which I have not joined." This I gave to the town clerk; and he has it. The State, having thus learned that I did not wish to be regarded as a member of that church, has never made a like demand on me since; though it said that it must adhere to its original presumption that time. If I had known how to name them, I should then have signed off in detail from all the societies which I never signed on to; but I did not know where to find a complete list.

26   I have paid no poll-tax[4] for six years. I was put into jail once on this account, for one night; and, as I stood considering the walls of solid stone, two or three feet thick, the door of wood and iron, a foot thick, and the iron grating which strained the light, I could not help being struck with the foolishness of that institution which treated me as if I were mere flesh and blood and bones, to be locked up. I wondered that it should have concluded at length that this was the best use it could put me to, and had never thought to avail itself of my services in some way. I saw that, if there was a wall of stone between me and my townsmen, there was still a more difficult one to climb or break through before they could get to be as free as I was. I did not for a moment feel confined, and the walls seemed a great waste of stone and mortar. I felt as if I alone of all my townsmen had paid my tax. They plainly did not know how to treat me, but behaved like persons who are underbred. In every threat and in every compliment there was a blunder; for they thought that my chief desire was to stand the other side of that stone wall. I could not but smile to see how industriously they locked the door on my meditations, which followed them out again without let or hindrance, and *they* were really all that was dangerous. As they could not reach me, they had resolved to punish my body; just as boys, if they cannot come at some person against whom they have a spite, will abuse his dog. I saw that the State was half-witted, that it was timid as a lone woman with her silver spoons, and that it did not know its friends

---

[4]Tax assessed against a person (not property); payment was frequently prerequisite for voting.

from its foes, and I lost all my remaining respect for it, and pitied it.

Thus the State never intentionally confronts a man's 27 sense, intellectual or moral, but only his body, his senses. It is not armed with superior wit or honesty, but with superior physical strength. I was not born to be forced. I will breathe after my own fashion. Let us see who is the strongest. What force has a multitude? They only can force me who obey a higher law than I. They force me to become like themselves. I do not hear of *men* being *forced* to live this way or that by masses of men. What sort of life were that to live? When I meet a government which says to me, "Your money or your life," why should I be in haste to give it my money? It may be in a great strait, and not know what to do: I cannot help that. It must help itself; do as I do. It is not worth the while to snivel about it. I am not responsible for the successful working of the machinery of society. I am not the son of the engineer. I perceive that, when an acorn and a chestnut fall side by side, the one does not remain inert to make way for the other, but both obey their own laws, and spring and grow and flourish as best they can, till one, perchance, overshadows and destroys the other. If a plant cannot live according to its nature, it dies; and so a man.

The night in prison was novel and interesting enough. 28 The prisoners in their shirt-sleeves were enjoying a chat and the evening air in the doorway, when I entered. But the jailer said, "Come, boys, it is time to lock up;" and so they dispersed, and I heard the sound of their steps returning into the hollow apartments. My room-mate was introduced to me by the jailer as "a first-rate fellow and a clever man." When the door was locked, he showed me where to hang my hat, and how he managed matters there. The rooms were whitewashed once a month; and this one, at least, was the whitest, most simply furnished, and probably the neatest apartment in the town. He naturally wanted to know where I came from, and what brought me there; and, when I had told him, I asked him in my turn how he came there, presuming him to be an honest man, of course; and, as the world goes, I believe he was. "Why," said he, "they accuse me of burning a barn; but I never did it." As near as I could discover, he had probably gone to bed in a barn when drunk, and smoked his pipe there; and so a barn was burnt. He had the reputation of being a clever man, had been there some three months waiting for his trial to come on, and would have to wait as much longer; but he was quite domesticated and contented, since he got his board for nothing, and thought that he was well treated.

29   He occupied one window, and I the other; and I saw that if one stayed there long, his principal business would be to look out the window. I had soon read all the tracts that were left there, and examined where former prisoners had broken out, and where a grate had been sawed off, and heard the history of the various occupants of that room; for I found that even here there was a history and a gossip which never circulated beyond the walls of the jail. Probably this is the only house in the town where verses are composed, which are afterward printed in a circular form, but not published. I was shown quite a long list of verses which were composed by some young men who had been detected in an attempt to escape, who avenged themselves by singing them.

30   I pumped my fellow-prisoner as dry as I could, for fear I should never see him again; but at length he showed me which was my bed, and left me to blow out the lamp.

31   It was like traveling into a far country, such as I had never expected to behold, to lie there for one night. It seemed to me that I never had heard the town-clock strike before, nor the evening sounds of the village; for we slept with the windows open, which were inside the grating. It was to see my native village in the light of the Middle Ages, and our Concord was turned into a Rhine stream, and visions of knights and castles passed before me. They were the voices of old burghers that I heard in the streets. I was an involuntary spectator and auditor of whatever was done and said in the kitchen of the adjacent village-inn, — a wholly new and rare experience to me. It was a closer view of my native town. I was fairly inside of it. I never had seen its institutions before. This is one of its peculiar institutions; for it is a shire town. I began to comprehend what its inhabitants were about.

32   In the morning, our breakfasts were put through the hole in the door, in small oblong-square tin pans, made to fit, and holding a pint of chocolate, with brown bread, and an iron spoon. When they called for the vessels again, I was green enough to return what bread I had left; but my comrade seized it, and said that I should lay that up for lunch or dinner. Soon after he was let out to work at haying in a

neighboring field, whither he went every day, and would not be back till noon; so he bade me good-day, saying that he doubted if he should see me again.

When I came out of prison, — for some one interfered, and 33 paid that tax, — I did not perceive that great changes had taken place on the common, such as he observed who went in a youth and emerged a tottering and gray-headed man; and yet a change had to my eyes come over the scene, — the town, and State, and country, — greater than any that mere time could effect. I saw yet more distinctly the State in which I lived. I saw to what extent the people among whom I lived could be trusted as good neighbors and friends; that their friendship was for summer weather only; that they did not greatly propose to do right; that they were a distinct race from me by their prejudices and superstitions, as the Chinamen and Malays are; that in their sacrifices to humanity they ran no risks, not even to their property; that after all they were not so noble but they treated the thief as he had treated them, and hoped, by a certain outward observance and a few prayers, and by walking in a particular straight though useless path from time to time, to save their souls. This may be to judge my neighbors harshly; for I believe that many of them are not aware that they have such an institution as the jail in their village.

It was formerly the custom in our village, when a poor 34 debtor came out of jail, for his aquaintances to salute him, looking through their fingers, which were crossed to represent the grating of a jail window, "How do ye do?" My neighbors did not thus salute me, but first looked at me, and then at one another, as if I had returned from a long journey. I was put into jail as I was going to the shoemaker's to get a shoe which was mended. When I was let out the next morning, I proceeded to finish my errand, and, having put on my mended shoe, joined a huckleberry party, who were impatient to put themselves under my conduct; and in half an hour, — for the horse was soon tackled, — was in the midst of a huckleberry field, on one of our highest hills, two miles off, and then the State was nowhere to be seen.

This is the whole history of "My Prisons."   35

I have never declined paying the highway tax, because I 36 am as desirous of being a good neighbor as I am of being a bad subject; and as for supporting schools, I am doing my part to educate my fellow-countrymen now. It is for no particular item in the tax-bill that I refuse to pay it. I simply wish to refuse allegiance to the State, to withdraw and stand aloof from it effectually. I do not care to trace the course of my dollar, if I could, till it buys a man or a musket to shoot one with, — the dollar is innocent, — but I am concerned to trace the effects of my allegiance. In fact, I quietly declare war with the State, after my fashion, though I will still make what use and get what advantage of her I can, as is usual in such cases.

37   If others pay the tax which is demanded of me, from a sympathy with the State, they do but what they have already done in their own case, or rather they abet injustice to a greater extent than the State requires. If they pay the tax from a mistaken interest in the individual taxed, to save his property, or prevent his going to jail, it is because they have not considered wisely how far they let their private feelings interfere with the public good.

38   This, then, is my position at present. But one cannot be too much on his guard in such a case, lest his action be biased by obstinacy or an undue regard for the opinions of men. Let him see that he does only what belongs to himself and to the hour.

39   I think sometimes, Why, this people mean well, they are only ignorant; they would do better if they knew how: why give your neighbors this pain to treat you as they are not inclined to? But I think again, This is no reason why I should do as they do, or permit others to suffer much greater pain of a different kind. Again, I sometimes say to myself, When many millions of men, without heat, without ill will, without personal feeling of any kind, demand of you a few shillings only, without the possibility, such is their constitution, of retracting or altering their present demand, and without the possibility, on your side, of appeal to any other millions, why expose yourself to this overwhelming brute force? You do not resist cold and hunger, the winds and the waves, thus obstinately; you quietly submit to a thousand similar necessities. You do not put your head into the fire. But just in proportion as I regard this as not wholly a brute force, but partly a human force, and consider that I have relations to those millions as to so many millions of men, and not of mere brute or inanimate things, I see that appeal is possible, first and instantaneously, from them to the Maker of them, and, secondly, from them to themselves. But if I put my head deliberately into the fire, there is no

appeal to fire or to the Maker of fire, and I have only myself
to blame. If I could convince myself that I have any right
to be satisfied with men as they are, and to treat them
accordingly, and not according, in some respects, to my
requisitions and expectations of what they and I ought to
be, then, like a good Mussulman and fatalist, I should endeavor to be satisfied with things as they are, and say it is
the will of God. And, above all, there is this difference between resisting this and a purely brute or natural force,
that I can resist this with some effect; but I cannot expect,
like Orpheus, to change the nature of the rocks and trees
and beasts.

I do not wish to quarrel with any man or nation. I do   40
not wish to split hairs, to make fine distinctions, or set
myself up as better than my neighbors. I seek rather, I may
say, even an excuse for conforming to the laws of the land.
I am but too ready to conform to them. Indeed, I have
reason to suspect myself on this head; and each year, as
the tax-gatherer comes round, I find myself disposed to
review the acts and position of the general and State governments, and the spirit of the people, to discover a pretext
for conformity.

"We must affect our country as our parents,
And if at any time we alienate
Our love or industry from doing it honor,
We must respect effects and teach the soul
Matter of conscience and religion,
And not desire of rule or benefit."

I believe that the State will soon be able to take all my
work of this sort out of my hands, and then I shall be no
better a patriot than my fellow-countrymen. Seen from a
lower point of view, the Constitution, with all its faults, is
very good; the law and the courts are very respectable;
even this State and this American government are, in many
respects, very admirable, and rare things, to be thankful
for, such as a great many have described them; but seen
from a point of view a little higher, they are what I have
described them; seen from a higher still, and the highest,
who shall say what they are, or that they are worth looking
at or thinking of at all?

However, the government does not concern me much,   41
and I shall bestow the fewest possible thoughts on it. It is

not many moments that I live under a government, even in this world. If a man is thought-free, fancy-free, imagination-free, that which *is not* never for a long time appearing *to be* to him, unwise rulers or reformers cannot fatally interrupt him.

42   I know that most men think differently from myself; but those whose lives are by profession devoted to the study of these or kindred subjects content me as little as any. Statesmen and legislators, standing so completely within the institution, never distinctly and nakedly behold it. They speak of moving society, but have no resting-place without it. They may be men of a certain experience and discrimination, and have no doubt invented ingenious and even useful systems, for which we sincerely thank them; but all their wit and usefulness lie within certain not very wide limits. They are wont to forget that the world is not governed by policy and expediency. Webster[5] never goes behind government, and so cannot speak with authority about it. His words are wisdom to those legislators who contemplate no essential reform in the existing government; but for thinkers, and those who legislate for all time, he never once glances at the subject. I know of those whose serene and wise speculations on this theme would soon reveal the limits of his mind's range and hospitality. Yet, compared with the cheap professions of most reformers, and the still cheaper wisdom and eloquence of politicians in general, his are almost the only sensible and valuable words, and we thank Heaven for him. Comparatively, he is always strong, original, and, above all, practical. Still, his quality is not wisdom, but prudence. The lawyer's truth is not Truth, but consistency or a consistent expediency. Truth is always in harmony with herself, and is not concerned chiefly to reveal the justice that may consist with wrongdoing. He well deserves to be called, as he has been called, the Defender of the Constitution. There are really no blows to be given by him but defensive ones. He is not a leader, but a follower. His leaders are the men of '87.[6] "I have never made an effort," he says, "and never propose to make an effort; I have never countenanced an effort, and never mean to countenance an effort, to disturb the arrangement as

---

[5] Daniel Webster (1782–1852), American political leader.
[6] That is, the delegates who created and signed the Constitution of the United States in 1787.

originally made, by which the various States came into the Union." Still thinking of the sanction which the Constitution gives to slavery, he says, "Because it was a part of the original compact, — let it stand." Notwithstanding his special acuteness and ability, he is unable to take a fact out of its merely political relations, and behold it as it lies absolutely to be disposed of by the intellect, — what, for instance, it behooves a man to do here in America to-day with regard to slavery, — but ventures, or is driven, to make some such desperate answer as the following, while professing to speak absolutely, and as a private man, — from which what new and singular code of social duties might be inferred? "The manner," says he, "in which the governments of those States where slavery exists are to regulate it is for their own consideration, under their responsibility to their constituents, to the general laws of propriety, humanity, and justice, and to God. Associations formed elsewhere, springing from a feeling of humanity, or any other cause, have nothing whatever to do with it. They have never received any encouragement from me, and they never will."

They who know of no purer sources of truth, who have   43
traced up its stream no higher, stand, and wisely stand, by the Bible and the Constitution, and drink at it there with reverence and humility; but they who behold where it comes trickling into this lake or that pool, gird up their loins once more, and continue their pilgrimage toward its fountain-head.

No man with a genius for legislation has appeared in   44
America. They are rare in the history of the world. There are orators, politicians, and eloquent men, by the thousand; but the speaker has not yet opened his mouth to speak who is capable of settling the much-vexed questions of the day. We love eloquence for its own sake, and not for any truth which it may utter, or any heroism it may inspire. Our legislators have not yet learned the comparative value of free-trade and of freedom, of union, and of rectitude, to a nation. They have no genius or talent for comparatively humble questions of taxation and finance, commerce and manufactures and agriculture. If we were left solely to the wordy wit of legislators in Congress for our guidance, uncorrected by the seasonable experience and the effectual complaints of the people, America would not long retain her rank among the nations. For eighteen hundred years, though perchance I have no right to say it, the New Testa-

ment has been written; yet where is the legislator who has wisdom and practical talent enough to avail himself of the light which it sheds on the science of legislation?

45   The authority of government, even such as I am willing to submit to,—for I will cheerfully obey those who know and can do better than I, and in many things even those who neither know nor can do so well,—is still an impure one; to be strictly just, it must have the sanction and consent of the governed. It can have no pure right over my person and property but what I concede to it. The progress from an absolute to a limited monarchy, from a limited monarchy to a democracy, is a progress toward a true respect for the individual. Even the Chinese philosopher was wise enough to regard the individual as the basis of the empire. Is a democracy, such as we know it, the last improvement possible in government? Is it not possible to take a step further towards recognizing and organizing the rights of man? There will never be a really free and enlightened State until the State comes to recognize the individual as a higher and independent power, from which all its own power and authority are derived, and treats him accordingly. I please myself with imagining a State at last which can afford to be just to all men, and to treat the individual with respect as a neighbor; which even would not think it inconsistent with its own repose if a few were to live aloof from it, not meddling with it, nor embraced by it, who fulfilled all the duties of neighbors and fellow-men. A State which bore this kind of fruit, and suffered it to drop off as fast as it ripened, would prepare the way for a still more perfect and glorious State, which also I have imagined, but not yet anywhere seen.

Public Statement by Eight Alabama Clergymen

Letter from Birmingham Jail

Born in Atlanta and educated at Morehouse College, Martin Luther King, Jr. (1929–1968), was the leader of the movement for civil rights for blacks during the 1960s. An ordained minister with a doctorate in theology from Boston University, he worked especially in the South and through nonviolent means to overturn segregation statutes, to increase the number of black voters, and to support other civil rights initiatives. Reverend King won the Nobel Peace Prize in 1964. All America mourned when he was assassinated in 1968.

On April 12, 1963, in order to have himself arrested on a symbolic day (Good Friday), Reverend King disobeyed a court injunction forbidding demonstrations in Birmingham, Alabama. That same day, eight leading white Birmingham clergymen (Christian and Jewish) published a letter in the Birmingham News *calling for the end of protests and exhorting protesters to work through the courts for the redress of their grievances. On the morning after his arrest, while held in solitary confinement, King began his response to these clergymen — his famous "Letter from Birmingham Jail." Begun in the margins of newspapers and on scraps of paper and finished by the following Tuesday, the letter was widely distributed and then became a central chapter in King's* Why We Can't Wait *(1964).*

Public Statement by Eight Alabama Clergymen

April 12, 1963

We the undersigned clergymen are among those who, in   1
January, issued "An Appeal for Law and Order and Common Sense," in dealing with racial problems in Alabama. We expressed understanding that honest convictions in racial matters could properly be pursued in the courts, but urged that decisions of those courts should in the meantime be peacefully obeyed.

2 Since that time there had been some evidence of increased forbearance and a willingness to face facts. Responsible citizens have undertaken to work on various problems which cause racial friction and unrest. In Birmingham, recent public events have given indication that we all have opportunity for a new constructive and realistic approach to racial problems.

3 However, we are now confronted by a series of demonstrations by some of our Negro citizens, directed and led in part by outsiders. We recognize the natural impatience of people who feel that their hopes are slow in being realized. But we are convinced that these demonstrations are unwise and untimely.

4 We agree rather with certain local Negro leadership which has called for honest and open negotiation of racial issues in our area. And we believe this kind of facing of issues can best be accomplished by citizens of our own metropolitan area, white and Negro, meeting with their knowledge and experience of the local situation. All of us need to face that responsibility and find proper channels for its accomplishment.

5 Just as we formerly pointed out that "hatred and violence have no sanction in our religious and political traditions," we also point out that such actions as incite to hatred and violence, however technically peaceful those actions may be, have not contributed to the resolution of our local problems. We do not believe that these days of new hope are days when extreme measures are justified in Birmingham.

6 We commend the community as a whole, and the local news media and law enforcement officials in particular, on the calm manner in which these demonstrations have been handled. We urge the public to continue to show restraint should the demonstrations continue, and the law enforcement officials to remain calm and continue to protect our city from violence.

7 We further strongly urge our own Negro community to withdraw support from these demonstrations, and to unite locally in working peacefully for a better Birmingham. When rights are consistently denied, a cause should be pressed in the courts and in negotiations among local leaders, and not in the streets. We appeal to both our white and Negro citizenry to observe the principles of law and order and common sense.

Signed by:

C. C. J. Carpenter, D.D., LL.D.,
Bishop of Alabama
Joseph A. Durick, D.D.,
Auxiliary Bishop, Diocese of Mobile, Birmingham
Rabbi Milton L. Grafman,
Temple Emanu-El, Birmingham, Alabama
Bishop Paul Hardin,
Bishop of the Alabama-West Florida Conference
of the Methodist Church
Bishop Nolan B. Harmon,
Bishop of the North Alabama Conference
of the Methodist Church
George M. Murray, D.D., LL.D.,
Bishop Coadjutor, Episcopal Diocese of Alabama
Edward V. Ramage,
Moderator, Synod of the Alabama Presbyterian Church
in the United States
Earl Stallings,
Pastor, First Baptist Church, Birmingham, Alabama

Letter from Birmingham Jail

April 16, 1963

My Dear Fellow Clergymen:

While confined here in the Birmingham city jail, I came 1
across your recent statement calling my present activities
"unwise and untimely." Seldom do I pause to answer criticism of my work and ideas. If I sought to answer all the
criticisms that cross my desk, my secretaries would have
little time for anything other than such correspondence in
the course of the day, and I would have no time for constructive work. But since I feel that you are men of genuine good
will and that your criticisms are sincerely set forth, I want
to try to answer your statement in what I hope will be
patient and reasonable terms.

I think I should indicate why I am here in Birmingham, 2
since you have been influenced by the view which argues
against "outsiders coming in." I have the honor of serving
as president of the Southern Christian Leadership Conference, an organization operating in every southern state,

with headquarters in Atlanta, Georgia. We have some eighty-five affiliated organizations across the South, and one of them is the Alabama Christian Movement for Human Rights. Frequently we share staff, educational and financial resources with our affiliates. Several months ago the affiliate here in Birmingham asked us to be on call to engage in a nonviolent direct-action program if such were deemed necessary. We readily consented, and when the hour came we lived up to our promise. So I, along with several members of my staff, am here because I was invited here. I am here because I have organizational ties here.

3   But more basically, I am in Birmingham because injustice is here. Just as the prophets of the eighth century B.C. left their villages and carried their "thus saith the Lord" far beyond the boundaries of their home towns, and just as the Apostle Paul left his village of Tarsus and carried the gospel of Jesus Christ to the far corners of the Greco-Roman world, so am I compelled to carry the gospel of freedom beyond my own home town. Like Paul, I must constantly respond to the Macedonian call for aid.

4   Moreover, I am cognizant of the interrelatedness of all communities and states. I cannot sit idly by in Atlanta and not be concerned about what happens in Birmingham. Injustice anywhere is a threat to justice everywhere. We are caught in an inescapable network of mutuality, tied in a single garment of destiny. Whatever affects one directly, affects all indirectly. Never again can we afford to live with the narrow, provincial "outside agitator" idea. Anyone who lives inside the United States can never be considered an outsider anywhere within its bounds.

5   You deplore the demonstrations taking place in Birmingham. But your statement, I am sorry to say, fails to express a similar concern for the conditions that brought about the demonstrations. I am sure that none of you would want to rest content with the superficial kind of social analysis that deals merely with effects and does not grapple with underlying causes. It is unfortunate that demonstrations are taking place in Birmingham, but it is even more unfortunate that the city's white power structure left the Negro community with no alternative.

6   In any nonviolent campaign there are four basic steps: collection of the facts to determine whether injustices exist; negotiation; self-purification; and direct action. We have gone through all these steps in Birmingham. There can be

no gainsaying the fact that racial injustice engulfs this community. Birmingham is probably the most thoroughly segregated city in the United States. Its ugly record of brutality is widely known. Negroes have experienced grossly unjust treatment in the courts. There have been more unsolved bombings of Negro homes and churches in Birmingham than in any other city in the nation. These are the hard, brutal facts of the case. On the basis of these conditions, Negro leaders sought to negotiate with the city fathers. But the latter consistently refused to engage in good-faith negotiation.

Then, last September, came the opportunity to talk with   7
leaders of Birmingham's economic community. In the course of the negotiations, certain promises were made by the merchants — for example, to remove the stores' humiliating racial signs. On the basis of these promises, the Reverend Fred Shuttlesworth and the leaders of the Alabama Christian Movement for Human Rights agreed to a moratorium on all demonstrations. As the weeks and months went by, we realized that we were the victims of a broken promise. A few signs, briefly removed, returned; the others remained.

As in so many past experiences, our hopes had been   8
blasted, and the shadow of deep disappointment settled upon us. We had no alternative except to prepare for direct action, whereby we would present our very bodies as a means of laying our case before the conscience of the local and the national community. Mindful of the difficulties involved, we decided to undertake a process of self-purification. We began a series of workshops on nonviolence, and we repeatedly asked ourselves: "Are you able to accept blows without retaliating?" "Are you able to endure the ordeal of jail?" We decided to schedule our direct-action program for the Easter season, realizing that except for Christmas, this is the main shopping period of the year. Knowing that a strong economic-withdrawal program would be the by-product of direct action, we felt that this would be the best time to bring pressure to bear on the merchants for the needed change.

Then it occurred to us that Birmingham's mayoral elec-   9
tion was coming up in March, and we speedily decided to postpone action until after election day. When we discovered that the Commissioner of Public Safety, Eugene "Bull" Connor, had piled up enough votes to be in the run-off, we decided again to postpone action until the day after the

run-off so that the demonstrations could not be used to cloud the issues. Like many others, we waited to see Mr. Connor defeated, and to this end we endured postponement after postponement. Having aided in this community need, we felt that our direct action program could be delayed no longer.

10   You may well ask: "Why direct action? Why sit-ins, marches and so forth? Isn't negotiation a better path?" You are quite right in calling for negotiation. Indeed, this is the very purpose of direct action. Nonviolent direct action seeks to create such a crisis and foster such a tension that a community which has constantly refused to negotiate is forced to confront the issue. It seeks so to dramatize the issue that it can no longer be ignored. My citing the creation of tension as part of the work of the nonviolent-resister may sound rather shocking. But I must confess that I am not afraid of the word "tension." I have earnestly opposed violent tension, but there is a type of constructive, nonviolent tension which is necessary for growth. Just as Socrates felt that it was necessary to create a tension in the mind so that individuals could rise from the bondage of myths and half-truths to the unfettered realm of creative analysis and objective appraisal, so must we see the need for nonviolent gadflies to create the kind of tension in society that will help men rise from the dark depths of prejudice and racism to the majestic heights of understanding and brotherhood.

11   The purpose of our direct-action program is to create a situation so crisis-packed that it will inevitably open the door to negotiation. I therefore concur with you in your call for negotiation. Too long has our beloved Southland been bogged down in a tragic effort to live in monologue rather than dialogue.

12   One of the basic points in your statement is that the action that I and my associates have taken in Birmingham is untimely. Some have asked: "Why didn't you give the new city administration time to act?" The only answer that I can give to this query is that the new Birmingham administration must be prodded about as much as the outgoing one, before it will act. We are sadly mistaken if we feel that the election of Albert Boutwell as mayor will bring the millennium to Birmingham. While Mr. Boutwell is a much more gentle person than Mr. Connor, they are both segregationists, dedicated to maintenance of the status quo. I

have hope that Mr. Boutwell will be reasonable enough to see the futility of massive resistance to desegregation. But he will not see this without pressure from devotees of civil rights. My friends, I must say to you that we have not made a single gain in civil rights without determined legal and nonviolent pressure. Lamentably, it is an historical fact that privileged groups seldom give up their privileges voluntarily. Individuals may see the moral light and voluntarily give up their unjust posture; but, as Reinhold Niebuhr has reminded us, groups tend to be more immoral than individuals.

We know through painful experience that freedom is 13 never voluntarily given by the oppressor; it must be demanded by the oppressed. Frankly, I have yet to engage in a direct-action campaign that was "well timed" in the view of those who have not suffered unduly from the disease of segregation. For years now I have heard the word "Wait!" It rings in the ear of every Negro with piercing familiarity. This "Wait" has almost always meant "Never." We must come to see, with one of our distinguished jurists, that "justice too long delayed is justice denied."

We have waited for more than 340 years for our constitu- 14 tional and God-given rights. The nations of Asia and Africa are moving with jetlike speed toward gaining political independence, but we still creep at horse-and-buggy pace toward gaining a cup of coffee at a lunch counter. Perhaps it is easy for those who have never felt the stinging darts of segregation to say, "Wait." But when you have seen vicious mobs lynch your mothers and fathers at will and drown your sisters and brothers at whim; when you have seen hate-filled policemen curse, kick and even kill your black brothers and sisters; when you see the vast majority of your twenty million Negro brothers smothering in an airtight cage of poverty in the midst of an affluent society; when you suddenly find your tongue twisted and your speech stammering as you seek to explain to your six-year-old daughter why she can't go to the public amusement park that has just been advertised on television, and see tears welling up in her eyes when she is told that Funtown is closed to colored children, and see ominous clouds of inferiority beginning to form in her little mental sky, and see her beginning to distort her personality by developing an unconscious bitterness toward white people; when you have to concoct an answer for a five-year-old son who is

asking: "Daddy, why do white people treat colored people
so mean?"; when you take a cross-country drive and find
it necessary to sleep night after night in the uncomfortable
corners of your automobile because no motel will accept
you; when you are humiliated day in and day out by nagging
signs reading "white" and "colored"; when your first name
becomes "nigger," your middle name becomes "boy" (however old you are) and your last name becomes "John," and
your wife and mother are never given the respected title
"Mrs."; when you are harried by day and haunted by night
by the fact that you are a Negro, living constantly at tiptoe
stance, never quite knowing what to expect next, and are
plagued with inner fears and outer resentments; when you
are forever fighting a degenerating sense of "nobodiness" —
then you will understand why we find it difficult to wait.
There comes a time when the cup of endurance runs over,
and men are no longer willing to be plunged into the abyss
of despair. I hope, sirs, you can understand our legitimate
and unavoidable impatience.

15   You express a great deal of anxiety over our willingness
to break laws. This is certainly a legitimate concern. Since
we so diligently urge people to obey the Supreme Court's
decision of 1954 outlawing segregation in the public schools,
at first glance it may seem rather paradoxical for us consciously to break laws. One may well ask: "How can you
advocate breaking some laws and obeying others?" The
answer lies in the fact that there are two types of laws: just
and unjust. I would be the first to advocate obeying just
laws. One has not only a legal but a moral responsibility
to obey just laws. Conversely, one has a moral responsibility
to disobey unjust laws. I would agree with St. Augustine
that "an unjust law is no law at all."

16   Now, what is the difference between the two? How does
one determine whether a law is just or unjust? A just law
is a man-made code that squares with the moral law or the
law of God. An unjust law is a code that is out of harmony
with the moral law. To put it in the terms of St. Thomas
Aquinas: An unjust law is a human law that is not rooted
in eternal law and natural law. Any law that uplifts human
personality is just. Any law that degrades human personality is unjust. All segregation statutes are unjust because
segregation distorts the soul and damages the personality.
It gives the segregator a false sense of superiority and the
segregated a false sense of inferiority. Segregation, to use

the terminology of the Jewish philosopher Martin Buber, substitutes an "I–it" relationship for an "I–thou" relationship and ends up relegating persons to the status of things. Hence segregation is not only politically, economically and sociologically unsound, it is morally wrong and sinful. Paul Tillich has said that sin is separation. Is not segregation an existential expression of man's tragic separation, his awful estrangement, his terrible sinfulness? Thus it is that I can urge men to obey the 1954 decision of the Supreme Court, for it is morally right; and I can urge them to disobey segregation ordinances, for they are morally wrong.

Let us consider a more concrete example of just and un- 17 just laws. An unjust law is a code that a numerical or power majority group compels a minority group to obey but does not make binding on itself. This is *difference* made legal. By the same token, a just law is a code that a majority compels a minority to follow and that it is willing to follow itself. This is *sameness* made legal.

Let me give another explanation. A law is unjust if it is 18 inflicted on a minority that, as a result of being denied the right to vote, had no part in enacting or devising the law. Who can say that the legislature of Alabama which set up that state's segregation laws was democratically elected? Throughout Alabama all sorts of devious methods are used to prevent Negroes from becoming registered voters, and there are some counties in which, even though Negroes constitute a majority of the population, not a single Negro is registered. Can any law enacted under such circumstances be considered democratically structured?

Sometimes a law is just on its face and unjust in its 19 application. For instance, I have been arrested on a charge of parading without a permit. Now, there is nothing wrong in having an ordinance which requires a permit for a parade. But such an ordinance becomes unjust when it is used to maintain segregation and to deny citizens the First-Amendment privilege of peaceful assembly and protest.

I hope you are able to see the distinction I am trying to 20 point out. In no sense do I advocate evading or defying the law, as would the rabid segregationist. That would lead to anarchy. One who breaks an unjust law must do so openly, lovingly, and with a willingness to accept the penalty. I submit that an individual who breaks a law that conscience tells him is unjust, and who willingly accepts the penalty of imprisonment in order to arouse the conscience of the community over its injustice, is in reality expressing the highest respect for law.

21   Of course, there is nothing new about this kind of civil disobedience. It was evidenced sublimely in the refusal of Shadrach, Meshach and Abednego to obey the laws of Nebuchadnezzar, on the ground that a higher moral law was at stake. It was practiced superbly by the early Christians, who were willing to face hungry lions and the excruciating pain of chopping blocks rather than submit to certain unjust laws of the Roman Empire. To a degree, academic freedom is a reality today because Socrates practiced civil disobedience. In our own nation, the Boston Tea Party represented a massive act of civil disobedience.

22   We should never forget that everything Adolf Hitler did in Germany was "legal" and everything the Hungarian freedom fighters did in Hungary was "illegal." It was "illegal" to aid and comfort a Jew in Hitler's Germany. Even so, I am sure that, had I lived in Germany at the time, I would have aided and comforted my Jewish brothers. If today I lived in a Communist country where certain principles dear to the Christian faith are suppressed, I would openly advocate disobeying that country's antireligious laws.

23   I must make two honest confessions to you, my Christian and Jewish brothers. First, I must confess that over the past few years I have been gravely disappointed with the white moderate. I have almost reached the regrettable conclusion that the Negro's great stumbling block in his stride toward freedom is not the White Citizen's Counciler or the Ku Klux Klanner, but the white moderate, who is more devoted to "order" than to justice; who prefers a negative peace which is the absence of tension to a positive peace which is the presence of justice; who constantly says: "I agree with you in the goal you seek, but I cannot agree with your methods of direct action"; who paternalistically believes he can set the timetable for another man's freedom; who lives by a mythical concept of time and who constantly advises the Negro to wait for a "more convenient season." Shallow understanding from people of good will is more frustrating than absolute misunderstanding from people of ill will. Lukewarm acceptance is much more bewildering than outright rejection.

24   I had hoped that the white moderate would understand that law and order exist for the purpose of establishing justice and that when they fail in this purpose they become

the dangerously structured dams that block the flow of social progress. I had hoped that the white moderate would understand that the present tension in the South is a necessary phase of the transition from an obnoxious negative peace, in which the Negro passively accepted his unjust plight, to a substantive and positive peace, in which all men will respect the dignity and worth of human personality. Actually, we who engage in nonviolent direct action are not the creators of tension. We merely bring to the surface the hidden tension that is already alive. We bring it out in the open, where it can be seen and dealt with. Like a boil that can never be cured so long as it is covered up but must be opened with all its ugliness to the natural medicines of air and light, injustice must be exposed, with all the tension its exposure creates, to the light of human conscience and the air of national opinion before it can be cured.

In your statement you assert that our actions, even though 25 peaceful, must be condemned because they precipitate violence. But is this a logical assertion? Isn't this like condemning a robbed man because his possession of money precipitated the evil act of robbery? Isn't this like condemning Socrates because his unswerving commitment to truth and his philosophical inquiries precipitated the act by the misguided populace in which they made him drink hemlock? Isn't this like condemning Jesus because his unique God-consciousness and never-ceasing devotion to God's will precipitated the evil act of crucifixion? We must come to see that, as the federal courts have consistently affirmed, it is wrong to urge an individual to cease his efforts to gain his basic constitutional rights because the quest may precipitate violence. Society must protect the robbed and punish the robber.

I had also hoped that the white moderate would reject 26 the myth concerning time in relation to the struggle for freedom. I have just received a letter from a white brother in Texas. He writes: "All Christians know that the colored people will receive equal rights eventually, but it is possible that you are in too great a religious hurry. It has taken Christianity almost two thousand years to accomplish what it has. The teachings of Christ take time to come to earth." Such an attitude stems from a tragic misconception of time, from the strangely irrational notion that there is something in the very flow of time that will inevitably cure all ills.

Actually, time itself is neutral; it can be used either destructively or constructively. More and more I feel that the people of ill will have used time much more effectively than have the people of good will. We will have to repent in this generation not merely for the hateful words and actions of the bad people but for the appalling silence of the good people. Human progress never rolls in on wheels of inevitability; it comes through the tireless efforts of men willing to be co-workers with God, and without this hard work, time itself becomes an ally of the forces of social stagnation. We must use time creatively, in the knowledge that time is always ripe to do right. Now is the time to make real the promise of democracy and transform our pending national elegy into a creative psalm of brotherhood. Now is the time to lift our national policy from the quicksand of racial injustice to the solid rock of human dignity.

27   You speak of our activity in Birmingham as extreme. At first I was rather disappointed that fellow clergymen would see my nonviolent efforts as those of an extremist. I began thinking about the fact that I stand in the middle of two opposing forces in the Negro community. One is a force of complacency, made up in part of Negroes who, as a result of long years of oppression, are so drained of self-respect and a sense of "somebodiness" that they have adjusted to segregation; and in part of a few middle-class Negroes who, because of a degree of academic and economic security and because in some ways they profit by segregation, have become insensitive to the problems of the masses. The other force is one of bitterness and hatred, and it comes perilously close to advocating violence. It is expressed in the various black nationalist groups that are springing up across the nation, the largest and best-known being Elijah Muhammad's Muslim movement. Nourished by the Negro's frustration over the continued existence of racial discrimination, this movement is made up of people who have lost faith in America, who have absolutely repudiated Christianity, and who have concluded that the white man is an incorrigible "devil."

28   I have tried to stand between these two forces, saying that we need emulate neither the "do-nothingism" of the complacent nor the hatred and despair of the black nationalist. For there is the more excellent way of love and nonviolent protest. I am grateful to God that, through the influence of the Negro church, the way of nonviolence became an integral part of our struggle.

If this philosophy had not emerged, by now many streets 29
of the South would, I am convinced, be flowing with blood.
And I am further convinced that if our white brothers dismiss as "rabble-rousers" and "outside agitators" those of
us who employ nonviolent direct action, and if they refuse
to support our nonviolent efforts, millions of Negroes will,
out of frustration and despair, seek solace and security in
black-nationalist ideologies — a development that would inevitably lead to a frightening racial nightmare.

Oppressed people cannot remain oppressed forever. The 30
yearning for freedom eventually manifests itself, and that
is what has happened to the American Negro. Something
within has reminded him of his birthright of freedom, and
something without has reminded him that it can be gained.
Consciously or unconsciously, he has been caught up by
the *Zeitgeist*, and with his black brothers of Africa and his
brown and yellow brothers of Asia, South America and the
Caribbean, the United States Negro is moving with a sense
of great urgency toward the promised land of racial justice.
If one recognizes this vital urge that has engulfed the Negro
community, one should readily understand why public
demonstrations are taking place. The Negro has many pent-
up resentments and latent frustrations, and he must release
them. So let him march; let him make prayer pilgrimages
to the city hall; let him go on freedom rides — and try to
understand why he must do so. If his repressed emotions
are not released in nonviolent ways, they will seek expression through violence; this is not a threat but a fact of
history. So I have not said to my people: "Get rid of your
discontent." Rather, I have tried to say that this normal
and healthy discontent can be channeled into the creative
outlet of nonviolent direct action. And now this approach
is being termed extremist.

But though I was initially disappointed at being 31
categorized as an extremist, as I continued to think about
the matter I gradually gained a measure of satisfaction
from the label. Was not Jesus an extremist for love: "Love
your enemies, bless them that curse you, do good to them
that hate you, and pray for them which despitefully use
you, and persecute you." Was not Amos an extremist for
justice: "Let justice roll down like waters and righteousness
like an ever-flowing stream." Was not Paul an extremist for
the Christian gospel: "I bear in my body the marks of the
Lord Jesus." Was not Martin Luther an extremist: "Here I
stand; I cannot do otherwise, so help me God." And John

Bunyan: "I will stay in jail to the end of my days before I make a butchery of my conscience." And Abraham Lincoln: "This nation cannot survive half slave and half free." And Thomas Jefferson: "We hold these truths to be self-evident, that all men are created equal . . ." So the question is not whether we will be extremists, but what kind of extremists we will be. Will we be extremists for hate or for love? Will we be extremists for the preservation of injustice or for the extension of justice? In that dramatic scene on Calvary's hill three men were crucified. We must never forget that all three were crucified for the same crime—the crime of extremism. Two were extremists for immorality, and thus fell below their environment. The other, Jesus Christ, was an extremist for love, truth and goodness, and thereby rose above his environment. Perhaps the South, the nation and the world are in dire need of creative extremists.

32   I had hoped that the white moderate would see this need. Perhaps I was too optimistic; perhaps I expected too much. I suppose I should have realized that few members of the oppressor race can understand the deep groans and passionate yearnings of the oppressed race, and still fewer have the vision to see that injustice must be rooted out by strong, persistent and determined action. I am thankful, however, that some of our white brothers in the South have grasped the meaning of this social revolution and committed themselves to it. They are still all too few in quantity, but they are big in quality. Some—such as Ralph McGill, Lillian Smith, Harry Golden, James McBride Dabbs, Ann Braden and Sarah Patton Boyle—have written about our struggle in eloquent and prophetic terms. Others have marched with us down nameless streets of the South. They have languished in filthy, roach-infested jails, suffering the abuse and brutality of policemen who view them as "dirty nigger-lovers." Unlike so many of their moderate brothers and sisters, they have recognized the urgency of the moment and sensed the need for powerful "action" antidotes to combat the disease of segregation.

33   Let me take note of my other major disappointment. I have been so greatly disappointed with the white church and its leadership. Of course, there are some notable exceptions. I am not unmindful of the fact that each of you has taken some significant stands on this issue. I commend you, Reverend Stallings, for your Christian stand on this past Sunday, in welcoming Negroes to your worship service on a nonsegregated basis. I commend the Catholic leaders of

this state for integrating Spring Hill College several years ago.

But despite these notable exceptions, I must honestly   34
reiterate that I have been disappointed with the church. I
do not say this as one of those negative critics who can
always find something wrong with the church. I say this
as a minister of the gospel, who loves the church; who was
nurtured in its bosom; who has been sustained by its
spiritual blessings and who will remain true to it as long
as the cord of life shall lengthen.

When I was suddenly catapulted into the leadership of   35
the bus protest in Montgomery, Alabama, a few years ago,
I felt we would be supported by the white church. I felt
that the white ministers, priests and rabbis of the South
would be among our strongest allies. Instead, some have
been outright opponents, refusing to understand the freedom movement and misrepresenting its leaders; all too
many others have been more cautious than courageous and
have remained silent behind the anesthetizing security of
stained-glass windows.

In spite of my shattered dreams, I came to Birmingham   36
with the hope that the white religious leadership of this
community would see the justice of our cause and, with
deep moral concern, would serve as the channel through
which our just grievances could reach the power structure.
I had hoped that each of you would understand. But again
I have been disappointed.

I have heard numerous southern religious leaders ad-   37
monish their worshipers to comply with a desegregation
decision because it is the law, but I have longed to hear
white ministers declare: "Follow this decree because integration is morally right and because the Negro is your
brother." In the midst of blatant injustices inflicted upon
the Negro, I have watched white churchmen stand on the
sideline and mouth pious irrelevancies and sanctimonious
trivialities. In the midst of a mighty struggle to rid our
nation of racial and economic injustice, I have heard many
ministers say: "Those are social issues, with which the gospel has no real concern." And I have watched many churches
commit themselves to a completely otherworldly religion
which makes a strange, un-Biblical distinction between
body and soul, between the sacred and the secular.

I have traveled the length and breadth of Alabama, Mis-   38
sissippi and all the other southern states. On sweltering
summer days and crisp autumn mornings I have looked at

the South's beautiful churches with their lofty spires pointing heavenward. I have beheld the impressive outlines of her massive religious-education buildings. Over and over I have found myself asking: "What kind of people worship here? Who is their God? Where were their voices when the lips of Governor Barnett dripped with words of interposition and nullification? Where were they when Governor Wallace gave a clarion call for defiance and hatred? Where were their voices of support when bruised and weary Negro men and women decided to rise from the dark dungeons of complacency to the bright hills of creative protest?"

39   Yes, these questions are still in my mind. In deep disappointment I have wept over the laxity of the church. But be assured that my tears have been tears of love. There can be no deep disappointment where there is not deep love. Yes, I love the church. How could I do otherwise? I am in the rather unique position of being the son, the grandson and the great-grandson of preachers. Yes, I see the church as the body of Christ. But, oh! How we have blemished and scarred that body through social neglect and through fear of being nonconformists.

40   There was a time when the church was very powerful—in the time when the early Christians rejoiced at being deemed worthy to suffer for what they believed. In those days the church was not merely a thermometer that recorded the ideas and principles of popular opinion; it was a thermostat that transformed the mores of society. Whenever the early Christians entered a town, the people in power became disturbed and immediately sought to convict the Christians for being "disturbers of the peace" and "outside agitators." But the Christians pressed on, in the conviction that they were "a colony of heaven," called to obey God rather than man. Small in number, they were big in commitment. They were too God-intoxicated to be "astronomically intimidated." By their effort and example they brought an end to such ancient evils as infanticide and gladiatorial contests.

41   Things are different now. So often the contemporary church is a weak, ineffectual voice with an uncertain sound. So often it is an arch-defender of the status quo. Far from being disturbed by the presence of the church, the power structure of the average community is consoled by the church's silent—and often even vocal—sanction of things as they are.

42   But the judgment of God is upon the church as never

before. If today's church does not recapture the sacrificial spirit of the early church, it will lose its authenticity, forfeit the loyalty of millions, and be dismissed as an irrelevant social club with no meaning for the twentieth century. Every day I meet young people whose disappointment with the church has turned into outright disgust.

Perhaps I have once again been too optimistic. Is organized religion too inextricably bound to the status quo to save our nation and the world? Perhaps I must turn my faith to the inner spiritual church, the church within the church, as the true *ekklesia* and the hope of the world. But again I am thankful to God that some noble souls from the ranks of organized religion have broken loose from the paralyzing chains of conformity and joined us as active partners in the struggle for freedom. They have left their secure congregations and walked the streets of Albany, Georgia, with us. They have gone down the highways of the South on tortuous rides for freedom. Yes, they have gone to jail with us. Some have been dismissed from their churches, have lost the support of their bishops and fellow ministers. But they have acted in the faith that right defeated is stronger than evil triumphant. Their witness has been the spiritual salt that has preserved the true meaning of the gospel in these troubled times. They have carved a tunnel of hope through the dark mountain of disappointment.

I hope the church as a whole will meet the challenge of this decisive hour. But even if the church does not come to the aid of justice, I have no despair about the future. I have no fear about the outcome of our struggle in Birmingham, even if our motives are at present misunderstood. We will reach the goal of freedom in Birmingham and all over the nation, because the goal of America is freedom. Abused and scorned though we may be, our destiny is tied up with America's destiny. Before the pilgrims landed at Plymouth, we were here. Before the pen of Jefferson etched the majestic words of the Declaration of Independence across the pages of history, we were here. For more than two centuries our forebears labored in this country without wages; they made cotton king; they built the homes of their masters while suffering gross injustice and shameful humiliation— and yet out of a bottomless vitality they continued to thrive and develop. If the inexpressible cruelties of slavery could not stop us, the opposition we now face will surely fail. We will win our freedom because the sacred heritage of our

nation and the eternal will of God are embodied in our echoing demands.

45   Before closing I feel impelled to mention one other point in your statement that has troubled me profoundly. You warmly commended the Birmingham police force for keeping "order" and "preventing violence." I doubt that you would have so warmly commended the police force if you had seen its dogs sinking their teeth into unarmed, nonviolent Negroes. I doubt that you would so quickly commend the policemen if you were to observe their ugly and inhumane treatment of Negroes here in the city jail; if you were to watch them push and curse old Negro women and young Negro girls; if you were to see them slap and kick old Negro men and young boys; if you were to observe them, as they did on two occasions, refuse to give us food because we wanted to sing our grace together. I cannot join you in your praise of the Birmingham Police Department.

46   It is true that the police have exercised a degree of discipline in handling the demonstrators. In this sense they have conducted themselves rather "nonviolently" in public. But for what purpose? To preserve the evil system of segregation. Over the past few years I have consistently preached that nonviolence demands that the means we use must be as pure as the ends we seek. I have tried to make clear that it is wrong to use immoral means to attain moral ends. But now I must affirm that it is just as wrong, or perhaps even more so, to use moral means to preserve immoral ends. Perhaps Mr. Connor and his policemen have been rather nonviolent in public, as was Chief Pritchett in Albany, Georgia, but they have used the moral means of nonviolence to maintain the immoral end of racial injustice. As T. S. Eliot has said: "The last temptation is the greatest treason: To do the right deed for the wrong reason."

47   I wish you had commended the Negro sit-inners and demonstrators of Birmingham for their sublime courage, their willingness to suffer and their amazing discipline in the midst of great provocation. One day the South will recognize its real heroes. They will be the James Merediths, with the noble sense of purpose that enables them to face jeering and hostile mobs, and with the agonizing loneliness that characterizes the life of the pioneer. They will be old, oppressed, battered Negro women, symbolized in a seventy-two-year-old woman in Montgomery, Alabama, who rose up with a sense of dignity and with her people decided not

to ride segregated buses, and who responded with ungrammatical profundity to one who inquired about her weariness: "My feets is tired, but my soul is at rest." They will be the young high school and college students, the young ministers of the gospel and a host of their elders, courageously and nonviolently sitting in at lunch counters and willingly going to jail for conscience sake. One day the South will know that when these disinherited children of God sat down at lunch counters, they were in reality standing up for what is best in the American dream and for the most sacred values in our Judaeo-Christian heritage, thereby bringing our nation back to those great wells of democracy which were dug deep by the founding fathers in their formulation of the Constitution and the Declaration of Independence.

Never before have I written so long a letter. I'm afraid 48 it is much too long to take your precious time. I can assure you that it would have been much shorter if I had been writing from a comfortable desk, but what else can one do when he is alone in a narrow jail cell, other than write long letters, think long thoughts and pray long prayers?

If I have said anything in this letter that overstates the 49 truth and indicates an unreasonable impatience, I beg you to forgive me. If I have said anything that understates the truth and indicates my having a patience that allows me to settle for anything less than brotherhood, I beg God to forgive me.

I hope this letter finds you strong in the faith. I also hope 50 that circumstances will soon make it possible for me to meet each of you, not as an integrationist or a civil-rights leader but as a fellow clergyman and a Christian brother. Let us all hope that the dark clouds of racial prejudice will soon pass away and the deep fog of misunderstanding will be lifted from our fear-drenched communities, and in some not too distant tomorrow the radiant stars of love and brotherhood will shine over our great nation with all their scintillating beauty.

Yours for the cause of Peace and Brotherhood,
Martin Luther King, Jr.

Lewis H. Van Dusen, Jr.
Civil Disobedience: Destroyer of Democracy

Lewis H. Van Dusen, Jr. (born 1910), has practiced law in Philadelphia since 1935. Decorated for valor during World War II, he also served with the State Department during his distinguished career. He has written many essays for professional journals; the following one appeared in 1969 in the American Bar Association Journal.

1   As Charles E. Wyzanski, Chief Judge of the United States District Court in Boston, wrote in the February, 1968, *Atlantic:* "Disobedience is a long step from dissent. Civil disobedience involves a deliberate and punishable breach of legal duty." Protesters might prefer a different definition. They would rather say that civil disobedience is the peaceful resistance of conscience.

2   The philosophy of civil disobedience was not developed in our American democracy, but in the very first democracy of Athens. It was expressed by the poet Sophocles and the philosopher Socrates. In Sophocles's tragedy, Antigone chose to obey her conscience and violate the state edict against providing burial for her brother, who had been decreed a traitor. When the dictator Creon found out that Antigone had buried her fallen brother, he confronted her and reminded her that there was a mandatory death penalty for this deliberate disobedience of the state law. Antigone nobly replied, "Nor did I think your orders were so strong that you, a mortal man, could overrun the gods' unwritten and unfailing laws."

3   Conscience motivated Antigone. She was not testing the validity of the law in the hope that eventually she would be sustained. Appealing to the judgment of the community, she explained her action to the chorus. She was not secret and surreptitious — the interment of her brother was open and public. She was not violent; she did not trespass on another citizen's rights. And finally, she accepted without resistance the death sentence — the penalty for violation. By voluntarily accepting the law's sanctions, she was not a revolutionary denying the authority of the state. Antig-

one's behavior exemplifies the classic case of civil disobedience.

Socrates believed that reason could dictate a conscientious disobedience of state law, but he also believed that he had to accept the legal sanctions of the state. In Plato's *Crito*, Socrates from his hanging basket accepted the death penalty for his teaching of religion to youths contrary to state laws.

The sage of Walden, Henry David Thoreau, took this philosophy of nonviolence and developed it into a strategy for solving society's injustices. First enunciating it in protest against the Mexican War, he then turned it to use against slavery. For refusing to pay taxes that would help pay the enforcers of the fugitive slave law, he went to prison. In Thoreau's words, "If the alternative is to keep all just men in prison or to give up slavery, the state will not hesitate which to choose."

Sixty years later, Gandhi took Thoreau's civil disobedience as his strategy to wrest Indian independence from England. The famous salt march against a British imperial tax is his best-known example of protest.

But the conscientious law breaking of Socrates, Gandhi and Thoreau is to be distinguished from the conscientious law testing of Martin Luther King, Jr., who was not a civil disobedient. The civil disobedient withholds taxes or violates state laws knowing he is legally wrong, but believing he is morally right. While he wrapped himself in the mantle of Gandhi and Thoreau, Dr. King led his followers in violation of state laws he believed were contrary to the Federal Constitution. But since Supreme Court decisions in the end generally upheld his many actions, he should not be considered a true civil disobedient.

The civil disobedience of Antigone is like that of the pacifist who withholds paying the percentage of his taxes that goes to the Defense Department, or the Quaker who travels against State Department regulations to Hanoi to distribute medical supplies, or the Vietnam war protester who tears up his draft card. This civil disobedient has been nonviolent in his defiance of the law; he has been unfurtive in his violation; he has been submissive to the penalties of the law. He has neither evaded the law nor interfered with another's rights. He has been neither a rioter nor a revolutionary. The thrust of his cause has not been the might of coercion but the martyrdom of conscience.

Was the Boston Tea Party Civil Disobedience?

9   Those who justify violence and radical action as being
in the tradition of our Revolution show a misunderstanding
of the philosophy of democracy.

10   James Farmer, former head of the Congress of Racial
Equality, in defense of the mass action confrontation
method, has told of a famous organized demonstration that
took place in opposition to political and economic discrimination. The protesters beat back and scattered the law
enforcers and then proceeded to loot and destroy private
property. Mr. Farmer then said he was talking about the
Boston Tea Party and implied that violence as a method
for redress of grievances was an American tradition and a
legacy of our revolutionary heritage. While it is true that
there is no more sacred document than our Declaration of
Independence, Jefferson's "inherent right of rebellion" was
predicated on the tyrannical denial of democratic means.
If there is no popular assembly to provide an adjustment
of ills, and if there is no court system to dispose of injustices,
then there is, indeed, a right to rebel.

11   The seventeenth century's John Locke, the philosophical
father of the Declaration of Independence, wrote in his *Second Treatise on Civil Government:* "Wherever law ends,
tyranny begins . . . and the people are absolved from any
further obedience. Governments are dissolved from within
when the legislative [chamber] is altered. When the government [becomes] . . . arbitrary disposers of lives, liberties
and fortunes of the people, such revolutions happen. . . ."

12   But there are some sophisticated proponents of the revolutionary redress of grievances who say that the test of the
need for radical action is not the unavailability of democratic institutions but the ineffectuality of those institutions
to remove blatant social inequalities. If social injustice
exists, they say, concerted disobedience is required against
the constituted government, whether it be totalitarian or
democratic in structure.

13   Of course, only the most bigoted chauvinist would claim
that America is without some glaring faults. But there has
never been a utopian society on earth and there never will
be unless human nature is remade. Since inequities will
mar even the best-framed democracies, the injustice
rationale would allow a free right of civil resistance to be

available always as a shortcut alternative to the democratic way of petition, debate and assembly. The lesson of history is that civil insurgency spawns far more injustices than it removes. The Jeffersons, Washingtons and Adamses resisted tyranny with the aim of promoting the procedures of democracy. They would never have resisted a democratic government with the risk of promoting the techniques of tyranny.

Legitimate Pressures and Illegitimate Results

There are many civil rights leaders who show impatience 14 with the process of democracy. They rely on the sit-ins, boycott or mass picketing to gain speedier solutions to the problems that face every citizen. But we must realize that the legitimate pressures that won concessions in the past can easily escalate into the illegitimate power plays that might extort demands in the future. The victories of these civil rights leaders must not shake our confidence in the democratic procedures, as the pressures of demonstration are desirable only if they take place within the limits allowed by law. Civil rights gains should continue to be won by the persuasion of Congress and other legislative bodies and by the decision of courts. Any illegal entreaty for the rights of some can be an injury to the rights of others, for mass demonstrations often trigger violence.

Those who advocate taking the law into their own hands 15 should reflect that when they are disobeying what they consider to be an immoral law, they are deciding on a possibly immoral course. Their answer is that the process for democratic relief is too slow, that only mass confrontation can bring immediate action, and that any injuries are the inevitable cost of the pursuit of justice. Their answer is, simply put, that the end justifies the means. It is this justification of any form of demonstration as a form of dissent that threatens to destroy a society built on the rule of law.

Our Bill of Rights guarantees wide opportunities to use 16 mass meetings, public parades and organized demonstrations to stimulate sentiment, to dramatize issues and to cause change. The Washington freedom march of 1963 was such a call for action. But the rights of free expression cannot be mere force cloaked in the garb of free speech. As the courts have decreed in labor cases, free assembly does not mean mass picketing or sit-down strikes. These rights are subject to limitations of time and place so as to secure the rights of others. When militant students storm a college president's office to achieve demands, when certain groups plan rush-hour car stalling to protest discrimination in employment, these are not dissent, but a denial of rights to others. Neither is it the lawful use of mass protest, but rather the unlawful use of mob power.

17   Justice Black, one of the foremost advocates and defenders of the right of protest and dissent, has said:

> . . . Experience demonstrates that it is not a far step from what to many seems to be the earnest, honest, patriotic, kind-spirited multitude of today, to the fanatical, threatening, lawless mob of tomorrow. And the crowds that press in the streets for noble goals today can be supplanted tomorrow by street mobs pressuring the courts for precisely opposite ends.[1]

18   Society must censure those demonstrators who would trespass on the public peace, as it must condemn those rioters whose pillage would destroy the public peace. But more ambivalent is society's posture toward the civil disobedient. Unlike the rioter, the true civil disobedient commits no violence. Unlike the mob demonstrator, he commits no trespass on others' rights. The civil disobedient, while deliberately violating a law, shows an oblique respect for the law by voluntarily submitting to its sanctions. He neither resists arrest nor evades punishment. Thus, he breaches the law but not the peace.

19   But civil disobedience, whatever the ethical rationalization, is still an assault on our democratic society, an affront to our legal order and an attack on our constitutional government. To indulge civil disobedience is to invite anarchy, and the permissive arbitrariness of anarchy is hardly less tolerable than the repressive arbitrariness of tyranny. Too often the license of liberty is followed by the loss of liberty, because into the desert of anarchy comes the man on horseback, a Mussolini or a Hitler.

[1] In *Cox v. Louisiana*, 379 U.S. 536, 575, 584 (1965).

Violations of Law Subvert Democracy

Law violations, even for ends recognized as laudable, are   20
not only assaults on the rule of law, but subversions of the
democratic process. The disobedient act of conscience does
not ennoble democracy; it erodes it.

First, it courts violence, and even the most careful and   21
limited use of nonviolent acts of disobedience may help
sow the dragon-teeth of civil riot. Civil disobedience is the
progenitor of disorder, and disorder is the sire of violence.

Second, the concept of civil disobedience does not invite   22
principles of general applicability. If the children of light
are morally privileged to resist particular laws on grounds
of conscience, so are the children of darkness. Former Deputy Attorney General Burke Marshall said: "If the decision
to break the law really turned on individual conscience, it
is hard to see in law how [the civil rights leader] is better
off than former Governor Ross Barnett of Mississippi who
also believed deeply in his cause and was willing to go to
jail."[2]

Third, even the most noble act of civil disobedience as-   23
saults the rule of law. Although limited as to method, motive
and objective, it has the effect of inducing others to engage
in different forms of law breaking characterized by methods
unsanctioned and condemned by classic theories of law
violation. Unfortunately, the most patent lesson of civil
disobedience is not so much nonviolence of action as defiance of authority.

Finally, the greatest danger in condoning civil disobedi-   24
ence as a permissible strategy for hastening change is that
it undermines our democratic processes. To adopt the techniques of civil disobedience is to assume that representative
government does not work. To resist the decisions of courts
and the laws of elected assemblies is to say that democracy
has failed.

There is no man who is above the law, and there is no   25
man who has a right to break the law. Civil disobedience
is not above the law, but against the law. When the civil
disobedient disobeys one law, he invariably subverts all

---

[2]"The Protest Movement and the Law," *Virginia Legal Review* 51 (1965),
785.

law. When the civil disobedient says that he is above the law, he is saying that democracy is beneath him. His disobedience shows a distrust for the democratic system. He is merely saying that since democracy does not work, why should he help make it work. Thoreau expressed well the civil disobedient's disdain for democracy:

> As for adopting the ways which the state has provided for remedying the evil, I know not of such ways. They take too much time and a man's life will be gone. I have other affairs to attend to. I came into this world not chiefly to make this a good place to live in, but to live in it, be it good or bad.[3]

26   Thoreau's position is not only morally irresponsible but politically reprehensible. When citizens in a democracy are called on to make a profession of faith, the civil disobedients offer only a confession of failure. Tragically, when civil disobedients for lack of faith abstain from democratic involvement, they help attain their own gloomy prediction. They help create the social and political basis for their own despair. By foreseeing failure, they help forge it. If citizens rely on antidemocratic means of protest, they will help bring about the undemocratic result of an authoritarian or anarchic state.

27   How far demonstrations properly can be employed to produce political and social change is a pressing question, particularly in view of the provocations accompanying the National Democratic Convention in Chicago last August and the reaction of the police to them. A line must be drawn by the judiciary between the demands of those who seek absolute order, which can lead only to a dictatorship, and those who seek absolute freedom, which can lead only to anarchy. The line, wherever it is drawn by our courts, should be respected on the college campus, on the streets and elsewhere.

28   Undue provocation will inevitably result in overreaction, human emotions being what they are. Violence will follow. This cycle undermines the very democracy it is designed to preserve. The lesson of the past is that democracies will fall if violence, including the intentional provocations that will lead to violence, replaces democratic procedures, as

---

[3] Thoreau, "Civil Disobedience" (see page 607).

in Athens, Rome and the Weimar Republic. This lesson
must be constantly explained by the legal profession.

We should heed the words of William James: 29

> Democracy is still upon its trial. The civic genius of our
> people is its only bulwark and . . . neither battleships nor
> public libraries nor great newspapers nor booming stocks:
> neither mechanical invention nor political adroitness, nor
> churches nor universities nor civil service examinations can
> save us from degeneration if the inner mystery be lost.
>
> That mystery, at once the secret and the glory of our Eng-
> lish-speaking race, consists of nothing but two habits . . .
> [O]ne of them is the habit of trained and disciplined good
> temper towards the opposite party when it fairly wins its
> innings. The other is that of fierce and merciless resentment
> toward every man or set of men who break the public peace.[4]

[4] James, *Pragmatism* (1907), pp. 127–28.

Woody Allen

A Brief, Yet Helpful, Guide
to Civil Disobedience

*Woody Allen (born 1935) has won many Oscars for his
movies* — Annie Hall; Play It Again, Sam; Bananas; *and* Han-
nah and Her Sisters *(to name a few). He has also contributed
comic essays to* The New Republic, *the* New Yorker, Playboy,
and other publications. After the following essay appeared in
The New York Times *in 1972, it was collected in his book*
Without Feathers.

In perpetrating a revolution, there are two requirements: 1
someone or something to revolt against and someone to
actually show up and do the revolting. Dress is usually
casual and both parties may be flexible about time and
place but if either faction fails to attend, the whole enter-

prise is likely to come off badly. In the Chinese Revolution of 1650 neither party showed up and the deposit on the hall was forfeited.

2   The people or parties revolted against are called the "oppressors" and are easily recognized as they seem to be the ones having all the fun. The "oppressors" generally get to wear suits, own land, and play their radios late at night without being yelled at. Their job is to maintain the "status quo," a condition where everything remains the same although they may be willing to paint every two years.

3   When the "oppressors" become too strict, we have what is known as a police state, wherein all dissent is forbidden, as is chuckling, showing up in a bow tie, or referring to the mayor as "Fats." Civil liberties are greatly curtailed in a police state, and freedom of speech is unheard of, although one is allowed to mime to a record. Opinions critical of the government are not tolerated, particularly about their dancing. Freedom of the press is also curtailed and the ruling party "manages" the news, permitting the citizens to hear only acceptable political ideas and ball scores that will not cause unrest.

4   The groups who revolt are called the "oppressed" and can generally be seen milling about and grumbling or claiming to have headaches. (It should be noted that the oppressors never revolt and attempt to become the oppressed as that would entail a change of underwear.)

5   Some famous examples of revolutions are:

The French Revolution, in which the peasants seized power by force and quickly changed all locks on the palace doors so the nobles could not get back in. Then they had a large party and gorged themselves. When the nobles finally recaptured the palace they were forced to clean up and found many stains and cigarette burns.

6   **The Russian Revolution,** which simmered for years and suddenly erupted when the serfs finally realized that the Czar and the Tsar were the same person.

7   It should be noted that after a revolution is over, the "oppressed" frequently take over and begin acting like the "oppressors." Of course by then it is very hard to get them on the phone and money lent for cigarettes and gum during the fighting may as well be forgotten about.

8   Methods of Civil Disobedience:

Hunger Strike. Here the oppressed goes without food until his demands are met. Insidious politicians will often leave biscuits within easy reach or perhaps some cheddar cheese, but they must be resisted. If the party in power can get the striker to eat, they usually have little trouble putting down the insurrection. If they can get him to eat and also lift the check, they have won for sure. In Pakistan, a hunger strike was broken when the government produced an exceptionally fine veal cordon bleu, which the masses found was too appealing to turn down, but such gourmet dishes are rare.

The problem with the hunger strike is that after several   9
days one can get quite hungry, particularly since sound trucks are paid to go through the streets saying, "Um . . . what nice chicken—umm . . . some peas . . . umm . . ."

A modified form of the Hunger Strike for those whose   10
political convictions are not quite so radical is giving up chives. This small gesture, when used properly, can greatly influence a government, and it is well known that Mahatma Gandhi's insistence on eating his salads untossed shamed the British government into many concessions. Other things besides food one can give up are: whist, smiling, and standing on one foot and imitating a crane.

Sit-down Strike. Proceed to a designated spot and then   11
sit down, but sit all the way down. Otherwise you are squatting, a position that makes no political point unless the government is also squatting. (This is rare, although a government will occasionally crouch in cold weather.) The trick is to remain seated until concessions are made, but as in the Hunger Strike, the government will try subtle means of making the striker rise. They may say, "Okay, everybody up, we're closing." Or, "Can you get up for a minute, we'd just like to see how tall you are?"

Demonstration and Marches. The key point about a dem-   12
onstration is that it must be seen. Hence the term "demonstration." If a person demonstrates privately in his own home, this is not technically a demonstration but merely "acting silly" or "behaving like an ass."

A fine example of a demonstration was the Boston Tea   13
Party, where outraged Americans disguised as Indians dumped British tea into the harbor. Later, Indians disguised as outraged Americans dumped actual British into the water. Following that, the British, disguised as tea, dumped each other into the harbor. Finally, German mercenaries clad only in costumes from *The Trojan Women* leapt into the harbor for no apparent reason.

14   When demonstrating, it is good to carry a placard stating
      one's position. Some suggested positions are: (1) lower
      taxes, (2) raise taxes, and (3) stop grinning at Persians.
15   Miscellaneous methods of Civil Disobedience:
      Standing in front of City Hall and chanting the word
      "pudding" until one's demands are met.
      Tying up traffic by leading a flock of sheep into the shop-
      ping area.
      Phoning members of "the establishment" and singing
      "Bess, You Is My Woman Now" into the phone.
      Dressing as a policeman and then skipping.
      Pretending to be an artichoke but punching people as
      they pass.

Mia Klein Anderson
The *Other* Beauty
of Martin Luther King, Jr.'s
"Letter from Birmingham Jail"

*Mia Klein Anderson teaches English at Bergen Community
College in New Jersey. Her analysis of King's "Letter" was
published in 1981 in* College Composition and Communication, *a professional journal read by college writing teachers.
Note well: The version of King's letter that Professor Anderson
cites is not exactly the same as the one printed earlier on pages
631–647 of this book.*

1   Martin Luther King, Jr.'s "Letter from Birmingham Jail"
      is a document of great beauty. The arguments King makes
      for an end to the racial nightmare and for a new era of
      brotherhood are powerful in their intellectual appeal; just
      as powerfully persuasive in its ethical appeal is King's care-
      fully established *persona* as a wise, educated, and moderate
      proponent of peaceful civil disobedience. In an essay ap-
      pearing in *The Quarterly Journal of Speech,* "The Public Let-
      ter as Rhetorical Form: Structure, Logic, and Style in
      King's 'Letter from Birmingham Jail,'" Richard Fulkerson
      has thoughtfully and effectively discussed King's craft in
      structuring his "Letter" and in using logic as a major means

of argument. Fulkerson, however, makes only a beginning at examining King's prose style for its extraordinary emotional appeal to readers. I suggest that King's persuasiveness in this "Letter" as well as in his other speeches and essays may be attributed not only to his structure, logic, and ethos, but even more to his creative, eloquent, and commanding use of the English language.

"Letter from Birmingham Jail" is anthologized in nearly   2
a dozen college texts, and a group of black ministers from across the country aims to have it made a new book in the Bible. That the "Letter" enjoys such broad appeal and, indeed, has already become an American classic must be accounted for in a way other than that it rationally and ethically convinces its readers. When we examine King's prose style, we find paragraphs that are highly developed: not counting, for the moment, one paragraph that is 331 words long and one that is 118 words long, the average number of words per paragraph is thirty-eight (or nine sentences). We find a vocabulary that is highly polysyllabic; of the substantive words in paragraphs one through ten, 59% contain more than one syllable. We find sentences that are highly complex: of the 325 sentences in the "Letter," only 38% are simple sentences. And we find some twenty-eight educated allusions—to Greek philosophers, to persons and events in Christian history, to modern-day Christian and Jewish philosophers, and to others. Despite this sophistication of style, I submit, King's prose exerts a strong attraction—it is magnetic; and it is this quality that primarily accounts for the "Letter's" appeal beyond the audience of eight Southern clergymen to whom it is ostensibly addressed, beyond them to the much broader audience of lay readers.

Specifically, King's tone is engaging because of its candor   3
and its lack of affectation; he appeals, if you will, to the life-wish rather than to the death-wish that would be implied in a tone characterized by defiance and aggression. King's prose schemes—that is, his structural devices—are rhythmical, appealing to the reader's emotions on a level he or she may be only vaguely aware of. And his tropes—his figures of speech—appeal not so importantly to the intellect as to the imagination. Life-affirming in its tone, rhythmical in its schemes, and, in its tropes, challenging to the imagination—these are the characteristics of King's prose that captivate and persuade.

King establishes his tone in the introductory paragraph.   4

660 *MIA KLEIN ANDERSON*

Patience and reasonableness, he promises, will be maintained, and they are — to a degree of consistency which, to
readers already committed to his philosophy, may be maddening. Always he patiently notes the exceptions to his
generalizations; always he balances criticism with commendation (33).* He patiently describes his critical perspective
(34). Patiently he provides helpful historical background
(6–9). Patiently he offers both theoretical explanations and
concrete examples (15–22). In his conclusion, King humbly
expresses concern that he has taken too much of his readers'
time by writing at such length, begs their forgiveness if he
has overstated the truth or has been unduly impatient, begs
God's forgiveness if he has understated the truth or has
been unduly patient, and shares his vision of brotherhood.
Never, it should noted, does King sound coy or appear to
be using his patience and reasonableness as a manipulative
device; he manages to maintain that perfect balance between a commanding and authoritative argument on the
one hand and a humble and helpful tone on the other.

5   Fulkerson has demonstrated how carefully King, in establishing an identification with his audience and a conciliat-
ory tone, has moved among the personal pronouns *I, you,*
and *we.* But I think a somewhat different emphasis is important here. Many of the 139 "I" clauses in the "Letter" tell
of King's willingness to give, to act, to believe: "I would
like to answer," "I have earnestly worked and preached,"
"I am trying," "I continued to think," "I have watched," "I
have travelled," "I have looked," "I can assure," and "I hope"
are examples. Similarly, a perusal of King's topic sentences
reveals the same kind of willingness to consider, to be helpful, to dream of a better time. He writes, "I think I should
give the reason," "Let us turn to a more concrete example,"
"Let me give another explanation," "I hope you can see the
distinction I am trying to point out," "But as I continued
to think about the matter," and "I hope the Church as a
whole will meet the challenge." King's frequent use of allusions implies that he and his readers share a common heritage (Christianity, as detailed in the Bible) and that they
share a common knowledge (the knowledge of history and
philosophy). These characteristics of King's tone contribute
to an irresistible call for harmony — irresistible because pro-

*Where not otherwise noted, paragraph numbers will be provided in
parentheses.

duced justly, reasonably, and sincerely—the harmony that is unity of spirit and purpose among writer and readers.

Two powerful instances of understatement (litotes) help 6 establish King's lack of belligerence, his direct but unaggressive tone. In Paragraph 45, King graphically describes five instances of violence perpetrated by the Birmingham police against the Black community. He ends the paragraph by saying starkly, "I'm sorry that I can't join you in your praise for the police department." In Paragraph 14, he offers ten vivid illustrations of the "stinging darts of segregation," piling on detail after detail in a manner that suggests the list could go on endlessly. Then he closes the paragraph with this simple, direct statement: "I hope, sirs, you can understand our legitimate and unavoidable impatience." The restraint from attack is awesome.

Besides the emotionally appealing candor and unpreten- 7 tiousness of his tone, there is a second important element of King's prose style—the music of his schemes. King employs many structural devices, each of which produces an engaging beat or rhythm. Most notable are his use of balance in instances of parallelism and antithesis and his use of repetition in instances of anaphora, alliteration, and assonance.

King puts into parallel structure a wide variety of gram- 8 matical and syntactical units. He parallels nouns—here, four "-tion" nouns, with ascending and then descending numbers of syllables: "collection . . . negotiation . . . self-purification . . . direct action" (6). He parallels adverbs—here, four "-ally" adverbs, with ascending/descending syllable counts: "So segregation is not only politically, economically, and sociologically unsound, but it is morally wrong and sinful" (16). He parallels adjectives: "These are the hard, brutal, and unbelievable facts" (6). Verbs: "policemen curse, kick, brutalize, and even kill . . ." (14). Adjective/noun pairs—here, of equal numbers of syllables: "pent-up resentments and latent frustrations" (30). Clauses: "Some . . . have written . . . Others have marched . . . They have languished . . . They . . . have recognized . . . (32).

King's use of antithesis—notable because his juxtaposi- 9 tion of contrasting ideas is most often both of wording and of sense, and because he most often renders antithetical ideas in parallel structure—adds still more to the pleasing rhythm, however unconsciously the ear hears it. Many of King's antithetical expressions move from concepts of depth or darkness to concepts of height or light. Fulkerson rightly notes the archetypal appeal of these expressions, but he stops short of pointing to the rhythm that results from such constructions. For example:

> ... that will help men rise from the dark depths of prejudice to the majestic heights of understanding and brotherhood. (10)

> ... freedom is never voluntarily given by the oppressor; it must be demanded by the oppressed. (13)

> Any law that uplifts human personality is just. Any law that degrades human personality is unjust. (16)

> So I can urge men to obey the 1954 decision of the Supreme Court because it is morally right, and I can urge them to disobey segregation ordinances because they are morally wrong. (15)

> Shallow understanding from people of good will is more frustrating than absolute misunderstanding from people of ill will. (23)

> ... the transition from an obnoxious negative peace ... to a substance-filled positive peace ... (24)

> Now is the time to ... transform our pending national elegy into a creative psalm of brotherhood. (26)

> Where were their voices of support when tired, bruised, and weary Negro men and women decided to rise from the dark dungeons of complacency to the bright hills of creative protest? (38)

There are more than thirty such eminently quotable — because so strikingly rhythmic — instances of antithesis in the "Letter."

10   Contributing also to the music of King's prose is repetition. Instances of anaphora (repetition of the same word or group of words at the beginnings of successive clauses), for example, occur in the "Letter" more than a dozen times, often, as with other structural devices, in parallel units. Consider this series of anaphoristic clauses from Paragraph 23:

> ... the white moderate who is more devoted ...; who prefers ... ; who constantly says ... ; who paternalistically feels ... ; who lives ... and who constantly advises. ...

Or this series of interrogative sentences from Paragraph 25:

> Isn't this like condemning the robbed man because ... ?
> Isn't this like condemning Socrates because ... ? Isn't this
> like condemning Jesus because ... ?

Again in Paragraph 31 we find repetition at the openings
of successive rhetorical questions:

> Was not Jesus an extremist ... ? Was not Amos an extrem-
> ist ... ? Was not Paul an extremist ... ? Was not Martin
> Luther an extremist ... ? Was not John Bunyan an extrem-
> ist ... ? Was not Abraham Lincoln an extremist ... ? Was
> not Thomas Jefferson an extremist ... ?

Spanning Paragraphs 34 through 38, we find successive
clauses beginning, "I have ... ":

> I have been disappointed ... I have heard ... but I have
> longed to hear ... I have watched ... I have heard ... and
> I have watched ... I have travelled ... I have looked ...
> I have beheld ... I have found myself asking ... I have
> wept ...

Once such a rhythm is set in motion, the reader becomes
engaged — unconsciously engaged in awaiting the next beat
or refrain.

King makes music as well through alliteration, asso- 11
nance, and other sound combinations. Particularly alliteration. For example, the repeated d's, s's, and p's in "the
shadow of a deep disappointment settled upon us" (8) are
subtly pleasing to the ear, as are the b's in "So I am here
... because we were invited here. I am here because I have
basic organizational ties here. Beyond this, I am in Birmingham because injustice is here" (2–3). In this sentence, the
hard c's stand out: "Nonviolent direct action seeks to create
such a crisis and establish such creative tension that a community that has constantly refused to negotiate is forced
to confront the issue" (10). The following passage features
many s's and many vowel matches, but, even more importantly, it features a rapid fire of the "explosive" consonants,
d, t, p, k, and b: "When you suddenly find your tongue twisted
and your speech stammering as you seek to explain to your
six-year-old daughter why she can't go to the public amusement park that has just been advertised on television ..."

(14). The repeated explosive consonants, besides being musical, reflect the sharp-edged frustration that charges the speaker and thus add to the immediacy of the image.

12   Alliteration and assonance appear interwoven in such passages as these:

"... the South would be flowing with floods of blood" (29)

and " ... I have watched white churches stand on the sideline and merely mouth pious irrelevancies and sanctimonious trivialities" (37).

13   Others of the schemes may also be readily found in King's prose — more often than not, as we have already seen, simultaneously — and all combine to please the outer or inner ear. Polysyndeton is found in these passages:

> ... when you suddenly find your tongue twisted and your speech stammering as you seek to explain to your six-year-old daughter why she can't go to the public amusement park that has just been advertised on television, and see tears welling up in her little eyes when she is told that Funtown is closed to colored children, and see the depressing clouds of inferiority begin to form in her little mental sky, and see her begin to distort her little personality by unconsciously developing a bitterness toward white people ... (14)

> ... when your first name becomes "nigger" and your middle name becomes "boy" (however old you are) and your last name becomes "John," and when your wife and mother are never given the respected title "Mrs." ... (14) [emphasis in both passages is added]

Anastrophe is found:

> Seldom, if ever, do I pause ... (1)

> Never again can we afford ... (4)

> Then came the opportunity ... (6)

> Too long has our beloved Southland been bogged down ... (11)

Polyptoton is found:

> ... privileged groups seldom give up their privileges voluntarily. (12)

> Society must protect the robbed and punish the robber. (25)
>
> . . . write long letters, think strange thoughts, and pray long prayers? (48)

We must not underestimate the power of these devices to captivate readers. Granted, "Letter from Birmingham Jail" becomes more and more memorable each time it is "heard." Students relate easily to this concept, by the way, when I refer them to their experience with a new, good song. The point is that the "Letter's" musical arrangement of sounds plays a large part in its impact on readers.

Turning now to consider the role played by King's tropes   14 in broadening the appeal of the "Letter," I wish to emphasize that while his similes and metaphors certainly do engage the intellect, more importantly they engage the imagination and emotion. His similes and metaphors become the (serious) playthings of the imagination, and the play of the imagination has the effect on the emotions of readying the reader, making him or her more accepting and sympathetic toward the intellectual content of the figures of speech. I referred earlier to Fulkerson's correctly identifying the archetypal depth/height and dark/light element which pervades the tropes, but I would like to carry this observation a step further. Of the more than sixty readily noted similes and metaphors, almost four times as many come from the *organic* world — having to do with the body, with the sky and weather, and with the earth (topographical, as well as relating to water, plants, etc.) — as come from the world of *manufacture* or *technology*, though these, too, relate man to his largely familiar world.

Of King's two significant similes, one is "organic," and   15 one is not:

> Like a boil that can never be cured as long as it is covered up but must be opened with all its pus-flowing ugliness to the natural medicines of air and light, injustice must likewise be exposed, with all of the tension its exposing creates, to the light of human conscience and the air of national opinion before it can be cured. (24)
>
> So here we are moving toward the exit of the twentieth century with a religious community largely adjusted to the status quo, standing as a tail light behind other community agencies rather than a headlight leading men to higher levels of justice. (35)

King's organic metaphors of the body move back and forth between sickness and health:

> ... Suffered unduly from the disease of segregation. (13)

> ... plagued with inner fears and outer resentments ... (14)

> ... the need for powerful "action" antidotes to combat the disease of segregation. (32)

> ... the anesthetizing security of stained glass windows. (35)

> How we have blemished and scarred that body [the Church as the body of Christ] through social neglect and fear of being nonconformist. (39)

His organic metaphors of the sky and weather are seen in these instances:

> ... the dark shadow of a deep disappointment settled upon us. (8)

> ... so that the demonstrations could not be used to cloud the issues. (9)

His organic metaphors relating to the earth are seen here:

> These men have been the leaven in the lump of the race. Their witness has been the spiritual salt that has preserved the true meaning of the gospel in these troubled times. They have carved a tunnel of hope through the dark mountain of disappointment. (43)

> ... thus carrying our whole nation back to great wells of democracy which were dug deep by the founding fathers in the formulation of the Constitution and the Declaration of Independence. (47)

Most of the metaphors drawing from the world of manufacture and technology are quite uncomplicated:

> We are caught in an inescapable network of mutuality tied in a single garment of destiny. (4)

> ... the stinging darts of segregation ... (14)

> ... smothering in an air-tight cage of poverty ... (14)

> ... the cup of endurance runs over ... (14)

> We must come to see that human progress never rolls in on wheels of inevitability. (26)

> ... the paralyzing chains of conformity ... (43)

Two very memorable metaphors are decidedly technological (or scientific) but still are familiar:

> [The word "Wait!"] has been a tranquilizing thalidomide, relieving the emotional stress for the moment, only to give birth to an ill-formed infant of frustration. (11)

> In those days the Church was not merely a thermometer that recorded the ideas and principles of popular opinion; it was a thermostat that transformed the mores of society. (40)

Readers will want to make use of their dictionaries (for intellectual exercise) or apply their experience (gaining a more imaginative and emotional relationship to the matter of the trope) to appreciate precisely the difference between a thermometer and a thermostat, and then they will appreciate the distinction King is making between the Church of old and the Church of the 50's and 60's. They will want to make use of their reference books or apply their experience to explain the uses to which leaven and salt are put in cooking. They will want to explore why "air-tight cage" is uniquely appropriate for describing poverty, why despair can so aptly be said to "corrode," and why "stinging darts" so fittingly describes segregation. On the latter, my students surprised me with the subtlety of their insight: darts, they suggested, are purposely thrown, either as a weapon or for pleasure (sport); they enter quickly, penetrate deeply, and cause wounds more painful and slower to heal than surface wounds. My students' squirming and their facial expressions revealed that not only their minds but also their imaginations were fully engaged. Tropes of this caliber are exciting. 16

John Frederick Nims (in *Western Wind: An Introduction to Poetry*) tells the following story to illustrate the fact that "there are times when rhythm has a stronger hold on us than our most sacred concerns": 17

> A few years ago thousands of young people met in the gymnasium at Cornell to show their concern over vital issues of the day. But as time went on they became listless. Some

started throwing Frisbees, some fell asleep in each other's arms. Then a young Irishman took the platform to plead for contributions: "Spontaneously, without any musical backing," the *New York Times* account goes, "he sang an Irish rebel ballad. The words mattered little but the rhythm caught them. The youths rose and danced. They snakedanced in congas. They did jigs. It went on that way until early morning and it picked up again at noon. 'It's pretty bad,' said an editor of the *Cornell Daily Sun*. 'What does this have to do with politics or peace or any real issue?'"

Perhaps you have discussed with your students Alexander Solzhenitsyn's *One Day in the Life of Ivan Denisovich* and have seen how they are infinitely more repelled by the evils of that social system for having lived—via the imagination—through a day as one of its victims than they would have been had they read a factual document confronting them with essentially the same details. Rhythm and imagination, acting as they do on the emotion, are the key. Martin Luther King, Jr., knew that his effectiveness in reaching his wider audience would come both from what he said and from how he said it. The words can reach the mind, but the music and imagination can reach the heart and soul.

Mark Gardner
Appealing to White Moderates

Mark Gardner (born 1970), raised on a farm near Muncy, Pennsylvania, is studying agricultural engineering at Penn State; he plans to take over the family farm eventually or to pursue an engineering career. Gardner published this analysis of King's "Letter" in the 1989 Penn Statements, *a magazine of student writing produced for composition students at Penn State.*

1   On April 12, 1963, the Reverend Martin Luther King, Jr., was arrested in Birmingham, Alabama, for disobeying a court injunction against demonstrations. That same day,

eight white Birmingham clergymen—a Catholic priest, a Jewish rabbi, and five prominent Protestants—published a public letter in the *Birmingham News* that asked King and his fellow protesters to leave off their demonstrations and to pursue their grievances through established channels. That public letter was the occasion for King's famous response, his "Letter from Birmingham Jail." King's letter, therefore, is structured and addressed as a refutation to the eight clergymen. But because these clergymen represented a range of different faiths, King through them also had a chance to address a broader audience—the moderate white Catholics, Jews, and Protestants represented by these eight clergymen—especially when his letter was published in his 1964 book *Why We Can't Wait*.

Suppose that we are the white moderates who were living 2 in 1963 or 1964 and have just read "Letter from Birmingham Jail." After reading King's letter, we would probably now be very inclined to actively support his cause. But, why, after reading just fifteen pages written by a black man in jail, would we become so willing to become civil rights advocates? How did he manage to enliven our passive attitudes that have prevailed for decades? The answer is that King, by masterfully relating all three of the rhetorical appeals to us, his audience, successfully solicited our active support because he improved our image of him, logically proved his points to us, and skillfully appealed to our religious, moral, and patriotic beliefs.

King appreciated our social status and our code of ethics. 3 Knowing that we are lower- and middle-class people, King realized that we are moderately educated (most of us having a high school diploma) and know the history of his movement. He understood that we are simple, patriotic, God-fearing people with firm moral standards. King was also aware of our attitudes. He defined us as people who are "more devoted to 'order' than to justice" (paragraph 23). We agree with his views and see the need for change but do nothing to facilitate that change. Feeling that time is a "cure-all," we believe that justice will prevail through the passage of time. Although many of us do not like this description of us, through self-evaluation we must agree with him and are not offended.

King had to change our attitudes in order to achieve his 4 purpose of making us want to become actively involved in his movement. He needed vocal, active support, not silent, complacent agreement. But how did he make us, through words, want to become involved? To do this King launched a three-pronged attack of ethos, logos, and pathos.

5   The first step he took was to improve our image of him. King knew that because he was a black man in jail few of us would be willing to listen to him, let alone support him. So he established his credibility quite early in the letter. "My Dear Fellow Clergymen," he begins. Immediately, we realize that he is a man of God, someone with a high moral code. Also, he humbly states that he is the president of the Southern Christian Leadership Conference. This shows us that he is a leader. Other people trust his guidance, so why can't we? Finally, he explains that he is in Birmingham because he feels that it is "the most thoroughly segregated city in the United States" (paragraph 6). He feels that the need for reform is greatest here. We are led to understand that he is a man of logic, not whim or excessive passion. After the first few opening paragraphs, King has raised our image of him to the point that we believe we can trust what he says.

6   With this established worthiness, King can now begin logically to state his case to an attentive audience. He explains the four steps that his people took in determining the need for nonviolent campaigning. He gives reasons why they had to demonstrate immediately, and by philosophical deduction, King proves that segregation is an unjust, immoral law. But we are not the type of people to be quickly aroused by complicated philosophical deduction, you say. Correct! So, realizing this, King included a series of simple examples and analogies, just for us. He compares the surfacing tensions that have been exposed by the demonstrations to a boil. In order for the tensions to heal they must be exposed "to the light of human conscience and the air of national opinion" (paragraph 24). He proves that legal and moral do not always coincide by citing Hitler's Germany as an example. There it was legally, but not morally, right to persecute and kill Jews. By comparing the blacks to robbed men, to Socrates, and to Jesus, he refutes the accusation that their peaceful demonstrations were a direct cause of violence. Analogies such as these simplify King's complex deductions so that we can understand them easily.

7   This logical appeal has brought us into a complete agreement with King's points, but still only a few of us would be moved to action. But we haven't yet considered the strongest appeal that King used for us.

Emotionally, King causes us to develop a deep sense of   8
guilt and sympathy for blacks and their cause. Those of us
who are devout religious people are drawn to King's conclusions by a series of holy comparisons. He says that he is
"compelled to carry the gospel of freedom beyond my particular home town" (paragraph 3), just like the eighth-cen-
tury prophets and the apostle Paul. In paragraph twenty-
one the example of Shadrach, Meshach, and Abednego
peacefully disobeying the laws of Nebuchadnezzar helps
King to prove to us that civil disobedience is not a new and
immoral development. Admitting that he is an extremist,
King nobly compares himself to Jesus Christ. Christ "was
an extremist for love, truth and goodness" (paragraph 31),
but he was still persecuted and crucified for his beliefs.
King causes us to ask ourselves if we are going to let this
happen to his honorable movement for justice and freedom.

King also plays on our moral beliefs. In paragraph four-   9
teen King tells about the tears and "clouds of inferiority"
that his daughter forms when she is told that the public
amusement park is closed to black children. Do we want
to become guilty of the bitterness that is forming in this
dear, innocent child's mind? King explains how they must
sleep uncomfortably in their cars when they go on trips
because no motel will accept them. But as we are reading
this letter we might remember how wonderful and peaceful
our last vacation was. We wonder why we should be any
better than they. He also describes how vicious mobs and
policemen curse, beat, drown, and even lynch black people
at will without punishment. We can't understand how we
let these innocent human beings be treated so badly. He
makes us feel what it is like to be a black in a land full of
unfair prejudice.

To complete his emotional appeal King employs a group   10
of flag-waving techniques. He points out that segregation
is a violation of many of the convictions that Americans
take pride in. Segregation is smothering blacks "in an air-
tight cage of poverty" (paragraph 14) and is depriving them
of their freedom that is their birthright as an American
citizen. "We will reach the goal of freedom in Birmingham
and all over the nation, because the goal of America is freedom" (paragraph 44), says King. The ideals of freedom, justice, and equality are what this nation was founded on. King
reminds us of our duty to uphold these beliefs and to support
his movement. If we don't, then we will be guilty of not being
the true, patriotic Americans that we all want to be.

11   With these three appeals aimed directly at us, King made us want to help him in his "cause of Peace and Brotherhood" (paragraph 50). We logically realize that it is our moral duty to help blacks in their quest for the "promised land of racial justice" (paragraph 30). We want to be, as King strategically put it, the "real heroes" (paragraph 47) of the future.

AFFIRMATIVE ACTION

Affirmative Action: Cure or Contradiction?

In 1987, Center *magazine published the following "dialogue" on the issue of affirmative action. The participants include Gayle Binion, a professor of political science at the University of California, Santa Barbara; Virna Canson, from the National Association for the Advancement of Colored People; Joseph Duff, a lawyer from Los Angeles; Edward Erler, professor of political science at San Bernardino State University (California); Shirley Kennedy, who teaches in the Black Studies Department at the University of California, Santa Barbara; Sojourner Kincaid, who directs a rental housing mediation task force in Santa Barbara; Donald McDonald, formerly the director of the Center for the Study of Democratic Institutions; Clarence Thomas, chairman of the Equal Employment Opportunity Commission in Washington; and Anne Wortham, a scholar.*

1   CLARENCE THOMAS: Is the ideal of a fair society where there is equality of opportunity being vitiated by so-called progressive policies? Are there unintended consequences resulting from these policies?

2   I believe that our civil-rights policies should be based on fundamental American principles and on the assumption that Americans are basically decent and that they prize fairness. Unfortunately, much of what passes for civil-rights policies flies in the face of this common sense.

3   Martin Luther King was at his best when he emphasized

that the Civil Rights Movement would succeed only if it used the strengths of the American society, if it brought out what was good about America. To denounce America as corrupt, sick, or wicked was to cast away the greatest resource of the Civil Rights Movement — that is, the innate justice of the Constitution and the fundamental decency of the American people.

In his June 6, 1961 commencement address at Lincoln 4 University in Pennsylvania, Dr. King captured the utopianism of America: "For in a real sense, America is essentially a dream, a dream as yet unfulfilled. It is a dream of a land where men of all races, of all nationalities, and of all creeds can live together as brothers. The substance of the dream is expressed in these sublime words, words lifted to cosmic proportions: 'We hold these truths to be self-evident, that all men are created equal, that they are endowed by their Creator with certain unalienable rights, that among these are life, liberty, and the pursuit of happiness.'"

Dr. King, who would later speak of having a dream, went 5 on to reflect that the Declaration of Independence speaks not of "some men," but of "all men. It does not say all white men, but it says all men, which includes black men. It does not say all Gentiles, but it says all men, which includes Jews. It does not say all Protestants, but it says all men, which includes Catholics."

King noted further that the Declaration declares that 6 "each individual has certain basic rights that are neither conferred by nor derived from the state. To discover where they came from it is necessary to move back behind the dim mist of eternity, for they are God-given. Very seldom if ever in the history of the world has a sociopolitical document expressed in such profoundly eloquent and unequivocal language the dignity and the worth of human personality."

7   So here we have a sketch of the basis of American political 7 and moral life: because all men are created equal, and one is neither the natural nor the God-anointed ruler of the other, men can rule each other only through consent. Consent requires expression through representative institutions, and this in turn requires broad suffrage, fixed terms of office, and separation of powers to ensure not only that granted powers are not abused but also that government has sufficient power to perform the necessary task. Both slavery and its surrogate, segregation, denied Southern

blacks the right to be included in the scheme of the Declaration.

8   In his keynote address at the March on Washington, D.C., for Civil Rights, on August 28, 1963, Dr. King described the words of the Declaration and the Constitution as a "promissory note to which every American was to fall heir." But despite the "bad check" that America had written black Americans, Dr. King refused to believe that the bank of justice was bankrupt. He knew that the resources of America were great, because the dream he had had of a nation where his children would be judged not by the color of their skin but by the content of their character was deeply rooted in the American dream.

9   In his 1964 book, *Why We Can't Wait,* Dr. King, citing St. Thomas Aquinas, notes that "an unjust law is a human law that is not rooted in eternal law and natural law" and that "a just law is a man-made code that squares with the moral law or the law of God." This theme of a higher law behind the positive law is one that we today—we lawyers, we citizens who believe in the rule of law and we who honor Martin Luther King—need to take more seriously. For as King maintained, American politics and the American Constitution are unintelligible without the Declaration of Independence, and the Declaration is unintelligible without the notion of a higher law by which we fallible men and women can take our bearings.

10   The rule of law in America means nothing outside constitutional government and constitutionalism, and these are simply unintelligible without a higher law. Men cannot rule others by their consent unless their common humanity is understood in light of transcendent standards provided by the Declaration's "Laws of Nature and of Nature's God." Natural law provides a basis in human dignity by which we can judge whether human beings are just or unjust, noble or ignoble.

11   VIRNA M. CANSON: Advocacy requires that we use the broadest interpretation of affirmative action we can as we seek to redirect and counter various anti-civil-rights strategies. Affirmative action means taking extraordinary measures to remedy a condition that cannot be remedied through ordinary means.

12   The civil-rights strategies of the National Association for the Advancement of Colored People were honed with a

realistic view of conditions at the turn of the century. The interpretation of the Constitution by those in power at that time was different from that of the founders of the NAACP, and so we began intervention with extraordinary methods.

Our hearts have been lifted by the gains of blacks in   13 corporations. However, despite those gains, another front is emerging. Corporations, in the process of their restructurings, have become insensitive to their employees. The question for those of us in the civil-rights business is: What threat does this insensitivity pose to black executives, as well as to women? Does the possible demise of black executives send a message to black youth whom we are struggling to persuade to stay in school? The NAACP thinks that it does. The NAACP's Western Regional Office has therefore set up a task force to look at this particular problem.

A black vice-president of the Los Angeles unit of the Bank   14 of America lost his job when the company restructured itself. He recognized that he was a victim of the company's trying to survive. And we recognize that the company was not turning away from affirmative action. I believe that most corporations do not want to see their efforts to institutionalize affirmative action end abruptly. However, I question whether the first item on the agenda of the Bank of America's board was: "How do we protect our black executives?" A corporation's priority is its own survival. Our priority is the survival and advancement of blacks. I believe that the Bank of America has the resources to protect its priorities. The question is, how do we reconcile the needs and priorities of black professionals and the needs and priorities of the corporations?

The NAACP is mindful that the silver-tongued enemies   15 of black progress are using all forms of attack. Affirmative action and other approaches to healing the disease of racism are essential. And in this confusing but challenging struggle between the haves and the have-nots—between the white minority and people of color—we must continue.

EDWARD J. ERLER: Martin Luther King was looking fore-   16 ward to an ideal that would dispense with color-consciousness and race-consciousness, so that people could be judged on the content of their character. Insofar as affirmative action conditions rights upon a racial class, it is a denial of that ideal.

Judge A. Leon Higginbotham, Jr., a Federal Court of Ap-   17 peals judge, in his 1978 book, *In the Matter of Color, Race, and the American Legal Process: The Colonial Period,* said that Thomas Jefferson was something of a hypocrite when he wrote in the Declaration of Independence: "all men are created equal." Higginbotham said that Jefferson would have been more honest and less hypocritical if he had said that "all white men who own property were created equal," which would have been a more accurate expression of the time. He also said that it was lucky for us that Jefferson did not write the former statement because the statement "all men are created equal and are endowed with certain unalienable rights" established a moral standard by which we could forever judge our actions. Without that moral standard, Higginbotham said, we would have no guides, no goals, and no way to judge our political behavior.

18   In 1857, Abraham Lincoln said that the Declaration set up the standard maxim for us: All men are created equal. He said that the framers of the Constitution did not have the power to equalize all white people, let alone all black people. Their intention was to establish a moral standard by which we could judge ourselves. It perhaps might never be perfectly attained, but it could be constantly approximated.

19   We have used that standard almost from the beginning. Today it says that all men are created equal with the *a priori* notion that race classifications play no role in constitutional government. We used to believe that racial classifications had to be kept out of the law. We spent a hundred years putting the genii of race into the bottle where it belongs. Now, at the eleventh hour, everybody wants to take it out again and say, "We have not progressed enough. We have not progressed fast enough. Let's bring back racial consciousness. Let's make racial class consciousness legitimate again and let it be the standard."

20   JOSEPH H. DUFF: What is being addressed by affirmative action — and was being addressed by the Civil Rights Movement — is invidious racial discrimination, not race consciousness. Affirmative action starts from the premise that some racial classifications are not invidious.

21   GAYLE BINION: There are various forms of affirmative action. One is advertising that says: "Men and women, minorities and Caucasians, are all equally invited to apply." Another form is advertising that says: "We have three job

openings for blacks, six for women, and four for white
males." Still another is the statement: "We are going to do
a good job of looking for qualified people. We are going to
put time, money, energy, and resources into finding the
women and minorities that have been left out."

Those who oppose affirmative action assume that affir-   22
mative action means that *any* black or *any* woman has the
right to a particular job. I know of no affirmative-action
program that says that. Those who support affirmative action are saying: "We have a commitment to integrating and
weaving into our fabric of society all people, irrespective
of their race, religion, and gender. And unless institutions
can do that, they should reconsider how they function."

ERLER: On what ground is an unequal distribution based   23
on race or gender wrong?

BINION: The Fourteenth Amendment says that we are all   24
entitled to equal protection of the laws. The law ought to
embody principles that will allow people an equal shot at
things.

ERLER: But is equal protection compatible with race con-   25
sciousness? When you say that one form of affirmative action is quotas, you are considering equal-protection rights
exclusively in terms of class interests. The Fourteenth
Amendment says that all persons are entitled to equal protection of the laws. That implies that rights are individual
rights and that they are not conditioned by one's racial
class status. If you consider rights as being conditioned by
your racial class status or your gender class status, how
can you apply the law in any rational or intelligible way?

BINION: The misapplication here is the notion that one   26
has a right based on one's race. I am saying that institutions
have an obligation to create an equal-protection situation,
to see that persons, irrespective of their race, are woven
into the fabric of the institutions. I am saying that the
equal-protection law ought to be applied, and that we need
to define entitlements. And by entitlements I mean society's
system of so-called merit. For example, if someone has a
higher grade point average and a higher score on the Law
School Admission Test, that person has a higher entitlement
to go to law school. I am saying that we need to reevaluate
those kinds of entitlements.

27   SHIRLEY KENNEDY: The question is, are race-conscious remedies more dangerous than they are helpful and necessary? Even though race-conscious remedies may do some damage and violence to the ideals of the Constitution, I believe that the transcendent goal is important enough that we have to take that risk and minimize it in whatever way we can.

28   Race-conscious remedies are necessary because the continuing crisis in our country is getting worse, not better. Race-conscious remedies put pressure on the gatekeepers and the hiring people to resolve this crisis. These remedies also relieve the pressures that hirers who may be sympathetic to affirmative-action goals get from their peers to continue traditional patterns of hiring, such as the "old boy" network of hiring that goes on, for instance, in Chicago.

29   Some fear that affirmative action will result in unqualified people pushing out qualified people. None of us wants that. The black community does not want that. We do not want incompetent teachers, doctors, lawyers, and other professionals. We want to be judged as competent professionals.

30   THOMAS: Ultimately, any race-conscious remedy is not good. In any multiethnic, multiracial society, race-conscious remedies generate severe racial conflicts. Look at pre-World War II Germany. Look at India, Malaysia, South Africa, the Soviet Union. Look at this country — there was slavery and segregation.

31   In the context of the Equal Employment Opportunity Commission, when race is used as the basis for an individual or a class not being treated fairly or being discriminated against, the remedy is then based on race.

32   CANSON: What is a race-conscious law?

33   THOMAS: A race-conscious law is one that defines rights based on race. Segregation and apartheid are race-conscious laws.

34   DUFF: I was admitted to law school under the University of California's Equal Opportunity Program. I passed the bar exam, and now practice law in the community. That is a good race policy.

35   THOMAS: It is good for you.

DUFF: It is also good for the community and the society.   36

THOMAS: No, I think it is good for you. When I went to   37
college the problems with those policies were quite significant as were the animosities they generated.

DUFF: They were intended to be significant because the   38
problem — that is, a black could not be admitted because
of race — was significant.

SOJOURNER KINCAID: I was admitted to Boalt Hall, the   39
law school of the University of California, Berkeley, under
an affirmative-action program. Prior to that program in
1963, there was only a small number of blacks at Boalt Hall.
    Admission to law school is based on one's score on the   40
Law School Admission Test (LSAT) and on one's undergraduate scholastic record. If one meets that numerical
standard, one is admitted to law school. The affirmative-action program said that that standard was deciding not
whether one could do well in law school but that persons
from a certain segment of society were more likely to do
better in law school. The affirmative-action program said
that we will admit those who score below the LSAT standard because we are conscious of their race and of the need
to provide society with diversity in the overall population
of lawyers.
    That kind of affirmative-action policy benefits not only   41
the minority community but also society, which needs the
diversity that we are claiming it ought to have.
    As a law student, I was involved in a student group called   42
the Coalition for Diversified Faculty. Our claim against
Boalt Hall was that we were being harmed by not having
a diversified faculty, that we were being taught by faculty
who had only a specific attitude toward the law and who
were not involved with helping us who had come from
different communities return to our communities to help
them in their legal needs.

THOMAS: The school at which I was on the board of trus-   43
tees had a flunk-out rate anywhere from sixty to a hundred
percent.
    We brought in valedictorians, salutatorians, and kids   44
from the top twenty percent of the classes of the inner cities'
public schools. We hired a minority affairs director, who
gave us the Black Students Union and a bunch of money

and who tied us into the community. There was still a huge flunk-out rate. My question to the faculty and the administration was: Why are we bringing in these bright kids and turning them into anti-social people?

45   KINCAID: In that kind of situation, we should be saying: "We are bringing in these kids to produce a particular result. Now, how can we achieve that result?"

46   ANNE WORTHAM: Many minority students — particularly black students — are leaving universities such as the Harvard Business School because they want to succeed, they do not want to be a Harvard failure. They are choosing to enroll in Southern, traditionally black schools, in response to the situation in which admissions standards were lowered.

47   DUFF: I was admitted to a private college because I was black, not because admission standards were lowered. The innuendo here is that blacks are failing and that we should therefore not admit them because they will have to suffer the pain of being a Harvard failure.

48   THOMAS: I don't want to hear platitudes about affirmative action — I want to see progress. A seventy-nine percent flunk-out rate is not progress.

49   BINION: As to what kind of admissions programs succeed, law-school admissions provide a good example. Studies have shown that when admission to law school is based on the LSAT score and GPA, minority admission will be depressed because minorities do not score as high on the LSAT. However, studies have also shown that one's GPA is a far better predictor of how one will do in law school. Thus, if an admission standard emphasized one's GPA, not LSAT score, the number of blacks who would be eligible for admission to law school would rise substantially.

50   Also, the highest correlate with the Scholastic Aptitude Test in high school — the single best predictor of how well one will do — is family income.

51   KENNEDY: During the five years that I was in the College of Letters and Science at the University of California, Santa Barbara, students told me, "We are going to change

our majors. We are going to go to medical school." If those students had come from, say, Beverly Hills High School, I simply told them what courses they had to take. They took those courses, the Medical College Admission Test, and then they were admitted to medical school.

On the other hand, other students told me, "We think 52 we'd like to become doctors." I looked at their high school records and saw that they had not taken classes that would permit them to take the MCAT. I had to tell them that they had to go back to Santa Barbara City College and take biology and other courses. These students were graduating from schools that had no physics lab, no physics teachers, no chemistry teachers. Were these students — the majority of them black — really going to get into medical school?

WORTHAM: I think that an affirmative-action policy pro- 53 duces a stigma on those whom our government has put into special categories. I personally resent being one of the U.S. Labor Department's specially benefited or protected minorities. I would not like that kind of protection from my government.

KINCAID: I have no problem going into some place and 54 feeling that I am there because of a mandate for equal opportunity. I know that once I am there I will be recognized as an individual on my own. I do not feel that affirmative action produces a stigma — I am glad that I was given an opportunity.

THOMAS: Obviously, the education that minorities re- 55 ceive from kindergarten through twelfth grade is abysmal. It destroys them before they even get to where affirmative action means anything.

When discussing education for blacks, there is the issue 56 of busing. For example, black students in Montgomery County, Maryland — which has a fine school system — who were integrated into the school system as a result of court orders were doing worse than whites on the math portion of the exam. The almost immediate suggestion was that that was because of race. But it was simpler than that: whites were taking an average of three math courses while blacks were taking an average of one. Data show that blacks take fewer academic courses in their education from kinder- garten through twelfth grade than do whites. Blacks take less math, less history, less modern language. Instead they take more special studies, more physical education, and other courses that have nothing to do with training them for a career.

57   We can talk about the results and the compensations that should be made at the college level, but these are indicators of what is happening at the K–12 level, which is abysmal and which is where we ought to focus our attention.

58   DONALD MCDONALD: What should government do in the area of affirmative action?

59   THOMAS: I don't think that government should be in the business of parceling out rights or benefits. Rights emanate from the Constitution and from the Declaration. They are there, and they should be protected. I am not confident that Washington is any more moral or stronger than anyone else to assign rights, or even better able to do it. We should be careful not to concede the rights of individuals in our society in order to gain something such as parity. Ultimately that will do us a disservice.

60   The Equal Employment Opportunity Commission is mandated to protect people's individual rights to equal opportunity.

61   DUFF: Is the EEOC legally obligated to advocate and bring class actions? Does it provide for the use of affirmative-action remedies?

62   THOMAS: One of the remedies it uses—particularly in large class-action cases—is even more aggressive than quotas: the right to placement in the job one would have had but for discrimination.

63   DUFF: Then the EEOC decides when that so-called right is parceled out.

64   THOMAS: It is protecting one's right to be free from discrimination; it is not creating or parceling out that right. That right comes through the Constitution and is implemented by Title VII. If the government has any role in this matter, it is the protection of the rights of its citizens from foreign and domestic enemies.

DUFF: And the greatest domestic enemy we are dealing   65
with in this context is racism in the work force.

THOMAS: That is correct.   66

McDONALD: Can the EEOC initiate actions when it sus-   67
pects a violation of equal-opportunity laws? Or does it have
to wait until a case is brought to it?

THOMAS: It does initiate cases, and cases are brought to   68
it. More than fifty-five percent of its cases are class-action
cases, some of which are quite large and have resulted in
levels of monetary relief far more significant than any other
at any time in the history of the commission. There is also
far more litigation than at any other time in the history of
the commission.

Kurt Vonnegut, Jr.
Harrison Bergeron

*After graduating from Cornell University, Kurt Vonnegut, Jr.
(born in 1922 in Indianapolis), worked in journalism and public relations. Then he started publishing best-selling novels that
often feature imaginary (yet all too real) settings, a satiric edge,
and his characteristic narrative voice. Among them are* Cat's
Cradle, Slaughterhouse-Five, Breakfast of Champions, *and*
Jailbird. *"Harrison Bergeron" was published as part of his
collection of stories entitled* Welcome to the Monkey House.

The year was 2081, and everybody was finally equal. They   1
weren't only equal before God and the law. They were equal
every which way. Nobody was smarter than anybody else.
Nobody was better looking than anybody else. Nobody was
stronger or quicker than anybody else. All this equality was
due to the 211th, 212th, and 213th Amendments to the
Constitution, and to the unceasing vigilance of agents of
the United States Handicapper General.

2   Some things about living still weren't quite right, though. April, for instance, still drove people crazy by not being springtime. And it was in that clammy month that the H-G men took George and Hazel Bergeron's fourteen-year-old son, Harrison, away.

3   It was tragic, all right, but George and Hazel couldn't think about it very hard. Hazel had a perfectly average intelligence, which meant she couldn't think about anything except in short bursts. And George, while his intelligence was way above normal, had a little mental handicap radio in his ear. He was required by law to wear it at all times. It was tuned to a government transmitter. Every twenty seconds or so, the transmitter would send out some sharp noise to keep people like George from taking unfair advantage of their brains.

4   George and Hazel were watching television. There were tears on Hazel's cheeks, but she'd forgotten for the moment what they were about.

5   On the television screen were ballerinas.

6   A buzzer sounded in George's head. His thoughts fled in panic, like bandits from a burglar alarm.

7   "That was a real pretty dance, that dance they just did," said Hazel.

8   "Huh?" said George.

9   "That dance — it was nice," said Hazel.

10   "Yup," said George. He tried to think a little about the ballerinas. They weren't really very good — no better than anybody else would have been, anyway. They were burdened with sashweights and bags of birdshot, and their faces were masked, so that no one, seeing a free and graceful gesture or a pretty face, would feel like something the cat drug in. George was toying with the vague notion that maybe dancers shouldn't be handicapped. But he didn't get very far with it before another noise in his ear radio scattered his thoughts.

11   George winced. So did two out of the eight ballerinas.

12   Hazel saw him wince. Having no mental handicap herself, she had to ask George what the latest sound had been.

13   "Sounded like somebody hitting a milk bottle with a ball peen hammer," said George.

14   "I'd think it would be real interesting, hearing all the different sounds," said Hazel, a little envious. "All the things they think up."

"Um," said George.   15

"Only, if I was Handicapper General, you know what I   16
would do?" said Hazel. Hazel, as a matter of fact, bore a
strong resemblance to the Handicapper General, a woman
named Diana Moon Glampers. "If I was Diana Moon Glampers," said Hazel, "I'd have chimes on Sunday — just chimes.
Kind of in honor of religion."

"I could think, if it was just chimes," said George.   17

"Well — maybe make 'em real loud," said Hazel. "I think   18
I'd make a good Handicapper General."

"Good as anybody else," said George.   19

"Who knows better'n I do what normal is?" said Hazel.   20

"Right," said George. He began to think glimmeringly   21
about his abnormal son who was now in jail, about Harrison, but a twenty-one-gun salute in his head stopped that.

"Boy!" said Hazel, "that was a doozy, wasn't it?"   22

It was such a doozy that George was white and trembling,   23
and tears stood on the rims of his red eyes. Two of the eight
ballerinas had collapsed to the studio floor, [and] were
holding their temples.

"All of a sudden you look so tired," said Hazel. "Why don't 24
you stretch out on the sofa, so's you can rest your handicap
bag on the pillows, honeybunch." She was referring to the
forty-seven pounds of birdshot in a canvas bag, which was
padlocked around George's neck. "Go on and rest the bag
for a little while," she said. "I don't care if you're not equal
to me for a while."

George weighed the bag with his hands. "I don't mind   25
it," he said. "I don't notice it any more. It's just a part of me."

"You been so tired lately — kind of wore out," said Hazel.   26
"If there was just some way we could make a little hole in
the bottom of the bag, and just take out a few of them lead
balls. Just a few."

"Two years in prison and two thousand dollars fine for   27
every ball I took out," said George. "I don't call that a bargain."

"If you could just take a few out when you came home   28
from work," said Hazel. "I mean — you don't compete with
anybody around here. You just set around."

"If I tried to get away with it," said George, "then other   29
people'd get away with it — and pretty soon we'd be right
back to the dark ages again, with everybody competing
against everybody else. You wouldn't like that, would you?"

30   "I'd hate it," said Hazel.

31   "There you are," said George. "The minute people start cheating on laws, what do you think happens to society?"

32   If Hazel hadn't been able to come up with an answer to this question George couldn't have supplied one. A siren was going off in his head.

33   "Reckon it'd fall all apart," said Hazel.

34   "What would?" said George blankly.

35   "Society," said Hazel uncertainly. "Wasn't that what you just said?"

36   "Who knows?" said George.

37   The television program was suddenly interrupted for a news bulletin. It wasn't clear at first as to what the bulletin was about, since the announcer, like all announcers, had a serious speech impediment. For about half a minute, and in a state of high excitement, the announcer tried to say, "Ladies and gentlemen—"

38   He finally gave up, handed the bulletin to a ballerina to read.

39   "That's all right—" Hazel said of the announcer, "he tried. That's the big thing. He tried to do the best he could with what God gave him. He should get a nice raise for trying so hard."

40   "Ladies and gentlemen—" said the ballerina, reading the bulletin. She must have been extraordinarily beautiful, because the mask she wore was hideous. And it was easy to see that she was the strongest and most graceful of all the dancers, for her handicap bags were as big as those worn by two-hundred-pound men.

41   And she had to apologize at once for her voice, which was a very unfair voice for a woman to use. Her voice was a warm, luminous, timeless melody. "Excuse me—" she said, and she began again, making her voice absolutely uncompetitive.

42   "Harrison Bergeron, age fourteen," she said in a grackle squawk, "has just escaped from jail, where he was held on suspicion of plotting to overthrow the government. He is a genius and an athlete, is under-handicapped, and should be regarded as extremely dangerous."

43   A police photograph of Harrison Bergeron was flashed on the screen upside down, then sideways, upside down again, then right side up. The picture showed the full length of Harrison against a background calibrated in feet and inches. He was exactly seven feet tall.

The rest of Harrison's appearance was Halloween and 44
hardware. Nobody had ever borne heavier handicaps. He
had outgrown hindrances faster than the H-G men could
think them up. Instead of a little ear radio for a mental
handicap, he wore a tremendous pair of earphones, and
spectacles with thick wavy lenses. The spectacles were intended to make him not only half blind, but to give him
whanging headaches besides.

Scrap metal was hung all over him. Ordinarily, there 45
was a certain symmetry, a military neatness to the handicaps issued to strong people, but Harrison looked like a
walking junkyard. In the race of life, Harrison carried three
hundred pounds.

And to offset his good looks, the H-G men required that 46
he wear at all times a red rubber ball for a nose, keep his
eyebrows shaved off, and cover his even white teeth with
black caps at snaggle-tooth random.

"If you see this boy," said the ballerina, "do not — I repeat, 47
do not — try to reason with him."

There was the shriek of a door being torn from its hinges. 48

Screams and barking cries of consternation came from 49
the television set. The photograph of Harrison Bergeron on
the screen jumped again and again, as though dancing to
the tune of an earthquake.

George Bergeron correctly identified the earthquake, and 50
well he might have — for many was the time his own home
had danced to the same crashing tune. "My God —" said
George, "that must be Harrison!"

The realization was blasted from his mind instantly by 51
the sound of an automobile collision in his head.

When George could open his eyes again, the photograph 52
of Harrison was gone. A living, breathing Harrison filled
the screen.

Clanking, clownish, and huge, Harrison stood in the 53
center of the studio. The knob of the uprooted studio door
was still in his hand. Ballerinas, technicians, musicians,
and announcers cowered on their knees before him, expecting to die.

"I am the Emperor!" cried Harrison. "Do you hear? I am 54
the Emperor! Everybody must do what I say at once!" He
stamped his foot and the studio shook.

"Even as I stand here —" he bellowed, "crippled, hobbled, 55
sickened — I am a greater ruler than any man who ever
lived! Now watch me become what I *can* become!"

56   Harrison tore the straps of his handicap harness like wet tissue paper, tore straps guaranteed to support five thousand pounds.

57   Harrison's scrap-iron handicaps crashed to the floor.

58   Harrison thrust his thumbs under the bar of the padlock that secured his head harness. The bar snapped like celery. Harrison smashed his headphones and spectacles against the wall.

59   He flung away his rubber-ball nose, revealed a man that would have awed Thor, the god of thunder.

60   "I shall now select my Empress!" he said, looking down on the cowering people. "Let the first woman who dares rise to her feet claim her mate and her throne!"

61   A moment passed, and then a ballerina arose, swaying like a willow.

62   Harrison plucked the mental handicap from her ear, snapped off her physical handicaps with marvelous delicacy. Last of all, he removed her mask.

63   She was blindingly beautiful.

64   "Now—" said Harrison, taking her hand, "shall we show the people the meaning of the word dance? Music!" he commanded.

65   The musicians scrambled back into their chairs, and Harrison stripped them of their handicaps, too. "Play your best," he told them, "and I'll make you barons and dukes and earls."

66   The music began. It was normal at first—cheap, silly, false. But Harrison snatched two musicians from their chairs, waved them like batons as he sang the music as he wanted it played. He slammed them back into their chairs.

67   The music began again and was much improved.

68   Harrison and his Empress merely listened to the music for a while—listened gravely, as though synchronizing their heartbeats with it.

69   They shifted their weights to their toes.

70   Harrison placed his big hands on the girl's tiny waist, letting her sense the weightlessness that would soon be hers.

71   And then, in an explosion of joy and grace, into the air they sprang!

72   Not only were the laws of the land abandoned, but the law of gravity and the laws of motion as well.

73   They reeled, whirled, swiveled, flounced, capered, gamboled, and spun.

74   They leaped like deer on the moon.

The studio ceiling was thirty feet high, but each leap   75
brought the dancers nearer to it.

It became their obvious intention to kiss the ceiling.   76

They kissed it.   77

And then, neutralizing gravity with love and pure will,   78
they remained suspended in air inches below the ceiling,
and they kissed each other for a long, long time.

It was then that Diana Moon Glampers, the Handicapper   79
General, came into the studio with a double-barreled ten-
gauge shotgun. She fired twice, and the Emperor and the
Empress were dead before they hit the floor.

Diana Moon Glampers loaded the gun again. She aimed   80
it at the musicians and told them they had ten seconds to
get their handicaps back on.

It was then that the Bergerons' television tube burned out. 81

Hazel turned to comment about the blackout to George.   82
But George had gone out into the kitchen for a can of beer.

George came back in with the beer, paused while a handi-   83
cap signal shook him up. And then he sat down again. "You
been crying?" he said to Hazel.

"Yup," she said.   84

"What about?" he said.   85

"I forget," she said. "Something real sad on television."   86

"What was it?" he said.   87

"It's all kind of mixed up in my mind," said Hazel.   88

"Forget sad things," said George.   89

"I always do," said Hazel.   90

"That's my girl," said George. He winced. There was the   91
sound of a riveting gun in his head.

"Gee—I could tell that one was a doozy," said Hazel.   92

"You can say that again," said George.   93

"Gee—" said Hazel, "I could tell that one was a doozy."   94

Paul R. Spickard

Why I Believe in Affirmative Action

Paul R. Spickard, who teaches history at Capital University in Columbus, Ohio, published the following essay in Christianity Today, *an evangelical monthly magazine.*

1   Since the late 1960s, the federal government has required those with whom it does business to act positively to hire and promote people from groups that have been discriminated against. And affirmative action has helped bring a noticeable improvement in the life chances of many blacks, Hispanics, Asians, and white women.

2   More recently, Attorney General Edwin Meese mounted a campaign against affirmative action, calling it "reverse discrimination." Although the Supreme Court handed him a defeat in July, Justice Sandra Day O'Connor's concurring opinion and the justice department's hedging comments show that Meese is unlikely to surrender.

3   I, a white male, have suffered from affirmative action. In 1976, with degrees from Harvard and the University of California, and a teacher's credential, I applied to teach the history of China and Japan. I was told, "I think we'll hire an Asian-American." That stung. I was highly qualified: I spoke Japanese, had lived in Asia, and had studied Asian history for years. What would an American of Asian descent know about Asian history that I did not? The school could not find a qualified Asian, and I drove a truck for a living.

4   Five years later it happened again. A major university told me they would love to hire me. But the department was all white and all male, and they were looking to hire a minority woman.

5   I have been denied the chance to make a living because I am white and male. Yet I remain convinced that affirmative action is good social policy.

6   It is also a scriptural imperative in our social situation. Why? My understanding begins with Philippians 2:3–6, where Paul reminds us that Jesus did not look to his own benefit but spent himself for us, and he tells us that as Christians we have a responsibility to look out for other people's welfare before our own. Affirmative action is an appropriate way to do that.

America's initial push for equal opportunity resulted in 7 very little progress. Blacks and others had not just been shut out of jobs, but had also been shut out of the education necessary to qualify for jobs.

Then Lyndon Johnson argued that an equal race is not 8 necessarily a fair one. You don't starve somebody for a month, break both his legs, put him at the starting line and say, "May the best man win." The long history of oppression had left some categories of people unable to compete.

Fortunately, the federal government's commitment to af- 9 firmative action created a mentality in society that it was valuable to hire minorities. This wider conviction has played an important part in improving the life chances of some women and minorities.

Isn't all this unfair? It felt like discrimination to me. But 10 consider: I come from generations of moderate wealth. My family came over on the *Mayflower* and made money in the slave trade. Doctors, lawyers, judges, and comfortable business people go back several generations in my clan. I was never wealthy, but I could not have devoted myself to college and graduate school without support from my family and a timely inheritance. I am standing on the shoulders of my ancestors and their discriminatory behavior.

Contrast my experience with that of a Chicano friend, 11 whose immigrant father had a fourth-grade education and ran a grocery store. Without affirmative action and the social commitment it symbolizes, my friend might not have gone to Amherst, nor to Stanford law school. He might not have found a job with a major law firm, nor as a congressional aide. He is talented and has worked hard. But without affirmative action he might well be back in Modesto pumping gas. Our society would be poorer for the loss of his skills.

Affirmative action's job is not yet done. Black men still 12 earn only about 76 percent as much as white men in the same job categories. The gap between white males and others is far from closed.

Everything costs something. In the 1960s, when the econ- 13 omy was expanding, affirmative action seemed painless. But in the middle 1970s we realized that if some were to gain then others must lose. That was when affirmative action began to be called "reverse discrimination" (implying that there is a normal, proper direction for discrimination), and we white males began to defend our privileges.

14   Of course, affirmative action cannot do the whole job. It
can do little about residential, religious, and educational
segregation. But if genuine equal opportunity is to be
achieved, affirmative action must be part of the picture.
Some white males will get the short end of the stick, just
as we have given the short end to others for dozens of generations.

15   Affirmative action may not always be fair. But I'm willing
to take second best if overall fairness is achieved. After all,
for biblical Christians, fairness — often translated in our Bi-
bles as "justice" or "righteousness" — is a fundamental principle by which God calls us to live. And affirmative action
is an appropriate part of a larger program aimed at achieving the godly goal of putting others' welfare before my own.

Robert F. Drinan
Another Look at Affirmative Action

*Robert F. Drinan (born 1920), a Jesuit priest, was dean of the
law school at Boston College when he was elected to the U.S.
House of Representatives in 1970. A champion of humanitarian causes and advocate for civil rights, he retired from the
House in 1980. Currently professor of law at Georgetown University in Washington, D.C., he has written many books and
articles; the following one appeared in 1985 in* America, *a
magazine of Catholic thought.*

1   The controversy about affirmative action is becoming
more complex and confusing. It is uncertain whether the
negative attitude toward affirmative action on the part of
the Reagan Administration or the Supreme Court decision
concerning firefighters in Memphis last June will actually
deter specific, ongoing programs employing affirmative action. But the climate of general acceptance of affirmative
action may be shifting. It is therefore appropriate to discuss:
1) the meaning of the 6–3 Supreme Court decision in the
Memphis firefighters case, 2) the extensive use of affirmative action in other nations and its incorporation into international law and 3) the progress made by the use of affirmative action since 1965.

In 1974, the city of Memphis signed a consent decree that   2
settled a suit brought against the city by the Civil Rights
Division of the U.S. Department of Justice. The city agreed
to set aside 50 percent of all job vacancies for qualified
black applicants. In 1980, the city also agreed to ensure
that 20 percent of the promotions in each job classification
be given to blacks.

In neither decree was there any reference to what would   3
happen if some firefighters or others were laid off. In 1981,
the city announced that projected budget deficits required
a reduction in personnel and that the citywide seniority
system would be followed. Of the 40 firefighting employees
to be laid off, 25 were white and 15 were black.

The Federal District Court enjoined the city from follow-   4
ing the seniority rule since it would be in essence inconsistent with the consent decree agreed to by the city. The
Circuit Court of Appeals sustained the injunction, but on
June 12, 1984, the United States Supreme Court reversed,
holding that Federal courts had no power to impose on a
city a policy that preferred affirmative action to seniority.

The Supreme Court decision can be viewed narrowly as   5
not a curtailment of affirmative action but only as an insistence that Federal courts cannot go beyond their proper
mandate. Lawyers for black employees will henceforth insist that agreements involving affirmative action provide
specifically for the practices and priorities to be followed
if it becomes necessary to cut back the work force.

A few statements in the Memphis decision can be con-   6
strued as unfavorable to affirmative action. The fact is,
however, that all of the Federal courts of appeals throughout the country are unanimous in holding the view that
race-conscious affirmative relief is permissible under Title
VII of the Civil Rights Act of 1965; that law permits the
court to "order such affirmative action as may be appropriate, which may include, but is not limited to, reinstatement
or hiring of employees . . . or any other equitable relief as
the court deems appropriate."

It is also clear that the Memphis decision did not reverse   7
Bakke, the 1978 decision in which a majority of the Supreme
Court wrote that "executive, judicial and Congressional
action subsequent to the passage of Title VII did not bar
the remedial use of race."

That "remedial use" of race has been recommended on   8
the international level for many years and has become a

part of international law. In 1963, the General Assembly of the United Nations began the drafting of the Declaration on the Elimination of All Forms of Racial Discrimination. With active support from the United States, this document was completed in 1965. In 1969, after the requisite number of nations ratified the declaration, it entered into force as a part of international law. In 1984, 107 nations had ratified the declaration—more ratifications than for any of the treaties that have emerged from the United Nations. Even though the U.S. Senate has never ratified the declaration, it is arguably binding on the United States.

9   Article 1, 4 of this declaration approves of affirmative action in these carefully crafted words: "Special measures taken for the sole purpose of securing adequate advancement of certain racial or ethnic groups or individuals requiring such protection as may be necessary in order to ensure such groups or individuals equal enjoyment or exercise of human rights and fundamental freedoms shall not be deemed racial discrimination, provided, however, that such measures do not, as a consequence, lead to the maintenance of separate rights for different racial groups and that they shall not be continued after the objectives for which they were taken have been achieved."

10   This statement clearly enunciates the principle that measures designed to bring racial or ethnic groups into the mainstream shall *not* be deemed to be discrimination or reverse discrimination. The one qualification is the clear understanding that the privileges or preferences that have been extended will be removed as soon as they are no longer required.

11   It is unfortunate that this part of international law, which is the product of some of the finest legal minds around the world, has hardly ever entered into the heated discussion about affirmative action now going on in the United States.

12   This clear but careful endorsement of affirmative action agreed to by over two-thirds of the nations of the earth is a significant factor in the very valuable volume on affirmative action published in May by the Rockefeller Foundation. This collection of 10 papers on affirmative action, by experts from nations that include Malaysia, Nigeria, Israel and West Germany, demonstrates that in numerous nations, where leaders are trying to extend access to jobs to minorities hitherto locked out, they are utilizing various devices that could be called preferences, quotas, "special

measures" or set-asides. The objectives of affirmative action are somewhat different in various nations. In Peru, affirmative action is directed at enhancing the economic and educational status of Indians, who constitute the vast majority of the population. In India, affirmative action is targeted at 22 percent of the population consisting of castes, the best known of which are the untouchables. In Israel, affirmative action has been justified as a means of building the self-respect of groups, both Jews and Arabs, who are held in low esteem.

It is significant that in the new Canadian constitution   13
there is an acceptance of affirmative action since the document explicitly recognizes "any law, program or activity that has as its object the amelioration of conditions of disadvantaged individuals or groups."

In a summary of the papers and of the discussion on   14
which the Rockefeller report is based, the negative aspects of affirmative action are noted. Affirmative action, some feel, leads to low self-esteem of those who have been advanced pursuant to its use. Affirmative action may also, it is urged, benefit persons who were not personally victimized, at the expense of some who were not oppressors. It is also claimed that affirmative action can lead to economic inefficiency by placing unqualified persons in positions of responsibility.

Affirmative action has, nonetheless, the Rockefeller study   15
concludes, "made a positive difference where other measures have failed." The potential abuses in affirmative action, however, were warned against by Jack Greenberg, former general counsel to the N.A.A.C.P. Legal Defense Fund, who spent 25 years advancing various forms of affirmative action; he likened affirmative action to a "powerful drug that must be used for a serious illness but should be employed carefully to minimize objections and facilitate the goals it seeks to advance."

The American Association for Affirmative Action, a group   16
of administrators for colleges, corporations and government agencies, has the difficult task of increasing the number of minority employees while being careful not to dilute quality. They understandably like to point to the successes of affirmative action in the past. Medical schools, for example, in the 1960's had a minority enrollment of 2.6 percent; in the late 1970's that figure was up to 8.2 percent. In 1970, there were 4,084 black female bus drivers; in 1980, there were 22,652. In 1962, there were 750 black employees

at I.B.M.; in 1980, there were 16,546. In 1970, there were 962 black psychologists; in 1980, there were 6,756.

17   These amazing changes have many causes, but the official proponents and administrators of affirmative action programs understandably like to think that their objectives and their efforts have been important, if not crucial, in these developments. But the nation's administrators of affirmative action are wondering whether the next 10 years will bring new protests, or will the present controversies die down and the solid achievements of affirmative action in the years 1964 to 1984 be resumed? The answer to those questions depends in part on the future position of the Civil Rights Division of the Justice Department. Many of the top lawyers who directed that unit in 1981 have left—almost always in passionate dissent from the policies of Assistant Attorney General William Bradford Reynolds. The institutional memory of the Civil Rights Division may have been seriously damaged.

18   The future of affirmative action obviously also depends on what the courts decide in the next few months or years. But affirmative action probably depends more on the attitude that becomes dominant in American life during the balance of the 1980's. Up until the recent past, most individuals and corporations had welcomed affirmative action. It was a way to attract blacks into colleges and to places of employment. It was a reminder that women have been kept down in law firms, in industry and in higher education. And it taught a lesson that Hispanics had been discriminated against.

19   But now the consensus about affirmative action is less clear. An event in my class at Georgetown University Law Center revealed what a new generation is thinking about affirmative action.

20   Recently I put on the board for my class in constitutional law the median academic average and the scores on the law school admission test of the white and minority students at Georgetown Law Center. There is a difference of over 100 points between the scores of the white students and those of the minority. There is also a significant difference between the average grade quotient of these two types of students. Georgetown Law Center has 18 to 20 percent minority students—possibly the highest of any law school in the nation. The reactions of the class were very diverse. One black student said that she was "humiliated" that this information—routinely available to the faculty and to

others—was publicized in this fashion. Another student asked if Georgetown, a Catholic institution, could use what he characterized as a "double standard" to increase or maintain the number of Catholics in the student body. A white student said with some anger that now he knew why his roommate at college was denied admission to Georgetown. One white student who identified himself as a Catholic said that he was proud of what Georgetown was doing but felt that it could possibly be struck down by a court.

21   The lack of a consensus among these 120 students, soon to be lawyers, reflects the deep division that exists almost everywhere regarding the thorny questions of affirmative action. Morris Abram, a noted civil rights attorney, does not make his position on affirmative action any clearer despite his continuous attempts to do so. Thomas Sowell, a black scholar sometimes identified with conservative groups, apparently feels that blacks will gradually emerge into the middle class just as the children and grandchildren of Germans, Italians and Scandinavians did. The vehemence demonstrated in the rejections of this position by civil rights attorneys and black leaders is an indication of the depths of feeling existing in those who feel that the concept of affirmative action is the only available way by which blacks and other minorities can be helped to reverse decades and decades of segregation and discrimination.

22   In almost every discussion of affirmative action, the unspoken question centers on the issue of whether "innocent" white people must somehow be required to pay a penalty because other white people discriminated on the basis of race. In 1976 the U.S. Supreme Court, while sustaining a form of affirmative action, approached this question with these words: "The result which we reach today . . . establishes that a sharing of the burden of the past discrimination is presumptively necessary."

23   Those opposed to affirmative action have the burden of offering an alternative that will advance the position of blacks, at least as much as affirmative action has done. To many people they do not appear to have sustained that burden. After all the arguments have been made and the controversies aired, the central reality comes back to the words of Justice Harry A. Blackmun, who in the Bakke decision wrote that "to get beyond racism we must first take account of race."

Migdia Chinea-Varela
My Life as a "Twofer"

Migdia Chinea-Varela contributed this essay to Newsweek *on December 26, 1988.*

1   This Christmas I'll be celebrating my 10th anniversary as a card-carrying member of the film industry's Writers Guild. Ten brain-numbing years and a debilitating employment lull during the five-month-long writers' strike have taken their toll. Last week I'd awakened in what can only be described as profound financial melancholia and was taking inventory of my career alternatives when the phone rang. The caller was a friend at the Writers Guild of America, West. Great news, he said. Several production companies were starting "access" programs for minorities, women, the elderly and the disabled. They'd requested a sampler of scripts ASAP from which to fish out two, maybe *three* writers for free-lance assignments. It could even lead to staff jobs, he said.

2   My imagination flashes to a TV scene in which I grab the lifeline and submit my best script. I subsequently get chosen for a plum writing assignment that quickly turns into a staff position, where I do such a bang-up job that I become the show's producer and an Emmy award winner as well. In real life, however, I thank the guild rep for his good-faith efforts and tell him that my answer is no. Though I helped found and then chaired the Latino writer's committee, I don't want to send in my scripts.

3   Why? Why would anyone pass up such a sweet deal? Everyone knows how tough the film and television industry is. Yet contacts are everything, the insiders say. It helps if you have an agent with hot connections who believes in you and is willing to put in the time required to promote your career. It helps if you attended the "right" film school. It's a matter of timing. It's difficult for everyone. Yes, but consider this — if you're a member of a minority group, the equation should be multiplied by 10; and if you're a minority woman, then add 30 more points.

4   So what's my problem? Why not take advantage of every opportunity that comes my way? The answer is: I've been in this situation before and I don't like the way it makes

me feel. There's something almost insulting about these well-meaning affirmative-action searches. In the past I'd always rationalized my participation partly because I needed the break and even more because I needed the money. And as fate would have it, whenever a film- or TV-production company saw fit to round up minorities for a head count, I always came out on top. But the truth is that I've never felt good about it.

I've asked myself the obvious questions. Am I being   5
picked for my writing ability, or to fulfill a quota? Have I been selected because I'm a "twofer"—a female Hispanic, or because they were enthralled with my deftly drawn characters and strong, original story line? My writing career, it appears, has taken a particularly tortuous course. I've gone from being a dedicated writer to dedicated *minority* writer, which seems limiting for someone who was first inspired by Woody Allen.

Truth is, that even with the aid of special programs, job   6
assignments for writers who fit the "minority" category are inexplicably few and far between. The sad employment statistics reveal that ethnic minorities comprise less than 3 percent of our guild. Those who work do so less frequently and for a lot less money, yet the publicity harvested by the special programs creates the illusion of equal opportunity where very little exists. I don't want to seem overly gloomy. Nevertheless, my work's almost always seen on shows that have a minority star like "The Facts of Life," "What's Happening Now!" and "Punky Brewster."

Except for "The Cosby Show," minorities are not being   7
taken seriously enough to write about their real lives outside of the ghetto. Though few of us will admit to it—for fear of speaking out or being tagged as ungrateful—we're reminded of our status in not-so-subtle ways. I remember the time I was waiting for a story meeting where I wanted to pitch several ideas. As I chatted with the production secretary, an aspiring writer herself, I could hear laughter coming from inside the conference room. Finally, the executive in charge stepped outside, followed by five young men. Judging by the look of satisfaction on their faces, it had probably been a profitable session. The executive greeted me effusively by saying, as he turned to the rest of the group, "Meet M-I-G-D-I-A V-A-R-R-R-R-E-L-A. She's one of our minority writers." This comment drew a tight smile from my lips, as one and all present reacted with extrava-

gant expressions of support. Somehow I knew right then and there that my project would be down for the count. KO'd with kindness.

8   *Killer sharks*: More recently, I was spilling my guts to a friend with a recognizable name whose uncle was a famous writer. After sharing my woes and commiserating as fellow writers often do, we parted with that old cliché: "We're in the same boat." Suddenly it dawned on me that hell *no*, we're not even close. We're no doubt on the same ocean, but hardly in the same boat. From where I sit, my friend's being attended to on a luxury liner while I'm all alone paddling a canoe, surrounded by killer sharks and in the midst of a typhoon.

9   I'd like to think that after 10 years of paying my dues as a professional writer that I've earned the right to walk through the front door. After so many years, it's depressing to feel that I have to tag myself a minority as an incentive to those who may hire me. Why can't I get a job on my own merits? Am I destined to spend the rest of my writing career hooked up to these kinds of life-support systems?

10   I'm painfully aware that affirmative action, what little there is of it, may be the only way minorities are given a chance to compete. However, for me, it has become a stigma of sorts. In my view, there can be no affirmative action without segregation — nor any end to the segregation if our names must be kept on separate lists. I'd like to propose instead a simple scenario: a fair job market where employment is commensurate with ability regardless of gender, racial or ethnic background. I make a pitch, they like my story, I get the job. Why not?

Richard Rodriguez
None of This Is Fair

The following selection by Richard Rodriguez is excerpted from his 1982 book Hunger of Memory. *For more on Mr. Rodriguez — and for another selection of his work — see page 143.*

1   My plan to become a professor of English — my ambition during long years in college at Stanford, then in graduate

school at Columbia and Berkeley — was complicated by feelings of embarrassment and guilt. So many times I would see other Mexican-Americans and know we were alike only in race. And yet, simply because our race was the same, I was, during the last years of my schooling, the beneficiary of their situation. Affirmative Action programs had made it all possible. The disadvantages of others permitted my promotion; the absence of many Mexican-Americans from academic life allowed my designation as a "minority student."

For me opportunities had been extravagant. There were 2 fellowships, summer research grants, and teaching assistantships. After only two years in graduate school, I was offered teaching jobs by several colleges. Invitations to Washington conferences arrived and I had the chance to travel abroad as a "Mexican-American representative." The benefits were often, however, too gaudy to please. In three published essays, in conversations with teachers, in letters to politicians and at conferences, I worried the issue of Affirmative Action. Often I proposed contradictory opinions, though consistent was the admission that — because of an early, excellent education — I was no longer a principal victim of racism or any other social oppression. I said that but still I continued to indicate on applications for financial aid that I was a Hispanic-American. It didn't really occur to me to say anything else, or to leave the question unanswered.

Thus I complied with and encouraged the odd bureaucrat- 3 ic logic of Affirmative Action. I let government officials treat the disadvantaged condition of many Mexican-Americans with my advancement. Each fall my presence was noted by Health, Education, and Welfare department statisticians. As I pursued advanced literary studies and learned the skill of reading Spenser and Wordsworth and Empson, I would hear myself numbered among the culturally disadvantaged. Still, silent, I didn't object.

But the irony cut deep. And guilt would not be evaded 4 by averting my glance when I confronted a face like my own in a crowd. By late 1975, nearing the completion of my graduate studies at Berkeley, I was so wary of the benefits of Affirmative Action that I feared my inevitable success as an applicant for a teaching position. The months of fall — traditionally that time of academic job-searching — passed without my applying to a single school. When one of my professors chanced to learn this in late November, he was astonished, then furious. He yelled at me: Did I think that because I was a minority student jobs would just come looking for me? What was I thinking? Did I realize that he and several other faculty members had already written letters on my behalf? Was I going to start acting like some other minority students he had known? They struggled for success and then, when it was almost within reach, grew strangely afraid and let it pass. Was that it? Was I determined to fail?

5   I did not respond to his questions. I didn't want to admit to him, and thus to myself, the reason I delayed.

6   I merely agreed to write to several schools. (In my letter I wrote: "I cannot claim to represent disadvantaged Mexican-Americans. The very fact that I am in a position to apply for this job should make that clear.") After two or three days, there were telegrams and phone calls, invitations to interviews, then airplane trips. A blur of faces and the murmur of their soft questions. And, over someone's shoulder, the sight of campus buildings shadowing pictures I had seen years before when I leafed through Ivy League catalogues with great expectations. At the end of each visit, interviewers would smile and wonder if I had any questions. A few times I quietly wondered what advantage my race had given me over other applicants. But that was an impossible question for them to answer without embarrassing me. Quickly, several persons insisted that my ethnic identity had given me no more than a "foot inside the door"; at most, I had a "slight edge" over other applicants. "We just looked at your dossier with extra care and we like what we saw. There was never any question of having to alter our standards. You can be certain of that."

7   In the early part of January, offers arrived on stiffly elegant stationery. Most schools promised terms appropriate for any new assistant professor. A few made matters worse — and almost more tempting — by offering more: the use of university housing; an unusually large starting salary; a reduced teaching schedule. As the stack of letters mounted, my hesitation increased. I started calling department chairmen to ask for another week, then 10 more days — "more time to reach a decision" — to avoid the decision I would need to make.

8   At school, meantime, some students hadn't received a single job offer. One man, probably the best student in the department, did not even get a request for his dossier. He and I met outside a classroom one day and he asked about my opportunities. He seemed happy for me. Faculty mem-

bers beamed. They said they had expected it. "After all, not many schools are going to pass up getting a Chicano with a Ph.D. in Renaissance literature," somebody said laughing. Friends wanted to know which of the offers I was going to accept. But I couldn't make up my mind. February came and I was running out of time and excuses. (One chairman guessed my delay was a bargaining ploy and increased his offer with each of my calls.) I had to promise a decision by the 10th; the 12th at the very latest.

On the 18th of February, late in the afternoon, I was in   9
the office I shared with several other teaching assistants. Another graduate student was sitting across the room at his desk. When I got up to leave, he looked over to say in an uneventful voice that he had some big news. He had finally decided to accept a position at a faraway university. It was not a job he especially wanted, he admitted. But he had to take it because there hadn't been any other offers. He felt trapped, and depressed, since his job would separate him from his young daughter.

I tried to encourage him by remarking that he was lucky   10
at least to have found a job. So many others hadn't been able to get anything. But before I finished speaking I realized that I had said the wrong thing. And I anticipated his next question.

"What are your plans?" he wanted to know. "Is it true   11
you've gotten an offer from Yale?"

I said that it was. "Only, I still haven't made up my mind."   12

He stared at me as I put on my jacket. And smiling, then   13
unsmiling, he asked if I knew that he too had written to Yale. In his case, however, no one had bothered to acknowledge his letter with even a postcard. What did I think of that?

He gave me no time to answer.   14

"Damn!" he said sharply and his chair rasped the floor   15
as he pushed himself back. Suddenly, it was to *me* that he was complaining. "It's just not right, Richard. None of this is fair. You've done some good work, but so have I. I'll bet our records are just about equal. But when we look for jobs this year, it's a different story. You get all of the breaks."

To evade his criticism, I wanted to side with him. I was   16
about to admit the injustice of Affirmative Action. But he went on, his voice hard with accusation. "It's all very simple this year. You're a Chicano. And I am a Jew. That's the only real difference between us."

His words stung me: there was nothing he was telling   17 me that I didn't know. I had admitted everything already. But to hear someone else say these things, and in such an accusing tone, was suddenly hard to take. In a deceptively calm voice, I responded that he had simplified the whole issue. The phrases came like bubbles to the tip of my tongue: "new blood"; "the importance of cultural diversity"; "the goal of racial integration." These were all the arguments I had proposed several years ago — and had long since abandoned. Of course the offers were unjustifiable. I knew that. All I was saying amounted to a frantic self-defense. I tried to find an end to a sentence. My voice faltered to a stop.

18   "Yeah, sure," he said. "I've heard all that before. Nothing you say really changes the fact that Affirmative Action is unfair. You see that, don't you? There isn't any way for me to compete with you. Once there were quotas to keep my parents out of certain schools; now there are quotas to get you in and the effect on me is the same as it was for them."

19   I listened to every word he spoke. But my mind was really on something else. I knew at that moment that I would reject all of the offers. I stood there silently surprised by what an easy conclusion it was. Having prepared for so many years to teach, having trained myself to do nothing else, I had hesitated out of practical fear. But now that it was made, the decision came with relief. I immediately knew I had made the right choice.

20   My colleague continued talking and I realized that he was simply right. Affirmative Action programs *are* unfair to white students. But as I listened to him assert his rights, I thought of the seriously disadvantaged. How different they were from white, middle-class students who come armed with the testimony of their grades and aptitude scores and self-confidence to complain about the unequal treatment they now receive. I listen to them. I do not want to be careless about what they say. Their rights are important to protect. But inevitably when I hear them or their lawyers, I think about the most seriously disadvantaged, not simply Mexican-Americans, but of all those who do not ever imagine themselves going to college or becoming doctors: white, black, brown. Always poor. Silent. They are not plaintiffs before the court or against the misdirection of Affirmative Action. They lack the confidence (my confidence!) to assume their right to a good education. They lack the confidence and skills a good primary and secondary education provides and which are prerequisites for informed public life. They remain silent.

The debate drones on and surrounds them in stillness. 21
They are distant, faraway figures like the boys I have seen
peering down from freeway overpasses in some other part
of town.

RACE ON CAMPUS

Shelby Steele

The Recoloring of Campus Life

*Shelby Steele, professor of English at San Jose State University,
frequently writes essays on the subject of race. This essay
appeared in 1989 in* Harper's *magazine, a prestigious national
monthly.*

In the past few years, we have witnessed what the Na- 1
tional Institute Against Prejudice and Violence calls a "proliferation" of racial incidents on college campuses around
the country. Incidents of on-campus "intergroup conflict"
have occurred at more than 160 colleges in the last three
years, according to the institute. The nature of these incidents has ranged from open racial violence—most notoriously, the October 1986 beating of a black student at the
University of Massachusetts at Amherst after an argument
about the World Series turned into a racial bashing, with
a crowd of up to 3,000 whites chasing twenty blacks—to
the harassment of minority students, to acts of racial or
ethnic insensitivity, with by far the greatest number falling
in the last two categories. At Dartmouth College, three
editors of the *Dartmouth Review*, the off-campus right-wing
student weekly, were suspended last winter for harassing
a black professor in his lecture hall. At Yale University last
year a swastika and the words "white power" were painted
on the school's Afro-American cultural center. Racist jokes
were aired not long ago on a campus radio station at the
University of Michigan. And at the University of Wisconsin
at Madison, members of the Zeta Beta Tau fraternity held
a mock slave auction in which pledges painted their faces
black and wore Afro wigs. Two weeks after the president

of Stanford University informed the incoming freshman class last fall that "bigotry is out, and I mean it," two freshmen defaced a poster of Beethoven—gave the image thick lips—and hung it on a black student's door.

2   In response, black students around the country have rediscovered the militant protest strategies of the Sixties. At the University of Massachusetts at Amherst, Williams College, Penn State University, UC Berkeley, UCLA, Stanford, and countless other campuses, black students have sat in, marched, and rallied. But much of what they were marching and rallying about seemed less a response to specific racial incidents than a call for broader action on the part of the colleges and universities they were attending. Black students have demanded everything from more black faculty members and new courses on racism to the addition of "ethnic" foods in the cafeteria. There is the sense in these demands that racism runs deep.

3   Of course, universities are not where racial problems tend to arise. When I went to college in the mid-Sixties, colleges were oases of calm and understanding in a racially tense society; campus life—with its traditions of tolerance and fairness, its very distance from the "real" world—imposed a degree of broad-mindedness on even the most provincial students. If I met whites who were not anxious to be friends with blacks, most were at least vaguely friendly to the cause of our freedom. In any case, there was no guerrilla activity against our presence, no "mine field of racism" (as one black student at Berkeley recently put it) to negotiate. I wouldn't say that the phrase "campus racism" is a contradiction in terms, but until recently it certainly seemed an incongruence.

4   But a greater incongruence is the generational timing of this new problem on the campuses. Today's undergraduates were born after the passage of the 1964 Civil Rights Act. They grew up in an age when racial equality was for the first time enforceable by law. This too was a time when blacks suddenly appeared on television, as mayors of big cities, as icons of popular culture, as teachers, and in some cases even as neighbors. Today's black and white college students, veterans of *Sesame Street* and often of integrated grammar and high schools, have had more opportunities to know each other—whites and blacks—than any previous generation in American history. Not enough opportunities, perhaps, but enough to make the notion of racial tension on campus something of a mystery, at least to me.

5   To try to unravel this mystery I left my own campus,

where there have been few signs of racial tension, and talked
with black and white students at California schools where
racial incidents had occurred: Stanford, UCLA, Berkeley. I
spoke with black and white students — and not with Asians
and Hispanics — because, as always, blacks and whites represent the deepest lines of division, and because I hesitate
to wander onto the complex territory of other minority
groups. A phrase by William H. Gass — "the hidden internal-
ity of things" — describes with maybe a little too much grandeur what I hoped to find. But it *is* what I wanted to find,
for this is the kind of problem that makes a black person
nervous, which is not to say that it doesn't unnerve whites
as well. Once every six months or so someone yells "nigger"
at me from a passing car. I don't like to think that these
solo artists might soon make up a chorus or, worse, that
this chorus might one day soon sing to me from the paths
of my own campus.

I have long believed that trouble between the races is   6
seldom what it appears to be. It was not hard to see after
my first talks with students that racial tension on campus
is a problem that misrepresents itself. It has the same look,
the archetypal pattern, of America's timeless racial conflict —
white racism and black protest. And I think part of our
concern over it comes from the fact that it has the feel of
a relapse, illness gone and come again. But if we are seeing
the same symptoms, I don't believe we are dealing with
the same illness. For one thing, I think racial tension on
campus is the result more of racial equality than inequality.

How to live with racial difference has been America's   7
profound social problem. For the first 100 years or so following emancipation it was controlled by a legally sanctioned
inequality that acted as a buffer between the races. No
longer is this the case. On campuses today, as throughout
society, blacks enjoy equality under the law — a profound
social advancement. No student may be kept out of a class
or a dormitory or an extracurricular activity because of his
or her race. But there is a paradox here: On a campus where
members of all races are gathered, mixed together in the
classroom as well as socially, differences are more exposed
than ever. And this is where the trouble starts. For members
of each race — young adults coming into their own, often
away from home for the first time — bring to this site of
freedom, exploration, and now, today, equality very deep
fears and anxieties, inchoate feelings of racial shame, anger,

and guilt. These feelings could lie dormant in the home, in familiar neighborhoods, in simpler days of childhood. But the college campus, with its structures of interaction and adult-level competition—the big exam, the dorm, the "mixer"—is another matter. I think campus racism is born of the rub between racial difference and a setting, the campus itself, devoted to interaction and equality. On our campuses, such concentrated micro-societies, all that remains unresolved between blacks and whites, all the old wounds and shames that have never been addressed, present themselves for attention—and present our youth with pressures they cannot always handle.

8   I have mentioned one paradox: racial fears and anxieties among blacks and whites bubbling up in an era of racial equality under the law, in settings that are among the freest and fairest in society. And there is another, related paradox, stemming from the notion of—and practice of—affirmative action. Under the provisions of the Equal Employment Opportunity Act of 1972, all state governments and institutions (including universities) were forced to initiate plans to increase the proportion of minority and women employees—in the case of universities, of students too. Affirmative action plans that establish racial quotas were ruled unconstitutional more than ten years ago in *University of California Regents* v. *Bakke*. But quotas are only the most controversial aspect of affirmative action; the principle of affirmative action is reflected in various university programs aimed at redressing and overcoming past patterns of discrimination. Of course, to be conscious of patterns of discrimination—the fact, say, that public schools in the black inner cities are more crowded and employ fewer top-notch teachers than white suburban public schools, and that this is a factor in student performance—is only reasonable. However, in doing this we also call attention quite obviously to difference: in the case of blacks and whites, racial difference. What has emerged on campus in recent years—as a result of the new equality and affirmative action, in a sense, as a result of progress—is a *politics of difference*, a troubling, volatile politics in which each group justifies itself, its sense of worth and its pursuit of power, through difference alone.

9   In this context, racial, ethnic, and gender differences become forms of sovereignty, campuses become balkanized, and each group fights with whatever means are available. No doubt there are many factors that have contributed to the rise of racial tension on campus: What has been the

role of fraternities, which have returned to campus with their inclusions and exclusions? What role has the heightened notion of college as some first step to personal, financial success played in increasing competition, and thus tension? Mostly what I sense, though, is that in interactive settings, while fighting the fights of "difference," old ghosts are stirred, and haunt again. Black and white Americans simply have the power to make each other feel shame and guilt. In the "real" world, we may be able to deny these feelings, keep them at bay. But these feelings are likely to surface on college campuses, where young people are groping for identity and power, and where difference is made to matter so greatly. In a way, racial tension on campus in the Eighties might have been inevitable.

I would like, first, to discuss black students, their anxieties and vulnerabilities. The accusation that black Americans have always lived with is that they are inferior — inferior simply because they are black. And this accusation has been too uniform, too ingrained in cultural imagery, too enforced by law, custom, and every form of power not to have left a mark. Black inferiority was a precept accepted by the founders of this nation; it was a principle of social organization that relegated blacks to the sidelines of American life. So when today's young black students find themselves on white campuses, surrounded by those who historically have claimed superiority, they are also surrounded by the myth of their inferiority. 10

Of course it is true that many young people come to college with some anxiety about not being good enough. But only blacks come wearing a color that is still, in the minds of some, a sign of inferiority. Poles, Jews, Hispanics, and other groups also endure degrading stereotypes. But two things make the myth of black inferiority a far heavier burden — the broadness of its scope and its incarnation in color. There are not only more stereotypes of blacks than of other groups, but these stereotypes are also more dehumanizing, more focused on the most despised of human traits — stupidity, laziness, sexual immorality, dirtiness, and so on. In America's racial and ethnic hierarchy, blacks have clearly been relegated to the lowest level — have been burdened with an ambiguous, animalistic humanity. Moreover, this is made unavoidable for blacks by the sheer visibility of black skin, a skin that evokes the myth of inferiority on sight. And today this myth is sadly reinforced 11 for many black students by affirmative action programs, under which blacks may often enter college with lower test scores and high-school grade point averages than whites. "They see me as an affirmative action case," one black student told me at UCLA.

12   So when a black student enters college, the myth of inferiority compounds the normal anxiousness over whether he or she will be good enough. This anxiety is not only personal but also racial. The families of these students will have pounded into them the fact that blacks are not inferior. And probably more than anything, it is this pounding that finally leaves a mark. If I am not inferior, why the need to say so?

13   This myth of inferiority constitutes a very sharp and ongoing anxiety for young blacks, the nature of which is very precise: It is the terror that somehow, through one's actions or by virtue of some "proof" (a poor grade, a flubbed response in class), one's fear of inferiority—inculcated in ways large and small by society—will be confirmed as real. On a university campus, where intelligence itself is the ultimate measure, this anxiety is bound to be triggered.

14   A black student I met at UCLA was disturbed a little when I asked him if he ever felt vulnerable—anxious about "black inferiority"—as a black student. But after a long pause, he finally said, "I think I do." The example he gave was of a large lecture class he'd taken with more than 300 students. Fifty or so black students sat in the back of the lecture hall and "acted out every stereotype in the book." They were loud, ate food, came in late—and generally got lower grades than the whites in the class. "I knew I would be seen like them, and I didn't like it. I never sat by them." "Seen like what?" I asked, though we both knew the answer. "As lazy, ignorant, and stupid," he said sadly.

15   Had the group at the back been white fraternity brothers, they would not have been seen as dumb *whites*, of course. And a frat brother who worried about his grades would not worry that he would be seen "like them." The terror in this situation for the student I spoke with was that his own deeply buried anxiety would be given credence, that the myth would be verified, and that he would feel shame and humiliation not because of who he was but simply because he was black. In this lecture hall his race, quite apart from his performance, might subject him to four unendurable feelings—diminishment, accountability to the preconceptions of whites, a powerlessness to change these preconceptions, and, finally, shame. These are the feelings that make

up his racial anxiety, and that of all blacks on any campus. On a white campus a black is never far from these feelings, and even his unconscious knowledge that he is subject to them can undermine his self-esteem. There are blacks on every campus who are not up to doing good college-level work. Certain black students may not be happy or motivated or in the appropriate field of study—*just like whites*. (Let us not forget that many white students get poor grades, fail, drop out.) Moreover, many more blacks than whites are not quite prepared for college, may have to catch up, owing to factors beyond their control: poor previous schooling, for example. But the white who has to catch up will not be anxious that his being behind is a matter of his whiteness, of his being *racially* inferior. The black student may well have such a fear.

This, I believe, is one reason why black colleges in America turn out 34 percent of all black college graduates, though they enroll only 17 percent of black college students. Without whites around on campus the myth of inferiority is in abeyance and, along with it, a great reservoir of culturally imposed self-doubt. On black campuses feelings of inferiority are personal; on campuses with a white majority, a black's problems have a way of becoming a "black" problem. 16

But this feeling of vulnerability a black may feel in itself is not as serious a problem as what he or she does with it. To admit that one is made anxious in integrated situations about the myth of racial inferiority is difficult for young blacks. It seems like admitting that one *is* racially inferior. And so, most often, the student will deny harboring those feelings. This is where some of the pangs of racial tension begin, because denial always involves distortion. 17

In order to deny a problem we must tell ourselves that the problem is something different than what it really is. A black student at Berkeley told me that he felt defensive every time he walked into a class and saw mostly white faces. When I asked why, he said, "Because I know they're all racists. They think blacks are stupid." Of course it may be true that some whites feel this way, but the singular focus on white racism allows this student to obscure his own underlying racial anxiety. He can now say that his problem—facing a class full of white faces, *fearing* that they think he is dumb—is entirely the result of certifiable white racism and has nothing to do with his own anxieties, or even that this particular academic subject may not be his best. Now all the terror of his anxiety, its powerful energy, 18 is devoted to simply *seeing* racism. Whatever evidence of racism he finds — and looking this hard, he will no doubt find some — can be brought in to buttress his distorted view of the problem, while his actual deep-seated anxiety goes unseen.

19   Denial, and the distortion that results, places the problem *outside* the self and in the world. It is not that I have any inferiority anxiety because of my race; it is that I am going to school with people who don't like blacks. This is the shift in thinking that allows black students to reenact the protest pattern of the Sixties. Denied racial anxiety-distortion-reenactment is the process by which feelings of inferiority are transformed into an exaggerated white menace — which is then protested against with the techniques of the past. Under the sway of this process, black students believe that history is repeating itself, that it's just like the Sixties, or Fifties. In fact, it is the not yet healed wounds from the past, rather than the inequality that created the wounds, that is the real problem.

20   This process generates an unconscious need to exaggerate the level of racism on campus — to make it a matter of the system, not just a handful of students. Racism is the avenue away from the true inner anxiety. How many students demonstrating for a black "theme house" — demonstrating in the style of the Sixties, when the battle was to win for blacks a place on campus — might be better off spending their time reading and studying? Black students have the highest dropout rate and lowest grade point average of any group in American universities. This need not be so. And it is not the result of not having black theme houses.

21   It was my very good fortune to go to college in 1964, when the question of black "inferiority" was openly talked about among blacks. The summer before I left for college I heard Martin Luther King Jr. speak in Chicago, and he laid it on the line for black students everywhere. "When you are behind in a footrace, the only way to get ahead is to run faster than the man in front of you. So when your white roommate says he's tired and goes to sleep, you stay up and burn the midnight oil." His statement that we were "behind in a footrace" acknowledged that because of history, of few opportunities, of racism, we were, in a sense, "inferior." But this had to do with what had been done to our parents and their parents, not with inherent inferiority. And because it was acknowledged, it was presented to us as a challenge rather than a mark of shame.

Of the eighteen black students (in a student body of 1,000)   22
who were on campus in my freshman year, all graduated,
though a number of us were not from the middle class. At
the university where I currently teach, the drop-out rate
for black students is 72 percent, despite the presence of
several academic-support programs; a counseling center
with black counselors; an Afro-American studies department; black faculty, administrators, and staff; a general
education curriculum that emphasizes "cultural pluralism"; an Educational Opportunities Program; a mentor
program; a black faculty and staff association; and an
administration and faculty that often announce the need
to do more for black students.

It may be unfair to compare my generation with the cur-   23
rent one. Parents do this compulsively and to little end but
self-congratulation. But I don't congratulate my generation.
I think we were advantaged. We came along at a time when
racial integration was held in high esteem. And integration
was a very challenging social concept for both blacks and
whites. We were remaking ourselves—that's what one did
at college—and making history. We had something to
prove. This was a profound advantage; it gave us clarity
and a challenge. Achievement in the American mainstream
was the goal of integration, and the best thing about this
challenge was its secondary message—that we *could*
achieve.

There is much irony in the fact that black power would   24
come along in the late Sixties and change all this. Black
power was a movement of uplift and pride, and yet it also
delivered the weight of pride—a weight that would burden
black students from then on. Black power "nationalized"
the black identity, made blackness itself an object of celebration and allegiance. But if it transformed a mark of
shame into a mark of pride, it also, in the name of pride,
required the denial of racial anxiety. Without a frank account of one's anxieties, there is no clear direction, no concrete challenge. Black students today do not get as clear a
message from their racial identity as my generation got.
They are not filled with the same urgency to prove themselves, because black pride has said, You're already proven,
already equal, as good as anybody.

The "black identity" shaped by black power most power-   25
fully contributes to racial tensions on campuses by basing
entitlement more on race than on constitutional rights and
standards of merit. With integration, black entitlement was

derived from constitutional principles of fairness. Black power changed this by skewing the formula from rights to color—if you were black, you were entitled. Thus, the United Coalition Against Racism (UCAR) at the University of Michigan could "demand" two years ago that all black professors be given immediate tenure, that there be special pay incentives for black professors, and that money be provided for an all-black student union. In this formula, black becomes the very color of entitlement, an extra right in itself, and a very dangerous grandiosity is promoted in which blackness amounts to specialness.

26   Race is, by any standard, an unprincipled source of power. And on campuses the use of racial power by one group makes racial or ethnic or gender *difference* a currency of power for all groups. When I make my difference into power, other groups must seize upon their difference to contain my power and maintain their position relative to me. Very quickly a kind of politics of difference emerges in which racial, ethnic, and gender groups are forced to assert their entitlement and vie for power based on the single quality that makes them different from one another.

27   On many campuses today academic departments and programs are established on the basis of difference—black studies, women's studies, Asian studies, and so on—despite the fact that there is nothing in these "difference" departments that cannot be studied within traditional academic disciplines. If their rationale truly is past exclusion from the mainstream curriculum, shouldn't the goal now be complete inclusion rather than separateness? I think this logic is overlooked because these groups are too interested in the power their difference can bring, and they insist on separate departments and programs as a tribute to that power.

28   This politics of difference makes everyone on campus a member of a minority group. It also makes racial tensions inevitable. To highlight one's difference as a source of advantage is also, indirectly, to inspire the enemies of that difference. When blackness (and femaleness) becomes power, then white maleness is also sanctioned as power. A white male student at Stanford told me, "One of my friends said the other day that we should get together and start up a white student union and come up with a list of demands."

29   It is certainly true that white maleness has long been an unfair source of power. But the sin of white male power is precisely its use of race and gender as a source of entitlement. When minorities and women use their race, ethnicity,

and gender in the same way, they not only commit the same sin but also, indirectly, sanction the very form of power that oppressed them in the first place. The politics of difference is based on a tit-for-tat sort of logic in which every victory only calls one's enemies to arms.

This elevation of difference undermines the communal 30 impulse by making each group foreign and inaccessible to others. When difference is celebrated rather than remarked, people must think in terms of difference, they must find meaning in difference, and this meaning comes from an endless process of contrasting one's group with other groups. Blacks use whites to define themselves as different, women use men, Hispanics use whites and blacks, and on it goes. And in the process each group mythologizes and mystifies its difference, puts it beyond the full comprehension of outsiders. Difference becomes an inaccessible preciousness toward which outsiders are expected to be simply and uncomprehendingly reverential. But beware: In this world, even the insulated world of the college campus, preciousness is a balloon asking for a needle. At Smith College, graffiti appears: "Niggers, Spics, and Chinks quit complaining or get out."

Most of the white students I talked with spoke as if from 31 under a faint cloud of accusation. There was always a ring of defensiveness in their complaints about blacks. A white student I spoke with at UCLA told me: "Most white students on this campus think the black student leadership here is made up of oversensitive crybabies who spend all their time looking for things to kick up a ruckus about." A white student at Stanford said: "Blacks do nothing but complain and ask for sympathy when everyone really knows they don't do well because they don't try. If they worked harder, they could do as well as everyone else."

That these students felt accused was most obvious in 32 their compulsion to assure me that they were not racists. Oblique versions of some-of-my-best-friends-are stories came ritualistically before or after critiques of black students. Some said flatly, "I am not a racist, but ..." Of course, we all deny being racists, but we only do this compulsively, I think, when we are working against an accusation of bias. I think it was the color of my skin, itself, that accused them.

This was the meta-message that surrounded these conver- 33 sations like an aura, and in it, I believe, is the core of white

American racial anxiety. My skin not only accused them, it judged them. And this judgment was a sad gift of history that brought them to account whether they deserved such an accounting or not. It said that wherever and whenever blacks were concerned, they had reason to feel guilt. And whether it was earned or unearned, I think it was guilt that set off the compulsion in these students to disclaim. I believe it is true that in America black people make white people feel guilty.

34   Guilt is the essence of white anxiety, just as inferiority is the essence of black anxiety. And the terror that it carries for whites is the terror of discovering that one has reason to feel guilt where blacks are concerned — not so much because of what blacks might think but because of what guilt can say about oneself. If the darkest fear of blacks is inferiority, the darkest fear of whites is that their better lot in life is at least partially the result of their capacity for evil — their capacity to dehumanize an entire people for their own benefit, and then to be indifferent to the devastation their dehumanization has wrought on successive generations of their victims. This is the terror that whites are vulnerable to regarding blacks. And the mere fact of being white is sufficient to feel it, since even whites with hearts clean of racism benefit from being white — benefit at the expense of blacks. This is a conditional guilt having nothing to do with individual intentions or actions. And it makes for a very powerful anxiety because it threatens whites with a view of themselves as inhuman, just as inferiority threatens blacks with a similar view of themselves. At the dark core of both anxieties is a suspicion of incomplete humanity.

35   So the white students I met were not just meeting me; they were also meeting the possibility of their own inhumanity. And this, I think, is what explains how some young white college students in the late Eighties can so frankly take part in racially insensitive and outright racist acts. They were expected to be cleaner of racism than any previous generation — they were born into the Great Society. But this expectation overlooks the fact that, for them, color is still an accusation and judgment. In black faces there is a discomforting reflection of white collective shame. Blacks remind them that their racial innocence is questionable, that they are the beneficiaries of past and present racism, and that the sins of the father may well have been visited on the children.

36   And yet young whites tell themselves that they had noth-

ing to do with the oppression of black people. They have a
stronger belief in their racial innocence than any previous
generation of whites, and a natural hostility toward anyone
who would challenge that innocence. So (with a great deal
of individual variation) they can end up in the paradoxical
position of being hostile to blacks as a way of defending
their own racial innocence.

I think this is what the young white editors of the *Dartmouth*   37
Review were doing when they shamelessly harassed William
Cole, a black music professor. Weren't they saying, in effect,
I am so free of racial guilt that I can afford to ruthlessly
attack blacks and still be racially innocent? The ruthless-
ness of that attack was a form of denial, a badge of innocence. The more they were charged with racism, the more
ugly and confrontational their harassment became. Racism
became a means of rejecting racial guilt, a way of showing
that they were not ultimately racists.

The politics of difference sets up a struggle for innocence   38
among all groups. When difference is the currency of power,
each group must fight for the innocence that entitles it to
power. Blacks sting whites with guilt, remind them of their
racist past, accuse them of new and more subtle forms of
racism. One way whites retrieve their innocence is to dis-
credit blacks and deny their difficulties, for in this denial
is the denial of their own guilt. To blacks this denial looks
like racism, a racism that feeds black innocence and encourages them to throw more guilt at whites. And so the cycle
continues. The politics of difference leads each group to
pick at the sore spots of the other.

Men and women who run universities — whites, mostly —   39
also participate in the politics of difference, although they
handle their guilt differently than many of their students.
They don't deny it, but still they don't want to *feel* it. And
to avoid this *feeling* of guilt they have tended to go along
with whatever blacks put on the table rather than work
with them to assess their real needs. University administrators have too often been afraid of their own guilt and have
relied on negotiation and capitulation more to appease that
guilt than to help blacks and other minorities. Administrators would never give white students a racial theme house
where they could be "more comfortable with people of their
own kind," yet more and more universities are doing this
for black students, thus fostering a kind of voluntary segregation. To avoid the anxieties of integrated situations,

blacks ask for theme houses; to avoid guilt, white administrators give them theme houses.

40   When everyone is on the run from his anxieties about race, race relations on campus can be reduced to the negotiation of avoidances. A pattern of demand and concession develops in which each side uses the other to escape itself. Black studies departments, black deans of student affairs, black counseling programs, Afro houses, black theme houses, black homecoming dances and graduation ceremonies — black students and white administrators have slowly engineered a machinery of separatism that, in the name of sacred difference, redraws the ugly lines of segregation.

41   Black students have not sufficiently helped themselves, and universities, despite all their concessions, have not really done much for blacks. If both faced their anxieties, I think they would see the same thing: Academic parity with all other groups should be the overriding mission of black students, and it should also be the first goal that universities have for their black students. Blacks can only *know* they are as good as others when they are, in fact, as good — when their grades are higher and their dropout rate lower. Nothing under the sun will substitute for this, and no amount of concessions will bring it about.

42   Universities and colleges can never be free of guilt until they truly help black students, which means leading and challenging them rather than negotiating and capitulating. It means inspiring them to achieve academic parity, nothing less, and helping them see their own weaknesses as their greatest challenge. It also means dismantling the machinery of separatism, breaking the link between difference and power, and skewing the formula for entitlement away from race and gender and back to 'constitutional rights.

43   As for the young white students who have rediscovered swastikas and the word "nigger," I think they suffer from an exaggerated sense of their own innocence, as if they were incapable of evil and beyond the reach of guilt. But it is also true that the politics of difference creates an environment which threatens their innocence and makes them defensive. White students are not invited to the negotiating table from which they see blacks and others walk away with concessions. The presumption is that they do not deserve to be there because they are white. So they can only be defensive, and the less mature among them will be ag-

gressive. Guerrilla activity will ensue. Of course this is wrong, but it is also a reflection of an environment where difference carries power and where whites have the wrong "difference."

I think universities should emphasize commonality as a 44
higher value than "diversity" and "pluralism" — buzzwords for the politics of difference. Difference that does not rest on a clearly delineated foundation of commonality not only is inaccessible to those who are not part of the ethnic or racial group but is antagonistic to them. Difference can enrich only the common ground.

Integration has become an abstract term today, having 45
to do with little more than numbers and racial balances. But it once stood for a high and admirable set of values. It made difference second to commonality, and it asked members of all races to face whatever fears they inspired in each other. I doubt the word will have a new vogue, but the values, under whatever name, are worth working for.

Ruth Conniff
Racism 101

Ruth Conniff was an undergraduate editorial intern studying at Yale University when she wrote the following article for The Progressive *in 1988.*

At the University of Wisconsin in Madison, the brothers 1
of Phi Gamma Delta fraternity are known as Fijis, and each spring they throw what they call a Fiji Island Party. For the festivities of May 1987, they painted themselves in blackface and set up, on the lawn outside their fraternity house, a large caricatured cutout of a black man with a bone through his nose.

At about the same time, black students at the University 2
of Michigan found fliers slipped under their doors declaring "open hunting season on jigaboos and porch monkeys." At the University of Massachusetts, white students attacked an interracial couple and several black students on campus.

These incidents and others like them have been widely 3

reported as evidence of a resurgence of racism on campus. University administrators have responded to the outcry by announcing plans to combat the problem.

4   But for minorities, the news is old. Long after the civil-rights movement and desegregation, black students worry about their safety at universities all over the country. Name-calling and even violent threats are routine. And campus racism is no new phenomenon. The Fiji party, for example, had been going on every spring for years before anyone called attention to it.

5   But tensions between black and white students are just the most visible part of the problem. Hispanics, Asians, and native Americans, as well as blacks, struggle against racism deeply rooted in the universities. It starts when they apply for admission and financial aid, continues in the classroom, and extends to daily life on campus.

6   "You have to look at the mindset of minority students when they get here," says Charles Holly of the University of Wisconsin's Black Student Union. "You're going to class on the first day, and you're the only black in with 300 white students, all staring at you like, 'What are you doing here?' My first football game here, freshman year, I had garbage thrown at me and was called 'nigger.' That was my last football game, too."

7   Many white students, however, resent the recent surge of attention to issues of race.

8   "We've been stabbed from all sides," says Dan Mose, a Wisconsin Fiji.

9   "It seems like the way the university and the black students went after them was just for attention," says a member of a sorority on campus. "They always pick on the Greek system. It's gotten to the point now where you hear so much about it [racism] that people are watching everything they say."

10   Fewer nonwhites are enrolling in college these days, and fewer can stay. Blacks and Hispanics are increasingly un-derrepresented on campus — 26,000 fewer blacks attend col-lege now than in 1980 — because cuts in financial aid and the shift from grants to loans under the Reagan Administra-tion make tuition unaffordable for most minorities.

11   More black students graduate from high school now than ten years ago, but more and more blacks and Hispanics join the military or enroll in vocational schools instead of

going to college. The current emphasis on "raising standards" at universities, rather than on opening doors to students from ethnically and economically diverse backgrounds, has aggravated this trend.

In Albuquerque last year, the University of New Mexico 12 began referring students who once qualified for the school's General College, or remedial program, to local community colleges. The state legislature imposed the plan to raise standards at the university by phasing out a special-admissions program for students who don't meet the regular grade and test-score requirements.

Going to the nearby Technical Vocational Institute is 13 more reasonable for students than paying university tuition for basic courses, says Gary Kerkendal, assistant head of admissions at the university. "We feel very comfortable that there is an alternative for students to come back to us better prepared."

The alternatives are less comfortable for New Mexico's 14 low-income Hispanic, native American, and black students. Extra years in school mean a bigger accumulation of loans to pay off and more time before beginning careers. These factors, plus rising tuition rates, push the state university beyond the reach of many.

"The thing is," says Maximiliano Madrid, a senior at UNM 15 who was admitted as a General College student, "now you're told you're going to have to take two years at the community college and then comes the university and it takes four or five more years. You're behind to start off with and you're going to stay behind."

In Albuquerque's public high schools, the Industrial 16 Cooperative Training Program encourages low-income students to learn job skills and start working before they graduate. Most continue in their jobs afterwards or go on to the Technical Vocational Institute.

At the University of California at Berkeley, Asian-Ameri- 17 can students are engaged in a different kind of struggle with the administration.

Enrollment by Asians has not declined, but in the last 18 few years it has leveled off. Students charge that some admissions policies are deliberately designed to keep them out. Berkeley awards extra points, for example, to students who pass achievement tests in European foreign languages, but no points are awarded to students who know Chinese or Vietnamese. Asian students, like Hispanics and blacks, also say they feel alienated and receive inadequate support while at the university.

19   Chancellor Ira Michael Heyman denies that the university's admissions policies are discriminatory, but he recently made a public apology for not responding "more openly and less defensively" to Asian students' concerns.

20   One major bone of contention is the English-language program. More than half of the Asian students at Berkeley are recent immigrants, and they represent 80 per cent of those enrolled in the three-semester English as a Second Language sequence. As with all the university's remedial programs, a student who fails more than one ESL course flunks out, regardless of grade-point average. Many Asian immigrants who pass their other classes do not graduate because of the English requirement.

21   "U.C. Berkeley considers that there are too many Asians on campus in the first place, and not enough are flunking out to need help," says Richard Ehara, a tutor at Berkeley and a member of a committee protesting the university's Asian policies. "There are no Asian counselors and they are not considered a priority for tutoring."

22   Student activists claim the ESL program is culturally discriminatory.

23   "That's why a lot of Asians flunk out of Berkeley," says Nam Nguyen, a Vietnamese-American student, "not because they can't do the work. You have to write an essay on a subject that you don't understand because of cultural differences. For instance, they ask you to debate a point in the Constitution. First of all, if you're a recent immigrant, you might not know the Constitution as well. And secondly, if it's someone from an Asian culture, most people don't debate in Asian culture. When you write a paper, it's more of a discussion. You use a lot of philosophy and a lot of quotes and stuff. And teachers don't understand why the students are writing this way."

24   In New Mexico, students also complain about ethnocentrism in the classroom.

25   "There are certain pieces of literature that are very offensive," says Madrid. "You study long enough and all of a sudden you say, 'Hey, maybe that's not right,' even the way the Pulitzer Prize-winning authors depict things in Southwest Studies. You're from the area and you're proud of your people and you're sitting here reading something by Willa Cather about fat, greasy Mexicans who, all they want

to do is have kids. And you know, it may be written so it sounds kind of nice, but you're sitting there saying, 'God, this is offensive.' That's what your professors want you to read. They don't want you to read something by Raulfo Acuna, talking about occupied America. And you don't study people like Rejes Tijerina, or the disputes over the treaty of Guadalupe Hidalgo land grants. You've got to teach yourself that stuff."

Institutional callousness to nonwhites fosters an at-   26
mosphere among students that is hostile to minorities in several ways:

- White students don't see or know much about other cultures and ethnic groups because groups are underrepresented on campus.
- White culture dominates the curriculum, and that reinforces white students' assumption that theirs is the only legitimate culture.
- With the tightening of educational funds and the conservative political climate, many white students resent such measures as affirmative action, which seem to coddle minorities.

Given this set of circumstances, it is not surprising that   27
white students are confused by and resentful of the sudden surge of attention to issues of race.

Many of the gains achieved by the civil-rights movement   28
in the 1960s and 1970s are slipping away. Cultural centers and special programs set up to accommodate nonwhite students have dwindled or disappeared.

Gerald Thomas, who now conducts race-awareness train-   29
ing sessions at the University of Wisconsin, has watched the atmosphere on campus change since he started teaching Afro-American studies in 1970.

"We had the sensitivity and the awareness of racial issues   30
culminating toward the end of the 1960s," he says. "The white community was sensitized and the minority community's interest was heightened. And then it died out. Students moved on, and administrators and institutions got weary of dealing in a half-assed way with racism."

After recent racist incidents, black student activists have   31
rallied to demand that university administrators protect their safety and address the declines in enrollment, financial aid, and supportive resources.

The United Coalition Against Racism at Michigan played   32 host in the summer of 1987 to students from twenty other campuses to discuss building a new movement. At several such conferences held that summer, students discussed strategies for dealing with a racism that is more subtle and insidious than that confronted by their predecessors a generation ago. Members of UCAR are working to form a national student movement against racism.

33   "Mainly, we're not talking about white students," says Barbara Ransby of the Michigan coalition, "but rather a racist administration." Efforts to combat racism among students can be useful, she says, "but it's really not the crux of the problem. If whites are nicer and more polite to black students, it doesn't change the underlying oppressive power structure."

34   Although student activists have made some gains recently in the struggle against campus racism, it will take a deep revision of universities' structures and values to make a lasting change.

35   Mandatory ethnic-studies programs, which would teach students about a variety of cultures, are a big item among the reforms student activists are demanding and university administrators are discussing on various campuses, including Stanford, Berkeley, Wisconsin, Michigan, and Massachusetts.

36   In Madison, University of Wisconsin chancellor Donna Shalala, with the help of student and faculty committees, has formulated a plan to combat racism that includes awareness training for students, a cross-departmental ethnic-studies requirement, and a pledge to increase recruitment of minority students and faculty. The university has instituted workshops and classes on race relations, a pledge to recruit more minority staff and students, and stricter penalties for racial harassment. After the Fiji party, the university temporarily suspended the fraternity. It was reinstated last spring with the understanding that members would attend one of the new racism-awareness sessions.

37   "The model for these training sessions describes racism as a series of stages varying between ignorance and intentional discrimination," says Roger Howard, associate dean of students. "If you go by that model, then, yes, the members of the Fiji fraternity were racist in that they were ignorant and insensitive. But what feels like racism from the point of view of a minority doesn't seem like racism to white students."

Charles Holly, who attended the fraternity's training ses-   38
sion, has a different view.

"The university's idea was just to parade black students   39
in there," Holly says. "They said, 'Okay, we have this racial
ignorance, you go in and educate them.' It was like when
you're four years old and your parents sit you down and
try to make you learn your multiplication tables. One guy
stood up and said, 'I don't know why we're here.' That set
the tone. 'We don't think we need to be here. We just had
a party, and they're making us into villains.'

"It was the whole blame-the-victim thing. We [black stu-   40
dents] were wrong for even raising the issue, because it had
been going on for years. If it was okay then, why not now?
There was this alumnus standing there in the background
clapping and saying, 'Yeah!' The whole thing was based on
the idea that the fraternity guys were ignorant. But their
idea was that what they do shouldn't offend anyone. That's
racist. It's one thing to say, 'Damn, I'm sorry, Charles, I
didn't know that would offend you,' and another to say, 'I
don't care if it does.' That's the attitude the fraternity has:
'I don't know and I don't care.'"

The same attitude is evident in the argument that Stan-   41
ford's Pulitzer Prize-winning historian Carl Degler makes
against multicultural education: "It is difficult, to say the
least, to name the important institutions and values in modern American culture that can be shown to have been derived from Africa, China, Japan. . . ."

Changes like those made by Stanford in its required study   42
of Western civilization — which is now called "Culture and
Ideas" and includes works by minorities and women — are
still the subject of much debate. Many academics fear that
in embracing such a diverse program of studies, universities
may fail to educate students in the foundations of American
society. While this is a legitimate concern, it must be considered alongside the all-too-visible failings of a university
atmosphere traditionally hostile to minorities.

Before they can hope to combat campus racism, students,   43
professors, and administrators must change the deeply ingrained attitude that Western culture is the most important
culture, that nonwhite cultures are separate from "real"
American culture.

Real change requires a reevaluation of the basic   44
philosophy of college education — who is qualified to be
educated and what constitutes an education? When white
students say there is no reason for them to challenge their

racist assumptions, they merely reflect a world view fostered by the university.

45   Meanwhile, back in Madison at the University of Wisconsin, in late October, the Zeta Beta Tau fraternity dressed its pledges up in Afro wigs and blackface and held a slave auction. Eight students who protested were arrested. The fraternity has been suspended by the Interfraternity Council. Its president told one of the protesters the event "wasn't intended to be racist."

Victor Hao Li

Asian Discrimination: Fact or Fiction?

Victor Hao Li is president of the East-West Center at Stanford University. He published the following analysis in 1988 in The College Board Review, *a periodical designed chiefly for academic administrators.*

1   Universities have always faced a difficult task. From a pool of fully qualified candidates, how can a fraction be selected for admission? In making this selection, universities must meet many criteria and deal with many constituencies. They must admit leaders and scholars, artists and athletes, alumni legacies and minority members. The process of identifying the most meritorious does not by nature lend itself to simple solutions or test score rankings. It calls for the making of judgments, and these judgments must be based on clearly articulated principles which are objectively applied.

2   In recent decades, another admissions task has been added: How can fair opportunity be given to able students whose backgrounds, for one reason or another, have adversely affected their educational achievements or aspirations?

3   The American higher education system has made tremendous progress in extending the opportunity to attend college to all groups in our society, poor as well as rich, blacks and

other races as well as white. There was an earlier, shameful time when some universities discriminated against Jewish applicants. The methods used were sometimes blunt, and sometimes subtle gentlemen's agreements. Nevertheless, the result was that principles concerning the definition and value of merit were violated, often in the guise of seeking diversity or avoiding overrepresentation.

I especially appreciate the efforts made by many univer-   4
sities to increase opportunities for able people from educationally disadvantaged backgrounds. In this regard, Asian applicants have posed some complex new questions for universities. Asians, though clearly a separate and minority ethnic group, do not fit into traditional categories. Indeed, a number of universities do not regard Asian-Americans as "minority" for many reasons.

What we must deal with is how to handle the large   5
number of Asian-Americans applying — and being admitted — to universities. These numbers often exceed by far the comparable proportion of Asian-Americans in the total national or regional college-age population. The success of such students is usually attributed to cultural factors that stress education, discipline, and achievement.

Asian-American communities are worried that de facto   6
quotas or other limitations on admissions have been or might be established. They want assurances that Asian-American applicants are not denied admission simply because an above-average number of such applicants may be qualified.

Universities deny that they discriminate against Asian-   7
Americans, or that they use racial quotas in any form. On the other hand, some California studies have suggested that Asian-American applicants have been accepted at a somewhat lower rate than whites. Some universities could conceivably worry that enrolling too large a concentration of Asian-Americans might harm their educational efforts by decreasing diversity, or might lead to political problems, especially in public institutions.

Questions concerning discrimination — we are speaking   8
here, after all, about discrimination and not about affirmative action — can be answered directly and readily. At the level of fundamental principle, there cannot be disagreement: No person should suffer any disadvantage because of race.

At the practical level, there should also be no controversy.   9
In the normal admissions process, applicants should be

accepted on the basis of merit. Merit should have a direct and substantial bearing on academic performance and promise, although factors such as diversity of background and interests are legitimate concerns. In any case, the definition of merit and the criteria and process by which applicants are accepted should be clearly and publicly spelled out. All are entitled to know the rules of the game, and to attempt to measure performance against the stated norms.

10   I begin with the assumption that admissions officers are honorable and conscientious people. I also recognize that selection is — and ought to be — partly subjective, as much art as science. From time to time, a valedictorian-student class president-bassoon player may be rejected for legitimate reasons. There is no doubt that mistakes will be made in some cases. But until a clear and undeniable pattern is shown, allegations of discriminatory practices are unfair.

11   Having said that, I do believe that some admissions officers and selection processes are insensitive to Asian-American conditions and issues. I am not trying to assign fault, but simply to state a fact. Each of us is most sensitive to the familiar, and most insensitive to the unfamiliar. For large numbers of people, Asian-Americans still fall in the category of unfamiliar. The solutions to this problem are tried and true, but also take some time to implement: good will, education, training where necessary, inclusion of Asian-Americans in the admissions process, and open dialogue on all issues. I suspect that much of the criticism from Asian-American communities ultimately is aimed at insensitivity rather than discrimination.

Asian and American Communities

12   There is in this country a misconception — or at least, a partial conception — of Asian-Americans. It causes far more serious problems than the possible discrimination in college admissions. Indeed, the misconception may lie at the heart of the insensitivity issue.

13   To begin with, many subgroups are labeled "Asian-Americans." These persons originally came from a very large number of countries having highly distinct cultures, languages, and histories. To be sure, many from East and Southeast Asia share a Sinitic cultural heritage. Nevertheless, a Japanese is very different from a Chinese or a Vietnamese, much less an Indian or an Indonesian.

Some Asian-Americans are quite well-established in 14
American society. The families of these persons may have
arrived in the United States some time ago (Hawaii is celebrating in 1989 the 200th anniversary of the first Chinese
immigrants); others may have come as graduate students
and remained to hold good professional positions; still
others may have been wealthy at the time they immigrated.

The children of such families may find that their physical 15
appearance and perhaps some cultural traits set them
apart. The Nisei who were interned in World War II suffered
a special disability. Others encountered discrimination,
both overt and subtle, or had language and other social
deficiencies. But taken as a whole, this group of young
people were well-educated and were beginning good
careers. They often needed extra nurturing and understanding, but that is quite different from needing affirmative
action. To a significant degree, these are the persons who
are pointed to as the "model minority," who exemplify the
American success story, the *Time* magazine "whiz kids," or
the Westinghouse science winners.

To be sure, some children of poor families or recent im- 16
migrants are also high achievers. I have no doubt that the
cultural factors mentioned earlier plus the hunger for survival or acceptance motivate such persons. My point is that
when thinking of Asian-Americans as a group, we usually
picture the high achievers from good backgrounds.

But there is an underside, a very substantial one. For 17
many years, large numbers of Asian-Americans lived in true
"ghetto" circumstances. In many Chinatowns or Japan-
towns around the country, one could find abject poverty,
abominable living conditions, little English spoken, and
even less hope. These persons truly needed affirmative action programs and many other forms of assistance. But
they tended to get little attention because we all were
watching the "model minority" segment.

For universities, dealing with two distinctly different 18
types of Asian-Americans posed a special dilemma. If
Asian-Americans were regarded as a "minority" for various
affirmative action purposes, the beneficiaries undoubtedly
would be the well-off group that did not need such assistance. If Asian-Americans were not regarded as a minority
requiring affirmative action (because enough members of
the "model minority" were part of the mainstream), then
the disadvantaged would never get the opportunity to break
out. And if a distinction were made between the two groups

so that socio-economic (rather than ethnic) factors carried paramount weight, then complaints would likely be heard from others.

19   This situation was further complicated by the immigration law changes of the late 1960s. Immigration quotas had previously been based on the size of a particular national origin group then in the United States. Since most of the settlers of this country came from Europe, the formal quota for almost all Asian countries was 100 persons per year. The new immigration law raised this figure to 20,000 per year, and has fundamentally changed immigration patterns in this country. Since that time, the number of immigrants from China, the Philippines, Korea, and other Asian countries has increased dramatically, and has been augmented by a large influx of refugees from Indochina. These newcomers include both "the best and the brightest" of the region and the economically and socially worst-off. In addition, huge numbers of college and graduate students have come from Asia, and many have remained in the United States after completing their studies.

20   How well do these newcomers do? Many excel, but again I would like to draw attention to the underside. We have all read about cultural problems encountered by the Hmong people settling in Minnesota, ethnic conflict between Vietnamese and other fishermen in Louisiana, and poverty and crime among newcomers in Southern California.

21   Hawaii has none of these overt and festering social sores, and hence is one of the better places. But even in Hawaii, the situation is alarming. About 8,000 new persons arrive there each year, mostly immigrants from China, the Philippines and Korea, plus several hundred Indochinese refugees. Again, many excel, and we are proud of our success stories. But very many do not, or at least they have a long and difficult adjustment. For example, Hawaii's department of education found that the public schools had 9,000 persons identified as "students of limited English proficiency" (SLEP), with another 1,000 added each year.

22   These people must be reached by college and university admissions personnel. Because of their achievement and their background, these are individuals who would be model candidates for an affirmative action program. They require, I believe, a greater share of our attention and caring than do the overachievers at the top of the scale.

VI.

CRIME AND PUNISHMENT

You've heard all the statistics.

According to the Department of Justice, a violent crime occurs somewhere in the United States every twenty seconds. A murder occurs every half hour (about 23,000 in 1990). Someone is raped every six minutes. Almost fourteen million arrests were made in 1988, over a million of them for drug abuse violations. More Americans are in prison, per capita, than any other "developed" nation. The point is this: crime has become an inescapable fact of American life. And what to do about it has become a perennial issue, as the selections in this part demonstrate.

What is the source of crime, anyway? This central question is addressed by the first set of readings. Do economic circumstances cause crime? Are most people driven to crime, desperate to meet their daily needs, or determined to strike out against a system that keeps them attached permanently to an underclass? Is crime a blow against "the system"? Then again, if economic circumstances cause crime, why were crime rates lower during the Great Depression than during the economic boom years of the 1960s or 1980s? Or does crime have a social explanation? Is it an outgrowth of our society's rootlessness, or our fragmented families, or impersonal "value-free" schools? Is crime an inevitable by-product of a national identity that prizes nonconformity and anti-authoritarianism? (Think of Billy the Kid and Bonnie and Clyde.) Or is crime glorified and perpetuated by the media — by newspaper sensationalism and television shows? (In this connection, you may wish to read or reread earlier selections in this book on the effects of television and on pornography.) Is crime somehow encouraged by the justice itself? Is it the result of our national addiction to drugs? Or is crime much simpler to explain — as a manifestation of our human fallibility, our human sinfulness, that Americans are simply unwilling to face up to?

Our collective perplexity about the causes of crime is matched by our uneasiness about what to do about it. No country has a prison system as extensive as ours, yet we seem not to have reached consensus about the goal of the system. Are prisons primarily designed for punishment — demanded by our sense of justice? Is the motive self-preservation, to remove dangerous people from society? Are prisons designed to deter others from committing crimes? Or is our motive mercy: to rehabilitate people so that they can live more productive lives? Or is the prison system something more sinister: a subtle form of brainwashing or social conditioning designed to bring rebels into conformity? The second set of readings in this part discuss those questions.

The third group of readings debate the ultimate incarceration, capital punishment. Is capital punishment an expression of justice, "an eye for an eye"? Is it a useful deterrent to other would-be murderers? Or does it feed one of our basest instincts—for revenge? Is the death penalty cruel and unusual punishment? Is it unfairly applied to minority criminals, especially for crimes against majority members? If so, is this an argument for abolition, or for improving our system of justice?

This part concludes with a discussion of whether illegal drugs should be regulated or made legal. As you know, the last two American presidents have declared war on drugs, but the war remains unwon. In the face of persistent and debilitating drug use, some have proposed legalization—not because they see drugs as less than a menace, but because they trust in other measures than law to fight it. Those who would legalize drugs propose that we approach drug abuse as an economic and medical problem rather than as a legal one. Legalizers wish to minimize the effects of illegal drugs by eliminating black market profits; legalization would drive down drug prices, the argument goes, and therefore reduce secondary crime motivated by the need to finance the drug habit. Legalizers would regulate and tax drugs, as liquor is regulated and taxed; the revenues could be used for education and drug prevention campaigns, and for treatment of drug addicts. Those who would legalize drugs argue by analogy to the prohibition of alcohol in the 1920s, a prohibition that made average citizens into criminals, made gangsters and rumrunners into millionaires, and reduced respect for law throughout the land. But those against legalization also point to Prohibition—to the end of Prohibition in 1930, when alcohol use skyrocketed. They argue that legalizing drugs would result in an inevitable spread in the use of cocaine and heroin, and an inevitable increase in cocaine babies, child abuse, wrecked automobiles and airplanes, and wrecked lives. And they contend that it is against the American grain to legalize immoral acts, no matter how often the acts are being committed.

In any case, what to do about drugs—and what to do about crime and criminals in general—will continue to engage our national attention for the remainder of this century. At least.

WHAT CAUSES CRIME?

Clarence Darrow

Address to the Prisoners in the Cook County Jail

Clarence Darrow (1857–1928) was the most famous American lawyer of the early twentieth century. An eloquent speaker from Youngstown, Ohio, who practiced mostly in Chicago, Darrow defended Eugene V. Debs and other controversial labor leaders, Nathan Leopold and Richard Loeb (two notorious murderers), and John Scopes in the famous Monkey Trial of 1925. The following is a transcript of a speech that Darrow delivered to prisoners in Chicago in 1902.

1   If I looked at jails and crimes and prisoners in the way the ordinary person does, I should not speak on this subject to you. The reason I talk to you on the question of crime, its cause and cure, is that I really do not in the least believe in crime. There is no such thing as a crime as the word is generally understood. I do not believe there is any sort of distinction between the real moral conditions of the people in and out of jail. One is just as good as the other. The people here can no more help being here than the people outside can avoid being outside. I do not believe that people are in jail because they deserve to be. They are in jail simply because they cannot avoid it on account of circumstances which are entirely beyond their control and for which they are in no way responsible.

2   I suppose a great many people on the outside would say I was doing you harm if they should hear what I say to you this afternoon, but you cannot be hurt a great deal anyway, so it will not matter. Good people outside would say that I was really teaching you things that were calculated to injure society, but it's worth while now and then to hear something different from what you ordinarily get from preachers and the like. These will tell you that you should

be good and then you will get rich and be happy. Of course we know that people do not get rich by being good, and that is the reason why so many of you people try to get rich some other way, only you do not understand how to do it quite as well as the fellow outside.

There are people who think that everything in this world   3
is an accident. But really there is no such thing as an accident. A great many folks admit that many of the people in jail ought to be there, and many who are outside ought to be in. I think none of them ought to be here. There ought to be no jails; and if it were not for the fact that people on the outside are so grasping and heartless in their dealings with the people on the inside, there would be no such institution as jails.

I do not want you to believe that I think all you people   4
here are angels. I do not think that. You are people of all kinds, all of you doing the best you can — and that is evidently not very well. You are people of all kinds and conditions and under all circumstances. In one sense everybody is equally good and equally bad. We all do the best we can under the circumstances. But as to the exact things for which you are sent here, some of you are guilty and did the particular act because you needed the money. Some of you did it because you are in the habit of doing it, and some of you because you are born to it, and it comes to be as natural as it does, for instance, for me to be good.

Most of you probably have nothing against me, and most   5
of you would treat me the same way as any other person would, probably better than some of the people on the outside would treat me, because you think I believe in you and they know I do not believe in them. While you would not have the least thing against me in the world, you might pick my pockets. I do not think all of you would, but I think some of you would. You would not have anything against me, but that's your profession, a few of you. Some of the rest of you, if my doors were unlocked, might come in if you saw anything you wanted — not out of any malice to me, but because that is your trade. There is no doubt there are quite a number of people in this jail who would pick my pockets. And still I know this — that when I get outside pretty nearly everybody picks my pocket. There may be some of you who would hold up a man on the street, if you did not happen to have something else to do, and needed the money; but when I want to light my house or my office

the gas company holds me up. They charge me one dollar for something that is worth twenty-five cents. Still all these people are good people; they are pillars of society and support the churches, and they are respectable.

6   When I ride on the streetcars I am held up—I pay five cents for a ride that is worth two and a half cents, simply because a body of men have bribed the city council and the legislature, so that all the rest of us have to pay tribute to them.

7   If I do not want to fall into the clutches of the gas trust and choose to burn oil instead of gas, then good Mr. Rockefeller holds me up, and he uses a certain portion of his money to build universities and support churches which are engaged in telling us how to be good.

8   Some of you are here for obtaining property under false pretenses—yet I pick up a great Sunday paper and read the advertisements of a merchant prince—"Shirtwaists for 39 cents, marked down from $3.00."

9   When I read the advertisements in the paper I see they are all lies. When I want to get out and find a place to stand anywhere on the face of the earth, I find that it has all been taken up long ago before I came here, and before you came here, and somebody says, "Get off, swim into the lake, fly into the air; go anywhere, but get off." That is because these people have the police and they have the jails and the judges and the lawyers and the soldiers and all the rest of them to take care of the earth and drive everybody off that comes in their way.

10   A great many people will tell you that all this is true, but that it does not excuse you. These facts do not excuse some fellow who reaches into my pocket and takes out a five-dollar bill. The fact that the gas company bribes the members of the legislature from year to year, and fixes the law, so that all you people are compelled to be "fleeced" whenever you deal with them; the fact that the streetcar companies and the gas companies have control of the streets; and the fact that the landlords own all the earth—this, they say, has nothing to do with you.

11   Let us see whether there is any connection between the crimes of the respectable classes and your presence in the jail. Many of you people are in jail because you have really committed burglary; many of you, because you have stolen something. In the meaning of the law, you have taken some other person's property. Some of you have entered a store

and carried off a pair of shoes because you did not have the price. Possibly some of you have committed murder. I cannot tell what all of you did. There are a great many people here who have done some of these things who really do not know themselves why they did them. I think I know why you did them — every one of you; you did these things because you were bound to do them. It looked to you at the time as if you had a chance to do them or not, as you saw fit; but still, after all, you had no choice. There may be people here who had some money in their pockets and who still went out and got some more money in a way society forbids. Now, you may not yourselves see exactly why it was you did this thing, but if you look at the question deeply enough and carefully enough you will see that there were circumstances that drove you to do exactly the thing which you did. You could not help it any more than we outside can help taking the positions that we take. The reformers who tell you to be good and you will be happy, and the people on the outside who have property to protect — they think that the only way to do it is by building jails and locking you up in cells on weekdays and praying for you Sundays.

I think that all of this has nothing whatever to do with 12 right conduct. I think it is very easily seen what has to do with right conduct. Some so-called criminals — and I will use this word because it is handy, it means nothing to me — I speak of the criminals who get caught as distinguished from the criminals who catch them — some of these so-called criminals are in jail for their first offenses, but nine tenths of you are in jail because you did not have a good lawyer and, of course, you did not have a good lawyer because you did not have enough money to pay a good lawyer. There is no very great danger of a rich man going to jail.

Some of you may be here for the first time. If we would 13 open the doors and let you out, and leave the laws as they are today, some of you would be back tomorrow. This is about as good a place as you can get anyway. There are many people here who are so in the habit of coming that they would not know where else to go. There are people who are born with the tendency to break into jail every chance they get, and they cannot avoid it. You cannot figure out your life and see why it was, but still there is a reason for it; and if we were all wise and knew all the facts, we could figure it out.

14   In the first place, there are a good many more people who go to jail in the wintertime than in the summer. Why is this? Is it because people are more wicked in winter? No, it is because the coal trust begins to get in its grip in the winter. A few gentlemen take possession of the coal, and unless the people will pay seven or eight dollars a ton for something that is worth three dollars, they will have to freeze. Then there is nothing to do but to break into jail, and so there are many more in jail in the winter than in summer. It costs more for gas in the winter because the nights are longer, and people go to jail to save gas bills. The jails are electric-lighted. You may not know it, but these economic laws are working all the time, whether we know it or do not know it.

15   There are more people who go to jail in hard times than in good times—few people, comparatively, go to jail except when they are hard up. They go to jail because they have no other place to go. They may not know why, but it is true all the same. People are not more wicked in hard times. That is not the reason. The fact is true all over the world that in hard times more people go to jail than in good times, and in winter more people go to jail than in summer. Of course it is pretty hard times for people who go to jail at any time. The people who go to jail are almost always poor people—people who have no other place to live, first and last. When times are hard, then you find large numbers of people who go to jail who would not otherwise be in jail.

16   Long ago, Mr. Buckle, who was a great philosopher and historian, collected facts, and he showed that the number of people who are arrested increased just as the price of food increased. When they put up the price of gas ten cents a thousand, I do not know who will go to jail, but I do know that a certain number of people will go. When the meat combine raises the price of beef, I do not know who is going to jail, but I know that a large number of people are bound to go. Whenever the Standard Oil Company raises the price of oil, I know that a certain number of girls who are seamstresses, and who work night after night long hours for somebody else, will be compelled to go out on the streets and ply another trade, and I know that Mr. Rockefeller and his associates are responsible and not the poor girls in the jails.

17   First and last, people are sent to jail because they are poor. Sometimes, as I say, you may not need money at the

particular time, but you wish to have thrifty forehanded habits, and do not always wait until you are in absolute want. Some of you people are perhaps plying the trade, the profession, which is called burglary. No man in his right senses will go into a strange house in the dead of night and prowl around with a dark lantern through unfamiliar rooms and take chances of his life, if he has plenty of the good things of the world in his own home. You would not take any such chances as that. If a man had clothes in his clothes-press and beefsteak in his pantry and money in the bank, he would not navigate around nights in houses where he knows nothing about the premises whatever. It always requires experience and education for this profession, and people who fit themselves for it are no more to blame than I am for being a lawyer. A man would not hold up another man on the street if he had plenty of money in his own pocket. He might do it if he had one dollar or two dollars, but he wouldn't if he had as much money as Mr. Rockefeller has. Mr. Rockefeller has a great deal better hold-up game than that.

18   The more that is taken from the poor by the rich, who have the chance to take it, the more poor people there are who are compelled to resort to these means for a livelihood. They may not understand it, they may not think so at once, but after all they are driven into that line of employment.

19   There is a bill before the legislature of this state to punish kidnaping children with death. We have wise members of the legislature. They know the gas trust when they see it and they always see it—they can furnish light enough to be seen; and this legislature thinks it is going to stop kidnaping children by making a law punishing kidnapers of children with death. I don't believe in kidnaping children, but the legislature is all wrong. Kidnaping children is not a crime, it is a profession. It has been developed with the times. It has been developed with our modern industrial conditions. There are many ways of making money—many new ways that our ancestors knew nothing about. Our ancestors knew nothing about a billion-dollar trust; and here comes some poor fellow who has no other trade and he discovers the profession of kidnaping children.

20   This crime is born, not because people are bad; people don't kidnap other people's children because they want the children or because they are devilish, but because they see a chance to get some money out of it. You cannot cure this

crime by passing a law punishing by death kidnapers of
children. There is one way to cure it. There is one way to
cure all these offenses, and that is to give the people a
chance to live. There is no other way, and there never was
any other way since the world began; and the world is so
blind and stupid that it will not see. If every man and
woman and child in the world had a chance to make a
decent, fair, honest living, there would be no jails and no
lawyers and no courts. There might be some persons here
or there with some peculiar formation of their brain, like
Rockefeller, who would do these things simply to be doing
them; but they would be very, very few, and those should
be sent to a hospital and treated, and not sent to jail; and
they would entirely disappear in the second generation, or
at least in the third generation.

21   I am not talking pure theory. I will just give you two or
three illustrations.

22   The English people once punished criminals by sending
them away. They would load them on a ship and export
them to Australia. England was owned by lords and nobles
and rich people. They owned the whole earth over there,
and the other people had to stay in the streets. They could
not get a decent living. They used to take their criminals
and send them to Australia — I mean the class of criminals
who got caught. When these criminals got over there, and
nobody else had come, they had the whole continent to run
over, and so they could raise sheep and furnish their own
meat, which is easier than stealing it. These criminals then
became decent, respectable people because they had a
chance to live. They did not commit any crimes. They were
just like the English people who sent them there, only better. And in the second generation the descendants of those
criminals were as good and respectable a class of people
as there were on the face of the earth, and then they began
building churches and jails themselves.

23   A portion of this country was settled in the same way,
landing prisoners down on the southern coast; but when
they got here and had a whole continent to run over and
plenty of chances to make a living, they became respectable
citizens, making their own living just like any other citizen
in the world. But finally the descendants of the English
aristocracy who sent the people over to Australia found out
they were getting rich, and so they went over to get possession of the earth as they always do, and they organized

land syndicates and got control of the land and ores, and then they had just as many criminals in Australia as they did in England. It was not because the world had grown bad; it was because the earth had been taken away from the people.

Some of you people have lived in the country. It's prettier 24 than it is here. And if you have ever lived on a farm you understand that if you put a lot of cattle in a field, when the pasture is short they will jump over the fence; but put them in a good field where there is plenty of pasture, and they will be law-abiding cattle to the end of time. The human animal is just like the rest of the animals, only a little more so. The same thing that governs in the one governs in the other.

Everybody makes his living along the lines of least resis- 25 tance. A wise man who comes into a country early sees a great undeveloped land. For instance, our rich men twenty-five years ago saw that Chicago was small and knew a lot of people would come here and settle, and they readily saw that if they had all the land around here it would be worth a good deal, so they grabbed the land. You cannot be a landlord because somebody has got it all. You must find some other calling. In England and Ireland and Scotland less than five per cent own all the land there is, and the people are bound to stay there on any kind of terms the landlords give. They must live the best they can, so they develop all these various professions — burglary, picking pockets, and the like.

Again, people find all sorts of ways of getting rich. These 26 are diseases like everything else. You look at people getting rich, organizing trusts and making a million dollars, and somebody gets the disease and he starts out. He catches it just as a man catches the mumps or the measles; he is not to blame, it is in the air. You will find men speculating beyond their means, because the mania of money-getting is taking possession of them. It is simply a disease — nothing more, nothing less. You cannot avoid catching it; but the fellows who have control of the earth have the advantage of you. See what the law is: when these men get control of things, they make the laws. They do not make the laws to protect anybody; courts are not instruments of justice. When your case gets into court it will make little difference whether you are guilty or innocent, but it's better if you have a smart lawyer. And you cannot have a smart lawyer unless you have money. First and last it's a question of money. Those men who own the earth make the laws to protect what they have. They fix up a sort of fence or pen around what they have, and they fix the law so the fellow on the outside cannot get in. The laws are really organized for the protection of the men who rule the world. They were never organized or enforced to do justice. We have no system for doing justice, not the slightest in the world.

27   Let me illustrate: Take the poorest person in this room. If the community had provided a system of doing justice, the poorest person in this room would have as good a lawyer as the richest, would he not? When you went into court you would have just as long a trial and just as fair a trial as the richest person in Chicago. Your case would not be tried in fifteen or twenty minutes, whereas it would take fifteen days to get through with a rich man's case.

28   Then if you were rich and were beaten, your case would be taken to the Appellate Court. A poor man cannot take his case to the Appellate Court; he has not the price. And then to the Supreme Court. And if he were beaten there he might perhaps go to the United States Supreme Court. And he might die of old age before he got into jail. If you are poor, it's a quick job. You are almost known to be guilty, else you would not be there. Why should anyone be in the criminal court if he were not guilty? He would not be there if he could be anywhere else. The officials have no time to look after all these cases. The people who are on the outside, who are running banks and building churches and making jails, they have no time to examine 600 or 700 prisoners each year to see whether they are guilty or innocent. If the courts were organized to promote justice the people would elect somebody to defend all these criminals, somebody as smart as the prosecutor—and give him as many detectives and as many assistants to help, and pay as much money to defend you as to prosecute you. We have a very able man for state's attorney, and he has many assistants, detectives, and policemen without end, and judges to hear the cases— everything handy.

29   Most all of our criminal code consists in offenses against property. People are sent to jail because they have committed a crime against property. It is of very little consequence whether one hundred people more or less go to jail who ought not to go—you must protect property, because in this world property is of more importance than anything else.

How is it done? These people who have property fix it so 30
they can protect what they have. When somebody commits
a crime it does not follow that he has done something that
is morally wrong. The man on the outside who has committed no crime may have done something. For instance: to
take all the coal in the United States and raise the price
two dollars or three dollars when there is no need of it, and
thus kill thousands of babies and send thousands of people
to the poorhouse and tens of thousands to jail, as is done
every year in the United States—this is a greater crime
than all the people in our jails ever committed; but the law
does not punish it. Why? Because the fellows who control
the earth make the laws. If you and I had the making of
the laws, the first thing we would do would be to punish
the fellow who gets control of the earth. Nature put this
coal in the ground for me as well as for them and nature
made the prairies up here to raise wheat for me as well as
for them, and then the great railroad companies came along
and fenced it up.

Most all of the crimes for which we are punished are 31
property crimes. There are a few personal crimes, like murder—but they are very few. The crimes committed are
mostly those against property. If this punishment is right
the criminals must have a lot of property. How much money
is there in this crowd? And yet you are all here for crimes
against property. The people up and down the Lake Shore
have not committed crime; still they have so much property
they don't know what to do with it. It is perfectly plain
why these people have not committed crimes against property; they make the laws and therefore do not need to break
them. And in order for you to get some property you are
obliged to break the rules of the game. I don't know but
what some of you may have had a very nice chance to get
rich by carrying a hod for one dollar a day, twelve hours.
Instead of taking that nice, easy profession, you are a burglar. If you had been given a chance to be a banker you
would rather follow that. Some of you may have had a
chance to work as a switchman on a railroad where you
know, according to statistics, that you cannot live and keep
all your limbs more than seven years, and you can get fifty
dollars or seventy-five dollars a month for taking your lives
in your hands; and instead of taking that lucrative position
you chose to be a sneak thief, or something like that. Some
of you made that sort of choice. I don't know which I would
take if I was reduced to this choice. I have an easier choice.

32   I will guarantee to take from this jail, or any jail in the
world, five hundred men who have been the worst criminals
and law-breakers who ever got into jail, and I will go down
to our lowest streets and take five hundred of the most
abandoned prostitutes, and go out somewhere where there
is plenty of land, and will give them a chance to make a
living, and they will be as good people as the average in
the community.

33   There is one remedy for the sort of condition we see here.
The world never finds it out, or when it does find it out it
does not enforce it. You may pass a law punishing every
person with death for burglary, and it will make no difference. Men will commit it just the same. In England there
was a time when one hundred different offenses were
punishable with death, and it made no difference. The English people strangely found out that so fast as they repealed
the severe penalties and so fast as they did away with
punishing men by death, crime decreased instead of increased; that the smaller the penalty the fewer the crimes.

34   Hanging men in our county jails does not prevent murder.
It makes murderers.

35   And this has been the history of the world. It's easy to
see how to do away with what we call crime. It is not so
easy to do it. I will tell you how to do it. It can be done by
giving the people a chance to live — by destroying special
privileges. So long as big criminals can get the coal fields,
so long as the big criminals have control of the city council
and get the public streets for streetcars and gas rights — this
is bound to send thousands of poor people to jail. So long
as men are allowed to monopolize all the earth, and compel
others to live on such terms as these men see fit to make,
then you are bound to get into jail.

36   The only way in the world to abolish crime and criminals
is to abolish the big ones and the little ones together. Make
fair conditions of life. Give men a chance to live. Abolish
the right of private ownership of land, abolish monopoly,
make the world partners in production, partners in the
good things of life. Nobody would steal if he could get something of his own some easier way. Nobody will commit
burglary when he has a house full. No girl will go out on
the streets when she has a comfortable place at home. The
man who owns a sweatshop or a department store may not
be to blame himself for the condition of his girls, but when
he pays them five dollars, three dollars, and two dollars a
week, I wonder where he thinks they will get the rest of

their money to live. The only way to cure these conditions is by equality. There should be no jails. They do not accomplish what they pretend to accomplish. If you would wipe them out there would be no more criminals than now. They terrorize nobody. They are a blot upon any civilization, and a jail is an evidence of the lack of charity of the people on the outside who make the jails and fill them with the victims of their greed.

Richard J. Herrnstein and James Q. Wilson

Are Criminals Made or Born?

Richard J. Herrnstein and James Q. Wilson work at Harvard University — Herrnstein as a professor of psychology, Wilson as a professor of government. The following article, adapted from their book Crime and Human Nature, *appeared in* The New York Times Magazine *in 1985.*

A revolution in our understanding of crime is quietly overthrowing some established doctrines. Until recently, criminologists looked for the causes of crime almost entirely in the offenders' social circumstances. There seemed to be no shortage of circumstances to blame: weakened, chaotic or broken families, ineffective schools, antisocial gangs, racism, poverty, unemployment. Criminologists took seriously, more so than many other students of social behavior, the famous dictum of the French sociologist Emile Durkheim: Social facts must have social explanations. The sociological theory of crime had the unquestioned support of prominent editorialists, commentators, politicians and most thoughtful people.

Today, many learned journals and scholarly works draw a different picture. Sociological factors have not been abandoned, but increasingly it is becoming clear to many scholars that crime is the outcome of an interaction between social factors and certain biological factors, particularly for the offenders who, by repeated crimes, have made public places dangerous. The idea is still controversial, but increasingly, to the old question "Are criminals born or made?" the answer seems to be: both. The causes of crime

lie in a combination of predisposing biological traits channeled by social circumstance into criminal behavior. The
traits alone do not inevitably lead to crime; the circumstances do not make criminals of everyone; but together
they create a population responsible for a large fraction of
America's problem of crime in the streets.

3   Evidence that criminal behavior has deeper roots than
social circumstances has always been right at hand, but
social science has, until recent years, overlooked its implications. As far as the records show, crime everywhere and
throughout history is disproportionately a young man's
pursuit. Whether men are 20 or more times as likely to be
arrested as women, as is the case in Malawi or Brunei, or
only four to six times as likely, as in the United States or
France, the sex difference in crime statistics is universal.
Similarly, 18-year-olds may sometimes be four times as
likely to be criminal as 40-year-olds, while at other times
only twice as likely. In the United States, more than half
of all arrests for serious property crimes are of 20-year-olds
or younger. Nowhere have older persons been as criminal
as younger ones.

4   It is easy to imagine purely social explanations for the
effects of age and sex on crime. Boys in many societies are
trained by their parents and the society itself to play more
roughly and aggressively than girls. Boys are expected to
fight back, not to cry, and to play to win. Likewise, boys
in many cultures are denied adult responsibilities, kept in
a state of prolonged dependence and confined too long in
schools that many of them find unrewarding. For a long
time, these factors were thought to be the whole story.

5   Ultimately, however, the very universality of the age and
sex differences in crime have alerted some social scientists
to the implausibility of a theory that does not look beyond
the accidents of particular societies. If cultures as different
as Japan's and Sweden's, England's and Mexico's, have sex
and age differences in crime, then perhaps we should have
suspected from the start that there was something more
fundamental going on than parents happening to decide to
raise their boys and girls differently. What is it about boys,
girls and their parents, in societies of all sorts, that leads
them to emphasize, rather than overcome, sex differences?
Moreover, even if we believed that every society has arbitrarily decided to inculcate aggressiveness in males, there
would still be the greater criminality among *young* males

to explain. After all, in some cultures, young boys are not denied adult responsibilities but are kept out of school, put to work tilling the land and made to accept obligations to the society.

But it is no longer necessary to approach questions about 6 the sources of criminal behavior merely with argument and supposition. There is evidence. Much crime, it is agreed, has an aggressive component, and Eleanor Emmons Maccoby, a professor of psychology at Stanford University, and Carol Nagy Jacklin, a psychologist now at the University of Southern California, after reviewing the evidence on sex differences in aggression, concluded that it has a foundation that is at least in part biological. Only that conclusion can be drawn, they said, from data that show that the average man is more aggressive than the average woman in all known societies, that the sex difference is present in infancy well before evidence of sex-role socialization by adults, that similar sex differences turn up in many of our biological relatives — monkeys and apes. Human aggression has been directly tied to sex hormones, particularly male sex hormones, in experiments on athletes engaging in competitive sports and on prisoners known for violent or domineering behavior. No single line of evidence is decisive and each can be challenged, but all together they convinced Drs. Maccoby and Jacklin, as well as most specialists on the biology of sex differences, that the sexual conventions that assign males the aggressive roles have biological roots.

That is also the conclusion of most researchers about the 7 developmental forces that make adolescence and young adulthood a time of risk for criminal and other nonconventional behavior. This is when powerful new drives awaken, leading to frustrations that foster behavior unchecked by the internalized prohibitions of adulthood. The result is usually just youthful rowdiness, but, in a minority of cases, it passes over the line into crime.

The most compelling evidence of biological factors for 8 criminality comes from two studies — one of twins, the other of adopted boys. Since the 1920's it has been understood that twins may develop from a single fertilized egg, resulting in identical genetic endowments — identical twins — or from a pair of separately fertilized eggs that have about half their genes in common — fraternal twins. A standard procedure for estimating how important genes are to a trait is to compare the similarity between identical twins with that between fraternal twins. When identical twins are clearly more similar in a trait than fraternal twins, the trait probably has high heritability.

9   There have been about a dozen studies of criminality using twins. More than 1,500 pairs of twins have been studied in the United States, the Scandinavian countries, Japan, West Germany, Britain and elsewhere, and the result is qualitatively the same everywhere. Identical twins are more likely to have similar criminal records than fraternal twins. For example, the late Karl O. Christiansen, a Danish criminologist, using the Danish Twin Register, searched police, court and prison records for entries regarding twins born in a certain region of Denmark between 1881 and 1910. When an identical twin had a criminal record, Christiansen found, his or her co-twin was more than twice as likely to have one also than when a fraternal twin had a criminal record.

10   In the United States, a similar result has recently been reported by David Rowe, a psychologist at the University of Oklahoma, using questionnaires instead of official records to measure criminality. Twins in high school in almost all the school districts of Ohio received questionnaires by mail, with a promise of confidentiality as well as a small payment if the questionnaires were filled out and returned. The twins were asked about their activities, including their delinquent behavior, about their friends, and about their co-twins. The identical twins were more similar in delinquency than the fraternal twins. In addition, the twins who shared more activities with each other were no more likely to be similar in delinquency than those who shared fewer activities.

11   No single method of inquiry should be regarded as conclusive. But essentially the same results are found in studies of adopted children. The idea behind such studies is to find a sample of children adopted early in life, cases in which the criminal histories of both adopting and biological parents are known. Then, as the children grow up, researchers can discover how predictive of their criminality are the family histories of their adopting and biological parents. Recent studies show that the biological family history contributes substantially to the adoptees' likelihood of breaking the law.

12   For example, Sarnoff Mednick, a psychologist at the Uni-

versity of Southern California, and his associates in the United States and Denmark have followed a sample of several thousand boys adopted in Denmark between 1927 and 1947. Boys with criminal biological parents and noncriminal adopting parents were more likely to have criminal records than those with noncriminal biological parents and criminal adopting parents. The more criminal convictions a boy's natural parents had, the greater the risk of criminality for boys being raised by adopting parents who had no records. The risk was unrelated to whether the boy or his adopting parents knew about the natural parents' criminal records, whether the natural parents committed their crimes before or after the boy was given up for adoption, or whether the boy was adopted immediately after birth or a year or two later. The results of this study have been confirmed in Swedish and American samples of adopted children.

Because of studies like these, many sociologists and [13] criminologists now accept the existence of genetic factors contributing to criminality. When there is disagreement, it is about how large the genetic contribution to crime is and about how the criminality of biological parents is transmitted to their children.

Both the twin and adoption studies show that genetic [14] contributions are not alone responsible for crime — there is, for example, some increase in criminality among boys if their adopted fathers are criminal even when their biological parents are not, and not every co-twin of a criminal identical twin becomes criminal himself. Although it appears, on average, to be substantial, the precise size of the genetic contribution to crime is probably unknowable, particularly since the measures of criminality itself are now so crude.

We have a bit more to go on with respect to the link that [15] transmits a predisposition toward crime from parents to children. No one believes there are "crime genes," but there are two major attributes that have, to some degree, a heritable base and that appear to influence criminal behavior. These are intelligence and temperament. Hundreds of studies have found that the more genes people share, the more likely they are to resemble each other intellectually and temperamentally.

Starting with studies in the 1930's, the average offender [16] in broad samples has consistently scored 91 to 93 on I.Q.

tests for which the general population's average is 100. The typical offender does worse on the verbal items of intelligence tests than on the nonverbal items but is usually below average on both.

17   Criminologists have long known about the correlation between criminal behavior and I.Q., but many of them have discounted it for various reasons. Some have suggested that the correlation can be explained away by the association between low socioeconomic status and crime, on the one hand, and that between low I.Q. and low socioeconomic status, on the other. These criminologists say it is low socioeconomic status, rather than low I.Q., that fosters crime. Others have questioned whether I.Q. tests really measure intelligence for the populations that are at greater risk for breaking the law. The low scores of offenders, the argument goes, betray a culturally deprived background or alienation from our society's values rather than low intelligence. Finally, it is often noted that the offenders in some studies have been caught for their crimes. Perhaps the ones who got away have higher I.Q.s.

18   But these objections have proved to be less telling than they once seemed to be. There are, for example, many poor law-abiding people living in deprived environments, and one of their more salient characteristics is that they have higher I.Q. scores than those in the same environment who break the law.

19   Then, too, it is a common misconception that I.Q. tests are invalid for people from disadvantaged backgrounds. If what is implied by this criticism is that scores predict academic potential or job performance differently for different groups, then the criticism is wrong. A comprehensive recent survey sponsored by the National Academy of Sciences concluded that "tests predict about as well for one group as for another." And that some highly intelligent criminals may well be good at eluding capture is fully consistent with the belief that offenders, in general, have lower scores than nonoffenders.

20   If I.Q. and criminality are linked, what may explain the link? There are several possibilities. One is that low scores on I.Q. tests signify greater difficulty in grasping the likely consequences of action or in learning the meaning and significance of moral codes. Another is that low scores, especially on the verbal component of the tests, mean trouble

in school, which leads to frustration, thence to resentment, anger and delinquency. Still another is that persons who are not as skillful as others in expressing themselves verbally may find it more rewarding to express themselves in ways in which they will do better, such as physical threat or force.

For some repeat offenders, the predisposition to criminality may be more a matter of temperament than intelligence. Impulsiveness, insensitivity to social mores, a lack of deep and enduring emotional attachments to others and an appetite for danger are among the temperamental characteristics of high-rate offenders. Temperament is, to a degree, heritable, though not as much so as intelligence. All parents know that their children, shortly after birth, begin to exhibit certain characteristic ways of behaving—they are placid or fussy, shy or bold. Some of the traits endure, among them aggressiveness and hyperactivity, although they change in form as the child develops. As the child grows up, these traits, among others, may gradually unfold into a disposition toward unconventional, defiant or antisocial behavior.   21

Lee Robins, a sociologist at Washington University School of Medicine in St. Louis, reconstructed 30 years of the lives of more than 500 children who were patients in the 1920's at a child guidance clinic in St. Louis. She was interested in the early precursors of chronic sociopathy, a condition of antisocial personality that often includes criminal behavior as one of its symptoms. Adult sociopaths in her sample who did not suffer from psychosis, mental retardation or addiction, were, without exception, antisocial before they were 18. More than half of the male sociopaths had serious symptoms before they were 11. The main childhood precursors were truancy, poor school performance, theft, running away, recklessness, slovenliness, impulsiveness and guiltlessness. The more symptoms in childhood, the greater the risk of sociopathy in adulthood.   22

Other studies confirm and extend Dr. Robins's conclusions. For example, two psychologists, John J. Conger of the University of Colorado and Wilbur Miller of Drake University in Des Moines, searching back over the histories of a sample of delinquent boys in Denver, found that "by the end of the third grade, future delinquents were already seen   23 by their teachers as more poorly adapted than their class-mates. They appeared to have less regard for the rights and feelings of their peers; less awareness of the need to accept responsibility for their obligations, both as individuals and as members of a group, and poorer attitudes toward authority."

24   Traits that foreshadow serious, recurrent criminal be-havior have been traced all the way back to behavior pat-terns such as hyperactivity and unusual fussiness, and neurological signs such as atypical brain waves or reflexes. In at least a minority of cases, these are detectable in the first few years of life. Some of the characteristics are sex-linked. There is evidence that newborn females are more likely than newborn males to smile, to cling to their mothers, to be receptive to touching and talking, to be sen-sitive to certain stimuli, such as being touched by a cloth, and to have less upper-body strength. Mothers certainly treat girls and boys differently, but the differences are not simply a matter of the mother's choice—female babies are more responsive than male babies to precisely the kind of treatment that is regarded as "feminine." When adults are asked to play with infants, they play with them in ways they think are appropriate to the infants' sexes. But there is also some evidence that when the sex of the infant is concealed, the behavior of the adults is influenced by the conduct of the child.

25   Premature infants or those born with low birth weights have a special problem. These children are vulnerable to any adverse circumstances in their environment—includ-ing child abuse—that may foster crime. Although nurturing parents can compensate for adversity, cold or inconsistent parents may exacerbate it. Prematurity and low birth weight may result from poor prenatal care, a bad diet or excessive use of alcohol or drugs. Whether the care is due to poverty, ignorance or anything else, here we see criminal-ity arising from biological, though not necessarily genetic, factors. It is now known that these babies are more likely than normal babies to be the victims of child abuse.

26   We do not mean to blame child abuse on the victim by saying that premature and low-birth-weight infants are more difficult to care for and thus place a great strain on the parents. But unless parents are emotionally prepared for the task of caring for such children, they may vent their frustration at the infant's unresponsiveness by hitting or

neglecting it. Whatever it is in parent and child that leads to prematurity or low birth weight is compounded by the subsequent interaction between them. Similarly, children with low I.Q.s may have difficulty in understanding rules, but if their parents also have poor verbal skills, they may have difficulty in communicating rules, and so each party to the conflict exacerbates the defects of the other.

The statement that biology plays a role in explaining 27 human behavior, especially criminal behavior, sometimes elicits a powerful political or ideological reaction. Fearful that what is being proposed is a crude biological determinism, some critics deny the evidence while others wish the evidence to be confined to scientific journals. Scientists who have merely proposed studying the possible effects of chromosomal abnormalities on behavior have been ruthlessly attacked by other scientists, as have those who have made public the voluminous data showing the heritability of intelligence and temperament.

Some people worry that any claim that biological factors 28 influence criminality is tantamount to saying that the higher crime rate of black compared to white Americans has a genetic basis. But no responsible work in the field leads to any such conclusion. The data show that of all the reasons people vary in their crime rates, race is far less important than age, sex, intelligence and the other individual factors that vary within races. Any study of the causes of crime must therefore first consider the individual factors. Differences among races may have many explanations, most of them having nothing to do with biology.

The intense reaction to the study of biological factors in 29 crime, we believe, is utterly misguided. In fact, these discoveries, far from implying that "criminals are born" and should be locked up forever, suggest new and imaginative ways of reducing criminality by benign treatment. The opportunity we have is precisely analogous to that which we had when the biological bases of other disorders were established. Mental as well as physical illness—alcoholism, learning disabilities of various sorts, and perhaps even susceptibilities to drug addiction—now seem to have genetic components. In each case, new understanding energized the search for treatment and gave it new direction. Now we know that many forms of depression can be successfully treated with drugs; in time we may learn the same of Alzheimer's disease. Alcoholics are helped when they understand that some persons, because of their predisposition toward addiction to alcohol, should probably never consume it at all. A chemical treatment of the predisposition is a realistic possibility. Certain types of slow learners can already be helped by special programs. In time, others will be also.

30   Crime, admittedly, may be a more difficult program. So many different acts are criminal that it is only with considerable poetic license that we can speak of "criminality" at all. The bank teller who embezzles $500 to pay off a gambling debt is not engaging in the same behavior as a person who takes $500 from a liquor store at the point of a gun or one who causes $500 worth of damage by drunkenly driving his car into a parked vehicle. Moreover, crime, unlike alcoholism or dyslexia, exposes a person to the formal condemnation of society and the possibility of imprisonment. We naturally and rightly worry about treating all "criminals" alike, or stigmatizing persons whom we think might become criminal by placing them in special programs designed to prevent criminality.

31   But these problems are not insurmountable barriers to better ways of thinking about crime prevention. Though criminals are of all sorts, we know that a very small fraction of all young males commit so large a fraction of serious street crime that we can properly blame these chronic offenders for most such crime. We also know that chronic offenders typically begin their misconduct at an early age. Early family and preschool programs may be far better repositories for the crime-prevention dollar than rehabilitation programs aimed—usually futilely—at the 19- or 20-year-old veteran offender. Prevention programs risk stigmatizing children, but this may be less of a risk than is neglect. If stigma were a problem to be avoided at all costs, we would have to dismantle most special-needs education programs.

32   Having said all this, we must acknowledge that there is at present little hard evidence that we know how to inhibit the development of delinquent tendencies in children. There are some leads, such as family training programs of the sort pioneered at the Oregon Social Learning Center, where parents are taught how to use small rewards and penalties to alter the behavior of misbehaving children.

There is also evidence from David Weikart and Lawrence Schweinhart of the High/Scope Educational Research Foundation at Ypsilanti, Mich., that preschool education programs akin to Project Head Start may reduce later delinquency. There is nothing yet to build a national policy on, but there are ideas worth exploring by carefully repeating and refining these pioneering experimental efforts.

Above all, there is a case for redirecting research into the   33
causes of crime in ways that take into account the interaction of biological and social factors. Some scholars, such as the criminologist Marvin E. Wolfgang and his colleagues at the University of Pennsylvania, are already exploring these issues by analyzing social and biological information from large groups as they age from infancy to adulthood and linking the data to criminal behavior. But much more needs to be done.

It took years of patiently following the life histories of   34
many men and women to establish the linkages between smoking or diet and disease; it will also take years to unravel the complex and subtle ways in which intelligence, temperament, hormonal levels and other traits combine with family circumstances and later experiences in school and elsewhere to produce human character.

Stephen Jay Gould

Of Crime, Cause, and Correlation

Stephen Jay Gould (born 1941), a celebrated paleontologist and historian of science, has won many awards for his essays and books on science, in large part because of his conscious decision to write for a broad audience. Among his best known works are The Panda's Thumb *(1977),* The Mismeasure of Man *(1980),* Time's Arrow, Time's Cycle *(1987) and* Wonderful Life *(1989). Particularly interested in the conduct of science and its relationship to larger societal and cultural issues, he has been an outspoken opponent of creation science. The following short essay appeared in 1983 in* Discover, *a science magazine designed for the general reader.*

1   Since sex can be gentle and a thing of great beauty, it may seem peculiar that so many animals are most touchy and aggressive during their mating seasons. Nonetheless, this apparent paradox makes sense in light of evolutionary theory. An organism's success in the evolutionary race may be measured by the number of offspring raised to carry its genes into future generations. For a male, more copulations with more females mean more offspring, and this biological imperative can engender severe competition among males and zealous defense of females within a male's orbit — hence the link of sex with aggression. Females may also struggle among themselves to win the attention of best fit males or to discourage inappropriate suitors.

2   In most mammals, sex is seasonal — and periods of nastiness and aggression therefore ebb and flow in correlation with mating activity throughout the year. Yet writings on human evolution usually cite a loss of seasonality in mating as a key feature of our biological history. Human females ovulate at regular intervals throughout the year and both males and females seem interested in and capable of indulging in sexual activity at any time. Indeed, the invention of adaptive reasons for this loss of seasonality forms a common theme in treatises on human evolution — the advantages of monogamy and a strong pair bond for raising children, for example, and the role of continual sexual receptivity among females in maintaining a male's interest in sticking around. I regard most of these scenarios as pretty silly and purely speculative, but they do attempt to explain a fact of evident importance — why humans are the most persistently sexy of primates.

3   Yet this very loss of evident seasonality has prompted many scientists to wonder whether some small or subtle remnant of our evolutionary past might still be preserved in modern humans. Does any vestigial seasonality of sexual behavior and its correlates in aggression still remain with us? Does the animal still lurk beneath a human guise?

4   Since we have no direct evidence for seasonality in human sexual behavior, scientists who seek some sign of it must search the dossier of human activity for conduct that cycles with the seasons and might be linked with sexuality. Various types of aggressive behavior form a promising area for investigation.

5   This style of research faces, unfortunately, one enormous and daunting problem — it falls so easily into what

is probably the most common error of human reasoning, the confusion of correlation with cause. We may illustrate the fallacy with some simple examples. Halley's comet is approaching the earth and has been steadily drawing nearer to us for many years. During the same time, my pet hamster has been ageing continually and the price of an ice cream cone has risen steadily in Boston. If I computed what scientists call a correlation coefficient between any two of these events (comet distances, hamster ages, and cone prices), I would get a nearly perfect relationship—a quantitative value near the maximum of 1. Yet everyone understands intuitively that none of these correlations has any causal meaning—lots of things are moving in the same direction independently.

Even more difficult to interpret are correlations between 6 phenomena that seem to have some causal relationship, but in which the potential causal pathways are both great in number and varied in style. The simple existence of a correlation does not permit a distinction among these myriad pathways. Seasonality, for example, has numerous consequences—variation in temperature and length of daylight are the most direct and prominent. When we find a kind of human behavior that cycles with the seasons, and not by accident, how can we know which of the astronomical number of facets of seasonality it reflects? The causal pathways are often subtle, indirect, and complex. Why, for example, do we play baseball in the summer and football in the fall and winter? Nothing intrinsic to the games dictates such a custom, especially in our modern all-weather domed stadiums. The reason is linked with seasonality, but by a most indirect and historical route. Baseball has old and populist origins as a game of ordinary folk in rural and urban communities. Our great-grandfathers played it when they could, and when their families would enjoy watching— when it was warm enough, in summer. But football had its origin as a collegiate sport, and colleges (for reasons originally and indirectly linked to the warmth of seasons and the timing of agriculture) are not in session until the fall.

Thus the problem in using correlation with seasons as a 7 method for making inferences about the vestigial existence of human sexual cycles: we may expect to find many seasonal fluctuations in potentially indirect correlates of sex— aggressive behavior most prominently—but we cannot infer cause, because the simple correlation cannot, by itself, tell us which of the numerous aspects of seasonality has engendered the behavioral cycle. The discovery of yearly cycles in aggressive behavior does not permit the inference that human biology still records a vestige of primate mating seasons, for two reasons: first, too many unrelated aspects of seasonality may be causing the correlation, and these must be identified and eliminated before we have any right to assert an evolutionary hypothesis; second, underlying sexual cycles are not (by far) the only cause of human aggression. Nonetheless, psychiatrist Richard Michael and ethologist Doris Zumpe recently published a study in the *American Journal of Psychiatry* that made just such a claim and elicited a flurry of press commentary about our vestigial animality (*Sexual Violence in the United States and the Role of Season*, July 1983). Michael and Zumpe fall right into the fallacy of confusing correlation with cause: they find a simple correlation of aggression to season and ascribe its cause to vestigial sexual cyclicism without any supporting evidence and without even discussing an old and sensible alternative explanation that fits the data far better.

8   Michael and Zumpe considered the frequency of four crimes — forcible rape, aggravated assault, murder, and robbery — throughout the year in 16 American localities from Maine to Honolulu. They found that rape and assault showed nearly the same pattern in all but two localities for rape and all but four for assault: the greatest number occurred in summer, within an eight-week period between July 7 and September 8. They conclude: "Because of the close relationship between assault and rape, and because rapes are invariably less numerous than assaults, we postulate that rape comprises a subcategory of assaultive behavior." Robberies, on the other hand, tend to show a reversed pattern, with the greatest number in winter, while murders are scattered throughout the year and display no seasonal peaks. The authors also found no significant differences in frequencies of the various crimes among their 16 places — especially no tendency toward more violence in hotter climates.

9   Michael and Zumpe's data provide nothing more than a correlation between frequency of some crimes (but not others) and seasonal fluctuations of climate. They clearly do not have enough information to make causal asser-

tions—for the correlation of crime and season may have a host of potential reasons (or even no reason at all), and the correlation itself does not permit a distinction among numerous possibilities.

Nonetheless, Michael and Zumpe present a single hypothesis about cause, providing no alternative at all, and implying that their data are sufficient to make such an assertion. They claim that seasonal fluctuations in hormone levels probably underlie cycles of crime—and suggest that these fluctuations record a vestige of primate mating cycles. They write: "The view that environmental factors may act via neuroendocrine pathways in the human to influence our behavior is consistent with the known role of these factors in socially living, nonhuman primates, which show increased aggressivity at the start of the mating season." 10

I believe that two debilitating objections can be raised against this far-fetched conclusion: first, some of the authors' own data contradict it (or at least fit uncomfortably within their hypothesis); second, an explanation that they never consider—the old and "classical" explanation for crime's well known seasonal cycles—fits all the data, and fits them better and more simply than the hormonal hypothesis. 11

If rape correlates with assault because it constitutes "a subcategory of assaultive behavior," and aggression cycles with the season as a result of environmentally entrained variation in hormone levels, then why does murder show no seasonal pattern? Surely murder is aggression. Moreover, though we may regard robbery as premeditated behavior for gain and not, therefore, as another category of aggression expected to cycle with rape and assault, we still cannot understand, on Michael and Zumpe's hypothesis, why robbery shows a reversed seasonal pattern. If their hypothesis has general merit, it should explain the cycles of all the crimes they consider. Michael and Zumpe's batting average, in short, is poor. Their speculation fits only half their data; a third crime (murder) does not show the expected pattern, while a fourth (robbery) displays a different cycle, which they do not attempt to explain at all. 12

Michael and Zumpe have discovered nothing new. The four patterns that they cite "have been known by criminologists and the beat cop for many years" (to quote Mark Fox, who outlined the same objections in a letter to *Science News*, September 24, commenting on a previous favorable 13 report of Michael and Zumpe's article). The same criminologists and policemen have a standard explanation that fits all four patterns—not just two of them—and seems eminently direct and reasonable to me. It relies upon an immediate, nonbiological reason for correlations between seasons and crime. Quite simply, and to put it somewhat crudely, rapes and assaults peak in summer because winter is a hell of a time to lurk in alleyways—more contact and greater availability in summer provide more opportunity. Robberies show a reversed pattern because weapons are more easily concealed under winter attire. Murders show no pattern because most are unplanned acts of violence committed against friends and family members at moments of extreme stress. I do not assert that this classical explanation must be correct, but it explains everything simply and should not be omitted from discussion. Yet Michael and Zumpe ignored it in favor of exclusive speculations about evolutionary vestiges. The potential pathways from correlation to cause are always numerous.

14   Michael and Zumpe seem to think that their demonstration of similar peaks in rape and assault for their coldest (Maine) and warmest (Hawaii and Puerto Rico) regions argues for biology and against the idea that "higher temperatures facilitate increased social interaction." But this fact is irrelevant to the debate because both explanations predict it. In particular, the social hypothesis simply requires that summers be warm—and it is hot enough during a Maine summer to populate the alleyways. Similarly, Michael and Zumpe's demonstration that regions with greater seasonal change in temperature show greater annual fluctuations in frequency of rape and assault, if anything, fits the social hypothesis better—it really is too cold during a Maine winter, but quite possible in Honolulu.

15   I wrote this essay primarily to illustrate, by egregious example, the cardinal fallacy of confusing correlation with cause. But Michael and Zumpe's article raises two other interesting and general points about scientific explanation.

16   Why, first of all, do so many scientists show a preference for arcane, complex, indirect, and implausible causal pathways when simple (if less intriguing) explanations are so clearly available? (I have previously argued that the higher batting averages of lefties really can be explained by the unexciting and classical observation that lefties hit right-

handed pitching better, and that most pitchers, like most of us, are right-handed — and not by newfangled, high-falutin notions about differences between left and right brains, as two overenthusiastic doctors have suggested.) We should start with the immediate and obvious (they usually work), and move to the complex and indirect when our initial efforts fail. Have a healthy respect for simple answers; the world is not always a deep conundrum fit only for consideration by certified scholars.

Second, why are we so fascinated by explanations that invoke innate and inherited biology (vestigial mating cycles in this case), when simpler hypotheses based upon the interaction of a flexible personality with the immediate environment explain things better and more fully? We seem drawn, in the absence of good evidence, to biological hypotheses for differences in social and intellectual behavior between men and women, or the activities of criminal and law-abiding citizens. I suspect that this preference reflects one of the oldest and most unfortunate biases of Western thought, dating back at least to Plato's search for essences. We want to know what we are "really" like, why we behave as we do. Somehow, we feel that a claim for something inborn and inherited must be more fundamental or essential than an undetermined response to an immediate environment. We prefer to believe that more men are driven to rape in summer by a rise in hormones reflecting an evolutionary past than by a simple increase in availability of targets. But if humans have an essence, it surely lies in the remarkable flexibility that permits such an enormous range of unprogrammed responses to environment. This flexibility defines us and makes us human. We should not only cherish and foster it, but also learn to recognize and take interest in its manifestations.

Garrison Keillor
The Current Crisis in Remorse

Garrison Keillor, born in 1942 in Anoka, Minnesota, is a writer and broadcaster. He founded and hosted "A Prairie Home Companion," an award-winning radio variety show offered on National Public Radio. A droll and funny storyteller who spins affectionate yarns of small-town life, he published in 1985 the best-selling Lake Wobegon Days, *named for the fictional locale of his broadcasts. The following sketch appeared in* The New Yorker *and in his 1989 collection* We Are Still Married.

1   Remorse is a fairly new area in social work so it's no wonder we get the short end when it comes to budget and staffing. Take me, for example. For three years, I was the *only professional remorse officer* in a Department of Human Services serving a city of *more than 1.5 million*, and not so long ago my supervisor Mitch (a man with no remorse background at all) told me I was "expendable" and that he would "shed no tears" if remorse was eliminated from the Department entirely. I had no office, only a desk across from the elevators, and I shared a phone with the director of the Nephew Program in Family Counseling. And it's not only me! Around the country, morale in remorse has never been lower.

2   We in remorse are a radical minority within the social-work community. We believe that not every wrong in our society is the result of complex factors such as poor early-learning environment and resultative dissocialized communication. Some wrong is the result of *badness*. We believe that some people act like jerks, and that when dealing with jerks one doesn't waste too much time on sympathy. They're jerks. They do bad things. They should feel sorry for what they did and stop doing it. Of course, I'm oversimplifying here, trying to state things in layman's terms, and I should add that we are professionals, after all, who are trained in behavioral methodology *including* remorse, but also a lot more — if you're interested, read "Principles of Deductive Repentance," by Morse and Frain, or Professor Frain's excellent "Failure and Fault: Assignment and Acceptance."

3   I did my training under Frain and graduated in 1976, just as remorse was coming to the forefront. People in the

helping professions had begun to notice a dramatic increase in the number of clients who did terrible things and didn't feel one bit sorry. It was an utterly common phenomenon for a man who had been apprehended after months of senseless carnage to look at a social worker or psychologist with an expression of mild dismay and say, "Hey, I know what you're thinking, but that wasn't *me* out there, it wasn't *like* me at all. I'm a caring type of guy. Anyway, it's over now, it's done, and I got to get on with my own life, you know," as if he had only been unkind or unsupportive of his victims and not dismembered them and stuffed them into mailboxes. This was not the "cold-blooded" or "hardened" criminal but, rather, a cheerful, self-accepting one, who looked on his crime as "something that happened" and had a theory to explain it.

"I'm thinking it was a nutritional thing," one mass murderer remarked to me in 1978. "I was feeling down that day. I'd been doing a lot of deep-fried foods, and I was going to get a multi-vitamin out of the medicine chest when I noticed all those old ladies in the park and — well, one thing just led to another. I've completely changed my food intake since then. I really feel *good* now. I know I'm never going to let myself get in that type of situation again!" 4

It wasn't only vicious criminals who didn't feel sorry, though. It was a regretless time all around. Your own best friend might spill a glass of red wine on your new white sofa and immediately *explain* it — no spontaneous shame and embarrassment, just "Oh, I've always had poor motor skills," or "You distracted me with your comment about Bolivia." People walked in and stole your shoes, they trashed your lawn and bullied your children and blasted the neighborhood with powerful tape machines at 4:00 A.M. and got stone drunk and cruised through red lights, smashing your car and ruining your life for the next six months, and if you confronted them about these actions they told you about a particularly upsetting life-experience they'd gone through recently, such as condemnation, that caused them to do it. 5

In 1976, a major Protestant denomination narrowly defeated an attempt to destigmatize the Prayer of Confession by removing from it all guilt or guilt-oriented references: "Lord, we approach Thy Throne of Grace, having committed acts which, we do heartily acknowledge, must be very difficult for Thee to understand. Nevertheless, we do be- 6 seech Thee to postpone judgment and to give Thy faithful servants the benefit of the doubt until such time as we are able to answer all Thy questions fully and clear our reputations in Heaven."

7   It was lack of remorse among criminals, though, that aroused public outrage, and suddenly we few professionals in the field were under terrible pressure to have full-fledged remorse programs in place in weeks, even days. City Hall was on the phone, demanding to see miscreants slumped in courtrooms, weeping, shielding their faces while led off to jail.

8   Fine, I said. Give me full funding to hire a staff and I'll give you a remorse program you can be proud of. Mitch sneered. "Ha!" he said. He said, "Get this straight, showboat, 'cause I'll only say it once. You work for me, and I say remorse is Number Last on the list around here. Cosmetics! That's all City Hall wants and that's what we give them. A few tears. You can twist arms, step on toes, or use raw onions, but forget about funding."

9   His insensitivity shocked me. Remorselessness is a fundamental flaw, a crack in the social contract, and repair requires a major commitment. One man simply couldn't keep up with the caseload.

10   I spent two months on the president of AmTox, who was sent to me after his conviction for dumping tons of deadly wastes into a scenic gorge and killing thousands of trout and who took a Who—me? attitude toward the deed until finally I elicited a small amount of shame by requiring him to spend Saturdays panhandling in the bus depot, wearing a sign that said "Help Me. I'm Not Too Bright." But meanwhile hundreds of others got off scot-free. I'd put the screws to the guy who enjoyed touching pedestrians with his front fender, but meanwhile the guys who bilked hundreds of elderly women of their life savings walked out the door saying, "Hey, what's the big deal? So we exaggerated a little. No need to get huffy about it."

11   It depressed the hell out of me. Here I was, swimming in paperwork with my hands tied, and out on the street were jerks on parade: unassuming, pleasant, perfectly normal people except that they had an extra bone in their head and less moral sense than God gave badgers. And the ones I did put through remorse didn't improve a lot. Six months ago, thirty-seven former clients of mine filed a class-action suit against the state demanding millions in restitution for the ethically handicapped and arguing neglect on the state's

part in failing to provide remorse counseling earlier. "We have suffered terrible remorse," the brief said, "as we begin to recognize the enormity of our sins, including but not limited to: pure selfishness, vicious cruelty, utter dishonesty, blind insensitivity, gross neglect, overweening pride, etc. And that's fine. But where was this program ten years ago? Nowhere to be found! That was the Me Decade! Is that our fault? Therefore, in consideration of the vast black abyss of guilt to which we have been suddenly subjected, we demand that the court order . . ." My heart sank as I read it. They had even quoted my speech to the Council on Penitential Reform in 1981:

> Criminal nonremorse is the tip of a very large iceberg, and unless we initiate broad-based remorse reforms on the community level and start talking about an overhaul of our entire moral system—church, media, education, the parental system, personal networking, the entire values-delivery infrastructure—and recognize that it requires major investment by private *and* public sectors in professional training and research and that we're looking at a time frame of years, not months, and that we must begin now, we simply *must*, because, believe me, if we don't, that is a mistake we're going to live to regret!

The state, they said further, had failed to exercise due care in neglecting to warn them earlier and to inform them of the urgent necessity of changing their ways.

Three days later, the order came down that I was reas- 12
signed. By offering remorse assistance, it said, I had needlessly raised people's expectations of inner peace.

"That means you, lamebrain," Mitch cackled, leaning 13
across his desk and poking an index finger into my rib cage. "Let's see how you like it in the basement." He assigned me to "assist in the assembly and assessment" of ancient and dusty ascertainment files in a dim, airless room deep in the bowels of Human Services—useless and demeaning work that left me weak and dispirited after only a day, but I held on and did the work and didn't complain. He plugged the ventilator, reduced light-bulb wattage, denied me a radio. I spent three weeks in that hellhole, reading lengthy case histories of clients long since deceased and sorting them into meaningless piles and attaching gummed labels that tasted like dead socks.

Suddenly, one afternoon, he appeared in the doorway, 14

his face drawn, his eyes filled with tears. "I read Frain last night," he said. "All night. Why—I—You should have told me. Oh God, oh God! What have I done to you? How can I make it up? You want my job? Take it."

15   "No, thanks. That's all right. No problem," I said. "I'm quitting."

16   He begged me to stay. "I can't live with my conscience if you won't let me do something for you. Let me at least take you to lunch. There's a terrific little seafood place a block from here that I've been keeping to myself—"

17   "Don't bother," I said. "Come five o'clock you'll never see me again."

18   I was true to my word. I'm a vice-president of Yakamoto now, where I've designed a remorse program for assembly-line workers to build stronger emotional responses to poor workmanship, tardiness, false sick days, and excessive lunch breaks. The job is challenging, the people pleasant, the fringe benefits outstanding, and the salary is three hundred and ninety-five thou a year. The Japanese place a high premium on shame. You don't see them treating other people like dirt. They even feel contrition for things that someone standing next to them did! They treat me like a prince. I'm a lucky man. I'm extremely happy here.

Roger Rosenblatt

Why the Justice System Fails

Roger Rosenblatt (born 1940) is a writer and editor at Time *magazine. He wrote the following cover story for* Time *in 1981.*

1   Anyone who claims it is impossible to get rid of the random violence of today's mean streets may be telling the truth, but is also missing the point. Street crime may be normal in the U.S., but it is not inevitable at such advanced levels, and the fact is that there are specific reasons for the nation's incapacity to keep its street crime down. Almost all these reasons can be traced to the American criminal justice system. It is not that there are no mechanisms in place to deal with American crime, merely that the existing

ones are impractical, inefficient, anachronistic, uncoopera-
tive, and often lead to as much civic destruction as they
are meant to curtail.

Why does the system fail? For one thing, the majority of   2
criminals go untouched by it. The police learn about one-
quarter of the thefts committed each year, and about less
than half the robberies, burglaries and rapes. Either victims
are afraid or ashamed to report crimes, or they may conclude gloomily that nothing will be done if they do. Murder
is the crime the police do hear about, but only 73% of the
nation's murders lead to arrest. The arrest rates for lesser
crimes are astonishingly low — 59% for aggravated assault
in 1979, 48% for rape, 25% for robbery, 15% for burglary.

Even when a suspect is apprehended, the chances of his   3
getting punished are mighty slim. In New York State each
year there are some 130,000 felony arrests; approximately
8,000 people go to prison. There are 94,000 felony arrests
in New York City; 5,000 to 6,000 serve time. A 1974 study
of the District of Columbia came up with a similar picture.
Of those arrested for armed robbery, less than one-quarter
went to prison. More than 6,000 aggravated assaults were
reported; 116 people were put away. A 1977 study of such
cities as Detroit, Indianapolis and New Orleans produced
slightly better numbers, but nothing to counteract the
exasperation of New York Police Commissioner Robert
McGuire: "The criminal justice system almost creates incentives for street criminals."

It is hard to pinpoint any one stage of the system that is   4
more culpable than any other. Start with the relationship
between police and prosecutors. Logic would suggest that
these groups work together like the gears of a watch since,
theoretically, they have the same priorities: to arrest and
convict. But prosecutors have enormous caseloads, and too
often they simply focus on lightening them. Or they work
too fast and lose a case; or they plea-bargain and diminish
justice. The police also work too fast too often, are concerned with "clearing" arrests, for which they get credit.
They receive no credit for convictions. Their work gets
sloppy — misinformation recorded, witnesses lost, no fol-
low-up. That 1974 study of the District of Columbia indicated that fully one-third of the police making arrests failed
to process a single conviction. A study released this week
of 2,418 police in seven cities showed that 15% were credited
with half the convictions; 31% had no convictions whatever.

The criminal justice system is also debased by plea bar-   5 gaining. At present nine out of ten convictions occur because of a guilty plea arrived at through a deal between the state and defendant, in which the defendant forgoes his right to trial. Of course, plea bargaining keeps the courts less crowded and doubtless sends to jail, albeit for a shorter stretch, some felons who might have got off if judged by their peers. And many feel that a bargain results in a truer level of justice, since prosecutors tend to hike up the charge in the first place in anticipation of the defendant's copping a plea. Still, there are tricks like "swallowing the gun" — reducing the charge of armed robbery to unarmed robbery — that are performed for expediency, not for justice.

6   "Justice delayed is justice denied," is a root principle of common law, but nowadays the right to a speedy trial is so regularly denied that the thought seems antique. Last Aug. 1, a witness was prepared to testify that Cornelius Wright, 18, shot him five times in the chest, stomach and legs. Because of a series of mishaps and continuances, Wright has been stewing in the Cook County jail for more than eight months. In fact, Wright's delay is the norm; eight months is the average time between arrest and trial. Continuances have so clogged Chicago's courts that the city's Crime Commission issues a monthly "Ten Most Wanted Dispositions" list in an effort to prod the system.

7   Detroit Deputy Police Chief James Bannon believes that trial delays work against the victim. "The judge doesn't see the hysterical, distraught victim. He sees a person who comes into court after several months or years who is totally different. He sees a defendant that bears no relationship to what he appeared to be at the time of the crime. He sits there in a nice three-piece suit and keeps his mouth shut. And the judge doesn't see the shouting, raging animal the victim saw when she was being raped, for example. Both the defendant and victim have lawyers, and that's what the court hears: law. It doesn't hear the guts of the crime."

8   Procedural concerns can cause delays, and in rare cases defendants' rights can be carried to absurd extremes. California Attorney General George Deukmejian tells of Willie Edward Level, who was convicted of beating a Bakersfield College woman student to death with a table leg. Level was informed of his right to remain silent and/or have an attorney present (the *Miranda* ruling). He waived these rights and confessed the murder. Yet the California Court of Appeals threw out the conviction because Level

had asked to speak to his mother at the time of his arrest
and had not been permitted to; had he been able to do so,
it was argued, he might not have made his confession.

"There's nothing in *Miranda* that says a defendant has   9
the right to talk with his mother or a friend," says Deukmejian. "It says he can talk to a lawyer or not at all. It's so
much of this kind of thing that makes a mockery of the
system. And every time you have one of these rulings it has
the effect of dragging out the length of cases, which builds
in more and more delays. We've got a murder case in Sacramento that's been in the pretrial state for four years."

Add to this the fact that witnesses are discouraged and   10
lost by trial delays. In New York the average number of
appearances a witness has to make in a given disposition
is 17. Few people have the time or stamina to see a case
through.

Then there is the matter of bail. In a recent speech before   11
the American Bar Association, Chief Justice Warren Burger
argued for tightening the standards for releasing defendants
on bail, which seems justifiable. But the subject is complicated. Technically, judges are supposed to base their decisions about bail strictly on the likelihood of a defendant's
appearing for trial. In practice, however, this is mere
guesswork, and a great many serious crimes are committed
by people out on bail or by bail jumpers, who are often
given bail when rearrested. One sound reason for a bail
system is to avoid locking up anyone before he is proved
guilty. But it is simply unrealistic to disregard the criterion
of likely dangerousness, even though it raises serious constitutional questions. It has probably resulted in more
tragedies than a different standard would result in denials
of civil liberties.

Judges blame the cops, and cops blame the judges. Patrick   12
F. Healy, executive director of the Chicago Crime Commission, says judges are plain lazy. "Last year we did a spot
check, and the judges' day on the bench totaled 3 hours 49
minutes." The judges will not concede laziness, but several
of the nation's best, like Marvin Frankel, former federal
judge in the District Court of Manhattan, admit to a "remarkable lack of consistency" in the judiciary. Judge Lois
Forer, a most respected criminal-court justice in Philadelphia, contends that it "simply isn't true" that defendants
get off on technicalities. It is just that "the system is over-
loaded." She also emphasizes the problem of sloppy prepa-

rations: "It's truly painful when there's someone you're pretty sure committed a crime, and they [police, prosecutors] don't bring in the evidence."

13   Almost every critic of the system cites the lack of prison space. Despite the enormously high operating costs ($4 billion annually for all U.S. penal institutions), more prison space is an absolute necessity. New York State has between 22,000 and 24,000 jail cells. All are filled, some beyond proper capacity. Twice this year local officials in Missouri were asked not to send any more inmates to the state penitentiary. As a result the St. Louis county jail had to retain seven prisoners who ought to have been in the state pen, even though it meant holding eleven more inmates than the jail was intended to hold. Florida, which already has a higher proportion of its citizenry under lock and key than any other state, may need to spend $83 million on new prison construction and staff. This month 223 supposedly nonviolent inmates of Illinois' 13 prisons were given early release to make room for 223 newcomers. New York Police Inspector Richard Dillon, one of the nation's most thoughtful law officers, cites lack of prison space as the primary cause of city crime—the ultimate reason for inappropriate plea bargains, premature paroles, careless bail and too brief sentences.

14   Finally, the criminal justice system fails at its most sensitive level, that of juvenile crime. Until recently few juvenile courts admitted there was such a thing as a bad boy, restricting their vision of youthful offenders to memories of Father Flanagan's Boys Town or to Judge Tom Clark's quaint view that "every boy, in his heart, would rather steal second base than an automobile." In fact, there are several boys these days who would prefer to kill the umpire, and who have done so, only to receive light sentences or none at all. A study by Marvin Wolfgang at the University of Pennsylvania traced the criminal careers of 10,000 males born in 1948. By the age of 16, 35% had one arrest, but then almost all stopped committing crimes. A small group, however, did not: 627 had five arrests by the time they were adults. They accounted for two-thirds of all the violent crime attributed to the group and almost all the homicides. "This is the group that society is afraid of, and rightly so," says Wolfgang. He is now studying a new group, born in 1958, which is "even nastier and more violent. We should concentrate on them and capture them as soon as possible."

Of course, there is no place to put this hard core, and 15
that is part of the problem. The main difficulty, however,
is a Pollyannish, outdated vision of youth, one that results
in treating a child not as a potentially responsible human
being but rather as some vague romantic entity, capable
of continuous regeneration. An underage murderer may be
put away for a few months or not at all. As Harvard's James
Q. Wilson says, "The adult system is harsh, but before that
it's a free ride." The ride is not only free, but clean. At the
age of 18, juvenile criminals in many states start all over
with unblemished records no matter how many crimes they
have committed earlier.

In short, the criminal justice system is not really a sys- 16
tem—at least not one in which the individual parts work
well on their own or mesh effectively with each other. Few
of the participants deny this, and while there is a natural
tendency for each stratum—police, lawyers, prosecutors,
judges, prison officials—to lay the blame for the system's
failures on one another, nobody is happy with the current
situation. Reforming the system, however, is a tricky business, especially when reforms are likely to tend toward
severity. "For my part," said Oliver Wendell Holmes in
Olmstead vs. *U.S.*, "I think it a less evil that some criminals
should escape than that the Government should play an
ignoble part." Whatever reforms are contemplated, Justice
Holmes will preside.

WHAT'S A PRISON FOR?

Warren Burger
Prisons Are Designed to Rehabilitate

Warren Burger, born in 1907 in St. Paul, Minnesota, was appointed by President Nixon as the fourteenth Chief Justice of the United States. He served from 1969 until his retirement in 1987 and was known for his efforts to reform judicial practice. Since he was known to be tough on criminals and a supporter of the death penalty, his comments here on prisons may surprise you; they were delivered in a commencement address for the Pace University Law School class of 1983.

1 The ancient and honorable American custom of commencement speeches is an innocuous one that has done very little harm to those who are graduating, and it may even have the beneficial consequence of teaching the graduates the virtue of patience. With the problems you are about to confront in the disturbed world of today, you will need patience. And the parents, who are now to be released from paying the high costs of keeping a student in college, are bound to be in such a happy mood that no speech could depress them. . . .

2 Today I want to discuss with you a grave problem which my generation and those who went before me have failed to solve and as a result, you inherit the consequences of that failure. In one sense we can say that it is a "torch" you are being handed, one that will singe your pocketbooks and affect your lives from now on.

3 Since I have been a member of the federal judiciary I have thought and spoken on the subject of penal and correctional institutions and those policies and practices that ought to be changed. I see this as part of the administration of justice. People go to prisons only when judges send them there and judges should have a particular concern about

the effectiveness of the prisons and the correctional process, even though we have no responsibility for their management. Based on my observations as a judge for more than twenty-five years and from visiting prisons in the United States and in most of the countries of Europe—and in the Soviet Union and The People's Republic of China—I have long believed that we have not gone about the matter in the best way.

This is one of the unresolved problems on your agenda   4 and today I will propose some changes in our approach to prisons. But before doing that, let me suggest why the subject has a special relevance, even a special urgency, right now. Our country is about to embark on a multi-billion dollar prison construction program. At least one billion dollars of construction is already underway. The question I raise is this: are we going to build more "human warehouses" or should we change our thinking and create institutions that are training schools and factories with fences around them where we will first train the inmates and then have them engage in useful production to prepare them for the future and to help pay for their confinement?

One thoughtful scholar of criminal justice described the   5 state of affairs in much harsher terms than I have ever used. Four years ago he wrote this:

> Criminal justice in the United States is in a state of spreading decay. . . . The direct costs of crime include loss of life and limb, loss of [earnings], . . . physical and mental suffering by the victims and their families. . . . [1]

These direct losses, he continued, run into many billions   6 of dollars annually. But indirect losses are vastly more and reach the astonishing figure of 100 billion dollars a year. These indirect costs include higher police budgets, higher private security measures, higher insurance premiums, medical expenses of the victims, and welfare payments to dependents of prisoners and victims. In the immediate future these astounding figures and the great suffering that underlies them can be reduced. This can be done by more effective law enforcement which in turn will produce a demand for more and more prison facilities. But more prisons of the kind we now have will not solve the basic prob-

[1] J. Gorecki, *A Theory of Criminal Justice* (1979), page xi.

lem. Plainly, if we can divert more people from lives of crime we would benefit those who are diverted and the potential victims. All that we have done in improved law enforcement, in new laws for mandatory minimum sentences, and changes in parole and probation practices has not prevented thirty percent of America's homes from being touched by crime every year.

7   Twenty years ago I shared with such distinguished penologists as the late James V. Bennett, longtime Director of the Federal Bureau of Prisons, Torsten Eriksson, his counterpart in Sweden, and Dr. George K. Sturrup in Denmark and others, high hopes for rehabilitation programs. These hopes now seem to have been based more on optimism and wishful thinking than on reality. During that period of time we have seen that even the enlightened correctional practices of Sweden and other northern European countries have produced results that, although better than ours, have also fallen short of expectations.

8   On several occasions I have stated one proposition to which I have adhered to for the twenty-five years that I have worked on this problem and it is this:

> When society places a person behind walls and bars it has an obligation—a moral obligation—to do whatever can reasonably be done to change that person before he or she goes back into the stream of society.

9   If we had begun twenty-five, thirty-five, or fifty years ago to develop the kinds of correctional programs that are appropriate for an enlightened and civilized society, the word "recidivist" might not have quite as much currency as it does today. This is not simply a matter of compassion for other human beings, it is a hard common sense matter for our own protection and our own pocketbooks.

10   In just the past ten years the prison population in America has doubled from less than 200,000 inmates to more than 400,000. This reflects, in part, the increase in crime, better law enforcement, and the imposition of longer sentences and more stringent standards of parole and probation. Budgets for law enforcement, for example, like the rates for theft insurance have skyrocketed.

11   If we accept the idea that the most fundamental obligation of government in a civilized society is the protection of people and homes, then we must have more effective law

enforcement, but equally important, we must make fundamental changes in our prison and correctional systems. Just more stone, mortar and steel for walls and bars will not change this melancholy picture. If we are to make progress and at the same time protect the persons and property of people and make streets and homes safe from crime, we must change our approach in dealing with people convicted of crimes. Our system provides more protection and more safeguards for persons accused of crime, more appeals and more reviews than any other country in the world. But once the judicial process has run its course we seem to lose interest. The prisoner and the problem are brushed under the rug.[2]

It is predictable that a person confined in a penal institution for two, five or ten years, and then released, yet still unable to read, write, spell or do simple arithmetic and not trained in any marketable vocational skill, will be vulnerable to returning to a life of crime. And very often the return to crime begins within weeks after release. What job opportunities are there for an unskilled, functional illiterate who has a criminal record? The recidivists who return to our prisons are like automobiles that are called back to Detroit. What business enterprise, whether building automobiles in Detroit or ships in Norfolk, Virginia, or airplanes in Seattle, could continue with the same rate of "recall" of its "products" as our prisons? 12

The best prisons in the world, the best programs that we can devise will not totally cure this dismal problem for, like disease and war, it is one that the human race has struggled with since the beginning of organized societies. But improvements in our system can be made and the improvements will cost less in the long run than the failure to make them. 13

I have already said that today one billion dollars in new prison facilities is actually under construction. More than thirty states have authorized construction programs for 14

[2]The Federal Bureau of Prisons under the leadership of the late James V. Bennett and now Norman Carlson, the present Director, has performed extremely well, given legislative restraints on production of goods in prisons and archaic attitudes of business and labor. But the Federal Bureau of Prisons deals with barely seven percent of the 400,000 prisoners now confined.

new prison facilities that over the next ten years will cost as much as ten billion dollars.

15   If these programs proceed, and we must assume they will, it is imperative that there be new standards that will include the following:

> a. Conversion of prisons into places of education and training and into factories and shops for the production of goods.
> b. Repeal of statutes which limit the amount of prison industry production or the markets for such goods.
> c. Repeal of laws discriminating against the sale or transportation of prison-made goods.
> d. The leaders of business and organized labor must cooperate in programs to permit wider use of productive facilities in prisons.

16   On the affirmative side I have every reason to believe that business and labor leaders will cooperate in more intelligent and more humane prison programs. Of course, prison production programs will compete to some extent with the private sector, but this is not a real problem. With optimum progress in the programs I have outlined, it would be three to five years, or even more, before these changes would have any market impact and even then it will be a very small impact. I cannot believe for one moment that this great country of ours, the most voracious consumer society in the world, will not be able to absorb the production of prison inmates without significant injury to private employment or business. With the most favorable results, the production level of prison inmates would be no more than a tiny drop in the bucket in terms of the Gross National Product. Yet, we find prisons in the United States with limited production facilities which are lying idle because of statutory limitations confining the sale of their products to city and county governments within the state. . . .

17   Prison inmates, by definition, are for the most part maladjusted people. From whatever cause, whether too little discipline or too much; too little security or too much; broken homes or whatever, these people lack self-esteem. They are insecure, they are at war with themselves as well as with society. They do not share the work ethic that made this country great. They did not learn, either at home or in the schools, the moral values that lead people to have respect

and concern for the rights of others. But if we place that person in a factory, rather than a "warehouse," whether that factory makes ballpoint pens, hosiery, cases for watches, parts for automobiles, lawnmowers or computers; pay that person reasonable compensation, charge something for room and board, I believe we will have an improved chance to release from prison a person better able to secure gainful employment and to live a normal, productive life. If we do this, we will have a person whose self-esteem will at least have been improved so that there is a better chance that he or she can cope with life.

There are exceptions of course. The destructive arrogance 18 of the psychopath with no concern for the rights of others may well be beyond the reach of any programs that prisons or treatments can provide. Our prison programs must aim chiefly at the others — those who want to change.

There is nothing really new in this concept. It has been 19 applied for years in northern Europe, and in my native state of Minnesota there are important beginnings. Special federal legislation authorized pilot programs for contracts with private companies to produce and ship merchandise in interstate commerce. Even though Minnesota's pilot program involves only a fraction of the inmates it represents a significant new start. In that program prisoners were identified by tests to determine their adaptability for training. After that they were trained and now there are approximately fifty-two prisoners in one section of the Minnesota prison engaged in assembling computers for Control Data Corporation. These prisoners will have a job waiting for them when they leave prison. Is it not reasonable to assume that the temptation to return to a life of crime will be vastly reduced?

On my first visit to Scandinavian prisons twenty-five 20 years ago, I watched prison inmates constructing fishing dories, office furniture, and other products. On my most recent visit six years ago, prisoners in one institution were making components for prefabricated houses, under the supervision of skilled carpenters. Those components could be transported to a building site and assembled by semi-skilled workers under trained supervision. Two years ago in a prison I visited in The People's Republic of China, 1000 inmates made up a complete factory unit producing hosiery and casual sport shoes. Truly that was a factory with a fence around it. In each case, prisoners were learning a trade and paying at least part of the cost of their confinement.

21   Today the confinement of the 400,000 inmates in American prisons costs the taxpayers of this country, including the innocent victims of crimes, who help pay for it, more than twelve million dollars a day! I will let you convert that into billions. We need not try in one leap to copy fully the Scandinavian model of production in prison factories. We can begin with the production of machine parts for lawnmowers, automobiles, washing machines or refrigerators. This kind of limited beginning would minimize the capital investment for plant and equipment and give prisoners the opportunity to learn relatively simple skills at the outset.

22   We do not need the help of behavioral scientists to understand that human beings who are taught to produce useful goods for that marketplace, and to be productive are more likely to develop the self-esteem essential to a normal, integrated personality. This kind of program would provide training in skills and work habits, and replace the sense of hopelessness that is the common lot of prison inmates. Prisoners who work and study forty-five to fifty-five hours a week — as you graduates have done — are also less prone to violent prison conduct. Prisoners given a stake in society, and in the future, are more likely to avoid being part of the "recall" process that today sends thousands of repeat offenders back to prisons each year.

23   One prison in Europe, an institution for incorrigible juvenile offenders from fourteen to eighteen years of age who had been convicted of serious crimes of violence, has on the wall at the entrance to the institution four challenging statements in bold script with letters a foot high. Translated they read approximately this way:

1. You are here because you need help.
2. We are here to help you.
3. We cannot help you unless you cooperate.
4. *If you don't cooperate, we will make you.*

24   Here is an offer of a compassionate helping hand coupled with the kind of discipline that, if missing in early life in homes and schools that ignored moral values, produces the kind of maladjusted, incorrigible people who are found in prisons. Some voices have been raised saying that prisoners

should not be coerced into work and training programs. Depending upon what these speakers mean by "coerced," I might be able to agree. But I would say that every prisoner should be "induced" to cooperate by the same methods that are employed in many other areas. Life is filled with rewards for cooperation and penalties for noncooperation. Prison sentences are shortened and privileges are given to prisoners who cooperate. What I urge are programs in which the inmate can earn and learn his way to freedom and the opportunity for a new life. . . .

J. J. Maloney

The J. B. Factor

J. J. Maloney spent thirteen years in the Missouri State Penitentiary for a murder he committed as a teenager. Paroled in 1972, he then went to work as a reporter for the Kansas City Star. *He wrote the following article in 1983 for* Saturday Review, *a magazine of the arts and public affairs.*

J.B. was a street kid from South St. Louis, a nice-looking,   1 bright kid with a drive to be somebody. But he was impatient. Working for a living took too much time. He wanted some money immediately. One night he and a friend walked into a tavern to rob it. A cop came in and went for his gun. J.B. shot him. The cop died, and J.B. was sentenced to life imprisonment.

J.B. was tough and became a minor legend in prison. He   2 tried to escape, and his status rose among the convicts. For a while he was poor, so he robbed other convicts of their cigarettes and commissary books. Then a friend got out of prison and started sending dope to him through a guard. He was getting amphetamine in by the ounce and selling it to other convicts. That made him a king. He used this income to start poker games and lending operations. He eventually was making more than $1,000 a month, a staggering sum in a world where the average convict might have $15 a month to spend. The average guard's salary then was only a third of what J.B. was making.

3   J.B. had settled in for the long haul. He no longer thought
about escaping.

4   Personal furniture was permitted in the prison, and J.B.
had the best: a big mirror, a dresser, a bedspread. He also
had a locker full of tuna, candy bars, and cookies. He had
an Omega watch, a diamond ring, and other jewelry in his
dresser. He had a good-looking young boy to take care of
his baser needs. His cell door was often left open, and he
would wander around the cell block. He had guards on his
payroll. If someone wanted a cell change, he could arrange
it. In time he became a major legend. Ex-convicts would
sit in South St. Louis taverns and regale each other with
stories of J.B.'s exploits in the joint.

5   After a scandal that culminated in the suicide of the warden, new officials were hired to run the prison. One of the
ways they decided to demonstrate their control was to
"break" J.B.

6   They boldly moved him from cell 52, where he had lived
for years. They confiscated his dresser and broke it into
kindling. In a dramatic move, they cut the diamond ring
from his finger.

7   J.B. took it all good-humoredly. The attention was flatter-
ing. He had never stood higher in the eyes of the convicts.
The officials changed the shape but not the substance of
his existence. He now wore a Timex watch (the only kind
permitted). He wore the most bedraggled sweat shirt he
could find, in an effort to convince the officials he had been
pauperized. He became more tractable. He even joshed with
the warden on occasion. The warden bragged to visiting
journalists that J.B. would call him on the phone from the
powerhouse and shoot the breeze with him. Without realizing it, the very warden who had set out to "break" J.B. was
now wallowing in his shadow.

8   J.B. still sold dope, had a punk, and accumulated cigarettes and candy bars; he was still somebody.

9   He began to feed the officials tidbits of information to
convince them he was rehabilitated. J.B. would even tell
the warden where to find a gallon of hooch, that sort of
thing—never anything that would get another convict in
trouble. He probably planted the hooch himself, then told
the prison officials where to find it.

10   Finally he convinced them he had changed, and he was
paroled.

11   In the free world he quickly learned there is no market

for a consummate prison hustler. He may have had the brains, but he lacked the education to get a high-paying job. Instead he took a menial job and scraped by. He probably stared wistfully at the people driving Mercedes and wearing Brooks Brothers suits.

Here was a man who had everything in prison and nothing outside of it. The only people who respected him were ex-convicts. 12

Prison was on his mind. He periodically called the warden, probably sensing he would be going back, and wanting to ensure a job and good treatment when he did. No one expressed it better than Milton when he wrote, "Better to reign in hell than serve in heav'n." 13

Not long after his release, J.B. was shot and killed while attempting a robbery. 14

J.B. is a classic example of what is wrong with American prisons. For him, prison became an acceptable alternative, as it does for the young convicts who aspire to be like him. 15

Thirty percent of those who go to prison become recidivists. In 1968 there were about 200,000 convicts; 60,000 of them fell into the recidivist category. By the end of this decade there will be 1 million convicts, giving us a recidivist pool of 300,000, and growing at the rate of more than 30,000 a year. 16

Prison officials across the country are stunned by the number of convicts flooding in. America has been in the right-wing mood for a decade, as demonstrated by efforts to roll back civil rights legislation—affirmative action in particular—and by a chipping away at welfare programs. It is most visible in the current get-tough policy toward social malefactors. Several states have abolished parole, or have passed laws requiring a wait of fifty years. Sentences for virtually all crimes have been lengthened, and legislation defining new crimes is created almost daily. 17

In response to this surge in incarceration, John Sullivan, the Delaware correction commissioner, commented in the June 1983 issue of *Corrections Magazine*, "If we continue to grow at the rate we have for the last twenty months, in twenty years the entire population of the state will be incarcerated." 18

In Texas, more than 4,000 convicts are living in tents at fifteen of the state's twenty-five prisons. California is getting ready to build tent cities at San Quentin and Chino. Prison officials in the South are scurrying to find Quonset huts, 19 but most have been bought by prison systems elsewhere. In Missouri the prison population has jumped from 3,300 in 1972 to 7,800, and the system is gaining 100 convicts a month.

20   By the end of 1982, there were 412,000 men and women in American prisons, an increase of 11.6 percent over the previous year. The actual increase was higher, because many prisons were refusing to admit new convicts until they had room. Instead people are crowded in jails waiting for prison space.

21   If the Reagan administration's efforts to abolish parole nationally are successful, the system could collapse overnight. While 622,000 people were serving time in jails and prisons in 1982, an additional 1.4 million were on probation or parole. In 1972 ninety-three out of every 100,000 adults were in prison in the United States, the highest rate in the Western world. By 1982 this figure had risen to 170.

22   An overcrowded prison is a small city filled with desperate people, finagling, manipulating, trying to get dope, booze, and sex, trying to beat the system, trying to prove themselves, trying, above all, to survive. The following incidents occurred while I was incarcerated. They don't even scratch the surface of what goes on in a maximum-security prison.

- A 21-year-old boy was stabbed to death with a large ice pick and sodomized while he was dying. He had less than a month to serve.
- A 16-year-old black boy refused to let a group sodomize him. He was stabbed to death in the shower and rolled up in a piece of rug.
- A young convict who had been hounded by an older convict for sex finally stabbed the older man to death. While he was in solitary for the killing, his cellmate raped him.
- A man working in the kitchen killed a convict with a meat cleaver. He told the guards Moses told him to do it.
- A convict worker in the school was stabbed to death. The killer had just been returned from a state hospital and thought the victim was staring at him.
- A man was stabbed in the eye when he failed to pay a debt. He owed four packs of cigarettes.
- A 20-year-old convict broke both of his hands fighting off sexual assaults in the receiving unit. While

he was in the prison hospital, with both hands in casts, he was raped at knife point.

- A convict went to a movie and was stabbed in the back. He lost a lung and two ribs. The man who stabbed him later apologized, saying he had mistaken the victim for someone else.

Rehabilitation is not possible in this kind of setting. And   23
neither are extended sentences a solution to crime.

The modern prison system developed over a period of   24
two centuries. As long ago as 1831, it was declared a failure.
Alexis de Tocqueville said then, after surveying U.S. prisons, "Nowhere was this system of imprisonment crowned
with the hoped-for success. It never effected the reformation
of the prisoners."

From that point on there has never been a consensus on   25
what a prison should be like, who should go to prison, what
prisons can be expected to accomplish, or how they should
accomplish it.

Rehabilitation itself is a much abused word. At various   26
times it was thought that solitude was the answer, or back-
breaking work, or psychoanalysis, or education, or simply
understanding. When all was said and done, none of them
worked.

Instead, we need to understand the dual development in   27
prisons of this century: they have become more lenient as
sentences have grown longer. At the urging of well-meaning
people, prisons have been infused with amenities, ostensibly to make them more humane. They now have liberties
such as correspondence and visiting rules that in some
states extend to conjugal visits, weekly telephone calls,
commissary privileges, furlough programs, radios, televisions, personalized clothing, magazines, extended yard
time, beards and mustaches, and private rooms.

These are not available at all prisons, but that is the   28
trend. Prison reform has been confused with increasing
comforts. Many prisons offer more comfort than the U.S.
Army offered its soldiers in 1959.

This is one of the primary factors behind the increased   29
length of prison sentences. These amenities have clouded
the public's judgment. As people perceive prison becoming
luxurious, they assume it will take longer to accomplish
punishment and rehabilitation. The true nature of prison,
the terrifying underbelly of it, is only visible to the people

who are there. Those outside, as well as the convicts, must know that prison is a major deprivation, inconceivable as an alternative to life outside.

30   We need a simultaneous development: radically short-ened sentences and elimination of all amenities. No fac-tories or jobs, thereby cutting off the source of weapons. No commissary: no cigarettes, coffee, or candy bars. This would eliminate gambling, loan sharking, the trappings of success. No personal radios or televisions. No phone calls, unless the phone call is substituted for a visit. Curtailed correspondence and one visit a month.

31   In this prison convicts would be given coveralls, under-wear, socks, and tennis shoes. They would have a flexible toothbrush so it couldn't be sharpened into a weapon, a flexible comb, liquid soap, a towel, and toilet paper. They would be allowed one library book in their cells. No per-sonal property whatever, which alone would eliminate half the violence in prison. No one could smoke, which would eliminate fires and reduce lung cancer. Prisoners would spend more time in their cells, as convicts in solitary do now. Convicts hate solitary; it's boring.

32   At the end of six months, prisoners could enroll in the prison school, which would get them out of their cells four hours a day. They wouldn't have to enroll in school, but given the alternative, most probably would.

33   Failure to apply themselves in school or disruptive be-havior would be grounds for revoking the privilege. Those who didn't go to school would be housed separately to pre-vent them from harassing or intimidating those who did.

34   Every moment that a man was out of his cell, he would be under the direct scrutiny of guards. No rapes. No homosexuality. No maneuvering. There would be less guard-on-inmate brutality. Such brutality often springs from fear. In prisons as they are now, the guards are at the mercy of the inmates. In the proposed prison, the guards would know they had total control. A law would mandate imprisonment for any guard who assaults an inmate, except in self-defense. A second law would mandate imprisonment for any prison employee who conceals knowledge of such an assault. Such prisons would have to be of manageable size.

35   A year in such a prison would be like three years in a current prison. Five years would be hard to take. Ten years would be almost too much.

The cost factor of such a prison would be higher, because 36
all the food service, school, and hospital employees would
be civilians instead of convicts. On the other hand, there
would be far fewer people in these prisons, and for shorter
periods of time.

The only people who would need to go to prison would 37
be violent, dangerous offenders: killers, rapists, kidnappers,
armed robbers. Fifty-three percent of the people now in
prison are convicted of non-violent offenses: forgery, em-
bezzlement, non-sufficient funds checks, gambling, prostitution, petty theft, shoplifting, bribery, confidence games,
pickpocketing, fraud, pornography, drug use, burglary, car
theft, and sex acts between consenting adults.

As a nation we can't afford to send these people to the 38
penitentiary. When a man steals $100 and spends two years
in prison—at a cost of thousands of dollars a year—we are
committing fiscal folly. The only non-violent crimes that
merit a prison term are those in the category of "criminal
enterprise": professional forgery rings, burglary rings, fenc-
ing operations, and drug rings.

The rest of these people should be treated as misdemean- 39
ants, facing a term in a rigorous local jail. Under this kind
of setup, it would be necessary for the rural counties to
build regional jails, so that no one county would have to
maintain such an expensive institution. It might be necessary for the state to bear part of the cost.

What are the logistics of turning the system we now have 40
into the envisioned one? It's easier than you might think.
The governor has the power of clemency. He can decree
that all people with no violent crimes on their records are
to have their sentences reduced to two years, and that all
those with two years are to be given 120 days good time.
That would open up an enormous amount of prison space
in a relatively short time.

The second step is to devise a sentencing structure for 41
all new convicts. An essential ingredient is fairness. The
same crime should carry the same penalty for the rich and
the poor, black and white, the educated and the ignorant.

Contemporary theory, however, is going in the other di- 42
rection. The way we do it now, a mildly retarded defendant
from a poor family, with little education, is punished much
more harshly than an honor student from a good family.
The honor student is seen as a potential asset to society,
the other defendant as more likely to be a lifelong liability.

Most courts now use "pre-sentence evaluations." When 43

sentencing, they consider the defendant's familial stability, his education, his prior record, his marital status, etc. If the defendant has a good profile, the recommendation may be that he not go to prison at all. The poor defendant I described probably would receive a much longer sentence. A kid from a white-collar family probably would be granted probation the first time around, even for armed robbery. Many people steal knowing they have one free slide coming. By punishing the crime rather than the individual, the courts could eliminate such thinking. It is common in every prison for one man to be serving two years for a crime, and another to be serving twenty years for a similar crime. That is a great source of bitterness. Judicial discretion breeds judicial abuse.

44   Most importantly, once the prisoner had served his time and completed parole, he should be done with it forever. All rights as a citizen should be restored to him. Five years after completion of parole, his criminal record should be expunged.

45   The current system is obviously not working. It's time to try something radically new.

Allan C. Brownfeld
Putting Killers on the Streets

Allan C. Brownfeld is a syndicated columnist whose work frequently appears in conservative publications. He wrote "Putting Killers on the Streets" for the Washington Times *in 1984.*

1   Recently, in a typical case, a man free on parole after a manslaughter conviction was arrested and charged with murdering a New York City Police officer and wounding two others. Twenty-four-year-old George Acosta had a long history of arrests, beginning when he was 16 years old. The last two came while he was on parole after serving three years of a 5-to-15 year sentence in the 1977 slaying of an 18-year-old youth in a Bronx social club. Bronx District Attorney Mario Merola described Acosta as "a career criminal."

Mr. Acosta was paroled in August 1982, arrested on a gun 2
possession charge the next January and then arrested on a
burglary charge. He pleaded guilty to burglary and served
a four-month sentence. But his parole on the manslaughter
sentence remained in effect. He was free to kill again. And
he did.

In another much publicized case in California Theodore 3
Streleski was paroled after serving only five years for murder. On a summer day in 1978, Streleski, then a Stanford
University graduate student, crept silently into the office
of his faculty adviser and bludgeoned him to death with a
hammer. After taping the victim's head inside a plastic bag,
he calmly placed a sign on the door saying "No Office Hours
Today." He told police that he had plotted the killing of
Professor Karel de Leeuw over a period of years as "a political statement" against the university's treatment of
graduate students and as "a logically and morally correct
action."

Under California's 1976 determinate sentencing law, 4
Streleski received the maximum sentence of seven years
with one additional year for the use of a deadly weapon —
hardly a sentence commensurate with the crime. After serving two-thirds of that time, according to the law, he had
to be paroled. He was arrested three hours after being
released for refusing to abide by the terms of the parole —
fortunately before he killed again, which he has said he
would do.

Releasing Threats to Society

Clearly, prison systems throughout the U.S. are releasing 5
prisoners who are obvious threats to society. In eleven
states, including California, parole release has now been
abolished for most offenders in favor of a fixed or "determinate" sentencing system. Under it, a judge must impose
punishment from a narrow range of options set by the legislature or some administrative body, and an offender must
serve all of the sentence, minus time off for good behavior.
Such states have eliminated the old "one-to-20-year" sentences, which left parole boards to decide the real length
of time.

In recent years, New York's parole commissioners have 6
annually considered the cases of 15,000 inmates seeking
early release from prison. Last year, the board decided to

parole 8,300 inmates, with two-thirds being released to New York City's streets—including George Acosta. "Right now we have judges supposedly doing the sentencing," said Lawrence T. Kurlander, Governor Mario Cuomo's criminal justice coordinator, "but the real sentencing is being done by the Parole Board within the confines of prison walls, by what criteria we don't know."

7   The president of the United Probation Officer's Association in New York, Wallace Cheatham, declares: "A significant number of offenders on probation are every day committing robberies, assaults, murders and other serious crimes. One-third of all offenders being placed on probation instead of being supervised, merely have to call in once a month to a clerk. The unconscionable high case loads means that anyone placed on probation in New York City receives little or no supervision. Almost fifty per cent of offenders placed on probation are re-arrested within the first eight months of their sentence."

8   Our criminal justice system seems to have forgotten that its goal is to protect honest citizens from criminals—and that men and women must be held responsible for their actions. For too long, the alleged "well-being" of the perpetrators of crime seems to have been of more concern than the protection of society. What has been the result of this approach? Our crime rate is by far the highest in the industrial world. Violent crimes of assault or rape and of burglary now touch more than 10 per cent of U.S. households. If the lesser crime of larceny is included, the number of households involved is 30 per cent. The chances of being a victim of violent crime nearly tripled in the last 25 years, as did the possibility of being the victim of a serious crime such as burglary or auto theft. According to the F.B.I.'s Crime Clock, one crime is committed every two seconds, one violent crime every twenty-four seconds, one murder every 23 minutes, one rape every six minutes.

9   While crime has increased, our criminal justice system has made it easier for perpetrators to escape punishment. For every 500 serious crimes, just 20 adults and 5 juveniles on average, are sent to jail—a ratio of 1 in 20. Of some 2 million serious criminal cases filed each year, only 1 in 5 actually goes to trial. In New York State in 1980, of the 130,000 men and women arrested for felonies, only about 8,000 actually went to prison. Sociologists calculate that if the robbery rate in large cities continues to grow as it did

between 1962 and 1974, by the year 2024 each man, woman and child in a large city would be robbed by force or threat of force 2.3 times per year.

Insightful Rapists

Rather than putting murderers and rapists in prison— and preventing them from murdering and raping again— we seek to "treat" their alleged "problems." In his important book, "Inside The Criminal Mind," psychologist Stanton E. Samenow recalls his work with Dr. Samuel Yochelson at St. Elizabeth's Hospital: "Dr. Yochelson treated rapists using psychoanalytic concepts and techniques, and what he found was, he then had rapists with psychiatric insight." Criminals, Dr. Samenow points out, love the Freudian approach: "They learn to fool the psychiatrists by playing the psychiatric game of mouthing insights. . . . By taking the position that the criminal is a victim, society has provided him with excuses and supported his contention that he is not to blame."

10

To argue that men are not responsible for what they do is to deny all of us our humanity. We should recall the point made by G.K. Chesterton in his classic work, "Orthodoxy": "The fallacy to the torrent of model talk about treating crime as a disease, about making a prison merely a hygienic environment like a hospital, of healing sin by slow scientific methods . . . is that evil is a matter of active choice, whereas disease is not."

11

George Jackson

A Letter from Prison

George Jackson, arrested several times as a teenager, at nineteen was given a one-year-to-life sentence for burglary. He spent the next eleven years in prison, seven in solitary confinement. Jackson considered himself a political prisoner because at San Quentin he studied Marx and Mao, espoused revolution, and tried to politicize other prisoners. At the age of twenty-nine, in 1971, during an alleged escape attempt, he was shot and killed. The following description of prison life at San Quentin appeared in Soledad Brother: The Letters of George Jackson *(1970). "Fay" refers to Fay Stender, Jackson's attorney.*

April 1970

Dear Fay,

1   On the occasion of your and Senator Dymally's tour and investigation into the affairs here at Soledad, I detected in the questions posed by your team a desire to isolate some rationale that would explain why racism exists at the prison with "particular prominence." Of course the subject was really too large to be dealt with in one tour and in the short time they allowed you, but it was a brave scene. My small but mighty mouthpiece, and the black establishment senator and his team, invading the state's maximum security row in the worst of its concentration camps. I think you are the first woman to be allowed to inspect these facilities. Thanks from all. . . .

2   To determine how men will behave once they enter the prison it is of first importance to know that prison. Men are brutalized by their environment—not the reverse.

3   I gave you a good example of this when I saw you last. Where I am presently being held, they never allow us to leave our cell without first handcuffing us and belting or chaining the cuffs to our waists. This is preceded always by a very thorough skin search. A force of a dozen or more pigs can be expected to invade the row at any time searching and destroying personal effects. The attitude of the staff toward the convicts is both defensive and hostile. Until the convict gives in completely it will continue to be so. By giving in, I mean prostrating oneself at their feet. Only then does their attitude alter itself to one of paternalistic condescension. Most convicts don't dig this kind of relationship (though there are some who do love it) with a group of individuals demonstrably inferior to the rest of the society in regard to education, culture, and sensitivity. Our cells are so far from the regular dining area that our food is always cold before we get it. Some days there is only one meal that can be called cooked. We *never* get anything but cold-cut sandwiches for lunch. There is no variety to the menu. The same things week after week. One is confined to his cell 23½ hours a day. Overt racism exists unchecked.

It is not a case of the pigs trying to stop the many racist attacks; they actively encourage them.

They are fighting upstairs right now. It's 11:10 A.M., June 4 11. No black is supposed to be on the tier upstairs with anyone but other blacks but — mistakes take place — and one or two blacks end up on the tier with nine or ten white convicts frustrated by the living conditions or openly working with the pigs. The whole ceiling is trembling. In hand-to-hand combat we always win; we lose sometimes if the pigs give them knives or zip guns. Lunch will be delayed today, the tear gas or whatever it is drifts down to sting my nose and eyes. Someone is hurt bad. I hear the meat wagon from the hospital being brought up. Pigs probably gave them some weapons. But I must be fair. Sometimes (not more often than necessary) they'll set up one of the Mexican or white convicts. He'll be one who has not been sufficiently racist in his attitudes. After the brothers (enraged by previous attacks) kick on this white convict whom the officials have set up, he'll fall right into line with the rest.

I was saying that the great majority of the people who 5 live in this area of the state and seek their employment from this institution have overt racism as a *traditional* aspect of their characters. The only stops that regulate how far they will carry this thing come from the fear of losing employment here as a result of the outside pressures to control the violence. That is O Wing, Max (Maximum Security) Row, Soledad — in part anyway.

Take an individual who has been in the general prison 6 population for a time. Picture him as an average convict with the average twelve-year-old mentality, the nation's norm. He wants out, he wants a woman and a beer. Let's say this average convict is white and has just been caught attempting to escape. They may put him on Max Row. This is the worst thing that will ever happen to him. In the general population facility there are no chains and cuffs. TVs, radios, record players, civilian sweaters, keys to his own cell for daytime use, serve to keep his mind off his real problems. There is also a recreation yard with all sorts of balls and instruments to strike or thrust at. There is a gym. There are movies and a library well stocked with light fiction. And of course there is work, where for two or three cents an hour convicts here at Soledad make paper products, furniture, and clothing. Some people actually like this

work since it does provide some money for the small things
and helps them to get through their day—*without thinking*
about their real problems.

7   Take an innocent con out of this general population setting (because a pig "thought" he may have seen him attempting a lock). Bring him to any part of O Wing (the
worst part of the adjustment center of which Max Row is
a part). He will be cuffed, chained, belted, pressured by the
police who think that every convict should be an informer.
He will be pressured by the white cons to join their racist
brand of politics (they *all* go under the nickname "Hitler's
Helpers"). If he is predisposed to help black he will be
pushed away—by black. Three weeks is enough. The
strongest hold out no more than a couple of weeks. There
has been *one* white man only to go through this O Wing
experience without losing his balance, without allowing
himself to succumb to the madness of ribald, protrusive
racism.

8   It destroys the logical processes of the mind, a man's
thoughts become completely disorganized. The noise, madness streaming from every throat, frustrated sounds from
the bars, metallic sounds from the walls, the steel trays,
the iron beds bolted to the wall, the hollow sounds from a
cast-iron sink or toilet.

9   The smells, the human waste thrown at us, unwashed
bodies, the rotten food. When a white con leaves here he's
ruined for life. No black leaves Max Row walking. Either
he leaves on the meat wagon or he leaves crawling licking
at the pig's feet. . . .

10   One can understand the depression felt by an inmate on
Max Row. He's fallen as far as he can into the social trap,
relief is so distant that it is very easy for him lose his holds.
In two weeks that little average man who may have ended
up on Max Row for *suspicion* of *attempted* escape is so
brutalized, so completely without holds, that he will never
heal again. It's worse than Vietnam.

11   He's dodging lead. He may be forced to fight a duel to the
death with knives. If he doesn't sound and act more zealous
than everyone else he will be challenged for not being loyal
to his race and its politics, fascism. Some of these cons
support the pigs' racism without shame, the others support
it inadvertently by their own racism. The former are white,
the latter black. But in here as on the street black racism
is a forced *reaction*. A survival adaptation.

The picture that I have painted of Soledad's general popu- 12
lation facility may have made it sound not too bad at all.
That mistaken impression would result from the absence
in my description of one more very important feature of
the main line — terrorism. A frightening, petrifying diffusion of violence and intimidation is emitted from the offices
of the warden and captain. How else could a small group
of armed men be expected to hold and rule another much
larger group except through *fear*?

We have a gym (inducement to throw away our energies 13
with a ball instead of revolution). But if you walk into this
gym with a cigarette burning, you're probably in trouble.
There is a pig waiting to trap you. There's a sign "No Smoking." If you miss the sign, trouble. If you drop the cigarette
to comply, trouble. The floor is regarded as something of
a fire hazard (I'm not certain what the pretext is). There
are no receptacles. The pig will pounce. You'll be told in
no uncertain terms to scrape the cigarette from the floor
with your hands. It builds from there. You have a gym but
only certain things may be done and in specified ways.
Since the rules change with the pigs' mood, it is really safer
for a man to stay in his cell.

You have to work with emoluments that range from noth- 14
ing to three cents an hour! But once you accept the pay job
in the prison's industrial sector you cannot get out without
going through the bad conduct process. When workers are
needed, it isn't a case of accepting a job in this area. You
take the job or you're automatically refusing to work, even
if you clearly stated that you would cooperate in other
employment. The same atmosphere prevails on the recreation yard where any type of minor mistake could result
not in merely a bad conduct report and placement in adjustment center, but death. A fistfight, a temporary, trivial loss
of temper will bring a fusillade of bullets down on the
darker of the two men fighting.

You can't begin to measure the bad feeling caused by the 15
existence of one TV set shared by 140 men. Think! One TV,
140 men. If there is more than one channel, what's going
to occur? In Soledad's TV rooms there has been murder,
mayhem, and destruction of many TV sets. . . .

An official is allowed full range in violent means because 16
a convict can be handled no other way. Fay, have you ever
considered what type of man is capable of handling absolute
power? I mean how many would not abuse it? Is there any

way of isolating or classifying generally who can be trusted with a gun and *absolute* discretion as to who he will kill? I've already mentioned that most of them are KKK types. The rest, all the rest, in general, are so stupid that they shouldn't be allowed to run their own bath. A *responsible* state government would have found a means of weeding out most of the savage types that are drawn to gunslinger jobs long ago. . . .

17   These prisons have always borne a certain resemblance to Dachau and Buchenwald, places for the bad niggers, Mexicans, and poor whites. But the last ten years have brought an increase in the percentage of blacks for crimes that can *clearly* be traced to political-economic causes. There are still some blacks here who consider themselves criminals — but not many. Believe me, my friend, with the time and incentive that these brothers have to read, study, and think, you will find no class or category more aware, more embittered, desperate, or dedicated to the ultimate remedy — revolution. The most dedicated, the best of our kind — you'll find them in the Folsoms, San Quentins, and Soledads. They live like there was no tomorrow. And for most of them there isn't. Somewhere along the line they sensed this. Life on the installment plan, three years of prison, three months on parole; then back to start all over again, sometimes in the same cell. Parole officers have sent brothers back to the joint for selling newspapers (the Black Panther paper). Their official reason is "Failure to Maintain Gainful Employment," etc. . . . It is such things that explain why California prisons produce more than their share of Bunchy Carters and Eldridge Cleavers.

18   Fay, there are only two types of blacks ever released from these places, the Carters and the broken men.

19   The broken men are so damaged that they will never again be suitable members of any sort of social unit. Everything that was still good when they entered the joint, anything inside of them that may have escaped the ruinous effects of black colonial existence, anything that may have been redeemable when they first entered the joint — is gone when they leave.

20   This camp brings out the very best in brothers or destroys them entirely. But none are unaffected. None who leave here are normal. If I leave here alive, I'll leave nothing behind. They'll never count me among the broken men, but I can't say that I am normal either. I've been hungry too

long. I've gotten angry too often. I've been lied to and insulted too many times. They've pushed me over the line from which there can be no retreat. I *know* that they will not be satisfied until they've pushed me out of this existence altogether. I've been the victim of so many racist attacks that I could never relax again. My reflexes will never be normal again. I'm like a dog that has gone through the K–9 process.

This is not the first attempt the institution (camp) has 21 made to murder me. It is the most determined attempt, but not the first.

I look into myself at the close of every one of these pretrial 22 days for any changes that may have taken place. I can still smile now, after ten years of blocking knife thrusts and pick handles of faceless sadistic pigs, of anticipating and reacting for ten years, seven of them in solitary. I can still smile sometimes, but by the time this thing is over I may not be a nice person. And I just lit my seventy-seventh cigarette of this twenty-one-hour day. I'm going to lay down for two or three hours, perhaps I'll sleep . . .

Seize the Time.   23

James Wright
American Twilights, 1957

to Caryl Chessman

James Wright (1927–1980) wrote many volumes of poetry and is frequently anthologized; more details about him are included on page 798. The following poem (written in 1957) concerns Caryl Chessman, a Los Angeles-area rapist who was executed in 1960 after a long and well-publicized legal battle, for crimes committed before 1948.

1

The buckles glitter, billies lean   1
Supple and cold as men on walls.

The trusties' faces, yawning green,
Summon up heart, as someone calls
For light, for light! and evening falls.

2   Checking the cells, the warden piles
Shadow on shadow where he goes
Beyond the catwalk, down the files,
Sneering at one who thumbs his nose.
One weeps, and stumbles on his toes.

3   Tear and tormented snicker and heart
Click in the darkness; close, and fade.
Clean locks together mesh and part,
And lonely lifers, foot and head,
Huddle against the bed they made.

2

4   Lie dark, beloved country, now.
Trouble no dream, so still you lie.
Citizens drawl their dreams away;
Stupored, they hid their agony
Deep in the rock; but men must die.

5   Tall on the earth I would have sung
Heroes of hell, could I have learned
Their names to marvel on my tongue;
The land is dark where they have turned,
And now their very names are burned.

6   But buried under trestled rock
The broken thief and killer quake:
Tower by tower and clock by clock
Citizens wind the towns asleep.
God, God have pity when they wake.

7   Haunted by gallows, peering in dark,
I conjure prisons out of wet
And strangling pillows where I mark
The misery man must not forget,
Though I have found no prison yet.

8   Lo now, the desolation man
Has tossed away like a gnawed bone

Will hunt him where the sea began,
Summon him out of tree and stone,
Damn him, before his dream be gone: —

Seek him behind his bars, to crack   9
Out the dried kernel of his heart.
God, God have pity if he wake,
Have mercy on man who dreamed apart.
God, God have pity on man apart.

.

CAPITAL PUNISHMENT

James Wright
At the Executed Murderer's Grave

for J. L. D.

James Wright (1927–1980), educator, translator, and poet, frequently wrote about his native Midwest. (See another of his poems on page 795.) Born in Martin's Ferry, Ohio, and educated at Kenyon College and the University of Washington, he won the Pulitzer Prize for poetry in 1972. The following poem is a response to the execution of George L. Doty, a convicted rapist and murderer who was electrocuted in 1957.

> Why should we do this? What good is it to
> us? Above all, how can we do such a thing?
> How can it possibly be done?
>
> — *Freud*

1   My name is James A. Wright, and I was born
    Twenty-five miles from this infected grave,
    In Martins Ferry, Ohio, where one slave
    To Hazel-Atlas Glass became my father.
    He tried to teach me kindness. I return
    Only in memory now, aloof, unhurried,
    To dead Ohio, where I might lie buried,
    Had I not run away before my time.
    Ohio caught George Doty. Clean as lime,
    His skull rots empty here. Dying's the best
    Of all the arts men learn in a dead place.
    I walked here once. I made my loud display,
    Leaning for language on a dead man's voice.
    Now sick of lies, I turn to face the past.
    I add my easy grievance to the rest:

Doty, if I confess I do not love you,   2
Will you let me alone? I burn for my own lies.
The nights electrocute my fugitive,
My mind. I run like the bewildered mad
At St. Clair Sanitarium, who lurk,
Arch and cunning, under the maple trees,
Pleased to be playing guilty after dark.
Staring to bed, they croon self-lullabies.
Doty, you make me sick. I am not dead.
I croon my tears at fifty cents per line.

Idiot, he demanded love from girls,   3
And murdered one. Also, he was a thief.
He left two women, and a ghost with child.
The hair, foul as a dog's upon his head,
Made such revolting Ohio animals
Fitter for vomit than a kind man's grief.
I waste no pity on the dead that stink,
And no love's lost between me and the crying
Drunks of Belaire, Ohio, where police
Kick at their kidneys till they die of drink.
Christ may restore them whole, for all of me.
Alive and dead, those giggling muckers who
Saddled my nightmares thirty years ago
Can do without my widely printed sighing
Over their pains with paid sincerity.
I do not pity the dead, I pity the dying.

I pity myself, because a man is dead.   4
If Belmont County killed him, what of me?
His victims never loved him. Why should we?
And yet, nobody had to kill him either.
It does no good to woo the grass, to veil
The quicklime hole of a man's defeat and shame.
Nature-lovers are gone. To hell with them.
I kick the clods away, and speak my name.

This grave's gash festers. Maybe it will heal,   5
When all are caught with what they had to do
In fear of love, when every man stands still
By the last sea,
And the princes of the sea come down
To lay away their robes, to judge the earth

And its dead, and we dead stand undefended everywhere,
And my bodies — father and child and unskilled criminal —
Ridiculously kneel to bare my scars,
My sneaking crimes, to God's unpitying stars.

6 Staring politely, they will not mark my face
From any murderer's, buried in this place.
Why should they? We are nothing but a man.

7 Doty, the rapist and the murderer,
Sleeps in a ditch of fire, and cannot hear;
And where, in earth or hell's unholy peace,
Men's suicides will stop, God knows, not I.
Angels and pebbles mock me under trees.
Earth is a door I cannot even face.
Order be damned, I do not want to die,
Even to keep Belaire, Ohio, safe.
The hackles on my neck are fear, not grief.
(Open, dungeon! Open, roof of the ground!)
I hear the last sea in the Ohio grass,
Heaving a tide of gray disastrousness.
Wrinkles of winter ditch the rotted face
Of Doty, killer, imbecile, and thief:
Dirt of my flesh, defeated, underground.

George Orwell

A Hanging

George Orwell (born Eric Arthur Blair in India in 1903) was England's most prominent political writer in the decade before his death in 1950. A socialist but no communist, he wrote numerous books of fiction and nonfiction; but he is best known for Animal Farm *(1945) and* 1984 *(1949) — novels that contributed mythic terms like Big Brother and doublespeak and "1984" to our culture. His fictional description of "A Hanging" appeared in his* Shooting an Elephant and Other Essays *(1950).*

It was in Burma, a sodden morning of the rains. A sickly   1
light, like yellow tinfoil, was slanting over the high walls
into the jail yard. We were waiting outside the condemned
cells, a row of sheds fronted with double bars, like small
animal cages. Each cell measured about ten feet by ten and
was quite bare within except for a plank bed and a pot for
drinking water. In some of them brown, silent men were
squatting at the inner bars, with their blankets draped
round them. These were the condemned men, due to be
hanged within the next week or two.

One prisoner had been brought out of his cell. He was a   2
Hindu, a puny wisp of a man, with a shaven head and vague
liquid eyes. He had a thick, sprouting mustache, absurdly
too big for his body, rather like the mustache of a comic
man on the films. Six tall Indian warders were guarding
him and getting him ready for the gallows. Two of them
stood by with rifles and fixed bayonets, while the others
handcuffed him, passed a chain through his handcuffs and
fixed it to their belts, and lashed his arms tight to his sides.
They crowded very close about him, with their hands always on him in a careful, caressing grip, as though all the
while feeling him to make sure he was there. It was like
men handling a fish which is still alive and may jump back
into the water. But he stood quite unresisting, yielding his
arms limply to the ropes, as though he hardly noticed what
was happening.

Eight o'clock struck and a bugle call, desolately thin in   3
the wet air, floated from the distant barracks. The superintendent of the jail, who was standing apart from the rest
of us, moodily prodding the gravel with his stick, raised
his head at the sound. He was an army doctor, with a gray
toothbrush mustache and a gruff voice. "For God's sake,
hurry up, Francis," he said irritably. "The man ought to
have been dead by this time. Aren't you ready yet?"

Francis, the head jailer, a fat Dravidian in a white drill   4
suit and gold spectacles, waved his black hand. "Yes sir,
yes sir," he bubbled. "All iss satisfactorily prepared. The
hangman iss waiting. We shall proceed."

"Well, quick march, then. The prisoners can't get their   5
breakfast till this job's over."

We set out for the gallows. Two warders marched on   6
either side of the prisoner, with their rifles at the slope;
two others marched close against him, gripping him by

arm and shoulder, as though at once pushing and supporting him. The rest of us, magistrates and the like, followed
behind. Suddenly, when we had gone ten yards, the procession stopped short without any order or warning. A dreadful
thing had happened — a dog, come goodness knows whence,
had appeared in the yard. It came bounding among us with
a loud volley of barks and leapt round up wagging its whole
body, wild with glee at finding so many human beings
together. It was a large woolly dog, half Airedale, half
pariah. For a moment it pranced around us, and then, before
anyone could stop it, it had made a dash for the prisoner,
and jumping up tried to lick his face. Everybody stood
aghast, too taken aback even to grab the dog.

7   "Who let that bloody brute in here?" said the superintendent angrily. "Catch it, someone!"

8   A warder detached from the escort charged clumsily after
the dog, but it danced and gamboled just out of his reach,
taking everything as part of the game. A young Eurasian
jailer picked up a handful of gravel and tried to stone the
dog away, but it dodged the stones and came after us again.
Its yaps echoed from the jail walls. The prisoner, in the
grasp of the two warders, looked on incuriously, as though
this was another formality of the hanging. It was several
minutes before someone managed to catch the dog. Then
we put my handkerchief through its collar and moved off
once more, with the dog still straining and whimpering.

9   It was about forty yards to the gallows. I watched the
bare brown back of the prisoner marching in front of me.
He walked clumsily with his bound arms, but quite steadily,
with that bobbing gait of the Indian who never straightens
his knees. At each step his muscles slid neatly into place,
the lock of hair on his scalp danced up and down, his feet
printed themselves on the wet gravel. And once, in spite of
the men who gripped him by each shoulder, he stepped
lightly aside to avoid a puddle on the path.

10   It is curious; but till that moment I had never realized
what it means to destroy a healthy, conscious man. When
I saw the prisoner step aside to avoid the puddle, I saw the
mystery, the unspeakable wrongness, of cutting a life short
when it is in full tide. This man was not dying, he was alive
just as we are alive. All the organs of his body were working — bowels digesting food, skin renewing itself, nails
growing, tissues forming — all toiling away in solemn fool-
ery. His nails would still be growing when he stood on the

drop, when he was falling through the air with a tenth-of-a-second to live. His eyes saw the yellow gravel and the gray walls, and his brain still remembered, foresaw, reasoned — even about puddles. He and we were a party of men walking together, seeing, hearing, feeling, understanding the same world; and in two minutes, with a sudden snap, one of us would be gone — one mind less, one world less.

The gallows stood in a small yard, separate from the main grounds of the prison, and overgrown with tall prickly weeds. It was a brick erection like three sides of a shed, with planking on top, and above that two beams and a crossbar with the rope dangling. The hangman, a gray-haired convict in the white uniform of the prison, was waiting beside his machine. He greeted us with a servile crouch as we entered. At a word from Francis the two warders, gripping the prisoner more closely than ever, half led, half pushed him to the gallows and helped him clumsily up the ladder. Then the hangman climbed up and fixed the rope round the prisoner's neck. **11**

We stood waiting, five yards away. The warders had formed in a rough circle round the gallows. And then, when the noose was fixed, the prisoner began crying out to his god. It was a high, reiterated cry of "Ram! Ram! Ram! Ram!" not urgent and fearful like a prayer or cry for help, but steady, rhythmical, almost like the tolling of a bell. The dog answered the sound with a whine. The hangman, still standing on the gallows, produced a small cotton bag like a flour bag and drew it down over the prisoner's face. But the sound, muffled by the cloth, still persisted, over and over again: "Ram! Ram! Ram! Ram! Ram!" **12**

The hangman climbed down and stood ready, holding the lever. Minutes seemed to pass. The steady, muffled crying from the prisoner went on and on, "Ram! Ram! Ram!" never faltering for an instant. The superintendent, his head on his chest, was slowly poking the ground with his stick; perhaps he was counting the cries, allowing the prisoner a fixed number — fifty, perhaps, or a hundred. Everyone had changed color. The Indians had gone gray like bad coffee, and one or two of the bayonets were wavering. We looked at the lashed, hooded man on the drop, and listened to his cries — each cry another second of life; the same thought was in all our minds; oh, kill him quickly, get it over, stop that abominable noise! **13**

Suddenly the superintendent made up his mind. Throw- **14** ing up his head he made a swift motion with his stick. "Chalo!" he shouted almost fiercely.

15   There was a clanking noise, and then dead silence. The prisoner had vanished, and the rope was twisting on itself. I let go of the dog, and it galloped immediately to the back of the gallows; but when it got there it stopped short, barked, and then retreated into a corner of the yard, where it stood among the weeds, looking timorously out at us. We went round the gallows to inspect the prisoner's body. He was dangling with his toes pointed straight downwards, very slowly revolving, as dead as a stone.

16   The superintendent reached out with his stick and poked the bare brown body; it oscillated slightly. "*He's* all right," said the superintendent. He backed out from under the gallows, and blew out a deep breath. The moody look had gone out of his face quite suddenly. He glanced at his wristwatch. "Eight minutes past eight. Well, that's all for this morning, thank God."

17   The warders unfixed bayonets and marched away. The dog, sobered and conscious of having misbehaved itself, slipped after them. We walked out of the gallows yard, past the condemned cells with their waiting prisoners, into the big central yard of the prison. The convicts, under the command of warders armed with lathis, were already receiving their breakfast. They squatted in long rows, each man holding a tin pannikin, while two warders with buckets marched around ladling out rice; it seemed quite a homely, jolly scene, after the hanging. An enormous relief had come upon us now that the job was done. One felt an impulse to sing, to break into a run, to snigger. All at once everyone began chattering gaily.

18   The Eurasian boy walking beside me nodded towards the way we had come, with a knowing smile: "Do you know sir, our friend (he meant the dead man) when he heard his appeal had been dismissed, he pissed on the floor of his cell. From fright. Kindly take one of my cigarettes, sir. Do you not admire my new silver case, sir? From the boxwallah, two rupees eight annas. Classy European style."

19   Several people laughed—at what, nobody seemed certain.

20   Francis was walking by the superintendent, talking garrulously: "Well, sir, all has passed off with the utmost satisfactoriness. It was all finished—flick! Like that. It iss not always so—oah, no! I have known cases where the doctor

wass obliged to go beneath the gallows and pull the prisoner's legs to ensure decease. Most disagreeable!"

"Wriggling about, eh? That's bad," said the superintendent.   21

"Ach, sir, it iss worse when they become refractory! One   22
man, I recall, clung to the bars of hiss cage when we went
to take him out. You will scarcely credit, sir, that it took
six warders to dislodge him, three pulling at each leg. We
reasoned with him, 'My dear fellow,' we said, 'think of all
the pain and trouble you are causing to us!' But no, he
would not listen! Ach, he wass very troublesome!"

I found that I was laughing quite loudly. Everyone was   23
laughing. Even the superintendent grinned in a tolerant
way. "You'd better all come out and have a drink," he said
quite genially. "I've got a bottle of whiskey in the car. We
could do with it."

We went through the big double gates of the prison into   24
the road. "Pulling at his legs!" exclaimed a Burmese magistrate suddenly, and burst into a loud chuckling. We all
began laughing again. At that moment Francis' anecdote
seemed extraordinarily funny. We all had a drink together,
native and European alike, quite amicably. The dead man
was a hundred yards away.

H. L. Mencken
The Penalty of Death

*Newspaperman, linguist, satirist, and editor, H. L. Mencken
(1880–1956) received more public attention than any other
American journalist of his day. Known for his iconoclastic
opinions and for his opposition to puritanical norms, Mencken
was at the height of his popularity in the 1920s, when he wrote
the following article.*

Of the arguments against capital punishment that issue   1
from uplifters, two are commonly heard most often, to wit:

1. That hanging a man (or frying him or gassing him)
   is a dreadful business, degrading to those who have
   to do it and revolting to those who have to witness it.

2. That it is useless, for does not deter others from the same crime.

2   The first of these arguments, it seems to me, is plainly too weak to need serious refutation. All it says, in brief, is that the work of the hangman is unpleasant. Granted. But suppose it is? It may be quite necessary to society for all that. There are, indeed, many other jobs that are unpleasant, and yet no one thinks of abolishing them — that of the plumber, that of the soldier, that of the garbage-man, that of the priest hearing confessions, that of the sand-hog, and so on. Moreover, what evidence is there that any actual hangman complains of his work? I have heard none. On the contrary, I have known many who delighted in their ancient art, and practiced it proudly.

3   In the second argument of the abolitionists there is rather more force, but even here, I believe, the ground under them is shaky. Their fundamental error consists in assuming that the whole aim of punishing criminals is to deter other (potential) criminals — that we hang or electrocute A simply in order to so alarm B that he will not kill C. This, I believe, is an assumption which confuses a part with the whole. Deterrence, obviously, is *one* of the aims of punishment, but it is surely not the only one. On the contrary, there are at least half a dozen, and some are probably quite as important. At least one of them, practically considered, is *more* important. Commonly, it is described as revenge, but revenge is really not the word for it. I borrow a better term from the late Aristotle: *katharsis. Katharsis*, so used, means a salubrious discharge of emotions, a healthy letting off of steam. A school-boy, disliking his teacher, deposits a tack under the pedagogical chair; the teacher jumps and the boy laughs. This is *katharsis*. What I contend is that one of the prime objects of all judicial punishments is to afford the same grateful relief *(a)* to the immediate victims of the criminal punished, and *(b)* to the general body of moral and timorous men.

4   These persons, and particularly the first group, are concerned only indirectly with deterring other criminals. The thing they crave primarily is the satisfaction of seeing the criminal actually before them suffer as he made them suffer. What they want is the peace of mind that goes with the feeling that accounts are squared. Until they get that satis-

faction they are in a state of emotional tension, and hence unhappy. The instant they get it they are comfortable. I do not argue that this yearning is noble; I simply argue that it is almost universal among human beings. In the face of injuries that are unimportant and can be borne without damage it may yield to higher impulses; that is to say, it may yield to what is called Christian charity. But when the injury is serious Christianity is adjourned, and even saints reach for their sidearms. It is plainly asking too much of human nature to expect it to conquer so natural an impulse. A keeps a store and has a bookkeeper, B. B steals $700, employs it in playing at dice or bingo, and is cleaned out. What is A to do? Let B go? If he does he will be unable to sleep at night. The sense of injury, of injustice, of frustration will haunt him like pruritus. So he turns B over to the police, and they hustle B to prison. Thereafter A can sleep. More, he has pleasant dreams. He pictures B chained to the wall of a dungeon a hundred feet underground, devoured by rats and scorpions. It is so agreeable that it makes him forget his $700. He has got his *katharsis*.

The same thing precisely takes place on a larger scale 5 when there is a crime which destroys a whole community's sense of security. Every law-abiding citizen feels menaced and frustrated until the criminals have been struck down — until the communal capacity to get even with them, and more than even, has been dramatically demonstrated. Here, manifestly, the business of deterring others is no more than an afterthought. The main thing is to destroy the concrete scoundrels whose act has alarmed everyone, and thus made everyone unhappy. Until they are brought to book that unhappiness continues; when the law has been executed upon them there is a sigh of relief. In other words, there is *katharsis*.

I know of no public demand for the death penalty for 6 ordinary crimes, even for ordinary homicides. Its infliction would shock all men of normal decency of feeling. But for crimes involving the deliberate and inexcusable taking of human life, by men openly defiant of all civilized order — for such crimes it seems, to nine men out of ten, a just and proper punishment. Any lesser penalty leaves them feeling that the criminal has got the better of society — that he is free to add insult to injury by laughing. That feeling can be dissipated only by a recourse to *katharsis*, the invention of the aforesaid Aristotle. It is more effectively and economically achieved, as human nature now is, by wafting the criminal to realms of bliss.

7   The real objection to capital punishment doesn't lie against the actual extermination of the condemned, but against our brutal American habit of putting it off so long. After all, every one of us must die soon or late, and a murderer, it must be assumed, is one who makes that sad fact the cornerstone of his metaphysic. But it is one thing to die, and quite another thing to lie for long months and even years under the shadow of death. No sane man would choose such a finish. All of us, despite the Prayer Book, long for a swift and unexpected end. Unhappily, a murderer, under the irrational American system, is tortured for what, to him, must seem a whole series of eternities. For months on end he sits in prison while his lawyers carry on their idiotic buffoonery with writs, injunctions, mandamuses, and appeals. In order to get his money (or that of his friends) they have to feed him with hope. Now and then, by the imbecility of a judge or some trick of juridic science, they actually justify it. But let us say that, his money all gone, they finally throw up their hands. Their client is now ready for the rope or the chair. But he must still wait for months before it fetches him.

8   That wait, I believe, is horribly cruel. I have seen more than one man sitting in the death-house, and I don't want to see any more. Worse, it is wholly useless. Why should he wait at all? Why not hang him the day after the last court dissipates his last hope? Why torture him as not even cannibals would torture their victims? The common answer is that he must have time to make his peace with God. But how long does that take? It may be accomplished, I believe, in two hours quite as comfortably as in two years. There are, indeed, no temporal limitations upon God. He could forgive a whole herd of murderers in a millionth of a second. More, it has been done.

Edward I. Koch
Death and Justice

*Outspoken and controversial, Edward I. Koch served as mayor
of New York from 1978 to 1989. In 1985 he contributed the
following essay to* The New Republic, *an influential public
affairs magazine generally considered liberal in outlook.*

Last December a man named Robert Lee Willie, who had   1
been convicted of raping and murdering an 18-year-old
woman, was executed in the Louisiana state prison. In a
statement issued several minutes before his death, Mr.
Willie said: "Killing people is wrong. . . . It makes no difference whether it's citizens, countries, or governments.
Killing is wrong." Two weeks later in South Carolina, an
admitted killer named Joseph Carl Shaw was put to death
for murdering two teenagers. In an appeal to the governor
for clemency, Mr. Shaw wrote: "Killing is wrong when I
did it. Killing is wrong when you do it. I hope you have
the courage and moral strength to stop the killing."

It is a curiosity of modern life that we find ourselves   2
being lectured on morality by cold-blooded killers. Mr.
Willie previously had been convicted of aggravated rape,
aggravated kidnapping, and the murders of a Louisiana
deputy and a man from Missouri. Mr. Shaw committed
another murder a week before the two for which he was
executed, and admitted mutilating the body of the 14-year-
old girl he killed. I can't help wondering what prompted
these murderers to speak out against killing as they entered
the death-house door. Did their newfound reverence for life
stem from the realization that they were about to lose their
own?

Life is indeed precious, and I believe the death penalty   3
helps to affirm this fact. Had the death penalty been a real
possibility in the minds of these murderers, they might well
have stayed their hand. They might have shown moral
awareness before their victims died, and not after. Consider
the tragic death of Rosa Velez, who happened to be home
when a man named Luis Vera burglarized her apartment
in Brooklyn. "Yeah, I shot her," Vera admitted. "She knew
me, and I knew I wouldn't go to the chair."

During my 22 years in public service, I have heard the   4

pros and cons of capital punishment expressed with special intensity. As a district leader, councilman, congressman, and mayor, I have represented constituencies generally thought of as liberal. Because I support the death penalty for heinous crimes of murder, I have sometimes been the subject of emotional and outraged attacks by voters who find my position reprehensible or worse. I have listened to their ideas. I have weighed their objections carefully. I still support the death penalty. The reasons I maintain my position can be best understood by examining the arguments most frequently heard in opposition.

5   1. *The death penalty is "barbaric."* Sometimes opponents of capital punishment horrify with tales of lingering death on the gallows, of faulty electric chairs, or of agony in the gas chamber. Partly in response to such protests, several states such as North Carolina and Texas switched to execution by lethal injection. The condemned person is put to death painlessly, without ropes, voltage, bullets, or gas. Did this answer the objections of death penalty opponents? Of course not. On June 22, 1984, *The New York Times* published an editorial that sarcastically attacked the new "hygienic" method of death by injection, and stated that "execution can never be made humane through science." So it's not the method that really troubles opponents. It's the death itself they consider barbaric.

6   Admittedly, capital punishment is not a pleasant topic. However, one does not have to like the death penalty in order to support it any more than one must like radical surgery, radiation, or chemotherapy in order to find necessary these attempts at curing cancer. Ultimately we may learn how to cure cancer with a simple pill. Unfortunately, that day has not yet arrived. Today we are faced with the choice of letting the cancer spread or trying to cure it with the methods available, methods that one day will almost certainly be considered barbaric. But to give up and do nothing would be far more barbaric and would certainly delay the discovery of an eventual cure. The analogy between cancer and murder is imperfect, because murder is not the "disease" we are trying to cure. The disease is injustice. We may not like the death penalty, but it must be available to punish crimes of cold-blooded murder, cases in which any other form of punishment would be inadequate and, therefore, unjust. If we create a society in

which injustice is not tolerated, incidents of murder — the most flagrant form of injustice — will diminish.

2. *No other major democracy uses the death penalty.* No other major democracy — in fact, few other countries of any description — are plagued by a murder rate such as that in the United States. Fewer and fewer Americans can remember the days when unlocked doors were the norm and murder was a rare and terrible offense. In America the murder rate climbed 122 percent between 1963 and 1980. During that same period, the murder rate in New York City increased by almost 400 percent, and the statistics are even worse in many other cities. A study at M.I.T. showed that based on 1970 homicide rates a person who lived in a large American city ran a greater risk of being murdered than an American soldier in World War II ran of being killed in combat. It is not surprising that the laws of each country differ according to differing conditions and traditions. If other countries had our murder problem, the cry for capital punishment would be just as loud as it is here. And I daresay that any other major democracy where 75 percent of the people supported the death penalty would soon enact it into law.

3. *An innocent person might be executed by mistake.* Consider the work of Adam Bedau, one of the most implacable foes of capital punishment in this country. According to Mr. Bedau, it is "false sentimentality to argue that the death penalty should be abolished because of the abstract possibility that an innocent person might be executed." He cites a study of the 7,000 executions in this country from 1893 to 1971, and concludes that the record fails to show that such cases occur. The main point, however, is this. If government functioned only when the possibility of error didn't exist, government wouldn't function at all. Human life deserves special protection, and one of the best ways to guarantee that protection is to assure that convicted murderers do not kill again. Only the death penalty can accomplish this end. In a recent case in New Jersey, a man named Richard Biegenwald was freed from prison after serving 18 years for murder; since his release he has been convicted of committing four murders. A prisoner named Lemuel Smith, who, while serving four life sentences for murder (plus two life sentences for kidnapping and robbery) in New York's Green Haven Prison, lured a woman corrections of-

ficer into the chaplain's office and strangled her. He then mutilated and dismembered her body. An additional life sentence for Smith is meaningless. Because New York has no death penalty statute, Smith has effectively been given a license to kill.

9   But the problem of multiple murder is not confined to the nation's penitentiaries. In 1981, 91 police officers were killed in the line of duty in this country. Seven percent of those arrested in the cases that have been solved had a previous arrest for murder. In New York City in 1976 and 1977, 85 persons arrested for homicide had a previous arrest for murder. Six of these individuals had two previous arrests for murder, and one had four previous murder arrests. During those two years the New York police were arresting for murder persons with a previous arrest for murder on the average of one every 8.5 days. This is not surprising when we learn that in 1975, for example, the median time served in Massachusetts for homicide was less than two-and-a-half years. In 1976 a study sponsored by the Twentieth Century Fund found that the average time served in the United States for first-degree murder is ten years. The median time served may be considerably lower.

10   4. *Capital punishment cheapens the value of human life.* On the contrary, it can be easily demonstrated that the death penalty strengthens the value of human life. If the penalty for rape were lowered, clearly it would signal a lessened regard for the victims' suffering, humiliation, and personal integrity. It would cheapen their horrible experience, and expose them to an increased danger of recurrence. When we lower the penalty for murder, it signals a lessened regard for the value of the victim's life. Some critics of capital punishment, such as columnist Jimmy Breslin, have suggested that a life sentence is actually a harsher penalty for murder than death. This is sophistic nonsense. A few killers may decide not to appeal a death sentence, but the overwhelming majority make every effort to stay alive. It is by exacting the highest penalty for the taking of human life that we affirm the highest value of human life.

11   5. *The death penalty is applied in a discriminatory manner.* This factor no longer seems to be the problem it once was. The appeals process for a condemned prisoner is lengthy and painstaking. Every effort is made to see that the verdict and sentence were fairly arrived at. However, assertions of discrimination are not an argument for ending the death

penalty but for extending it. It is not justice to exclude everyone from the penalty of the law if a few are found to be so favored. Justice requires that the law be applied equally to all.

6. *Thou Shalt Not Kill.* The Bible is our greatest source of 12 moral inspiration. Opponents of the death penalty frequently cite the sixth of the Ten Commandments in an attempt to prove that capital punishment is divinely proscribed. In the original Hebrew, however, the Sixth Commandment reads, "Thou Shalt Not Commit Murder," and the Torah specifies capital punishment for a variety of offenses. The biblical viewpoint has been upheld by philosophers throughout history. The greatest thinkers of the 19th century — Kant, Locke, Hobbes, Rousseau, Montesquieu, and Mill — agreed that natural law properly authorizes the sovereign to take life in order to vindicate justice. Only Jeremy Bentham was ambivalent. Washington, Jefferson, and Franklin endorsed it. Abraham Lincoln authorized executions for deserters in wartime. Alexis de Tocqueville, who expressed profound respect for American institutions, believed that the death penalty was indispensable to the support of social order. The United States Constitution, widely admired as one of the seminal achievements in the history of humanity, condemns cruel and inhuman punishment, but does not condemn capital punishment.

7. *The death penalty is state-sanctioned murder.* This is the 13 defense with which Messrs. Willie and Shaw hoped to soften the resolve of those who sentenced them to death. By saying in effect, "You're no better than I am," the murderer seeks to bring his accusers down to his own level. It is also a popular argument among opponents of capital punishment, but a transparently false one. Simply put, the state has rights that the private individual does not. In a democracy, those rights are given to the state by the electorate. The execution of a lawfully condemned killer is no more an act of murder than is legal imprisonment an act of kidnapping. If an individual forces a neighbor to pay him money under threat of punishment, it's called extortion. If the state does it, it's called taxation. Rights and responsibilities surrendered by the individual are what give the state its power to govern. This contract is the foundation of civilization itself.

Everyone wants his or her rights, and will defend them 14 jealously. Not everyone, however, wants responsibilities, especially the painful responsibilities that come with law enforcement. Twenty-one years ago a woman named Kitty Genovese was assaulted and murdered on a street in New York. Dozens of neighbors heard her cries for help but did nothing to assist her. They didn't even call the police. In such a climate the criminal understandably grows bolder. In the presence of moral cowardice, he lectures us on our supposed failings and tries to equate his crimes with our quest for justice.

15   The death of anyone—even a convicted killer—diminishes us all. But we are diminished even more by a justice system that fails to function. It is an illusion to let ourselves believe that doing away with capital punishment removes the murderer's deed from our conscience. The rights of society are paramount. When we protect guilty lives, we give up innocent lives in exchange. When opponents of capital punishment say to the state: "I will not let you kill in my name," they are also saying to murderers: "You can kill in your *own* name as long as I have an excuse for not getting involved."

16   It is hard to imagine anything worse than being murdered while neighbors do nothing. But something worse exists. When those same neighbors shrink back from justly punishing the murderer, the victim dies twice.

Henry Schwarzschild

In Opposition to Death Penalty Legislation

Henry Schwarzschild, director of the National Coalition Against the Death Penalty, gave the following testimony in 1978 before the U.S. House of Representatives subcommittee on Criminal Justice.

1   You know the classic arguments about the merits of the death penalty:

- Its dubious and unproved value as a deterrent to violent crime;

- The arbitrariness and mistakes inevitable in any system of justice instituted and administered by fallible human beings;
- The persistent and ineradicable discrimination on grounds of race, class, and sex in its administration in our country's history (including the present time);
- The degrading and hurtful impulse toward retribution and revenge that it expresses;
- The barbarousness of its process (whether by burning at the stake, by hanging from the gallows, by frying in the electric chair, by suffocating in the gas chamber, by shooting at the hands of a firing squad, or by lethal injection with a technology designed to heal and save lives);
- Even the deeply distorting and costly effect the death penalty has upon the administration of the courts, upon law enforcement, and upon the penal institutions of the country.

Let me therefore concentrate my remarks upon a few 2
selected issues about which much unclarity exists in the public mind, in the media, and even in many legislative chambers.

I want to discuss these issues in the context of the evident 3
support of public opinion for the reintroduction of capital punishment in the country. Let me be candid: For the past few years, public opinion polls, whether national or regional, have tended to reflect a substantial majority of the American people affirming their support for the death penalty, to the level of between 65 percent and 75 percent — enough to make many an elected official surrender his or her religious or moral principles against capital punishment. As little as twenty years ago, the polls reflected almost precisely the opposite distribution of views in the country. It is not hard to infer what has turned the American people back toward support of so atavistic and demonstrably useless a criminal sanction. The causes are (a) the rising rate of violent crime in the past two decades, (b) the increasing panic about the rising crime rate, together with a justified (as well as exaggerated) fear for the safety of lives and property, (c) the understandable reaction to a terrible series of assassinations and attempted assassinations of our national leaders and other prominent personalities (President John Kennedy, Senator Robert Kennedy, the Rev. Dr. Martin Luther King Jr., Governor George Wallace, Malcolm X,

Medgar Evers, and others), (d) the rise of international terrorism, including aircraft hijackings and the murder of
prominent political and business leaders as well as the random political killings of innocent victims, (e) many years
of the effective discontinuation of capital punishment and
the remoteness from actual experience of its horrors, and
finally (f) a largely subliminal but sometimes almost articulated racism that attributes most violent criminality to the
minority community, that knows quite well that the poor
and the black are most often the subjects of the death penalty, and that thinks that's just the way it ought to be.

4   What, then, are the rational answers to this series of
partly understandable and partly impermissible misconsi-
ceptions in the American public?

5   True, violent crime has risen sharply in the past two
decades, but to begin with it has been abundantly demonstrated by social research that the availability of the death
penalty has no effect whatsoever upon the rate of violent
crime; to the contrary, there is some scientific evidence
that death sentences imposed and carried out may, for
peculiar reasons of social and psychic pathology, be an
incentive to further acts of violence in the society. Furthermore, while the rates of most major, violent felonies have
been rising — most probably by reason of increased urbani-
zation, social mobility, economic distress, and the like —
the rate of non-negligent homicide has been rising at a rate
slower than the other major felonies, and non-negligent
homicide is, of course, the only crime for which the death
penalty has been declared constitutionally permissible by
the Supreme Court. The crisis in violent crime, such as it
is, has therefore been least acute in the area of homicide.
Indeed, in the past three years, the murder rate in this
country has actually been declining. Thirdly, there is an
appalling number of about 20,000 non-negligent homicides
in this country per year. But we would have to return to
the condition of the mid-1950s to execute as many as one
hundred persons per year, and even that would constitute
only one in every two hundred murderers. In other words,
we have always picked quite arbitrarily a tiny handful of
people among those convicted of murder to be executed,
not those who have committed the most heinous, the most
revolting, the most destructive murders, but always the
poor, the black, the friendless, the life's losers, those without
competent, private attorneys, the illiterate, those despised
or ignored by the community for reasons having nothing

to do with their crime. Ninety-nine and one-half percent of all murderers were never executed—and the deterrent value (which very likely does not exist at all in any case) is reduced to invisibility by the overwhelming likelihood that one will not be caught, or not be prosecuted, or not be tried on a capital charge, or not be convicted, or not be sentenced to death, or have the conviction or sentence reversed on appeal, or have one's sentence commuted.

And if we took the other course and eliminated those high chances of not being executed, but rather carried out the death penalty for every murder, then we should be executing 400 persons per week, every week of the month, every month of the year—and that, Mr. Chairman, should strike even the most ardent supporters of the death penalty as a bloodbath, not as a civilized system of criminal justice. 6

Assassinations and terrorism are well known to be undeterrable by the threat of the death penalty. They are acts of political desperation or political insanity, always committed by people who are at least willing, if not eager, to be martyrs to their cause. Nor would executing terrorists be a preventive against the subsequent taking of hostages for the purpose of setting political assassins or terrorists free. There would of course be a considerable interval of time between arrest and execution, at least for the purpose of trial and the accompanying processes of law, and during that time their fellow activists would have a far more urgent incentive for taking hostages, since not only the freedom but the very lives of their arrested and sentenced colleagues would be at stake. Let me only respectfully add that distinguished fellow citizens of ours such as Senator Edward Kennedy and Ms. Coretta King, who have suffered terrible sadness in their lives at the hands of assassins, are committed opponents of the death penalty. 7

There has been only one execution in the United States since 1967, that of Gary Mark Gilmore, by a volunteer firing squad in Utah on January 17, 1977. Gilmore's execution troubled the public conscience less than it might have otherwise because of his own determination to die. The public and perhaps the legislators of our states and in the Congress have forgotten in a decade that was virtually without executions what sort of demoralizing and brutalizing spectacle executions are. There are now enough people on death row in the country to stage one execution each and every single day for more than a year, to say nothing of the other people who are liable to be sentenced to death during that time. 8

We will again know the details of men crazed with fear, screaming like wounded animals, being dragged from the cell, against their desperate resistance, strapped into the electric chair, voiding their bowels and bladder, being burned alive, almost breaking the restraints from the impact of the high voltage, with their eyeballs popping out of their sockets, the smell of their burning flesh in the nostrils of the witnesses. The ghastly experience of men being hanged, their heads half torn off their bodies, or of the slow strangulation in the gas chamber, or of the press sticking their fingers into the bloody bullet holes of the chair in which Gilmore sat to be executed by rifles, or the use of forcible injection by a paralyzing agent — these reports will not ennoble the image of the United States of America that wants to be the defender of human rights and decency in a world that has largely given up the death penalty as archaic.

9   No one in this Committee surely is guilty of that shoddiest of all impulses toward capital punishment, namely the sense that white, middle-class people, irrespective of their crime, in fact hardly ever get sentenced to death and in such an extremely rare case are virtually never executed. You, Mr. Chairman and Members, and I and probably everyone in this hearing room are in fact absolutely immune, no matter what ghastly crime we might commit, from the likelihood of being executed for it. The penalty of death is imposed almost entirely upon members of what the distinguished social psychologist Kenneth B. Clark has referred to as "the lower status elements of American society."

10   Blacks have always constituted a dramatically disproportionate number of persons executed in the United States, far beyond their share of capital crimes, and even as we sit here today they represent half of the more than 500 persons on the death rows of our state prisons. Indeed, not only the race of the criminal is directly proportional to the likelihood of his being sentenced to death and executed but the race of the victim of the crime a well. The large majority of criminal homicides are still disasters between people who have some previous connection with each other (as husband and wife, parent and child, lovers, business associates, and the like), and murder is therefore still largely an intra-racial event, i.e. black on black or white on white. Yet while half the people under sentence of death right now are black (showing egregious discrimination on the grounds of the race of the murderer), about 85 percent of their victims were white.

11   In other words, it is far more likely to get the murderer

into the electric chair or the gas chamber if he has killed a white person than if he had killed a black person, quite irrespective of his own race. (I say "he" in this context for good reason: the death penalty is also highly discriminatory on grounds of sex. Of the 380 death-row inmates in the country today, only two are women, and even they are far more likely objects of executive commutation of their death sentences than their male counterparts.)

Let me add here that, to the extent to which fear of crime 12 and greater exposure to it, combined with inadequate police protection and more callous jurisprudence, has made the minority communities also voice increasing support for the death penalty, they have not yet fully realized that the death penalty will not protect them from what they (and all of us) rightly fear but that their support of capital punishment will only put their brothers and husbands and sons in jeopardy of being killed by the same state that has been unable properly to protect their lives, their rights, or their property to begin with.

In sum: The public is deeply uninformed about the real 13 social facts of the death penalty and is responding to the seemingly insoluble problem of crime by a retreat to the hope that an even more severe criminal penalty will stem the tide of violence. But it will not. We do not know what will. Judges and lawyers do not know, philosophers and criminologists don't, not even civil libertarians or legislators know the answer—if any of us did, we would have long since accomplished our purpose of reducing crime to the irreducible minimum. But legislators are not therefore entitled to suborn illusory solutions merely because they would garner widespread though uninformed public approval, in order to signal to the electorate that they are "tough on crime." Capital punishment does not deal with crime in any useful fashion and in fact deludes the public into an entirely false sense of greater security about that complex social problem. The death penalty is a legislative way of avoiding rather than dealing with the problem of crime, and the American public will come to learn this very dramatically and tragically if the Congress should unwisely enact the bill before you today.

Two final words about public support for the death 14 penalty.

There are strong indications that the public in great num- 15 bers answers in the affirmative when asked whether they support capital punishment because they want a death penalty law on the books in the hope that this threat will deter criminals from committing violent crimes. Many, perhaps most, of the people who support the enactment of the death penalty do not want executions and would be horrified at being asked to sentence a living human being to a premeditated, ceremonial, legally sanctioned killing. They want deterrence, not electrocutions; prevention, not lethal injections; safety, not firing squads. But a re-enactment by this Congress of a federal death penalty statute will give them at best only electrocutions or lethal injections or firing squads, but neither deterrence nor crime prevention nor safety from violence.

16   The last stand of supporters for the death penalty, when all the other arguments have been rebutted or met, is that of retribution or revenge, the proposition that a murderer has forfeited his life and that we should kill him as an act of abstract equity, irrespective of whether executions serve any social purpose whatsoever. We do not need to preach to each other here this morning, but it is important to have it said once more that civilized societies have instituted systems of justice precisely in order to overcome private acts of retribution and revenge and that they have done so with the understanding that social necessity and social usefulness will be the guideposts of their punishments. Since there has never been and cannot be a showing of social usefulness or social necessity for capital punishment, the virtually unanimous voices of the religious community of our land, our leading thinkers and social analysts, in unison with enlightened opinion for hundreds, perhaps thousands, of years should guide your actions on this matter. Whatever the understandable, bitter, vengeful impulses might be of any of us who suffer the disastrous tragedy of having someone we love or respect murdered by pathological or cruel killers, the society's laws are written not to gratify those impulses but to channel them into helpful, healing, and life-sustaining directions. Gratifying the impulse for revenge is not the business of a government that espouses the humane and liberating ideas expressed in our Declaration of Independence and Constitution. It would be rather a return to the darkest instincts of mankind. It would be arrogating unto the state, unto government, either the godlike wisdom to judge who shall live and who shall die or else the totalitarian arrogance to make that judgment. We, as a nation, have foresworn that idolatry of the state that would justify either of these grounds for the legally

sanctioned killing of our fellow citizens, of any human being, except perhaps in personal or national self-defense.

Mr. Chairman: The question before the country and before the Congress ultimately is whether it is the right of the state, with premeditation, with the long foreknowledge of the victim, under color of law, in the name of all of us, with great ceremony, and to the approval of many angry people in our land, to kill a fellow citizen, a fellow human being, to do that which we utterly condemn, which we utterly abhor in him for having done. What does the penalty, after all, say to the American people and to our children? That killing is all right if the right people do it and think they have a good enough reason for doing it! That is the rationale of every pathological murderer walking the street: he thinks he is the right person to do it and has a good reason for doing his destructive deed. How can a thoughtful and sensible person justify killing people who kill people to teach that killing is wrong? How can you avert your eyes from the obvious: that the death penalty and that executions in all their bloody and terrible reality only aggravate the deplorable atmosphere of violence, the disrespect for life, and brutalization of ourselves that we need to overcome?

If the death penalty were shown, or even could be shown, to be socially necessary or even useful, I would personally still have a deep objection to it. But those who argue for its re-enactment have not and cannot meet the burden of proving its necessity or usefulness. At the very least, before you kill a human being under law, do you not have to be absolutely certain that you are doing the right thing? But how can you be sure that the criminal justice system has worked with absolute accuracy in designating this single person to be the guilty one, that this single person is the one that should be killed, that killing him is the absolutely right thing to do? You cannot be sure, because human judgment and human institutions are demonstrably fallible. And you cannot kill a man when you are not absolutely sure. You can (indeed sometimes you must) make sure that he is incapacitated from repeating his crime, and we obviously accomplish that by ways other than killing him. And while there is fallibility there also, death is different: it is final, irreversible, barbarous, brutalizing to all who come into contact with it. That is a very hurtful model for the United States to play in the world; it is a very hurtful model for a democratic and free government to play for its people.

SHOULD DRUGS BE LEGALIZED?

Kurt Schmoke

A War for the Surgeon General,
Not the Attorney General

One of the most outspoken advocates of legalizing drugs has been Kurt Schmoke, mayor of Baltimore since 1987. Previously, as Assistant U.S. Attorney and as State's Attorney for Baltimore, Schmoke was a highly visible prosecutor of drug cases. The following argument appeared in New Perspectives Quarterly, *a public affairs forum, in the summer of 1989. It was adapted from his testimony before a congressional committee on September 29, 1988.*

1   In the last ten years, the US has become absolutely awash in illegal drugs. Tougher laws, greater efforts at interdiction, and stronger rhetoric at all levels of government and from both political parties have not and will not be able to stop the flow. That is why we must begin to consider what heretofore has been beyond the realm of consideration: decriminalization.

Addiction Is a Disease

2   The violence brought about by the black market in drugs is attributable in large part to the fact that we have chosen to make criminals out of millions of people who have a disease. In the words of the American Medical Association, "It is clear that addiction is not simply the product of a failure of individual will-power. . . . It is properly viewed as a disease, and one that physicians can help many individuals control and overcome."

3   The nature of addiction is very important to the argument in favor of decriminalization. The sad truth is that heroin and morphine addiction is, for most users, a lifetime afflic-

tion that is impervious to any punishment that the criminal-justice system could reasonably mete out.

Given the nature of addiction — whether to narcotics or   4
cocaine — and the very large number of Americans using drugs (the National Institute on Drug Abuse estimates that one in six working Americans has a substance abuse problem), laws restricting their possession and sale have had predictable consequences — most of them bad.

Crimes Committed by Addicts

Addicts commit crimes in order to pay for their drug   5
habits. According to the Justice Department, 90 percent of those who voluntarily seek treatment are turned away. In other words, on any given day, nine out of every ten addicts have no legal way to satisfy their addiction. And, failing to secure help, an untreated addict will commit a crime every other day to maintain his habit.

Whether one relies on studies, or on simple observation,   6
it is indisputable that drug users are committing vast amounts of crime. Baltimore, the city with which I am most familiar, is no exception. According to James A. Inciardi, of the Division of Criminal Justice at the University of Delaware, a 1983 study of addicts in Baltimore showed that ". . . there were high rates of criminality among heroin users during those periods that they were addicted and markedly lower rates during times of nonaddiction." The study also showed that addicts committed crimes on a persistent day-to-day basis and over a long period of time. And the trends are getting worse. Thus, while the total number of arrests in Baltimore remained almost unchanged between 1983 and 1987, there was an approximately 40 percent increase in the number of drug-related arrests.

On the other hand, statistics recently compiled by the   7
Maryland Drug and Alcohol Abuse Administration indicate that crime rates go down among addicts when treatment is available. Thus, for example, of the 6,910 Baltimore residents admitted to drug-abuse treatment in fiscal 1987, 4,386 or 63 percent had been arrested one or more times in the 24-month period prior to admission to treatment, whereas of the 6,698 Baltimore residents who were discharged from drug treatment in fiscal 1987, 6,152 or 91.8 percent were not arrested during the time of their treat-

ment. These statistics tend to support the view that one
way to greatly reduce drug-related crime is to assure addicts legal access to methadone or other drugs.

Overload of the Criminal-Justice System

8   We cannot prosecute our way out of the drug problem.
There are several reasons for this, but the most basic reason
is that the criminal-justice system cannot—without sacrificing our civil liberties— handle the sheer volume of drug-related cases.

9   Nationwide last year, over 750,000 people were arrested
for violating drug laws. Most of these arrests were for possession. In Baltimore, there were 13,037 drug-related arrests in 1987. Between January 1, 1988 and July 1, 1988,
there were 7,981 drug-related arrests. Those numbers are
large, but they hardly reflect the annual total number of
drug violations committed in Baltimore. Should we, therefore, try to arrest still more? Yes—as long as the laws are
on the books. But as a practical matter, we don't have any
place to put the drug offenders we are now arresting. The
population in the Baltimore City Jail is currently 2,900
inmates, even though its inmate capacity is only 2,700. This
shortage of prison space has led to severe overcrowding,
and Baltimore is now under court order to reduce its jail
population.

10   Will more prisons help? Not in any significant way. We
simply cannot build enough of them to hold all of America's
drug offenders—which number in the millions. And even
if we could, the cost would far exceed what American taxpayers would be willing to pay.

11   Decriminalization is the single most effective step we
could take to reduce prison overcrowding. And with less
crowded prisons, there will be less pressure on prosecutors
to plea bargain and far greater chance that non-drug criminals will go to jail—and stay in jail.

12   The unvarnished truth is that in our effort to prosecute
and imprison our way out of the drug war, we have allowed
the drug lords to put us exactly where they want us: wasting
enormous resources—both in money and in personnel—
attacking the fringes of the problem (the drug users and
small-time pushers), while the heart of the problem—the
traffickers and their profits—goes unsolved.

Failed Supply-Side Policies

Not only can we not prosecute our way out of our drug   13
morass, we cannot interdict our way out of it either. Lately,
there have been calls for stepped-up border patrols, increased use of the military and greater pressure on foreign
governments.

Assuming these measures would reduce the supply of   14
illegal drugs, that reduction would not alleviate the chaos
in our cities. According to statistics recently cited by the
American Medical Association, Latin American countries
produced between 162,000 and 211,400 metric tons of
cocaine in 1987. That is five times the amount needed to
supply the US market. Moreover, we are probably only
interdicting 10 to 15 percent of the cocaine entering this
country. Thus, even if we quadrupled the amount of cocaine
we interdict, the world supply of cocaine would still far
outstrip US demand.

If the drug laws in the US simply didn't achieve their   15
intent, perhaps there would be insufficient reason to get
rid of them. But these laws are doing more than not working — they are violating Hippocrates' famous admonition:
First, do no harm.

The legal prohibition of narcotics, cocaine and marijuana   16
demonstrably increases the price of those drugs. For example, an importer can purchase a kilogram of heroin for
$10,000. By the time that kilogram passes through the
hands of several middlemen, its street value can reach
$1,000,000. Such profits can't help but attract major crimi-
nal entrepreneurs willing to take any risk to keep their
product coming to the American market.

Victimization of Children

Perhaps the most tragic victims of our drug laws are   17
children. Many, for example, have been killed as innocent
bystanders in gun battles among traffickers. Furthermore,
while it is true that drug prohibition probably does keep
some children from experimenting with drugs, almost any
child who wants drugs can get them. Keeping drugs outlawed has not kept them out of children's hands.

Recent statistics in both Maryland and Baltimore prove   18
the point: In a 1986–87 survey of Maryland adolescents, 13

percent of eighth graders, 18.5 percent of tenth graders and 22.3 percent of twelfth graders report that they are currently using drugs. In Baltimore, the percentages are 16.6, 16.5 and 20.3, respectively. It should be noted that these numbers exclude alcohol and tobacco, and that current use means at least once a month. It should also be noted that these numbers show a decrease from earlier surveys in 1982 and 1984. Nevertheless, the fact remains that drugs are being widely used by students. Moreover, these numbers do not include the many young people who have left school or who failed to report their drug use.

19   A related problem is that many children, especially those living in the inner city, are frequently barraged with the message that selling drugs is an easy road to riches. In Baltimore, as in many other cities, small children are acting as lookouts and runners for drug pushers, just as they did for bootleggers during Prohibition. Decriminalization and the destruction of the black market would end this most invidious form of child labor.

20   As for education, decriminalization will not end the *Just Say No* and similar education campaigns. On the contrary, more money will be available for such programs. Decriminalization will, however, end the competing message of "easy money" that the drug dealers use to entice children. Furthermore, decriminalization will free up valuable criminal-justice resources that can be used to find, prosecute and punish those who sell drugs to children.

21   This said, if there has been one problem with the current drug-reform debate, it has been the tendency to focus on narrow problems and narrow solutions. That is, we talk about the number of people arrested, the number of tons of drugs entering our ports, the number of available treatment centers, and so on, but there is a bigger picture out there. We, as a nation, have not done nearly enough to battle the social and economic problems that make drug abuse an easy escape for the despairing, and drug trafficking an easy answer to a lack of education and joblessness.

22   Adolescents who take drugs are making a not-so-subtle statement about their confidence in the future. Children without hope are children who will take drugs. We need to give these children more than simple slogans. We need to give them a brighter tomorrow, a sense of purpose, a chance at economic opportunity. It is on that battlefield that the real war against drugs must be fought.

Spread of AIDS

The 1980s have brought another major public health 23
problem that is being made still worse because of our drug
laws: AIDS. Contaminated intravenous drug needles are
now the principal means of transmission for the HIV infection. The users of drug needles infect not only those with
whom they share needles, but also their sex partners and
their unborn children.

One way to effectively slow this means of transmission 24
would be to allow addicts to exchange their dirty needles
for clean ones. However, in a political climate where all
illicit drug use is condemned, and where possession of a
syringe can be a criminal offense, few jurisdictions have
been willing to initiate a needle exchange program. This is
a graphic example, along with our failure to give illegal
drugs to cancer patients with intractable pain, of our blind
pursuit of an irrational policy.

The Mixed Message of Tobacco and Alcohol

The case for the decriminalization of drugs becomes even 25
stronger when illegal drugs are looked at in the context of
legal drugs.

It is estimated that over 350,000 people will die this year 26
from tobacco-related diseases. Last year the number was
equally large. And it will be again next year. Why do millions of people continue to engage in an activity which has
been proven to cause cancer and heart disease? The answer
is that smoking is more than just a bad habit. It is an
addiction. In 1988, Surgeon General C. Everett Koop called
nicotine as addictive as heroin and cocaine. And yet, with
the exception of taxes and labeling, cigarettes are sold without restriction.

By every standard we apply to illicit drugs, tobacco 27
should be a controlled substance. But it is not, and for good
reason. Given that millions of people continue to smoke—
many of whom would quit if they could—making cigarettes
illegal would be an open invitation to a new black market.

The certain occurrence of a costly and dangerous illegal 28
tobacco trade (if tobacco were outlawed) is well understood
by Congress, the Bush Administration and the criminal-
justice community. No rationally thinking person would

want to bring such a catastrophe down upon the US—even if it would prevent some people from smoking.

29   Like tobacco, alcohol is a drug that kills thousands of Americans every year. It plays a part in more than half of all automobile fatalities; and is also frequently involved in suicides, non-automobile accidents, domestic disputes and crimes of violence. Millions of Americans are alcoholic, and alcohol costs the nation billions of dollars in health care and lost productivity. So why not ban alcohol? Because, as almost every American knows, we already tried that. Prohibition turned out to be one of the worst social experiments this country has ever undertaken.

30   I will not review the sorry history of Prohibition except to make two important points. The first is that in repealing Prohibition, we made significant mistakes that should not be repeated in the event that drug use is decriminalized. Specifically, when alcohol was again made legal in 1934, we made no significant effort to educate people as to its dangers. There were no (and still are no) *Just Say No* campaigns against alcohol. We allowed alcohol to be advertised and have associated it with happiness, success and social acceptability. We have also been far too lenient with drunk drivers.

31   The second point is that, notwithstanding claims to the contrary by critics of decriminalization, there are marked parallels between the era of Prohibition and our current policy of making drugs illegal, and important lessons to be learned from our attempts to ban the use and sale of alcohol.

32   During Prohibition, the government tried to keep alcohol out of the hands of millions of people who refused to give it up. As a result, our cities were overrun by criminal syndicates enriching themselves with the profits of bootleg liquor and terrorizing anyone who got in their way. We then looked to the criminal-justice system to solve the crime problems that Prohibition created. But the criminal-justice system—outmanned, outgunned and often corrupted by enormous black market profits—was incapable of stopping the massive crime wave that Prohibition brought, just as it was incapable of stopping people from drinking.

33   As a person now publicly identified with the movement to reform our drug laws through the use of some form of decriminalization, I consider it very important to say that I am not soft on either drug use or drug dealers. I am a soldier in the war against drugs. As Maryland's State Attorney, I spent years prosecuting and jailing drug traffickers,

and had one of the highest rates of incarceration for drug convictions in the country. And if I were still State's Attorney, I would be enforcing the law as vigorously as ever. My experience as a prosecutor did not in any way alter my passionate dislike for drug dealers, it simply convinced me that the present system doesn't work and cannot be made to work.

During the Revolutionary War, the British insisted on 34 wearing red coats and marching in formation. They looked very pretty. They also lost. A good general does not pursue a strategy in the face of overwhelming evidence of failure. Instead, a good general changes from a losing strategy to one that exploits his enemy's weakness, while exposing his own troops to only as much danger as is required to win. The drug war can be beaten and the public health of the US can be improved if we are willing to substitute common sense for rhetoric, myth and blind persistence, and to put the war in the hands of the Surgeon General, not the Attorney General.

Milton Friedman

Prohibition and Drugs

When he was on the faculty of the University of Chicago, Milton Friedman won the Nobel Prize for his "monetarist" school of economics, one that stresses stable growth in the supply of cash and credit in an economy. A conservative—he influenced the policies of Ronald Reagan—he enjoys writing about a range of public issues. Now a senior research fellow at the Hoover Institute at Stanford University, he wrote the two following articles on the legalization of drugs for Newsweek *(1972) and* The Wall Street Journal *(1989).*

The Wall Street Journal piece, which contains a reference in paragraph five to the Newsweek essay, is an "open letter" to William Bennett, an outspoken secretary of education during the Reagan administration who in 1988 became President Bush's "drug czar"—his Director of the Office of National Drug Control Policy. Bennett's response to Milton Friedman (below) also appeared in The Wall Street Journal in 1989—as did the counterresponses printed after it.

1   "The reign of tears is over. The slums will soon be only
a memory. We will turn our prisons into factories and our
jails into storehouses and corncribs. Men will walk upright
now, women will smile, and the children will laugh. Hell
will be forever for rent."

2   That is how Billy Sunday, the noted evangelist and leading crusader against Demon Rum, greeted the onset of Prohibition in early 1920. We know now how tragically his
hopes were doomed. New prisons and jails had to be built
to house the criminals spawned by converting the drinking
of spirits into a crime against the state. Prohibition undermined respect for the law, corrupted the minions of the
law, created a decadent moral climate—but did not stop
the consumption of alcohol.

3   Despite this tragic object lesson, we seem bent on repeating precisely the same mistake in the handling of drugs.

Ethics and Expediency

4   On ethical grounds, do we have the right to use the
machinery of government to prevent an individual from
becoming an alcoholic or a drug addict? For children, almost everyone would answer at least a qualified yes. But
for responsible adults, I, for one, would answer no. Reason
with the potential addict, yes. Tell him the consequences,
yes. Pray for and with him, yes. But I believe that we have
no right to use force, directly or indirectly, to prevent a
fellow man from committing suicide, let alone from drinking alcohol or taking drugs.

5   I readily grant that the ethical issue is difficult and that
men of goodwill may well disagree. Fortunately, we need
not resolve the ethical issue to agree on policy. *Prohibition
is an attempted cure that makes matters worse—for both the
addict and the rest of us.* Hence, even if you regard present
policy toward drugs as ethically justified, considerations
of expediency make that policy most unwise.

6   *Consider first the addict.* Legalizing drugs might increase
the number of addicts, but it is not clear that it would.
Forbidden fruit is attractive, particularly to the young.
More important, many drug addicts are deliberately made
by pushers, who give likely prospects their first few doses
free. It pays the pusher to do so because, once hooked, the
addict is a captive customer. If drugs were legally available,

any possible profit from such inhumane activity would disappear, since the addict could buy from the cheapest source.

Whatever happens to the number of addicts, the individual addict would clearly be far better off if drugs were legal. Today, drugs are both incredibly expensive and highly uncertain in quality. Addicts are driven to associate with criminals to get the drugs, become criminals themselves to finance the habit, and risk constant danger of death and disease.   7

Consider next the rest of us. Here the situation is crystal-clear. The harm to us from the addiction of others arises almost wholly from the fact that drugs are illegal. A recent committee of the American Bar Association estimated that addicts commit one-third to one-half of all street crime in the U.S. Legalize drugs, and street crime would drop dramatically.   8

Moreover, addicts and pushers are not the only ones corrupted. Immense sums are at stake. It is inevitable that some relatively low-paid police and other government officials—and some high-paid ones as well—will succumb to the temptation to pick up easy money.   9

Law and Order

Legalizing drugs would simultaneously reduce the amount of crime and raise the quality of law enforcement. Can you conceive of any other measure that would accomplish so much to promote law and order?   10

But, you may say, must we accept defeat? Why not simply end the drug traffic? That is where experience under Prohibition is most relevant. We cannot end the drug traffic. We may be able to cut off opium from Turkey—but there are innumerable other places where the opium poppy grows. With French cooperation, we may be able to make Marseilles an unhealthy place to manufacture heroin—but there are innumerable other places where the simple manufacturing operations involved can be carried out. So long as large sums of money are involved—and they are bound to be if drugs are illegal—it is literally hopeless to expect to end the traffic or even to reduce seriously its scope.   11

In drugs, as in other areas, persuasion and example are likely to be far more effective than the use of force to shape others in our image.   12

Milton Friedman
An Open Letter to Bill Bennett

Dear Bill:

1   In Oliver Cromwell's eloquent words, "I beseech you, in the bowels of Christ, think it possible you may be mistaken" about the course you and President Bush urge us to adopt to fight drugs. The path you propose of more police, more jails, use of the military in foreign countries, harsh penalties for drug users, and a whole panoply of repressive measures can only make a bad situation worse. The drug war cannot be won by those tactics without undermining the human liberty and individual freedom that you and I cherish.

2   You are not mistaken in believing that drugs are a scourge that is devastating our society. You are not mistaken in believing that drugs are tearing asunder our social fabric, ruining the lives of many young people, and imposing heavy costs on some of the most disadvantaged among us. You are not mistaken in believing that the majority of the public share your concerns. In short, you are not mistaken in the end you seek to achieve.

3   Your mistake is failing to recognize that the very measures you favor are a major source of the evils you deplore. Of course the problem is demand, but it is not only demand, it is demand that must operate through repressed and illegal channels. Illegality creates obscene profits that finance the murderous tactics of the drug lords; illegality leads to the corruption of law enforcement officials; illegality monopolizes the efforts of honest law forces so that they are starved for resources to fight the simpler crimes of robbery, theft and assault.

4   Drugs are a tragedy for addicts. But criminalizing their use converts that tragedy into a disaster for society, for users and non-users alike. Our experience with the prohibition of drugs is a replay of our experience with the prohibition of alcoholic beverages.

5   I append excerpts from a column that I wrote in 1972 on "Prohibition and Drugs." The major problem then was heroin from Marseilles; today, it is cocaine from Latin America. Today, also, the problem is far more serious than it was 17 years ago: more addicts, more innocent victims; more drug

pushers, more law enforcement officials; more money spent to enforce prohibition, more money spent to circumvent prohibition.

Had drugs been decriminalized 17 years ago, "crack" 6 would never have been invented (it was invented because the high cost of illegal drugs made it profitable to provide a cheaper version) and there would today be far fewer addicts. The lives of thousands, perhaps hundreds of thousands of innocent victims would have been saved, and not only in the U.S. The ghettos of our major cities would not be drug-and-crime-infested no-man's lands. Fewer people would be in jails, and fewer jails would have been built.

Colombia, Bolivia and Peru would not be suffering from 7 narco-terror, and we would not be distorting our foreign policy because of narco-terror. Hell would not, in the words with which Billy Sunday welcomed Prohibition, "be forever for rent," but it would be a lot emptier.

Decriminalizing drugs is even more urgent now than in 8 1972, but we must recognize that the harm done in the interim cannot be wiped out, certainly not immediately. Postponing decriminalization will only make matters worse, and make the problem appear even more intractable.

Alcohol and tobacco cause many more deaths in users 9 than do drugs. Decriminalization would not prevent us from treating drugs as we now treat alcohol and tobacco: prohibiting sales of drugs to minors, outlawing the advertising of drugs and similar measures. Such measures could be enforced, while outright prohibition cannot be. Moreover, if even a small fraction of the money we now spend on trying to enforce drug prohibition were devoted to treatment and rehabilitation, in an atmosphere of compassion not punishment, the reduction in drug usage and in the harm done to the users could be dramatic.

This plea comes from the bottom of my heart. Every 10 friend of freedom, and I know you are one, must be as revolted as I am by the prospect of turning the United States into an armed camp, by the vision of jails filled with casual drug users and of an army of enforcers empowered to invade the liberty of citizens on slight evidence. A country in which shooting down unidentified planes "on suspicion" can be seriously considered as a drug-war tactic is not the kind of United States that either you or I want to hand on to future generations.

William Bennett
A Response to Milton Friedman

Dear Milton:

1   There was little, if anything, new in your open letter to
me calling for the legalization of drugs (*The Wall Street
Journal*, Sept. 7). As your 1972 article made clear, the legalization argument is an old and familiar one, which has recently been revived by a small number of journalists and
academics who insist that the only solution to the drug
problem is no solution at all. What surprises me is that you
would continue to advocate so unrealistic a proposal without pausing to consider seriously its consequences.

2   If the argument for drug legalization has one virtue it is
its sheer simplicity. Eliminate laws against drugs, and
street crime will disappear. Take the profit out of the black
market through decriminalization and regulation, and poor
neighborhoods will no longer be victimized by drug dealers.
Cut back on drug enforcement, and use the money to wage
a public health campaign against drugs, as we do with
tobacco and alcohol.

Counting Costs

3   The basic premise of all these propositions is that using
our nation's laws to fight drugs is too costly. To be sure,
our attempts to reduce drug use do carry with them enormous costs. But the question that must be asked—and
which is totally ignored by the legalization advocates—is,
what are the costs of *not* enforcing laws against drugs?

4   In my judgment, and in the judgment of virtually every
serious scholar in this field, the potential costs of legalizing
drugs would be so large as to make it a public policy disaster.

5   Of course, no one, including you, can say with certainty
what would happen in the U.S. if drugs were suddenly to
become a readily purchased product. We do know, however,
that wherever drugs have been cheaper and more easily
obtained, drug use—and addiction—has skyrocketed. In
opium and cocaine producing countries, addiction is ram-
pant among the peasants involved in drug production.

6   Professor James Q. Wilson tells us that during the years

in which heroin could be legally prescribed by doctors in Britain, the number of addicts increased forty-fold. And after the repeal of Prohibition — an analogy favored but misunderstood by legalization advocates — consumption of alcohol soared by 350%.

Could we afford such dramatic increases in drug use? I doubt it. Already the toll of drug use on American society — measured in lost productivity, in rising health insurance costs, in hospitals flooded with drug overdose emergencies, in drug caused accidents, and in premature death — is surely more than we would like to bear.   7

You seem to believe that by spending just a little more money on treatment and rehabilitation, the costs of increased addiction can be avoided. That hope betrays a basic misunderstanding of the problems facing drug treatment. Most addicts don't suddenly decide to get help. They remain addicts either because treatment isn't available or because they don't seek it out. The National Drug Control Strategy announced by President Bush on Sept. 5 goes a long way in making sure that more treatment slots are available. But the simple fact remains that many drug users won't enter treatment until they are forced to — often by the very criminal justice system you think is the source of the problem.   8

As for the connection between drugs and crime, your unswerving commitment to a legalization solution prevents you from appreciating the complexity of the drug market. Contrary to your claim, most addicts do not turn to crime to support their habit. Research shows that many of them were involved in criminal activity before they turned to drugs. Many former addicts who have received treatment continue to commit crimes during their recovery. And even if drugs were legal, what evidence do you have that the habitual drug user wouldn't continue to rob and steal to get money for clothes, food or shelter? Drug addicts always want more drugs than they can afford, and no legalization scheme has yet come up with a way of satisfying that appetite.   9

The National Drug Control Strategy emphasizes the importance of reclaiming the streets and neighborhoods where drugs have wrought havoc because, I admit, the price of having drug laws is having criminals who will try to subvert them. Your proposal might conceivably reduce the amount of gang- and dealer-related crime, but it is fanciful to suggest that it would make crime vanish. Unless you are willing   10 to distribute drugs freely and widely, there will always be a black market to undercut the regulated one. And as for the potential addicts, for the school children and for the pregnant mothers, all of whom would find drugs more accessible and legally condoned, your proposal would offer nothing at all.

11   So I advocate a larger criminal justice system to take drug users off the streets and deter new users from becoming more deeply involved in so hazardous an activity. You suggest that such policies would turn the country "into an armed camp." Try telling that to the public housing tenants who enthusiastically support plans to enhance security in their buildings, or to the residents who applaud police when a local crack house is razed. They recognize that drug use is a threat to the individual liberty and domestic tranquility guaranteed by the Constitution.

12   I remain an ardent defender of our nation's laws against illegal drug use and our attempts to enforce them because I believe drug use is wrong. A true friend of freedom understands that government has a responsibility to craft and uphold laws that help educate citizens about right and wrong. That, at any rate, was the Founders' view of our system of government.

Liberal Ridicule

13   Today this view is much ridiculed by liberal elites and entirely neglected by you. So while I cannot doubt the sincerity of your opinion on drug legalization, I find it difficult to respect. The moral cost of legalizing drugs is great, but it is a cost that apparently lies outside the narrow scope of libertarian policy prescriptions.

14   I do not have a simple solution to the drug problem. I doubt that one exists. But I am committed to fighting the problem on several fronts through imaginative policies and hard work over a long period of time. As in the past, some of these efforts will work and some won't. Your response, however, is to surrender and see what happens. To my mind that is irresponsible and reckless public policy. At a time when national intolerance for drug use is rapidly increasing, the legalization argument is a political anachronism. Its recent resurgence is, I trust, only a temporary distraction from the genuine debate on national drug policy.

Responses: Letters to the Editor by Milton Friedman and Others

William Bennett is entirely right (editorial page, Sept. 1 19) that "there was little, if anything, new in" my open letter to him — just as there is little, if anything, new in his proposed program to rid this nation of the scourge of drugs. That is why I am so disturbed by that program. It flies in the face of decades of experience. More police, more jails, more-stringent penalties, increased efforts at interception, increased publicity about the evils of drugs — all this has been accompanied by more, not fewer, drug addicts; more, not fewer, crimes and murders; more, not less, corruption; more, not fewer, innocent victims.

Like Mr. Bennett, his predecessors were "committed to 2 fighting the problem on several fronts through imaginative policies and hard work over a long period of time." What evidence convinces him that the same policies on a larger scale will end the drug scourge? He offers none in his response to me, only assertion and the conjecture that legalizing drugs would produce "a public policy disaster" — as if that is not exactly what we already have.

Legalizing drugs is not equivalent to surrender in the 3 fight against drug addiction. On the contrary, I believe that legalizing drugs is a precondition for an effective fight. We might then have a real chance to prevent sales to minors; get drugs out of the schools and playgrounds; save crack babies and reduce their number; launch an effective educational campaign on the personal costs of drug use — not necessarily conducted, I might add, by government; punish drug users guilty of harming others while "under the influence"; and encourage large numbers of addicts to volunteer for treatment and rehabilitation when they could do so without confessing to criminal actions. Some habitual drug users would, as he says, "continue to rob and steal to get money for clothes, food or shelter." No doubt also there will be "a black market to undercut the regulated one" — as there now is bootleg liquor thanks to high taxes on alcoholic beverages. But these would be on a far smaller scale than at present. Perfection is not for this world. Pursuing the unattainable best can prevent achievement of the attainable good.

As Mr. Bennett recognizes, the victims of drugs fall into 4

two classes: those who choose to use drugs and innocent victims — who in one way or another include almost all the rest of us. Legalization would drastically reduce the number of innocent victims. That is a virtual certainty. The number of self-chosen victims might increase, but it is pure conjecture that the number would, as he asserts, skyrocket. In any event, while both groups of victims are to be pitied, the innocent victims surely have a far greater claim on our sympathy than the self-chosen victims — or else the concept of personal responsibility has been emptied of all content.

5 A particular class of innocent victims generally overlooked is foreigners. By what right do we impose our values on the residents of Colombia? Or, by our actions undermine the very foundations of their society and condemn hundreds, perhaps thousands, of Colombians to violent death? All because the U.S. government is unable to enforce its own laws on its own citizens. I regard such actions as indefensible, entirely aside from the distortions they introduce into our foreign policy.

6 Finally, he and I interpret the "Founders' view of our system of government" very differently. To him, they believed "that government has a responsibility to . . . help educate citizens about right and wrong." To me, that is a totalitarian view opening the road to thought control and would have been utterly unacceptable to the Founders. I do not believe, and neither did they, that it is the responsibility of government to tell free citizens what is right and wrong. That is something for them to decide for themselves. Government is a means to enable each of us to pursue our own vision in our own way so long as we do not interfere with the right of others to do the same. In the words of the Declaration of Independence, "all Men are . . . endowed by their Creator with certain unalienable Rights, that among these are Life, Liberty, and the pursuit of Happiness. That to secure these Rights Governments are instituted among Men, deriving their just powers from the consent of the Governed." In my view, Justice Louis Brandeis was a "true friend of freedom" when he wrote, "Experience should teach us to be most on our guard to protect liberty when the government's purposes are beneficial. Men born to freedom are naturally alert to repel invasions of their liberty by evil-minded rulers. The greater dangers to liberty lurk in

insidious encroachment by men of zeal, well meaning, but without understanding."

Milton Friedman
Hoover Institution
Stanford, Calif.

Mr. Friedman ("An Open Letter to Bill Bennett," Sept. 7) 1
traces the drug crisis to a decision to continue criminalization of narcotics: "Had drugs been decriminalized 17 years ago, 'crack' would never have been invented (it was invented because the high cost of illegal drugs made it profitable to provide a cheaper version) and there would today be far fewer addicts."

It's always more profitable for drug producers (or any 2
other producer) to make a substitute that is cheaper to produce. Moreover, the incentive to produce the cheaper substitute is greater in a decriminalized environment in which monopoly profits are absent than in a criminalized environment with its constricted supply and higher prices and profits.

Criminalization, in short, restricts both the supply and 3
demand for narcotics by penalizing drug-related behavior, while raising economic profits to those successful in avoiding prosecution. By restricting supply, both through deterrence and the incarceration of producers, criminalization limited the number of potential producers and no doubt delayed the invention of "crack" rather than accelerating it as Mr. Friedman has contended.

Robert N. Ray
Economist
U.S. Small Business Administration
Washington

Messrs. Friedman and Bennett limited themselves to economic 1
nomic and crime issues and ignored the moral question.

While I agree with Mr. Friedman that relegalization will 2
reduce the harm stemming from drugs, I fear repeal will be delayed until Christians wake up to a simple fact: We've overrendered to Caesar again. In the Inquisition we rendered unto Caesar the health of the soul. Two centuries ago, Americans saw the mistake and separated Church and

State. Now Christians are becoming Inquisitors again by rendering unto Caesar the health of the body.

3   We Christians call the body the "Temple of the Holy Spirit," never the "Temple of Congress." If the body belongs to God, we Christians must call for the separation of Health and State. Period. This includes the relegalization of drugs (they were legal until 1914).

4   When the Church stops playing fulcrum to "Kaiser Bill" Bennett, we'll see both political parties come round to the libertarian position.

Marshall Fritz
President
Advocates for Self-Government
Fresno, Calif.

VII.

SCIENCE AND
SOCIETY

No one doubts that science and technology have become central enterprises in our culture. But this doesn't mean that everything science does is accepted uncritically. In fact, as science and technology become more central to our society, it is inevitable that conflicts between science and technology (on the one hand) and society and nature (on the other) will become more important and more complicated.

The first readings in this part introduce the contestants in these conflicts. For central to discussions concerning the relationships among science, nature, and society is an old argument in our culture about the nature of nature: Is nature something fallen, something subordinate to humanity, something to be subdued and exploited? Or is nature unspoiled—an unfallen Eden that restores fallen humanity and that requires a custodial role from us? Should we live in harmony with nature and be ennobled by it, as Thomas Jefferson and Wendell Berry would have it? Or is nature to be used by us for our own ends? Are we locked into some kind of mortal competition with nature, or is cooperation the only proper attitude? Are science and technology means of subduing and subordinating nature? Are they specialized enterprises separate from nature and human values? Or must the distance between science and the humanities— science and society—be bridged?

The contemporary controversy over genetic engineering works out of the same basic conflicts between science, nature, and society; only this time the controversy has specific, practical applications. Are scientists justified in intervening in the very genetic codes that define a species? Is it legitimate to invent and patent new life forms, and to market these products for a profit, as Harvard scientists did when they created a "new" mouse in 1988 for the sake of cancer research? Is it acceptable to control the processes of nature, to manipulate living things for our human advantage? Or should we worry about the ethical and practical implications of genetic engineering? Some articles in the section on genetic engineering contend that genetic engineering is a moral imperative because it can lead to breakthroughs in the management of sickle cell anemia, Huntington's disease, Tay-Sachs disease, or other genetic disorders. But others wonder about the safety of manufacturing and managing life forms, or about the ethics of eugenics. After all, the Nazis espoused eugenics half a century ago. And after all, who will determine which traits count as "deformities" to be stamped out through genetic engineering? And what are the implications of "using" genetically engineered animals to serve us?

The last question brings up the matter of animal rights. As the next set of readings makes clear, over the past decade many people have wondered about the ethics of "using" animals, whether for clothing or cosmetics, or for food or laboratory experiments. Do animals really have rights? If so, what are they? Do people have any rights that animals do not have? Is it legitimate to put people before animals — or animals before people? Do animals comprise another kind of American minority in need of protection from a stronger and exploitative majority? Is it a form of discrimination — "specieism" — to exploit animals, or do human beings by virtue of their special attributes have the right to do just that? Do the benefits of using animals for food, clothing, and medical science outweigh the liabilities? Does the controversy over animal rights come down to a conflict of rights that pits the rights of animals against the rights of people — including the rights of scientists to pursue their work? Should the animal rights movement be less focused on abstract rights and more concerned about treating animals decently while they are "used"? According to some estimates, 50 million animals — cats, dogs, pigs, mice, rats, chimpanzees, rabbits, and more — are experimented on each year, very probably some on your own campus. And very probably the use of animals is an issue someplace on your campus as well.

Members of your community are also no doubt involved in some kind of local environmental controversy. And no doubt that controversy dramatizes in a particular way the same abstract issue articulated in the selections from Jefferson and Cooper: Do we have an adversarial relationship to nature? Is nature inevitably at odds with science and technology? Or do we have a custodial responsibility toward the environment that derives both from morality and from a practical desire for long-term self-preservation? The environmental issue presented in this part involves the complex question of acid rain. Is acid rain a serious problem? What criteria do we use to decide if it is serious? And if it is serious, what should be done about it? Does the responsibility for reducing acid rain fall on the industries that produce it or on society in general? Is there any way to compromise between technology and nature, between "the machine and the garden"? Can technology be employed to clean up the disruption and waste caused by other technology?

This part ends with a discussion of one of the most controversial questions related to science and society today: the matter of euthanasia. Again, the question comes up because of advances in technology—because medical science has extended life expectancies and because medical technology can extend the life of the grievously ill and injured. But what are society's responsibilities to the very ill and incapacitated? Under what circumstances is it permissible to deny or remove medical treatment from a patient? And is it ever permissible to use medical technology actively to end a life—when someone is suffering for example? Who should decide when euthanasia is permissible—family or physicians? Will an acceptance of euthanasia bring out our worst prejudices toward the aged, toward the mentally disadvantaged, toward the insane or deviant?

The advances brought by science and technology solve many human problems, but with these advances come a number of perplexing ethical dilemmas. This is the lesson of this final part, and this is the challenge to all citizens, whether they are scientists or not, in this last decade of the twentieth century.

NATURE, SCIENCE, AND SOCIETY: IS PEACEFUL COEXISTENCE POSSIBLE?

Thomas Jefferson

Query XIX: Manufactures (from *Notes on the State of Virginia*)

In 1781, a French diplomat asked Thomas Jefferson, then governor of Virginia and later the third president of the United States, a series of questions about the state. Notes on the State of Virginia *is Jefferson's official and extended reply. In twenty-three sections, Jefferson (himself a scientist, plantation owner, architect, and statesman—among other things) dealt with the geography, resources, government, education, customs, and inhabitants of his state. In Query XIX, Jefferson addressed the appropriateness of manufacturing industries in the new nation—and articulated his own commitment to an agriculture-based economy.*

We never had an interior trade of any importance. Our 1
exterior commerce has suffered very much from the beginning of the present contest. During this time we have manufactured within our families the most necessary articles of clothing. Those of cotton will bear some comparison with the same kinds of manufacture in Europe; but those of wool, flax and hemp are very coarse, unsightly, and unpleasant: and such is our attachment to agriculture, and such our preference for foreign manufactures, that be it wise or unwise, our people will certainly return as soon as they can, to the raising of raw materials, and exchanging them for finer manufactures than they are able to execute themselves.

The political economists of Europe have established it as 2
a principle that every state should endeavor to manufacture for itself: and this principle, like many others, we transfer

to America, without calculating the difference of circumstance which should often produce a difference of result. In Europe the lands are either cultivated, or locked up against the cultivator. Manufacture must therefore be resorted to of necessity not of choice, to support the surplus of their people. But we have an immensity of land courting the industry of the husbandman. Is it best then that all our citizens should be employed in its improvement, or that one half should be called off from that to exercise manufactures and handicraft arts for the other? Those who labor in the earth are the chosen people of God, if ever He had a chosen people, whose breasts He has made his peculiar deposit for substantial and genuine virtue. It is the focus in which He keeps alive that sacred fire, which otherwise might escape from the face of the earth. Corruption of morals in the mass of cultivators is a phenomenon of which no age nor nation has furnished an example. It is the mark set on those, who not looking up to heaven, to their own soil and industry, as does the husbandman, for their subsistence, depend for it on the casualties and caprice of customers. Dependence begets subservience and venality, suffocates the germ of virtue, and prepares fit tools for the designs of ambition. This, the natural progress and consequence of the arts, has sometimes perhaps been retarded by accidental circumstances: but, generally speaking, the proportion which the aggregate of the other classes of citizens bears in any state to that of its husbandmen is the proportion of its unsound to its healthy parts, and is a good enough barometer whereby to measure its degree of corruption. While we have land to labor then, let us never wish to see our citizens occupied at a workbench, or twirling a distaff. Carpenters, masons, smiths are wanting in husbandry; but, for the general operations of manufacture, let our workshops remain in Europe. It is better to carry provisions and materials to workmen there, than bring them to the provisions and materials, and with them their manners and principles. The loss by the transportation of commodities across the Atlantic will be made up in happiness and permanence of government. The mobs of great cities add just so much to the support of pure government as sores do to the strength of the human body. It is the manners and spirit of a people which preserve a republic in vigor. A degeneracy in these is a canker which soon eats to the heart of its laws and constitution.

Wendell Berry
A Good Scythe

*Wendell Berry is living out the Jeffersonian "agrarian ideal" in
Kentucky, where he was born, where he now teaches, and where
he farms and lives with his family. His award-winning poetry
and prose celebrate the virtues of living in harmony with the
land. The following selection (written in 1979) is a chapter in
his 1981 book,* The Gift of the Good Land.

When we moved to our little farm in the Kentucky River   1
Valley in 1965, we came with a lot of assumptions that we
have abandoned or changed in response to the demands of
place and time. We assumed, for example, that there would
be good motor-powered solutions for all of our practical
problems.

One of the biggest problems from the beginning was that   2
our place was mostly on a hillside and included a good deal
of ground near the house and along the road that was too
steep to mow with a lawn mower. Also, we were using some
electric fence, which needed to be mowed out once or twice
a year.

When I saw that Sears Roebuck sold a "power scythe,"   3
it seemed the ideal solution, and I bought one. I don't remember what I paid for it, but it was expensive, considering
the relatively small amount of work I needed it for. It consisted of a one-cylinder gasoline engine mounted on a frame
with a handlebar, a long metal tube enclosing a flexible
drive shaft, and a rotary blade. To use it, you hung it from
your shoulder by a web strap, and swept the whirling blade
over the ground at the desired height.

It did a fairly good job of mowing, cutting the grass and 4
weeds off clean and close to the ground. An added advantage
was that it readily whacked off small bushes and tree sprouts.
But this solution to the mowing problem involved a whole
package of new problems:

1. The power scythe was heavy.
2. It was clumsy to use, and it got clumsier as the
   ground got steeper and rougher. The tool that was
   supposed to solve the problem of steep ground
   worked best on level ground.

3. It was dangerous. As long as the scythe was attached
    to you by the shoulder strap, you weren't likely to
    fall onto that naked blade. But it *was* a naked blade,
    and it did create a constant threat of flying rock
    chips, pieces of glass, etc.
4. It enveloped you in noise, and in the smudge and
    stench of exhaust fumes.
5. In rank growth, the blade tended to choke — in which
    case you had to kill the engine in a hurry or it would
    twist the drive shaft in two.
6. Like a lot of small gas engines not regularly used,
    this one was temperamental and undependable. And
    dependence on an engine that won't run is a plague
    and a curse.

5   When I review my own history, I am always amazed at
how slow I have been to see the obvious. I don't remember
how long I used that "labor-saving" power scythe before I
finally donated it to help enlighten one of my friends — but
it was too long. Nor do I remember all the stages of my
own enlightenment.

6   The turning point, anyhow, was the day when Harlan
Hubbard showed me an old-fashioned, human-powered
scythe that was clearly the best that I had ever seen. It was
light, comfortable to hold and handle. The blade was very
sharp, angled and curved precisely to the path of its stroke.
There was an intelligence and refinement in its design that
made it a pleasure to handle and look at and think about. I
asked where I could get one, and Harlan gave me an address:
The Marugg Company, Tracy City, Tennessee 37387.

7   I wrote for a price list and promptly received a sheet
exhibiting the stock in trade of the Marugg Company: grass
scythes, bush scythes, snaths, sickles, hoes, stock bells, carrying yokes, whetstones, and the hammers and anvils used
in beating out the "dangle" cutting edge that is an essential
feature of the grass scythes.

8   In due time I became the owner of a grass scythe, hammer
and anvil, and whetstone. Learning to use the hammer and
anvil properly (the Marugg Company provides a sheet of
instructions) takes some effort and some considering. And
so does learning to use the scythe. It is essential to hold
the point so that it won't dig into the ground, for instance;
and you must learn to swing so that you slice rather than
hack.

Once these fundamentals are mastered, the Marugg grass   9
scythe proves itself an excellent tool. It is the most satisfying
hand tool that I have ever used. In tough grass it cuts a
little less uniformly than the power scythe. In all other
ways, in my opinion it is a better tool:

1. It is light.
2. It handles gracefully and comfortably even on steep
   ground.
3. It is far less dangerous than the power scythe.
4. It is quiet and makes no fumes.
5. It is much more adaptable to conditions than the
   power scythe: in ranker growth, narrow the cut and
   shorten the stroke.
6. It always starts — provided the user will start. Aside
   from reasonable skill and care in use, there are no
   maintenance problems.
7. It requires no fuel or oil. It runs on what you ate for
   breakfast.
8. It is at least as fast as the power scythe. Where the
   cutting is either light or extra heavy, it can be appreciably faster.
9. It is far cheaper than the power scythe, both to buy
   and to use.

Since I bought my power scythe, a new version has come   10
on the market, using a short length of nylon string in place
of the metal blade. It is undoubtedly safer. But I believe
the other drawbacks remain. Though I have not used one
of these, I have observed them in use, and they appear to
me to be slower than the metal-bladed power scythe, and
less effective on large-stemmed plants.

I have noticed two further differences between the power   11
scythe and the Marugg scythe that are not so practical as
those listed above, but which I think are just as significant.
The first is that I never took the least pleasure in using the
power scythe, whereas in using the Marugg scythe, whatever the weather and however difficult the cutting, I always
work with the pleasure that one invariably gets from using
a good tool. And because it is not motor driven and is quiet
and odorless, the Marugg scythe also allows the pleasure
of awareness of what is going on around you as you work.

The other difference is between kinds of weariness. Using   12
the Marugg scythe causes the simple bodily weariness that

comes with exertion. This is a kind of weariness that, when not extreme, can in itself be one of the pleasures of work. The power scythe, on the other hand, adds to the weariness of exertion the unpleasant and destructive weariness of strain. This is partly because, in addition to carrying and handling it, your attention is necessarily clenched to it; if you are to use it effectively and safely, you *must* not look away. And partly it is because the power scythe, like all motor-driven tools, imposes patterns of endurance that are alien to the body. As long as the motor is running there is a pressure to keep going. You don't stop to consider or rest or look around. You keep on until the motor stops or the job is finished or you have some kind of trouble. (This explains why the tractor soon evolved headlights, and farmers began to do daywork at night.)

13   These differences have come to have, for me, the force of a parable. Once you have mastered the Marugg scythe, what an absurd thing it makes of the power scythe! What possible sense can there be in carrying a heavy weight on your shoulder in order to reduce by a very little the use of your arms? Or to use quite a lot of money as a substitute for a little skill?

14   The power scythe—and it is far from being an isolated or unusual example—is *not* a labor saver or a shortcut. It is a labor maker (you have to work to pay for it as well as to use it) and a long cut. Apologists for such expensive technological solutions love to say that "you can't turn back the clock." But when it makes perfect sense to do so—as when the clock is wrong—of *course* you can!

James Fenimore Cooper
The Slaughter of the Pigeons

The following passage is a chapter from James Fenimore Cooper's The Pioneers, *an 1823 novel whose protagonist is Natty Bumppo, "Leather-stocking," a prototype of the American western hero who Cooper would include in four other novels (e.g.,* The Last of the Mohicans, The Deerslayer*). In this novel Natty Bumppo is in his early seventies; clad in deerskin and*

in a foxskin hat, and carrying a long rifle, his demeanor is the
one that captured and captivated the American imagination.
The episode of this chapter is set in spring 1794, at Otsego
Lake in central New York, about fifty miles west of Albany.
The passenger pigeons described in the passage are now extinct.

From this time to the close of April, the weather continued   1
to be a succession of great and rapid changes. One day, the
soft airs of spring would seem to be stealing along the valley,
and, in unison with an invigorating sun, attempting,
covertly, to rouse the dormant powers of the vegetable
world; while on the next, the surly blasts from the north
would sweep across the lake, and erase every impression
left by their gentle adversaries. The snow, however, finally
disappeared, and the green wheat fields were seen in every
direction, spotted with the dark and charred stumps that
had, the preceding season, supported some of the proudest
trees of the forest.[1] Ploughs were in motion, wherever those
useful implements could be used, and the smokes of the
sugar-camps[2] were no longer seen issuing from the summits
of the woods of maple. The lake had lost all the characteristic beauty of a field of ice, but still, a dark and gloomy
covering concealed its waters, for the absence of currents
left them yet hid under a porous crust, which, saturated
with the fluid, barely retained enough of its strength to
preserve the contiguity of its parts. Large flocks of wild
geese were seen passing over the country, which would
hover, for a time, around the hidden sheet of water, apparently searching for an opening, where they might obtain a
resting-place; and then, on finding themselves excluded by
the chill covering, would soar away to the north, filling the
air with their discordant screams, as if venting their complaints at the tardy operations of nature.

For a week, the dark covering of the Otsego was left to   2
the undisturbed possession of two eagles, who alighted on
the centre of its field, and sat proudly eyeing the extent of
their undisputed territory. During the presence of these
monarchs of the air, the flocks of migrating birds avoided

[1]The practice was to chop timber down in the spring, let it dry through
the summer, then burn the cleared area so that only blackened logs and
stumps remained. Nothing was salvaged except some ashes used as the
basis for potash.

[2]Where sugar was made from maple sap.

crossing the plain of ice, by turning into the hills, and apparently seeking the protection of the forests, while the white and bald heads of the tenants of the lake were turned upward, with a look of majestic contempt, as if penetrating to the very heavens, with the acuteness of their vision. But the time had come, when even these kings of birds were to be dispossessed. An opening had been gradually increasing, at the lower extremity of the lake, and around the dark spot where the current of the river had prevented the formation of ice, during even the coldest weather; and the fresh southerly winds, that now breathed freely up the valley, obtained an impression on the waters. Mimic waves begun to curl over the margin of the frozen field, which exhibited an outline of crystallizations, that slowly receded towards the north. At each step the power of the winds and the waves increased, until, after a struggle of a few hours, the turbulent little billows succeeded in setting the whole field in an undulating motion, when it was driven beyond the reach of the eye, with a rapidity, that was as magical as the change produced in the scene by this expulsion of the lingering remnant of winter. Just as the last sheet of agitated ice was disappearing in the distance, the eagles rose over the border of crystals, and soared with a wide sweep far above the clouds, while the waves tossed their little caps of snow into the air, as if rioting in their release from a thraldom of five months duration.

3   The following morning Elizabeth[3] was awakened by the exhilarating sounds of the martins, who were quarrelling and chattering around the little boxes which were suspended above her windows, and the cries of Richard,[4] who was calling, in tones as animating as the signs of the season itself—

4   "Awake! awake! my lady fair! the gulls are hovering over the lake already, and the heavens are alive with the pigeons. You may look an hour before you can find a hole, through which, to get a peep at the sun. Awake! awake! lazy ones! Benjamin[5] is overhauling the ammunition, and we only

[3]Elizabeth Temple, daughter of Judge Marmaduke Temple, the founder of Templeton and its chief landowner.

[4]Richard (Dickon) Jones, the sheriff, a cousin of Judge Temple.

[5]Benjamin Penguillan (called Ben Pump), a steward under Jones. In the next paragraph Pump is called "the ex-steward" because he had been a steward to the captain in his seagoing years. One of his charges at the Templeton house is to keep the stove in the parlor hot in winter.

wait for our breakfasts, and away for the mountains and pigeon-shooting."

There was no resisting this animated appeal, and in a few minutes Miss Temple and her friend[6] descended to the parlor. The doors of the hall were thrown open, and the mild, balmy air of a clear spring morning was ventilating the apartment, where the vigilance of the ex-steward had been so long maintaining an artificial heat, with such unremitted diligence. All of the gentlemen . . . were impatiently waiting their morning's repast, each being equipt in the garb of a sportsman. Mr. Jones made many visits to the southern door, and would cry— 5

"See, cousin Bess! see, 'duke![7] the pigeon-roosts of the south have broken up! They are growing more thick every instant. Here is a flock that the eye cannot see the end of. There is food enough in it to keep the army of Xerxes for a month, and feathers enough to make beds for the whole county. Xerxes, Mr. Edwards,[8] was a Grecian king, who— no, he was a Turk, or a Persian, who wanted to conquer Greece, just the same as these rascals will overrun our wheat-fields, when they come back in the fall.—Away! away! Bess; I long to pepper them from the mountain." 6

In this wish both Marmaduke and young Edwards seemed equally to participate, for really the sight was most exhilarating to a sportsman; and the ladies soon dismissed the party, after a hasty breakfast. 7

If the heavens were alive with pigeons, the whole village seemed equally in motion, with men, women, and children. Every species of fire-arms, from the French ducking-gun, with its barrel of near six feet in length, to the common horseman's pistol, was to be seen in the hands of the men and boys; while bows and arrows, some made of the simple stick of a walnut sapling, and others in a rude imitation of the ancient cross-bows, were carried by many of the latter. 8

The houses, and the signs of life apparent in the village, drove the alarmed birds from the direct line of their flight, towards the mountains, along the sides and near the bases of which they were glancing in dense masses, that were equally wonderful by the rapidity of their motion, as by their incredible numbers. 9

We have already said, that across the inclined plane 10

[6]Louisa Grant, daughter of the Episcopal minister.
[7]Short for "Marmaduke," the judge.
[8]Oliver Edwards, a mysterious young stranger.

which fell from the steep ascent of the mountain to the banks of the Susquehanna, ran the highway, on either side of which a clearing of many acres had been made, at a very early day. Over those clearings, and up the eastern mountain, and along the dangerous path that was cut into its side, the different individuals posted themselves, as suited their inclinations; and in a few moments the attack commenced.

11   Amongst the sportsmen was to be seen the tall, gaunt form of Leather-stocking,[9] who was walking over the field, with his rifle hanging on his arm, his dogs following close at his heels, now scenting the dead or wounded birds, that were beginning to tumble from the flocks, and then crouching under the legs of their master, as if they participated in his feelings, at this wasteful and unsportsmanlike execution.

12   The reports of the fire-arms became rapid, whole volleys rising from the plain, as flocks of more than ordinary numbers darted over the opening, covering the field with darkness, like an interposing cloud; and then the light smoke of a single piece would issue from among the leafless bushes on the mountain, as death was hurled on the retreat of the affrighted birds, who would rise from a volley, for many feet into the air, in a vain effort to escape the attacks of man. Arrows, and missiles of every kind, were seen in the midst of the flocks; and so numerous were the birds, and so low did they take their flight, that even long poles, in the hands of those on the sides of the mountain, were used to strike them to the earth.

13   During all this time, Mr. Jones, who disdained the humble and ordinary means of destruction used by his companions, was busily occupied, aided by Benjamin, in making arrangements for an assault of a more than ordinarily fatal character. Among the relics of the old military excursions, that occasionally are discovered throughout the different districts of the western part of New-York, there had been found in Templeton, at its settlement, a small swivel,[10] which would carry a ball of a pound weight. It was thought to have been deserted by a war-party of the whites, in one of their inroads into the Indian settlements, when, perhaps, their convenience or their necessities induced them to leave

[9]I.e., Natty Bumppo.
[10]Small cannon capable of being swung higher or lower.

such an encumbrance to the rapidity of their march, behind them in the woods. This miniature cannon had been released from the rust, and mounted on little wheels, in a state for actual service. For several years, it was the sole organ for extraordinary rejoicings that was used in those mountains. On the mornings of the Fourth of July, it would be heard, with its echoes ringing among the hills, and telling forth its sounds, for thirteen times, with all the dignity of a two-and-thirty pounder. . . . It was somewhat the worse for the service it had performed, it is true, there being but a trifling difference in size between the touch-hole and the muzzle. Still, the grand conceptions of Richard had suggested the importance of such an instrument, in hurling death at his nimble enemies. The swivel was dragged by a horse into a part of the open space, that the sheriff thought most eligible for planting a battery of the kind, and Mr. Pump proceeded to load it. Several handfuls of duck-shot were placed on top of the powder, and the Major-domo soon announced that his piece was ready for service.

The sight of such an implement collected all the idle   14
spectators to the spot, who, being mostly boys, filled the air with their cries of exultation and delight. The gun was pointed on high, and Richard, holding a coal of fire in a pair of tongs, patiently took his seat on a stump, awaiting the appearance of a flock that was worthy of his notice.

So prodigious was the number of the birds, that the scat-   15
tering fire of the guns, with the hurling of missiles, and the cries of the boys, had no other effect than to break off small flocks from the immense masses that continued to dart along the valley, as if the whole creation of the feathered tribe were pouring through that one pass. None pretended to collect the game, which lay scattered over the fields in such profusion, as to cover the very ground with the fluttering victims.

Leather-stocking was a silent, but uneasy spectator of all   16
these proceedings, but was able to keep his sentiments to himself until he saw the introduction of the swivel into the sports.

"This comes of settling a country!" he said—"here have   17
I known the pigeons to fly for forty long years, and, till you made your clearings, there was nobody to scare or to hurt them. I loved to see them come into the woods, for they were company to a body; hurting nothing; being, as it was, as harmless as a garter-snake. But now it gives me sore

thoughts when I hear the frighty things whizzing through the air, for I know it's only a motion to bring out all the brats in the village at them. Well! the Lord won't see the waste of his creaters for nothing, and right will be done to the pigeons, as well as others, by-and-by. — There's Mr. Oliver, as bad as the rest of them, firing into the flocks as if he was shooting down nothing but the Mingo[11] warriors."

18   Among the sportsmen was Billy Kirby,[12] who, armed with an old musket, was loading, and, without even looking into the air, was firing, and shouting as his victims fell even on his own person. He heard the speech of Natty, and took upon himself to reply —

19   "What's that, old Leather-stocking!" he cried; "grumbling at the loss of a few pigeons! If you had to sow your wheat twice, and three times, as I have done, you wouldn't be so massyfully[13] feeling'd to'ards the divils. — Hurrah, boys! scatter the feathers. This is better than shooting at a turkey's head and neck, old fellow."

20   "It's better for you, maybe, Billy Kirby," returned the indignant old hunter, "and all them as don't know how to put a ball down a rifle-barrel, or how to bring it up ag'in with a true aim; but it's wicked to be shooting into flocks in this wastey manner; and none do it, who know how to knock over a single bird. If a body has a craving for pigeon's flesh, why! it's made the same as all other creaters, for man's eating, but not to kill twenty and eat one. When I want such a thing, I go into the woods till I find one to my liking, and then I shoot him off the branches without touching a feather of another, though there might be a hundred on the same tree. But you couldn't do such a thing, Billy Kirby — you couldn't do it if you tried."

21   "What's that you say, you old, dried cornstalk! you sapless stub!" cried the wood-chopper. "You've grown mighty boasting, since you killed the turkey; but if you're for a single shot, here goes at that bird which comes on by himself."

22   The fire from the distant part of the field had driven a single pigeon below the flock to which it had belonged, and, frightened with the constant reports of the muskets,

[11]In the *Leather-Stocking* novels set in New York, the Mingos (Iroquois) are made out to be the "bad Indians" while the Delawares are the "good Indians."

[12]A woodchopper.

[13]Mercifully.

it was approaching the spot where the disputants stood, darting first from one side, and then to the other, cutting the air with the swiftness of lightning, and making a noise with its wings, not unlike the rushing of a bullet. Unfortunately for the wood-chopper, notwithstanding his vaunt, he did not see his bird until it was too late for him to fire as it approached, and he pulled his trigger at the unlucky moment when it was darting immediately over his head. The bird continued its course with incredible velocity.

Natty had dropped his piece from his arm, when the   23 challenge was made, and, waiting a moment, until the terrified victim had got in a line with his eyes, and had dropped near the bank of the lake, he raised his rifle with uncommon rapidity, and fired. It might have been chance, or it might have been skill, that produced the result; it was probably a union of both; but the pigeon whirled over in the air, and fell into the lake, with a broken wing. At the sound of his rifle, both his dogs started from his feet, and in a few minutes the "slut"[14] brought out the bird, still alive.

The wonderful exploit of Leather-stocking was noised   24 through the field with great rapidity, and the sportsmen gathered in to learn the truth of the report.

"What," said young Edwards, "have you really killed a   25 pigeon on the wing, Natty, with a single ball?"

"Haven't I killed loons before now, lad, that dive at the   26 flash?" returned the hunter. "It's much better to kill only such as you want, without wasting your powder and lead, than to be firing into God's creaters in such a wicked manner. But I come out for a bird, and you know the reason why I like small game, Mr. Oliver, and now I have got one I will go home, for I don't like to see these wasty ways that you are all practysing, as if the least thing was not made for use, and not to destroy."

"Thou sayest well, Leather-stocking," cried Marmaduke,   27 "and I begin to think it time to put an end to this work of destruction."

"Put an ind, Judge, to your clearings. An't the woods his   28 work as well as the pigeons? Use, but don't waste. Wasn't the woods made for the beasts and birds to harbour in? and when man wanted their flesh, their skins, or their feathers, there's the place to seek them. But I'll go to the hut with my own game, for I wouldn't touch one of the harmless

[14]Bitch, female dog.

things that kiver the ground here, looking up with their eyes at me, as if they only wanted tongues to say their thoughts."

29   With this sentiment in his mouth, Leather-stocking threw his rifle over his arm, and, followed by his dogs, stepped across the clearing with great caution, taking care not to tread on one, of the hundreds of the wounded birds that lay in his path. He soon entered the bushes on the margin of the lake, and was hid from view.

William Wordsworth

The Tables Turned

William Wordsworth, one of the greatest English poets, dramatized the tension between science and nature in "The Tables Turned," published in 1798.

1   Up! up! my friend, and quit your books,
      Or surely you'll grow double;
      Up! up! my friend, and clear your looks;
      Why all this toil and trouble?

2   The sun, above the mountain's head,
      A freshening luster mellow
      Through all the long green fields has spread,
      His first sweet evening yellow.

3   Books! 'tis a dull and endless strife;
      Come, hear the woodland linnet,
      How sweet his music! on my life,
      There's more of wisdom in it.

4   And hark! how blithe the throstle sings!
      He, too, is no mean preacher;
      Come forth into the light of things,
      Let Nature be your teacher.

She has a world of ready wealth, 5
Our minds and hearts to bless —
Spontaneous wisdom breathed by health,
Truth breathed by cheerfulness.

One impulse from a vernal wood 6
May teach you more of man,
Of moral evil and of good,
Than all the sages can.

Sweet is the lore which Nature brings; 7
Our meddling intellect
Misshapes the beauteous forms of things;
We murder to dissect.

Enough of Science and of Art; 8
Close up those barren leaves;
Come forth, and bring with you a heart
That watches and receives.

C. P. Snow

The Two Cultures

C. P. Snow (1905–1980) wrote the following essay in the British periodical The New Statesman and Nation *in 1956. It immediately became famous as a characterization of emerging post-war culture, and it remains frequently referenced today. Snow himself bridged "the two cultures" quite well: he was a physicist at Cambridge from 1930 to 1950, and he wrote many novels.*

"It's rather odd," said G. H. Hardy, one afternoon in the 1
early Thirties, "but when we hear about 'intellectuals' nowadays, it doesn't include people like me and J. J. Thomson and Rutherford." Hardy was the first mathematician of his generation, J. J. Thomson the first physicist of his; as for Rutherford, he was one of the greatest scientists who have

ever lived. Some bright young literary person (I forget the exact context) putting them outside the enclosure reserved for intellectuals seemed to Hardy the best joke for some time. It does not seem quite such a good joke now. The separation between the two cultures has been getting deeper under our eyes; there is now precious little communication between them, little but different kinds of incomprehension and dislike.

2   The traditional culture, which is, of course, mainly literary, is behaving like a state whose power is rapidly declining—standing on its precarious dignity, spending far too much energy on Alexandrian intricacies, occasionally letting fly in fits of aggressive pique quite beyond its means, too much on the defensive to show any generous imagination to the forces which must inevitably reshape it. Whereas the scientific culture is expansive, not restrictive, confident at the roots, the more confident after its bout of Oppenheimerian self-criticism, certain that history is on its side, impatient, intolerant, creative rather than critical, good-natured and brash. Neither culture knows the virtues of the other; often it seems they deliberately do not want to know. The resentment which the traditional culture feels for the scientific is shaded with fear; from the other side, the resentment is not shaded so much as brimming with irritation. When scientists are faced with an expression of the traditional culture, it tends (to borrow Mr. William Cooper's eloquent phrase) to make their feet ache.

3   It does not need saying that generalisations of this kind are bound to look silly at the edges. There are a good many scientists indistinguishable from literary persons, and vice versa. Even the stereotype generalisations about scientists are misleading without some sort of detail—e.g., the generalisation that scientists as a group stand on the political Left. This is only partly true. A very high proportion of engineers is almost as conservative as doctors; of pure scientists, the same would apply to chemists. It is only among physicists and biologists that one finds the Left in strength. If one compared the whole body of scientists with their opposite numbers of the traditional culture (writers, academics, and so on), the total result might be a few per cent. more towards the Left wing, but not more than that. Nevertheless, as a first approximation, the scientific culture is real enough, and so is its difference from the traditional. For anyone like myself, by education a scientist, by calling

a writer, at one time moving between groups of scientists and writers in the same evening, the difference has seemed dramatic.

The first thing, impossible to miss, is that scientists are 4 on the up and up; they have the strength of a social force behind them. If they are English, they share the experience common to us all—of being in a country sliding economically downhill—but in addition (and to many of them it seems psychologically more important) they belong to something more than a profession, to something more like a directing class of a new society. In a sense oddly divorced from politics, they are the new men. Even the staidest and most politically conservative of scientific veterans, lurking in dignity in their colleges, have some kind of link with the world to come. They do not hate it as their colleagues do; part of their mind is open to it; almost against their will, there is a residual glimmer of kinship there. The young English scientists may and do curse their luck; increasingly they fret about the rigidities of their universities, about the ossification of the traditional culture which, to the scientists, makes the universities cold and dead; they violently envy their Russian counterparts who have money and equipment without discernible limit, who have the whole field wide open. But still they stay pretty resilient: they are swept on by the same social force. Harwell and Winscale have just as much spirit as Los Alamos and Chalk River: the neat petty bourgeois houses, the tough and clever young, the crowds of children: they are symbols, frontier towns.

There is a touch of the frontier qualities, in fact, about 5 the whole scientific culture. Its tone is, for example, steadily heterosexual. The difference in social manners between Harwell and Hampstead, or as far as that goes between Los Alamos and Greenwich Village, would make an anthropologist blink. About the whole scientific culture, there is an absence—surprising to outsiders—of the feline and oblique. Sometimes it seems that scientists relish speaking the truth, especially when it is unpleasant. The climate of personal relations is singularly bracing, not to say harsh: it strikes bleakly on those unused to it, who suddenly find that the scientists' way of deciding on action is by a full-dress argument, with no regard for sensibilities and no holds barred. No body of people ever believed more in dialectic as the primary method of attaining sense; and if you want a picture of scientists in their off-moments it could be just one of a knock-about argument. Under the argument there glitter egotisms as rapacious as any of ours: but, unlike ours, the egotisms are driven by a common purpose.

6   How much of the traditional culture gets through to them? The answer is not simple. A good many scientists, including some of the most gifted, have the tastes of literary persons, read the same things, and read as much. Broadly, though, the infiltration is much less. History gets across to a certain extent, in particular social history: the sheer mechanics of living, how men ate, built, travelled, worked, touches a good many scientific imaginations, and so they have fastened on such works as Trevelyan's *Social History*, and Professor Gordon Childe's books. Philosophy, the scientific culture views with indifference, especially metaphysics. As Rutherford said cheerfully to Samuel Alexander: "When you think of all the years you've been talking about those things, Alexander, and what does it all add up to? *Hot air*, nothing but *hot air*." A bit less exuberantly, that is what contemporary scientists would say. They regard it as a major intellectual virtue, to know what not to think about. They might touch their hats to linguistic analysis, as a relatively honourable way of wasting time; not so to existentialism.

7   The arts? The only one which is cultivated among scientists is music. It goes both wide and deep; there may possibly be a greater density of musical appreciation than in the traditional culture. In comparison, the graphic arts (except architecture) score little, and poetry not at all. Some novels work their way through, but not as a rule the novels which literary persons set most value on. The two cultures have so few points of contact that the diffusion of novels shows the same sort of delay, and exhibits the same oddities, as though they were getting into translation in a foreign country. It is only fairly recently, for instance, that Graham Greene and Evelyn Waugh have become more than names. And, just as it is rather startling to find that in Italy Bruce Marshall is by a long shot the best-known British novelist, so it jolts one to hear scientists talking with attention of the works of Nevil Shute. In fact, there is a good reason for that: Mr. Shute was himself a high-class engineer, and a book like *No Highway* is packed with technical stuff that is not only accurate but often original. Incidentally, there

are benefits to be gained from listening to intelligent men, utterly removed from the literary scene and unconcerned as to who's in and who's out. One can pick up such a comment as a scientist once made, that it looked to him as though the current preoccupations of the New Criticism, the extreme concentration on a tiny passage, had made us curiously insensitive to the total flavour of a work, to its cumulative effects, to the epic qualities in literature. But, on the other side of the coin, one is just as likely to listen to three of the most massive intellects in Europe happily discussing the merits of *The Wallet of Kai-Lung*.

When you meet the younger rank-and-file of scientists,   8
it often seems that they do not read at all. The prestige of the traditional culture is high enough for some of them to make a gallant shot at it. Oddly enough, the novelist whose name to them has become a token of esoteric literary excellence is that difficult highbrow Dickens. They approach him in a grim and dutiful spirit as though tackling *Finnegan's Wake*, and feel a sense of achievement if they manage to read a book through. But most young technicians do not fly so high. When you ask them what they read—"As a married man," one says, "I prefer the garden." Another says: "I always like just to use my books as tools." (Difficult to resist speculating what kind of tool a book would make. A sort of hammer? A crude digging instrument?)

That, or something like it, is a measure of the incom-   9
municability of the two cultures. On their side the scientists are losing a great deal. Some of that loss is inevitable: it must and would happen in any society at our technical level. But in this country we make it quite unnecessarily worse by our educational patterns. On the other side, how much does the traditional culture lose by the separation?

I am inclined to think, even more. Not only practically—   10
we are familiar with those arguments by now—but also intellectually and morally. The intellectual loss is a little difficult to appraise. Most scientists would claim that you cannot comprehend the world unless you know the structure of science, in particular of physical science. In a sense, and a perfectly genuine sense, that is true. Not to have read *War and Peace* and *La Cousine Bette* and *La Chartreuse de Parme* is not to be educated; but so is not to have a glimmer of the Second Law of Thermodynamics. Yet that case ought not to be pressed too far. It is more justifiable to say that those without any scientific understanding miss a whole

body of experience: they are rather like the tone deaf, from whom all musical experience is cut off and who have to get on without it. The intellectual invasions of science are, however, penetrating deeper. Psycho-analysis once looked like a deep invasion, but that was a false alarm; cybernetics may turn out to be the real thing, driving down into the problems of will and cause and motive. If so, those who do not understand the method will not understand the depths of their own cultures.

11　　　But the greatest enrichment the scientific culture could give us is — though it does not originate like that — a moral one. Among scientists, deep-natured men know, as starkly as any men have known, that the individual human condition is tragic; for all its triumphs and joys, the essence of it is loneliness and the end death. But what they will not admit is that, because the individual condition is tragic, therefore the social condition must be tragic, too. Because a man must die, that is no excuse for his dying before his time and after a servile life. The impulse behind the scientists drives them to limit the area of tragedy, to take nothing as tragic that can conceivably lie within men's will. They have nothing but contempt for those representatives of the traditional culture who use a deep insight into man's fate to obscure the social truth — or to do something pettier than obscure the truth, just to hang on to a few perks. Dostoevski sucking up to the Chancellor Pobedonostsev, who thought the only thing wrong with slavery was that there was not enough of it; the political decadence of the *avant garde* of 1914, with Ezra Pound finishing up broadcasting for the Fascists; Claudel agreeing sanctimoniously with the Marshal about the virtue in others' suffering; Faulkner giving sentimental reasons for treating Negroes as a different species. They are all symptoms of the deepest temptation of the clerks — which is to say: "Because man's condition is tragic, everyone ought to stay in their place, with mine as it happens somewhere near the top." From that particular temptation, made up of defeat, self-indulgence, and moral vanity, the scientific culture is almost totally immune. It is that kind of moral health of the scientists which, in the last few years, the rest of us have needed most; and of which, because the two cultures scarcely touch, we have been most deprived.

Loren Eiseley

The Illusion of the Two Cultures

Loren Eiseley (1907–1970) grew up in Nebraska. A well-known anthropologist who worked at the University of Pennsylvania, he gained even greater renown by writing many books about nature and his own relationship to it. This essay contests C. P. Snow's assertion that the humanities and sciences are necessarily antagonistic. It was published in 1964 in The American Scholar, *a respected journal that considers American intellectual life.*

Not long ago an English scientist, Sir Eric Ashby, remarked that "to train young people in the dialectic between orthodoxy and dissent is the unique contribution which universities make to society." I am sure that Sir Eric meant by this remark that nowhere but in universities are the young given the opportunity to absorb past tradition and at the same time to experience the impact of new ideas — in the sense of a constant dialogue between past and present — lived in every hour of the student's existence. This dialogue, ideally, should lead to a great winnowing and sifting of experience and to a heightened consciousness of self which, in turn, should lead on to greater sensitivity and perception on the part of the individual. 1

Our lives are the creation of memory and the accompanying power to extend ourselves outward into ideas and relive them. The finest intellect is that which employs an invisible web of gossamer running into the past as well as across the minds of living men and which constantly responds to the vibrations transmitted through these tenuous lines of sympathy. It would be contrary to fact, however, to assume that our universities always perform this unique function of which Sir Eric speaks, with either grace or perfection; in fact our investment in man, it has been justly remarked, is deteriorating even as the financial investment in science grows. 2

More than thirty years ago, George Santayana[1] had already sensed this trend. He commented, in a now-forgotten 3

[1]George Santayana (1863–1952), Spanish-American poet and philosopher and Harvard professor.

essay, that one of the strangest consequences of modern science was that as the visible wealth of nature was more and more transferred and abstracted, the mind seemed to lose courage and to become ashamed of its own fertility. "The hard-pressed natural man will not indulge his imagination," continued Santayana, "unless it poses for truth; and being half-aware of this imposition, he is more troubled at the thought of being deceived than at the fact of being mechanized or being bored; and he would wish to escape imagination altogether."

4   "Man would wish to escape imagination altogether." I repeat that last phrase, for it defines a peculiar aberration of the human mind found on both sides of that bipolar division between the humanities and the sciences, which C. P. Snow has popularized under the title of *The Two Cultures*. The idea is not solely a product of this age. It was already emerging with the science of the seventeenth century; one finds it in Bacon.[2] One finds the fear of it faintly foreshadowed in Thoreau. Thomas Huxley[3] lent it weight when he referred contemptuously to the "caterwauling of poets."

5   Ironically, professional scientists berated the early evolutionists such as Lamarck and Chambers for overindulgence in the imagination. Almost eighty years ago John Burroughs observed that some of the animus once directed by science toward dogmatic theology seemed in his day increasingly to be vented upon the literary naturalist. In the early 1900s a quarrel over "nature faking" raised a confused din in America and aroused W. H. Hudson to some dry and pungent comment upon the failure to distinguish the purposes of science from those of literature. I know of at least one scholar who, venturing to develop some personal ideas in an essay for the layman, was characterized by a reviewer in a leading professional journal as a worthless writer, although, as it chanced, the work under discussion had received several awards in literature, one of them international in scope. More recently, some scholars not indifferent to humanistic values have exhorted poets to

---

[2]Francis Bacon (1561–1626), philosopher and author whose works were instrumental in furthering the development of modern science.

[3]Thomas Henry Huxley (1825–1895), English biologist, best known in his own day for his spirited defense of evolutionary theory.

leave their personal songs in order to portray the beauty and symmetry of molecular structures.

Now some very fine verse has been written on scientific subjects, but, I fear, very little under the dictate of scientists as such. Rather there is evident here precisely that restriction of imagination against which Santayana inveighed; namely, an attempt to constrain literature itself to the delineation of objective or empiric truth, and to dismiss the whole domain of value, which after all constitutes the very nature of man, as without significance and beneath contempt.   6

Unconsciously, the human realm is denied in favor of the world of pure technics. Man, the tool user, grows convinced that he is himself only useful as a tool, that fertility except in the use of the scientific imagination is wasteful and without purpose, even, in some indefinable way, sinful. I was reading J. R. R. Tolkien's great symbolic trilogy, *The Fellowship of the Ring*, a few months ago, when a young scientist of my acquaintance paused and looked over my shoulder. After a little casual interchange the man departed leaving an accusing remark hovering in the air between us. "I wouldn't waste my time with a man who writes fairy stories." He might as well have added, "or with a man who reads them."   7

As I went back to my book I wondered vaguely in what leafless landscape one grew up without Hans Christian Andersen, or Dunsany, or even Jules Verne.[4] There lingered about the young man's words a puritanism which seemed the more remarkable because, as nearly as I could discover, it was unmotivated by any sectarian religiosity unless a total dedication to science brings to some minds a similar authoritarian desire to shackle the human imagination. After all, it is this impossible, fertile world of our imagination which gave birth to liberty in the midst of oppression, and which persists in seeking until what is sought is seen. Against such invisible and fearful powers, there can be found in all ages and in all institutions — even the institutions of professional learning — the humorless man with the sneer, or if the sneer does not suffice, then the torch, for the bright unperishing letters of the human dream.   8

[4]Andersen (1805–1875), Edward Plunkett (1878–1957), eighteenth baron of Dunsany, and Verne (1828–1905) all wrote fairy tales or adventure stories popular with children.

9   One can contrast this recalcitrant attitude with an 1890 reminiscence from that great Egyptologist Sir Flinders Petrie, which steals over into the realm of pure literature. It was written, in unconscious symbolism, from a tomb:

10   "I here live, and do not scramble to fit myself to the requirements of others. In a narrow tomb, with the figure of Néfermaat standing on each side of me — as he has stood through all that we know as human history — I have just room for my bed, and a row of good reading in which I can take pleasure after dinner. Behind me is that Great Peace, the Desert. It is an entity — a power — just as much as the sea is. No wonder men fled to it from the turmoil of the ancient world."

11   It may now reasonably be asked why one who has similarly, if less dramatically, spent his life among the stones and broken shards of the remote past should be writing here about matters involving literature and science. While I was considering this with humility and trepidation, my eye fell upon a stone in my office. I am sure that professional journalists must recall times when an approaching deadline has keyed all their senses and led them to glance wildly around in the hope that something might leap out at them from the most prosaic surroundings. At all events my eyes fell upon this stone.

12   Now the stone antedated anything that the historians would call art; it had been shaped many hundreds of thousands of years ago by men whose faces would frighten us if they sat among us today. Out of old habit, since I like the feel of worked flint, I picked it up and hefted it as I groped for words over this difficult matter of the growing rift between science and art. Certainly the stone was of no help to me; it was a utilitarian thing which had cracked marrow bones, if not heads, in the remote dim morning of the human species. It was nothing if not practical. It was, in fact, an extremely early example of the empirical tradition which has led on to modern science.

13   The mind which had shaped this artifact knew its precise purpose. It had found out by experimental observation that the stone was tougher, sharper, more enduring than the hand which wielded it. The creature's mind had solved the question of the best form of the implement and how it could be manipulated most effectively. In its day and time this hand ax was as grand an intellectual achievement as a rocket.

As a scientist my admiration went out to that unidentified 14
workman. How he must have labored to understand the
forces involved in the fracturing of flint, and all that involved practical survival in his world. My uncalloused
twentieth-century hand caressed the yellow stone lovingly.
It was then that I made a remarkable discovery.

In the mind of this gross-featured early exponent of the 15
practical approach to nature — the technician, the no-non-
sense practitioner of survival — two forces had met and
merged. There had not been room in his short and desperate
life for the delicate and supercilious separation of the arts
from the sciences. There did not exist then the refined distinctions set up between the scholarly percipience of reality
and what has sometimes been called the vaporings of the
artistic imagination.

As I clasped and unclasped the stone, running my fingers 16
down its edges, I began to perceive the ghostly emanations
from a long-vanished mind, the kind of mind which, once
having shaped an object of any sort, leaves an individual
trace behind it which speaks to others across the barriers
of time and language. It was not the practical experimental
aspect of this mind that startled me, but rather that the
fellow had wasted time.

In an incalculably brutish and dangerous world he had 17
both shaped an instrument of practical application and
then, with a virtuoso's elegance, proceeded to embellish
his product. He had not been content to produce a plain,
utilitarian implement. In some wistful, inarticulate way,
in the grip of the dim aesthetic feelings which are one of
the marks of man — or perhaps I should say, some men — this
archaic creature had lingered over his handiwork.

One could still feel him crouching among the stones on a 18
long-vanished river bar, turning the thing over in his hands,
feeling its polished surface, striking, here and there, just one
more blow that no longer had usefulness as its criterion.
He had, like myself, enjoyed the texture of the stone. With
skills lost to me, he had gone on flaking the implement
with an eye to beauty until it had become a kind of rough
jewel, equivalent in its day to the carved and gold-inlaid
pommel of the iron dagger placed in Tutankhamen's tomb.

All the later history of man contains these impractical 19
exertions expended upon a great diversity of objects, and,
with literacy, breaking even into printed dreams. Today's
secular disruption between the creative aspect of art and

that of science is a barbarism that would have brought lifted eyebrows in a Cro-Magnon cave. It is a product of high technical specialization, the deliberate blunting of wonder, and the equally deliberate suppression of a phase of our humanity in the name of an authoritarian institution, science, which has taken on, in our time, curious puritanical overtones. Many scientists seem unaware of the historical reasons for this development or the fact that the creative aspect of art is not so remote from that of science as may seem, at first glance, to be the case.

20   I am not so foolish as to categorize individual scholars or scientists. I am, however, about to remark on the nature of science as an institution. Like all such structures it is apt to reveal certain behavioral rigidities and conformities which increase with age. It is no longer the domain of the amateur, though some of its greatest discoverers could be so defined. It is now a professional body, and with professionalism there tends to emerge a greater emphasis upon a coherent system of regulations. The deviant is more sharply treated, and the young tend to imitate their successful elders. In short, an "Establishment" — a trade union — has appeared.

21   Similar tendencies can be observed among those of the humanities concerned with the professional analysis and interpretation of the works of the creative artist. Here too, a similar rigidity and exclusiveness make their appearance. It is not that in the case of both the sciences and the humanities standards are out of place. What I am briefly cautioning against is that too frequently they afford an excuse for stifling original thought or constricting much latent creativity within traditional molds.

22   Such molds are always useful to the mediocre conformist who instinctively castigates and rejects what he cannot imitate. Tradition, the continuity of learning, are, it is true, enormously important to the learned disciplines. What we must realize as scientists is that the particular institution we inhabit has its own irrational accretions and authoritarian dogmas which can be as unpleasant as some of those encountered in sectarian circles — particularly so since they are frequently unconsciously held and surrounded by an impenetrable wall of self-righteousness brought about because science is regarded as totally empiric and open-minded by tradition.

23   This type of professionalism, as I shall label it in order

to distinguish it from what is best in both the sciences and humanities, is characterized by two assumptions: that the accretions of fact are cumulative and lead to progress, whereas the insights of art are, at best, singular, and lead nowhere, or, when introduced into the realm of science, produce obscurity and confusion. The convenient label "mystic" is, in our day, readily applied to men who pause for simple wonder, or who encounter along the borders of the known that "awful power" which Wordsworth characterized as the human imagination. It can, he says, rise suddenly from the mind's abyss and enwrap the solitary traveler like a mist.

We do not like mists in this era, and the word imagination is less and less used. We like, instead, a clear road, and we abhor solitary traveling. Indeed one of our great scientific historians remarked not long ago that the literary naturalist was obsolescent if not completely outmoded. I suppose he meant that with our penetration into the biophysical realm, life, like matter, would become increasingly represented by abstract symbols. To many it must appear that the more we can dissect life into its elements, the closer we are getting to its ultimate resolution. While I have some reservations on this score, they are not important. Rather, I should like to look at the symbols which in the one case denote science and in the other constitute those vaporings and cloud wraiths that are the abomination, so it is said, of the true scientist but are the delight of the poet and literary artist.

Creation in science demands a high level of imaginative insight and intuitive perception. I believe no one would deny this, even though it exists in varying degrees, just as it does, similarly, among writers, musicians, or artists. The scientist's achievement, however, is quantitatively transmissible. From a single point his discovery is verifiable by other men who may then, on the basis of corresponding data, accept the innovation and elaborate upon it in the cumulative fashion which is one of the great triumphs of science.

Artistic creation, on the other hand, is unique. It cannot be twice discovered, as, say, natural selection was discovered. It may be imitated stylistically, in a genre, a school, but, save for a few items of technique, it is not cumulative. A successful work of art may set up reverberations and is, in this, just as transmissible as science, but there is a qualitative character about it. Each reverberation in another mind is unique. As the French novelist François Mauriac has remarked, each great novel is a separate and distinct world operating under its own laws with a flora and fauna totally its own. There is communication, or the work is a failure, but the communication releases our own visions, touches some highly personal chord in our own experience.

27   The symbols used by the great artist are a key releasing our humanity from the solitary tower of the self. "Man," says Lewis Mumford, "is first and foremost the self-fabricating animal." I shall merely add that the artist plays an enormous role in this act of self-creation. It is he who touches the hidden strings of pity, who searches our hearts, who makes us sensitive to beauty, who asks questions about fate and destiny. Such questions, though they lurk always around the corners of the external universe which is the peculiar province of science, the rigors of the scientific method do not enable us to pursue directly.

28   And yet I wonder.

29   It is surely possible to observe that it is the successful analogy or symbol which frequently allows the scientist to leap from a generalization in one field of thought to a triumphant achievement in another. For example, Progressionism in a spiritual sense later became the model contributing to the discovery of organic evolution. Such analogies genuinely resemble the figures and enchantments of great literature, whose meanings similarly can never be totally grasped because of their endless power to ramify in the individual mind.

30   John Donne gave powerful expression to a feeling applicable as much to science as to literature when he said devoutly of certain Biblical passages: "The literall sense is always to be preserved; but the literall sense is not always to be discerned; for the literall sense is not always that which the very letter and grammar of the place presents." A figurative sense, he argues cogently, can sometimes be the most "literall intention of the Holy Ghost."

31   It is here that the scientist and artist sometimes meet in uneasy opposition, or at least along lines of tension. The scientist's attitude is sometimes, I suspect, that embodied in Samuel Johnson's remark that, wherever there is mystery, roguery is not far off.

32   Yet surely it was not roguery when Sir Charles Lyell[5]

---

[5]Lyell's (1795–1875) *Principles of Geology* (1830–1833) earned him the popular title of "father of geology."

glimpsed in a few fossil prints of raindrops the persistence of the world's natural forces through the incredible, mysterious aeons of geologic time. The fossils were a symbol of a vast hitherto unglimpsed order. They are, in Donne's sense, both literal and symbolic. As fossils they merely denote evidence of rain in a past era. Figuratively they are more. To the perceptive intelligence they afford the hint of lengthened natural order, just as the eyes of ancient trilobites tell us similarly of the unchanging laws of light. Equally, the educated mind may discern in a scratched pebble the retreating shadow of vast ages of ice and gloom. In Donne's archaic phraseology these objects would bespeak the principal intention of the Divine Being—that is, of order beyond our power to grasp.

Such images drawn from the world of science are every 33 bit as powerful as great literary symbolism and equally demanding upon the individual imagination of the scientist who would fully grasp the extension of meaning which is involved. It is, in fact, one and the same creative act in both domains.

Indeed evolution itself has become such a figurative sym- 34 bol, as has also the hypothesis of the expanding universe. The laboratory worker may think of these concepts in a totally empirical fashion as subject to proof or disproof by the experimental method. Like Freud's doctrine of the subconscious, however, such ideas frequently escape from the professional scientist into the public domain. There they may undergo further individual transformation and embellishment. Whether the scholar approves or not, such hypotheses are now as free to evolve in the mind of the individual as are the creations of art. All the resulting enrichment and confusion will bear about it something suggestive of the world of artistic endeavor.

As figurative insights into the nature of things, such em- 35 bracing conceptions may become grotesquely distorted or glow with added philosophical wisdom. As in the case of the trilobite eye or the fossil raindrop, there lurks behind the visible evidence vast shadows no longer quite of that world which we term natural. Like the words in Donne's Bible, enormous implications have transcended the literal expression of the thought. Reality itself has been superseded by a greater reality. As Donne himself asserted, "The substance of the truth is in the great images which lie behind."

It is because these two types of creation—the artistic and 36 the scientific—have sprung from the same being and have

their points of contact even in division that I have the te-
merity to assert that, in a sense, the "two cultures" are an
illusion, that they are a product of unreasoning fear, professionalism, and misunderstanding. Because of the emphasis
upon science in our society, much has been said about the
necessity of educating the layman and even the professional
student of the humanities upon the ways and the achievements of science. I admit that a barrier exists, but I am
also concerned to express the view that there persists in
the domain of science itself an occasional marked intolerance of those of its own membership who venture to pursue
the way of letters. As I have remarked, this intolerance can
the more successfully clothe itself in seeming objectivity
because of the supposed open nature of the scientific society.
It is not remarkable that this trait is sometimes more manifest in the younger and less secure disciplines.

37   There was a time, not too many centuries ago, when to
be active in scientific investigation was to invite suspicion.
Thus it may be that there now lingers among us, even in
the triumph of the experimental method, a kind of vague
fear of that other artistic world of deep emotion, of strange
symbols, lest it seize upon us or distort the hard-won objectivity of our thinking—lest it corrupt, in other words, that
crystalline and icy objectivity which, in our scientific guise,
we erect as a model of conduct. This model, incidentally,
if pursued to its absurd conclusion, would lead to a world
in which the computer would determine all aspects of our
existence; one in which the bomb would be as welcome as
the discoveries of the physician.

38   Happily, the very great in science, or even those unique
scientist-artists such as Leonardo, who foreran the emergence of science as an institution, have been singularly
free from this folly. Darwin decried it even as he recognized
that he had paid a certain price in concentrated specialization for his achievement. Einstein, it is well known, retained
a simple sense of wonder; Newton felt like a child playing
with pretty shells on a beach. All show a deep humility and
an emotional hunger which is the prerogative of the artist.
It is with the lesser men, with the institutionalization of
method, with the appearance of dogma and mapped-out
territories, that an unpleasant suggestion of fenced preserves begins to dominate the university atmosphere.

39   As a scientist, I can say that I have observed it in my own
and others' specialties. I have had occasion, also, to observe

its effects in the humanities. It is not science *per se;* it is, instead, in both regions of thought, the narrow professionalism which is also plainly evident in the trade union. There can be small men in science just as there are small men in government or business. In fact it is one of the disadvantages of big science, just as it is of big government, that the availability of huge sums attracts a swarm of elbowing and contentious men to whom great dreams are less than protected hunting preserves.

The sociology of science deserves at least equal consideration with the biographies of the great scientists, for powerful and changing forces are at work upon science, the institution, as contrasted with science as a dream and an ideal of the individual. Like other aspects of society, it is a construct of men and is subject, like other social structures, to human pressures and inescapable distortions.   40

Let me give an illustration. Even in learned journals, clashes occasionally occur between those who would regard biology as a separate and distinct domain of inquiry and the reductionists who, by contrast, perceive in the living organism only a vaster and more random chemistry. Understandably, the concern of the reductionists is with the immediate. Thomas Hobbes was expressing a similar point of view when he castigated poets as "working on mean minds with words and distinctions that of themselves signify nothing, but betray (by their obscurity) that there walketh . . . another kingdome, as it were a kingdome of fayries in the dark." I myself have been similarly criticized for speaking of a nature "beyond the nature that we know."   41

Yet consider for a moment this dark, impossible realm of "fayrie." Man is not totally compounded of the nature we profess to understand. He contains, instead, a lurking unknown future, just as the man-apes of the Pliocene contained in embryo the future that surrounds us now. The world of human culture itself was an unpredictable fairy world until, in some pre-ice-age meadow, the first meaningful sounds in all the world broke through the jungle babble of the past, the nature, until that moment, "known."   42

It is fascinating to observe that, in the very dawn of science, Francis Bacon, the spokesman for the empirical approach to nature, shared with Shakespeare, the poet, a recognition of the creativeness which adds to nature, and which emerges from nature as "an art which nature makes." Neither the great scholar nor the great poet had renounced   43 this "kingdome of fayries." Both had realized what Henri Bergson was later to express so effectively, that life inserts a vast "indetermination into matter." It is, in a sense, an intrusion from a realm which can never be completely subject to prophetic analysis by science. The novelties of evolution emerge; they cannot be predicted. They haunt, until their arrival, a world of unimaginable possibilities behind the living screen of events, as these last exist to the observer confined to a single point on the time scale.

44   Oddly enough, much of the confusion that surrounded my phrase, "a nature beyond the nature that we know," resolves itself into pure semantics. I might have pointed out what must be obvious even to the most dedicated scientific mind — that the nature which we know has been many times reinterpreted in human thinking, and that the hard, substantial matter of the nineteenth century has already vanished into a dark, bodiless void, a web of "events" in space-time. This is a realm, I venture to assert, as weird as any we have tried, in the past, to exorcise by the brave use of seeming solid words. Yet some minds exhibit an almost instinctive hostility toward the mere attempt to wonder or to ask what lies below that microcosmic world out of which emerge the particles which compose our bodies and which now take on this wraithlike quality.

45   Is there something here we fear to face, except when clothed in safely sterilized professional speech? Have we grown reluctant in this age of power to admit mystery and beauty into our thoughts, or to learn where power ceases? I referred earlier to one of our own forebears on a gravel bar, thumbing a pebble. If, after the ages of building and destroying, if after the measuring of light-years and the powers probed at the atom's heart, if after the last iron is rust-eaten and the last glass lies shattered in the streets, a man, some savage, some remnant of what once we were, pauses on his way to the tribal drinking place and feels rising from within his soul the inexplicable mist of terror and beauty that is evoked from old ruins — even the ruins of the greatest city in the world — then, I say, all will still be well with man.

46   And if that savage can pluck a stone from the gravel because it shone like crystal when the water rushed over it, and hold it against the sunset, he will be as we were in the beginning , whole — as we were when we were children, before we began to split the knowledge from the dream.

All talk of the two cultures is an illusion; it is the pebble which tells man's story. Upon it is written man's two faces, the artistic and the practical. They are expressed upon one stone over which a hand once closed, no less firm because the mind behind it was submerged in light and shadow and deep wonder.

Today we hold a stone, the heavy stone of power. We 47 must perceive beyond it, however, by the aid of the artistic imagination, those humane insights and understandings which alone can lighten our burden and enable us to shape ourselves, rather than the stone, into the forms which great art has anticipated.

GENETIC ENGINEERING

Lewis Thomas
The Hazards of Science

Lewis Thomas has served as president of the Sloan-Kettering Cancer Center in New York, as dean of the Yale Medical School, and as a member of the National Academy of Sciences, among other things. But he is best known as an essayist about science. His collection of essays The Lives of a Cell *(1974) won a National Book Award. "The Hazards of Science" appeared in a similar collection,* Medusa and the Snail, *in 1977; it originally appeared in* The New England Journal of Medicine.

1   The code word for criticism of science and scientists these days is "hubris." Once you've said that word, you've said it all; it sums up, in a word, all of today's apprehensions and misgivings in the public mind — not just about what is perceived as the insufferable attitude of the scientists themselves but, enclosed in the same word, what science and technology are perceived to be doing to make this century, this near to its ending, turn out so wrong.

2   "Hubris" is a powerful word, containing layers of powerful meaning, derived from a very old word, but with a new life of its own, growing way beyond the limits of its original meaning. Today, it is strong enough to carry the full weight of disapproval for the cast of mind that thought up atomic fusion and fission as ways of first blowing up and later heating cities as well as the attitudes which led to stripmining, offshore oil wells, Kepone, food additives, SSTs, and the tiny spherical particles of plastic recently discovered clogging the waters of the Sargasso Sea.

3   The biomedical sciences are now caught up with physical science and technology in the same kind of critical judgment, with the same pejorative word. Hubris is responsible, it is said, for the whole biological revolution. It is hubris that has given us the prospects of behavior control, psychosurgery, fetal research, heart transplants, the cloning of

prominent politicians from bits of their own eminent tissue, iatrogenic disease, overpopulation, and recombinant DNA. This last, the new technology that permits the stitching of one creature's genes into the DNA of another, to make hybrids, is currently cited as the ultimate example of hubris. It is hubris for man to manufacture a hybrid on his own.

So now we are back to the first word again, from "hybrid"   4
to "hubris," and the hidden meaning of two beings joined unnaturally together by man is somehow retained. Today's joining is straight out of Greek mythology: it is the combining of man's capacity with the special prerogative of the gods, and it is really in this sense of outrage that the word "hubris" is being used today. That is what the word has grown into, a warning, a code word, a shorthand signal from the language itself: if man starts doing things reserved for the gods, deifying himself, the outcome will be something worse for him, symbolically, than the litters of wild boars and domestic sows were for the ancient Romans.

To be charged with hubris is therefore an extremely seri-   5
ous matter, and not to be dealt with by murmuring things about antiscience and antiintellectualism, which is what many of us engaged in science tend to do these days. The doubts about our enterprise have their origin in the most profound kind of human anxiety. If we are right and the critics are wrong, then it has to be that the word "hubris" is being mistakenly employed, that this is not what we are up to, that there is, for the time being anyway, a fundamental misunderstanding of science.

I suppose there is one central question to be dealt with,   6
and I am not at all sure how to deal with it, although I am quite certain about my own answer to it. It is this: are there some kinds of information leading to some sorts of knowledge that human beings are really better off not having? Is there a limit to scientific inquiry not set by what is knowable but what we *ought* to be knowing? Should we stop short of learning about some things, for fear of what we, or someone, will do with the knowledge? My own answer is a flat no, but I must confess that this is an intuitive response and I am neither inclined nor trained to reason my way through it.

There has been some effort, in and out of scientific quar-   7
ters, to make recombinant DNA into the issue on which to settle this argument. Proponents of this line of research are accused of pure hubris, of assuming the rights of gods, of

arrogance and outrage; what is more, they confess themselves to be in the business of making live hybrids with
their own hands. The mayor of Cambridge and the attorney
general of New York have both been advised to put a stop
to it, forthwith.

8   It is not quite the same sort of argument, however, as
the one about limiting knowledge, although this is surely
part of it. The knowledge is already here, and the rage of
the argument is about its application in technology. Should
DNA for making certain useful or interesting proteins be
incorporated into *E. coli* plasmids or not? Is there a risk of
inserting the wrong sort of toxins or hazardous viruses, and
then having the new hybrid organisms spread beyond the
laboratory? Is this a technology for creating new varieties
of pathogens, and should it be stopped because of this?

9   If the argument is held to this level, I can see no reason
why it cannot be settled, by reasonable people. We have
learned a great deal about the handling of dangerous microbes in the last century, although I must say that the
opponents of recombinant-DNA research tend to down-
grade this huge body of information. At one time or another,
agents as hazardous as those of rabies, psittacosis, plague,
and typhus have been dealt with by investigators in secure
laboratories, with only rare instances of self-infection of
the investigators themselves, and no instances at all of
epidemics. It takes some high imagining to postulate the
creation of brand-new pathogens so wild and voracious as to
spread from equally secure laboratories to endanger human
life at large, as some of the arguers are now maintaining.

10   But this is precisely the trouble with the recombinant-
DNA problem: it has become an emotional issue, with too
many irretrievably lost tempers on both sides. It has lost
the sound of a discussion of technological safety, and begins
now to sound like something else, almost like a religious
controversy, and here it is moving toward the central issue:
are there some things in science we should not be learning
about?

11   There is an inevitably long list of hard questions to follow
this one, beginning with the one which asks whether the
mayor of Cambridge should be the one to decide, first off.

12   Maybe we'd be wiser, all of us, to back off before the
recombinant-DNA issue becomes too large to cope with. If
we're going to have a fight about it, let it be confined to
the immediate issue of safety and security, of the recombi-

nants now under consideration, and let us by all means have regulations and guidelines to assure the public safety wherever these are indicated or even suggested. But if it is possible let us stay off that question about limiting human knowledge. It is too loaded, and we'll simply not be able to cope with it.

By this time it will have become clear that I have already 13 taken sides in the matter, and my point of view is entirely prejudiced. This is true, but with a qualification. I am not so much in favor of recombinant-DNA research as I am opposed to the opposition to this line of inquiry. As a longtime student of infectious-disease agents I do not take kindly the declarations that we do not know how to keep from catching things in laboratories, much less how to keep them from spreading beyond the laboratory walls. I believe we learned a lot about this sort of thing, long ago. Moreover, I regard it as a form of hubris-in-reverse to claim that man can make deadly pathogenic microorganisms so easily. In my view, it takes a long time and a great deal of interliving before a microbe can become a successful pathogen. Pathogenicity is, in a sense, a highly skilled trade, and only a tiny minority of all the numberless tons of microbes on the earth has ever involved itself in it; most bacteria are busy with their own business, browsing and recycling the rest of life. Indeed, pathogenicity often seems to me a sort of biological accident in which signals are misdirected by the microbe or misinterpreted by the host, as in the case of endotoxin, or in which the intimacy between host and microbe is of such long standing that a form of molecular mimicry becomes possible, as in the case of diphtheria toxin. I do not believe that by simply putting together new combinations of genes one can create creatures as highly skilled and adapted for dependence as a pathogen must be, any more than I have ever believed that microbial life from the moon or Mars could possibly make a living on this planet.

But, as I said, I'm not at all sure this is what the argument 14 is really about. Behind it is that other discussion, which I wish we would not have to become enmeshed in.

I cannot speak for the physical sciences, which have 15 moved an immense distance in this century by any standard, but it does seem to me that in the biological and medical sciences we are still far too ignorant to begin making judgments about what sorts of things we should be learning or not learning. To the contrary, we ought to be grateful for whatever snatches we can get hold of, and we ought to be out there on a much larger scale than today's, looking for more.

16   We should be very careful with that word "hubris," and make sure it is not used when not warranted. There is a great danger in applying it to the search for knowledge. The application of knowledge is another matter, and there is hubris in plenty of our technology, but I do not believe that looking for new information about nature, at whatever level, can possibly be called unnatural. Indeed, if there is any single attribute of human beings, apart from language, which distinguishes them from all other creatures on earth, it is their insatiable, uncontrollable drive to learn things and then to exchange the information with others of the species. Learning is what we do, when you think about it. I cannot think of a human impulse more difficult to govern.

17   But I can imagine lots of reasons for trying to govern it. New information about nature is very likely, at the outset, to be upsetting to someone or other. The recombinant-DNA line of research is already upsetting, not because of the dangers now being argued about but because it is disturbing, in a fundamental way, to face the fact that the genetic machinery in control of the planet's life can be fooled around with so easily. We do not like the idea that anything so fixed and stable as a species line can be changed. The notion that genes can be taken out of one genome and inserted in another is unnerving. Classical mythology is peopled with mixed beings—part man, part animal or plant—and most of them are associated with tragic stories. Recombinant DNA is a reminder of bad dreams.

18   The easiest decision for society to make in terms of this kind is to appoint an agency, or a commission, or a subcommittee within an agency to look into the problem and provide advice. And the easiest course for a committee to take, when confronted by any process that appears to be disturbing people or making them uncomfortable, is to recommend that it be stopped, at least for the time being.

19   I can easily imagine such a committee, composed of unimpeachable public figures, arriving at the decision that the time is not quite ripe for further exploration of the transplantation of genes, that we should put this off for a while, maybe until next century, and get on with other affairs that make us less discomfited. Why not do science on something more popular, say, how to get solar energy more cheaply? Or mental health?

The trouble is, it would be very hard to stop once this 20
line was begun. There are, after all, all sorts of scientific
inquiry that are not much liked by one constituency or
another, and we might soon find ourselves with crowded
rosters, panels, standing committees, set up in Washington
for the appraisal, and then the regulation, of research. Not
on grounds of the possible value and usefulness of the new
knowledge, mind you, but for guarding society against scientific hubris, against the kinds of knowledge we're better
off without.

It would be absolutely irresistible as a way of spending 21
time, and people would form long queues for membership.
Almost anything would be fair game, certainly anything to
do with genetics, anything relating to population control,
or, on the other side, research on aging. Very few fields
would get by, except perhaps for some, like mental health,
in which nobody really expects anything much to happen,
surely nothing new or disturbing.

The research areas in the greatest trouble would be those 22
already containing a sense of bewilderment and surprise,
with discernible prospects of upheaving present dogmas.

It is hard to predict how science is going to turn out, and 23
if it is really good science it is impossible to predict. This
is in the nature of the enterprise. If the things to be found
are actually new, they are by definition unknown in advance, and there is no way of telling in advance where a
really new line of inquiry will lead. You cannot make
choices in this matter, selecting things you think you're
going to like and shutting off the lines that make for discomfort. You either have science or you don't, and if you have
it you are obliged to accept the surprising and disturbing
pieces of information, even the overwhelming and upheaving ones, along with the neat and promptly useful bits.
It is like that.

The only solid piece of scientific truth about which I feel 24
totally confident is that we are profoundly ignorant about
nature. Indeed, I regard this as a major discovery of the
past hundred years of biology. It is, in its way, an illuminat-
ing piece of news. It would have amazed the brightest minds
of the eighteenth-century Enlightenment to be told by any
of us how little we know, and how bewildering seems the
way ahead. It is this sudden confrontation with the depth
and scope of ignorance that represents the most significant
contribution of twentieth-century science to the human intellect. We are, at last, facing up to it. In earlier times, we

either pretended to understand how things worked or ignored the problem, or simply made up stories to fill the gaps. Now that we have begun exploring in earnest, doing serious science, we are getting glimpses of how huge the questions are, and how far from being answered. Because of this, these are hard times for the human intellect, and it is no wonder that we are depressed. It is not so bad being ignorant if you are totally ignorant; the hard thing is knowing in some detail the reality of ignorance, the worst spots and here and there the not-so-bad spots, but no true light at the end of any tunnel nor even any tunnels that can yet be trusted. Hard times, indeed.

25   But we are making a beginning, and there ought to be some satisfaction, even exhilaration, in that. The method works. There are probably no questions we can think up that can't be answered, sooner or later, including even the matter of consciousness. To be sure, there may well be questions we can't think up, ever, and therefore limits to the reach of human intellect which we will never know about, but that is another matter. Within our limits, we should be able to work our way through to all our answers, if we keep at it long enough, and pay attention.

26   I am putting it this way, with all the presumption and confidence that I can summon, in order to raise another, last question. Is this hubris? Is there something fundamentally unnatural, or intrinsically wrong, or hazardous for the species in the ambition that drives us all to reach a comprehensive understanding of nature, including ourselves? I cannot believe it. It would seem to me a more unnatural thing, and more of an offense against nature, for us to come on the same scene endowed as we are with curiosity, filled to overbrimming as we are with questions, and naturally talented as we are for the asking of clear questions, and then for us to do nothing about it or, worse, to try to suppress the questions. This is the greater danger for our species, to try to pretend that we are another kind of animal, that we do not need to satisfy our curiosity, that we can get along somehow without inquiry and exploration and experimentation, and that the human mind can rise above its ignorance by simply asserting that there are things it has no need to know. This, to my way to thinking, is the real hubris, and it carries danger for us all.

Nathaniel Hawthorne
The Birth-mark

*Nathaniel Hawthorne (1804–1864), one of America's greatest
fiction writers, lived most of his life near Boston. He first published "The Birth-mark" in 1843.*

In the latter part of the last century, there lived a man   1
of science — an eminent proficient in every branch of natural
philosophy — who, not long before our story opens, had
made experience of a spiritual affinity, more attractive than
any chemical one. He had left his laboratory to the care of
an assistant, cleared his fine countenance from the furnace-
smoke, washed the stain of acids from his fingers, and persuaded a beautiful woman to become his wife. In those
days, when the comparatively recent discovery of electricity, and other kindred mysteries of nature, seemed to open
paths into the region of miracle, it was not unusual for the
love of science to rival the love of woman, in its depth and
absorbing energy. The higher intellect, the imagination,
the spirit, and even the heart, might all find their congenial
aliment in pursuits which, as some of their ardent votaries
believed, would ascend from one step of powerful intelligence to another, until the philosopher should lay his hand
on the secret of creative force, and perhaps make new
worlds for himself. We know not whether Aylmer possessed
this degree of faith in man's ultimate control over nature.
He had devoted himself, however, too unreservedly to scientific studies, ever to be weaned from them by any second
passion. His love for his young wife might prove the stronger
of the two; but it could only be by intertwining itself with
his love of science, and uniting the strength of the latter to
its own.

Such a union accordingly took place, and was attended   2
with truly remarkable consequences, and a deeply impressive moral. One day, very soon after their marriage, Aylmer
sat gazing at his wife, with a trouble in his countenance
that grew stronger, until he spoke.

"Georgiana," said he, "has it never occurred to you that   3
the mark upon your cheek might be removed?"

"No, indeed," said she, smiling; but perceiving the seri-   4
ousness of his manner, she blushed deeply. "To tell you the

truth, it has been so often called a charm, that I was simple enough to imagine it might be so."

5   "Ah, upon another face, perhaps it might," replied her husband. "But never on yours! No, dearest Georgiana, you came so nearly perfect from the hand of Nature, that this slightest possible defect—which we hesitate whether to term a defect or a beauty—shocks me, as being the visible mark of earthly imperfection."

6   "Shocks you, my husband!" cried Georgiana, deeply hurt; at first reddening with momentary anger, but then bursting into tears. "Then why did you take me from my mother's side? You cannot love what shocks you!"

7   To explain this conversation, it must be mentioned, that, in the centre of Georgiana's left cheek, there was a singular mark, deeply interwoven, as it were, with the texture and substance of her face. In the usual state of her complexion,—a healthy, though delicate bloom,—the mark wore a tint of deeper crimson, which imperfectly defined its shape amid the surrounding rosiness, When she blushed, it gradually became more indistinct, and finally vanished amid the triumphant rush of blood, that bathed the whole cheek with its brilliant glow. But, if any shifting emotion caused her to turn pale, there was the mark again, a crimson stain upon the snow, in what Aylmer sometimes deemed an almost fearful distinctness. Its shape bore not a little similarity to the human hand, though of the smallest pigmy size. Georgiana's lovers were wont to say, that some fairy, at her birth-hour, had laid her tiny hand upon the infant's cheek, and left this impress there, in token of the magic endowments that were to give her such sway over all hearts. Many a desperate swain would have risked life for the privilege of pressing his lips to the mysterious hand. It must not be concealed, however, that the impression wrought by this fairy sign-manual varied exceedingly, according to the difference of temperament in the beholders. Some fastidious persons—but they were exclusively of her own sex—affirmed that the Bloody Hand, as they chose to call it, quite destroyed the effect of Georgiana's beauty, and rendered her countenance even hideous. But it would be as reasonable to say, that one of those small blue stains, which sometimes occur in the purest statuary marble, would convert the Eve of Powers to a monster. Masculine observers, if the birth-mark did not heighten their admiration, contented themselves with wishing it away, that the world might possess one living specimen of ideal loveliness, with-

out the semblance of a flaw. After his marriage—for he thought little or nothing of the matter before—Aylmer discovered that this was the case with himself.

Had she been less beautiful—if Envy's self could have found aught else to sneer at—he might have felt his affection heightened by the prettiness of this mimic hand, now vaguely portrayed, now lost, now stealing forth again, and glimmering to-and-fro with every pulse of emotion that throbbed within her heart. But, seeing her otherwise so perfect, he found this one defect grow more and more intolerable, with every moment of their united lives. It was the fatal flaw of humanity, which Nature, in one shape or another, stamps ineffaceably on all her productions, either to imply that they are temporary and finite, or that their perfection must be wrought by toil and pain. The Crimson Hand expressed the ineludible gripe, in which mortality clutches the highest and purest of earthly mould, degrading them into kindred with the lowest, and even with the very brutes, like whom their visible frames return to dust. In this manner, selecting it as the symbol of his wife's liability to sin, sorrow, decay, and death, Aylmer's sombre imagination was not long in rendering the birth-mark a frightful object, causing him more trouble and horror than ever Georgiana's beauty, whether of soul or sense, had given him delight. **8**

At all the seasons which should have been their happiest, he invariably, and without intending it—nay, in spite of a purpose to the contrary—reverted to this one disastrous topic. Trifling as it at first appeared, it so connected itself with innumerable trains of thought, and modes of feeling, that it became the central point of all. With the morning twilight, Aylmer opened his eyes upon his wife's face, and recognized the symbol of imperfection; and when they sat together at the evening hearth, his eyes wandered stealthily to her cheek, and beheld, flickering with the blaze of the wood fire, the spectral Hand that wrote mortality, where he would fain have worshipped. Georgiana soon learned to shudder at his gaze. It needed but a glance, with the peculiar expression that his face often wore, to change the roses of her cheek into a deathlike paleness, amid which the Crimson Hand was brought strongly out, like a bas-relief of ruby on the whitest marble. **9**

Late, one night, when the lights were growing dim, so as hardly to betray the stain on the poor wife's cheek, she herself, for the first time, voluntarily took up the subject. **10**

"Do you remember, my dear Aylmer," said she, with a **11**

feeble attempt at a smile—"have you any recollection of a dream, last night, about this odious Hand?"

12   "None!—none whatever!" replied Aylmer, starting; but then he added in a dry, cold tone, affected for the sake of concealing the real depth of his emotion:—"I might well dream of it; for before I fell asleep, it had taken a pretty firm hold of my fancy."

13   "And you did dream of it," continued Georgiana, hastily; for she dreaded lest a gush of tears should interrupt what she had to say—"A terrible dream! I wonder that you can forget it. Is it possible to forget this one expression?—'It is in her heart now—we must have it out!'—Reflect, my husband; for by all means I would have you recall that dream."

14   The mind is in a sad note, when Sleep, the all-involving, cannot confine her spectres within the dim region of her sway, but suffers them to break forth, affrighting this actual life with secrets that perchance belong to a deeper one. Aylmer now remembered his dream. He had fancied himself, with his servant Aminadab, attempting an operation for the removal of the birth-mark. But the deeper went the knife, the deeper sank the Hand, until at length its tiny grasp appeared to have caught hold of Georgiana's heart; whence, however, her husband was inexorably resolved to cut or wrench it away.

15   When the dream had shaped itself perfectly in his memory, Aylmer sat in his wife's presence with a guilty feeling. Truth often finds its way to the mind close-muffled in robes of sleep, and then speaks with uncompromising directness of matters in regard to which we practise an unconscious self-deception, during our waking moments. Until now, he had not been aware of the tyrannizing influence acquired by one idea over his mind, and of the lengths which he might find in his heart to go, for the sake of giving himself peace.

16   "Aylmer," resumed Georgiana, solemnly, "I know not what may be the cost to both of us, to rid me of this fatal birth-mark. Perhaps its removal may cause cureless deformity. Or, it may be, the stain goes as deep as life itself. Again, do we know that there is a possibility, on any terms, of unclasping the firm gripe of this little Hand, which was laid upon me before I came into the world?"

17   "Dearest Georgiana, I have spent much thought upon the subject," hastily interrupted Aylmer—"I am convinced of the perfect practicability of its removal."

18   "If there be the remotest possibility of it," continued Geor-

giana, "let the attempt be made, at whatever risk. Danger is nothing to me; for life—while this hateful mark makes me the object of your horror and disgust—life is a burthen which I would fling down with joy. Either remove this dreadful Hand, or take my wretched life! You have deep science! All the world bears witness of it. You have achieved great wonders! Cannot you remove this little, little mark, which I cover with the tips of two small fingers? Is this beyond your power, for the sake of your own peace, and to save your poor wife from madness?"

"Noblest—dearest—tenderest wife!" cried Aylmer, rap-   19
turously. "Doubt not my power. I have already given this matter the deepest thought—thought which might almost have enlightened me to create a being less perfect than yourself. Georgiana, you have led me deeper than ever into the heart of science. I feel myself fully competent to render this dear cheek as faultless as its fellow; and then, most beloved, what will be my triumph, when I shall have corrected what Nature left imperfect, in her fairest work! Even Pygmalion, when his sculptured woman assumed life, felt not greater ecstasy than mine will be."

"It is resolved, then," said Georgiana, faintly smiling,—   20
"And, Aylmer, spare me not, though you should find the birth-mark take refuge in my heart at last."

Her husband tenderly kissed her cheek—her right   21
cheek—not that which bore the impress of the Crimson Hand.

The next day, Aylmer apprized his wife of a plan that he   22
had formed, whereby he might have opportunity for the intense thought and constant watchfulness, which the proposed operation would require; while Georgiana, likewise, would enjoy the perfect repose essential to its success. They were to seclude themselves in the extensive apartments occupied by Aylmer as a laboratory, and where, during his toilsome youth, he had made discoveries in the elemental powers of nature, that had roused the admiration of all the learned societies in Europe. Seated calmly in this laboratory, the pale philosopher had investigated the secrets of the highest cloud-region, and of the profoundest mines; he had satisfied himself of the causes that kindled and kept alive the fires of the volcano; and had explained the mystery of fountains, and how it is that they gush forth, some so bright and pure, and others with such rich medicinal virtues, from the dark bosom of the earth. Here, too, at an earlier period, he had studied the wonders of the human

frame, and attempted to fathom the very process by which Nature assimilates all her precious influences from earth and air, and from the spiritual world, to create and foster Man, her masterpiece. The latter pursuit, however, Aylmer had long laid aside, in unwilling recognition of the truth, against which all seekers sooner or later stumble, that our great creative Mother, while she amuses us with apparently working in the broadest sunshine, is yet severely careful to keep her own secrets, and, in spite of her pretended openness, shows us nothing but results. She permits us indeed, to mar, but seldom to mend, and, like a jealous patentee, on no account to make. Now, however, Aylmer resumed these half-forgotten investigations; not, of course, with such hopes or wishes as first suggested them; but because they involved much physiological truth, and lay in the path of his proposed scheme for the treatment of Georgiana.

23   As he led her over the threshold of the laboratory, Georgiana was cold and tremulous. Aylmer looked cheerfully into her face, with intent to reassure her, but was so startled with the intense glow of the birth-mark upon the whiteness of her cheek, that he could not restrain a strong convulsive shudder. His wife fainted.

24   "Aminadab! Aminadab!" shouted Aylmer, stamping violently on the floor.

25   Forthwith, there issued from an inner apartment a man of low stature, but bulky frame, with shaggy hair hanging about his visage, which was grimed with the vapors of the furnace. This personage had been Aylmer's under-worker during his whole scientific career, and was admirably fitted for that office by his great mechanical readiness, and the skill with which, while incapable of comprehending a single principle, he executed all the practical details of his master's experiments. With his vast strength, his shaggy hair, his smoky aspect, and the indescribable earthiness that incrusted him, he seemed to represent man's physical nature; while Aylmer's slender figure, and pale, intellectual face, were no less apt a type of the spiritual element.

26   "Throw open the door of the boudoir, Aminadab," said Aylmer, "and burn a pastille."

27   "Yes, master," answered Aminadab, looking intently at the lifeless form of Georgiana; and then he muttered to himself: — "If she were my wife, I'd never part with that birth-mark."

28   When Georgiana recovered consciousness, she found herself breathing an atmosphere of penetrating fragrance, the

gentle potency of which had recalled her from her deathlike
faintness. The scene around her looked like enchantment.
Aylmer had converted those smoky, dingy, sombre rooms,
where he had spent his brightest years in recondite pursuits,
into a series of beautiful apartments, not unfit to be the
secluded abode of a lovely woman. The walls were hung
with gorgeous curtains, which imparted the combination
of grandeur and grace, that no other species of adornment
can achieve; and as they fell from the ceiling to the floor,
their rich and ponderous folds, concealing all angles and
straight lines, appeared to shut in the scene from infinite
space. For aught Georgiana knew, it might be a pavilion
among the clouds. And Aylmer, excluding the sunshine,
which would have interfered with his chemical processes,
had supplied its place with perfumed lamps, emitting
flames of various hue, but all uniting in a soft, empurpled
radiance. He now knelt by his wife's side, watching her
earnestly, but without alarm; for he was confident in his
science, and felt that he could draw a magic circle round
her, within which no evil might intrude.

"Where am I? — Ah, I remember!" said Georgiana, faintly;   29
and she placed her hand over her cheek, to hide the terrible
mark from her husband's eyes.

"Fear not, dearest!" exclaimed he. "Do not shrink from   30
me! Believe me, Georgiana, I even rejoice in this single
imperfection, since it will be such rapture to remove it."

"Oh, spare me!" sadly replied his wife — "Pray do not look   31
at it again. I never can forget that convulsive shudder."

In order to soothe Georgiana, and, as it were, to release   32
her mind from the burthen of actual things, Aylmer now
put in practice some of the light and playful secrets, which
science had taught him among its profounder lore. Airy
figures, absolutely bodiless ideas, and forms of unsubstan-
tial beauty, came and danced before her, imprinting their
momentary footsteps on beams of light. Though she had
some indistinct idea of the method of these optical
phenomena, still the illusion was almost perfect enough to
warrant the belief, that her husband possessed sway over
the spiritual world. Then again, when she felt a wish to
look forth from her seclusion, immediately, as if her
thoughts were answered, the procession of external existence flitted across a screen. The scenery and the figures of
actual life were perfectly represented, but with that be-
witching, yet indescribable difference, which always makes
a picture, an image, or a shadow, so much more attractive

than the original. When wearied of this, Aylmer bade her
cast her eyes upon a vessel, containing a quantity of earth.
She did so, with little interest at first, but was soon startled,
to perceive the germ of a plant, shooting upward from the
soil. Then came the slender stalk — the leaves gradually un-
folded themselves — and amid them was a perfect and lovely
flower.

33   "It is magical!" cried Georgiana, "I dare not touch it."

34   "Nay, pluck it," answered Aylmer, "pluck it, and inhale
its brief perfume while you may. The flower will wither in
a few moments, and leave nothing save its brown seed-ves-
sels — but thence may be perpetuated a race as ephemeral
as itself."

35   But Georgiana had no sooner touched the flower than
the whole plant suffered a blight, its leaves turning coal-
black, as if by the agency of fire.

36   "There was too powerful a stimulus," said Aylmer
thoughtfully.

37   To make up for this abortive experiment, he proposed to
take her portrait by a scientific process of his own invention.
It was to be effected by rays of light striking upon a polished
plate of metal. Georgiana assented — but, on looking at the
result, was affrighted to find the features of the portrait
blurred and indefinable; while the minute figure of a hand
appeared where the cheek should have been. Aylmer
snatched the metallic plate, and threw it into a jar of cor-
rosive acid.

38   Soon, however, he forgot these mortifying failures. In the
intervals of study and chemical experiment, he came to
her, flushed and exhausted, but seemed invigorated by her
presence, and spoke in glowing language of the resources
of his art. He gave a history of the long dynasty of the
Alchemists, who spent so many ages in quest of the universal solvent, by which the Golden Principle might be elicited
from all things vile and base. Aylmer appeared to believe,
that, by the plainest scientific logic, it was altogether within
the limits of possibility to discover this long-sought
medium; but, he added, a philosopher who should go deep
enough to acquire the power, would attain too lofty a wisdom to stoop to the exercise of it. Not less singular were
his opinions in regard to the Elixir Vitae. He more than
intimated, that it was his option to concoct a liquid that
should prolong life for years — perhaps interminably — but
that it would produce a discord in nature, which all the

world, and chiefly the quaffer of the immortal nostrum, would find cause to curse.

"Aylmer, are you in earnest?" asked Georgiana, looking   39
at him with amazement and fear; "it is terrible to possess such power, or even to dream of possessing it!"

"Oh, do not tremble, my love!" said her husband, "I would   40
not wrong either you or myself by working such inharmonious effects upon our lives. But I would have you consider how trifling, in comparison, is the skill requisite to remove this little Hand."

At the mention of the birth-mark, Georgiana, as usual,   41
shrank, as if a red-hot iron had touched her cheek.

Again Aylmer applied himself to his labors. She could   42
hear his voice in the distant furnace-room, giving directions to Aminadab, whose harsh, uncouth, misshapen tones were audible in response, more like the grunt or growl of a brute than human speech. After hours of absence, Aylmer reappeared, and proposed that she should now examine his cabinet of chemical products, and natural treasures of the earth. Among the former he showed her a small vial, in which, he remarked, was contained a gentle yet most powerful fragrance, capable of impregnating all the breezes that blow across a kingdom. They were of inestimable value, the contents of that little vial; and, as he said so, he threw some of the perfume into the air, and filled the room with piercing and invigorating delight.

"And what is this?" asked Georgiana, pointing to a small   43
crystal globe, containing a gold-colored liquid. "It is so beautiful to the eye, that I could imagine it the Elixir of Life."

"In one sense it is," replied Aylmer, "or rather the Elixir   44
of Immortality. It is the most precious poison that ever was concocted in this world. By its aid, I could apportion the lifetime of any mortal at whom you might point your finger. The strength of the dose would determine whether he were to linger out years, or drop dead in the midst of a breath. No king, on his guarded throne, could keep his life, if I, in my private station, should deem that the welfare of millions justified me in depriving him of it."

"Why do you keep such a terrific drug?" inquired Geor-   45
giana in horror.

"Do not mistrust me, dearest!" said her husband, smiling;   46
"its virtuous potency is yet greater than its harmful one. But, see! here is a powerful cosmetic. With a few drops of

this, in a vase of water, freckles may be washed away as
easily as the hands are cleansed. A stronger infusion would
take the blood out of the cheek, and leave the rosiest beauty
a pale ghost."

47   "Is it with this lotion that you intend to bathe my cheek?"
asked Georgiana anxiously.

48   "Oh, no!" hastily replied her husband—"this is merely superficial. Your case demands a remedy that shall go deeper."

49   In his interviews with Georgiana, Aylmer generally made
minute inquiries as to her sensations, and whether the
confinement of the rooms, and the temperature of the
atmosphere, agreed with her. These questions had such a
particular drift, that Georgiana began to conjecture that
she was already subjected to certain physical influences,
either breathed in with the fragrant air, or taken with her
food. She fancied, likewise—but it might be altogether
fancy—that there was a stirring up of her system,—a
strange indefinite sensation creeping through her veins, and
tingling, half painfully, half pleasurably, at her heart. Still,
whenever she dared to look into the mirror, there she beheld
herself, pale as a white rose, and with the crimson birth-
mark stamped upon her cheek. Not even Aylmer now hated
it so much as she.

50   To dispel the tedium of the hours which her husband
found it necessary to devote to the processes of combination
and analysis, Georgiana turned over the volumes of his
scientific library. In many dark old tomes, she met with
chapters full of romance and poetry. They were the works
of the philosophers of the middle ages, such as Albertus
Magnus, Cornelius Agrippa, Paracelsus, and the famous
friar who created the prophetic Brazen Head. All these antique naturalists stood in advance of their centuries, yet
were imbued with some of their credulity, and therefore
were believed, and perhaps imagined themselves, to have
acquired from the investigation of nature a power above
nature, and from physics a sway over the spiritual world.
Hardly less curious and imaginative were the early volumes
of the Transactions of the Royal Society, in which the members, knowing little of the limits of natural possibility, were
continually recording wonders, or proposing methods
whereby wonders might be wrought.

51   But, to Georgiana, the most engrossing volume was a
large folio from her husband's own hand, in which he had
recorded every experiment of his scientific career, with its

original aim, the methods adopted for its development, and its final success or failure, with the circumstances to which either event was attributable. The book, in truth, was both the history and emblem of his ardent, ambitious, imaginative, yet practical and laborious, life. He handled physical details, as if there were nothing beyond them; yet spiritualized them all, and redeemed himself from materialism, by his strong and eager aspiration towards the infinite. In his grasp, the veriest clod of earth assumed a soul. Georgiana, as she read, reverenced Aylmer, and loved him more profoundly than ever, but with a less entire dependence on his judgment than heretofore. Much as he had accomplished, she could not but observe that his most splendid successes were almost invariably failures, if compared with the ideal at which he aimed. His brightest diamonds were the merest pebbles, and felt to be so by himself, in comparison with the inestimable gems which lay hidden beyond his reach. The volume, rich with achievements that had won renown for its author, was yet as melancholy a record as ever mortal hand had penned. It was the sad confession, and continual exemplification, of the short-comings of the composite man— the spirit burthened with clay and working in matter—and of the despair that assails the higher nature, at finding itself so miserably thwarted by the earthly part. Perhaps every man of genius, in whatever sphere, might recognize the image of his own experience in Aylmer's journal.

So deeply did these reflections affect Georgiana, that she 52 laid her face upon the open volume, and burst into tears. In this situation she was found by her husband.

"It is dangerous to read in a sorcerer's books," said he, 53 with a smile, though his countenance was uneasy and displeased. "Georgiana, there are pages in that volume, which I can scarcely glance over and keep my senses. Take heed lest it prove as detrimental to you!"

"It has made me worship you more than ever," said she. 54

"Ah! wait for this one success," rejoined he, "then worship 55 me if you will. I shall deem myself hardly unworthy of it. But, come! I have sought you for the luxury of your voice. Sing to me, dearest!"

So she poured out the liquid music of her voice to quench 56 the thirst of his spirit. He then took his leave, with a boyish exuberance of gaiety, assuring her that her seclusion would endure but a little longer, and that the result was already certain. Scarcely had he departed, when Georgiana felt irresistibly impelled to follow him. She had forgotten to inform Aylmer of a symptom, which, for two or three hours past, had begun to excite her attention. It was a sensation in the fatal birth-mark, not painful, but which induced a restlessness throughout her system. Hastening after her husband, she intruded, for the first time, into the laboratory.

57   The first thing that struck her eye was the furnace, that hot and feverish worker, with the intense glow of its fire, which, by the quantities of soot clustered above it, seemed to have been burning for ages. There was a distilling apparatus in full operation. Around the room were retorts, tubes, cylinders, crucibles, and other apparatus of chemical research. An electrical machine stood ready for immediate use. The atmosphere felt oppressively close, and was tainted with gaseous odors, which had been tormented forth by the processes of science. The severe and homely simplicity of the apartment, with its naked walls and brick pavement, looked strange, accustomed as Georgiana had become to the fantastic elegance of her boudoir. But what chiefly, indeed almost solely, drew her attention, was the aspect of Aylmer himself.

58   He was pale as death, anxious, and absorbed, and hung over the furnace as if it depended upon his utmost watchfulness whether the liquid, which it was distilling, should be the draught of immortal happiness or misery. How different from the sanguine and joyous mien that he had assumed for Georgiana's encouragement!

59   "Carefully now, Aminadab! Carefully, thou human machine! Carefully, thou man of clay!" muttered Aylmer, more to himself than his assistant. "Now, if there be a thought too much or too little, it is all over!"

60   "Hoh! hoh!" mumbled Aminadab—"look, master, look!"

61   Aylmer raised his eyes hastily, and at first reddened, then grew paler than ever, on beholding Georgiana. He rushed towards her, and seized her arm with a gripe that left the print of his fingers upon it.

62   "Why do you come hither? Have you no trust in your husband?" cried he impetuously. "Would you throw the blight of that fatal birth-mark over my labors? It is not well done. Go, prying woman, go!"

63   "Nay, Aylmer," said Georgiana, with the firmness of which she possessed no stinted endowment, "it is not you that have a right to complain. You mistrust your wife! You have concealed the anxiety with which you watch the de-

velopment of this experiment. Think not so unworthily of me, my husband! Tell me all the risk we run; and fear not that I shall shrink, for my share in it is far less than your own!"

"No, no, Georgiana!" said Aylmer impatiently, "it must not be." 64

"I submit," replied she calmly. "And, Aylmer, I shall quaff whatever draught you bring me; but it will be on the same principle that would induce me to take a dose of poison, if offered by your hand." 65

"My noble wife," said Aylmer, deeply moved, "I knew not the height and depth of your nature, until now. Nothing shall be concealed. Know, then, that this Crimson Hand, superficial as it seems, has clutched its grasp into your being, with a strength of which I had no previous conception. I have already administered agents powerful enough to do aught except to change your entire physical system. Only one thing remains to be tried. If that fail us, we are ruined!" 66

"Why did you hesitate to tell me this?" asked she. 67

"Because, Georgiana," said Aylmer, in a low voice, "there is danger!" 68

"Danger? There is but one danger—that this horrible stigma shall be left upon my cheek!" cried Georgiana. "Remove it! remove it!—whatever be the cost—or we shall both go mad!" 69

"Heaven knows, your words are too true," said Aylmer, sadly. "And now, dearest, return to your boudoir. In a little while, all will be tested." 70

He conducted her back, and took leave of her with a solemn tenderness, which spoke far more than his words how much was now at stake. After his departure, Georgiana became wrapt in musings. She considered the character of Aylmer, and did it completer justice than at any previous moment. Her heart exulted, while it trembled, at his honorable love, so pure and lofty that it would accept nothing less than perfection, nor miserably make itself contented with an earthlier nature than he had dreamed of. She felt how much more precious was such a sentiment, than that meaner kind which would have borne with the imperfection for her sake, and have been guilty of treason to holy love, by degrading its perfect idea to the level of the actual. And, with her whole spirit, she prayed, that, for a single moment, she might satisfy his highest and deepest conception. 71

Longer than one moment, she well knew, it could not be; for his spirit was ever on the march — ever ascending — and each instant required something that was beyond the scope of the instant before.

72   The sound of her husband's footsteps aroused her. He bore a crystal goblet, containing a liquor colorless as water, but bright enough to be the draught of immortality. Aylmer was pale; but it seemed rather the consequence of a highly wrought state of mind, and tension of spirit, than of fear or doubt.

73   "The concoction of the draught has been perfect," said he, in answer to Georgiana's look. "Unless all my science have deceived me, it cannot fail."

74   "Save on your account, my dearest Aylmer," observed his wife, "I might wish to put off this birth-mark of mortality by relinquishing mortality itself, in preference to any other mode. Life is but a sad possession to those who have attained precisely the degree of moral advancement at which I stand. Were I weaker and blinder, it might be happiness. Were I stronger, it might be endured hopefully. But, being what I find myself, methinks I am of all mortals the most fit to die."

75   "You are fit for heaven without tasting death!" replied her husband. "But why do we speak of dying? The draught cannot fail. Behold its effect upon this plant!"

76   On the window-seat there stood a geranium, diseased with yellow blotches, which had overspread all its leaves. Aylmer poured a small quantity of the liquid upon the soil in which it grew. In a little time, when the roots of the plant had taken up the moisture, the unsightly blotches began to be extinguished in a living verdure.

77   "There needed no proof," said Georgiana, quietly. "Give me the goblet. I joyfully stake all upon your word."

78   "Drink, then, thou lofty creature!" exclaimed Aylmer, with fervid admiration. "There is no taint of imperfection on thy spirit. Thy sensible frame, too, shall soon be all perfect!"

79   She quaffed the liquid, and returned the goblet to his hand.

80   "It is grateful," said she, with a placid smile. "Methinks it is like water from a heavenly fountain; for it contains I know not what of unobtrusive fragrance and deliciousness. It allays a feverish thirst, that had parched me for many days. Now, dearest, let me sleep. My earthly senses are

closing over my spirit, like the leaves round the heart of a
rose, at sunset."

She spoke the last words with a gentle reluctance, as if   81
it required almost more energy than she could command
to pronounce the faint and lingering syllables. Scarcely had
they loitered through her lips, ere she was lost in slumber.
Aylmer sat by her side, watching her aspect with the emotions proper to a man, the whole value of whose existence
was involved in the process now to be tested. Mingled with
this mood, however, was the philosophic investigation,
characteristic of the man of science. Not the minutest
symptom escaped him. A heightened flush of the cheek—a
slight irregularity of breath—a quiver of the eyelid—a
hardly perceptible tremor through the frame—such were
the details which, as the moments passed, he wrote down
in his folio volume. Intense thought had set its stamp upon
every previous page of that volume; but the thoughts of
years were all concentrated upon the last.

While thus employed, he failed not to gaze often at the   82
fatal Hand, and not without a shudder. Yet once, by a
strange and unaccountable impulse, he pressed it with his
lips. His spirit recoiled, however, in the very act, and Georgiana, out of the midst of her deep sleep, moved uneasily
and murmured, as if in remonstrance. Again, Aylmer resumed his watch. Nor was it without avail. The Crimson
Hand, which at first had been strongly visible upon the
marble paleness of Georgiana's cheek now grew more
faintly outlined. She remained not less pale than ever; but
the birth-mark, with every breath that came and went, lost
somewhat of its former distinctness. Its presence had been
awful; its departure was more awful still. Watch the stain
of the rainbow fading out of the sky; and you will know
how that mysterious symbol passed away.

"By Heaven, it is well nigh gone!" said Aylmer to himself,   83
in almost irrepressible ecstasy. "I can scarcely trace it now.
Success! Success! And now it is like the faintest rose-color.
The slightest flush of blood across her cheek would overcome it. But she is so pale!"

He drew aside the window-curtain, and suffered the light   84
of natural day to fall into the room, and rest upon her cheek.
At the same time, he heard a gross, hoarse chuckle, which
he had long known as his servant Aminadab's expression
of delight.

"Ah, clod! Ah, earthly mass!" cried Aylmer, laughing in   85 a sort of frenzy. "You have served me well! Matter and Spirit—Earth and Heaven—have both done their part in this! Laugh, thing of senses! You have earned the right to laugh."

86   These exclamations broke Georgiana's sleep. She slowly unclosed her eyes, and gazed into the mirror, which her husband had arranged for that purpose. A faint smile flitted over her lips, when she recognized how barely perceptible was now that Crimson Hand, which had once blazed forth with such disastrous brilliancy as to scare away all their happiness. But then her eyes sought Aylmer's face, with a trouble and anxiety that he could by no means account for.

87   "My poor Aylmer!" murmured she.

88   "Poor? Nay, richest! Happiest! Most favored!" exclaimed he. "My peerless bride, it is successful! You are perfect!"

89   "My poor Aylmer!" she repeated, with a more than human tenderness. "You have aimed loftily!—you have done nobly! Do not repent, that, with so high and pure a feeling, you have rejected the best that earth could offer. Aylmer— dearest Aylmer—I am dying!"

90   Alas, it was too true! The fatal Hand had grappled with the mystery of life, and was the bond by which an angelic spirit kept itself in union with a mortal frame. As the last crimson tint of the birth-mark—that sole token of human imperfection—faded from her cheek, the parting breath of the now perfect woman passed into the atmosphere, and her soul, lingering a moment near her husband, took its heavenward flight. Then a hoarse, chuckling laugh was heard again! Thus ever does the gross Fatality of Earth exult in its invariable triumph over the immortal essence, which, in this dim sphere of half-development, demands the completeness of a higher state. Yet, had Aylmer reached a profounder wisdom, he need not thus have flung away the happiness, which would have woven his mortal life of the self-same texture with the celestial. The momentary circumstance was too strong for him; he failed to look beyond the shadowy scope of Time, and living once for all in Eternity, to find the perfect Future in the present.

Jonathan King

New Genetic Technology: Prospects and Hazards

Jonathan King, who holds a doctorate in genetics, teaches biology at Massachusetts Institute of Technology. He wrote the following essay in 1980 for Technology Review, *a product of the MIT alumni association.*

During the past 30 years we have witnessed extraordinary advances in knowledge of fundamental biological processes, particularly at the cellular and molecular level. These advances have derived in large part from the major investment of public funds in the training of biomedical scientists and support for biomedical research, conducted by the governments of the industrialized countries since the end of World War II. The 1978 budget for biomedical research in the U.S. is about 3 billion dollars. This is one thousand times the federal expenditure for biomedical research in 1948.

In the U.S., these programs originated in the pressing need for coordinated biomedical research to deal with the immense damage suffered by soldiers during and after World War II. The federal funding and encouragement of cooperative, organized research ventures was highly successful and continued after the war, when public pressure overcame opposition from the private medical sector.

The well-financed program of training and research has led to: the elucidation of the chemical structure of the genetic material, DNA; the understanding of the organization of the genetic material in linear segments, the genes; the recognition that genes are blueprints for the structure of protein molecules, which form both the building blocks and working parts of cells; the understanding of the roles of the thin membranes that divide cells into different compartments; and enhanced knowledge of the organization and functions of the complex ribosomes, themselves composed of more than 70 different kinds of protein molecules, which serve as the factories for assembling new proteins according to the instructions of the genes. Thus, the mental and physical labors of tens of thousands of laboratory workers have revealed the extraordinary richness and creativity of the mechanisms by which living things reproduce themselves and interact with their environment.

4   In the industrialized nations, the major steps in cutting infant mortality, increasing the life span, and controlling infectious disease occurred earlier in this century. These resulted from economic struggles, led principally by the trade unions, for an improved standard of living—notably the shorter working day, increased wages, and improved working conditions. They were aided by public health professionals who fought for improved sanitation, water supplies, and food, thereby helping to eliminate cholera, diphtheria, scarlet fever, and other scourges of the urban poor.

5   The more recently acquired understanding of the biochemistry of bacteria and the role of viruses in human disease, and the development of tissue culture technology for growing cells and viruses in the test tube, laid the basis for eliminating a further set of diseases: poliovirus infections in the 1950s; rinderpest virus, a major killer of African cattle, in the 1960s; and more recently, the dramatic eradication of smallpox. (Twenty years ago in India alone there were 150,000 cases of smallpox, causing 41,000 deaths.) The elimination of rinderpest and smallpox viruses resulted from campaigns organized and coordinated by the United Nations.

6   The scientific basis now exists for mounting research campaigns against viral diseases such as Rift Valley fever in North Africa, yellow fever in Central Africa, and hemorrhagic fever in Asia, as well as such widespread parasitic diseases as schistosomiasis and filariasis, including one of its more tragic forms, river blindness.

7   Of course many of these diseases are intimately associated with particular conditions of life—local housing, agriculture, water supplies and sanitation, and nutrition. Increased knowledge of the biochemistry and physiology of particular organisms does not substitute for the need to study the interrelationships of organisms within ecosystems as well as the social and economic conditions of human society.

8   Smallpox infects only humans for example, enabling all potential hosts to be identified and vaccinated. Many of the other viruses that affect humans also live in insects or animals and other parts of the ecosystem. These cannot be eradicated by the same strategies used for smallpox. Chol-

era provides another example: it is still a major problem in Calcutta, where the virus was first isolated in 1817. Indian scientists understand the microbiology of cholera, but the poverty that is partly the legacy of British imperialism must be overcome before the disease can be eradicated.

Another major contribution of modern molecular genet- 9 ics and cell biology is the recognition that much of human cancer is due to damage by external agents to the genes of human somatic cells. These agents include industrial chemicals such as aniline dyes, which cause bladder cancer, vinyl chloride, which causes liver cancer, and most forms of ionizing radiation. For example, high levels of leukemia and bone cancer are found among survivors of the Hiroshima and Nagasaki holocausts and among people repeatedly exposed to nuclear testing. Other cancers from excessive medical irradiation and exposure to mismanaged nuclear waste will likely manifest themselves in coming years.

These major breakthroughs have led to the recognition 10 among a sector of the scientific community that much human cancer is preventable. Unfortunately, powerful economic forces have vested interests in the continued production and sale of these agents. Therefore, the prevention of cancer will involve a social struggle similar to those earlier in the century for better working conditions.

In the United States, we do not have a national system 11 of comprehensive medical care. This limits our ability to realize the fullest fruits of our biomedical research. Without a comprehensive health care system, it is difficult to couple research to health care needs. When substantial advances occur, they are sometimes available only to economically advantaged groups. Farm workers in Texas, for example, have an average life span many years less than the national average.

Recombinant DNA Technology

The growth of biological knowledge has engendered the 12 development of very sophisticated biochemical genetic technologies. These technologies, which are today tools for the accumulation of knowledge of organisms, are also the tools for the genetic and biochemical modification of those organisms.

The most dramatic and revolutionary of these tech- 13

nologies is recombinant DNA technology, or genetic engineering — the ability to incorporate segments of DNA, i.e., genetic material, derived from one organism into the cells of another organism. The donor and recipient may be closely related (for example, two strains of bacteria), or they may be very different (for example, a mouse and a bacterium).

14   Members of the same species exchange segments of genetic material regularly; this is the biological basis of mating and sex — the exchange of equivalent segments of genetic material of parents, generating new genetic combinations in the offspring, which may prove advantageous in adapting to a changing environment.

15   However, exchange of genetic material between members of unrelated species is rare. Organisms adapting to different environments — to different niches, to use the ecologists' term — evolve different "instructions": different genes. Exchange between such organisms is generally not useful, and therefore rarely observed in nature.

16   Recombinant DNA technology is useful in biological research, however. Suppose I am studying how pancreatic cells produce insulin and why liver cells do not. I might remove the pancreas from a mouse, and extract from the pancreas cells the long, stringy DNA molecules that represent the blueprints for being a mouse. By treating the isolated DNA molecules with a special protein catalyst, the DNA can be cut into shorter pieces, with the cut ends left sticky. Using similar techniques, I can isolate DNA molecules from a bacterium, whose cut ends are also sticky. Usually this bacterium will be common in the human gut, and called E. coli. On mixing the two tubes of DNA, the sticky ends of mouse DNA will join with lengths of bacterial DNA. Such molecules, containing the genetic material of two different organisms, are termed "recombinant DNA" molecules.

17   These recombinant molecules can then be reincorporated into a living, growing bacterium. When the bacterium divides, it will reproduce its own DNA, and also reproduce the piece of mouse DNA, or gene. If we isolate the bacterium and incubate it in some beef broth, the next morning we will have 100 billion daughter cells. Each of these will have an identical copy of the mouse gene. Molecular biologists speak of this as "cloning" a mouse gene.

18   Because bacteria, despite their complexity, are vastly

simpler than mouse cells, the techniques of chemistry and biochemistry can be used to study the mouse gene and sometimes the protein whose structure it encodes. From these studies, we might learn about what signals turn this gene on in some cells and off in others. We might also get some hint as to how the genetic information stored in the nucleus of a cell provides the blueprint for the three-dimensional structure and function of the cell.

This technology requires no more equipment than is [19] found in a common college microbiology laboratory. Therefore, it is being used in a vast variety of research situations. Furthermore, recently developed techniques make it possible to transfer in the *other* direction to introduce DNA of a bacterium into a mouse cell. Similarly, one can introduce DNA from one species of mouse into another, or transfer small segments of DNA from human cells to mouse cells or other human cells. This technology, developed originally from microbiology and molecular genetics, provides the technological basis for human genetic manipulation. Because of the intense level of research—hundreds of laboratories are using these techniques to study the genes of animal cells—experiments labelled "impossible" become routine six months later.

Commercial Exploitation and Biological Hazards

Though the scientific community generally views recom- [20] binant DNA technology as a research tool, private corporations have moved rapidly to construct and market strains of economically or agriculturally valuable organisms and their byproducts. In addition to the activities of small venture firms and most of the pharmaceutical industry, substantial investments have been made by transnational corporations such as International Nickel, Standard Oil, and Imperial Chemical Industries. A well-publicized case in the drug industry is Eli Lilly Corp.'s plan to grow strains of E. coli bacteria containing insulin for sale to diabetics. Strains have already been constructed or isolated that contain the human insulin gene and that synthesize the protein and export a version of it outside the cell. Lilly believes this will be less expensive than its current practice of extracting insulin from the pancreas of beef cattle. The sale of insulin to diabetics is a $100-million-a-year business.

21   As most people know, there has been substantial debate
over recombinant DNA technology. The debate has centered
on whether bacteria incorporating foreign DNA constitute
new hazards to humans or to other species in the ecosystem.
For example, though E. coli is a normal inhabitant of our
intestinal tract, certain strains are the cause of infantile
meningitis and diarrhea, urinary tract infections in women,
and serious bloodstream infections in hospital patients. In
many cases, the pathogenicity of these strains stems from
the parasites — derivations of wild strains — that they harbor. Were such strains to synthesize and export insulin,
they could well cause additional damage.

22   To the extent that such strains escape into the environment
and establish themselves in some niche, they constitute a
form of pollution, an unwanted byproduct of technology.
But such biological pollution is qualitatively different from
other forms of pollution such as heavy metals, oil, and synthetic chemicals. Organisms reproduce themselves and cannot easily be removed from the ecosystem. This self-repro-
ducing potential of the byproducts of recombinant DNA
technology is the reason for the special concern of many
scientists and the public.

23   After considerable internal debate and controversy, the
scientific community adopted guidelines requiring that recombinant DNA experiments be performed with weakened
strains of bacteria unlikely to survive outside the laboratory, and that physical containment procedures be used,
making it even less likely that such strains would escape.

24   These guidelines are now referred to as the NIH (National
Institutes of Health) guidelines. A controversy arose in Cambridge, Mass. over the adequacy of these guidelines, and
whether compliance should be left to scientists or overseen
by the community and laboratory workers. Cambridge and
a few other communities subsequently passed ordinances
making the NIH guidelines mandatory. However, they do
not apply to private industry or non-federally funded research. Thus, no laws regulate the activities of private companies engaged in genetic engineering in the U.S., although
some have been proposed by a number of legislators. These
were defeated by the combined influence of the corporations and a wing of the scientific community more interested in exploiting the technology than in protecting the
public. In Great Britain, however, these guidelines apply
to the entire country, and are supported by the Trade Union

Congress and strengthened by representation of the workers involved.

Unfortunately during 1979 the guidelines were severely weakened by the efforts of a group of scientists actively engaged in the development of recombinant DNA technology in alliance with commercial interests. These scientists first argued that the risks are trivial, since the guidelines prevent the construction or release of hazardous strains. This argument was then switched around: since the risks are trivial, there is no need for strong guidelines. The negative outcomes of a few risk-assessment experiments were widely publicized, while the positive results reported in the same studies were actively ignored and suppressed. The guidelines have now been so weakened that rather than protecting public health, they in fact protect those engaged in the technology from public inquiry and regulation. The few within the scientific community who understand the major misrepresentations that have occurred, and are inclined to critique them, are inhibited by the fact that we receive our funding from the NIH.

Some observers have found it difficult to understand why scientists should be concerned about community-imposed safety standards on laboratory work. Many safety constraints are inconvenient but have a relatively minor effect, as one can see by the rate at which work proceeds. However, safety procedures that are a minor inconvenience on work involving 10 milliliters of cells have a very different impact on the production of 1000 liters at the commercial scale. If concerned scientists, citizens, and workers demand strong safety standards, these will not only decrease profit margins but will also result in greater community and worker control over the production process.

New technologies often result in human casualties, such as respiratory damage in coal miners after the development of deep mining, the induction of bladder cancer in workers in British and German chemical industries, and lung cancer among uranium miners. And the costs, as well as the suffering, have generally been borne by the workers themselves. In the case of recombinant DNA technology, we must insist that such costs be reckoned with from the beginning as part of the production process, and not be passed on to an unwilling or unknowing population. It is not just a question of costs versus benefits, but who gets the benefits and who bears the costs.

28   Attempts to protect capital investments and profit margins distort certain features of the scientific process. A
number of corporations involved in exploiting recombinant
DNA technology have obtained patents on organisms and
processes, even though all of the developmental work was
publicly financed. The scientists involved simply disas-
sociated themselves from public funding and entered into
relations with private companies, thus appropriating public knowledge for private accumulation of wealth not generally available to academic scientists.

29   Although some scientific/industrial spokespersons have
called for the unfettered (and unregulated) "search for
truth," the controversy over recombinant DNA technology
is not about freedom of enquiry; it is about regulating those
who want to rashly exploit for private gain the fruits of
knowledge that should belong to all.

Agricultural and Microbial Productivity

30   A potentially productive application of recombinant DNA
and other molecular genetic technologies is the development of new strains of plants and microorganisms. The
danger here is familiar: the strains developed in the industrialized countries will be designed for capital-intensive
agriculture, thus requiring chemical fertilizer, pesticides,
and the destruction of many indigenous ecosystems. But
the most productive uses with respect to preservation of
human and natural resources will probably involve less
manipulative technologies.

31   For example, in India, China, and Pakistan, microbial
technologies for converting manure and waste into clean
gas for cooking, heating, and transportation have been developed with existing bacterial strains. And the residue provides a good source of fertilizer. Similarly in India, Burma,
and Nepal, very successful projects to fertilize rice paddies
have utilized strains of nitrogen-fixing blue-green algae.

32   If local education and know-how are not commensurate
with the sophistication of the imported technologies, proper
investigation will be unlikely, and it will be difficult for
the people of the developing countries to assert control.

33   A second danger derives from corporations who move
production facilities for modified organisms from industrialized countries to developing countries to escape regu-

lation. Of course, this is done in the name of technology transfer. Ironically, the health hazards of recombinant DNA technology are much more acute in developing countries, where conditions for the spread of disease still exist.

Human Genetic Engineering

The new biological technologies make possible the ulti-   34
mate modification: the "engineering" of human beings. There is a great deal of research with small mammals such as mice and rabbits, both in introducing segments of DNA into their cells and analyzing the DNA by taking pieces out of the cells and cloning them in bacteria. For example, attempts are now being made to remove bone marrow cells (which form blood cells) from an animal and insert into those cells the DNA segment coding for hemoglobin. The cell with the added segment can be transplanted back into the animal. This is a model for gene therapy of inherited blood diseases such as sickle cell anemia and thalassemia.

The use of genetic technologies on human beings will   35
expand in the medical sector far more rapidly than anyone can accurately predict. This will alleviate the suffering of a small number of individuals but will also generate many moral and social dilemmas.

The development of human *in vitro* fertilization by Ed-   36
wards and Steptoe has vastly increased the potential for human genetic manipulation. One can obtain in the test tube the earliest stages of a human embryo. By introducing DNA, or cells altered in the laboratory, into this embryo and then reimplanting the embryo into the womb, the possibility exists for introducing genetic change in most of the cells of the body—including the germ-line cells. Thus, changes would be passed on to subsequent generations.

Prior to the genetic manipulation itself, the use of DNA   37
technology to physically analyze the DNA of human cells will vastly increase. Some of this analysis will be used for screening purposes, as in rare cases where the change in the DNA and the relationship to disease is known (in certain rare inherited blood diseases, for example). Instead of examining the blood in the already mature fetus, we will examine the DNA of the cells of the early embryo or the parents.

Researchers will be confronted by the full range of genetic   38
variation among individuals. What constitutes a genetic

defect and what constitutes genetic variation? Historically, the value of many genetically determined features such as skin color and hair character were socially determined. What is a defect in one society is a desirable characteristic in another. At the biological level, the sickle cell trait is considered by some a genetic defect in the United States. But in central Africa it is necessary for survival in malaria-infested areas, rendering the blood cells resistant to the malarial parasite.

39   Another problem is the distortion of the true causes of human disease. Genetic engineering technology will focus attention on affected individuals and their genes. As a result there will be a strong tendency to lose sight of the agents that caused the damage in the first place, such as mutagenic and carcinogenic chemicals and radiation. Most problems are not with our genes; they are in recreating a society in which the genes of individuals are protected from unnecessary damage. It is critically important that the ability to identify genetic damage serves as a first step in identifying the *cause* of the damage wherever possible, and removing it from the ecosphere.

40   Note that not all conditions resulting from damage to genes are inherited. If the egg is damaged, resulting in altered chromosome compositions, as in Down's syndrome, this is not passed on to the next generation.

Reordering Priorities

41   We must support every effort to expand and increase knowledge of the functioning of living things and their interactions with the environment, and of the effect of human society on these interactions. This knowledge must be available to all the peoples of the earth and not just a technocratic elite.

42   At present, a number of the most potent biological technologies are being developed by transnational corporations and institutions who serve private gain rather than social and economic justice. To select what is needed in a particular area will require very broad biological, ecological, and agricultural education. The same lessons that many peoples of the world have learned with respect to the import of technologies of resource exploitation will have to be applied in this field if the fruits of biological knowledge

are to be used to attain an equitable, participatory, and sustainable society.

Citizen participation in the decision-making processes, 43 whether on biohazards committees, protection-of-human-subjects committees, or other appropriate forms, must be encouraged. Appropriate support on an international level might be achieved through efforts of the International Labor Organization, the World Health Organization, and the United Nations Agency for Development. In the United States, it is critically important to involve the Environmental Protection Agency and the Occupational Safety and Health Agency in the regulation of genetic technologies. NIH lacks the experience and inclination to regulate a burgeoning multimillion-dollar industry.

In the area of human experimentation and genetic ma- 44 nipulation, we must ensure that the development of very sophisticated technologies for helping a small number of individuals does not obscure the pressing need for eliminating widespread causes of disease and genetic damage. An appropriate form might be task forces on protection of the genetic inheritance from environmental and social damage. This will entail input into the setting of priorities in biomedical research (i.e., what technologies to develop) and not just into the use of technology that is *already* developed. Today we can transplant kidneys, but we cannot prevent kidney disease.

Public health, social ethics, and the problems of underde- 45 veloped rural societies are not the highest priority of experts in molecular genetics and antibiotic production. We must insure the fullest participation of different sectors of society in the development of biological technologies, not as a cosmetic nod to democracy, but because this is the only way to maximize the social benefits and minimize the risks. We are entering a new era of direct modification and design of organisms. These endeavors will require new social forms and the development of a much higher level of democratic process within the technological sphere.

The following advertisement was devised by ICI AMERICAS, Inc.,
and appeared in a number of weekly news magazines in 1989.

© 1989 ICI Americas, Inc., Wilmington, DE 19897

Susan Wright

Genetic Engineering: The Risks

Susan Wright, a consultant to the National and World Councils of Churches, directs the Science and Society program at the University of Michigan. The following essay appeared in 1983 in Christianity and Crisis, *a Christian journal of opinion. It was adapted from an article written with Robert L. Sinsheimer for the* Bulletin of the Atomic Scientists, *1983.*

1   Media coverage of genetic engineering has painted a picture of an optimistic and benign future: industrialized bacteria meekly pumping out lifesaving quantities of insulin and interferon; a combination of genetic engineering and fetal surgery ultimately eradicating genetic diseases; self-fertilizing plants ending hunger and famine. But the media picture may be too optimistic, too benign. As research and development (R and D) in genetic engineering accelerates, two questions need critical attention.

> 1. What hazards to workers, the environment, and the general population will be generated by research and full-scale industrial activities?
> 2. What are the real goals of new military interest in this field?

2   Recombinant DNA, or gene splicing, techniques were developed in 1972, in a few California biological research laboratories. Gene splicing is a method of chemically cutting and joining DNA, the hereditary material of living things. Because DNA usually has the same structure regardless of its source, the techniques can be used to remove genes from a donor organism and transfer them into a recipient, where, under appropriate conditions, they can function. For example, in 1978, the human insulin gene was introduced into the bacterium *Escherichia coli* so that the bacterium was "programmed" to make human insulin. More recently, recombinant DNA containing the gene for growth hormone was inserted into fertilized mouse cells. In some cases, the gene functioned, and mice bearing this gene grew to twice their normal size.

3   In a word, gene splicing offers the potential to redesign

life (in genetic terms), to construct new combinations of genes, and new organisms with new functions.

Because it signified different potentialities to different 4
sectors of society, it was clear from the first that this technology would be controversial. Biologists had at hand a set of powerful research tools and it seemed likely that these tools would yield a new understanding of the structure and function of genes. (And, indeed they have.) Industrial and commercial interests foresaw a wide range of applications in techniques that could be used to transform bacteria into miniscule "factories" for producing substances not easily manufactured through conventional processes. It also seemed likely that in the future the techniques could be applied to commercially important plants and animals. Plants might be endowed with their own nitrogen-fixing genes; cows might be endowed with extra growth hormone genes; and surely some task would be found for the giant mice.

It was equally clear that the techniques might generate 5
a broad range of problems. Concerns about health hazards and hazards to the environment were expressed. If microorganisms, or other organisms, were endowed with new functions, might they not find new ecological niches, and with what impact on the rest of the living world? For example, could an *E.coli* bacterium, endowed with the gene for *cellulase*, the enzyme that breaks down cellulose, find a niche in the human intestine? If so, would such an organism cause epidemics of chronic diarrhea? Could a plant endowed with nitrogen-fixing genes, and thus self-fertilizing, become a persistent weed, threatening the survival of other plants? The potential for military application was apparent. If gene splicing could find application in commerce, why not in warfare? For example, could the technology be used for toxin manufacture, or for construction of novel pathogens against which an adversary would have no defense?

Concern also focused on: 6

- the potential for *human genetic engineering*. If gene splicing could be used to redesign mice, why not human beings? Who would decide whether this would be desirable, and for what purpose?
- the *proprietary status* of redesigned forms of life. Was it ethically acceptable for corporations to patent redesigned genes, or organisms containing such genes, or the progeny of such organisms?

- the *terms of development* of this technology: Whose priorities and values should determine how this potent technology would be applied, and toward what ends? Should the reshaping of life be left to market forces to determine?

7   Many of these issues were either recognized at the outset or emerged shortly after the first gene-splicing experiments, and as they were aired, it became apparent that perceptions were mixed. Many of those close to the development of the techniques saw mainly the advantages they would yield for science and industry. But others saw a possibly highly destructive impact on society and on the environment. These critics focused on the power of the new techniques and argued that increasing the power to intervene in natural processes had frequently brought the power to disrupt them as well. They pointed to the history of nuclear fission and synthetic organic chemicals. Would the technology of genetic manipulation likewise generate serious hazards? Furthermore, would these hazards be uncontrollable since they would be borne by living organisms that could reproduce themselves? And even if the techniques turned out to be safe when used in research or industry, could they be deliberately applied in biological warfare, or in unethical forms of genetic treatment?

8   The first response to these concerns came from the community of molecular biologists in whose midst the techniques had been developed. In 1974, at an international conference held in Asilomar, California, leading molecular biologists called on governments in countries where research was underway to assess the risks and to develop controls.

9   This meeting is interesting as much for what was *not* addressed as for what it achieved: The only issue addressed in depth was the question of the hazards of research. Other concerns were either not raised or quickly dropped from the agenda. Health hazards, and controls to protect against them, quickly became the center of concern. This led eventually to the promulgation of guidelines for recombinant DNA research in most countries involved in this work. In the United States, guidelines were written by an advisory committee to the National Institutes of Health.

10   In 1976, these guidelines were quite strict. Six different

categories of R and D were prohibited; much other research could proceed only under rigorous containment conditions; all research was screened both nationally and locally. There was, however, always a major loophole: the guidelines applied only to government-supported R and D; R and D supported by other sources, such as pharmaceutical companies or companies founded by molecular biologists themselves, was not covered.

Only six years after the promulgation of those guidelines, 11 a dramatic shift of attitude has taken place. (This has been particularly striking in the United States.) Within the scientific community, initial fears of potential harm have been widely (although not completely) dismissed. For the general public, the controversy has all but faded away. Controls have been progressively dismantled. At the present time, there are effective controls for only the most hazardous experiments. For other work—the vast majority of recombinant DNA experiments and processes—there is virtually no provision for oversight or containment.

The new "biobusiness," based on recombinant DNA and 12 other forms of genetic manipulation, is now booming. Production processes using genetically manipulated organisms are functioning, and their first products are being marketed. Most major oil, chemical, and pharmaceutical corporations are investing heavily in the field. A race to achieve technological dominance began to accelerate in 1978, and continues today. It is this side of recombinant DNA technology that is constantly reflected in the press: Commercial applications—usually portrayed as "benefits"—are highlighted; hazards and social problems are played down or—what is more usual—ignored.

But have the problems been resolved? Is it really the case 13 that we can now sit back and wait for the new genetic paradise to come to us, complete with giant mice?

I shall argue no: the problems are still there, some, now, 14 in a more acute form than before. I strongly disagree with the conventional wisdom: that the questions surrounding recombinant DNA activities are "non-issues," or, in other words, that the recombinant DNA issue has been decided largely "on its merits" (that is, it has been "scientifically," and "objectively" resolved).

First, the question of hazards that may arise *inadver-* 15 *tently*—as side effects of recombinant DNA activities—is largely unresolved. Second, the question of *deliberate* construction of hazardous organisms has not been addressed; further, there are now pressing reasons to do so.

16   The question of hazards arising inadvertently in the course of recombinant DNA research or industrial production has long been the focus of concern and the primary reason for development of controls. At one end of the spectrum are gene combinations which would almost certainly produce a fearsome organism. (For example, introduction of the botulinus toxin gene into *E.coli* would likely pose serious hazard.) At the other end of the spectrum are procedures which everyone would agree are innocuous. (For example, the insertion into *E.coli* of a gene from an organism that naturally exchanges genes with *E.coli*.)

17   Between these two extremes, there is an enormous number of possible gene combinations and their implications have been marked by a great deal of controversy and very little solid scientific consensus based on good evidence. Would it be safe, for example, to be exposed to *E.coli* bacteria programmed to make insulin, or interferon, or growth hormone? We have little evidence to draw on, certainly nothing that scientists would call "definitive."

18   Those who claim that the recombinant DNA "problem" has been solved agree that we now have "new evidence" which shows that the procedures are safe, that the original fears were unfounded, and that controls are unnecessary (see Sheldon Krimsky, *Genetic Alchemy*, MIT Press, 1982). Note that the scope of this claim is large: it applies not only to the techniques used today, but to future refinements as well. I would argue that while this "new evidence" is applicable to considerations of hazard, it is applicable only in a limited way in which major issues are left unresolved.

19   Let me briefly indicate two examples:

20   **1. The "epidemic pathogen" argument**. One of the arguments used most extensively to downplay hazards is that the bacterium often used for recombinant DNA experiments (*E.coli* K-12) cannot be converted into an epidemic pathogen (i.e., a disease-causing organism that spreads throughout a human population). There is solid consensus that this generalization is correct: K-12 is a weakly bug (usually), and it is unlikely to survive in competition with the normal gut flora. So it is unlikely to be transmitted from one person to another.

It is important to understand what this argument does 21
not say:

First, the argument says nothing about what happens to 22
the individual unfortunate enough to be the first to be exposed to *E.coli* bacteria manipulated to make a harmful
substance. It doesn't matter that the bacteria would all die
out in 24 hours: by that time, the damage might be done.

Second, the argument does not apply to organisms other 23
than *E.coli* K-12. It does not apply, for example, to the
relatives of K-12 — the strains of *E.coli* that live in the
human intestine, which under some circumstances can survive and colonize the guts of human beings quite effectively.
It does not apply to all the other organisms being used for
recombinant DNA activities: *Salmonella* (a food contami-
nant), *Pseudomonas* (an organism responsible for a wide
range of hospital-acquired and other infections), viruses,
etc. So there is a wide range of possibilities that the
"epidemic pathogen" argument does not cover.

2. The "intervening sequence" argument. In 1977, new 24
evidence on the structure of genes of higher organisms
showed that most DNA of higher organisms would not be
automatically processed by bacteria. This meant that the
possibility of accidentally constructing bacteria capable of
synthesizing proteins encoded in the genes of higher organisms was remote.

This argument, too, is limited in scope. It does not apply 25
to the whole range of recombinant DNA activities *deliberately* aimed at enabling bacteria to make proteins usually
made only by higher organisms. It does not apply to experiments in which genes from bacterial species are transferred
into other bacteria, where expression of these genes may
occur.

Arguments like these — all partial, with a limited range 26
of applicability — have provided a veneer of scientific objectivity for the position that controls for recombinant DNA
activities are no longer necessary. They have been used
repeatedly since 1977 to justify progressive dismantling of
controls to the point where there are now virtually no controls whatever. I think that detailed analysis of these and
other arguments shows that, in fact, the recombinant DNA
issue was not "decided on its merits": The decision to dismantle controls was political, not scientific.

A more objective assessment would conclude that in fact 27

we still know very little about possible recombinant DNA hazards, particularly those involved in industrial processes. New biotechnologies will use very large volumes of microorganisms such as *E.coli, B.subtilis, Pseudomonas* and yeast in fermentation processes. Within the workplace, possible occupational hazards include exposure to microorganisms containing recombinant DNA, exposure to the products of such organisms, and exposure to hazardous chemicals used in extraction and purification. Outside the workplace, hazards may be generated by spills and leaks, improper ventilation, and improper disposal of wastes. For example, organisms released in large quantities into surface waters or sewer systems might transfer harmful characteristics to other organisms capable of infecting humans or animals. There is very little hard evidence, at present, concerning such possibilities. But the evidence we do have is not particularly reassuring. For example, it has been shown that even a weakened strain of *E.coli* not only survives in sewage but also survives secondary sewage treatment. But perhaps more importantly in the long run, the direction of recombinant DNA research and development is toward increasing both the variety of organisms used for synthesis of new products and the efficiency with which they can function. Genetic manipulation techniques, if they are to compete effectively with existing production methods, must be made more efficient than they are at present. Thus, if there are hazards, it is likely that they will increase as the commercial potential of recombinant DNA technology is realized.

28   If the issue of hazards that arise inadvertently is unresolved, few would argue against the possibility of *deliberate* design and construction of a hazardous organism with recombinant DNA techniques. That, one might say, is the ultimate biohazard, and the obvious applications are for military and terrorist purposes.

29   The question of military application of recombinant DNA technology has always been in the background of the controversy. There are several reasons why the issue needs to be addressed, and why, in the last three years, this need has become pressing. (See Robert Sinsheimer and Susan Wright, "Recombinant DNA and Biological Warfare," *Bulletin of the Atomic Scientists*, November 1983.)

30   First, the progressive weakening of controls for recombinant DNA technology in the last few years means that it is

now permissible to do experiments which were originally seen as so hazardous that they were prohibited. Consequently, a variety of experiments are now being planned to introduce into bacteria genes for some of the most potent toxins known to science. We may expect that the number of such experiments will increase. And while these experiments are being undertaken in the civilian sector for scientific and medical reasons, they may be of equal if not greater interest to the military. Thus an unintended consequence of the weakening of controls is likely to be the provision of a body of knowledge on the behavior of novel biological agents which could find military application.

Second, since 1980, new military interests in biological research in general and in recombinant DNA technology in particular have emerged: [31]

1. Data on support for biological research by the Department of Defense (DOD) and the National Institutes of Health (NIH) show that in the past few years, DOD support has increased substantially whereas NIH support has declined. In 1980–82, defense obligations for all biological research and for biological research in the universities increased in real terms by 15 percent and 24 percent respectively. (The percentages in terms of current dollars are, of course, more dramatic: 36 percent vs. 47 percent.) On the other hand, the corresponding changes for NIH were decreases of 4.1 percent and 3.6 percent respectively. We may expect that biologists will feel increased pressure to seek support from military sources. [32]

2. In FY 1980, the DOD initiated programs of research using recombinant DNA technology. There are at present some 15 unclassified projects underway and an expansion of this program is planned. Many of these projects focus on cloning of genes for pathogenic organisms in order to make vaccines against them. No fewer than six of these projects focus on making the enzyme acetylicholinesterase, a neural transmitter attacked by nerve gas. (The DOD frankly acknowledges that the teams of scientists involved in these projects are competing with one another for results.) All of these projects are justified as "defensive" research (a point of legal importance since, as I will discuss later, the United States is a party to the Biological Weapons Convention). [33]

3. In addition, the DOD has recognized that recombinant [34]

DNA (as well as other newer biological techniques) could also present new military problems because of its potential to enhance such factors as the selectivity, lethality, and stability of microorganisms. DOD reports to Congress for FY 1980 and FY 1981 characterize this possibility as a "new threat." And in response to this perception, the DOD contemplates new lines of research, the objective of this research being: "to provide a better understanding of . . . [disease-causing organisms] *with or without* genetic manipulation." That passage suggests that DOD planners contemplate projects using recombinant DNA techniques to change or accentuate the properties of disease-causing organisms: For how else could a "better understanding" of such organisms be derived? Statements of DOD officials have confirmed this interpretation: Under certain circumstances, the DOD is prepared to initiate programs aimed at making novel pathogens.

35   4. The DOD also anticipates that recombinant DNA technology may be applied for the production of toxins or other toxic agents. A report commissioned by the department in 1981 concludes that "toxins could probably be manufactured by newly created bacterial strains under controlled laboratory conditions."

36   DOD officials insist that no work on novel harmful agents — either toxins or organisms — is currently in progress.

37   Finally, there are potential loopholes in the international treaty covering biological research and development for military purposes, the Biological Weapons Convention. The convention bans development, construction, and stockpiling of biological weapons. For many years, the fact that the convention existed, and that it had been signed by the major world powers (including the U.S. and the Soviet Union), served to assuage concern about the development of recombinant DNA technology for weapons purposes.

38   It is not clear, however, that the treaty covers all aspects of the newer forms of genetic engineering. For example, it is unclear how much "research" is prohibited by the convention's ban on "development," whether this ban covers the construction of novel harmful agents, and whether it would cover manufacture of novel toxins. Furthermore, the treaty makes no provision for verification of compliance.

39   The enhanced capability made possible by the new technology might provide the incentive to use such loopholes. And that possibility is increased in the present climate of deepening suspicion and deteriorating international relations.

In the face of these problems, what can we do, first, to 40
ensure that the new biology is directed exclusively for
peaceful applications; and second, to ensure that those
peaceful applications are safe?

With respect to the industrial application of genetic en- 41
gineering, the situation seems comparable to the development of synthetic organic chemicals by 1950. By that point,
advances in chemistry had made possible the invention of
thousands of novel substances the impact of which on
health and environment was unknown. Only now are we
facing the full consequences of that ignorance: the overwhelming costs to human health and the environment of
dioxin, PBB, PCBs, kepone, and the thousands of other lethal chemicals we have recklessly released. Can we afford
to make the same mistake again, this time with self-repro-
ducing novel organisms?

We need to regulate this field. The costs of regulation 42
will be minute compared to the possible costs of damage
wrought by an unregulated industry. We need to ensure
that wastes are adequately treated and monitored. We need
to monitor the health of workers. And we need meaningful
involvement of workers and communities in decision making.

With respect to the military application of the new biol- 43
ogy, the situation seems comparable to that in nuclear
physics in 1940. Novel biological weapons have not yet
been invented; yet it is likely that they could be as the
result of determined effort on the part of military establishments. The critical question is whether we can learn from
the experience of nuclear physics. The application of that
field for weapons purposes, fueled by the logic of protection
and counter-protection, has brought us to the brink of nuclear annihilation. Unless we renounce that logic, we run
the risk of being swept up into a new weapons race, this
time based on biology. Efforts directed toward negotiation
and control of biological weapons are surely less hazardous
than the alternative of *not* attempting to take this step.

Before the nations begin to build major military dependen- 44
cies on the new biological technologies, we need to intervene
to ensure that these technologies are directed exclusively into
peaceful applications. All the nations should be encouraged
to sign the existing treaty and to incorporate its provisions
into their domestic law. And all nations should renounce
secret biological research.

Beyond these steps, the entire subject of biological weapons 45 disarmament needs to be reopened. Collectively, the United States and other nations should seek to strengthen the Biological Weapons Convention to ensure that any research on novel harmful agents is screened nationally and internationally, that all appropriate research is conducted in the open, in internationally approved facilities, and that all such work is directed toward peaceful ends.

46   I am not advocating that we stop the development of the new biology. I believe that we can achieve wonderful and important results with it. But we do need to ensure that its application is both peaceful and safe. We have to learn from the history of nuclear physics and organic chemistry. Indeed, I believe we have no real choice. We cannot afford to develop the new biological technologies without controlling them.

DO ANIMALS HAVE RIGHTS?

Tom Regan
Religion and Animal Rights

Tom Regan, a philosopher and educator, is president of the Culture and Animals Foundation in Raleigh, North Carolina. He presented the following argument before the Conference on Creation Theology and Environmental Ethics at the World Council of Churches in Annecy, France, in 1988. It was reprinted in The Animals' Voice *magazine.*

In its simplest terms the animal rights position I uphold 1 maintains that such diverse practices as the use of animals in science, sport and recreational hunting, the trapping of furbearing animals for vanity products, and commercial animal agriculture are categorically wrong—wrong because these practices systematically violate the rights of the animals involved. Morally, these practices ought to be abolished. That is the goal of the *social* struggle for animal rights. The goal of our *individual* struggle is to divest ourselves of our moral and economic ties to these injustices— for example, by not wearing the skins of dead animals and by not eating their decaying corpses.

Not a few people regard the animal rights position as 2 extreme, calling, as it does, for the abolition of certain well-entrenched social practices rather than for their "humane" reform. And many seem to imagine that once this label ("extreme") is applied, the need for further refutation evaporates. After all, how can such an "extreme" moral position be correct?

I addressed this question in a recent speech, reminding 3 my audience of a few "extreme" moral positions we all accept:

Rape is *always* wrong.   4
Child pornography is *always* wrong.   5
Racial and sexual discrimination are *always* wrong.   6
I went on to note that when an injustice is absolute, as   7

is true of each of the examples just cited, then one must oppose it absolutely. It is not reformed, more humane child pornography that an enlightened ethic calls for; it is its abolition that is required—it is this *extreme* position we must uphold. And analogous remarks apply in the case of the other examples.

8   Once this much is acknowledged, it is evident (or at least it should be) that those who oppose or resist the animal rights position will have to do better than merely attach the label "extreme" to it. Sometimes "extreme" positions about what is wrong are right.

9   Of course, there are two obvious differences between the animal rights position and the other examples of extreme views I have given. The latter views are very generally accepted, whereas the former position is not. And unlike these very generally accepted views, which concern wrongful acts done to human beings, the animal rights position concerns the (alleged) wrongfulness of treating animals (nonhuman animals, that is) in certain ways. Those who oppose or resist the animal rights position might seize upon these two differences in an effort to justify themselves in accepting extreme positions regarding rape and child abuse, for example, while rejecting the "extremism" of animal rights.

10   But neither of these differences will bear the weight of justification. That a view (whether moral or otherwise) is very generally accepted is not a sufficient reason for accepting it as true. There was a time when the shape of the earth was very generally believed to be flat, and when the presence of physical and mental handicaps was very generally thought to make the people who bore them morally inferior. That very many people believed these falsehoods obviously did not make them true. We won't discover or confirm what's true by taking a vote.

11   The reverse of the preceding also can be demonstrated. That a view (moral or otherwise) is not generally accepted is not a sufficient reason for judging it to be false. When those lonely few first conjectured that the earth is round and that women are the moral equals of men, they conjectured truly, notwithstanding how grandly they were outnumbered. The solitary person who, in Thoreau's enduring image, marches to a different drummer, may be the only person to apprehend the truth.

12   The second difference noted above is more problematic. That difference cites the fact that child abuse and rape, for

example, involve evils done to human beings, while the animal rights position claims that certain (alleged) evils are done to nonhuman animals. Now, there is no question that this does constitute a difference. The question is, is this a *morally relevant difference* — a difference, that is, that would justify us in accepting the extreme opposition we judge to be appropriate in the case of child abuse and rape, for example, but, which most people resist or abjure in the case of, say, vivisection. For a variety of reasons I do not myself think that this difference is a morally relevant one. Permit me to explain why.

Viewed scientifically, this second difference succeeds 13 only in citing a biological difference: The victims of rape and child abuse belong to one species (the species *Homo sapiens*) whereas the (alleged) victims of vivisection and trapping belong to other species (the species *Canis lupus*, for example). But biological differences *inside* the species *Homo sapiens* do not justify radically different treatment among those individual humans who differ biologically (for example, in terms of sex, or skin color, or chromosome count). Why, then, should biological differences *outside* our species count morally? If having one eye or deformed limbs does not disqualify a human being from moral consideration equal to that given to those humans who are more fortunate, how can it be rational to disqualify a rat or a wolf from equal moral consideration because, unlike us, they have paws and a tail?

Some of those who resist or oppose the animal rights 14 position might have recourse to "intuition" at this point. They might claim that one either "sees" that the principal biological difference at issue (namely, species membership) *is* a morally relevant one, or does *not* see this. No *reason* can be given as to why belonging to the species *Homo sapiens* gives one a superior moral status, just as no *reason* can be given as to why belonging to the species *Canis lupus* gives wolves an inferior moral status (if wolves have a moral status at all). This difference in moral status can only be grasped immediately, without making an inference, by an exercise of intuitive reason. This moral difference is "self-evident"–or so it will be claimed by those who claim to "intuit" it.

However attractive this appeal to intuition may seem to 15 some, it woefully fails to bear the weight of justification. The plain fact is, people have claimed to "intuit" differences in the comparative moral standing of individuals and groups *inside* the human species, and these alleged "intuitions," we all would agree, are painful symptoms of unquestioned and unjustifiable prejudice. Over the course of history, for example, many men have "intuited" the moral superiority of men when compared with that of women, and many white-skinned humans have "intuited" the moral superiority of white-skinned humans when compared with humans having different skin colors. If this is a matter of intuition, then no reason can be given for this superiority. No inference is (or can be) required, no evidence adduced. One either "sees" it, or one doesn't. It's just that those who do "see" it (or so they will insist) apprehend the truth, while those whose deficient intuitive faculties prevent them from "seeing" it fail to do so.

16   I cannot believe that any thoughtful person will be taken in by this ruse. Appeals to "intuition" in these contexts are symptomatic of unquestioned and unjustifiable moral prejudices. What prompts or encourages men to "see" their moral superiority over women are the sexual prejudices men bring with them, not what is to be found in the existence of sexual differences themselves. And the same is true, *mutatis mutandis*, of "seeing" moral superiority in racial or other biological differences between humans.

17   That much established, the weakness of appeals to intuition in the case at hand should be apparent. Since intuition is not to be trusted when questions of the comparative moral standing of biologically different individuals *inside* the species *Homo sapiens* are at issue, it cannot be rational to assume or insist that such appeals can or should be trusted when questions of the comparative moral standing of individuals *outside* the species are at issue. Moreover, since appeals to intuition in the former case turn out to be symptomatic of unquestioned and unjustifiable moral prejudices, rather than being revelatory of some important moral truth, it is not unreasonable to suspect that the same diagnosis applies to appeals to intuition in the latter case. If true, then those who "intuit" the moral superiority of all members of the species *Homo sapiens* over all members of every other species, also emerge as the unwitting victims or the willful perpetrators of an unquestioned and unjustifiable moral prejudice.

18   "Speciesism" is the name given to this (alleged) prejudice. This idea has been characterized in a variety of ways.

For present purposes let us begin with the following two-fold characterization of what I shall call "categorical speciesism."

Categorical speciesism is the belief that (1) the inherent 19 value of an individual can be judged solely on the basis of the biological species to which that individual belongs, and that (2) all the members of the species *Homo sapiens* have equal inherent value, while all the members of every other species lack this kind of value, simply because all and only humans are members of the species *Homo sapiens*.

In speaking of inherent value, both here and throughout 20 what follows, I mean something that coincides with Kant's famous idea of "end-in-itself." Individuals who have inherent value, in other words, have value in their own right, apart from their possible utility for others; as such, these individuals are never to be treated in ways that reduce their value to their possible usefulness for others; they are always to be treated as "ends-in-themselves," not as "means merely." Categorical speciesism, then, holds that all and only humans have this kind of value precisely because all and only humans belong to the species *Homo sapiens*.

I have already indicated why I believe that appeals to 21 intuition cannot succeed in establishing the truth of categorical speciesism as so characterized. How, then, might the prejudicial character of speciesism be established?

Part of that answer is to be found when we pause to 22 consider the nature of the animals we humans hunt, trap, eat and use for scientific purposes. Any person of common sense will agree that these animals bring the mystery of consciousness to the world. These animals, that is, not only are *in* the world, they are aware *of it* — and also of their "inner" world. They see, hear, touch and feel; but they also desire, believe, remember and anticipate.

If anyone questions my assessment of the common sense 23 view about these animals, then I would invite them to speak with people who share their lives with dogs or cats or horses, or others who know the ways of wolves or coyotes, or still others who have had contact with any bird one might wish to name. Common sense clearly is on the side of viewing these animals as unified psychological beings, individuals who have a biography (a psychological life-story), not merely a biology. And common sense is not in conflict with our best science here. Indeed, our best science offers a scientific corroboration of the common sense view.

24   That corroboration is to be found in a set of diverse but related considerations. One is evolutionary theory, which implies that (1) the more complex has evolved from the less complex, that (2) members of the species *Homo sapiens* are the most complex life form of which we are aware, that (3) members of our species bring a psychological presence to the world, that (4) the psychological capacities we find in humans have evolved over time, and that (5) these capacities would not have evolved at all and would not have been passed on from one generation to the next if they (that is, these capacities) failed to have adaptive value—that is, if they failed to offer advantages to our species in its ongoing struggle to survive in an ever-changing environment.

25   Given these five points, it is entirely consistent with the main thrust of evolutionary theory, and is, indeed, required by it, to maintain that the members of some species of nonhuman animals are like us in having the capacity to see and hear and feel, for example, as well as to believe and desire, to remember and anticipate.

26   Certainly this is what Darwin thinks, as is evident when he writes of the animals we humans eat and trap, to use just two instances, that they differ psychologically (or mentally) from us in degree, not in kind.

27   A second, related consideration involves comparative anatomy and physiology. Everything we know about nature must incline us to believe that a complex structure has a complex reason for being. It would therefore be an extraordinary lapse of form if we humans had evolved into complicated psychological creatures, with an underlying anatomical and physiological complexity, while other species of animals had evolved to have a more or less complex anatomy and physiology, very much like our own in many respects, and yet lacked—*totally* lacked—any and every psychological capacity. If nature could respond to this bizarre suggestion, the verdict we would hear would be, "Nonsense!"

28   Thus it is, then, that both common sense and our best science speak with one voice regarding the psychological nature we share with the nonhuman animals I have mentioned—those, for example, many people stew, roast, fry, broil and grill for the sake of their gustatory desires and delights. When the dead and putrefying bodies of these animals are eaten, our psychological kin are consumed.

29   Recall the occasion for this review of relevant scientific

considerations. Categorical speciesism, which I characterized earlier, is not shown to be a moral prejudice merely because those who accept it are unable to prove its truth. This much has been conceded and, indeed, insisted upon. What more, then, would have to be established before the charge of moral prejudice could be made to stick? Part of that answer is to be found in the recent discussion of what common sense and our best science contribute to our understanding of the nonhuman animals we have been discussing. Both agree that these animals are fundamentally like ordinary human beings — like you and me. For, like us, these animals have a unified psychological presence in the world, a life-story that is uniquely their own, a separate biography. In the simplest terms *they are somebody, not something*. Precisely because this similarity is so well established, grounded in the opinions, as Aristotle would express this, of both "the many and the wise," any substantive moral position at odds with it seems dubious to say the least.

And categorical speciesism, as I have characterized it, *is* 30 at odds with the joint verdict of common sense and our best science. For once the appeal to intuition is denied (and denied for good reasons), the onus of justification must be borne by the speciesist to cite some unique feature of being human that would ground the attribution of inherent value exclusively to human beings, a task that we now see is all but certain to end in failure, given the biographical status humans share with those nonhuman animals to whom I have been referring. Rationally considered, we must judge similar cases similarly. This is what the principle of formal justice requires, what respect for logical consistency demands. Thus, since we share a biographical presence in the world with these animals, it seems arbitrary and prejudicial in the extreme to insist that all humans have a kind of value that every other animal lacks.

In response to this line of argument people who wish to 31 retain the spirit of speciesism might be prompted to alter its letter. This position I shall call modified speciesism. According to this form of speciesism those nonhuman animals who, like us, have a biographical presence in the world have *some* inherent value, it's just that the degree of inherent value they have *always is less* than that possessed by human beings. And if we ask why this is thought to be so, the answer modified speciesism offers is the same as categorical speciesism: The degree of value differs because humans belong to a particular species to which no other animal belongs — the species *Homo sapiens*.

32   I think it should be obvious that modified speciesism is open to many of the same kinds of damaging criticisms as categorical speciesism. What, we may ask, is supposed to be the basis of the alleged superior value of human beings? Will it be said that one simply "intuits" this? Then all the same difficulties this appeal faced in the case of categorical speciesism will resurface and ultimately swamp modified speciesism. To avoid this, will it be suggested that the degree of inherent value an individual possesses depends on the relative complexity of that individual's psychological repertoire — the greater the complexity, the greater the value? Then modified speciesism simply will not be able to justify the ascription of superior inherent value to all human beings when compared with every nonhuman animal. And the reason it will not be able to do this is simple: Some nonhuman animals bring to their biography a degree of psychological complexity that far exceeds what is brought by some human beings. One need only to compare, say, the psychological repertoire of a healthy two year old chimp, or dog, or hog, or robin to that of a profoundly handicapped human of any age, to recognize the incontrovertible truth of what I have just said. Not all human beings have richer, more complex biographies than every nonhuman animal.

33   How are speciesists to get around this fact — for get around it they must, because fact it is. There is a familiar theological answer to this question; at least it is familiar to those who know something of the Judeo-Christian religious traditions, as these traditions sometimes have been interpreted. That answer states that human beings — all of us — are inherently more valuable than any other existing individual because we are spiritually different and, indeed, unique. This uniqueness stems from our having been created in the image of God, a status we share with no other creature. If, then, it is true that all humans uniquely image God, then we are able to cite a real (spiritual) difference between every member of our species and the countless numbers of the millions of other species of creaturely life. And, if, moreover, this difference is a morally relevant one, then speciesists might seem to be in a position to defend their speciesism (and this is true whether they are categorical or moderate speciesists) in the face of the demands of formal justice.

After all, that principle requires that we judge similar cases similarly, whereas any two individuals—the one human, the other of some other species—will not be relevantly similar, given the hypothesis of the unique spiritual worth of all human beings.

Now I myself am not ill-disposed to the idea of there 34 being something about us humans that gives us a unique spiritual worth, nor am I ill-disposed to the idea that the ground of this worth is to be found or explicated in the idea that we humans uniquely "image" God. Not surprisingly, therefore, the interpretation of these ideas I favor, while it concedes this (possible) difference between humans and the rest of creation, does not yield anything like the results favored by speciesism, whether categorical or moderate. Let me explain.

The position I favor is the one that interprets our divine 35 "imaging" in terms of our moral responsibility: By this I mean that we are expressly chosen by God to be God's vice-regent in the day-to-day affairs of the world; we are chosen by God, that is, to be as loving in our day-to-day dealings with the created order, as God was in creating that order in the first place. In *this* sense, therefore, there *is* a morally relevant difference between human beings and every other creaturely expression of God. For it is only members of the human species who are given the awesome freedom and responsibility to be God's representative within creation. And it is, therefore, only we humans who can be held morally blameworthy when we fail to do this, and morally praiseworthy when we succeed.

Within the general context of this interpretation of our 36 unique "imaging" of God, then, we find a morally relevant difference between God's creative expression in the human and God's creative expression in every other aspect of creation. But—as should be evident—this difference *by itself* offers neither aid nor comfort to speciesism, of whatever variety. For to agree that only humans image God, in the sense that only humans have the moral responsibility to be loving toward God's creation, in no way entails either that all and only humans have inherent value (so-called categorical speciesism) or that all and only humans have a superior inherent value (modified speciesism, as I have called it). It is perfectly consistent with our unique status as God's chosen representative within creation that *other* creatures have inherent value and possess it to a degree equal to that possessed by human beings. Granted, our uniqueness lies in our moral responsibility to God and to God's creation, including, of course, all members of the human family. But this fact, assuming it to be a fact, only answers the question, "Which among God's creatures are capable of acting rightly or wrongly (or, as philosophers might say, 'are moral agents')?" What this fact, assuming it to be one, does not answer are the questions, "To which creatures can we act rightly or wrongly?" and "What kind of value do other creatures have?"

37   Every prejudice dies hard. Speciesism is no exception. That it is a prejudice and that, by acting on it, we humans have been, and continue to be, responsible for an incalculable amount of evil, an amount of truly monumental proportions, is, I believe, as true as it is regrettable. In my philosophical writings over the past fifteen years I have endeavored to show how this tragic truth can be argued for on wholly secular grounds. On this occasion I have looked elsewhere for support — have in fact looked to the original saga of creation we find in *Genesis* — in the hope that we might there find a religious or theological account that resonates with the secular case for animal rights. Neither case — not the secular and not the religious — has, or can have, the conclusiveness of a proof in, say, geometry. I say "can have" because I am reminded of Aristotle's astute observation, that it is the mark of an educated person not to demand "proof" that is inappropriate for a given subject matter. And whatever else we might think of moral thought, I believe we at least can agree that it is importantly unlike geometry.

38   It remains true, nonetheless, that my attempt to explain and defend as egalitarian this view of the inherent value of humans and other animals must face a number of important challenges. For reasons of length, if for no other, I cannot on this occasion characterize or respond to all these challenges, not even all the most fundamental ones. The best I can do, before concluding, is describe and defuse two of them.

39   The first begins by observing that, within the traditions of Judaism and Christianity, *every form of life*, not simply humans and other animals, is to be viewed as expressive of God's love. Thus, to attempt to "elevate" the value of nonhuman animals, as I might be accused of having done, could be viewed as having the unacceptable consequence of negating or reducing the value of everything else.

I think this objection misses the mark. There is nothing 40
in the animal rights philosophy (nothing, that is, in the
kind of egalitarianism I have endeavored to defend) that
either denies or diminishes the value of fruits, nuts, grains
and other forms of vegetative life, or that refuses to accept
the possibility that these and the rest of creation are so
many ways in which God's loving presence is manifested.
Nor is there anything in this philosophy that disparages
the wise counsel to treat all of creation gently and apprecia-
tively. It is an arrogant, unbridled anthropocentrism, often
aided and abetted in our history by an arrogant, unbridled
Christian theology, not the philosophy of animal rights,
that has brought the earth to the brink of ecological disaster.

Still, this philosophy does find in humans and other ani- 41
mals, because of our shared biographical status in creation,
a kind of value—inherent value—which other creatures fail
to possess, either not at all or at least not to the degree in
which humans and other animals possess it. Is it possible to
defend this view? I believe it is, both on the grounds of a
purely secular moral philosophy and by appeal to Biblical
authority. The secular defense I have attempted to offer elsewhere and will not repeat here. As for the Christian defense,
I shall merely reaffirm the vital importance (in my view) of
Genesis 1, as well as (to my mind) the more than symbolic
significance of the covenant, and note that in both we find
Biblical sanction for viewing the value of animals to be
superior to that of vegetables. After all, we do not find carrots
and almonds included in the covenant, and we do find God
expressly giving these and other forms of vegetative life to
us, as our food, in *Genesis'* first creation saga. In a word, then,
vegetative life was meant to be used by us, thus giving it
utility value for us (which does not mean or entail that we
may use these life forms thoughtlessly or even irreverently).

So much for the first challenge. The second one emanates 42
from quite a different source and mounts a quite different
objection. It begins by noting the large disparities that exist
in the quality of life available to those who are affluent (the
"haves") and those who are poor (the "have-nots"), especially those who live in the so-called "Third World." "It is
all fine and good to preach the gospel of animal rights to
those people who have the financial and other means to
practice it, if they choose to do so," this objection states,
"but please do spare us your self-righteous denunciation of
the struggling (and often starving) masses of people in the
rest of the world, who really have no choice but to eat

animals, wear their skins, and use them in other ways. To condemn these people is to value animal life above human life. And this is misanthropy at its worst."

43   Now, this particular variation on the familiar theme of misanthropy (at least this is familiar to advocates of animal rights) has a point, up to a point. The point it has, is that it would be self-righteous to condemn the people in question for acting as they do, especially if we are acting worse than they are (as well we may be). But, of course, nothing in what I have argued supports such a condemnation, and this for the simple reason that I have nowhere argued that people who eat animals, or who hunt and trap them, or who cut their heads off or burst their intestines in pursuit of "scientific knowledge," either are or must be *evil* people. The position I have set forth concerns the moral wrongness of what people do, not the *vileness of their character*. In my view, it is entirely possible that good people sometimes do what is wrong, and evil people sometimes do what is right.

44   Indeed, not only is this possible, it frequently happens, and among those circumstances in which it does, some concern the actions performed by people in the Third World. At least this is the conclusion we reach if we take the philosophy of animal rights seriously. To make my meaning clearer, consider the following example. Suppose we chance upon a tribe of hunter-gatherers who annually, on a date sacred to their tradition, sacrifice the most beautiful female child to the gods, in the hope that the tribe will prosper in the coming year. In my view this act of human sacrifice is morally wrong and ought to be stopped (which does *not* mean that we should invade with tanks and flame-throwers to stop it!). From this moral assessment of what these human beings do, however, it does not follow that we should judge them to be evil, vicious people. It could well be that they act from only the best intentions and with nothing but the best motives. Nevertheless, what they do, in my judgment, is morally wrong.

45   What is true of the imaginary case of this tribe, is no less true of real-life cases where people in the Third World raise and kill animals for food, cruelly subject other animals to forced labor, and so on. Anytime anyone reduces the inherent value of a nonhuman animal to that animal's utility value for human beings, what is done, in my view, is morally wrong. But it does not follow from this that we should make a negative moral judgment about the character of the human moral agents involved, especially if, as is true in

the Third World, there are mitigating circumstances. For it often happens that people who do what is morally wrong should be *excused* from moral blame and censure. A person who shoots a family member, for example, in the mistaken belief that there is a burglar in the house, does what is wrong and yet may well *not* be morally blameworthy. Similarly, those people in the Third World who act in ways that are prohibited by respect for the rights of animals, do what is wrong. But because of the harsh, uncompromising exigencies of their life, where they are daily faced with the demand to make truly heroic sacrifices, where indeed it often is a matter of their life or their death that hangs in the balance, the people of the Third World in my view should be excused from our harsh, uncompromising judgments of moral blame. The circumstances of their life, one might say, are as mitigating as any circumstances can be.

In light of the preceding remarks, I hope it is clear why 46 it would be a bad reading of the philosophy of animal rights, to charge its proponents with a hearty appetite, if not for animal flesh then at least for self-righteousness. When we understand the difference between morally assessing a person's act and that person's character, and when we take cognizance of the appropriateness of reducing or erasing moral blame in the face of mitigating circumstances, then the proponents of animal rights should be seen to be no more censorious or "self-righteous" than the proponents of any other moral philosophy.

The challenge to lead a good, respectful, loving life just 47 in our dealings within the human family is onerous and demanding. How much more onerous and demanding must it be, therefore, if we widen the circle of the moral community to include the whole of creation. How might we begin to meet this enlarged challenge? Doubtless there are many possible places to begin, some of which will be more accessible to some than to others. For my part, however, I cannot help believing that an appropriate place to begin is with the food on our plates. For here we are faced with a direct personal choice, over which we exercise absolute sovereign authority. Such power is not always within our grasp. How little influence we really have, you and I, on the practices of the World Bank, the agrarian land-reform movement, the call to reduce armed conflicts, the cessation of famine and the evil of abject poverty! These large-scale evils stand beyond the reach of our small wills.

But not the food on our plates. Here we are at liberty to 48 exercise absolute control. And here, then, we ought to be asking ourselves, "Which of those choices I can make are most in accord with the idea of the integrity of creation?"

49   When we consider the biographical and, I dare say, the spiritual kinship we share with those billions of animals raised and slaughtered for food; when, further, we inform ourselves of the truly wretched conditions in which most of these animals are raised, not to mention the deplorable methods by which they are transported and the gruesome, blood-soaked reality of the slaughterhouse; and when, finally, we take honest stock of our privileged position in the world, a position that will not afford us the excuse from moral blame shared by the desperately poor who, as we say, "really have no choice" — when we consider all these factors, then the case for abstaining from animal flesh has the overwhelming weight of both impartial reason and a spiritually-infused compassion on its side.

50   True, to make this change will involve some sacrifices — in taste perhaps, in convenience certainly. And yet the whole fabric of Christian *agape* is woven from the threads of sacrificial acts. To abstain, on principle, from eating animals, therefore, although it is not the end-all, can be the begin-all of our conscientious effort to journey back to (or toward) Eden, can be one way (among others) to re-establish or create that relationship to the earth which, if *Genesis 1* is to be trusted, was part of God's original hopes for and plans in creation. It is the integrity of this creation we seek to understand and aspire to honor. In the choice of our food, I believe, we see, not in a glass darkly, but face to face, a small but not unimportant part of both the challenge and the promise of Christianity and animal rights.

Teresa K. Rye
How I Benefited from Animal Research

A registered nurse, Teresa K. Rye in 1984 offered the following personal testimony to a national symposium sponsored by the U.S. Department of Health and Human Services.

As I am listening to these proceedings and talking to you 1
today, my emotions are of deep gratitude for the work that
has been done by medical researchers and practitioners.
Had I been born 20 years earlier I would not be alive
now. Had the research not been performed to develop the
knowledge base and sophisticated techniques to support
the surgery that I had, I would have only a short life to
look forward to.

I was asked to come and speak at this symposium as I 2
have directly received the benefits of animal research. A
year-and-a-half ago I had open-heart surgery at the Brigham
and Women's Hospital in Boston performed by Doctor
Cohn. I am 28 years old. I am a registered nurse and an
instructor for nursing education and research at University
Hospital at Boston University Medical Center. In October
1982 I underwent surgery for repair of a very rare congenital
heart defect called the scimitar syndrome. In spite of my
education as a nurse, I had never heard of this syndrome.
The name is derived from the appearance of the chest X-ray
which shows the veins connecting the lungs to the heart in
a semi-curved pattern around the right side of the heart.

The very name "scimitar syndrome" frightened me. I felt 3
doomed. My cardiologist said this defect is so rare, he would
be surprised if he saw three or four more cases of this type
in his entire career. I was told I would need open-heart
surgery. The alternative would have been to develop pulmo-
nary artery hypertension and almost certain death around
age 35.

My operation was unique. Part of my surgery required 4
the heart-lung by-pass machine to be turned off. It was a
chilling experience for me to learn my body was frozen to
15° centigrade and that I had been clinically dead for 30
minutes during the operation. I hope that legislators, lob-
byists, and research agencies appreciate that these kinds
of procedures would be impossible to perform had there
not been an animal research model. No number of
mathematical, statistical, analytical, and engineering techniques could replace the animal model in my case. I am
deeply fortunate to have the opportunity of a normal life
expectancy now. Death at 35 seems much too close for me.

I was admitted for surgery and stayed in the hospital for 11 5
days. I recuperated at home and returned to work 6 weeks
after my surgery, working 4 hours a day. Two weeks later,
just 2 months after the operation, I was working full-time.

Not only was my successful surgery due to the techniques 6

developed from animal research, but also the diagnostic testing was possible because of animal modeling. I required a cardiac catheterization as well as a nuclear scan with injections of dye to diagnose my abnormality.

7   It was by chance that this problem was discovered. I had begun a new job and had a routine chest X-ray as a pre-employment screen to rule out tuberculosis. I was called to the employee health department to discuss the findings of my film. The physician told me my right heart was enlarged and the blood vessels over my right lung were quite prominent. He said the film suggested that I had a congenital heart defect with signs of an abnormal left to right shunting of blood. He urged me to see a cardiologist.

8   I was shocked, confused, and scared. At the time I was working as a surgical intensive care unit nurse. I felt absolutely fine and led a physically active life. I had no other symptoms of cardiac disease aside from what had been described as a benign heart murmur that I had known about since age 12. As a surgical intensive care unit nurse I was familiar with the battery of tests I would have to undergo. I was aware of the life-threatening risks that could arise during a cardiac catheterization as well as from open-heart surgery. As a nurse I was caring for patients who did, indeed, develop serious — sometimes fatal — complications. I found myself experiencing maximum stress.

9   Once again, animal research had a direct benefit for me. I was able to use medication to ease my anxiety and continue to be productive at work while I waited 6 weeks between my cardiac catheterization and my open-heart surgery.

10   The first day after my surgery I developed a life-threatening complication. My left lung collapsed from positive pressure on the mechanical ventilator. I needed a chest tube emergently inserted into my lung to re-expand it. This procedure also could not have been performed without prior animal testing.

11   At times I experienced intense pain. One of my friends, also a nurse, came to visit me in the intensive care unit and asked me "How is the pain?" I did not remember this, but later she told me I said, "It's killing me. I don't want to move." She asked, "Does the medication help?" I said, "Yes, it does." I am thankful for the amnesia of some of my experience. I sincerely hope and have to believe that animals are given the same kind of relief.

Six years ago I adopted a kitten from the Boston Animal 12
Shelter. She has grown into a beautiful affectionate cat.
She has given me much happiness and feelings of love. Her
picture was on my bedside table at the hospital. Even
though I am a pet owner and animal lover, there is no question in my mind that animal research must be continued.

I have tremendous appreciation for the advances in sci- 13
ence, the skill and care from my doctors and nurses and
the gift of life from animals that allow my continued good
health.

Ten years ago, Lane Potter, in the *Proceedings of the* 14
Royal Society of Medicine, posed five questions for animal
researchers: Is the animal the best experimental system for
the problem? Must the animal be conscious at any time
throughout the experiment? Can pain or discomfort associated with the experiment be lessened or eliminated?
Could the number of animals be reduced? Is the problem
worth solving anyhow?

For me, it is clear that some research involving the use 15
of animals similar to man must continue if mankind is to
continue to advance and survive. For me, it is clear that
these animals deserve the utmost respect and care that we
can give them. They give so much to us. Antivivisectionist
legislation which, in some cases, would absolutely prohibit
animal research, would cause irreparable damage to the
advancement of medical science. If these measures were in
place 20 years ago, surgery involving an open chest and
heart would not be possible. I would probably be experiencing the beginning signs and symptoms of chronic pulmo-
nary artery hypertension. I would be unable to work in my
early thirties. I would have high medical care costs and
would be facing almost certain death at age 35.

But today I am looking forward to turning 29 next week 16
and intend to have a big celebration when I turn 35. I hope
that research using animals continues so that children who
are presently in life-threatening situations will also have a
chance to look forward to birthdays, anniversaries and a
healthy, productive life.

Edward C. Melby, Jr.
A Statement from the Association for Biomedical Research

Edward C. Melby, Jr., is dean of the College of Veterinary Medicine at Cornell University. In 1981, while he was president of the Association for Biomedical Research, he offered the following testimony before a congressional committee that was considering laws to restrict animal research.

1   Mr. Chairman, Members of the Subcommittee, I am Edward C. Melby, Jr., President of the Association for Biomedical Research. I am also Dean of the Faculty and Professor of Medicine of the College of Veterinary Medicine at Cornell University. Prior to accepting that appointment in 1974, I served 12 years as a Professor and Director of the Division of Comparative Medicine of the Johns Hopkins University School of Medicine.

2   The Association for Biomedical Research (ABR), established in 1979, represents nearly 200 universities, hospitals, medical schools, veterinary schools, research institutes, animal producers and suppliers, pharmaceutical, chemical, petroleum and contract testing companies. ABR's primary objective is to help assure the continuation of responsible biomedical research.

3   It is our understanding that we are here today to discuss the use of live animals in medical research and laboratory testing. Perhaps one of the most significant steps taken in the past few years was the passage of the Laboratory Animal Welfare Act, Public Law 89-544, in 1966, for it marked a new era in research regulation. Amendments in 1970 as well as subsequently have broadened the Act to its present form known as the "Animal Welfare Act" and it now protects show horses, zoo and aquarium species, and other categories of animals as well as those used in laboratories. Ironically, the two largest categories of animals in the United States — largest by far — are not covered by the present Act: pet dogs and cats, and farm animals. It is important to understand this dichotomy perhaps best expressed through citing the numbers of animals involved. In FY 1980,

188,700 dogs were studied in research in the United States according to official U.S. Department of Agriculture figures. This can be compared to over three billion—that is three billion—chickens raised for food each year in the United States or the thirteen million—that is thirteen million—dogs killed each year by public pounds, municipal animal shelters, and "humane" societies, according to reliable estimates. There are believed to be about 35 million pet dogs in the United States at any moment, yet the Animal Welfare Act does not cover them. We will return to this point in a moment. But think about those numbers because it is important to put these data into proper perspective; 188,700 dogs studied in medicine and science compared to over thirteen million killed as unclaimed, unwanted dogs each year by towns and cities across America.

ABR was established precisely because no private, non-profit, non-governmental organization seemed to exist which would interact in *a positive way* with scientists, animal welfare organizations, science-based industries in medicine and health, universities and research institutions, and government regulators. ABR has, therefore, in its mere two years of existence, established lines of communication among these varied organizations and, in a more formal way, met with USDA officials to hold serious discussions on improving the Animal Welfare Act. These efforts are ongoing and have been very useful, we believe.

ABR here wishes to emphasize that it welcomes proposals, questions, and discussions with representatives of any interest in the field of animal use in biomedical research. Surprisingly, no animal welfare organization or "humane" society has presented any written proposal to us, nor has any legislator sought the views of the constituency ABR represents through contacting ABR. We hope such representations will be made in the future and assure the Subcommittee that ABR will respond thoughtfully and reliably to any consultation requested. We offer our services as a sounding board to all concerned with biomedical research.

The Subcommittee has expressed an interest in whether laboratory animals are studied unnecessarily or inappropriately. ABR has no reason to believe that in science as in politics or law, there is perfection. The difficulty with words like "unnecessary" or "inappropriate" is that what seems unnecessary to one person from one vantage point, may seem absolutely necessary to another from a different vantage point. Had a Pasteur or a Madame Curie in France, or a Fleming or a Lister in England, or a Salk or a DeBakey in the United States been prevented from following their studies on vaccines, X-rays, penicillin, antiseptics, polio or heart surgery because they were judged "unnecessary," these advances and concepts so taken for granted would not have been developed as they were. Verification of their results by a certain amount of replication was and is an essential part of the scientific process.

7   Having said that, it is clear to us that endless repetition and duplication without purpose is to be avoided. It is our opinion that the peer review system of the major granting agencies, such as the National Institute of Health, the editorial review process for originality of thought by scientific journals, and the cost effectiveness of private industry, prevent most so-called "unnecessary" animal experiments. Those persons and organizations opposed to *all* studies of animals will, of course, consider all such studies as "unnecessary"—a view far from that of mainstream America, we believe. Nevertheless, any improvements which would prevent unnecessary experiments without preventing those which turn out, sometimes unexpectedly, to have been very necessary, would be welcome. The Association for Biomedical Research believes that none of the legislative proposals now in the Congress succeed in making this distinction, but ABR is anxious to work toward this goal.

8   The use of techniques labelled by some as "alternatives" to animals is as old as chemistry, physics, astronomy and modern science itself. Recent NIH studies have shown that roughly one third of its current budget is spent on research using mammals and about one fourth on research using humans themselves, the remainder being in research which studies neither people nor mammals directly. In other words, NIH's average yearly support over the last three fiscal years for projects which do not involve laboratory mammals constitutes 55% of total research dollars expended. Further in FY 1980, approximately 28% of NIH funds were committed to projects using neither humans or mammals. In dollars this translates into $704.8 million. This, combined with the finding that animal use declined by 40% in the decade 1968 through 1978 in the United States by a National Research Council–Institute of Laboratory Animal Resources survey published in 1980, must be taken by any reasonable person as strong evidence of sci-

ence incorporating non-animal techniques as soon as they become scientifically reliable. So-called "alternatives" are consistently incorporated into research, education and testing requirements as the particular medical or scientific field warrants. In addition, the significant pressures of inflation on scientific endeavors have made acquisition and use of animals increasingly expensive. As a result, universities and private industry have experienced considerable motivation to replace animals with less expensive, non-animal techniques wherever possible. A significant percentage of industry's research and development budget is dedicated to the search for in vitro techniques as standard procedures. It must be emphasized, however, that the criterion of scientific excellence must remain the principal determinant of any research method. Where appropriate alternatives to the use of living animals have and will continue to be developed; the benefits obtained through their precision and reproducibility certainly make alternatives a most attractive choice. Several of the present legislative proposals before the Congress in respect to these so-called "alternatives" are therefore redundant and, in our view, dangerous to the conduct of science by the time-tested, scientific peer review process in this country. The Soviet Union, it should be recalled, has still not recovered in medicine and biology from the period of "Lysenkoism" when the government dictated false biological information as a mandated approach to science.

The appropriate care, acquisition and maintenance of laboratory animals is of continuing interest and concern to all responsible scientists. ABR therefore supports efforts to amend those components of the Animal Welfare Act in need of improvement, to which I referred earlier. Indeed, ABR would recommend expansion of the present Act's coverage to pet dogs and cats, and those in municipal pounds or animal shelters, whose municipalities or owning organizations receive federal funds. ABR would be pleased to interact with Congressional sponsors of bills related to animal welfare to insure participation of the larger biomedical community, including the major research and teaching organizations and research-based industries of America. 9

We would be pleased to respond to any questions or comments you may have, and hope that members of the Congress or their staff will contact our office at any time information from the biomedical perspective is required. 10

11   As part of these hearings we wish to offer specific comment on four bills (HR 556, HR 4406, HR 930 and HR 220) now under consideration by the Subcommittee on Science, Research and Technology. For purposes of clarity I list these according to the specific points identified by the Committee for review:

12   1. Excessive, unnecessary, uneconomic or inappropriate use of animals in current practice:

13   Biomedical research institutions in this country operate under a peer review system comprised of before-the-fact reviews of applications and subsequent reviews of data and results in scientific meetings as well as by reviewers and editors of scientific journals. In 1966 the Animal Welfare Act (Public Law 89-547) was enacted. At about the same time, the scientific community sponsored an independent, peer review accreditation program under the auspices of the American Association for Accreditation of Laboratory Animal Care which now accredits some 440 institutions. Institutions now follow guidelines prescribed by the NIH Office of Protection of Research Risks, and a signed statement by each investigator is prepared in making application for research funds that principles for the proper use of animals are being followed.

14   According to studies carried out under the auspices of the National Academy of Sciences–National Research Council, reported in 1980, there was a 40% decrease in total animal use in the decade 1968 through 1978. Although the reasons are varied, there is good evidence to indicate that the supply and use of healthier animals has reduced loss as well as variation in results and hence, reduced the need for confirmation through repetitive studies. Additionally, there has been the ongoing process of incorporating "new technologies" including tissue culture, computer modeling, in vitro diagnostic and assay instrumentation and, most recently, the advent of recombinant DNA techniques. This has been an ongoing process. For example, records of the College I head indicate that tissue culture techniques were introduced on this campus in the mid-1940's. The very nature of science requires that such new technologies be implemented as soon as they are demonstrated to be the equal or superior to existing technologies. Furthermore, economic pressures require that more effective substitutions be introduced wherever possible.

2. Ways to promote more humane and appropriate use of   15
animals, including alternatives to animal use:

   Concurrent with the enormous expansion of biomedical   16
research following World War II, the scientific community
has made a major commitment to the improvement of laboratory animal science. Indeed, an entirely new area of scientific specialization and the infrastructure to support it,
has evolved to meet that need. Training programs have
evolved in both the two and four year colleges to train animal
technicians and technologists; a new specialty board recognized by the American Veterinary Medical Association, the
American College of Laboratory Animal Medicine, certifies
veterinarians with advanced training and experience in that
specialty; and most institutions provide in-house training
programs for animal technicians and graduate students,
many following the programs fostered by the American Association for Laboratory Animal Science. Through these and
related efforts the personnel directly involved in the care
and use of laboratory animals have gained significant understanding of the humane care and specialized requirements
of the various animal species used.

   I believe it is important to repeat observations made ear-   17
lier in this testimony. So-called "alternatives" are consistently incorporated into research, education and testing requirements as the particular medical or scientific field warrants. In recent years, the significant pressures of inflation
on scientific endeavors have made acquisition and use of
animals increasingly expensive. As a result, universities and
private industry have experienced considerable motivation
to replace animals with less expensive, non-animal techniques wherever possible. It must be emphasized, however,
that the criterion of scientific excellence must remain the
principal determinant of any research method. Where appropriate alternatives to the use of living animals have been
developed, the benefits obtained through their precision and
reproducibility certainly make alternatives a most attractive choice. Both HR 930 and HR 220 have been written in
such a manner as to be a constructive force and we generally
support that approach.

3. Incentives for development of more and improved alterna-   18
tives to animal use:

   The object of all research must be that of uncovering facts   19
and truths, regardless of the approach. In science there are
enumerable "incentives for excellence and accuracy," in-

cluding various awards, recognition by learned societies, research grant support, authorship of books and scientific papers and perhaps most importantly, the acceptance and recognition of one's peers. As mentioned previously, alternatives to animal use have continually been developed, accepted and implemented based upon scientific validity, improvement of effectiveness, cost reduction and efficiency. It is questionable whether or not additional "incentives" can really be granted to stimulate the development of meaningful alternatives to animal use, especially if this is carried out without reference to whether or not such methods are scientifically useful in the understanding of human or animal disease or for predicting safety of drugs. If the approach necessitates the use of animals, the scientist must be sensitive to the animal's requirements. It is our belief that the continuing progress of scientific knowledge will continue, as it has in the past, to recognize, develop and implement such alternatives without artificial stimulants.

20 4. Responses from academic, private and public research institutions to problems raised by pending legislative proposals:

21 In reviewing the several bills now before the Congress, two are particularly worthy of comment. HR 556 is, in our opinion, an intrusion into the scientist's ability to use a wide variety of approaches based upon experience, experimental design and intended objectives. To artificially require deviation from accepted scientific principles would create a situation not unlike the Lysenko era in the Soviet Union. As presented, the bill would mandate a wholesale diversion of 30% to 50% of *all* federal research funds from existing, peer reviewed projects, thus jeopardizing the entire scientific research program of the nation. As objectionable as that mandate might be, the fundamental issue with the approach taken by the bill is that it fails to recognize innovative and creative scientific inquiry, mandating restrictions on what have proven to be the most fruitful approaches to biological and medical research since the advancement of the germ theory of disease.

22 HR 4406 proposes to amend the existing animal welfare act in a number of ways. Perhaps of greatest concern is the attempt to modify section 3(a) which would attempt to define "pain" in animals. It has been clearly demonstrated that the concept and interpretation of pain is exceptionally complex and clarification is not amendable by the sort of

definition proposed. In section 10, we object strongly to the recommendation that inspectors be given authority to "confiscate or destroy" animals which, in the sole judgment of the inspector are "suffering as a result of failure to comply with any provision—" unless the institution's animal care committee is convened. In the day to day working situation of a complex institution such as the University I serve, such a provision for the convening of a committee for immediate action is clearly fraught with impossible problems. Furthermore, the scientific qualifications of individual "inspectors" is and will probably always remain a questionable aspect.

5. Areas in which animal-based research or testing remains crucial to protection or enhancement of human health: 23

This topic must be addressed in a variety of ways and to adequately respond to the question would require a voluminous amount of data. I will, therefore, limit my observations but would be pleased to provide members of the Committee with additional information should that be helpful.   24

In the area of infectious disease, prior to advances in chemotherapy and vaccines, such diseases were the cause of most deaths in the industrialized world. Today, many have been reduced to the point where infectious disease ranks among the lowest causes of death. Biologic production and testing has always been dependent on animal use since only the complex, biologically interrelated systems of the whole animal can respond in a fashion indicative to that of man. Certain aspects of testing have been delegated to "alternatives" and where proven efficacious, these practices will continue and expand. Similarly, the toxic effects of many antibiotics and other chemotherapeutic agents have first been recognized through their application in animals. This method of testing is the only one endorsed by the FDA for human use and the USDA for animal use, for no acceptable alternatives currently exist which embody the total host response provided by animals. Relatively recent examples of the importance of such testings and the use of a variety of systems are found in the development of polio vaccine and the identification of thalidomide as a teratogen.   25

In the underdeveloped countries, many infectious diseases still account for tremendous morbidity and mortality. According to the 1980 World Health Organization Summary Reports, 200,000,000 people are affected by schistosomiasis; 100,000,000 by leishumaniasis with 400,000 new cases developing annually; 300–400,000,000 cases of malaria which   26 kills in excess of 1,000,000 children each year, and, 100,000,000 humans are affected by trypanosomiasis. It is estimated that the morbidity from these four diseases alone is four times the entire population of the United States. At the present time, there are no alternatives to the use of animals in demonstrating the host response to these infectious agents. Any severe reduction in the use of animals to continue important studies on these diseases, aimed at treatment and prevention, would severely impede the progress being made by many U.S. research institutions, including Cornell, thus prolonging the suffering and death of millions of humans throughout the world.

27   In the United States, hepatitis B infection remains an important cause of death and illness. Recent evidence indicates that infected individuals demonstrate a very high rate of developing cancer of the liver in later life. Outside of the United States, hepatitis is a major contributor to human suffering. At the present time, Cornell University, under contract from NIH, is developing an important animal model for hepatitis B virus research and vaccine testing using the feral woodchuck, *Marmota monax*. Should attempts be made to eliminate the use of this or other valuable animal models for hepatitis B research, it will severely impact the ability to develop a protective vaccine for man.

28   In spite of significant progress in treatment and control, leprosy remains a major world-wide disease with many cases occurring here in the United States. To date, the only method for studying the growth and establishment of infection of the causative agent is through the use of the armadillo. Continued research in this disease will be dependent on the use of this animal model.

29   The above examples are directed to human disease, yet it is important to recognize that millions of domestic animals are saved in the United States each year through the use of prophylactic vaccination. Recent United States Department of Agriculture figures show that in 1970, for every 10,000 poultry sent to slaughter, 158 poultry had Marek's Disease. In 1979, as the result of the development of a new vaccine, the incidence of Marek's Disease was reduced to 11 cases per 10,000 poultry. As an example of other control measures, in 1950, there were 1.4 cases of hog cholera per 10,000 animals. In 1979, this figure was reduced to zero. Hog cholera has been virtually eliminated. In 1950, there were .86 cases of cattle tuberculosis per 10,000 animals

slaughtered. This disease is transmissible to man. In 1979, cattle tuberculosis was reduced to .008 cases per 10,000, thus decreasing the prevalence of this disease by 1000-fold. A significant number of vaccines used in control of diseases of animals were developed and tested at Cornell University, the most recent being the canine parvovirus vaccine to protect against a new disease which simultaneously occurred in several parts of the world in 1978. Recognizing the tremendous number of dogs lost to this disease since 1978, and the significant distress this brought to animal owners, we question the wisdom of mandating discontinuing the use of living animals in such research.

In the area of non-infectious disease, the major cause of 30 mortality in the United States is that of diseases associated with the cardiovascular system. During the past three decades, animals have played an instrumental role in the development of new surgical, therapeutic and electronic devices which have played an enormous role in decreasing both mortality and morbidity. As an example, it is estimated that 50,000 coronary bypass operations take place annually in this country, thus relieving thousands suffering from pain and for many, prolonging their lives.

Cancer ranks second, after cardiovascular disease, as a 31 cause of death in America. Tremendous advances have been made in cancer chemotherapy and the public is just recognizing that permanent cures are now possible for many forms of cancer. Granted, much remains to be done in solving the ravages of this disease, but I must point out that all chemotherapeutic agents have first been tested in animals for signs of toxicity. Indeed, animals remain the key for further progress in our conquest of cancer.

Other diseases of significance in the United States have 32 likewise benefited from animal experimentation. Animal "models," or those animals in which similar if not identical disease syndromes exist, obviously represent a fertile source of investigation. In many instances, the information gained can be of direct benefit to the animal populations involved, thus preventing death or improving the quality of their lives. As examples, one can cite spontaneous systematic lupus erythematosus, rheumatoid arthritis, and hemolytic anemia. In the field of endocrinology we have benefited immensely from the use of animals to delineate the growth changes and bodily responses altered through disorders of the endocrine system. Such studies have shed new light on diseases such as thyroiditis, pituitary giantism, Cushing's syndrome, Addison's disease, and many others. The isolation, purification, testing and synthesis of a number of hormones have significantly influenced the lives of millions. Again, because of the complexities of the systems involved, only living animals manifest the full range of physiologic changes needed to develop, test and produce such compounds.

33   In diseases of the central nervous system, significant advances have been made in products such as lithium for patients with manic depression. At the present time, investigators at Cornell are testing several new synthetic lithium compounds in animals which promise to bring beneficial therapeutic effects without the severe toxicity currently encountered with the parent compound.

34   Chronic debilitating diseases, such as rheumatoid and osteoarthritis, have benefited greatly from animal research. During the past two decades, surgical procedures developed in animals have led to the production and implantation of total hip joint prosthetic devices, knees, and other bone replacements in man. Such devices have provided pain-free locomotion in thousands of Americans who were previously immobile.

35   The examples cited above are chosen merely to illustrate the importance of animal experimentation to relieve pain, suffering and death in both man and animals. The listing is representative of only a small portion of those diseases and disorders in which animals have made useful contributions to human medicine; most were selected because they are currently used or are under study at Cornell University; thus, I have personal knowledge concerning this work.

36   The Subcommittee should also be aware of the fact that, since World War II, there have been 52 Nobel Prize winners in medicine and physiology. Thirty-seven of these awards were achieved with NIH grants. We have had 21 Nobel Prize winners in chemistry; twelve of these received NIH support. Within the past few days, this year's Nobel Prize recipients were announced. Their scientific observations and discoveries were made by utilizing animal models — non-human primates. The science being conducted in this country is perhaps the finest in the world. Congress must strive to preserve the right of scientific freedom to insure continued creativity and excellence.

37   In this correspondence I have intended to be informative, yet to constructively criticize the various bills currently before the Subcommittee on Science, Research and Tech-

nology. We are aware that under certain conditions our research animals are subjected to painful procedures, yet we do everything possible to minimize the number of such procedures and to use drugs to abrogate pain. Rest assured that we agree that alternatives to living animals should be employed whenever appropriate and that science will continue, as it has in the past, the development of new alternative methods. It is our opinion that enactment of HR 930 or HR 220 would promote such alternatives without disrupting biomedical research. We wish to emphasize to the Committee the significant past achievements in biomedical science, many of which have been accomplished through the use of living animals, and stress the importance of their use in ongoing and future studies. Attempts to reduce the use of animals through restrictive legislation or through the imposition of unnecessary bureaucratic authority which extends beyond the time-tested, peer review system, would seriously impede efforts to improve the lives of both man and animals.

On behalf of the Association for Biomedical Research, 38 thank you for permitting me to comment on these issues.

Neal D. Barnard

Letter from the Physicians Committee for Responsible Medicine

The Physicians Committee for Responsible Medicine, an organization comprised mainly of physicians and dedicated to saving animals from pain and suffering in needless laboratory experiments, in 1990 sent out the following letter asking for support.

My Dear Friend:

If you're a friend of animals and oppose their unnecessary 1 suffering, I have good news for you. There's an effective force now working to end the needless, senseless cruelty against animals in laboratory experiments.

And *that growing force is coming from the medical commu-* 2 *nity itself.* It's called the Physicians Committee for Responsible Medicine.

3   With over 1,900 participating physicians, many believe PCRM is the vital ingredient needed to make the turnaround from animal experimentation to animal protection. Finally, *we have a powerful way to dispel — once and for all — the myth that good human health hinges upon animal testing.*

4   Even though you may not be a physician, you can take an important personal role in helping this precedent-setting group succeed. I'll tell you how you can do this in just a moment.

5   But first, please let me tell you about my own personal experiences as a physician. I have witnessed first-hand how medical research and training subject a wide variety of animals to cruel, even sadistic treatment. And I regret to say that what I have seen occurs in medical schools and research laboratories all across the country.

6   In medical school I was supposed to take part in a course where dogs were experimented on and killed — dogs just like 'Betsy,' a stray who I found one day on my way home from class. Seeing what I saw in these experiments and knowing what I knew about their results, I couldn't help but realize *how pointless was the extreme suffering these laboratory animals went through.*

7   I couldn't help but feel that *more humane methods could teach me exactly what I needed to know* from my studies. In fact, I actually devised an alternative using my textbook diagrams . . . passed the course . . . and am now on the faculty of that same medical school.

8   I have become more and more aware that *many* doctors share my concern. We *care about human health* and we know that *inhumane research on animals is simply not necessary* to protect it.

9   I hope you share our feelings about animal cruelty. That is why I have written to you today. You have a choice. You could either throw away this letter and turn a deaf ear and a blind eye to the matter . . . or you could learn the truth.

10   The facts you'll read in this letter are all true. *I challenge anyone in laboratory research to show otherwise.*

11   It's a fact, for example, that *animal experimentation has often misled experimenters.* Medications like thalidomide — which appeared safe in animals — have caused birth defects, disease, and death in humans.

12   It's a fact that there are existing *alternatives to animal*

testing that are safer, more economical, more effective, and far more humane.

It's a fact that *animals used in testing feel emotions* like 13 fear, anxiety, stress, pain, and loneliness—just as we do.

It's also a fact that many U.S. medical colleges don't 14 require students to experiment on animals in order to earn a degree.

Far too often, lab animals are caged in filthy, unhealthy 15 surroundings. Too often, they're ill-fed and treated with abuse. Too often, the laboratories in which they are kept are maintained in sub-standard conditions.

Imagine yourself witnessing experiments on animals in 16 such a laboratory. You watch as a chimpanzee is strapped onto a table and given electric shock. You watch as a cat has her head cut open and an implant set in her brain. You watch as a goat is shot with high velocity bullets so medical students can learn how to take care of wounds.

You watch as a dog has his limbs broken and reset . . . 17 or is force fed . . . or is made radioactive. Other animals are heartlessly burned, blinded, gassed, poisoned, infected with diseases. And in most cases, *no pain relief is given.*

The list of outrages goes on and on. 18

In this country alone, tens of millions of animals are used 19 *in laboratory experiments in such ways.* TENS OF MIL-LIONS! It's time for every man and woman of conscience to act to put a stop to this cruelty once and for all.

These laboratory experiments do not only produce inac- 20 curate, skewed results, *they're simply not necessary.* Thousands of physicians throughout the nation and the world (and their number is constantly growing!) are con-vinced that such cruelty is unessential.

As one distinguished cancer researcher put it, "While con- 21 flicting animal results have often delayed and hampered advances in the war on cancer, they have never produced a single substantial advance either in prevention or in the treatment of human cancer."

What's more, *EFFECTIVE ALTERNATIVE METHODS* 22 *can and have been used to teach physicians and conduct research without inflicting pain and death on animals.*

The Physicians Committee for Responsible Medicine is 23 leading the way in awakening both the medical community and the public to this fact.

Did you know, for example, that simulators and computer 24 models can be far more useful as teaching tools for medical students than operating on innocent animals? In fact, these models are among the most important advances in recent years in medical training programs.

25   Did you know that scientists can now test potential anti-cancer drugs on actual human cancer cells rather than on animals? Or that vaccines can now be produced in cell cultures rather than in animals? Yes, all true!

26   Until PCRM was formed, no animal protection group had reached out to rank and file physicians to use their expertise to fight animal experimentation. *Leaders in the drive for animal protection are convinced that this involvement by physicians is what is needed if we're going to bring about change.*

27   We know that when there's a proposed new law involving animals in laboratory work, decision-makers in Congress and in state legislatures heed the expert testimony of doctors.

28   Now, doctors from the Physicians Committee for Responsible Medicine can provide that testimony. We've already testified in several states and on Capitol Hill, and met with officials of the National Institutes of Health. (Up to now, labs have been able to get away with mistreating their animals because animal welfare laws have given no guidelines for animal experiments. None!)

29   We know that television and other media pay special attention to physicians' statements on matters of animal experimentation.

30   Now when the media need information, they turn to the Physicians Committee for Responsible Medicine for valid views. We've already appeared on many national television and radio shows enlightening millions about the issue of laboratory animal abuse.

31   We know that if there's any way to organize medical students against the use of animals in their lab work, it's through the Physicians Committee for Responsible Medicine.

32   *PCRM is, in fact, contacting ALL U.S. medical students, supporting their right to make their own decision regarding animal research.* Before, animal protection was not a subject students talked about in medical schools.

33   Now *for the first time*, thanks to PCRM, it's an issue medical students not only talk about, but *act on*. What's more, PCRM offers special fellowships for medical and veterinary student projects that will develop non-animal lab techniques.

34   There's no question about it. In just a few short years

since PCRM was formed in 1984, we've made extraordinary inroads in garnering support from medical circles.

Until recently, medical organizations have been uni-   35
formly against animal protection. PCRM has already had success in changing one leading medical association's attitude toward animal protection. And our network of physicians is calling and writing to their own professional organizations to get them to improve their policies about animal research.

But that's just the beginning.   36

We know that if we're going to succeed, we need to rein-   37
force the efforts of PCRM with public support—to unite ourselves with everyone in this country who cares about animal protection.

I hope that includes you—and that you will become a   38
Charter Sponsor of the Physicians Committee for Responsible Medicine.

PCRM *will* be effective. We know that already. How effec-   39
tive we'll be depends on caring people like you.

As a PCRM Charter sponsor, you'll be part of the impor-   40
tant team that *utilizes proven medical facts and expertise to stop the inhumane treatment of lab animals . . . to end needless animal experimentation . . . and to develop other methods that are effective in teaching and research.*

When you hear about the suffering of laboratory animals,   41
you can't help but feel angry and frustrated. "What can *I* do to stop it?" you ask yourself. Well, now there *is* something you can do. *It's one of the most effective things you can do.*

You can mail back the enclosed reply form today with   42
your tax-deductible contribution and become a Charter Sponsor of the Physicians Committee for Responsible Medicine. You'll find a postage-free return envelope provided for your convenience.

Your $50 contribution—or $25 or $100 or whatever   43
amount you can send—will be put to work immediately in our fight. And on behalf of all the animals you'll be saving from cruelty and death, allow me to say a very heartfelt "thank you."

Sincerely,

Neil D. Barnard, M.D.
Chairman

Jane Goodall
A Plea for the Chimpanzees

Jane Goodall, born in 1934 in London, from childhood aspired to study animals in Africa. Since the early 1960s she has studied chimpanzees and other primates in their natural habitat — the wilds of Tanzania. Now world-renowned for her books and articles, she makes television shows in cooperation with the National Geographic Society and continues to do research. The following essay appeared in The New York Times *in 1985.*

1   The chimpanzee is more like us, genetically, than any other animal. It is because of similarities in physiology, in biochemistry, and in the immune system that medical science makes use of the living bodies of chimpanzees in its search for cures and vaccines for a variety of human diseases.

2   There are also behavioral, psychological, and emotional similarities between chimpanzees and humans, resemblances so striking that they raise a serious ethical question: Are we justified in using an animal so close to us — an animal, moreover, that is highly endangered in its African forest home — as a human substitute in medical experimentation?

3   In the long run, we can hope that scientists will find ways of exploring human physiology and disease, and of testing cures and vaccines, that do not depend on the use of living animals of any sort. A number of steps in this direction already have been taken, prompted in large part by a growing public awareness of the suffering that is being inflicted on millions of animals. More and more people are beginning to realize that nonhuman animals — even rats and guinea pigs — are not just unfeeling machines but are capable of enjoying their lives, and of feeling fear, pain, and despair.

4   But until alternatives have been found, medical science will continue to use animals in the battle against human disease and suffering. And some of those animals will continue to be chimpanzees.

5   Because they share with us 99 percent of their genetic material, chimpanzees can be infected with some human diseases that do not infect other animals. They are currently being used in research on the nature of hepatitis non-A non-B, for example, and they continue to play a major role in the development of vaccines against hepatitis B.

Many biomedical laboratories are looking to the chim-   6
panzee to help them in the race to find a vaccine against
acquired immune deficiency syndrome. Chimpanzees are
not good models for AIDS research; although the AIDS virus
stays alive and replicates within the chimpanzee's
bloodstream, no chimp has yet come down with the disease
itself. Nevertheless, many of the scientists involved argue
that only by using chimpanzees can potential vaccines be
safely tested.

Given the scientists' professed need for animals in re-   7
search, let us turn aside from the sensitive ethical issue of
whether chimpanzees *should* be used in medical research,
and consider a more immediate issue: How are we treating
the chimpanzees that are actually being used?

Just after Christmas I watched, with shock, anger, and   8
anguish, a videotape—made by an animal rights group during a raid—revealing the conditions in a large biomedical
research laboratory, under contract to the National Institutes
of Health, in which various primates, including chimpanzees, are maintained. In late March, I was given permission
to visit the facility.

It was a visit I shall never forget. Room after room was   9
lined with small, bare cages, stacked one above the other,
in which monkeys circled round and round and chimpanzees sat huddled, far gone in depression and despair.

Young chimpanzees, three or four years old, were crammed,   10
two together, into tiny cages measuring 57 cm by 57 cm
and only 61 cm high. They could hardly turn around. Not
yet part of any experiment, they had been confined in these
cages for more than three months.

The chimps had each other for comfort, but they would   11
not remain together for long. Once they are infected, probably with hepatitis, they will be separated and placed in
another cage. And there they will remain, living in conditions of severe sensory deprivation, for the next several
years. During that time, they will become insane.

A juvenile female rocked from side to side, sealed off from   12
the outside world behind the glass doors of her metal isolation chamber. She was in semidarkness. All she could hear
was the incessant roar of air rushing through vents into
her prison.

In order to demonstrate the "good" relationship the lab's   13
caretaker had with this chimpanzee, one of the scientists
told him to lift her from the cage. The caretaker opened

the door. She sat, unmoving. He reached in. She did not greet him — nor did he greet her. As if drugged, she allowed him to take her out. She sat motionless in his arms. He did not speak to her, she did not look at him. He touched her lips briefly. He returned her to her cage. She sat again on the bars of the floor. The door closed.

14   I shall be haunted forever by her eyes, and by the eyes of the other infant chimpanzees I saw that day. Have you ever looked into the eyes of a person who, stressed beyond endurance, has given up, succumbed utterly to the crippling helplessness of despair? I once saw a little African boy whose whole family had been killed during the fighting in Burundi. He too looked out at the world, unseeing, from dull, blank eyes.

15   Though this particular laboratory may be one of the worst, from what I have learned, most of the other biomedical animal-research facilities are not much better. Yet only when one has some understanding of the true nature of the chimpanzee can the cruelty of these captive conditions be fully understood.

An Isolating Cage

16   Chimpanzees are very social by nature. Bonds between individuals, particularly between family members and close friends, can be affectionate and supportive, and can endure throughout their lives. The accidental separation of two friendly individuals can cause them intense distress. Indeed, the death of a mother may be such a psychological blow to her child that even if the child is five years old and no longer dependent on its mother's milk, it may pine away and die.

17   It is impossible to overemphasize the importance of friendly physical contact for the well-being of the chimpanzee. Again and again one can watch a frightened or tense individual relax if she is patted, kissed, or embraced reassuringly by a companion. Social grooming, which provides hours of close contact, is undoubtedly the single most important social activity.

18   Chimpanzees in their natural habitat are active for much of the day. They travel extensively within their territory, which can be as large as 50 km^2 for a community of about 50 individuals. If they hear other chimpanzees calling as

they move through the forest, or anticipate arriving at a good food source, they typically break into excited charging displays, racing along the ground, hurling sticks and rocks and shaking the vegetation. Youngsters, particularly, are full of energy, and spend long hours playing with one another or by themselves, leaping through the branches and gamboling along the ground. Adults sometimes join these games. Bunches of fruit, twigs, and rocks may be used as toys.

19   Chimpanzees enjoy comfort. They construct sleeping platforms each night, using a multitude of leafy twigs to make their beds soft. Often, too, they make little "pillows" on which to rest during a midday siesta.

20   Chimps are highly intelligent. They display cognitive abilities that were, until recently, thought to be unique to humans. They are capable of cross-modal transfer of information — that is, they can identify by touch an object they have previously only seen, and vice versa. They are capable of reasoned thought, generalization, abstraction, and symbolic representation. They have some concept of self. They have excellent memories and can, to some extent, plan for the future. They show a capacity for intentional communication that depends, in part, on their ability to understand the motives of the individuals with whom they are communicating.

21   Chimpanzees are capable of empathy and altruistic behavior. They show emotions that are undoubtedly similar, if not identical, to human emotions — joy, pleasure, contentment, anxiety, fear, and rage. They even have a sense of humor.

22   The chimpanzee child and the human child are alike in many ways: in their capacity for endless romping and fun; their curiosity; their ability to learn by observation, imitation, and practice; and, above all, their need for reassurance and love. When young chimpanzees are brought up in a human home and treated like human children, they learn to eat at table, to help themselves to snacks from the refrigerator, to sort and put away cutlery, to brush their teeth, to play with dolls, to switch on the television and select a program that interests them and watch it.

23   Young chimpanzees can easily learn over 200 signs of the American language of the deaf and use these signs to communicate meaningfully with humans and with one another. One youngster in the laboratory of Roger S. Fouts, a psychologist at Central Washington University, has picked up

68 signs from four older signing chimpanzee companions, with no coaching from humans. The chimp uses the signs in communication with other chimpanzees and with humans.

24   The chimpanzee facilities in most biomedical research laboratories allow for the expression of almost none of these activities and behaviors. They provide little — if anything — more than the warmth, food and water, and veterinary care required to sustain life. The psychological and emotional needs of these creatures are rarely catered to, and often not even acknowledged.

25   In most labs the chimpanzees are housed individually, one chimp to a cage, unless they are part of a breeding program. The standard size of each cage is about 7.6 m^2 and about 1.8 m high. In one facility, a cage described in the catalogue as "large," designed for a chimpanzee of up to 25 kg, measures 0.76 by 1.1 m, with a height of 1.6 m. Federal requirements for cage size are dependent on body size; infant chimpanzees, who are the most active, are often imprisoned in the smallest cages.

26   In most labs, the chimpanzees cannot even lie with their arms and legs outstretched. They are not let out to exercise. There is seldom anything for them to do other than eat, and then only when food is brought. The caretakers are usually too busy to pay attention to individual chimpanzees. The cages are bleak and sterile, with bars above, bars below, bars on every side. There is no comfort in them, no bedding. The chimps, infected with human disease, will often feel sick and miserable.

A Harmful System

27   What of the human beings who administer these facilities — the caretakers, veterinarians, and scientists who work at them? If they are decent, compassionate people, how can they condone, or even tolerate, the kind of conditions I have described?

28   They are, I believe, victims of a system that was set up long before the cognitive abilities and emotional needs of chimpanzees were understood. Newly employed staff members, equipped with a normal measure of compassion, may well be sickened by what they see. And, in fact, many of them do quit their jobs, unable to endure the suffering they see inflicted on the animals yet feeling powerless to help.

But others stay on and gradually come to accept the 29 cruelty, believing (or forcing themselves to believe) that it is an inevitable part of the struggle to reduce human suffering. Some become hard and callous in the process, in Shakespeare's words, "all pity choked with custom of fell deeds."

A handful of compassionate and dedicated caretakers and 30 veterinarians are fighting to improve the lot of the animals in their care. Veterinarians are often in a particularly difficult position, for if they stand firm and try to uphold high standards of humane care, they will not always be welcome in the lab.

Many of the scientists believe that a bleak, sterile, and 31 restricting environment is necessary for their research. The cages must be small, the scientists maintain, because otherwise it is too difficult to treat the chimpanzees — to inject them, to draw their blood, or to anesthetize them. Moreover, they are less likely to hurt themselves in small cages.

The cages must also be barren, with no bedding or toys, 32 say the scientists. This way, the chimpanzees are less likely to pick up diseases or parasites. Also, if things are lying about, the cages are harder to clean.

And the chimpanzees must be kept in isolation, the scien- 33 tists believe, to avoid the risk of cross-infection, particularly in hepatitis research.

Finally, of course, bigger cages, social groups, and elaborate 34 furnishings require more space, more caretakers — and more money. Perhaps, then, if we are to believe these researchers, it is not possible to improve conditions for chimpanzees imprisoned in biomedical research laboratories.

I believe not only that it *is* possible, but that improve- 35 ments are absolutely necessary. If we do not do something to help these creatures, we make a mockery of the whole concept of justice.

Quality of Life in the Laboratory

Perhaps the most important way we can improve the 36 quality of life of the laboratory chimps is to increase the number of carefully trained caretakers. These people should be selected for their understanding of animal behavior and their compassion and respect for, and dedication to, their charges. Each caretaker, having established a relationship

of trust with the chimpanzees in his care, should be allowed
to spend time with the animals over and above that required
for cleaning the cages and providing the animals with food
and water.

37   It has been shown that a chimpanzee who has a good
relationship with his caretaker will cooperate calmly during experimental procedures, rather than react with fear
or anger. At the Dutch Primate Center in Rijswijk, for example, some chimpanzees have been trained to leave their
group cage on command and move into small, single cages
for treatment. At the Stanford Primate Center in California,
a number of chimpanzees were taught to extend their arms
for the drawing of blood. In return they were given a food
reward.

38   Much can be done to alleviate the pain and distress felt
by younger chimpanzees during experimental procedures.
A youngster, for example, can be treated when in the presence of a trusted human friend. Experiments have shown
that young chimps react with high levels of distress if subjected to mild electric shocks when alone, but show almost
no fear or pain when held by a sympathetic caretaker.

39   What about cage size? Here we should emulate the ani-
mal-protection regulations that already exist in Switzerland. These laws stipulate that a cage must be, at minimum,
about 20 m^2 and 3 m high for pairs of chimpanzees.

40   The chimpanzees should never be housed alone unless
this is an essential part of the experimental procedure. For
chimps in solitary confinement, particularly youngsters,
three to four hours of friendly interaction with a caretaker
should be mandatory. A chimp taking part in hepatitis research, in which the risk of cross-infection is, I am told,
great, can be provided with a companion of a compatible
species if it doesn't infringe on existing regulations—a
rhesus monkey, for example, which cannot catch or pass
on the disease.

41   For healthy chimpanzees there should be little risk of
infection from bedding and toys. Stress and depression,
however, can have deleterious effects on their health. It is
known that clinically depressed humans are more prone to
a variety of physiological disorders, and heightened stress
can interfere with immune function. Given the chimpanzee's similarities to humans, it is not surprising that the
chimp in a typical laboratory, alone in his bleak cage, is
an easy prey to infections and parasites.

Thus, the chimpanzees also should be provided with a 42 rich and stimulating environment. Climbing apparatus should be obligatory. There should be many objects for them to play with or otherwise manipulate. A variety of simple devices designed to alleviate boredom could be produced quite cheaply. Unexpected food items will elicit great pleasure. If a few simple buttons in each cage were connected to a computer terminal, it would be possible for the chimpanzees to feel they at least have some control over their world — if one button produced a grape when pressed, another a drink, another a video picture. (The Canadian Council on Animal Care recommends the provision of television for primates in solitary confinement, or other means of enriching their environment.)

Without doubt, it will be considerable more costly to 43 maintain chimpanzees in the manner I have outlined. Should we begrudge them the extra dollars? We take from them their freedom, their health, and often their lives. Surely, the least we can do is try to provide them with some of the things that could make their imprisonment more bearable.

There are hopeful signs. I was immensely grateful to of- 44 ficials of the National Institutes of Health for allowing me to visit the primate facility, enabling me to see the conditions there and judge them for myself. And I was even more grateful for the fact that they gave me a great deal of time for serious discussions of the problem. Doors were opened and a dialogue begun. All who were present at the meetings agreed that, in light of present knowledge, it is indeed necessary to give chimpanzees a better deal in the labs.

I have had the privilege of working among wild, free 45 chimpanzees for more than 26 years. I have gained a deep understanding of chimpanzee nature. Chimpanzees have given me so much in my life. The least I can do is to speak out for the hundreds of chimpanzees who, right now, sit hunched, miserable and without hope, staring out with dead eyes from their metal prisons. They cannot speak for themselves.

The following excerpts from Garry B. Trudeau's "Doonesbury" appeared around Christmas 1989. For more of his work, and more on Mr. Trudeau, see page 70.

WHAT TO DO ABOUT
ACID RAIN?

Dixy Lee Ray
The Great Acid Rain Debate

Dixy Lee Ray, former governor of Washington and former chair of the Atomic Energy Commission, wrote the following essay for The American Spectator *in 1987.*

The Great Acid Rain Debate has been going on for more 1 than a decade. Public alarm in the United States probably dates from a widely publicized 1974 report which concluded that "the northeastern U.S. has an extensive and severe acid precipitation problem." Does it? Probably not. Is rain really acidic? Yes. Does acid rain, or preferably, acid precipitation, really damage forests, lakes and streams, fish, buildings and monuments? Yes, in some instances, but not as the primary or only cause. Can the adverse environmental effects that have been attributed to acid rain — whatever the real cause — be mitigated by reducing the amount of sulfur dioxide emitted to the atmosphere from industrial sources? No, what evidence there is suggests that it cannot be. Is enough known, and understood, about acid precipitation to warrant spending billions of dollars of public funds on supposed corrective measures? Certainly not.

Clearly, the U.S. Environmental Protection Agency agrees 2 with this assessment, for the agency's administrator, Lee M. Thomas, said in 1986: "Current scientific data suggest that environmental damage would not worsen materially if acidic emissions continued at their present levels for ten or twenty more years. Acid rain is a serious problem, but it is not an emergency."

That rain is acidic has been known for a long time. Among 3 the first records are a reference to acid rain in Sweden in 1848 and a discussion on the chemistry of English rain in 1872. Sulfur dioxide was established as a possible cause of

967

damage to trees and other plants in Germany in 1867. The commonly repeated alarm that rainfall has become increasingly acidic over the past twenty-five years rests for its validity on an influential and oft-cited series of articles by G. E. Likens and his co-workers published in the 1970s. Careful evaluation by a group of scientists at Environmental Research and Technology Inc. reveals that Likens's research suffered from problems in data collection and analysis, errors in calculations, questionable averaging of some data, selection of results to support the desired conclusions, and failure to consider all the available data. In a more recent study, Vaclav Smil of the University of Manitoba reached similar conclusions. Besides analyzing Likens's methods of determining rain acidity, Smil examined maps of the distribution of acid precipitation in the eastern U.S. between the mid-1950s and the mid-1960s, prepared by Likens et al. and publicized as providing "unassailable proofs" of rising acidity. "In reality," Smil concludes, "the measurement errors, incompatibility of collection and analytical procedures, inappropriate extrapolations, weather effects and local interferences, make such maps very dubious."

4   Rain forms when molecules of water vapor condense on ice crystals or salt crystals or minute particles of dust in clouds and then coalesce to form droplets that respond to the force of gravity. As rain falls through the atmosphere it can "pick up" or "wash out" chemicals or other foreign materials or pollutants that may be present. Because water is such a good solvent, even in the cleanest air, rainwater dissolves some of the naturally present carbon dioxide, forming carbonic acid. Hence, rainwater is *always acidic* or if you like, acid rain is normal. There is no such thing as naturally neutral rainwater. Scientific studies generally distinguish between "acid rain," i.e., the acidity of rainwater itself, and "acid deposition," i.e., the fallout of sulfates, nitrates, and other acidic substances. Acid deposition may be "wet" if washed out of the atmosphere with rain, or "dry" if gases or particles simply settle out.

5   How acidic is pure water? Despite the fact that water molecules are very stable, with a chemical composition of two parts hydrogen to one part oxygen (H_2O), the molecular structure or architecture is somewhat asymmetrical; the molecules tend both to clump and to dissociate in response to intermolecular forces. Dissociation leads to a few hydrogen ions carrying a positive charge and an equal number

of OH or hydroxyl ions with a negative charge. Under normal conditions, in pure distilled water only a few molecules are dissociated, in fact, about two–ten millionths of one percent. Now 2/10,000,000 of 1 percent is an awkward numerical expression. Therefore, for greater ease in expressing the number of dissociated molecules, which is the measure of relative acidity, a method called pH has been adopted. The pH of pure water is 7, the numerical expression of neutrality. Any pH measure below 7 is acidic, any above 7 is basic or alkaline. The pH scale is logarithmic (like the Richter scale for measuring intensity of earthquakes); therefore a change of one pH unit, for example, from pH 5 to pH 6, is a ten-fold change.

Water in the atmosphere normally contains some carbonic acid from dissolved carbon dioxide, and the pH of clean rainwater even in pristine regions of the earth is about pH 5.0 to 5.5.[1] Any lower pH is believed to be environmentally damaging. Lakes, streams, rivers, ponds, indeed all bodies of fresh water may and usually do receive dissolved material, either acidic or alkaline, from runoff and from the soil or earthen basin in which the water stands or flows. Both acid and alkaline lakes are natural phenomena, and exist without intervention by humans.   6

Getting an accurate measure of the pH of rainwater is more difficult than it may at first seem. Certainly it is no simple litmus test; accurate procedures require careful laboratory analyses. For example, early work — that is, measurements taken before 1968 — generally used soft glass containers; it is now known that even when the containers were carefully cleaned and when the analysis was done very soon after collection, the soft glass contributed alkalinity to the sample, and this increased with time in storage. Indeed the range of error attributable to the use of soft glass is sufficient so that it might account for the difference in pH measurements between 1955–56 and 1965–66 reported by Coghill and Likens. Rainwater collection made in metal gauges, a common procedure before the 1960s, also influenced the results. An experiment to test this difference, using a dilute solution of sulfuric acid with a pH of 4.39, gave a reading of pH 5.9 when held for a short time in a metal gauge.   7

It is also now known that a rainwater sample taken at   8

[1]The pH of clean rainwater compares to that of carrots (pH 5.0), and lies between the acidity of spinach (pH 5.4) and bananas (pH 4.6). Rainwater is far less acidic, for example, then cola drinks (pH 2.2).

the beginning of a storm will give a pH reading different from that taken during and at the end of the rainfall; that measurements may differ widely at different locales within a region; and that weather and climate affect the results. With regard to this last phenomenon, it may be that the more alkaline results reported by Likens for the northeast U.S. in the 1950s were related to the drought conditions that prevailed during those years. By contrast, the 1960s were rainy. When dry conditions persist, dust particles are more prevalent, and if they are present in the rain samples, they can neutralize some of the acidity and shift the pH toward the alkaline end of the scale.

9   For several reasons, then, it now appears that the historical data, on which so much of the alarm and worry has been based, are of insufficient quality and quantity to establish as indisputable a trend toward higher acidity in the rainfall of the northeastern United States.

10   Complicating the acid rain picture still further are results of samples recently collected from ice frozen in the geological past, and from rainfall in remote regions of the earth. These results suggest that the relationship between acidity and the industrial production of sulfur dioxide emissions is at best extremely tenuous.

11   Analysis of ice pack samples in the Antarctic and in the Himalayas indicates that precipitation deposited at intervals hundreds and thousands of years ago in those pristine environments had a pH value of 4.4 to 4.8. Some measurements were as low as 4.2. Examination of Greenland icepack samples shows that many times in the last 7,000 years the acidity of the rain was as high as pH 4.4. In some cases the periods of extremely high acidity lasted for a year or more. Coal burning utilities spewing out sulfur dioxide could not have been responsible, but these periods of high acidity do correspond to times of major volcanic eruptions. Also remarkable is the period of low acidity in the ice lasting from 1920 to 1960, when no major volcanic eruptions occurred but industrial pollution increased.

12   Recent measurements taken by the National Oceanic and Atmospheric Administration on Mauna Loa in Hawaii at 3,500 meters above sea level gave average pH values of 4.9 regardless of wind direction. Moreover, sampling at Cape Matatula on American Samoa, a monitoring site selected for its extreme cleanliness, resulted in measurements from pH 4.5 to 6.0 in the rainwater.

To gather more systematic data on the pH of rain in   13
remote areas, a Global Precipitation Chemistry Project was
set up in 1979. Samples of rainwater were tested from five
sites: Northern Australia, Southern Venezuela, Central
Alaska, Bermuda, and Amsterdam Island in the southern
Indian Ocean halfway between Africa and Australia. The
first results were published in 1982. Precipitation was
everywhere acidic, pH values averaging between 4.8 and
5.0. Now it is possible to imagine that the Bermuda results
could have been affected by long range transport of sulfate
aerosols or other atmospheric pollution from the U.S., or
that Alaskan atmosphere is polluted from coal burning in
the Midwest, but that does not appear to be reasonable. At
the remaining sites, including American Samoa, clearly
man-made emissions could not have caused the measured
acidity.

Conversely, in some areas where one might expect a low   14
pH, actual measurements of the rainwater reveal higher
than anticipated pH values. Twelve sites in Mexico, for
example, measured pH 6.2 to 6.8; nine inland sites in India
gave a median pH of 7.5 (range 5.8 to 8.9). It turns out that
the expected natural acidity of the rain is neutralized by
suspended alkaline particles, mainly dust from dry fields,
unpaved streets, and so on.

In China seventy percent of the basic energy comes from   15
burning coal; sulfur dioxide releases are very high, particularly in urban areas. Rainwater in Peking is nevertheless
close to neutral, most values falling between pH 6.0 and
7.0. Interestingly, the same samples have heavy concentrations of sulfate and nitrate ions as well as suspended alkaline matter, probably dust blown from desert regions.
The pH is determined by complex interaction among these
aerosols, ions, and particles.

Acid rain can also be buffered or neutralized by soil con-   16
ditions. Recent studies at nearly 200 sites in the United
States show that in the northern Great Plains high levels
of calcium and magnesium ions occur, along with ammonia
associated with animal husbandry and fertilizers. These
combine to neutralize acidic precipitation. In the western
half of North America 75 to 96 percent of all acid anions
are so neutralized. By way of contrast, in the northeastern
U.S. 52 percent of all acid anions are not so neutralized.

It might be that lower levels of alkaline dust, especially   17
in the northeast, are a consequence of successful air pollution control, resulting in the effective capture of particulate

matter from industrial smoke. This possibility was investigated in 1985 by Smil, who reports a great loss of airborne alkaline material between the mid-1950s and mid-1960s. This loss resulted from large scale replacement of coal as fuel for homes, transportation, and industrial boilers, as well as highly efficient removal of fly ash from flue gases. Although exact and accurate calculations are not possible, reasonable estimates of the largely alkaline particulate emissions were about nine million tons annually in the 1950s; this fell to about four million tons by 1975. Actually the total loss of man-made alkaline material over the northeast was probably much larger than the estimates indicate since emission controls were also applied to the iron, steel, and cement industries. And the amount of barren, dusty land shrank with advancing settlements, paved roads, lawns, and considerable re-growth of forests. Another contributing factor to loss of alkaline materials may have been the practice of prompt extinction of forest fires. Wildfires, when left to burn themselves out, result in an accumulation of alkaline ash, which, together with the minerals it contains, acts to buffer natural acidity in the soil and redress the mineral imbalance.

18   One final point should be made about natural acidity and alkalinity. Soils along the North Pacific coast tend to be quite acidic, a usual feature in areas that had been glaciated. Peat bogs are common; cranberries, huckleberries, blueberries, and Douglas Fir trees — all requiring acid soil — are abundant. For comparison, soils in the arid west and southwest are alkaline, and rarely measure a pH below 9.0. By contrast the soils in New England are among the most acid in the world. Representative Adirondack soil measures pH 3.4. Soils in southeast Canada are similar. That region also was glaciated, and the thin poor soil overlays acid granitic material. In other words, the soils of the northeast United States are by nature acidic, and always have been, environmentalist claims notwithstanding.

19   There is an extensive and growing body of scientific literature on atmospheric chemistry, much of it highly technical. Gradually, understanding is also growing, but many areas of uncertainty remain. Experts are divided on exactly how acids are formed in clouds, in rainwater, and upon deposition. There is some disagreement too on the relative amount and importance of acid precursors from man-made

versus natural sources. Most knowledgeable scientists tend to take a middle view, that the amount of pollutants in the air, particularly of sulfates and nitrates, on a global scale comes about equally from natural and human sources, but even this is a supposition or educated guess.

Natural Sources

Sulfur and nitrogen compounds—the "acid" in acid rain— 20 are produced naturally by the decay of organic matter in swamps, wetlands, intertidal areas, and shallow waters of the oceans. How much is contributed to the atmosphere from these sources is not known for certain, but it is considerable. Estimates of naturally produced sulfates and other sulfur compounds are from 35 percent to 85 percent of the total—a rather wide range!—and naturally occurring nitrogen compounds are generally believed to be 40 percent to 60 percent of the total. Some experts go further and claim that nature contributes over 90 percent of the global nitrogen. Considering the additional sulfur that emanates from volcanoes and fumaroles and hot springs and ocean spray, and the nitrogen fixed by lightning, the generally accepted contribution from natural sources may be underestimated.

The contribution of lightning to the acidity of rain is 21 significant. Two strokes of lightning over one square kilometer (four-tenths of a square mile) produce enough nitric acid to make eight-tenths of an inch of rain with a pH of 3.5. In fact, it has been estimated that lightning creates enough nitric acid so that annual rainfall over the world's land surfaces would average pH 5.0 even without taking into account other natural sources of acidity.

The contribution of volcanoes to atmospheric sulfur diox- 22 ide seems never to have been taken seriously; acknowledged, yes—but then dismissed as trivial. Perhaps this is related to the fact that volcanoes are studied by geologists and vulcanologists rather than by atmospheric scientists. Or perhaps it's because volcanic mountains tend to be where meteorologists are not. Predicting exactly when an eruption will occur is notoriously undependable, and obtaining direct measurements or samples of ejecta during eruptions is dangerous and can be fatal. During the daylong eruption of Mt. St. Helens on May 18, 1980, over four billion tons of material were ejected. Although large quantities of gases, including sulfur dioxide, were released to the atmosphere, no direct measurements could be made during the major eruption itself. Before May 18, in the period March 29 to May 14, spectroscopic measurements revealed about forty tons per day of sulfur dioxide. By May 25 measuring was resumed and showed 130 to 260 tons per day. On June 6 this increased abruptly to 1,000 tons per day. From the end of June through December of that year the rates of sulfur dioxide ranged from 500 tons per day to 3,400 tons per day. Sulfur dioxide, hydrogen sulfide, carbon disulfide, and other sulfur compounds continue to be released from the crater floor and dome, and arise also from fumaroles and the debris of pyroclastic flows.

23　　El Chicon, an exceptionally acidic and sulfurous mountain in Mexico, erupted in early 1982, far more violently than Mt. St. Helens. Materials ejected reached the stratosphere and will probably affect the atmosphere for many years. Again no direct measurements were possible, but it is estimated that twenty million tons of sulfur dioxide were released. Also in the northern hemisphere, Mt. St. Augustine in Alaska erupted twice in 1986 with sulfur fumes detectable in Anchorage many miles away. Sulfur fumes continue to seep from both El Chicon and St. Augustine.

24　　In 1973 two scientists, Stoiber and Jepson, reported data on sulfur dioxide emissions from Central American volcanoes, obtained both by remote sensing and by calculation. They conclude that 10,000 metric tons of sulfur dioxide are released to the atmosphere daily. Extrapolating worldwide, they calculate that volcanoes are responsible for emitting annually about 100 million metric tons of sulfur compounds. Thus nature is responsible for putting large quantities of sulfates and nitrates into the atmosphere.

Man-Made Sources

25　　But so, of course, is man. Industrial activity, transportation, and burning fossil fuel for commercial and domestic purposes all contribute sulfate, nitrates, and other pollutants to the atmosphere. Since passage of the Clean Air Act in 1970 there has been an overall reduction of more than 40 percent in factory and utility sulfur dioxide production. But as sulfur dioxide emissions decrease, nitrogen emissions are increasing, primarily from oil burning and oil used in transportation. Industrial society also produces other air pollutants, including volatile organic compounds, ammonia, and hydrocarbons. Any of these may contribute to the formation of acid rain, either singly or in combination. Further, some man-made pollutants can undergo photo-oxidation in sunlight, leading, for example, to the conversion of sulfur dioxide to highly toxic sulfur trioxide. But even this compound, should it be deposited over the ocean, loses its toxicity due to the extraordinarily high buffering capacity of sea water.

26   Another photo oxidant, ozone, is possibly the most damaging of all air pollutants derived from human activity. Ozone accumulates in quantities toxic to vegetation in all industrial regions of the world. Ozone is a product of photochemical oxidation between oxides of nitrogen and volatile organic substances. The latter may be unburned hydrocarbons (e.g., from automobile exhaust in cars not equipped with catalytic converters) or various organic solvents. Ozone is known to cause severe injury and even death to certain forest trees. The best known cases are the decline of white pine in much of eastern North America and ponderosa and Jeffrey pine in the San Bernardino Mountains of California. Ozone acts synergistically with other pollutants and has been shown to cause damage to agricultural crops when exposure occurs along with sulfur and nitrogen oxides.

27   Thus, singling out sulfur dioxide produced by human activities as the major cause of acid rain is not only a gross over-simplification, but probably wrong.

Effects on Forests

28   What about the dying forests? Here again the acid rain activists blame sulfur dioxide produced by industry.

29   Trees, like every other living thing, are not immortal. They too grow old and die. The decline of a forest may be part of the slow but natural process of plant succession, or it may be initiated by any of several stress-causing factors. Each forest and each tree species responds differently to environmental insults, whether natural or human. As Professor Paul D. Mannion of the State University of New York has said: "If one recognizes the complex array of factors that can contribute to the decline of trees, it is difficult to

accept the hypothesis that air pollutants are the basis of our tree decline problems today . . . [although] to question the popular opinion on the cause of our decline problems is not to suggest that pollutants do not produce any effect."

30   Widespread mortality of forest trees has occurred at times and places where pollution stress was probably not a factor. Declines of western white pine in the 1930s and yellow birch in the 1940s and fifties, for example, were induced by drought, while secondary invasion by insects or other disease organisms is most often the ultimate cause of fatality.

31   Currently the most widely publicized forest decline problem in the U.S. is the red spruce forest in the northern Appalachian Mountains. Few people now cite the widespread mortality in red spruce between 1871 and 1890. The dieback occurred at roughly the same time in West Virginia, New York, Vermont, New Hampshire, Maine and New Brunswick, and was then attributed to the invasion of a spruce beetle that followed some other stress. What that was is not clear.

32   Today the dieback symptoms of the red spruce are most pronounced above 900 meters in an environment that is subject to natural stresses such as wind, winter cold, nutrient-poor soils, and possible high levels of pollutants, heavy metals, and acidity in the clouds that often envelop the forest. The relative importance of each of these stresses has not been rigorously investigated.

33   The affected trees grow in one of the windiest locations in North America. It is known that wind can dry out or even remove red spruce foliage, especially if rime ice has formed; it can also cause root damage by excessive tree movements. Tree ring analyses indicate a possible relation between recent cold winters and decline. The abnormal cold extending into spring may have caused the trees to be more susceptible to the adverse effects of pollutants. Arthur H. Johnson and Samuel B. MacLaughlin, who have studied tree rings and the red spruce forest decline, conclude in *Acid Deposition: Long Term Trends* (National Academy Press, 1986) that "there is no indication now that acidic deposition is an important factor in red spruce decline . . . . The abrupt and synchronous changes in ring width and wood density patterns across such a wide area seem more likely to be related to climate than to air pollution." Air borne chemicals might play a role, but they will have to be further assessed.

And then there are the dying forests of Germany. Whereas 34
originally the focus was on acid precipitation and deposition of sulfur dioxide and to a lesser extent nitrogen oxides,
emphasis has now shifted to the oxides of nitrogen, hydrocarbons, soil minerals such as aluminum and magnesium,
and photo oxidants, chiefly ozone. Sulfur dioxide emissions
have been declining in Germany since the mid-1970s, due
mainly to the substitution of nuclear energy for coal burning in the production of electricity. But this decline was
not accompanied by improvement in the health of forests,
suggesting that other factors may be implicated. It is now
believed that only in exceptional cases does sulfur dioxide
cause direct damage to forests in Germany. But motor vehicle pollution from more than 27 million autos and trucks
is among the highest in the world in density per area, and
is considered to be a contributing factor to the formation
of ozone. Indeed, ozone levels in Germany's damaged forests
are often remarkably high. Long-term measurements indicate that the mean value of ozone concentration has increased by one-third over the last twenty years. And the
investigators at the Norwegian Forest Research Institute
have reached similar conclusions about the importance of
ozone in forest declines.

The adoption of the catalytic converter for automobiles 35
in America was primarily to control the release of unburned
hydrocarbons in order to reduce the photochemical production of ozone. In this it has functioned well, although it has
also led to formation of formaldehyde and larger amounts
of acid, especially sulfuric acid. But there is another source
of atmospheric hydrocarbons that has not been controlled —
cows! American cows burp about fifty million tons of hydrocarbons to the atmosphere annually! There is no known control technology for these emissions. Whether they contribute
to ozone formation is also not known, but their presence helps
to emphasize the complexity of atmospheric chemistry.

Effects on Lakes and Fish

There are three kinds of naturally occurring acidic lakes: 36
1) those associated with inorganic acids in geothermal areas
(i.e., Yellowstone Park) and sulfur springs (pH 2.0 to 3.0);
2) those found in peat lands, cypress swamps, and rain
forests where the acidity is derived from organic acids

leached from humus and decaying vegetation (pH 3.5 to
5.0); and 3) those located in areas of weather resistant granitic or silicious bedrock. Only the last-named are involved
in the acid rain question. In these lakes and streams, the
absence of carbonate rocks means little natural buffering
capacity. This type of naturally acidic lake is common in
large areas of eastern Canada and the northeastern United
States, where glaciers exposed granitic bedrock during the
last period of glaciation. The lakes are called "sensitive"
because they may readily become further acidified with
adverse impacts on aquatic organisms, of which fish are
the most important to man. Indeed the most widely proclaimed complaint about the consequence of acid deposition is the reduction or elimination of fish populations in
response to surface water acidification.

37   But again, this is not a recent phenomenon. Dead lakes
are not new. A study by the New York State Department
of Environmental Conservation reveals that the stocking of
fish in twelve lakes was attempted and failed as early as
the 1920s. Of course, many people did catch fish in the
1920s and 1930s in lakes where fish are not available today.
But the fact is that during those years many of the Adirondack lakes were being stocked annually by the Fish and
Game Commission; fish did not propagate, and the stocking
program was discontinued about 1940.

38   In the United States 219 lakes have been identified as
too acidic to support fish. Two hundred and six of these
lakes are in the Adirondacks, but they account for only four
percent of the lake surface of New York state alone. This,
then, is hardly a national problem; it is local. The same
applies to southeast Canada, where the highest percentage
of acid lakes is located.

39   Uncertainty continues whether these acid lakes have always had a low pH or whether human activities have reduced
the neutralizing capability of the waters, or the lake basin.
A range of human activities could be to blame: use of chemical
pesticides to control spruce budworm or black fly infestations,
changes in fish hatchery production, change in angler pressure, lumbering, burning of watersheds. On the other hand,
declining fish populations were noted in some New York
lakes as early as 1918, and bottom sediments deposited
eight hundred years ago in Scandinavian lakes are more
acid than today's sediments.

40   To conclude that a decline in fish population is caused

by atmospheric acid deposition, it must be established that the lake formerly supported a viable fish population; one or more species of fish formerly present has been reduced or lost; the lake is more acidic now than it was when the fish were present; the increased acid level was not caused by local factors; and other factors, e.g., toxic chemicals, are not present or are unimportant.

Such data are rare. Studies on three lakes in the Adiron- 41 dacks—Panther, Sagamore, and Woods Lake, which are remote but close enough together to be affected by the same rainfall—disclosed radically different degrees of acidity, large differences that can be accounted for by the varying geological makeup of the three lake beds and local, surrounding soils and vegetation.

Outside the Adirondack Mountains and New York state, 42 many emotional claims have been made about fish kills in Canada, Norway, and Sweden. Most of the losses are reported in the spring; in Scandinavia fish kills have been reported annually in the springtime for more than one hundred years. This recurring natural phenomenon is likely due to oxygen depletion or to snow melt and rain runoff carrying sudden high concentrations of many materials into lakes and streams, and in fact, the acidity of most waters is greatest in the spring. Modern findings call into question the claim that distant sources of sulfur dioxide are responsible for the growing acidity of waters hundreds of miles away.

Using trace elements, Dr. Kenneth Rahn of the University 43 of Rhode Island has found that it is local pollution sources, mostly residual fuel oil burned for domestic, commercial, and industrial purposes in New England, that are the main cause of added acidity in rain and snow. A meteorological team from the University of Stockholm cautioned the Swedish people not to blame acid rain on emissions from England; they found that local sources accounted for local acid rain. Great Britain, incidentally, has reduced sulfur dioxide emissions by more than 30 percent since 1970 with no effect whatever on the acidity of lakes or rain in Scandinavia. In New York City, EPA scientists traced elevated sulfur dioxide and sulfuric acid in the wintertime to the burning of oil in the 35,000 oil burners of the city's apartment houses. European scientists at the Organization for Economic and Cooperative Development, in Paris, have reached the same conclusion; the most revealing result of

an extensive project is that every source region affects itself
more than any other region.

Effects on Man-Made Structures

44   The impact of air borne pollutants and acid rain on deterioration of buildings, monuments, and man-made materials
is also predominantly a local phenomenon. It is at least as
complex as the effects on the natural environment. And,
like forests and lakes, every site is specific and every material different. Few generalizations are possible; fewer still
stand up under careful scrutiny. Of course metals corrode,
marble and limestone weather, masonry and concrete de-
teriorate, paint erodes, and so on; but the conditions and
substances that lead to loss of integrity vary widely. Perhaps
the only statement that can be made is that moisture is
essential, that deterioration results more from acid deposition than from acid rain, and that local sources are more
important than possible long-range transport of pollutants.

45   Yet belief persists that acid rain from "someplace else"
is destroying cultural monuments. Perhaps the most egregious example is the damage to the granite Egyptian
obelisk, "Cleopatra's Needle," located since 1881 in New
York City's Central Park. It has been claimed that "the city's
atmosphere has done more damage than three and one half
millennia in the desert, and in another dozen years the
hieroglyphs will probably disappear." A careful study of
the monument's complex history, however, makes it clear
that the damage can be attributed to advanced salt decay,
the high humidity of the New York climate, and unfortunate
attempts at preservation. There is no question but that acid
deposition causes incremental damage to materials, but far
more research is needed before reliable surface protection
systems can be developed.

46   At the very least, the historical record of dramatic fluctuations in rain acidity, and episodes of environmental damage that cannot be attributed to industrial pollution; the
evidence that natural events such as drought and abnormal
cold can be important factors in environmental deterioration; the probability that compounds other than sulfur
dioxide (e.g., ozone) are responsible for causing damage to
plant life; the complex interactions among the many chem-

icals, aerosols, and other substances in the atmosphere and upon deposition; the likelihood that local sources are responsible for local effects; and the fact that there is no real, direct evidence that long distance transport of sulfur dioxide causes acid rain problems in New England, should make Congress very cautious about committing public funds to ill-conceived "solutions" to an ill-defined problem. At best, proposed federal programs constitute, in the words of Dr. S. Fred Singer of the National Advisory Committee on Oceans and Atmosphere, a multibillion dollar solution to a multimillion dollar problem.

One federal program that fits this description is a plan developed last summer by Drew Lewis and William Davis, special envoys for the United States and Canada, respectively. Under this plan, the U.S. will spend $2.5 billion of federal funds and $2.5 billion from U.S. industry to demonstrate how to burn high sulfur coal and release less sulfur dioxide to the atmosphere. Burning low sulfur coal was not proposed because that would "impose significant socioeconomic costs on high sulfur coal miners, their families and their communities." According to EPA administrator Lee N. Thomas, the $5 billion program will be a proper "first step toward the goal of a solution to North America's acid rain problem."[2] There is no reason to believe that the proposed solution will solve or even contribute to solving the perceived problem.   47

Despite reports to the contrary in the popular press, the Committee on Atmosphere and Biosphere of the National Research Council–National Academy of Sciences did *not* conclude in its 1981 report that a 50 percent reduction in sulfur dioxide from factories and utilities in the Midwest would significantly reduce environmental problems attributed to acid rain in the northeast. This misinterpretation was pointed out in the 1983 NRC-NAS report for the Environmental Studies Board, which concluded: "The relative contributions of such long range effects and of more local regional effects are currently unknown and cannot be reliably estimated using currently available models." The only   48

---

[2]This statement, which appeared in the *EPA Journal* (June/July 1986), is particularly curious, since in the same article Mr. Thomas also says: "it is difficult, if not impossible, to predict with any certainty to what extent acid deposition in any specific area would be reduced by emission controls on any specific sources."

change since this position was reached is the growing evidence of the past three years that local sources predominantly influence local effects.

49   Nevertheless, industrial activities generally and coal burning in particular put pollutants into the atmosphere, and what goes up must come down — somewhere. It is reasonable therefore to require, as the Clean Air Act does, that emissions of sulfur dioxide and other pollutants be reduced. It is also reasonable to spend federal funds to collect accurate data and to continue efforts to understand the problem of acid deposition in all its complexity. What is not reasonable is the requirement by a Congress impatient for immediate results that all coal-burning utilities must use expensive flue gas scrubbers regardless of whether the coal complies with federal standards or not. With even less reason the 1977 amendments to the Clean Air Act require that the sulfur content of all coal be reduced by the same specified percentage. It seems not to matter, under this law, that low sulfur western coal still goes into the scrubbers cleaner than high sulfur eastern coal comes out of them. What apparently does matter is that the top eight polluting states have large high sulfur coal reserves and high economic dependence on mining it. They are represented in the House of Representatives by about 105 votes. By contrast western, low sulfur coal is dominated by two states, Montana with two votes and Wyoming with one.

50   But even this pales to insignificance beside legislation considered by the 99th Congress, HR 4567. This bill had about 160 co-sponsors and was approved by the House Energy Subcommittee on Health and the Environment on July 20, 1986. It called for significant further reductions of sulfur dioxide emissions from utilities, industries, and motor vehicles, and nitrogen oxides were also to be reduced along with hydrocarbons, particulates, and carbon monoxide. The greatest burden would have fallen on utilities, and therefore the greatest effect would have been to drive up electricity rates. For this reason subsidies were to be provided to keep rates from rising more than 10 percent. Also proposed was a nationwide fee on all electrical generation. Department of Energy estimates put the cost of HR 4567 at a minimum of $2.5 billion to $8 billion annually. Others calculated that the costs could exceed $15 billion a year. TVA reported that the bill would drive up their electric rates by 12–14 percent, while Ohio Power's residential cus-

tomers would pay 34 percent more and industry 44 percent more. The bill was opposed by the Administration, utilities, industry including coal mining, automobile manufacturers, and some members of Congress. Although the 99th Congress adjourned without taking action on this or other acid rain bills, the sponsors have vowed to try again when the new Congress convenes in January.

Department of Energy Secretary Herrington, in tes-   51
timony before Congress in June 1986, pointed out (as have all responsible scientific reports) that "there is no evidence to suggest that the problem [of acid rain] is urgent or getting worse." Why then the big push to spend billions — not on research so that we may know what we're doing, but on supposed controls that no one can say will be effective? The Great Acid Rain Debate goes on . . . and on.

George Reiger

What Can Be Done About Acid Rain?

George Reiger (born in 1939 in Brooklyn) has written several books and a great many articles for outdoor magazines. Marine conservation is a particular interest of his. Currently he serves as an editor for Field and Stream, *where he published the following essay in 1987.*

All major environmental crises seem to go through four   1
stages. The first is one of discovery. A research team or a solitary worker perceives a problem and begins accumulating data about its causes and effects. Acid rain historian Robert H. Boyle writes that "acid rain as such was first described as a local phenomenon in England in 1852 by Robert Angus Smith, who did his research in and around the industrialized city of Manchester. Smith blamed the sulfuric acid in the city air for the rusting of metals and the fading of colors in dyed goods."

The next stage occurs when the problem is acknowledged   2

by a majority of the scientific community. In the case of acid rain, this took more than a century after Smith's initial work, but today's research has come to involve everyone from meteorologists to microbiologists.

3   As early as 1895, Norwegian observers began documenting a decline in fish populations in the southern lakes of their country, and as early as 1905, trout had vanished completely from several lakes where they had flourished before the industrial revolution. However, it wasn't until after World War II that Swedish soil, forestry, and meteorological scientists proved the connection between industrialization, acid rain, and the resulting deterioration of · "downstream" air and water.

4   Still, as Bob Boyle writes, "a thundering silence" greeted the evidence. Additional findings in the 1950's and 1960's on both sides of the North Atlantic did little to alter public apathy. Most people seem to feel that since our modern economy depends on an ever-increasing human population educated from birth to be better consumers than citizens, and that since a visionary has not yet shown us how we can satisfy both our appetite for more things and our need for a healthy environment, we'll simply put off worrying about our need while catering to our appetite.

5   As long as pollution is reckoned to be part of the cost of upward mobility and national security, people seem to display an amazing tolerance for degraded land, air, and water, even though scientists warn of the dangers of complacency.

6   It is at this stage in the evolution of the environmental crisis that the press begins to play an increasingly important role by publicizing each new scientific finding and each new example of environmental degradation. In the case of the present acid rain crisis, now in this third phase of development, concerned technicians and economists are placing increasing emphasis on the overall social cost of worsening air quality. Their understanding of the problem has moved many of them from positions of "scientific objectivity" to partisan commitment, and it is from such concerned scientists that we journalists get much of our information.

7   Actually, this third stage was entered a few years ago as more and more agricultural publications featured articles about the harm that acid rain causes plant life; architectural magazines began to concentrate on the damage inflicted by acid rain on buildings and historic monuments; and outdoor journals such as *Field & Stream* focused on the subtle harm of acid rain to gamefish fry, which need to

feed on microorganisms and invertebrates that can no longer live in acidified watersheds. More recently, the equally harmful effects of acid rain on waterfowl production has also been recognized as a major cause in the decline of species that breed in areas hard hit by the high acidity.

At this stage, a businessman who is also a sportsman 8 may not *want* to think about acid rain in his workaday existence, but he is increasingly *forced* to face the issue because of his interest in sport. He may tell himself for a while that the decline of black ducks and Atlantic salmon, for example, is due to many factors. But as we better regulate the commercial harvest of salmon or eliminate the incidental mortality of black ducks due to lead shot ingestion and still see these species declining, it becomes increasingly evident that acid rain is a major stumbling block to the restoration of any sport linked to productive freshwater. No matter how much money a businessman has, there is no place left in the Northern Hemisphere where he can find recreation that is not impacted to one degree or another by acid rain.

The final phase in the evolution of an environmental crisis 9 comes about when the public is finally persuaded that it will cost society far more to continue ignoring the problem than it will to try to do something about it. We should be entering this phase now, except that first our political leaders and press must convince the public that something *can* be done about the problem. Unfortunately, so far as acid rain is concerned, the public is not yet convinced.

It does no good for conservationists to point to the partial 10 restoration of the Great Lakes as an example of what can be done through a large-scale regional effort. The partial restoration of the Great Lakes was largely a matter of cleaning up point sources of pollution in selected areas of a relatively few states and provinces.

By contrast, although most sources of acid rain can also 11 be pinpointed, they include petroleum-powered vehicles, coal-fired power plants, and Freon-associated refrigerators and air-conditioners. Unfortunately, every modern economy is based on a growing demand for transportation, refrigeration, and electricity. As the dream of safe and inexpensive nuclear energy fades, and as the cost of oil again begins to climb, most nations will find themselves burning more coal which, with our presently inadequate anti-pollution devices, will mean more acid rain.

There is no longer any doubt that since the advent of the 12 industrial age, carbon dioxide levels have risen everywhere in the world. The only question is how long it will take (or has it already occurred?) for the increasing levels of CO_2 to affect global climate, possibly causing the polar icecaps to melt and flooding *billions* of people presently living on the coastal plains.

13   Likewise, there is no longer any doubt that ozone, which helps screen the earth from excessive solar radiation but which also damages many forms of life, is decreasing where it is most needed (in the stratosphere) and increasing where it is least wanted (in the troposphere, the lower reaches of the atmosphere). The only debate among scientists is whether the growing "ozone hole" above Antarctica is a result of industrial pollution or whether it is caused by a changing climate, perhaps resulting from the CO_2-inspired "greenhouse effect."

14   This debate seems as irrelevant as asking which came first, the chicken or the egg, since the point is that both chickens and eggs exist as well as, unfortunately, increasing CO_2 and decreasing stratospheric ozone.

15   Until recently, acid rain was perceived as exclusively a product of industrial smokestacks and vehicular exhaust pipes. Today, however, many atmospheric chemists suggest that acid rain is only one effect of a global alteration of the air we breathe.

16   "We see about a 2 percent increase in smog ozone from a 1 percent decrease in stratospheric ozone," says Gary Z. Whitten of Systems Applications Inc. of San Raphael, California. This suggests that the risks to plants, fish, wildlife, and human health from acid rain may be growing much faster than what is implied by the gradual increase of sulfur dioxide, nitrogen oxides, and other chemical pollutants in the atmosphere.

17   It also suggests that the escalating increase in the atmospheric production of hydrogen peroxide due to the increase of smog ozone will lead to dramatically increased acid rain over the next quarter century. Our children may look back on our presently poor air quality as a standard to which they aspire in their own efforts to restore the environment.

18   Michael Gery, also with Systems Applications Inc., reports that there might be as much as "an 80 percent increase in hydrogen peroxide production for each 1 percent decrease in stratospheric ozone." If this is so, most other researchers have grossly underestimated not only the extent

of our smog and acid rain dilemma, but the eventual cost of rehabilitation.

Indeed, much of the damage currently assumed to be the work of regional acid rain may actually be the result of stratospheric ozone depletion. Researchers at the Yale School of Forestry and at Michigan Technological University discovered a 16 to 19 percent stunting in the growth of several key species of trees exposed to outdoor ozone levels well within the current federal air-quality limit. Such stunting is alarming to foresters around the world, not only because it is happening around the world, but because, as Deane Wang of the University of Washington's Center for Urban Horticulture in Seattle notes, ozone- and acid-rain-damaged trees have less capacity than "normal" trees to resist stress—be it in the form of harsh weather, insects, or disease. 19

Although some people still insist that the entire acid rain issue is inconsequential—Dixy Lee Ray, former chairperson of the Atomic Energy Commission and former Governor of Washington State, recently wrote that "rainwater is *always acidic*, or if you like, acid rain is normal"—most scientists and engineers now argue only over what can be done to alleviate the problem. So far, the consensus seems to be "not very much" as long as we continue with "business as usual." 20

What does this mean? Basically, the same thing it has meant for years. We must stop talking and begin to do what we can to eliminate sources of acid rain where we can. We must reduce the emission of acid rain precursors at smokestacks and exhaust pipes. However, this is not going to be easy. 21

Two years ago, David C. Pierce of Rome, New York, sent a letter to *Field & Stream*'s "Cheers & Jeers" pointing out that the electrostatic precipitators promoted by utility companies and the federal government as the surest way to reduce air pollution were actually contributing to greater unseen air pollution by removing the soot and fly ash that had formerly helped neutralize much of the acid-forming oxides generated by coal burning. 22

When this letter was brought to the attention of the Environmental Protection Agency, administrators indicated that they were officially skeptical about the existence of acid rain and felt cleaning up the visible problems of soot and ash was sufficient. This Administration continues to 23 trickle a few million dollars a year into "more research" on whether or not there is a problem in order to avoid spending the billions of dollars that an increasing army of scientists feels must eventually be spent to correct the rapidly escalating problem of air pollution. This past January, for example, the U.S. Forest Service provided a grant, which could eventually amount to $1.7 million, to Penn State University to study the effects of acid rain on Pennsylvanian forests over the next four years.

24   We don't need any more redundant research designed to muzzle scientists and placate critics. And we don't need any more cosmetic solutions like electrostatic precipitators. Had we spent as much time studying the viability of space exploration as we have in reconfirming what researchers understood about acid rain half a century ago, we would still be contemplating a mission to the moon!

25   Surely a nation that has sent space probes to the farthest reaches of the solar system can come up with an effective way to remove the oxides of sulfur and nitrogen from industrial exhausts. And surely a nation that is now planning manned missions to Mars can find some substitute for Freon in refrigerators and air conditioners.

26   Of course, we must demand greater knowledge and better conscience from our politicians and journalists about what's at stake. So long as our opinion makers do not question the traditional parameters of Gross National Production, we will go on thinking that paving more farm fields for more roads for more cars and clearing more woods and filling more swamps for more housing is our only proper course when it is now abundantly clear that short-term profit and convenience lead to long-term environmental decay and human disease.

27   Can something be done about atmospheric pollution and acid rain?

28   Yes, but not so long as we keep on spending our research dollars on studies of the problem rather than searches for some solutions, and imagining that there is no middle road between mindless mass production and economic stagnation.

29   Obviously, we cannot return to a "state of nature," free of cars, power plants, air conditioners, and the like. Our entire society is built around these technological entities. But we must recognize the damage being done by the residues of this technology, and put all our intelligence and resources to work finding less harmful substitutes or remedies.

30   First, however, it must be acknowledged that a problem

exists, and that a "middle road" solution can be sought. Judging by the amount of official foot-dragging that has been going on for years, getting any real movement on this issue will be difficult. Yet with enough pressure from ordinary citizens it can be done. The sooner all of us move into the final stage of environmental awareness, the sooner the job of rehabilitating our fragile atmospheric envelope can begin.

The Latest Official Report on Acid Rain

In response to growing concern about acid rain, Congress in 1980 created the National Acid Precipitation Assessment Program (NAPAP). Its purpose is to coordinate research efforts and to assess the extent of acid rain. Excerpts from NAPAP's 1986 and 1987 annual reports follow; they were published in Consumers' Research *in 1988.*

1   Acid rain in the amounts and concentrations that occur over the entire United States would appear to have no significant effects on the yield of most, if not all, agricultural crops.

2   Levels of sulfur dioxide and nitrogen dioxide gases (the two main ingredients of acid rain) that have been reported to cause crop damage in controlled studies rarely occur in the rural United States. The interactive effects of the two pollutants may cause damage to some crops in a few local situations such as near a smelter with uncontrolled emissions.

3   Acidic deposition at present levels may have a modest net benefit to cropland by providing needed nitrogen and sulfur to the soil.

4   According to data from the National Crop Loss Assessment Network (NCLAN), ozone at current levels in the United States reduces the yield of most agricultural crops compared to yields in charcoal-filtered air. National agricultural crop production is estimated to be reduced on average by at least 5% due to anthropogenically-produced ozone. According to the NCLAN Program, this translates to a loss of potential crop value on the order of $1 billion.

Effects on Forests

5   As with agricultural crops, there appears to be no significant foliar effect on seedlings. Because seedlings have, pro-
portionally, more sensitive leaf or needle tissue than mature
trees, foliar effects on mature trees would not be expected
to be more severe than on seedlings. Therefore, forests are
probably relatively unaffected by ambient acidity in rain
on their foliage at low elevations or even in the mist of
above-cloud base forests. However, effects of acidic deposition mediated through soils have not been resolved.

6   Forests in the United States are probably stressed to some
extent by ambient ozone levels. At low elevation, this may
be reflected in growth suppression without visible injury.
In the Northeast, growth reductions are reported for red
spruce at lower elevations. Tree ring and standard plot
studies of pines in coastal plain and piedmont provinces of
the Southeast, and on hardwood and conifers in large areas
of the Northeast show a reduction of growth over the past
few decades. There are differences of opinion whether this
can be accounted for solely by natural processes or whether
air pollution makes a contribution.

7   The growth of the loblolly pine seedlings is reduced by
ozone, and the magnitude of this response varies among
families. But generally, the height, diameter, and total
biomass decreased as ozone concentrations increased.

8   The mountaintop forests in the Appalachians (above
cloud base), which show obvious decline, experience a
higher average daily ozone concentration than adjacent
forests at low elevation. Further, the trees are enshrouded
in mist about half the time. Experiments with crops have
shown that ozone damage increases with average humidity,
reaching a maximum with continuous nightly mist.

9   Hydrogen peroxide may cause additional significant
stress contributing to the decline of the above-cloud-base
in forests.

10   Historical data on high elevation spruce-fir forests of the
Southeast show that major disturbances in the past were
caused by railroad logging, windstorms, slash fires, grazing,
and balsam woolly aphid. These disturbances can change
species composition, age distribution, site quality, and
forest health in general, depending on the time and location.
The more that is known about each one and its effects, the
clearer the role of air pollutants will be.

All low-elevation New England forest tree species inves- 11
tigated are growing at rates equal to or exceeding those
prior to 1960, with the exception of the red spruce and
balsam fir. Recent studies have identified a definite decline
in basal area growth rates of stands (60 to 75 years old) of
red spruce and balsam fir starting about 1960. It was once
suspected that the decline was associated with acid rain.

However, a recent analysis of tree ring data indicated 12
that stand aging is playing a major role in these growth
declines in low-elevation forests. These data showed that
most low-elevation red spruce stands are functionally even-
aged as the result of harvesting and spruce budworm infestations after the turn of the century. These stands have now
attained an age when a natural reduction in growth rate
is expected.

Effects on Lakes

The current chemical condition of Eastern lakes is now 13
known on a broad regional scale for the first time. Based
on the number of low pH (the lower the pH, the higher the
acidity) in several subregions also receiving high sulfur deposition, it is expected that acidic deposition has played a
role in their current condition. There is currently no evidence to suggest that regional scale chronic acidification
has occurred in Western lakes.

There is increasingly clear evidence that sulfate deposition 14
influences sulfate concentrations in surface waters. However,
the relationship may be quite different in areas receiving
similar deposition, for example, the Adirondacks versus
the Southern Appalachians, suggesting the importance of
watershed characteristics in controlling acidification.

Bedrock composition appears to be the major watershed 15
property affecting surface water chemistry in five watersheds in western Maryland and Virginia. One small stream
flowing on pure quartzite bedrock and overlying quartz
sand soil showed the stream pH at 4.5 with average local
rain at 4.2. For these watersheds, the less reactive the bedrock and associated soil, the more acidic a system will become under similar deposition levels.

Episodic inputs of acidic deposition from snow-melt or 16
storm events can produce short-term pulses of reduced pH
in streams and lakes. In well-buffered lake systems, these

episodes may not be injurious to fish health. In other cases, the pH may be lowered enough for a sufficient period to reduce fish populations. Peaks due to heavy rainfall from naturally acid soil have also been observed and have caused fish mortality in a fish hatchery.

17   For lakes and streams with low pH, the chemical environment can be improved by periodic liming to provide a suitable habitat for brook trout and lake sports fish. Experiments in the United Kingdom and Scandinavia and model studies in Wisconsin have shown that liming a watershed has more long-term benefit to the condition of an acidic lake system than direct liming of the lakes. In most instances, healthy fish populations can be restocked.

Effects on Materials

18   A wide variety of man-made and naturally occurring materials are used in all types of building projects. These materials are subjected to fluctuating natural environmental factors, including temperature, wind, humidity, rain, dew, snow, and solar radiation, all of which may contribute to their gradual deterioration.

19   In addition, in many locations these materials are also subjected to variable quantities of man-made oxidants (such as ozone), acid precursor gases (such as oxides of sulfur and nitrogen), particulate matter, and acidic rainfall. Depending on their concentration, some of these pollutants may add a significant increment to the deterioration of certain materials.

20   The problem is first to measure quantitatively the incremental effect on a particular material and second, to determine if this effect causes a significant decrease in the normal time of replacement or repair. If this is the case, an economic value can be placed on the reduction of the pollutant. This process is a complicated one, and, to date, has not been completed for any material.

Acid Rain's Sources

21   Within the United States, sulfur dioxide (SO_2) and oxides of nitrogen (NO_x) are emitted mainly by electricity generation, transportation, and other fuel-burning processes.

Transportation, petroleum refining, chemical manufacturing, and paint and solvent use are the major sources of volatile organic compounds (VOCs), some of which help transform sulfur dioxide and nitrogen oxides to acidic compounds in the atmosphere.

Natural sources such as soils, tidal areas, ocean waters, dust storms, and lightning discharges may also be important contributors to these emissions. Natural sources contribute significantly to the total VOC emissions, and possibly to NO_x emissions. 22

Sulfur dioxide emissions in the United States increased from about 10 million tons per year in 1900 to more than 20 million tons per year in 1925. After peaks in 1944 and the early 1970's, SO_2 emissions in 1986 are about the same as 1930–21 million metric tons per year. 23

Man-made emissions of SO_2 in the United States have decreased by about 28% since reaching a peak in 1973. Since 1975, national SO_2 emissions from coal-fired power plants have decreased by 10%, while coal consumption has increased by 70%. In the Northeast, these emissions have dropped by 19% while coal consumption has increased by 24%. 24

Seventy percent of SO_2 emissions come from the utility sector, and in 1980 about 94% of these emissions came from plants that were not subject to the EPA New Source Performance Standards (NSPS), which require use of lower sulfur flues or flue-gas desulfurization. As old power plants reach the end of their economic life and are repowered or replaced by new NSPS plants, the emissions of SO_2 will decrease. 25

Atmospheric Chemistry

The total amount of SO_2 derived from natural emissions is estimated to be about 2 million tons. In the Eastern United States, natural source contributions to the total emissions of sulfur are negligible (approximately 0.1%). 26

The total natural NO_x emissions are estimated to be about 3 million tons per year. At present, natural sources of NO_x are a minor contributor to the total in the Eastern United States. In more remote areas (e.g., the Northwest), natural sources of NO_x play a more important role. 27

Results of studies in Pennsylvania emphasized the influence of natural emissions, primarily of VOC, on the produc- 28 tion of ozone at a rural site in the East. Most ozone in the lower atmosphere is produced through photochemical reactions that involve simultaneously both NO_x and VOC as the major precursors. Previous studies have established that anthropogenic emissions are the major source of NO_x over rural areas in the Eastern United States.

29   The dominant source of hydrogen peroxide (H_2O_2) is photochemical reactions in the atmosphere. Hydrogen peroxide is a compound of considerable interest because it may affect tree growth and because of its role in the oxidation of SO_2 in cloud water. Hydrogen peroxide concentrations can be relatively high in summer, sometimes greater, sometimes less than sulfur dioxide concentrations. In winter, H_2O_2 concentrations are typically quite low.

30   In the Northeastern United States, the acidity of rain is two to three times greater in the summer than the winter due primarily to increased concentrations of hydrogen peroxide in the clouds. The nitric acid component of wet deposition is relatively constant through the seasons.

31   The annual average concentrations of SO_2 and NO_x in the urban environment are at least a factor of 10 greater than in rural areas. The average acidity of rain in the New York City area is about 50% greater than in surrounding rural areas, according to a recent study. This may be true for other cities as well.

Jon R. Luoma
Acid Murder No Longer a Mystery

Jon R. Luoma, a native of Michigan's Upper Peninsula and now Director of Public Information for the Pollution Control Agency in Minnesota, often writes about acid rain; a book on the subject was published in 1984. Many of his essays—including the one printed here (1988)—have appeared in Audubon *magazine, a publication on nature and the environment.*

It's been nearly a decade since acid rain surged into news 1
media and public consciousness with reports from scientists that the rains and snows — once symbols of purity —
could quite literally poison entire freshwater ecosystems.
Captured in huge weather systems, acid-forming pollutants
could travel hundreds, or even thousands, of miles from
their sources to pollute waters across state or national boundaries.

Now, a near-decade and hundreds of millions of research 2
dollars later, concerns about acid rain have broadened to
include threats to wider regions of freshwater lakes and
streams, threats to forests, and threats to public health. A
clear scientific consensus that acid rain is at least a long-
term threat to some aquatic ecosystems has solidified.

In many other ways, very little has changed. The key 3
sources of acid rain remain sulfur dioxide from poorly controlled fossil-fuel-burning powerplants and nitrogen oxides
from a range of combustion sources, including industrial
furnaces and cars. The responsible industries, citing high
costs, steadfastly oppose tighter controls, instead calling
for more research.

Attempts at federally legislating new controls may have 4
faltered because the pathways of acidification are initially
so subtle that widespread damage is not evident. Chemical
compounds naturally present in even some of the most sensitive lakes, streams, and watersheds can neutralize acids,
often for many years. Only when those neutralizers are used
up will a lake quite suddenly begin to turn acid. And although lakes with little remaining neutralizing capacity
number in the tens of thousands in North America, lakes
actually acidified to date number only in the hundreds.
Similarly, research scientists have learned that visible
symptoms of forest destruction become obvious only after
damage is well under way.

What follows is a compendium of new developments on 5
the acid rain front.

News from Mount Mitchell

When *Audubon* last visited Mount Mitchell in North 6
Carolina ("Forests Are Dying, but Is Acid Rain to Blame?"
March 1987), plant pathologist Robert I. Bruck was specu-
lating that it might be many years before he had enough

data to make clear projections about whether acid rain — or any kind of air pollution — was causing the forest devastation there, so complex was the issue. He said that he'd let us know when he felt scientifically confident to make a bold statement — maybe a decade hence.

7   "Time's up," Bruck fairly growled in a telephone interview from his prefab headquarters on the 6,684-foot mountain this summer. "You would not believe how this place has changed even in the time since you were up here."

8   As it turns out, Bruck and a team of scientists, with their networks of towers, collectors, monitors, tubes, and wires laced through the skeletal trees, have discovered persistent high levels of pollutants — notably ozone and atmospheric acids — that appear to correlate strongly to a forest die-off that has increased by some 30 percent since we visited the mountain.

9   "It's plain," he says, "that no one has proved, or ever will, that air pollution is killing the trees up here. But far more quickly than we ever expected, we've ended up with a highly correlated bunch of data — high levels of air pollution correlated to a decline we're watching in progress."

10   A trip up Mount Mitchell, eastern North America's highest peak, is a thumbnail experience of the kind of biotic transition one might see on a 1,500-mile automobile journey northward from the sultry southeastern United States to frigid Labrador. Although Mount Mitchell sits at about the same latitude as California's Mojave Desert, the trees on and around the blustery mountaintop are hardy near-Arctic species, red spruce and Fraser fir.

11   And like many of the ridgetop trees along the entire stretch of the Appalachians — like trees in many of the forests of Europe — they are in evident decline. During my 1986 visit, the fir forest at the summit was eerily dominated by death — stark, brown hulks and deadfalls creaking in the ever-present wind.

12   According to Bruck, it has gotten worse. The damage extends even further down the mountain into more of the pure red spruce stands and, in some cases, all the way down to the line where hardwood forests begin. According to other reports, Appalachian spruce–fir forests from the White Mountains in New Hampshire to the Great Smokies south of Mount Mitchell are showing signs of reduced growth and general decline.

13   The information gathered during the federally funded

mega-study that Bruck has been coordinating on Mount Mitchell has him saying that he is "ninety percent certain" that air pollutants are killing the southern Appalachian ridgetop spruce and fir forests.

Two years ago Bruck was wondering if some other factor 14 or complex of factors — insects, fungi, climate, or even forest management practices — might be responsible.

But his data now show that more than half of the time 15 ozone levels on the mountain exceed those at which tree damage has been proven to occur in controlled laboratory studies. Frequently, levels increase to more than double the minimum damage limit. Acidity in the clouds that bathe the summit of the mountain eight out of every ten days has also been extraordinary: ranging from a worst case of pH 2.12 to a best case of 2.9. In other words, on the *best* days of cloud cover, acidity has been somewhat more than that of vinegar.

"Let me tell you about an experiment thirty yards from 16 where I'm sitting on top of the mountain," Bruck said. He described a set of large outdoor chambers, sealed in clear plastic to create a controlled greenhouse, in which young trees have been placed. The usual, and apparently polluted, mountain air is pumped into one chamber without alteration. A second chamber receives mountain air filtered through activated carbon, which removes ozone and some other pollutants. "We set up that experiment only six weeks ago. We're already getting fifty percent growth suppression in the chamber receiving ambient [unfiltered] air."

He also reports that the research team noted widespread 17 burning of new needle-tips on conifers after particularly acid air masses passed through. Analysis of the burnt needles in Environmental Protection Agency laboratories revealed extremely high levels of sulfate, a compound associated with acid rain.

Mountaintops are subject to greater pollutant deposits 18 because they are frequently bathed in polluted cloud water. Extensive forest destruction in Europe began in the 1970s on the mountaintops but has extended to stands at lower altitudes. Many scientists studying the problem feel that air pollution does not kill trees directly but rather weakens them to the point where, like punch-drunk fighters, they are no longer able to withstand normal episodes of moderate drought or insects or diseases that they could otherwise easily resist.

Killer Moss, Acid Soils

19   Now come reports from field researchers of problems stemming from acid mosses and acid soils.

20   Lee Klinger, working with the National Center for Atmospheric Research in Boulder, Colorado, claims to have correlated forest diebacks with the presence of three kinds of mosses: sphagnum, polystrichum, and aulocomnium. He says that the mosses alone are not killing trees but were virtually always present in more than a hundred dying forests that he examined, and that they appear to be a key part of a forest death syndrome.

21   The mosses produce organic acids which appear to gang up with inorganic acids in polluted rain to mobilize aluminum naturally present but harmlessly bound up in most soils. Additional aluminum appears to be falling out of the atmosphere bound to dust particles. The mobilized aluminum is toxic to the fine feeder roots of most trees. In fact, says Klinger, mats of killer mosses inevitably overlay networks of dead feeder roots. Furthermore, sphagnum acts as a sponge, saturating the soil just beneath the moss and creating an anaerobic, or oxygen-starved, soil environment, which also helps kill roots. The mosses, he says, occur naturally in forests and may even be part of an extremely slow plant-succession process that, over centuries or millennia, turns old forests to bogs. But the present moss invasion appears to be promoted and greatly speeded up by acidic rainfall.

22   "In general," Klinger says, "mosses require acid conditions for their establishment — so it appears that as the soils become acidified, there are more places for the mosses to get established." He also suggests that nitrates that form from nitrogen oxide pollutants in the rain fertilize the mosses, which have no roots but are entirely nourished by atmospheric chemicals.

23   Meanwhile, some scientists have begun to change their minds about acid soils. Until recently, most researchers looking into acid rain's terrestrial effects have assumed that trees and other plants growing in naturally acid soils — including trees found in many northern coniferous forests— had more resistance to pollutants.

24   But now Daniel Richter of Duke University reports that his laboratory experiments show that naturally acid soils, such as those often found at high elevations in parts of the

Appalachians, are highly sensitive to chemical imbalances caused by the addition of more acids from precipitation. According to Richter, highly acid forest soils that become further acidified can become virtually "infertile" through a complex series of chemical reactions that deprives them of nutrients. At the same time, the soils are assaulted by an overload of mobilized and root-toxic aluminum.

It Keeps Getting Worse

New York was one of the first states to become deeply   25
concerned about the effects that acid rain could have on its surface waters, and particularly on the pristine but poorly buffered lakes of the huge and beautiful Adirondack Park. In the 1970s the New York Department of Environmental Conservation jolted the conservation community by reporting that more than two hundred lakes, most of them in the western Adirondacks, had already become too acidic for fish to survive, and that many more appeared to be threatened.

In a new study, three years in the making, the New York   26
DEC reports that fully 25 percent of the lakes and ponds in the Adirondack Mountains are now so acidic that they cannot support fish life. Another 20 percent have lost most of their acid-buffering capacity and therefore appear doomed if acid input continues.

Massachusetts has reported that almost 20 percent — or   27
about eight hundred — of the state's ponds, lakes, and rivers are vulnerable to acid deposition and could become acidified within the next forty years. Already, according to Environmental Affairs Secretary James Hoyte, surveys have located 217 acidified bodies of water that cannot support natural communities. Particularly alarming to state officials is data showing that more than 50 percent of the state's thirty-four drinking-water reservoirs have lost much of their acid-buffering capacity since 1940. The largest of these, Quabbin Reservoir, has lost about three-fourths of its buffering capacity, and the Massachusetts Executive Office of Environmental Affairs now estimates that twenty years remain before the reservoir loses all of its capacity to handle acids. Acidification tends to occur within a few years after buffering capacity is lost.

Meanwhile, Environmental Protection Agency research-   28

ers, in a recent report, have identified new and surprising acidification sites in the mid-Atlantic states of Virginia, Delaware, Pennsylvania, Maryland, and West Virginia. The report shows that 2.7 percent of sampled stream miles in the mid-Atlantic region are already acidic, with the afflicted number as high as 10 percent at higher elevations. Despite the fact that rain acidity levels in the region are among the highest in the nation, it has long been assumed that soils in much of the mid-Atlantic could buffer the acidity effectively. The study notes that the stream damage is "probably associated with atmospheric acid deposition."

29   The Pennsylvania Fish Commission estimated in 1987 that half the state's streams will not be able to support fish life by the year 2000 unless acid deposits decline. Now seventy-eight of the two hundred members of the Pennsylvania House of Representatives are co-sponsoring a bill to slash emissions of sulfur dioxide by more than half, in a program that would be phased in over a period of thirteen years.

30   Pennsylvania has long been in an acid rain quandary. Its emissions of sulfur dioxide are the second worst in the nation, and both its industrial emitters and its powerful coal industry have strongly opposed regulation. But unlike many other high-emission areas, which contain few easily acidified waters, the state has long recognized that many of its woodland streams are acid-sensitive. Pennsylvania government insiders expect vigorous opposition from the pollution lobby on the bill: The state coal association issued a statement immediately after the bill was introduced pointing to government "facts" that watershed acidification was not going to get any worse.

Fertilizing Chesapeake Bay

31   Two-thirds of the excess acidity in precipitation falling on the eastern United States comes from sulfur dioxide. So SO_2 has long occupied the attention of most of those concerned with the problem.

32   But a new study from the Environmental Defense Fund points out that there are plenty of reasons to be concerned about oxides of nitrogen, which not only produce the other one-third of the acid rain problem but are key to the formation of ground-level ozone. (While ozone in the stratosphere is, indeed, necessary to shield the Earth from excess ul-

traviolet radiation, low-level ozone is not only a health hazard but a proven multibillion-dollar destroyer of agricultural crops and, possibly, forests.)

The EDF study looked at neither of those aspects of nitrogen oxides, but rather at their ability also to function as fertilizers — in this case, unwanted fertilizers of the already pollution-ravaged Chesapeake Bay. The resulting report, based on data from government studies, calculated that one-fourth of the total nitrogen entering Chesapeake Bay comes from excess atmospheric nitrogen oxides, which are produced by combustion in automobile engines, in powerplant furnaces, and in virtually all high-temperature burners. 33

The deposited nitrogen, in turn, is one of the key nutrient pollutants feeding algae in the waters of Chesapeake Bay — to such an extent that biological oxygen demand is up and water quality and fish and shellfish survival are down. The entire process is accelerating eutrophication, a rapid and premature aging process in the bay. 34

According to EDF's analysis, the nitrogen input to the bay from air pollution exceeds the contribution from sewage-treatment-plant effluents and, in fact, exceeds the contribution from all sources but agricultural fertilizer runoff. Although the study was limited to Chesapeake Bay, it suggests that other bays and estuaries may also be suffering from the fertilizing effects of nitrogen raining from the skies. 35

An Honest Federal Summary?

In the history of acid rain research, surely the strangest few days came in September 1987, when the National Acid Precipitation Assessment Program finally released a long awaited "interim report." 36

NAPAP, set up late in the Carter Administration to coordinate federal acid rain research, had already been criticized by the General Accounting Office for foot-dragging. When the interim assessment was finally released — two years late — it ignited a veritable firestorm of scientific protest. 37

There were few complaints about the veracity of the three main volumes of the study. But the slim fourth volume, an "executive summary," was at the heart of the heat. J. Lawrence Kulp, then the NAPAP director and a former Weyerhaeuser executive appointed by Ronald Reagan, had written much of the summary himself. 38

39   Critics were especially disturbed that the summary's tally of "acid lakes" counted only those so acid that adult fish could not survive, with far less emphasis on the more numerous acidified waters where amphibian and insect life are harmed, fish reproduction is destroyed, and ecosystem food webs are disrupted.

40   Further, some critics were outraged that the summary promoted as fact an unproven chemical "steady state" theory, favored by Kulp, that lakes in the Northeast would not become more acidic.

41   Some prominent researchers spoke out, including several vociferously in the pages of *Science*, which had obtained a pre-release copy. Just days after the summary's release, J. Lawrence Kulp resigned.

42   The new NAPAP director is one James R. Mahoney. Last April, Mahoney offered a pleasant surprise to many conservationist observers. Testifying before a congressional subcommittee, he offered to prepare a new summary. "I believe the executive summary can and should be expanded to be more representative of all the data available," he said, adding that he "would not subscribe . . . at this time" to Kulp's assertion that acid rain would not harm more northeastern lakes.

43   Mahoney and Representative James Scheuer, chairman of the subcommittee, later agreed that a shorter report responding to the scientific criticisms would make more practical sense than a wholly republished "interim" summary. That because Mahoney has agreed to gear up his staff to accelerate the massive final assessment to meet the original 1990 deadline, despite the previous delays.

44   NAPAP plans, this time around, to be more active in soliciting criticisms and comments, according to staff ecologist Patricia Irving. "We want this to be a [scientific] consensus document in every sense," she says.

45   Scheuer, the congressman, appears to agree that the summary, at least, needs some work. He called that 1987 version "intellectually dishonest."

Wait for Clean Coal?

46   A broad and bipartisan coalition of representatives and senators has introduced compromise legislation in an attempt to break through the political blockade that has stalled

all attempts to control acid rain at its source. The new legislation scales back on earlier calls for an annual reduction of 12 million tons of sulfur dioxide. The new target would be 10 million tons per year, or about a 35 percent decrease from current levels.

Connie Mahan of National Audubon Society's government relations office says the society is supporting the bill "even though we are not happy with scaling back by two tons. We went into the 100th Congress believing that the political will for solving this problem was finally taking shape. We continue to hope that by the 101st Congress we'll have acid rain legislation." [47]

The coal and electric power lobbies are continuing to fight legislation which would require them to reduce sulfur dioxide emissions at costs that could exceed $100 million for each poorly controlled fossil-fuel-burning powerplant. Instead, they are promoting "clean coal technologies" now in the research and testing stage that could control pollution in the combustion process at much lower costs. However, they have not suggested that large-scale clean coal technology will be available in the foreseeable future. [48]

"We're very suspicious that the promise of future technological improvements is being used as an excuse for not introducing technology that's already known," says Jan Beyea, National Audubon Society senior staff scientist. Beyea points out that the dirtiest powerplants, in terms of acid gas emissions, are pre-1980s facilities that were grandfathered at high emission rates by the Clean Air Act. "The real need is for control technology on these older plants. A technology that's useful by the year 2010 isn't going to be of much use. And we don't want to see North America's forests go the way of the European forests." [49]

From his mountaintop headquarters in western North Carolina, Bob Bruck would seem to agree. "People are going to have to start understanding that this is not like some kind of disease where we're going to give all the trees a pill and cure it. We are going to have to decide as a society how to come up with the most logical and reasonable way of implementing what looks like the best solution." [50]

The following cartoon by Leo Cullum appeared in 1989 in the
New Yorker. *Is it purely for laughs, or does it make some kind*
of comment about the acid rain controversy?

EUTHANASIA

It's Over, Debbie

In 1988 the Journal of the American Medical Association *published the following anonymous contribution to its "A Piece of My Mind" opinion column. Nothing ever published there has been more controversial.*

The call came in the middle of the night. As a gynecology 1
resident rotating through a large, private hospital, I had
come to detest telephone calls, because invariably I would
be up for several hours and would not feel good the next
day. However, duty called, so I answered the phone. A nurse
informed me that a patient was having difficulty getting
rest, could I please see her. She was on 3 North. That was
the gynecologic-oncology unit, not my usual duty station.
As I trudged along, bumping sleepily against walls and
corners and not believing I was up again, I tried to imagine
what I might find at the end of my walk. Maybe an elderly
woman with an anxiety reaction, or perhaps something
particularly horrible.

I grabbed the chart from the nurses station on my way 2
to the patient's room, and the nurse gave me some hurried
details: a 20-year-old girl named Debbie was dying of ovar-
ian cancer. She was having unrelenting vomiting apparently as the result of an alcohol drip administered for seda-
tion. Hmm, I thought. Very sad. As I approached the room
I could hear loud, labored breathing. I entered and saw an
emaciated, dark-haired woman who appeared much older
than 20. She was receiving nasal oxygen, had an IV, and
was sitting in bed suffering from what was obviously severe
air hunger. The chart noted her weight at 80 pounds. A
second woman, also dark-haired but of middle-age, stood
at her right, holding her hand. Both looked up as I entered.
The room seemed filled with the patient's desperate effort
to survive. Her eyes were hollow, and she had suprasternal
and intercostal retractions with her rapid inspirations. She
had not eaten or slept in two days. She had not responded

to chemotherapy and was being given supportive care only. It was a gallows scene, a cruel mockery of her youth and unfulfilled potential. Her only words to me were, "Let's get this over with."

3   I retreated with my thoughts to the nurses station. The patient was tired and needed rest. I could not give her health, but I could give her rest. I asked the nurse to draw 20 mg of morphine sulfate into a syringe. Enough, I thought, to do the job. I took the syringe into the room and told the two women I was going to give Debbie something that would let her rest and to say good-bye. Debbie looked at the syringe, then laid her head on the pillow with her eyes open, watching what was left of the world. I injected the morphine intravenously and watched to see if my calculations on its effects would be correct. Within seconds her breathing slowed to a normal rate, her eyes closed, and her features softened as she seemed restful at last. The older woman stroked the hair of the now-sleeping patient. I waited for the inevitable next effect of depressing the respiratory drive. With clocklike certainty, within four minutes the breathing rate slowed even more, then became irregular, then ceased. The dark-haired woman stood erect and seemed relieved.

4   It's over, Debbie.

Name Withheld by Request

Charles Colson
It's Not Over, Debbie

Charles Colson (born 1931) was converted to Christianity while serving a prison term for his role in the Watergate scandal of the Nixon administration. He has written five books on Christian topics and contributes regularly to the evangelical publication Christianity Today, *where the following column appeared in 1988.*

1   The scene is a darkened hospital ward. An intern stands over Debbie, a young woman with terminal cancer. Her breathing is labored as she struggles for oxygen. She weighs 80 pounds. She is in horrible pain.

The doctor has never seen Debbie before, but a glance at   2
her chart confirms she is not responding to treatment. He
leans down to hear her whisper, "Let's get this over with."

Most doctors would have hurried to give relief against   3
the pain, or tried to offer some solace to the anguished
relative standing near the bed. But this intern measured
out 20 milligrams of morphine into a syringe — enough, he
wrote later, "to do the job" — and injected it. Four minutes
later, Debbie was dead. The doctor's only comment: "It's
over, Debbie."

Stories like this, publicized a few months back, are shock-   4
ing but should not surprise us. While no one likes to admit
it, active euthanasia is not uncommon. It has been closeted
in hospital ethics committees, cloaked in euphemisms spoken to grieving relatives. It is the unnamed shadow on an
unknown number of death certificates — of handicapped newborns; sickly, aged parents; the terminally ill in critical pain.

No, Debbie's case is something new only because of the   5
public nature of both its telling and the debate that has
followed.

This story was first written, anonymously but without   6
apology, by the intern himself, and published in the *Journal
of the American Medical Association* (JAMA) — one of the
most respected medical journals in the world.

Following the article's publication, the commentary   7
came fast and furious. Some experts dismissed the incident
as fictional. Others believed it, but focused their criticism
on the young doctor's lack of familiarity with Debbie's medical history.

But the article's greatest effect was to yank euthanasia   8
out of the closet and thrust it into the arena of national
debate. On the surface that might seem healthy, getting
the whole ugly issue into the open. But there's a subtle
danger here: The JAMA article and the impassioned discussion it provoked offer a case study of a recurring process
in American life by which the unthinkable in short order
becomes the unquestionable.

Usually it works like this: Some practice so offensive that   9
it could scarcely be discussed in public is suddenly advocated by a respected expert in a respected forum. The public
is shocked, then outraged. The very fact that such a thing
could be publicly debated becomes the focus of the debate.

But in the process, the sheer repetition of the shocking   10
gradually dulls its shock effect. No longer outraged, people
begin to argue for positions to moderate the extreme; or

they accept the premise, challenging instead the means to achieve it. (Note that in Debbie's debate, many challenged not the killing, but the intern's failure to check more carefully into the case.)

11   And gradually, though no one remembers quite how it all happened, the once unspeakable becomes tolerable and, in time, acceptable.

12   An example of how this process works is the case of homosexuality. Not long ago it was widely regarded, even in secular society, as a perversion. The gay-rights movement's first pronouncements were received with shock; then, in the process of debate, the public gradually lost its sense of outrage. Homosexuality became a cause — and what was once deviant is today, in many jurisdictions, a legally protected right. All this in little more than a decade.

13   Debbie's story appears to have initiated this process for euthanasia. Columnist Ellen Goodman welcomed the case as "a debate that should be taking place."

14   So what was once a crime becomes a debate. And, if history holds true, that debate will usher the once unmentionable into common practice.

15   Already the stage is set. In a 1983 poll, 63 percent of Americans approved of mercy killing in certain cases. In a 1988 poll, more than 50 percent of lawyers favored legal euthanasia. The Hemlock Society is working to put the issue on the ballot in several states.

16   I don't intend to sound alarmist; legal euthanasia in this country is still more a threat than a reality. But 20 years ago, who would have thought abortion would one day be a constitutional right, or that infanticide would be given legal protection?

17   The path from the unmentionable to the commonplace is being traveled with increasing speed in medical ethics. Without some concerted resistance, euthanasia is likely to be the next to make the trip. As Ellen Goodman concluded her column, "The Debbie story is not over yet, not by a long shot."

18   Indeed.

19   Novelist Walker Percy, in *The Thanatos Syndrome*, offers one vision of where such compromising debates on the value of life might take us.

20   The time is the 1990s. Qualitarian Life Centers have sprung up across the country after the landmark case of *Doe* v. *Dade* "which decreed, with solid scientific evidence, that the human infant does not achieve personhood until

18 months." At these centers one can conveniently dispose of unwanted young and old alike.

An old priest, Father Smith, confronts the narrator, a   21
psychiatrist, in this exchange:

> "'You are an able psychiatrist. On the whole a decent, gener-   22
> ous humanitarian person in the abstract sense of the word.
> You know what is going to happen to you."
>
> "What?"   23
>
> "You are a member of the first generation of doctors in   24
> the history of medicine to turn their backs on the oath of
> Hippocrates and kill millions of old, useless people, unborn
> children, born malformed children, for the good of man-
> kind—and to do so without a single murmur from one of
> you. Not a single letter of protest in the august *New England
> Journal of Medicine*. And do you know what you are going
> to end up doing?"
>
> "No," I say . . .   25
>
> The priest aims his azimuth squarely at me and then ap-   26
> pears to lose his train of thought . . . .
>
> "What is going to happen to me, Father?" I ask before he   27
> gets away altogether.
>
> "Oh," he says absently, appearing to be thinking of some-   28
> thing else, "you're going to end up killing Jews."

James Rachels
Active and Passive Euthanasia

James Rachels (born 1941), a philosopher and teacher at New York University, University of Miami, and the University of Alabama at Birmingham (where he currently works), is particu-larly interested in ethics. He contributed the following essay to The New England Journal of Medicine *in 1975.*

The distinction between active and passive euthanasia is   1
thought to be crucial for medical ethics. The idea is that it
is permissible, at least in some cases, to withhold treatment
and allow a patient to die, but it is never permissible to
take any direct action designed to kill the patient. This

doctrine seems to be accepted by most doctors, and it is endorsed in a statement adopted by the House of Delegates of the American Medical Association on December 4, 1973:

> The intentional termination of the life of one human being by another—mercy killing—is contrary to that for which the medical profession stands and is contrary to the policy of the American Medical Association.
>
> The cessation of the employment of extraordinary means to prolong the life of the body when there is irrefutable evidence that biological death is imminent is the decision of the patient and/or his family. The advice and judgment of the physician should be freely available to the patient and/or his immediate family.

However, a strong case can be made against this doctrine. In what follows I will set out some of the relevant arguments, and urge doctors to reconsider their views on this matter.

2   To begin with a familiar type of situation, a patient who is dying of incurable cancer of the throat is in terrible pain, which can no longer be satisfactorily alleviated. He is certain to die within a few days, even if present treatment is continued, but he does not want to go on living for those days since the pain is unbearable. So he asks the doctor for an end to it, and his family joins in the request.

3   Suppose the doctor agrees to withhold treatment, as the conventional doctrine says he may. The justification for his doing so is that the patient is in terrible agony, and since he is going to die anyway, it would be wrong to prolong his suffering needlessly. But now notice this. If one simply withholds treatment, it may take the patient longer to die, and so he may suffer more than he would if more direct action were taken and a lethal injection given. This fact provides strong reason for thinking that, once the initial decision not to prolong his agony has been made, active euthanasia is actually preferable to passive euthanasia, rather than the reverse. To say otherwise is to endorse the option that leads to more suffering rather than less, and is contrary to the humanitarian impulse that prompts the decision not to prolong his life in the first place.

4   Part of my point is that the process of being "allowed to die" can be relatively slow and painful, whereas being given a lethal injection is relatively quick and painless. Let me

give a different sort of example. In the United States about one in 600 babies is born with Down's syndrome. Most of these babies are otherwise healthy — that is, with only the usual pediatric care, they will proceed to an otherwise normal infancy. Some, however, are born with congenital defects such as intestinal obstructions that require operations if they are to live. Sometimes, the parents and the doctor will decide not to operate, and let the infant die. Anthony Shaw describes what happens then:

> . . . When surgery is denied [the doctor] must try to keep the infant from suffering while natural forces sap the baby's life away. As a surgeon whose natural inclination is to use the scalpel to fight off death, standing by and watching a salvageable baby die is the most emotionally exhausting experience I know. It is easy at a conference, in a theoretical discussion, to decide that such infants should be allowed to die. It is altogether different to stand by in the nursery and watch as dehydration and infection wither a tiny being over hours and days. This is a terrible ordeal for me and the hospital staff — much more so than for the parents who never set foot in the nursery.

I can understand why some people are opposed to all euthanasia, and insist that such infants must be allowed to live. I think I can also understand why other people favor destroying these babies quickly and painlessly. But why should anyone favor letting "dehydration and infection wither a tiny being over hours and days"? The doctrine that says that a baby may be allowed to dehydrate and wither, but may not be given an injection that would end its life without suffering, seems so patently cruel as to require no further refutation. The strong language is not intended to offend, but only to put the point in the clearest possible way.

My second argument is that the conventional doctrine 5 leads to decisions concerning life and death made on irrelevant grounds.

Consider again the case of the infants with Down's syn- 6 drome who need operations for congenital defects unrelated to the syndrome to live. Sometimes, there is no operation, and the baby dies. But when there is no such defect, the baby lives on. Now, an operation such as that to remove an intestinal obstruction is not prohibitively difficult. The reason why such operations are not performed in these cases is, clearly, that the child has Down's syndrome and the parents and doctor judge that because of that fact it is better for the child to die.

7   But notice that this situation is absurd, no matter what view one takes of the lives and potential of such babies. If the life of such an infant is worth preserving, what does it matter if it needs a simple operation? Or, if one thinks it better that such a baby should not live on, what difference does it make that it happens to have an unobstructed intestinal tract? In either case, the matter of life and death is being decided on irrelevant grounds. It is the Down's syndrome, and not the intestines, that is the issue. The matter should be decided, if at all, on that basis, and not be allowed to depend on the essentially irrelevant question of whether the intestinal tract is blocked.

8   What makes this situation possible, of course, is the idea that when there is an intestinal blockage, one can "let the baby die," but when there is no such defect there is nothing that can be done, for one must not "kill" it. The fact that this idea leads to such results as deciding life or death on irrelevant grounds is another good reason why the doctrine should be rejected.

9   One reason why so many people think that there is an important moral difference between active and passive euthanasia is that they think killing someone is morally worse than letting someone die. But is it? Is killing in itself worse than letting die? To investigate this issue, two cases may be considered that are exactly alike except that one involves killing whereas the other involves letting someone die. Then it can be asked whether this difference makes any difference to the moral assessments. It is important that the cases be exactly alike, except for this one difference and not some other that accounts for any variation in the assessments of the two cases. So, let us consider this pair of cases:

10   In the first, Smith stands to gain a large inheritance if anything should happen to his six-year-old cousin. One evening while the child is taking his bath, Smith sneaks into the bathroom and drowns the child, and then arranges things so that it will look like an accident.

11   In the second, Jones also stands to gain if anything should happen to his six-year-old cousin. Like Smith, Jones sneaks in planning to drown the child in his bath. However, just

as he enters the bathroom Jones sees the child slip and hit his head, and fall face down in the water. Jones is delighted; he stands by, ready to push the child's head back under if it is necessary. With only a little thrashing about, the child drowns all by himself, "accidentally," as Jones watches and does nothing.

Now Smith killed the child, whereas Jones "merely" let   12
the child die. That is the only difference between them. Did either man behave better, from a moral point of view? If the difference between killing and letting die were in itself a morally important matter, one should say that Jones's behavior was less reprehensible than Smith's. But does one really want to say that? I think not. In the first place, both men acted from the same motive, personal gain, and both had exactly the same end in view when they acted. It may be inferred from Smith's conduct that he is a bad man, although that judgment may be withdrawn or modified if certain further facts are learned about him—for example, that he is mentally deranged. But would not the very same thing be inferred about Jones from his conduct? And would not the same further considerations also be relevant to any modification of this judgment? Moreover, suppose Jones pleaded, in his own defense, "After all, I didn't do anything except just stand there and watch the child drown. I didn't kill him; I only let him die." Again, if letting die were in itself less bad than killing, this defense should have at least some weight. But it does not. Such a "defense" can only be regarded as a grotesque perversion of moral reasoning. Morally speaking, it is no defense at all.

Now, it may be pointed out, quite properly, that the cases   13
of euthanasia with which doctors are concerned are not like this at all. They do not involve personal gain or the destruction of normal healthy children. Doctors are concerned only with cases in which the patient's life is of no further use to him, or in which the patient's life has become or will soon become a terrible burden. However, the point is the same in these cases: the bare difference between killing and letting die does not, in itself, make a moral difference. If a doctor lets a patient die, for humane reasons, he is in the same moral position as if he had given the patient a lethal injection for humane reasons. If his decision was wrong—if, for example, the patient's illness was in fact curable—the decision would be equally regrettable no matter which method was used to carry it out. And if the doc-

tor's decision was the right one, the method used is not in itself important.

14   The AMA policy statement isolates the crucial issue very well; the crucial issue is "the intentional termination of the life of one human being by another." But after identifying this issue, and forbidding "mercy killing," the statement goes on to deny that the cessation of treatment is the intentional termination of a life. This is where the mistake comes in, for what is the cessation of treatment, in these circumstances, if it is not "the intentional termination of the life of one human being by another"? Of course it is exactly that, and if it were not, there would be no point to it.

15   Many people will find this judgment hard to accept. One reason, I think, is that it is very easy to conflate the question of whether killing is, in itself, worse than letting die, with the very different question of whether most actual cases of killing are more reprehensible than most actual cases of letting die. Most actual cases of killing are clearly terrible (think, for example, of all the murders reported in the newspapers), and one hears of such cases every day. On the other hand, one hardly ever hears of a case of letting die, except for the actions of doctors who are motivated by humanitarian reasons. So one learns to think of killing in a much worse light than of letting die. For it is not the bare difference between killing and letting die that makes the difference in these cases. Rather, the other factors — the murderer's motive of personal gain, for example, contrasted with the doctor's humanitarian motivation — account for the different reactions to the different cases.

16   I have argued that killing is not in itself any worse than letting die; if my contention is right, it follows that active euthanasia is not any worse than passive euthanasia. What arguments can be given on the other side? The most common, I believe, is the following:

17   "The important difference between active and passive euthanasia is that in passive euthanasia, the doctor does not do anything to bring about the patient's death. The doctor does nothing, and the patient dies of whatever ills already afflict him. In active euthanasia, however, the doctor does something to bring about the patient's death: he kills him. The doctor who gives the patient with cancer a lethal injection has himself caused his patient's death; whereas if he merely ceases treatment, the cancer is the cause of the death."

18   A number of points need to be made here. The first is

that it is not exactly correct to say that in passive euthanasia the doctor does nothing, for he does do one thing that is very important: he lets the patient die. "Letting someone die" is certainly different in some respects, from other types of action—mainly in that it is a kind of action that one may perform by way of not performing certain other actions. For example, one may let a patient die by way of not giving medication, just as one may insult someone by way of not shaking his hand. But for any purpose of moral assessment, it is a type of action nonetheless. The decision to let a patient die is subject to moral appraisal in the same way that a decision to kill him would be subject to moral appraisal: it may be assessed as wise or unwise, compassionate or sadistic, right or wrong. If a doctor deliberately let a patient die who was suffering from a routinely curable illness, the doctor would certainly be to blame for what he had done, just as he would be to blame if he had needlessly killed the patient. Charges against him would then be appropriate. If so, it would be no defense at all for him to insist that he didn't "do anything." He would have done something very serious indeed, for he let his patient die.

Fixing the cause of death may be very important from a   19
legal point of view, for it may determine whether criminal charges are brought against the doctor. But I do not think that this notion can be used to show a moral difference between active and passive euthanasia. The reason why it is considered bad to be the cause of someone's death is that death is regarded as a great evil—and so it is. However, if it had been decided that euthanasia—even passive euthanasia—is desirable in a given case, it has also been decided that in this instance death is no greater an evil than the patient's continued existence. And if this is true, the usual reason for not wanting to be the cause of someone's death simply does not apply.

Finally, doctors may think that all of this is only of   20
academic interest—the sort of thing that philosophers may worry about but that has no practical bearing on their own work. After all, doctors must be concerned about the legal consequences of what they do, and active euthanasia is clearly forbidden by law. But even so, doctors should also be concerned with the fact that the law is forcing upon them a moral doctrine that may well be indefensible, and has a considerable effect on their practices. Of course, most doctors are not now in the position of being coerced in this matter, for they do not regard themselves as merely going

along with what the law requires. Rather, in statements such as the AMA policy statement that I have quoted, they are endorsing this doctrine as a central point of medical ethics. In that statement, active euthanasia is condemned not merely as illegal but as "contrary to that for which the medical profession stands," whereas passive euthanasia is approved. However, the preceding considerations suggest that there is really no moral difference between the two, considered in themselves (there may be important moral differences in some cases in their consequences, but, as I pointed out, these differences may make active euthanasia, and not passive euthanasia, the morally preferable option). So whereas doctors may have to discriminate between active and passive euthanasia to satisfy the law, they should not do any more than that. In particular, they should not give the distinction any added authority and weight by writing it into official statements of medical ethics.

Sidney Hook

In Defense of Voluntary Euthanasia

Sidney Hook (born 1902) studied philosophy under John Dewey and became an outspoken, controversial, daring social thinker. A prolific essayist who also published some thirty books, a champion of Marx in the 1930s but of individual freedoms as well, Hook remains iconoclastic and independent. He wrote the following essay for The New York Times *in 1987.*

1   A few short years ago, I lay at the point of death. A congestive heart failure was treated for diagnostic purposes by an angiogram that triggered a stroke. Violent and painful hiccups, uninterrupted for several days and nights, prevented the indigestion of food. My left side and one of my vocal cords became paralyzed. Some form of pleurisy set in, and I felt I was drowning in a sea of slime. At one point, my heart stopped beating; just as I lost consciousness, it was thumped back into action again. In one of my lucid

intervals during those days of agony, I asked my physician to discontinue all life-supporting services or show me how to do it. He refused and told me that someday I would appreciate the unwisdom of my request.

A month later, I was discharged from the hospital. In six months, I regained the use of my limbs, and although my voice still lacks its old resonance and carrying power I no longer croak like a frog. There remain some minor disabilities and I am restricted to a rigorous, low sodium diet. I have resumed my writing and research. 2

My experience can be and has been cited as an argument against honoring requests of stricken patients to be gently eased out of their pain and life. I cannot agree. There are two main reasons. As an octogenarian, there is a reasonable likelihood that I may suffer another "cardiovascular accident" or worse. I may not even be in a position to ask for the surcease of pain. It seems to me that I have already paid my dues to death — indeed, although time has softened my memories they are vivid enough to justify my saying that I suffered enough to warrant dying several times over. Why run the risk of more? 3

Secondly, I dread imposing on my family and friends another grim round of misery similar to the one my first attack occasioned. 4

My wife and children endured enough for one lifetime. I know that for them the long days and nights of waiting, the disruption of their professional duties and their own familial responsibilities counted for nothing in their anxiety for me. In their joy at my recovery they have been forgotten. Nonetheless, to visit another prolonged spell of helpless suffering on them as my life ebbs away, or even worse, if I linger on into a comatose senility, seems altogether gratuitous. 5

But what, it may be asked, of the joy and satisfaction of living, of basking in the sunlight, listening to music, watching one's grandchildren growing into adolescence, following the news about the fate of freedom in a troubled world, playing with ideas, writing one's testament of wisdom and folly for posterity? Is not all that one endured, together with the risk of its recurrence, an acceptable price for the multiple satisfactions that are still open even to a person of advanced years? 6

Apparently those who cling to life, no matter what, think so. I do not. 7

8   The zest and intensity of these experiences are no longer
what they used to be. I am not vain enough to delude myself
that I can in the few remaining years make an important
discovery useful for mankind or can lead a social movement
or do anything that will be historically eventful, no less
event-making. My autobiography, which describes a record
of intellectual and political experiences of some historical
value, already much too long, could be posthumously published. I have had my fill of joys and sorrows and am not
greedy for more life. I have always thought that a test of
whether one had found happiness in one's life is whether
one would be willing to relive it — whether, if it were possible, one would accept the opportunity to be born again.

9   Having lived a full and relatively happy life, I would
cheerfully accept the chance to be reborn, but certainly not
to be reborn again as an infirm octogenarian. To some extent, my views reflect what I have seen happen to the aged
and stricken who have been so unfortunate as to survive
crippling paralysis. They suffer, and impose suffering on
others, unable even to make a request that their torment
be ended.

10   I am mindful too of the burdens placed upon the community, with its rapidly diminishing resources, to provide the
adequate and costly services necessary to sustain the lives
of those whose days and nights are spent on mattress graves
of pain. A better use could be made of these resources to
increase the opportunities and qualities of life for the young.
I am not denying the moral obligation the community has
to look after its disabled and aged. There are times, however, when an individual may find it pointless to insist on
the fulfillment of a legal and moral right.

11   What is required is no great revolution in morals but an
enlargement of imagination and an intelligent evaluation
of alternative uses of community resources.

12   Long ago, Seneca observed that "the wise man will live
as long as he ought, not as long as he can." One can envisage
hypothetical circumstances in which one has a duty to prolong one's life despite its costs for the sake of others, but such
circumstances are far removed from the ordinary prospects
we are considering. If wisdom is rooted in the knowledge of
the alternatives of choice, it must be reliably informed of the
state one is in and its likely outcome. Scientific medicine is
not infallible, but it is the best we have. Should a rational
person be willing to endure acute suffering merely on the

chance that a miraculous cure might presently be at hand? Each one should be permitted to make his own choice — especially when no one else is harmed by it.

The responsibility for the decision, whether deemed wise   13 or foolish, must be with the chooser.

May Sarton

From *Recovering: A Journal 1978–1979*

May Sarton (born 1912 in Belgium, which her family fled when World War I broke out) has been writing poems and novels for over half a century. She has over thirty-five books to her credit. Old age has been the subject of some of her most moving novels. Lately she has been publishing her journals: Recovering: A Journal *(1980),* At Seventy: A Journal *(1984), and* After the Stroke *(1988). The following excerpts are from* Recovering *and* At Seventy.

Thursday, December 28th, 1978

I had thought not to begin a new journal until I am se-   1 venty, four years from now, but perhaps the time has come to sort myself out, and see whether I can restore a sense of meaning and continuity to my life by this familiar means.

Also I need to communicate with something better than   2 tears my long companionship with Judy that began thirty-five years ago in Santa Fe and ended on Christmas Day. Our last Christmas together; it was a fiasco. I wasn't feeling well and had a low fever when I went to fetch her on Christmas Eve at the Walden Nursing Home where she has been for seven years. I had been warned that she had changed for the worse in her slow progress toward complete senility, but I hoped that after twenty-four hours with me here, she would begin to relate again. That is the way it has been for the last few years and when she was here for her eightieth birthday in September, we did have a few moments of communion.

. . .

3   Over the years we have always opened our stockings in bed but Judy no longer enjoys opening presents so I had given up on stockings and brought up a present from faithful Emily Huntington for her to unwrap. She showed no interest in an elegant pair of gray slacks after refusing to unwrap the package. It was "downhill all the way," and I began to wonder how I was going to manage. I made fires in both fireplaces downstairs and got Judy dressed in a warm sweater and slacks and settled her in an armchair with a rug over her knees beside the fire in the library. But she was very restless and was soon up, moving around in the curious shuffle that has replaced walking now. She never once looked at the tree, poignantly beautiful this year, and—as it has been for thirty years—decorated with the many ornaments we have collected together.

4   It is often a small thing that shatters hope. For me it came when a male pheasant appeared close to the porch window—such a dazzling sight in all the gloom that I called out, "Come Judy, come quickly!" She didn't come, of course. I found her shuffling about in the library and by the time I had dragged her to the window, the pheasant was out of sight. At that moment I knew that Judy had gone beyond where being with me in this house means anything.

. . .

5   Yesterday I took the day off and took the making of an oyster stew to Eleanor Blair. She has graduated from her walker to a four-pronged cane that makes her far more mobile with less effort. She told me triumphantly that she has even climbed the stairs. What joy it was to be in her dear house, so full of life, geraniums in flower in a small window greenhouse, books everywhere, light and peace. At eighty-five she is a marvelous "role model" as today's fashion has the phrase, and I hated to cut the visit short but I wanted to stop and see Judy. Since the disaster of Christmas I have not seen her.

6   I think she recognized me but I am not sure. Two nurses were making her bed and laughed with real merriment when they forgot, because we were talking, to put in the rubber sheet and had to begin again. Their presence was a help as Judy was totally unresponsive, except that she

noticed my green jacket when I took off my coat. I stayed only a quarter of an hour. When I left I turned back at the door and saw her sitting in the only chair in her room, her face still so distinguished, but now a blank mask. She is not lonely, but the isolation of her state struck me like a blow to the heart. To be so helpless to help, and to leave her there lost. She did not look up even as I said goodbye.

Tuesday, July 10th

I am happy to hear that Judy's family, so sensitive to her needs, so much on the job, came to the decision two weeks ago or more, to move her to a smaller nursing home where she is in a less institutional atmosphere. Connie, her sister, went to see her around two one day and found her eating strawberry shortcake with evident relish, sitting in her wheelchair in the parlor there. The best news is that she is now off tranquilizers (overused no doubt in the larger place) and as soon as I can drive that far, I long to see her, and perhaps to erase my last vision of her some months ago, sitting alone in her room, her face turned away, with a look of tragic emptiness in it. I have thought of Judy so much since the operation, benign star in my firmament, she who could and did love me for what I am and accepted the flaws. The never-failing support and friend. 7

Friday, August 24th

The day before yesterday I went down to Cambridge and stopped on the way to see Judy in her new "home." Her windows look out on trees and the atmosphere is sunny and peaceful. The move has been a wise one. She did not recognize me, "babbles of green fields," and I shall leave it there. 8

. . .

Judy's senility throws me. There is no way to transcend it except through the memory of what she was. I suppose I have been honest about all the horror of senility because there are many people who have to face it alone. I have wished *to be present* to their pain. To be honest. Not to deny the physical facts which make transcendence difficult if not impossible. I have thought of those who share my pain, rather than of Judy who does not care, does not know, and is not in pain. 9

10   What of the nurses who deal with all this every day? How
do they keep on being loving and care-full of a stranger
who cannot respond? It takes superior love and superior
detachment and I honor them for both, more than I can
say. But for them there is the consolation of doing what
has to be done, and they are not betrayed in their inmost
hearts by what cannot be changed and can only get worse,
as the families of loved ones are.

From *At Seventy: A Journal*

Wednesday, September 8th

1   But then I had to go shortly after lunch to drive to Concord
to see Judy for the first time in months, since before Christmas. There she was, there she will be until she slips away,
in her wheelchair, singing to herself. I know now that she
will not recognize me, but I held her cold little hand and
talked about old times. I gave her the duck feathers and
reminded her of our walks at Mt. Auburn and for thirty
seconds I thought she was enjoying the silky feathers, and
perhaps listening, but then she put them into her mouth,
and I had to try to take them away. She held on fiercely
and only let them go when I gave her a brownie to eat. Her
face is still so distinguished, the dark eyes, the cap of white
hair, that it seems incredible that she herself is far away
and what is left is a baby, for whom food is the only real
pleasure. The truth is I go to see her for me, not for her.
After a time I feel a strong compulsion to touch base, as it
were. True love does not die.

Wednesday, December 22nd

2   I feel I have been climbing the Christmas mountain for
weeks, so many things I longed to record here and didn't.
But now that I have come to a good pause I can lay down
my knapsack and look at the view.

The tree is up and it is a dream. Last year I took a great   3
dislike to the tree, which was enormous and rather ferocious
looking. I felt it was so German! This one is beautifully pro-
portioned and smaller, and Edythe and I had a lovely afternoon decking it, as we have done now twice, so it is becoming
a ritual. Of course, almost every ornament brings memories
of Judy and our trees at 14 Wright Street in Cambridge, and
the little front parlor where it stood on a table, and where
we invited our friends in, one by one or in small groups, for
champagne and to sit by the Franklin stove. There Anne Thorp
and Agnes Swift came bearing jars of wild cranberry jelly
from Greenings Island; there we heard Dorothy Wallace with
her daughter Anne and her husband, bearing Anne's tiny
daughter in a basket, singing "Go Tell It on the Mountain,"
and there on one memorable occasion Barbara Hawthorne
came with (of all singular and magical things) a bunch of
violets, so forever after I have associated Christmas Eve with
that scent. There Judy's cousin Nancy Carey came with her
two small children and Ruth Harnden and so many other
friends—and after the guests left we had restful lamb stew,
which I always made for the holidays.

Later there were the Christmases of Nelson when the   4
Warners came down from the farm on the Eve for chocolate
ice cream with ginger ale poured over it and a cake Sally
baked shaped like a tree with green frosting, and Mildred
and Quig crossed the street, and Judy was with me. And
now—it is hard to believe—it is the tenth Christmas here.

Why is it, I wonder, that Christmas brings so much depres-   5
sion with it, so many people struggle against an undertow?
It is partly because this moment of light shines out of the
darkest and shortest days of the year, the lowest ebb of the
cycle when wise animals dig themselves in for a long sleep,
while we, driven creatures, spend immense energy on wrapping presents, sending off packages, baking cookies (this I
used to do but have stopped doing myself, so other people's
cookies are specially welcome). Partly it is that memories
well up and not all are happy ones. We are dealing with a
host of faces and times and sorrows and joys, and there is
no time to sort them out.

Every year Christmas becomes a real creation for each   6
of us, and as it is created we are re-creating the moment
when Love is born again, Love that will know pain as well
as joy.

As I was writing that last sentence Tim Warren, Judy's   7

nephew, called — it is 8 A.M. — to tell me that Judy died last night. I have prayed that she might be allowed to slip away, and now she has. But it is always so sudden, so unexpected — death — and so final. When I went to see her last September and held her ice-cold hand in mine, at the very end of the half-hour when she had made no sign of recognition, she reached over and patted my hand and held it over her other one for a moment. I must remember that and that she is free at last of the failing body and mind and is wherever spirits dwell.

Author/Title Index

Acid Murder No Longer a Mystery (Luoma), 994

Active and Passive Euthanasia (Rachels), 1009

Address to the Prisoners in the Cook County Jail (Darrow), 734

Advertisement: To Fight World Hunger, 912

Advertisement for Babson College, 100

Advertisement for Hofstra University, 99

Affirmative Action: Cure or Contradiction?, 672

Ain't I a Woman? (Truth), 236

Allen, Margot, *Huck Finn:* Two Generations of Pain, 571

Allen, Woody, A Brief, Yet Helpful, Guide to Civil Disobedience, 655

American Twilights, 1957 (Wright), 795

Amy Kelley, Machinist (Schroedel), 340

Anderson, Mia Klein, The *Other* Beauty of Martin Luther King, Jr.'s "Letter from Birmingham Jail", 658

Anonymous, It's Over, Debbie, 1005

Another Look at Affirmative Action (Drinan), 692

Appealing to White Moderates (Gardner), 668

Are Criminals Made or Born? (Herrnstein and Wilson), 745

Aria: A Memoir of a Bilingual Childhood (Rodriguez), 143

Asian Discrimination: Fact or Fiction? (Li), 726

At the Executed Murderer's Grave (Wright), 798

Baldwin, James, If Black English Isn't a Language, Then Tell Me, What Is?, 112

Banashek, Mary Ellen, Bruce Springsteen: Why He Makes Us Feel So Good, 473

Barnard, Neal D., Letter from the Physicians Committee for Responsible Medicine, 953

Being a Man (Theroux), 302

Belly Dancer (Wakoski), 276

Benbow, Camilla Persson, Sex Differences in Mathematical Reasoning Ability: More Facts, 306

Bennett, William, A Response to Milton Friedman, 834

Berry, Wendell, A Good Scythe, 847

Biondolillo, Deborah, Letter to the Editor, 370

Bird, Caroline, College Is a Waste of Time and Money, 79

Birth-mark, The (Hawthorne), 885

Bleier, Ruth, Gender and Mathematical Ability, 310

Brief, Yet Helpful, Guide to Civil Disobedience, A (Allen), 655

Brownfeld, Allan C., Putting Killers on the Streets, 786

Brownmiller, Susan, Emotion, 277; Let's Put Pornography Back in the Closet, 544; Pornography Hurts Women, 552

Bruce Springsteen: Why He Makes Us Feel So Good (Banashek), 473

Bruuuuuce (Will), 471

Burger, Warren, Prisons Are Designed to Rehabilitate, 772

Canby, Vincent, How an All-American Boy Went to War and Lost His Faith, 504

Case Against Bilingualism, The (Sundberg), 187

Child's Other World, A (Paradis), 403

Chinea-Varela, Migdia, My Life as a 'Twofer', 698

Civil Disobedience (Thoreau), 607

Civil Disobedience: Destroyer of Democracy (Van Dusen), 648

Claiming an Education (Rich), 65

College Is a Waste of Time and Money (Bird), 79

Colson, Charles, It's Not Over, Debbie, 1006

Conniff, Ruth, Racism 101, 719

Conway, Jill, Letter to the Editor, 374

Cooper, James Fenimore, The Slaughter of the Pigeons, 850

Cousins, Norman, How to Make People Smaller Than They Are, 71

Cruz, Ramon, Letter to the Editor, 94

Cullum, Leo, cartoon, 1004

Current Crisis in Remorse, The (Keillor), 762

Darrow, Clarence, Address to the Prisoners in the Cook County Jail, 734

Death and Justice (Koch), 809

deJong, John, Letter to the Editor, 93

Dickens, Charles, What Is a Horse?, 23

Different Take on the Ol' Bump and Grind, A (Gillespie), 272

Doe, Glen, Letter to the Editor, 92

Doonesbury (Trudeau), 70, 966

Drinan, Robert F., Another Look at Affirmative Action, 692

Dudash, Susan, We've Come a Long Way, but Magazines Stayed Behind, 376

Education (White), 20

Efron, Edith, The Soaps—Anything But 99-44/100 Percent Pure, 384

Eiseley, Loren, The Illusion of the Two Cultures, 865

Emotion (Brownmiller), 277

Engineering and the Female Mind (Florman), 325

English Language Amendment: Examining Myths, The (Gonzalez, Schott, and Vasquez), 189

Erotica and Pornography (Steinem), 531

Everyday Use (Walker), 56

Examination, The (Snodgrass), 107

Far Side, The (Larson), 142

Feiffer, Jules, cartoon, 415

Fernsler, Kurt, Why I Want a Husband, 300

First Amendment Pixillation, Editorial (anonymous), 551

Florman, Samuel C., Engineering and the Female Mind, 325

Four-Letter Words Can Hurt You (Lawrence), 217

Friedman, Milton, Prohibition and Drugs, 829; An Open Letter to Bill Bennett, 832; Letter to the Editor, 837

Fritz, Marshall, Letter to the Editor, 839

Galazzi, Stefan, Letter to the Editor, 92
Gardner, Mark, Appealing to White Moderates, 668
Geiger, Karen, Letter to the Editor, 371
Gender and Mathematical Ability (Bleier), 310
Genetic Engineering: The Risks (Wright), 914
Gilbertson, Susan, Letter to the Editor, 92
Gillespie, Marcia Ann, A Different Take on the Ol' Bump and Grind, 272
Gilligan, Carol, Images of Relationships, 289
Glaspell, Susan, *Trifles*, 238; Jury of Her Peers, A, 251
Glazer, Nathan, Some Very Modest Proposals for the Improvement of American Education, 38
Gonzalez, Roseann Duenas, The English Language Amendment: Examining Myths, 189
Good Scythe, A (Berry), 847
Goodall, Jane, A Plea for the Chimpanzees, 958
Gould, Stephen Jay, Of Crime, Cause, and Correlation, 755
Great Acid Rain Debate, The (Ray), 967
Greenberg, Peter, Making of a Rock Star, The, 456
Groening, Matt, Life in Hell, 46

Hanging, A (Orwell), 800
Harrison Bergeron (Vonnegut), 683
Hawthorne, Nathaniel, The Birthmark, 885
Hazards of Science, The (Thomas), 878
Hentoff, Nat, Huck Finn Better Get Out of Town by Sundown, 584

Herrnstein, Richard J., Are Criminals Made or Born?, 745
Hofstadter, Douglas R., A Person Paper on Purity in Language, 220
Hook, Sidney, In Defense of Voluntary Euthanasia, 1016
Horgesheimer, Jerry, Letter to the Editor, 91
How an All-American Boy Went to War and Lost His Faith (Vincent), 504
How I Benefited from Animal Research (Rye), 938
How to Make People Smaller Than They Are (Cousins), 71
Huck Finn Better Get Out of Town by Sundown (Hentoff), 584
Huck Finn: Two Generations of Pain (Allen), 571
Huckleberry Finn Is a Moral Story (Nadeau), 581
Huckleberry Finn Is Offensive (Wallace), 579
Huddleston, Walter D., Speech on Behalf of a Constitutional Amendment to Make English the Official Language of the United States, 165

If Black English Isn't a Language, Then Tell Me, What Is? (Baldwin), 112
Illusion of the Two Cultures, The (Eiseley), 865
I'm a First Amendment Junkie (Jacoby), 547
Images of Relationships (Gilligan), 289
In Opposition to Death Penalty Legislation (Schwarzschild), 814
In Defense of Voluntary Euthanasia (Hook), 1016
It's Not Over, Debbie (Colson), 1006
It's Over, Debbie (Anonymous), 1005

J.B. Factor, The (Maloney), 779

Jackson, George, A Letter from Prison, 789

Jacoby, Susan, I'm a First Amendment Junkie, 547

Janowitz, Tama, You and The Boss, 496

Jefferson, Thomas, Query XIX: Manufactures, 845

Jester, Christopher, Not Just a Diploma Factory, 95

Jones, Rachel L., What's Wrong with Black English, 115

Jury of Her Peers, A (Glaspell), 251

Keillor, Garrison, The Current Crisis in Remorse, 762

Keller, Evelyn Fox, Women in Science: An Analysis of a Social Problem, 314

King, Jonathan, New Genetic Technology: Prospects and Hazards, 901

King, Martin Luther, Jr., Letter from Birmingham Jail, 631

Klawans, Stuart, On *Born on the Fourth of July*, 502

Koch, Edward I., Death and Justice, 809

Larson, Gary, Far Side, The (cartoon), 142

Latest Official Report on Acid Rain, The, 989

Lawrence, Barbara, Four-Letter Words Can Hurt You, 217

Let's Put Pornography Back in the Closet (Brownmiller), 544

Letter from Birmingham Jail (King), 631

Letter from Prison, A (Jackson), 789

Letters to the Editor, 90–94, 369–378, 837

Li, Victor Hao, Asian Discrimination: Fact or Fiction?, 726

Life in Hell (Groening), 46

Lombardi, John, St. Boss, 478

Los Vendidos (Valdez), 519

Lowden, Janet, Letter to the Editor, 375

Luoma, Jon R., Acid Murder No Longer a Mystery, 994

McGarvey, Jack, To Be or Not to Be as Defined by TV, 416

MacKnight, Eric, Letter to the Editor, 93

Macoby, Michael, Letter to the Editor, 373

McWilliams, Wilson Carey, A Republic of Couch Potatoes: The Media Shrivel the Electorate, 446

Making of a Rock Star, The (Orth, Thuck, and Greenberg), 456

Maloney, J. J., The J. B. Factor, 779

Management Women and the New Facts of Life (Schwartz), 353

Mannes, Marya, Television Advertising: The Splitting Image, 407

Maravich, Sam, Letter to the Editor, 91

Marrow, Victor, Letter to the Editor, 93

Masi, Christine, Letter to the Editor, 92

Melby, Edward C., Jr., A Statement from the Association for Biomedical Research, 942

Mencken, H. L., The Penalty of Death, 805

Meyrowitz, Joshua, No Sense of Place, 422; Whither "1984"?, 432

Michelsen, John, Letter to the Editor, 91

Miller, Casey, One Small Step for Genkind, 205

Morley, Jefferson, The Phenomenon, 466

My Life as a "Twofer" (Chinea-Varela), 698

Nadeau, Robert, *Huckleberry Finn* Is a Moral Story, 581

NCTE Resolution on English as the "Official Language" (1986), 203

New Genetic Technology: Prospects and Hazards (King), 901

1992—A New Proposal (Zuckerman), 453

No Sense of Place (Meyrowitz), 422

None of This Is Fair (Rodriguez), 700

Not Just a Diploma Factory (Jester), 95

Of Crime, Cause, and Correlation (Gould), 755

Official English or English Only? (Stalker), 176

"Official Language" Resolution (NCTE), 203

On Born on the Fourth of July (Klawans), 502

One Small Step for Genkind (Miller and Swift), 205

Open Letter to Bill Bennett, An (Friedman), 832

Order in the Classroom (Postman), 47

Orth, Maureen, Making of a Rock Star, The, 456

Orwell, George, A Hanging, 800

Other Beauty of Martin Luther King, Jr.'s, "Letter from Birmingham Jail," The (Anderson), 658

Paradis, Tom, A Child's Other World, 403

Pauline Kael, Potency, 507

Penalty of Death, The (Mencken), 805

Person Paper on Purity in Language, A (Hofstadter), 220

Phenomenon, The (Morley), 466

Plea for the Chimpanzees, A (Goodall), 958

Pornography Hurts Women (Brownmiller), 552

Postman, Neil, Order in the Classroom, 47

Potency (Kael), 507

President's Commission on Obscenity and Pornography, Majority Report, 536

President's Commission on Obscenity and Pornography, Minority Report, 541

Prisons Are Designed to Rehabilitate (Burger), 772

Professions for Women (Woolf), 335

Prohibition and Drugs (Friedman), 829

Public Statement by Eight Alabama Clergymen, 629

Putting Killers on the Streets (Brownfeld), 786

Query XIX: Manufactures (Jefferson), 845

Rachels, James, Active and Passive Euthanasia, 1009

Racism 101 (Conniff), 719

Ray, Dixy Lee, The Great Acid Rain Debate, 967

Ray, Robert, Letter to the Editor, 839

Recoloring of Campus Life, The (Steele), 705

Regan, Tom, Religion and Animal Rights, 925

Reiger, George, What Can Be Done About Acid Rain, 983

Religion and Animal Rights (Regan), 925

Remaking of the Presidents, The (Wills), 437

Republic of Couch Potatoes: The Media Shrivel the Electorate, A (McWilliams), 446

Response to Milton Friedman, A (Bennett), 834

Responses to Caroline Bird (letters to the editor), 90

Reviews of Born on the Fourth of July (Klawans, Canby, and Kael), 502

Rich, Adrienne, Claiming an Education, 65

Rodriguez, Richard, Aria: A Memoir of a Bilingual Childhood, 143; None of This Is Fair, 700

Rosenblatt, Roger, Why the Justice System Fails, 766

Rye, Teresa K., How I Benefited from Animal Research, 938

Sachs, Judith, Letter to the Editor, 91

St. Boss (Lombardi), 478

Sarton, May, journal entries, 1019

Schmoke, Kurt, A War for the Surgeon General, Not the Attorney General, 822

Schott, Alice A., The English Language Amendment: Examining Myths, 189

Schroedel, Jean Reith, Amy Kelley, Machinist, 340

Schwartz, Felice N., Management Women and the New Facts of Life, 353

Schwarzschild, Henry, In Opposition to Death Penalty Legislation, 814

Seneca Falls Declaration, The (Stanton), 232

Sex Differences in Mathematical Reasoning Ability: More Facts (Benbow and Stanley), 306

Shea, Robert, Women at War, 557

Simon, John, Why Good English Is Good for You, 130

Sizer, Theodore, What High School Is, 25

Slaughter of the Pigeons, The (Cooper), 850

Slepicka, Linda, Letter to the Editor, 94

Smitherman, Geneva, White English in Blackface, or Who Do I Be?, 118

Snodgrass, W. D., The Examination, 107

Snow, C. P., The Two Cultures, 859

So Who Needs College? (Tuhy) 74

Soaps — Anything But 99-44/100 Percent Pure, The, (Efron), 384

Some Very Modest Proposals for the Improvement of American Education (Glazer), 38

Speech on Behalf of a Constitutional Amendment to Make English the Official Language of the United States (Huddleston), 165

Spickard, Paul R., Why I Believe in Affirmative Action, 690

Stalker, James C., Official English or English Only?, 176

Stanley, Julian, Sex Differences in Mathematical Reasoning Ability: More Facts, 306

Stanton, Elizabeth Cady, The Seneca Falls Declaration, 232

Statement from the Association for Biomedical Research, A (Melby), 942

Steele, Shelby, The Recoloring of Campus Life, 705

Steinem, Gloria, Erotica and Pornography, 531

Stern, Jerome, What They Learn in School, 54

Sundberg, Trudy J., The Case Against Bilingualism, 187

Swift, Kate, One Small Step for Genkind, 205

Syfers, Judy, Why I Want a Wife, 298

Tables Turned, The (Wadsworth), 858

Television Advertising: The Splitting Image (Mannes), 407

Television Violence Act of 1989, The, 391

Theroux, Paul, Being a Man, 302

Thomas, Lewis, The Hazards of Science, 878

Thoreau, Henry David, Civil Disobedience, 607

Thuck, Jane, Making of a Rock Star, The, 456

Thurber, James, University Days, 101

Thurow, Lester, Why Women Are Paid Less Than Men, 350

To Fight World Hunger (Advertisement), 912

To Be or Not to Be as Defined by TV (McGarvey), 416

Trifles (Glaspell), 238

Trisko, Karen, Letter to the Editor, 94

Trudeau, Garry B., cartoon from Doonesbury, 70, 966

Truth, Sojourner, Ain't I a Woman?, 236

Tuhy, Carrie, So Who Needs College?, 74

Two Cultures, The (Snow), 859

University Days (Thurber), 101

Valdez, Luis, *Los Vendidos*, 519

Van Dusen, Lewis H., Jr., Civil Disobedience: Destroyer of Democracy, 648

Vasquez, Victoria F., The English Language Amendment: Examining Myths, 189

Villanueva, Victor, Jr., Whose Voice Is It Anyway? Rodriguez's Speech in Retrospect, 155

Vonnegut, Kurt, Harrison Bergeron, 683

Wakoski, Diane, Belly Dancer, 276

Walker, Alice, Everyday Use, 56

Wallace, John H., *Huckleberry Finn* Is Offensive, 579

War for the Surgeon General, Not the Attorney General, A (Schmoke), 822

We've Come a Long Way, But Magazines Stayed Behind (Dudash), 376

What Can Be Done About Acid Rain (Reiger), 983

What High School Is (Sizer), 25

What Is a Horse? (Dickens), 24

What They Learn in School (Stern), 54

What's Wrong with Black English (Jones), 115

White, E. B., Education, 20

White English in Blackface, or Who Do I Be? (Smitherman), 118

Whither "1984" (Meyrowitz), 432

Whose Voice Is It Anyway? Rodriguez's Speech in Retrospect (Villanueva), 155

Why Good English Is Good for You (Simon), 130

Why the Justice System Fails (Rosenblatt), 766

Why I Believe in Affirmative Action (Spickard), 690

Why I Want a Wife (Syfers), 298

Why I Want a Husband (Fernsler), 300

Why Women Are Paid Less Than Men (Thurow), 350

Will, George F., Bruuuuuce, 471

Wills, Garry, The Remaking of the Presidents, 437

Wilson, James Q., Are Criminals Made or Born?, 745

Women in Science: An Analysis of a Social Problem (Keller), 314

Women at War (Shea), 557

Woolf, Virginia, Professions for Women, 335

Wordsworth, William, The Tables Turned, 858

Wright, James, American Twilights, 1957, 795; At the Executed Murderer's Grave, 798

Wright, Susan, Genetic Engineering: The Risks, 914

You and The Boss (Janowicz), 496

Zuckerman, Mortimer B., 1992— A New Proposal, 453